THIRD EDITION

Handbook of Social Psychology

VOLUME I
Theory and Method

Gardner Lindzey
Center for Advanced Study in the Behavioral Sciences

Elliot Aronson
University of California, Santa Cruz

 RANDOM HOUSE

New York

Distributed exclusively by
Lawrence Erlbaum Associates, Inc., Publishers
Hillsdale, New Jersey, and London

Third Edition

987654321

Library of Congress Cataloging in Publication Data
Main entry under title:

The Handbook of social psychology.

Includes index.
Contents: v. 1. Theory and method—v. 2. Special fields and applications.
1. Social psychology. I. Lindzey, Gardner.
II. Aronson, Elliot.
HM251.H224 1985 302 84-18509
ISBN 0-394-35049-9 (v. 1)
ISBN 0-394-35050-2 (v. 2)

Manufactured in the United States of America

The editors wish to thank a number of publishers and copyright holders for permission to reproduce tables, figures, and excerpts from the following sources:

American Psychological Association, *Ethical Guidelines for Psychologists*. Copyright © 1982. Reprinted by permission.

Aberle, D. F. et al. "The functional prerequisites of a society." *Ethics, 60,* pp. 110–111. Copyright © 1950. Reprinted by permission of the University of Chicago Press.

Alevizos, P. N., and P. L. Berck. "Communication: an instructional aid for staff training in behavioral assessment." *J. of Applied Behavior Analysis, 7,* pp. 472, 660. Copyright © 1975 by the Society for the Experimental Analysis of Behavior, Inc. Reprinted by permission.

Bales, R. F., and S. P. Cohen, *SYMLOG: A system for the multiple level observation of groups.* Copyright © 1979 by The Free Press, a Division of Macmillan Publishing Co., Inc. Adapted with permission of Macmillan, Inc.

Benjamin, L. S. "Structural Analysis of Differentiation Failure." *Psychiatry, 42,* 1–23. Copyright © 1979 by The William Alanson White Psychiatric Foundation, Inc. Reprinted by special permission of The William Alanson White Psychiatric Foundation, Inc.

Berry, W. *Sayings and doings.* Gnomon Press. Copyright © 1975. Quotes from *Sayings and doings* by Wendell Berry used by permission of Gnomon Press.

Brandt, R. M. *Studying behavior in natural settings.* Copyright © 1982. Reprinted by arrangement with University Press of America, Inc.

Cavan, S. "Seeing social structure in a rural setting." *Urban Life Culture, 3,* 334–335. Copyright © 1974. Reprinted by permission of Sage Publications, Inc.

Coombs, C. H. "Thurstone's measurement of social values revisited 40 years later." *J. Personality and Social Psychology, 6,* 85–90. Copyright © 1967. Reprinted by permission.

Dawes, R. M., and M. Moore. "Guttman scaling orthodox and randomized responses." In F. Peterman (Ed.), *Attitude measurement.* Gottingen: Verlag für psychologie. Pp. 129–131. Copyright © 1980. Reprinted by permission.

Douglas. J. D. *Investigative social research.* Pp. 15–16. Copyright © 1976. Reprinted by permission of Sage Publications.

Goffman, E. *Frame analysis.* New York: Harper & Row. Pp. 1–2. Copyright © 1974. Reprinted by permission.

Goodman, L. A. "A modified regression approach to the analysis of dichotomous variable." *American Sociological Review, 39,* Table p. 29. Copyright © 1972. Reprinted by permission of The American Sociological Association.

Kahneman, D., and A. Tversky. "The psychology of preferences." *Scientific American, 246,* 160–173. Copyright © 1982 by Scientific American, Inc. All rights reserved.

Lofland, J. *Doing social life.* New York: Wiley. Copyright © 1976. Reprinted by permission.

(Cont. on page xvi)

Preface to the Third Edition

This is the fourth *Handbook of Social Psychology*—the third involving one or both of the current editors. To examine these four *Handbooks* for constancy and change is a revealing exercise.

In introducing his 1935 *Handbook* Carl Murchison remarked, "The social sciences at the present moment stand naked and feeble in the midst of the political uncertainty of the world. The physical sciences seem so brilliant, so clothed with power by contrast. Either something has gone all wrong in the evolution of the social sciences, or their great day in court has not yet arrived. It is with something akin to despair that one contemplates the piffling, trivial, superficial, damnably unimportant topics that some social scientists investigate with agony and sweat. And at the end of all these centuries, no one knows what is wrong with the world or what is likely to happen to the world" (p. ix). A mere decade later this paragraph already seemed to many observers archaic and poorly informed. Even more remarkable is the fact that more than one-third the chapters in the 1935 *Handbook* dealt with the social psychology of bacteria, plants, and lower animals. Moreover, four chapters dealt with the social history of the negro, the red man, the white man, and the yellow man—labels that if used today would create a wave of revulsion. These chapters and others not mentioned, strike no note of resonance with contemporary social psychology.

Are there any traces in Murchison's *Handbook* of what has emerged as social psychology fifty years later? Clearly, the answer is yes, although the number of such continuities is not large. Perhaps the most dramatic example of anticipating the future is Gordon Allport's chapter on attitudes. In the 1954 *Handbook* there were to be two chapters on attitudes—one on measurement, and the other on attitude theory and research—and it was a last-minute withdrawal that led to omission of the chapter on attitude theory and research. In subsequent volumes we have observed a very heavy emphasis on attitude research as a cornerstone of social psychology. A second line of continuity is represented by Esper's chapter on language, which has been reflected and elaborated on in each of the subsequent editions. Moreover, Dashiell's chapter on human social experiments remarkably anticipates the industrious experimental social psychologists who to date have played an increasingly dominant role in American social psychology. Chapters on gender differences and the behavior of children in social situations are also reflected in subsequent *Handbooks*.

The 1954 edition fell naturally into two volumes: Volume I was devoted to prominent theories and major methods; Volume II dealt entirely with the most active substantive research areas of the time. The theoretical positions represented in the 1954 edition were almost identical to those in the 1968–1969 edition. In 1954, separate chapters were devoted to S–R theory (including reinforcement and contiguity), cognitive theory, psychoanalytic theory, field theory, and role theory. In the 1968–1969 edition each of those theoretical positions was again represented, and in addition, separate chapters were devoted to organization theory and mathematical models. In the current edition we have reverted to five theoretical positions. We retained S–R theory but broadened it to include the wider issues implied by the title "learning theory." Our chapter on cognitive theories acknowledges the continuing development of exciting systematic positions in that area. Similarly, our decision to retain a chapter on organization theory indicates the continued impact of that position. Our chapter on role theory has now been expanded to include symbolic interactionism in order to provide stronger representation of sociological perspectives. Although we have dropped specific chapters on mathematical models and field theory, work in these areas is very much in evidence in our new chapters on decision theory and cognitive theories. Our decision not to include a chapter on psychoanalytic theory was difficult. Although we appreciate the riches that social psychologists have extracted from this particular mine of ideas, it seems clear that over the past two decades very little research by social psychologists has been directly stimulated by this theory.

With regard to methods, we find few changes in chapter titles over the past thirty years. Social psychologists are still interested primarily in experimentation, attitude and opinion measurement, survey research, systematic observation, and quantitative analysis. Needless to say, the *content* of the chapters has changed dramatically over the years as our colleagues have become increasingly sophisticated in their use of these methods. The one new chapter that has been added concerns evaluation—reflecting a body of techniques that has become increasingly important since the late 1960s and has resulted in a new psychological specialty.

It is particularly interesting to compare the substantive research areas across the three modern editions of the handbook. Some areas have been a major focus of social psychological research since World War II and seem destined to remain so for the foreseeable future. Thus since the war all three handbooks have included chapters

on attitude change, leadership, the media, prejudice and racism, anthropological social psychology, psycholinguistics, and political behavior.

Some content areas have undergone a shift in emphasis over the years that has been great enough to require a major change in the title of the chapter. Thus our current chapter on social influence covers some of the same issues and kinds of research contained in chapters from earlier editions on group problem solving, but with a much wider range. Similarly, social psychologists have been interested in the socialization process for a very long time. The title of the current chapter emphasizes that the socialization process is not confined to infants, children, and adolescents, and reflects the increase in research on socialization throughout the life cycle. Likewise, the new chapter on social factors in cognition combines and expands earlier chapters on person perception and social and cultural factors in perception. The current edition also continues some trends that were initiated in the 1968–1969 edition. These include a special emphasis on interpersonal attraction and on the interaction between personality and social psychology.

Finally, there are some substantive chapters that are either totally new to this edition or that bear only slight resemblance to anything that has appeared in previous editions. These include chapters on sex roles, environmental psychology, social deviance, prosocial and antisocial behavior, and applications of social psychology. The chapters on sex roles and environmental psychology reflect issues and interests that were simply not factors in 1954, were barely on the horizon in 1968–1969, but are very much a part of our lives in the 1980s. Social psychologists have been playing a major role in increasing our understanding of these issues. In one sense, the handbook has been involved with applied social psychology throughout its existence. Thus the 1954 edition included a chapter on industrial social psychology; the 1968 edition included a revised version of that chapter but also included separate chapters on the social psychology of education, social psychological aspects of international relations, the social psychology of mental health, and others. But in another sense, the current chapter is innovative in that its focus is not on "applied social psychology" but on the broader issue of "the application" of social psychological knowledge and methods to a wide variety of contemporary problems such as health care, the legal system, and the classroom.

The only author to appear in all four *Handbooks* is Allport, who has written both on attitudes (1935) and on the history of social psychology (1954, 1968, 1985). His contribution to the present volume appears posthumously and is a slightly abridged version of the chapter that appeared in the last edition. No other author has appeared in more than two editions, although one was involved with four chapters in the 1954 and 1968–1969 editions, and a substantial number (twenty-five) have contributed to two editions. There are forty-five contributors to the current edition only seven of whom contributed to the last edition. As these figures indicate, the current volumes represent a decidedly fresh perspective on the field of social psychology. Many of our colleagues continued to find the 1954 edition useful after the appearance of the 1968–1969 edition, and we have little doubt that both the previous editions will continue to be of utility even with the appearance of this revision.

Because the *Handbook* is generally regarded as a kind of "standard," it is sometimes used to gauge current interests in social psychology or even to predict the health and direction of social psychology. For this reason we feel the editors have an obligation to make certain that our decisions (implicit and explicit) are not misinterpreted. For example one reviewer, in noting that the 1954 edition did not contain a chapter on "Attitude Theory and Research," concluded that social psychologists were losing interest in the concept of attitude. As noted earlier, the absence of that chapter was no more meaningful than the delinquency of one of our contributors! A final *Handbook* is almost never a precise reflection of the intentions of the editors and their advisors, and consequently readers should be cautious in interpreting trends or the current state of the field from the contents of the various editions.

With these concerns in mind, it is clearly important to discuss changes we have made in the format of the *Handbook*. The 1954 edition consisted of two volumes. The 1968–1969 edition was expanded to five volumes. For the current edition we decided to return to the two-volume format. A facile (but incorrect) interpretation might be that social psychology reached its peak in the 1960s and is now declining. We do not hold this view. We believe social psychology is as vital today as it was twenty years ago. Our decisions regarding format were based on more mundane issues—utility, convenience, and cost. Specifically, in 1967–1968 we believed that the five-volume format would make it easier for social psychologists interested in specific topics to purchase one or two

small volumes rather than the entire set. This proved to be a poor prediction: sales figures indicated that most users purchased all five volumes simultaneously. Moreover, we noted with dismay that the five-volume format changed the way the *Handbook* was being used. Apparently there is a tendency for a work in five volumes to be seen and used as if it were an encyclopedia. That is, our graduate students and colleagues tended to place their *Handbooks* on a shelf and to pull down a volume only when they needed a reference book. This was not the case with the 1954 edition, which was used both as a text and as a portable companion. Moreover, the cost of producing a five-volume set today would place the *Handbook* beyond the financial grasp of all but libraries and the very well-to-do. In short, our decision to return to a two-volume format was made because we believe the *Handbook* is more vital if it is off the shelf and priced at the lowest possible level.

The current volumes had their beginnings in May 1978, when we sent more than 130 letters to well-known social psychologists, including all contributors to the previous edition of the *Handbook*. We enclosed a tentative outline for the current *Handbook* and asked for comments about both topics and potential authors. We also pointed to a reorganization that in both number of volumes and chapters implied a product that would be more like the 1954 volumes than the 1968–1969 *Handbook*. We received more than seventy-five replies. All but one of the respondents felt a revision was timely. All but one respondent also approved, explicitly or implicitly, the reduction in number of volumes from five to two. Virtually all had suggestions for changes in our outline and roster of potential authors. The outline was substantially altered as a result of these suggestions, and in October 1978 we began to solicit authors. We will not take you through the tortuous path of changing deadlines, authors, and (very slightly) chapters. Actually, of the thirty-two chapters included in our outline, only two have been lost through attrition.

Some readers may be surprised to discover that these volumes have been published by Random House rather than Addison-Wesley. Certainly the editors were surprised when informed in the late stages of production that Addison-Wesley was transferring all of its social science publications to Random House. We were assured that there would be no delay in the appearance of the volumes and that Random House was looking forward eagerly to the production and promotion of the *Hand-*

book. We see no reason to doubt these statements and look forward to an amicable and rewarding relationship with Random House.

The facilities of the Center for Advanced Study in the Behavioral Sciences played a very significant role in the production of these volumes. In particular, the pa-tience and skill of Joyce McDonald were indispensable and are deeply appreciated.

September 1984
Stanford, California   G. L.
Santa Cruz, California   E. A.

Preface to the Second Edition

In the fourteen years that have elapsed since the last edition of this *Handbook,* the field of social psychology has evolved at a rapid rate. The present volumes are intended to represent these changes as faithfully as possible and at a level appropriate for the beginning graduate student as well as the fully trained psychologist.

The reader familiar with the previous *Handbook* will realize that we have employed the same general outline in the present volumes. The many new chapters reflect the increased quantitative and methodological sophistication of social psychologists, the development of certain specialized areas of research, and the increased activity in a variety of applied areas. In some instances we have attempted to compensate for known deficiencies in the coverage of the previous edition.

One can never be certain of portraying adequately the changes in a large and diverse area of scholarship, but we can be certain that this *Handbook* is very different from its predecessor. It is substantially larger—instead of one million words, two volumes, and 30 chapters, there are now approximately two-and-one-half million words, five volumes, and 45 chapters. We are convinced that our decision to present this material in five volumes will increase its utility for those who have specialized interests linked to either teaching or research activities. But the difference goes beyond mere size. The list of contributors has a decidedly new flavor—of the 45 authors in the previous edition, only 22 have contributed to this volume. Viewed from another vantage, of the 68 authors contributing to the current volume, 46 are represented in the *Handbook* for the first time. Only one chapter is reprinted without a thorough revision, and this, an essay (Hebb and Thompson) presenting a point of view that seems little affected by recent research and formulation. There are 15 chapters that are completely new and, in addition, a number of the replacements bear little resemblance to the chapter of the same, or similar, title that appeared earlier.

Plans for the current revision were begun in January of 1963. By July of that year a tentative chapter outline had been prepared and distributed to an array of distinguished social scientists, including the previous contributors to the *Handbook.* We benefited materially from the advice of dozens of persons in regard to both the chapter outline and the nomination of potential authors; we are grateful for their efforts on behalf of the *Handbook.* By fall of 1963 we had succeeded in constructing a final outline and a list of contributors. Our initial letters of invitation asked that completed manuscripts be submitted by January 1, 1965. We managed to obtain the bulk of the chapters eighteen months and several deadlines later, and the first two volumes were sent to the publishers early in 1967. The final chapters were secured the following July, when the remaining volumes went to press.

In selecting contributors we made every effort, within the general constraints of technical competence and availability, to obtain scholars of diverse professional and institutional backgrounds. Thus we take special pleasure in the fact that almost all areas of the country are well represented, that six of the contributors are affiliated with institutions outside the United States, and that the authors include political scientists, sociologists, and anthropologists as well as psychologists.

We consider it extremely fortunate that of the chapters listed in our working outline, all of those that we regarded as "key" or central chapters are included here. Indeed, there are only three chapters from that list that are not a part of the present volumes; this includes one (attitude change) that was deliberately incorporated within another chapter because such an arrangement seemed to offer a greater likelihood of satisfactory integration and coverage. It should be noted that this success is in marked contrast to the previous *Handbook,* where such essential areas as attitudes and social perception were omitted because of last-minute delinquencies. Although a few invited contributors did withdraw from the present *Handbook* after initially having agreed to prepare a chapter, in all cases we were fortunate in being able to find equally qualified replacements who were willing to take on this assignment on relatively short notice. To these individuals we owe a special debt of gratitude.

We wish to acknowledge the indispensable assistance of Judith Hilton, Shirley Cearley, and Leslie Segner in connection with the final preparation of the manuscript. Finally, we would like to express our gratitude to Mary Jane Whiteside for her tireless efforts in the final indexing of all volumes of the *Handbook.*

February 1968   G. L.
Austin, Texas   E. A.

Preface to the First Edition

The accelerating expansion of social psychology in the past two decades has led to an acute need for a source book more advanced than the ordinary textbook in the field but yet more focused than scattered periodical literature. Murchison's *Handbook of Social Psychology* (1935), the only previous attempt to meet this need, is out of date and out of print. It was this state of affairs that led us to assemble a book that would represent the major areas of social psychology at a level of difficulty appropriate for graduate students. In addition to serving the needs of graduate instruction, we anticipate that the volumes will be useful in advanced undergraduate courses and as a reference book for professional psychologists.

We first considered the possibility of preparing a *Handbook* three years ago. However, a final decision to proceed with the plan was not reached until the fall of 1951. During the interval we arranged an outline of topics that represented our convictions concerning the present state of social psychology. We then wrote to a large number of distinguished social psychologists asking them whether they felt our venture was likely to be professionally valuable and asking for criticisms of the outline we had prepared. The response to these letters was immensely gratifying—social psychologists as a group appear sufficiently altruistic to spend large amounts of time criticizing and commenting on a project of which they approve even though they may be unable to participate in it themselves. We also asked for specific recommendations of people who seemed best qualified to prepare the various chapters. After receiving answers we drastically revised our outline and proceeded to invite authors to prepare the various chapters. It was not until the spring of 1952 that we completed our list of contributors and even this list later underwent change. We first suggested (tongue in cheek) that the manuscripts be submitted by September 15, 1952. However, as we secretly expected, we were forced to change this due date to January 1, 1953. This "deadline" we tried hard to meet. But of course we failed and shifted our aspiration to June 15, 1953. Again we failed, although by now we were making substantial progress. By early in the fall of 1953 we had all the chapters excepting two, and the first volume was completed and in the hands of the publishers. The last two chapters were not received until early in 1954, when the second volume went to press.

Something should be said concerning the basis for the organization of the subject matter of these volumes. It became apparent early that there are many ways to subdivide social psychology but very little agreement concerning just which is best. Although we sought the advice of others, we found for almost every compelling suggestion an equally compelling countersuggestion. Thus, in the end, it was necessary to make many arbitrary decisions. So much for our knowledge that the *Handbook* could have been organized in many different ways. There is no single scheme that would satisfy all readers.

We early discovered that the subject matter was too voluminous to be contained in a single volume. Given this decision it seemed quite natural to present in one volume the chapters that dealt primarily with theoretical convictions or systematic positions, and also the methods and procedures commonly employed in social psychology. Likewise it seemed wise to present in one volume those chapters that focus upon the substantive findings and applications of social psychology. The decision to place the historical introduction, theory, and method chapters in the first volume reflects a bias in favor of investigation that begins with an awareness of the message of the past, an attempt at theoretical relevance, and finally with a full knowledge of the procedural or measurement alternatives. All of the content of the first volume is seen, at least by the editor, as a necessary preparation for good investigation. These are the things the social psychologist should know before he lifts a single empirical finger. The second volume, then, can be seen as a justification of the contents of the first volume. Here are the empirical fruits stemming from the theories and methods summarized in the first volume.

But does this ideal scheme mirror common practice? Are the major empirical advances summarized in the second volume in reality a legitimate by-product of theoretical conceptions and sophisticated method? In fairness to science in action (as opposed to science on the books) we are afraid the answer is No. Social psychology has made its advances largely on the shoulders of random empiricists and naive realists. Inability to distinguish between analytic and synthetic and a tendency toward reification of concepts has accompanied many of the most significant advances in this field. Who would say that those who view an attitude as a "construct" created by the investigator have made more of a contribution to this area of psychology than those who naively view attitudes as real and concrete entities? Thus we sorrowfully admit the organization we have imposed upon the *Handbook* may bear little relation to the path thus far trod in the development of social psychology. Nevertheless, it stands as a suggestion of the manner in which future development may well take place and as a reminder that the powerful

weapon of systematic theory is now more nearly within the grasp of the wise psychologist than formerly. Where yesterday the theoretically oriented investigator and the random realist may have been on even terms, recent developments within the field may well have destroyed this equality. An approach efficient in the wilderness may be foolish in a more carefully mapped region. In summary, the precedence we give to theoretical positions reflects our conviction of the importance of theories as spurs to research, but may also represent a program for the future rather than a reflection of the past.

It must be conceded that not all areas of social psychology are covered in these volumes with equal thoroughness. Some gaps are due to the blind spots of the editor while others are the result of contributors failing to cover an area they originally agreed to cover and, in a few cases, to contributors who withdrew altogether. In spite of these shortcomings, the volumes in their present state provide the most comprehensive picture of social psychology that exists in one place today.

While deficiencies of the final product are my own responsibility, they exist in spite of a number of advisors who gave their time and energy generously throughout the venture. Of these collaborators none was nearly so important as Gordon Allport. In fairness he should be co-editor of the volume, as he contributed immeasurably both in matters of policy and in matters of detail. I owe a very special debt of gratitude to my wife Andrea for her tolerance, encouragement, and detailed assistance. Likewise of great importance is the contribution of Shirley H. Heinemann, who has been of constant help throughout the editorial process and in preparing the Index. Crucial to the success of this work were various additional colleagues who served as referees, reading individual chapters and suggesting changes and deletions. On this score I express my gratitude to Raymond Bauer, Anthony Davids, Edward E. Jones, Kaspar Naegele, David Schneider, and Walter Weiss. In addition, many of the contributors served as referees for chapters other·than their own. I am indebted to E. G. Boring, S. S. Stevens, and Geraldine Stone for many helpful suggestions based on their experience in arranging the *Handbook of Experimental Psychology*. Mrs. Olga Crawford of Addison-Wesley played an indispensable role in final preparation of the manuscripts.

April 1954   G. L.

Contents

VOLUME I: THEORY AND METHODS

CHAPTER 1   The Historical Background of Social Psychology   1

Gordon W. Allport
Harvard University

CHAPTER 2   Major Developments in Social Psychology During the Past Five Decades   47

Edward E. Jones
Princeton University

CHAPTER 3   Learning Theory in Contemporary Social Psychology   109

Bernice Lott
University of Rhode Island

Albert J. Lott
University of Rhode Island

CHAPTER 4   The Cognitive Perspective in Social Psychology   137

Hazel Markus
University of Michigan

R. B. Zajonc
University of Michigan

CHAPTER 5   Decision Making and Decision Theory   231

Robert P. Abelson
Yale University

Ariel Levi
Teachers College, Columbia University

CHAPTER 6   Symbolic Interaction and Role Theory   311

Sheldon Stryker
Indiana University

Anne Statham
University of Wisconsin at Parkside

CHAPTER 7   Organizations and Organization Theory   379

Jeffrey Pfeffer
Stanford University

CHAPTER 8   Experimentation in Social Psychology   441

Elliot Aronson
University of California, Santa Cruz

Marilynn Brewer
University of California, Los Angeles

J. Merrill Carlsmith
Stanford University

CHAPTER 9   Quantitative Methods for Social Psychology   487

David A. Kenny
The University of Connecticut

CHAPTER 10   Attitude and Opinion Measurement   509

Robyn M. Dawes
University of Oregon

Tom L. Smith
Research and Education Institute of Denver (REID)

CHAPTER 11   Systematic Observational Methods   567

Karl E. Weick
University of Texas at Austin

CHAPTER 12   Survey Methods   635

Howard Schuman
University of Michigan

Graham Kalton
University of Michigan

CHAPTER 13   Program Evaluation   699

Thomas D. Cook
Northwestern University

Laura C. Leviton
University of Pittsburg

William R. Shadish, Jr.
Memphis State University

VOLUME II: SPECIAL FIELDS AND APPLICATIONS

CHAPTER 14   Altruism and Aggression   1

Dennis L. Krebs
Simon Fraser University

Dale T. Miller
Simon Fraser University

CHAPTER 15   Attribution and Social Perception   73

Michael Ross
University of Waterloo

Garth J. O. Fletcher
Illinois State University

CHAPTER 16   Socialization in Adulthood   123

Karen K. Dion
University of Toronto

CHAPTER 17   Sex Roles in Contemporary American Society   149

Janet T. Spence
University of Texas at Austin

Kay Deaux
Purdue University

Robert L. Helmreich
University of Texas at Austin

CHAPTER 18   Language Use and Language Users   179

Herbert H. Clark
Stanford University

CHAPTER 19   Attitudes and Attitude Change   233

William J. McGuire
Yale University

CHAPTER 20   Social Influence and Conformity   347

Serge Moscovici
Ecole des Hautes Etudes En Sciences Sociales

CHAPTER 21   Interpersonal Attraction   413

Ellen Berscheid
University of Minnesota

CHAPTER 22   Leadership and Power   485

Edwin P. Hollander
State University of New York at Buffalo

CHAPTER 23   Effects of Mass Communication   539

Donald F. Roberts
Stanford University

Nathan Maccoby
Stanford University

CHAPTER 24   Intergroup Relations   599

Walter G. Stephan
New Mexico State University

CHAPTER 25   Public Opinion and Polical Action   659

Donald R. Kinder
University of Michigan

David O. Sears
University of California, Los Angeles

CHAPTER 26   Social Deviance   743

Dane Archer
University of California, Santa Cruz

CHAPTER 27 — The Application of Social Psychology — 805

Judith Rodin
Yale University

CHAPTER 28 — Personality and Social Behavior — 883

Mark Snyder
University of Minnesota

William Ickes
University of Texas at Arlington

CHAPTER 29 — Social Psychological Aspects of Environmental Psychology — 949

John M. Darley
Princeton University

Daniel T. Gilbert
Princeton University

CHAPTER 30 — Cultural Psychology — 993

D. R. Price-Williams
University of California, Los Angeles

Lott, B. E., and A. J. Lott. "The formation of positive attitudes toward group members." *J. Abnormal and Social Psychology,* 298. Copyright © 1960 by the American Psychological Association. Reprinted by permission of the publisher and the author.

McHugh, P. *Defining the situation: the organization of meaning in social integration.* Copyright © 1968 by The Bobbs-Merrill Company. Reprinted by permission of the publisher.

MacNeil, M. K., L. E. Davis, and D. J. Pace. "Group status displacement under stress: a serendipitous finding." *Sociometry, 38,* 294, 303–305. Copyright © 1975. Reprinted by permission of the American Sociological Association.

Marceil, J. C. "Implicit demensions of idiography and nomothesis: a reformulation." *American Psychologist, 32,* 1046–1055. Copyright © 1977 by the American Psychological Association. Reprinted by permission of the author.

Mehan, H., and H. Wood. *The reality of ethnomethodology.* New York: Wiley. Copyright © 1975. Reprinted by permission.

Mitroff, I. I., and R. H. Kilmann. *Methodological approaches to social science.* San Francisco: Jossey-Bass. Copyright © 1978. Reprinted by permission.

Morgan, G., and L. Smircich. "The case for qualitative research." *Academy of Management Review, 5,* Table 1, 492. Copyright © 1980. Reprinted by permission of *The Academy of Management Review* and the authors.

Pfeffer, J., and R. Salancik. Figure 4.1 from *The external control of organizations.* Copyright © 1978. Reprinted by permission of Harper & Row, Publishers, Inc.

Sainsbury, T., R. K. Sharma, S. Iyengar, and B. Overman. "A preliminary study of home health care in Allegheny County, Pennsylvania." University of Pittsburgh Graduate School of Public Health, 1979. Reprinted by permission of the author.

Schwartz, H., and J. Jacobs. *Qualitative sociology: a method to the madness.* Copyright © 1979 by The Free Press, a Division of Macmillan Publishing Co., Inc. Reprinted with permission of Macmillan Inc.

Spradley, J. P. *The Ethnographic Interview,* p. 178. Copyright © 1979 by Holt, Rinehart and Winston. Reprinted by permission of Holt, Rinehart and Winston, CBS College Publishing.

Spradley, J. P. *Participant Observation,* pp. 43–44, 93, 108. Copyright © 1980 by Holt, Rinehart and Winston. Reprinted by permission of Holt, Rinehart and Winston, CBS College Publishing. ·

Thurstone, L. L., "Attitudes can be measured." *American J. of Sociology, 33,* 524–529. Copyright © 1928. Reprinted by permission of The University of Chicago Press.

Tversky, A., and D. Kahneman. "The framing of decisions and the psychology of choice." *Science, 211,* 453–458. Figs. 1 and 2. Copyright © 1981 by the American Association for the Advancement of Science. Reprinted by permission.

Webb, E., and K. E. Weick. Reprinted from "Unobtrusive measures in organizational theory: a reminder," published in *Administrative Science Quarterly, 24,* copyright © 1979, by permission of the *Administrative Science Quarterly.*

Whyte, W. T. Reprinted from *Street Corner Society,* pp. 303–304, 318–120, by W. T. Whyte by permission of the University of Chicago Press. Copyright © 1955.

CHAPTER 1

The Historical Background of Social Psychology

Gordon W. Allport
Harvard University

Social psychology is an ancient discipline. It is also modern—ultramodern and exciting. So much so that we are tempted to disregard the past, and to brush aside the thoughts of our intellectual ancestors. Why let the rust of their old-fashioned theories clog the gears of a new and vital science? Why bother with the "metaphysical stage" of speculation, as Comte called it, when a new era of positivism and progress has now dawned?

But there is another and wiser way to view the matter. Our intellectual ancestors, for all their fumbling, were asking precisely the same questions that we are asking today. How does one generation, they wanted to know, impose its culture and its thought forms upon the next? What happens to the mental life of the individual when he enters into association with others? And long before social psychology became a science, political philosophers sought an answer to the question, What is the social nature of man? They well knew, as Vico (1725) observed, that *"governments must conform to the nature of the men governed."* Hence interest in the key problem of social psychology—man's social nature—is both ancient and persistent.

This chapter has been lightly abridged by Gardner Lindzey but otherwise is unchanged from the version published in the Second Edition of the Handbook of Social Psychology.

It is true that our intellectual forefathers lacked tools of precision for empirical research and that they were sometimes naive in their theories; yet they bequeathed to us an important store of shrewd insights that have stood the test of time. Even their errors and blind alleys are instructive. It has been well said that those who do not know history are doomed to repeat its mistakes. And the history of science shows that both the accomplishments and the blunders of one generation of scholars may become building stones in the hands of the next.

While the argument in favor of historical perspective is compelling, it is not all-compelling. It does not, for example, require us to make a conducted tour through a museum of oddities and antiquities. Nor does it hold us to a series of dust-covered portraits. A study of the history of social psychology can be justified only if it shows the relevance of historical backgrounds to present-day foregrounds. To this end the present essay lays stress not upon curios and portraits, but upon those psychological topics of current concern that receive genuinely helpful illumination from the past.

THE SOIL OF SOCIAL PSYCHOLOGY

If we ask an apparently simple question, "Who founded social psychology?" we run headfirst into one of the major problems of the science itself—the problem of so-cial invention. Can we ever say that a single person turns the tide of history? If we favor the "great man" type of explanation we can single out several candidates for the honor of founding social psychology: Plato, Aristotle, Hobbes, Comte, Hegel, Lazarus and Steinthal, Tarde, E. A. Ross, and others, depending on the criteria and the time perspective we choose to adopt. A good case could be made for each of these men. Several of them have actually been called "the father of social psychology." But the truest answer to the question asserts that the roots of modern social psychology lie in the distinctive soil of western thought and civilization.

While the roots of social psychology lie in the intellectual soil of the whole western tradition, its present flowering is recognized to be characteristically an American phenomenon. One reason for the striking upsurge of social psychology in the United States lies in the pragmatic tradition of this country. National emergencies and conditions of social disruption provide special incentive to invent new techniques, and to strike out boldly for solutions to practical social problems. Social psychology began to flourish soon after the First World War. This event, followed by the spread of Communism, by the great depression of the 1930s, by the rise of Hitler, the genocide of the Jews, race riots, the Second World War and the atomic threat, stimulated all branches of social science. A special challenge fell to social psychology. The question was asked: How is it possible to preserve the values of freedom and individual rights under conditions of mounting social strain and regimentation? Can science help provide an answer? This challenging question led to a burst of creative effort that added much to our understanding of the phenomena of leadership, public opinion, rumor, propaganda, prejudice, attitude change, morale, communication, decision-making, race relations, and conflicts of value.

Reviewing the decade that followed World War II, Cartwright (1961) speaks of the "excitement and optimism" of American social psychologists, and notes "the tremendous increase in the total number of people calling themselves social psychologists." Most of these, we may add, show little awareness of the history of their field.

Practical and humanitarian motives have always played an important part in the development of social psychology, not only in America but in other lands as well. Yet there have been discordant and dissenting voices. In the opinion of Herbert Spencer in England, of Ludwig Gumplowicz in Austria, and of William Graham

Sumner in the United States, it is both futile and dangerous for men to attempt to steer or to speed social change. Social evolution, they argue, requires time and obeys laws beyond the control of man. The only practical service of social science is to warn men not to interfere with the course of nature (or society). But these authors are in a minority. Most social psychologists share with Comte an optimistic view of man's chances to better his way of life. Has he not already improved his material welfare via natural science, and his health via biological science? Why should he not better his social relationships via social science? For the past century this optimistic outlook has persisted even in the face of slender accomplishment to date. Human relations seem stubbornly set. Wars have not been abolished, labor troubles have not abated, and racial tensions are still with us. Give us time and give us money for research, the optimists say.

There is a more formal way of viewing the recent upsurge of interest in social psychology. It could be explained in terms of Comte's theory of three stages (1830, Chapter 1). Comte would say that only recently have the social sciences left the constraints of the first two stages, the *theological* and *metaphysical* respectively, and entered fully into the third stage of *positivism*. While Comte himself endeavored to inaugurate the third stage, it is clear that the fruit of his effort was delayed for nearly a century until the positivistic tools of experiment—statistics, survey methods, and like instruments—were more adequately developed. Hornell Hart (1949) plotted convincingly the recent upswing in the productions of social science, and argued that the acceleration marks the delayed entrance of social science into the era of positivism. Even so, technological developments are dangerously far in front of social advances. Man can change matter into energy but cannot yet socially control the energy he creates.

Whether social science, under proper ethical guidance, can eventually reduce or eliminate the cultural lag may well be a question upon which human destiny depends.

DEFINING SOCIAL PSYCHOLOGY

No sharp boundaries demarcate social psychology from other social sciences. It overlaps political and economic science and cultural anthropology, and in many respects it is indistinguishable from general psychology. Likewise, its tie with sociology is close. It was a sociologist, E. A. Ross, who wrote the first book to bear the title

Social Psychology (1908), but most of the subsequent textbooks have been written by psychologists.

In spite of this apparent lack of autonomy, social psychology has its own core of theory and data and its own special viewpoint. Its focus of interest is upon the social nature of the individual person. By contrast, political science, sociology, and cultural anthropology take as their starting points the political, social, or cultural systems in which an individual person lives.

With few exceptions, social psychologists regard their discipline as *an attempt to understand and explain how the thought, feeling, and behavior of individuals are influenced by the actual, imagined, or implied presence of others.* The term "implied presence" refers to the many activities the individual carries out because of his position (role) in a complex social structure and because of his membership in a cultural group.

Sociology, anthropology, and political science are "higher-level" disciplines; they seek inclusive laws of social structure, social change, cultural patterning. They wish to know the course of society with the individual extracted. What happens when all citizens of the United States are gradually replaced by other citizens? The English language continues to be spoken; the form of government is not fundamentally altered; the cycles of economic behavior and the existence of social classes continue to be pretty much as they were. By contrast, social psychology wishes to know how any given member of a society is affected by all the social stimuli that surround him. How does he learn his native language? Whence come the social and political attitudes that he develops? What happens when he becomes a member of a group or of a crowd?

Social psychology is above all else a branch of general psychology. Its center of emphasis is the same: human nature as localized in the person. Some writers argue that since personal mental life is always influenced by "the actual, imagined, or implied presence of others" then all psychology must be social. The point is tenable if we wish to press it. But in practice it has little value. There are many problems of human nature that need to be solved apart from social considerations: problems of psychophysics, sensory processes, emotional functions, memory span, the nature of personality integration. Social psychology overlaps general psychology, but is not identical with it.

In tracing the history of social psychology we are in the uncomfortable position of having to abstract from the total context of each author's thought those ideas that bear specifically on the social nature of the individual. We shall not, for example, examine the entire political philosophy of Bentham, or the entire sociology of Herbert Spencer. We pick out only those psychological assumptions upon which the remainder of their social theory rests. As for psychologists, we do not describe the total contribution of Wundt or McDougall or Freud to psychological science, but only those portions that are especially relevant to the explanation of social conduct.

Thus to write a history of social psychology requires a special type of lightfingeredness. One extracts a finding here, an idea there, and tries to show how these threads have woven themselves into the fabric of present-day social psychology.

SECONDARY SOURCES

The only way the student can achieve an accurate sense of history is to dig into the original writings of the leading authors of the past. But as the shadow of history lengthens it becomes increasingly difficult to consult primary sources exclusively. Secondary sources, if used with discrimination, have their uses. Not only do they save time, but they allow the student of history to check one interpretation against another.

While there are many histories of sociological and political thought, there is no definitive history of social psychology. Selected portions of the subject are treated by Sprowls (1927) and by Dr. Karpf in her *American Social Psychology* (1932) and in her more recent addendum (1952). Cottrell and Gallagher (1941) have surveyed the decade 1930–1940, Cartwright the decade 1948–1958. Few of these authors maintain a distinction between sociology and social psychology. Among the histories of sociology we sometimes find an antipsychological bias, as in Becker and Barnes's *Social Thought from Lore to Science* (1952). But in this book as well as in Sorokin (1928), Rice (1931), L. L. Bernard (1934), House (1936), and Barnes (1965), we find helpful interpretations of the thought of past authors, including their basic psychological assumptions.

The history of cultural anthropology is still a neglected subject. Some assistance may be obtained from Haddon (1910, 1949), and even more from Kroeber and Kluckhohn (1952), who give a painstaking review of the concept of culture, giving due weight to its psychological connotations.

Political theories have received many historical treatments, some of which include an extensive consideration of the social nature of man. A useful source in this connection is G. Engelmann, *Political Philosophy from Plato to Jeremy Bentham* (1927). This volume contains a series of pastiches that summarize each author's views of "the nature of men governed" in the author's own style. Other sources include Sabine (1961), Wolin (1960), and Catlin (1947). Catlin makes the interesting observation that while political *philosophy* has flourished for two millennia, we are only now witnessing the beginnings of a political *science,* because the development of a science of politics would have been "too dangerous to the powers that be." The same reasoning may help to explain why it is only in recent years that the soil has been favorable for the unimpeded growth of a science of social psychology; and why it is only in certain western lands that the growth has taken place.

We must not forget the history of philosophy. Until a century ago all social psychologists were at the same time philosophers, and many philosophers were social psychologists. Surveys that aid in tracing this relationship have been written by Windelband (1935), Vaughan (1939), Russell (1945), and Baker (1947). Historians of intellectual movements also have much to offer, for example, M. E. Curti in *The Growth of American Thought* (1943).

To these sources must be added historical treatments of general psychology, for above all else social psychology depends upon the basic orientations and methods of experimental and theoretical psychology. In Boring (1950) there is much of value. Other historians of psychology, for example, Murphy (1949), devote special chapters to social psychology.

SIMPLE AND SOVEREIGN THEORIES: THEIR SIGNIFICANCE

Most social psychologists of the nineteenth century thrived on unitary explanations. Each tended to select and develop one simple and sovereign formula that seemed to him to hold the key to social behavior. The phrase "simple and sovereign" is borrowed from Henry George, who declared in 1879 that the single tax would be a "simple and sovereign remedy for the ills of mankind." In the nineteenth century both social scientists and reformers sought unitary solutions of social riddles. Favorite among the psychological open sesames were *pleasure-pain, egoism, sympathy, gregariousness, imitation,* and *suggestion.*

The year 1908 may be said to mark a turn away from such monistic explanations and toward pluralistic expla-

nations. In that year the first two textbooks in social psychology appeared. The earlier, by Ross, continued to place the burden of explanation upon a single principle, sometimes called by him "imitation," sometimes "suggestion." The latter text, McDougall's, called upon a plural array of instincts as prime movers of mankind. While the instinct doctrine may, in a sense, seem to represent only another simplicist type of causal force, still the instincts were regarded by McDougall as varied in type and diversified in the social behavior they provoked.

It is easy to inveigh against the fallacy of unitary explanation, or the *simplicist fallacy,* as it is sometimes called. Few modern writers focus on a single motive or mechanism and claim it as an all-sufficient explanation of social behavior. Yet even today we find authors who favor some one predominant factor to the *relative* neglect of others. Among these factors are such favorites as *conditioning, reinforcement, anxiety, sexuality, guilt, frustration, cognitive organization, role, identity, alienation,* and *social class.* Thus it is difficult for even a modern author to keep a balance in his repertoire of explanations. The reason seems to be that every writer aspires to a coherent system of explanation and wishes to reduce the number of variables in his system to the minimum.

The following pages examine in some detail the leading simple and sovereign conceptions of the nineteenth century. Our purpose is not to resurrect discredited theories, or even to warn modern authors against their own obsessive tendencies in system building. Rather we hope to demonstrate that the unitary principles of the past still represent live issues in contemporary social psychology. While our present-day approach is certainly more cautious and more pluralistic, yet the phenomena described by earlier writers are still with us, and in some cases it is doubtful whether today's conceptualizations improve upon those of yesterday.

HEDONISM

We take first a simple and sovereign theory that reaches from the time of Greek philosophy into the present day. Psychological hedonism (or as Jeremy Bentham, 1748–1832, prefers to call it, the Principle of Utility) maintains that pain and pleasure are our "sovereign masters" (Bentham, 1789, p. 1).

While Bentham had the hedonistic doctrines of Epicurus, Aristippus, Hobbes, Adam Smith, and many others on which to draw, the credit for the first extensive formulation of hedonism in relation to social psychology is his. He denies the importance of sympathy in social life. The basic fact is that men act simply to secure pleasure (sometimes called happiness) and to avoid pain. On the occasion of every act a person is led to pursue that line of conduct which, according to his view of the case taken by him at the moment, will be in the highest degree contributory to his own happiness. John Stuart Mill (1863) agreed with Bentham that to desire anything except in proportion as the idea of it is pleasant is a physical impossibility.

Starting with this basic assumption, Bentham evolved his *hedonistic calculus*. It maintains that the degree of pleasure and of pain can be measured if we analyze any given affective state with the aid of certain dimensions. Pleasures (and pains) have differing degrees of *duration, intensity, certainty, propinquity* (or *remoteness*), *fecundity* (will pleasure or pain follow?), *purity* (will the pleasure be mixed with pain?), and *extent* (will other people be involved pleasurably or painfully?). Such an analytic scheme reminds us of Wundt's, Titchener's, and Osgood's later attempts to establish the attributes of feelings, though the dimensions they chose are different from Bentham's.

To Bentham all pleasures were measurable. Their motivational power, also their utility, could be computed. He did not deny that pleasures had differing qualities; there were, he admitted, pleasures of sense, wealth, skill, amity, good name, power, piety, benevolence, malevolence, memory, imagination, expectation, association, and relief (1789, Chapter 5). But one was "as good as" another. A bottle of pickles is as good as a book of poetry if it yields equal pleasure. (On this point John Stuart Mill disagreed.) All that mattered to Bentham was the maximizing of total pleasure. To reach a rational decision regarding a course of conduct—and psychological hedonism has a heavily rationalistic cast—one would simply compute the probable hedonic consequences of the proposed act in terms of the resulting duration, intensity, certainty, and so forth, of pleasure. He would (and should) act so as to bring himself the greatest hedonic good.

At this point psychological hedonism merges into ethical hedonism. Not only is it true that men do tend to act in such a way as to maximize pleasure but they *should* so act. To be sure, other people's pleasure may enter into the person's calculations, in the dimension of *extent*. He should try to maximize the happiness of others along with his own. And the policy of government and of all social agencies should be to facilitate "the greatest good (happiness) to the greatest number."

Thus Utilitarian ethics is simply an extension of a psychological theory into the domain of morals. To apply these ethics one must in general follow a policy of *laissez-faire* ("hands off"). It was customary to ask the question, "How much government should we have?" and to give the answer, "As little as possible." For if men instinctively seek pleasure, then they need very little guidance or constraint. Let each serve his own good. While an occasional law may be needed, still laissez-faire is the surest way to achieve the greatest good for the greatest number.

Here is a case where a psychological assumption had far-reaching practical consequences in society. Its proponents—and there were many—fought against social legislation. Why, they asked, should we curtail the good resulting from the industrial revolution? For example, if under sweatshop conditions ten thousand men obtain factory-made pants at a cheaper price, the "greatest good" is served; for their pleasure in the aggregate probably exceeds the pain caused to the relatively few sweatshop (or child) laborers involved in the process of mass production.

The doctrine of the "economic man" is likewise a direct outgrowth of the same hedonistic assumption. Man, it was held, basically works for monetary gain, because money is pleasure *in abstracto*. With it he buys the utilities that yield him maximum good according to his conception of the matter (and no one else's conception counts). To take only one example from the classic economic laws founded on this assumption, it was held that "man will buy in the lowest market and sell in the highest market." For many years this "law" of behavior underlay economic theory. To a considerable extent it still does so. Yet exceptions are numerous. In times of panic, the reverse rule holds. Further, a man who is temperamentally generous or temperamentally pessimistic may act contrary to the law. And Pareto tells of a superstitious banker who lost money by refusing to sit at a table with thirteen people to consummate a sale "in the highest market." Thus a host of noneconomic motives enter into economic conduct. It is true that many modern economists have abandoned the rigid formulas that derived from rationalistic hedonism. The "economic man" is becoming extinct. A newer, pluralistic conception of economic behavior is arising that takes into account many more factors than are included in the hedonistic assumption (Parsons, 1949; Katona, 1951).

Herbert Spencer (1820–1903) gave support to the hedonistic theory and to laissez-faire by tying both to the doctrine of evolution. He pointed out that pleasurable activities, for the most part, make for survival. Pain betokens danger and death. It is therefore natural to seek pleasure and avoid pain. To the obvious objection that some destructive activities are also pleasurable (drunkenness and other vices) Spencer replied that this dislocation is only a reflection of the imperfect state of society. When social life is fully regulated by evolutionary principles, then pleasure and survival value will be identical.

Spencer joined the opponents of social legislation, likewise on psychological grounds. The state must respect rugged individualism and, as far as possible, allow every pleasure seeker to attain his own good in his own way. Man's motives, like nature herself, are often "red in tooth and claw," but even so a premium must be put on these natural impulses. To be sure, Spencer recognized the affiliative (sympathetic) motives in men. But these, he thought, should be expressed not in the activities of the state, but only within the circle of the family. For him there was a sharp distinction between the *ethics of the state* and the *ethics of the family*. On this ground he opposed the advent of free public education in Britain, which was finally achieved over his protests in 1873. Let the family plan for, and pay for, the education of its children. The state should never put a premium on weakness.

We have dwelt on the relationship between psychological hedonism and social policy in the nineteenth century for two special reasons. First, we wish to show that here is a psychological hypothesis that was, in a sense, put to the test, and failed. In the long run the state could not leave men alone to seek their own good, relying on their instinct for pleasure and their reason. The cry of protest from Dickens, Ruskin, Kingsley, and the socialists finally prevailed. Their argument was that only one side of human nature and only one portion of the population were being favored by Utilitarian ethics. Human life is too complex to rely on the manifestly narrow doctrine of Utility. The tide turned toward social welfare policies, toward what today is called *welfare state*. The claims of simon-pure hedonism, when tested in the crucible of social policy, proved inadequate.

A second reason for dwelling on this matter is to provide illustration for another significant fact. The theories of social psychology are rarely, if ever, chaste scientific productions. They usually gear into the prevailing political and social atmosphere. Dewey (1899) has shown that this is so. For example, an aristocracy produces no psychology of individual differences, for the individual is unimportant unless he happens to belong to the higher classes. Dewey has likewise pointed out that dualistic psychology flourishes best when one group holds a mo-

nopoly of social power and wishes to do the thinking and planning, while others remain the docile, unthinking instruments of execution. And apologists for the status quo, he added in another context, are those who most readily declare human nature to be unalterable (1917, p. 273):

> The ultimate refuge of the standpatter in every field, education, religion, politics, industrial and domestic life, has been the notion of an alleged fixed structure of mind.

Our point is that laissez-faire was in part the consequence of a psychological theory, and in part a product of the prevailing social ethos. The thinking of Bentham, Mill, Spencer, and other hedonists was inevitably molded by the prevailing practices of the era of the industrial revolution. Their psychological theory meshed into the social situation of the day, and became to some extent what Marx and Engels (1846) and Mannheim (1936) called *ideology*.

In recent years we have had more spectacular samples of the dependence of scientific theory upon the prevailing political and social conditions, specifically in the surrender of German psychology to Nazi thought and of Russian psychology to Communist thought.

Hedonism Today

Yet hedonism is more than a culture-bound and time-linked ideology. It is a basic theory of the prime motivation of men. In various guises it is held today as tenaciously as in the past. Freud, especially in his earlier writing, insisted that all instincts "seek pleasure." While they may be overlaid, repressed, or controlled, they still strive unconsciously, and in disguised ways, for pleasure. To seek for such gratification is the "primary process" of the mind.

At the present time, however, the term "pleasure" is not popular with psychologists, chiefly because it implies a dualism in the relation of body and mind. (Pleasure is a conscious state, and it is considered unscientific to claim that consciousness "causes" behavior.) Hence other labels for current hedonism have been devised. For example, Dollard and Miller (1950, p. 9) wrote:

> The principle of reinforcement has been substituted for Freud's pleasure principle. The concept of "pleasure" has proved a difficult and slippery notion in the history of psychology.

As we shall see, "reinforcement" refers to past pleasure (or satisfaction) rather than to future pleasure (which the classical hedonists stressed), but the hedonistic flavor is still present.

Another disguised version of hedonism is the prevailing dictum, found in most present-day psychological texts, that all motives tend to achieve *tension reduction.* Thus Kluckhohn and Murray wrote that "the nearest thing to an all-embracing principle" is the concept of "need, drive, or vectorial force." Such a force leads the individual to "re-establish equilibrium, reduce the tensions, appease the need" (1948, p. 14). This view is at bottom a variant of hedonism, because the act of escaping tension is also an escape from anxiety, from frustration, from distention—in brief, from pain. To be sure, the stress here is on negative hedonism (Epicurean) rather than a positive pleasure-seeking hedonism (Cyrenaic), but it is hedonism all the same. Since *all* motives are said to be of this tension-reducing order, the position is not unlike Bentham's contention that "pleasure and pain are our sovereign masters." Thus hedonism, as an overall conceptualization of human motivation, is neither dead nor discredited. Perhaps its longevity certifies that it contains a core of truth.

Critique

There are, however, many arguments raised against hedonism, some of which apply to modern as well as to classical formulations. To assist our survey of these criticisms, we shall adopt the analytical scheme proposed by Troland (1928). This author advises us to distinguish between hedonism of the *present,* of the *future,* and of the *past.*

Hedonism of the present would hold that each individual now, in the present moment, is acting in such a way as to obtain maximum present pleasure. This is clearly an untenable position, excepting perhaps in the case of a vegetative, psychotic patient. Most people do submit themselves to the dentist's chair; they do wash dishes, save money, and forego present pleasures. No hedonistic writer makes any contrary claim.

Hedonism of the future, however, is the doctrine of Bentham and Mill and, in some respects, of the tension-reduction school of thought. The individual is doing now what is designed to gain happiness or relief from pain in the future. Here many criticisms are relevant:

1. We recall that when recast in terms of social policy (laissez-faire) the assumptions of classical hedonism failed to hold up. Men do not in fact act so as to maximize pleasure in the long run for themselves or for others.

2. Troublesome too is the interactionist position implied. How can "ideas" of future pleasure motivate present conduct?

3. Especially serious is the charge that men cannot aim at pleasure in the abstract. They can only seek concrete goals (a job, a mate, food, shelter). At best the feeling tone is a by-product of reaching the goal; it does not constitute the motive itself. In this connection, employing the evidence of introspection, Titchener found that pleasure and pain are not the sole determinants of action. Indeed, he wrote, "I do not consider that they can be numbered at all among the conditions of action" (1908, pp. 297f).

4. Similar is McDougall's argument that pleasure and pain are nonmotivational; they are nothing more than signposts, guides, indicators that instincts are successfully or unsuccessfully running their course (1923). A mother cannot help but care for her offspring through thick and thin (if she has a normal parental instinct). Pleasure and unpleasure merely tell her that the instinct is, or is not, fulfilling its basic purpose of successfully caring for her young. Instincts are the prime movers; at most they are guided by the signals of pleasure and unpleasure to select instrumental activities that will fulfill their purposes.

Freud, we recall, identified instincts with pleasure seeking. His earlier view of the matter was thus very different from McDougall's. In later years, however, Freud modified his hedonistic position considerably, and in *Beyond the Pleasure Principle* (1920) postulated Thanatos, a death instinct, which ultimately negates Eros and pleasure seeking.

5. If we appeal to common observation, doubts increase. While hedonism may seem a good "fit" to the self-seeking activities of childhood and youth, it seems less appropriate to the activities of parents, teachers, artists, and above all, martyrs. In mature conduct there is often an overwhelming sense of duty, loyalty, or commitment to a way of life, and these motives seem to take control of the personality. When pleasure or pain are encountered, they may be regarded as "twin impostors," and the motive may run its course regardless of the affect involved. To this line of argument the hedonists reply that duty-ridden people are after all merely avoiding the pain of not doing their duty; and martyrs too are selecting the least painful course of conduct, or perhaps seeking the pleasure of the next world. It is a question whether at this point hedonists are not overextending their terms. Can the bomber who crash-dives into his target be said, in any reasonable sense, to be seeking plea-

sure and avoiding pain? His motive seems remote from such affective considerations. It is easy to stretch the meanings of pleasure and pain until they lose significance.

Hedonism of the past escapes some of these criticisms, but is open to others. Its most succinct statement comes from Thorndike's dictum that "pleasure stamps in; pain stamps out" (1898). He was referring, of course, to the learning process, and defining what he called the Law of Effect, which in the present day is usually rendered as *reinforcement theory*. This form of hedonism says merely that each person is now acting according to the mode of conduct he has in the past found pleasurable (satisfying, effective, tension reducing). Good consequences have reinforced his habits, his opinions, his ways of seeking goals, so that now he maintains them. To argue this position in detail would take us too far afield. Suffice it to say that studies of memory have failed to show convincingly that pleasurable memories are significantly more often retained than unpleasurable, as the theory would predict (Meltzer, 1930). And the existence of satiation, boredom, risk taking, cognitive learning, and other phenomena make trouble for the theory (Hoppe, 1930; Allport, 1946).

At the present time no conclusion seems justified, other than that pleasure and unpleasure have some important relationship to motivation. Just what it is we do not yet know. It may be as central as Bentham claimed, or as incidental as McDougall claimed. It may be a principle appropriate to childhood but less so to maturity. In any case, the role of affect needs vastly more empirical and theoretical study before it finds its rightful place in an improved science of social behavior.

EGOISM (POWER)

Hedonism is a doctrine of self-centeredness. A person who seeks pleasure and avoids pain is inevitably serving his own affective interest. Even though, as Mill eloquently argued, he can sometimes gain happiness from contributing to the welfare of others, it is still the pursuit of his own pleasure that motivates him.

Thomas Hobbes (1588–1679) was likewise a hedonist, but unlike Bentham and Mill he reduced pleasure seeking to a more basic passion of egoism. The conflict of egos was, to his mind, so prominent that mankind must be regarded as in a state of "war of all against all." To obtain pleasure it is necessary first and foremost to have

power. For power gives one the means to obtain ease and sensual pleasure; it brings admiration and flattery from others, and it thus conduces to "the greatest joy of the human soul," which is to have a high opinion of oneself. Therefore, man's most basic motive is "the desire of power after power that ceaseth only in death" (1651, p. 63):

> So that in the first place, I put for a generall inclination of all mankind, a perpetuall and restlesse desire of Power after power, that ceaseth only in Death. And the cause of this, is not alwayes that a man hopes for a more intensive delight, than he has already attained to; or that he cannot be content with a moderate power; but because he cannot assure the power and means to live well which he hath present, without the acquisition of more.

Since life in society would be impossible if the insatiable desire for power were not curbed, men yield to the "common power" of the state, which Hobbes calls the *Leviathan*. Through a form of "social contract" each person obtains protection from other power-seeking mortals, and obtains a chance to utilize his leisure for the arts of peace and for the acquisition of knowledge.

Hobbes gives an analysis of the power motive which is surprisingly modern in several respects. The following passage indicates the extent to which power holders may corrupt communication and create an ideology favorable to themselves (1651, p. 67):

> For I doubt not, but if it had been a thing contrary to any man's right of dominion, that the three Angles of a Triangle should be equall to two Angles of a Square; that doctrine should have been, if not disputed, yet by the burning of all books of Geometry, suppressed, as farre as he whom it concerned was able.

Extravagant as the example may seem, its resemblance to the deeds of the Nazis and the Soviets is close.

Equally shrewd is his observation of the way in which each man thinks very highly of his own particular ego (1651, p. 82):

> For such is the nature of men, that howsoever they may acknowledge many others to be more witty, or more eloquent, or more learned; Yet they will hardly believe there be many so wise as themselves.

Since all men have a maximum feeling of self-worth and self-satisfaction, then men are by nature equal. "For there is not ordinarily a greater signe of the equall distribution of any thing, than that every man is contented with his share.'' In many respects Hobbes foreshadows modern doctrines of self-esteem, status seeking, and self-regard as pivotal motives, and at the same time perceived the sly operation of what today are called ego-defensive mechanisms.

Many variants of the power doctrine can be found in the nineteenth and twentieth centuries. In Germany two influential proponents were Max Stirner and Nietzsche. Stirner's book, *The Ego and his Own* (1845), anticipated the works of Nietzsche. The latter in his *The Will to Power* (1912 ed., Sec. 702), gives a crisp statement of his position:

> What man wills, what every smallest part of a living organism wills, is a plus of power. Both pleasure and unpleasure are consequences of striving for it.

To Nietzsche, as to McDougall, hedonic states were incidental to a more basic form of motivation. All social behavior, according to Nietzsche, is a direct or disguised reflection of power seeking. Affect is a ''consequence.'' Even the emotion of gratitude is nothing more than a ''good revenge'' one takes to reestablish his own potency in a social relationship. When viewed in the light of man's will to power, his alleged motives of altruism, love of truth, and religion turn out to be hollow shams.

A generation later the doctrine received an empirical and clinical rendering at the hands of the Austrian psychiatrist Alfred Adler (1917), who felt that his teacher and associate, Freud, was neglecting the role of inferiority feelings so often engendered by poor physique or organic defects. The striving for masculinity, overcompensation, a desire ''to confirm one's own value,'' loomed large in Adler's thought. Still later another psychoanalyst, deviating from Freud, declared competition to be even more important than sex striving in causing personality disorders (Horney, 1939), and the philosopher Bertrand Russell (1938) emphasizes the same motive. While present-day psychologists avoid a unitary conceptualization, much current work features the status motive (Williams, 1920), the ego level (Hoppe, 1930), ego involvement (Allport, 1943), self-image (Lecky, 1945). These, and many other writings, lay heavy emphasis upon self-esteem.

The most uncompromising and exhaustive treatment of the ego motive is found in *L'Egoisme,* written by the French biologist, Felix Le Dantec (1918). His approach is evolutionary. Le Dantec argues that fairly stable levels of matter and life have evolved: atoms, molecules, cells, organisms. Each tenaciously seeks to maintain itself. A phagocyte in the bloodstream does not devour disease bacteria ''in order to'' serve the organism as a whole, but simply to maintain itself. Similarly, each individual organism pursues its own good, without reference to society. Try as hard as we may, we cannot evolve a social unit to supplant the individual ego. Each person is interested exclusively in himself; altruism is an illusion. ''To exist at all is to struggle; to survive is to conquer.'' All social varnish is superficial; at bottom the caveman remains. Even the most pious Christian is thrilled and excited by battle and by brute victory.

If this stark account of human motivation is true, one naturally asks, ''How are we to account for society at all, especially for the social institutions that seem to foster cooperation and mutual aid?'' Le Dantec answers: By the existence of common enemies. The basis of all society is *l'ennemi commun*. Even the family is at bottom merely a serviceable unit for common protection. Parents take care of children in order to benefit later, for example, to gain financial support in their old age. The basis of friendships and of ingroups is not love so much as a common fear or common hate. The easiest way to get along with a stranger is to find some person, some group, or some object that both dislike. Allies in wartime place their own selfish interests in abeyance until the common enemy is defeated; then the allies fall out with one another. Indeed, even a single nation has genuine unity only in wartime, when the lives of all its members are threatened. For this reason governments provoke wars.

Yet, Le Dantec continues, we cannot afford to admit that our motives are purely egoistic and that the only basis of social solidarity is common hate and distrust. To do so would weaken further the already precarious fabric of society. Hence a fantastic superstructure of *metaphysical absolutes* has grown up. A metaphysical absolute is any doctrine, taught with the sanctity of tradition, that masks the basic egoism of human life. Conscience is the carrier of such doctrines, and is created by parents and teachers in children in order to preserve the hypocrises that are so essential in social life.

Take, for example, the metaphysical absolutes of religion. The Decalogue, so it seems to Le Dantec, provides a transparent example of social hypocrisy. The first three Commandments require men's obedience to God, and this initial obedience provides the sanction for all remaining Commandments. Le Dantec would agree with Voltaire, who held that no parent could bring up a child without invoking divine sanction. The postulated power of a deity is essential to achieve social control. The Fourth Commandment reveals the point: it says, "Honor thy father and thy mother"—a rule of extreme convenience to parents. The utilitarian nature of this Commandment is betrayed in its additional phrase, "in order that thy days may be long...."

"Thou shalt not kill" is likewise an egoistic rule, meaning, naturally, that thou shalt not kill *me*. Similarly, "Thou shalt not steal" protects the property of the one who teaches the rule. "Thou shalt not bear false witness" grew out of necessity for the ingroup to be relatively truthful. Likewise, the prohibition against coveting is psychologically adroit, for the place to block transgressions is in the attitudes of the would-be transgressor before they issue into action. "Thou shalt not commit adultery" is a Commandment taught with special enthusiasm by those who have sexual partners to those who have not.

Le Dantec's view of human motivation and of social values may seem to an extreme degree to be cynical and dyspeptic. But is it wrong?

Critique
Common to all theories of egoism is one precarious assumption, namely, that the process of social learning never results in a genuine transformation of motives; that is to say, the process of socialization is never truly effective. Le Dantec views socialization as a matter of "deformations of the ego resulting from life in common." "Why 'deformation'?" one may ask. May not social learning result in formation, in conformation, or even in re-formation? Comte held a more optimistic view of socialization, expressed in his Law of Affective Evolution, which says that with time there comes a diminution in the preponderance and intensity of personal inclinations, and a genuine growth and extension of altruistic sentiments.

May it not be that the picture of egoism is more appropriate to the unsocialized being (including the child) than to adults with socialized personalities? Hobbes wrote, "the wicked man is the child grown strong." Unbridled self-assertion may be natural at an early stage in the development of personality, but abnormal at a later stage. Theories of socialization today are split on this same issue: Some hold that the primitive egoistic drives are never modified but only overlaid, or channeled, or "cathected." Others argue for a changing ego structure, wherein new interests become functionally independent of their origins, or where productiveness and maturity effectively inhibit earlier instinctive aggression and pleasure seeking.

It is difficult to strike a proper balance in this matter. On the one hand, we cannot deny that hypocrisies and rationalizations of men concerning their own motives are common. On the other hand, who can say with certainty that the original nature of man does not include some strongly affiliative dispositions? Or that the course of social learning does not result in thoroughgoing transformations of the character structure? While self-love remains positive and active in every man, is it necessary that it should be sovereign with him? We shall resume consideration of these questions in our discussion of sympathy.

SYMPATHY

It is not only rationalists who object to hedonism and egoism as sole explanations of social conduct. Some irrationalists (believers in instinct, urge, inborn nature) join the protest. They argue that self-love is a grossly one-sided principle. Granted that self-love is present in every man, they say it is not necessarily dominant in his nature.

Some even reverse the formula and insist that the human relationship of love or symbiosis is primary; see, for example, Kropotkin (1902), Suttie (1935), and Ashley-Montagu (1950). A basic groundwork of love and trust is established in the early mother-child relationship, and this is essential to all survival. So fundamental is this fact that it is often overlooked by psychologists, who are inclined to glue their attention upon the pattern of hostility and aggression which is perceptible only because it contrasts with the underlying ground of affiliation (see Sorokin, 1950, especially Chapter 5).

Other theorists do not insist that sympathy or affiliation is sovereign, but they agree in giving it a prominent place among social motives. In this section we shall consider the history of this motive, regardless of whether or not it is advanced as the sole explanation of social conduct.

Sympathy, Imitation, Suggestion
First let us note that there is good historical reason why we ought to examine these three fundamental concepts in close succession. In a sense, they compose the principal triumvirate of theories in social psychology. The reason

for their close relationship goes back to Plato. As everyone knows, Plato, like Freud, conceived the human mind as made up of three faculties or "institutions." For Plato, the abdomen was the seat of emotions or feeling; the breast the seat of striving and action; the head the seat of reason and thought. (Society had three parallel classes—slaves, warriors, philosophers.) Throughout the ages this Platonic trichotomy has persisted. Mind, it is said, is constituted of:

> Affection (feeling),
>
> Conation (striving),
>
> Cognition (thought).

Now, it is possible for a psychologist to stress one of these faculties at the expense of others. When a social psychologist does so, seeking in any one of these functions an exclusive (or almost exclusive) explanation of social conduct, he is likely to end up with a simple and sovereign system based on one of three principles:

> Sympathy (affective),
>
> Imitation (conative),
>
> Suggestion (cognitive).

In a certain sense these concepts are interchangeable, in that the phenomena one author would explain by one principle, a different author would explain by another. And occasionally a given author combines two, as when Ross (1908) speaks of the *suggestion-imitation principle*.

Because of this historical linkage, we shall consider the three concepts *seriatim,* starting with the doctrine of sympathy in its various forms.

Proponents of Sympathy

Adam Smith, in his *Wealth of Nations* (1776), gave marked impetus to hedonism and to laissez-faire. Yet his total system of thought demanded an equal emphasis upon human sympathy. The opening sentence of his *Theory of Moral Sentiments* (1759) reads:

> How selfish soever man may be supposed, there are evidently some principles in his nature which interest him in the fortune of others, and render their happiness necessary to him....

Smith distinguished two basic forms of sympathy which most subsequent writers have preserved. First there is the quick, almost reflex, type of response. When we see a person struck with a stick we cringe; when we watch a tightrope walker we grow tense. In these cases we feel as the other person feels and do as he does. Some writers have regarded this mimicry as instinctive. But today we might say that the conditioned-reflex formula covers it well enough: At first we cringe when we are hit, and later we cringe at the visual cues that were initially associated with our own cringing.

The second type of sympathy is more intellectualized. We are able to sympathize with a person even though we do not feel as he feels. We may congratulate the successful and condole the afflicted at times when we feel neither success nor affliction. There are sympathetic bonds between friends even when they are viewing a given situation with unlike emotions.

Smith derived man's sense of justice from the operation of sympathy. Our capacity for sympathy leads us to feel with both the aggressor and the aggrieved. The resulting balance of sympathy determines our final judgment as to where justice lies. Similarly, our judgments of propriety or good taste are the result of weighing a person's emotional expression against the exciting fact. If it seems disproportionate we cannot sympathize, and therefore we judge his response to be improper. These instances indicate how Smith used his favorite principle to explain a large and diversified range of social behavior.

Herbert Spencer. Spencer (1870) distinguished the same two basic forms of sympathy. He called them, respectively, *presentative* (immediate, reflexive) and *representative* (conscious, reflective). For a still more highly intellectualized sentiment (for example, the abstract idea of love as a proper way of life) he coined the term "*re-representative* sympathy." Also, like Smith, he felt that the hedonism and laissez-faire he espoused needed to be softened by a principle that would explain affiliative urges. Society originates in the sex instinct. It leads to the institution of the family, which is the essential unit of survival. Within the family the principle of sympathy takes over: a child survives not because he is strong and fit but because his defenselessness arouses sympathy in others. Spencer, as we have previously seen, argued strongly that this feeling should find its expression only in the family circle and not be allowed to weaken the rugged fiber of the state, which ought to give its rewards to the strong and never to the weak. Gregarious propensities are a mutation in the evolutionary struggle. While they are essential to human survival, they must not lead to coddling. Spencer, as we have said, had no use for the welfare state;

he even opposed free public schools. Let education, he said, be a product of family sympathy, not of public policy.

Peter Kropotkin. The harshness of the "red in tooth and claw" doctrine of evolution led to a marked reaction. In *Mutual Aid* (1902) Kropotkin argued that the mutation of sympathy to which Spencer called attention is the *primary* fact in human evolution. It represents the neglected aspect of Darwinism. Kropotkin's evidence rests chiefly upon anecdotes collected both in time of war and in time of peace. He argued that the mutual aid we see around us is not based upon love for specific individuals, but rather upon a broad instinct of *human solidarity*. A more modern book that in many respects restates Kropotkin's position is Ashley-Montagu's *On Being Human* (1950).

Gregariousness. Many authors have postulated, as Kropotkin did, a protean social instinct. Sociologists especially have done so, in order that this broad psychological foundation might support their differentiated theories of social structure and functioning. For Giddings there was a basic *consciousness of kind* compounded of organic sympathy, the perception of resemblance, conscious or reflective sympathy, affection, and the desire for recognition. "To trace the operation of the consciousness of kind through all its social manifestations is to work out a complete subjective interpretation of society" (1896, p. 19).

During the First World War, Trotter published his *Instincts of the Herd in Peace and War* (1916), which postulated a similar basic explanatory propensity. In it Trotter argued somewhat chauvinistically in favor of the English variant of this instinct as against the German. While McDougall (1908) likewise postulated a gregarious instinct, he did not derive all social conduct from this single source. The parental instinct, the instinct of appeal, and other instincts too have social reference. When about 1920 a sharp reaction set in against the instinct doctrine, gregariousness all but disappeared as a postulate from social psychology. Virtually no writer today employs it as an explanatory principle. The present trend is toward an experimental analysis of affiliative behavior (see Schachter, 1959).

Primitive Passive Sympathy
Before leaving instinctivist explanations, it is necessary to call attention to McDougall's theory of the *sympathetic induction of emotion* or, as he preferred to call it, *primitive passive sympathy* (1908). He states his views as follows (14th edition, p. 98):

> We must not say, as many authors have done, that sympathy is due to an instinct, but rather that sympathy is founded upon a special adaptation of the receptive side of each of the principal instinctive dispositions, an adaptation that renders each instinct capable of being excited on the perception of the bodily expressions of the excitement of the same instinct in other persons.

In other words, if I perceive expressions of rage in another, this perception is likely to arouse my own instinct of anger. There are two keys that will unlock every instinct: one is the "biologically adequate" cause; the other is the perception of the instinct in action in another person. The reader may rightly ask, "Would not this formula lay all of us open to too much induced emotion? Should we not constantly be suffering instinctive seizures vicariously?" McDougall escapes this dilemma in an interesting fashion. He brings laughter into the picture. Laughter is a device by which we avoid excessive sympathy. Byron wrote, "If I laugh at any mortal thing, 'tis that I may not weep." McDougall heartily agrees, and adds that laughter saves us not only from depression and grief, but from all other forms of vicarious sympathy as well.

The Phenomenological Approach
Theodore Ribot, in his *Psychology of the Emotions* (1897), gave great prominence to sympathy, which he called "the foundation of all social existence." He was not content with the two forms which most writers recognize, but postulated three. The first is the primitive or automatic type that we have suggested might be regarded as an instance of conditioned response. The second is reflective in that the individual is self-conscious concerning his state of mind. He knows that he feels for the other person even if the suffering is not his. The third is an intellectualized sentiment of loyalty, tolerance, or philanthropy, far broader in type than any specific instance of fellow-feeling. His three grades are similar to, if not identical with, Spencer's.

Ribot's approach was phenomenological. He asked: What are the diverse forms of experience or "intentions" that men have, to which the single and inadequate label *sympathy* is applied? Are we dealing here with a simple unitary process, or with a term covering various types of mental acts?

Max Scheler. The phenomenological approach reaches its climax in Max Scheler's *Wesen und Formen der Sympathie* (1923). The German language is far more flexible than the English or French in dealing with this particular subject. A secondary account may be found in Becker (1931). There are, according to Scheler, eight forms of sympathetic orientation (or acts). For most of them clear English equivalents are lacking.

The first three are of a low grade, really *pseudosympathy,* since in these cases the focus is upon the subject's own feeling and not upon his feeling *with* or *for* others.

1. *Einfühlung* is the primitive, reflex process mentioned by Smith, Spencer, Ribot, and others. The term "empathy" is a fair translation, provided it is understood to mean only elementary motor mimicry and is not employed in the broad sense of "an ability to understand people," as is sometimes the case today.

2. *Miteinanderfühlung* calls attention to a condition of "simultaneous feeling," as in the case of two or more people reacting in a similar way to the same stimulus (for example, an attentive and emotional cinema audience).

3. *Gefühlsansteckung* refers to the spread of feeling through social induction and facilitation, as in a mob, panic, or throng. It likewise includes McDougall's sympathetic induction of emotion. Such "transpathy" is still focused upon the affective experience of the individual, and is not truly sympathetic.

Higher levels of sympathy are found in:

4. *Einsfühlung,* wherein occurs an identification of feeling: the child playing with a doll identifies with her mother; citizens in wartime feel united in suffering and in aim. There is an especially high degree of such "unipathy" between lovers who feel keenly the joys and sorrows of each other.

5. *Nachfühlung* is far more conscious and detached. We encounter it in the statement, "I know just how you feel." In such a case, however, we distinguish clearly our own feeling from another's. We may even add, "I know how you feel, but I wouldn't act as you are acting." This state of mind is Adam Smith's *intellectualized* or Ribot's *reflective* sympathy.

6. *Mitgefühl,* or fellow-feeling, refers to an act of participation in another's emotional state. If my friend has lost his mother through death I can experience an affiliative sorrow. But *my* commiseration (*Mitleid*) and *his* suffering are phenomenologically two different facts.

7. *Menschenliebe* is the level of sentiment recognized explicitly by Ribot and McDougall. One not only senses the other person's state of mind, but prizes it and respects it. Altruism and philanthropy belong to this class.

8. *Akosmistische Person- und Gottesliebe* ("unworldly sympathy") refers to the sense of mystical sympathy that characterizes some people's religious orientation to life as a whole: "a unity of all finite spirits in God."

Scheler's phenomenological analysis has not been surpassed in subtlety. Besides being valuable in its own right, it illustrates the important fact that psychological analysis depends to a considerable degree upon the categories of language available to the analyst.

Empirical Work

It was not until the decade of the 1930s that sustained attempts were made to study the problems of sympathy on an empirical basis. Freudian theory, World War I, and the prevailing temper of irrationalist theories had focused attention earlier upon aggressive behavior. But during the business depression, interest in cooperative conduct rose. A summary of work prior to the late 1930s is found in May and Doob (1937), and pertinent anthropological evidence is presented by Mead (1937).

Employing the method of observation, Lois Murphy (1937) analyzed five thousand episodes of behavior in a nursery school. While aggressive acts were much more numerous than sympathetic acts, she found that the latter occurred with considerable frequency, chiefly among children who felt psychologically secure, who themselves had had an experience similar to that evoking their sympathy, and among children who came from certain types of cultural surroundings.

In recent years considerable relevant work has been added, although the concept of *sympathy* or even of *cooperation* is seldom used, probably because their flavor is moralistic rather than scientific. But much of the current research in group dynamics, in industrial relations, in the psychological aspects of group tensions, and in psychotherapy represents an empirically action-oriented extension of the movement we have here surveyed. The interested reader will find guidance in Leighton (1945), Pear (1950), Chase (1951), Maier (1952), Sorokin (1950), and Schachter (1959).

It still remains true, however, that psychologists, in their research and in their theory, devote far more attention to aggressive, hostile, prejudiced behavior than to the softer acts of sympathy and love, which are equally important ingredients of social life. As Suttie (1935) says, there has been a strange "flight from tenderness."

IMITATION

Social psychologists are required to explain the overwhelming fact of social conformity in human behavior. Parents set models to which children conform; fashions are models to which adults conform; and culture itself is a model to which everyone (or nearly everyone) conforms. No problem in social psychology is more insistent. The term *imitation* designates the problem, but does not solve it.

Certain nineteenth-century writers, however, saw in imitation a simple and sovereign principle suited to explain all conformity. One single force was thought to provide both the motive and the means. Walter Bagehot (1826–1877) represents this point of view (1875, p. 36):

> At first a sort of "chance predominance" made a model, and then invincible attraction, the necessity which rules all but the strongest men to imitate what is before their eyes, and to be what they are expected to be, moulded men by that model.

Imitation is thus the conserving agency in society accounting for the "cake of custom" that binds all but the strongest men. It accounts for the "sameness" in savage societies, for the mimicry of children, for the gregariousness of species. Since conformity behavior is the result of "invincible attraction" the really critical problem lies in invention and novelty. Inventive departures from conformity Bagehot accounted for by the activity of "strong men," whom he also called "nation builders."

More extended was the treatment given by the French author Tarde (1843–1904). For him, as for his British contemporary, imitation was "the key to the social mystery." Enthusiastically he asserts, "Society is imitation" (1903, p. 74). Among Tarde's famous laws of imitation are those listed below.

1. The *law of descent* maintains that superior classes are imitated by the socially inferior. Fads, we might note today, start in Paris or on Park Avenue and die on the counters of the dime stores.

2. The *law of geometrical progression* calls attention to the rapid dissemination of a fashion, rumor, or craze from the point of origin.

3. The *law of the internal before the exotic* helps to account for the fact that one's own culture is imitated in preference to foreign cultures.

About the process of imitation itself Tarde has little to say. He likens it to a hypnotic dream state—to somnambulism, which runs its course under the dominance of photographic images formed by the model in people's minds. This formulation runs parallel to the concept of *suggestion,* equally prominent in French social psychology of the same period (for example, Charcot, Le Bon).

Novelty and invention, according to Tarde, are the result of conflicting imitations. All opposition is a matter of clash between contrary models. Competition, discussion, war are the three great forms of social opposition; they arise because contrary models are being imitated simultaneously.

Unlike his countryman Durkheim, Tarde was an individualist. He once wrote to Baldwin in America, "your point of arrival is my point of departure," by which he meant that Baldwin's treatment of imitation as a specific mechanism in each individual person is the foundation upon which Tarde himself would build his more sweeping sociology of imitation.

Baldwin found in imitation the key to mental development in the child (1895, 1897). His account calls attention to the fact that there seem to be at least two forms of imitation—nondeliberate and deliberate (we might say today conditioned reflex and insightful). This process of development involves three stages. In the *projective* stage the child receives impressions of a model as a photographic plate receives an image. (The meaning of "projective" here differs from the modern use of the term.) In the *subjective* stage the child tends to assume the movements, strains, and attitudes of the model. He is "a veritable copying machine" and cannot help doing so. It should be noted that at this crucial stage in the process Baldwin seems to rely on the little understood tendency to elementary motor mimicry. He also calls attention to the large amount of self-imitation in infancy (circular reflex activity) which contributes to the repetitiousness of a child's behavior. Finally, in the *ejective* stage the child reaches a comprehension of the model—he may recognize that he is acting like the other; he knows how the other feels. Here imitation is an avenue to knowledge of the *alter.*

Mead (1934) went beyond Baldwin's ejective stage. We do more than imitate, he said. We perceive what the other is doing (through ejective imitation) but we also perceive our own response to it. What occurs is an interweaving process. Each act is the resultant both of our role assumption and of our self-perceptions. There follows, therefore, a "conversation of gestures" from which emerge mutual understanding and continual accommodation and adjustment of two people's sets of interests. In the process, language is of the highest importance, and "significant symbols" become a substitute for gross motor adjustment. Mead's theory of socialization is not exclusively "imitationist"; yet his point of departure lies in the same tradition.

Reference should be made to the tendency of many writers to include an *instinct of imitation* among the potpourri of motives postulated in man's original nature. William James did so (1890). Bernard (1926) shows that the acceptance of an instinct of imitation, as one innate motive among many others, has been a common but sterile practice in the history of social and psychological science.

The writers we have mentioned, with the possible exception of Mead, regard imitation as having motivational force. Later writers tended to shift their attention away from the "why" of imitative behavior to the "how." Imitation is regarded merely as a means by which other motives reach their goal. McDougall perceived this issue clearly. He felt that, unlike true instincts, imitation has little or no "urge" character, and no specific goal. It seemed to him to be rather a *nonspecific innate tendency* (1908, Chapter 4). In this respect it should be classed with play, and also with *primitive passive sympathy* which we have previously discussed. Yet McDougall was much troubled by the process of precision which enables a child (or a parrot) to accommodate his vocal sounds to a model, as well as by the manifest tendency of spectators to assume the postural strains of the dancers or athletes they are watching, and also by the child's tendency to take over the tensions of an adult into his own motor (and emotional) conduct. Blanton and Blanton (1927) emphasize the importance of postural tensions in the mother which tend to be assumed even by an infant in arms, so that a mother's fear becomes the child's fear.

This process of *empathy* remains a riddle in social psychology. It would seem to be genetically and conceptually basic to social learning and to lie at the heart of any theory of imitation. Some motor mimicry, as we have said, seems reducible to previous conditioning, but in other cases it appears to precede and to be a precondition of learning. The nature of the mechanism is not yet understood. It is obvious that the process of perception itself entails motor adjustments (for example, of the eyes) that are *imitative* of certain properties of the perceived object. This fact may give the clue we need. The problem is discussed further by Lipps (1907) and by G. W. Allport (1961, pp. 533–537).

Most accounts of the "how" of imitation do not reach back to this simple empathic phenomenon. Many authors lean on the *ideomotor theory,* which Cooley (1902, pp. 62f) states as follows:

> It is a doctrine now generally taught by psychologists that the idea of an action is itself a motive to that action and tends intrinsically to produce it unless something intervenes to prevent it. This being the case, it would appear that we must always have some impulse to do what we see done, provided it is something we understand sufficiently to be able to form a definite idea of doing it.

The ideomotor theory is no longer "generally taught." But its potential value as an explanation of imitation, if it were true, would be great. It says, simply, that all "ideas" press toward expression. Since many of our ideas come while we are observing other people (or things), it follows that we tend to act out (imitate) our perception of the stimulus pattern. Although we cannot say that this theory is without merit, it is coarse and needs considerable refinement and modernization.

When idea psychology declined and behaviorism arose, an explanation of imitative behavior was sought in the properties of the *conditioned reflex.* Classical (Pavlovian) conditioning is represented in the theories of Humphrey (1921), F. H. Allport (1924), and Holt (1931). Let us take Holt's statement of the matter in his formulation (1931, p. 112) of what he calls the "echo principle":

> A child will learn to echo back any action of another provided that another's performance of the act stimulates any of the child's sense organs at a moment when the child is engaged in a (random) performance of the same act.

To illustrate, let us take the infant's early game of pat-a-cake. The theory assumes that first the child is moving his hands randomly in a clapping manner. The fact that he does so repetitively is an important initial fact, for the circular reflex involved provides a longer base in time for the conditioning to take hold. Perceiving this action, the parent likewise claps his hands (note that the parent is the first "imitator") and says "pat-a-cake." Thereafter the child tends to clap his hands when he sees the action or hears the words "pat-a-cake."

While trying to keep the simplicity of a stimulus-response view of the matter, later authors regard the formula of classical conditioning as inadequate, and prefer to look at the phenomenon in terms of *instrumental* (also called *operant*) *conditioning,* or "*reinforcement.*" According to this approach, imitation is learned because it brings rewards and satisfactions. The young boy, for example, will develop a generalized tendency to imitate his brother when he finds that candy, comfort, and other desirable consequences follow his (at first accidental) imitation of his brother's behavior. This *matched-dependent relationship* is regarded by Miller and Dollard (1941) as accounting for most forms of imitation. It encounters some difficulties when applied to the process of deliberate, conscious copying; and it does not seem to apply to the elementary phenomenon of motor mimicry in infants, that is, mimicry prior to reward or satisfaction.

Gestalt psychologists (Köhler, 1927; Asch, 1952, Chapter 16) doubt that a conditioned imitative tendency can be established even with the aid of reward. Apes as well as human beings seem normally to require a *comprehension* of the means-end relationship represented by a model before they adopt it. An organism directed to a goal will reproduce in the motor sphere what he sees in a model *only* if he has familiarity with the situation and sees the relevance of the model for his goal. In this type of theory we are dealing with conscious and deliberate copying, which to some psychologists presumes "insight" or some other "cognitive" principle of learning.

Turning from the cognitive to the emotional level, we encounter the familiar concept *identification.* The term obviously refers to *affective* imitation. The boy identifies with the father, the bobby-soxer with an actress, the Negro with his race, and the humanitarian with mankind. This broad term is the key concept in psychoanalytic explanations of socialization (conformity) of the child. He is said to learn his morality and basic character structure through emotional imitation of the parent and other authority figures. Freud (1921) makes the interesting suggestion that people who have no particular emotional significance for us are understood through empathy, but those who are of emotional value to us are understood through identification.

Finally, we call attention to the importance of imitation in cultural anthropology. Wissler has said that without assuming some imitative process it would be hard to imagine how men could possess a culture, "for it must be perpetuated by the imitation of the older by the younger members of the group" (1923, p. 206). The *diffusionists* in anthropology are accused of exaggerating the extent of imitative adoption of culture traits. Anthropologists who argue for "multiple origin" say that much apparent imitation is specious. They say that similarly constructed people with similar needs will do the same things and produce the same inventions, without imitation being involved. The same caution can extend to everyday behavior. Children and adults may do the same thing under similar provocation without in reality imitating at all.

SUMMARY

The reader who finds this survey uncomfortably condensed will profit from reading the second Appendix to Miller and Dollard, *Social Learning and Imitation* (1941).

Imitation is a protean concept. Its definition must inevitably remain exceedingly broad. *The term refers to any occasion where a stimulus situation gives rise to motor activity of a sort that resembles the stimulus situation.* Since various types of processes may have this broad result, we may well suspect that there is no single entity. Investigators and writers have called attention to at least five apparently distinct mechanisms that may be involved:

1. Motor mimicry (empathy), basically a perceptual motor reaction at present not fully understood (Lipps, McDougall, Blanton and Blanton).

2. Classical conditioning, including the echo principle (Holt, Humphrey, F. H. Allport).

3. Instrumental conditioning, emphasizing the rewards involved in engendering either specific or generalized imitative habits (Miller and Dollard).

4. Cognitive structuring, including all instances of deliberate copying and insightful reproduction (Köhler, Asch).

5. Identification, having at present various meanings, but emphasizing the emotional disposition of the whole person to resemble some model (Freud; White, 1963).

Although it is not impossible that these processes may in time be successfully reduced to a single formula, the prospect seems most unlikely.

As for earlier writers on the subject, we may declare that their interest lay primarily in the societal consequences of imitation. Though they tended to postulate a sovereign motive and mechanism, their real concern was with the social results of conformity (Bagehot, Tarde, and to some extent Baldwin, Mead, Cooley). Eventually, of course, the sociology of conformity will receive illumination from the mechanisms of imitation when these are more fully understood, but for the time being it is well to view the problems as distinct. The sociology of conformity must wait for an improved psychology of the processes that result in similar or same behavior.

SUGGESTION

As we have pointed out, sympathy, imitation, and suggestion are the "big three." Between them, these concepts have dominated much of the systematic social psychology of the past. The differences among them, as we have said, reflect the preference of authors for emphasizing the functions of *affection, conation,* or *cognition,* respectively.

The cognitive flavor of the term *suggestion* stands out clearly in McDougall's definition (1908, p. 100):

> Suggestion is a process of communication resulting in the acceptance with conviction of the communicated proposition in the absence of logically adequate grounds for its acceptance.

McDougall held that the dynamics of the process lay in man's instinct of *submission;* this instinct is aroused by any person or symbol having prestige, and accounts for our yielding to communicated propositions "in the absence of logically adequate grounds."

Historically considered, suggestion is the most important of the three concepts. This is true even though its impact on social psychology was not felt until about 1890. But so persuasive at that time was the work of Charcot, Le Bon, Sighele, Sidis, and others, that nearly all the problems in social psychology became formulated both for scientists and for laymen in terms of suggestion. Even today the layman inclines to think of the whole field of social behavior as a matter of "mass mind," "mob hysteria," "power of suggestion." The concept brought about a marriage between abnormal and social psycholo-

gy. While the union has cooled, it has not entirely dissolved.

The process of suggestion has been explained in various ways, chiefly in terms of the following:

1. Animal magnetism (mesmerism).

2. Ideomotor response.

3. Dissociation of consciousness.

4. Association of ideas, redintegration, conditioning.

5. Reduction of determining tendencies.

6. Identification.

7. Cognitive restructuring.

Such explanations pertain to both suggestion and hypnotism, for most writers regard hypnotism as nothing more than an extreme instance of the suggestive process. The early history of these concepts is well reviewed by Boring (1929, 1950).

Animal Magnetism

This was the vague formula offered by Mesmer (1779). By "magnetizing" a wand or a tube Mesmer found that when subjects in his seances touched these instruments they fell into trances and became obedient to his voice. Even in his day Mesmer's magnetic explanation was severely questioned. Yet his subjects did go into trances, and cures of neurotic ills did result. Mesmerism was a fact, however queer its trappings and theory.

Ideomotor Response

Braid (1843) rejected Mesmer, and invented the term *hypnotism* to describe the phenomenon under dispute. He noted the importance of sensory fixation. Hypnotism must start with a limitation of the field of consciousness. Sensory fixation is followed by a restriction of ideas, a process he called *monoideism.* An idea firmly planted in the patient's mind takes root and issues into motor behavior. Surgeons of the day were greatly interested, for in the era prior to anesthetics it seemed a hopeful possibility that ideas planted in a patient's mind through hypnosis might dull the pain of the knife.

It is important to recall here that much nineteenth-century psychology was dominated by the concept of *idea.* One heard of the mechanics of ideas, of the association of ideas, and of ideomotor action. Herbart, Kant's successor at Königsberg, was a dominating figure. His influence on educational practice was immense. Because of it, nineteenth-century educational psychology became largely a matter of planting the right ideas (for example, by means of copybooks) in children's minds, the hope being that such ideas would issue into right actions. In this period Michael Faraday (1853) tried to improve "the morbid condition of public thought" by pointing out that table tipping and other spiritualistic phenomena could easily be explained by the subtle effects of the idea upon physical movement. The direct issuing of ideas of movement into action became known as *dynamogenesis,* and was regarded as a special case of the ideomotor theory. The high repute of the theory as late as the time of William James is seen in his enthusiastic endorsement (1890, II, p. 526):

> We may then lay it down for certain that every representation [idea] of a movement awakens in some degree the actual movement which is its object.

Liébeault (1866) published an important work in which he explicitly introduced the concept of *suggestion,* insisting that the process was identical with hypnotism, and that all people could under favorable conditions be hypnotized. To him suggestion was merely the acting out of an idea planted with *rapport* in a field of limited attention. This emphasis on rapport anticipates McDougall's claim that the submissive instinct is aroused in all cases of suggestibility, and also Freud's still heavier stress on identification as essential to the state of rapport that makes suggestible behavior possible.

Bernheim (1884) followed Liébeault in his thinking, and through his direction of the Nancy school of psychiatry he was influential in establishing suggestive psychotherapy based on the view that suggestion is an essentially normal ideomotor process. It is interesting to note that Freud himself translated Bernheim's book into German, although his own thinking later departed widely from Bernheim's.

Dissociation of Consciousness

Opposition to the theories of the Nancy school sprang up in Paris at the school of Salpêtrière, headed by Jean Martin Charcot (*Oeuvres complètes,* 1888–1894). As a persuasive and dramatic clinician, Charcot demonstrated to gaping audiences the phenomenon of the hysteric splitting of personality under hypnosis. Unlike the Nancy school, he maintained that only hysteric personalities could be hypnotized (hence hypnosis and normal

suggestion do not form a continuum). Some of Charcot's students, Pierre Janet and Boris Sidis, for example, modified this extreme position. Sidis (1898) regarded hypnotism as *abnormal suggestibility,* marked by deep dissociation and disaggregation of consciousness. By contrast, *normal suggestibility* falls short of true hypnotism, but is also a matter of splitting off, to a slighter extent, the waking, guiding, controlling, guardian consciousness from the automatic, reflex, subconscious self. Abnormal suggestibility can be induced through direct commands ("You are falling asleep"); the normal person, however, tends to resist direct command and to respond only to subtle indirect suggestions introduced at the "psychological moment" ("Tommy, it's bedtime"). Sidis sums up his views under three laws:

1. Suggestibility varies directly with dissociation of consciousness and inversely with unification of consciousness.

2. Normal suggestibility varies directly with indirectness of suggestion and inversely with directness of suggestion.

3. Abnormal suggestibility, that is, hypnotizability, varies directly with directness of suggestion and inversely with indirectness of suggestion.

Charcot's influence on clinical psychiatry was, of course, very great, both through students who followed his teaching closely (Morton Prince), and those who departed from it or reacted against it (Janet, Sidis, Binet, Freud). Equally great was his influence upon social psychologists, who found in the doctrine of dissociation an explanation for crowd phenomena, mobs, mass hysteria, and demagogic leadership. Perhaps the most influential book ever written in social psychology is Le Bon's *The Crowd* (1895); it is a direct product of Charcot's teaching. Later we shall speak of it more fully.

This school of thought took a grim view of man's subconscious nature. Whether released through hypnosis, hysteric seizure, or mob conditions, the automatic, subconscious self is an antisocial actor. In 1886 Robert Louis Stevenson immortalized the Charcotian view in *The Strange Case of Dr. Jekyll and Mr. Hyde,* clear evidence that the dramatic teachings of the Salpêtrière school had by that time become international public property. A decade or two later, in spite of Freud's rejection of Charcot's formulations, his concept of the unconscious *id* took over the same essential function as

Charcot's split-off subconscious self. This concept like-wise became public property, and has helped maintain the supremacy of irrationalism in clinical, academic, and popular psychology to the present day.

Starting about 1890, many writers, as we have said, enthusiastically applied the concept of dissociation to social behavior, thus bringing about the marriage between abnormal and social psychology. Charcot's pupil, Morton Prince, found it entirely natural to enlarge the scope of the *Journal of Abnormal Psychology* which he had established in 1908, and to rechristen it in 1922 as the *Journal of Abnormal and Social Psychology.* He regarded the two fields as indissolubly linked. For practical reasons of size, and not on theoretical grounds, the *Journal* split into two separate periodicals in 1965—one reverting to the original title, the other becoming the *Journal of Personality and Social Psychology.*

Association, Redintegration, Conditioning
A more conventional type of theorizing keeps suggestion safely within the confines of simple associationism. A stimulus *suggests,* that is, touches off, a particular idea (determining tendency, brain path) which leads to a particular response. For a fisherman a sunny day in springtime suggests fishing. The Scottish psychologist, Thomas Brown (1820), employed the term "suggestion" as wholly equivalent to "association." Bernheim (1884) of the Nancy school, although he recognized the importance of rapport and of ideomotor response, also agreed that every impression, every mental picture, every association was a suggestion. Only slightly different is Titchener's statement that "a suggestion is any stimulus, external or internal, accompanied or unaccompanied by consciousness, which touches off a determining tendency" (1916, p. 450).

A variant of this view makes suggestion a matter of *redintegration.* A previously formed disposition of a highly complex order can be rearoused as a whole by an associated cue. The sunny springtime day is the cue; "going fishing" is the complex activated response. Hamilton (1859) first called attention to this "part-arousing-the-whole" relationship in association. More recently Hollingworth (1920) used it extensively to account for suggestibility in both normal and abnormal subjects.

The concept of the *conditioned response* is closely related to this line of thought. Suggestions are conditioned cues, and the process involved is simply the reacti-

vation of a motor pathway to which the cue has been conditioned. "Tom, go to bed" (direct suggestion) and "Tom, it is bedtime" (indirect suggestion) are cues intended to reactivate Tom's nocturnal habits. This view is found in all behavioristic treatments of social phenomena, such as those of F. H. Allport (1924), Bechterew (1932), and Hull (1934).

The manifest difficulty with these treatments is that they fail to distinguish suggestion from any other process of association of ideas, or from any other stimulus-response sequence. While it is undoubtedly true that suggestion should properly be viewed as a type of associative phenomenon, how are we to distinguish it from other types of association?

Reduction of Determining Tendencies
The distinction required is offered in Warren's (1934) *Dictionary of Psychology,* where he indicates that a suggestion is a

> . . . stimulus, usually verbal in nature, by which one individual seeks to arouse action in another by circumventing the critical, integrative functions.

We have already cited McDougall's similar definition, which refers to the acceptance of a proposition without logically adequate grounds. In these and in similar definitions, attention is called to a restriction in the determinants of behavior. The individual is not employing all relevant ideas, nor his full intelligence. He is for the moment acting without full self-determination. Granted that suggestion proceeds according to the laws of association (conditioning), still we must also allow for the *blocking* of normal associations; thus the end result in behavior is due to a selected field of determinants. Braid, we have noted, labeled this restriction *monoideism.* When we speak of "reduction of determining tendencies" we are not, of course, referring to the sheer number of associations present, but to a functional restriction of the brain field by which the "critical, integrative" functions are circumvented.

Let us take the case of a man who buys a suit of clothes under the persuasion of a silver-tongued salesman. The seller points out its virtues in terms of fashion, flattering fit, and comfort. Bombarded by these arguments the customer yields to persuasion; but he has not given due weight to equally relevant considerations that might have blocked the purchase—expense, specific wardrobe needs, and personal preference. Even though the salesman may have introduced *more* determining tendencies than the buyer initially possessed, yet, functionally speaking, the salesman has reduced the *effective* determinants. The buyer's purchase is therefore partly, if not altogether, the result of suggestion.

Around the turn of the century a great deal of psychological thought and writing was ordered in accordance with the concept of suggestion. Many books and articles dealt with automatisms, dissociation, hysteria, and similar matters. Against this background Binet (1900) made two significant contributions. He reacted against hypnosis, agreeing with Wundt that its use was immoral, and sought instead for "inoffensive" methods by which to explore "normal suggestibility." In so doing he leaned away from Charcot and toward Bernheim. His second contribution had to do with his invention of experimental methods. He presented children with lines, with drawings, with questionnaires in such a way that some strong *idées directrices* were planted in their minds. Later they were asked to reproduce the stimuli, with the result that specific distortions occurred in the direction of the implanted idea. In group behavior he observed the effects of prestige among children. The leaders in his experimental groups of children proved to be less suggestible than the followers. Owing largely to Binet's efforts, suggestion became a standard problem for academic as well as clinical psychology.

One favorite problem had to do with the conditions of suggestibilty. Who is suggestible? The answers given, as summarized by Ross (1908), include several dubious assertions. Certain species of animals (sheep, for example) are more suggestible than others; certain "races" (Frenchmen and Slavs) are more suggestible than others (Anglo-Saxons); children more so than adults; women more so than men. People are suggestible if they are temperamentally absent-minded or in a state of emotion (Othello's jealousy). They are vulnerable toward sources possessing prestige, and toward often repeated assertions; and they are especially suggestible in crowds.

These are bold and unproved propositions. Only in recent years have detailed studies been made (employing the term *persuasibility* rather than *suggestibility*). Hovland and Janis (1959) conclude that to some extent persuasibility is content-bound. Thus a woman may be persuasible with respect to investments, but not with respect to keeping her house. At the same time there is good evidence that suggestibility is often a general trait. A person who yields to verbal persuasion in one direction is

likely (but by no means certain) to yield to other verbal persuasions.

Cantril has clarified the dynamics of the process. He states that suggestion occurs especially when the individual is confronted by a *critical situation* in which he cannot readily make a decision. He will accept the suggested proposition for belief (and action) (1941, pp. 64f):

> (1) if he has no adequate mental context of his own for the interpretation of the event; or (2) when his mental context is so rigidly fixed that the suggestion automatically arouses this context (e.g., a prejudice) and the person fails to examine the situation in its own right. The first condition results from bewilderment; the second from the "will to believe."

To paraphrase this view, a person will act uncritically (with a reduction of determining tendencies) if he is relatively unfamiliar with a topic, unaccustomed or unable to check up on the suggestion offered to him—in short, if his mental organization is *unstructured*. He is likewise prone to accept the suggestion if it fits with his *rigidly structured* stereotypes, thus nourishing and calling into action preexisting attitudes, prejudices, beliefs. An "unstuck" mind and an "overstuck" mind both favor suggestibility.

Within this framework we can fashion an entire psychology of crowd control, demagoguery, and propaganda. Sometimes, for example, leaders try by various devices to "unstructure" people's minds. Demagogues start off by calling attention to the bad state of affairs, to the malfeasance of government, or to the threat of poverty, ill health, failure. When people are sufficiently unsettled by this barrage, the propagandist states his remedy. It is then likely to be accepted as a way out of the confusion. Or, still more frequently, demagogues appeal directly to people's "overstuck" convictions. The propagandist, orator, or advertiser simply associates his product (or message) with preexisting idols (sentiments, prejudices, convictions). It is accepted because it is congruent with the person's preexisting desires and aversions. George Bernard Shaw once defined propaganda as "the organization of idolatry" (the organization of the propagandist's message with an old idol).

Identification

McDougall, as we have seen, invoked the submissive instinct as a necessary link in the suggestion process. The Nancy school felt that good rapport was necessary between *suggestionneur* and *suggestionné*. Freud felt both these views to be pallid. Thoroughly familiar with the theories and therapy of Nancy and Salpêtrière, he rejected completely their concepts of suggestion and hypnosis. There is a deeper reason why a leader attracts followers and is able to mold their behavior—it is because they find in him a love object, one who relates himself to their thwarted sex needs (Freud, 1921). In the case of male groups and crowds (for example, Nazi storm troopers) a deeply repressed homosexual interest is revealed through their passivity toward, and identification with, the leader. What has been called suggestion, especially in mass situations, is in reality a consequence of identification. The theory has been more fully explained, with special reference to the leader-follower relation in wartime, by Waelder (1939). Its merit lies in calling attention to the importance of emotional attachments in bringing about obedient behavior.

Cognitive Restructuring

In recent years considerable skepticism has been expressed concerning the utility, and even the validity, of the concept of suggestion. Asch, for example, has declared flatly that "the case for the doctrine of suggestion has not been proven" (1948, p. 251).

The argument turns on the question whether there is any real difference between conduct that is said to show suggestibility and conduct that is said to show critical ability or full self-determination. Another way to state the issue is in terms of *rationality*. Is the person who seems to us to be suggestible behaving any less rationally, in reality, than the person who seems to us to be nonsuggestible? From their own points of view, both are probably acting in an intelligent way, making the best use they can of the totality of information that confronts them.

One experimental example will suffice to etch this new point of view (which derives from phenomenology and Gestalt psychology). Subjects are asked to think about the following passage, and are told that its author is Thomas Jefferson:

> I hold it that a little rebellion, now and then, is a good thing, and as necessary in the political world as storms are in the physical.

When asked whether they agree with the sentiment expressed, and what it really means to them, subjects generally approve it, and interpret the word "rebellion"

to mean somewhat minor agitation. But when subjects are told that the author is Lenin, they ordinarily repudiate the statement, and interpret the word "rebellion" to mean violent revolution (Asch, 1952, pp. 419–425).

Just what is happening here? The doctrine of suggestion would say that people hold previous emotional attitudes toward Jefferson and Lenin, the former being "good," the latter "bad." Hence the statement when ascribed to Lenin is rejected, for it is not viewed critically in its own right but is responded to only in terms of one's prejudice against Lenin. The selfsame statement is accepted when it "redintegrates" one's veneration for Jefferson. Thus the person is suggestible, reacting not to the statement in its own right but on the basis of preformed attitudes toward its presumed author.

The cognitive theorist, however, points out that the author's name altered the whole meaning of the stimulus. This fact is shown by the subject's tendency to interpret "rebellion" in different ways. If Jefferson wrote the passage he could only have meant by it mild agitation; if Lenin, he surely had in mind violent revolution. Hence it is *not* the "selfsame" passage, evaluated differently because of the suggestive force of the supposed authors' names. Rather, two dissimilar stimuli are evaluated rationally (that is, according to the true meaning of the stimulus in context). As Asch puts it, it is not the judgment of the object that is altered (through suggestion), but the object of judgment is itself altered, and interpreted objectively and rationally.

Whether this line of argument can be extended so far as to eliminate the need for the distinctive concept of suggestion is doubtful. Even in the case cited it seems clear that people's prejudices for Jefferson or against Lenin are active factors in the process of interpretation, and that there is a tendency therefore to react to the statement, not with all one's critical associations, but primarily on the basis of the pattern of reduced determining tendencies activated by the supposed author's name.

The term *cognitive restructuring* does indeed describe (phenomenologically) what seems to happen in all cases of suggestion. We perceive and interpret matters differently in different circumstances. But whether cognitive restructuring is an *explanatory* concept is a question. It serves to warn us that much behavior that seems suggestible and irrational to others is not so from the actor's point of view. He is doing what he can in the given circumstances. Yet the fact remains that in *certain* circumstances his behavior is far more critical and self-determined than in *other* circumstances. Hence, we still need the concept of suggestion to designate behavior that results from a narrow, rather than a full, set of determinants.

Summary

Most, if not all, of the views here surveyed contain some truth. We start with the simple observation that in certain circumstances people act with less critical capacity than in others. When their critical sense is wholly or partly in abeyance we are likely to find a high degree of dominance of one idea or image (monoideism). Dynamogenic tendencies may also be present. Redintegration and conditioning help touch off the decisive determiners of conduct. In extreme cases there may be a hysteric splitting of the personality. In all cases a cognitive restructuring takes place, in the sense that the individual organizes the determinants that are acting upon him. This organization can often be controlled from outside if the proper conditions are present (for example, an unstuck or overstuck mind) and if leaders or manipulators use adroit appeals, aided perhaps by bright trappings (sensory fixation) and eloquence. Rapport, identification, a submissive attitude, and habits of obedience greatly facilitate the process. And as Hovland and Janis (1959) show, insecure personalities are in general suggestion-prone.

Thus suggestion is a complex phenomenon. We need all the insights that history has bequeathed us to construct an adequately comprehensive theory.

THE CROWD

Plato feared democracy because he feared the irrationality of men. In relative solitude they may deliberate wisely, but in the herd their reasoning is defective. "Had every Athenian citizen been a Socrates, every Athenian assembly would still have been a mob." While this suspicion of human collectivities is ancient and recurrent, it was not until the 1890s that a systematic theory of crowd behavior became available.

Le Bon's reliance on suggestion, considered as a hysteric splitting of personality, is seen in the following quotation. In a crowd, he writes (1895, p. 34),

> . . . the individual may be brought into such a condition that, having entirely lost his conscious personality, he obeys all the suggestions of the operator who has deprived him of it, and commits acts in utter contradiction with his character and habits.

Crowd conditions release deep prejudices, racial tradition, and brute instinct. The crowd man (p. 35)

> . . . is no longer conscious of his acts. In his case, as in the case of the hypnotized subject, at the same time that certain faculties are destroyed, others may be brought to a high degree of exaltation. Under the influence of a suggestion, he will undertake the accomplishment of certain acts with irresistible impetuosity.

People in crowds and crowd leaders are given to *action,* never to critical *thought.* When a man joins a crowd he "descends several rungs in the ladder of civilization. Isolated, he may be a cultivated individual; in a crowd, he is a barbarian, that is, a creature acting by instinct" (p. 35). Since Le Bon believed in the excessive suggestibility of women and of certain races, he adds, "Crowds are everywhere distinguished by feminine characteristics, but Latin crowds are the most feminine of all" (p. 44).

Having applied the theory of dissociation to crowd members, Le Bon next considers the attributes of the crowd leader. He is a person who knows how to invoke pointed and clear images "freed from all accessory explanation." Crowds act only on the basis of *image-like ideas.* While these may be accidental and passing, such as an auctioneer or barker might employ to make a sale, more often they are fundamental, deep-lying convictions of an instinctive or quasi-religious order. But in any event the leader will deal only in image-like ideas that point directly to action (ideomotor theory). The leader's immediate tool in the control of ideas is the well-chosen word: "The word is merely the button of an electric bell that calls them up" (p. 118). The word evokes the image, the image evokes a sentiment, the sentiment leads to action. Crowds "are not influenced by reasoning, and can only comprehend rough-and-ready associations of ideas. . . . The laws of logic have no action on crowds" (p. 128). The clever leader will obey the principles of affirmation and repetition. He will assert, not argue; and above all he will, as Hitler later also advised, give his proposition thousandfold repetition. In discussing the elementary principles of crowd control Le Bon set the stage for modern work on demagogic leadership (*cf.* Lowenthal and Guterman, 1949) and on the rules of propaganda (*cf.* Doob, 1935).

It is obvious that Le Bon had a low opinion of the crowd man. He saw crowds as a menace to established institutions. Crowds flourish as civilization declines. He wrote: "The age we are about to enter will in truth be the era of crowds." Masses are bent on destroying society as we know it and harking back to "primitive communism." Was Le Bon thinking prophetically of the fascist and communist upsurges of the twentieth century? Yet for all his apprehension and conservatism Le Bon was unwilling to condemn democracy. While he deplores the irrationality of electoral crowds, of juries, of parliaments, he thinks it well to risk their errors, for in their way crowds do express the basic aspirations of the race, and at times act with a rough heroism.

Sighele's evaluation differed. This Italian writer—whose basic theories were so much like Le Bon's that the two authors fell into a great dispute over priority—said that democracy, because of its crowdish tendency, was an evil. As an Appendix to his *Psychologie des sectes* (1895) he published an essay "Contre le Parlementairisme" which laid one of the cornerstones for later fascistic ideology. Parliaments are crowdish—away with them! Curiously enough Sidis (1898), an American, drew opposite conclusions from similar premises. Like Le Bon and Sighele, he held suggestion to be a basic evil, but he felt that democracy could and should combat its ravages through proper education, so that eventually the decisions of the electorate and of parliaments might be reached on a more rational basis.

There is a systematic character in Sighele's work which merits attention. His three volumes form a logical series: *Le crime à deux* (1893), *La foule criminelle* (1891), and *Psychologie des sectes* (1895). All are saturated with the evils of suggestion. Man's subconscious nature is bestial and criminal. Hence suggestion and criminality are inevitably linked. Like Lombroso and many of his countrymen, Sighele was captivated by the study of crime and other abnormal manifestations of social life. But what is noteworthy about this author is his orderly conception of social psychology. He deals with the dyadic relationship—two individuals bound together as *suggestionneur* and *suggestionné;* with the larger transitory collective of the crowd; and eventually with more organized and enduring groups or *sectes*. No other social psychologist seems to have focused his work at the basic level of the dyad, and then tested his views in relation to progressively larger groupings. The idea is a good one. The dyadic relationship has, however, received extensive treatment by Simmel (1950) and by Heider (1958).

Both Le Bon and Sighele maintain that crowd phenomena do not necessarily require physical proximity.

While most crowds are *congregate,* they may (especially in these days of radio communication) be *consociate.* Even in his day Le Bon observed (1895, p. 27):

> Thousands of isolated individuals may acquire at certain moments, and under the influence of certain violent emotions—such, for example, as a great national event—the characteristics of a psychological crowd.

While it is certainly true that mass phenomena are ordinarily found only in congregate crowds, we must allow for exceptions. There are on record at least two cases of a consociate panic—the result of Orson Welles's broadcast *The War of the Worlds* in the United States in October, 1938 (Cantril, 1940), and in Ecuador in February, 1949 (Britt, 1950, Section 31).

The combined influence of Charcot, Le Bon, Sidis, Sighele, and Tarde blew like a gale upon the American sociologist, E. A. Ross. His *Social Psychology* (1908) brought to a climax this whole vigorous movement. While Ross deals with many of the consequences of suggestion (fashions, crazes, conformity, custom), he regards crowds as the crowning mass phenomenon. In them the strength of *multiplied suggestion* is at its maximum. The individual is "helpless to control his position or movements." Ross's account of crowds is strictly in the tradition we have described, and shares its atmosphere of melodramatic exaggeration.

Turning our attention for a moment from congregate crowds to the cognate phenomenon of "crazes," let us list briefly Ross's laws (1908, p. 76):

1. A craze takes time to develop to its height.

2. The more extensive its ravages, the stronger the type of intellect that will fall prey.

3. The greater its height, the more absurd the propositions that will be believed.

4. One craze is frequently followed by another.

5. Dynamic society (for example, American) is more craze-ridden than one in the ruts of custom.

6. The higher the craze, the sharper the reaction against it.

7. Ethnic or mental homogeneity is favorable to the craze.

Let the reader ask himself the following questions. What would be a good example to illustrate each of these various laws? On what basis did Ross devise them? Are they well-framed scientific propositions? Why, or why not? If the reader will take the time and trouble to carry through this exercise, he will then be in a position to evaluate properly the influential suggestion-imitation school of thought which we have been discussing.

E. D. Martin's *The Behavior of Crowds* (1920) leans on both the Le Bon-Ross tradition and on Freud. From the former the author derives the conviction that "the crowd mind is a phenomenon which should best be classed with dreams, delusions, and the various forms of automatic behavior" (p. 19). From the latter he derives his belief that crowds are agents for the release of repressed impulses. There are hunger crowds, fear crowds (panics), aggressive crowds (mobs), and other emotional masses, each one corresponding to some one long-standing repression that is struggling for an outlet. Under favorable conditions crowds offer a channel for their release. In this sense, therefore, crowds are a safe way for men to "go crazy together." While Freud (1921) would agree in part, we have seen that his theory of suggestion and crowd requires the added attribute of *identification* between the members and their leader.

Panic behavior is surveyed by Schultz (1964), who also gives a useful bibliography of the subject. A broader modern treatment of crowds is offered by Smelser (1963). And finally, the reader is referred to Chapter 35, by Milgram and Toch, in Volume 4 of the present *Handbook*.

THE GROUP MIND

Many authors, past and present, would agree that the interaction of individual minds produces a common manner of thinking, feeling, and willing, different from that of single minds in isolation, and from that of a mere summation of minds.

Yet the phrase "a common manner of thinking, feeling, and willing" is susceptible of various interpretations. In the period 1850–1930, roughly delimited, these interpretations were regarded as so many attempts to solve the problem of the *group mind*. Solutions were offered by sociologists, philosophers, and anthropologists, as well as by psychologists. In recent years the label "group mind" has fallen into disuse, but the same issues remain in new guises. For instance, what is today called a *social institution* is manifestly a common manner of thinking, feeling, willing; so too is a *culture,* and also a *nation*. The problem of the group and the individual, of the one and the many, is still with us. And the solutions of the past, often only thinly disguised, may be found in current theorizing.

A MODERN EXAMPLE

A team of five contemporary authors set out to discover "the functional prerequisites of a society" (Aberle *et al.,* 1950). They defined society (p. 101) as

> . . . a group of human beings sharing a self-sufficient system of action which is capable of existing longer than the life span of an individual, the group being recruited at least in part by the sexual reproduction of the members.

A nation or tribe is an excellent example of a society thus defined. Such a society, the authors argue, cannot endure unless the following conditions are met:

1. There must be provision for adequate relationship to the environment and for sexual recruitment of new members.

2. There must be role differentiation and role assignment, that is, a division of labor to carry out the intricacies of the social organization.

3. Means of communication must exist.

4. The members must share a body of "cognitive orientations," that is, have common modes of thinking.

5. They must share certain goals, that is, have common modes of feeling and willing.

6. There must be normative regulation of means (for example, laws, ceremonials, and customs).

7. Affective states must be regulated (because "the ungoverned expression of lust and rage leads to the disruption of relationships and ultimately to the war of all against all").

8. Socialization must occur (that is, new members must learn the accepted modes of behavior).

9. There must be effective control of disruptive forces (crime, fraud, promiscuity).

These authors write in an ahistorical vein; they make no mention of the venerable problem of the group mind. Yet the issues they treat are precisely those that have led many of their predecessors to argue for the existence of a group mind.

A close parallel may be seen between this list of functional prerequisites for a society and the criteria established for the group mind by McDougall (1920). (Numbers in parentheses refer to items in the above list that parallel McDougall's criteria.):

- Continuity of existence, with the individual replaceable (1).

- Existence of an idea of the group in the minds of members (4, 5).

- Interaction with other groups, especially rivalry and conflict, promoting a group self-sentiment (implied in 3, 4, 5).

- Existence of a body of tradition and customs in the minds of members (implied in 3, 4, 5, 6, 7, 8, 9).

- Specialization of functions and division of labor (2).

Whether we have made an exact parallel with these two sets of criteria is not important. Our point is simply that historical formulations of the group-mind problem are still relevant to current theorizing. Earlier writers struggled to place the individual and his group in proper perspective—so do modern authors. Earlier writers sensed a continuity in the ideas, motives, and habits of the group that was not dependent on the ideas, motives, and habits of any particular individual—and so do modern authors.

The social psychologist is not particularly concerned with the vast amount of ethnological and sociological evidence that may be adduced in support of the social mind. The existence of language, religion, tradition, and nationalism is enough to convince him that a problem exists. What he wants to know is just how the social mind is supposed to operate. *Mind* is his province, and if in any sense at all there is a social or group mind he wants to know its nature and functioning. What then are the leading historical views from which he may make his selection—or upon which he must improve?

While any classification of theories is somewhat arbitrary, it seems helpful to distinguish seven types of emphasis:

1. Analogical doctrines.

2. The collective unconscious.

3. The objective mind.

4. Folk mind.

5. Collective representations.

6. Cultural determinism.

7. Common-segment doctrines.

Occasionally a single author will be found to embrace more than one of these conceptions.

ANALOGICAL DOCTRINES

Throughout the ages men have likened society to an organism. We have already called attention to Plato's psychosocial analogy:

the head—*cognition*—the ruling class

the breast—*conation*—the warrior class

the abdomen—*affection*—the slave class

The first edition of Hobbes's *Leviathan* (1651) carried as its frontispiece a picture of a gigantic human figure made up of smaller men. This simple imagery serves to arouse in our minds the problem that has troubled writers from Plato to the present day. How are we little men related to the Great Being of society? The first relationship that strikes us is one of *similarity*. Little men have thoughts, feelings, will; so too in a sense does the Great Being.

Herbert Spencer (1876) pressed the analogy much further. The nutritive system of society includes agriculture and the productive industries; the circulatory system includes traffic, communication, and the stock exchange; the regulating "brain" consists of the organs of government. With what we may suspect to be wry humor, Spencer ascribed to the House of Commons the functions of the cortex, to the House of Lords the functions of the medulla oblongata. Such analogies were vastly popular among nineteenth-century social theorists.

Some writers, Spencer among them, pointed to limitations in the analogy: society lacks the specific external form that every organism possesses; its parts or "organs" are not in contact with one another and show greater freedom of mobility. Yet more convincing, these writers felt, are the similarities. The social organism, like the individual, has a continuous life history from birth to death; an increasing complexity marks its growth, along with an increasing specialization and differentiation of parts. What is most important of all, one cell (person) may die without disrupting the continuity of the whole. Individuals are replaceable—one perishes and one is born—but the common mental content and functioning of the group continue.

Analogical thinking is by no means a thing of the past. The organismic model still attracts many types of writers. One often reads such statements as the following: "Religion is the heart in the organism of the group mind. If this heart ceases to beat, decay and decomposition set in."—mere metaphor, but helpful in making a point. A more subtle example of current analogical doctrine is seen in Wiener's conception of *cybernetics* (1948). The initial model employed is modern mechanics. The "feedback" machines (for instance, the thermostat) have servomechanisms similar to those of the human body. Both may, for example, become "jammed" through overloading or through faulty clearing. Similarly in society, systems of communication can be overloaded and clog, resulting in "noise." And just as neuroses and compulsions may obtain a monopoly on the nervous system of the individual, so may selfish tycoons buy up and dominate the communication channels of society. Enthusiasts for cybernetics might say that Wiener is really stating universal laws and thus forging a "unity of science"; the same laws of servomechanisms, communication, and noise apply to machines, to man, and to society. But others may see in cybernetics nothing much more than an artful revival of Spencerian thinking.

The same issue arises when we consider General Systems Theory (see von Bertalanffy, 1962). Can all behavior (of the atom, the organism, the group) be ordered to the same basic laws of systems? Or will the attempt end in vague analogizing?

THE COLLECTIVE UNCONSCIOUS

In a sense, all psychologists hold that our conscious mental life is continuous with a subconscious mental life. A few (not many) assert that this subconscious mental life reaches out to embrace more than our own personal experiences. Each person's mind is like an island. While it seems to stand alone, there are subterranean connections via the ocean floor with other islands. The ocean floor can be conceived in a variety of ways. Perhaps it is a "racial unconscious," as Jung would say (1922); perhaps it is the *altman* (the universal soul) of Hindu psychology. Perhaps it is "objective mind" (*objektiver Geist* of

Hegel), the island formations representing so many individuations of one universal psychic system.

William James, though certainly not a Hegelian, employed a similar postulate to account for certain religious experiences, especially the apparent inrush of religious conviction and comfort during moments of prayer or meditation (1902, p. 506):

> The further limits of our being plunge, it seems to me, into an altogether other dimension of existence from the sensible and merely "understandable" world. Name it the mystical region, or the supernatural region, whichever you choose.

To James this metaphysical assumption did not seem farfetched. He wrote at a time when the subconscious self had become an accredited phenomenon. Who could tell the limits of its subliminal reach? He felt that the concept was "exactly the mediating term required" to relate the scientific study of the individual to the superindividual verities of religion. In terms of consciousness we are single individuals, but in terms of subconsciousness each of us has a wider self than he knows.

The metaphysical view here represented is not popular in present-day social psychology. Yet there are those who argue that without some similar doctrine it is hard to explain certain common ideas that occur in the race. Jung's contention, for example, is that certain symbols recur especially in dreams, regardless of specific contact between cultures (1922). For instance, an individual entirely ignorant of Egyptian lore may in his dreams or fantasy employ the scarab as a symbol of immortality. In so doing he dips into a racial unconscious.

THE OBJECTIVE MIND

We need to look more closely at the Hegelian conception of *objektiver Geist,* for it has seeped into much sociological and psychological thinking. Some writers argue that we owe to Hegelian philosophy the beginning of social psychology; for Hegel's system is the true antecedent of all theories that pass beyond individuals and claim that in some sense the social mind is an entity.

According to Hegel's idealistic philosophy there is only one Mind (1807). It is absolute, all-embracing, divine. It works itself out in the course of history. Individual men are but its agents. Its principal focus is in the state, which is therefore the chief agent of divine life on earth. Each state has, in fact *is,* a group mind. It has its own laws of growth and development (the dialectic), and while it makes much use of individuals, it is by no means reducible to their transitory mental life. Hitler, as well as Marx, was among the spiritual children of Hegel. Like Hegel, they equated personal freedom with obedience to the group, morality with discipline, personal growth with the prosperity of the party, class, or state. *Du bist nichts: dein Volk ist alles* was the Nazi rallying cry.

We can trace Hegel's psychological influence in several directions. As we have said, it underlay Karl Marx's exaltation of social class as a superindividual entity. All contemporary Soviet psychology reflects this view (Bauer, 1952). In Britain, Bosanquet (1899) and Green (1900) were among the political philosophers who, following Hegel, viewed the state as an organic mind transcending the component minds of individuals and demanding "sober daily loyalty." It is hardly necessary to point out that psychological apologists for racism and nationalism tend no less than Hegel to apotheosize the group mind, as represented by the state, race, folk, or *Kultur*. Schaeffle (1878), while approaching the matter by way of the organic analogy, went the limit in accepting the nation as an organism in the fullest sense of the word, as capable of having its own goals and purposes, its own pleasures and pains, its own consciousness, and its own right to demand obedience from the individual.

Even without subscribing to the moral aspects of Hegelian philosophy, many social psychologists in Germany have taken up his concept of *Volksgeist*. To them it seems self-evident that a people has a mental unity. In the following section we shall consider *Völkerpsychologie*, which especially busied itself with this problem.

In France, Espinas (1877) set forth a theory of an objective group mind, apparently uninfluenced by Hegel. Individual minds, he held, fuse into a *collective consciousness*. They do so because presentations (ideas) pass rapidly from mind to mind by means of language and gestures; impulses (emotions) are similarly contagious. Thus it is from the normal processes of communication that a group mind is generated. While individual minds are multiple, yet there is engendered a social consciousness capable of knowing itself, and in which each individual participates.

FOLK PSYCHOLOGY

In addition to Hegel, several writers, such as Fichte and von Humboldt, laid the philosophical ground for the concept of *Volk* which gradually emerged in the course of Germany's struggle for unification. By 1860 the concept was ripe for psychological exploitation. At that time three programs for research and theory were laid down, all of them aiming to combine ethnological study with psychological interpretations. Bastian (1860) introduced his concept of *Elementargedanken*—thought forms so basic to the life of a folk that they supply the units of analysis needed for a study of any form of human society. Lazarus and Steinthal (1860) inaugurated the *Zeitschrift für Völkerpsychologie und Sprachwissenschaft*, which had an influential life of thirty years, ceasing publication in 1890. Wundt (1862) wrote his remarkable *Beiträge*, in which he laid down a program of writing and research for himself that should (and did) occupy him for sixty years, reaching its culmination in the publication of ten volumes of his *Völkerpsychologie* (1910–1920). Although these authors worked from the armchair (or "at the green table," as the Germans say), the movement they represented had a lasting influence on social science. In Germany, Thurnwald (1925–1935), and in America, Judd (1926) and Goldenweiser (1933) are at least in part representatives of the tradition.

Some years later England picked up the thread with empirically skilled fingers. The conviction that anthropology needs psychology found its first expression in authentic collaborative field work. In 1898 the Cambridge Anthropological Expedition to Torres Straits enlisted in its field staff three trained experimental psychologists, W. H. R. Rivers, W. McDougall, and C. S. Myers. Here for the first time a study with laboratory equipment was made of preliterate peoples under their ordinary conditions of life. The expedition was a landmark in the collaboration of social scientists. The spirit of this historic research is still alive and expanding. Today ethnologists often borrow both theory and methods from psychology, and psychologists in turn are growing more and more aware of the need for testing their hypotheses cross-culturally. In this connection one thinks of the work of Freud (1913), Bartlett (1923), Roheim (1925), Rivers (1926), Malinowski (1944), and Kluckhohn and Strodtbeck (1961), to mention only a few. It is not difficult to account for the interdependence of social psychology and ethnology (cultural anthropology). Taken by itself, ethnology lacks a theory of the motives and capacities of men; whereas social psychology by itself cannot state the cultural models to which men's motives and capacities tend to conform.

Lazarus and Steinthal were a collaborative pair, an anthropologist and a philologist, primarily interested in a comparative characterology of peoples. Each people, they held, has its own *Volksgeist*. This *Geist* they defined in the opening volume of their Journal (1860) as "a similar consciousness of many individuals, plus an awareness of this similarity, arising through similar descent and spatial proximity." In this definition we may, if we wish, see merely a mild nominalism. The reality of the group mind is not transcendental, it is only a matter of similarities of individual minds plus a recognition of these similarities. But, unfortunately, this easily intelligible concept was not consistently maintained. In most of their discourse Lazarus and Steinthal spoke of the *Volksgeist* in true Hegelian fashion as a metaphysical entity standing over against the individual mind. This type of double-talk was apparently encouraged by the influence of Herbart, whom the authors followed. Herbart had written an essay proposing that the static and dynamic conditions of the individual mind have parallels in the statics and dynamics of the state (1821). Just as ideas might rise above, or sink below, the threshold of an individual's consciousness, so too they may grow active or fall into disuse in society. Just as ideas may conflict in an individual's mind, so too may there be a war of ideas in society. Strictly speaking, Herbart's own position is merely analogical, but it was interpreted as establishing an independent self-active *Geist* of the people.

The embodiment of the folk mind lies in speech, mythology, religion, folklore, art, literature, morality, custom, and law. Hence the appropriate methods for its study are those familiar to ethnologists and to philologists. With this starting point, it is not surprising that little progress was made in developing a social psychology as distinct from traditional ethnology. In spite of programmatic fanfare, psychological analysis did not advance. When, on rare occasions, psychology was invoked it was invariably the idea psychology of Herbart.

Wilhelm Wundt (1832–1921), in spite of his controversies with Lazarus and Steinthal, was much like them in his conception of *Völkerpsychologie*. The chief systematic difference between them was that Wundt was not a Herbartian but a Wundtian. Having evolved his own fundamental concepts in general psychology, he drew upon them freely in his social psychology. Wundt decided early in his career (1862) that there were two branches of psychology—physiological and social (folk). He planned to devote the first part of his life to the former subject, and the second part to the latter. He kept to his plan, writing prodigiously—an average of two and two-tenths pages per day over a span of sixty-eight years, for a total of 53,735 pages (Boring, 1950, p. 345).

The most significant fact about Wundt is his insistence that the study of all higher mental processes falls within the province of *Völkerpsychologie*. He did not believe that individual psychology, especially as pursued in the psychological laboratory, could account for man's thought. Thinking is heavily conditioned by *language,* by *custom,* and by *myth,* which to him were the three primary problem areas of *Völkerpsychologie*. The argument runs as follows: When an individual receives sensations from the outer world these commence to combine according to the laws of association, but association depends upon the absorption of an impression into the individual's apperceptive mass. Impressions enter into a creative relation with memories and contexts stored in this apperceptive mass. But this apperceptive mass is itself largely a product of culture. The apperceptive mass is furnished with linguistic habits, moral ideas, and ideological convictions that compose the *Volksseele*. Wundt would have felt at home in modern-day discussions of "social perception."

He preferred the term *Volksseele* to *Volksgeist* which, he insisted, was too objective, implying an entity entirely apart from, and over and above, individuals. Semantically at least Wundt leaned somewhat away from the substantive group mind implied by Hegel and by Lazarus and Steinthal. Yet, like all group-mind theorists, Wundt seems to temporize. He says that, while it is true that the folk soul presupposes component individuals, yet it is more than the sum of their mental activities. Interaction brings about new qualities. A language, for example, is a psychic product and a determining force that cannot possibly be accounted for except in terms of a social mind. Josiah Royce was following Wundt when he wrote (1913, p. 27):

> The creator of the English speech is the English people. Hence the English people is itself some sort of mental unit with a mind of its own.

The case for the folk soul rests to a large extent upon Wundt's concept of *psychic actuality*. Although in a broad way Wundt subscribed to psychophysical parallelism, yet he believed that mental events can be regarded as lying in a causal chain. Man's experience is not identical with the activity of nerves. One state of consciousness may lead directly to another, and one man's conscious life may interact with another's. Thus by employing a somewhat loose hypothesis of the body-mind relationship Wundt is able, without serious difficulty, to claim a kind of autonomy for *group* mental life.

We have said that, to Wundt, the primary ingredients of the *Volksseele* were language, myth, and custom. By the time he had exhausted these topics in his ten-volume *Völkerpsychologie* he had, however, embraced art, religion, law, and social organization. But he omitted altogether the material and technological aspects of culture. He found no use for the skills, tools, or potsherds that fascinate anthropologists. Why? Because as a psychologist Wundt identified the mind of a folk only with its *immaterial culture,* that is, with the habits and ideas that lead to activity, not with the *products* of activity.

Summary.   The movement we have been discussing is a curious blend of Hegelian idealism, Herbartian idea psychology, Wundtian concepts, and library ethnology. While its central intent was to discover the nature and laws of the group mind, the actual accomplishment in theory was meager and confused. The movement did, however, succeed in preparing the ground for fruitful collaboration between psychology and social anthropology. Today this tide of collaboration is still rising, and has not yet reached its crest. An important clarification of concepts has occurred, as Kroeber and Kluckhohn (1952) point out. What was formerly ascribed to the mind of the *Volk* is now largely subsumed under the current concept of *culture.* "Personality in culture" promises to be a far more productive concept than "the mind of the group" has been.

COLLECTIVE REPRESENTATIONS

Emile Durkheim (1858–1917) was a French contemporary of Wundt. In many ways the views of the two authors were similar. Both felt keenly "the reality of the social." Both insisted that individual minds are in some sense compounded into a collective mind. Each had a favorite example of the force that this collective mind may exert upon the individual: Wundt chose language, Durkheim religion. Both tended toward intellectualism, regarding the social mind as furnished with ideas, representations, apperceptions (rather than with emotions, passions, volitions). Of the two, however, Wundt was the more voluntaristic.

In one respect, however, Durkheim was more extreme than Wundt. He rejected the parallelistic view that men's bodies and men's minds are somehow closely bound together. Wundt, with his concept of "psychic actuality," had taken liberties with this doctrine, perhaps more than he knew. But Durkheim repudiated it altogether. To him events in the nervous system were one

thing, events in the individual mind something entirely different, and events in the social mind a third distinctive type of reality.

His argument, as set forth in the *Revue de métaphysique* (1898, transl. 1953), is trenchant. He first sets out to demolish the epiphenomenal view that images, memories, and thoughts are merely excrescences of brain activity. William James had identified memory with brain traces, and denied that memory was a fact of the mental order at all. Huxley had likened thought to the shadow cast by the machinery of the brain. Durkheim ridicules the claim. If mental states are only an echo of the physical, why do we have conscious mental states at all? And this was a question that perplexed William James as well, and drove him, ultimately and inconsistently, to argue as Durkheim did for a certain independence of the psychic.

Durkheim claimed that only sensations, the primary elements of individual states of mind, are referable directly to cerebral states. But once existing, we find that sensations compound themselves by the laws of association into images and ideas. These are no longer referable to brain states. Why not? For one thing the basic law of association is similarity (similar ideas form larger clusters or concepts), and there is no mechanism in the brain for producing similarity. While the point is too technical to discuss here, Durkheim's attack on the identical-element theory of similarity is still cogent. It is only whole ideas, he argues, that are similar to one another; they are not decomposable into elements, and therefore not accounted for by specific brain traces.

Having established to his satisfaction that individual representations (ideas) are not reducible to nervous operation, he then continues his case for emergence (1898, p. 296):

> Just as you cannot specify the contribution of each brain cell to an image, so you cannot specify the contribution of an individual to the collective representation.

Thus having leaped the physiological-psychological gulf, he then leaps the psychological-social gulf. While individuals contribute to the *conscious collective,* this final emergent is exterior to, and independent of, any specified individual (p. 293):

> When we have said that social facts are in a sense independent of individuals, and exterior to individual consciousness, we have only affirmed in the social realm what we have established in the psychic realm.

Whenever higher levels emerge from lower, there is a new autonomy achieved at each stage:

brain cells → sensations → images → individual representations → collective representations

Not only is Durkheim a dualist in his separation of mind and body, but from the point of view of monists, he compounds the felony by arguing for the independence of the social and the individual. There are two consciousnesses in each of us, he insists: one pertains to our own private experience, the other to all portions of experience attributable to the fact of human association. This association of human beings produces thoughts and manners and practices that are external to, and independent of, any single human being. Religion (1912) is a collective representation to which the individual in his course of growth is exposed. The division of labor (1902) is similarly a fact of the social mind, not of the individual. Social disruption (*anomie*), even the causes of suicide (1897), are exterior to any one member of the group.

Besides having the property of exteriority, collective representations have likewise the property of *constraint*. There is a compelling force in society that requires the individual to think and behave according to its rules. Often, of course, we cooperate and conform gladly. The concept of constraint covers both cooperation and coercion.

Durkheim, it is true, was a sociologist, yet the line of reasoning by which he achieves his "sociological sociology" is of special interest to the psychologist. His argument is more painstaking, more sophisticated, than that of most writers who have postulated a group mind. There are many secondary sources that give fuller treatment of Durkheim's contributions, among them Gehlke (1915), Goldenweiser (1933), and Parsons (1937). Durkheim's influence upon anthropological theory may be seen strikingly in Lévy-Bruhl's work, *La mentalité primitive* (1922).

While the concept *collective representations* is peculiarly Durkheim's, other authors—psychologists among them—have shown its influence. Take, for example, Fouillée's key concept of the *idées-forces* (1908). While this writer believed that Durkheim had pushed the criteria of exteriority and constraint too far, yet he accepted the basic fact that much of each person's mental life is of social origin. He proposed that the so-called constraint of social ideas lies in the psychologically anchored mechanism of ideomotor action. Fouillée saw no need to break with psychology as drastically as Durkheim had done.

The latter's influence may be traced also in Piaget (1932), who regards the *moral realism* of the child as the result of the child's exposure to, and unquestioning acceptance of, prevailing conceptions of right and wrong, good and bad. Similar is Bartlett (1932), who regards memory as heavily conditioned by the thought forms current in a social group. While Piaget and Bartlett would not subscribe to Durkheim's view as a whole, the problems they treat and their manner of approach show a Durkheimian respect for the reality of the social.

CULTURAL DETERMINISM

Strictly speaking, cultural determinism is not a theory of the group mind. It is, however, a doctrine that makes much of the exteriority and constraint of cultural factors. Extreme advocates seem at times to be saying that psychology can explain nothing of importance concerning social behavior. They quote with favor Durkheim's adage: "Every time a social phenomenon is directly explained by a psychological phenomenon, we may be sure that the explanation is false." The following passage, written by White (1949, pp. 143–144), presents the argument:

> To the culturologist the reasoning that says that one people drinks milk because they like it, another does not because they loathe it, is senseless. It explains nothing at all. Why does one people like, another loathe, milk? *This* is what we want to know. And the psychologist cannot give us the answer. Nor can he tell us why a people does or does not avoid mothers-in-law, practice monogamy, inhumation, the couvade, or circumcision; use chopsticks, forks, the pentatonic scale, hats, or microscopes; form plurals by affixation—or any of the other thousands of customs known to ethnography.

White favors a *cultural* explanation even for the existence of nonconformists, as this quotation illustrates:

> A revolutionist is a human organism that is held and wielded by certain cultural elements and forces that are moving in the direction of profound change.

This manner of thinking about social behavior is at a high level of abstraction. Only gross changes, broad trends, and long-range effects are considered. Culturologists happen to be interested in wide horizons; to them the individual is unimportant. They do not worry about the fact that all cultures have plenty of men who deviate from the picture they create of a *modal personality*. Even in a milk-drinking culture, plenty of individuals loathe mild. Nor do culturologists worry about the extreme selectivity individuals show in responding to this or that feature of their own culture. Nor are they concerned with the process of communication and learning by which children within a culture acquire its ways. Cultural determinism says in effect that children in English-speaking countries will learn to speak English, but it does not explain why they learn to speak at all, or how they learn, or why among them there are almost infinite variations in habits of speech.

The quarrel, of course, is unprofitable. Let us admit that cultural models prescribe what types of conformity will (probably) be learned; also that over long periods of time, language and other cultural forms seem to go through cycles of change independently of what any particular individual may do or think. Yet within this cultural matrix certain psychological factors are presupposed: motivation, learning, the process of perception, concept formation, and the organization of attitudes and sentiments. Only when the cultural and the psychological factors are treated together is a full explanation of social behavior likely to be achieved.

COMMON AND RECIPROCAL SEGMENTS OF BEHAVIOR

We have pointed out that the term "group mind" disappeared from the scene after the 1920s, even though the problem it represents has persisted. Boredom had much to do with dropping the label. Everyone seemed wearied following the climax of the controversy in the decade of the twenties.

Certain nominalists attacked the *group fallacy* with vigor. Thus F. H. Allport wrote (1924, p. 9):

> Nationality, Free-masonry, Catholicism, and the like are not group minds . . . they are sets of ideals, thoughts, and habits repeated in each individual mind and existing only in those minds. . . . All theories which partake of the group fallacy have the unfortunate consequence of diverting attention from the true locus of cause and effect, namely, the behavior mechanism of the individual.

This same author expanded and fortified his argument in *Institutional Behavior* (1933). Opposing views, based largely on the argument of cultural determinism, were stated by Wallis (1925) and Judd (1926). A judicious weighing of evidence, pro and con, came from the pens of the philosophers Perry (1922a, 1922b) and Hocking (1926).

Best known among the disputants is McDougall (1920). The first edition of his *Group Mind* seemed to affirm, with qualifications, his belief in its existence; the second edition (1928) bewailed the reader's misunderstanding of his position. Earlier in this section we stated McDougall's criteria for the existence of a group mind. He found these fulfilled most clearly in the case of nations, for nations have a permanent and highly organized character. McDougall did not regard his criteria as leading to the postulation of a social consciousness for "there is no consciousness excepting in individuals"; yet, he insisted, "we may still speak of collective minds, for we have defined mind as an organized system of interacting mental or psychical forces" (p. 66).

In spite of their disagreements, there is a common thread in the thinking of McDougall and of F. H. Allport. What is called the group mind, they said, is essentially the abstraction of certain attitudes and beliefs from the personal mental life of individuals. We may, if we wish, regard all the common (comparable) attitudes of Englishmen as comprising the group mind of the English nation. McDougall, in the preface (p. ix) to the 1928 edition, explicitly stated that he viewed the group mind

> . . . as consisting in the similarities of structure of the individual minds which render them capable of responding in similar fashion to the common features of the environment, social and physical.

Social institutions, thus regarded, become abstractions from the behavior and consciousness of individuals. People are not parts of institutions, but institutions are parts of people. Figure 1 represents the situation diagrammatically.

It should be noted in Fig. 1 that *common* segments (that is, similar habits and attitudes) are clearly represented, but that the *reciprocal relation* of these segments —also essential to a group mind or *institution*—is not well represented. As it stands, the diagram overstresses *conformity* (which is indeed an important aspect of institutionalism), but understresses the *reciprocity of roles,* which is an equally important aspect. Both McDougall and F. H. Allport (1940) admitted that both aspects are vital. The latter author considered conformity and reci-

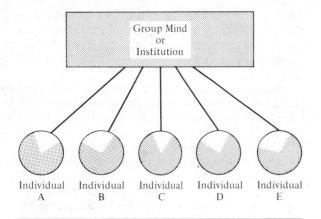

FIGURE 1
Common and reciprocal segment theory

procity to be the essential features of operationally denotable *event structures* that have in the past been called group minds or institutions.

Such a view preserves the strictly individual locus of mind, yet enables us for certain purposes to examine segments of the mental life of individuals in relation to comparable, or reciprocal, segments of the mental life of others. This method permits culturologists to affirm the importance of custom, viewed as common conformity. It allows the sociologist to affirm the independence (in a sense) of institutions, the activity of social systems, and the viability of role relations.

FINAL WORD

After McDougall had wrestled with the problem for a time, he bewailed his "tactical error" in using the phrase *group mind*. Probably it is regrettable that the concept was ever used by anyone. We see now that it has unnecessarily imposed metaphysical blocks in the path of constructive conceptualization. It is important, however, for the student of social science to understand this historical background. Corporate groups have been multiplying at a spectacular rate throughout modern society. An individual is a member of many publics, of many institutions, of many social systems. Each of these memberships poses afresh the ancient question. The problem of the group mind will not be downed.

But at the present time theories are being recentered. Writers realize that the integrity of the personality system can be preserved even while we affirm the existence and

action of social structures which are transindividual. It was Sapir who advised all social and psychological scientists to form the habit of looking at their data both from the concrete individual point of view and from the abstract social point of view. It enriches research and theory to do so. As we have said, the approach now growing in favor combines the idea of *common segment* with that of *role*. Parsons and Shils (1951, p. 23) write:

> Personality as a system has a fundamental and stable point of reference, the acting organism. It is organized around the one organism and its life processes. But ego and alter in interaction with each other also constitute a system. This is a system of a new order, which, however intimately dependent on them, does not simply consist of the personalities of the two members.

Having thus restated the problem in terms of "systems," the authors proceed to say that "the most significant unit of social structures is not the person but the role." Both the actor and those with whom he interacts possess certain expectations due to their places in the social structure. The final essential step in the argument, obviously akin to the common-segment theories, is stated as follows:

> The abstraction of an actor's role from the total system of his personality makes it possible to analyze the articulation of personality with the organization of social systems. The structure of a social system and the functional imperatives for its operation and survival or orderly change as a system are moreover different from those of personality.

Thus what was formerly called the group mind becomes a matter of abstracted role segments, both common and reciprocal. These segments or aspects of personality provide the raw material for the social system. While this mode of conceptualization is still incomplete, it provides a promising new attack upon the venerable riddle of the group mind.

We end this discussion with a warning concerning a certain semantic trap. Many modern writers, in dealing with this troublesome problem, employ the word "share." They speak of "shared ideas," "shared attitudes," "shared norms," "shared values." The trap is obvious. Whenever we share something there is an objective *thing* to share. Hence the term tips the writer's implicit theory of the nature of his collective toward Hegel and toward Durkheim. He implies that ideas, attitudes, norms, values have an outer existence, external to the individual who merely "shares" them. If a writer (or a student) prefers a more individualistic position—for example, the *common and reciprocal segment* theory—he should avoid using the term "share," however convenient it may be.

UNITS OF ANALYSIS

Every science works with units of analysis. The complex order of nature gives way to the quantum in physics, to the element in chemistry, to the cell in biology, and to the nerve impulse in neurophysiology. Psychology has tried out, and in part discarded, a wide variety of units: for example, *sensation, image, idea, reflex*. Social psychology has had a similar experience and, as in the case of general psychology, the search has met with frustrations. Some writers (for example, Lewin, 1951; Asch, 1952) say that the search for elements is doomed to failure because the individual acts in a whole field of forces, and does not react to stimuli in fixed ways.

Still, historically, the postulation of units has played an important part in the development of social psychology, and it is by no means clear that they can be, or should be, dispensed with. Most important among the assumed units are *instinct, habit, attitude,* and *sentiment.*

INSTINCT

While faculty psychologists since the time of Descartes affirmed and classified the *passions* of men, their efforts led to no systematic discussion of the nature of these faculties or of their social consequences. Darwin's doctrine of natural selection changed the situation. It gave grounds for believing that all behavior—animal and human, individual and social—lay in the evolutionary array of instincts that serve the survival of the species. Following Darwin's lead, naturalists immediately began to prepare lists of animal instincts. It was not long before writers of psychological textbooks (for example, James, 1890) set forth with more abandon than reflection long schedules of the presumable basic motivational units underlying human behavior (*cf*. Bernard, 1926). But it remained for McDougall to clarify the implications of Darwinism and build a completely coherent system of social psychology upon the instinct hypothesis. His definition of instinct, if fully understood word by word, adumbrates his entire system of social psychology (1908, p. 30):

We may, then, define an instinct as an inherited or innate psycho-physical disposition which determines its possessor to perceive, and to pay attention to, objects of a certain class, to experience an emotional excitement of a particular quality upon perceiving such an object, and to act in regard to it in a particular manner, or, at least, to experience an impulse to such action.

Under the broad tent of this definition McDougall was able to order many, if not most, social phenomena. The process of suggestion is a consequence of the instinct of self-abasement. Primitive passive sympathy, as we have seen, is an induced instinctive seizure which occurs when one person sees another behaving in an instinctive manner. Laughter is an antidote to such sympathetic induction. Emotion is lockstitched to instinct. Instincts may form compounds: thus a person's religious orientation may be a blend of curiosity, self-abasement, flight (fear), and the tender emotion which accompanies the parental instinct. McDougall believed that the whole story of social behavior could be based on his hormic (urge-like) view of instincts. He readily admitted that the force of learning and integration creates complex units (sentiments) which are often of more immediate concern than instincts to social psychologists. But sentiments, he insisted, are not the ultimate units of behavior. Only instincts are ultimate.

The decade following the appearance of McDougall's *Introduction to Social Psychology* was almost wholly dominated by instinct theory. We have already called attention to G. Wallas' *Human Nature and Politics* (1908) and Trotter's *Instincts of the Herd in Peace and War* (1916). We may add Thorndike's *The Original Nature of Man* (1913), Woodworth's *Dynamic Psychology* (1918), and Dewey's presidential address to the American Psychological Association, in which he declared that the science of social psychology must be founded on a doctrine of instincts (1917).

The same decade was marked by the worldwide spread of Freud's theories. While Freud's instinctivism differs in many ways from McDougall's, it too helped fix the attention of social psychologists upon the primacy of impulses in social conduct. During the decade 1910–1920, however, Freud's influence on *social* psychology was not as marked as McDougall's, probably because the instincts Freud postulated were far less definite and manipulable than McDougall's. By 1932 McDougall had given up the term "instinct" (in response to violent attack by behaviorists), but maintained all essential features of his doctrine under the label "propensities." Between 1908 and 1932 he had considerably expanded his list of native propensities. Its final form includes eighteen items (1932, Chapter 7):

> Food-seeking; disgust; sex; fear; curiosity; protective or parental propensity; gregariousness; self-assertion; submission; anger; appeal; constructive propensity; acquisitive propensity; laughter; comfort; rest or sleep; migratory propensity; a cluster of specific bodily needs—coughing, sneezing, breathing, elimination.

In 1919 Knight Dunlap hurled the first anti-instinct bombshell. From that time onward the whole theory came under attack. Objections to it are many. For one thing, there is no factual proof for the existence of instincts in McDougall's sense of the term. For another, the doctrine brings with it a curious sterility in theorizing. It implies that what is given by heredity is final. Having discovered "first causes" and "prime movers" there is no incentive to look further and discover additional basic principles of human behavior. Furthermore, instinct doctrines inevitably regard certain motives as primary, and all others as secondary, derived, and less basic. It is questionable whether such a distinction can be sustained. McDougall himself felt compelled to supplement instincts by sentiments, but he held that these merely borrow their energy from a handful of original and unchanging instincts. Finally, American social scientists generally have a distaste for nativism (the view that human nature is fixed and at bottom unalterable). The American intellectual climate favors environmentalism.

But it must not be thought that instincts were discarded altogether. How could they be? Elementary motives and reflex adjustments are manifestly present in infancy prior to training and independent of experience. Even parsimonious behaviorists had to admit innate pushes of some sort, variously called "tissue changes," "prepotent reflexes," or "primary drives." But these initial motives were not viewed, as in McDougall's case, as enduring and changeless units of human nature; they became incorporated through learning into a chain of *habits* which constituted the "true" unit.

Besides behaviorism, which represents a distinct countertrend to instinctivism, there is a somewhat colorless middle position that many authors today prefer to hold. They, like McDougall, feel the necessity for dynamic units, and variously affirm the existence of *desires, wishes, needs, vectors,* or simply *motives.* Such units are employed as building blocks in various contemporary systems, but they differ from instinctive units in that they try to sidestep the thorny question of innateness. Modern writers seem not to care whether a motivational unit is inborn or learned. Likewise, they tend to hold their postulated units in a tentative, heuristic way—as mere constructs—and not to regard them as eternally fixed in the person or in the species. Some of these "middle ground" views are defended in Lindzey (1958).

HABIT

Although James affirmed the existence and importance of instinct, he gave chief weight to the habit unit. Instincts as such never endure. Strictly speaking, they manifest themselves only once in a lifetime; thereafter learning immediately sets in. This doctrine of the *transitoriness of instinct* prepared the way for James's famous apotheosis of habit. It is more than second nature, he insisted, it is "ten times nature" (1890, I, p. 121):

> Habit is thus the enormous flywheel of society, its most precious conservative agent. It alone is what keeps us all within the bounds of ordinance, and saves the children of fortune from the envious uprisings of the poor. . . . It keeps different social strata from mixing. Already at the age of twenty-five you see professional mannerisms settling down on the young commercial traveller, on the young doctor, on the young minister, on the young counsellor-at-law. . . . It is well for the world that in most of us, by the age of thirty, the character has set like plaster, and will never soften again.

The social and ethical consequences of this view of habit are, according to James, "numerous and momentous." Since in his view we acquire habits primarily through repetition of actions, it behooves us to pay alert attention to the formation of right habits. In building good habits never let an exception occur. Whether they are good or bad, all habits are a ball and chain.

It was partly due to the eloquence of James that the habit unit came to be taken for granted during the following three or four decades. To be sure, it became recast in terms of *conditioned response* in the hands of behaviorists, but this unit is only another version of the habit doctrine (Holt, 1915; Watson, 1919; F. H. Allport, 1924). Somewhat later, in conjunction with what is sometimes known as "Yale learning theory," the concepts *re-*

sponse and *habit-family hierarchy* became preferred (for example, Miller and Dollard, 1941). But while the habit theory has grown more sophisticated than that depicted by James, the unit is of the same genre.

A somewhat different conception of habit was employed systematically by Dewey "as the key to social psychology" (1922), only a few years after he forsook his advocacy of the instinct unit. In two important respects Dewey's view differs from most others. In the first place, the unit is more flexible: it is not merely a frozen connection in motor pathways, but includes general attitudes, outlooks, purposes, interests. A man may commit murder only once in his lifetime. The act is, however, due to habit—to a habit of hatred. Furthermore, habit has a motivational character (1922, p. 25):

> We may think of habits as means, waiting, like tools in a box, to be used by conscious resolve. But they are something more than that. They are active means, means that project themselves, energetic and dominating ways of action.

In the second place, Dewey tried to include *situationism* within his conception of habit. The neural mechanism alone does not anchor the habit. The environment helps to sustain it. If the environment changes, the habit will change. Every manifestation of a habit is altered by other people who are concerned in the act. "Conduct is always shared; this is the difference betweeen it and the physiological process" (p. 17).

Dewey was attempting to claim too many attributes for the habit unit (fixity and change, neural impulse and situation, motivation and instrumentality). As a result, the unit seemed vague. Later writers did not follow his lead or attempt to refine the concept for systematic use. The reason, no doubt, is that the concept *attitude* was already established. For all intents and purposes it filled the need that Dewey felt.

ATTITUDE

The following brief historical survey of the attitude concept is adapted from the author's earlier and more extended treatment of "Attitudes" (1935).

This concept is probably the most distinctive and indispensable concept in contemporary American social psychology. No other term appears more frequently in experimental and theoretical literature. Its popularity is not difficult to explain. It has come into favor, first of all, because it is not the property of any one psychological school of thought, and therefore serves admirably the purposes of eclectic writers. Furthermore, it is a concept which escapes the controversy concerning the relative influence of heredity and environment. Since an attitude may combine both instinct and habit in any proportion, it avoids the extreme commitments of both the instinct theory and environmentalism. The term likewise is elastic enough to apply either to the dispositions of single, isolated individuals or to broad patterns of culture (*common* attitudes). Psychologists and sociologists therefore find in it a meeting point for discussion and research. This useful, one might almost say peaceful, concept has been so widely adopted that it has virtually established itself as the keystone in the edifice of American social psychology. In fact, several writers, starting with Thomas and Znaniecki (1918), have *defined* social psychology as "the scientific study of attitudes."

Like most abstract terms in the English language, *attitude* has more than one meaning. Derived from the Latin *aptus*, it has on the one hand the significance of "fitness" or "adaptedness," connoting, as does its by-form "aptitude," a subjective or mental state of preparation for action. Through its use in the field of art, however, the term came to have a quite independent meaning; it referred to the outward or visible posture (the bodily position) of a figure in statuary or painting. The first meaning is clearly preserved in the phrase *mental attitudes,* and the second meaning in *motor attitudes*. Since mentalistic psychology historically precedes response psychology, it is only natural to find that mental attitudes are given recognition earlier than motor attitudes. One of the earliest psychologists to employ the term was Herbert Spencer. In his *First Principles* (1862), he wrote (I, 1, i):

> Arriving at correct judgements on disputed questions, much depends on the attitude of mind we preserve while listening to, or taking part in, the controversy; and for the preservation of a right attitude it is needful that we should learn how true, and yet how untrue, are average human beliefs.

Somewhat later, when psychologists were forsaking their exclusively mentalistic point of view, the concept of motor attitudes became popular. In 1888, for example, N. Lange developed a motor theory wherein the process of a perception was considered to be in large part a consequence of muscular preparation or *set*. At about the same time Münsterberg (1889) developed his action theory of attention, and Féré (1890) maintained that a balanced condition of tension in the muscles was a determining condition of selective consciousness.

In recent years it is uncommon to find explicit labeling of an attitude either as *mental* or as *motor.* Such a practice smacks of body-mind dualism, and is therefore distasteful to contemporary psychologists. In nearly all cases today the term appears without a qualifying adjective, and implicitly retains both its original meanings: a mental aptness and a motor set. "Attitude" connotes a *neuropsychic state of readiness for mental and physical activity.*

Perhaps the first explicit recognition of attitudes within the domain of laboratory psychology was in connection with a study of reaction time. In 1888, L. Lange discovered that a subject who was consciously prepared to press a telegraph key immediately upon receiving a signal reacted more quickly than did one whose attention was directed mainly to the incoming stimulus and whose consciousness was therefore not directed primarily upon the expected reaction. After Lange's work, the task attitude, or *Aufgabe,* as it came to be called, was discovered to play a decisive part in nearly all psychological experiments. Not only in the reaction experiment, but in investigations of perception, recall, judgment, thought, and volition, the central importance of the subjects' *preparedness* became universally recognized. In Germany, where most of the early experimental work was done, there arose a swarm of technical expressions to designate the varieties of mental and motor sets that influence the subjects' trains of thought or behavior during the experiment. In addition to the *Aufgabe,* there was the *Absicht* (conscious purpose), the *Zielvorstellung* (idea of the goal), the *Bezugsvorstellung* (idea of the relation between the self and the object to which the self is responding), the *Richtungsvorstellung* (idea of direction), the *determinierende Tendenz* (any disposition that brings in its train related ideas and tendencies to action), the *Einstellung* (a more general term, roughly equivalent to "set"), the *Haltung* (with a more behavioral connotation), and the *Bewusstseinslage* (the "posture or lay of consciousness"). It was perhaps the lack of a general term equivalent to "attitude" that led the German experimentalists to discover so many types and forms. The lack may also explain why no systematic social psychology was written in Germany based upon a unified concept of attitude.

Then came the lively controversy over the place of attitudes in consciousness. The "Würzburg school" was agreed that attitudes were neither sensation not imagery nor affection, nor any combination of these states. Time and again attitudes were studied by the method of introspection, always with meager results. Often an attitude seemed to have no representation in consciousness other than as a vague sense of need, or some indefinite and unanalyzable feeling of doubt, assent, conviction, effort, or familiarity (Titchener, 1909).

As a result of the Würzburg work all psychologists came to accept attitudes, but not all believed them to be impalpable and irreducible mental elements. In general, the followers of Wundt believed that attitudes could be accounted for adequately as *feelings,* particularly as some blend of striving and excitement. Clarke (1911), a pupil of Titchener, found that attitudes in large part *are* represented in consciousness through imagery, sensation, and affection, and that where no such states are reported there is presumably merely a decay or abbreviation of these same constituents.

However they might have disagreed upon the nature of attitudes as these appear in consciousness, all investigators came to admit attitudes as an indispensable part of their psychological armamentarium. Titchener is a case in point. His *Outline of Psychology* in 1899 contained no reference to attitude; ten years later, in his *Textbook of Psychology,* several pages are given to the subject, and its systematic importance is fully recognized.

Many authors have reduced the phenomena of perception, judgment, memory, learning, and thought largely to the operation of attitudes (see, for example, Ach, 1905; Bartlett, 1932). Without guiding attitudes the individual is confused and baffled. Some kind of preparation is essential before he can make a satisfactory observation, pass suitable judgment, or make any but the most primitive reflex type of response. Attitudes determine for each individual what he will see and hear, what he will think and what he will do. To borrow a phrase from William James, they "engender meaning upon the world"; they draw lines about, and segregate, an otherwise chaotic environment; they are our methods for finding our way about in an ambiguous universe. It is especially when the stimulus is not of great intensity, nor closely bound with some reflex or automatic response, that attitudes play a decisive role in the determination of meaning and of behavior.

The meagerness with which attitudes are represented in consciousness resulted in a tendency to regard them as manifestations of brain activity or of the unconscious mind. The persistence of attitudes which are totally unconscious was demonstrated by Müller and Pilzecker

(1900), who called the phenomenon "perseveration." The tendency of the subject to slip into some frame of mind peculiar to himself led Koffka (1912) to postulate "latent attitudes." Washburn (1916) characterized attitudes as "static movement systems" within the organs of the body and the brain. Other writers, still more physiologically inclined, subsumed attitudes under neurological rubrics: traces, neurograms, incitograms, brain patterns, and the like. The contribution of the *Würzbürger* and of all other experimental psychologists was in effect the demonstration that the concept of attitude is indispensable.

But it was the influence of Freud that endowed attitudes with vitality, equating them with longing, hatred and love, with passion and prejudice, in short, with the onrushing stream of unconscious life. Without the painstaking labors of the experimentalists, attitudes would not today be an established concept in the field of psychology; but also, without the influence of psychoanalytic theory they would certainly have remained relatively lifeless, and would not have been of much assistance to social psychology. For the explanation of prejudice, loyalty, patriotism, crowd behavior, control by propaganda, no anemic conception of attitudes will suffice.

As we have said, the instinct hypothesis did not satisfy social scientists for long, for the very nature of their work forced them to recognize the importance of custom and environment in shaping social behavior. What social scientists required was a new psychological concept that would escape, on the one hand, the hollow impersonality of *custom* and *social force* and, on the other, nativism. They gradually adopted the concept of *attitude*.

The credit for instituting the concept as a permanent and central feature in sociological writing must be assigned to Thomas and Znaniecki (1918), who gave it systematic priority in their monumental study of Polish peasants. Before this time the term had made only sporadic appearances in sociological literature, but immediately afterward it was adopted with enthusiasm by scores of writers.

According to Thomas and Znaniecki, the study of attitudes is *par excellence* the field of social psychology. Attitudes are individual mental processes which determine both the actual and potential responses of each person in the social world. Since an attitude is always directed toward some object, it may be defined as a "state of mind of the individual toward a value." Values are usually social in nature, that is to say, they are objects of common regard on the part of socialized men. Love of

money, desire for fame, hatred of foreigners, and respect for a scientific doctrine are typical attitudes. It follows that money, fame, foreigners, and a scientific theory are all *values*. A *social value* is defined as "any datum having an empirical content accessible to the members of some social group and a meaning with regard to which it is or may be an object of activity." To be sure, there are numerous attitudes corresponding to every social value —there are, for example, many attitudes regarding the church or the state. There are also numerous possible values for any single attitude—the iconoclast may direct his attacks quite at random upon all established social values; the Philistine may accept them all uncritically. Hence, in the social world, as studied by the sociologist, both values and attitudes must have a place.

Park (see Young, 1931), who is in essential agreement with this school of thought, suggests four criteria for an attitude:

1. It has definite orientation in the world of objects (or values), and in this respect differs from simple and conditioned reflexes.

2. It is not an altogether automatic and routine type of conduct, but displays some tension even when latent.

3. It varies in intensity, sometimes being regnant, sometimes relatively ineffective.

4. It is rooted in experience, and therefore is not simply a social instinct.

The following are typical definitions of *attitude:*

. . . the specific mental disposition toward an incoming (or arising) experience, whereby that experience is modified; or, a condition of readiness for a certain type of activity. (Warren, 1934)

. . . a mental disposition of the human individual to act for or against a definite object. (Droba, 1933)

. . . a mental and neural state of readiness, organized through experience, exerting a directive or dynamic influence upon the individual's response to all objects and situations with which it is related. (G. W. Allport, 1935)

To sum up: The attitude unit has been the primary building stone in the edifice of social psychology. Although there have been attempts to dislodge it on the part of some field theorists, phenomenologists, and learning theorists, it is questionable whether their criticisms can do more than refine the concept for continued use. Recent literature shows that the concept is still in high favor. It has a prominent place in textbooks (for example, Newcomb, Turner, and Converse, 1965), and still invites fresh technical inspection and analysis (for example, Katz and Stotland, 1959).

SENTIMENT

McDougall did not like the term "attitude." It seemed to him to reflect a transient and superficial level of organization. Yet he staunchly argued that some conception of "tendency" must forever serve as "the basic postulate of all psychology." So far as social behavior is concerned his own preference was for the unit *sentiment.* According to McDougall (1932, p. 211):

> The theory of sentiments is the theory of the progressive organization of the propensities (instincts) in systems which become the main sources of all our activities; systems which give consistency, continuity and order to our life of striving and emotion; systems which in turn become organized in larger systems, and which, when harmoniously organized in one comprehensive system, constitute what we properly call *character.*

Thus conceived, sentiment differs from attitude in four respects:

1. A sentiment presupposes underlying propensities, whereas attitude is a disposition within the organism without regard to its origins or source of energy.

2. An attitude may be either specific or diffuse in its reference, whereas a sentiment is centered on some definite object. One can speak, for example, of an antisocial attitude but scarcely of an antisocial sentiment.

3. Sentiments are conceived as more lasting and hierarchical than attitudes need be. The transitory *Aufgabe* is an attitude as truly as is an enduring philosophy of life, but it is not a sentiment.

4. A sentiment is conscious and benign, in contrast to a complex, which is a morbid and repressed sentiment. "Attitude" could cover both wholesomely conscious and morbidly repressed dispositions.

The concept of sentiment received its first systematic use in the hands of Shand (1896), whose theory that human character is composed of sentiments was adopted and elaborated by McDougall. Not only did sentiment seem to these authors to provide a proper unit for characterizing man's social attachments, but also to provide a proper unit for the theory of personality. To McDougall the unity of personality was guaranteed by its possession of the crowning *self-regarding sentiment* at the top of the hierarchical structure.

Certain other authors likewise have expressed strong preference for the concept of sentiment and strong dislike for the attitude unit. To Murray and Morgan (1945), for example, "attitude" seems too superficial, too motor, to represent the basic organization of needs and cathexes that is, to their minds, the core of "sentiment."

FINAL WORD

The four types of units we have discussed—instinct, habit, attitude, sentiment—all claim that dynamic dispositions of some type underlie social behavior. They all have the weakness of assuming a fixity of disposition in the person, and overlook the flexibility of behavior that is exhibited when environmental situations alter.

Field theorists and other critics say that human behavior is immensely variable, depending upon the situation in which a person finds himself. Some critics go so far as to deny generalized attitudinal dispositions and to put all weight upon the specific tendency to react in a specific way in each situation (for example, Coutu, 1949). And yet individuals do not behave in altogether different ways as they move from one situation to another. If there is danger of implying an exaggerated fixity in the units we have described, it is surely not necessary to abandon them altogether in favor of momentary situationism or in favor of an extreme version of field theory.

THE BEGINNINGS OF OBJECTIVE METHOD

EXPERIMENTATION

The year 1879 saw the formal establishment of the first laboratory of psychology. Credit goes to Wundt at Leipzig, although both James at Harvard and Wundt had demonstrational (not research) laboratories as early as 1875. But it took several years longer for social variables to enter the laboratory. The first experimental problem—indeed the only problem studied in the first three decades of experimental research—was formulated as follows: *What change in an individual's normal solitary performance occurs when other people are present?*

The first laboratory answer to this question came from Triplett (1897). While examining the official records of bicycle races, Triplett noted that a rider's maximum speed was approximately 20 percent greater when he was paced by a visible multicycle. Desiring to learn more about the matter, he set up an experiment with children in the age range of ten to twelve, giving them the task of winding fishing reels. Alternating situations *alone* and *together,* he found that when working together 20 of his 40 subjects excelled their own solitary record, while 10 did less work (apparently because they were overstimulated by the desire to win) and 10 were essentially unaffected. All in all, he concluded that the group situation must normally be thought of as producing greater output of energy and achievement. His explanation is of interest (p. 533):

> The bodily presence of another contestant participating simultaneously in the race serves to liberate latent energy not ordinarily available.... The sight of the movements of the pacemakers or leading competitors, and the idea of higher speed furnished by this or other means, are probably in themselves dynamogenic factors of some consequence.

In his experimental design, as well as in his explanation, Triplett fails to distinguish two causal factors: emotional competitiveness, on the one hand, and the simple dynamogenic effect resulting from the sights and sounds of coworkers, on the other.

The reader will recall from our discussion of suggestion that the concept of *dynamogenesis* is a special case of ideomotor theory. Automatic and unconscious movements resulting from sensory or affective stimulation were matters of considerable interest. Féré (1900), a physician in Charcot's clinic, Binet (1900), and others had great faith in the explanatory value of the concept. Hence it was natural for Triplett to explain the "plus" production of his subjects in terms of dynamogenesis.

The same problem was an early concern of pedagogics. A. Mayer (1903) studied both the quantity and quality of schoolchildren's homework and classwork with respect to memorization, composition, arithmetic, and other tasks. On the whole, his results clearly favored group over solitary work, although he found, as Triplett did, that conditions of overkeen competition in congre-

gate groups affected the quality of the production adversely.

It was a full generation later that the important distinction was drawn between emulation or competition, on the one hand, and simple *social facilitation* (whether or not explained in terms of dynamogenesis), on the other. F. H. Allport (1924), who drew this distinction, also pointed to the existence of two kinds of small groups: the *coacting* and the *face-to-face.* In the former one finds the simplest psychology operating. People working side by side receive their social stimulation almost wholly from "contributory" social stimuli and thus most clearly display the effects of simon-pure social facilitation. In face-to-face groups, on the other hand, entirely new problems arise: conversation, interaction, circular social behavior, "group thinking," and all manner of direct (not merely contributory) social effects. Accepting this distinction, we may say that early work dealt entirely with coacting groups. It took a longer time for face-to-face groups to become a central focus of interest. Bechterew and de Lange (1924), G. Watson (1928), and especially Kurt Lewin (see collections of his studies, 1948, 1951) gave incentive to research in face-to-face groups.

In 1913 Moede outlined a monumental program of research on coacting groups. He decided that a systematic attempt should be made to introduce the social variable into all, or nearly all, standard psychological experiments. If thresholds for the intensity of audible sound can be determined for the individual working alone, why not for two, four, six, or any number of subjects working in the presence of one another? Also, why should not the available instrumental devices for recording involuntary muscular movements be used in the study of imitation? The subject's involuntary movements can, for example, be measured while he is watching similar movements of the experimenter's arm. Also, associative processes, shifts in the fixation of attention, learning and forgetting—all well-known phenomena in experimental psychology—can be studied (and were studied, using groups of Leipzig school and college students as subjects). Moede published his results in *Experimentelle Massenpsychologie* (1920), but his pioneer conception had less influence than it should have, partly because he failed to generalize his findings into systematic theory, and partly because his stimulating book was not translated into English.

Moede's experimental program was, however, known to Münsterberg at Harvard. It was he who, in

1915, encouraged F. H. Allport to undertake work in this area. The latter confirmed the principal findings of Moede and his predecessors and formulated a series of generalizations (1920). Even when the effects of competitiveness are minimized the mere presence of coworkers seems ordinarily to increase the quantity of output (*social increment*); it tends, however, to make judgments conservative, to make associations less personal, and to diminish the quality of reasoning (*social subvaluent*). This work was systematically extended by Whittemore (1924), who added the variable of competitiveness and found in general that it enhanced all these social effects. Unlike Triplett, these authors explained their results in terms of *contributory social stimulation*—a summation of cues and innervations resulting from previous conditioning and leading to the excess output. When the variable of competition is added, emotional reinforcement from within summates with the contributory cues from without.

This type of work, with many elaborations, was carried on by subsequent investigators. Travis, for example, found that some of the effects were reversed in the case of stutterers, whose social shyness seemed to be an inhibiting variable (1925). Dashiell (1935) summarized all this work and added his own research on the *imagined* as compared with the *actual* presence of others. Among early experiments on group influence was that of H. T. Moore, who gauged the relative effect of expert opinion and majority opinion upon moral and esthetic judgments (1921). Moore's research initiated a new method. Instead of having "experts" or a "majority" physically present, he merely reported their judgments to his subjects. In this way it was discovered that the effects of social prestige can be measured simply through instructions that induce an attitude. Countless subsequent investigations have taken advantage of this fact, and have measured social effects through the artificial arousal of preexisting attitudes.

Russian psychology, also employing the experimental method, soon after the Bolshevik revolution turned its attention to problems of collective versus individual behavior. Bechterew and de Lange (1924), using face-to-face (not merely coacting) groups, reported on the effects of discussion in modifying previous individual judgments. Collective thinking, they concluded, is not less efficient than private thinking; often it is superior in terms of the accuracy of judgments. Russian investigations centered attention likewise on the relative merits of competitive and cooperative social situations. Later Bauer

(1952) showed that Soviet psychology had shifted from its earlier emphasis on the exclusive power of environmental forces to an emphasis on the duties and obligations of the individual. The superiority of group thinking, teamwork, and reliance on collectivities became less essential to Communist ideology.

In America a widening of experimental interest took place. Group influence upon the mental processes of the individual was no longer the sole focus. Lewin, Lippitt, and White (1939) introduced the concept of *social climate* or *group atmosphere*. In particular they showed that styles of leadership (autocratic, laissez-faire, democratic) profoundly influenced the conduct of group members. This work, in effect, opened the gates to floods of research in group dynamics, group structure, group decision, group cohesion—in short, to the many-sided investigation of small groups. For a final account of this historic experiment see White and Lippitt (1960).

CONTROLLED OBSERVATION

While the experimental method approaches the ideal design for social research, it is not adapted to all the problems with which social psychology must wrestle. No doubt most investigators, from the earliest days, would have insisted that their theories and dicta were based on the solid foundation of "facts." Comte, Spencer, Tarde, Durkheim—all theorists—were interpreting social data as they *observed* them. What they lacked was a method for checking and extending their unaided observation.

Perhaps the earliest attempt to improve private observation was through the adoption of questionnaire procedures. Boring (1950) reports uses of this method as early as 1869 in the Berlin schools. Galton (1883) leaned upon questionnaires in his famous study of imagery. Its use on a vast scale commenced with G. Stanley Hall (1891), chiefly in his studies of child psychology. Soon Starbuck (1899) adapted the method for investigations of the religious beliefs and practices of adults. James's work of genius, *Varieties of Religious Experience* (1902), was aided by Starbuck's study. In the course of time the need for refinements and safeguards brought special methodological researches in matters of wording, interviewing, coding of responses, and scaling. Originally a loose, naive instrument, the questionnaire has gradually been forged into a tool of considerable precision.

Gradually, too, statistical aids, invented by Quetelet, Galton, Pearson, Fisher, and others, came to serve as safeguards for research in social psychology. Devoting himself specifically to the problem of attitude measurement, Thurstone (1927) first introduced statistical sophistication into this important area of investigation. Sociometry, a quasi-quantitative technique invented by Moreno (1934), enabled social psychologists to assess the personal attractions and rejections among members of a group. Following Gallup's first signal success with public opinion polling in the Presidential elections of 1936, an elaborate special branch of survey research rapidly developed.

Since most of these long strides in method are of recent date, they do not form a part of our historical account. The fact is that empiricism and positivism did not enter social psychology to any appreciable extent until the decade of the 1920s. The ideals of objectivity and precision then rapidly assumed a dominant position. By 1931 Murphy and Murphy, in the first edition of their *Experimental Social Psychology,* were able to list over eight hundred relevant studies, and in a revised edition (Murphy, Murphy, and Newcomb, 1937) expanded the entries by several hundred additional titles.

Today the outstanding mark of social psychology as a discipline is its sophistication in method and in experimental design. It has come a long way from the days of "simple and sovereign" speculation. To appreciate the range, power, and marked originality of modern controlled methods of research, the reader should consult the impressive surveys offered by Berelson and Steiner (1964), Berkowitz (1964), Proshansky and Seidenberg (1965), and Steiner and Fishbein (1965). The many chapters of the present *Handbook* tell the same story. Comte would say that now, at long last, social psychology has entered the "positive stage" with a vengeance.

TEXTBOOKS

One may learn something about the history of a discipline by surveying its textbooks. In the first (1954) edition of this *Handbook* an approximately complete list of available texts appeared—52 of them, extending from the Ross and McDougall texts of 1908 through the year 1952. Perhaps two-thirds of the texts are written by authors who consider themselves to be psychologists, about one-third by sociologists. This fact calls attention to the persistent bipolarity of the science. Emphasis ranges from individual processes (for example, how a child learns to talk) to the constraining influences in the social system (for example, social class differences in speech). One author may treat creativity as an attribute of the individual, another as a feature of the *Zeitgeist.* One regards attitudes as personal and private dispositions, another as incidental to the role, sex, and cultural setting of the individual.

The definition of the field offered in the present chapter may be said to have a psychological slant: "an attempt to understand and explain how the thought, feeling, and behavior of individuals are influenced by the actual, imagined, or implied presence of others." Ellwood (1925, p. 16) offers a more typical sociological definition:

> Social psychology is the study of social interaction. It is based upon the psychology of group life. It begins with an interpretation of group-made types of human reactions, of communication, and of instinctive and habitual actions.

No doubt it is a wholesome thing to look at the rich problem areas of social psychology from both points of view.

CONCLUSION

Without doubt the current trend in social psychology is toward the objective, not speculative, study of social behavior. Watchwords are *experimentation, automatic computation, statistical reliability, replicability.* Noteworthy scientific gains result from this "hard-nosed" approach. There is, however, one serious disadvantage: neat and elegant experiments often lack generalizing power. Trade with his simple and sovereign concept of imitation had too much generalizing power. But, by contrast, many contemporary studies seem to shed light on nothing more than a narrow phenomenon studied under specific conditions. Even if the experiment is successfully repeated there is no proof that the discovery has wider validity. It is for this reason that some current investigations seem to end up in elegantly polished triviality —snippets of empiricism, but nothing more.

Here surely lies the current challenge to social psychology. Can the improved objectivity in method be brought to serve broad theory and practical application? Early in this chapter we noted how the burning issues of war and peace, education for life in a world community, population control, effective democracy, all urgently call for assistance from social psychology. Such assistance is unlikely to come from small gemlike researchers, however exquisite their perfection. The question at issue is whether the present preoccupation with method, with miniature models, will in the near future lead to a new emphasis on theory and application.

Integrative theories are not easy to come by. Like all behavioral science, social psychology rests ultimately upon broad metatheories concerning the nature of man and the nature of society. This high level of conceptualization was of greater concern to the Machiavellis, Benthams, Comtes of yesteryear than to the empiricists of today. The arrival of the positivism that Comte advocated has led to an essentially nontheoretical orientation. The result has been that journals and textbooks are filled with specific and particular investigations, with a minimum of theorizing.

The tide, however, may turn. Scattered empirical research may increasingly cloy scientific taste. Interest in broad theory may again have its day. If so, investigators who are familiar with the history of social psychology will be able to strike out with firm assurance. They will be able to distinguish what is significant from what is trivial, to progress from platitude, and to borrow selectively from the past in order to create a cumulative and coherent science of the future.

REFERENCES

Aberle, D. F., A. K. Cohen, A. K. Davis, M. J. Levy, and F. X. Sutton (1950). The functional prerequisites of a society. *Ethics, 60,* 100–111.

Ach, N. (1905). *Über die Willenstätigkeit und das Denken.* Göttingen: Vanderhoeck and Ruprecht.

Adler, A. (1917). A study of organ inferiority and its psychic compensations. Transl. *Nerv. ment. Dis. Monogr., 24.*

Allport, F. H. (1920). The influence of the group upon association and thought. *J. exp. Psychol., 3,* 159–182.

_____ (1924). *Social psychology.* Boston: Houghton Mifflin.

_____ (1933). *Institutional behavior.* Chapel Hill: Univ. of North Carolina Press.

_____ (1940). An event system theory of collective action: with illustrations from economic and political phenomena and the production of war. *J. soc. Psychol., 11,* 417–445.

Allport, G. W. (1935). Attitudes. In C. M. Murchison (Ed.), *Handbook of social psychology.* Worcester, Mass.: Clark Univ. Press. Pp. 798–844.

_____ (1943). The ego in contemporary psychology. *Psychol. Rev., 50,* 451–478.

_____ (1946). Effect: a secondary principle of learning. *Psychol. Rev., 53,* 335–347.

_____ (1961). *Pattern and growth in personality.* New York: Holt, Rinehart, and Winston.

Asch, S. E. (1948). The doctrine of suppression, prestige, and imitation in social psychology. *Psychol. Rev., 55,* 250–276.

_____ (1952). *Social psychology.* New York: Prentice-Hall.

Ashley-Montagu, M. F. (1950). *On being human.* New York: H. Schuman.

Bagehot, W. (1875). *Physics and politics.* New York: D. Appleton.

Baker, H. (1947). *The dignity of man.* Cambridge, Mass.: Harvard Univ. Press.

Baldwin, J. M. (1895). *Mental development in the child and in the race.* New York: Macmillan.

_____ (1897). *Social and ethical interpretations in mental development.* New York: Macmillan.

Barnes, H. E. (1965). *An intellectual and cultural history of the western world* (3rd rev. ed.). New York: Dover.

Bartlett, F. C. (1923). *Psychology and primitive culture.* Cambridge: Cambridge Univ. Press.

_____ (1932). *Remembering.* Cambridge: Cambridge Univ. Press.

Bastian, A. (1860). *Der Mensch in der Geschichte: zur Begründung einer psychologischen Weltanschauung* (3 vols.). Leipzig: O. Wigand.

Bauer, R. A. (1952). *The new man in Soviet psychology.* Cambridge, Mass.: Harvard Univ. Press.

Bechterew, V. M. (1932). *General principles of human reflexology* (transl. from 4th Russian ed., 1928). New York: International Publishers.

Bechterew, V. M., and M. de Lange (1924). Die Ergebnisse des Experiments auf dem Gebiete der kollektiven Reflexologie. *Z. angew. Psychol., 24,* 305–344.

Becker, H. (1931). Some forms of sympathy: a phenomenological analysis. *J. abnorm. soc. Psychol., 26,* 58–68.

Becker, H., and H. E. Barnes (1952). *Social thought from lore to science* (2nd ed.). Washington: Hansen Press.

Bentham, J. (1789). *An introduction to the principles of morals and legislation.* (Oxford: Clarendon Press, 1879.)

Berelson, B., and G. A. Steiner (1964). *Human behavior: an inventory of scientific findings.* New York: Harcourt, Brace, and World.

Berkowitz, L., Ed. (1964). *Advances in experimental social psychology.* New York: Academic Press.

Bernard, L. L. (1926). *Instinct: a study in social psychology.* New York: Henry Holt.

_____ (1934). Social psychology. In *Encyclopedia of social science.* Vol. 14. New York: Macmillan. Pp. 151–157.

Bernheim, H. (1884). *De la suggestion dans l'état hypnotique et dans l'état de veille.* Paris: O. Doin.

Bertalanffy, L. von (1962). General system theory. *Gen. Systems* (Yearbook of the Society for General Systems Research), *7,* 1–20.

Binet, A. (1900). *La suggestibilité.* Paris: Schleicher.

Blanton, S., and M. Blanton (1927). *Child guidance.* New York: Century.

Boring, E. G. (1929). *A history of experimental psychology.* New York: D. Appleton-Century.

_____ (1950). *A history of experimental psychology* (rev. ed.). New York: Appleton-Century-Crofts.

Bosanquet, B. (1899). *Philosophical theory of the state.* New York: Macmillan.

Braid, J. (1843). *Neurypnology.* (Rev. ed. London: G. Redway, 1899.)

Britt, S. H. (1950). *Selected readings in social psychology.* New York: Rinehart.

Brown, T. (1820). *Lectures on the philosophy of the human mind* (4 vols.). Edinburgh: J. Ballantyne for W. Tait and C. Tait.

Cantril, H. (1940). *The invasion from Mars.* Princeton: Princeton Univ. Press.

_____ (1941). *The psychology of social movements.* New York: Wiley.

Cartwright, D. (1961). A decade of social psychology. In R. Patton (Ed.), *Current trends in psychological theory.* Pittsburgh: Univ. of Pittsburgh Press. Pp. 9–30.

Catlin, G. (1947). *The story of the political philosophers* (rev. ed.). New York: Tudor.

Charcot, J. M. (1888–1894). *Oeuvres complètes* (9 vols.). Paris: Bureaux du progrès médical.

Chase, S. (1951). *Roads to agreement.* New York: Harper.

Clarke, H. M. (1911). Conscious attitudes. *Amer. J. Psychol., 32,* 214–249.

Comte, A. (1830). *The positive philosophy.* Vol. 1. (Transl. London: Trubner, 1853.)

Cooley, C. H. (1902). *Human nature and the social order.* New York: Scribner's.

Cottrell, L. S., and R. Gallagher (1941). Developments in social psychology, 1930–1940. *Sociom. Monogr.,* No. 1. New York: Beacon House.

Coutu, W. (1949). *Emergent human nature.* New York: Knopf.

Curti, M. (1943). *The growth of American thought.* New York: Harper.

Darwin, C. (1859). *On the origin of species.* London: J. Murray.

Dashiell, J. F. (1935). Experimental studies of the influence of social situations on the behavior of individual human adults. In C. C. Murchison (Ed.), *Handbook of social psychology.* Worcester, Mass.: Clark Univ. Press. Pp. 1097–1158.

Dewey, J. (1899). *Psychology as philosophic method.* Berkeley: University Chronicle.

_____ (1917). The need for social psychology. *Psychol. Rev., 24,* 266–277.

_____ (1922). *Human nature and conduct: an introduction to social psychology.* New York: Henry Holt.

Dollard, J., and N. E. Miller (1950). *Personality and psychotherapy.* New York: McGraw-Hill.

Doob, L. W. (1935). *Propaganda: its psychology and techniques.* New York: Henry Holt.

Droba, D. D. (1933). The nature of attitude. *J. soc. Psychol., 4,* 444–463.

Dunlap, K. (1919). Are there any instincts? *J. abnorm. Psychol., 14,* 307–311.

Durkheim, E. (1897). *Le suicide.* Paris: F. Alcan. (Transl. Glencoe, Ill.: Free Press, 1951.)

_____ (1898). Représentations individuelles et représentations collectives. *Rev. de métaphysique, 6,* 275–302. (Transl. D. F. Pocock, *Sociology and philosophy.* New York: Free Press, 1953.)

_____ (1902). *De la division du travail social.* Paris: F. Alcan. (Transl. New York: Macmillan, 1933.)

_____ (1912). *Les formes élémentaires de la vie religieuse.* Paris: F. Alcan. (Transl. New York: Macmillan, 1915.)

Ellwood, C. A. (1925). *The psychology of human society.* New York: Appleton.

Engelmann, G. (1927). *Political philosophy from Plato to Jeremy Bentham* (transl.). New York: Harper.

Espinas, A. (1877). *Des sociétés animales.* Paris: G. Baillière.

Faraday, M. (1853). Experimental investigation of table-moving. *Athenaeum, 1340* 801–803.

Féré, C. (1890). Note sur la physiologie de l'attention. *Rev. phil., 30,* 393–405.

_____ (1900). *Sensation et mouvement.* Paris: F. Alcan.

Fouillée, A. (1908). *Morale des idées-forces* (2nd ed.). Paris: F. Alcan.

Freud, S. (1913). *Totem and taboo.* (Transl. New York: Moffat, Yard, 1918.)

_____ (1920). *Beyond the pleasure principle.* (Transl. London: International Psychoanalytical Press, 1922.)

_____ (1921). *Group psychology and the analysis of the ego.* (Transl. London: International Psychoanalytical Press, 1922.)

Galton, F. (1883). *Inquiries into human faculty and its development.* London: Macmillan.

Gehlke, C. E. (1915). *Emile Durkheim's contributions to sociological theory.* New York: Columbia Univ. Press.

Giddings, F. H. (1896). *The principles of sociology.* New York: Macmillan.

Goldenweiser, A. (1933). *History, psychology, and culture.* New York: Knopf.

Green, T. H. (1900). Lectures on the principles of political obligation. In *Collected works.* Vol. 2. London: Longmans, Green.

Haddon, A. C. (1910). *History of anthropology.* London: Watts.

_____ (1949). *History of anthropology* (rev. ed.). London: Watts.

Hall, G. S. (1891). The contents of children's minds on entering school. *Ped. Sem., 1,* 139–173.

Hamilton, W. (1859–1860). *Lectures on metaphysics* (H. Maurel and J. Veitch, Eds.). Boston: Gould and Lincoln.

Hart, H. (1949). The pre-war upsurge in social science. *Amer. sociol. Rev., 14,* 599–607.

Hegel, G. W. F. (1807). *Phänomenologie des Geistes.* (Transl. *The phenomenology of mind.* London: Allen and Unwin, 1910.)

Heider, F. (1958). *The psychology of interpersonal relations.* New York: Wiley.

Herbart, J. F. (1821). Über einige Beziehungen zwischen Psychologie und Staatswissenschaft. In Vol. 5 (1890) of *Sämtliche Werke* (19 vols.). Langensalza: Hermann Beyer, 1887–1912.

Hobbes, T. (1651). *Leviathan.* (Reprint of 1st ed. Cambridge: Cambridge Univ. Press, 1904.)

Hocking, W. E. (1926). *Man and the state.* New Haven: Yale Univ. Press.

Hollingworth, H. L. (1920). *Psychology of the functional neuroses.* New York: D. Appleton.

Holt, E. B. (1915). *The Freudian wish and its place in ethics.* New York: Holt.

_____ (1931). *Animal drive and the learning process.* New York: Holt.

Hoppe, F. (1930). Das Anspruchsniveau. In "Untersuchungen zur Handlungsund Affektpsychologie": IX. Erfolg und Misserfolg. *Psychol. Forsch., 14,* 1–62.

Horney, K. (1939). *New ways in psychoanalysis.* New York: Norton.

House, F. N. (1936). *Development of sociology.* New York: McGraw-Hill.

Hovland, C. I., and I. L. Janis, Eds. (1959). *Personality and persuasibility.* New Haven: Yale Univ. Press.

Hull, C. L. (1934). *Hypnosis and suggestibility.* New York: D. Appleton-Century.

Humphrey, G. (1921). Imitation and the conditioned reflex. *Ped. Sem., 28,* 1–21.

James, W. (1890). *Principles of psychology* (2 vols.). New York: Holt.

———— (1902). *The varieties of religious experience.* New York: Longmans, Green. (The quotation is from the Modern Library edition.)

Judd, C. H. (1926). *The psychology of social institutions.* New York: Macmillan.

Jung, C. G. (1922). *Collected papers on analytical psychology* (2nd ed.). Transl. London: Baillière, Tindall, and Cox.

Karpf, F. B. (1932). *American social psychology.* New York: McGraw-Hill.

———— (1952). American social psychology—1951. *Amer. J. Sociol., 2,* 187–193.

Katona, G. (1951). *Psychological analysis of economic behavior.* New York: McGraw-Hill.

Katz, D., Ed. (1951). *Handbuch der Psychologie.* Transl. Basel: Schwabe.

Katz, D., and E. Stotland (1959). A preliminary statement to a theory of attitude structure and change. In S. Koch (Ed.), *Psychology: a study of a science.* Vol. 3. New York: McGraw-Hill.

Kluckhohn, C., and H. A. Murray, Eds. (1948). *Personality in nature, society, and culture.* New York: Knopf. (Rev. ed., 1953.)

Kluckhohn, F. R., and F. L. Strodtbeck (1961). *Variations in value orientations.* Evanston, Ill.: Row, Peterson.

Koffka, K. (1912). *Zur Analyse der Vorstellungen und ihren Gesetze.* Leipzig: Quelle and Meyer.

Köhler, W. (1927). *The mentality of apes* (transl.). New York: Harcourt, Brace.

Kroeber, A. L., and C. Kluckhohn (1952). *Culture: a critical review of concepts and definitions.* Cambridge, Mass.: Peabody Museum Papers, *47,* No. 1.

Kropotkin, P. A. (1902). *Mutual aid, a factor of evolution.* New York: McClure, Phillips.

Lange, L. (1888). Neue Experimente über den Vorgang der einfachen Reaktion auf Sinneseindrücke. *Phil. Stud., 4,* 472–510.

Lange, N. (1888). Beiträge zur Theorie der sinnlichen Aufmerksamkeit und der aktiven Apperception. *Phil. Stud., 4,* 390–422.

Lazarus, M., and H. Steinthal (1860–1890). *Zeitschrift für Völkerpsychologie und Sprachwissenschaft* (20 vols.). Berlin: F. Dümmler.

Le Bon, G. (1895). *Psychologie des foules.* Paris: F. Olean. (Transl. *The crowd.* London: T. Fisher Unwin, 1896. Quotations are from the 12th English impression, 1920.)

Lecky, P. (1945). *Self-consistency: a theory of personality.* New York: Island Press.

Le Dantec, F. (1918). *L'égoisme: seul base de toute société.* Paris: Flammarion.

Leighton, A. H. (1945). *The governing of men.* Princeton: Princeton Univ. Press.

Levy-Bruhl, L. (1922). *La mentalité primitive.* Paris: F. Alcan. (Transl. *How natives think.* London: Allen and Unwin, 1926.)

Lewin, K. (1948). *Resolving social conflict: selected papers on group dynamics.* New York: Harper.

———— (1951). *Field theory in social science.* New York: Harper.

Lewin, K., R. Lippitt, and R. White (1939). Patterns of aggressive behavior in experimentally created 'social climates.' *J. soc. Psychol., 10,* 271–299.

Liébeault, A. A. (1866). *Du sommeil et des états analogues, considérés surtout au point de vue de l'action de la morale sur le physique.* Paris: V. Masson.

Lindzey, G., Ed. (1954). *Handbook of social psychology* (2 vols.). Cambridge, Mass.: Addison-Wesley.

————, Ed. (1958). *Assessment of human motives.* New York: Rinehart. (Evergreen ed., 1960.)

Lipps, T. (1907). Das Wissen von fremden Ichen. *Psychol. Untersuch., 1,* 694–722.

Lowenthal, L., and N. Guterman (1949). *Prophets of deceit.* New York: Harper.

McDougall, W. (1908). *Introduction to social psychology.* London: Methuen.

———— (1920). *The group mind.* New York: G. P. Putnam's Sons. (Rev. ed., 1928.)

———— (1923). *Outline of psychology.* New York and Chicago: C. Scribner's.

———— (1932). *The energies of men: a study of the fundamentals of dynamic psychology.* London: Methuen.

Maier, N. R. F. (1952). *Principles of human relations.* New York: Wiley.

Malinowski, B. (1944). *A scientific theory of culture and other essays.* Chapel Hill: Univ. of North Carolina Press.

Mannheim, K. (1936). *Ideology and utopia.* (transl.). New York: Hartcourt, Brace.

Martin, E. D. (1920). *The behavior of crowds.* New York: Harper.

Marx, K., and F. Engels (1846). *The German ideology.* (Written 1846; first portions published 1903–1904. Transl. New York: International, 1937.)

May, M. A., and L. W. Doob (1937). *Competition and cooperation.* New York: Social Science Research Council. Bull. No. 25.

Mayer, A. (1903). Über Einzel- und Gesamtleistung des Schulkindes. *Arch. ges. Psychol., 1,* 276–416.

Mead, G. H. (1934). *Mind, self and society* (posthumous; C. M. Morris, Ed.). Chicago: Univ. of Chicago Press.

Mead, M. (1937). *Cooperation and competition among primitive peoples.* New York: McGraw-Hill.

Meltzer, H. (1930). Present status of experimental studies on the relationship of feeling to memory. *Psychol. Rev., 37,* 124–129.

Mesmer, F. A. (1779). *Mémoire sur la découverte du magnétisme animal.* (Transl. *Mesmerism.* London: MacDonald, 1948.)

Mill, J. S. (1863). *Utilitarianism.* London: Parker, Son, and Bourn. (Reprint from *Fraser's Magazine,* 1861.)

Miller, N. E., and J. Dollard (1941). *Social learning and imitation.* New Haven: Yale Univ. Press.

Moede, W. (1920). *Experimentelle Massenpsychologie.* Leipzig: S. Hirzel.

Moore, H. T. (1921). The comparative influence of majority and expert opinion. *Amer. J. Psychol., 32,* 16–20.

Moreno, J. L. (1934). *Who shall survive?* Washington, D.C.: Nervous and Mental Disease Publ. Co.

Müller, G. E., and A. Pilzecker (1900). Experimentelle Beiträge zur Lehre vom Gedächtniss. *Z. Psychol.,* Ergbd. 1.

Münsterberg, H. (1889). *Beiträge zur experimentellen Psychologie.* Vol. 1. Freiburg: Mohr.

Murray, H. A., and C. Morgan (1945). A clinical study of sentiments. *Genet. Psychol. Monogr., 32,* 3–149.

Murphy, G. (1949). *Historical introduction to modern psychology* (rev. ed.). New York: Harcourt, Brace.

Murphy, G., and L. B. Murphy (1931). *Experimental social psychology.* New York: Harper.

Murphy, G., L. B. Murphy, and T. M. Newcomb (1937). *Experimental social psychology* (rev. ed.). New York: Harper.

Murphy, L. B. (1937). *Social behavior and child personality: an exploratory study of some roots of sympathy.* New York: Columbia Univ. Press.

Newcomb, T. M., R. H. Turner, and P. E. Converse (1965). *Social psychology: the study of human interaction.* New York: Holt, Rinehart, and Winston.

Neitzsche, F. (1912 ed.). *Der Wille zur Macht.* Book 3. In *Werke,* Vol. 16. Leipzig: Alfred Kröner.

Parsons, T. (1937). *The structure of social action.* New York: McGraw-Hill.

_____ (1949). The rise and decline of economic man. *J. gen. Educ., 4,* 47–53.

Pear, T. H., Ed. (1950). *Psychological factors of peace and war.* London: Hutchinson.

Perry, R. B. (1922a). Is there a social mind? *Amer. J. Sociol., 27,* 561–572.

_____ (1922b). Is there a social mind? *Amer. J. Sociol., 27,* 721–736.

Piaget, J. (1932). *The moral judgment of the child* (transl.). London: Kegan Paul, Trench, Trubner.

Proshansky, H. M., and B. Seidenberg, Eds. (1965). *Basic studies in social psychology.* New York: Holt, Rinehart, and Winston.

Ribot, T. (1897). *The psychology of the emotions* (transl.). London: W. Scott.

Rice, S. A., Ed. (1931). *Methods in social science.* Chicago: Univ. of Chicago Press.

Rivers, W. H. R. (1926). *Psychology and ethnology.* New York: Harcourt, Brace.

Roheim, G. (1925). *Australian totemism: a psychoanalytic study in anthropology.* London: Allen and Unwin.

Ross, E. A. (1908). *Social psychology.* New York: Macmillan.

Royce, J. (1913). *The problem of Christianity.* Vol. 2. New York: Macmillan.

Russell, B. (1938). *Power.* New York: Norton.

_____ (1945). *History of western philosophy.* New York: Simon and Schuster.

Sabine, G. H. (1961). *A history of political theory* (3rd ed.). New York: Holt, Rinehart, and Winston.

Schachter, S. (1959). *The psychology of affiliation: experimental studies of the sources of gregariousness.* Stanford: Stanford Univ. Press.

Schaeffle, A. (1875–1878). *Bau und Leben des sozialen Körpers* (4 vols.). Tübingen: H. Laupp.

Scheler, M. (1923). *Wesen und Formen der Sympathie* (2nd ed.). Bonn: Friedrich Cohen. (Transl. P. Heath, *The nature of sympathy.* New Haven: Yale Univ. Press, 1954.)

Schultz, D. P. (1964). *Panic behavior: discussion and readings.* New York: Random House.

Shand, A. (1896). Character and the emotions. *Mind, 21,* 203–342.

Sidis, B. (1898). *The psychology of suggestion.* New York: D. Appleton.

Sighele, S. (1891). *La foule criminelle.* Transl. Paris: Baillière, 1892.

_____ (1893). *Le crime à deux.* Transl. Lyon: A. Storck, 1893.

_____ (1895). *Psychologie des sectes.* Transl. Paris: V. Girard et E. Brière, 1898.

Simmel, G. (1950). *The sociology of Georg Simmel* (K. H. Wolff, Transl. and Ed.). Glencoe, Ill.: Free Press.

Smelser, N. J. (1963). *Theory of collective behavior.* New York: Free Press.

Smith, A. (1759). *The theory of moral sentiments.* London: A. Miller.

_____ (1776). *An inquiry into the nature and causes of the wealth of nations.* London: W. Strahan and T. Cadell.

Sorokin, P. A. (1928). *Contemporary sociological theories.* New York: Harper.

_____, Ed. (1950). *Explorations in altruistic love and behavior: a symposium.* Boston: Beacon Press.

Spencer, H. (1862). *First principles.* (Preface dated 1862.) New York: Appleton, 1895.

_____ (1870). *The principles of psychology* (2nd. ed.). Vol. 1. London: Williams and Norgate.

_____ (1872). *The principles of psychology* (2nd. ed.). Vol. 2. London: Williams and Norgate.

_____ (1876). *The principles of sociology* (2 vols.). (Reissued New York: D. Appleton, 1900.)

Sprowls, J. W. (1927). *Social psychology interpreted.* Baltimore: Williams and Wilkins.

Starbuck, E. D. (1899). *The psychology of religion.* London: W. Scott.

Steiner, I. D., and M. Fishbein (1965). *Current studies in social psychology.* New York: Holt, Rinehart, and Winston.

Stirner, M. (J. K. Schmidt) (1845). *Der Einzige und sein Eigenthum.* Leipzig: O. Wigand. (Transl. *The ego and his own.* New York: B. R. Tucker, 1907.)

Suttie, I. D. (1935). *The origins of love and hate.* London: Kegan Paul, Trench, Truber.

Tarde, G. (1903). *The laws of imitation* (transl.). New York: Henry Holt.

Thomas, W. I., and F. Znaniecki (1918–1920). *The Polish peasant in Europe and America* (5 vols.). Boston: Badger.

Thorndike, E. L. (1898). Animal intelligence: an experimental study of the associative process in animals. *Psychol. Rev., Monogr. Suppl.* No. 8.

_____ (1913). *Educational psychology.* Vol. 2: The original nature of man. New York: Columbia Univ. Teachers College.

Thurnwald, R., Ed. (1925–1935). *Forschungen zur Völkerpsychologie und Soziologie* (14 vols.). Leipzig: C. L. Hirschfeld.

Thurstone, L. L. (1927–1928). Attitudes can be measured. *Amer. J. Sociol., 33,* 529–554.

Titchener, E. B. (1908). *Lectures on the elementary psychology of feeling and attention.* New York: Macmillan.

_____ (1909). *Experimental psychology of the thought processes.* New York: Macmillan.

_____ (1916). *A textbook of psychology* (new ed.). New York: Macmillan. (First published 1910.)

Travis, L. E. (1925). The influence of the group upon the stutterer's speed in free association. *J. abnorm. soc. Psychol., 20,* 142–146.

Triplett, N. (1897). The dynamogenic factors in pacemaking and competition. *Amer. J. Psychol., 9,* 507–533.

Troland, L. T. (1928). *Fundamentals of human motivation.* New York: Van Nostrand.

Trotter, W. (1916). *Instincts of the herd in peace and war.* New York: Macmillan.

Vaughan, C. E. (1939). *Studies in the history of political philosophy before and after Rousseau* (2 vols.). Manchester, Eng.: University Press.

Vico, G. (1725). *The new science of Gianbattista Vico.* (Transl. from 3rd ed., 1744. Ithaca: Cornell Univ. Press, 1948.)

Waelder, R. (1939). *Psychological aspects of war and peace.* Geneva: Geneva Research Centre.

Wallas, G. (1908). *Human nature in politics.* London: A. Constable.

Wallis, W. D. (1925). The independence of social psychology. *J. abnorm. soc. Psychol., 20,* 147–150.

Ward, H. C. (1926). *Thobbing.* Indianapolis: Bobbs-Merrill.

Warren, H. C., Ed. (1934). *Dictionary of psychology.* Boston: Houghton Mifflin.

Washburn, M. F. (1916). *Movement and mental imagery.* Boston: Houghton Mifflin.

Watson, G. (1928). Do groups think more efficiently than individuals? *J. abnorm. soc. Psychol., 23,* 328–336.

Watson, J. B. (1919). *Psychology from the standpoint of a behaviorist.* New York: J. B. Lippincott.

White, L. A. (1949). *The science of culture.* New York: Farrar, Straus. (Also reprinted in paperback form by Grove Press.)

White, R. K., and R. Lippitt (1960). *Autocracy and democracy.* New York: Harper.

White, R. W. (1963). *Ego and reality in psychoanalytic theory.* New York: International Univ. Press.

Whittemore, I. C. (1924). Influence of competition on performance: an experimental study. *J. abnorm. soc. Psychol., 19,* 236–253.

Wiener, N. (1948). *Cybernetics.* New York: Wiley.

Williams, W. (1920). *What's on the worker's mind.* New York: Scribner's.

Windelband, W. (1935). *A history of philosophy.* Transl. (2nd rev. ed.). New York: Macmillan.

Wissler, C. (1923). *Man and culture.* New York: Thomas Y. Crowell.

Wolin, S. S. (1960). *Politics and vision: continuity in western political thought.* Boston: Little, Brown.

Woodworth, R. S. (1918). *Dynamic psychology.* New York: Columbia Univ. Press.

Wundt, W. (1862). *Beiträge zur Theorie der Sinneswahrnehmung.* Leipzig: C. F. Winter.

_____ (1910–1920). *Völkerpsychologie: eine Untersuchung der Entwicklungsgesetze von Sprache, Mythus und Sitte* (10 vols.). Leipzig: Engelmann. (Transl. Vols. 1–3, *Elements of folk psychology.* New York: Macmillan, 1916.)

Young, K., Ed. (1931). *Social attitudes.* New York: Henry Holt.

CHAPTER 2

Major Developments in Social Psychology During the Past Five Decades

Edward E. Jones
Princeton University

Chapter 1 by G. W. Allport sets the stage for the following review of the past five decades of social psychology. We need not recapitulate, then, the celebrated event of Triplett's (1898) experiment, the coincidental publication of social psychology texts by the sociologist Ross and the psychologist McDougall in 1908, or the defining impact on psychology of F. H. Allport's 1924 text. In addition, we accept G. W. Allport's definition of social psychology with its emphasis on "the thought, feeling, and behavior of individuals" as shaped by the "actual, imagined, or implied presence of others." Finally, we concur that social psychology (or at least the field as currently defined) is largely a North American phenomenon. The reasons why this is so will be explored later in this chapter. This chapter will concentrate on American social psychology with only occasional references to European developments. Although European social psychology (at least until quite recently) has been largely

Preparation of this chapter was supported in part by the National Science Foundation. Portions of the chapter were written while the author was a Fellow at the Center for Advanced Study in the Behavioral Sciences. The author is indebted to the many readers of early drafts who helped to shape the present version. They are, unfortunately, too numerous (and no doubt in some cases too reluctant) to be mentioned.

derived from American models and methods, it should be noted that many outstanding contributors to the field were European refugees, a fact that lead Cartwright (1979) to name Adolph Hitler as the one person who had the greatest impact on the development of social psychology. Without the influence of Lewin, Heider, Lazarsfeld, the Brunswiks, and Katona; and without the upheaval of the Second World War and the political events preceding it, the history of social psychology would be different indeed.

INTERDISCIPLINE OR SUBDISCIPLINE?

Perhaps it is curious that a subject matter focusing on the "thought, feeling, and behavior of individuals" should have strong roots in the field of sociology as well as psychology. G. W. Allport has noted the lack of clearly defined boundaries among the various social sciences, and social psychology seems like an excellent candidate for an interdisciplinary field. In 1951 Newcomb argued that social psychology is the study of interaction in its own right, and thus requires a field separate from either psychology or sociology.

In general, however, proponents of both the interdisciplinary and the separate disciplinary approaches have failed in their efforts and social psychology has clearly evolved as a subdiscipline of psychology—with some resonating pockets of highly compatible interest in sociology. This judgment is supported by the history of failed interdisciplinary administrative arrangements in U.S. universities, by the increasing domination by psychologists of the social psychology textbook market (and the allied college course market), and by the proportionate volume of social psychological literature in psychological journals.

Undoubtedly the boldest and most celebrated early effort to break down the barriers between social science disciplines was Harvard's formation of the Department of Social Relations in 1946. Here social psychology was to exist as one of four component parts, the other three being clinical psychology, sociology, and cultural anthropology. Though the department was born in an atmosphere of heady exhilaration, it was soon subject to the inexorable pressures of regression toward the parent disciplines of psychology, sociology, and anthropology. This regression may have had more to do with the academic job market, publication opportunities, and internal politics than with intellectual concerns. Nevertheless, for a variety of tangled reasons the study of social relations became increasingly fractionated and the label is now a concession to nostalgia that is attached to a reconstructed psychology department.

An alternative arrangement emerged at the University of Michigan when a joint psychology-sociology doctoral program in social psychology was established in 1946. Psychologists always outnumbered sociologists in this program, however, and it was eventually abandoned in 1967, not without some bitterness on the part of representatives from both departments (Newcomb, 1973). Columbia University exemplified the separate discipline alternative when it authorized the formation of the De-

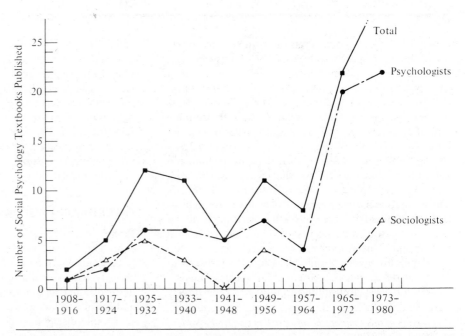

FIGURE 1
Introductory Social Psychology Textbooks Published in the United States, 1908–1980, Written by Psychologists and by Sociologists.

Figures for "total" include collaborations by psychologists and sociologists as well as texts authored by neither group. A full list of titles is available from the author.

partment of Social Psychology in 1961. Shortly after its formation, however, the small faculty of this new department worked to re-establish itself with the psychology department, an endeavor accomplished eight years after the initial split.

Interdisciplinary institutes and research groupings have been more common and more viable. Yale's Institute of Human Relations was an early and important example of such a grouping, lasting from 1929 until its gradual demise in the early 1960s. The University of Michigan's Institute for Social Research, a more durable prototype, still thrives after more than thirty years. Typically, however, such institutes or laboratories or research groups have had more to do with funding and with space than with fundamental intellectual convergence.

If one considers social psychology textbooks, a different kind of case may be made for viewing social psychology primarily as a psychological subdiscipline. In the early 1950s G. W. Allport noted that somewhat more than half of the dozens of social psychology textbooks were written by psychologists. This trend has accelerated, as Fig. 1 clearly shows. Out of seventy-three textbooks appearing between 1947 and 1980 fully 75 percent were written by psychologists, 22 percent were written by sociologists, and 3 percent were collaborative efforts capitalizing on the overlap between the two fields.

Those who question the value of such frequency counts may be somewhat mollified by the realization that textbooks in social psychology have played a distinctive role in shaping and integrating the field. This has been particularly true of a handful of systematic and original texts written by psychologists. It is hard to think of another field in which textbooks have served as such an important vehicle for theorizing about, and generating influential distinctions within, their subject matter. Two examples suffice to make the point. The highly original textbook of Krech and Crutchfield (1948), with its organizing propositions, influenced a generation of social psychologists and several generations of subsequent textbook authors. Asch's (1952) textbook represents an elegant and articulate advocacy of a neogestalt approach to social psychology, emphasizing humankind's rational capacities and the primacy of the individual's search for understanding. It, too, has had a lasting impact on the field and represents a major contribution to our understanding of social psychological processes.

In addition, empirical journals in social psychology are more likely to be edited by psychologists than by sociologists or to be sponsored by psychological organiza-

tions. The following major journals publish almost the entire empirical literature of social psychology in the United States:

- *Basic and Applied Social Psychology*
- *Journal of Applied Social Psychology*
- *Journal of Experimental Social Psychology*
- *Journal of Personality*
- *Journal of Personality and Social Psychology*
- *Journal of Social Issues*
- *Journal of Social Psychology*
- *Personality and Social Psychology Bulletin*
- *Social Cognition*
- *Social Psychology Quarterly*

Of these, only *Social Psychology Quarterly* (formerly *Sociometry*) is edited and sponsored by sociologists (The American Sociological Association), and many of the articles in this journal are written by psychologists.

Despite the quantitative dominance by psychologists and psychological organizations in the conduct of social psychology's intellectual business, it is not surprising that sociologists usually reject Allport's definition of social psychology and the assumption that it is a psychological subdiscipline. Stryker (1977) distinguishes between psychological and sociological social psychologies, arguing that the latter is more explicitly concerned with reciprocity of the society and the individual and with social interaction per se. He points specifically to developments of the symbolic interactionist model, identity theory, and ethnomethodology. House (1977) adds a third face to social psychology, namely, the study of social structure and personality. He notes that each of the three faces of social psychology is associated with a characteristic method: psychological social psychology with the experimental method, symbolic interactionism with participant observation and informal interviewing, and sociological social psychology (or social structure and personality) with survey methods. Both Stryker and House argue for increased cross-fertilization and interchange among the social psychologies.

Examples of such cross-fertilization can be seen in the impact of Erving Goffman (1959) and other symbolic interactions (Mead, 1934; Manis and Meltzer, 1962), on psychological accounts of self-presentation (cf. Schlenker, 1980), and in how the work of B. F. Skinner (1953) influenced the behavioral sociology approach to interaction (Homans, 1961, 1974; Burgess and Bushell, 1969). Although these instances of interdisciplinary influence are important, it remains the case that the literatures of the social aspects of psychology and of the psychological aspects of sociology are remarkably sealed off from each other. Take, for example, the relatively self-contained literatures of medical sociology and labeling approaches on the one hand and behavioral medicine and attributional approaches on the other. Such mutual isolation and disciplinary inbreeding is not entirely irrational, however, because the central foci and traditions of the two disciplines are quite divergent. For the sociological social psychologist the proccesses of interaction are viewed largely from a social function or a system maintenance point of view. Processes of conformity, for example, may be viewed by the sociologist in the broader institutional context of social control and normative stability. The psychologist, on the other hand, is more likely to treat conformity as a process of reality definition or a personal adaptation to affiliative pressures.

In conclusion, there is some interweaving between psychological and sociological approaches to interpersonal behavior, but the ultimate interests of the two approaches are distinctive. Therefore much of the overlap in empirical content may reflect superficial similarities that gloss over distinct analytic differences. Moreover, the sheer volume of work on interpersonal processes in psychology relative to sociology sustains our claim that most of social psychology may be treated as a subdiscipline of the field of psychology, though much research by psychologists has some homologous ties to microsociological concerns with the details of social interaction and the processes of social control.

THE SOCIAL PSYCHOLOGY-PERSONALITY INTERFACE

As much of psychology became increasingly austere in the 1930s and 1940s, pushing toward a more refined understanding of molecular learning, sensory, and perceptual processes, a more molar, integrative thrust also evolved into the psychology of personality. Personality theories vied with each other to provide comprehensive accounts of the motivational dynamics of the "whole person."

Many of these theories were heavily influenced by psychoanalysis (e.g., Murray, 1938; Erickson, 1950).

Others fused dynamic motivational ideas to strong social psychological concerns (e.g., Horney, 1939; Sullivan, 1947). G. W. Allport (1937) specifically rejected many major psychoanalytic assumptions, formulating a sophisticated trait theory of personality and a conception of motivation that was liberated from infantile fixations. Other personality theories were elaborations of reinforcement and conditioning propositions central to research in learning (Dollard and Miller, 1950; McClelland, 1951; Rotter, 1954).

Although all personality theories focus primarily on more or less stable internal structures and processes, personality theorists have generally acknowledged that a comprehensive view of human action requires some specification of the actor's social environment. Since it is even more generally understood that personality structures reflect individualized social experiences, it is not surprising that personality psychologists and social psychologists have often fallen into symbiotic relationships. One view, at least, is that each needs the other to achieve reasonable precision in the prediction of decisions and choices in the complex natural environment. Without a recognition of individual differences, the social psychologist must be content with low-level actuarial predictions of responses to representative settings. On the other hand, without taking into account the requirements and cue values of situations, the personality psychologist can only talk about the most generalized trans-situational response tendencies. And the existence of such tendencies in other than ability and stylistic domains is highly debatable (Mischel, 1968).

Perhaps some such awareness of mutual dependence prompted Morton Prince to change the name of the publication, *Journal of Abnormal Psychology,* to that of the *Journal of Abnormal and Social Psychology* in 1921 and to invite F. H. Allport to serve as a cooperating editor. In 1965, now under the auspices of the American Psychological Association, a new alignment resulted once again in a revived *Journal of Abnormal Psychology,* and a new *Journal of Personality and Social Psychology.* Another sign of integrative pull is the fact that the Society of Personality and Social Psychology is one of the largest and most active divisions in the American Psychological Association, with a total of more than 4,000 members, fellows, and associates. A journal sponsored by this division is called the *Personality and Social Psychology Bulletin.* Though a 1980 referendum approved a reorganization of the society into sections, 60 percent of the members chose affiliation with the section called "Both

Personality and Social Psychology." In addition to this evidence at the organizational level of the integration of personality and social psychology, the independedent *Journal of Personality* has published articles for many years, to use Sechrest's (1976) description, "in the mainstream of social psychology." Finally, the fact that there are many graduate programs labeled "personality and social psychology" across the country suggests at least some consensus regarding an intellectual affinity between the two approaches to molar behavior.

Within the history of psychology, many individuals defy an easy classification as being either a social or a personality psychologist and have theorized about one in such a way as to incorporate the other. The names of G. W. Allport, Gardner Murphy, and Daniel Katz stand out in this regard. Many other self-identified social psychologists have developed dispositional measures to capture important individual difference dimensions. The Authoritarian Personality scales provide one well-known example (Adorno, Frenkel-Brunswik, Levinson, and Sanford, 1950). Others include "Machiavellianism" (Christie and Geis, 1970) and "self-monitoring" (Snyder, 1974).

Undoubtedly there are those who would insist that a comprehensive social psychology must include relevant dispositional constructs as manifested by persistent complaints in the "personality" chapters of recent *Annual Reviews of Psychology* that social psychologists have taken over or at least "dominate" the field of personality. Sechrest (1976), in particular, complains that social psychologists have "nabbed off" a number of personality-relevant concerns that are therefore now identified as parts of the domain of social psychology: for example, attribution, aggression, emotion, obesity. Helson and Mitchell (1978) express similar concerns about the identity of the field of personality, wondering whether parts of the field will disappear and, because of the absence of "a viable center and core problems," whether the field itself will disappear with them.

In addition to the combinatorial, integrationist forces and incorporative, imperialistic forces within social psychology there have also been strong separatist forces. These forces were in part mobilized by the metatheoretical statements of Kurt Lewin, but they have also been strengthened by the methodological distinction between experimental (S–R) and correlational (R–R) approaches (cf. Cronbach, 1957). In his persistent advocacy of the relational or constructive versus the classificatory or taxonomic approach to conceptual development,

Lewin argued explicitly against explanations involving individual differences (1951a, p. 61). This argument was part of a more general opposition of Galilean versus Aristotelian science and was no doubt heavily influenced by Cassirer's (1923) distinction between *thing* concepts and *relation* concepts.

An outgrowth of this way of thinking was Lewin's preference for systematic versus historical explanations and his emphasis on contemporaneous, situational causation. Since personality theory has almost invariably included developmental accounts and featured historically flavored determinism, Lewin's "Dynamic Theory of Personality" hardly seems like a theory of personality at all. Though he did have his own ideas of intrapersonal structure, the emphasis of his writings is on the deterministic potency of the concrete situation in which the individual found himself.

Perhaps as a legacy of the strong Lewinian influence on social psychology, many opinion leaders of social psychology have tended to view the inclusion of individual difference variables in experimental research as an unimaginative concession to ignorance or to poor experimental planning. In their view of "personality and social interaction" in the second edition of this handbook, Marlowe and Gergen (1968) distinguish between researchers primarily interested in situational effects who use individual difference measures to account for some of the variance and those researchers concerned with the manifestations within social interaction contexts of single personality dimensions. Those in the former group often treat the interactive or main effects of their individual difference variables with apologetic demurrers, as if conceding that accounting for variance is not necessarily an act of scientific enlightenment. Those in the latter group may wish to dissociate themselves from clinical or psychometric approaches to personality study, but they presumably are comfortable attempting to predict behavior in meaningful social settings from indices based on penciled responses to brief inventories. Their comfort no doubt suggests the absence of a strong Lewinian introject, but it is hard to gainsay the heuristic fruitfulness of the best examples of this approach (Adorno *et al.*, 1950; Christie and Geis, 1970; Snyder, 1974, 1979).

The intellectual, almost ideological, battle between what has been called situationism (Bowers, 1973) and what might be called dispositionism, flared into the open at the beginning of the 1970s. In a series of books and papers, Mischel (1968, 1973, 1977) criticized those trait psychologists who search for trans-situational dispositions, claiming that behavioral consistencies across settings are empirically rare. He also discussed some reasons why the level of consistency is thought to be higher than it really is. The presumption of exaggerated *perceived* consistency resonated with developments in attribution theory was featured in a paper on actor-observer differences by Jones and Nisbett (1971) and later became celebrated as the "fundamental attribution error" (Ross, 1977). The error referred to is the tendency of observers to underestimate the power of situations in shaping a target person's behavior and to overestimate the correspondence between behavior and dispositions.

It can reasonably be argued that the proposal of this particular form of attribution error, along with Mischel's advocacy of a stimulus-oriented social learning view of personality, drove a deeper wedge between the traditionalists in social psychology and those favoring the explorations of systematic individual differences. The "Establishment" social psychologists could now claim that the individual difference approach was not only causally uninformative but also based on an illusory assumption. The reliability of dispositional differences, in this view, was vastly overrated by personality psychologists who were victimized by the fundamental attribution error. It mattered little that some personality psychologists took strong exception to this line of argument (cf. Block 1977; Hogan, DeSoto, and Solano, 1977).

It mattered more, perhaps, that Daryl Bem sought a constructive rapprochement in several papers combining empirical data with theoretical argument. Bem and Allen (1974) take us back to G. W. Allport's advocacy of an idiographic approach to personal consistency. They argue that people are only consistent when the specified dispositional dimensions apply to them or are personally relevant. Bem and Allen contend that individual differences reside primarily in *which* personality traits are important, central, or salient for the individual, and they report a demonstration study that supports this position.

In subsequent papers Bem (Bem and Funder, 1978; Bem, 1980a; Bem, 1980b) has advocated the development of assessment techniques for characterizing both persons and situations in comparable terms. Bem and Lord's study (1979) provides one example of the use of an assessment technique to predict response preferences in a prisoners' dilemma game. Judges provided Q-sort ratings of the kind of person who would adopt competitive, independent, or joint outcome strategies in the game. Roommates' ratings of individual subjects' tendencies to be competitive in the natural environment were found to be significantly related to the strategy actually chosen by the subject. Bem and Lord thus provided evidence for the ecological validity of a particular laboratory setting, that involving a mixed-motive game. The flexibility of what Bem has called the "template matching" approach seems to promise renewed pressures toward the integration of social and personality approaches in predicting behavior.

The question of how best to characterize the interplay between personalities and situations remains a matter of considerable controversy, however. In spite of their general sympathy with idiographic approaches and strong situational influences, Mischel and Peake (1982) criticize Bem's approach as too empirical and produce some evidence to support their contention that "atheoretical approaches yield results that tend to seem promising at first but are notoriously difficult to replicate."

It is not surprising that someone (Endler and Magnuson, 1976) has proposed that the only reasonable position to take with regard to persons and situations is a strong interactionism. The argument is that person, situation, and behavior all affect each other continuously. They are so causally intertwined that it is impossible to separate out the effects of one, the other, or even their statistical interactions by conventional analysis of variance techniques. These and other issues are discussed in Chapter 15 in greater detail, but it is obvious that the relations between social and personality psychology are very much in ferment at the present time.

In summary, no one has ever argued that behavior is entirely determined by the actor's pre-existing dispositions or that all variance in behavior can be accounted for by an analysis of situational cues or requirements. It is both popular and truistic to emphasize the importance of the person-situation interaction term. However, social and personality psychologists have historically placed their bets on different elements in the Lewinian $B = f(P,E)$ equation. Social psychologists not strongly infected by the Field Theory virus have generally emphasized the complementarity of approaches emphasizing settings and approaches emphasizing dispositions. The strong experimental model emerging from the Lewinian camp attached secondary importance, at best, to individual differences. The individual difference approach has been further eroded within social psychology by the emphasis on attributional error that involves assigning too much weight to internal dispositions. In addition, it has been eroded within personality psychology itself by those who favor a social learning approach, since this approach emphasizes distinctive learning histories and current reinforcement contingencies. It seems possible that methods based on idiographic considerations and parallel analyses of perceived situations will revive interest in personality psychology and strengthen its now fragile ties with social psychology. It also seems likely that separatist pressures will be more persistent if personality is conceived exclusively in terms of individual differences than if it is conceived in terms of general cognitive and motivational processes. Social psychological research must invariably include explicit or implicit theorizing about persons, but that theorizing is likely to be strongly oriented to the role of situational or contextual influences, as perceived and interpreted by the person involved.

THE GEOGRAPHY OF SOCIAL PSYCHOLOGY

The field of social psychology grew out of the recognition of human diversity within cultural uniformity. The social psychologist typically seeks a level of generalization that falls between broad cultural abstractions and accounts of individual learning experiences. If personality were merely the subjective side of culture or if uniqueness always overwhelmed the variance attributable to cultural constraints, the concept of a social psychology would hardly be salient. The individual must be seen as the intersection point of a variety of pressures: immediate situational demands, conflicting social expectations, and internalized beliefs and values. It is the social psychologist's task to understand how the conflict among these pressures is resolved. Though social psychologists typically work with samples that are culturally homogeneous and adapt the content of their inquiry to the concerns of the sample members, they hope to uncover relationships that can be stated in general and fundamental terms.

These considerations have some bearing on the "geography" of social psychology's development. It seems to follow from the intersecting pressures model that social psychology would be less prominent, if it existed at all, in more homogeneous and traditional cultures. In such cultures behavior priorities within settings are rather well established by unquestioned cultural norms. Conflict is minimal as everyone more or less follows the traditional ways. The presence of competing normative options may account, in part, for the distinctive flowering of social psychology in the United States,

and for the distribution of social psychologists and programs within our states and regions.

The development of social psychology encompasses a very short time span. Cartwright (1979) estimates that 90 percent of all social psychologists who have ever lived are alive at the present time. He also suggests that social psychology truly became a field only after the Second World War when it exploded into prominence in America at a time when European and Asian universities were reeling from the exhausting global struggle. Within the United States, however, the emergence of social psychology was strongly linked to universities in metropolitan regions: Columbia, Yale, Harvard, and the University of Michigan. Until the postwar explosion Cartwright describes, vast areas of the country were innocent of any contact with academic social psychology. Psychology departments in midwestern universities—with the notable exception of the University of Michigan—were almost exclusively involved in "brass instrument" methodology, research on traditional problems of learning and sensory processes, and in the applications of aptitude and interest measurement. This traditionalism was at least as pronounced in the southeastern region of the United States where most prewar psychology departments viewed themselves as closely tied to the natural sciences on the one hand or to philosophy on the other. It is tempting to propose that just as the United States, the melting pot of world cultures, was a natural context for the emergence of social psychology, so for similar reasons within the United States, social psychology emerged most vigorously in the universities of metropolitan urban areas. It was here that problems of intergroup conflict, prejudice, deviance, and attitudinal differences were the most salient. Indeed, a rural social psychology is almost a contradiction in terms, at least in comparison to a psychology based on animal behavior.

Added to this rather benign view of urban versus rural impact is the likelihood that ideology, prejudice, and economics may have also been involved in the distribution of social psychology programs. Cartwright suggests (personal communication) that it was difficult for social psychology to penetrate the Old South because of the volatile conditions of racial ferment that prevailed there from 1930 to 1960. Many administrators (and legislators) probably viewed social psychology as a troublesome disrupter of the status quo. In addition, Cartwright proposes, social psychology may have come sooner to the prosperous schools of the Northeast not because they were urban, but because they could afford this "luxury" of adding a social component to the more traditional areas of learning, sensory processes, and physiological psychology.

Although social psychology was nurtured until the mid 1940s in only a handful of prestigious metropolitan universities, the end of the Second World War clearly accelerated its growth in these universities and in other institutions influenced by them. Nevertheless, the growth of the field was still largely contained in a few universities large enough to support diverse interests within a psychology department. Until well into the 1950s, only a small number of university departments had anything approaching a program of study in social psychology.

During the next fifteen years, however, social psychology spread into every region of the country, and social psychology doctoral programs began to multiply. A proliferation of undergraduate offerings is also apparent in the upsurge in social psychology textbooks in the late 1960s. This striking diffusion of social psychology and social psychologists may be seen as a product of the general academic expansion affecting all academic fields plus an additional impetus stemming from a new perception of social psychology as constructively linked to the experimental method and therefore entitled to a place in the psychological mainstream. This respectability was not universally accorded, but there was enough of an increment to make a difference in an expanding academic economy.

Summary remarks. In summary, the growth of social psychology has been shaped by the intertwining of accident with broader socio-political events. We have argued that social psychology was, for an important period at least, not only largely confined to the United States but largely an urban phenomenon. This does not explain why Lewin was invited to the Iowa Child Welfare Station in 1934, or why attribution theory flowered in Kansas, to which Fritz Heider moved in 1947. In general, however, social psychology can be accurately described as the understandable intellectual by-product of normative complexity. It is thus not surprising that historically the major urban centers were the spawning ground for social psychology in its early formative years, though the picture now is one of widespread geographical and regional diffusion. It is interesting to speculate whether social psychology will maintain its newly gained footing in the more traditional, culturally homogeneous regions of the United States when, as seems likely, many universities will be forced to trim their programs and faculty rosters.

THE SOCIAL PSYCHOLOGY OF RESEARCH CONCERNS IN SOCIAL PSYCHOLOGY

This section might be labeled "bandwagons and sinking ships" for it deals with the waxing and waning of research fashions in social psychology. Many social psychologists feel that their field is uniquely or especially vulnerable to faddism. Since the grounds for such feelings are largely matters of definition and involve developments that evade easy documentation, it would be hard to prove that social psychology is unique in this respect. Surely there are bandwagons upon which graduate students and more established scholars climb in all research fields. However, it may be that such labels as "fad" or "fashion" are more easily applied to the social sciences than to the natural sciences because developments in the social sciences tend to be less cumulative and each research concern is therefore more limited by time. In any event, any student of social psychology knows that particular theories or methods or paradigms gain favor, dominate segments of the literature for a period of time, and then recede from view. Taking a look at the history of social psychology, a historical analysis should have something to offer about why the field is vulnerable to faddism.

THE "WAXING" OF RESEARCH INTERESTS

To avoid the pejorative connotations of "fads and fashions," let us speak more neutrally of *dominating research themes* to characterize rather self-contained spurts of interests in a particular topic or in a particular way of looking at an old topic in the research literature. We suspect there would be fairly wide agreement on the following examples: social facilitation effects, prestige suggestion effects, authoritarian personality studies, the forced-compliance paradigm in dissonance research, Asch's conformity research paradigm, the "risky shift" phenomenon, bystander intervention, mixed motive game research, overjustification effects, and actor-observer attribution differences. A consideration of these examples suggests that there is no single determinant of "waxing." Indeed, we can identify six determinants that might reasonably be relevant and important.

The first is the social and political Zeitgeist. Social psychology is obviously affected more than most disciplines by the surrounding social milieu. As Cartwright (1961) notes, it depends on society for financial support, it obtains its data from society, and its finding may be used to influence the course of societal events. The data-providing function needs amplification because it is true in so many respects. Society provides not only our subjects but also many of the themes and problems that challenge and instigate the research progress. For example, the study of attitude change received enormous impetus from concerns during the Second World War with propaganda, military morale, and the potential integration of ethnic minorities into established military units. Authoritarian personality research obviously grew out of the Nazi experience as did, in a quite different way, Milgram's later research on obedience. It seems more than a coincidence that the widespread interest in the determinants of peer conformity reached its peak shortly after the rise of Senator McCarthy and associated public concerns with social deviance in the form of "card-carrying Communists" and "fellow travelers." Much of the interest in mixed-motive games derived from concerns about international disarmament negotiations in a nuclear age. While specifically citing the Kitty Genovese murder as its starting point, bystander intervention research was nurtured by a broader public concern with urban alienation, apathy, and anomie. Undoubtedly many other connections between social problems and research themes can be traced but these examples are probably clear enough to make the point without further elaboration.

A more subtle and yet related source of research themes can be found in the personal interests and concerns of the innovating researcher and of others who resonate to the theme he or she introduces. We assume that most researchers work on problems that interest them personally. Though the sources of this interest are undoubtedly numerous, an important determinant may be the motivational dynamics of the researcher. It would be extremely mischievous (and just plain wrong) to assert that all aggression researchers are personally troubled by the management of their own aggressive impulses, that reactance theorists are especially touchy about their personal freedom, that students of bargaining have a deathly fear either of being outmaneuvered in negotiations or of being too ruthlessly exploitative. Nevertheless, a research problem that is endlessly fascinating to one group of psychologists may seem totally trivial to another. It stands to reason that one source of this fascination is the salience of the problem in the researcher's personal life space. If Professor X is totally unconcerned with his own appearance, he is not likely to spend a lifetime doing research on the effects of physical attractiveness. Victims of prejudice are probably more likely than nonvictims to end up as its students. Certainly the number of males who are interested in sex roles and in sexist discrimination is eclipsed by female counterparts. Students of inequity, locus of control, and achievement motivation may also have become involved in these problems because of personal concerns.

Although our intent is not to minimize the complexity that may underlie personal concerns, it is probable that only a very small minority of researchers attempt to resolve their own hidden conflicts or neurotic problems through their own research. More have chosen research problems that are natural and open reflections of their past experiences in the absence of hidden motivational dynamics. Still others, perhaps a definite majority, choose to work on problems bearing no particular relation to their own unique social or personal history. Nevertheless we feel confident in asserting that *sometimes* a cluster of empirical studies is spawned by a researcher attempting to illuminate a personal enigma. In the process, the researcher develops propositions to which a significant group of other researchers resonate.

A second determinant of dominant research themes is theoretical power. The classic or conventional image of scientific deduction embraces a sequence running from assumptions, to theoretical propositions, to experimental tests. Though it has, perhaps, become fashionable to note the many exceptions to this idealized sequence in the real world of social science research, it remains true that a good theory can provide a powerful stimulus for research. Almost by definition, *good* theories are likely to get involved in bandwagon effects as claims, qualifications, and counterclaims dominate a segment of the literature. This involvement ends when the theory becomes part of accepted social science wisdom, is demonstrated to have little or no predictive utility, or is supplanted by a better theory more congruent with existing data. (At appropriate points in this chapter documentation about the role that theories have played in the recent history of social psychology will be presented.)

Convenient research paradigms constitute a third determinant. Unlike the natural sciences where advances are often dependent on technical innovations in measurement or detection, there is no such applicable technology to mark advances in the social sciences. However, there are new measuring instruments that have often facilitated clusters of research because of their convenience and availability. This is particularly obvious in the case of personality measures. We have seen the waxing and waning of research on authoritarianism, need for achievement, social desirability, locus of control, and Machiavellianism. In addition, dominant research themes can also emerge from convenient research designs or experimental scenarios. Some of the attractiveness of Asch's path-breaking studies of impression formation stems from the fact that they involve the extremely simple procedure of giving subjects lists of adjectives and asking them to rate or describe the person characterized by them. Thus it is not surprising that his "warm-cold" study (see page 87) was soon followed by dozens of replications with slight variations. Norman Anderson later gave this paradigm an even more solid footing by developing all-purpose lists of adjectives scaled for evaluative direction and potency. In addition, an argument can be made that one reason for the shift in interest from dissonance research to attribution research in the late 1960s and early 1970s is the fact that much attribution research could be performed without having to construct elaborate scenarios involving complex cover stories. In contrast, research in such areas as personal attraction, social comparison, and aggression has persisted more because of the practical and theoretical importance of these problems than because of the development of convenient research paradigms for their investigation. Elaborate, impactful experiments such as those conducted by Aronson and Linder (1965), Walster (1965), or Milgram (1974) are very costly to replicate and do not readily form the cornerstones of dominating themes.

The fourth determinant is the prestige of the innovator and his institution or laboratory. More than most areas of psychology, social psychology is a personalized subdiscipline. People are often more concerned with "what Arbuthnot is up to" than with the state of knowledge on a particular topic. Prestigious researchers can be very influential in elevating the perceived importance of a research topic or claiming it for social psychology. For example, Schachter's prestige was an important determinant of the sudden upsurge of interest in the effects of birth order that occurred in the 1960s, and the facts that Osgood became interested in attitude change, Kelley in attribution, Freedman in crowding, and Thibaut in procedural justice no doubt enhanced the legitimacy and interest value of these areas for other scholars.

Funding priorities are a fifth important determinant of research themes. Availability of funding surely plays a role in the choice of research area for many people.

"Health-related" research is obviously more fundable than research on language usage or on self-presentational strategies. In the middle and late 1970s, those applying for support to do research on alcoholism or drug abuse tended to receive a particularly warm reception. It would be hard if not impossible to calculate the subtle effects of funding priorities on the choice of research area, but it seems reasonable to include such external incentive factors in this list of bandwagon facilitators.

Because funding priorities are not always obvious, researchers must sometimes learn from their own bitter experiences with granting agencies and editors just what fields of study are valued by their peers. They may or may not decide to continue their lonely pursuit of arcane truth, but feedback from peers and powerful gatekeepers can be an important determinant of choices among reasonably intriguing options. The role of students should also not be ignored. The enthusiasm that both undergraduates and graduate students have for some topics and not others has some influence on research directions. It is difficult to persist in one's research when students and colloquium audiences convey nothing but somnolent disinterest.

A sixth determinant is the fact that certain scholars are attracted by the freedom available at the frontiers of unexplored scientific terrain. The researcher who follows up previous work may be performing an important service in the advancement of knowledge, but he or she is necessarily constrained by procedures and by a scholarly literature provided by others. Such a researcher may receive modest commendations for competence displayed but will typically be by-passed when more spectacular kudos are issued. It is perhaps inevitable that those who, through accident or through shrewd forecasting, get in on the problem-posing phases of a research theme, are more likely to reap the accolades of academic success. The accolades for innovation in social psychology may indeed be differentially higher than in better established scientific fields. This might be true because the field is still expectantly waiting for its true intellectual messiah, since there is a common recognition that the field is still in a problem-posing rather than problem-solving phase. In any event, social psychologists appear to have a peculiar penchant for being impatiently critical of their own field. No doubt for very complex reasons, it might be hypothesized that compared to other fields of science, social psychology is unusually oriented toward, and responsive to, new approaches, new conceptualizations, and new openings.

The appeal of working at the frontiers, of course, is not at all specific to social psychology. Work in undercultivated areas is in many ways much easier than work on problems characterized by heavy research traffic. Any contribution, no matter how modest, is likely to seem more of an increment than the result of comparable effort expended on a well-researched problem. Lack of rigor in the design of the research and in the analysis of its data can more readily be excused when one is searching for problem definition, for hypotheses rather than for confirmation of problem solutions. The researcher has more to gain and less to lose when operating in unexplored terrain. No one can be too critical if the researcher fails to make headway on a problem that no one else has addressed or solved. Of course, the terrain may be so ill-chosen that the innovative researcher works in isolation and confronts an indifferent audience when presenting his or her contribution. But at the very least he or she will gain credit for daring to leave the beaten path.

THE "WANING" OF RESEARCH INTERESTS

Dominant research themes wane when the more active and prestigious researchers turn their attention to new problems. Four reasons for the waning of research interests may be identified. The discussion is brief because in many ways "sinking ships" are the opposite of "bandwagons."

The first is the fact that the problem is solved. Though some may think problem solutions are an empty category in the social sciences, there are cases where work on a problem declines because the main outlines of a solution have become clear and a point of diminishing returns has been reached. When this happens the task that remains is to "dot the i's and cross the t's"—that is, to fill in the outline with more detailed information predictable from what already exists. Thus a theory may be extended to new areas where it accounts for some, but not an important amount of the variance. In another case, researchers may test the empirical generality of a finding by using larger and more representative samples than those used in the launching stages. In still another example, mediating variables may be introduced that mute or exaggerate the established effects. All these may be important endeavors, but they are the kinds of efforts that many researchers hope will be done by others. A clean-up hitter in baseball is highly regarded; a clean-up person in research is likely to be tolerated at best with patronizing,

supercilious praise. Laborers in the replication vineyard are needed but are not well paid in the coin of academic prestige. Given the existing incentive structure in social psychology, it is very understandable that people move away from a research area when the prestige payoffs loom larger elsewhere. Once the alternatives become more attractive, positive or confirming results in the waning area may add at best a small increment to our knowledge whereas disconfirming results tend to be ignored or attributed to poor research procedures.

Perhaps the best example of this reason for a declining volume of research can be found in the cognitive dissonance area (well summarized in a recent volume by Wicklund and Brehm, 1976). Because the main propositions of dissonance theory have been confirmed with sufficient regularity, there is not a great deal to be gained from further research in this area. Although there is, of course, still room for debate about the mechanisms involved and about the role of dissonance reduction in various naturalistic settings, much is already known about the determinants of dissonance and its various contexts of manifestation. Research on dissonance continues but no longer holds the center stage.

The second reason behind the decline of research in a formerly lively area is the existence of an empirical dead end. Sometimes a promising theory ultimately proves untestable or a dominant research theme becomes stymied in empirical confusion or in failures to replicate. Empirical confusion presumably results when researchers are asking the wrong question, have misidentified the appropriate controlling variables, or have been too inflexible in the application of procedures that are appropriate in one setting but not in another. Some examples of empirical confusion include research on the effects of drawing conclusions from attitude change, order effects and first-impression formation, the role of prior expectancy in response to performance feedback, self-esteem and the response to being liked, postdecisional exposure to relevant information, and aggression as a precursor of catharsis or more aggression. Some of these research problems will be resuscitated when conceptualized in more fruitful ways or when better measurement techniques emerge. At present, however, research in these areas of empirical confusion is relatively quiescent—not because the problems are seen as trivial, but because the evidence refuses to order itself into stable, consistent patterns.

A third reason for declining research interest is the discovery of methodological flaws leading to artifactual re-explanations. Perhaps the most fundamental single advantage of the scientific method is that it is self-correcting. Some may argue that authoritarian personality theory, certainly a dominant research theme in the 1950s, did not really survive the methodological attacks epitomized by the definitive critique of Hyman and Sheatsley (in Christie and Jahoda, 1954). Such a proposition, we believe, overstates the case, but the serious methodological flaws in authoritarian personality research certainly contributed to a decline in research employing the various interrelated scales. Interrelationships among the scales measuring antisemitism, ethnocentrism, and antidemocratic ideology were crucial to theoretical arguments about the nature of the authoritarian personality. When it became apparent that these interrelationships were to some unknown degree inflated by acquiescent response bias (the simple tendency to agree with any statement), many felt that the entire concept of authoritarianism was based on an artifact of scale construction. Other flaws in sampling and content analysis procedures contributed to this pessimistic conclusion. Sophisticated young researchers tended to accept the validity of such criticisms; authoritarian research became a tainted enterprise; and budding social psychologists began to look elsewhere for dissertation topics (cf. Brewster Smith, 1979).

Another fascinating case of the rapid emergence and geometric spread of a research paradigm, followed by an even more rapid decline, is the investigation concerned with group decisions involving risk. Cartwright (1973) offers a discerning discussion of the factors contributing to the compelling attractiveness of this aspect of research for so many experimenters. As early as 1924 F. H. Allport reported that individuals tend to produce more common or popular verbal associations in a group than in an individual context. This and similar findings on conformity and opinion convergence in groups contributed to a widely accepted assumption that group interaction would produce conservative problem solutions and that compromise would lead the group normally to the average or modal final position. Stoner's (1961) observation that group discussion led the members to take a riskier stance on a variety of issues therefore came as a considerable surprise. His study, dealing with hypothetical dilemmas, launched a series of experiments that generally replicated the so-called "risky shift" effect, and it seemed that an important and very general social phenomenon had been discovered. After researchers had accepted the validity of the risky shift, they tried in their research to discriminate among the hypothetical reasons behind the shift. Ironically, it was at this point that they began to find that the phenomenon was not so robust after all. As Cartwright (1973) notes, "Instead of providing an explanation of why 'groups are riskier than individuals,' they in fact cast serious doubt on the validity of the proposition itself. And since this proposition was such a central part of the risky-shift paradigm, they undermined the confidence in the very paradigm that led to their discovery" (p. 225).

Teger and Pruitt (1967), among others, began to notice that for some choice dilemmas the shift was in the cautious or conservative direction. Furthermore, the direction of the shift was found to be a function of the group members' initial position on the item. If they were initially on the risky side, they became riskier after group discussion. If initially conservative, they became more cautious. Thus in spite of the illusion of generality born in the many risky-shift replications, using different subject samples in different experimental contexts, it was belatedly recognized that the standard measure of risk (Kogan and Wallach's, 1964, choice dilemma questionnaire) contained a biased sample of dilemmas favoring initial riskiness. If the research had broken away earlier from the choice dilemma questionnaire initially used by Stoner, progress toward a clearer understanding of the complexities involved would have been more rapid. However, the ease of relying on such a readily administered instrument, coupled with the high replicability of results obtained when the scale's total scores were used, proved highly seductive. The rise and fall of this self-contained tradition of risky-shift studies covered a ten-year period. Cartwright's (1973) review of the risky-shift paradigm identified 196 bibliographic items, representing the work of 187 investigators from 8 different countries. Though reaching a realistic conclusion about the complexity of risk-taking behavior took a long time and involved many now forgotten words, the research does represent progress toward greater understanding of how groups function and how they influence individual decision making. At the very least it represents progress in learning about some of the ways in which researchers can be misled by an overly psychometric orientation. Others have salvaged the idea of *group polarization* (Moscovici and Zavalloni, 1969) from the wreckage of risky-shift research, and this endeavor may eventually prove to be an important step forward.

The fourth determinant of "waning" is the possibility that research paradigms may prove vulnerable to changes in ethical standards and the increasing pervasiveness of institutional monitoring of research practices. As already noted, one explanation for the shift from dissonance as a dominant research theme to attribution research may have been the greater appropriateness of straightforward, nondeceptive procedures to explore attributional questions. Part of the appeal of attribution-based research may simply be that experiments in the cognitive realm are easier to conduct and replicate because they lend themselves more naturally to simple paper-and-pencil implementation. In addition, however, it is also probable that attribution-based research tends to involve only the most benign deceptions, if it involves any deceptions at all. Many problems on which dissonance researchers focused, on the other hand, required elaborate staging and convoluted deceptions. The most extreme instance of this, undoubtedly, was the infiltration of a doomsday group to study what happens when strongly held beliefs are dramatically disconfirmed (Festinger, Riecken, and Schachter, 1956). Literature generated by the so-called forced-compliance paradigm within dissonance theory abounds with instances in which subjects were promised rewards that were never actually granted, manipulated into decisions they would have preferred to avoid, and subjected to various forms of stress and suffering in the process of arousing dissonance. Undoubtedly, many of these procedures would be ruled out or severely diluted by contemporary institutional committees designed to protect the welfare of human subjects (cf. Festinger, 1980).

It is even more likely that today experimental investigations involving physically invasive procedures would be proscribed in the ethical review process. Thus Schachter's work involving the injection of epinephrine (1964) would probably fail to pass ethical muster today in many human subjects committees. The decline of stress research involving electric shock is undoubtedly also attributable in part to the difficulty of getting such research past review committees. In discussing this fourth reason for the waning of research, one must mention not only abort the immediate effect of committee decisions in constraining research but also the more insidious ripple effects whereby whole classes of research are not even considered by rising generations of researchers because of the anticipated difficulty of institutional review. Regardless of whether one celebrates or laments this state of affairs, the point is that shifting ethical concerns are clearly important determinants of the kinds of problems tackled as well as the specific procedures used to tackle them.

In summary, there are many factors involved in the rise and fall of particular research paradigms or investigative traditions—whether these are defined narrowly by such self-contained research clusters as the risky-shift studies or more broadly by such comprehensive programs of research as those concerning cognitive dissonance. This discussion has mentioned only the more obvious of these factors and those that are easiest to exemplify. In doing so, reference to prestige and status considerations has been unavoidable. Some bandwagons become bandwagons because they are bandwagons. Just as surely, prestige factors can cause researchers to turn a bandwagon into a sinking ship when the traffic becomes too heavy and the increments to knowledge too slight or improbable. Prestige factors become directly relevant in the choice of research topics and indirectly relevant through the operation of editorial review processes. In addition to such extrinsic motivational factors, however, the research process has its own internal dynamics. Sometimes problems do get solved, and there is little payoff in further research. Sometimes it takes a certain number of studies before it becomes clear that the wrong question is being asked. The study of research innovation, of paradigm development and paradigm shifts, has become an important offshoot of the philosophy of science literature. We have tried to show the specific applicability of the more general determinants to lines of investigation in social psychology.

SOCIAL PSYCHOLOGY AS METHOD

The identity of social psychology in the 1930s was clearly strengthened by the development of distinctive methods. However, the ambitious agenda of a social psychology poses severe methodological problems. Conventional social psychology textbooks have often defined their subject matter as the study of responses made to social stimuli. The definer usually goes on to elaborate on both the independent variable and the dependent variable side. Social stimuli, it is noted, may be and are often "implicit"; the individual's behavior may be conditioned by his or her consideration of how significant others or reference groups might react if they were present. On the response side, the social psychologist is interested in more than "overt behavior." In fact, overt behavior—what a person says or does at a moment in time—often is considered transient and so multiply determined that it is not a reliable basis for psychological understanding. More important and more stable may be the underlying dispositions that guide complex molar behavior; that is, the values, attitudes, and beliefs that persist as influences on the things we say and do in diverse settings.

Thus social psychologists inevitably find themselves dealing with inferred dispositions influencing responses not only to ongoing stimuli but also to implicit or imagined stimuli. Such a state of affairs could lead to the avoidant reductionism of animal experimentation, to the metaphoric syntheses of the humanities, or to methodological invention. The advance of the kind of social psychology celebrated in this chapter was clearly dependent on the latter.

The problem of access to subtle social stimulus values was eventually addressed by the followers of Kurt Lewin, and various solutions to the problem of stimulus identification became triumphant achievements within the experimental movement in social psychology. Historically, however, priority was assigned to the measurement of social responses and their attitudinal underpinnings. In fact, social psychology's progress during much of the 1930s is reflected in the ascendant muscle flexing of attitudinal measurement.

By the end of the 1920s, social psychology had become an area capable of textbook demarcation, but it was a field lacking in relevant theory or distinctive methodology. As for theory, Cottrell and Gallagher (1941) argued, the early "social psychologists conducted a kind of a clearing house for the theoretical output of other social scientists. They battened on the research efforts in other fields but offered little in the way of research return from their own field" (p. 48). The methodology was also derivative. Investigators used quantitative measures of performance or other measures of attention, learning, or forgetting that had been developed in the field of educational testing or in the experimental laboratories of "natural science psychology." It was becoming increasingly clear, however, that the attitude concept was the distinctive domain of social psychology and that the development of reliable and valid attitudinal measures was an important contribution to the growing identity of the field.

ATTITUDE MEASUREMENT

In 1929 Thurstone and Chave published a classic monograph, "The Measurement of Attitude." In it they espoused the application of psychophysical methods to the measurement of a person's position along an attitudinal dimension such as pro- or anti-religion. Their adaptation of the law of comparative judgment was ingenious. The purpose of their method was to develop a collection of statements falling at different points along a particu-

lar pro-con dimension. The problem was how to determine with any degree of precision what the "scale value" or location of a given statement should be. This was done by applying the logic that the distance between two statements was a function of the number of people who agreed that they were different. If 90 percent of a group of judges rated statement A as more proreligion than statement B, whereas 65 percent rated A as more pro than C, then C not only could be placed between A and B but also the distance between these statements could be stated as a conversion of the percentage of judged difference figures. Through variants of this basic method (the most popular being the "method of equal-appearing intervals") a group of statements could be developed by judges to form a scale. This scale could in turn be administered to subjects whose own position on the dimension could be scored as the median scale value of endorsed items or as a similar measure of central tendency.

Thurstone's scaling procedures were essentially rational and required a separation of judges from eventual subjects. It was assumed that a judge's own opinion would not bias his or her relative placement of items, and the method required that the items be straightforward and clearly related to the belief or issue in question. In 1932, however, Likert employed a very different and more clearly empirical approach to the measurement of attitudes. His method was to generate statements about the target issue without any necessary restriction that the statements were on their face related to the issue. The items could then be administered to groups of pretest subjects with instructions to indicate the degree of agreement or disagreement with each one. Total scores for each subject could be gained by scoring each item in terms of degree of agreement (reversing those phrased in the negative) and summing these item scores. Each item could then be evaluated for each pretest subject sample in terms of its contribution to the total score. If the items were concerned with political liberalism, for example, endorsement of some items would correlate more highly with the total score than others. The diagnostic (high correlating) items could then be retained for further use. This procedure could be repeated over several pretest samples until a relatively robust and purified scale resulted, a scale built by the subjects themselves rather than by a group of presumably objective judges. The Likert approach proved to be more suitable than Thurstone's approach for detecting unpopular or prejudiced attitudes because the items did not need an obvious surface relationship to the issue involved. The advantages of this approach were exploited in building the authoritarian personality scales in the early 1950s. For example, the investigators in this project predicted and found that subjects who endorse the item "people are born with an urge to jump from high places" tend to endorse statements reflecting authoritarianism and antisemitism. It is hard to imagine how this finding could have been discovered or confirmed with the Thurstone method.

The 1930s marked the beginnings of a concern with the structure and functioning of attitudes and an accounting of their distribution in different classes or groups. The former emphasis is reflected in Gordon Allport's chapter on attitudes in Murchison's 1935 *Handbook of Social Psychology*. Allport analyzes the history of usage of the terms and considers, for example, whether attitudes have their own motive power (concluding that at least some do) and whether attitudes can be either individual, defying nomothetic measurement, or common and measurable (yes they can be either, he concludes).

A more strictly empirical approach is reflected in many of the chapters of Murphy, Murphy, and Newcomb's *Experimental Social Psychology,* published in 1937 (as a very extensive revision of Murphy and Murphy's 1931 edition). Much of the research described in this book amounts to a mapping of the terrain—a charting of sex, age, and educational level differences in such attitudes as liberalism versus conservatism. The correlates of attitudes toward ethnic and national groups are also extensively reviewed in this useful compendium. Because of the emphasis on straightforward description, however, most of the conclusions presented by Murphy, Murphy, and Newcomb are time and context specific. Nevertheless, one has to be impressed with the variety of early approaches to the study of attitudes and the high level of interest in exploring attitudinal correlates. The range of attitude studies reported before the outbreak of the Second World War reflected both a substantive interest in the social determinants of specific attitudes and a flexing of methodological muscles.

PUBLIC OPINION RESEARCH

Though the academic study of attitudes focused to some extent on the basic questions of dispositional structure raised by Allport in his handbook chapter, a related but separate development focused more directly on the distribution of politically or economically consequential opinion in the society at large. The growth of public opinion

studies was in turn highly dependent on the refinement of population sampling techniques. The American Institute of Public Opinion was founded in 1934, the first major practitioner of the form of opinion assessment that is now so commonplace in journalism, campaign strategy, and marketing research. Other survey research operations soon followed. George Gallup, Elmo Roper, and Archibald Crosley each used the sample survey method to forecast correctly the outcome of the 1936 presidential election. This method became widespread not only in the political prediction arena and in the commercial sphere where opinions about consumer products and advertising campaigns were systematically gathered, but also in the U.S. government where bodies such as the Department of Agriculture made extensive use of sample surveys. The public opinion industry has clearly mushroomed during the past twenty years, although the results of many subsidized surveys are used for competitive economic or political advantages and have not become part of the social science literature. There are, of course, many surveys addressed to important theoretical issues. However, the development of appropriate sampling and questioning techniques has had a much greater impact on the growth of empirical sociology than on social psychology itself. This was particularly true when, in the 1950s, the sample survey was wedded to computer processing.

SOCIOMETRY

Of somewhat greater relevance for psychology was the introduction of sociometric measurement by J. L. Moreno in 1934. His technique involved the simple questioning of group members regarding those fellow members with whom they would choose to associate in some activity. More generally, the sociometric method is now defined as including any procedure that involves choice, preference, or liking among group members. From such statements of preference certain aspects of group structure can be readily derived. For example, groups can be characterized in terms of the presence of clique cleavages, the degree of mutuality of choice, or the concentration of attraction directed toward a few members. In addition, individuals can be readily identified as sociometric "stars" (heavily chosen by others) or isolates. The addition of dislike dimensions provides many further possibilities of group characterization.

Sociometric measures have become so ubiquitous in social psychology that they are now viewed as one among many measures of attraction or social preference (cf.

Chapter 9). They have been widely used in applied research on morale and leadership as well as in basic research on such topics as the rejection of opinion deviates (Schachter, 1951), the measurement of in-group cohesion (Sherif, Harvey, White, Hood, and Sherif, 1961), and the study of hysterical contagion (Kerckhoff and Back, 1968).

SYSTEMATIC OBSERVATIONAL METHODS

The development of systems for recording and quantifying social behavior has a number of ancient antecedents, certainly including the training of behavioral observation in medicine. In 1933 Dorothy Thomas made the first explicit attempts to systematize and quantify the observation of social behavior. Interestingly enough, the development of systematic observational techniques beginning in the 1930s parallels the development of other measures of complex molar behavior in psychology. First there were competing attempts to develop all-purpose instruments that yielded high observer agreement. Enthusiasm in the early stages was fed by a naive realism that there was something "there" to be measured and observed. The task was to measure that something accurately and without bias. Eventually, however, whether dealing with general attitude measures in which the name of the issue was plugged in or with all-purpose observational systems of group behavior, researchers began to realize that the possible gains of reliability were offset by the empty, formalistic character of the measurement procedures themselves. In the case of systematic observational systems, for example, researchers began to realize how unproductive it was to divorce observer systems from theories of interaction or group functioning.

All such systems clearly involve selection and embody theoretical assumptions whether these are explicit or implicit. The heyday of general observational systems linked to theories about the way in which people behave toward each other was in the 1950s, though many of these systems were inductively derived in part. The best known and most widely used of the observational schemes was Bales's Interaction Process Analysis (1950). Bales wanted to develop a set of categories that could be applied to groups varying in size, composition, and function. The final set of twelve categories was a compromise between pressures of theory and practicality. Bales wanted the category system to be a set of hypotheses about face-to-face interaction, although the categories emerged in part from long and tedious hours of observing *ad hoc* laboratory groups. The Interaction Process Analysis system instructs the observer to place individual statements or idea units in one of the twelve categories, noting who made the remark and to whom it was directed. The categories are basically divided into expressive social-emotional actions and instrumental task-oriented actions. It was Bales's belief that successful groups moved from defining the situation (orientation), to developing a consensual value system (evaluation), to a phase of mutual influence attempts (control), and hence to a final decision. Along the way there were problems of tension management and group maintenance.

Bales's Interaction Process Analysis system was more influential than other category systems that appeared at about the same time (Steinzor, 1949; Coffey, Freedman, Leary and Ossorio, 1950; Carter, 1951a; 1951b) though its influence has been primarily felt in the sociological literature. In their review of laboratory experimentation featuring sociological investigators, Bonacich and Light (1978) suggest that Bales set the agenda for much current research on group participation rates and role differentiation, although many of his early findings and conjectures about group interaction have since been rejected. The impact of Bales's three dimensional conceptualization of personality (1970), derived from factor analytic studies of interaction process and inter-member perceptions, has been less profound. In general, the approach to systematic observation has changed from a main-force assault into a more sophisticated recognition that observation is merely a part of complex research procedures in the laboratory or field. Thus Weick (1968) stresses the importance of setting selection and of subtle interventions that facilitate reliable and meaningful observations. Perhaps the major holdover in social psychology from the early attempts to quantify social interaction (most particularly Chapple's "interaction chronograph" 1940, 1949) is the work of Darren Newtson (1973, 1976). The basic procedure in his work is to ask subjects to break behavior into units—to observe ongoing action and press a recording button when one meaningful segment of action ends and another begins. Thus far, Newtson has generated some interesting data concerning the high level of agreement over "break points" and the effects of such variables as behavioral predictability on unit size. (When behavior becomes unpredictable, the units recorded become smaller and smaller in duration.) The theoretical significance of Newtson's work is difficult to evaluate at present, but it is clear that his efforts raise some interesting possibilities concerning the perceptual organization of behavioral stimuli.

THE EVOLUTION OF AN EXPERIMENTAL SOCIAL PSYCHOLOGY

Though the emphasis on method in the 1930s struck first on the response side with the measurement of social behavior and behavior-linked attitudes, toward the end of the decade there was increasing interest in identifying and manipulating social stimuli. This increasing interest coincided with the vigorous development of experimental approaches to animal learning and undoubtedly borrowed part of its impetus from the dominant concern with discovering the laws of stimulus-response relationships. However, the full implementation of an experimental social psychology depended more directly on a combination of technical and theoretical developments that will be discussed in this and the following section. In order for the idea of an experimental social psychology to take hold, social stimulus variables had to be identified and techniques developed so they could be realized empirically. The main development in social psychology between 1930 and 1945 was movement toward the solution of these two problems. As a consequence, experimentation in the postwar period began to exert a dominant influence on the methodology of the field.

The idea of experimentation in social psychology did not suddenly emerge. By the time of Murchison's *Handbook of Social Psychology* in 1935, there were already a substantial number of studies dealing with the effects on individual performance of the presence of other people—what today we call "social facilitation." As Haines and Vaughan (1979) note, scattered experiments on suggestibility even preceded the Triplett (1898) experiment on the effects of competition. However, the variables chosen were typically restricted to concrete conditions that could be easily (often physically) specified, such as the presence or absence of other people, the difficulty level of the task, or the high versus low prestige of a communicator. The possibilities of creating complex and realistic social situations in the laboratory were essentially ignored until the contributions of Sherif (1936) and Lewin (with Lippitt and White, 1939; with Barker and Dembo, 1941).

If Murchison's *Handbook* can be cited to affirm the antiquity of experimental research in the one area of social facilitation effects, it may also be cited as a clear indication of the status of social psychology as a nonexperimental discipline in the mid 1930s. With the exception of Dashiell's chapter, the remainder of the handbook consists of essays in comparative psychology. It does offer, however, separate treatments concerning the social history of the white man, the yellow man, the black man, and the red man. As Farr (1976) notes (p. 226):

> Social psychology was very broadly concerned with the study of social aggregates (whether of birds, insects, or even bacteria) as well as with studying the varieties of human nature resulting from growing up in widely different cultures.

This interest in the cultural variability of psychological states remained a prominent theme in social psychology well into the 1940s as typified by Klineberg's (1940) text.

Murchison's *Handbook of Social Psychology* marked the end of the preexperimental era in social psychology. The development of a distinctive experimental methodology in social psychology was forecast and facilitated by three important landmarks: the social memory studies of F. C. Bartlett (1932), the group influence studies of Sherif (1936, 1947), and the leadership atmosphere studies of Lewin, Lippitt, and White (1939).

Bartlett's "Experimental" Work
In 1932 Frederick C. Bartlett's *Remembering* was published in England. This classic book may be viewed as a major precursor of contemporary cognitive psychology. It specifically set the stage for studies of the role of motivation and expectancy in perception (Bruner and Goodman, 1947), introduced many of the procedures and concepts used by G. W. Allport and Postman in their study of rumor (1947), and even may be credited with an important role in the development of dissonance theory. Festinger (1957) was clearly impressed by the Indian rumor studies of two of Bartlett's students (Sinha, 1952; Prasad, 1950) in developing his theory. In the present context, we emphasize Bartlett's contribution to an experimental orientation in social psychology. This contribution was essentially a liberating one, for Bartlett was intent on resisting "the artificiality which often hangs over laboratory experiments in psychology" (p. 47) and boldly attempted to cope with subjects' verbal accounts

of their perceptions, imagery, and memory in all their complexity. His reports of these accounts come across as faithfully accurate descriptions. He moved somewhat reluctantly to inductive generalizations, so impressed was he by the variety and uniqueness of responses to complex verbal and pictorial materials. He was essentially an experimental naturalist.

In Bartlett's best-known study, subjects were asked to read a 300-word folk story containing unfamiliar ideas and obscure connections and then to report on what they had read. In their reproductions, the subjects (who were British) assimilated the story to their own culturally determined cognitive categories, or as Bartlett called them, *schemata.* Bartlett's subjects condensed, highlighted, and rationalized the story to enhance its apparent coherence and consistency. His systematic observations were similar to those that had often been made by students of the psychology of courtroom testimony. As far back as the turn of the century, psychologists had been interested in showing how witnesses assimilate recalled experiences to their own expectations and distort them to agree with their motives. Bartlett, however, brought such considerations into the mainstream of psychological research and provided a number of useful descriptive labels for summarizing common cognitive tendencies.

Today, we readily accept the idea that our recollections and interpretations of events are biased by our cultural history and our current motives, but such a point of view came rather late to a psychology concerned with "pure memory" and therefore concentrating on the remembering of nonsense syllables—supposedly uncontaminated by "meaning." Thus Bartlett's contribution has to be weighed against the constricting earlier work typified by Ebbinghaus (1885) whose influence dominated the approach to the study of memory until the appearance of *Remembering.*

Most of the research listed by Bartlett in Part I of *Remembering,* under the heading "experimental studies," was not experimental at all. The studies typically did not feature the hallmarks of control, comparison, and random assignment that are usually considered the defining criteria of an experiment (cf. Campbell and Stanley, 1966; Carlsmith, Ellsworth, and Aronson, 1976). They did feature procedures in which materials were presented under controlled conditions to subjects in laboratory settings. Responses were faithfully and carefully recorded. There was little or no attempt, however, to compare experimental with control conditions. Al-

though in the experiments on repeated and serial reproduction, successive renderings of recall were compared with each other, in the remainder of the research the only comparisons were between total accuracy and subjects' recollections. Thus statisticians and compulsive methodologists would not refer to Bartlett's work as a model of scientific research. Nevertheless, Bartlett's faithful attention to the rich associative imagery of his subjects left an important legacy for the cognitive psychologist, showing that processes heavily infused with motivational, affective, and experiential variables can be elicited in a laboratory and preserved for scrutiny and reflection.

In his comments on experimental procedure, Bartlett left a more controversial legacy. It was *not* important to him that the same procedural sequences or instructional wordings be followed for each succesive subject. The important thing, rather, was to establish comparable conditions for his subjects. Thus, he tells us in introducing the experimental studies (p. 12):

> I have not hesitated to vary [the presentation of material] from person to person, or from time to time, and to adapt the conditions of its presentation, if it appeared to me that by doing so I could best get comparable conditions on the subjective side.

The issue of procedural consistency versus impact comparability is still a matter of debate among experimental social psychologists (e.g., Aronson and Carlsmith, 1968, p. 48). Though his role as an experimenter may be questioned, Bartlett was certainly important methodologically as a spokesman against reductionism on both the stimulus and the response side. He took his subjects seriously and was eager to let them tell their own stories in their own vernacular.

The Group Influence Studies of Sherif

Bartlett argued vigorously that the subjects' cultural backgrounds should be the frames of reference for interpreting events. In an important series of experiments done shortly after Bartlett's book, Sherif (1936) dramatically showed how such frames of reference can be bred in the laboratory. Subjects, either alone or in groups of two or three, were exposed to a stationary light in an otherwise dark room. They were asked to indicate when the light started moving and to estimate how far it moved. It is a common illusion ("autokinetic effect") that such a light will appear to move, but the situation is obviously very ambiguous. When an individual faced the light alone, he or she rather quickly developed a personally characteristic range within which his or her judgments fell. Sherif referred to this as the individual's "norm." When the subject was exposed to the judgments of others (in some cases preinstructed accomplices of the experimenter), his or her judgments converged toward a group norm. When the individual was then re-exposed to the light in isolation, he or she retained the group-established norm, which continued to influence judgments made.

Sherif proposed that "the psychological basis of the established social norms, such as stereotypes, conventions, customs and values, is the formation of common frames of reference as a product of the contact of individuals" (1947, p. 85). Though this particular generalization may be debatable, his experiments beautifully dramatized the cognitive interdependence of persons confronting an ambiguous situation and set the stage for hundreds of conformity experiments in the following two decades. Sherif's experiments also showed how a social situation could be constructed in the laboratory by the occasional use of experimental confederates. Such deception in the interest of combining impact with control later became a common feature of social psychology experiments.

The Leadership Atmosphere Studies

Both Bartlett and Sherif made imaginative use of laboratory settings to bring crucial features of the natural social environment under experimental control. They championed the idea that experiments do not have to deal only with variables definable in terms of centimeters, seconds, or grams. This idea was more audaciously illustrated by the leadership atmosphere experiments of Lewin, Lippitt, and White (1939), experiments undoubtedly stimulated by Lewin's strong belief in the psychological fruits of democracy. In these experiments, groups of five boys were formed to carry out such extracurricular activities as making masks. The boys were assigned to groups that were as comparable as possible in terms of the personality and level of popularity of each member. Each group was led by an adult who played, initially, one of two carefully constructed roles: He or she was either consistently autocratic or democratic. In subsequent experiments a third leader, who played a laissez-faire role, was added to the design. Unlike the democratic leader who solicit-

ed agreement and helped guide the group along its chosen course of action, the laissez-faire leader was a passive resource person available for consultation.

Five observers took continuous notes on the behavior of the leader and the boys in each group. Observation categories were devised so that quantitative indexes of such actions as "hostile criticism," "friendly cooperation," or "giving instructions" could be developed to compare the different leadership atmospheres. Different experimental events were arranged to explore the reactions of the children in the different experimental groups. At times the leader was deliberately late; at other times the leader left the group, and a janitor entered to make standard hostile comments. In order to study out-group scapegoating, groups sometimes met at the same time in adjacent areas.

The autocratic leadership produced both aggressive and apathetic reactions. The democratic leadership was uniformly preferred to both autocratic and laissez-faire styles. Scapegoating and blowing off steam in the absence of the leader were minimal in the democratic groups, but very apparent in the others. Productivity was approximately the same in the democratic and autocratic groups but considerably lower in the laissez-faire group. From the perspective of current experimental designs, the Lewin-Lippitt-White experiments were rather crude and confounded. Many compromises were made in an attempt to get more information from fewer groups than a fully counter-balanced design would require. However, the experiment had a number of features later more generally associated with the Lewinian approach:

1. A complex situational variable, in this case leadership atmosphere, was manipulated, and systematic observations provided a quantitative check on the success of that manipulation. This procedure represented a breaking away from the constraints of purely physical specification of independent variables.

2. Every effort was made to keep the setting as natural as possible and to inhibit self-consciousness in the subjects. One can speculate about the impact of observers, unobtrusive though they tried to be, but the boys apparently did not know that they were experimental subjects. The report suggests that their behavior was quite natural, implying that they adapted readily to the potentially distracting observers.

3. Theoretical considerations led to the initial choice of independent variables, but changes and additions were

made in follow-up experiments as a function of initial observations.

4. The detailed observation of social behavior reflected an interest in interpersonal processes rather than merely in the products or outcomes of interaction. Thus there was only an incidental interest in such things as ratings of satisfaction and the number of masks made.

5. Follow-up interviews were conducted to assess each child's phenomenal perceptions of the experience in accord with Sherif's interest in how aware subjects are of their own responses to social influence pressures.

Though it is difficult to assess the actual effects of such an experimental demonstration on subsequent developments, perhaps it is no coincidence that so many experiments in the 1950s, 1960s, and 1970s also involved the use of preinstructed role players, an emphasis on nonreactive behavioral measures, a concern with validation of experimental manipulations, and a retrospective examination of the subject's phenomenal experiences while going through the experiments. In addition, the attempt of Lewin and his colleagues to realize empirically such a nebulous concept as leadership atmosphere may have served to challenge future investigators and to provoke them to think about similar nebulous concepts that might be realized through the construction of creative role-playing scenarios.

Probability Statistics and Experimental Design

The sine qua non of experimentation is comparison —looking at the differential consequences of systematically varied antecedents. Physical scientists of the 1920s and 1930s pressed toward purification of the materials used, the procedures followed, and the measurements made so as to produce unequivocal and uniform effects. In their pure research efforts, they did not have to worry unduly about experimental settings, samples and populations, and individual differences. The prospects of a true experimental science involving reactions to complex social settings must have seemed remote as long as one held up the idea of uniform experimental effects. After all, common sense tells us that the more complex the environment, the greater the likelihood that individuals will differ in their responses to it.

Clinical and personality psychologists converted their recognition of this fact into the search for stable dimensions of individual differences. To some extent, this search represented an ultimate optimism about the development of penetrating measures of predictive disposi-

tions as well as a certain sense of defeat about the specification or measurement of environmental features. Since the ultimate objective of social psychology is to predict behavior in the natural environment and the natural environment is too complicated to control with precision in the laboratory, the personality-clinical approach emphasized a strategy of extrapolating from an individual's standing on a psychometric instrument his response in a meaningful social situation. Insofar as statistical techniques were involved, this approach relied on correlational measures and, in some cases, factor analysis. During the 1930s an alternative approach focused on an increased understanding of the role of situational contexts. The popularity of this alternative was undoubtedly elevated as social psychologists began to understand the relevance of probability statistics to an experimental approach. With the development of the "critical ratio" and the more flexible and sophisticated *t*-test, it became possible to reach consensus about whether an experimental effect was or was not substantial enough to be meaningful. One could concede the inevitable role of individual differences and unmeasured sources of error variance while still being able to tease out the effects of sufficiently powerful experimental variables. Never mind that not all members of condition A give the same uniform response, the central tendency can be assessed and differences in such tendencies can be measured against the degree of noise or variance associated with the condition. The idea that one could accurately assess the probability of a true difference between experimental conditions was enormously important in paving the way for an experimental social psychology. Although well-established correlational techniques were derived from the same model of variance, the particular format of the *t*-test (and similar measures of differences between groups) undoubtedly facilitated its influence in the development of experimental procedures.

Also of great importance, especially since the Second World War, was the increasing use of analysis of variance procedures. The potential of such procedures naturally affected the planning of experiments and decisions about feasible experimental designs. If the *t*-test was liberating in permitting the assessment of group differences in the face of "error," analysis of variance techniques were liberating in permitting the assessment of multiply determined effects. Not only could more than two groups be compared in one analysis, but cross-cutting factorial designs made possible investigations of the effects of one variable at different levels of other variables. Statistical interaction effects, an intriguing yield of analysis of variance procedures, became the hallmark of sophisticated theorizing about nonobvious effects in social psychology. Though lending itself to an almost unlimited potential complexity of experimental design, analysis of variance procedures proved most informative with designs of no more than moderate complexity. In particular, the advent of analysis of variance techniques highlighted the beauties of the four-fold table or the two-by-two design, beauties that had only been hinted at with chi square and tetrachoric correlation approaches. Without the many two-by-two designs developed to test theoretical hypotheses, the literature of social psychology in the 1960s and 1970s would have been considerably thinner.

All this, however, gets ahead of our story. We have tried to isolate certain methodologically important examples of experimentation during the thirties and to acknowledge the role of statistical innovations applied to comparisons of experimentally contrived conditions. One can argue, however, that experimental demonstrations in social psychology would have been isolated and selective without the metatheoretical underpinning provided by Lewinian Field Theory. We turn next to the role of Kurt Lewin in fathering a coherent experimental social psychology.

THE LINKAGE OF THEORY WITH EXPERIMENTATION

To some extent, the development of theory in social psychology awaited the generation of reliable data that needed to be explained and integrated. But the reverse was even more true. Social psychology was very slow to develop indigenous theory, and this fact unquestionably handicapped its emergence as an experimental science. Without some kind of bridging theory of interpersonal process, would-be experimenters were thwarted by what might be called the generalization question. How could an experimenter claim that his findings on thirty male college sophomores were in any important sense generalizable to a broader population of human beings or even to college males? Sociology essentially confronted the generalization question by abjuring the laboratory experiment and constructing or testing theories through survey methods in which sample representativeness was an important consideration. Psychologists, on the other hand, developed and refined experimental techniques that would test the plausibility of general process theories in restricted concrete contexts. In the late 1920s and 1930s this effort increased particularly in studies of animal behavior in which psychologists like Hull and Tolman attempted to theorize about general learning processes from data produced by rats in mazes. Thus there developed a broad context in U.S. psychology nurturing the importance of theory as a bridge between concrete experimental findings. As the experimental tradition developed in social psychology, researchers became more preoccupied with the conceptual generality of their findings than with the representativeness of their samples. Theories were useful to the extent that they predicted superficially different but conceptually similar relations in a variety of contexts. It was Kurt Lewin who, more than anyone else, stimulated and provided the philosophical rationale for this approach.

LEWINIAN FIELD THEORY

Lewin was a refugee from the Nazis who arrived in this country to stay in 1933, making the rather remarkable shift from Berlin's Psychological Institute to Cornell's Department of Home Economics. He moved shortly thereafter to the Iowa Child Welfare Research Station where he began to apply his basic theoretical predilections to the study of group dynamics and to train a number of students who were to play an important role in social psychology. In 1945 he moved to the Massachusetts Institute of Technology where he organized the Research Center for Group Dynamics. He died prematurely in 1947. Lewin was to an extent influenced by the Gestalt psychology triumvirate Wertheimer, Kohler, and Koffka, but he was by no means a classic Gestaltist. Whereas Gestalt psychologists traditionally emphasized perceptual and cognitive structures, Lewin was much more intrigued with questions of motivation and the dynamics of feeling and action. If a Gestaltist, he was a "hot" Gestaltist.

At least as important as his contact with the leading Gestalt psychologists was Lewin's assimilation of Cassirer's philosophical teachings. These he wove into his own field theory, which is described in a variety of publications appearing from 1937 to 1947. Unlike the usual set of assumptions and propositions from which empirical hypotheses could be deduced, this theory was more like a language or point of view. Lewin himself described the theory as "a method: namely a method of analyzing causal relations and building scientific constructs" (1951a, p. 45, orig. 1943). Lewin did use a terminology borrowed from force-field physics. Instead of behaving or responding, organisms "locomoted" through a field of bounded "regions" impelled by "forces" or drawn by "valences" along power "vectors." Much more important than the specific terminology was Lewin's movement away from conceiving man as a bundle of propensities confronting a structured social system. For certain purposes he conceived of a person as a point in psychological space, constrained to move in certain directions by the field of forces operating in that space. The imagery evoked by this conceptualization offers an invitation to experimentation or at least an invitation to the kind of theorizing that in turn could lead to experimentation. A view of a human being as the product of long developmental history emphasizes the uniqueness and the distinctiveness of his or her responses to a common environment. On the other hand, a view of a human being as a point at the intersection of environmental forces emphasizes the contemporaneous perceptions and related actions he or she shares with others in that same position. Through experimentation, one hopes that such common action patterns can be determined.

Lewin had glimmerings of an ultimate theory that was highly abstract and expressible in the new mathematics of topology. Of much greater historical importance, however, was his recognition that one must initially proceed with crude approximations, with what he called "quasi-concepts" like hope, expectancy, and frustration. Lewin openly and persistently advocated the experimental method, but at least as important an influence on the evolution of experimental social psychology were the research examples provided by him and his students.

The path-breaking studies of Bluma Zeigarnik (1927), under Lewin's direction, provide excellent examples of the bold use of psychological theory in generating an experimental program. We have already described the impact of the leadership atmosphere studies of Lewin, Lippitt, and White (1939), stressing the innovative methodology. Other influential examples included Lewin's studies of regression with Barker and Dembo (1941), of group decision and social change (1947), and his work with several associates on level of aspiration (Lewin, Dembo, Festinger, and Sears, 1944).

In spite of the interesting substantive issues raised by these examples, Lewin's contribution was basically atmospheric. His mode of conceptualizing fed easily into experimental interventions. He also provided a rationale for theory-based experimentation and for the idea of conceptual generality of a relationship across contexts rather than simple empirical generality across samples.

As early as 1926 Lewin said, "the quantitative level most propitious for experimental analysis varies from case to case and laws shift little as a function of this level" (1951b, p. 83). And fourteen years later he made more specific the way to implement conceptual generality (1951a, p. 9, orig. 1940):

> to prove or disprove the theory of tension systems, it seems much more important to find a variety of derivations from this theory which should be as different as possible from each other, and to test as many as possible of these derivations, even if this test should be rather crude quantitatively at the beginning.

In addition to his contribution to an experimental social psychology, Lewin made numerous others to applied social psychology and was himself a consultant to industry, government, and social service organizations. He was the founder of group dynamics, an approach to interactions in groups that laid the ground work for such subsequent movements as T-groups and certain kinds of encounter groups. In addition to writing a variety of influential books and articles (see Chapter 8 for a complete bibliography), Lewin attracted a distinguished group of students who played a vital role in the evolution of social psychology. Prior to his emigration to the United States, Lewin's students included Dembo, Hoppe, Ovsiankina, and Zeigarnik. His Iowa years were shared with Bavelas, Festinger, Lippitt, and White. The next generation joined the Center for Group Dynamics at the Massachusetts Institute of Technology. Dorwin Cartwright and Leon Festinger helped to form a faculty nucleus for a student group that included Kurt Back, Morton Deutsch, Murray Horwitz, Harold Kelley, Stanley Schachter, and John Thibaut. After Lewin's death and the Center's move to the University of Michigan, a number of students working with Festinger began to tackle the challenges posed by his theory of social comparison processes. Festinger went on to become the dominant figure in social psychology for a period roughly spanning the two decades from 1950 to 1970.

THE THEORY OF SOCIAL COMPARISON PROCESSES

Festinger's first highly influential achievement was the publication of a theory of social comparison processes in 1954. Festinger presented his theory in the form of postulates and corollaries, reminiscent of Hull's earlier theoretical efforts, and probably intended to emphasize that social psychology had "come of age." In addition to offering the most formal theorizing yet to appear in social psychology, Festinger reported the results of many experiments specifically designed to test hypotheses about our sensitivity to others' opinions and our abilities in coming to terms with our own. He proposed that there are large areas of judgment in which "reality" cannot be reliably measured by conventional physical devices. In these areas reality must be socially defined. When a person finds himself or herself in disagreement with others about the nature of this reality, he or she will be motivated to handle the discrepancy in some way. The individual may either change his or her own opinion, persuade others to change theirs, or decide that the others are irrelevant as comparison persons. Festinger spelled out in some detail the independent variables that should affect the resolution of opinion and ability discrepancies. Many of his students conducted experiments manipulating group cohesiveness (the attraction of the group to its members), issue relevance, degree of discrepancy, and other sources of pressure toward uniformity in a group. Most of these studies are included in a bibliography of social comparison studies collected by Radloff and Bard (1966). A more recent volume edited by Suls (1977) extends and refines many of the theory's hypotheses.

The theory was a tour de force in tying together conformity, rejection of deviates, and instrumental communication and in illustrating the role comparison processes play in evaluating our abilities as well as our opinions. Festinger's theory was generally compatible with previous formulations such as those of James (1890), Cooley (1902), and Mead (1934) in its emphasis on the social derivation and maintenance of one's self-concept. The form and particulars of the theory, however, seem to have been more specifically influenced by Lewin's (1936) theory about the spread of tension within systems. Festinger's 1950 essay on informal communication was a bridging paper in which he conceived of small groups as systems tending toward equilibrium. Since differences of opinion are disequilibrating, they generate "pressures toward uniformity" and result in influence attempts, opinion change, and/or social rejection (cf. Jones and Gerard, 1967, p. 340). In addition, the ideas of judgmental relativity from level of aspiration theory (Lewin *et al.,* 1944) were prominently carried over into social comparison theory.

Although the pervasive influence of social comparison theory is difficult to document, certainly social comparison ideas have played a prominent role in subsequent research on equity (Adams, 1965), attribution (Kelley,

1967) and social interaction (Thibaut and Kelley, 1959). A specific, closely related offshoot from the theory of social comparison was Schachter's (1959) work on the need for self-appraisal as a determinant of affiliation. In a series of realistic experiments, subjects were threatened with electric shock and given the choice of waiting alone or with others in a similar predicament. Schachter's major finding was that highly anxious subjects preferred to affiliate with others before being given electric shocks (they in fact never were) in order to calibrate through social comparison their own level of fear. Schachter's student Wrightsman found, in addition, that experienced anxiety became more homogeneous in groups of subjects waiting together in anticipation of a drug injection. Thus the effects of social comparison on emotional experience were similar to those predicted for the evaluation of one's own opinions and abilities.

Schachter followed the implications of the Wrightsman finding into a broader theory of emotional experience. He proposed (1964) that emotional states are a combination of physiological arousal and cognitive labeling and showed that vastly different emotional states could result from the same physiological arousal in different social contexts. Schachter's subsequent research into obesity and nicotine addiction has removed him from social psychology proper—in fact he has recently (1980) expressed considerable skepticism about the role of psychological and social factors in addictive patterns. Nevertheless, his approach to emotional experience, as we shall see, played a vital role in the emergence of attributional approaches to social explanation.

COGNITIVE DISSONANCE THEORY

Although Festinger's theory of social comparison was a dramatic integrative attempt, it did not clearly exemplify the evolution of understanding through the interplay of theorizing and experimenting. The theory certainly spawned research, yet many of its postulates and propositions have proved relatively intractable or exceedingly difficult to confirm. The issues raised by social comparison theory will be with us for a long time, but progress toward their solutions seems sporadic and generally indirect. The theory of cognitive dissonance, on the other hand, comes closer to the prototypic middle-range theory that Lewin idealized. It is generally recognized as Festinger's greatest creative contribution, and research related to dissonance theory dominated the journals of social psychology from the late 1950s to the early 1970s. This period presents the historian with the fruits of a flexible, abstract theory being tested in a variety of socially interesting content domains.

The idea that people are more comfortable with consistent than with inconsistent cognitions has been proclaimed by many psychologists and philosophers. People are not only rational most of the time but also (as Freud especially noted) rationalizers. We want our attitudes and beliefs to support rather than contradict our behavior, and we want our cognitions tied together in a coherent, mutually reinforcing system. Such basic assumptions characterize a variety of consistency theories that appeared in the 1940s and 1950s (Lecky, 1945; Heider, 1946; Newcomb, 1953; Osgood and Tannenbaum, 1955). What Festinger did was to consider the motivational implication of those inconsistencies that are from time to time thrust upon us; the result of his work was the firm establishment of the experimental method in discriminating among theoretical alternatives in social psychology.

Festinger's theory can be very simply stated: Two cognitions can be either relevant or irrelevant. If they are relevant, then they must be consonant or dissonant. To say that two cognitions are dissonant is to say that one does not follow from the other or that one follows from the converse of the other. Dissonant cognitions produce an aversive state which the individual will try to reduce by changing one or both of the cognitions. If a heavy smoker is exposed to statistics showing that smoking leads to lung cancer, he or she can change the cognition about how much he smokes ("I'm really only a light smoker.") or perceive the statistical data as hysterical environmentalist propaganda and discount it. Festinger went beyond the other consistency formulations in recognizing and exploiting the recognition that some cognitions are more resistant to change than others. Cognitions about behavior, in particular, are resistant to change. It is hard to convince ourselves that we did not just knock over our wine glass when we did, that we did not vote for a particular candidate when we just pulled the lever, and so on. Putting together the combined ideas of inconsistency-generated motivation and the fact that cognitions are differentially resistant to change, Festinger and his students were able to derive a number of diverse and often counter-intuitive propositions.

A sampling of these shows the versatility and power of cognitive dissonance theory in its applications to decision processes, social influence attempts, classic learning phenomena, moral developments, and attitude change:

1. *Postdecision changes in the desirability of alternatives.* Choosing between two equally desirable alternatives creates dissonance, which can be reduced by seeing the chosen alternative as more desirable and the unchosen alternative as less desirable than initially judged (Brehm, 1956).

2. *Bolstering belief through the recruitment of social consensus.* Irrevocable commitment to a belief that is later disconfirmed fosters attempts to persuade others to share the disconfirmed belief (Festinger, Riecken, and Schachter, 1956).

3. *Learning to love that for which you have suffered.* Resistance to extinction by partially reinforced rats may be explained in terms of dissonance reduction. Running in a maze to an empty goal box on nonreinforced trials creates dissonance, which can be reduced by developing an extra attraction for the goal box or other features of the correct paths (Lawrence and Festinger, 1962).

4. *Internalization of prohibitions under insufficient deterrence.* Children who obey a weak injunction not to play with a desirable toy will subsequently like the toy less than those who obey a completely sufficient injunction (Aronson and Carlsmith, 1963).

5. *The energizing quality of cognitive dissonance.* Conditions known to produce dissonance also increase the emission of responses governed by strong habits at the expense of responses governed by weak habits (Cottrell, 1972).

6. *The inducement of attitude change by counter attitudinal behavior.* Cajoling subjects to speak out against cherished beliefs for insufficient justification encourages them to change those beliefs in a moderating direction (Festinger and Carlsmith, 1959; Brehm and Cohen, 1962). The contributions of dissonance theory to our understanding of attitude change are so substantial that we shall return to the "induced compliance paradigm" in a subsequent section.

Much of the more recent research on dissonance theory specifies the precise conditions under which cognitive dissonance is or is not aroused. In particular, research on the role of foreseeability, personal responsibility, and aversive consequences has led to a new emphasis on implications of behavior for the self-concept (Aronson, 1968, 1980). Thus, inconsistency between behavior and attitudes is not sufficient for dissonance arousal unless the attitudes are firmly anchored in the self-concept and the behavior produces aversive consequences that could have been foreseen.

In summary, cognitive dissonance theory and research not only made a substantive contribution to our understanding of human nature but also served as a clear example of the promise offered by theory-based experimental research in social science. From Festinger's extremely simple, rather vague theoretical statement, the theory evolved with the aid of experimental feedback to include a set of well-articulated systematic relationships. Inherent in this development were many of the features encouraged by Lewin in the construction of a theory of behavior causation: Here was a middle-range theory being used to generate testable propositions. Although these findings were conceptually replicable in a variety of superficially different domains, they were not self-evident without the theory to house them. Many of these experiments involved the kind of stage management first noted in the Lewin, Lippitt, and White studies discussed earlier. Although most of the research was done in the laboratory, there were also many excursions into field settings to check on the empirical utility of the developing theory.

Dissonance research aroused considerable controversy in the middle and late 1960s for a variety of complex reasons. The fact that the major terms of the theory (cognition, importance, relevance, obverse implication) were defined in only the most sketchy way did not help matters. Because the theory did not contain specific operational rules, much was left to the imagination and creativity of the researcher. Thus individual experiments purporting to confirm the theory could be dismissed with some justification as triumphs of clever experimental engineering. The presentation of the theory contrasted sharply with the formal elegance of Hullian behavior theory and the detailed empirical linkages of Skinner's formulation. These departures might have gone unnoticed and unlamented by other psychologists if dissonance researchers had restricted their concern to the "soft" domains of cognitive selectivity and attitude change. However, as Aronson (1980) notes, in flexing their theoretical muscles, dissonance researchers took on the conventional wisdom at many points. In particular, dissonance theorists challenged the reigning importance of secondary reinforcement notions in proposing that action to obtain a small reward will stamp in associative cognitions more than actions to obtain a large reward. When Lawrence and Festinger (1962) invaded the domain of animal learning by suggesting that rats possessed something like cog-

nitions and that dissonance theory could explain response persistence and resistance to extinction better than the established learning theories, their claims were challenged.

The methodological style of the dissonance proponents also contributed to the controversy. No one denied the rather bold inventiveness of the early dissonance researchers, but this inventiveness was usually coupled with procedural complexities that made precise replication difficult. Those bred in the tradition of cumulative research in experimental psychology thought they saw serious vulnerability in this complexity and in the apparent disregard of standardized dependent variable measurement. Also, almost without exception, dissonance experiments involved deceptive scenarios that often enticed subjects into doing things they would not normally do—presumably a sine qua non for studying adjustments to counter-attitudinal activites. An ethical reaction against deception developed in the late 1960s (e.g., Kelman, 1968) which chose as its target the form of laboratory deception research typical of that deriving from dissonance theory.

Such controversy and criticisms are not entirely a thing of the past (e.g., Fishbein and Ajzen, 1975) and debate still continues about the generality and replicability of dissonance phenomena. Nevertheless, it is probably fair to say that dissonance theory has reached a stage of middle-aged respectability and that most social psychologists accept the fact (however reluctantly in some quarters) that the insights gained through dissonance-related research are important and lasting.

STIMULUS-RESPONSE (BEHAVIOR) THEORY

Lewinian metatheory, particularly as a backdrop for Festinger's productive theorizing, was directly instrumental in converting social psychology into a primarily experimental discipline. The impact of stimulus-response (S–R) theory over the past fifty years is more ubiquitous and therefore more difficult to trace. Certainly S–R theorists like Miller and Dollard, Mowrer, Sears, Rotter, Campbell, Aronfreed, Bandura, and Mischel reached out in an attempt to incorporate responses to social stimuli. They did this, by and large, through the expansion of mediational constructs, such as response-produced stimulation. Clearly contemporary approaches that partake of the S–R legacy have increasingly featured complex cognitive, affective, and motivational processes. However, it is probably accurate to say that S–R formulations were extended more naturally and gracefully into the areas of personality and developmental psychology than into social psychology per se. It is worth a little space to speculate on why this might be so.

An important impediment to extending S–R formulations to the social arena is the difficulty in specifying the social stimulus in clear, objective, noncircular terms. The major reference experiments of Thorndike, Pavlov, Guthrie, Hull, Tolman, and Skinner involved animals interacting with various features of the physical environment. This environment could be described objectively in terms of centimeters, grams, or seconds. The everyday social behavior of human beings, of course, defies description in these terms. To extend the S–R analysis to such behavior episodes requires reference to some internal set of mechanisms encompassing attention, perception, memory, and complex cognitive transformations. Almost since its inception, the S–R approach has really been a stimulus-organism-response approach. By elaborating the organism (O) term within the classical S–O–R paradigm, behavior theorists were able to account for complex social behavior—at least after the fact. The problem has always been that of specifying independently of observed behavior the social stimulus conditions of which that behavior is a function. The fact that each organism confronts each social situation with a history of prior learning that is ultimately unique and unrecoverable by the behavior analyst (except, perhaps, in the individualized settings of psychotherapy), makes specification of stimuli very difficult.

There are three basic responses to this dilemma: reductionism (which might take the form of a researcher dealing only with schedules of reinforcement in the pigeon while speculating about analogies to complex human functioning), working with personality differences as intervening variables to predict responses to representative situations, and "bootstrapping" the definition of social stimuli. The latter procedure typically involves creating an experimental situation designed to mean roughly the same thing to different human subjects and checking on the validity of this intended construction by a variety of direct and indirect postexperimental probes. The early behavior theorists traditionally placed great emphasis on an objective, independent stimulus definition. It is not surprising, therefore, that those coming out of this tradition would feel uneasy, to say the least, with complex social stimulus configurations that can only be summarily described and that are specified through some joint combination of experimenter intentions and subject

response. Hullians and Skinnerians found the circularity lurking in such definitional bootstrapping disturbing and pseudoscientific.

In comparison, personality approaches involving the exploitation of measurable individual differences have two major advantages. First, personality can be readily conceptualized in terms of learning processes and products—whether the major constructs used are habits, operants, traits, or secondary drives. Secondly, useful measures of individual differences in personality (learning history?) can be exploited in conjunction with standardized stimulus settings. In Spence's (1944), Kimble's (1953), or Cronbach's (1957) terms, one shifts from S–R laws to R–R laws, from experimental to correlational approaches. In this way the purity of experimentation with independent variables anchored in replicable operations can be supplemented by a differential personality approach in which predictive variance in response can be attributed to measurable differences in learning history.

Whether or not these speculations have any validity, it is our impression that S–R psychologists in the 1950s and 1960s were much less sympathetic to the Lewin-Festinger approach to experimentation than they were to research developments in personality and clinical psychology. Perhaps a rather cruel way to put it is to state that the behaviorist had a respectable "applied" category for clinicians—they were R–R, correlational psychologists—whereas the experimental social psychologists of that period encroached on the turf of objective science with independent variables that were not truly independent. Thus the experimental social psychologists in the Lewinian tradition seemed to be subverting the rules against subjectivity that had been so laboriously fought for within the behavioristic tradition.

Though the behaviorist tradition has had more of an impact on personality and developmental research than on the central problems of social influence within social psychology, there are many important exceptions. One area where theorizing has historically partaken of (usually liberated) S–R concepts is that of *aggression*. The importance of frustration-aggression theory to social psychology in particular and to the social sciences in general cannot be overestimated. In 1939, Dollard, Doob, Miller, Mowrer, and Sears proposed a hypotheses linking aggression with frustration that allegedly was derived from "common sense observation, from clinical case histories, from experimental investigations, from sociological studies, and from the results of anthropological field work" (Miller, 1941, p. 337). However, the hypothesis was clearly couched in the Hullian idiom of the time.

Frustration was defined as an "interrupted behavior sequence," and aggression as one of a hierarchy of responses that are instigated by frustration, and so on. The ideas of displacement and catharsis were also heavily influenced, presumably, by psychoanalytic formulations of motivational dynamics, although the theory departed from Freud in avoiding any reference to the instinctual origins of aggression. Frustration-aggression theory has been criticized for the circularity of its major terms and maligned for its apparent invulnerability to disconfirmation. Nevertheless, the theory, when joined to Miller's subsequent theory of conflict and displacement (1944, 1948), represented an important advance that exposed a variety of social problems to experimental attack. Among other things, the approach opened up a much more sophisticated set of possibilities for dealing with the "scapegoat theory of prejudice." Extrapolating from animal maze-running behavior in approach and avoidance learning situations, Miller developed a theoretical basis for predicting the displacement of responses when the most strongly instigated approach response is inhibited by even stronger avoidance tendencies. This conceptual relation offered some promise to those who wanted to predict the conditions under which particular minority group targets would be chosen as scapegoats by members of the majority. In theory, if an aggressive response to life's frustrations must be displaced from more powerful instigating sources to less relevant and less powerful substitutes (e.g., a minority group), this displacement should be a function of the shapes of the instigation and inhibition gradients and of the degree of similarity between instigator and substitute target. Unfortunately, the problems of specifying gradients and sorting out appropriate dimensions of similarity have proved to be insurmountable. Nevertheless, the scapegoat notion lay at the heart of authoritarian personality theory (Adorno *et al.*, 1950), and Miller's work provided a behavior theory underpinning for the looser displacement idea of Freudian psychoanalysis.

In general, more recent theorizing about aggression has underplayed psychoanalytic drive-displacement ideas while placing greater emphasis on a combination of cognitive and attributional considerations within the hospitable confines of contemporary behavior theory. The two most influential spokesmen for a neo-behavioral view have been Berkowitz and Bandura. In particular, Berkowitz has emphasized the combination of emotional arousal (generally because of some form of frustration) with cues that have been previously associated with reinforced aggression. This view has been given some support by several provocative (albeit controversial) experiments in which an experimental frustration occurs in conjunction with cues that either have or have not been associated with aggressive acts in the past (e.g., Berkowitz and Geen, 1966; Berkowitz and LePage, 1967). Bandura's (1973) theoretical account of aggression also emphasizes learned determinants and incentives and takes the position that aggression is one of a number of responses linked to aversive experiences and controlled by anticipated consequences. Bandura's experimental research has focused on the imitation of aggressive models, although his flexible theoretical housing may be more adaptable to therapeutic intervention than to basic experimental research. A basic problem, as Bandura (1973) notes, is that aggression is a complex synthesis of emotion, attitude, and action, each of which can be linked in different ways to instigating conditions. Because our learning histories are so diverse, it is likely that research on aggression will continue to be more promising with young children than with adults. Nevertheless, a considerable amount of experimental research on aggression (both with children and adults) has been spawned within the S–R, reinforcement framework.

Imitation and vicarious learning are two closely related areas where S–R behavior theories have contributed to informative experimental research. Miller and Dollard's (1941) *Imitation and social learning* was unquestionably an important book that liberalized S–R theory in proposing that the behavior of a model can serve as a discriminative cue for an observer. (A very similar view was later proposed by Skinner, 1953.) The authors also conducted a number of experiments demonstrating "matched-dependent" learning, in which a rat or a child learns to make the correct (rewarded) response by paying attention to the rewarded response of another rat or child. Bandura and Walters (1963) were later to argue that Miller and Dollard focused on only one form of imitation and a trivial form at that. They presented many examples of complex imitation going well beyond the simple discriminative learning identified by Miller and Dollard. Nevertheless, from a historical point of view, Miller and Dollard's work was important in distinguishing among different forms of imitation-like behavior, releasing the concept from its instinctual and reflexive origins and showing how empirical progress can be made through a program combining human and animal experimentation.

Vacarious learning phenomena have been distinguished from imitation because they do not necessarily involve any direct reinforcement to the observer. They would include, therefore, the spontaneous and elaborate imitative responses singled out by Bandura and Walters. As is true with his work on aggression, Bandura has made significant contributions to our understanding of imitation, identification, and vicarious learning through a series of complex and ingenious experiments. This work is important in understanding some of the subprocesses of socialization. Yet progress in our understanding of imitation and vicarious learning over the past forty years has been surprisingly modest, given the importance of the topic. One reason may be that even a liberalized S–R approach is too static because it fails to deal with the active role of the model (parent) in shaping the observer's (child's) behavior. The importance of such active shaping has been emphasized by Brown and Bellugi (1964) in their work on language acquisition. Another reason for this lack of progress is that social psychologists have expended more of their energies on processes of social influence and conformity, thus treating many of the phenomena of imitation in a radically different, but quite heuristic, context.

Important aspects of the S–R behavior theory approach have been treated in many other research contexts in social psychology. Hovland and his Yale colleagues' approach to attitude change was initially framed in terms of learned "implicit responses" that may change under the normal conditions of learning, controlled by incentives conveyed by persuasive communications. (This approach will be discussed in greater detail in the next section.) A number of attempts have been made to incorporate social interaction within an S–R framework (most explicitly Homans, 1961, 1974, but also Thibaut and Kelley, 1959). Since many other theoretical elements are also involved in these treatments, they will be dealt with subsequently as separate descriptive frameworks.

Zajonc's (1965) analysis of social facilitation, one of the oldest empirical phenomenon in experimental social psychology, is explicitly derived from Hull-Spence behavior theory. The mere presence of others, according to Zajonc, provides a nonspecific drive stimulus that energizes responses. As in Spence's theory (1956) the stronger or more dominant responses in a hierarchy are energized more than the weaker responses. Zajonc and his colleagues present suggestive support for this view by showing that well-learned responses are strengthened by the presence of others, whereas weaker responses are disrupted.

Byrne (1971) has provided a model showing how reinforcements influence evaluations of people and ob-

jects. His extensive research relating attraction to perceived similarity in others has produced remarkably stable and consistent results. However, his research has been criticized as being derived from highly restricted and artificial settings, and his theory has been cited as too restricted in its explanatory power (West and Wicklund, 1980).

Finally, researchers within the S–R tradition have raised questions concerning the automatic and "unconscious" operations of reinforcements in dyadic interaction. Sidowski (1957; with Wykoff and Tabori, 1956) investigated the "minimal social situation" in which two physically isolated subjects have the means to provide reinforcing points for each other by pressing a button in their respective booths. In the classic minimal information case, neither subject is aware that he or she controls the outcomes of the other. In fact neither knows that another subject is present in the experiment. Posed with the problem of obtaining the maximum number of points, each subject is free to press the button in his or her booth as often or as seldom as he or she wishes. In these early studies, the authors found that the subjects generally "learned" to reinforce each other whether or not they were aware of the contingency between their button presses and their hidden partner's outcomes. However, later studies by Kelley, Thibaut, Radloff, and Mundy (1962) did show that explicit information about the nature of the subjects' mutual dependence significantly improves learning in a similar, minimal social situation. Comparable issues of "learning without awareness" received considerable attention in the 1960s (e.g., Eriksen, 1962). If one person shapes another's behavior through such subtle reinforcements as head nods and verbal "uh-huhs," does this occur without the target person's awareness? Though this question has never been clearly resolved because of the insurmountable difficulties involved in recapturing awareness after the behavioral fact, similar problems of behavioral decisions without awareness are embedded in contemporary treatments of naive cognition (e.g., Nisbett and Wilson, 1977).

In summary, experimentation without theory presents severe generalization problems. Lewin clearly saw that testing theories of sufficient abstraction in different empirical domains would help to resolve questions of conceptual generality. Festinger became the creative executor of Lewin's metatheoretical estate, first with his theory of social comparison processes and then even more clearly with his theory of cognitive dissonance. In the 1960s and 1970s the clearly dominant paradigm in social psychology became the laboratory experiment in which complex independent variables were embedded in systematically varied, realistic scenarios designed to eliminate inapplicable theoretical alternatives. Though the idea of theoretical advance through the elimination of alternatives is a very general one in science, the particular style and expression of this goal within social psychology owes much to the exhortations of Lewin and the exemplifications of Festinger.

The traditions of S–R behavior theory, on the other hand, have had a less specific, secondary impact on social psychological research and theory. In the study of the complexity of human social behavior, the pronouncements of reinforcement psychologists can have the banal ring of truisms. The classic behavior theory paradigm emphasized temporal relations between stimuli in restricted settings where relevant incentives could be easily specified in terms of deprivation operations. Sloppy generalizations from such reference experiments to the complex human scene have not been helpful in furthering our understanding. Nevertheless, as behavior theorists have become more sophisticated about internal mediating processes in the human organism, they have had more and more to say to social psychologists. Although the impact of behavior theory has been more apparent in the specific areas of socialization and personality functioning than in social psychology, this area also has benefited in both general and specific ways from the traditional concepts and analytic procedures of behavior theory. At the very least, reinforcement concepts have often provided an ever-present alternative to more subtle, cognitive explanations. In addition, however, behavior theory has advanced our understanding of imitation, vicarious behavior, social interaction decisions, attitude change, attraction, and aggression.

CENTRAL RESEARCH AREAS

COMMUNICATION AND PERSUASION: ATTITUDE CHANGE

Social psychologists were remarkably slow to turn their attention to the study of attitude and opinion change. Though the study of attitudes had been almost equated with social psychology by Watson's work in 1925 and even earlier by Thomas and Znaniecki's endeavor in 1918, one finds there were only a handful of studies dealing with the processes of attitude change until the Second World War. Instead, as McGuire (1969) points out,

from 1920 to 1945 attitude theorizing had "become top heavy with conceptual elaboration including contentious questions of definition, analysis into components, and distinctions between attitudes and related concepts" (p. 137). Perhaps the reverence for the attitude concept during the 1930s—for the sovereign role of attitudes as crucial determinants of behavior—impeded experimental research into the conditions under which attitudes can and do change.

The Second World War shifted many priorities within social psychology, as it did within the other social sciences. In particular, the Information and Education branch of the U. S. Army conducted a number of surveys and experimental studies to assess the impact of morale films and internal Army "propaganda" (e.g., concerning the likelihood of a long war with Japan after V. E. day) on soldiers. One psychologist heavily involved in many of these studies was Carl I. Hovland. Prior to the war Hovland had been primarily interested in conditioned generalization and rote learning, though he also played a role in the development of the frustration-aggression hypothesis and had become increasingly receptive to the liberalization of Hullian behavior theory. Hovland became fascinated by the potential of studying the determinants of attitude change with the use of carefully developed experimental designs, and his contributions to *Experiments on Mass Communication* (with Lumsdaine and Sheffield, 1949), a summary of the army research that he directed, alone marks him as a significant figure in the history of social psychology. His contribution to this volume was both substantive and methodological; it clearly showed that it was possible to disentangle experimentally the effects of different components of the persuasion process. Hovland returned to Yale after the war and established a project studying persuasion and attitude change that activated a whole new tradition of empirical research.

The Yale Communication Research Program, as it was officially called, attracted young scholars from a variety of universities and generated a stream of collaborative research under Hovland's general direction. The classic *Communication and Persuasion* (Hovland, Janis, and Kelley, 1953) clearly established the value of an experimental paradigm that Laswell had earlier anticipated by his didactic phrase: "who says what to whom with what effect." Hovland and his colleagues explored a number of communicator variables (such as prestige, expertise, and credibility), communication variables (such as whether or not a conclusion is drawn in the persuasive message), and context variables (whether a particular reference group is made salient) and examined the effects of these variables on changes in opinion. The experiments involved exposing undergraduates to persuasive communications in laboratory or classroom settings, although Hovland later (1959) compared laboratory experiments with field research in an important analysis. The hypotheses of the various experiments derived from diverse theoretical origins. Hovland was clearly most comfortable with a view of attitude change as a special instance of human learning. He was especially interested in the implications for learning and retention of exposure to verbal symbols and made distinctive contributions in his chapters dealing with the organization of persuasive arguments and the retention of opinion change. Janis was a personality psychologist intrigued with the effects on motivation of messages having different arousal potential. His work in *Communication and Persuasion* on fear-arousing messages and the consequences of participative role playing established a research area that is still active thirty years later. Kelley brought to the collaboration the approach of Lewinian group dynamics, contributing research on the role of membership and reference groups in the resistance to persuasive communications. In retrospect, perhaps, the great importance of the Hovland, Janis, and Kelley volume is its emphasis on the importance of theory, the effective use of controlled experimentation, and the example of the friendly coexistence of different viewpoints in shedding light on an important and ubiquitous social phenomenon.

Until his premature death in 1961 Hovland continued to attract gifted young researchers from different theoretical backgrounds to work on problems within the attitude change framework. Jack Brehm, fresh from working with Festinger in the formative stages of dissonance theory, joined the group and soon was collaborating with Arthur R. Cohen on the implications of that theory for attitude change. Their work began to take form as the "induced compliance paradigm" (as labeled by Worchel and Cooper, 1979), and the many subsequent studies within this paradigm represent the central showpiece of dissonance research. The induced compliance paradigm was essential for capturing and portraying the vital switch on common sense: Although everyone knows that attitudes affect behavior, it may be more important to realize the circumstances under which behavior affects attitudes. The induced compliance paradigm involved a crucial experimental condition in which subjects were cajoled to engage in some action that would

normally be dishonest, embarrasing, or at least counter to their own prior attitudes. However, the induction was subtle enough to leave the subject with a feeling that he or she had a choice and was behaving voluntarily. The experimenters were able to show convincingly that such subtle behavior inductions lead to accommodating changes in belief, attitude, or values. For example, if a subject previously opposed to nuclear war was induced to write an essay favoring it, a subsequent measure would typically show a moderation of the antiwar stand. If, however, he or she was merely assigned such an essay (with no choice), there would be no such attitude change. In theoretical terms, the "freely chosen" behavior would be dissonant with existing attitudes; since perception of behavior is especially resistant to change, a change in attitude would be the most convenient way to reduce dissonance.

Research within the induced compliance paradigm uncovered a number of basic issues concerning the relations between behavioral commitment, motivation, and cognitive processes. On a number of occasions arguments were precipitated between those who were convinced that induced compliance findings could best be explained by dissonance theory and those who held out for the more traditional reinforcement view, patched up with assumptions about "self-persuasion." Janis himself, along with M. Rosenberg and other members of the Yale group, argued for variations of the reinforcement alternative in a number of papers (e.g., Janis and Gilmore, 1965; Elms and Janis, 1965; Rosenberg, 1965). Their former colleague Brehm (1965) remained unconvinced, and the controversy eventually receded as researchers began to identify more clearly the proper domains for the operation of dissonance reduction and secondary reinforcement processes (e.g., Linder, Cooper, and Jones, 1967).

The Yale program provided a vigorous continuing stimulus for the study of attitude change for approximately fifteen years. Following the pathbreaking Hovland, Janis, and Kelley book, the program spawned a series of more specialized volumes dealing with order effects (Hovland, 1957), personality and persuasibility (Hovland and Janis, 1959), cognitive consistency factors (Rosenberg, Hovland, McGuire, Abelson, and Brehm, 1960) and the role of assimilation and contrast (Sherif and Hovland, 1961). Research on attitude change through these and many other contributions moved from a strangely neglected area to the center stage of social psychology. By the end of the 1960s, attitude change took more space in social psychology textbooks than any other topic (McGuire, 1969, p. 138, estimates 25 percent).

This turned out, however, to be a high water mark of attitude change research. As the seventies began, the research flow receded into a steady but no longer torrential stream. Perhaps the Lasswell flowchart ("who says what to whom with what effect") was too unidirectional, too focused on messages delivered by speakers to an audience, to sustain the interest of psychological researchers indefinitely. In a broader sense, of course, an interest in attitude change is embodied in all studies of socialization, of person perception and attraction, of the self-concept, and of the transformations that take place in personal relationships over time. Studies with a more limited focus on communicator characteristics, message content, or audience features, however, gave way in the 1970s to the vigorous development of a strongly cognitive social psychology. Instead of focusing on communicator characteristics or features of the message, researchers increasingly turned to a consideration of consistency, dissonance, and attributional processes in the communication recipient. Before turning to these developments, we first return in time to discuss the impact of the 1940s and 1950s on investigation and theory dealing with group processes.

INTERDEPENDENCE AND GROUP DYNAMICS

In a curious way, social psychology has always been ambivalent about the study of groups per se. Some of this ambivalence may be traced to the heated controversies of the 1920s over the conceptualization of group properties. McDougall's 1920 treatment of group processes was dramatically titled *The Group Mind,* even though he later vigorously denied consciousness as a group property. The mystical idea that groups could be characterized by emergent anthropomorphic properties was mercilessly attacked by F. H. Allport and others in the mainstream of behaviorism, a fact that probably channeled subsequent psychological research toward the study of individual responses to group influences and away from the study of groups as groups.

In particular, the tradition of research comparing individual productivity and problem solving with those of the group (to which F. H. Allport was a major contributor) was seen as proper turf for an experimental social psychology. As we have already noted, this tradition was so well established by the 1950s that Kelley and

Thibaut could build on Dashiell's chapter in the *Handbook of Social Psychology* (1935) in writing their own for Lindzey's *Handbook of Social Psychology* (1954). However, Kelley and Thibaut correctly noted that a great proportion of the research on group functioning was quite innocent of penetrating theory. The research, though continuous during the 1920s, 1930s, and 1940s, was quite empirical and rarely grappled with the crucial processes in a group's "locomotions" toward a goal. The subtleties of social influence were not laid bare, and little was known or discovered about power strategies and the conditions affecting their successful employment. Conceptions of leadership were basically noninteractive and tended to avoid group dynamics considerations. Investigations in the 1930s and 1940s often involved a search for the personal characteristics of the effective leader. This search was not tied into a broader theory of influence processes.

Part of the problem was remedied by the success of the Lewinian group dynamics movement. Because of the abstract cast of his theorizing, Lewin had no trouble avoiding the anthropomorphic trap that had so bedeviled many of his predecessors. He approached the discussion of groups in a language that facilitated treating the group as a system of interrelated parts, and he personally advocated a concern with microprocesses rather than global descriptions or quantifications of group products. Many of Lewin's students in the Research Center for Group Dynamics at the Massachusetts Institute of Technology developed interesting theories about such different aspects of group process as identification with the group goal, communication as a substitute for mobility, and the dynamics of cooperative interaction.

Influential theoretical accounts of group functioning with a definite psychological flavor were also advanced by sociologists Homans (1950) and Bales (1950). In a tradition established by Barnard in 1938, both of these authors emphasized the distinction between task-oriented (external system) functions and social-emotional (internal system) functions in groups. Theoretical analysis was further advanced by Kelley and Thibaut's (1954) lucid identification of group problem-solving variables and their distinction between group influences on individual solution attempts on the one hand and factors influencing the combination or pooling of these attempts on the other. Their contribution provided a rational framework for organizing those portions of the social interaction literature concerned with group problem solving.

These same authors (Thibaut and Kelley, 1959) made a more basic and general contribution five years later in a book that introduced a framework for looking at the complexities of social interdependence in dyads and other small groups. Essentially, the framework dealt with the outcomes for the interacting parties that are consequences of their actual or potential responses to each other. By the ingenious use of "payoff matrixes" conceptualizing the response repertories of two or more individuals, Thibaut and Kelley were able to consider the response combinations that would provide the greatest satisfaction to each party and thus locate the most likely drift of the subjects' social behavior. In this way, Thibaut and Kelley developed a taxonomy of interpersonal power relations and provided the prototype of a social exchange model.

In their analyses of power and dependence, they crucially applied the ideas of social comparison. Thus a person's power in a given relationship depended on the attractiveness of alternative relationships into which he or she could conveniently enter. This feature of social comparison was missing in Homans' otherwise similar formulation that appeared two years later (1961). Nevertheless, it is interesting that Homans, Thibaut, and Kelley independently reached almost the same place from rather different origins. Thibaut and Kelley were influenced by Homans' earlier *The Human Group* (1950) and by developments in the economics of game and decision theory (Luce and Raiffa, 1957). They had also both been trained at the Research Center for Group Dynamics and were obviously influenced in a general way by the theorizing of Lewin and Festinger. Homans, on the other hand, was more explicitly influenced by the operant conditioning paradigm of B. F. Skinner. In any case, both formulations emphasized the exchange of reward and punishment in social interaction, and through this vehicle we are better able to understand norms, power, social dependence, and more generally group formation and maintenance. It is interesting, incidentally, that in the 1974 revision of his 1961 book, Homans explicitly incorporates many features of Thibaut and Kelley's analysis, including the exchange or payoff matrix.

In 1978 Kelley and Thibaut produced an extension and refinement of their earlier work in a book called *Interpersonal Relations: A Theory of Interdependence*. It offers a brilliant further analysis of matrix components and the dynamics of matrix transformations over time. The book contains a taxonomy of interdependent relations and could serve as the scaffold for a true social psychology of groups.

It is too early to assess the eventual impact of the Thibaut-Kelley and Kelley-Thibaut works on the transformation of investigative interests within social psychology. In spite of the elegance and originality of their 1959 treatment and the uniform critical acclaim with which both books have been received, there has not been a widespread embrace of mutual interdependence as a research and teaching focus in the United States. There are numerous graduate programs in social psychology where the study of small groups is given little attention, and where neither the students nor the faculty are familiar with the Thibaut and Kelley analysis. Given the elegance and profundity of this analysis, however, there is good reason to assume that its impact will indeed be durable.

The resistance of many social psychologists to full immersion in the study of groups has been noted by Steiner (1974) in his lament: "Whatever happened to the group in social psychology?" Steiner contrasts what he calls the "individualistic orientation" that characterizes most U.S. social psychologists and the "groupy approach." The latter differs from the former in attempting to treat the individual as an element in a larger external system. Individualists may focus on responses to group influence, but they ignore the "mutual responsivity of participants." Even the Lewinian group dynamics approach, Steiner argues, basically concentrated on the viewpoint of individuals confronting ad hoc groups operating under highly controlled and specialized conditions. Rather than deplore the individualists, Steiner calls for complementary pluralism of approaches and, of course, for more attention to the embedding dynamics of mutual interdependence. He links the neglect of group research to relative societal tranquility and predicts that group research will rise again when segments of society diverge or collide. But he also points to a "lack of nourishing theory." In this context, it is all the more surprising that his paper contains no reference to Thibaut and Kelley (1959) or to Homans (1961).

Though full-blown groupy research may have been the victim of relative neglect in the 1960s and 1970s, the same cannot be said for many of the component processes of small group dynamics. Several of these received lavish investigative attention. Two large clusters of experimental work can be singled out for brief review: social conformity and social conflict research. It is perhaps noteworthy and instructive that each of these clusters grew around convenient procedural paradigms, a fact that may well explain the heavy research traffic that brings these areas to our attention.

Social Conformity and Consensual Influence

Since social psychology can almost be defined as the study of social influence, it is hardly surprising that the conditions of this area's influence have received substantial research attention. Attitude change breaks away as one rather distinctive research cluster and judgmental or behavioral compliance as another. The attitude change paradigm exposes an individual (whose attitudes have been premeasured) to a persuasive communication by a source. The conformity paradigm, on the other hand, exposes the individual to a social consensus diverging from his or her presumed perception or judgment, the latter being usually inferred from the reports of control subjects responding in the absence of influence pressures. One of the earliest to exploit this paradigm was H. T. Moore in 1921. He exposed subjects to majority opinions on ethical judgment, language usage, and musical preferences and found these exerted a marked influence on the subjects' subsequent judgments. As noted earlier, Sherif (1936) showed how subjects when reporting their perceptions of a highly ambiguous stimulus situation were strongly influenced by the judgments of others. More than twenty years later the limits of ambiguity were tested in a series of conformity experiments by S. E. Asch (1956). His work established a simple and dramatic paradigm in tapping the conflict between consensus on the one hand and unambiguous perceptions or judgments on the other. Because of their intrinsic interest and the timing of their publication, Asch's studies rapidly became widely known in the social sciences, and their import began to be emphasized routinely in introductory psychology textbooks.

Asch's interests in the effects of social influence on individual cognitive judgments were very much influenced by his senior colleague Max Wertheimer, the eldest of the Gestalt triumvirate. Asch himself was (and remains) a "cold" Gestaltist, very much impressed with our needs to make "reasonable" sense out of experience. Although such influential authors as Fromm (1941) and Riesman (1950) had emphasized modern man's eagerness to hide among the consensus, Asch surmised that if subjects were exposed to several other subjects making unanimously erroneous judgments of unambiguous stimuli, they would reject any inherent pressures toward uniformity and report the correct answer. Thus he set out to study independence, not conformity. Asch was surprised when so many of his college student subjects denied the visual evidence in favor of the unanimous consensus. On the average, subjects made between four and five errors out of a possible twelve. Three-quarters of the subjects made at least one promajority error, and this turned out to be true in a variety of different samples of subjects. Though Asch's faith in the rationality and good sense of his subjects was somewhat shaken, his painstaking analyses of the subjective strain induced by the conformity conflict in many of his subjects inspired a number of investigators to pursue the determinants of conformity and independence.

Basically, this follow-up research established that people conformed either because they thought the majority was correct or because they were so reward- and punishment-oriented that they did not particularly care about accuracy. In fact, the underlying conditions of conformity, in perceptual judgment situations such as those studied by Asch, were essentially the same as those proposed by Festinger in a paper (1950) on informal social communication that presaged his social comparison theory. Social influence could be based either on considerations of social reality (influence oriented toward accuracy) or on those of group locomotion (influence oriented toward social reward). Under a variety of different labels (cf. Jones and Gerard, 1967) a number of other theorists emphasized this distinction between the individual's dependence on the group for information and his or her dependence on the group for rewards and acceptance.

Research within the Asch paradigm has waned during the past fifteen years, no doubt in part because of the very notoriety of the procedure and the necessary deceptions involved. However, conformity literature is sizable and rich, adding substantially to our understanding of what determines the average person's response when confronted with a conflict between his or her senses, perceptions, or convictions, and a strong contrasting social consensus. Of course, such conflict situations are rarely if ever experienced in anything like the dramatic form contrived by Asch. This line of research provides an excellent example of the value to be gained from procedures low in mundane realism (Aronson and Carlsmith, 1968) but sharply highlighting the issues to be studied.

A dramatic offshoot from the conformity conflict paradigm was the obedience research of Milgram (1963), who was very much influenced by the work of Asch. Milgram did strive for a certain kind of mundane realism in creating a laboratory analogue for the transmission of "totalitarian" orders to commit harmful actions. Subjects were induced to operate a device that they believed was transmitting electric shocks to another subject, ostensibly as part of corrective feedback in a teacher-learner situation. The typical subject, appointed to the teacher-shocker role, expressed extreme discomfort when told to raise the shock level to apparently dangerous heights. Many tried to refuse the order to do so. However, often under extreme and unrelenting pressure from the experimenter, many subjects acted against their own moral feelings in carrying out these potentially harmful commands.

The Milgram experiments generated an unusual amount of controversy. Much of this evolved around the serious ethical issues raised by the conduct of the research. Subjects not only were temporarily deceived but also had to live with the memory of their socially harmful experimental capitulation. There was also considerable disagreement concerning the importance and value of the research. Some of those who were normally critical of the trivial and artificial quality of experiments in social psychology (including a number of sociologists and clinicians) were enthusiastic about the fact that, at last, here was a set of experiments that shed light on something as important as the Nazi holocaust. Others felt that the research was theoretically barren and did not justify the psychological risks entailed. In their view, the findings were overdramatized and overpublicized. The degree of compliance could be readily understood once the extremely active role of the experimenter was fully detailed, something that was not at all clear in the earlier experimental reports. The jury is still out concerning the long-range value of the obedience paradigm in shedding new light on conditions controlling what Milgram (1974) has called "the agentic state." In any event, the research brought social psychology an unusual amount of attention in the popular media. The procedures and findings were the topics of feature articles in national magazines and served as the basis for a full-length prime time television drama.

Conflict Resolution in "Mixed-Motive" Settings

The early literature on problem-solving in groups concentrated on the social facilitation (and disruption) of individual performance and, to a lesser extent, on the coordination of individual actions to produce a group solution. Coordination studies were generally conducted within a framework of assumed cooperation as researchers posed questions about the relative effectiveness of cooperative groups versus comparable individuals working in isolation. An important development in the 1950s was the recognition that many group activities involved subtle mixtures of cooperation and competition, that the interests of the members generally converge in some respects and diverge in others.

This development was facilitated by two factors discussed together in Thibaut and Kelley's (1959) book. One of these was the matrix representation of interdependence borrowed from game theory (Von Neumann and Morgenstern, 1944). The other was a coordinate commitment to a "social exchange" view of interaction and relationship formation. The term *coordinate* is used because game theory deals in outcomes whose values are determined by the intersection of the responses of two or more persons. This model fit very nicely with a social exchange orientation that stressed the mutual delivery of rewards and punishments within a relationship, for it provided a precise way of defining the reward structure underlying various forms of interdependence.

Added to this promising convergence of a quantitative format and a particular view of interaction was a general concern in the late 1950s with international tension. As Pruitt and Kimmel (1977) note, many of the early users of experimental games were alarmed about world conditions and hoped to find ways of resolving them through laboratory experimentation.

> The experimental gaming and peace research movement were closely related at this time, as can be seen in the fact that the *Journal of Conflict Resolution: A Quarterly for the Study of War and Peace*, [founded in 1957] had a special section for articles based on experimental gaming. Hence there was an initial aura of urgency and even sacredness about the research, which probably contributed to its rapid proliferation (p. 367).

The game approach was especially adaptable to the kinds of mixed-motive situations (Schelling, 1960) that most intrigued social psychologists. There was a whole range of "non-zero-sum games" that lent themselves to the study of interactions featuring both convergent and divergent interests, such as those involved in real world disarmament negotiations and labor-management disputes.

The first social psychologist to exploit the possibilities of mixed-motive matrix games was Morton Deutsch. In his dissertation, published in 1949 (a,b), Deutsch launched a frontal theoretical assault on the process implications of cooperative and competitive goal structures in small groups. As he himself notes (1980), his ideas were influenced by Lewin's theorizing and research on tension systems and by the general atmosphere of the Research Center for Group Dynamics at the Massachusetts Institute of Technology, where the participants spoke of group goals and their interrelationship and of the various possibilities of vicarious gratification and the substitutability of one member's performance for another's. Deutsch's theory of promotive versus contrient interdependence has been widely cited because of the importance of the phenomena it addressed and because it represented a distinct advance over previous conceptions that were more typically focused on narrow issues of work output under the category of cooperation *versus* competition.

Deutsch's interest in the psychological consequences of interdependence made him highly receptive to the experimental possibilities of game theory and especially of the mixed-motive game. He used a version of the prisoner's dilemma game to study the determinants of interpersonal trust and suspicion (1958, 1962). His student Solomon (1960) also used a matrix game to study the development of trust, using a preprogrammed simulated other. Though matrix games had a number of attractive features, not the least of which was procedural convenience, the huge volume of subsequent research using such games has not substantially benefited social psychological understanding. The hundreds of prisoner's dilemma game studies have generated little more than a self-contained set of variations on a convenient procedure. Deutsch (1980) himself describes much of the game research as "mindless." Pruitt and Kimmell (1977) lament the slight impact such studies have had and propose that the lack of relevant theory has made it difficult to generalize from game behavior to important conflict situations in the natural world.

Though matrix games have generated a literature that is largely incestuous, the same cannot be said for other game settings designed to illuminate mixed-motive conflict and its resolution. Shortly after getting involved with matrix games himself, Deutsch (with Krauss, 1960) invented a simulated trucking game in which each of two subjects attempted to move a truck to a destination by manipulating electric switching devices. Since there was only a one-lane common path along the shortest route, the possibilities for confrontation and subsequent stalemate were clear. In some conditions, one or both subjects had control of a gate which could be used to bar access to the common path. The major finding was that the trucks of both subjects reached their destination more often and with higher joint payoffs when one player had control of the gate than when both players did.

This study became an instant classic, or at least it was soon widely cited and won the prestigious AAAS award for social science research. Unlike the relatively sterile setting of a matrix game, played over and over

again, the trucking scenario with its associated maps and apparatus posed an intriguing and highly involving dilemma for subjects, a dilemma that could be readily appreciated by the reader of the experimental report. The results seemed to support arguments of unilateral disarmament, though the authors were cautious about pushing their implications too far in that direction. As with most provocative and important studies, however, the specific meaning of the findings later became a subject of considerable dispute. Kelley (1965), in particular, questioned the definition of a gate as a genuine *threat* and suggested several possible alternative explanations for the results obtained. Kelley's student Gallo (1966) demonstrated that the results found by Deutsch and Krauss did not replicate if real money was involved as an incentive. When substantial sums of money were at stake, subjects were basically less competitive, and joint payoffs were higher. Apparently, when only imaginary sums were involved, there were no serious constraints to prevent the subjects from converting the game into a purely competitive one to make the experimental hour more interesting.

The debate over the significance of Deutsch and Krauss' findings highlights the central problem with all game research: how to use game behavior to make meaningful predictions in important naturalistic conflict settings. Obviously the role of stake or incentive may be crucially different in a laboratory situation than at most bargaining tables. In addition, it is easy to imagine the interactive role of many contextual variables in the real world that are typically excluded from the self-contained game situation. Although the problem of generalization is not unique to game research, of course, it is exacerbated here by the very seductiveness of generalization opportunities, coupled with the poverty of theoretical development in this area. Rapoport (1970), a major figure in game research, has argued that we should not extrapolate from laboratory games to situations of real-life conflict. Rather, the results should be conceptualized in their own terms and valued for the perspectives they suggest and the questions they raise. Although this position has served as one justification for an insular tradition of experimental game research, it has been clearly rejected by many investigators who feel that the only justification for game research is the continuity between the laboratory and the real world (cf. Pruitt and Kimmel, p. 367).

Within social psychology, at least, the trend over the past decade has been a greater concern with processes of negotiation and bargaining, coupled with a turning away from further variations on matrix game themes. The massive international experiment conducted by a committee of U.S. and European social psychologists (Kelley, Shure *et al.,* 1970) illustrates how sophisticated and complex the designs in this area have become: At eight laboratories, three in Europe and five in the United States, different investigators conducted essentially the same experiment featuring a complex negotiation game involving the choice of interdependent versus independent action. The negotiation game was played for either points or money, the difficulty level of the problems was varied, and in some conditions one subject was made systematically more dependent on reaching agreement than his or her partner. The major finding that held across the different experimental sites was that increasing the value of the stakes has a beneficial effect on negotiation when cooperation yields clear mutual gain and when exploitation is difficult. (There were also intriguing differences attributed to the meaning of cooperation in the different cultural contexts.)

The study of strategic conflict resolution has many origins, as we have seen, and many ramifications. A number of factors important in conflict resolution are relevant for understanding even the most casual sequences of social interaction. Thus, the social psychology of equity and justice (Berkowitz and Walster, 1976) is clearly involved in the conflict resolution process and remains an active area of theory and research. The study of self-presentation (Schlenker, 1980; Jones and Pittman, 1982) is often couched in power strategy terms and is clearly a crucial aspect of any conflict resolution situation. Finally, contemporary decision theories (Hammond, McClelland, and Mumpower, 1980) may ultimately have much to contribute to the debate on conflict resolution strategies, though as yet the communication links between social psychological and decision theory approaches are fragile and underdeveloped.

In summary, the study of group dynamics, or more generally social interdependence, has produced a voluminous literature of research, only a small portion of which we have mentioned here. The importance of the area is self-evident because most of our lives are conducted in groups and most of our important life decisions occur in contexts of social interdependence. It is easy to become discouraged by the bewildering complexities involved in the study of interdependent relations. As we have noted, useful theory has been difficult to develop, and much research has been inconclusive because the variables have been inadequately conceptualized. Nevertheless, it is clear that we have made substantial progress in organiz-

ing the interlocking concerns that influence group functioning and in identifying the crucial issues that merit intensive additional study. The differences between Kelley and Thibaut's two handbook chapters bear dramatic testimony to the growth of our knowledge and conceptual sophistication from 1954 to 1969. Much of the research bearing on problems of group dynamics has, reasonably enough, singled out component processes for intensive study. We have focused on two such areas by summarizing research developments in social conformity and social conflict. In both areas the importance of a convenient procedural paradigm is apparent. The problem of conformity is less complex than the ramified problems of social interdependence and social conflict. Whereas conformity research has waned, perhaps because many of the easy answers have been found, research in the latter area will probably continue to attract the interest of many social psychologists—especially those who are not intimidated by complexity and who are optimistic about extrapolating from experimental simulations to crucial human conflicts and their resolution. Useful framing models and taxonomies of interdependence are available. Perhaps what is most needed now are a series of subprocess theories that generate explicit disconfirmable hypotheses.

THE WAXING OF COGNITIVE SOCIAL PSYCHOLOGY

In a recent essay, Zajonc (1980) claimed that "cognition pervades social psychology, [that social psychology] has been cognitive for a very long time. It was cognitive long before the cognitive revolution in experimental psychology" (p. 181, 186). He traces the latter to Neisser's liberating treatment, *Cognitive Psychology* (1967) though Broadbent's *Perception and Communication* (1958) is certainly another important precursor along with Miller, Galanter, and Pribram's *Plans and the Structure of Behavior* (1960). Although we agree with this general assessment, we should also note that there have been peaks and valleys in the emphasis on cognitive factors and that, relative to earlier periods, social psychology has been undergoing its own less dramatic cognitive revolution since the ascendance of attributional approaches in the late 1960s. At present, there are abundant signs that a broader cognitive psychology is emerging to blur the boundary between social and nonsocial psychology. Social psychologists have reached out to borrow from, and argue with, cognitive psychologists.

And cognitive psychologists have more uniformly come to recognize that *nonsocial* cognition is really a special case of understandings typically incorporating social factors. This section will trace the evolution of this vigorous hybrid.

In order to understand clearly the rise of cognitive psychology and the forms it took, it is necessary to comment briefly on the traditional orientations that served as a backdrop and as a source of resistance to the "cognitivation" of psychology. A positivistic, natural science branch of experimental psychology was the dominant psychology of the U.S. "Establishment" from the 1930s to the 1950s. Basically, the orientation of experimental psychologists in this period was not merely noncognitive but anticognitive. The fear of mentalism was widespread as was the methodological conviction that science must deal only with observable, physically measurable variables. Sensation and perception research and theory were anchored in psychophysics and in the elegant functions relating physical stimulus variations to detection and estimation responses (which, in turn, were *not* treated as indices of thought or judgment). The study of learning was even more behavioristic, concentrating either on the locomotion of animals or on the retention of meaningless lists of rote-learned words, chosen especially because they supposedly had no affective or experiential significance for the subject.

It is commonly assumed that Gestalt psychology was much more receptive to mentalistic or cognitive concepts. To be sure, Koffka and Kohler spoke of pragnanz, of dynamic perceptual fields, of isomorphism, and of other constructs far removed from operational measurement. Both Koffka and Kohler, however, stressed nativistic or quasi-physiological determinants, and neither had much interest in dealing with the shaping of perception and thought by either current motivation or prior experience. The cognitive processes they wished to deal with were closely bound to lawful perceptual processes that were, in turn, linked to (in their terms, isomorphic with) properties of the stimulus environment or of electro-chemical brain fields. This proved to be a rather arbitrary restriction that is not, as we shall later note, fundamental to the Gestalt orientation. Lewin, Asch, and Heider eventually elaborated on the principles of Gestalt psychology in ways that were useful to social psychology. Prior to this elaboration, it was against the firmly established traditions of behaviorism, psychophysics, and classical Gestalt psychology that a cognitive psychology struggled to emerge after the Second

World War. A number of other developments, however, were setting the stage for a cognitive social psychology. Most of these had to do with the willingness to assume that the perceived world, and not the objective world, determines behavior.

THE RISE OF SUBJECTIVISM IN THE 1930s AND 1940s

Though the full development of a cognitive approach to social psychology may have been impeded by the conservative traditions of behaviorism and physiological reductionism, the concerns of social psychology inevitably required certain broad assumptions concerning cognitive structure. We have already cited Bartlett's classic work, *Remembering,* and Sherif's work on frames of reference as clear examples of experimentation in social psychology. Both works also exemplified a subjectivist tradition that had already been introduced in the late 1920s by the sociologist, W. I. Thomas. Thomas stressed the role of experience in shaping one's "definition of the situation" and insisted that situations are real if they are perceived as real (Thomas and Thomas, 1928, p. 572). We apply the label of subjectivism in the present context to the general position that events are interpreted in terms of internal information processing structures and that these, in turn, vary as a function of cultural and individual experience. Events are not passively registered on the perceptual apparatus. They are organized in categories shaped by past experiences, and they take on their meaning as part of an active, constructive process in dealing with reality.

Subjectivism was explicit not only in Thomas's concept of the definition of a situation, Barlett's notion of schema, and Sherif's frame of reference concept, but also in the idea of internal processing structures that was a part of many conceptualizations of attitude (G. W. Allport, 1935). Regardless of which particular processing construct one prefers, it is clear that social psychology was receptive to the relativism of values, motives, and perspectives that was promoted by the work of anthropologists. As Thomson (1968) points out, Margaret Mead's *Coming of Age in Samoa* (1928) and *Growing Up in New Guinea* (1930) "had a striking effect on social psychology in the 1930's" (p. 75). Athough he does not provide any further details, the general ideas that personality is shaped by culture and that different cultures produce citizens with different beliefs and orientations were clearly resonant with the early stirrings of a cognitive social psychology. Bartlett's observations on the recall biases of Swazi herdsmen forged an explicit historical linkage between cognitive psychology and cross-cultural comparison.

Kurt Lewin's conceptual approach represented an elaboration of what we have labeled the subjectivist view, though he was less concerned with the origin of cognitive framing structures than with their behavioral consequences. Thus, we take the unusual step of linking the Lewinian approach more to Thomas, Bartlett, and Sherif than to the classical Gestalt triumvirate, though there is no evidence that Lewin was explicitly influenced by these former sources. Still, Lewin is often classified as a Gestalt psychologist because of his early exposure to the Berlin triumvirate and because of some of the structural characteristics of his field theory. Lewin's most fundamental concept was that of the "life space," which is equivalent to the interdependent relationship between the person and his environment (thus, $B = f P, E = fLSp$). It is, therefore, the psychological or the interpreted environment that elicits or guides behavior, an idea that may seem self-evident to us now, but one that was met with considerable skepticism by psychologists in the grip of positivism. W. K. Estes (1954), for example, found Lewinian field theory incapable of *a priori* prediction and lacking in functional relationship statements that could be anchored in measurable stimuli and observable responses. Nevertheless, Lewin's grand truism $[B = f (PE)]$ and his emphasis on the psychological environment proved peculiarly adaptable to the concerns of social psychology where the most relevant governing stimuli must be defined in terms of their inferred meaning for the actor.

However, the question of how to penetrate an individual's life space, how to know his or her "definition of the situation," is almost overwhelming and partakes liberally of our earlier concern with how social stimuli can be defined independently of responses to them. Phenomenological inquiry seems called for, and indeed it seems reasonable to explain an actor's behavior in terms of his phenomenal world just prior to action. For Lewin, features of the life space need not be represented in consciousness. For him, "the phenomenal properties are to be distinguished from the conditional-genetic characteristics of objects and events, that is, from the properties that determine their causal relationship" (1936, p. 19). Thus the life space is a construct inferred to account for the individual's behavior. As Smith (1950) points out, the approach of directly tapping the actor's phenomenal representation of his current world is only one important kind of information about a subjective frame of reference. This frame may contain effective factors that are distorted or disguised in the subject's awareness. Even MacCleod (1947), in his classic paper advocating a phenomenological approach to social psychology, acknowledges that "the phenomenological method...can never be more than an approach to scientific inquiry" (p. 208).

Thus, very early in the development of a cognitive social psychology, it became important to distinguish between an actor's *conscious awareness* of his behavioral determinants and the fact that his behavior is shaped by cognitive structures that define reality for him. Such a distinction has reappeared in many guises in the subsequent decades so that there now seems to be a general consensus that cognitive determinants do not necessarily imply phenomenal awareness. Most would agree that one can gain valuable data about the determinants of an actor's behavior by eliciting his view of those determinants, although such phenomenological reports should not necessarily be taken at face value. Subjectivists, in the Thomas tradition, would argue that we are often unaware that there are perspectives alternative to our own. The world that we at least partially construct is perceived instead as the world given to us. To the extent that our perceptions are shaped by expectancies and other framing cognitions that we cannot explicitly identify, phenomenological accounts can clearly be little more than unwitting rationalizations.

The impact of more transitory motives and moods on cognitive processes has been somewhat more controversial, at least to the extent that one wants to argue for influences on perception itself in addition to influences on thought, interpretation, or memory. However, the "New Look" in perception after the Second World War explicitly argued that perception itself could be affected by motives and prior expectancies. This point of view too was an important line of theory and research that contributed to the development of a cognitive social psychology.

THE EFFECTS OF MOTIVATION ON PERCEPTION

Lewinian Field Theory initially developed outside the mainstream of U.S. psychology. Although Clark Hull's theoretical work held a certain morbid fascination for him, Lewin spent little time coming to terms with the theories and research data comprising the psychological literature. Instead, he wove together ideas borrowed from force-field physics and topological mathematics into a complex and highly original structure of terms and diagrammed relations. Both he and his first U.S. students relied mainly on intuition and each other for the ideas they converted into research on group dynamics. For a number of years the *apartheid* feeling was mutual. Although Lewin's contributions to the analysis of conflict and regression had an early impact on the fields of child development and personality, the broader theoretical issues he raised received spotty, belated, and skeptical reception in U.S. academic psychological circles. Social psychologists did not immediately flock to the banner of field theory when they dealt with topics of group psychology, leadership, and social influence. Mathematically inclined psychometricians tended to look upon his venture into topology with bemused derision. Positivistic learning and perception psychologists of the immediate postwar years seldom took Lewin seriously and responded as though whatever contribution he was making was to a discipline unrelated to their own.

In comparison, the new experimental approach to motivational effects on perception grew out of, and was in response to, traditional themes in perception research. Jerome Bruner did more than anyone else to render obsolete the idea that perception involves merely the passive registration of incoming stimulation. In doing so, he adopted a strong functionalistic position, looking at perception as an organismic process in the service of adaptive behavior. Bruner not only issued a verbal challenge to the staid perception establishment but also exploited through his experimental research variations in the classical methods of psychophysics in order to challenge the traditionalists in their very own backyard. The traditionalists fought back and won several local skirmishes; but in the end the research on motivational effects forced reformulations that were of crucial importance to the revolution of cognitive psychology. In this section we shall try to outline these developments.

Before the Second World War there had been suggestions that the study of perceptual processes could shed some light on the workings of personality. Social and personality psychologists generally agreed that people to some extent "see" what they want to see in the environment around them, but what the researchers usually meant was that the environment was *interpreted* differently by different people. Studies of perceptual discrimination, selectivity, and size judgment seldom if ever took social or personality factors into account. In the late

1940s such psychologists as Bruner, Ericksen, Klein, Lazarus, McClelland, McGinnies, Murphy, and Postman advocated a "new look" at the determinants of perception. The resulting volume of studies signified a radical departure in that they explored the effects of personal determinants on the most basic features of perceptual discrimination. Bruner and Postman, especially, wanted to move as far as current experimental methods would allow them from the metaphorical "see" of interpretation to the literal "see" of perception.

The basic argument of the new-look perception psychologists was that perceptions are often erroneous and that the errors bear some systematic relation to such interpersonal variables as expectancies, current motive states, stable value patterns, moods, and preferred defense mechanisms. The strategy was to inject these variables into the traditional settings of perceptual research and to measure the resulting distortions and differential sensitivities. Distortions in the estimation of size, color, and luminance were measured by such standard psychophysical techniques as the classic "method of average error." In addition, standard laboratory instruments, such as tachistoscopes, were routinely used to assess visual thresholds. F. H. Allport (1955) provides an excellent summary of this line of research on "directive state theory," and we shall present only the broadest outlines of the research here.

The new look in perception was really launched by experiments showing the increased salience of positively valued stimuli. A number of studies conducted by Gardner Murphy and his colleagues in the 1940s (e.g., Proshansky and Murphy, 1942; Schafer and Murphy, 1943) had shown that stimuli recently associated with reward were more salient and more readily perceived than stimuli associated with failure. A widely discussed study by Bruner and Goodman (1947) showed that subjects overestimated the size of valuable coins more than those of lower value and presented some data to show that this tendency was exaggerated with poor children. As controversial as some of these studies became, research concerning the perception of negatively valued stimuli generated considerably more controversy. Rather early in his research program, Bruner (with Postman and McGinnies, 1948) introduced the concepts of perceptual defense and vigilance to explain differential perceptual thresholds for value-charged words. The concept of perceptual defense was welcomed by many psychologists who were sympathetic to the psychoanalytic concept of repression and who saw its potential relevance for capturing the dynamics of personality functioning in the laboratory. Many others were both skeptical of the data and concerned about the paradox of having to see something before you can decide not to see it. Bruner and Postman's position was caricatured as involving the super ego, peering through the Judas eye, and scanning incoming percepts in order to decide which shall be permitted into consciousness. Nevertheless, the idea of the selective rating of personally relevant information touched on so many interests in psychology that a voluminous literature on perceptual defense and related issues was generated during the decade of the 1950s. Researchers tracked down artifacts, offered alternative explanations, and debated the Judas eye problem at length. Meanwhile, Bruner extricated himself from the controversy surrounding the perceptual defense idea by becoming more explicitly cognitive in his focus. His first step in this direction was the formulation of an expectancy or hypothesis theory of perception (1951). This theory emphasized the prepared or tuned state of the organism exposed to an informational input. The perceiver has a hypothesis that is either confirmed, or to varying degrees made infirm, by stimulus information. The stronger the hypothesis, the more it is likely to be confirmed by "unreliable" or ambiguous information. Hypothesis strength in turn is a function of both motivational and experiential factors. Thus the tuned organism is biased to perceive that which fulfills its needs, and strong hypotheses can also result from the frequency of past confirmations and the relative absence of alternatives. The reference to past experience was crucial here, for it marked a turn away from emphasis on the effects of motivation to a concern with probabilistic information processing. The idea that one's expectancies, based on the repeated contingencies of past experience, affect one's perceptual thresholds, proved easy to demonstrate in a variety of contexts. Such had not been the case with less stable motivational or attitudinal variables.

The role of the perceiver's personal history was even more heavily emphasized in Bruner's (1957) classic paper "On Perceptual Readiness." Here the language shifts from "hypotheses" to "categories," and this shift is critical because the prepared organism is now prepared with a cognitive structure of shaped expectations about the nature of the world. The cognitive category is for Bruner essentially a set of rules for classifying objects as equivalent. Bruner writes of the conditions affecting the "accessibility" of categories to stimulus input. He emphasizes the similarity between perceptual activity and problem solving in general. Perception always involves a decision process, a placement of incoming information into a network of meaningful categories developed largely from prior learning.

This paper was well ahead of its time, since many contemporary approaches to information processing and psycholinguistics are similarly concerned with category labels and the circumstances under which semantic and other codes produce assimilation to a typical instance or prototype. Bruner's essay can also serve as a useful framework for talking about stereotypes, a topic in which he had a long-term interest because of his early involvement in public opinion research and the study of propaganda. Subsequent to the perceptual readiness paper, Bruner moved on to the study of concept attainment, strategies of information packaging in classroom instruction, and problems of cognitive and linguistic development.

Though Bruner's work had largely stimulated the controversy over motivational effects on perception, that controversy continued in the 1950s without his active involvement in related research. In his very useful review, Erdelyi (1974) cites the year 1958 as a watershed marking the diminishing of publications on the new look. Lengthy critical papers by Ericksen and Goldiamond in that year seemed to take the steam out of the enterprise that had generated more than one thousand research publications. Erdelyi (1974) goes on to argue, convincingly, that "the New Look was to a large extent discredited on the basis of preconceptions about perception that were themselves on the verge of being superceded" (p. 2). In particular, much concern about the paradox of perceiving what not to perceive, inherent in the perceptual defense idea, loses its bite when one views perception as a multistage process. The distinction between perception and response also became usefully complicated as the research on motivational and experiential effects progressed. Since there is general agreement that perception involves going beyond the information given, what is the locus of this organismic elaboration? Do we talk here of internal responses to partial information (which certainly is consistent with perceptual defense ideas), or is it possible to distinguish still between perceptual elaboration and response selection? Bruner had argued (1957) that selective attention is a multiprocess phenomenon and, after Neisser's (1967) book, this view began to be widely accepted as part of an expanded information processing approach to cognitive functioning. This viewpoint is captured by the central theses of Erdelyi's paper, which rests on a view of multiple stages in the processing of information: "Selectivity is pervasive throughout the cognitive continuum, from input to output" (p.12). Though such a formulation hardly solves the problem of where bias enters in, the casting of new-look-in-perception issues in terms of selective attention and multiple information processing stages brought the problem back to the cognitive fold as a legitimate offspring.

Whereas the motivation and perception research of the 1940s and 1950s developed how traditional views of perception, the study of "person perception" had rather different historical origins. We turn next to review some of the early developments in impression formation research.

PERSON PERCEPTION RESEARCH

Motivation and perception research in the early postwar period was often referred to as *social perception,* meaning very generally the study of various social determinants of perceptual processes. This was not an appropriate term because many determinants being studied were not really social and also because the label promoted a confusion between social determinants of perception on the one hand and the perception of social stimuli (persons and groups) on the other. As the latter topic began to emerge as an explicit research focus in the early 1950s, the term *person perception* began to supplant *social perception* in designating research on the formation of first impressions. Person perception research was almost a syllogistic conclusion to the subjectivist premise: If people respond to the perceived environment and if other people are some of the most important entities in that environment, then it is important to study how people are perceived.

Despite the obvious importance to social psychology of knowledge about person perception processes, the development of such knowledge was delayed by a preoccupation with the accuracy of judgments about personality. Insofar as there was a tradition of person perception research before the Second World War, it lay in the literatures dealing with the identification of expressed emotions and with personality rating methodology. The recognition of emotions was seen as basically a side issue, a way of assessing the consistency or diagnosticity of emotional expression. Little attention was given to the process whereby perceivers relate facial expression to situational cues in the resultant perception of an emotion (cf. Bruner and Tagiuri, 1954). In the personality-rating literature, much of which appeared in educational psychology journals, the concern was with biasing proclivities (such as the "halo effect") that interfere with objectively accurate ratings of personality. How can such factors be checked or partialed out? What kinds of judges make accurate raters? What kinds of people and what kinds of traits are easy to rate accurately?

The naivete of this early assessment research was ultimately exposed by Cronbach's elegant critique in 1955. Cronbach showed that accuracy criteria are elusive and that the determinants of rating responses are psychometrically complex. Prior to this pivotal analysis, however, Asch solved the accuracy problem by by-passing it, thus ushering in a new era of impression formation experimentation. In a series of experiments published in 1946, Asch used an ingeniously simple procedure to explore some processes of forming a coherent impression of another person based on minimal, and sometimes conflicting, information about him or her. Asch presented subjects with adjective strings purported to describe a person. One such string, for example, was "The person is intelligent, skillful, industrious, warm, determined, practical, cautious." Subjects were asked to write a brief sketch of the person thus described and to check those traits among a list of additional adjectives that were judged as applicable to the person. Other subjects were confronted with an adjective string identical to the previous example, except that the word *cold* was substituted for the word *warm.* The resulting impressions were dramatically different due to the switch of these particular attributes. The *warm* person was described as much more generous, good-natured, and sociable than the *cold* person, who was generally described more negatively but was nevertheless judged to be slightly more reliable and restrained than the *warm* individual. Asch used these and other experimental results to argue for the dynamic interaction among trait qualities in the impression formation process. The meaning of each trait is modified by the context provided by the other traits, giving rise to an organized Gestalt of the entire person. This classic series of experiments spawned a crucial shift in the person perception area from a concern with judgmental outcome to a concern with perceptual process.

The simplicity of Asch's procedure was so seductive that a rash of impression formation studies followed. The idea that component bits of information are not necessarily additive, that the characteristics of a person are defined in relation to each other, was not initially challenged. Some years later, Wishner (1960) tried to make a refined analysis of the relation between stimulus traits and response lists. In doing so, he succeeded in dispelling much of the mystery generated by Asch's contention concerning emergent meaning. He also succeeded in showing how the centrality of a particular trait in a given context can be predicted on the basis of independent evidence. This was an important advance. Asch had merely argued that some traits are more central than others, without suggesting why this might be so. Shortly thereafter, Anderson (1962) published the first of a series of studies exploring the effects of the order of evaluative adjectives on the favorability of resulting impressions. Anderson sought to discriminate between different models of information processing, and his work is only an indirect contribution to the field of person perception. Nevertheless, he proposed a weighted average model based on the evaluation scale values of the individual traits, and for a time he challenged the Gestalt notion of interactive, emergent meaning. Many of his experiments showed that resultant judgments could be reliably predicted by adding or averaging the separately derived values of component adjectives. Later (with Jacobson, 1965) Anderson retreated somewhat to concede that (p. 539):

> Even though the averaging formulation shows promise in accounting for the impression response data *per se,* it cannot completely account for [the form of differential weighting observed]. In this respect it would appear that the adjectives do interact in forming the impression, a conclusion in harmony with the view of Asch (1946).

As we have intimated, however, Asch's contributions to the person perception area were more fundamental than creating a convenient research procedure to show how trait adjectives interact. By focusing on questions of process, he helped to launch or re-orient a whole field of study that was to become a standard chapter in social psychology textbooks. In the long run, however, the work of Fritz Heider became even more important in shaping the manner in which this chapter was written.

Heider evolved from an aspiring painter into a student of perception as he made the transition to adulthood in his native Austria. After receiving his doctoral degree at Graz in 1920, he moved to Berlin where he began to audit Kohler's and Wertheimer's courses and soon became acquainted with Kurt Lewin with whom he was in continuous contact for the next twenty-six years. Heider certainly absorbed many features of the Gestalt ap-

proach, but his first important paper in 1927 ("Thing and Medium") had more of the flavor of functionalism than of Gestalt psychology. In it he anticipated the main thrust of a later cognitive psychology by insisting that information from the external environment (the "thing" that reaches us through "the medium") must be read or interpreted through established organizing processes in the person. The distinction between thing and medium comes close to the distinction Brunswik later (1933) made between distal and proximal stimuli. In reading Heider's (1958) book, certainly his magnum opus, one is impressed with the use of Brunswikian notions in the development of attribution theory. However, the influence was at least mutual, and Heider contends that Brunswik "often said that he was influenced by *my* papers" (Harvey, Ickes, and Kidd, 1976). In any event, the two were close friends, and attribution theory is probably best described as synthesizing the tradition of perceptual functionalism and Gestalt psychology. The latter was more explicitly involved in Heider's development of cognitive balance theory that was clearly influenced by Wertheimer's ideas of unit formation.

Heider left his position in Hamburg, Germany, to visit the United States in 1930 at the request of Kurt Koffka who wanted his help in setting up a research department in a school for the deaf in Northampton, Massachusetts. There he remained, also teaching at Smith College, until moving to the University of Kansas in 1947. He stayed at the University of Kansas until his retirement some thirty years later. The careers of Heider and Asch have several things in common. Both were born in Europe, though Asch came to New York City as a thirteen-year-old in 1920. They were both heavily influenced by Gestalt psychology and clearly swam against the mainstream of American behaviorism. Neither was a prolific writer, both made each publication count. Because of the similarity of their interests, it is hardly surprising that they remain close friends who have spent much time in each other's company since their retirement from active teaching.

One of Heider's early contributions to person perception research was his effort in 1946 to conceptualize the relations between attitudes (incorporating affect) and cognitive organization. The history of subsequent person perception research reveals the intertwining of inferential and evaluative processes, and Heider's paper presented certain postulates along with a notational system for examining some of these relations. In particular, he argued that we tend to have the same positive or negative feelings about objects or persons who are cognitively associated with each other, who belong together. From such considerations a burgeoning interest in cognitive consistency was derived that was elaborated further in Heider's book (1958), in Newcomb's theorizing about communicative acts (1953), in Osgood and Tannenbaum's concern with the congruity of message source and content (1955), in Cartwright and Harary's elaboration of Heider's earlier notions (1956), and in Festinger's introduction of cognitive dissonance theory (1957).

Heider's formulation of balance theory is an important historical event, and there is no question that a large volume of research subsequently attempted to grapple with the issues he raised. However, contemporary hindsight indicates that the research value obtainable from assumptions of cognitive and affective unit formation was limited. Balance theory did not possess the clear motivational grounding that dissonance theory featured or the crucial ideas of commitment and differential cognitive resistance. In addition, the paradigmatic research (e.g., Jordan, 1953; Morrisette, 1958) was pallid, involving as it did hypothetical paper-and-pencil scenarios. Except for dissonance-related experimental reports, most balance theory publications had begun to subside by the mid 1960s, and the huge compendium edited by Abelson, Aronson, McGuire, Newcomb, Rosenberg, and Tannenbaum (1968) can almost be viewed as a capstone for this line of research. Nevertheless, the idea of a human preference for cognitive consistency is obviously an important and powerful one. Balance theory, in one form or another, has become a fundamental part of social psychological thinking.

In 1944, actually two years before his paper on attitudes and cognitive organization, Heider published a paper on "phenomenal causality" that became even more important for subsequent theorizing, though it did not have the immediate impact of his cognitive balance paper. In it he approached causal attributions as perceptual Gestalten linking motives or dispositions to action. Action is apprehended in a context that provides immediate meaning, and this meaning is heavily determined by causal attribution. In addition to laying the groundwork for attribution theory (see the following section) this paper directly influenced person perception research in the 1950s, research that further shaped our understanding of how we form impressions of others and interpret their actions. The experimental work of Thibaut and Reicken (1955) and of Jones and de Charms (1957) are examples of Heider's strong influence during this period.

Person perception research and research on the closely related topic of interpersonal attraction, continued steadily in the early 1960s. By the end of the decade, however, it was no longer possible even to talk about perceiving persons without coming to terms with attributional considerations. What started as the rather local impact of Heider's phenomenal causality ideas about person perception became a pervasive influence on almost all of social psychology. We now describe the sequence of events that culminated in this pervasive influence.

THE RISE OF ATTRIBUTIONAL APPROACHES

Heider's *The Psychology of Interpersonal Relations* was published in 1958. In active preparation for fifteen years, this book summarized Heider's insights and reflections on social behavior and its cognitive support systems. Specifically, it was an analysis of "common sense psychology" based on the conviction that if we can capture the naive understandings of the person on the street, we can accurately infer from them his other expectations and actions. In addition to this affirmation of functionalist subjectivism, Heider suggested that naive psychology may contain many experience-based truths and that scientific psychology has much to learn from the common sense intuitions of the everyday person. Heider's own approach to naive psychology was to break down the commonly offered reasons for actions, and the actions themselves, into their essential verbal prototypes. Thus, we have analyses of the concepts of *can, ought, try, harm, benefit, like, belong to,* and so on. To an extent, then, Heider presented an interpersonal psycholinguistics that traded on the reader's own understandings of the determinants of social behavior, while attempting to sharpen these understandings. Probably the most crucial distinction Heider drew, as far as future research and theory were concerned, was that between external or situational forces and internal or dispositional forces. People tend to explain human behavior by placing emphasis either on environmental causation or on the causal contributions of the actor's own beliefs, motives, or traits. Unraveling the determinants of internal versus external causal attribution was the central challenge for research. Armed with such information, one could better predict the circumstances of anger and aggression, of information seeking, of social influence, of various mood shifts, of task perseverence, and of many other crucial human states or activities.

Heider not only focused on the cognitions of others but also studiously cultivated the fruits of his own cognitive analyses. Never glib, he assimilated the data of interpersonal relations slowly, over a long and thoughtful lifetime, and carefully mulled their significance. Ambivalent toward laboratory experimentation, he was more comfortable dealing with literary plots and parables as repositories of naive wisdom concerning the drama of interpersonal relations. His book was a tangled skein of rich insights, consistently provocative, but only in the loosest sense programmatic. Its nuances enrich the reader's own naive psychology and its insights contain the sources of a thousand experiments.

Heider must surely be considered the father of attribution theory, though his assumptive framework was shaped by the broad traditions of functionalism, the subjectivism of Lewin, and the themes of cognitive organization and consistency implicit in Gestalt psychology. The attributional approach that became dominant in the 1970s was fed by other ideas as well.

A 1965 paper by Jones and Davis attempted to formalize some of Heider's attributional ideas in a "theory of correspondent inference." Drawing on Jones's early person perception research, which itself was influenced by Heider's paper on phenomenal causality, this essay considered the determinants of dispositional versus situational attributions and suggested that people infer intentions from behavioral effects to the extent that these effects are uniquely associated with the behavior chosen.

Although this paper launched a group of experiments on the attribution of attitudes, abilities, and emotions, it was Kelley's seminal paper two years later (1967) that finally began to generate momentum for the attributional approach. Kelley was able to integrate Heider's idea with Festinger's emphasis on social comparisons. He showed how Schachter's (1964) theory of emotion was basically an attributional account and noted that Bem's work (1967) provided an attributional alternative to dissonance theory. Kelley discussed the conditions under which we confidently attribute our perceptions and judgments to environmental entities. Our perception of such entities will be stable and unbiased to the extent that it is consistent over time, distinctive among entities, and in agreement with the perceptions of others. If not, the perception will be judged to be a function of perceiver dispositions or circumstances.

Self-Perception versus Dissonance Theory

A broad interest in the attributional approach began to emerge in the late 1960s just at the time that dissonance research was starting to wane. In addition to some of the reasons already discussed for this shift of interest from dissonance to attribution, another reason was the hospitality of the attributional approach to empirical phenomena generated in diverse theoretical contexts. The waxing of the attribution approach was due in part to the benign imperialism of attributionists themselves, as they reached out to provide attributional accounts of well-known psychological phenomena. In addition, there were many instances in which researchers starting with a different orientation ended up translating their findings into attributional terms, attempting to endow them with more general significance.

As noted, Schachter's theory of emotional experience, featuring a synthesis of cognitive labeling and physiological arousal, was essentially absorbed into attribution theory by Kelley (1967) and this was later facilitated by Schachter's own students Nisbett, Valins (in Jones *et al.,* 1972), Ross, and Rodin (Ross, Rodin, and Zimbardo, 1969; Rodin, 1976). The incorporation of Schachter's basic ideas as instances of self-attribution took place without a struggle. The attempt to incorporate the phenomena of cognitive dissonance met with considerably more resistance, however. Daryl Bem conducted a series of experiments for his dissertation at the University of Michigan, and the results of these were published in 1965—well before the impact of Heider's book was widely felt. Arguing from a Skinnerian "radical-behaviorist" position, Bem proposed that inferences about the self are fundamentally similar in process to inferences about someone else, that is, they are grounded in the observation of behavior. If our behavior is not "manded" (to use Skinner's term) by external requirements or incentives, we assume that it reflects our attitudes and desires. Thus, turning this around, it is reasonable that we infer our own beliefs (when asked to reflect on them) from observations of our own non-manded behavior. Bem applied this argument to well-established "attitude change" phenomena within the induced-compliance paradigm of dissonance research. He showed that observers could predict the obtained attitude results if informed about the subject's decision to comply and the circumstances under which the decision was elicited. Bem contended that subjects when asked about their attitudes after they had written counter-attitudinal essays for barely sufficient incentives would simply report an attitude that followed from their recent and therefore salient behavior. This alternative considerably reduced the "nonobviousness" of dissonance results and reasserted the relevance of behaviorism. Though Bem did not make the connection at the time, his finding also made dissonance theory a special case of attribution theory: We attribute behavior to dispositions (our own as well as others) when that behavior cannot readily be attributed to environmental forces.

Bem was immediately attacked for ignoring the fact that involved actor-subjects in traditional dissonance experiments brought a previous attitude to the experiment; Bem's observer-subjects were given no previous attitude information (Jones, Linder, Kiesler, Zanna, and Brehm, 1968). Bem countered by arguing that actor-subjects are essentially unaware of their previous attitudes by the time they are asked to state their final attitudes in the experiment. Controversy surrounded this issue for several years until a consensus began to emerge that the only grounds for choosing between dissonance theory and Bem's alternative were esthetic.

Since all this controversy was happening while the attributional approach was gathering impressive momentum, Bem began increasingly to describe his position in more cognitive attributional terms. He tired of the arguments with dissonance protagonists and tried to extricate himself with a general presentation of "self-perception" theory in 1972. In this elegant and thoughtful essay, although Bem paid appropriate tribute to Skinner, he essentially brought together the literature of self-knowledge under an attributional framework. In fact, this essay was a very important addition to the attributional literature because Bem raised sharp and well-formulated questions concerning the extent to which, and the conditions under which, attributions mediate behavior.

It is, perhaps, a final irony that the dissonance protagonists used a "misattribution" methodology to prove that Bem's self-attribution account of dissonance phenomena was inadequate. The basic theoretical divergence between dissonance theory and self-perception theory involved the assumption of motivational arousal. Dissonance theory assumed that counter-attitudinal behavior aroused an unpleasant affective state that, in turn, motivated the subject to reduce the dissonance in the most economical way. Self-perception theory argued that such motivational assumptions were superfluous.

Zanna and Cooper (1974) showed the relevance of affective arousal in the induced-compliance paradigm. Schachter and Singer (1962) had shown that subjects who were given a drug injection causing autonomic arousal and a correct description of what to expect were least likely to interpret the resulting experience as an emotion. Those who were given the injection and misinformed about the effects or not told there would be any attributed arousal to other features of the situation. Zanna and Cooper (1974) thought that these findings could be exploited to distinguish between the dissonance and the self-perception explanations of why people change their beliefs after compromising them for very little reason. They asked subjects to write a counter-attitudinal essay after participating first in an experiment supposedly dealing with the effect of drugs on memory. In that "prior experiment" subjects were given a placebo and told that the pill either would make them tense, relax them, or have no side-effects. Following the logic of Schachter and Singer, the results showed that post-essay attitude change was reduced when subjects could attribute the arousal presumably caused by writing a counter-attitudinal essay to the pill and enhanced when they thought the pill was supposed to relax them. Bem would have had difficulty incorporating this result into his version of attitude change, although more recent studies (Fazio, Zanna, and Cooper, 1977) have shown that Bem's explanation may be appropriate when the discrepancy between attitudes and behavior is mild, when the behavior is not sufficiently counterattitudinal to create dissonance.

More Examples of Attributional Hospitality

Other examples of the hospitability of an attributional approach are not hard to find. The learned helplessness model of depression (Seligman, 1975) was rather painlessly moved under the attributional rubric (cf. Abramson, Seligman and Teasdale, 1978) though many questions remain about just how attributional notions should be applied to helplessness phenomena (Wortman and Dintzer, 1978).

Our understanding of intrinsic versus extrinsic motivation has also been enhanced by the attributional framework. Considerable evidence has accumulated that activities performed for high incentives or under high external pressure will not be subsequently seen as enjoyable by the actor. The assumption is that the "over-justification" of a performance leads to an attribution that it would not have occurred in the absence of such external incentives. Therefore, the activity cannot be intrinsically enjoyable. As an elegant experimental demonstration of this point, Lepper, Greene, and Nisbett (1973) showed that children who performed an activity for an expected reward did not freely choose to perform the same activity later in a different setting. Those who were *not* initially rewarded for performing the activity were more likely to engage freely in the activity at a subsequent time.

Weiner and his colleagues have been engaged in a very self-conscious attempt to recast achievement motivation in attributional terms (1974). Weiner's basic argument is that the motivation to perform or to continue to perform an activity is closely linked to the actor's perception of the determinants of success. This reformulation has been very influential as a stimulus for both laboratory and classroom research.

The fact that it is relatively easy to use attributional terms to characterize different social phenomena suggests the importance of distinguishing between attribution theory and an attributional approach. There are attributional theories about inferring dispositions (Jones and Davis, 1965), about achieving stable inferences about the environment (Kelley, 1967), about actor-observer differences in explaining behavior (Jones and Nisbett, 1971), and about schemata used to handle partial data sets (Kelley, 1971). Much of the attributional literature, however, is not addressed to the testing of particular theoretical hypotheses; it can more accurately be described as attribution-based research and deals with diverse social phenomena in terms of various "local" or concrete determinants of causal allocation to persons versus situations. The flexibility of an attributional approach, as distinguished from attribution theory *per se,* is undoubtedly an important factor in its growth and staying power. The empirical literature exploiting this approach has been voluminous. Nelson and Hendrick's survey in 1974 showed that, at that time, attribution-based studies formed by far the largest category in the social psychology research literature. Some decline thereafter was inevitable, but the amount of attributional research remains considerable. In addition, the volumes edited by Harvey, Ickes, and Kidd (entitled *New Directions in Attribution Research,* Volume 1, 1976; Volume 2, 1978; and Volume 3, 1981) were important as forums for the discussion and consolidation of attribution research. And finally, it should be noted that an entire so-

cial psychology textbook has been written from an attributional approach (Harvey and Smith, 1977). The fact that the text is not obviously deviant or idiosyncratic is testimony once again to the flexibility of the approach and its basic compatibility with other orientations.

In summary, the attributional approach became dominant in social psychology for a variety of reasons, including the decline of specific interest in dissonance theory, the general momentum of cognitive approaches within psychology at large, the hospitable flexibility of the approach, and its capacity to offer a reasonable alternative explanation for important results generated by other theories. By and large, the waxing of the attributional approach was not an imperialistic putsch engineered by aggressive attribution theorists. In many cases (including those of Bem and Seligman), an attributional approach was adopted by those whose research began under different premises. Once again, the attributional approach is not a theory. In fact, it has become practically synonymous with research based on the premise that people act with reference to their conception of causal forces in the environment. Such a premise covers a very large terrain.

Inference Shortcomings

As far as research specifically relevant to attribution theory is concerned, the formulations of Heider, Jones, Kelley, and Weiner have primarily served as normative models of rational inference that are often honored by real subjects only in the breach. Correspondent inference theory (Jones and Davis, 1965), especially, has been used to identify such pervasive inference biases as the "fundamental attribution error" (Ross, 1977). This is the tendency to overattribute causation to dispositions and/or to underattribute causation to the situation.

The work on bias has been extended recently into the broader domain of general inference processes and judgmental heuristics. Building on the data of attributional biases as well as the work of Tversky and Kahneman (1974), Nisbett and Ross (1980) have identified a variety of human shortcomings in reaching conclusions from available evidence about the self, other persons, and events. Their approach suggests that many processing short cuts that have survived because of their general usefulness can lead to serious errors of understanding when misapplied. This provocative review constructs a wide and inviting bridge between the domains of social and cognitive psychology.

The Role of Affect

The 1970s have been characterized as a period in which cognitive approaches to the understanding of interpersonal relations have become ascendant. Is it likely that "this, too, shall pass?" There are more than a few signs that the cognitive revolution will be at least moderated by an increasing interest in affect and arousal. As long as cognitivists could buy the strong version of Schachter's theory of emotion—that nonspecific, uninformative, autonomic arousal becomes "emotion" when attached to a cognitive label—affect could be confined to glandular subservience. However, any evidence of separate affective systems, operating with some independence of the cognitive sphere, cries for a theoretical orientation that gives affect its own place in the conceptual realm. Tomkins (1981) is convinced that such evidence is abundant in pan-cultural consistencies of facial response mediation as well as in our own phenomenal experience. He argues that "affect can determine cognition at one time, be determined by cognition at another time, and be independent under other circumstances" (p. 324). Although he hopes that reality confirms the rumors that the next decade or so belongs to affect he fears that affect will continue to be co-opted by "the hypertrophy of cognitive imperialism" (p. 328). Thorough, sensitive reviews like Leventhal's (1980), however, may help to keep such imperialism in its place. Leventhal's formulation provides a comprehensive housing for emotions built around "innate motor scripts" and their separate cognitive representations. However, in emphasizing the enormous complexity of cognitive-affective interactions, his view will perhaps dismay those who would rather cling to a simpler version. Indeed, it is quite possible that more one-sided formulations may prove to be heuristic, even though they are obviously incomplete or even wrong.

An important paper by Zajonc (1980) pleads for the recognition of independent affective and cognitive response systems. Though we normally think of affect as following from cognition (believing that one must identify or discriminate before evaluating or preferring), Zajonc argues persuasively for the temporal primacy of affective response systems and for their relative independence from cognitive recognition response systems. Affect may be generated by the most primitive or minimal discriminations, and the subsequently elaborated cognitions typically incorporate the affective response and are, to an extent, determined by it.

The works of Zajonc and of Nisbett and Ross converge to raise considerable doubt about the accuracy of self-knowledge in determining our actions, beliefs, and feelings. Although interest in attribution was originally premised on the causal role that attributions play as determinants of behavior, there are increasing signs that, in many important respects, we are out of touch with many determinants of our behavior and are readily seduced into offering salient cultural stereotypes and rationalizations in answer to Why questions. In any event, the precise relations between cognition, affect, and behavior remain very much a mystery—a fact that must certainly have been sensed by both Lewin and Heider, who refused to equate subjectivism with phenomenological validity. It seems reasonable to predict that there will be much more to say in the near future about the complex relations between attributions and behavior, and the role of affect is likely to receive greater attention by social psychologists than has been the case up to now.

THE ANALYSIS OF SOCIAL PROBLEMS

Our discussion thus far has emphasized the major lines of theoretical development in social psychology and the clusters of research (primarily experimental) relating to them. This portrayal presents a distorted picture of the total range of social psychology's contribution, since it omits the extensive literature growing out of, and responding to, social problems. This literature is difficult to characterize historically, since the research tends to be triggered by contemporary circumstances and interpretations of the findings weave together both new and old theoretical trends. One can visualize a continuum ranging from theory-driven research at one extreme to research focused on social problems at the other. Some researchers tend to operate with a theory in search of exemplification, whereas others begin with a phenomenon and try to conceptualize its features, often with reference to one or more existing theories. However, the two approaches are often in various stages of transition so that the distinction between them may become easily blurred.

Social psychology has always straddled the line between theory and application. Many natural science psychologists would no doubt (privately if not publicly) cast most of social psychology in the "applied" camp. On the other hand, those in the applied fields of clinical and organizational psychology often look to social psychology for basic concepts and general principles. To an important extent, then, what is basic and what is applied are functions of the observer's orientation. Furthermore, the same research can often be titled and described in basic or applied terms. (Presentational format may be at least partly determined by the state of the external reward system in the social sciences.)

No doubt social relevance is always "in," but sometimes it is more "in" than at other times. The Second World War was a clear and obvious stimulus for applied research in the social sciences. It precipitated an urgent need for problem solutions, resources were ample, and the accessibility of large numbers of military subjects was often a researcher's dream. Many social psychologists turned their attention to such things as the analysis of propaganda, methods of inducing attitude change on vital war-related issues, and the determinants of high versus low morale, especially as linked to the concept of relative deprivation (cf. Cartwright, 1948). In the relatively quiet Eisenhower years, the cry for social relevance was muted in favor of the development of basic research paradigms that would separate the conceptual gold from the idiosyncratic complexities of interpersonal behavior episodes. This was the Rodney Dangerfield era, with social psychology attempting to gain respect as a coherent field with its own powerful theoretical and investigative tools. The Kennedy and King assassinations and our tragic Vietnam involvement were important factors that changed all this as they changed so many other features of our society.

The early 1970s witnessed dramatic shifts in the teaching of undergraduates in psychology courses. Students demanded and generally received larger amounts of relevance in their courses. New courses were added and instructors in the traditional courses turned to textbooks that featured a greater concern with the problems of society. Such textbooks began to be the rule rather than the exception, and it is hard to find a contemporary text without obligatory treatments of the determinants of violence, helping behavior, crowding, environmental psychology, love and attraction, and the psychology of women.

Though textbooks have, quite understandably, reflected the perceived demands for relevance in their packaging of available research data, problem-driven research has itself grown substantially in the past fifteen years. It is a commentary on the nature of the field that problem-focused research articles appear in the same journals with theory-driven research, though it is also true that the *Journal of Applied Social Psychology* was explicitly founded in 1971 as an outlet for the applications of behavioral science research to the problems of society. In order to redress, ever so slightly, the balance of the present chapter, we shall briefly mention some major clusters of social problem research that have received particular attention in the past fifteen years.

PREJUDICE AND STEREOTYPY

Research on ethnic prejudice, stereotypes, and intergroup relations has persistently attracted the attention of social psychologists. LaPiere's classic study in 1934 raised the intriguing and still unanswered question, "When does prejudice toward an out-group lead to discrimination toward individual out-group members?" Many measures of attitudes developed during the 1930s and 1940s focused on social distance preferences toward various ethnic groups (e.g., Hartley, 1946). As early as 1933, Katz and Braly showed the striking consensus of Princeton students concerning their ethnic stereotypes. In *The Nature of Prejudice,* G. W. Allport (1954) provided a comprehensive view of the patterning and determinants of prejudice, summarizing the state of our knowledge at that point in time. His review gave impetus to the idea that prejudice grows out of normal cognitive processes; thus Allport directed the field away from the emphasis on abnormality and individual differences conveyed by authoritarian personality theory (Adorno *et al.,* 1950) and from the motivated irrationality implied by frustration-aggression theory (Dollard *et al.,* 1939). Interest in the cognitive bases of stereotypy has accelerated in recent years as a natural consequence of the upsurge of interest in cognitive biases of all sorts. Brigham's (1971) useful review marks a convenient starting point for this accelerated interest which, ten years later, was exemplified in a volume edited by Hamilton (1981) on cognitive processes in stereotyping and inter-group behavior.

The affective side of prejudice has also been recently highlighted in Katz's (1981) book, *Stigma,* which presents an analysis of reactions to black or disabled target persons in a series of experiments. Clearly, the study of affective biasing factors in interpersonal relations lies at the heart of the social psychology domain and is likely to remain a topic of research concern.

THE IMPACT OF TELEVISION VIOLENCE

Social psychologists have also participated in the wave of research on the effects of television on its viewers. Much of this research has centered on the role exposure to violence on television plays in the induction of crime and aggressive behavior. Though some researchers (e.g., Feshbach and Singer, 1971) have found that watching violence reduces aggressive behavior, the general consensus, as expressed in the conclusions of the Eisenhower Commission on the Causes and Prevention of Violence, is that "violence on television encourages violent forms of behavior." For the time being, at least, the imitation or modeling approach seems to have won out over catharsis theory.

HELPING BEHAVIOR

A classic example of phenomena-driven research was the series of studies conducted by Latané and Darley that investigated bystander intervention in emergency situations (summarized in their 1970 book). Undoubtedly, the Zeitgeist was an important background factor in alerting them to the social problems that they addressed. Post-assassination years of the 1960s brought an increasing societal concern with alienation and the fragmentation of social bonds. The urban environment, in particular, was portrayed as an anarchic jungle characterized by a decline in human compassion and in feelings of social involvement. In this general context of concern, the brutal courtyard murder of Kitty Genovese, featuring the failure of thirty-eight witnesses to intervene, became a critical stimulus for launching a program of experimental research. In a series of ingenious and realistic experiments, conducted both in the laboratory and in the field, Latané and Darley were able to show that intervention is the final step in a complex sequence of interpretations. How these interpretations resolve the issue of personal responsibility is a critical feature in the decision process.

The themes of the Latané and Darley research resonated with the heightened concern that social psychology should be more relevant, and a large literature on bystander intervention has developed over the past decade. An even larger literature has developed dealing with more general issues of helping and altruism and touching on the role of perceived equity, the desire for justice, and evocation of the social responsibility norm (cf. Macauley and Berkowitz, 1970). Although the general area of prosocial behavior has long been a concern of social psychologists, the specific twist provided by Latané and Darley accelerated research in the treacherous theoretical briar patch where considerations of morality are tangled with reward-cost calculations, with probability assessments, and with questions of courage and fear.

CROWDING AND STRESS

Reflections on urban life in the late 1960s and 1970s also generated a cluster of research on the relations between crowding and stress. Much of this research was done by social psychologists, and much of it has been rather doggedly empirical. Because useful theoretical formulations have been difficult to develop, the thrust of the research has been to dramatize the lack of any simple connection between crowding and density on the one hand and stress or performance decrements on the other. Indeed, the major conclusion of the most widely known treatment of crowding (Freedman, 1975) is that the destructive effects of high urban density have been vastly exaggerated. According to Glass and Singer (1972), however, the stressful effects of urban noise have not been. In their important and ingenious experimental program, Glass and Singer were able to show that the after-effects of noise pollution can be as debilitating on performance as the concurrent ones. In particular, Glass and Singer stressed the "therapeutic" importance of predictability and of control over the onset of such potential stressors as noise and shock.

The research on crowding, noise, and other factors contributing to urban stress form part of the rapidly developing field of environmental psychology. The relations between this field and social psychology are not entirely clear. In addition to the work of such social psychologists as Freedman, Glass, and Singer, environmental psychology clearly owes much to the research and intellectual orientation of such pioneers as Roger Barker (e.g., 1968), who prefers the label of "ecological psychology." Many if not most environmental psychologists are also identified as social psychologists, though some would prefer to be called *former* social psychologists, perhaps to strengthen their sense of identification with what they perceive as a new field. In fact, two (former?) social psychologists have expressed their strong disagreement with each other concerning the relationship between social and environmental psychology. Altman

(1976) feels that social psychological methods and theories are highly relevant in developing the field of environmental psychology. Proshansky (1976) disagrees and contends that social psychology "broke its promise" and has not really solved the problems it had set out to solve. Its methods, he claims, are too restrictive and violate the "environmental assumption of person-environment integrity." Obviously there are aspects of environmental psychology rather far removed from traditional social psychological concerns, but the historical, if not also the theoretical and methodological, affinity between the two fields is clear.

HEALTH AND MEDICINE

Especially in the wake of developments in attribution theory, social psychologists have devoted considerable attention to the behavioral aspects of health and medicine. Though the label "behavioral medicine" tends to connote a behavior modification approach, the last decade has seen important contributions by social psychologists to such problems as the analysis of doctor-patient relations, reactions to diagnostic information, placebo effects, "illness management" by patients, and some of the relations between causal attribution and the experience of pain (cf. Taylor, 1978). Much of the research in this area centers around the concept of personal responsibility and control in the adjustment of the aged. Other research has dealt with consequences of personal responsibility or control in the prevention of illness as well as in the rehabilitation process.

SOCIAL PSYCHOLOGY AND LAW

Finally, there has been a growing involvement of social psychologists in the study of problems posed by the legal system. This is hardly surprising in view of the general pressure toward relevance and the many easily identifiable social psychological problems embedded in the administration of justice. An interest in the psychology of testimony goes back at least to the turn of the century, and many experimental studies of selective retention and attitude change have used the jury-trial setting to promote mundane realism. It is hard to imagine a more fertile setting than jury deliberations for the study of social influence processes at work. Because the sanctity of such deliberations cannot be directly breached, social scientists have had to content themselves with simulated jury situations. Perhaps the closest approximation to true

jury deliberations was the study of Strodtbeck, James, and Hawkins (1958) in which jurors drawn by lot from the regular jury pool of Chicago and St. Louis courts were exposed to recordings of two civil trials and then proceeded to discuss each case as a mock jury. Many other jury simulation experiments have since been conducted, focusing on the role of juror attitudes and personality factors as well as on different features of case presentation or characteristics of the defendant. As social psychologists have become more familiar with the kinds of legal issues that recur in the adjudication process, there has been a shift from using legal contexts in pursuing general psychological questions to the analysis of legal procedures themselves. Thus, a recent issue of the *Journal of Personality and Social Psychology* (1978, *36*, no. 12) presents a collection of experimental studies focusing on such questions as the role of sentencing strategies, plea bargaining, the severity of prescribed penalties, and the consequences of adversarial versus inquisitorial procedures. An acceleration of this trend toward law-tailored research may generate findings that begin to have an impact on judicial decisions as well as on procedural arrangements. Tanke and Tanke (1979) point out, however, that the actual use of social science findings in courtroom proceedings is rare. They note that the role of social science findings in the historic 1954 Supreme Court desegregation ruling has been highly exaggerated. Following Kalven and Zeisel (1961), they refer to the citation of social science work in the *Brown vs. Board of Education* ruling as a pedagogical sideshow and argue that these works were not a moving force in the decision.

RELEVANCE AND FUNDING PRIORITIES

As noted earlier, the flow of research traffic in and out of various topic areas is partly determined by the funding priorities of foundations and governmental agencies. An important question for the future is the level of specification these agencies use in defining relevance. Natural scientists appear to have better control than social scientists over the setting of relevant research agendas. Perhaps natural scientists, because their procedures and findings are relatively immune to evaluations by lay overseers, are in a better position to insure that available funds support research on tractable problems of their own choosing. In contrast, because their findings and procedures are more open to lay evaluations, social scientists are likely to be pressed into working on problems defined as urgent or important by those outside the profession. Some of these problems may be much less tractable than others, and yet the lay evaluator may uniformly expect results in proportion to the money spent. Not surprisingly, some social scientists have acquiesced in, if not promoted, the raising of unrealistic expectations about the potential value for society of social science research. Failure to fulfill these expectations is then used by Congress or the administration in power to justify funding restrictions or cutbacks in times of economic distress. As Homans (1967) has said, "I sometimes think that the social sciences are criticized as sciences for failing to do what a respectable physical science would not have ever tried to do" (p. 96).

Perhaps it is too much to expect that social scientists will ever approach the degree of control the natural science community has over its own research priorities, at least not until the unlikely event that a basic "breakthrough" can be utilized to support successful social change. In the meantime, our best hope may lie in the gradual accumulation of results on a variety of fronts, results that enter by osmosis into important forms of social decision making. Indeed, many definite changes in society brought about by social science findings quickly become such an integral part of the cultural background that it is easy to forget their origins. For example, consider the ever-growing number of social psychological principles currently embedded in political campaigning, industrial management, and mixed motive negotiations. In any event, quite independently of funding opportunities and considerations of disciplinary prestige, many social psychologists were attracted to the field in the first place because of their interest in understanding and solving social problems, and a large number of them are members of the Society for the Psychological Study of Social Issues, a group emphasizing involvement in contemporary social problems. Undoubtedly a high proportion of social psychological research will continue to be generated by contemporary social issues, and social psychological findings will eventually work their way into the solution strategies of some policy and decision makers.

REPRISE AND FORECAST

All behavioral science disciplines share a strong tendency to examine and criticize themselves periodically. We have already noted the self-doubts of contemporary personality psychologists. Elms (1975), among others, has cited the widespread self-doubts about goals, methods, and accomplishments in developmental and clinical psychol-

ogy, in sociology, in anthropology, and in economics. Social psychology has certainly not escaped this tendency toward self-flagellation, and criticism has taken a variety of forms. Asch (1951) was neither the first nor the last to complain of the reductionistic tendencies of those who would emulate the techniques of the natural sciences without noticing the limits of their applicability. Through the years other internal critics have commented on various theoretical or methodological shortcomings in social psychology. A unique convergence of events in the late 1960s brought about an exacerbation of self-criticism that became identified as "the crisis in social psychology." To some extent, this despairing rhetoric fed on itself. The research literature continued to grow during the 1970s at a fast rate, and it is hard to detect any direct effects of malaise in the journals carrying this prime research. However, enough people were disturbed by developments in their field to organize symposia and generate essays proclaiming social psychology as a field in moral and methodological disarray. The events converging to bring this about generally fell in three areas: ethics, artifacts, and relevance (cf. Rosnow, 1981).

THE RISE OF ETHICAL CONCERN

The linkage of deceptive scenarios with experimentation grew stronger and stronger as social psychology moved into the 1960s. Conformity research, whether in the Asch or the social comparison paradigm, inevitably involved deceptive information about the opinions or judgments of others. It also involved a kind of entrapment of subjects who would later have to deal with the implications on their self-concept of their particular resolution of the conformity conflict. As dissonance research gained momentum in the 1960s, hundreds of experiments were published in which subjects were induced to do things, or to commit themselves to do things, that they would ordinarily avoid doing. The ethical problems inherent in the use of deception were especially highlighted by Festinger, Riecken, and Schachter's (1956) infiltration of a doomsday group and by Milgram's (1963) obedience research. It was perhaps inevitable that the widespread adoption of deception techniques, especially those that embarrassed subjects or lowered their self-esteem, would elicit a chorus of concerned comment. A strong early criticism was voiced by Baumrind (1964) concerning Milgram's research. This resulted in a debate that constituted the first truly public airing of the pros and cons of deception in social psychological research. Kelman (1967) was also an early critic of the unbridled use of deception, and the title and thrust of his subsequent book (*A Time to Speak,* 1968) may have reinforced the picture of social scientists involved in a silent conspiracy to manipulate and humiliate subjects.

Although the full impact of such criticisms is difficult to assess, they undoubtedly sensitized psychologists and the public to the ethical dilemmas inherent in social psychological experimentation and stimulated considerable debate about alternative (i.e., nondeceptive) procedures. In this atmosphere of ethical concern, the federal government began to extend its monitoring of the protection of human subjects from medical to behavioral science research. Under pressure from federal granting agencies—especially the Department of Health Education and Welfare—universities established or reorganized committees to monitor all human subjects research conducted by their personnel or on their premises. Though there has undoubtedly been considerable variation in how individual committees have viewed deception research, it is fair to say that the range of available procedures has been restricted by ethical concerns enforceable by human subjects committees.

ARTIFACTS AND EXPERIMENTER EFFECTS

In the rush to consolidate the experimental triumphs of Lewin and Sherif in the 1930s, many investigators lost sight of the fact (first emphasized by Rosenzweig in 1933) that the contact between an experimenter and his subjects involves a complex social interaction. The work of Robert Rosenthal reminded them (even while it was annoying them). As early as 1956, in his doctoral dissertation, Rosenthal suggested that experimenters may exert subtle influence within the experimental setting to confirm their theoretical hypotheses or expectancies. At the time he wrote of "unconscious experimenter bias" to indicate that experimenters might be quite unaware of their contributions to self-fulfilling prophecies in interacting with subjects. Although Rosenthal's research has itself been severely criticized on many grounds (cf. Barber and Silver, 1968), the cumulative impact of his experimenter bias studies was to improve decidedly the methodology of experimentation. His research, combined with Orne's (1962) demonstrations of "experimenter demand" artifacts, were important determinants of the increasing inclusion of sophisticated precautions within experimental

designs. In particular, investigators have become much more sensitive to the need to keep experimenters blind to the experimental condition of the subject being run.

THE "ETHOGENIC APPROACH"

Whereas the artifact crisis was basically self-corrective, resulting in clear methodological advances, more fundamental and disturbing criticisms raised fundamental doubts about the status of social psychology as a quantitative empirical science. These criticisms have involved a convergence of British linguistic philosophy, micro-sociology (especially, "ethno-methodology"), and good old-fashioned humanism. This convergence is especially apparent in the writings of Harré (with Secord 1972, 1977), who has tried to urge an "ethogenic approach" on restless, dissatisfied social psychologists. This approach is considerably clearer about what it is against than what it is for. It is against a mechanistic model of man, antipositivistic, and skeptical of the naive determinism implicit in stimulus-response causal models. Experimentation embodies all these evils, according to Harré and his group, and should be replaced by methods appropriate to an anthropomorphic view of humankind, emphasizing the human being's capacity to initiate action, monitor his or her performances, and monitor his or her monitorings. The only method described in detail is "account analysis" defined by Harré (1977) with characteristic opacity (p. 284):

> It is the analysis of both the social force and explanatory content of the speech produced by social actors as a guide to the structure of the cognitive resources required for the genesis of intelligible and warrantable social action by those actors.

Above all else, account analysis involves a reliance on the negotiation of explanations between actors and observers until satisfactory concordance is achieved.

The ethogenic approach has much in common with the "descriptive psychology" approach of Peter Ossorio (1981). Both approaches emphasize structural linguistic features and shared assumptions about the meaning of social behavior. Though they both have raised interesting possibilities about future research formats, neither has yet proved itself as an alternative to the mix of existing empirical approaches. It seems especially unfortunate that the ethogenic approach involves an exclusionary stance, arguing for replacing experimental approaches with a loose assortment of observational techniques and "negotiation" by interview. As Schlenker (1977) points out, social psychologists are not forced to rely exclusively on either a rigorous quantitative or a more sensitive qualitative methodology. Each has its place, and the contributions of a Goffman or a Garfinkel can enrich, without replacing or superceding, the contributions of a Kelley or a Zajonc.

Exclusionary arguments may originate from the misplaced assumption that social psychology's so-called "crisis" is actually a paradigmatic crisis in the sense proposed by Kuhn (1962). Kuhn has argued that major scientific advances emerge only after the normal problem-solving activities have for the time being failed. Thus, crises are healthy; they lead to paradigm shifts. As Elms (1975) notes, however, this may be wishful thinking, based on the fallacious assumption that there is a genuine scientific paradigm in social psychology, a well-developed and widely shared version of normal science. In his view, a crisis of confidence does not necessarily denote a shattering of an old orthodoxy (that in the case of social psychology never existed) in preparation for a new one (that is unlikely to arrive in the near future).

SOCIAL PSYCHOLOGY AS HISTORY?

The most controversial aspect of an experimental approach in social psychology has always been the problem of generalization or ecological validity. How does one proceed from a context-bound finding to a statement about the condition of human nature? Kenneth Gergen (1973, 1976) tackled this problem and produced a sweeping indictment of social psychology's scientific pretensions. First, Gergen argued that the data of human behavior are culturally and historically relative, at best characterizing a particular sample of subjects in a particular setting at a particular time. Secondly, and with more than a trace of self-contradiction, he stated that social psychological findings enlighten the public and can thus generate oppositional tendencies that render the observed behavior less likely in the future. In a recent book, Gergen (1982) has adumbrated these themes and incorporated them into a sophisticated attack on positivism in general and hypothesis-testing empiricism in particular. In this treatment, Gergen argues for a "sociorationalistic" position that emphasizes collective sources of knowledge as an alternative both to the "exogenous" view of science as a mapping of nature and to the completely "endogenous" view of knowledge as entirely relative to the individual knower. It remains to be seen whether appropriate methods can be developed to implement this orientation and to make it more than a vaguely shimmering promissory note.

Though Gergen is clearly trying in this recent work to sketch the outlines of a paradigm shift, many social psychologists viewed his earlier statements as intellectually irresponsible invitations to despair. Schlenker has provided strong rebuttals not only to Gergen (1974, 1976) but also to Harré (1977).

Putting aside the particular merits of the argument, the response to Gergen's 1973 paper poses interesting problems for this historical review. Since Gergen's pessimistic conclusions are not particularly novel, one can wonder why contemporary social psychologists paid such lavish attention to them. Countless symposia during the 1970s were built around a debate of his thesis. It seems likely that his paper is as widely known as any single essay on the general subject published in the past decade. A widespread need for self-flagellation, perhaps unique to social psychologists, may account for some of the mileage of the Gergen message. It is also the case that the message (especially in this early paper) has the advantage of rhetorical simplicity; the rejoinders are perforce more complex and therefore more forgettable, partly because it would be difficult simply to stand up for the straw men that Gergen attacks.

It is not too surprising that those who hope to change the ways of social psychologists create such straw men to substitute for the actual heterogeneity of research approaches and objectives within social psychology. Thus there is a tendency to caricature past social psychological research and to consign it to a simple positivistic trash bin along with reductionistic learning experiments. Such a caricature may be easily lampooned to make the experimental approach to the complexities of social behavior appear irrelevant and derivative. Perhaps more attention should be paid to the varieties of experimentation that actually have generated our literature and to the diverse roles that experiments can play in illuminating the nature of a problem and the ways of thinking about it. Perhaps, as Kaplan (1964) has suggested, we do not have to believe that laws exist to believe that they are worth looking for. Even Gergen (1976) acknowledges that "theories of social behavior may play a number of very useful roles other than improving prediction" (p. 375). And even if we concede, along with Gergen (1982), that the main function of research is to lend rhetorical power to theoretical interpretation, this is a vastly important function that hardly deserves belittlement.

The crisis of social psychology has begun to take its place as a minor perturbation in the long history of the social sciences. The intellectual momentum of the field has not been radically affected by crisis proclamations, though some of the broader institutional consequences should be considered and eventually assessed. A case can be made that the severity of the self-doubting criticisms, along with the publicity they received, played into the hands of political and academic forces poised to put social psychology in its place. There is a clear sense in which the apparent malaise affecting social psychology was seen as more devastating by outsiders than by social psychologists themselves. Other psychologists and other social scientists are more likely to know social psychology through its current self-depictions than through its prime research literature. Perhaps it is not surprising that some of them thought the malaise was terminal.

From a long-range perspective, the educational reproduction of social psychologists will ebb and flow with shifts in social and economic priorities. The number of social psychologists will expand rapidly at times and contract at others. Graduate programs will emerge, and others will disappear. But as this handbook testifies, the progress in our understanding has been remarkable in the short period of little more than a decade since the preceding edition. The progress should not be measured either in terms of neat cumulative linear increments or in terms of great re-orienting breakthroughs but rather in the increased insights that gradually work their way into our cultural wisdom. It is a person's very nature to understand himself or herself in relation to others. The future of social psychology is assured not only by the vital importance of its subject matter but also by its unique conceptual and methodological strengths that permit the identification of underlying processes in everyday social life.

REFERENCES

Abelson, R. P., E. Aronson, W. J. McGuire, T. M. Newcomb, M. J. Rosenberg, and P. H. Tannenbaum (Eds.), (1968). *Theories of cognitive consistency: a source book*. Chicago: Rand McNally.

Abramson, L. Y., M. E. P. Seligman, and J. D. Teasdale, (1978). Learned helplessness in humans: critique and reformulation. *J. abnorm. Psychol., 87,* 49–74.

Adams, J. S. (1965). Inequity in social exchange. In L. Berkowitz (Ed.), *Advances in Experimental Social Psychology*. Vol. 2. New York: Academic Press.

Adorno, T. W., E. Frenkel-Brunswik, D. J. Levinson, and R. N. Sanford (1950). *The authoritarian personality*. New York: Harper & Row.

Allport, F. H. (1924). *Social psychology*. Boston: Houghton Mifflin.

_____ (1955). *Theories of perception and the concept of structure*. New York: Wiley.

Allport, G. W. (1935). Attitudes. In C. Murchison (Ed.), *A handbook of social psychology*. Worcester, Mass.: Clark Univ. Press. Pp. 798–844.

_____ (1937). *Personality: a psychological interpretation*. New York: Henry Holt.

_____ (1954a). *The nature of prejudice*. Reading, Mass.: Addison-Wesley.

_____ (1954b). The historical background of modern social psychology. In G. Lindzey (Ed.), *The handbook of social psychology*. (Vol. I). Cambridge, Mass.: Addison-Wesley. Pp. 3–56.

Allport, G. W., and L. Postman (1947). *The psychology of rumor*. New York: Henry Holt.

Altman, I. (1976). Environmental psychology and social psychology. *Pers. and soc. Psychol. Bull., 2,* 96–113.

Anderson, N. H. (1962). Application of an attitude model to impression formation. *Science, 138,* 817–818.

Anderson, H., and A. Jacobson (1965). Effect of stimulus inconsistency and discounting instructions in personality impression formation. *J. Pers. soc. Psychol., 2,* 531–539.

Aronson, E. (1968). Dissonance theory: progress and problems. In R. P. Abelson, E. Aronson, W. J. McGuire, T. M. Newcomb, M. J. Rosenberg, and P. H. Tannenbaum, (Eds.). *Theories of cognitive consistency: a source book*. Chicago: Rand McNally. Pp. 5–27.

_____ (1980). Persuasion via self-justification: large commitments for small rewards. In L. Festinger (Ed.), *Retrospections on social psychology*. New York: Oxford Univ. Press. Pp. 3–21.

Aronson, E., and J. M. Carlsmith (1963). The effect of the severity of threat on the devaluation of forbidden behavior. *J. abnorm. soc. Psychol., 66,* 584–588.

_____ (1968). Experimentation in social psychology. In G. Lindzey and E. Aronson (Eds.), *Handbook of social psychology* (2nd ed.). Vol. 2. Reading, Mass.: Addison-Wesley.

Aronson, E., and D. Linder (1965). Gain and loss of esteem as determinants of interpersonal attractiveness. *J. exp. soc. Psychol., 1,* 156–172.

Asch, S. E. (1946). Forming impressions of personality. *J. abnorm. soc. Psychol., 41,* 258–290.

_____ (1952). *Social psychology*. New York: Prentice-Hall.

_____ (1956). Studies of independence and conformity: a minority of one against a unanimous majority. *Psychol. Monogr., 70,* No. 9 (Whole No. 416).

Bales, R. F. (1950). *Interaction process analysis*. Cambridge, Mass.: Addison-Wesley.

_____ (1970). *Personality and interpersonal behavior*. New York: Holt, Rinehart and Winston.

Bandura, A. (1973). *Aggression: A social learning analysis.* Englewood Cliffs, N.J.: Prentice-Hall.

Bandura, A., and R. H. Walters (1963). *Social learning and personality development.* New York: Holt, Rinehart and Winston.

Barber, T. X., and M. J. Silver (1968). Fact, fiction, and the experimenter bias effect. *Psychol. Bull.* Monogr. Suppl., 70, 1–29.

Barker, R. (1968). *Ecological psychology: concepts and methods for studying the environment of human behavior.* Stanford: Stanford Univ. Press.

Barker, R., T. Dembo, and K. Lewin (1941). Frustration and regression: an experiment with young children. *Univ. of Iowa Studies in Child Welfare, 18,* No. 1.

Bartlett, F. C. (1932). *Remembering.* Cambridge: Cambridge Univ. Press.

Baumrind, D. (1964). Some thoughts on ethics of research: After reading Milgram's "behavioral study of obedience," *Amer. Psychologist, 19,* 421–423.

Bem, D. (1965). An experimental analysis of self-persuasion. *J. exp. soc. Psychol., 1,* 199–218.

_____ (1967). Self-perception: an alternative interpretation of cognitive dissonance phenomena. *Psychol. Rev., 74,* 183–200.

_____ (1972). Self-perception theory. In L. Berkowitz (Ed.), *Advances in experimental social psychology.* Vol. 6. New York: Academic Press.

_____ (1980a). Assessing situations by assessing persons. In D. Magnusson (Ed.), *Toward a psychology of situations: an interactional perspective.* Hillsdale, N.J.: Erlbaum.

_____ (1980b). Assessing persons and situations with the template-matching technique. In L. Kahle (Ed.), *New directions in the methodology of behavioral research: methods for studying person situation interactions.* San Francisco: Jossey-Bass.

Bem, D., and A. Allen (1974). On predicting some of the people some of the time: the search for cross-situational consistencies in behavior. *Psychol. Rev., 81,* 506–520.

Bem, D. J., and D. C. Funder (1978). Predicting more of the people more of the time: assessing the personality of situations. *Psychol. Rev., 85,* 485–501.

Bem. D., and C. J. Lord (1970). Template matching: a proposal for probing the ecological validity of experimental settings in social psychology. *J. Pers. soc. Psychol., 37,* 833–846.

Berkowitz, L., and R. Geen (1966). Film violence and cue properties of available targets. *J. Pers. soc. Psychol., 3,* 525–530.

Berkowitz, L., and A. Lepage (1967). Weapons as aggression-eliciting stimuli. *J. Pers. soc. Psychol., 7,* 202–207.

Berkowitz, L., and E. Walster (1976). Equity theory: toward a general theory of social interaction. *Advances in experimental social psychology.* Vol. 9. New York: Academic Press.

Block, J. (1977). Advancing the psychology of personality: paradigmatic shift or improving the quality of research? In D. Magnusson and N. S. Endler (Eds.), *Personality at the crossroads: current issues and interactional psychology.* Hillsdale, N.J.: Erlbaum.

Bonacich, P., and J. Light (1978). Laboratory experimentation in sociology. In *Ann. Rev. Sociol., 4,* 145–170.

Bowers, K. S. (1973). Situationism in psychology: an analysis and critique. *Psychol. Rev., 80,* 307–336.

Brehm, J. W. (1956). Post decision changes in the desirability of alternatives. *J. abnorm. soc. Psychol., 52,* 384–389.

_____ (1965). Comment on "counternorm attitudes induced by consonant versus dissonant conditions of role-playing." *J. exp. Res. Pers., 1,* 61–64.

Brehm, J. W., and A. R. Cohen (1962). *Explorations in cognitive dissonance.* New York: Wiley.

Brigham, J. C. (1971). Ethnic stereotypes. *Psychol. Bull., 76,* 15–38.

Broadbent, D. E. (1958). *Perception and communication.* London: Pergamon Press.

Brown, R., and U. Bellugi (1964). Three processes in the child's acquisition of syntax. In E.H. Lennenberg (Ed.), *New directions in the study of language.* Cambridge, Mass.: MIT Press. Pp. 131–161.

Bruner, J. S. (1951). Personality dynamics and the process of perceiving. In R. R. Blake and G. B. Ramsey (Eds.), *Perception: an approach to personality.* New York: Ronald Press.

_____ (1957). On perceptual readiness. *Psychol. Rev., 64,* 123–152.

Bruner, J. S., and C. C. Goodman (1947). Value and need as organizing factors in perception. *J. abnorm. soc. Psychol., 42,* 33–44.

Bruner, J. S., and R. Tagiuri (1954). The perception of people. In G. Lindzey (Ed.), *Handbook of social psychology.* Vol. 2. Cambridge, Mass.: Addison-Wesley. Pp. 634–654.

Brunswik, E. (1933). Die Zuganglichkeit Von Gegenstanden Fur Vie Wahrnehmung. *Archives of Gestalt Psychology, 88,* 377–418.

Burgess, R. L., and D. Bushell (1969). *Behavioral sociology: the experimental analysis of social process.* New York: Columbia Univ. Press.

Byrne, D. (1971). *The attraction paradigm.* New York: Academic Press.

Campbell, D. T., and J. C. Stanley (1966). *Experimental and quasi-experimental designs for research.* Chicago: Rand McNally.

Carlsmith, J. M., P. C. Ellsworth, and E. Aronson (1976). *Methods of research in social psychology.* Reading, Mass.: Addison-Wesley.

Carter, L., W. Haythorn, B. Meirowitz, and J. Lanzetta (1951a). The relation of categorization and ratings in the observation of group behavior. *Hum. Relat., 4,* 239–254.

_____ (1951b). A note on a new technique of interaction recording. *J. abnorm. soc. Psychol., 46,* 258–260.

Cartwright, D. (1948). Social psychology during World War II. *Hum. Relat., 1,* 333–352.

_____ (1973). Determinants of scientific progress: the case of research on the risky shift. *Amer. Psychologist, 28,* 222–231.

_____ (1979). Contemporary social psychology in historical perspective. *Soc. Psychol. Quart., 42,* 82–93.

_____ (1961). In W. Dennis (Ed.), *Current trends in psychological theory: a bicentennial program.* Pittsburgh: Univ. of Pittsburgh Press.

Cartwright, D., and F. Harary (1956). Structural balance: a generalization of Heider's theory. *Psychol. Rev., 63,* 277–293.

Cassirer, E. (1923). *Substance and function, and Einstein's theory of relativity.* Chicago: Open Court.

Chapple, E. D. (1940). Measuring human relations: an introduction to the study of the interaction of individuals. *Genetic Psychol. Monogr., 22,* 1–147.

———— (1949). The interaction chronograph: its evolution and present application. *Personnel, 25,* 295–307.

Christie, R., and F. L. Geis (1970). *Studies in Machiavellianism.* New York: Academic Press.

Christie, R., and M. Jahoda (1954). *Studies in the scope and method of the "authoritarian personality."* Glencoe, Ill.: Free Press.

Coffey, H. S., M. B. Freedman, T. F. Leary, and A. G. Ossorio (1950). Community service and social research—group psychotherapy in a church program. *J. soc. Issues, 6,* 1–65.

Cooley, C. H. (1902). *Human nature and social order.* New York: Scribner.

Cottrell, L. S., and R. Gallagher (1941). Developments in social psychology, 1930–1940. *Sociometry* Monogr. No. 1. New York: Beacon House.

Cottrell, N. B. (1972). Social facilitation. In C. B. McClintock (Ed.), *Experimental social psychology.* New York: Holt, Rinehart, and Winston. Pp. 185–236.

Cronbach, L. J. (1955). Processes affecting scores on "understanding of others" and "assumed similarity." *Psychol. Bull., 52,* 177–193.

———— (1957). The two disciplines of scientific psychology. *Amer. Psychologist, 12,* 671–684.

Deutsch, M. (1949a). A theory of cooperation and competition. *Hum. Relat., 2,* 129–152.

———— (1949b). An experimental study of the effects of cooperation and competition upon group process. *Hum. Relat., 2,* 199–232.

———— (1958). Trust and suspicion. *J. Conflict Resolution, 21,* 265–279.

———— (1962). Cooperation and trust: some theoretical notes. In M. R. Jones (Ed.), *Nebraska Symposium on Motivation.* Lincoln: Univ. of Nebraska Press.

Deutsch, M., and R. M. Krauss (1960). The effect of threat on interpersonal bargaining. *J. abnorm. soc. Psychol., 61,* 181–189.

Deutsch, M. (1980). Fifty years of conflict. In L. Festinger (Ed.), *Retrospections on social psychology.* New York: Oxford Univ. Press. Pp. 46–77.

Dollard, J., L. W. Doob, N. E. Miller, O. H. Mowrer, and R. R. Sears (1939). *Frustration and aggression.* New Haven: Yale Univ. Press.

Dollard, J., and N. E. Miller (1950). *Personality and psychotherapy.* New York: McGraw Hill.

Ebbinghaus, H. (1885). *Memory.* (Trans. H. A. Ruger and C. E. Bussenius) New York: Teachers College (1913). Originally *Uber das Gedachtnis.* Leipzig, Germany: Duncker.

Elms, A. C. (1975). The crisis of confidence in social psychology. *Amer. Psychol., 30,* 967–976.

Elms, A. C., and I. L. Janis (1965). Counternorm attitudes induced by consonant versus dissonant conditions of role playing. *J. exp. Res. Pers., 1,* 50–60.

Endler, N., and D. Magnusson (1976). Toward an interactional psychology of personality. *Psychol. Bull., 83,* 956–974.

Erdelyi, M. H. (1974). A new look at the new look: perceptual defense and vigilance. *Psychol. Rev., 81,* 1–25.

Eriksen, C. W., Ed. (1962). *Behavior and awareness.* Durham, N.C.: Duke Univ. Press.

Eriksen, C. W. (1958). Unconscious processes. In M. R. Jones (Ed.), *Nebraska symposium on motivation.* Lincoln: Univ. of Nebraska Press, 169–227.

Erickson, E. H. (1950). *Childhood and society.* New York: Norton.

Estes, W. K. (1954). Kurt Lewin. In W. K. Estes, S. Koch, K. MacCorquodale, P. Muhl, C. G. Mueller, W. N. Schoenfeld, and W. S. Verplanck, *Modern learning theory.* New York: Appleton-Century-Crofts. Pp. 317–344.

Farr, R. M. (1976). Experimentation: a social psychological perspective. *Brit. J. soc. clinic. Psychol., 15,* 225–238.

Fazio, R. H., M. P. Zanna, and J. Cooper (1977). Dissonance and self-perception: an integrative view of each theory's proper domain of application. *J. exp. soc. Psychol., 13,* 464–479.

Feshbach, S., and R. C. Singer (1971). *Television and aggression: an experimental field study.* San Francisco: Jossey-Bass.

Festinger, L. (1950). Informal social communication. *Psychol. Rev., 57,* 271–282.

———— (1954). A theory of social comparison processes. *Hum. Relat., 7,* 117–140.

———— (1957). *A theory of cognitive dissonance.* Evanston, Ill.: Row-Peterson.

———— (1980). Looking backward. In L. Festinger (Ed.), *Retrospections on social psychology.* New York: Oxford Univ. Press. Pp. 236–254.

Festinger, L., and J. M. Carlsmith (1959). Cognitive consequences of forced compliance. *J. abnorm soc. Psychol., 58,* 203–211.

Festinger, L., H. W. Riecken, and S. Schachter (1956). *When prophecy fails.* Minneapolis: Univ. of Minnesota.

Fishbein, M., and I. Ajzen (1975). *Belief, attitude, intention and behavior: an introduction to theory and research.* Reading, Mass.: Addison-Wesley.

Freedman, J. L. (1975). *Crowding and human behavior.* New York: Viking Press.

Fromm, E. (1941). *Escape from freedom.* New York: Rinehart.

Gallo, P. S. (1966). Effects of increased incentives upon the use of threat in bargaining. *J. Pers. soc. Psychol., 4,* 14–20.

Gergen, K. (1973). Social psychology as history. *J. Pers. soc. Psychol., 26,* 309–320.

Gergen, K. J. (1976). Social psychology, science, and history. *Pers. soc. Psychol. Bull., 2,* 373–383.

———— (1982). *Toward transformation in social knowledge.* New York: Springer-Verlag.

Glass, D. C., and J. E. Singer (1972). *Urban stress.* New York: Academic Press.

Goffman, E. (1959). *The presentation of self in everyday life.* Garden City, N.Y.: Doubleday, Anchor Books.

Goldiamond, I. (1958). Indicators of perceptions: I. subliminal perception, subception, unconscious perception: an analysis in terms of psychophysical indicator methodology. *Psychol. Bull., 55,* 373–411.

Haines, H., and G. M. Vaughan, (1979). Was 1898 a "great date" in the history of experimental social psychology? *J. Hist. behav. Sci., 15,* 323–332.

Hammond, K. R., G. H. McClelland, and J. Mumpower (1980). *Human judgment and decision making.* New York: Praeger.

Hamilton, D. L., Ed. (1981). *Cognitive processes in stereotyping and intergroup behavior.* Hillsdale, N.J.: Erlbaum.

Harré, R. (1977). The ethogenic approach: theory and practice. In L. Berkowitz (Ed.), *Advances in experimental social psychology.* Vol. 10. New York: Academic Press. Pp. 283–314.

Harré, R., and P. F. Secord (1972). *The explanation of social behavior.* Oxford: Blackwell.

Hartley, E. L. (1946). *Problems in prejudice.* New York: King's Crown Press.

Harvey, J. H., W. J. Ickes, and R. F. Kidd (1976). *New directions in attribution research.* Vol. 1. Hillsdale, N.J.: Erlbaum. Vol. 2 (1978); Vol. 3 (1981).

Harvey, J. H., and W. P. Smith (1977). *Social psychology: an attributional approach.* St. Louis: Mosby.

Heider, F. (1944). Social perception and phenomenal causality. *Psychol. Rev., 51,* 358–374.

———— (1946). Attitudes and cognitive organization. *J. Psychol., 21,* 107–112.

———— (1958). *The psychology of interpersonal relations.* New York: Wiley.

Helson, R. and V. Mitchell (1978). Personality. *Ann. Rev. Psychol., 29,* 555–586.

Hogan, R., C. B. DeSoto, and C. Solans (1977). Traits, tests, and personality research. *Amer. Psychologist, 32,* 255–264.

Homans, G. C. (1950). *The human group.* New York: Harcourt, Brace.

———— (1961, 1974, Rev.). *Social behavior: its elementary forms.* New York: Harcourt Brace Jovanovich.

———— (1967). *The nature of social science.* New York: Harcourt, Brace and World.

Horney, K. (1939). *New ways in psychoanalysis.* New York: Norton.

House, J. (1977). The three faces of social psychology. *Sociometry, 40,* 161–177.

Hovland, C. I., Ed. (1957). *The order of presentation in persuasion.* New Haven: Yale Univ. Press.

———— (1959). Reconciling results derived from experimental and survey studies of attitude change. *Amer. Psychologist, 14,* 8–17.

Hovland, C. I., and I. L. Janis (1959). *Personality and persuasibility.* New Haven: Yale Univ. Press.

Hovland, C. I., I. L. Janis, and H. H. Kelley (1953). *Communication and persuasion.* New Haven: Yale Univ. Press.

Hovland, C. I., A. A. Lumsdaine, and F. D. Sheffield (1949). *Experiments on mass communications.* Princeton: Princeton Univ. Press.

James, W. (1890). *The principles of psychology.* New York: Henry Holt.

Janis, I. L., and J. Gilmore (1965). The influence of incentive conditions on the success of role playing in modifying attitudes. *J. Pers. soc. Psychol., 1,* 17–27.

Jones, E. E., and K. E. Davis (1965). From acts to dispositions: the attribution process in person perception. In L. Berkowitz (Ed.), *Advances in experimental social psychology.* Vol. II. New York: Academic Press. Pp. 219–266.

Jones, E. E., and R. deCharms (1957). Changes in social perception as a function of the personal relevance of behavior. *Sociometry, 20,* 75–85.

Jones, E. E., and H. B. Gerard (1967). *Foundations of social psychology.* New York: Wiley.

Jones, E. E., D. Kanouse, H. H. Kelley, R. Nisbett, S. Valins, and D. Weiner (1971, 1972). *Attribution: perceiving the causes of behavior.* Morristown, N.J.: General Learning Press.

Jones, E. E., and R. E. Nisbet (1971–1972). The actor and the observer: divergent perceptions of the cause of behavior. In E. E. Jones, D. Kanouse, H. H. Kelley, R. E. Nisbett, S. Valins, B. Weiner. *Attribution: perceiving the causes of behavior.* Morristown, N.J.: General Learning Press.

Jones, E. E., and T. S. Pittman (1982). Toward a general theory of strategic self presentation. In J. Suls (Ed.), *Psychological perspectives on the self.* Vol. I. Hillsdale, N.J: Erlbaum. Pp. 231–262.

Jones, R. A., D. E. Linder, C. A. Kiesler, M. P. Zanna, and J. W. Brehm (1968). Internal states or external stimuli: observers' attitude judgments and the dissonance theory—self-persuasion controversy. *J. exp. soc. Psychol., 4,* 247–269.

Jordan, N. (1953). Behavioral forces that are a function of attitudes and of cognitive organization. *Hum. Relat., 6,* 273–288.

Kalven, H., and H. Zeisel (1961). Science and humanism. In J. Huxley (Ed.), *The humanist frame.* New York: Harper.

Kaplan, A. (1964). *The conduct of inquiry: methodology for behavioral science.* San Francisco: Chandler.

Katz, D., and K. W. Braly (1933). Racial stereotypes of 100 college students. *J. abnorm. soc. Psychol., 28,* 280–290.

Katz, I. (1981). *Stigma: a social psychological analysis.* Hillsdale, N.J.: Erlbaum.

Kelley, H. H. (1965). Experimental studies of threats in interpersonal negotiations. *J. Conflict Resolution, 9,* 79–105.

———— (1967). Attribution theory in social psychology. In D. Levine (Ed.), *Nebraska symposium on motivation.* Lincoln: Univ. of Nebraska Press, 192–241.

———— (1971, 1972). Causal schemata and the attribution process. In E. E. Jones, D. Kanouse, H. H. Kelley, R. E. Nisbett, S. Valins, B. Weiner. *Attribution: perceiving the causes of behavior.* Morristown, N.J.: General Learning. Pp. 151–174.

Kelley, H. H., G. H. Shure, M. Deutsch, C. Faucheux, J. T. Lanzetta, S. Moscovici, J. M. Nutting Jr., J. M. Rabbie, and J. W. Thibaut (1970). A comparative experimental study of negotiation behavior. *J. Pers. soc. Psychol., 16,* 411–438.

Kelley, H. H., and J. W. Thibaut (1954). Experimental studies of group problem solving and process. In G. Lindzey (Ed.), *Handbook of social psychology.* Vol. 2. Cambridge, Mass.: Addison-Wesley. Pp. 735–785.

Kelley, H. H., and J. W. Thibaut (1978). *Interpersonal relations: a theory of interdependence.* New York: Wiley.

Kelley, H. H., J. W. Thibaut, R. Radloff, and D. Mundy (1962). The development of cooperation in the "minimal social situation." *Psychol. Monogr., 76,* No. 19 (Whole No. 538).

Kelman, H. C. (1967). Human use of human subjects: the problem of deception in social psychological experiments. *Psychol. Bull., 67,* 1–11.

_____ (1968). *A time to speak.* San Francisco: Jossey-Bass.

Kerckhoff, A. C., and K. W. Back (1968). *The junebug.* New York: Appleton-Century-Crofts.

Kimble, G. A. (1953). Psychology as a science. *Scientific Monthly.* New York, *77,* 156–160.

Klineberg, O. (1940). *Social Psychology.* New York: Henry Holt.

Krech, D., and R. S. Crutchfield (1948). *Theory and problems of social psychology.* New York: McGraw-Hill.

Kogan, N., and N. W. Wallach (1964). *Risk taking: a study in cognition and personality.* New York: Holt, Rinehart, Winston.

Kuhn, T. S. (1962). *The structure of scientific revolutions.* Chicago: Univ. of Chicago Press.

LaPiere, R. T. (1934). Attitudes versus actions. *Social Forces, 13,* 230–237.

Latané, B., and J. M. Darley (1970). *The unresponsive bystander: why doesn't he help?* New York: Appleton-Century-Crofts.

Lawrence, D. H., and L. Festinger (1962). *Deterrents and reinforcement: the psychology of insufficient reward.* Stanford: Stanford Univ. Press.

Lecky, P. (1945). *Self-consistency: a theory of personality.* New York: Island Press.

Lepper, M. R., D. Greene, and R. E. Nisbett (1973). Undermining children's intrinsic interests with extrinsic reward: a test of the overjustification hypothesis. *J. Pers. soc. Psychol., 28,* 129–137.

Leventhal, H. (1980). Toward a comprehensive theory of emotion. In L. Berkowitz (Ed.), *Advances in experimental social psychology.* Vol. 13. New York: Academic Press.

Lewin, K. (1936). *Principles of topological psychology.* New York: McGraw-Hill.

_____ (1947). Group decision and social change. In T. M. Newcomb and E. L. Hartley (Eds.), *Readings in social psychology.* New York: Henry Holt.

_____ (1951a). *Field theory in social science* (D. Cartwright, Ed.). New York: Harper & Bros.

_____ (1951b). Comments concerning psychological forces and energies, and the structure of the psyche. In D. Rapaport (Ed.), *Organization and pathology of thought.* New York: Columbia Univ. Press. Pp. 76–94 (Orig. Publ. 1926).

Lewin, K., T. Dembo, L. Festinger, and P. Sears (1944). Level of aspiration. In J. McV Hunt (Ed.), *Personality and the behavior disorders.* New York: Ronald Press. Pp. 333–378.

Lewin, K., R. Lippitt, and R. K. White (1939). Patterns of aggressive behavior in experimentally created "social climates." *J. soc. Psychol., 10,* 271–299.

Likert, R. (1932). A technique for the measurement of attitudes. *Archives of Psychol.,* No. 140.

Linder, D. E., J. Cooper, and E. E. Jones (1967). Decision-freedom as a determinant of the role of incentive magnitude in attitude change. *J. Pers. soc. Psychol., 6,* 245–254.

Luce, R. D., and H. Raiffa (1957). *Games and decisions.* New York: Wiley.

Macauley, J., and L. Berkowitz (1970). *Altruism and helping behavior.* New York: Academic Press.

McClelland, D. C. (1951). *Personality.* New York: William Sloane.

Macleod, R. B. (1947). The phenomenological approach to social psychology. *Psychol. Rev., 54,* 193–210.

McDougall, W. (1908). *An introduction to social psychology.* London: Methuen.

_____ (1920). *The group mind.* New York: Putnam's.

McGuire, W. J. (1969). The nature of attitudes and attitude change. In G. Lindzey and E. Aronson (Eds.), *Handbook of social psychology.* Vol. 3. (2nd ed.) Reading, Mass.: Addison-Wesley. Pp. 136–314.

Manis, J. G., and B. N. Meltzer, Eds. (1962, Rev. 1972). *Symbolic interaction.* Boston: Allyn and Bacon.

Marlowe, D., and K. J. Gergen (1969). Personality and social interaction. In G. Lindzey and E. Aronson (Eds.), *Handbook of social psychology.* Vol. 3. (2nd ed.). Reading, Mass.: Addison-Wesley. Pp. 590–665.

Mead, G. H. (1934). *Mind, self and society.* Chicago: Univ. of Chicago Press.

Mead, M. (1928). *Coming of age in Samoa: a psychological study in primitive youth for western civilization.* New York: Morrow.

_____ (1930). *Growing up in New Guinea: a comparative education.* New York: Morrow.

Milgram, S. (1963). Behavioral study of obedience. *J. abnorm. soc. Psychol., 67,* 371–378.

_____ (1974). *Obedience to authority.* New York: Harper & Row.

Miller, G. A., E. Galanter, and K. H. Pribram (1960). *Plans and the structure of behavior.* New York: Holt, Rinehart, and Winston.

Miller, N. E. (1941). Frustration-aggression hypothesis. *Psychol. Rev., 48,* 337–342.

_____ (1944). Experimental studies in conflict. In J. McV Hunt (Ed.), *Personality and the behavior disorder.* New York: Ronald Press. Pp. 431–465.

_____ (1948). Theory and experiment relating psychoanalytic displacement to stimulus-response generalization. *J. abnorm. soc. Psychol., 43,* 155–178.

Miller, N. E., and J. Dollard (1941). *Social learning and imitation.* New Haven: Yale Univ. Press.

Mischel, W. (1968). *Personality and assessment.* New York: Wiley.

_____ (1973). Toward a cognitive social learning reconceptualization of personality. *Psychol. Rev., 80,* 252–283.

_____ (1977). The interaction of person and situation. In D. Magnusson and N. S. Endler (Eds.), *Personality at the* crossroads: current issues in interactional psychology. Hillsdale, N.J.: Erlbaum.

Mischel, W., and P. K. Peake (1982). Beyond déjà vu in the search for cross-situational consistency. *Psychol. Rev., 89,* 730–755.

Moore, H. T. (1921). The comparative influence of majority and expert opinion. *J. Psychol., 32,* 16–20.

Morrisette, J. O. (1958). An experimental study of the theory of structural balance. *Hum. Relat., 11,* 239–254.

Moreno, J. L. (1934). *Who shall survive?* Washington, D.C.: *Nervous and mental disease monograph,* No. 58.

Moscovici, S., and M. Zavalloni (1969). The group as a polarizer of attitudes. *J. Pers. soc. Psychol., 12,* 125–135.

Murchison, C., Ed. (1935). *Handbook of social psychology.* Worcester, Mass.: Clark Univ. Press.

Murphy, G., and L. B. Murphy (1931). *Experimental social psychology.* New York: Harper.

Murphy, G., L. B. Murphy, and T. M. Newcomb (1937). *Experimental social psychology* (rev. ed.). New York: Harper.

Murray, H. A. (1938). *Explorations in personality.* New York: Oxford Univ. Press.

Neisser, U. (1967). *Cognitive Psychology.* New York: Appleton-Century-Crofts.

Nelson, C. A., and C. Hendrick (1974). Bibliography of journal articles in social psychology. Mimeo. Kent State Univ.

Newcomb, T. M. (1951). Social psychological theory: integrating individual and social approaches. In Rohrer, J. H. and M. Sherif (Eds.), *Social psychology at the crossroads.* New York: Harper. Pp. 31–49.

_____ (1953). An approach to the study of communicative acts. *Psychol. Rev., 60,* 393–404.

_____ (1954). Sociology and psychology. In J. Gillin (Ed.), *For a science of social man: convergences in anthropology.* New York: Macmillan.

_____ (1973). In G. Lindzey (Ed.), *A history of psychology in autobiography.* Vol. 6. New York: Prentice-Hall.

Newtson, D. (1973). Attribution and the unit of perception of ongoing behavior. *J. Pers. soc. Psychol., 28,* 28–38.

_____ (1976). Foundations of attribution: the perception of ongoing behavior. In J. H. Harvey, W. J. Ickes, and R. F. Kidd, (Eds.), *New directions in attribution research.* Vol. 1. Hillsdale, N.J.: Erlbaum.

Nisbett, R. E., and L. Ross (1980). *Human inference: strategies and shortcomings of social judgment.* Englewood Cliffs, N.J.: Prentice-Hall.

Nisbett, R. E., and T. D. Wilson (1977). Telling more than we can know: verbal reports on mental processes. *Psychol. Rev., 84,* 231–259.

Orne, M. T. (1962). On the social psychology of the psychological experiment: with particular reference to demand characteristics and their implications. *Amer. Psychologist, 17,* 776–783.

Osgood, C. E., and P. H. Tannenbaum (1955). The principle of congruity in the prediction of attitude change. *Psychol. Rev., 62,* 42–55.

Ossorio, P. (1981). Foundations of descriptive psychology. In K. Davis (Ed.), *Advances in descriptive psychology.* Vol. 1. Greenwich, Conn.: JAI Press. Pp. 13–135.

Postman, L., J. S. Bruner, and E. McGinnies (1948). Personal values as selective factors in perception. *J. abnorm. soc. Psychol., 43,* 142–154.

Prasad, J. A. (1950). A comparative study of rumors and reports and earthquakes. *Brit. J. Psychol., 41,* 129–144.

Proshansky, H. M. (1976). Environmental psychology and the real world. *Amer. Psychologist, 31,* 303–310.

Proshansky H. M., and G. Murphy (1942). The effects of reward and punishment on perception. *J. Psychol., 13,* 295–305.

Pruitt, D. G., and M. J. Kimmel (1977). Twenty years of experimental gaming: critique, synthesis, and suggestions for the future. *Ann. Rev. Psychol., 28,* 363–392.

Radloff, R., and L. Bard (1966). A social comparison bibliography. *J. exp. soc. Psychol.,* Supplement *1,* 111–115.

Rapoport, A. (1970). Conflict resolution in the light of game theory and beyond. In P. Swingle (Ed.), *The structure of conflict.* New York: Academic Press. Pp. 1–42.

Reisman, D. (1950). *The lonely crowd: a study of the changing American character.* New Haven: Yale Univ. Press.

Rodin, J. (1976). Menstruation, reattribution and competence. *J. Pers. soc. Psychol., 33,* 345–353.

Rosenberg, M. J. (1965). When dissonance fails: on eliminating evaluation apprehension from attitude measurement. *J. Pers. soc. Psychol., 1,* 28–43.

Rosenberg, M. J., C. I. Hovland, W. J. McGuire, R. T. Abelson, and J. W. Brehm (1960). *Attitude organization and change.* New Haven: Yale Univ. Press.

Rosenthal, R. (1956). An attempt at the experimental induction of the defense mechanism of projection. Unpublished doctoral dissertation. University of California, Los Angeles.

Rosenzweig, S. (1933). The experimental situation as a psychological problem. *Psychol. Rev., 40,* 337–354.

Rosnow, R. L. (1981). *Paradigms in transition.* New York: Oxford Univ. Press.

Ross, E. A. (1908). *Social psychology: an outline and a source book.* New York: Macmillan.

Ross, L. (1977). The intuitive psychologist and his shortcomings: distortions in the attribution process. In L. Berkowitz (Ed.), *Advances in experimental social psychology.* Vol. 10. New York: Academic Press.

Ross, L., J. Rodin, and P. Zimbardo (1969). Toward an attribution therapy: the reduction of fear through induced cognitive-emotional misattribution. *J. Pers. soc. Psychol., 12,* 279–288.

Rotter, J. B. (1954). *Social learning and clinical psychology.* Englewood Cliffs, N.J.: Prentice-Hall.

Schachter, S. (1951). Deviation, rejection, and communication. *J. abnorm. soc. Psychol., 46,* 190–207.

_____ (1959). *The psychology of affiliation.* Stanford: Stanford Univ. Press.

_____ (1964). The interaction of cognitive and physiological determinants of emotional state. In L. Berkowitz (Ed.), *Advances in experimental social psychology.* New York: Academic Press. Pp. 49–80.

_____ (1980). Non-psychological explanations of behavior. In L. Festinger (Ed.), *Retrospections on social psychology.* New York: Oxford Univ. Press. Pp. 131–157.

Schachter, S., and J. E. Singer (1962). Cognitive, social, and physiological determinants of emotional state. *Psychol. Rev., 69,* 379–399.

Schafer, E., and G. Murphy (1943). The role of autism in a visual figureground relationship. *J. exp. Psychol., 32,* 335–343.

Schelling, T. C. (1960). *The strategy of conflict.* Cambridge, Mass.: Harvard Univ. Press.

Schlenker, B. R. (1974). Social psychology and science. *J. Pers. soc. Psychol., 29,* 1–15.

―――― (1977). On the ethogenic approach: etiquette and revolution. In L. Berkowitz (Ed.), *Advances in experimental social psychology.* Vol. 10. New York: Academic Press. Pp. 315–330.

―――― (1980). *Impression management.* Monterey, Calif.: Brooks/Cole.

Sechrest, L. (1976). Personality. *Ann. Rev. Psychol., 27,* 1–28.

Seligman, M. E. P. (1975). *Helplessness.* San Francisco: Freeman.

Sherif, M. (1936). *The psychology of social norms.* New York: Harper Bros.

―――― (1947). Group influences upon the formation of norms and attitudes. In T. M. Newcomb and E. L. Hartley (Eds.), *Readings in social psychology.* New York: Henry Holt. Pp. 77–90.

Sherif, M., O. J. Harvey, B. White, W. Hood, and C. Sherif (1961). *Intergroup conflict and cooperation: the robbers' cave experiment.* Norman: Institute of Group Relations, Univ. of Oklahoma.

Sherif, M., and C. I. Hovland (1961). *Social judgment.* New Haven: Yale Univ. Press.

Sidowski, J. B. (1957). Reward and punishment in a minimal social situation. *J. Exp. Psychol., 54,* 318–326.

Sidowski, J. B., L. B. Wykoff, and L. Tabori (1956). The influence of reinforcement and punishment in a minimal social situation. *J. abnorm. soc. Psychol., 52,* 115–119.

Sinha, D. (1952). Behavior in a catastrophic situation: a psychological study of reports and rumors. *Brit. J. Psychol., 43,* 200–209.

Skinner, B. F. (1953). *Science and human behavior.* New York: Macmillan.

Smith, M. B. (1950). The phenomenological approach in personality theory: some critical remarks. *J. abnorm. soc. Psychol., 45,* 516–522.

―――― (1979). Attitudes, values, and selfhood. In H. E. Howe, Jr. and M. M. Page (Eds.), *Nebraska Symposium on Motivation.* Lincoln: Univ. of Nebraska Press. Pp. 305–350.

Snyder, M. (1974). Self-monitoring of expressive behavior. *J. Pers. soc. Psychol., 30,* 526–537.

―――― (1979). Self-monitoring processes. In L. Berkowitz (Ed.), *Advances in experimental social psychology.* Vol. 12. New York: Academic Press. Pp. 86–128.

Solomon, L. (1960). The influences of some types of power relationships and game strategies upon the development of interpersonal trust. *J. abnorm. soc. Psychol., 61,* 223–230.

Spence, K. W. (1944). The nature of theory construction in contemporary psychology. *Psychol. Rev., 51,* 47–68.

―――― (1956). *Behavior theory and conditioning.* New Haven: Yale Univ. Press.

Steiner, I. D. (1974). Whatever happened to the group in social psychology? *J. exp. soc. Psychol., 10,* 94–108.

Steinzor, B. (1949). The development and evaluation of a measure of social interaction. *Hum. Relat., 2,* 103–122.

Stoner, J. A. F. (1961). A comparison of individual and group decisions involving risk. Unpublished M.A. thesis, M.I.T.

Strodtbeck, F. L., R. M. James, and C. Hawkins (1958). Social status in jury deliberations. In E. Maccoby, T. M. Newcomb, and E. L. Hartley (Eds.), *Readings in social psychology* (3rd Edition). New York: Henery Holt. Pp. 379–388.

Stryker, S. (1977). Development in "two social psychologies": toward an appreciation of mutual relevance. *Sociometry, 40,* 145–160.

Sullivan, H. S. (1947). *Conceptions of modern psychiatry.* Washington, D.C.: W. A. White Foundation.

Suls, J. M., and R. L. Miller, Eds. (1977). *Social comparison processes: theoretical and empirical perspectives.* New York: Washington Hemisphere Pub. Corp.

Tanke, E. D., and T. J. Tanke (1979). Getting off the slippery slope: social science in the judicial process. *Amer. Psychologist, 34,* 1130–1138.

Taylor, S. E. (1978). A developing role for social psychology in medicine and medical practice. *Pers. and soc. Psychol. Bull., 4,* 515–523.

Teger, A. I., and D. G. Pruitt (1967). Components of group risk taking. *J. exp. soc. Psychol., 3,* 189–205.

Thibaut, J. W., and H. H. Kelley (1959). *The social psychology of groups.* New York: Wiley.

Thibaut, J. W., and H. W. Riecken (1955). Some determinants and consequences of the perception of social causality. *J. Pers., 24,* 113–133.

Thibaut, J. W., and L. Walker (1975). *Procedural justice: a psychological analysis.* Hillside, N.J.: Erlbaum.

Thomas, D. (1933). An attempt to develop precise measurement in the social behavior field. *Sociologus, 9,* 1–21.

Thomson, R. (1968). *The Pelican history of psychology.* Baltimore: Penguin.

Thomas, W. I., and D. S. Thomas (1928). *The child in America: behavior problems and programs.* New York: Knopf.

Thomas, W. I., and F. Znaniecki (1918–1920). *The Polish peasant in Europe and America,* (5 vols.). Boston: Badger.

Thurstone, L. L., and E. J. Chave (1929). *The measurement of attitude.* Chicago: Univ. of Chicago Press.

Tomkins, S. S. (1981). The quest for primary motives: biography and autobiography of an idea. *J. Pers. soc. Psychol., 41,* 306–329.

Triplett, N. (1898). The dynamogenic factors in pacemaking and competition. *Amer. J. Psychol., 9,* 507–533.

Tversky, A., and D. Kahneman (1974). Judgment under uncertainty: heuristics and biases. *Science, 185,* 1124–1131.

Von Neumann, J., and O. Morgenstern (1944). *The theory of games and economic behavior.* Princeton: Princeton Univ. Press.

Walster, E. (1965). The effect of self-esteem on romantic liking. *J. exp. soc. Psychol., 1,* 184–198.

Watson, J. B. (1925). *Behaviorism.* New York: Norton.

Weick, K. E. (1968). Systematic observational methods. In G. Lindzey and E. Aronson (Eds.), *Handbook of social psy-*

chology Vol. 2. (2nd ed.). Reading, Mass.: Addison-Wesley. Pp. 357–451.

Weiner, B. (1974). *Achievement motivation and attribution theory*. Morristown, N.J.: General Learning.

West, S. G., and R. A. Wicklund (1980). *A primer of social psychological theories*. Monterey, Calif.: Brooks/Cole.

Wicklund, R. A., and J. W. Brehm (1976). *Perspectives on cognitive dissonance*. Hillsdale, N.J.: Erlbaum.

Wishner, J. (1960). Reanalysis of "impressions of personality." *Psychol. Rev., 67,* 96–112.

Worchel, S. and J. Cooper (1979). *Understanding social psychology*. Homewood, Ill.: Dorsey Press.

Wortman, C. B., and L. Dintzer (1978). Is an attributional analysis of the learned helplessness phenomenon viable?: a critique of the Abramson-Seligman-Teasdale reformulation. *J. abnorm. Psychol., 87,* 75–90.

Zajonc, R. B. (1965). Social Facilitation. *Science, 149,* 269–274.

Zajonc, R. B. (1980). Feeling and thinking: preferences need no inferences. *Amer. Psychologist, 35,* 151–175.

Zajonc, R. B. (1980). Cognition and social cognition: a historical perspective. In L. Festinger (Ed.), *Retrospections on social psychology*. New York: Oxford Univ. Press. Pp. 180–204.

Zanna, M. P., and J. Cooper (1974). Dissonance and the pill: an attribution approach to studying the arousal properties of dissonance. *J. Pers. soc. Psychol., 29,* 703–709.

Zeigarnik, B. (1927). Uber das leehalten von Erledigten und unerleighten Handbegen. *Psycholische Forschung, 9,* 1–85.

CHAPTER 3

Learning Theory in Contemporary Social Psychology

Bernice Lott
Albert J. Lott
University of Rhode Island

INTRODUCTION

In previous editions of this handbook Lambert (1954) and then Berger and Lambert (1968) carefully described and detailed the essential elements of what has come to be known as S–R theory and identified the contributions that this perspective has made to empirical and analytical development in social psychology. We interpret our task for this third edition as one of beginning where the discussion ended in the mid sixties, that is, re-identifying the significant strands of S–R thinking that continue to vitalize our research and that find their way into our primary journals, monographs, and textbooks. In preparing this chapter, we have focused on work published between 1965 and 1980 in which *social behavior is treated primarily as particular or general responses acquired through classical or instrumental conditioning.* Although such interpretations may be widespread on the level of covert assumption, we have directed our attention, for the most part, to explicit explanations of social behaviors that articulate their learned response nature with minimal ambiguity and that relate social acts to broader categories of human behavior and to general principles

of learning. In such analyses of social behavior the concepts of discriminable environmental stimuli (situational cues), drive (as a general arousal state), and reinforcement (primarily as drive reduction) typically play central roles in accounting for acquisition and maintenance of observable responses. The language used in describing independent and dependent variables and in interpreting their relationships is that of learning theory, and the hypotheses tested are either derived directly from general learning principles or findings are explained in terms of these principles.

The fundamental objectives of the learning-oriented social psychologist are to predict a person's social behavior from knowledge of situational events and from the individual's previous experiences with these (or similar) events and to relate S and R variables in a reliable and lawful manner, that is, to investigate, as Skinner (1975) has put it, the relation between behavior and the environment without being "diverted from, and blocked in our inquiries...by an absorbing interest in the organism itself," a temptation to which cognitive social psychologists have succumbed. Skinnerian and Hull-Spencian descriptions of such S–R relations differ primarily in the exclusion by the former and inclusion by the latter of drive as a significant internal response that mediates overt behavior.

We wish to thank Seymour Berger, Leonard Berkowitz, and Jerry Cohen for their constructive criticism of a preliminary draft of this chapter.

Although descriptive concepts having cognitive or phenomenological significance may sometimes appear in the theoretical formulations of learning-oriented social psychologists, it is the language of observables that is preferred. Cognitive variables play a minimal role in the vocabulary utilized to describe and explain the behavior under study. Where concepts are used that do not denote immediately observable events, such concepts are defined as mediating conditions (also stimulus and response in nature, but covert), intervening between, and having predictable relationships with, firmly anchored antecedents and consequents.

All human behavior, according to the S–R view, can ultimately be explained by means of one set of general and interrelated principles. Although the content of what is learned in diverse situations may be almost infinite in its variety, the process is always the same. Thus, the behavior of a legislator who votes against the Equal Rights Amendment is explained by utilizing and adapting the same general principles that are relevant to the maintenance of any response instrumental in avoiding an aversive stimulus and in increasing the probability of positive reinforcement. Miller (1959) has called such use of general learning principles in the interpretation of complex human behavior, the "extension of liberalized S–R theory."

In social psychology, learning theorists use the individual, and not the group, as the major unit of analysis even when group variables like cohesiveness are explained in learning theory terms (e.g., B. Lott, 1961). The emphasis is on understanding the conditions preceding the acquisition of a particular behavior, and those which are necessary to maintain it, rather than on fully describing the on-going behavior in process. The learning approach is historical and deterministic, and the reinforcement consequences of behavior play, by far, the major explanatory role.

Despite criticism from other theoretical positions that learning-oriented social psychology is too narrow and omits consideration of meaningful and necessary information, few behaviors have been considered too complex for analysis within an S–R framework by learning-oriented psychologists themselves. Over fifty years ago, for example, Hull (1930) recognized the difficulty that scientists have in maintaining "a thoroughly naturalistic attitude toward the complex forms of human behavior" and proposed an objective interpretation of "knowledge" and "purpose," identifying them as "pure stimulus acts" that are implicit responses or "acts whose sole function is to serve as stimuli for other acts." Later, Hull (1943) envisaged a hierarchy of principles that would "parallel all of the objectively observable phenomena of the behavior of higher organisms," and that would deal with human skills, language, problem solving, economic and moral values, intelligence, education, psychogenic disorders, delinquency, personality, acculturation, religion, custom, politics, and government. This endeavor he called the "great task," the replacing of "anthropomorphic intuition" with meticulous experiments and imaginative field studies. The historical record, contained in the first two editions of this handbook, attests to the fact that Hull's challenge was quickly accepted, with learning theorists finding no realm of human behavior too formidable for their analysis.

Our look at the contemporary literature reveals that objective stimulus-response learning formulations continue to be applied for all the behaviors that represent the central core of concern in our field. These are the behaviors that all social psychologists attempt to explain, the sine qua non of our inquiries, the heart of historical and current questions about social relationships and social life. They include both ends of the social relationship dimension, that is, aggression (destructive antisocial acts) and altruism (prosocial helping) as well as competition, dependency, communication, and other behaviors interpreted as instrumental acts acquired and maintained in accordance with the principles of learning. Of central concern, as well, are the general phenomena relevant to wide areas of social interaction, such as imitation of models and attitudes toward persons and socially significant objects and events. In addition, attention has also been directed to the role of particular arousal factors, most notably the presence of persons as drive activators, and the consequences of fear.

The following discussion is in no way intended to be a thorough review of all relevant contemporary literature. Our objective instead is to highlight, through use of selected illustrative work, examples of the theoretical and empirical contributions that a general learning theory perspective (primarily within the Hull-Spence tradition) is currently making to the understanding of complex social behavior.

SOCIAL BEHAVIOR AS A LEARNED RESPONSE

AGGRESSION

Albert Bandura (1973) and Leonard Berkowitz (1962, 1965, 1974) can be credited with advancing the position that treats aggression, like other responses, as an explicit consequence of motivational, stimulus, and reinforcement conditions. Their work, along with that of their colleagues and others, shifted the focus in aggression research from a study of individual differences in the tendency to hurt others (assumed to be a relatively stable disposition) and from explorations of frustrations as the major determinant to a concern with specifying the various situational conditions that increase the probability or the strength of aggressive behavior.

Bandura (1973) proposed that knowledge of the social contexts and cues that specify actual or potential consequences of aggressive acts provides a better assessment of when persons will or will not behave aggressively than an analysis of the personal motive of the actor. Furthermore, he stated that there is a continuous interaction between social setting and person that determines and controls all behavior, including aggression. This approach suggests that aversive treatment leads to a general state of arousal that can facilitate a variety of responses depending upon the person's learning history, the particular cues in the current setting, and the general incentive value of aggression (the benefits it has mediated in the past). Once an aggressive response has been performed, feedback from its consequences will form the basis of reinforcement control in the form of direct, vicarious, or self-administered reward. Self-monitoring and self-evaluation are added to the external outcomes that influence later behavior through the anticipation of consequences.

Berkowitz has made less use of cognitive mediators in explaining aggressive behavior in particular settings. In his early view (1965), anger evoked by frustration was said to generate "only a *readiness* for aggressive acts," something that can also be created by previously acquired "aggressive habits," established by a history of positive reinforcement for aggression. Such reinforcements may have included "tangible benefits such as social approval," the avoidance or prevention of mistreatment from others, and success in inflicting hurt or damage or in attaining some other goal (Berkowitz, 1974). The probability that an aggressive response will occur in a particular situation will be low "even given this readiness, unless there are suitable cues, stimuli associated with the present or previous anger instigators [or] having some connection with aggression" (Berkowitz, 1965).

Berkowitz (1974) elaborated further on the nature of these stimuli and suggested that because of their association with the positive reinforcement of aggression, they acquire "the ability to elicit components of the behavior

that had led to the reinforcement." Through association with aggression *and* its positive consequences, any cue (object, event, or person) can acquire discriminative cue properties and evoke aggressive reactions. (Berkowitz did not distinguish between the secondary reinforcing properties of these cues, which should be acquired under the conditions he outlined, and their discriminative functions.) Aggressive habits can be acquired in the absence of frustration and will be evoked in a situation, with or without frustration-induced arousal if suitable cues are present. Aggression, in other words, is "learned much as other instrumental actions are learned—because the actor has found the behavior pays off" (1978). The strength of the aggressive response will vary with the "aggressive cue value" of the stimuli (determined by the strength of prior associations) and with "the degree of aggression readiness—anger intensity or strength of the aggressiveness habits" (1965). Although internal excitation (e.g., anger) is not necessary, it serves, if present, to increase general drive and thus to " 'energize' the individual's habitual reactions to the environmental stimuli" (1974). When such internal excitation is present, however, Berkowitz (1978, 1981) now maintains that aggressive behavior is *likely* to be evoked. Aversive conditions, that is, the negative affect generated by pain, frustration, or other noxious stimuli, are said not only to increase general drive but also to produce a *specific* instigation to aggression. Without the facilitation of external cues, the instigating conditions may be too weak to lead to overt aggressive responses, but environmental stimuli "are not necessary for frustrations or other painful occurrences to lead to" what Berkowitz calls "angry" or "emotional" aggression (1978). Aggressive behavior is thus a consequence of either contemporary aversive instigating conditions and/or environmental stimuli associated with previous frustration or pain or with prior reinforcement for aggression. Overt aggression is, nevertheless, a more probable response when both sets of conditions are acting together than when either is present alone.

Berkowitz recognized that the tendency to flee or escape is also generated by aversive events and that this will compete with aggressive reactions. "Which of these instigations will dominate in overt behavior probably varies with a number of situational conditions, including . . . ability to get away from or even eliminate the noxious occurrence. This ability, in turn, can be a function of prior learning and also the availability of escape routes" (Berkowitz, 1981).

Although many of the empirical implications of this approach to aggression have been described previously (cf. Berkowitz, 1962, 1965, 1974; Berger and Lambert, 1968), their systematic exploration continues to occupy a prominent place in the literature. In this line of research, aggression is typically operationalized as behavior producing nonaccidental pain or injury to another person, and the independent variables are manipulated either to directly vary the strength of this behavior or to vary the anxiety assumed to inhibit it. The assumption that anxiety is a well-learned immediate response to aggression-evoking (or aggression-related) situations is often made, particularly when there is reason to believe that persons have previously, and relatively consistently, experienced pain or punishment in such situations as victim, observer, or negatively reinforced aggressor.

Reinforcement of Aggressive Behavior

Some studies illustrate the role of direct reinforcement in the maintenance of aggressive responses. Brown and Rogers (1965), for example, had nursery school teachers systematically ignore aggressive acts by three- and four-year-old boys, while at the same time they paid attention to acts incompatible with aggression. Two independent raters observed significant decreases in the number of physical and verbal aggressive responses following such treatment during the course of two weeks. In this study the likelihood of aggressive acts was decreased through the withholding of positive consequences. Geen and Stonner (1971) have demonstrated the other side of the phenomenon. Adult males who were verbally reinforced (with the word "fine" or "good" from the experimenter) for delivering electric shocks to another person each time that person made an "incorrect" response significantly increased the intensity of the shocks they gave over a long series in comparison with a group of nonreinforced males. The reinforced men also gave more intense shocks when aggressive words (e.g., "choke," "stab") were flashed on a screen than when neutral words appeared. The investigators suggested that the experimenter's approval seemed to weaken anxiety-related restraints against aggression as well as to contribute directly to an increase in the habit strength of such behavior. A different experimental situation investigated by Geen, Stonner, and Shope (1975) yielded results that may be interpreted in a similar way. A group of male students who had been shocked (and disagreed with) by a confederate and who were subsequently able to shock him in return gave shocks of greater intensity to that confederate later in a new situation than did comparable males who had not been given the previous opportunity to shock the confederate. In this study, as in the earlier one, the previous practice of aggressive behavior accompanied by no negative consequences and most likely positive ones (since the aggression was directed against an attacker) can be said to have weakened "socialized restraints" against violence and/or to have increased the strength of previously learned behavior. The authors themselves suggest still another, more cognitive possibility, namely, "having aggressed once against the confederate [the participants may have] felt compelled to behave consistently."

Buss (1966) manipulated reinforcement for aggressive behavior in a somewhat indirect manner but with similar results. Some participants were told that their ability to help a "learner" reduce incorrect responses in a concept formation task by delivering shock feedback would be taken into account by the course instructor in determining their final grades (if they were borderline cases). These "instrumental instructions" were significantly related to the intensity of the shocks delivered, and Buss concluded that "aggression that helps the aggressor to reach his [sic] goal is significantly more intense than aggression that has no instrumental value." It is important to note that in research of this kind the targets of shock (i.e., the intended recipients of aggression) never actually receive it although participants are led to believe otherwise; yet participants themselves are sometimes mildly shocked in instigation-inducing conditions or as a means of enhancing the situation's credibility. The aggressive response monitored in such research, by a frequency or intensity measure, is typically shock delivery inferred from the pressing of a button or the pulling of a lever.

Other studies have manipulated the consequences of aggressive behavior by having it occur in situations in which it could be observed by others who might be expected to react in predictable ways or who react in a prearranged manner. For example, Richardson, Bernstein and Taylor (1979) had women compete against an unseen male opponent in a reaction time task under conditions in which they were alone (private) or in the presence of a silent female observer (public), or with a woman who verbally supported the retaliative acts of shocking the opponent. Shock was deliverable at any of five different intensities in response to provocations (shocks) by the male opponent. The investigators report that "as the trials progressed, women in the private and supportive other conditions responded in an increasingly more aggressive manner than did the women in the public condition.'' It is assumed that the latter probably anticipated, in the absence of contrary indications, that aggressive behavior on their part would be disapproved. In two other investigations concerned with the same general variable, Borden (1975) found that one group of male college students gave more intense shocks to an opponent in a reaction time situation when they were observed by a man than by a woman and another group of males aggressed with greater intensity when observed by a brown belt Karate club member (either male or female) than by a member of a pacifist, antinuclear organization who was wearing a peace symbol. In neither of these studies did the participants receive "overt indications of approval or disapproval from the observer.'' Their behavior was modified, according to the investigator, "merely by the anticipation of approval.'' Rogers (1980) has reported complementary findings from a study in which some participants in a shock-delivery situation were observed by the investigator and others were not observed. Participants were free to choose among seven different shock intensities to be administered to a confederate. Under the condition in which male and female participants were led to believe that the confederate would not have an opportunity to retaliate, those who were anonymous (not observed) delivered shocks of stronger intensity than those who were not anonymous (were observed).

Aggression-evoking Stimuli

Aggression learned as a response to a specific situation can be generalized to other situations containing similar cues. The probability that an aggressive response will be made in a new situation (assuming neutral or nonaversive consequences) should vary with the strength of the previously acquired behavior and with the nature (and number) of relevant discriminable cues, that is, whether they have been associated with positive consequences for aggression or with punishment or pain. One investigation relating to this general proposition was reported by Buss, Booker and Buss (1972). In one of five experiments exploring the relationship between the firing of weapons and consequent aggressive behavior in a shock-delivery situation, the investigators found that persons with long-time gun use experience differed from people without such experience (after both groups were given some target shooting practice with guns) in that the experienced gun users delivered shock at higher intensities initially and increased the intensity of shock more over trials than the inexperienced users. Short-run laboratory experience with guns, provided by target-shooting practice, was found not to be effective in influencing subsequent shock-delivery behavior but long-time gun use experience was. The generalization in this case was from aggressive behavior with guns to the same category of behavior with shock.

Other studies have been concerned with generalization from verbal aggression to physical aggression. Loew (1967) reported that persons trained to choose words with aggressive connotations subsequently delivered more intense shocks to another person (in a laboratory setting) than persons trained to choose words with nonaggressive connotations. Loew suggested that the shock delivery behavior was mediated by the covert response of hostility, strengthened by the previous "training of aggressive verbalizations.'' Such verbalizations are assumed to evoke a hostile attitude (a response-produced-stimulus or r–s) that serves as a cue for aggressive acts under appropriate conditions of instigation. Parke, Ewall, and Slaby (1972) repeated Loew's study and added a neutral word condition. Like Loew, they found greater subsequent aggressive behavior (shock delivery) by persons who had been previously reinforced for choosing (and speaking) aggressive words than by those reinforced for speaking either neutral or helpful words (semantically incompatible with aggression). In addition, the speaking of "helpful'' words was associated with less subsequent shock aggression than the speaking of neutral words. The authors interpreted their findings as indicating "that verbal cues can serve to inhibit as well as elicit aggressive motor behavior'' by producing, in the former case, tendencies toward helpful behavior (which is incompatible with hurting behavior) and in the latter case, tendencies to hurt; what mechanisms underlie these tendencies were not specified.

That cues, generally, are effective in evoking (or restraining) aggressive behavior as a consequence of their previous association with aggression is a proposition that Berkowitz and others have empirically validated in a variety of situations. In one study, Berkowitz and Geen (1966) gave male students an opportunity to administer shocks to a confederate who had either angered them earlier (by giving them seven shocks for "poor answers'') or not angered them (gave them only one shock). The confederate was named Kirk or Bob. More shocks were given to Kirk by those men who had been angered by him and who had also witnessed, in the interim, a seven-minute filmed prize-fight sequence in which Kirk Douglas received a beating than by men who had watched a filmed horse-racing sequence. The confederate's name mediated behavior from the unpunished film violence to the socially approved shock situation because of cue properties acquired in association with aggression. In a subsequent study Berkowitz and LePage (1967) utilized a cue (weapon) that they did not differentially associate with aggression for different participants but assumed was so associated for most persons. They found that angered men (provoked in the same manner as described in the Berkowitz and Geen study) gave a greater number of shocks to their instigator when a rifle and revolver were in full view on a table near the shock key than when the weapons were absent. This "weapons effect" has since proved to be relatively "elusive," in the words of Page and Scheidt (1971) whose investigations have failed to confirm it (except as a function of demand characteristics and participant "cooperativeness").

In response to some of the criticisms of Page and Scheidt (1971), Berkowitz (1974) has re-examined the assumptions implicit in the original weapons study. Although weapons in our culture are assuredly associated with aggression, for some persons, depending upon their previously encountered reinforcement consequences, a weapon will serve as a conditioned stimulus for aggression while for others it will serve as a conditioned stimulus for "anxiety and suffering," inhibiting aggression. The previously cited work of Buss, Booker and Buss (1972) is relevant here; firing a weapon enhanced subsequent aggression among persons with long-time gun handling experience but not among others. Turner, Simons, Berkowitz and Frodi (1977) cite a number of recent studies across a wide variety of participants, including groups in other countries, which have supported the weapons effect. They suggest that the replication failures were obtained in situations in which participants "were not naive about deception studies" or "were very apprehensive about the impression they might create if they were highly punitive to their partner." Such sophistication or apprehension would serve to inhibit aggressive responses in the presence of a weapon, as would other mediators of "aggression-related anxiety" such as fear of retaliation or previous experience as a victim.

Like weapon cues, pain cues should evoke aggression in some persons and anxiety in others. For those who have been positively rewarded for aggression (by approval, gain, etc.) the associated pain of a victim will acquire secondary rewarding properties. Such pain cues not only should subsequently serve to reinforce other behavior but also should serve an incentive function and, as proposed by Berkowitz (1974), should "evoke impulsive

aggressive responses from those who, for one reason or another, are prepared to attack someone." As a test of this general hypothesis, Swart and Berkowitz (1976) paired a white light with pain experienced by a confederate who had either provoked or not provoked participants who witnessed, but were not the cause of, the confederate's suffering. The participants were then asked to deliver shocks to a second confederate with whom they had had no prior contact; for some the shock signal was the same light previously associated with the pain of the first confederate, and for others the shock signal was a new stimulus. Among the previously angered men, more intense shocks were delivered to the new confederate by those for whom the shock signal was the same stimulus previously associated with the pain of the person who had angered them. Thus, a pain cue served to evoke and maintain aggressive behavior in a new situation on the part of the previously angered men.

For persons who have not been positively reinforced for aggression and who have been punished or rebuked as victims or aggressors, pain cues should evoke not aggressive responses but anxiety and aggression inhibition. Demonstrating the aggression-diminishing effect of pain cues has been the objective of several experiments. Buss (1966), for example, found that pain feedback (moans and groans) from a target of shock delivery significantly reduced the intensity of the shocks, and Baron (1971a), using different feedback, a "pain meter" (deflection of a needle indicating magnitude of a victim's pain), also found that persons delivered less intense shocks to a confederate as his signs of suffering increased, despite having been previously angered by him. In this study both aggressors (participants) and victim (confederate) were college students similar in such respects as age, dress, and sex. Baron suggested that this similarity "may have facilitated the occurrence of empathic arousal among aggressors in response to the victim's apparent pain, and so tended to inhibit further attacks against this individual." In a subsequent study, Baron (1971b) varied the similarity between aggressor and victim and found that this variable had no effect. Signs of high pain on the victim's part were related to significantly less intense shock given by male participants than were signs of low pain.

Imitation of Aggression

Aggressive behavior has been shown to vary with reinforcement, with anticipated consequences, and with stimulus conditions and to generalize across situations. In addition, it has been found that observers after viewing models engaged in aggressive behavior tend to imitate that behavior. Whether viewing an unpunished aggressive model increases the probability of the observer's aggressive behavior by lowering inhibitions or by increasing the strength of particular cues to evoke aggression (or both) remains unclear. Similarly, viewing a nonaggressive model may be said to decrease the probability of aggressive responses as a result of strengthening alternative behaviors or increasing the strength of aggression inhibitors. Hanratty, O'Neal and Sulzer (1972), for example, working with first-grade children, found that among those who had been frustrated by the experimenter (but not among those who were not) there was more aggressive behavior directed toward a live "clown" by those children who had witnessed a film of a model attacking the clown than by those who had not seen the film. Similarly, Baron (1971c) demonstrated that previously angered male students delivered less severe shocks to their instigator if they had first observed both a nonaggressive model and an aggressive live model (confederate) deliver shocks than if they had observed only an aggressive one. Persons who had watched only a nonaggressive model later delivered shocks of lowest intensity and least duration. Working with students who were not instigated to aggression by anger but by instructions in an obedience situation, Powers and Geen (1972) found obedient aggression to be a more likely response by those who had first observed an obedient live model who was nervous or by those who had observed no model. Observation of a disobedient model was associated with the tendency not to deliver shocks to the victim/learner. Using a verbal measure of aggression (vile cursing) Wheeler and Smith (1967) varied the conditions under which male participants (navy men) responded to the tape-recorded opinions of a target person after first listening to the tape-recorded response of a confederate (model). Participants responded more aggressively after hearing an aggressive response by the confederate and responded least aggressively when the confederate's abusive language had been censured by the experimenter (a scientist and high-ranking naval officer).

Other investigators have varied different aspects of aggression-relevant situations observed by persons. For example, Meyer (1972) had male students, who were angered by a confederate, view film violence that was presented as either "justified" or "unjustified." When given an opportunity to shock the confederate, those who had seen the justified aggression gave significantly more shocks, and of greater intensity, than those who had viewed unjustified violence, seen a nonviolent film, or no film. Viewing a film villian who is deservedly punished serves to positively reinforce aggressive responses (a simpler explanation, according to Meyer, than suggesting that such an experience lowers inhibitions against aggression), while viewing a film in which punishment is not justifiable or deserved serves to restrain aggression, presumably because such aggression is socially disapproved and therefore is potentially punishable.

Drive Factors

Some instigation of arousal has been assumed to be a necessary, but not sufficient, condition for aggression, and numerous investigations have demonstrated that previous provocation (e.g., frustration or attack) increases the likelihood of aggressive behavior in the laboratory. In addition, stimuli previously associated with aggression may function as incentives, thereby increasing drive or arousal. Illustrative of studies that focus primarily and directly on the relationship between aggression and drive factors is one by Fitz (1976). Some participants were not angered by a confederate; others were angered; and still others were both angered and led to fear that he might later shock them. The latter participants were thus placed in an approach-avoidance conflict situation when given the opportunity to aggress (produce loud noise) against the confederate, a friend of the confederate, and someone unassociated with the confederate. As predicted from Neal Miller's conflict theory of aggression displacement, angered participants who were not also frightened produced the most intense noise for their previous annoyer and the least intense noise for the target least associated with him. Participants "who were both angered and frightened were more likely than ... [those] who were only angered to give their most intense aggression to a displaced target" (least similar to the annoyer). Rocha and Rogers (1976), working with kindergarten and first-grade children, varied drive by manipulating competition. One prize was offered to the one member of a face-to-face pair (participant and a confederate) who could build the highest tower from an abundant supply of one-hundred blocks (low competition) or from a restricted supply of thirteen blocks (high competition). Using three separate measures of aggression (physical, interference, and verbal), children in the high-competition condition were found to display a greater frequency of such behavior.

ALTRUISM

Like aggression, altruism, in the context of a learning theory approach to social behavior, is interpreted as an instrumental response that is acquired and maintained in direct relationship to the consequences it mediates. The implication here is that acts of helping others that bring no direct or obvious benefit to the helper and that may incur some costs (the standard definition of altruism) nevertheless also have positively rewarding consequences, albeit subtle or indirect. Such a position maintains that altruistic behavior is teachable and modifiable and subject to control by cue and reinforcement variables.

Reward for Altruistic Behavior

Illustrative of this approach is a study by Midlarsky and Bryan (1967) in which children were asked to donate anonymously M&M candies to needy peers. Those who had previously received explicit expressions of pleasure from an adult for giving up their candy during a training session later donated more candy than other children. In this instance the strength of an altruistic response can be said to have increased directly through previous positive reinforcement. Also working with children, Miller, Brickman and Bolen (1975) demonstrated the effectiveness of a more subtle reinforcer. Fifth graders who were told in advance that they *were* neat and tidy children responded positively to an antilitter program by more frequently depositing candy wrappers in waste baskets and picking up littered items than children who were told they *should* be neat and tidy. Altruistic responses on the part of the former, the investigators suggested, were reinforced by the match between socially desirable behavior and assumptions by adults that it would be forthcoming.

Reinforcement was manipulated somewhat differently by Darlington and Macker (1966), who provided some persons with an opportunity to relieve feelings of guilt. Participants led to believe that they had harmed another person were found to agree more often to donate blood in a subsequent situation than participants who were not led to believe that they had caused harm to another. In this case it is assumed that a helping response is accompanied by self-reinforcement and that the doers of harm are more highly motivated to seek it. The self-reinforcing consequences of helping another person may be said to derive from previous associations between altruistic acts and the receipt of praise, approval, or other positive consequences from others. As Aronfreed (1968,

1970) has suggested, cues of "relief from distress" have acquired secondary reinforcing properties from their association with the positive consequences of such relief directly experienced by a person in similar situations. Thus, an act that appears to an external observer to have no observable rewarding consequence may, in fact, be reinforcing for the actor who makes empathic or vicarious responses to social cues provided by other persons and who has learned to associate positive outcomes with helping. The actor's altruistic behavior is dependent upon the actor's empathic experience and is controlled by anticipation of the consequences of helping another individual. Rosenhan (1972) and Bandura (1977) have taken similar positions, with Bandura's emphasis more on the intervening cognitive mediators. Cues previously associated with the positive consequences of helping behavior signal its implicit representation in the potential helper.

Kanfer (1979), too, views the learning of altruism as similar to the learning of self-control. Following Skinner's proposal, as elaborated by Kanfer (1971), that self-control is evidenced by the making of a response that changes the probability that another response (reinforcement) will occur, Kanfer and Seidner (1973) note that "the execution of self-controlling behavior is...not only...a result of the person's past history and personality processes but also of particular situational variables." In the case of altruism, social approval or social recognition is posited as necessary to establish incentives for such responses. When accompanied by self-reinforcing statements, as suggested by Bandura (1977), this condition provides the mechanism for self-control, and both external and internal cues can elicit altruistic behavior that, in turn, can be reinforced by external or internal reinforcements. The most durable altruistic response, according to Kanfer, is one that has a history of both kinds of reinforcement. Self-reinforcement as well as reinforcement from an adult are variables in a study by Rosenhan and White (1967). Children who observed a model donate gift certificates to charity later made more such donations when alone, particularly if they had previously practiced making donations in the model's presence, than children who had not observed the model.

Arousal Factors

Goranson and Berkowitz (1966) have demonstrated the influence of still another related antecedent condition, the receipt of previous help from a person who later is in need of it. College women who had received voluntary assistance from a confederate later worked harder in her behalf than those who had not previously been assisted. Krebs (1975) has shown a direct relationship between empathy and helping. Persons who indicated the strongest empathic responses (as indicated by psychophysiological and verbal measures) to a similar or dissimilar confederate presumably experiencing pain and pleasure were most willing to help him at some cost to themselves. Krebs (pp. 1144–1145) suggested that

> When the pains and pleasures of others become intrinsically tied to the affective state of observers, it can be in their best interest to maximize the favorableness of the hedonic balance of others in order to maximize the favorableness of their own hedonic state.

A number of other investigators have been concerned with the effect of one's "affective state," manipulated differently, on tendencies to behave in a prosocial or altruistic manner. Under certain conditions "feeling good" and "feeling bad" have both been predicted and found to increase the probability of helping behavior, while "feeling bad" has sometimes been shown to be negatively associated with helping. The "goodness" or "badness" of participants' feelings is typically assumed to follow from particular experiences and is sometimes independently assessed by verbal report. In the language of S–R theory these are intrinsic responses having both response and stimulus properties (r–s).

Berkowitz and Connor (1966) found that previous failure on a task lessened willingness to help a dependent other, while previous success increased it, and they suggested that "the success experience had produced a glow of good will." Since success had been experienced in the presence of the experimenter and the person who subsequently required help, the increased attractiveness of these two people (as a function of success) may also have been a factor. In two studies by Isen and Levin (1972) good feelings were separated from previous association with the persons requesting or needing assistance but were again found to increase altruism. College students volunteered more as helpers (in a creativity task) and less as distractors following receipt of free and unexpected cookies, and persons were more likely to pick up papers dropped by a stranger if they had just found a dime in a coin-return slot of a public telephone. Bad feelings, or negative mood, on the other hand, have also been found to be associated with increased generosity by Kenrick, Bauman and Cialdini (1979). Primary school children asked to reminisce about a sad experience later donated more of their winnings to other children when in the presence of an adult (but not in his absence) than children who had imagined something neutral. Helping, suggested the investigators (p. 760), is a way for persons

> in a lowered mood state . . . to relieve their negative affective state. For adults, who have internalized the reward value of benevolence, the help may occur in private and still retain its self-gratifying function. For young children . . . altruism . . . will be gratifying only when it is instrumental to an extrinsic form of reward like public approval.

Thus, helping, if it is not too much effort, is a probable response when one feels bad if the particular response involved is likely to make one feel better either through self-reward or reward from other sources. Weyant (1978), for example, found that although college students in a positive-mood condition volunteered more, in general, to collect donations (for both a highly worthwhile and less worthwhile cause) than did neutral- or negative-mood participants, the latter volunteered more than neutral-mood participants when the charity was very worthwhile and when the effort involved was low. Cunningham, Steinberg and Grev (1980) have argued that positive and negative moods function differently with respect to their influence on altruistic behavior. Positive mood serves to "increase motivation to seek reward stimuli," and negative mood (e.g., failure or guilt) serves to "increase behaviors oriented toward avoiding or reducing punishment." In accord with this proposition, they found that persons in a positive mood (after finding a dime in a phone slot) made more contributions to a children's fund when the request was positive ("help keep the children smiling") than when it was negative ("you owe it to the children"). Conversely, persons in a negative mood (after being told they did not use a camera properly) made more contributions under the negative request condition.

Helping as Self-Reinforcement

The investigations cited previously varied antecedent conditions to study their effects on the frequency or strength of altruistic behavior. Implied in the explanations has been the assumption that an altruistic response, because it relieves someone's suffering or promotes someone's pleasure, is a source of reward for the person who makes it. This reinforcement property of altruism has been the focus of investigation by Weiss and his co-workers who, in a series of studies (Weiss, Buchanan, Altstatt, and Lombardo, 1971; Weiss, Boyer, Lombardo, and Stich, 1973), demonstrated that adults would learn to push one or several buttons if this response was followed by the cessation of suffering simulated by a confederate. Furthermore, the speed with which this response is made was shown to be greater under continuous rather than under partial reinforcement; when reinforcement is immediate than when it is delayed by five seconds; and under high magnitude of reinforcement (high relief from suffering) rather than under low magnitude. What Weiss and his colleagues have shown is that instrumental responses can be learned solely through the rewarding effect of altruism and that varying standard parameters of reward (e.g., partial versus continuous, delayed versus immediate, and high magnitude versus low magnitude) where the reinforcement is an altruistic outcome has the same effect on learning as varying these parameters of more conventional rewards.

That altruistic behavior has positive consequences for the responder has also been reported by Geer and Jarmecky (1973). In their study college men learned to throw a switch at the sound of a tone. Those who were told that this response would terminate a shock being delivered to another person (confederate) responded increasingly more quickly than those who were not led to believe that their behavior affected the shock received by the confederate. Neither these investigators nor Weiss and his coworkers specified the source of altruism's reinforcement properties, but the latter note the compatibility of their findings with a variety of views: that altruism is an innate human need, that it has acquired secondary reinforcing properties through association with directly experienced relief from stress or with other rewards such as approval, that it reduces guilt or the anticipation of guilt, or that it provides a means to adhere to the cultural norm of social responsibility.

IMITATION

From a learning theory perspective imitation is not simply a means by which persons acquire new behavior; that is, it is not a process (e.g., observational learning) that occupies a position equal to classical and operant conditioning but is a general response tendency that has been learned. Thus, imitation is treated as a learned habit. A clear statement of this position has been provided by Gewirtz and Stingle (1968). Their analysis begins

with the definition of copying proposed by Miller and Dollard (1941), that is, a response that has been learned as a result of the experience of reward for similarity (matching) and punishment for dissimilarity. Copying becomes a general response because anxiety will be evoked when one's behavior is different from a model's and reduced when one's behavior is the same or, following Mowrer's (1960) position, because cues associated with a model's behavior have acquired reinforcing value (through their association with reinforcement), therefore responses that produce such cues are likely to be made. Gewirtz and Stingle propose a simpler model that does not depend on the use of mediational constructs. They suggest that imitative responses are learned instrumentally, occurring in a child's experience first by chance or by direct parental assistance or training. Thus they are "strengthened and maintained by direct extrinsic reinforcement." After the establishment of several specific imitative responses, "a class of diverse but functionally equivalent behaviors is acquired and is maintained by extrinsic reinforcement on an intermittent schedule." Thus, "one must *learn* to learn" through exposure to models, and positive consequences for copying a model are likely to follow, albeit intermittently, throughout one's life and especially during childhood. Gewirtz and Stingle further propose that identification can be understood as "generalized imitation"; the behaviors subsumed by identification are then viewed not as unchangeable or necessarily long term but as "potentially subject to acquisition, discrimination, extinction, and other modifications, according to well-established laws of behavior."

Bandura (1969), too, has suggested that imitation and identification (as well as observational learning) are equivalent concepts, each referring to "behavioral modifications resulting from exposure to modeling stimuli." His analysis, however, differs sharply from that of Gewirtz and Stingle. Whereas the latter predict a generalized tendency to imitate (or match one's behavior against that of a model) as a function of previous and continued intermittent reinforcement, Bandura explains the acquisition of "matching behavior" as independent of reinforcement, invoking only the principle of contiguity that produces an association between the "modeling of stimulus consequences and symbolic verbal coding of observational inputs. These representational symbolic events, in conjunction with appropriate environmental cues, later guide overt enactment of appropriate matching responses." Bandura regards imaginal coding, as well as verbal coding, as significant symbolic and internal representations of observations. According to Bandura, reinforcement theories fail to account for imitation under conditions of no practice of the behavior by the observer, no reinforcement to model or observer, and delayed performance of the behavior. Reinforcement, however, is said to be a primary determinant of the performance (not the acquisition) of imitative responses whether "externally applied, self-administered, or vicariously experienced."

Bandura explains observational learning (new behavior by an observer following exposure to a model) by the mediation of imaginal and verbal codes that become conditioned to external stimuli. In addition, Berger and his colleagues (e.g., Bernal and Berger, 1976; Berger, Carli, Hammersla, Karshmer, and Sanchez, 1979) have demonstrated the occurrence of a third type of mediating process, spontaneous motor mimicry (an overt vicarious response). These mimetic responses have been shown to occur during observation under certain conditions and to be conditionable to environmental stimuli.

Learning to Imitate

Relatively little research on imitation has focused on the conditions under which such a general response is learned or on demonstrating that imitation ("matching") is a teachable behavior. Evidence has come primarily from related areas. If conformity, for example, is defined as the matching of a response, not to that of a single model but to a group consensus, then the work of Endler (1966) and Endler and Hoy (1967) appears relevant. They regard conformity behavior as a learned instrumental response leading to goal attainment and have demonstrated that it can be modified as a function of its consequences. Reinforcement was provided by the experimenter agreeing with the participant's response in social pressure situations requiring selection of light switches. In both investigations, 100 percent reinforcement produced greater conformity than 50 percent reinforcement, and conformity was greater in the situation in which rewards were present than in a later situation in which they were absent (extinction phase), although the fact that the previous learning carried over into the postsession indicated the stability of the matching response. Another study, by Grusec and Brinker (1972), has also demonstrated that positive consequences received *for matching* one's responses to that of another person are predictably related to subsequent behavior. The subsequent behavior measured, however, was not imitation but

verbal recall of a model's act. Children who had been rewarded for imitating the behavior of one of two possible adult models and who were later given another opportunity to observe the models in a different situation recalled more of the behaviors of the model they had earlier been rewarded for copying.

Variables Influencing Overt Imitation

The empirical study of imitation has most frequently been concerned with specifying the conditions under which persons are more likely, and less likely, to match a model's response, with imitation assumed to be already a part of the observer's response repertoire. Many studies, for example, have shown that the observed reinforcement consequences to the model influence the probability that the model's behavior will be imitated. Bandura (1965) found that children who observed a filmed model punished for aggressive behavior later performed fewer matching responses than children who had seen the model rewarded. This difference disappeared when the children were offered attractive rewards for imitating the model's aggressive acts. Britt (1971) reported the results of three experiments in which adult students in ambiguous situations tended to imitate "competent" models (i.e., persons who obtained positive reinforcement) more than less competent ones. Lerner and Weiss (1972) varied the quality of the reward and the model's affective response to the reinforcement and found that seven-year-old boys exposed to a model who responded positively to rewards subsequently imitated the model in play with toys more than boys exposed to a model who responded negatively to rewards. As in Bandura's study, however, all observers could reproduce the model's behavior under performance conditions in which they were rewarded for doing so. Lerner and Weiss suggest that the affective cues displayed by a model elicit comparable cues in an observer and that the latter becomes "conditioned to the modeled activities, which when subsequently imitated by the observer, generate in him positive (or negative) emotional arousal as he now performs...the modeled activities." Similarly, Masters, Gordon, and Clark (1976) reported that regardless of whether reward to a live adult model was self-dispensed or external, children who had observed the model were more likely to show spontaneous imitation of the adult's behavior in the " 'context' of reward...than of punishment." Schedule of reward obtained by a model has also been shown to influence subsequent imitation of the model's behavior by an observer. Braun (1972) varied the reward given to college learners (20 percent versus 80 percent variable ratio) and found that the behavior of learners and peer observers was similarly affected during a period when neither received reinforcement (i.e., an extinction phase) with respect to resistance to extinction (rate of emission of response). Braun argues that covert stimuli "provided by the observer on a symbolic and imaginal level" may function like the overt stimuli provided by the model (i.e., as discriminative stimuli) and that symbolic or imaginal reinforcers can function like overt rewards in reinforcing "covert responses as well as overt matching responses." The schedule with which a model received reward was also shown by Kerns (1975) to have a predictable effect on the behavior of boys who observed the model. Observers who had seen a videotape of a peer obtaining variable ratio reward for a marble dropping response later emitted more responses and persisted longer in the task (without reward) than children who had observed a continuously reinforced model. In the latter study, observers of partially rewarded models appear to have leaned a "response strategy."

In addition to observed consequences to the model, other model characteristics have been found to affect significantly the likelihood that the model's behavior will be imitated by observers. One such model characteristic is typically operationalized by varying the previous interaction between model and observer in terms of the warmth, pleasantness, or reward of the interaction. Mussen and Parker (1965) found that five-year-old daughters who observed highly nurturing mothers in a maze-solving situation imitated more of their mother's incidental behavior than daughters of less nurturing mothers. The authors suggest that the more nurturing parent had acquired greater secondary reward value leading to greater self-rewards experienced by the daughters following the matching of responses to those of their mothers. In two other studies with preschool children, Mischel and Grusec (1966) and Grusec and Mischel (1966) varied both the reward value of interaction between children and an adult and the extent to which the adult had control over future rewards. Both variables were effective in influencing later imitation of the adult's behavior. In the first study, more children displayed both the aversive and neutral responses modeled by an adult woman in a game situation if that adult had earlier been highly rewarding and had future control than if she had been minimally rewarding and had little control over resources. In the second study, the same results were obtained with a dependent measure of recall, not active

imitation, under conditions in which children were rewarded for remembering the model's behavior. Hetherington and Frankie (1967) also investigated imitation as a function of the model's warmth and dominance (control over resources). Children alternately watched each parent (who had earlier been categorized as high or low in warmth and dominance) perform in a free-play situation, and then the imitative responses of the children were observed. As in the studies reported previously, children tended in general to match their behavior to the model (parent) who was judged to be warmer (i.e., more nurturing and rewarding) and more dominant (i.e., powerful). Both variables influenced the behavior of girls and boys, but the latter were more influenced by the model's power than warmth. In an earlier investigation, Hetherington (1965) had found that children of both sexes imitated the choice behavior of their more dominant parent, regardless of the parent's sex. In a study in which adults' degree of dominance (power or control over resources) was manipulated directly by the investigators, Chartier and Weiss (1974) obtained further evidence that children tend to imitate previously rewarding adults and adults who have power to dispense rewards.

Still another model characteristic, similarity to the observer, has been shown to affect the probability that the model will be imitated. Rosekrans (1967), for example, reported that among a group of boy scouts who watched a filmed model play an army game, greater imitation was observed on the part of those who were similar in background and interests to the model than on the part of those who were dissimilar. Bussey and Perry (1976) varied model-observer similarity by manipulating the consequences which children received for performing the same responses as an adult in an earlier task. Some children received the same consequence as the adult, while other children received different consequences. In two studies, the results indicated greater subsequent imitation by children of "a model who had been subject to the same reinforcement contingencies as themselves" than of "a model whose contingencies had been uncorrelated with their own."

Concordance between models and observers has been enhanced in two other ways by Berger (1971), namely, through peer (versus nonpeer) status or opinion similarity (versus dissimilarity). Observers first watched models respond to an ESP task under conditions of 25 percent or 75 percent correct, and then they were presented with the same task under a no-reward (extinction) condition. A differential effect on observer perseverance (greater if the model had been successful 25 percent of the time) was found only for observers who had watched a similar or, as Berger suggests, a "relevant" or "appropriate" model. Such observers should be more likely than those who watched models different from themselves, Berger argues, to develop "higher expectancies for success and a lower tolerance for frustration" under the condition of more frequent model reward. They should subsequently experience greater frustration on no-success trials of their own and therefore persist less on the task. Berger (1979), moving beyond explanatory concepts from learning theory, has introduced Festinger's social comparison theory into the imitation-modeling literature, suggesting that models may provide standards to which observers can later compare their own performance and that this is most likely when the model is similar in some way to the observer. Although a "model's performance may have instrumental relevance for the observer without necessarily involving social comparison processes...a model's performance may have attributional relevance as well."

Other research has varied the consistency of reinforcement consequences received by the model (e.g., Rosekrans and Hartup, 1967), the consistency of behavior in more than one model (e.g., Fehrenbach, Miller, and Thelen, 1979), and the consistency of the model's behavior with expectations for that behavior such as its sex role appropriateness (Perry and Bussey, 1979). In each case, consistency was found to increase the likelihood that observed behavior would be imitated by children.

Learning through Imitation

The previously cited studies have investigated the conditions or variables that tend to increase (or decrease) imitative behavior, that is, the matching of an observer's responses (of varied types, verbal or nonverbal) to that of a model who has previously performed them. Many investigations of imitation have had a different focus—simply the demonstration that behavior *can* be modified by exposing persons to a model. Such demonstrations indicate the value of imitation as a process for learning new responses or altering old ones but do not elucidate the conditions under which imitation is most likely to occur. Thus Bandura and Mischel (1965), for example, showed that children who initially preferred to delay rewards were significantly influenced by exposure to either live or symbolic models to change their behavior in favor of immediate gratification. Bandura, Grusec, and Menlove (1967) demonstrated that children who were fearful of

dogs displayed greater approach behavior and more intimate interactions with dogs following their repeated observation of a fearless peer model interacting with a dog. Similarly, Geer and Turteltaub (1967) found that college women who were very fearful of snakes approached one closely after observing a "calmly acting confederate." Bandura, Blanchard, and Ritter (1969), also working with snake-phobic persons, found that live modeling with guided participation was the most effective condition of all in extinguishing snake-avoidance behavior. They describe the change process as follows (p. 198):

> Repeated modeling of approach responses and the anxiety-mitigating influence of physical contact and physical protection decrease the arousal potential of aversive stimuli below the threshold for activating avoidance responses, thus enabling persons to engage, albeit somewhat anxiously, in approach behavior.

The literature on modification of behavior as a consequence of exposure to models is an extensive one that has profited from, but gone beyond, the basic proposition that imitation is a response acquired and maintained, like other responses, in accordance with the principles of learning.

Contagion

Wheeler (1966) has also proposed a learning model to explain imitation under the particular conditions in which a behavior is instigated by some external cues, is part of a person's response repertoire, but is not performed until the person observes someone else making the response. The behavior involved is typically a socially undesirable one or is, for some other reason, associated with consequent pain or punishment; the imitation, under these conditions, is labeled contagion. Wheeler assumes that the person who does not immediately respond to the instigating conditions "is experiencing an approach-avoidance conflict" and that observing another person responding in the same situation "changes the relative strengths" of the approach and avoidance tendencies. The conflict has not been created by the action of the other person (as may occur, for example, in a social pressure situation), but exists previous to, and independently of, the behavior of others. It is the latter that "contributes to conflict resolution" by reducing fear and lowering the observer's avoidance gradient for the modeled response when the behavior performed by the other person has gone unpunished. Bandura (1969) might explain contagion similarly by invoking the concept of disinhibition; the observer behaves like the model as a consequence of the weakening of the observer's inhibitory responses.

OTHER SOCIAL BEHAVIOR

Persuasion

Weiss (1968) has proposed that being persuaded by a communication is analogous to the learning of other responses (such as running in a straight alley maze). He has systematically related the variables relevant to instrumental learning with those relevant to persuasive communication and suggested that communication cues correspond to "stimulus," stating an opinion corresponds to "response," and argument corresponds to the "reinforcement." A number of experimental tests of the model found that speed of agreement and forced-choice behavior varied predictably with such learning-relevant independent variables as number of reinforced persuasion trials and delay of reinforcement (argument). Also, arguing within a reinforcement theory framework "that individuals are motivated to accept conclusions that will lead to reward," Maddux and Rogers (1980) predicted that persons will be more persuaded on an issue by an expert than by a nonexpert and if arguments are provided for the conclusion than if no arguments are provided. Both variables proved to be independently significant in increasing the persuasive effect of communication.

A number of investigators have been particularly concerned with the use of fear appeals in persuasive communication. Higbee (1969), in summarizing fifteen years of research on "threat appeals," concluded that much evidence (although not all) supported a positive relationship between level of fear arousal and persuasiveness of communication, as typically measured by the extent to which persons agree to follow, or actually follow, a recommended course of action. The work of Leventhal and his colleagues (e.g., Leventhal and Singer, 1966; Dabbs and Leventhal, 1966) illustrates this line of research. Weiss, following the fear reduction model earlier proposed by the Yale researchers led by Hovland, has argued that fear appeals are effective in persuading persons to adopt a course of action or a particular belief because the recommendation *reduces the fear*. In a study by Cecil, Weiss, and Feinberg (1978), participants first read a threatening communiciation and then, upon presentation of a signal, pressed a switch that permitted them to hear "reassuring recommendations effective in avoiding

the danger." The speed with which the instrumental response of pressing the switch was performed was found to vary with the delay in presentation of the recommendations. In addition, communications with less of a reinforcing component were not as effective as the communication with the highest reinforcement score, indicating that "although a consistent amount of drive was being induced by the threatening portion of the different communications, there were significant differences in the degree to which this drive was diminished by the recommendations." It was this reward variable that was related to the speed of the instrumental response upon which the hearing of the recommendation was contingent.

Independence

Behaviors varying in dominance or independence have been shown to be related to, or modifiable by, their reinforcement consequences. Hilton (1967) had judges observe mother and four-year-old child pairs working together on puzzles and found that the behavior of mothers of first-born (and only) children differed significantly from the behavior of mothers of later-born children. First-born children, who had also been rated as more dependent than later-born children, had mothers who were more likely to be involved with and interfere with the child's activity, signal the start of the activity, and reward success with demonstrative love and reduce demonstrative love for failure. The learning of dependency responses was thus more likely for the first-born children than for the others whose mothers behaved differently. In an analogous situation, Barton, Baltes, and Orzech (1980) found from sequential observation of interactions between nursing home residents and staff workers during "morning care" periods, that "resident dependence was most frequently followed by dependent-supported behavior by staff," and that, in general, dependence-support was the most frequent staff response to all resident behavior. The authors conclude that the nursing home patients receive "a schedule of frequent, continuous staff reinforcement for dependent behavior."

In some studies the reinforcement consequences for dominant-independent behavior have been experimentally manipulated and found to be effective variables in influencing the probability of such responses. Blum and Kennedy (1967), for example, obtained initial measures of dominance from the behavior of third- and fourth-grade children who made joint decisions in same-sex pairs. On each of several trials the child "whose individual preference prevailed" in the collective answer was said to have made the more dominant response. Children who tended to make few dominant responses were subsequently reinforced for dominance (with candy and a light) over twenty trials, and previously dominant children were punished for such behavior (by withdrawal of candy), with the result that significant changes occurred in this behavior in the predicted directions. Similarly, Serbin, Connor, and Citron (1978) successfully modified independence behaviors of preschool children. For a twenty-minute period during each of five consecutive weeks, teachers praised one group of children for their exploration and persistence (independent behavior) but ignored proximity-seeking and the soliciting of teacher attention (dependent behaviors). When compared with another group of children who were randomly praised, the training was found to be effective in increasing independence and decreasing dependency in both girls and boys.

Conversation

Weiss and his colleagues have compared the response of replying to a disagreeing other person to the learning of instrumental escape responses, on the assumption that disagreement is a drive-inducing aversive stimulus. In four studies, Weiss, Lombardo, Warren, and Kelley (1971) demonstrated that the speed with which a button-pressing response was made was predictably related to the number of times the responder was able to reply to a disagreeing other person following the button press, to the delay in this reinforcement, and to whether the reinforcement was continuous or partial. The authors concluded that they had "revealed a striking point-for-point correspondence between the effects of a reinforcer in escape conditioning and the effects of speaking in reply in conversation." In a later investigation, Lombardo, Weiss, and Stich (1973) found that subsequent liking for disagreeing strangers was highest under the condition in which persons could fully reply to them (on several trials) and lowest under conditions that permitted no reply, confirming in an indirect manner the proposition that replying to disagreement is drive reducing.

Prophesied Behavior

That behavior is acquired and maintained as a direct result of the consequences received by the persons exhibiting the behavior is a general principle invoked by some investigators interested in explaining the "prophecy fulfillment" phenomenon. Persons who expect or anticipate certain interpersonal responses from others have been found to be more likely than persons without these

expectations to reinforce them promptly and directly and to thereby influence the frequency with which the expected responses occur. In one study, Meichenbaum, Bowers, and Ross (1969) found that the interaction of teachers with adolescents at a training school was affected by the differential identification of some of the students as "late bloomers." Three out of four teachers either increased their positive interactions or decreased their negative interactions with these students, and the latter significantly improved their academic performance and the appropriateness of their classroom behavior. Similarly, Rubovitz and Maehr (1971) found that college students acting as teachers made more requests of, and gave more praise to, sixth- and seventh-grade students labeled as "gifted" in comparison to those labeled "nongifted." Chaiken, Sigler, and Devlega (1974), utilizing a similar experimental design, found that college students who tutored a boy described as "bright" differed from those who tutored a boy described as "dull" on a number of socially reinforcing (approving) behaviors: smiling more often, exhibiting more direct eye contact, leaning forward more, and nodding their heads more. In a more complex study, Snyder, Tanke, and Berscheid (1977) instructed male students to engage in a ten-minute telephone conversation with an "attractive" or "unattractive" woman (as operationalized by prejudged photographs). Observers later listened to the taped conversations and rated the verbal behavior of the callers and of the persons called. Men who telephoned women they believed to be physically attractive were judged to be significantly different on a wide variety of dimensions from men who telephoned presumably unattractive women. For example, the former were judged to be more sociable, interesting, outgoing, humorous, socially adept, and animated in their conversation; to take initiative more often; and to use their voices more effectively. In addition, the targets who were identified as attractive behaved in reciprocally positive ways toward their callers ("in a friendly, likeable, and sociable manner") and differed in their verbal behavior from the targets identified as unattractive.

DRIVE-RELATED SOCIAL PHENOMENA

COGNITIVE DISSONANCE

In an extension of Festinger's early suggestion that cognitive dissonance was a "motivating factor," some investigators have predicted that dissonance, like hunger or frustration, acting as a source of general arousal (drive), would serve an energizing function and facilitate performance on tasks unrelated to it. Thus, Waterman and Katkin (1967) found that cognitive dissonance, induced by the writing of attitude-discrepant essays, facilitated the performance of students on symbol-substitution tasks. Cottrell and Wack (1967) induced dissonance by having some students commit themselves to a task without adequate justification. Subsequently, participants learned strong and weak verbal responses (pronunciation of Turkish words). On a test, it was found that "the strongest habits were emitted more frequently in the high-dissonance condition than in the low-dissonance condition," as predicted by learning theory. Drive is said to facilitate behavior and therefore to enhance responses that are strong but not those that are weak, because in the latter case there is usually competition among previously acquired responses of relatively equal strength. Complementary findings were reported by Pallak and Pittman (1972) from two studies in which high-dissonance participants made more errors than low-dissonance participants in a verbal task high in response competition (and therefore considered difficult); however, they made fewer errors than low-dissonance participants in a task low in response competition (i.e., an easy task). The investigators concluded that "dissonance arousal may have properties similar to those of more general motivational constructs," such as drive.

COMPETITION

Weiss and his colleagues have proposed, within the framework of liberalized S–R theory, that competition is a noxious drive. Thus, persons should learn responses that are followed by the termination of competition just as they learn behavior that reduces pain or other aversive stimuli. Steigleder, Weiss, Cramer, and Feinberg (1978) reported five experiments that suggest a clear "correspondence between the effects of a reinforcer in escape conditioning and the effects of competition cessation." Termination of competition functioned as a reinforcer, and the speed with which participants threw a switch in response to a cue was found to increase with increased numbers of reinforced trials, with lower levels of delay in reinforcement, with continuous as compared to partial reinforcement, and with improved quality of reinforcement (longer periods of noncompetition). The investigators suggest that more socially relevant responses "such as resignation or devalued self-esteem" might, perhaps,

also be learned by persons "to escape or avoid competition." In additional studies using the same procedure, Steigleder, Weiss, Balling, Wenninger, and Lombardo (1980) varied drive intensity (by varying the number of competitors) and the percentage of trials on which persons competed. As predicted, speed of the instrumental responses (throwing a switch in response to a light) "was an increasing function of the number of reinforced ...trials (cessation of competition) and an increasing function of drive intensity." Participants were faster when competing in groups of four than in groups of two. In addition, groups competing on 100 percent of the trials were faster than those competing on 66 percent, and these were faster than groups competing on 33 percent of the trials. In a third study, the investigators found that a person associated with the noxious drive of competition (i.e., one's competitor) will "acquire the capacity to elicit noxious drive." Performance on a complex list of paired associates, as measured by trials required to learn, errors, and omissions, was found to be impaired for those participants who were required to learn the list in the presence of a previous competitor as compared to the performance of those who learned the list in the presence of a neutral person or alone.

SOCIAL FACILITATION

Learning theorists view persons not only as responding organisms but also as cues for the responses of others. Persons are said to function as discriminative stimuli or as generalized stimuli to which responses have been conditioned. In addition, as proposed by Zajonc (1965), persons may be drive arousing. In his view the "mere presence" of other persons is sufficient to arouse drive; the "other persons" present need not engage in any particular behavior. It is the drive-arousing nature of other persons which is said to produce their "facilitative" effect (i.e., to enhance behavior as measured by such quantitative indices as speed and frequency). This effect will be of greatest benefit to those responses (performed in the presence of others) that are already well learned or easy (i.e., involve few competitive responses), since generalized drive energizes all learned responses in a given situation, whether correct or incorrect. Cottrell (1968) has elaborated on this view and proposed that the drive aroused by persons has been *acquired* under conditions in which persons have been associated with evaluation and that their subsequent arousal properties are attributable to elicited anxiety (anticipation of negative consequences, e.g., negative appraisal, failure, or frustration). The presence of persons will be facilitative, therefore, under conditions in which the fear of evaluation is most likely to be evoked. As summarized by Weiss and Miller (1971), the Cottrell position assumes that "the audience...is a conditioned stimulus for a learned drive of fear or anticipatory frustration." Both Weiss and Miller (1971) and Geen and Gange (1977), after reviewing the accumulated theory and research, concluded that available evidence tended to support Cottrell's learned drive hypothesis and the primary importance of an "evaluative stance on the part of the audience" (Weiss and Miller, 1971). What is particularly important is that there is a possibility of negative evaluation.

Weiss, Miller, Langan, and Cecil (1971) predicted that opinions could be conditioned to cue statements and that the strength of an agreeing response would be positively related to the number of persuasion trials and to the presence of an evaluative audience (two male peers who rated each male participant on "personality and speech characteristics"). Agreement, measured by latency—the speed a lever was moved in a particular direction, was found to be greater under the evaluative audience condition than under the no-audience condition. In this study, participants did not know whether their evaluations were favorable or unfavorable. In an investigation by Good (1973), however, some participants were led to anticipate that they would perform well in the presence of others (on a free association task) and were positively evaluated by the experimenter, while other participants were led to believe that they would perform poorly. Social facilitation effects were found only for those "in the positive anticipation—immediate evaluation condition," supporting an alternative hypothesis that the presence of others is effective in enhancing performance because other persons are a source of *positive reinforcement.* According to Good, social facilitation will occur in those situations in which other persons can "potentially provide social reinforcement contingent on...[the performer's] behavior."

Still another interpretation of the social facilitation phenomenon attributes the arousal effects of an audience, or the presence of other persons, to their tendency to distract performers from their task. Sanders and Baron (1975) have suggested that "social facilitation effects may be merely a subcategory of a more general phenomenon involving the motivational effects of distraction." Like other distractors, an audience should heighten drive because performers will experience con-

flict between attending to the task and attending to others present. As predicted, distraction was found to facilitate performance on simple tasks but to impair performance on more complex tasks. Similarly, Baron, Moore and Sanders (1978) found a significant facilitative effect on a simple, noncompetitive, paired-associative task performed in the presence of one observer and introduced after practice on the task (and a trend toward impairment on a complex task). Participants who were observed "indicated on self-report and recall measures that they were more distracted than isolated subjects."

In those cases where other persons are coactors, that is, performing the same tasks as the participants and not simply present as potential evaluators, reinforcers, or distractors, their arousal effect (and consequent facilitation of simple behavior) can be attributed to competition. This hypothesis was tested by Beck and Seta (1980) by putting two coactors in a situation in which they received feedback on their performance but could also observe feedback to the other; each coactor received a tone after making four or seven (button pressing) responses in the presence of another person who was also on a four- or seven-response schedule. It was predicted that the competitive cues would serve to increase drive level in the performers and that "drive level should be greater the more often competitive cues occur." Thus, "drive induced by feedback to the subject should summate with arousal produced by feedback given the other coacter...[and] social facilitation should be greater the more often the subjects receive feedback concerning their own or the other coactor's performance." As predicted, performance was enhanced when both coactors received feedback after every four responses in comparison to every seven responses and was at an intermediate level when one coactor was on a four-response schedule and the other on a seven-response schedule.

In an attempt to isolate "mere presence" from all other possibilities, that is, to eliminate conditions in which "the present other" provides the chance for imitation or competition, for controlling the performer's reinforcement, for evaluating the performer's task behavior, or for giving any relevant information, Markus (1978) devised a clever situation that would permit a test of Zajonc's original position that "the mere presence of others is a source of nonspecific and nondirective arousal that enhances the dominant responses of the performer." Participants were required to perform a well-learned response (putting on shoes and socks) and a new response (putting on unfamiliar clothing) in preparation presumably for a later experiment in the presence of a watching confederate, in the presence of a nonwatching confederate busy repairing equipment in a corner, or alone. Both the watching confederate and the non-watching "incidental audience" produced the same effect: they enhanced performance on the well-learned task and impaired performance on the new task in comparison with the alone condition. Perhaps, suggests Markus, it is the unpredictability of situations in which others are present that is the drive-arousing factor, a suggestion earlier made by Zajonc.

ATTITUDES AND INTERPERSONAL ATTRACTION

ATTITUDES AS LEARNED RESPONSES

A learning-theory interpretation of attitudes by Doob was among the first of the significant extensions of Hullian theory in the area of social behavior. Doob (1947) argued that attitudes are acquired in the same way as other habits and should be interpretable in S–R terms. He defined attitudes as learned covert anticipatory responses having both stimulus and drive properties and suggested that they differ from other such covert responses, such as a rat's learned aversion to a grid, only by being "socially significant." Both aversion to a grid and a socially significant attitude like a child's aversion to school are learned as a result of associating stimuli with response consequences, and like other covert anticipatory responses, attitudes need to be tied to antecedent stimulus conditions on the one hand and to observable behavior on the other. Utilizing a mediated generalization paradigm, Eisman (B. Lott, 1955) tested Doob's formulation. Children were taught to attach the same verbal label to two otherwise different stimuli; then, after experiencing reward in association with one of the stimuli, they manifested a preference for the other of the same name as well as for stimuli physically resembling the latter. The children were tested for their preference (attitudes) in situations that differed in context, complexity, and social significance. Later, Staats and Staats (1958), using as their point of departure S–R interpretations of "meaning" (as suggested by Cofer and Foley, 1942; Osgood, 1952; and Mowrer, 1954), demonstrated that attitudes could also be acquired through classical conditioning.

Staats (1968) proposed that attitude acquisition is the result of classical conditioning that most typically oc-

curs within the context of an operant reward situation. Attitudes are defined as emotional (affective) responses, and stimuli that come to elicit such responses are called attitudinal stimuli. When a neutral stimulus is paired with an unconditioned stimulus that elicits an emotional response, it is expected that this response will be conditioned to the neutral stimulus. In a study by Staats, Minke, Martin and Higa (1972), for example, food words (assumed to elicit positive attitudes through previous pairing with food) were associated with trigrams under conditions of food deprivation or satiation. Food-deprived participants acquired a stronger positive attitude toward the trigrams (as measured by semantic differential rating scales) than the satiated participants. Variation in food-associated drive thus affected the attitudinal potency of the food words ("secondary stimuli") and the conditioning of attitudinal responses to previously neutral stimuli paired with the food words.

In another investigation, Staats, Gross, Guay and Carlson (1973) demonstrated that trigrams paired with items of positive interest to students later elicited positive ratings on a scale of pleasantness versus unpleasantness, whereas those paired with items of negative interest were later rated negatively. Staats's conditioning analysis, developed with respect to attitudes in general, is also applicable to attitudes toward persons.

Interpersonal attitudes have been the specific focus of a series of theoretical and empirical papers on "liking" by Lott and Lott (beginning in 1960), who have elaborated a learning theory approach to attraction utilizing general behavior principles to specify the conditions under which persons will learn to like (or dislike) one another (i.e., the antecedents of liking) and the consequences of liking (or disliking) for subsequent behavior. Interpersonal attraction, it is argued, is learned in the same way as attitudes are, and the primary proposition relevant to this learning is that if a person is positively or negatively reinforced in the presence of another, a positive or negative attitude toward that other will be formed. This proposition rests upon the following assumptions (B. Lott and A. Lott, 1960, p. 298):

1. Persons may be conceptualized as discriminable stimuli to which responses may be learned.

2. A person who experiences reinforcement or reward for some behavior will react to the reward, i.e., will perform some observable or covert goal response (R_g or r_g).

3. This response to reward will become conditioned, like any other response, to all discriminable stimuli present at the time of reinforcement.

4. A person... who is present at the time that individual X, for example, is rewarded thus becomes able in a later situation to evoke R_g, or, what is more likely, its fractional and anticipatory component, $r_g - s_g$. This latter response, which Hull has called "expectative"... was... interpreted by Doob... as the underlying mechanism of an attitude."

No instrumental relationship between the discriminable stimulus person and reward is implied or necessary; the sufficient condition for the development of liking is merely the consistent presence of the stimulus person during receipt of some positive state of affairs. Learning to like a person is essentially learning to anticipate reward in that person's presence. Subsequently, the liked person can raise general drive level in the liker and can function as a secondary reward. Liking can also mediate between the stimulus person evoking this implicit response and a variety of overt approach behaviors.

ANTECEDENTS AND CONSEQUENTS OF LIKING

Summarized in Lott and Lott (1968) are a series of experiments that demonstrated the particular conditions under which learning to like other persons can occur. Being in the presence of a discriminable person when satisfaction is experienced was shown to be a sufficient condition for the acquisition of liking for that person; in addition, frequency of reward, vicarious reinforcement, immediate versus delayed reward, high versus low drive, and quality of reward were all shown to affect significantly the development of interpersonal attitudes in a theoretically predictable way. A later review of studies in which reward was investigated as a factor in the formation of positive interpersonal attitudes led to the conclusion that although "only a small number of investigators unabashedly make systematic use of reinforcement-related principles to generate testable hypotheses regarding interpersonal attraction, a great many... actually manipulate conditions of reward in their investigations and utilize the concept of reward to explain their empirical results" (Lott and Lott, 1974). The major sources of reward manipulated or experimentally isolated were identified as direct reward provided by another person, the characteristics of another person, another person's

attitude similarity as evidence for one's own competence, and the receipt of reward in another person's presence.

Hypotheses relevant to the consequences of attraction have also been derived and tested by Lott and Lott (1972) who propose that liked persons and disliked persons will function as positive and negative secondary reinforcers. Certain consequences for behavior theoretically follow from this approach and, in a number of empirical demonstrations, support has been obtained for the following predictions (Lott and Lott, 1974; p. 173):

> As positive secondary reinforcing stimuli, people we like should have consequences for perception and memory, stemming from their heightened salience and distinctiveness; consequences for performance, stemming from their incentive or drive-arousing quality; and consequences for learning, because they can function as rewards. If the presence of a liked person is made contingent upon some behavior, that behavior should be strengthened.

Confirming evidence for these predictions has been reported in Lott and Lott (1966, 1969), Lott, Lott, Reed, and Crow (1970), and Lott, Lott, and Walsh (1970).

Another approach to interpersonal attraction that makes explicit use of the concept of reinforcement and S–R learning principles is that of Byrne (Byrne and Clore, 1970; Clore and Byrne, 1974). Beginning with empirical demonstrations that persons are positively attracted to strangers having similar attitudes in direct proportion to the extent of that similarity (e.g., Byrne and Nelson, 1965), Byrne attempted to account for this relationship by use of a classical conditioning model (similar to that of Staats, previously cited). Attitude similarity was interpreted as an unconditional stimulus that evokes an implicit affective response. This response is automatically evoked because attitude similarity is "reinforcing," and positively valued by virtue of its being able to satisfy a need for effectance. A stimulus person, through association with similar attitude statements (the UCS), can be conditioned to evoke the same positive affect. Byrne's model, originally formulated to account for the specific relationship between attitude similarity and interpersonal attraction, has contributed to the larger and more general literature that relates interpersonal attitudes to concepts within reinforcement learning theory. Although allied, the position of Lott and Lott differs from those of Staats and of Bryne and Clore in that the former makes explicit use of learning principles associated with the Yale-Iowa model (e.g., Hull, Spence, Mowrer) and identifies attitudes (liking or disliking) as anticipatory goal responses and liked or disliked persons as secondary reinforcers.

Other investigators have made empirical contributions to a general learning model of attitude acquisition and the prediction of behavioral consequences of attitudes. For example, a sizable number of studies have demonstrated, in a variety of different conditions, that a verbal or written statement of opinion is strengthened when it is followed by some positive state of affairs (reward). Rosenberg (1965) found that when the writing of a counterattitudinal essay, followed by the giving of a monetary reward, was separated from the situation in which attitude change was measured, undergraduates manifested change in their views (about the behavior of police officers at a previous campus riot) from negative to positive in direct proportion to the magnitude of the reward received for writing a positive essay. Insko and his colleagues have successfully modified the opinions of students on a range of issues by verbally reinforcing some statements and not others in telephone interviews. The use of the word "good" to signify agreement positively affected opinions during a phone conversation as well as responses to a "local issue" questionnaire one week later (Insko, 1965), was found to be a more potent reinforcer when the person signifying agreement to an expressed opinion was mildly ingratiating as opposed to mildly insulting (Insko and Butzine, 1967), and was found to be more effective than a nonevaluative "huh" (Insko and Cialdini, 1969).

In a study by Schlenker, Brown and Tedeschi (1975), dealing not with opinions but persons, a confederate delivered shocks to male participants who varied in their initial liking of him. Liking was found to increase in the low-attraction condition after the confederate delivered only one shock in contrast to a possible five or nine shocks, whereas in the high attraction condition, liking for the confederate decreased when he delivered more than one shock. Similarly, the mere expectation that a person will provide positive or negative reinforcement was found by Griffitt (1968b) to influence attitudinal responses to that person. Students indicated greater liking for a stranger from whom they expected to receive money for correct responses on a laboratory task than for a stranger from whom they expected to receive shock for incorrect responses.

Other studies have investigated change in attitudes toward impersonal or personal stimuli as a function of mere association with positive or negative reinforcement,

that is, situations in which the attitude was not directly instrumental to receipt of consequences and in which person stimuli were not the direct mediators of consequences. Janis, Kaye and Kirschner (1965) reported that college students exposed to a persuasive communication (supporting an unpopular point of view) while eating desirable snack food subsequently manifested more opinion change than students exposed to the same communication in the absence of food. Similarly, Griffitt (1968a) found that students indicated greater attraction to an unseen stranger in a situation in which they received five points (applicable to their course grade) for participating in an investigation than when they received only one point. Utilizing a more complex design, Bleda (1976) separated participants into three teams of same-sex pairs and arranged conditions so that one team (A) received unfavorable evaluations from a second team (B) but no feedback from the third team (C). On subsequent ratings of the members of the other teams, persons in group A were found to manifest the greatest level of dislike for group B members and an intermediate level of dislike for group C members; the latter had not been responsible for the negative reinforcement received by persons in the A team but were a competing group like group B that had administered the negative feedback to group A. The author follows Clore and Byrne, and Lott and Lott, in assuming that "through temporal association with... affect [evoked by a reinforcing event] previously unknown and presumably neutral persons...become capable of eliciting a conditioned response that mediates various forms of approach-avoidance responses including verbal evaluations of attraction." As Bleda notes, this process is applicable not only to social behavior at the interpersonal level but also to responses we acquire to groups.

Arguing that disagreement with a person's attitudes or opinions is aversive and a source of tension, arousal, or drive and that subsequent agreement is therefore drive reducing, Stapert and Clore (1969) demonstrated that attraction toward agreeing persons increased following exposure to disagreement. Lombardo, Weiss and Buchanan (1972), in two separate experiments, found that response speeds (for pressing a switch) were greater for participants whose responses were followed by hearing another person yield (i.e., change from initial disagreement to agreement) than for participants whose responses were followed by either agreement or disagreement (on current controversial issues). The authors note that "since both item interest and number of reinforcements were equated in the yield and agree groups, the observed differences in response speed could only be attributed to the differences in the magnitude of the drive aroused (by disagreement) and consequently reduced by...agreement." In addition to affecting the strength of an instrumental response, yielding was also shown to positively influence liking of the yielder.

Kenrick and his colleagues have been concerned with a related phenomenon, that is, the reduction of aversive drive, not by agreement but by the physical presence of another person, and the consequent increase in that person's attractiveness. As Kenrick and Cialdini (1977) have argued, "Enhanced attraction under aversive circumstances does not contradict reinforcement principles but can instead be seen as due to the effects of...the termination or reduction of aversive stimuli," produced by the presence of another person. Mere presence of another person should, under ordinary circumstances, reduce an aversive state, and "it is the *reduction* of this aversive arousal that is associated with strengthening interpersonal bonds," since it is this reduction of arousal which is rewarding. Liking for a person should increase under conditions of negative arousal only if the person is physically present, since it is the actual presence of another person that is assumed to be anxiety reducing. This hypothesis was tested by Kenrick and Johnson (1979) who found that participants working in pairs rated a nonpresent fictional stranger more negatively in an aversive high-noise condition that under a low-noise condition but rated the other member of the pair more positively under high than low noise. These data suggest that other persons in general function as *generalized* reinforcers and can reduce drive. It is to be expected, however, that continued and frequent association between specific persons (or categories of persons) and aversive conditions would change the reinforcing potential of that person from positive (through generalization from other persons) or neutral to negative; such a person would become a stimulus for the anticipation of aversive (painful, punishing, or frustrating) consequences and elicit the negative attitude of dislike.

The consequences of interpersonal attraction for performance on learning tasks have been explored by Lott and Lott and their coworkers and by other recent investigators. In a study utilizing small groups of children who liked or did not like each other and who were learning Spanish equivalents for English words, Lott and Lott (1966) found that on a number of measures high IQ children did better in the presence of liked classmates than in the presence of less liked ones. These data were interpreted as supporting the proposition that the presence of liked others enhances drive. For the low IQ children, for whom the experimental tasks were difficult, the drive increment served to decrease learning efficiency because high drive strengthens competing incorrect as well as correct responses. For the high IQ children, on the other hand, the task was relatively simple; because there was little response competition, drive improved performance. Complementary data have been reported by Reiter and DeVellis (1976) who studied the effect on performance of the presence of a person previously paired with an unpleasant, aversive event and who evoked unpleasant feelings in participants. The amount of time to complete a task increased sharply in the presence of the disliked person (but not in the presence of a control person) and then returned to baseline after his departure. The authors interpret their findings as indicating that "response suppression in human subjects" can be produced by the presence of a person who evokes anxiety.

That liked and disliked persons not only are drive arousing but also are positive and negative reinforcers, respectively, has been demonstrated experimentally. Lott and Lott (1969) had ninth graders learn a moderately difficult discrimination problem under conditions where correct or incorrect responses were followed by photographs of differentially liked peers or blank cards. Students were found to perform in the following order, from best to poorest: those whose correct responses were reinforced with the printed word "right" and incorrect ones with a blank card, those whose correct responses were reinforced with the photograph of a liked peer and incorrect ones with a blank card, those whose correct responses were followed by a blank card and incorrect ones with a photo of a disliked peer, those whose correct responses were reinforced with a photo of a neutral peer, and those whose correct responses were reinforced with the photo of a disliked peer. Using a similar paradigm but in the investigation of the reinforcing properties of liked and disliked "interest items" rather than persons, Staats, Gross, Guay and Carlson (1973) obtained similar results. Participants learned the particular response in a visual discrimination task that was followed by liked items. Kian, Rosen, and Tesser (1973) also presented a discrimination task to participants but used similar or dissimilar (relevant to own) attitude statements from liked or disliked international figures as reinforcers. They found that persons who received similar statements from liked sources, contingent upon a correct response, tended to show greater improvement in their performance than persons who received similar statements from disliked sources or dissimilar statements from liked ones.

CONCLUSIONS

In comparison with their colleagues of twenty years ago, today's social psychologists who find learning principles useful in their interpretations and predictions of social behavior have decreased in number, visibility, and representation in our major journals. Cognitive concepts, variables that emphasize interpretation of events, attributions, and perceptions are found far more often in our contemporary social psychological literature than the learning relevant concepts of stimulus, drive, response, and reinforcement. This state of affairs, however, represents what has always been the modal position; the dominant voice in social psychology has never been that of the learning theorist. Doob's (1947) redefinition of attitudes in S-R language was greeted with skepticism (e.g., Chien, 1948), and Gordon Allport had earlier (1947) spoken out sharply against the use of "machine models" in psychology, decrying theories that ascribe behavior "wholly to past experience, to learned cues, and to mechanical reinforcements." To traditional social psychologists like Gordon Allport and Solomon Asch, behavioristic psychology appeared narrow and sterile, reflecting what they considered to be an egoistic view of human beings.

The learning-theory perspective has never really enjoyed a solid position within the mainstream of social psychological thought, although there was greater receptivity to, and encouragement of, such "deviant" views in the 1950s and 1960s than in the earlier years or in the current period. S-R theorists like Mowrer, Miller, Dollard, and Hovland have proposed explanations of complex interpersonal behavior that have been widely praised, popularized, and incorporated into the body of social psychological wisdom, and bold learning proposals such as those on language, utopian societies and culture from B. F. Skinner (e.g., 1971) have sparked interdisciplinary debates about significant and far-reaching social issues. Nevertheless, the general tenor of theory in social psychology has remained consistently cognitively oriented, while our research is primarily topical and atheoretical.

Despite the intermittent charge of narrowness leveled at them, and their status as relative outsiders, learning-oriented social psychologists have shown no limitation of their objectives nor decrease in their vitality during the contemporary period covered by this present review. Previous extensions of learning principles into analyses of personality, psychotherapy, thinking, language, interpersonal behavior, and group processes have continued, although they are now represented by a smaller group of investigators.

In addition to a general decrease in the number of learning-oriented papers, it appears that contemporary investigators more often invoke the terminology of learning theory than vigorously attempt to derive hypotheses from learning principles for explaining results in terms of these basic propositions. Paralleling this trend is the more frequent use of learning terms in tandem with cognitive concepts. Sometimes the latter are presented unabashedly as necessary adjuncts; at other times they are redefined in more traditional learning-theory terms as implicit, internal responses (r-s) having stimulus and affective (drive) properties that can therefore function as cues or contributors to general arousal. Concepts that relate to interpretations or judgments of persons have always been welcome within learning theory as verbal reports, enjoying the same logical status as other observable behavior.

The contribution of the stimulus-response learning model of behavior to social psychology has been, from the beginning, one of providing convenient, theoretically related, descriptive parameters that permit us to treat social behavior as the behavior of individuals in a social context (i.e., having social antecedents and/or consequences). Basic principles verified in one behavioral context are assumed to be applicable to all, and tests of this assumption continue to be made. One of our colleagues, in reading a first draft of this chapter asked us, "How liberalized has learning theory become?" The intention has been wide application, it seems to us, from the start. Recall Hull's (1943) vision, referred to earlier, of a hierarchy of principles relevant to all human activity. Recall that it was in 1941 that Miller and Dollard presented a brilliant analysis of the lynching of a black man by a white mob by carefully relating the four key concepts of drive, cue, response, and reinforcement within the S-R nomothetic framework. The behavior of individuals that makes up the "group response" is predictable, they argued, if we understand their past histories, habits, and needs as well as characteristics of the present situation. The behavior of a lynch mob is no less complex than the behavior that contemporary social psychologists endeavor to explain with learning principles or any other set of propositions and concepts. An attempt to explain behavior which occurs outside of the learning laboratory has characterized S-R theory from the beginning. If we interpret liberalization, however, as referring to a shift from "strict constructionism," or conservative application of learning concepts, to a freer, more expanded set of definitions, then a conclusion of greater liberalization is warranted.

In our view, learning theory continues to make a significant and necessary contribution to social psychology. S-R analyses of social behavior have proven to be vigorous and tenacious and to have a positive effect by expanding research questions and stimulating alternative explanations of old and new social phenomena. The ongoing effort to understand social behavior is enriched by debates over useful concepts and principles and by empirical contests among rival positions.

REFERENCES

Allport, G. W. (1947). Scientific models and human morals. *Psychol. Rev., 54,* 182–192.

Aronfreed, J. (1968). *Conduct and conscience: the socialization of internalized control over behavior.* New York: Academic Press.

_____ (1970). The socialization of altruistic and sympathetic behavior: some theoretical and experimental analyses. In J. Macauley and L. Berkowitz (Eds.), *Altruism and helping behavior.* New York: Academic Press.

Bandura, A. (1965). Influence of models' reinforcement contingencies on the acquisition of imitative responses. *J. Pers. soc. Psychol., 1,* 589–595.

_____ (1969). Social-learning theory of identificatory processes. In D. A. Goslin (Ed.), *Handbook of socialization theory and research.* Chicago: Rand McNally.

_____ (1973). *Aggression: a social learning analysis.* Englewood Cliffs, N.J.: Prentice-Hall.

_____ (1977). *Social learning theory.* Englewood Cliffs, N.J.: Prentice-Hall.

Bandura, A., E. B. Blanchard, and B. Ritter (1969). Relative efficacy of desensitization and modeling approaches for inducing behavioral, affective, and attitudinal changes. *J. Pers. soc. Psychol., 13,* 173–199.

Bandura, A., J. E. Grusec, and F. L. Menlove (1967). Vicarious extinction of avoidance behavior. *J. Pers. soc.Psychol., 5,* 16–23.

Bandura, A., and W. Mischel (1965). Modification of self-imposed delay of reward through exposure to live and symbolic models. *J. Pers. soc. Psychol., 2,* 698–705.

Baron, R. A. (1971a). Magnitude of victim's pain cues and level of prior anger arousal as determinants of adult aggressive behavior. *J. Pers. soc. Psychol., 17,* 236–243.

_____ (1971b). Aggression as a function of magnitude of victim's pain cues, level of prior anger arousal, and aggressor-victim similarity. *J. Pers. soc. Psychol., 18,* 48–54.

_____ (1971c). Reducing the influence of an aggressive model: the restraining effects of discrepant modeling cues. *J. Pers. soc. Psychol., 20,* 240–245.

Baron, R. S., D. Moore, and G. S. Sanders (1978). Distraction as a source of drive in social facilitation research. *J. Pers. soc. Psychol., 36,* 816–824.

Barton, E. M., M. M. Baltes, and M. J. Orzech (1980). Etiology of dependence in older nursing home residents during morning care; the role of staff behavior. *J. Pers. soc. Psychol., 38,* 423–431.

Beck, H. P., and J. J. Seta (1980). The effects of frequency of feedback on a simple coaction task. *J. Pers. soc. Psychol., 38,* 75–80.

Berger, S. M. (1971). Observer's perseverance as related to a model's success: a social comparison analysis. *J. Pers. soc. Psychol., 19,* 341–350.

_____ (1979). Social comparison, modeling, and perseverance. In J. Suls and R. Miller (Eds.), *Recent advances in social comparison processes.* New York: Halsted Press.

Berger, S. M., L. L. Carli, K. S. Hammersla, J. F. Karshmer, and M. E. Sanchez (1979). Motoric and symbolic mediation in observational learning. *J. Pers. soc. Psychol., 37,* 735–746.

Berger, S. M., and W. W. Lambert (1968). Stimulus-response theory in contemporary social psychology. In G. Lindzey and E. Aronson (Eds.), *The handbook of social psychology.* (2nd ed.). Vol. 1. Reading, Mass.: Addison-Wesley.

Berkowitz, L. (1962). *Aggression: a social psychological analysis.* New York: McGraw-Hill.

_____ (1965). The concept of aggressive drive: some additional considerations. In L. Berkowitz (Ed.), *Advances in experimental social psychology.* Vol. 2. New York: Academic Press.

_____ (1974). Some determinants of impulsive aggression: role of mediated associations with reinforcements for aggression. *Psychol. Rev., 81,* 165–176.

_____ (1978). Whatever happened to the frustration-aggression hypothesis? *Amer. behav. Scient., 21,* 691–708.

_____ (1981). Aversive conditions as stimuli to aggression. Invited address to Midwestern Psychological Association.

Berkowitz, L., and W. H. Connor (1966). Success, failure, and social responsibility. *J. Pers. soc. Psychol., 4,* 664–669.

Berkowitz, L., and R. G. Geen (1966). Film violence and the cue properties of available targets. *J. Pers. soc. Psychol., 3,* 525–530.

Berkowitz, L., and A. LePage (1967). Weapons as aggression-eliciting stimuli. *J. Pers. soc. Psychol., 7,* 202–207.

Bernal, G., and S. M. Berger (1976). Vicarious eyelid conditioning. *J. Pers. soc. Psychol., 34,* 62–68.

Bleda, P. R. (1976). Conditioning and discrimination of affect and attraction. *J. Pers. soc. Psychol., 34,* 1106–1113.

Blum, E. R., and W. A. Kennedy (1967). Modification of dominant behavior in school children. *J. Pers. soc. Psychol., 7,* 275–281.

Borden, R. J. (1975). Witnessed aggression: influence of an observer's sex and values on aggressive responding. *J. Pers. soc. Psychol., 31,* 567–573.

Braun, S. H. (1972). Effects of schedules of direct or vicarious reinforcement and modeling cues on behavior in extinction. *J. Pers. soc. Psychol., 22,* 356–365.

Britt, D. W. (1971). Effects of probability of reinforcement and social stimulus consistency on imitation. *J. Pers. soc. Psychol., 18,* 189–200.

Brown, P., and E. Rogers (1965). Control of aggression in a nursery school class. *J. exp. child Psychol., 2,* 103–107.

Buss, A. H. (1966). Instrumentality of aggression, feedback, and frustration as determinants of physical aggression. *J. Pers. soc. Psychol., 3,* 153–162.

Buss, A. H., A. Booker, and E. Buss (1972). Firing a weapon and aggression. *J. Pers. soc. Psychol., 22,* 296–302.

Bussey, K., and D. G. Perry (1976). Sharing reinforcement contingencies with a model: a social-learning analysis of similarity effects in imitation research. *J. Pers. soc. Psychol., 34,* 1168–1176.

Byrne, D., and G. L. Clore (1970). A reinforcement model of evaluative responses. *Pers. int. J., 1,* 103–128.

Byrne, D., and D. Nelson (1965). Attraction as a linear function of proportion of positive reinforcements. *J. Pers. soc. Psychol., 1,* 659–663.

Cecil, J. S., R. F. Weiss, and R. A. Feinberg (1978). The reinforcing effects of the recommendation in threatening communication. *J. gen. Psychol., 98,* 65–77.

Chaikin, A. L., E. Sigler, and V. J. Devlega (1974). Non-verbal mediators of teacher expectancy effects. *J. Pers. soc. Psychol., 30,* 144–149.

Chartier, G. M., and R. L. Weiss (1974). Comparative test of positive control, negative control, and social power theories of identificatory learning in disadvantaged children. *J. Pers. soc. Psychol., 29,* 724–730.

Chien, I. (1948). Behavior theory and the behavior of attitudes: some critical comments. *Psychol. Rev., 55,* 175–188.

Clore, G. L., and D. Byrne (1974). A reinforcement-affect model of attraction. In T. L. Huston (Ed.), *Foundations of interpersonal attraction.* New York: Academic Press.

Cofer, C. N., and J. P. Foley (1942). Mediated generalization and the interpretation of verbal behavior: I. Prologemena. *Psychol. Rev., 49,* 513–540.

Cottrell, N. B. (1968). Performance in the presence of other human beings: mere presence, audience, and affiliation effects. In E. C. Simmel, R. A. Hoppe, and G. A. Milton (Eds.), *Social facilitation and imitative behavior.* Boston: Allyn and Bacon.

Cottrell, N. B., and D. L. Wack (1967). Energizing effects of cognitive dissonance upon dominant and subordinate responses. *J. Pers. soc. Psychol., 6,* 132–138.

Cunningham, M. R., J. Steinberg, and R. Grev (1980). Wanting to and having to help: separate motivations for positive mood and guilt-induced helping. *J. Pers. soc. Psych., 38,* 181–192.

Dabbs, J. M., and H. Leventhal (1966). Effects of varying the recommendations in a fear-arousing communication. *J. Pers. soc. Psychol., 4,* 525–531.

Darlington, R. B., and C. E. Macker (1966). Displacement of guilt-produced altruistic behavior. *J. Pers. soc. Psychol., 4,* 442–443.

Doob, L. W. (1947). The behavior of attitudes. *Psychol. Rev., 54,* 135–156.

Eisman (Lott) B. (1955). Attitude formation: the development of a color preference response through mediated generalization. *J. abnorm. soc. Psychol., 50,* 321–326.

Endler, N. S. (1966). Conformity as a function of different reinforcement schedules. *J. Pers. soc. Psychol., 4,* 175–180.

Endler, N. S., and E. Hoy (1967). Conformity as related to reinforcement and social pressure. *J. Pers. soc. Psychol., 7,* 197–202.

Fehrenbach, P. A., D. J. Miller, and M. H. Thelen (1979). The importance of consistency of modeling behavior upon imitation: a comparison of single and multiple models. *J. Pers. soc. Psychol., 37,* 1412–1417.

Fitz, D. (1976). A renewed look at Miller's conflict theory of aggression displacement. *J. Pers. soc. Psychol., 33,* 725–732.

Geen, R. G., and J. J. Gange (1977). Drive theory of social facilitation: twelve years of theory and research. *Psychol. Bull., 84,* 1267–1288.

Geen, R. G., and D. Stonner (1971). Effects of aggressiveness habit strength on behavior in the presence of aggression-related stimuli. *J. Pers. soc. Psychol., 17,* 149–153.

Geen, R. G., D. Stonner, and G. L. Shope (1975). The facilitation of aggression by aggression: evidence against the catharsis hypothesis. *J. Pers. soc. Psychol., 31,* 721–726.

Geer, J. H., and L. Jarmecky (1973). The effect of being responsible for reducing another's pain on subjects' response and arousal. *J. Pers. soc. Psychol., 26,* 232–237.

Geer, J. H., and A. Turteltaub (1967). Fear reduction following observation of a model. *J. Pers. soc. Psychol., 6,* 327–331.

Gewirtz, J. L., and K. G. Stingle (1968). Learning of generalized imitation as the basis for identification. *Psychol. Rev., 75,* 374–397.

Good, K. J. (1973). Social facilitation: effects of performance anticipation, evaluation, and response competition on free associations. *J. Pers. soc. Psychol., 28,* 270–275.

Goranson, R. E., and L. Berkowitz (1966). Reciprocity and responsibility reactions to prior help. *J. Pers. soc. Psychol., 3,* 227–232.

Griffitt, W. B. (1968a). Attraction toward a stranger as a function of direct and associated reinforcement. *Psychon. Sci., 11,* 147–148.

———— (1968b). Anticipated reinforcement and attraction. *Psychon. Sci., 11,* 355.

Grusec, J. E., and D. B. Brinker, Jr. (1972). Reinforcement for imitation as a social learning determinant with implications for sex-role development. *J. Pers. soc. Psychol., 21,* 149–158.

Grusec, J., and W. Mischel (1966). Model's characteristics as determinants of social learning. *J. Pers. soc. Psychol., 4,* 211–215.

Hanratty, M. A., E. O'Neal, and J. L. Sulzer (1972). Effect of frustration upon imitation of aggression. *J. Pers. soc. Psychol., 21,* 30–34.

Hetherington, E. M. (1965). A developmental study of the effects of sex of the dominant parent on sex-role preference, identification, and imitation in children. *J. Pers. soc. Psychol., 2,* 188–194.

Hetherington, E. M., and G. Frankie (1967). Effects of parental dominance, warmth, and conflict on imitation in children. *J. Pers. soc. Psychol., 6,* 119–125.

Higbee, K. L. (1969). Fifteen years of fear arousal: research on threat appeals: 1953–1968. *Psychol. Bull., 72,* 426–444.

Hilton, I. (1967). Differences in the behavior of mothers toward first- and later-born children. *J. Pers. soc. Psychol., 7,* 282–290.

Hull, C. L. (1930). Knowledge and purpose as habit mechanisms. *Psychol. Rev., 6,* 511–525.

Hull, C. L. (1943). *Principles of behavior.* New York: Appleton-Century-Crofts.

Insko, C. A. (1965). Verbal reinforcement of attitudes. *J. Pers. soc. Psychol., 2,* 621–623.

Insko, C. A., and K. W. Butzine (1967). Rapport, awareness, and verbal reinforcement of attitude. *J. Pers. soc. Psychol., 6,* 225–228.

Insko, C. A., and R. B. Cialdini (1969). A test of three interpretations of attitudinal verbal reinforcement. *J. Pers. soc. Psychol., 12,* 333–341.

Isen, A. M., and P. F. Levin (1972). Effect of feeling good on helping: cookies and kindness. *J. Pers. soc. Psychol., 21,* 384–388.

Janis, I. L., D. Kaye, and P. Kirschner (1965). Facilitating effects of "eating-while-reading" on responsiveness to persuasive communications. *J. Pers. soc. Psychol., 1,* 181–186.

Kanfer, F. H. (1971). The maintenance of behavior by self-generated stimuli and reinforcement. In A. Jacobs and L. B. Sachs (Eds.), *The psychology of private events.* New York: Academic Press.

_____ (1979). Personal control, social control, and altruism: can society survive the age of individualism? *Amer. Psychologist, 34,* 231–239.

Kanfer, F. H., and M. L. Seidner (1973). Self-control: factors enhancing tolerance of noxious stimulation. *J. Pers. soc. Psychol., 25,* 381–389.

Kenrick, D. T., D. J. Baumann, and R. B. Cialdini (1979). A step in the socialization of altruism as hedonism: effects of negative mood on children's generosity. *J. Pers. soc. Psychol., 37,* 747–755.

Kenrick, D. T., and R. B. Cialdini (1977). Romantic attraction: misattribution versus reinforcement explanations. *J. Pers. soc. Psychol., 35,* 381–391.

Kenrick, D. T., and G. A. Johnson (1979). Interpersonal attraction in aversive environments: a problem for the classical conditioning paradigm? *J. Pers. soc. Psychol., 37,* 572–579.

Kerns, C. D. (1975). Effects of schedule and amount of observed reinforcement on response persistence. *J. Pers. soc. Psychol., 31,* 983–991.

Kian, M., S. Rosen, and A. Tesser (1973). Reinforcement effects of attitude similarity and source evaluation on discrimination learning. *J. Pers. soc. Psychol., 27,* 366–371.

Krebs, D. (1975). Empathy and altruism. *J. Pers. soc. Psychol., 32,* 1134–1146.

Lambert, W. W. (1954). Stimulus-response contiguity and reinforcement theory in social psychology. In G. Lindzey (Ed.), *Handbook of social psychology.* Vol. I. Reading, Mass.: Addison-Wesley.

Lerner, L., and R. L. Weiss (1972). Role of value of reward and model affective response in vicarious reinforcement. *J. Pers. soc. Psychol., 21,* 93–100.

Leventhal, H., and R. P. Singer (1966). Affect arousal and positioning of recommendations in persuasive communication. *J. Pers. soc. Psychol., 4,* 137–146.

Loew, C. A. (1967). Acquisition of a hostile attitude and its relationship to aggressive behavior. *J. Pers. soc. Psychol., 5,* 335–341.

Lombardo, J. P., R. F. Weiss, and W. Buchanan (1972). Reinforcing and attracting functions of yielding. *J. Pers. soc. Psychol., 21,* 359–368.

Lombardo, J. P., R. F. Weiss, and M. H. Stich (1973). Effectance reduction through speaking in reply and its relation to attraction. *J. Pers. soc. Psychol., 28,* 325–332.

Lott, A. J., and B. E. Lott (1966). Group cohesiveness and individual learning. *J. educ. Psychol., 57,* 61–73.

_____ (1968). A learning theory approach to interpersonal attitudes. In A. G. Greenwald, T. C. Brock, and T. M. Ostrom (Eds.), *Psychological foundations of attitudes.* New York: Academic Press.

_____ (1969). Liked and disliked persons as reinforcing stimuli. *J. Pers. soc. Psychol., 11,* 129–137.

_____ (1972). The power of liking: consequences of interpersonal attitudes derived from a liberalized view of secondary reinforcement. In L. Berkowitz (Ed.), *Advances in experimental social psychology.* Vol. 6. New York: Academic Press.

_____ (1974). The role of reward in the formation of positive interpersonal attitudes. In T. L. Huston (Ed.), *Foundations of interpersonal attraction.* New York: Academic Press.

Lott, A. J., B. E. Lott, T. Reed, and T. Crow (1970). Personality-trait descriptions of differentially liked persons. *J. Pers. soc. Psychol., 16,* 284–290.

Lott, A. J., B. E. Lott, and M. L. Walsh (1970). Learning of paired associates relevant to differentially liked persons. *J. Pers. soc. Psychol., 16,* 274–283.

Lott, B. E. (1961). Group cohesiveness: a learning phenomenon. *J. soc. Psychol., 55,* 275–286.

Lott, B. E., and A. J. Lott (1960). The formation of positive attitudes toward group members. *J. abnorm. soc. Psychol., 61,* 297–300.

Maddux, J. E., and R. W. Rogers (1980). Effects of source expertness, physical attractiveness, and supporting arguments on persuasion: a case of brains over beauty. *J. Pers. soc. Psychol., 39,* 235–244.

Markus, H. (1978). The effect of mere presence on social facilitation: an unobtrusive test. *J. exp. soc. Psychol., 14,* 389–397.

Masters, J. C., F. R. Gordon, and L. V. Clark (1976). Effects of self-dispensed and externally dispensed model consequences on acquisition, spontaneous and oppositional imitation and long-term retention. *J. Pers. soc. Psychol., 33,* 421–430.

Meichenbaum, D. H., K. S. Bowers, and R. R. Ross (1969). A behavioral analysis of teacher expectancy effect. *J. Pers. soc. Psychol., 13,* 306–316.

Meyer, T. P. (1972). Effects of viewing justified and unjustified real film violence on aggressive behavior. *J. Pers. soc. Psychol., 23,* 21–29.

Midlarsky, E., and J. H. Bryan (1967). Training charity in children. *J. Pers. soc. Psychol., 5,* 408–415.

Miller, N. E. (1959). Extensions of liberalized S-R theory. In S. Koch (Ed.), *Psychology: a study of a science.* Vol. 2. New York: McGraw-Hill.

Miller, N. E., and J. Dollard (1941). *Social learning and imitation.* New Haven: Yale Univ. Press.

Miller, R. L., P. Brickman, and D. Bolen (1975). Attribution versus persuasion as a means for modifying behavior. *J. Pers. soc. Psychol., 31,* 430–441.

Mischel, W., and J. Grusec (1966). Determinants of the rehearsal and transmission of neutral and aversive behaviors. *J. Pers. soc. Psychol., 3,* 197–205.

Mowrer, O. H. (1954). The psychologist looks at language. *Amer. Psychologist, 9,* 660–694.

—— (1960). *Learning theory and the symbolic processes.* New York: Wiley.

Mussen, P. H., and A. L. Parker (1965). Mother nurturance and girls' incidental imitative learning. *J. Pers. soc. Psychol., 2,* 94–97.

Osgood, C. E. (1952). The nature and measurement of meaning. *Psychol. Bull., 49,* 197–237.

Page, M. M., and R. J. Scheidt (1971). The elusive weapons effect: demand awareness, evaluation apprehension, and slightly sophisticated subjects. *J. Pers. soc. Psychol., 20,* 304–318.

Pallak, M. S., and T. S. Pittman (1972). General motivational effects of dissonance arousal. *J. Pers. soc. Psychol., 21,* 349–358.

Parke, R. D., W. Ewall, and R. G. Slaby (1972). Hostile and helpful verbalizations as regulators of nonverbal aggression. *J. Pers. soc. Psychol., 23,* 243–248.

Perry, D. G., and K. Bussey (1979). The social learning theory of sex differences: imitation is alive and well. *J. Pers. soc. Psychol., 37,* 1699–1712.

Powers, P. C., and R. G. Geen (1972). Effects of the behavior and the perceived arousal of a model on instrumental aggression. *J. Pers. soc. Psychol., 23,* 175–183.

Reiter, L. A., and B. M. DeVellis (1976). Conditioned suppression in humans produced by a human stimulus. *J. Pers. soc. Psychol., 34,* 223–227.

Richardson, D. C., S. Bernstein, and S. P. Taylor (1979). The effect of situational contingencies on female retaliative behavior. *J. Pers. soc. Psychol., 37,* 2044–2048.

Rocha, R. F., and R. W. Rogers (1976). Ares and Babbitt in the classroom. Effects of competition and reward on children's aggression. *J. Pers. soc. Psychol., 33,* 588–593.

Rogers, R. W. (1980). Expressions of aggression: aggression-inhibiting effects of anonymity to authority and threatened retaliation. *Pers. soc. Psychol. Bull., 6,* 315–320.

Rosekrans, M. A. (1967). Imitation in children as a function of perceived similarity to a social model and vicarious reinforcement. *J. Pers. soc. Psychol., 7,* 307–315.

Rosekrans, M. A., and W. W. Hartup (1967). Imitative influences of consistent and inconsistent response consequences to a model on aggressive behavior in children. *J. Pers. soc. Psychol., 7,* 429–434.

Rosenberg, M. J. (1965). When dissonance fails: on eliminating evaluation apprehension from attitude measurement. *J. Pers. soc. Psychol., 1,* 28–42.

Rosenhan, D. L. (1972). Learning theory and prosocial behavior. *J. soc. Issues, 28,* 151–163.

Rosenhan, D., and G. M. White (1967). Observation and rehearsal as determinants of prosocial behavior. *J. Pers. soc. Psychol., 5,* 424–431.

Rubovitz, P. C., and M. L. Maehr (1971). Pygmalion analyzed: toward an explanation of the Rosenthal-Jacobson findings. *J. Pers. soc. Psychol., 19,* 197–203.

Sanders, G. S., and R. S. Baron (1975). The motivating effects of distraction on task performance. *J. Pers. soc. Psychol., 32,* 956–963.

Schlenker, B. R., R. C. Brown, Jr., and J. T. Tedeschi (1975). Attraction and expectations of harm and benefits. *J. Pers. soc. Psychol., 32,* 664–670.

Serbin, L. A., J. M. Connor, and C. C. Citron (1978). Environmental control of independent and dependent behaviors in preschool girls and boys: a model for early independence training. *Sex Roles, 4,* 867–875.

Skinner, B. F. (1971). *Beyond freedom and dignity.* New York: Knopf.

—— (1975). The steep and thorny way to a science of behavior. *Amer. Psychologist, 30,* 42–49.

Snyder, M., E. D. Tanke, and E. Berscheid (1977). Social perception and interpersonal behavior: on the self-fulfilling nature of social stereotypes. *J. Pers. soc. Psychol., 35,* 656–666.

Staats, A. W. (1968). Social behaviorism and human motivation: principles of the attitude-reinforcer-discriminative system. In A. G. Greenwald, T. C. Brock, and T. M. Ostrom (Eds.), *Psychological foundations of attitudes.* New York: Academic Press.

Staats, A. W., M. C. Gross, P. F. Guay, and C. C. Carlson (1973). Personality and social systems and attitude-reinforcer-discriminative theory: interest (attitude) formation, function, and measurement. *J. Pers. soc. Psychol., 26,* 251–261.

Staats, A. W., K. A. Minke, C. H. Martin, and W. R. Higa (1972). Deprivation-satiation and strength of attitude conditioning: a test of attitude-reinforcer-discriminative theory. *J. Pers. soc. Psychol., 24,* 178–185.

Staats, A. W., and C. K. Staats (1958). Attitudes established by classical conditioning. *J. abnorm. soc. Psychol., 57,* 37–40.

Stapert, J. C., and G. L. Clore (1969). Attraction and disagreement-produced arousal. *J. Pers. soc. Psychol., 13,* 64–69.

Steigleder, M. K., R. F. Weiss, S. S. Balling, V. L. Wenninger, and J. P. Lombardo (1980). Drivelike motivational properties of competitive behavior. *J. Pers. soc. Psychol., 38,* 93–104.

Steigleder, M. K., R. F. Weiss, R. E. Cramer, and R. A. Feinberg (1978). Motivating and reinforcing functions of competitive behavior. *J. Pers. soc. Psychol., 36,* 1291–1301.

Swart, C., and L. Berkowitz (1976). Effects of a stimulus associated with a victim's pain on later aggression. *J. Pers. soc. Psychol., 33,* 623–631.

Turner, C. W., L. S. Simons, L. Berkowitz, and A. Frodi (1977). The stimulating and inhibiting effects of weapons on aggressive behavior. *Aggressive Behav., 3,* 355–378.

Waterman, C. K., and E. S. Katkin (1967). Energizing (dynamogenic) effect of cognitive dissonance on task performance. *J. Pers. soc. Psychol., 6,* 126–131.

Weiss, R. F. (1968). An extension of Hullian learning theory to persuasive communication. In A. G. Greenwald, T. C. Brock, and T. M. Ostrom (Eds.), *Psychological foundations of attitudes*. New York: Academic Press.

Weiss, R. F., J. L. Boyer, J. P. Lombardo, and M. H. Stich (1973). Altruistic drive and altruistic reinforcement. *J. Pers. soc. Psychol., 25,* 390–400.

Weiss, R. F., W. Buchanan, L. Altstatt, and J. P. Lombardo (1971). Altruism is rewarding. *Science, 171,* 1262–1263.

Weiss, R. F., J. P. Lombardo, D. R. Warren, and K. A. Kelley (1971). Reinforcing effects of speaking in reply. *J. Pers. soc. Psychol., 20,* 186–199.

Weiss, R. F., and F. G. Miller (1971). The drive theory of social facilitation. *Psychol. Rev., 78,* 44–57.

Weiss, R. F., F. G. Miller, C. J. Langan, and J. S. Cecil (1971). Social facilitation of attitude change. *Psychon. Sci., 22,* 113–114.

Weyant, J. M. (1978). Effects of mood states, costs, and benefits in helping. *J. Pers. soc. Psychol., 36,* 1169–1176.

Wheeler, L. (1966). Toward a theory of behavioral contagion. *Psychol. Rev., 73,* 179–192.

Wheeler, L., and S. Smith (1967). Censure of the model in the contagion of aggression. *J. Pers. soc. Psychol.,* 693–698.

Zajonc, R. B. (1965). Social facilitation. *Science, 149,* 269–274.

CHAPTER 4

The Cognitive Perspective in Social Psychology

Hazel Markus
R. B. Zajonc
University of Michigan

THE GROWTH OF THE COGNITIVE PERSPECTIVE IN SOCIAL PSYCHOLOGY

The social psychology of the fifties and sixties was characterized by a diversity of approaches. Some research was framed in stimulus-response language, some in the field-theoretical and Gestalt traditions, and the remainder was conceptualized in cognitive terms. The change since then has been of revolutionary proportions, impelling nearly all investigators to view social psychological phenomena from the cognitive perspective. Social psychology and cognitive social psychology are today nearly synonymous. The cognitive approach is now clearly the dominant approach among social psychologists, having virtually no competitors.

Even those approaches thoroughly identified with the S-R position, such as social learning theory (Bandura, 1977), are now transformed so that their conceptual language, like the language of verbal learning (J. R. Anderson and Bower, 1973), is increasingly cognitive. This adoption of the cognitive view among social psychologists has been so complete that it is extremely difficult for most of the workers in the field to conceive of a viable alternative. Given a problem, the tendency to frame it in cognitive terms—to begin by inquiring how the situation, the stimuli, and the variables controlling the responses are represented in the minds of the participants—is nearly automatic. The result is that one can no longer view today's social psychology as the study of social behavior. It is more accurate to define it as the study of the social mind.

The traditional way of distinguishing the cognitive approach from its immediately preceding competitor, the stimulus-response (S-R) approach, was to insist on the participation of an active organism (O) that intervened between the stimulus and the response. The formula for the cognitive approach was written S-O-R. The organism performed operations that transformed the stimulus, and it was the stimulus thus transformed that mediated the response. The role assigned to O in the S-O-R chain was at first quite modest and limited, and the transformations performed by the undefined and unspecified O were seldom of critical consequence. The major contributions of O were studied in the problems of

The work on this chapter was supported by National Institute for Mental Health Grant MH29753 to Hazel Markus and National Science Foundation Grant BS-8117977 to R. B. Zajonc. We wish to thank E. Tory Higgins, Darrin Lehman, Paula S. Nurius, and Thomas M. Ostrom for their helpful comments.

inaccurate perception, selective attention and memory, and context effects.

In this S–O–R formulation, one was compelled to view both S (the stimulus) and R (the response) as having existence *outside* the organism. This, of course, was as it should be for the Skinnerians. The hallmark of their approach was a commitment to the external nature of stimulation and to the overt nature of responses. The purpose of the analysis of behavior, according to their view, was to identify the parameters of control that specifiable stimuli in the environment exercise over observable responses of the organism.

Eventually, however, O assumed a more significant role. It became an acceptable euphemism for *mind,* eclipsing the S–R bond and absorbing it into hypothetical internal organizations such as associative networks, schemas, scripts, and other not directly verifiable structures. Operationalism's credo that dictated a primary commitment to observable processes was supplanted by the explicit affirmation of the mind as the most important and significant link in the entire behavioral process. The concern with stimuli, with their psychophysical properties, and with responses and their topography, receded into the background and was replaced by a focus on internal representational states.

The essential link in the behavioral process became an active cognitive construction of the environment—a product of individual and social factors. The earlier S–R view of the organism as simply an arena where stimuli select among responses is now without advocates. The social psychology of the seventies and of the eighties takes it for granted that internal representations mediate between the stimulus and its behavioral consequences and that these representations dominate the entire process. The implicit idea is that we can understand social behavior only if we understand the precise nature of these representations. Much of the research in social psychology is, therefore, concerned with identifying the properties of these representations, examining their stability in memory, and assessing their vulnerability to change as a result of new information. Strictly speaking, today's approach to behavior must be represented as O–S–O–R. It is now recognized that the internal states not only mediate between the stimuli of the environment and the responses but that what stimuli are attended to and what stimuli are ignored is under the selective control of the organism as well. A clear shift of focus has thus taken place. Interest in the contribution of the *stimulus* to the variability of individual's responses has been replaced with a much

more consuming interest in the contribution of the cognizing *organism* (cf. Lewin, 1946, 1951).

This fundamental shift in emphasis toward the cognitive view was foreshadowed for decades. Most definitions of social psychology, even those proposed quite early, reflect the incipient dominance of the cognitive approach. G. W. Allport (1968), whose definition has been cited and paraphrased most often, defined social psychology as "an attempt to understand and explain how thought, feeling, and behavior of individuals are influenced by the actual, imagined, or implied presence of others" (p. 3). Note that among the phenomena to be explained, *thought* occupies the dominant position—*before* action and feeling. And among the independent variables the influence of the presence of others may be *imagined* and *implied*—processes of purely cognitive form. Other early writers also acknowledged the heavy reliance of social psychological concepts and formulations on cognitive processes. For example, Krech and Crutchfield (1948) insisted that "if we are to understand social behavior, we must know how all perceptions, memories, fantasies are combined or integrated or organized into...*cognitive structures*" (p. 77).

When viewed in historical context, the dominance of the cognitive emphasis in social psychology is nearly inevitable. The factors that contributed to the field's reliance on the cognitive perspective are numerous, and they converged to make the social psychologists' choice of a paradigm a highly determined one. The heavy emphasis on attitudes, the apparent complexity of social behavior and its antecedents, the nearly exclusive concern with adult humans, the extensive use of verbal responses and of judgments and opinions as measures of the dependent variables—all required a cognitive approach. Moreover, the two major competitors to the cognitive view in social psychology, the stimulus-response and the psychoanalytic positions, did not lend themselves to the type of experimental work that became central in social psychological research.

The psychoanalytic approach did not yield experimental applications because its variables were even more inaccessible to direct measurement or manipulation than those of the cognitive approach. The S–R approach, in contrast, did provide precision of measurement and standard ways of manipulating the experimental variables, but it required units of observation and a level of analysis that were so fine-grained that it could adequately represent only a limited range of social behavior. The S–R microanalysis invoked S–R bonds, habits, generalization gradients, and fractional anticipatory goal responses. It necessitated a decomposition of social behavior into units that were unsatisfyingly constricted.

The Miller and Dollard (1941) liberalization of the Hull-Spence position tried to render it more accessible for social psychology, but this revision also required the observation of behavior in its primitive and restricted form. Finally, a feature that made the cognitive approach especially attractive to a very wide group of researchers—a feature that conceivably could have made it *less* attractive—was the relative invulnerability of the cognitive analysis to empirical falsification. Experiments in cognitive social psychology are often easy to run and their conclusions hard to disprove.

There were thus hardly any viable theoretical alternatives to the cognitive view, and today's social psychology is nearly completely cognitive. While the exact point of emphasis or the level of analysis may vary, the focus is nearly always cognitive. It is concerned with attributions, inferences, judgments and decisions, and the cognitive structures and processes that are implicated in them. The experimental tasks are cognitive and involve measures of categorization, recall, recognition, and reaction time. The experimental context is created through cognitive means by allowing subjects to form anticipations about the nature and purpose of the experiment through instructions. Even the critique of social psychological experimentation is cognitive in nature. In studies of experimenter effects or demand characteristics, the emphasis is on what the subjects *think* they are expected to do or accomplish in a given experiment (Zajonc, 1980a).

The cognitive perspective, however, invites a new concern absent in our other approaches. We do not ask of an S–R bond if it is "true" or "valid." But cognitions are *about* the world, and questions of veridicality necessarily arise. And so do questions about rationality. Now that O contributes of its own to the behavioral process, is this contribution producing a closer correspondence between stimuli and cognitions or does it cause divergence (Gibson and Gibson, 1955)?

THE COGNITIVE REVOLUTION

The corresponding chapter in the second edition of the *Handbook* (Lindzey and Aronson, 1968, p. 391) ended with the expectation that the emphasis on cognitive *dynamics* prevalent during the sixties, with its particular focus on cognitive dissonance and balance, would soon be combined with the earlier descriptive approaches that focused on the *structural* and substantive properties of cognitions. This expectation for an integrated approach to social cognition was definitely not realized. Not only have the seventies and the early eighties failed to achieve a synthesis of the dynamic and descriptive approaches, but for the most part they have abandoned cognitive dynamics altogether. Today's cognitive approaches in social psychology show little concern with the dynamic properties of cognitions—those that posit forces and interdependence among cognitions and produce changes over time. Until quite recently, extracognitive dynamics, such as motivation and emotion, were also shunned. In fact, the consequence of the major theoretical effort of the last two decades was to produce a motivation-free and emotion-free explanation of social behavior.

What happened to the emphasis on dynamic factors prevalent during the sixties? Two sources of forces were analyzed in social cognition of this period: structural dynamics and motivational dynamics. From Gestalt psychology came the notion of structural and configurational forces invoked to explain interdependence and interaction among cognitions—a trend beginning with the early work of Lewis (1941), Heider (1944, 1946), and Asch (1946). From behaviorism came motivational forces, external to structural dynamics. The motivational forces consisted mainly of the demands placed on the behaving and adapting organism in the form of goals, needs, incentives, and attitudes, all of which were factors assumed to have a profound driving and reinforcing influence on cognitive processes (F. H. Allport, 1955). The first set of forces were what the New Look in perception classified as *autochthonous factors*. The second set of forces were called *behavioral factors*. Autochthonous factors (Bruner, 1951) derived from the features of the stimulus and from the structure of information. They reflected objective reality that existed independently of the perceiver. The behavioral factors imposed the individual's fears, wishes, and passions on this vulnerable reflection of objective reality and thus constituted the individual's own construction of that reality.

Note that both structural and motivational concepts were the basic classes of concepts of field theory (Deutsch, 1968). The presence of structural tension systems assumed to pervade interacting cognitions afforded an explanatory basis for cognitive change and for resistance to change, i.e., for the maintenance and stability of structures. Congruity, dissonance, and balance were dynamics that were indigenous to cognitions themselves. Motivational dynamics derived from the individuals' commerce with the environment. Individuals' needs, motives, values, incentives, and relationships to objects in the environment were assumed to have an independent influence on cognitions. These latter factors, therefore, formed a conceptual bridge between cognitions and the environment by postulating behavioral mechanisms that were engaged when the individual confronted information.

The New Look challenged a previous view of perception and cognition as passive and dispassionate processes and conceptualized them as useful functions of an adapting organism. Individuals were regarded as willing to forgo perceptual veridicality if they could thereby avoid embarrassment and displeasure. They were viewed as able to defend themselves from threatening perceptions. They were thought to be highly selective in representing their own environment, seeking to achieve and maintain a coherent view of the world. Perception and cognition were thus obedient to goals, needs, and fears and were at times more subservient to these inner states than to the constraints of reality (Bruner and Goodman, 1947; Bruner, 1951). By postulating such needs as exploration (Montgomery, 1954), curiosity (Berlyne, 1955, 1960), intolerance for ambiguity (Adorno *et al.*, 1950), desire for uncertainty reduction (Berlyne, 1957), avoidance of cognitive conflict (G. W. Allport, 1937), open and closed minds (Rokeach, 1960), the social psychologist hoped to understand such phenomena as selective perception (Bruner and Krech, 1950), distortion (Bruner and Goodman, 1947), biasing (Lorge, 1936), and selective forgetting (Meltzer, 1930).

The dynamic approach to social cognition produced a rich conceptual base for the analysis of numerous social psychological phenomena and spawned a vast empirical literature (F. H. Allport, 1955). Toward the end of the sixties, however, the concern with the dynamic forces underlying the interactions among cognitions was replaced by a concern with the products of more complex cognitive processes, such as inference and attribution, and with a focus on the nature of cognitive representations. This change in emphasis resulted in part from the difficulties encountered in understanding *simultaneously* both the *internal* cognitive dynamics and the relations of *behavioral* dynamics to cognitions. The understanding of the dynamics of cognitions seemed to require an understanding of the cognitions themselves and how they were represented or structured. The voluminous research effort directed to the analysis of consistency phenomena, for example, failed to reveal much specific information

about the cognitive dynamics that held structures together or led to separation of elements. This failure stems from our lack of understanding of what comprised units of cognition and from the ambiguity regarding the psychological nature of the presumed noxious states of imbalance.

Moreover, it never became clear *how* causal contact was made between needs, drives, and emotions on the one hand and cognitions on the other. In general, consistency theories relied on constructs such as needs, goals, drives, tensions, and conflict to generate the energy that guided, directed, and produced behavior. Unfortunately, these were inaccessible variables about which there was little theoretical sophistication and for which measurement instrumentation was practically nonexistent. In what systems—cognition, motivation, affect—were the underpinnings of these dynamics to be found and how were they activated and represented? With respect to dissonance, for example, researchers experienced considerable difficulty in finding empirical confirmation for the existence of tension and for the aversive nature of dissonant states (Greenwald, 1975), although such evidence was eventually supplied (Cottrell and Wack, 1967; Zanna and Cooper, 1974; Kiesler and Pallak, 1976; Zanna, Higgins, and Taves, 1976). There was so little information about the elements of cognitive structures and about their properties that the elusiveness of the dynamics and the vagueness surrounding their mechanisms soon began to impede progress.

The inflection point of the transition from dynamic to descriptive perspective can be fixed to 1965 and the publication of Jones and Davis's (1965) theory of inference and attribution and D. Bem's (1965, 1967, 1972) self-perception critique of cognitive dissonance. These approaches sought to provide a direct link between cognition and behavior (although in the new conception cognition and behavior traded their roles as the independent and dependent variables). The assumption of dynamic processes, such as aversive tension and drive, was considered unnecessary. The individual's own behavior and that of others became the data base from which inferences about internal states could be drawn by that individual. At the same time the very internal states that were inferred by the individual from his or her own behavior were accorded only negligible influence over behavior. From this perspective the response thus became the stimulus for social perception and cognition.

Bem's (1965) paper was written from the point of view of radical behaviorism and was based on Skinner's distinction between mands and tacts as forms of stimulus control over behavior. Like Schachter and Singer (1962), Bem argued that internal events are interpreted by observing external outcomes. Thus individuals know their own attitudes through observing their own behavior and the reactions of the social environment to it. But observing behavior is not a simple or a singular process. New questions thus emerged: How was the behavior encoded; how was it organized, retained, retrieved, and utilized in forming attitudes and preferences?

Bem's paper tried to replace the inaccessible "hot" internal states postulated by the theory of cognitive dissonance (and basically inimical to the Skinnerian position) with *observable* features of stimulus control. Ironically, the paper did not succeed either in eliminating the emphasis on covert internal states or in promoting a greater reliance on stimulus control. On the contrary, these ideas on self-perception coupled with the growth of attribution theory (Jones and Davis, 1965; Kelley, 1967) led to an ever-increasing cognitive imperialism—the postulating of a *new* variety of internal states and processes, all as inaccessible to direct observation as needs, goals, and conflicts among cognitions.

The emphasis on self-perception and attribution marked the beginning of a decreasing concern with cognitive dynamics and with motivational and emotional variables—in short, with all "hot" cognition. From this point on, cognitive and perceptual phenomena that involved distortion, inaccuracy, or selectivity were explained parsimoniously without invoking values, needs, tensions, emotions, anxiety, arousal, or any other "hot" factors. In fact, according to the prevalent conception, these "hot" factors had little influence on anything at all. The idea was that all behavior could be explained entirely by its "cold" information-processing antecedents. The link, however, between individuals' cognitions of their own behavior (or that of others) and their present ongoing overt behavior was decidedly ambiguous. And this ambiguity remains in current social cognition research (Watson, 1982).

A number of other developments also led the field away from its preoccupation with cognitive dynamics. First, within the field of learning and memory there was a vigorous concern with the way stimulus information was represented in memory. The idea of the human organism as an information processor became popular. The mind came to be viewed by many as a computerlike apparatus that registered the incoming information and then subjected it to a variety of transformations before ordering a

response. This information transformation, which eventually influenced overt behavior (in ways still to be determined), was seen as an orderly linear process that could be modeled by a flowchart. The information-processing analogy was viewed as the "cool" alternative to the "hot" consistency theories.

The computer analogy led away from a concern with cognitive dynamics and to an emphasis on how social information gleaned from the environment was represented and how it was processed, stored, and retrieved for the purpose of inference, attribution, judgment, evaluation, and other forms of cognitive operations. Prediction and explanation of behavior were completely dependent on the outcome of the analysis of cognition. If the individual engaged in behavior A rather than B, it was because the individual in some way (conscious or unconscious) *evaluated* A to be the preferred course of action. And conversely, if A was seen by the person as preferable to B, then behavior A would surely be executed.

The following literature review focuses on research that is formulated in terms of cognitive processes. And as was the case in the second edition of the *Handbook* (Lindzey and Aronson, 1968), we focus primarily on material that is of theoretical significance. The literature explosion in social cognition makes an exhaustive review of the field, with its wealth of empirical findings, impossible within the scope of this chapter. Therefore only some of the important basic issues can be considered.

COGNITIVE REPRESENTATIONS

Most of the critical questions of social cognition cannot be definitively resolved until we understand how social knowledge is represented. It is still a matter of some conjecture how knowledge *in general*—even quite elementary knowledge—is represented by the individual, and the problem of the representation of social knowledge is even more complex.

What is a *representation?* Empirical and theoretical work in social and in experimental cognition has occupied itself primarily with mental representations, focusing, in the vast majority of instances, on verbally rooted representations. In part, the nearly exclusive emphasis on linguistic and propositional representations is a consequence of the adoption of the computer model of information processing.

At the minimum a *representation* is some event within the organism that *stands for* some object or event. The referent object or event can be external to the organism or internal. It can be the neighbor's cat or one's own bladder pressure. And it must be arbitrarily specified by the experimenter. If it was not so specified, there would always be confusion about what it is that is being represented by the individual. It is not always certain what the individual is in fact attending to. But even if we know what the individual is attending to, the problem is not solved. Some cognitions are direct transformations of a sensory input, and one could achieve experimental control over sensory input so that there would be little question about the object of a given cognition. But there are also higher-order cognitions, such as our thoughts of a false impression we once had. Here the problem of experimental control over the referent is much more serious.

Representational events can assume a variety of forms—many of them in parallel and partially independent. We can speak of neural representations, mental representations, or motor representations, and there is no reason why various other processes of the organism could not perform representational functions as well (Zajonc and Markus, 1982, 1983). Thus an accelerated heart rate that occurs as a result of a fear-arousing stimulus may well become a partial representation of the stimulus object, such that the organism would have a tendency to experience some, however minimal, acceleration of the heart on future confrontations of the same or a similar fear-producing object. Note that this minimal form of representation is simply one aspect of classical conditioning and of stimulus generalization.

Note also from the above example that *at the minimum* a cognitive representation need not be verbal, iconic, sensory, or neural, but it can assume all and any of these forms. Moreover, there need not be a one-to-one correspondence between the representational event and the referent event, nor need there be an isomorphism. A one-to-one correspondence is not given in language since any one word can have several meanings and any one object can assume a variety of verbal designations. And except for onomatopoeia, no isomorphism is to be found in language. Thus those cognitive representations that are studied most extensively by social psychologists—namely, verbal representations—require neither a one-to-one correspondence nor isomorphism with their referent objects and events.

The analysis of cognitive processes, both in general experimental and in social psychology, has proceeded without waiting until we discover the precise nature of representations—a problem that is beyond today's knowledge and techniques (J. R. Anderson, 1978). For the time being the assumption has been that whatever a representation might be and whatever its units, they must be somehow organized and related to each other. It has also been assumed that the process of retrieval of these units would follow the constraints of cognitive organization and that the conditions of input would determine the way in which newly acquired information is represented and organized. By constraining the conditions of input and observing the time relations, pattern, order, and grouping of the person's responses, one can make fair guesses both about the nature of the cognitive organization and about the units of which it must consist. It is, to be sure, a bootstrapping operation, because observing correspondence and systematic discrepancy between input and output requires inferences about both the nature of the transformation of the input and the process that transpires to extract the particular output from the transformed input. Nevertheless, considerable progress has been made, and while there are a variety of theories about the cognitive structure of representations, they have a great deal in common.

COGNITIVE STRUCTURES

HISTORICAL BACKGROUND AND RECENT EXAMPLES

In the voluminous attribution literature that began with the work of Bem (1965), Jones and Davis (1965), and Kelley (1967), some of the most intriguing findings were those showing significant departures from the normative model of causal explanation. Investigators repeatedly found instances of errors, bias, and distortion (Jones and Nisbett, 1971; L. Ross, Bierbrauer, and Polly, 1974; Miller and M. Ross, 1975; L. Ross, 1977b). Very often people did not seem to conform to the model of the individual as "naive scientist." However reasonable the assumptions of Heider (1958) and Kelley (1967), it was apparent that the perceiver did not attend to all the available information and was not particularly adept at evaluating, in an impartial manner, the independent contributions of persons, situations, and entities to the observed effect. Perceivers are selective in what they notice, learn, remember, or infer in any situation. These selective tendencies, these departures from the normative model of how and what information is eventually achieved from the environment, are not random, however. The pervasive errors and biases that result from such selective information processing are very often quite systematic.

The explanation of these systematic biases or selective tendencies required investigators to postulate the existence of internal cognitive structures and mechanisms. Systematic errors imply systematic origins. If there were regularity in the biases, the sources generating them must also have some regularity—there had to be some structure that had properties likely to produce these biases. A primary role of these cognitive structures and mechanisms was to determine what information from the social environment would eventually be represented and how it would be categorized and stored. With a focus on these mediating structures it became possible to understand what and why departures from the normative models of attribution theory might be expected and how they can be predicted.

The cognitive view asserted that information could only be processed if the perceiver had some type of internal perceptual or cognitive structure with which to receive and organize it. Neisser (1976) called these internal mechanisms "schemas" and suggested that they were necessary components of all perception and cognition. He wrote, "Perceivers pick up only what we have schemas for and willy-nilly ignore the rest" (p. 80). Not all investigators studying cognitive structure assumed such a strong position about the necessity of cognitive schemas, but there was little argument with the idea that some events, situations, behavior, and aspects of people were much more likely to be attended to and processed than others because of the perceiver's cognitive structures.

In earlier work Bruner's (1951) concept of "hypotheses" played such a role, and he wrote insightfully of perceiving as taking "place in a 'tuned organism' " (p. 124). Woodworth (1947) aptly noted that we not only see but look for, and we not only hear but listen to. These structures, called "cognitive structures" in early social psychological writings and now often referred to as "knowledge structures," were assumed to be organizations of stored information achieved as a result of prior information processing. They were thought to operate as frameworks for organizing and interpreting the social environment.

Once investigators allowed for the possibility of these internal structures, it was readily evident that not all information potentially available in the environment was diagnostic, useful, or equally likely to be processed. The usefulness of a particular set of stimuli was dependent, in large part, on the nature of the relationship between the internal structure and the experienced event. If the data associated with a particular event were relevant to a perceiver's internal "theory" or schema, they assumed a special status within the range of stimuli. An event, a concept, an object, or a behavior that "fit" a particular internal structure was more likely to be attended to and processed than one that did not. This approach assumed an active perceiver or cognizer—an individual heavily involved in constructing his or her own social reality (Moscovici, 1983).

An emphasis on cognitive structures has implications for attribution theory. Perceivers do not always experience "effects" (persons, behaviors, situations) in similar ways. The effect perceived depends on the available internal structures and how they have been used during processing. Both the "effect" and the range of "causes" that are invoked for understanding it are importantly determined by the internal structures that were initially activated to comprehend the event.

Internal structures were given a variety of names including *inferential sets* (e.g., Jones and Thibaut, 1958), *hypotheses* (e.g., Bruner, 1951), *theories* (e.g., Epstein, 1973), *scripts* (e.g., Abelson, 1976), *themes* (Lingle and Ostrom, 1981), *frames* (e.g., Minsky, 1975), *categories* (e.g., Rosch, 1973; Smith and Medin, 1981), *prototypes* (e.g., Cantor and Mischel, 1977, 1979), *attitudes* (e.g., Tesser and Cowan, 1975, 1977), and *schemas* (e.g., Stotland and Canon, 1972; Neisser, 1976). Although distinct in some aspects, these concepts shared a set of important structural and functional properties.

Cognitive structures are organizations of conceptually related representations of objects, situations, events, and of sequences of events and actions. What is stored in a cognitive structure can be the specific elements and features defining the object, event, or situation or it can be the rules defining the interrelationships among the elements, or both. Cognitive structures derive from past experiences with many instances of the complex concepts they represent. Cognitive structures simplify when there is too much, and thus they allow the perceiver to reduce an enormously complex environment to a manageable number of meaningful categories. They fill in where there is too little and allow the perceiver to go beyond the information given. These structures help the perceiver achieve some coherence in the environment and in the most general sense provide for the construction of social reality. They are built up in the course of information processing and they function as interpretive frameworks.

The memory system is assumed to contain countless such cognitive structures (cf. Neisser, 1976; Rummelhart and Ortony, 1977). Moreover, the organism can construct on-the-spot structures never previously generated.

An understanding of how perceivers process information in the social environment, how they categorize, evaluate, and assign causality, or what they remember or infer from a situation depends on an understanding of the cognitive structures that are responsible for selectivity in information processing. In developing their ideas about the construction of social reality, investigators have employed a diversity of methods, many borrowed from experimental cognitive psychology. At the conceptual level, however, these investigators have returned to their theoretical roots and to the ideas of the New Look, to Gestalt theory, and to the general insights of Bartlett (1932), Bruner (1951, 1957a, 1957b), and F. H. Allport (1955).

In the last edition of the *Handbook of Social Psychology* (Zajonc, 1968), each hypothesized type of cognitive structure (e.g., attributes, categories, schemas, etc.) was reviewed separately. The research of the past fifteen years has made it clear, however, that cognitive structures are more alike than they are different. What has emerged from the research is an understanding of social information processors, of their capabilities and shortcomings, and a view of the general function of cognitive structures in the social information-processing sequence. It is from this perspective that the research will be discussed. In the following subsections the internal-structure concepts (schemas, prototypes, and scripts) that have received the most empirical attention within social psychology will be discussed, and a few examples of the type of research associated with each will be given. In the subsequent section the function of cognitive structures in information processing will be reviewed. We shall then turn to inference processes and finally to cognitive dynamics.

Schemas

One of the most often used terms for cognitive structures is *schema*. Current notions of a schema range from the highly structured perceptual schemas (Neisser, 1976) that are ephemeral and constantly changing to the very general idea of a schema as a world view. In between are story schemas that help one comprehend text or narrative discourse (Thorndyke, 1977; J. Mandler, 1978), and higher order principles summarizing likely patterns of causality (Kelley, 1972a, 1972b). The appeal of the schema term

seems to rest primarily with its sound historical precedent (Head, 1920; Bartlett, 1932; Oldfield and Zangwill, 1942; Piaget, 1954).

The term was first applied to psychological phenomena by Head (1920) and was developed to explain the capacity of humans to appreciate both the position and direction of the movement of bodies. For Head a schema was a type of continuous standard that permitted an integration of what is currently occurring with what went on before. Head's concept of schemas represented them as fundamental standards in the individual's judgment system for categorizing and interpreting objects and events in the environment.

Bartlett (1932) used the term in reference both to overt actions and to cognitive processes. In his theory a schema was an organized representation of past behavior and experience that guided an individual in construing new experience. Schemas were viewed as the determinants of any form of organized behavior. Bartlett spoke of the individual's capacity "to go directly to that portion of the organized setting of past responses which is most relevant to the needs of the moment" (p. 206). The concept of schema was also basic to the work of Piaget, who suggested that the "cognizing organism...actually constructs his world by assimilating it to schemas while accommodating these schemas to its constraints" (Flavell, 1963, p. 71). For Piaget schemas were "mobile frames" successively applied to various actions and objects during cognitive functioning. They also contained significant sensorimotor elements.

In an analysis of the functions of schema principles in memory, Hastie (1981) identified three types of schemas:

1. Central-tendency schemas, which refer to a member of a stimulus set that is in the statistical middle of a distribution.

2. Template schemas, which are filing systems for classifying and organizing incoming sensory data.

3. Procedural schemas, which in Neisser's (1976) terms refer to "that portion of the entire perceptual cycle which is internal to the perceiver, modifiable by experience, and somehow specific to what is being perceived" (p. 54).

The functions of these three types of schemas are not assumed to be mutually exclusive, and many of the conceptualizations of schemas as used by social psychologists subsume all three. Drawing attention to the variety of meaning incorporated within the schema term, however, and the wealth of assumptions that accompany these meanings makes it easier to comprehend why the notion has been so difficult to operationalize and why it has been the source of some unresolved (and perhaps unresolvable) theoretical and empirical controversy.

Although schema was not a well-specified concept, it was both conceptually rich and conceptually familiar to most social psychologists. Many social psychological theories have included one or another form of cognitive structure concept. The term was thus readily embraced without excessive concern for its definition, and the primary research emphasis within social psychology has been on the functions that schemas serve in an individual's perceptual and memory system. For cognitive and experimental psychologists, however, adoption of the schema view was more radical because it was seen as a challenge to the simple, associationist analyses of memory (cf. Landman and Manis, in press).

The schema approach was viewed as a viable alternative to these associationist accounts. To be sure, cognitive psychologists were relatively more interested in the precise nature and form of the internal representation than the social psychologists preceding them. For example, Norman and Bobrow (1975, p. 125) wrote that a

> schema consists of a framework for tying together the information about any given event, with specification about the types of interrelationships and procedures upon the way things fit together. Schemata can activate procedures capable of operating upon local information and a common pool of data.

J. R. Anderson (1980) also viewed schemas as packages of data; in fact, in his theorizing, a schema is seen as a complex cognitive unit—a set of related propositions that the cognitive processes treat in an all-or-none manner.

There is still relatively little direct empirical work on the structure and the representational nature of schemas. For the most part social psychologists who have used the term *schemas* have viewed them as subjective "theories" about how the social world operates. These "theories" are derived from generalizing across one's experiences with the social world. Some of the earliest experimental work on schemas was done by DeSoto and Kuethe (1958, 1959) and follows the footsteps of Heider's (1944) work on structural balance. DeSoto and Kuethe attempted to discover what some of these subjective "theories" were.

Schemas were viewed by them as the abstract "residue" of social experience. Their approach grew out of a series of studies (DeSoto, 1960; DeSoto and Bosley, 1962) that sought to determine whether interpersonal relationships such as liking, trusting, dominating, and hating are perceived according to some specified formal properties such as symmetry or transitivity.

DeSoto hypothesized that structures characterized by formal properties consistent with the prevalent social schemas are easier to learn than structures inconsistent with these schemas. Thus, for instance, a liking structure is relatively easy to learn if it includes a good deal of reciprocation. But the prevalence of reciprocated relationships would impair the learning of structures of influence relationships. The presence of transitive relationships, on the other hand, would enhance the learning of hierarchies.

In these studies individuals were usually given information about relationships among a set of hypothetical persons; for example, "Bill likes Norman, and Norman likes Glenn." They were then asked to estimate the probability that "Bill likes Glenn" on the basis of the above information alone. The general findings of these experiments indicated that interpersonal relations are indeed perceived according to stable formal properties, with *liking,* for instance, being subject to transitivity (given that "Bill likes Norman and Norman likes Glenn," subjects estimated the probability that "Bill likes Glenn" to be high) and to symmetry (given that "Bill likes Norman," subjects tended to guess that "Norman likes Bill" rather than "Norman does not like Bill").

Further work on social schemas about influence led Henley, Horsfall, and DeSoto (1969) to postulate a linear-ordering schema—a tendency for individuals to impose a sequential order on those situations where dominance and influence are assumed to be important. Using a memory paradigm, Potts (1974) investigated this linear-ordering schema by presenting subjects with an incomplete story about influence relationships among people. He found that in a recognition test subjects tended to fill in the relationships that were missing from the story as if they expected these social relationships to form a linear order. Moreover, response time to questions about relationships between people was positively associated with the hierarchical distance between them.

A study by Tsujimoto, Wilde, and Robertson (1978) pursued this line of investigation and demonstrated an actual memory bias toward linear ordering. They showed slides of athletes finishing in an athletic event. Each slide depicted one of the six athletes. The slides were arranged in episodes consisting of two to five slides, the first slide representing first place in the event, the second slide second place, etc. During the initial phase of the study episodes consistent with a linear order of athletic skill were presented. During a recogntion memory test subjects were presented with episodes they had already seen as well as new episodes that either were consistent with the skill order or violated it. Old episodes were confidently recognized, but two types of memory distortion were noted in response to new episodes. False alarms were made on new episodes of length five that were consistent with the ordering, and the subjects' confidence in these judgments was very high—in fact, greater than in their judgments of previously seen episodes of length two. Tsujimoto *et al.* (1978) interpreted these results by claiming that subjects were constructing an all-encompassing linear-ordering schema that represented the relationships among the athletes and mediated recognition performance.

Kuethe (1962) developed a somewhat different technique for the substantive analysis of social schemas. Subjects were given silhouettes of human figures cut out of felt and asked to place them on a felt board. Observations were made of the ways the individuals arranged silhouettes of man, woman, and child in comparison with the way they arranged rectangles. Kuethe's findings indicated a strong tendency to arrange the rectangles in descending order of height. In the case of human figures the man's silhouette was placed on the extreme left most of the time, while the woman's and boy's silhouettes were placed in the middle or on the right equally often.

A variation of Kuethe's technique involved placing two figures 30 inches apart on a felt board and allowing the subject to look at them for five seconds. The figures were then taken off the board, and the subjects were asked to replace them as accurately as they could. For rectangles there were relatively few errors, and if errors were made, they were errors of both over- and underestimations of the original separation between the rectangles. When silhouettes of man and woman were substituted for rectangles, a systematic error in replacement was found; the distance between the figures was consistently underestimated. Given that, in reality, close spatial proximity among people is usually associated with positive feelings, Kuethe's results suggest that in the absence of information about people, a social schema is activated that assumes affiliation or attraction among them. These initial findings were replicated and extended

by Kuethe and Stricker (1963) and by Little (1968). Fischer (1968), using this same technique, found that these social schemas are quite powerful and have an impact not only on the response that is made but on the initial perception of human figures as well.

Later work on social schemas explored a variety of other theories that individuals might hold to help them organize and interpret the stimuli from the social environment. Markus (1977), for example, conducted a series of studies concerned with schemas about the self. Self-schemas were viewed as generalizations or theories about the self in particular domains, derived from past experience, that are used to guide the processing of social information relevant to these domains. Presumably, these cognitive structures developed from the repeated similar categorization and evaluation of behavior by one's self and others in important or salient domains. Self-schemas enabled individuals to understand their own social experiences and to integrate a variety of stimulus information about the self into meaningful patterns.

A major focus of the study by Markus (1977) was to link the schema idea with a converging set of information-processing consequences. Thus the emphasis was less on the content of the schemas and more on their selective function in the information-processing sequence; it was assumed that all self-schemas would operate in a fairly similar way regardless of content. Specifically, individuals thought to have self-schemas with respect to various domains such as independence, creativity, gender, or body weight (schematics) were compared with individuals thought not to have self-schemas in these domains (aschematics). Individuals are schematic for a domain if they judge that it is highly self-descriptive and that it is important for overall self-evaluation. Aschematics judge the domain neither self-descriptive nor important for self-evaluation. The schematics and the aschematics were compared for their cognitive performance on a variety of tasks.

In one study, for example, subjects with self-schemas in the domain of independence were presented with a series of trait adjectives related to independence and dependence and asked to indicate, by responding ''me'' or ''not me,'' whether or not each adjective described them. The results indicated that subjects showed a clear differentiation both in their responses and in their response times to schema-consistent and schema-inconsistent traits. Those individuals who thought of themselves as ''independent'' responded ''me'' to a large proportion of the ''independent'' adjectives and required a shorter time to make their judgments of independence than they did for judgments of dependence. Individuals with dependent self-schemas showed a similar pattern of results, responding faster to the "dependent" adjectives than they did to the "independent" adjectives. Individuals assumed not to have schemas, the aschematics, did not differ in their processing times for independent and dependent qualities.

In further research Markus and her colleagues (Markus and Smith, 1981; Markus and Sentis, 1982; Markus *et al.*, 1982) have investigated the range of possible information-processing consequences associated with these self-schemas. They concluded that individuals with schemas in particular domains (Markus and Sentis, 1982, p. 62):

1. can evaluate new information with respect to its relevance for this domain.

2. can process information about the self in the given domain (e.g., make judgments and decisions) with relative ease or certainty.

3. are consistent in their responses.

4. have relatively better recognition memory and recall for information relevant to this domain.

5. can predict future behavior in these areas.

6. can resist information that is counter to the prevailing schema.

In these studies Markus used the term *self-schemas* in part as a stand-in for the most traditional term of self-concept. The schema terminology is particularly useful, however, because it suggests the type of selective influences that might be associated with the cognitive aspect of self and, in fact, the type of influence that was claimed in the theories of the self developed by Kelly (1955) and Rogers (1951).

Similarly, in related studies many investigators searched for the cognitive consequences of other types of internal structures. A variety of cognitive constructs that had previously gone by other labels were now interpreted in schema terms. C. E. Cohen (1981a), for example, referred to implicit personality theories (Tagiuri and Petrullo, 1958) as high-level *implicit personality schemas* that represent the perceiver's assumptions about the

interrelationships among traits. In turn, each trait comprising the implicit personality schema is assumed to be a low-level schema summarizing the variety of behaviors that are associated with the trait. Although the term *schema* was often used promiscuously, for the most part the strategy of couching many of the older cognitive structure concepts in terms of schemas enriched the original concepts and instigated new lines of research. The schema conceptualization served primarily as an important heuristic for guiding research and for generating somewhat more specific hypotheses about the cognitive functions of various internal structures.

Prototypes

Another concept that has been productively employed in research on the nature and function of internal cognitive structures is prototype. A *prototype* is defined as an "abstract set of features commonly associated with members of a category, with each feature assigned a weight according to the degree of association with the category" (Cantor, 1981, p. 27). Thus a prototype of a *jock* contains a large and varied set of features that through experience have come to be associated with very athletic types. The jock prototype allows perceivers to distinguish jocks from other person types, such as criminals or businesspeople (Cantor and Mischel, 1979; Cantor *et al.*, 1980). Building on the techniques developed by Rosch (1973) to understand the natural categories of object perception, Cantor and Mischel (1979) had students list attributes of a number of categories, like geniuses, introverts, and phobics. They found that individuals could list attributes with relative ease and that there was a great deal of agreement. They interpreted their findings as evidence of rich and well-structured "consensual prototypes." Cantor, Mischel, and Schwartz (1982) also found that consensual prototypes can be generated for standard, clinical diagnostic categories, such as paranoid schizophrenic, and that these prototypes often revealed features that were not included in standard psychiatric manuals. Moreover, this approach has been expanded to include the examination of prototypes for everyday social situations such as *parties* and *classes,* and these social situation prototypes appear as orderly as those for objects or persons.

In exploring some of the specific information-processing consequences of prototypes, Cantor and Mischel (1977) used the recognition memory method. Subjects were presented with a list of traits that were consistent either with introversion or with extroversion. On a subsequent recognition memory test subjects were presented with traits displayed earlier as well as a new set of traits that were consistent with either introversion or extroversion. A clear bias was evident in that subjects were quite confident that they had in fact seen many of the foils that were congruent with extroversion/introversion. This did not occur for prototype-incongruent items. According to Cantor and Mischel, subjects evidenced a false confidence for the congruent foils because these stimuli matched the prototype for extroversion or introversion. As with schemas, the prototype terminology is useful because it allows researchers to speculate about a set of specific information-processing functions associated with knowledge structures.

Scripts

In yet another attempt to characterize the cognitive structures that contain the individual's expectations or theories about events in the social world, Schank and Abelson (1977) developed the notion of a *script*. A script is a conceptual structure outlining the roles, objects, conditions and results that occur in a stereotyped sequence of events such as eating in a restaurant, visiting a doctor, or taking a plane flight. Scripts differ from schemas or prototypes in that scripts are concerned with actions and with the temporal sequence of events.

For example, Bower, Black, and Turner (1979) gave the elements of the getting-up-and-going-to-work script in an unconventional order (she started the car, drank coffee, got up, and put on her coat). When asked to recall these elements, subjects did so in the typical scripted order, i.e., she got up, drank coffee, etc. The temporal structure of the script is a result of the action sequence that is required by the goal and by the environmental constraints.

In another study the same investigators gave subjects events that were congruent, incongruent, or irrelevant for particular scripts. Incongruent events were interruptions in the script that appeared to block the normal goal sequence (e.g., in the restaurant script the waiter does not bring the menu), while irrelevant events were those that were descriptions or details that were unrelated to the theme of the script. The results indicated that memory was best for script interruptions, relatively good for incongruent events, and least good for irrelevant events. A study by Nottenburg and Shoben (1980) using a reaction time paradigm found that scripts function in memory very much like linear orderings.

COGNITIVE STRUCTURE RESEARCH: PROGRESS AND PROBLEMS

The work on schemas, prototypes, and scripts was the foremost interest of cognitive social psychologists in the last half of the 1970s. Studies of cognitive structures and their functions in information processing proliferated. Investigators chose the concept—category, script, prototype, frame—that suited them. Yet there was actually very little conceptual or empirical basis on which to choose among them. For the most part researchers took it upon themselves to make a case for the value of a particular cognitive structure in understanding a set of findings.

Several reviews of this literature have attempted to impose some order on the variety of research relevant to cognitive structures. Thus Taylor and Crocker (1981) termed all of these internal structures *schemas* and identified three general classes of social schemas: (1) person schemas, schemas of one's self or other people; (2) role schemas, schemas for occupations or social roles or social groups; and (3) event schemas, action schemas or practiced behavioral scripts. In another review by Hastie (1981) schemas were divided into linguistic schemas, visual schemas, social group schemas, individual person schemas, point-of-view or perspective schemas, and self-concept schemas.

Some investigators decried the free and easy manner in which these terms were used and the lack of specific definition (e.g., Fiske and Linville, 1980). It is interesting in this regard to recall an often-cited paper by Gibson (1941) in which he despaired over the multiplicity of meanings given the concept of set. He wrote (p. 781):

> The concept of set or attitude is a nearly universal one in psychological thinking despite the fact that the underlying meaning is indefinite, the terminology chaotic, and the usage by psychologists highly individualistic. For almost 40 years, since the first employment of the concept in research problems, the meaning which clusters around such words as readiness, preparation, disposition, and intention has scarcely been refined beyond the common-sense level to be found in the dictionary. By some experimenters, particularly those working on conditioning, the meaning is felt to be unsatisfactory, and the concept is employed reluctantly and only because the facts make it absolutely unavoidable. By other experimenters, particularly those interested in

thinking, the concept is used freely, but with great variations in terminology (direction, need, hypothesis, schema). . . . Apparently the term *set* denotes a large and heterogeneous body of experimental facts and connotes rather different things to different psychologists. The scientific problem involved—if it is a single problem—is obscured by confusions and contradictions.

With very slight changes in wording, the same could be said about the concept of schema in contemporary psychology. The fact that forty years later the field is again experiencing a definitional crisis over a similar concept has no doubt a diversity of implications. The general concept of schema is probably a "right" one, but it has yet to be properly characterized or formulated.

Because most cognitive social psychologists have felt that a theory of cognitive structure was premature and that one could not sensibly develop a cognitive structure theory apart from a complete theory of social information processing, investigators have been content, for the time being, with making conjectures about a variety of cognitive structures and postulating the scope and range of their influence on information processing. These speculations, however, led to imaginative and productive research that employed a diversity of techniques from cognitive psychology: recognition and recall memory paradigms, impression formation tasks, lexical decision tasks, sentence verification tasks, and a range of judgment, decision, inference, and attribution tasks. A variety of response parameters including latency, confidence, accuracy, and organization also have been examined.

Although one can fault these studies for paying greater attention to the particular technique employed than to the content ostensibly investigated, for the lack of a priori specificity, or for their invulnerability to falsification, it is important to realize that in the course of this work many of the assumptions routinely held about the effects of cognitive structures were empirically evaluated for the first time.

During the New Look era in social perception, a spate of similar claims was made about the power of hypotheses, sets, or preexisting configurations of needs and values on subsequent thinking. In large part these statements went far beyond what the relatively meager data base could support. For this reason much of the initial New Look fervor about perceivers' abilities to construct their own reality was eventually lost. Experiments that were rife with methodological flaws gradually dampened enthusiasm for and interest in the notion of an active, constructive perceiver. This second round of empirical work on the functions of cognitive structures has renewed the long-term concern of social psychologists with the power of past experiences to shape one's understanding of the present reality and, moreover, has given it a firmer empirical base.

One of the best examples of the better understanding created by the application of new terms and techniques to old ideas can be found in an article by Erdelyi (1974) entitled "New Look at the New Look." This paper pointed out that in the years since the first New Look our ideas about perception and cognition have radically changed and that the phenomena of perception and cognition are no longer regarded as all-or-none events. Instead, they are each conceived of as multistage processes. Earlier notions of perception regarded it as a single, unitary event. Given such an assumed unitary process, it was difficult to explain, for example, why individuals would manifest galvanic skin reactions to stimuli they could not see (Lazarus and McLeary, 1951).

Erdelyi succeeded in demonstrating how an application of a general information-processing model to the problem of perceptual defense can clarify this apparent paradox. The clarification rests with the ideas that all input is subjected to a series of cognitive transformations and that selectivity is pervasive throughout the entire series. If a unitary process is replaced by multiple encoding of stimulus input, some of which may be preattentive or precognitive, we can begin to understand how the organism can defend itself against a threatening stimulus it has not yet seen.

In fact, the early and much-maligned perceptual defense and subception research has been thoroughly vindicated (perhaps more in substance than in method, however) by recent results. Thus, for example, Posner (1982) has shown effects of stimuli that the subject could not detect, Marcel (1980) demonstrated that a lexical decision involving complex semantic processing was considerably facilitated by a subliminal presentation of a related word, and Kunst-Wilson and Zajonc (1980) have shown that affective discriminations are possible in the absence of discriminations at the level of recognition memory.

Another important development besides the reconceptualization of perception and cognition has been a methodological one. Researchers are no longer constrained by a single liking or identification judgment, as was the case in earlier social cognition experiments. Instead, it is now commonplace to analyze responses for their content, structure, accuracy, latency, and confidence. As noted by Hastie and Carlston (1980) and Taylor and Fiske (1981), this has been one of the most important advantages of the cognitive approach in social psychology. The studies to be reviewed in the next sections allow us today to be decidedly more specific about how perceivers actively construct their social realities.

THE INFLUENCE OF SCHEMAS ON INFORMATION PROCESSING

Research of the past decade considered knowledge to be represented in memory in structures, which are bundles or packages of information. In the present context these knowledge structures will be all called schemas, although as noted earlier, they have been labeled in a variety of ways. Schemas are most often investigated as if they were in verbal or image form, yet there is no reason that the representation of past experience should not take other forms as well. Few researchers would assume that individuals can verbalize the exact contents of their schemas or have conscious access to all of their elements. It is not possible today to be very specific about the structure of schemas, and the conceptualization of how schemas function is already somewhat more precise than the data can justify. Yet providing a general framework for how schemas might serve as the building blocks of information processing gives some organization for the large number of studies of schema operation. Toward this end, a few further general statements about schemas can be made.

It is generally held that schemas can be activated (aroused, elicited) as a result of both internal and external activity. That is, schemas can be externally activated by some aspects of the stimulus information in the environment (person, event, message situation) or by the response requirements, goals, or processing objectives that are directly given to the individual or implied by the constraints of the social environment. Other schemas can be internally activated by information or goals that the perceiver generates or by schemas already active at a given moment, quite apart from what is directly implied or required by the stimulus situation.

Once activated, these schemas become ongoing information-processing units that allow the perceiver to provide structure and to achieve meaning and understanding. In general, *information processing may be seen as consisting of schema formation or activation, of the integration of input with these schemas, and of the updating or revision of these schemas to accommodate new input.* Accordingly, it should be possible to observe the influence of schemas at every *stage* of information processing (e.g., encoding, storage, retrieval, inference), at all *levels* of processing (conscious, preconscious), and on all *parameters* of the response (speed, confidence, accuracy, etc.).

There have been several extensive reviews of the schema literature (Hastie *et al.,* 1981; Taylor and Crocker, 1981), and it is now evident that some broad statements can be made about the influence of schemas. Generally, the studies that are reviewed below concern themselves with how social knowledge directs future information processing. The findings can be divided into four broad sections:

1. The effects of schemas on the initial encoding and organization of stimuli.

2. The effects of schemas on retrieval of these stimuli.

3. The effects of schemas on evaluation, judgment, prediction, and inference.

4. The effects of schemas on overt behavior.

This organization of the schema literature will guide the subsequent discussion of empirical work and highlight the areas of theoretical controversy.

The schemas involved in the studies to be reviewed are of a wide-ranging variety and are implicated in a number of ways. Most often a label, a category, a theme, or an instructional set is given that the experimenter assumes will activate a knowledge structure or schema. Thus if the subject is told that the stimulus film he or she is about to see is of two burglars in a conversation, it is assumed that schemas associated with burglary, housebreaking, theft, and illegal activities will be activated to encode and organize the unfolding events (Zadny and Gerard, 1974). It is important to note that given the general schema perspective outlined here, some schemas are always active. Information processing cannot be carried out without them. These may be schemas for words, for actions, for events, for social relationships, etc.

The goal of most of these studies is to explore the effect of *particular* schemas that are assumed to have been activated and to be appropriate for the stimulus input or the context. Generally, the schemas of concern here are those viewed as critical for person perception, person memory, or impression formation. Thus when subjects do not receive some information designed to prime a particular schema or are described as aschematic, it does not mean that they are without schemas of any type. Rather, they are assumed not to have available or not to have the particular schema of interest.

Schemas Influence What Information Will Receive Attention and How It Will Be Encoded and Organized

Evidence for this generalization is indirect, and it comes primarily from research showing that memory for stimuli is enhanced if they are preceded by or presented together with a category, label, or concept that imposes some coherence or organization on them. For example, the symbol "9W" is incomprehensible by itself. But when it follows the question "Is your name spelled with a V, Herr Wittgenstein?" it becomes perfectly clear. Bransford and Johnson (1973) gave subjects the apparently disjointed stimulus paragraph that began as follows (p. 400):

> The procedure is quite simple. First you arrange things into different groups. Of course, one pile may be sufficient, depending on how much there is to do. If you have to go somewhere else due to lack of facilities, that is the next step; otherwise you are pretty well set.

Subjects who were given the idea of "washing clothes" at the time they read the paragraph had no difficulty understanding it, and later they recalled more propositions from it than did subjects who read it without the initial organizing idea. It appears in studies like this one that the schema activated by the initial clue allows the perceiver to attend selectively to some common essential aspects of the stimulus set while ignoring others and thus achieve a more coherent and unified understanding of the stimulus input. As a result, subsequent cognitive performance is facilitated.

A study by C. E. Cohen (1977), for example, required subjects to observe a videotape of an individual going through a daily routine. Some subjects were told that she was a waitress, while others were told that she was a librarian. A subsequent recall test showed that information recalled from the tape was consistent with the label they had been provided. This recall of schema-consistent information was superior to their recall of ir-

relevant or inconsistent information. The inference here is that the schema associated with the occupational label influenced what common features of the various segments of the film received attention from the subject. There are numerous similar studies: (Dooling and Lachman, 1971; Bransford and Johnson, 1973; Dooling and Mullet, 1973; Sulin and Dooling, 1974; Picek, Sherman, and Shiffrin, 1975; Cantor and Mischel, 1977; Owens, Bower, and Black, 1978; Taylor, Crocker, and D'Agostino, 1978; Woll and Yopp, 1978; Rothbart, Evans, and Fulero, 1979; Hamilton and Rose, 1978; Weldon and Malpass, 1981).

One of the most often cited studies on this point is by Zadny and Gerard (1974). They were among the first social psychologists to investigate how a schema influences the encoding of events. They showed subjects a videotape of two people exploring a room in a house talking about drug use, the police, and theft. Subjects were given one of three schemas with which to understand the behavior of the two men: two burglars, two students waiting for a friend, or two friends attempting to conceal illegal drugs. The results indicated a tendency for subjects given the two-burglars schema to recall more theft-relevant objects and comments than subjects in the other two conditions. Here, again, the inference is that the schema influenced the initial organization of the input so that the subject could more completely comprehend the discussion featured in the stimulus film.

A systematic series of studies reported by Ostrom *et al.* (1980) made a deliberate attempt to understand whether the selective influence of the schema was indeed on the initial encoding or organization of the stimulus as suggested by some investigators or whether, in contrast, it had its impact at the point of retrieval when the subject was asked questions about the stimulus. In these studies subjects were given a set of trait terms describing an individual. The subjects' task was to predict the target person's success at a particular occupation. Of the trait terms provided, half were chosen to be relevant to the occupation and half were irrelevant. In the next stage of the experiment the subjects were asked to recall as many traits as they could. The investigators found that subjects recalled significantly more traits that were relevant to the activated occupational schema than traits that were irrelevant to it.

In a second study using the same paradigm, subjects were required to make a second occupational judgment about the person without going over the initial characteristics again. The difference was that the traits in the list that were originally irrelevant with respect to the first occupational judgment were now relevant to this second occupational judgment. However, the judgments made following the initial encoding of the trait terms failed to affect recall of the traits. This second judgment did not enhance recall for the originally irrelevant traits. From this set of studies Ostrom *et al.* concluded that the first occupation label had an important influence on the initial encoding and that any retrieval process that may have had an influence on recall must have been mediated by this encoding.

In another set of experiments Lingle and Ostrom (1979) used decision time to explore the influence of an activated schema on information processing. They employed the same paradigm in which subjects rated the suitability of a target person described by a set of traits for a certain occupation. Following this rating the trait set was removed from subjects' view, and they were asked to make a judgment about the target's suitability for a second occupation. The similarity between the two occupations was varied and decision time was measured. So that the basis of the second judgment could be explored, the size of the trait set was varied from one to seven, and the homogeneity of the trait set with respect to negativity or positivity of the trait was also varied. If during the second judgment subjects were reviewing the whole list of traits when deciding about the suitability of the target individual, the number of traits in the set should have had a marked influence on decision time. In fact, although the second-judgment times were a direct function of the similarity of the second occupation to the first occupation (the more similar, the faster the latency), neither set size nor homogeneity of the traits within a set had an impact on judgment time.

These data suggest that the initial encoding of the traits with respect to the occupational schema had a major impact on the organization and retention of these traits and consequently on the future judgments that were relevant to them. This finding implies that the schema-driven first impressions of the target individual were a more important source of influence on later judgments of the target individual than were the occupationally relevant traits that were included in the list. Furthermore, these results are significant for generalizations about the influence of schemas on judgments and inference, yet they are included here because they demonstrate the influence that schemas may exert on the initial organization of stimulus input. Finally, they point to the in-

terdependence of encoding and retrieval. Thus many impressions of other people may be based primarily on the memory of the inferences made when the initial schemas were activated to encode their behavior rather than on memory for the actual behavioral inputs (Carlston, 1980).

The interpretation of some of these findings varies with the researcher's theoretical framework. Ebbesen (1980), for example, disagrees that subjects in the type of studies done by Lingle and Ostrom (1979) have no representations of the irrelevant traits. He suggests that they actually do, but that they are not activated because the subject finds it easier to use the global, impressionistic representations. The implication is that other more specific and detailed representations could be activated if necessary.

In an effort to explore these questions, C. E. Cohen and Ebbesen (1979) used the unitizing task developed by Newtson (1976). In this task the subject is asked to watch a film, usually of a person engaging in a variety of routine activities, and is asked to press a button each time a meaningful unit of behavior occurs. Cohen and Ebbesen's subjects performed this task after they were given one of two observational goals. In one condition they were told to form a "detailed impression of the actress' personality;" in another they were told to "remember what the actress did." The implicit assumption was that subjects in the impression condition would activate a person schema within which to structure the stimulus events. Subjects in the memory condition would activate an events schema. Following the unitizing task all subjects were given a recognition memory test for the behaviors in the film and asked to describe the woman in the film on a series of trait adjectives. With respect to accuracy those given the memory goal remembered more details of the film than those trying to form an impression of the woman's behavior. They also divided the film into smaller units than subjects in the impression condition.

In interpreting these results, Ebbesen (1980) is careful to note that unitizing does not necessarily reflect a primary-encoding process; rather, he suggests that it reflects a secondary organization process. In contrast to Newtson (1976), Ebbesen does not equate the number of divisions with the number of action units that have been encoded. It is Ebbesen's view that the perceiver constructs a number of different types of representations while watching the film, one of which seems to be a detailed representation of the behavior and one of which is a more general, global representation. These two encodings seem to occur regardless of one's observational goals. The difference in the number of units made appears to result from the encoding of different types of information rather than from different amounts. The person schema may produce its selective effects by influencing the way the information is retrieved, that is, which representation—the detailed or the global—is accessed first at the time of the memory or inference task.

An investigation by Markus, Smith, and Moreland (1983) compared the unitizing judgments of individuals with self-schemas for masculinity (schematics) and individuals without such self-schemas (aschematics). With respect to a neutral film of a college student performing a number of mundane activities, the two groups did not differ in the number of units formed. However, in a film containing stereotypically masculine behavior, the schematics formed substantially fewer units than did the aschematics. Markus *et al.* suggest that the self-schema enabled these subjects to construct a global impression of the target with respect to masculinity. The aschematics—those without a relevant schema for interpreting the events—could not organize the film in this same way, presumably because they had some difficulty in comprehending the events. Markus *et al.* also found that the larger units of the schematics are related to more extreme descriptions, more positive evaluations, and more confident recall of the schema-relevant behavior.

Following the unitizing task the subjects in the above study were asked to reconstruct the film sequence by writing what they could remember about the target individual. Responses were coded for the amount of conjecture from the stimulus material involved in the inference. Markus *et al.* found that compared with the aschematics, the schematics made significantly more responses about the target individual that involved a great deal of conjecture. As suggested by the analysis of Lingle and Ostrom (1979), schematics probably made their initial judgments as a consequence of their self-schemas of masculinity and then later made inferences on the basis of these initial global judgments.

Together, these studies suggest that a label, a category, or a concept presented before or along with some stimulus input can, when relevant, have a significant impact on how a stimulus is processed. Apparently, this occurs because the label, category, or concept activates a schema that processes this input. The schema allows for additional organization and comprehension, beyond what is possible by virtue of just the stimulus alone. In this sense schemas allow individuals to "go beyond the information given" (Bruner, 1957a) and to "make more" of a given stimulus by bringing to bear the conceptual wealth contained in past knowledge. Whether this influence is one of encoding or retrieval is as yet unclear, and most studies suggest that the two are heavily interdependent.

The degree to which schematic organization may constrain processing is not revealed by these data. There is a suggestion from a number of these studies that the same stimulus may be represented in a variety of ways depending on the schemas available for processing. This multiplicity of organization of the same stimulus information is associated with flexibility and variability in subsequent response, depending on which representation of the stimuli best meets the processing requirements of a given situation.

Schemas Have a Selective Influence on Retention, Retrieval, and the Organization of Memory

The issue of the influence of schemas on retrieval from memory is a complex one. First, the majority of studies carried out in the testing of this generalization cannot be easily distinguished from those investigating the influence of schemas on the encoding of stimuli. It is often impossible to determine whether the memory effect in question indicates an acquisition or a retrieval bias. Second, the influence of schemas on retrieval entails a number of different questions, including the influence of schemas on the amount and accuracy of recall and on type of information recalled (i.e., consistent, inconsistent, relevant, or irrelevant).

The earliest studies on the influence of schemas on memory pitted remembering with a schema against remembering without a schema. In regard to sheer amount of recall it is a fair generalization that relevant schemas always facilitate recall; that is, individuals always remember more with a relevant schema than without one (e.g., Dooling and Mullet, 1973; Kintsch and Van Dijk, 1978; Bower, Black, and Turner, 1979; Weldon and Malpass, 1981). Yet this generalization must not be stated without qualifications. What is meant by a "relevant" schema? What happens to memory when the information being processed is inconsistent with a schema? Are both recognition and recall affected in similar ways? And what influence does the individual's processing goal or instructional set have on how schemas are likely to influence memory? In recent years all of these questions have been broached, some more systematically than others.

Despite the fact that the numerous studies on the effects of schemas on memory do not form a coherent whole, some generalizations can be drawn. The most often cited studies concerning the effects of schematic processing on memory suggest that individuals remember best those stimulus events that fit their prevailing schemas. In a study by Snyder and Uranowitz (1978) subjects read a short life history of a woman named Betty K. Immediately following the story the subjects were told either that Betty K. was a lesbian or that she was a heterosexual. Another group of subjects was not told anything about her sexual preferences. In a recognition-memory test subjects who were presented with the lesbian label showed a tendency to make more false alarms on items that fit the lesbian stereotype than did those who were not told about her sexual preference. While the heterosexual label did not produce a similar false-alarm pattern, the bias did occur for hits, so subjects in the heterosexual label condition were more correct on the heterosexual than the lesbian items.

A study by Rothbart, Evans, and Fulero (1979) was also concerned with memory for information that was consistent and inconsistent with a stereotypic schema of a group. Subjects received information that the members of a group "tended to be more friendly and sociable than average" or that the members of a group "tended to be more intellectual than average" (p. 347). Subjects were then given individual items that were either consistent or inconsistent with this initial expectancy. The results indicated that subjects recalled more behaviors that were consistent with their expectancies or schemas for the group than behaviors that were inconsistent with their schemas. Other studies showing schema-consistent recall include those by C. E. Cohen (1977; 1981b), Howard and Rothbart (1980), and Bem (1981).

Those concerned with the role of self-schemas on information processing also have repeatedly shown that individuals remember information that is schema-consistent. In a simple convincing demonstration of the power of self-reference, Rogers, Kuiper, and Kirker (1977) asked subjects to respond yes or no depending on whether particular adjectives like *independent* described them. They also were asked to answer yes or no to questions about the structural, phonemic, and semantic qualities of the same adjectives. Of the four types of

judgments that were made (self-descriptive, structural, semantic, and phonemic), the self-referent decisions resulted in superior recall, and within the self-referent decisions those given yes answers were particularly well recalled, presumably because they were consistent with the self-schema. Similar results showing enhanced recall of material consistent with self-schemas have been found by Lord (1980), Markus *et al.* (1982), and Swann and Read (1981).

On the basis of these studies many researchers asserted that individuals discount information that does not fit with their initial schemas. The conclusion usually is that individuals remember best information that is consistent with a prevailing schema. Such a generalization was particularly important because many of the studies were done from a stereotyping perspective and were seeking an empirical undergirding for the compelling notion that people selectively remember more information that "fits" with their stereotype than information that does not fit. This conclusion is doubtlessly a valid one under some conditions, but as a number of other empirical studies were soon to make clear, it could not stand as the whole story about the effects of schemas on retrieval.

Two studies published simultaneously reported failures to confirm the Snyder and Uranowitz (1978) finding that the label of lesbian or heterosexual had a significant impact on recognition memory for information about Betty K. Clark and Woll (1981) found no biasing effects of the schema or label on their subjects' recognition memory. They also manipulated the instructions that were given to the subjects such that one group was told to "be as accurate and precise as possible" in their judgments about Betty K. and another was told "to choose the alternative that gives the best answer or is most correct" (p. 1067). No differences in recognition memory were found as a result of these strict or lenient instructions either.

Bellezza and Bower (1981) also performed the Betty K. experiment, using a signal detection model in an attempt to examine the separate effects of the schema on the amount of information available in memory and on the subject's response bias. They found no enhancement of recognition memory as a result of the label, but they did find a response bias such that subjects were likely to guess in the direction of the label they had received. These two studies are useful in suggesting some caution in generalizing from the initial study of Snyder and Uranowitz. Neither study, however, gives any indication of why the intuitively appealing notion of reconstructive memory in the service of one's stereotypes did not hold under these conditions. Was the idea basically wrong, or were special conditions required before reconstructive memory would be evidenced? The question is still unanswered.

There also were other challenges to the conclusion that schematic material dominates in recall. A study by Hastie and Kumar (1979) produced opposite results, showing material that is *inconsistent* with a schema to be best remembered. Their study brought into sharp relief the question of whether individuals are most likely to recall schema-consistent or schema-inconsistent information. Hastie and Kumar's subjects were given traits that were all associated with a single characteristic, such as intelligence. Thus some subjects were told that a person was intelligent, clever, smart, bright, etc. Then they were given behavioral descriptions that were either consistent with, inconsistent with, or irrelevant to the intelligence schema that was presumably activated by the presentation of the set of traits. Subjects were told, for example, that the target individual won the chess tournament or had a cheeseburger. Subsequently, subjects were asked to recall the behavioral descriptions as accurately as possible. In contrast to many of the previous findings, Hastie and Kumar found that incongruent behaviors were recalled better than congruent ones. Further, both congruent and incongruent items were recalled better than irrelevant ones.

Judd and Kulik (1980), exploring the schematic effects of social attitudes on recall, also found substantial memory effects for inconsistent items. They proposed that when attitude-relevant information is processed, social attitudes function as schemas. They had subjects make pro/con and agree/disagree ratings of attitude statements on three issues. The next day these individuals were asked to recall the statements as close to the original as possible. Judd and Kulik found better recall for items that were extremely agreed with or extremely disagreed with than for items that produced less extreme responses. Recall of schema-inconsistent information was also found by Fiske, Kinder, and Larter (1983), who reported that political schematics (experts) remember some schema-inconsistent information at least as well as schema-consistent information; by Graesser and his colleagues (Graesser, Gordon, and Sawyer, 1979; Graesser *et al.*, 1980), who found greater recognition memory for atypical than for typical behavior; and by Bower, Black,

and Turner (1979), who found better recall for script-incongruent events.

A study by Wyer and Gordon (1982), replicating the Rothbart *et al.* (1979) study, found that only material that is *descriptively* inconsistent will be ignored. Stimuli that are *evaluatively* inconsistent with the initial expectation was quite likely to be remembered. Given the expectation that another person is honest, one may ignore the descriptively inconsistent fact that the person told a friend he liked a gift even though he thought it was tasteless but will not ignore the evaluatively inconsistent event that he sold a scratched album to a classmate after telling him it was almost new (cf. Lewicka, 1977, 1979; Wyer and Gordon, 1982).

There have been a number of attempts to reconcile these findings. Hastie (1981), for example, introduced a review chapter with the following question: "When a person perceives specific, concrete events that are related to a general, abstract schema, how will each event's relation to the schema affects its availability for later recall or cognitive utilization?" (p. 39). He answered his own question thus: "Information that is highly congruent or highly incongruent with reference to a currently active schema is best remembered. Information that is undiagnostic, or irrelevant to the applicability of the schema is worst remembered, all other factors being equal" (p. 75).

It appears, then, that schema-inconsistent information is quite likely to be recalled, but only if it competes with the information in the schema *and* if the cognitive task requires the subject to make use of it. These conditions would be met, for example, in an impression task where one must understand that a person is both intelligent and dull, or when a friendly person delivers a scathing criticism. The fact that schema-inconsistent information directly contradicts some knowledge in the schema gives the inconsistent information a structure of its own, calls for an explanation, and ensures that it will be noticed by the perceiver. If, on the other hand, the information is only slightly inconsistent such that the data does not conflict with the knowledge organized in the schema, or if the subject is not required to use the inconsistent information, it is likely that schema-consistent information will dominate in recall. Johnson and Judd (1983), for example, report good recall of incongruent items but only when they were extreme. Otherwise, these authors obtained superior recognition memory and accuracy judgments for congruent items.

Srull (1981) emphasized a number of other factors that may explain the divergent findings on the effects of schemas on memory. He noted, for example, that most of the studies that have found relatively better memory for schema-consistent information have used some form of a recognition task. Using Hastie's (1981) ideas about the origins of schematic effects in memory, he explained why a difference in recall and recognition memory with respect to consistency of information might be expected.

Hastie's theoretical model of why schema-incongruent items are remembered better than congruent ones is based on the idea that a behavior or a trait that is incongruent with a prior expectancy is difficult to understand and thus remains in working memory for a relatively long period of time. In an attempt to comprehend the incongruent event, the person keeps retrieving additional information from long-term memory until the item or event is adequately understood. Given a failure to comprehend, the person is likely to keep the event in working memory. As a result, Hastie hypothesized, the incongruent event makes contact with other behaviors (old ones or new ones yet to be learned), and a diversity of associative links are thus established. By this reasoning there are more associative pathways for incongruent behaviors than for congruent behaviors, which, by contrast, are relatively well understood. Events that do not fit the schema receive a great deal of cognitive work, or, in Hastie's words, "comprehension resources," and thus are relatively well remembered. Hastie's ideas on this issue are important because they imply that the advantage of schema-incongruent events derives from cognitive work at the acquisition stage of processing—the point at which perceivers are likely to expend cognitive effort assimilating the incongruent events to other events in memory.

Srull (1981) finds evidence for Hastie's theory in a number of studies and goes on to argue that the retrieval processes necessary for recall are bypassed with a recognition task and that is why better recall of inconsistency is often not found in recognition memory studies. In recall, however, the subject is assumed to reproduce the network that was created during encoding. The relatively greater number of links established during the initial processing of incongruent input are likely to have a direct influence on what is remembered. If this type of self-generated cognitive network is bypassed, as it may be in a recognition task, the special attention given the incongruent events will not have any impact, and schema-congruent events are likely to dominate in memory.

A study by Smith, Adams, and Schorr (1978) using response latency suggests that inconsistency may also influence some aspects of recognition memory, however. They presented subjects with sentences that were congruent with a schema, incongruent with a schema, and irrelevant to a schema. The task was to verify whether the sentence had been among previously presented material. Among the false alarms schema-incongruent sentences were associated with longer latencies than were schema-irrelevant sentences.

Srull (1981) also finds evidence for a number of other variables that have an important influence on whether an event will receive extra cognitive work at encoding and thereby increase the probability of links between the stimulus events and other events in memory. One of these factors is the learning condition. This is an obvious candidate, but it has only recently been systematically implicated in information processing (e.g., Wyer and Srull, 1980). Recently, for example, Berman, Read, and Kenny (1983) have demonstrated that consistency results must be viewed in terms of the expectations with which the subjects process the task information. They found that information consistent with expectations is judged by individuals to be more accurate. Moreover, the effect was found both at the encoding and at the retrieval stage of information processing.

The influence of learning conditions has been studied by examining the effects of what subjects think they are supposed to be doing in the experiment. Sometimes, subjects are instructed to form an impression of a particular target while processing the stimulus materials. At other times, they are required to remember as much as possible. In some studies they are required to do both. Given that present-day social cognition finds its historical roots in the New Look of the 1940s, and given that the hallmark of the New Look was a focus on how the perceiver's goals, values, and need states influence perception and cognition, it is extremely curious that modern cognitive social psychologists should come so late and so tentatively to the study of the influence of goals.

The limited work that has been done suggests quite clearly, as could be expected, that the perceiver's goals and requirements have a substantial impact on memory. Thus a program of research by Hamilton and his colleagues (Hamilton and Katz, 1975; Hamilton, Katz, and Leirer, 1980) used a paradigm in which subjects are given a list of fifteen behaviors performed by an individual and are asked either to form an impression or to memorize the items. Subjects given the impression instructions are found to have better memory for the behaviors than subjects in the memorize condition. In the impression condition, subjects apparently organize the stimulus materials primarily according to a person schema. This organizational strategy is not employed by subjects required simply to recall the behavioral information, and consequently their memory for the behaviors suffers by comparison.

A second factor outlined by Srull with respect to recall of incongruent material is the potential for modification in the perceiver's expectancy as more and more information is learned about the target person or persons. Thus the experimenter cannot blithely assume that the particular expectancy, label, or schema that has been initially instantiated will continue to be used unaltered throughout the processing sequence. Srull also noted that the amount of inconsistency experienced or tolerated may well depend on the nature of the target. Thus subjects who have difficulty with inconsistency in the case of a single individual may be willing to tolerate similar inconsistency if the target is a group, as in the Rothbart *et al.* (1979) study (e.g., three friendly and three unfriendly behaviors manifested by six different persons in a group).

Yet another issue concerning the effects of schemas on retrieval from memory is that of accuracy. Most studies dealing with schematic effects on memory have not reported accuracy of recall, choosing instead to examine relative recall of different types of information. Of those that have focused on accuracy, most report very few errors in memory as a consequence of schematic processing. There are some reports of intrusions into recall, but these seem to occur primarily with delay or in those circumstances where information from different contexts shares the same schema in memory. There do not appear to be any studies documenting serious distortions as a result of schematic processing. Perhaps such distortions do occur outside the confines of the laboratory (in those instances where it is extremely important for an individual to remember a stimulus event in a given manner), but blatant schema-driven distortion in recall remains to be demonstrated.

With respect to intrusions they are most likely to be evidenced in those situations where the experimental task requires the subject to summarize the situation or the stimulus information or where the instructions are not precise as to what the subject should try to remember.

When intrusions occur, they are thematic or consistent with the general ideas, dimensions, or concepts underlying the schema.

In general, the greater the knowledge and the more fully developed the schema, the greater is the number of thematic intrusions as a result of schematic processing. Spiro (1975), for example, found that if subjects are required to memorize stimuli, they may generate new schemas on the spot, and because the information is not then integrated with prior knowledge, it will remain unchanged over time. Without such memory instructions, they will show a gradual and a systematic distortion in the direction of a relevant schema. Recent attempts to differentiate reproductive or completely accurate recall from reconstructive recall (Hasher and Griffin, 1978) have concluded that what is found in the way of recall varies with (1) the demands placed on the recaller by himself or herself, (2) the target events, and (3) the recall situation.

In studies of recognition memory it initially appeared that schemas facilitate both the amount of recall and the accuracy. And if the focus is only on hit rates, it is almost always the case that schemas show this facilitation. But in the few studies that look not just at high hit rates but at false alarms as well, there are some results that question this generalization.

When a measure of sensitivity, such as A' or d' (Green and Swets, 1966), is employed, it becomes evident that memory may be impaired by schematic processing as the subject fills in the gaps in his or her memory by relying on the schema. For example, the previously cited studies by Cantor and Mischel (1977), Snyder and Uranowitz (1978), and Tsujimoto, Wilde, and Robertson (1978) all indicate a significant bias in recognition toward conceptually related foils. Attempts to draw conclusions about schematic effects on recognition accuracy must be tempered by the fact that some of these findings cannot be replicated and that many studies do not report false alarms and sensitivity results but only confidence scores for recognition. Overall, however, it seems that false-alarm rate is likely to be high in those instances where the perceiver is required to organize stimulus information into a whole or to form a global impression. Thus in experiments where subjects read a story about a person or are given traits about a person, the prevailing tendency is to integrate the information and to use it as a unit.

It is easy to see how this goal would lead quite naturally to a recognition bias for conceptually related but nonpresented items. A recent study by Burnstein and Schul (1983) found, for example, fewer false alarms in the recognition performance of those subjects who were asked to comprehend the information than for subjects who were required to form an impression. Instructions that lead subjects to use only one schema to process the stimulus situation and to achieve a single cognitive product, such as a single impression, are likely to show more intrusions and more false alarms. Instructions that call for comprehension, problem solving, understanding, or learning encourage the individual to use as many schemas as necessary to process the information. Hence false alarms are reduced, and as a result, recognition memory for details may be startlingly good.

Together, these studies suggest that schemas can have a variety of effects on retention and retrieval. Individuals are most likely to remember best and most confidently people, events, or situations as fitting their schemas when they are required to form a general impression and when memory is assessed by a recognition test. Just what proportion of naturally occurring memory situations meet these criteria remains to be determined. Most eyewitness situations are characterized by these conditions. And in many everyday events we are probably attempting to do little else than form a general impression and are not particularly vigilant for details that may conflict with our prevailing schemas about the world. What is most evident from these empirical investigations of schema-driven memory, however, is that the effects of schemas on memory vary dramatically with the nature of the stimulus material, the type of memory task, and the goals of the processing situation.

Schemas Function as Interpretive Frameworks and Thereby Influence Evaluations, Judgments, Predictions, and Inferences

In unstructured judgmental tasks schemas function as interpretive frameworks that influence inferences and predictions in schema-relevant domains and the confidence with which these judgments are made. Support for this generalization comes from a wealth of sources. Many of the studies described in the previous section also have included conditions that revealed the effects of schemas on judgments about others. For example, Lingle *et al.,* (1979) found that individuals not only rely on schemas for remembering information about people but are heavily dependent on schemas for future judgments and impressions as well. Subjects in their study were asked to

judge a set of individuals for intelligence and friendliness. For some of the judgments subjects made an intelligence-relevant occupational judgment ("Would this person make a good physicist?"). For others they made a friendliness-relevant occupational judgment ("Would this person make a good waiter?"). These first judgments were made while the stimulus descriptions were available for review. Subjects were then required to make a second set of judgments about the person's friendliness or intelligence just on the basis of their memory of the descriptions. In all cases the target individual was rated as more intelligent if he had been previously assessed for his suitability for an occupation that was stereotypically representative of intelligence. Similarly, a target individual was rated as more friendly if he had first been assessed for an occupation that was congruent with friendliness than if he had been evaluated for an occupation that was not congruent with friendliness.

The second judgments do not seem dependent on a review of the original stimulus elements; rather, they depend on memory for the initial impression that resulted from encoding the information about the target individual with a particular occupational schema. The nature of this process, which suggests that individuals rely on schema-driven judgments in their impressions of others, is particularly important for theorizing about the cognitive processes involved in stereotyping. Person impressions and judgments are very often influenced by the schemas that were active when the information about an individual was initially presented. If information about a shy or withdrawn person is processed with the label of "mental patient," the feature of shyness is likely to be seen as diagnostic of mental illness, and it is unlikely that it will be separately encoded. Such a tendency will be enhanced if the initial encoding or organization served some important or useful function for the subject. Given appropriate incentives, subjects are often capable of making this distinction (Lingle *et al.,* 1979), but unless it is especially required of them, they are unlikely to do so.

This notion harks back to Katz's (1960) functional approach to stereotypes because it implies that it is important to know what goal was active when a target person was initially perceived. It is the goal of the processing act that determines which schemas are activated and consequently which organization is likely to be the predominant one (Zajonc, 1960). Many impression studies have been done with only the most general goals of getting to know another person. As such, they may not adequately reflect the power that an initial interpersonal goal (to get a job, to become a friend, or to influence a police officer) may have on the initial interpretation of stimulus traits and thus on the subsequent evaluations and judgment of a target person.

The idea that many of our impressions and judgments are primarily a result of inference from earlier judgments has received support from other studies. Ebbesen and Allen (1979) had subjects view a videotape of a male and a female preparing and eating a meal. The tape was viewed at one of three exposures: at normal, twice-normal, and seven-times-normal playback speed. The subjects were given one of two instuctional sets; they were told to "remember what was done" or "to form an impression." They were given both a recognition memory test for behavioral details and a trait impression test. The latter consisted of some items that an independent group of judges had decided were characteristic of the actors in the film and items that they had judged as not characteristic. Subjects then answered yes or no to the trait impression test, as in the recognition test.

The rate of exposure of the film influenced the accuracy for actual behavioral details but had no effects on the personality impression test. Subjects seemed to remember the personality information equally well regardless of the speed of exposure. A further exploration sought to determine whether subjects were simply making their judgments on normative information or implicit personality schemas without taking into account the actual behavioral details.

Ebbesen, Cohen, and Allen (1979) varied the delay between the presentation of the film and the test. They also varied the instructional set. They found that with a short delay the structure of the trait inferences was more normative for those trying to form an impression than for those trying to remember what was done. This was determined by comparing the pattern of trait inferences made by subjects who had seen the videotape (depicting a man and a woman arguing) with the pattern of trait inferences made by subjects who were told to guess which traits and behaviors the two people would reveal, on the basis only of their knowledge of the sex of the actors and of the fact that the pair in the film had an argument. With a longer delay, however, the difference between the two instructional set conditions was not evident, and all of the ratings more closely matched the normative ratings.

As described earlier, these findings on retrieval are interpreted with the suggestion that subjects develop at least two representations when observing people. It appears that in addition to a specific representation, subjects always produce a global representation of a person regardless of the goal given them in instructions. This global representation is heavily influenced by implicit personality schemas and is used at all stages of processing but especially at the inference phase, unless the individual is forced to use the more detailed representation to make judgments.

The fact that individuals have common implicit personality theories need not imply that all their impressions of other people will be the same. There is indeed some overlap in the core elements, but the normative information summarized in one's personality schemas will probably vary considerably depending on one's social experience. For example, those with a great deal of experience with the concept of extroversion, perhaps those people who are themselves extroverts, are likely to have different implicit personality schema of extroversion than those without such experience.

Tesser (1978), in an innovative approach to attitudes, has elaborated the process by which implicit personality schemas shape our impressions of others. He suggests that if one has a view of another that includes, for example, the characteristics *gregarious, honest,* and *impolite* and has the occasion to think of this individual as a potential friend, then implicit personality schemas will be used to generate new ideas about the individual. On the basis of knowing that the person is gregarious, one might decide, for example, that the person has a lot of friends. *Impolite,* however, does not fit with *gregarious* according to the implicit personality schema, so *impolite* may be given a somewhat different cast. It may be interpreted as a tendency to say what one really thinks —being honest.

Tesser's idea is that thinking about a person with the implicit personality schema produces a set of salient cognitions that can turn a moderately attractive person into a very likable person. As a result of processing with a schema, one can change an initial positive feeling for a person to a very strong positive attitude. In this sense schematic processing produces systematic attitude change. The schema provides the rules for adding and ignoring ideas and for making inferences and interpretation. Tesser claims, then, that attitudes are not fixed products; rather, they change as a result of activation of a particular schema when thinking about the object. Specifically, Tesser (1978) says, "There is not a single attitude toward an object, but rather, any number of attitudes depending on the number of schemas available for thinking about the objects'' (p. 298).

Tesser and Leone (1977) conducted two studies to investigate the hypothesis that thought with a well-developed schema results in greater attitude change than thought with a less well developed schema. They compared the effects of thinking about the personality of individuals and thinking about the personality of a group. It was assumed that individuals have very well-developed schemas for the personality of individuals but much less well-developed schemas for the personality of groups. Subjects were given a description of either another person or a group, then were encouraged to think for ninety seconds or were distracted so as to be prevented from thinking, and then were asked for their attitudes.

The original hypothesis of Tesser and Leone (1977) received strong support. The difference in attitude polarization between the thought and the distraction groups was much stronger with persons as targets than with groups as targets. In another study they compared men and women for the effects of thinking about football and fashions. In this situation men were assumed to have a much more highly developed schema for football than for fashions, and the reverse was assumed to be true for women. Polarization in attitudes was found for male subjects processing items about sports and for female subjects processing items about fashion.

In a further set of studies Tesser and his colleagues pursued this line of reasoning and suggested that it was not enough to have a particular schema. It was necessary for this schema to be tuned in (cf. Zajonc, 1960). Building on earlier theoretical work (e.g., Jones and Thibaut, 1958), they hypothesized that the schema about another person depends on one's relationship to that person. In one study (Tesser and Danheiser, 1978) subjects gave a description of themselves and then heard a bogus description of their hypothetical partner. At this point the subjects gave their initial impression of the hypothetical partner. They were then led to believe that they would either be cooperating or competing with this partner and were encouraged to think about the target partner or were distracted from thinking. Finally, they rated the hypothetical partner again. In this case thinking about the target had no effect.

What mattered here was the relationship to the partner. Regardless of their initial opinion about the partner, activating a competitive schema led to a decrease in at-

raction. From these and other studies (Tesser and Cowan, 1975; Clary, Tesser, and Downing, 1978), Tesser and his colleagues claimed that changes in attitudes toward objects should be expected to occur only when individuals have well-differentiated schemas about the objects and when they are tuned in.

An extensive program of research carried out by Wyer (1974, 1975a, 1976) on the effects of previously formed beliefs on syllogistic inference processes also suggests that prior-knowledge structures are likely to have a significant impact on inferences. He found, for example, that even when subjects are provided with strong instructions encouraging them to attend only to the stimulus information presented and to ignore preconceptions about the stimuli, their prior beliefs still have substantial impact on their inferences.

Yet another way in which schemas have an influence on inferences and on impressions and evaluations of others is through the expectations they generate. The social cognition literature is replete with empirical work demonstrating the power of expectations (e.g., Kelley, 1950; Jones and McGillis, 1976; Eisen and McArthur, 1979). Thus Eisen and McArthur (1979) varied expectations about a social stimulus situation, leading some subjects to believe that they would see a trial and other subjects to believe that they would watch a social interaction. Those who expected a trial judged the target other to be more responsible for a crime than subjects who were primed for a social interaction. In this study the expectation for a trial led the subjects to organize the stimulus situation with a trial schema that presumably caused the guilt of the target person to be a focal concern. For those expecting a social interaction, however, the stimulus situation was constructed with the usual impression/personality schema that seems to be the default schema for the interpretation of people.

Taylor *et al.* (1978) found that expectations associated with sex role stereotypes had a pervasive influence on subjects' judgments of others. In their study subjects listened to tape recordings in which each speaker was identified by a slide shown while the individual was speaking. This manipulation allowed every participant's role in the discussion to be portrayed by both males and females. Following the discussion all subjects were rated.

Taylor *et al.* found that regardless of which roles the males played in the interaction, they were judged to be more confident, analytic, and influential than the females. These stereotypically masculine judgments may have been a result of the activation of gender schemas (Bem, 1981; Markus *et al.,* 1982) that led the subjects to interpret the comments of the speakers in terms that were congruent with them. Thus a seemingly perceptive comment may have contributed to the judgment of analytic for a male when processed with a masculinity schema. The same comment, however, may have generated the judgment of sensitive for a female when processed with a femininity schema.

Results quite similar to these were reported by Duncan (1976), who found that white subjects constructed the same stimulus event quite differently when the aggressor was black than when he was white. Specifically, the same shove was seen as violent when the target other was black and as aggressive or playing around when the target was white. Here, again, these results suggest that the stimulus event is constructed differently depending on which racial stereotypes are used to elaborate and comprehend the event. Additional studies that support this idea include Secord (1959), Gurwitz and Dodge (1977), and Ugwyebu (1979).

In an innovative study on individual differences in construct accessibility, Higgins, King, and Mavin (1982) demonstrated convincingly that the same objective stimulus can be processed quite differently by different individuals depending on one's previously activated cognitive structures. They found that a perceiver's impression of (and memory for) a target person involves greater omission of stimulus information related to the perceiver's inaccessible trait constructs than stimulus information related to the perceiver's accessible trait constructs. That is, individuals use their own easily accessible constructs to categorize the behavior of others. Moreover, these effects of construct accessibility on the impression of another were still evident a week later.

Schemas also have a systematic impact on the impressions and inferences about groups as well as about individuals. Massad, Hubbard, and Newtson (1979), for example, found that activating a schema involving an aggressor results in different impressions of the participants than activating a schema involving a guardian. The stimulus film was like the one originally used by Heider and Simmel (1944) in which geometrical shapes appear to interact with each other. As suggested by the work of Tesser and Danheiser (1978), the aggression/competition schema is a particularly powerful one. Subjects unitized the film (divided it into segments) in very different ways depending on which of two schemas were activated. And

once again there was evidence that schema-driven impressions were particularly difficult to change (cf. Lingle and Ostrom, 1979). Subjects in these studies were resistant to changing their impressions of the interactants and would only do so if they viewed the film again.

Linville and Jones (1980) examined the effects of schemas on perception of groups and found a polarization effect. In their study white subjects were asked to evaluate an applicant to law school who was either white or black and either well or poorly qualified. The white (in-group) members received the most moderate ratings; that is, the very well qualified whites were rated less well than the well-qualified blacks and less poorly than the poorly qualified blacks. Linville and Jones reasoned that schemas for in-group members may be more complex than out-group schemas, and thus any one piece of information about the in-group is unlikely to have a substantial impact on the overall evaluation of the group.

The greater complexity characterizing schemas associated with an in-group does not, however, seem to interfere with the generation of favorable evaluations for the group by in-group members. In fact, the hallmark of the in-group/out-group bias is a heightened discrimination between the two in favor of the in-group. These findings raise the general question of when schemas will lead to assimilation and the perception of similarity among elements and when they will lead to contrast and differentiation among elements. The pattern of effects appears a complex one and depends on the salience of the contrast, the goal of the evaluation, and the meaning of the differentiation or contrast. With respect to differentiation, for example, in-group members are viewed as more similar across traits than out-group members but more differentiated on any one trait. (See Chapter 24 in Volume Two of this *Handbook* for a full discussion of these issues.)

Together, these studies suggest that schemas have a number of systematic influences on the judgments and evaluations of others, whether individuals or groups. Personality schemas facilitate the production of global, general impressions of others. These impressions often become quite independent of the stimulus events that originally generated them, and they have a marked impact on subsequent judgments and predictions about target individuals. To the extent that a stimulus situation is ambiguous, inferences will be made in the direction fostered by the schema. Overall, schemas may have their most significant impact on the evaluation/inference stage of social information processing. This is the stage of processing that, as noted earlier in the chapter, may most clearly distinguish social perception from object perception.

As was evident in the previous sections, there is no compelling evidence that schemas markedly distort the initial perception and organization of stimuli, nor that they grossly distort recall or retrieval from memory. In other words, they do not have a dramatic impact on "the information given." Inferences and impressions, however, are much less constrained by the stimulus, and as a result, schemas can exert considerable power when going "*beyond* the information given." When stimulus information is impoverished, the default values of a schema allow for filling in so that a complete picture can be produced. This filling-in process is, of course, encouraged by behavioral situations that call for evaluations or impressions. When, in contrast, a stimulus event or situation in information-rich such that information can be gleaned from the environment or if the relevant cognitive tasks call for careful attention to the stimulus, the resultant inferences are less likely to be driven by a single schema.

Schemas Influence Overt Behavior

As might be expected, there are relatively few studies demonstrating overt behavioral effects of schemas. In principle, there should be no difficulty in finding evidence that schemas have an influence on schema-relevant behavior, except for the obvious greater difficulty of making precise behavioral observations. Of course, information-processing is also a form of behavior, albeit not readily accessible to direct observation. Schemas are assumed to include plans for action that, in large part, are the result of previous action or behavior. To the extent that some schemas are tied to particular goals (as the restaurant schema is tied to the goal of reducing hunger), the action components that accompany these plans should be readily accessible. Not all schemas, however, have clearly defined behavioral goals associated with them, and in these cases it is more difficult to predict the likely schematic effects on behavior.

In the view of Rummelhart and Ortony (1977), for example, there should be no discontinuity between plans and actions when describing schema functioning. Actions are simply plans that are "filled out" with motor values. These values may be themselves action schemas. Social cognition theories, however, appear to have overemphasized the potential difference between cognitive behavior and "real" behavior. To the extent that a schema includes action components, it should be possible to observe the influence of these schemas in shaping and constraining overt behavior.

At best, however, one could only expect some amount of behavior to be determined by any one schema because an overt behavior situation is most often a very rich one and comprehension of another's behavior requires activating a number of schemas. With respect to very general schemas, such as personality schemas, the nature of their impact on any overt behavior cannot be specified a priori. In fact, these types of schemas should only have impact on overt behavior to the extent that they are used in service of some specific behavioral purpose such as asking someone to go to the movies or choosing a person for a job.

The schema/behavior relationship is very like the attitude/behavior relationship, and predicting it involves the same general set of concerns (see Chapter 10 in this *Handbook*). How close should the relationship be? Given the multidetermined nature of most behavior, surely we cannot expect the relationship to be strong.

The role of schemas in mediating behavior has been studied in the case of the self-fulfilling prophecy (Merton, 1948; Darley and Fazio, 1980). The best-known studies of this phenomenon are by Rosenthal (1966), who has demonstrated that the expectancies of the behavioral scientist can have a substantial impact on the behavior of subjects in experiments. The ability of subjects to alter the behavior of other persons so as to make it consistent with their schemas was also investigated by Kelley and Stahelski (1970) and more recently by Snyder, Tanke, and Berscheid (1977). In the latter study the behavioral confirmation of a stereotype was investigated. Male subjects talked on the telephone with females they believed to be attractive or unattractive. Subjects who were in the unattractive condition rated their partners more negatively than subjects in the attractive condition. The behavior of the male subjects was evaluated by raters who were blind to the experimental condition. Those who believed their partner to be attractive were judged as having behaved in a more social, sexually warm, interesting, and humorous manner than those who believed their partner was unattractive. Also, the females who were in the attractive condition were rated as actually more animated, poised, sociable, and seemed to enjoy the conversation more. According to Snyder, Tanke, and Berscheid (1977), the schema that attractive people possess more socially desirable qualities was behaviorally confirmed.

In a related program of research Snyder and his colleagues (Snyder and Swann, 1978; Snyder and Campbell, 1980; Snyder, 1981) have studied the link between schemas and overt behavior by exploring the behavioral confirmation of hypotheses. These authors proposed that individuals engage in an hypothesis-confirming search strategy in which they seek out behavioral evidence that fits the hypothesis under scrutiny. In the attempt to gain evidence that fits the hypothesis, the behavior of others may be brought into line with the prevailing hypothesis and thereby succeed in confirming it. Thus in testing the hypothesis that another person is an extrovert, Snyder and Swann (1978) found that people ask questions that would be asked of people already known to be extroverts. It is hardly surprising that this line of questioning elicits behavior that often seems to confirm the hypothesis.

Trope and Bassok (1982) have sharply challenged this work on hypothesis testing and have claimed that people do not prefer questions that only confirm their hypothesis. Instead, Trope and Bassok suggest that information is gathered by a diagnosing strategy. Thus to test a hypothesis that a person is an extrovert, the information gatherer will ask about features that maximally discriminate between extrovert and nonextrovert. The results of their studies support this notion, revealing no tendency among their subjects toward hypothesis-confirming strategies.

It is likely that both explanations of how people gather information are valid. Which of the two best describes an individual's approach to social information no doubt depends on the goal of the information search. It is hardly ever the case that information is gathered in the absence of a strong organizing framework. If one is interested in detecting a particular type of individual so as to avoid forming a relationship with this person, it might be wise to follow a diagnosing strategy. In contrast, if one likes another and is hoping to discover similarities so as to pursue the relationship, a hypothesis confirmation strategy may be preferable. Fong and Markus (1982) found, for example, that when asked to form an impression, extrovert schematics ask questions that will reveal another person's extroversion, while introvert schematics ask questions designed to reveal another person's introversion.

Despite conflicting results the general line of work on information gathering is quite useful in spanning the gap between cognitive structures and action in social situations. As Trope and Bassok (1982) note, information gathering, unlike relatively passive information processing, entails social action. An understanding of the role of schemas in information gathering and in communication in general may begin to specify the role of schemas in social behavior.

SCHEMAS AND INFORMATION PROCESSING: AN INTEGRATION

From the preceding empirical generalizations about the effects of schemas on information processing, there is at least one conclusion that is readily apparent. A systematic statement of the role of cognitive structures will require linking these structures to cognitive processes, to the state of the perceiver, and to the nature of the stimulus information. It is now evident that schemas are multidetermined and multiply activated and that they have diverse and varied consequences depending on the goals of the perceiver and the content of the stimulus information.

In the preceding section all of the four summary statements include the phrase "schemas influence." To specify more precisely the nature of a schema's likely influence, one must know something about each of the following five factors: (1) the nature or content of the schema; (2) the nature or content of the input or stimulus information; (3) the fit between the schema and the stimulus information; (4) the state of the perceiver; and (5) the context of the information-processing situation or task. Each of these factors will be discussed separately below.

The Nature or Content of the Schema

There has been relatively less attention paid to the content of schemas than to their information-processing functions. The general assumption is that schemas differ in their complexity and level of generality. Of those who have attempted some specification of the nature of schemas, Rummelhart and Ortony (1977) have the most comprehensive, albeit not the most adroidtly worded, statement. They claim that schemas embed. The embedded schemas are called subschemas, and the schemas in which they appear are called the dominating schemas. The dominating schemas contain summary names or labels rather than all the conceptually related knowledge. The major advantage of embedding is that a stimulus event can be comprehended at a number of different levels.

An event, situation, or concept can be understood in terms of its major features and constituents, or it can be understood in terms of the more specific and detailed internal structure of these global features. To illustrate this point, Rummelhart and Ortony (1977) give the example of a face, which can be comprehended in terms of its global components (eyes, nose, ears, mouth, etc.) rather than in terms of the complex configuration of perceptual elements that determine each one of these parts of the face. A second assumption of these theorists about the nature of schemas is that there are countless schemas, each one referring to others, and that these schemas represent knowledge at all levels of abstraction ranging from "basic perceptual elements, such as the configuration of lines which form a square, to abstract conceptual levels which allow us to give cogent summaries of sequences of events occurring over substantial periods of time" (p. 110).

There is some theoretical controversy over whether schemas should be viewed just as structures that are activated and operated on by yet-to-be-specified cognitive processes or whether they are themselves to be considered processes. Neisser (1976) confronted this issue squarely and decided they were both. He stated (p. 56):

> In one sense, when it is viewed as an information accepting system, a schema is like a *format* in a computer-programming language. Formats specify that information must be of a certain sort if it is to be interpreted coherently. A schema is not merely a format, it also functions as a plan . . . ; schemata are plans for finding out about objects and events, for obtaining more information to fill in the format.
> . . . The information that fills in the format at one moment in the cyclic process becomes a part of the format in the next, determining how further information is accepted. The schema is not only the plan but also the executor of the plan. It is a pattern *of* action as well as a pattern *for* action.

This definition, like the Rummelhart and Ortony (1977) definition, is complex, and up to now there have been no empirical findings in the schema literature that would bolster the idea of a schema as a process or even as an essential component of the process. Yet these definitions are closest in spirit to Bartlett's (1932) original definitions of schema: "What is very essential to the whole notion, [is] that the organized mass results of past changes . . . are actively *doing* something all the time; are, so to speak, carried along with us, complete, though developing, from moment to moment" (p. 20).

Many current definitions of schemas also emphasize this same dynamic and fluid nature of thought. The alternative position holds that schemas are packages stored in memory that when necessary are activated by some cognitive process. A view of schemas as information-processing units that are continually assimilating stimuli in the environment as well as accommodating to its constraints provides some basis for conceptualizing the cognitive dynamics or the forces that presumably move thoughts around. There is no empirical foundation for these ideas, but they are useful as a set of guiding assumptions about the likely nature of schemas. Further progress in this area awaits a better understanding of the nature of representation in general.

In a review of the literature on the content and structure of social knowledge, Cantor, Mischel, and Schwartz (1982) noted that although little has been established about the structure of various schemas, evidence is growing about their likely contents. There is information, for example, about the contents of behavioral scripts for particular events (Schank and Abelson, 1977), occupational stereotypes (e.g., C. E. Cohen, 1977; Ostrom *et al.*, 1980), sex role stereotypes (Spence and Helmreich, 1978; S. Bem, 1981; Markus *et al.*, 1982), and political attitudes (e.g., Judd and Kulik, 1980).

With respect to the content of person schemas, Fiske and Cox (1979) performed a content analysis of subjects' free description of other people. They found that a set of descriptive responses they obtained could be ordered into four broad categories: appearance attributes, personality characteristics, relationships, and behavior. They also found, however, that the nature of these descriptions varied significantly with the perceiver's goal ["Find the person in Grand Central Station" versus "Describe what it is like to be around the person."].

Cantor, Mischel, and Schwartz (1982) used free-response techniques to investigate the knowledge structures of everyday situations. Such representations contain knowledge of the situation, details about the persons likely to be involved, and what is appropriate for them in these situations. Included also were the feelings of a person in particular situations and the appearance, traits, and behaviors of those who are typically present. Situation prototypes seem to consist of scriptlike structures of what to do in particular situations.

Cantor, Mischel, and Schwartz reason that the most naturally occurring content of social knowledge may be a compound structure that places persons within prototypic situations. Interestingly, this representation largely ignores the person/situation separation that has been assumed by personality and attribution theorists. Trzebinski (1984) views implicit personality schemas as containing action-goal-trait complexes. He suggests that person schemas, in general, are action-oriented in the sense that the "social entity in its general aspect is represented as chains of social events and actions, having actors with typical goals, occurring under certain typical conditions, and meeting obstacles that can be overcome in certain typical ways" (p. 3).

Schemas also differ in their coherence or integration. They may be tightly and permanently linked in a particular knowledge structure or they may be only loosely and temporarily connected. Although the conventional wisdom with respect to the content and organization of schemas is that they must be hierarchically structured, with concrete specifics in the lower levels of hierarchy and more abstract information at the top (Rummelhart and Ortony, 1977), there is little consensus on what actually happens to knowledge that becomes schematized. Theoretical opinion seems divided, for example, on whether schemas should best be viewed as cognitive units that are instantiated as a whole (Sentis and Burnstein, 1979; Thorndyke and Hayes-Roth, 1979) or whether certain aspects or components can be activated independently (Taylor and Crocker, 1981). There is slim empirical justification for either view, and continued speculation about the likely structure of schemas may serve only to emphasize the futility of trying to determine the exact nature of the cognitive unit (J. R. Anderson, 1980; Cantor, Mischel, and Schwartz, 1982).

A point well made by Neisser (1976) was that a schema should not be viewed as "a final constructed product in the perceiver's mind" (p. 57). The nature and characteristics of an activated schema probably depend on the perceiver's goal and on whether the input information comes from one's own memory and cognitive mechanisms or from the environment. The schema that becomes the on-line-processing unit is a consequence of a configuration of factors and is probably seldom the same from one time to another. In this sense no two instantiations of a schema can ever be the same, because at the minimum the latter carries in it the residue of the previous instantiation.

The Nature and Content
of the Input or Stimulus Information

Given the heavy emphasis on the ability of the perceiver to construct his or her own reality, the focus in much of social cognition research has been on the internal cognitive structures—the schemas—and much less on the nature of the stimulus input. There has been a pervasive tendency to celebrate the perceiver, to look inside the head

and—perhaps as an overreaction to the Skinnerian view—to assume that an analysis of the stimulus environment itself, without an understanding of how it was cognitively constructed, could not possibly reveal much of interest. Until quite recently, the Gibsonian charge of developing new and richer descriptions of the stimulus environment was largely ignored. This tendency to slight the stimulus has resulted in some rather unrealistic assumptions and expectations about the power of schemas to constrain the nature of information processing, as well as in a number of seemingly perplexing findings.

As described earlier, there are now two studies that fail to replicate the findings of Snyder and Uranowitz (1978). The results of these studies emphasize the necessity of considering the nature of the stimulus material when making predictions about the effects of particular schema. Instead of finding systematic reconstructive distortion of the memory of Betty K. in the direction of the label (lesbian or heterosexual) ascribed to her just before testing (as in the original study), Bellezza and Bower (1981) find a tendency to guess in the direction of the label but no evidence of schema-driven recall. Clark and Woll (1981), in fact, find an "unexpected" greater recognition accuracy by all subjects, regardless of the label, for neutral and lesbian items.

Here it is essential to note (cf. DeSilva, 1983) that as the subject is reading the story, the stimulus material *itself* may activate some very powerful schemas that may well mitigate or modify schemas activated by the labels. The story is constructed to be ambiguous with respect to sexual orientation. But given the strong normative expectations about sexual roles, subjects reading this ambiguous story are quite likely to activate a lesbian schema on their own. Under these conditions it is unreasonable to expect that the label "heterosexual" supplied by the experimenter after the reading will completely counteract the effects of schemas activated during reading, such that only information congruent with the experimenter's label will be remembered.

A socially ambiguous stimulus is quite unlike a nonsense syllable, which requires some structure to be processed meaningfully or efficiently. Because of the diverse and rich nature of our stored social knowledge, socially ambiguous stimuli will result in multiple interpretations or in different interpretations for different subjects. In this case the inconsistency present in the stimulus material itself, produced by some information that fits with one's normative expectations about other people and some that does not, is likely to activate schemas that successfully compete with those supplied by the experimenter. Research on the construction of causality, in fact, indicates that individuals are particularly fond of and remember well those events for which they can generate their own causal connections (Bower and Masling, 1981). The same may apply to organizations or encodings of stimulus material that are self-generated (Burnstein, 1962; Greenwald, 1982a).

Another example of the importance of the stimulus input is provided by Locksley, Borgida, Brekke, and Hepburn (1980). In an initial study they found that when categorical or irrelevant social information was given, subjects attributed assertiveness or passivity to male or female target persons in a manner completely congruent with sex role stereotypes. However, in a second study when behavioral information on the target's assertiveness was given, evaluations of the target person reflected this information even when it was clearly at odds with the expectations based on the sex of the individual. Here it appears that stimulus information about behavior activated schemas that accounted for the target's behavior better than did the sex role stereotypes, so powerful in the earlier study. Even the strongest schemas cannot resist stimulus information that is directly inconsistent and cannot overpower competing schemas that provide for a better fit with the stimulus events.

In developing his theory of how global impressions are generated from specific traits, N. H. Anderson (1981) has relied exclusively on the properties of the stimulus material rather than on the presumed properties of an internal structure. His information integration theory (N. H. Anderson, 1981) is the culminating development of an attempt to explicate the Asch (1946) work on impression formation begun some twenty years ago (N. H. Anderson and Barrios, 1961; N. H. Anderson, 1962, 1965a, 1965b; N. H. Anderson and Hubert, 1963; N. H. Anderson and Jacobson, 1965).

The essence of the theory seeks to determine how stimulus elements combine into wholes. It is able to specify the contributions of these elements to the total structure and to assess this contribution in precise algebraic form. Because information integration theory is a "cognitive algebra," it generates numerical solutions that can be compared with obtained data. The predictions of this theory have been quite accurate on the whole (N. H. Anderson, 1974).

The information integration theory holds that stimuli are integrated by simple algebraic rules that can be identified and specified. The basic concepts of the infor-

mation integration theory are three functions: valuation, integration, and response. The valuation function assigns psychological values to stimuli; the integration function specifies the rules whereby stimuli combine; and the response function represents the rules whereby the subject transforms an internal state (say a mental representation) into an overt judgmental response.

For the most part the integration rule is a weighted average. This rule has been challenged by the summation rule (Fishbein and Hunter, 1964), but the weight of evidence favored the weighted average (N. H. Anderson, 1965a; Hendrick, 1968). Both the averaging and the summation principles, however, are contradicted by Wyer's (1970) finding that the contribution of any one item to the overall impression varies with its redundancy with the previous items. The essential difference, however, between N. H. Anderson's approach and other current work on social cognition lies in his dependence on the stimulus materials. In his approach, relatively less attention is given to the antecedent states of the cognizer. The main specifications for the cognitive states that contribute to the cognitive product are to be found in the weights that are calculated for the stimuli that the subject combines into wholes.

The theory has been criticized by being too restrictive (Hastie, 1983), however. Yet it should be noted that Anderson sought a compromise between precision and generality. The precision criterion dictates that the input variables come in a numerical form, obeying formal measurement and scaling principles. These constraints limited the application of the theory to material that could be described numerically, such as trait adjectives. Hamilton (1981) criticized information integration theory (and similar attempts that seek to specify algebraic combination rules) for neglecting the cognitive process whereby information is combined by the individual. However, within these constraints a rich data base was generated that touches on a large variety of judgmental and attitudinal phenomena not only in social cognition but in many other fields as well. Thus while most information integration studies have been concerned with impression formation (see N. H. Anderson, 1981), there are important applications to psychophysics generally (N. H. Anderson and Jacobson, 1965; N. H. Anderson, 1967, 1970a; N. H. Anderson and Cuneo, 1978; Blankenship and N. H. Anderson, 1976), the size/weight illusion (N. H. Anderson, 1970b), equity (N. H. Anderson and Farkas, 1975; N. H. Anderson, 1976; N. H. Anderson and

Butzin, 1978), the motivation/incentive interaction (N. H. Anderson and Butzin, 1974), individual decision making (N. H. Anderson and Shanteau, 1970; Shanteau, 1970; Levin, 1975), group decision making (Kaplan, 1977; Ostrom, Werner, and Saks, 1978), social values (Leon, Oden, and N. H. Anderson, 1973), and others.

Although schemas can have a pronounced effect on how stimuli are organized initially, these effects are likely to be most evident when the stimulus itself is congruent with the schema or when the stimulus is ambiguous and does not suggest any particular structure. With respect to social stimuli, however, the latter is likely to be the rare instance. In a determination of the effects of a particular schema on processing, it is important, then, to consider the content of the stimulus material, the way it is likely to be represented, and what schemas it is likely to activate—all quite apart from the schemas that are induced by the experimenter. From a review of the studies on the effects of manipulated schemas on memory, for example, it is evident that they have some impact but that this impact is relatively weak in many cases. Only a small proportion of the complex of memory effects can be explained by their presence. Although social cognition literature is very often cited to suggest that individuals remember events that confirm their expectations or schemas, the majority of the findings show little beyond the fact that subjects "falsely" recognize foils that are consistent with their schemas.

This does not speak to the accuracy of memory. As noted by Ebbesen (1981), the number of errors that are consistent with one's schemas is most often much smaller than the number of schema-inconsistent correct responses. Thus subjects in the Rothbart, Evans, and Fulero (1979) study remembered many friendly behaviors even though they were given the schema "intelligent" with which to process the stimulus input. Subjects in C. E. Cohen's (1977) study remembered many waitress events even though they were given the "librarian" schema. And Snyder and Uranowitz's (1978) subjects remembered many lesbian items even though they were given the label "heterosexual." Mika (1966) found that arguments supporting one's attitudes are remembered better than contradictory arguments. But contradictory arguments are also remembered when they are quite silly or easy to reject. This evidence should not emphasize the failure of particular memory structures; rather, it should highlight the multiplicity of structures (those activated by the perceiver, those supplied by the experimenter, those activated by the stimulus, and those activated by the experimental context) that are likely to operate in any one processing act.

Srull and Wyer (1979) explicitly studied how stimulus input may prime particular categories that will be used in processing. Building on the work of Higgins, Rholes, and Jones (1977), they exposed subjects to behavioral statements that varied in the frequency with which a particular trait concept was implicitly invoked. Greater amount of priming led to a greater utilization of the trait concept in describing the person. They also found that once their subjects employed trait concepts that were implicitly suggested by the behavioral descriptions, they would continue to use them in their descriptions of the people and would generalize from these traits to other traits on the basis of implicit personality schemas.

It is the assumption of the cognitive structure approach that the activated schemas determine what is perceived in the social environment. As is evident from the above discussion, this is not always the case: Schemas are often activated by the on-line data. In this case processing becomes a data-driven or bottom-up process (Rummelhart and Ortony, 1977). Taylor and Fiske (1975, 1978) were first among social cognition researchers to make the case for the importance of stimulus salience in influencing perceivers' attention and employment of cognitive resources.

Salience "refers to the phenomenon that when one's attention is differentially directed to one portion of the environment rather than to others, the information contained in that portion will receive disproportionate weighting in subsequent judgments" (Taylor and Thompson, 1982, p. 175). Salient stimuli are more likely than peripheral stimuli to activate the schemas that are associated with them. With respect to social perception some categories appear to have an intrinsic salience. These include age, sex, race, and physical appearance. In undefined situations these features of people are nearly automatically salient and are ready to recruit the associated schemas. Attention may be drawn to individuals if they possess features that are likely to set them apart from others, such as a stigmatizing attribute (Langer *et al.*, 1976; Jones *et al.*, 1984).

Salience is also derived from the changing configurations of the social environment. Taylor *et al.* (1977) found that being the only male or only female in an otherwise opposite-sex group attracted greater attention than being in a more evenly mixed group. The same was found to be true for being the only black or white in a group situation. In reviewing these salience studies, Taylor and Fiske (1978) and McArthur (1981) conclude that individuals who attract attention are rated extremely, are better remembered, and are likely to be assigned a causal responsibility for behavior.

Similarly, in investigating determinants of the spontaneous self-concept, McGuire and McGuire (1982) find that if a category of a person is distinctive in a particular social environment, then this category is more likely to be used in self-description. Thus children, when describing themselves, mention their height if they are in a classroom filled with children shorter than they. The distinctiveness of a particular feature draws the perceiver's attention, and schemas associated with these features are thus activated. Recently, however, Borgida and Howard-Pitney (1983) have found that personal involvement may limit salience effects. Thus in their study highly involved perceivers showed extremely systematic processing of a message regardless of which discussant was visually salient.

There is some disagreement over whether salience effects occur during the initial encoding or during organization stages. McArthur (1980) takes a Gibsonian perspective and assumes that the structure is given by the stimuli themselves. Fiske *et al.* (1979), on the other hand, assume that perceivers impose the categorization on the stimuli once they are perceived. This debate, common in the 1940s, over the question of whether structure is imposed by the perceiver or given directly by the environment seems to be recurring in connection with a variety of social cognition problems and is likely to be a focus of research in the next decade.

Ostrom and his colleagues (Ostrom, Pryor, and Simpson, 1981; Pryor and Ostrom, 1981) have been directly concerned with the nature and content of the stimulus information. They have challenged the assumption implicit in much social psychological writing that the person is the fundamental unit of social perception. From data gathered using a speeded-sorting task, a recognition reaction time task, and a free-recall task, they suggest that the tendency to organize social stimuli according to person is importantly influenced by familiarity. When the information provided to subjects is about unfamiliar others, they will not always cluster the stimulus information according to persons. Instead, subjects may use a variety of temporal, semantic, or descriptor categories to cluster the information. Such results have led Ostrom

and his colleagues to question the generality of person perception studies that are all essentially focused on processing information about strangers.

To determine how "rich" a particular stimulus environment is, one needs to know how much structure is already present in the stimulus and how much is provided by the subject. In many schema studies the perceiver is presented with verbal descriptions of people or sets of trait adjectives that describe an individual. This form of presentation completely ignores the important questions of how the perceiver selects information from the stream of behavior. As C. E. Cohen (1981a) has suggested, this constraint on the natural situation has a number of consequences. The units of information supplied by the experimenter may not be the naturally occurring ones, and much of the range of behavioral information that is critical for person perception may not be available for investigation. She argues that a set of words or verbal descriptions provides less structure and constrains the constructive process much less than a stimulus such as a film that shows an individual engaging in a series of behaviors. Given shared linguistic and cultural conventions (P. Grice, 1967), subjects watching a film may be relatively more "stimulus bound" in their constructions than those given five adjectives to describe another person.

Investigations that are done outside of normally occurring, stimulus-rich social situations may well exaggerate the impact of schemas on the immediate course of information processing. In the laboratory setting the ambiguity of the stimulus input, of the situation, and of the perceiver's task may all invite a significant participation of a certain range of schemas. The results of many social cognition studies thus may well overestimate the power or robustness of a particular schema.

The Fit Between the Schema and the Stimulus Information

The previous section concerned the power of the input stimulus to activate schemas for its processing. This bottom-up or data-driven sequence occurs when the processing is not schema-driven or when the fit between the input and the available schemas is not a good one. What determines when a schema will fit the input situation is unclear and has been a central issue in the work of several research programs (cf. Rosch, 1973, 1975; Smith, Shoben, and Rips, 1974; Tversky, 1977; Tversky and Gati, 1978; Hastie, 1981). When a schema closely matches the structure of the input information, so that the stimulus is completely accounted for or comprehended, minimal processing will be necessary, and processing will occur effortlessly or automatically, perhaps outside conscious awareness. This seeming automaticity led Langer (1978) to brand this type of processing "mindlessness" and to suggest that there is a class of behavior that is not actively cognitively mediated. However, the case of a good fit between schema and input should actually be seen as an instance of heavily cognitively mediated behavior. It is in this instance that the schema has its most compelling, unimpeded influence on the construction of events (Cantor, Mischel, and Schwartz, 1982).

Very often, however, the fit between the input and the schema is less than perfect. Yet schemas can tolerate marked deviations and still have a powerful effect on processing. As Rummelhart and Ortony (1977) assert, the knowledge in our memory must be arranged in a manner that will allow that dead animals are still animals and that one-eyed faces are still faces. They also suggest that all of information processing can be viewed as a process of analogical reasoning. When individuals respond as if a particular stimulus event fit a particular schema, they appear to be determining that this stimulus event is analogous to those events from which the schema was originally derived. Analogies can be applied strictly and narrowly or rather broadly and loosely. It is this quality that produces flexibility in human thought, but it also makes it difficult to specify a priori the influence of a particular schema.

As discussed earlier, Hastie (1981) has specified what types of relationships between schemas and input events are likely to be associated with later recall and utilization of the input. He noted that events can be congruent, incongruent, or irrelevant to a schema. The consequence of an incongruent or an irrelevant relationship between a schema and an event is the deployment of additional cognitive resources. The individual will continue to process the stimulus input until an existing schema is made to account for it or until a new schema is generated.

Cantor (1978) has suggested that in person memory the fit between the stimulus and a particular schema may well vary with how familiar the individual is with the person being categorized. In a study in which subjects described people they knew well and whom they saw as good, moderate, and poor examples of an extrovert, Cantor found that the decision to categorize these people was based on three factors: the number of category-consistent features the person displayed, the ratio of category-consistent features to the total number of fea-

tures, and the number of features that were inconsistent with the category. These variables were related to how well an individual was perceived to fit a particular category and presumably to how likely the individual would be to activate a schema associated with this category. The weakest of these three predictors was the number of features that were inconsistent with the category.

Whether or not a schema will fit a particular input thus depends on both the perceiver's goals and the context within which the perceiver is processing the input, because both context and goals can generate different, perhaps competing schemas. And the presence of multiple schemas constrains the likelihood that any one schema will be activated to organize some input. Many of these types of issues are at the heart of the controversies over the strategies and shortcomings found to characterize the inference process. Many so-called biases, to be discussed in following sections, are the result of invoking schemas for information for which they are not appropriate. The pervasive influence of various biases and inference errors may be in some part a consequence of the experimenter contriving a situation by means of the questions that are asked (P. Grice, 1967) or the ways in which the stimulus materials are ordered or worded so that inappropriate schemas are in fact activated.

The State of the Perceiver

A critical factor in determining which schemas are activated and how well they fit the input is the state of perceiver. This includes the individual's knowledge base, motivational state, and the goals and processing objectives for the particular information-processing task. As noted previously, earlier research was very much concerned with understanding how the state of the perceiver—including his or her needs, desires, and motives—influences cognitions. Yet in more recent social cognition research only the perceiver's knowledge base has been given much consideration. All other aspects have been ignored. Recent research efforts have returned to the question of the state of perceiver with a focus on how goals or processing objectives influence the nature and course of schematic thinking.

Zajonc (1960) viewed the process of social cognition in the context of interpersonal communication. Thus the goals of information processing could be specified according to the requirements of the communication process. Two elementary communication goals were distinguished. Subjects were assigned either to the role of a receiver or to the role of a transmitter of information. It was expected that the transmitter, in order to form a clear and concise message, might represent the stimulus information in a streamlined or unified manner. In contrast, the receivers would try to understand as much of the message as possible and might "tune in" a loose structure or a number of structures so as to be prepared for all message contingencies. In other words, the transmitter might be more likely to assimilate the input information to a single schema so as to absorb the main information as accurately as possible. Receivers would be less likely to allow a single tight schema to dominate the organization of the input. This general idea was confirmed and has been replicated a number of times (A. R. Cohen, 1961; Leventhal, 1962; Brock and Fromkin, 1968; Mazias, 1973; Harvey, Harkins, and Kagenhiro, 1976; Harkins *et al.,* 1977, Higgins, McCann, and Fondacaro, 1982; Mora, 1983).

More recently, Higgins and his colleagues (Higgins, 1981; Higgins, Fondacaro, and McCann, 1981) have specified a number of particular information-processing goals and assumed that these goals can tune in various schemas. In their perspective, "communication is conceptualized as a 'game' in the sense of involving interdependent social roles and purposeful interpersonal interaction that occurs within socially defined contexts" (Higgins, McCann, and Fondacaro, 1982, p. 22). The role of speaker, for instance, is associated with a number of goals, including "[taking] the listener's characteristics into account," "[conveying] the truth as one sees it," "[trying] to be understood," "[being] relevant." Listeners, in contrast, are typically associated with a different set of goals. They are to "pay attention," "try to understand." These goals cannot all dominate at once, so one takes precedence at a given moment, and it becomes important in determining the schemas that are likely to be active. That goal then determines the fit between the schema and the data.

In the Higgins, McCann, and Fondacaro (1982) study, speakers were asked both to describe and to interpret information about another person. They were told that the listeners had either the same or different information about the stimulus person. It was expected that these speakers would pay more attention to the description goal than to the interpretation goal when they thought the listener's goal was different from their own. In support of this idea the messages of the speakers in the different condition included more unchanged descrip-

tions and evidenced less evaluation polarization of the stimulus information.

When subjects are given a goal of forming an impression of another, they also seem to organize the input within a schema and to use the schema as an interpretive framework to capture the gist of the person. They seem less concerned with reflecting the actual behavioral details. This was the conclusion of the Hamilton, Katz, and Leirer (1980) study cited earlier and the conclusion of Jeffrey and Mischel (1979), who reported that subjects organized behavior almost completely into trait categories when they were asked to form an impression of a person or to make a prediction about future behavior. They did not organize the behavioral information into situational constructs, although the experiment did not have a control group to determine what subjects would do in the absence of an impression goal. Given that it is the impression goal that most often dominates in person perception situations, it is likely that cognitions about other people are organized in terms of traits unless subjects are otherwise advised.

Wyer and Gordon (1982), in an elaborate set of studies on the recall of information about persons and groups, attempted to determine whether the trait information about a specific person is represented in a single configural representation of a target person or, alternatively, whether the information is represented according to separate traits that function as units of information about the target person. They conclude that the way in which trait and behavioral information is organized in memory and the factors that control retrieval are importantly dependent on the purpose for which the information is used when it is initially encoded. Thus different organizations of information may accompany a memory set, a person impression set, and a group impression set (cf. Gaborit, 1984).

In the investigation of the influence of goals, a number of researchers (Lingle *et al.,* 1979; Ebbesen, 1980; C. E. Cohen, 1981) have been careful to note that even though the goal of forming an impression may be preeminent in almost any social situation, it is necessary to investigate the nature of schematic processing driven by other goals before drawing conclusions about the nature of the schema or the information that is stored. C. E. Cohen (1981a), for example, draws on earlier theoretical work by Jones and Thibaut (1958) and identifies three general categories of observational goals that have been investigated empirically.

The first are information-seeking or learning goals. In this case the task seems to be one of gathering information about another or using that person's behavior to gain information for one's self, presumably about how to feel, think, or behave and what is appropriate. No interaction between the perceiver and the observed other is implied here. This could well be the goal of the individual who is scanning the social environment for cues as to appropriate social behavior (cf. M. Snyder, 1974). This goal is likely to be invoked when the subject is asked to try and remember as much about another's behavior as possible, as in the Hamilton, Katz, Leirer (1980) study discussed earlier. This recall goal also has been examined by N. H. Anderson and Hubert (1963) and by Dreben, Fiske, and Hastie (1979). In other studies that fit in this category, perceivers have been asked to take an empathy set presumably so that they could learn or understand how the target individual is feeling (Regan and Totten, 1975; Galper, 1976; Fiske *et al.,* 1979; Harvey *et al.,* 1980). Several of these studies indicate that this goal has a similar effect as the memory goal; that is, observers tend to recall more information relevant to the perspective they assume than do those who do not take this set.

The second broad category of goals identified by C. E. Cohen is personality analysis goals. This is the general goal of getting to know another person, and it includes going beyond the information given in making inferences about underlying qualities, attributes, and emotions for the target individual. This, as noted earlier, is probably the default goal for person perception, the naturally occurring goal that drives most of social cognition unless otherwise specified by the experimenter. The effects of this goal have been implicitly studied in all of the impression formation work (Asch, 1946; Wyer, 1974; N. H. Anderson, 1981) and have been explicitly studied in the behavior prediction study of Jeffrey and Mischel (1979).

The third general class of goals is that of judgment goals, where the perceiver is explicitly asked to evaluate the target persons on some characteristic or some dimension. For example, Lingle and Ostrom (1979) and Schul, Burnstein, and Martinez (1983) asked subjects to evaluate and to observe a person for suitability for particular occupations in order to decide whether he or she should be hired for a job. In those studies where observers are asked to evaluate another for likability, the goal is similar to that in impression formation or personality analysis. A liking judgment is assumed to be the consequence of a global, evaluative impression that is gained about another person. This list of goals is hardly complete. It focuses only on observational goals; it does not, for example, include the whole set of very important interpersonal and self-presentation goals.

The general idea of the C. E. Cohen (1981a) and Higgins (1981) research is that the goal is instrumental in determining which schemas are activated in a particular situation, and thus it influences the organization, retention, and retrieval of social information. Subjects given the goal of remembering another's behavior activate a schema that consists of expected actions and associations among them. Both encoding and retrieval are quite different when guided by this schema than when guided by a get-to-know-this-person schema. The major difference is that the former produces a representation of the input that stays fairly close to the specific observable details, while the second produces a representation whose details are unified and integrated into a whole. How the influence of these goals on schema activation is modified when the perceiver has the additional goals that emerge in interacting with others has not been investigated.

To understand how a goal affects the influence of schemas on information processing, one must know both the goal and the nature of the schema that is activated. Not all perceivers have the same schemas, and these schemas are not equally articulated. A study by Langer and Abelson (1972) illustrates this point. In their study therapists trained in the traditional manner and therapists with a behavioral orientation watched a videotape of a social interaction that was alternately labeled an interview with a mental patient or a job interview. The goal was to evaluate the interviewee. Presumably, the schemas of the behavioral therapists included categories or variables for specific behaviors, and the observation was then guided by this schema. Traditional therapists were more likely to invoke a person schema that included categories or variables for particular qualities of people. The person schema engaged a process of inference from the behavioral details. Accordingly, the results of this study indicated that the traditional therapists perceived the mental patient to be significantly more disturbed than the job applicant, while the behavioral therapists evaluated them similarly. It appears that the behavioral therapists attended primarily to the behavior and thus did not find differences between the two interviews. The traditional therapists, in an attempt to find the underlying qualities of the person, were probably considerably more influenced by the background informaton, allowing their schemas to fill in what they thought was missing information.

Markus, Smith, and Moreland (1983) also have explored the influence of goals on individuals assumed to have different schemas. Thus, for example, those with a self-schema for masculinity (schematics) were much more sensitive to different observational goals than were those without masculine self-schemas (aschematics). When told to form an impression of a target person engaged in a stereotypically masculine behavior, schematics made larger units and more inferences about the target than aschematics. When instructed to attend carefully to the detail of the target's behavior, schematics made more units than aschematics and reported behavioral details as well as inferences.

Although there are a substantial number of studies on the role of goals in information processing, they have only very recently been systematically examined. In the work of Schank and Abelson (1977) and in the earlier seminal work of Miller, Galanter, and Pribram (1960), goals were accorded a critical role. Similarly, Zajonc (1960) suggested that a transmitting goal activates structures whose elements are potential messages, whereas a receiving goal activates structures whose elements are classification and registration categories.

With the exception of C. E. Cohen (1981a), who has suggested that goals influence the course of information processing through their instrumental role in schema activation, there has been little speculation about what mechanisms might underlie the influence of goals. In a conceptual integration Wyer and Srull (1980) explicitly state that "information is typically processed in order to attain some objective" (p. 232)—seemingly, the most obvious of notions. Yet in the majority of social cognition studies information processing has been examined without particular regard for the goal. Given that a great deal of variance derives from goal effects, the failure to implicate goals and processing objectives in the information-processing framework is perhaps the most serious flaw of the social cognition work of the past ten or fifteen years.

In the work discussed thus far, the concern has been with goals that are presented prior to the required information processing. Other goals may be apparent, however, at different stages in the sequence. For example, Ebbesen (1980) has argued that investigators should consider the retrieval and decision processes that are invoked by the questions asked of subjects and the tasks required

of them *after* they have processed stimulus information. Some retrieval requirements or decision frameworks may lead the subject to employ a schema that is different from the one originally used to encode or organize the stimulus or to use a different component of the same schema.

The general notion is that schemas may have a greater influence on how observers construct answers to the various questions or decisions required of them than they do on the encoding or retention of the stimulus material. For example, if the perceiver is required to form a general impression of an individual, he or she may activate that schema or that portion of the schema that contains the global impressionistic or evaluative representation of the individual and may respond on the basis of this schema. It would, however, be incorrect to conclude from this cognitive performance that if given a different retrieval or decision task, the perceiver could not access a more detailed representation.

Ebbesen has used this idea to argue against the notion that personality features observed in others reflect a conceptual bias of the rater (Schweder, 1975; Schweder and D'Andrade, 1979). Schweder and D'Andrade claim that since the ratings of an individual known well to the rater often resemble the patterns for complete strangers, and since these ratings also match the perceiver's implicit personality theories, then the regularity or consistency perceived in other's behavior is little more than reflection of the perceiver's own conceptual system.

Ebbesen suggests, however, that if in giving a general impression of a target on a number of trait dimensions, the perceiver activates the same general, global impression schema for all of the questions asked, then the pattern of associations among different traits will be similar to the perceiver's beliefs about the associations among the traits themselves. That is, traits that are similar will be equally similar to the global impression schema and traits that are dissimilar will be equally dissimilar to the global impression schema. The general point is that the cognitive requirements of the personality-rating task may mask the fact that the subject has different cognitive representations of friends and strangers.

The Context of the Information-Processing Situation or Task

Context is a vague term. Generally, it refers to all the factors that are not directly relevant to the immediate processing act under scrutiny but that could predictably influence the process. In examining context, one generally considers the social nature of the situation. Is a communication directed to friends or strangers? Are subjects worried about how they will be perceived by these others? Are they anxious?

In principle, one could reduce the context to a set of subgoals. And all of these subgoals can have an influence on what schemas become most available during processing. The context of the particular processing act can influence the schema, the stimulus information, the schema/stimulus fit, and the state of the perceiver. For example, Trzebinski (1984) found different implicit personality structures when data were collected from subjects primed to think of "family life" than when collected from those primed to think of a "peer group." With respect to how context may influence schema activation, Higgins, Rholes, and Jones (1977) found that the immediately preceding task, even though unrelated, can have an effect on later cognitive performance by inadvertently priming certain categories. Specifically, they asked subjects to perform a color-naming task in which a set of traits were included. In one condition all of these traits were applicable to some behavior that the subjects would later evaluate. In others the traits were not related. After the color-naming task, subjects were given an ostensibly unrelated task that involved reading a story about a stimulus person and then describing that person.

Those who had been exposed to relevant traits in the earlier task framed their description of the target person in these terms. Those who had not been presented with these traits did not show this effect. Higgins, Rholes, and Jones concluded that the categories had been primed by the initial color-naming task and consequently were more available for use. The nature of the context may also have an influence on which stimuli are perceived as salient. Certain group compositions, for example, make some features of an individual decidedly more noticeable than others, as suggested by work on salience (Taylor and Fiske, 1978).

It is a reasonable conclusion from the Higgins, Rholes, and Jones study that certain contexts are likely to prime particular schemas and that these schemas are quite likely to be used when they are relevant to the task at hand. Bargh and Pietromonaco (1982) presented subjects with lists of words at subliminal-viewing levels. The lists of words varied in their composition; one list contained 20 percent hostile words, another 50 percent, and the third 80 percent. A recognition test indicated that these subjects showed no awareness of these words—recognition was at chance. Yet in a subsequent task involving the description of another person, these authors found that subjects in the 80 percent condition described the targets in substantially more negative terms than those in the other two conditions. A variety of other studies that reveal the influence of cognitive activity on stimuli processed outside of awareness also suggest that various features of the context may facilitate or impair the use of particular schemas (Bargh, 1982).

The larger social behavioral context also may have an impact on the fit between the schema and the stimulus. That is, different criteria may be used for schema activation when one is with a group of good friends than when one is getting to know a new co-worker. Cantor (1978) found, for example, that category placement may be determined by two quite different sets of heuristics depending on how familiar the individual is with the target.

Probably the most important influence that the context may have, however, is in determining which processing goals are being served. Most of the social cognition research reviewed in this section on cognitive structures has been done within a very limited range of social contexts. The experimental setup most often involves the subject and a hypothetical target simply in the form of a list of traits or a set of descriptions. In very few cases does the subject expect to confront the target. Consequently, the processing task is substantially simplified from what it might be in the naturally occurring situation. Subjects need only focus on the goal given by the experimenter: typically, to remember details or to form an impression. Subjects need not be concerned with a host of self-presentational concerns such as being accountable for their attitudes or behavior, creating a good impression, or presenting themselves as a particular type of person. Moreover, they need not worry about how the other person in the situation is reacting. That these expectations are important was shown by the differences in organization of information formed by subjects expecting to interact with people of similar opinion and those expecting to interact with people of contrary opinion (Zajonc, 1960).

Concerns of this type must necessarily consume a great deal of the perceiver's cognitive capacity, and hence less effort may be given to forming an impression of another person. If the social context is one in which the perceiver is trying to influence another person or is threatened by the other, it is even more likely to be the case that some aspects of content will be ignored or distorted. Just the presence of an actual stranger, as opposed to just a set of adjectives describing the other, may differentially constrain information processing.

In the current decade a great deal has been learned about the nature, organization, and function of knowledge structures, but further progress in this area may importantly depend on the realization that knowledge is structured and transmitted according to the goals, values, and motivations that are inherent in or suggested by the social context. The act of understanding is not an individual achievement; in large part it is a consequence of a social process. In a thoughtful discussion of these ideas Forgas (1981) suggests that many of the important problems of social cognition will not be understood with an exclusive focus on encoding, storage, and retrieval of information.

The current emphasis of knowledge structures provides an understanding of how the individual represents the social knowledge that is given by the society, but it does not lend insight into how social knowledge is constructed and negotiated in actual communication—factors that can only be investigated by varying the social context and examining the influence of information processing.

Which schemas will be used to comprehend events and situations at any given moment, and the influence they will have on the information-processing sequence, depends on all of the five factors outlined above. The schemas that are active at any one time are those that comprise the best fit to the needs created by these factors. One cannot, then, determine the nature or the function of a given cognitive structure until it has been established that its influence is invariant across stimuli, goals, and social context. On the basis of the research thus far, this type of invariance seems to be the exception rather than the rule.

The view of cognitive structures that emerges here is one that suggests multiple representations of stimuli—some representations being quite general and global, others being quite specific and faithful to the stimulus; some having stability, others being transitory. Moreover, it emphasizes flexibility and adaptability on the part of the perceiver in engaging these representations, depending on the needs created by the processing goals or implied by the social context.

In all the work on cognitive structures and in the attempts to analyze them, there has been very little concern with the individual's access to these processes and with the question of whether there is some awareness about them. In an important and provocative article Nisbett and T. Wilson (1977) argued convincingly that for the most part conscious access to cognitive processes is denied to the individual. In a more recent analysis, Wilson has pursued the awareness problem and argues that we have limited access to our attitudes and feelings and that self-analysis of the reasons of a given behavior serves only to confuse us and to lower the attitude behavior correlation (Wilson, Hull, and Johnson, 1981). Kellogg (1982) has tried to distinguish instances where conscious access to cognitive processes might exist. Thus he points out that when individuals are engaged in a complex inference process and test various hypotheses intentionally, introspective reports might be accurate in describing the internal process. However, the individuals may not be aware of simpler processes, such as how they detect and estimate the frequency of incidental events.

APPLICATIONS: SELF, ATTITUDES, STEREOTYPES

Many, perhaps the majority, of the studies described in the previous section were primarily concerned with social *information processing* and only secondarily interested in understanding a particular substantive problem of *social behavior*. Much of this research would, in fact, be difficult to distinguish from the standard fare of straight cognitive psychology. In attempts to examine the workings of internal cognitive structures, social psychologists have relied quite heavily on the computer metaphor. In the course of analyzing information storage and retrieval, we have very often ignored much of what is unique and special about the social stimulus and the social situation and, as a result, have done little to further our understanding of some of the essential psychological problems—aggression, competition, cooperation, conformity, group dynamics. There are, however, several important exceptions to this general statement. In the areas of self-concept theory, attitudes, persuasion, stereotyping, and intergroup behavior—all classic concerns of social psychological theory—some significant theoretical advances have been made that can be directly linked to the application of the cognitive perspective.

The self-concept, for example, has been returned to the realm of legitimate empirical study. Through a cognitive analysis of the self-concept and an emphasis on the nature of the knowledge structures relevant to the self, researchers have been able to empirically validate many of the assumptions of the early self theorists (e.g., Rogers, 1951; Kelly, 1955; Combs and Snygg, 1959; Sarbin, 1962) about the referencing, channeling, or distorting functions of the self. Many self-serving biases or distortions, for example, can be productively interpreted as the result of the greater availability and memorability of self-relevant stimuli (cf. D. T. Miller, 1978). Thus M. Ross and Sicoly (1979) find that the tendency to accord one's self the lion's share of credit for a joint product may be simply a function of the greater availability in memory of information about one's own contribution to a mutual endeavor, rather than a function of more mysterious ego-protective forces. Similarly, the tendency to implicate the situation to a greater extent in explaining one's own behavior than in explaining others' (Jones and Nisbett, 1971) can be seen as a consequence of one's perceptual perspective. In the examination of one's self what is figural is the situation. In the examination of others what is figural is the person, and the situation becomes the ground.

In this cognitive approach to the study of the self, the self-concept is viewed as a set of cognitive structures about the self used to recognize and interpret self-relevant stimuli in the individual's social experiences. From this perspective the self-concept functions just as any other cognitive structure is assumed to function. It influences what stimuli receive attention and has an effect on memory, prediction, inference, and behavior. Many of these results are described in Chapter 28 in this *Handbook,* and most have been thoroughly summarized in several recent volumes on the self in social psychology (see Wegner and Vallacher, 1980; Rosenberg and Kaplan, 1982; Suls, 1982). Some controversy exists over whether the self-concept should be viewed as a special or unique cognitive structure (cf. Rogers, 1951; Bower and Gilligan, 1979; Greenwald, 1982b; Markus and Sentis, 1982), but there is now substantial agreement among investigators that the self-concept does function as a selective mechanism in information processing and that the cognitive approach has succeeded in identifying the nature of this selectivity. Not all of the functions of the self, however, can be completely understood in terms of cognitive mechanisms. The defended nature of the self, for example, although somewhat illuminated by the cognitive perspective, seems to defy complete analysis in terms of cognitive factors.

A second major emphasis in the cognitive approach to the self has been more behavioral in nature and has focused on self-regulation and the control of behavior. Using information-processing concepts, Carver and Scheier (1981, 1982) have developed a complete theory of self-regulation that they call control theory. They suggest that an individual's focus of attention shifts back and forth between the environment and the self. The basic construct of their theory is the discrepancy-reducing feed-back loop. The loop consists of an input function that is the sensing of a present condition. This perception is then compared with a point of reference, and if a discrepancy is perceived between one's present state and the reference, an action is performed. The goal of this action is to reduce the discrepancy by having an impact on the system's environment. Carver and Scheier assume that knowledge about objects and events is organized in scripts and schemas and that these structures influence the way the environment and other people are construed.

In a systematic program of research (for reviews, see Carver and Scheier, 1981, 1982), they have tested the idea that some behavioral output will occur as a function of a discrepancy between a perceived state and a reference value. They have evidence in a variety of domains that experimental manipulations that increase self-focus result in increased conformity to standards that are situationally salient. Scheier, Fenigstein, and Buss (1974), for example, find that subjects in a learning experiment shocked women less intensely when self-directed attention was high than when it was low. The idea here was that the subjects high in self-focus were adhering to norms or standards of chivalry.

In general in these studies, attitudes and expectancies are reflected in behavior only when self-focus is relatively high. High self-focus promotes increased self-regulation, and thus social knowledge is directly linked to social behavior. Others, for example, Duval and Wicklund (1972), have interpreted these findings of enhanced or increased performance in various domains as reflecting an increase in drive as a result of failing to meet some internal standard (cf. Carver and Scheier, 1981). Carver and Scheier assume, however, that it is possible to explain all behavior in terms of discrepancy reduction, without invoking the concept of drive, and the issue is a matter of some controversy. On the one hand, it is important to ask why discrepancy generates instrumental behavior to reduce it. One obvious answer to this question is that discrepancy is aversive. But this is equivalent to accepting discrepancy as a drivelike state in the individual. On the other hand, discrepancy alone would be insufficient to explain the performance increments obtained in studies of objective self-awareness (e.g., Duval and Wicklund, 1972). For in these studies it is unlikely that a discrepancy was experienced by the subjects because standards of performance were often quite ambiguous.

In the general area of attitudes and persuasion, Greenwald (1968) and Petty, Ostrom, and Brock (1981) have used an information-processing approach to argue that persuasion can be best understood in terms of the thoughts that the recipient of a message generates in response to a particular communication. Their theory is called cognitive response theory and it views the thoughts that are invoked as a consequence of a message as the end result of information-processing activity. In their work they have emphasized that a great deal of the information that the individual uses in responding to a communication comes not from the communication itself but from the knowledge organized within the recipients' preexisting schemas. These self-generated cognitive responses may be at odds with the communication, may be irrelevant, or may be generally in agreement with it.

In attempts to validate the cognitive response theory, several studies have found that forewarning subjects of a subsequent attitude-discrepant communication has the effect of eliciting negative thoughts in anticipation of the message (Petty and Cacioppo, 1977; Cialdini and Petty, 1981). This counterargumentation leads to attitude polarization and finally to resistance to the persuasive message. In one study (Petty and Cacioppo, 1977) such forewarned subjects were compared with unwarned subjects. The unwarned subjects were simply asked to write their thoughts about an issue before hearing a message. They showed a resistance to the message that was equal to that of the warned groups. This finding led the cognitive response theorists to argue that it is not the forewarning itself that allows subjects to resist the persuasive message but rather the generation of cognitive responses or thoughts that will subsequently compete with those in the message.

Cognitive response theory has also produced several other findings of practical significance (Gillig and Greenwald, 1974; Petty and Cacioppo, 1981). When individuals are not involved with an issue or have little prior knowledge, highly credible speakers will be relatively more persuasive than low-credibility speakers. This occurs because low-involvement/knowledge recipients have more success in counterarguing or in generating negative cognitive responses to low-credibility than high-credibility sources. High credibility seems to inhibit the unfavorable thoughts that are likely to be the cognitive responses of these subjects.

Finally, in the area of stereotyping and prejudice, significant advances have been made with the application of the cognitive approach. G. W. Allport's (1954) early notion of categorization as the essence of stereotyping has been refined and developed by such researchers as Taylor, Hamilton, and Rothbart (see Hamilton, 1981,

for a review). Moreover, the concepts of schematic processing and illusory correlation (see Hamilton, 1981, pp. 181 ff.) have been productively employed to analyze some of the important features of prejudicial behavior. Finally, work by Tajfel (1970, 1981) and by Wilder (1981) has used the social categorization paradigm to explore the cognitive antecedents of intergroup conflict. This research is extensively reviewed in this *Handbook* in Chapter 24.

INFERENCE PROCESSES

As is evident in the previous section, schemas and the operations the individual performs on information have the most compelling effects in more complex cognitive tasks: judgments, decisions, and inferences. Hastie and Carlston (1980) characterized social cognition as being generally more complex than cognition as studied by experimental psychologists. A major source of this complexity stems from the fact that social cognition involves more than just questions of detection, recognition, retrieval, and comprehension. In complex cognitive tasks individuals "go beyond the information given." They form impressions, make judgments, and draw *inferences*. Moreover, cognitive *content* in itself is of interest.

It is in the process of inference and judgment that the individual makes the most significant contribution to the cognitive product, and conversely the nature of the stimulus information determines the cognitive product to a lesser extent. How some units of information are combined and processed to generate a cognitive product depends very much on what schemas, what premises, and what rules of combination the individual brings to the inference situation. A major area of empirical work in the cognitive social psychology of the past fifteen years has grown out of a concern with just these issues.

There seems to have been a cyclical series of swings peculiar to social psychology, from the view of the individual as a rational and efficient cognizer to one where the individual is irrational and quite imperfect. The thirties discovered the vulnerability of simple perceptual judgments to the pressures of group norms (Sherif, 1936). They revealed human irrationality in prestige and halo effects (Lorge, 1936), which demonstrated that aesthetic and political judgments are readily distorted by the assignment of prestige labels. During the forties Asch (1946) and Helen Block Lewis (1941) restored the dignity of the cognizer by explaining the embarrassing results on prestige suggestion in terms of search for meaning and

cognitive reorganization. The early work on informal social communication (Festinger, 1950), in which the individual was presented as seeking to achieve objective and
social reality, also had a distinctly rational cast. However, the fifties saw the pendulum swing back. Cognitive
dissonance research (Festinger, 1957) pictured individuals as quite ready to sacrifice their commitment to objective reality for the sake of psychological comfort. In a
reaction against this view of the cognizer as "rationalizing" rather than rational, attribution theory of the sixties
(Kelley, 1967) created the most rational individual
ever—an efficient inference machine capable of employing quasi-scientific methods. Finally, the most recent emphasis on inference, heuristics, and biases (Kahneman
and Tversky, 1973; Nisbett and Ross, 1980) represents
yet another swing. The individual is not so competent
after all; rather, the perceiver's logic is prone to fatal
flaws and self-deception. Christensen-Szalanski and
Beach (1984) have noted the enormous increase in articles
seeking to document human intellectual frailty. Between
1972 and 1981, they found more than five times as many
"poor performance" articles than "good performance"
articles. Shortly before active interest in heuristics and biases developed, Peterson and Beach (1967) compared the
average subject with a normative model and found that
"Inferences made by subjects are influenced by appropriate variables and in appropriate directions" (p. 42),
whereas only a few years later Slovic and Lichtenstein
(1971) concluded that "The Peterson and Beach view of
man's capabilities as an intuitive statistician is too
generous" (p. 79). If the cycles continue then the next
swing to come is sure to be a positive one.

Social psychology while almost always cognitive,
has in its short history at times paid tribute to the human
intellect and then in disdain turned against its frailty. A
correlate of these swings was a debate about the causes of
the individual's irrationality. Was faulty information
processing to be explained by assuming an interference
from "hot" factors, such as motives, moods, and emotions, or was it simply a matter of various inadequacies in
the programs that operated on information?

In the following section many of the biases found to
characterize human judgment and inference are reviewed. On many occasions these biases have heuristic
value and are, therefore, justifiable, useful, and entirely
proper. On other occasions, however, they can lead to serious errors in thinking. A compelling case has been
made by Nisbett and Ross (1980) for the failures of the
human mind with respect to inference and judgment and

for the social dangers these shortcomings invite. In their
book *Human Inference: Strategies and Shortcomings of
Social Judgment,* they illustrate the ways in which human
inferences depart from normative solutions. Although
acknowledging that people often fare quite well as intuitive scientists, Nisbett and Ross choose to focus on
human error and demonstrate that people's attempts to
understand and predict are often undermined by a diversity of inferential shortcomings. With a broad-ranging
set of anecdotes and empirical findings, Nisbett and Ross
link the source of inferential error to two general tendencies of the individual: (1) a willingness to overutilize
simplistic or intuitive inferential strategies and (2) a failure in everyday thinking to fully utilize a variety of formal, logical, and statistical strategies of the sort that
guide scientific analysis.

With respect to the first tendency named by Nisbett
and Ross, the primary concern is with the individual's excessive reliance on certain often-used schemas and causal
theories at the expense of other structures that might require more cognitive effort or time. To demonstrate the
second tendency, they compare the inference tasks of the
layperson with the inference tasks of the scientist. These
include characterization of events, samples, and populations, assessment of covariation, causal analysis, and
theory testing. Nisbett and Ross (1980, pp. 15–17) state:

> The laypersons' characterizations of events often
> are unduly influenced by prior beliefs or knowledge
> structures. Characterization of samples is distorted
> by the differential "availability" in experience and
> memory of various events. Characterization of the
> population is compromised by ignorance of statisti-
> cal considerations, chiefly those of sample size and
> sample bias. Covariation assessment is overly influ-
> enced by actual data configurations. Causal analysis
> suffers from similar overutilization of prior theories
> and from overreliance on the sheer conspicuousness
> of potential causal candidates. People have little
> knowledge of the regression considerations underly-
> ing prediction tasks and substitute simple similarity
> or representativeness judgments. Finally, people
> have little appreciation of strategies for disconfir-
> mation of theories and persist in adhering to a theo-
> ry when the number of exceptions to the theory
> exceeds the number of confirmations.

In their concluding chapters Nisbett and Ross speculate about the need to become aware of the inferential
shortcomings, and they point out the difficulty of doing

so. They worry that it is not the layperson who is so error-prone. Lawmakers, judges, and military decision makers may be equally susceptible to these shortcomings. Nisbett and Ross conclude with a set of maxims that should prevent the individual from falling prey to the most pernicious of the inferential errors. They advise that the individual's inferences should be guided by the following questions (Nisbett and Ross, 1980, pp. 283–285):

1. Is it an empirical question?

2. What hat did you draw that sample from?

3. Ok, what do the other three cells look like (referring to the tendency to ignore all cells in a contingency table except the present/present cell when judging the association between two variables)?

4. Did you ward off the fundamental attribution error?

5. Can you explain exceptions?

The terms *bias* and *heuristic* have often been used interchangeably in social cognition, but there are important differences between these concepts. Bias occurs when we are victims of the limitations of our own cognitive capacities. For example, if we are compelled by the salience of a particular stimulus to believe, without reflection, that it is the most likely cause of an event, we are subject to a bias. Heuristics, however, are inference tools used by the individual deliberately and purposefully. A tendency to guess heads more often than tails in a coin-tossing gamble may be a bias if the response "heads" has a higher probability of emission because it is easier to pronounce than "tails," for example. But it is a heuristic if the individual suspects the fairness of the coin and believes that heads have in fact a higher likelihood. Most of the phenomena to be discussed in the following section have elements of both heuristics and biases.

In principle, there are only two types of errors that can be made in drawing inferences. They can be made on the premises or the data, or on the operations of the inference process. Thus, on the one hand, in the case of deductive processes, the person might select inappropriate or false premises. In the case of inductive processes the person might consider the wrong data. Strictly speaking, selecting wrong premises or data is not always an error. Often it is a case of lack of foresight or simply bad luck. If we always knew to select the true and appropriate premises and if the "right" data were always available, we would be omniscient. Selecting wrong premises in deduction is equivalent to considering wrong data in induc-

tion. The second type of essential inference error can occur when the operations that derive conclusions from the premises are faulty.

Inferential, judgmental, and heuristic biases can be divided into those that affect the premises and those that affect the inference operations. However, those that have been studied do not fall neatly into these distinct categories, nor can they be ordered otherwise with much precision. There is a great deal of overlap and unclarity. Roughly, one can distinguish between (1) input biases, (2) output biases and, (3) operational biases and heuristics. An input bias exists when inference relies on data selectively such that some classes of data are given more weight than others. As a result, the individual may activate inappropriate schemas to deal with the information at hand. Input biases, such as availability, are thus data biases, and they reflect the individuals' preference for some data over other. Output biases, on the other hand, reflect response preferences. It is the study of input bias that reflects most clearly the contemporary O–S–O–R approach to the analysis of behavior (see p. 138). In the earlier S–O–R orientation, only the response was considered subject to bias because the stimulus was assumed to be under the experimenter's control and regarded as otherwise not free to vary. Thus, the study of output biases has a long theoretical history and derives from the S–R orientation. For example, acquiescence —the tendency to give a positive answer rather than a negative answer to a question—is such a bias. In the case of output bias, the individual does not evaluate data; the individual supplies guesses in the absence of data or when confronted with insufficient data. The third group—operational biases and heuristics—are largely operational rules of thumb for inference. Some of these operational biases and heuristics are general and apply to all inferences, whereas others are specifically social in that they apply only to inferences about people or about the self. A focus on these operational biases and heuristics is yet another manifestation of the general concern with the workings of the information-processing system that dominated the last two decades of research in social psychology. In the next section a variety of biases that fall within these categories are reviewed.

INPUT BIASES

Several decades ago Maier and Solem (1952) asked students how much money a person would make by buying a horse for $60, selling it for $70, buying it back for $80, and selling it again for $90. Only 45 percent of the undergraduate population was able to solve the problem at that time. When Hoffman and Maier (1961) used it again in a different context, only 40 percent solved it; and five years later (Hoffman and Maier, 1966) the proportion of correct solutions went down to 35 percent.

The problem has been used in a variety of settings, and correct answers seldom exceed 50 percent. It is revealing that when the question is modified such that in the second transaction the person, instead of buying the same horse back, buys an entirely different horse—or better yet, if the person buys a watch (for $80 and sells it for $90)—the solution is readily reached by nearly 100 percent of the population. Clearly, the two statements of the problem influence the subject to use the data differently, and they recruit different premises.

In the first form the "schema of *five* transactions" is activated, probably primed by the phrase "bought it *back*," and the person tends to subtract $70 − $80 = −$10 to mark the loss. The fact that the hypothetical horse trader bought the horse *back* is irrelevant and should have been ignored. In the second form of the problem the "schema of *four* transactions" is activated because the last two transactions appear to be independent of the first two, and for that matter they could have preceded them. Many input biases have the above form.

In general, data biases occur because some information is more available or accessible than other information, and the accessible information may at times activate an inappropriate schema, setting an inference process in motion that may lead to wrong conclusions.

Availability

Tversky and Kahneman (1973) state that an individual uses "the availability heuristic whenever he estimates frequency or probability by the ease with which instances or associations could be brought to mind" (p. 208). Commonly, it may well be that the more readily one can think of instances of a given event or of a class of objects or events, the more of these there may have been around or have occurred. And the heuristic of availability might serve us well. But not always.

The typical experiments on availability compare two groups or two conditions in one group. In one the subjects are asked to recall or to produce some information, for example, to name flowers or famous names of men and women. In another they are asked to estimate the level of their own performance. Thus, for example, in one study subjects were given two minutes to *recall* as

many as they could of city names beginning with F, Russian novelists, four-legged animals, etc. Another group was asked to *estimate* the number of instances they actually could name in a two-minute interval. The correlation between these two averaged for sixteen categories was .93.

Although never thought of as an instance of the availability heuristic, the phenomenon of increased truth value of statements achieved by sheer repetition *may well* involve some elements of this heuristic. The paradigm involves repeated presentation of assertions that are subsequently judged for their truth value. Hasher, Goldstein, and Toppino (1977), Bacon (1979), and Schwartz (1982) all found consistent increases in the rated truth value of uncertain statements presented repeatedly to the subjects—increases that were a monotone function of the number of repetitions. These results may involve the availability heuristic if subjects equate truth value with subjective familiarity. Statements repeated more frequently are readily available for recall and may thus be higher in subjective probability of being "true" than infrequent statements.

Even though these experiments were not ostensibly concerned with availability, they illustrate an important problem. The premise of the availability *heuristic* is that the individual instantiates the ease of recall as a problem-solving routine—utilizes it as a proxy for some other property of the stimulus world, such as frequency or probability. In the case of these last experiments the individual might have used ease of recall as a proxy for truth. But we do not know from the experimental data that ease of recall was in fact *used* by the subject at all. Nor do we know for experiments concerned with availability directly that ease of recall or any other internal symptom of availability was used by subjects *heuristically*. It is entirely conceivable, therefore, that many of the results on the availability heuristic are evidence only for the availability bias.

Availability bias has been invoked in the attitude/behavior consistency problem (Snyder and Kendzierski, 1982). Thus, for example, Fazio *et al.* (1982) have argued that if "an attitude is to guide behavior, the attitude must first be accessed from memory. Only when accessed, and consequently, salient, can attitudes exert any influence upon behavior" (p. 340). This is a rather strong statement, for it excludes habitual and automatic behavior that is guided by attitudes. Smokers have preferred brands, and they ask automatically for that brand when buying cigarettes. When they buy cigarettes, their attitudes toward the brand need not become especially salient. However, it is undeniably the case that when attitudes are made salient, related behavior is more likely to be consistent with these attitudes. This weaker hypothesis was demonstrated by Snyder and Swann (1976) in the case of judgments of sex discrimination.

Derivative experiments that invoke availability bias are not sufficient evidence for its operation as an *inference heuristic,* as Tversky and Kahneman (1973) defined it. However, up to now no research has demonstrated that such "shortcuts" are actually intended as deliberate heuristic devices. It does not suffice to demonstrate that there is a substantial correlation between individuals' actual performance and their estimate of their own performance. As a bias, however, it is clear that availability works primarily to promote the activation of schemas and attention to data that may often be inappropriate.

At the same time it cannot be assumed that just because the individual's choice agrees with the normative solution, the individual necessarily understands inferential rules (Evans, 1982). Kahneman and Tversky (1982) as well as their critic (L. J. Cohen, 1981) are both taken to task by Evans (1982) for making this implicit assumption.

Anchoring

As one example of the *anchoring heuristic,* Tversky and Kahneman (1973) asked subjects to estimate the product $8 \times 7 \times 6 \times 5 \times 4 \times 3 \times 2 \times 1$ or the product $1 \times 2 \times 3 \times 4 \times 5 \times 6 \times 7 \times 8$. The average estimate of the descending product was four times as large as that of the ascending sequence. The result was explained by suggesting that the subjects extrapolate the product on the basis of a few initial operations, e.g., $8 \times 7 \times 6$ or $1 \times 2 \times 3$. Since the basis of the extrapolation for the descending series was much larger than that for the ascending series, a larger product was estimated for the former. The core of the process in an anchoring heuristic (or bias) is that initial values play a more important role than they should (Poulton, 1968, 1977; Tversky and Kahneman, 1974; Fischhoff and MacGregor, 1980). Anchoring is thus a close relative of availability. Early data recruit a range of values that is too limited for the purposes at hand. It is thus the cognitive counterpart of anchoring effects in psychophysics (Helson, 1949).

Most of social psychological responses are obtained in forms of scale ratings, and it appears that individuals differ in the way they view the typical scales that are used in attitude and judgmental research. Individuals bring to the experimental situation their own "personal reference scales" that may vary with their background (Ostrom, 1966; Ostrom and Upshaw, 1970) and with context (Manis, 1960; Upshaw, 1962, 1965). These preferences, which may in one case favor one end of the scale and in another the opposite end, represent a form of anchoring in which, without knowing the "personal transformations" performed by the subjects, the meaning of the subjects' ratings cannot be understood.

Primacy

Asch (1946) was among the first to discover that the early items in an impression formation task contribute more significantly to the total impression than the later items. A person who is characterized as intelligent, slender, and suspicious is rated more positively than a person who is characterized as suspicious, slender, and intelligent. N. H. Anderson (1965a) has confirmed these results and described them precisely by means of information integration theory (N. H. Anderson, 1981). Vinokur and Ajzen (1982) have recently shown that prior causes are given greater weight in inferences than subsequent causes, a phenomenon they termed the *causal primacy effect.* And primacy has been shown in other phenomena as well (e.g., Feldman and Bernstein, 1978; Zenker *et al.,* 1982).

It may appear that the primacy effect in impressions depends entirely on the availability of items in the same way that the estimate of the product in the above example of anchoring depends on the availability of the early items. Such a conjecture, however, is contradicted by recall data in impression formation that suggest that it is not the early but the last items that are remembered best (N. H. Anderson and Hubert, 1963). If the early items recruited the main schema that operated on the ensuing adjectives, the individual should have remembered these early items quite well. N. H. Anderson and Hubert (1963) explain their results by assuming dual processing of the adjectives such that evaluative information is extracted from each adjective and stored separately from descriptive information. It would thus follow that if availability *bias* is at work, it is at work only for the evaluative aspect of information. However, the availability *heuristic* as defined by Tversky and Kahneman (1973) could not be invoked, because ease of recall of the items would lead the individual to consider last items as more important (and give them greater weight), since recall is dominated by recency, not primacy.

Why should primacy dominate impression formation? If we take the conversational conventions (P. Grice, 1967) into account and inquire what might be going on in the subject's mind, the primacy effect in impression formation might turn out to be a fairly reasonable phenomenon. It may be neither a matter of applying the availability heuristic nor a matter of an irrational primacy bias. The utterance "intelligent, slender, and suspicious" is understood not only for its components but for its sequence as well. The subject must automatically ask why *intelligent* is first in the list presented. The more significant information is, in fact, generally offered at the beginning. We *mean* to assign a greater weight to this information when we present it first.

Question order in survey research represents an interesting example of the effects of a conversational convention that changes meaning by virtue of order of presentation. Before the United States entered World War II, respondents were asked whether American citizens should be allowed to join the German army (Rugg and Cantril, 1944). Twenty-three percent answered in the affirmative when the question was first in the series of similar questions about the French army and the British army. A considerably greater proportion of positive answers was obtained (34 percent), however, when the question followed the two questions about Americans joining the French and the British troops. The first order of presentation activated a "loyalty and treason" schema, and without any other context an affirmative answer would have been interpreted as an expression of a pro-enemy attitude. The second order activated the "freedom of choice" schema. Americans should be allowed to fight in *any* army they chose. An affirmative answer was now more acceptable because the "loyalty and treason" considerations were mitigated by "freedom of choice." These differences demonstrate that the analysis of biases and heuristics requires precise information about the schema with which the subject approaches the information they were asked to process by the experimenter.

Perseverance

Ross, Lepper, and Hubbard (1975) have shown a powerful effect associated with postexperimental debriefing that is closely related to the primacy phenomenon. Subjects are asked to perform a task on which they ostensibly succeed or fail. Subsequent debriefing informs the subjects that the task performed was such that no real evaluation was possible and that the information they received about their own performance was entirely contrived. The subjects are told that no inferences should be drawn on the basis of the information they received from the experimenter because that information was previously contrived and was not contingent on the subjects' work.

Thus we have here clear and deliberate instructions for the subjects to ignore certain prior data. When later asked, however, how the subjects might have done on such a task had there been a way of evaluating their performance, the subjects *persevere* in their belief, accepting the prior data as valid and rejecting the subsequent discounting. Perseverance effects have also been found for abstract "theories" (C. Anderson, Lepper, and L. Ross, 1980), beliefs (Massad, Hubbard, and Newtson, 1979), and judgments (Walster *et al.*, 1967).

L. Ross (1977a) suggests that under the conditions of the experiment the subjects are prompted to construct antecedent-consequence linkages to deal with the feedback, and when the information previously given is revoked, the cognitions about the causal links are still salient and affect the subject's prediction for future similar tasks. Carroll (1978) argued that since it is easier to generate a cognition if the cognition has been generated on a recent occasion than if it has not been previously generated, it is availability in memory that best explains the perseverance effect. It should be noted, however, that perseverance effects may be avoided if the individual expects to justify decisions based on an early item of information (Tetlock, 1983). This form of accountability reduces primacy and perseverance effects and increases overall recall.

Strictly speaking, the perseverance paradigm combines in it a number of antecedent factors. First, there is a possible *primacy effect:* The information that the subject did well or poorly precedes the information that it was contrived. Why should the subject disbelieve the first and not the second? Second, the information that the subject did well or poorly comes in a *vivid* (see below) form—the discounting information is much less so. Third, there may be a *self-serving bias* (see below) such that success feedback is absorbed more readily than failure feedback, and most of the effect may come from that condition. That this may be the case is strongly suggested in a recent study by Sweeney and Moreland (1980).

Vividness

A number of experimental findings (Nisbett *et al.*, 1976; Borgida and Nisbett, 1977; Hamill, Wilson, and Nisbett, 1980) suggest that the subject might ignore statistical information in favor of a single highly vivid instance. Thus the person who is about to buy a car may discover that a particular brand is highly rated by a number of magazines and consumer organizations; yet upon hearing from her neighbor that the latter would not buy such a car because her brother-in-law had no end of troubles with his own car of that brand, the person may decide against the car. *Vividness* might be considered to be thus an availability bias that favors some data over others.

Evidence has been reported that vivid and salient events, because they are more available in memory, are taken to have greater causal potential than events that are pallid. Thus as noted previously, people who are in some way distinctive and demand the subject's attention are more likely to be viewed as causal agents. This effect apparently depends more on the "objective" salience of the stimulus person than on the subjects' perception of his or her salience (Arkin and Duval, 1975; Taylor *et al.,* 1979; Robinson and McArthur, 1982). McArthur and Ginsberg (1981) found no relationship between causal attribution and the amount of attention the subject deployed to a stimulus person, thus increasing its salience by subjective means, and Fiske, Kenny, and Taylor (1982) reported better recall of salient information only if these stimuli were perceived by the subject as implicated in the influence achieved.

Bizarreness—which is, of course, a form of vividness and salience—has been repeatedly found to facilitate learning, recall, and recognition (Wollen, Weber, and Lowry, 1972; Nappe and Wollen, 1973; Merry and Graham, 1978; Merry, 1980; Cox and Wollen, 1981; Wollen and Cox, 1981). A recent review of vividness literature by Taylor and Thompson (1982), however, claims that the evidence supporting the vividness phenomenon is questionable. They suggest that vividness effects may be obtained in within-subject designs, however. Most research on vividness employed between-subject comparison, which, as in the earlier work on contrasts in incentive effects (Crespi, 1942; G. R. Grice, 1966; Greenwald, 1976), may have been insensitive to differences produced by the experimental manipulations. Of course, if it were to be found that vividness works in within-subject designs but not in between-subject designs, we would still need to explain why this is so. And it remains also to be explained why between-subject designs do show vividness effects on memory (Taylor and Thompson, 1982) but fail to show these effects on inference.

Negativity Bias
The *negativity bias* has been studied primarily in the context of judgment and choice, and it consists of assigning relatively greater importance to negative features of the alternatives. Kanouse and Hanson (1971) have shown that under some circumstances negative information has more impact than positive information. This bias applies to all judgments, apparently. There is also another form of negativity bias, manifested primarily in social judgments, which consists of a tendency of people toward downward comparisons (Wills, 1981). That is, people seek out others less well off than themselves on some dimensions and thus experience a relative superiority.

In evaluating objects, people seem to protect themselves against eventual regret and weight negative attributes more than positive attributes. In postdecision experiments more cognitive "work" must be done on the rejected alternatives (Brehm, 1956). A similar tendency is found in other types of judgments (Birnbaum, 1972) and especially in risk taking, where anticipation of regret is especially salient (L. Katz, 1964; Rettig and Pasamanick, 1964; Slovic and Lichtenstein, 1968). Kanouse and Hanson (1971) interpreted negativity bias as a contrast phenomenon. They argued that since most information is positive, when we come across a negative item, it stands out against the positive information, and it is thus afforded more importance than it might otherwise deserve.

In the evaluation of persons it is commonly found that negative adjectives seem to contribute more to the overall impression than positive adjectives (N. H. Anderson, 1965a; Feldman, 1966; Richey, McClelland, and Shimkunas, 1967; Rokeach, 1968; Bolster and Springbett, 1972; Hamilton and Zanna, 1972; Hodges, 1974). In a sophisticated analysis of dispositional schemas, Reeder and Brewer (1979) show that "the performance of socially undesirable behavior will be dispositionally informative, whereas a single performance of socially desirable behavior will not" (p. 70). Amabile and Glazebrook (1982), however, describe social negativity bias as a more general tendency that has self-serving functions (see below). Judging someone in relatively derogatory terms has positive consequences for self-enhancement. This might be especially true when one's own self-esteem is threatened. Thus whereas Kanouse and Hanson (1971) explain the negativity bias in cognitive terms, Amabile and Glazebrook (1982) return to motivational antecedents. Note, however, that in the latter case only judgments of people are considered.

Negativity is a bias to the extent that in the drawing of inferences negative information is given more weight on the a priori false grounds that it leads to valid inferences or better decisions. However, if in general negative items are in fact more informative than positive items, then negativity may well be regarded not as a bias but as a useful and defensible heuristic that serves the individual well on appropriate occasions.

OUTPUT BIASES

On one of his programs Groucho Marx (G) had as participants an old man (O) and a woman teacher (T) of about thirty-five. The interview went something like this:

G. (*to the old man*): How old are you?

O.: Eighty-six years.

G.: Are you married?

O.: Yes.

G.: How long have you been married?

O.: Sixty-six years.

G.: Sixty-six years? This is fantastic! How can you be married for sixty-six years and look so good? What is your secret?

O.: I never argue with my wife.

G.: Hm. (*To the teacher*): Are you married?

T.: Yes.

G.: How long have you been married?

T.: Ten years.

G.: Do you ever argue with your husband? Did you hear what this old man just told us? He never argued with his wife. What do you think about it?

T.: He is quite wrong. When people live together they should feel free to have different views and they should feel free to disagree. If views are exchanged freely between husband and wife, their relationship will become stronger. It's no good to keep all this resentment inside of you.

G. (*to the old man*): Did you hear what she said? She doesn't agree with you at all! What do you think about her ideas?

O.: She is right.

This conversation illustrates a bias, called the *acquiescence bias,* that was extensively studied in the early fifties (Cronbach, 1950). It occurs here in an exaggerated form, but it illustrates an interpersonal strategy that may well qualify as one of the biases studied in social psychology. The output biases that are reviewed in this section are of this type and of similar types. They reflect the individual's preference, under uncertainty, to venture one class of responses—usually guesses—over another class.

Acquiescence

In the course of research on *The Authoritarian Personality* (Adorno *et al.,* 1950), it was found that subjects were more likely to answer a test question in the affirmative than in the negative. There was a greater likelihood of answering yes than no when these were the response alternatives. And more respondents tended to agree with an item than to disagree. Substantial acquiescence can be obtained when the scale items are ambiguous or difficult (Ray, 1983). The phenomenon became the basis of an individual difference (Jackson and Messick, 1958, 1961; Messick, 1962), and two types of persons were distinguished, "yea-sayers" and "nay-sayers" (Couch and Keniston, 1960). Subsequent research has shown that the person may tend to acquiesce in one type of test but not in another, and hence the hypothesis of acquiescence representing a stable personality trait was challenged (A. L. Edwards, 1963; Rorer, 1965). Again in contradiction, Pagano (1973) has shown systematic differences between repressors and sensitizers in the probability and reaction time of the yes and no responses in a Sternberg (1969) memory search task.

In the case of test questions, especially when they are directed at the person's character dispositions, the person very often has no solid and certain knowledge about the matter. How does one respond to the question "Were you an obedient child?" Not everybody knows precisely how *obedient* one was to one's parents. After all, how obedient must one be to be "obedient"? Given the uncertainty and given that discrete answers are called for, the subject must decide on a strategy. One strategy is to deny everything or as much as possible. After all, from denying that one was obedient it cannot be inferred that one was disobedient. When challenged, the denial could always be interpreted by the subject's saying, "What I meant was that I wasn't *especially* obedient." But because negative answers are more often challenged than positive answers, some people prefer the yea-saying strategy. Note, therefore, that this explanation is couched in terms of impression management (Schlenker, 1980), and thus it might belong in the realm of motivationally rooted biases.

Response Bias

A general form of bias that was identified more than three decades ago is the *response bias* (Howes and Solomon, 1950). The phenomenon was first discovered in the analysis and critique of perceptual defense research, and two kinds of response bias were distinguished. In the case of tachistoscopic presentations of taboo and neutral words, which served as stimuli whose recognition thresholds were measured by the ascending method of limits, the subject often refrained from offering taboo words as guesses. The phenomenon was explained by assuming that the subject would rather mistake a taboo word for a neutral one than the other way around. Thus even though the stimulus array for which recognition thresholds were collected consisted of an equal number of neutral and taboo words, there was a tendency to undercall taboo words. This form of bias was not cognitive but motivational in origin, for it involved a deliberate suppression of a reasonable response (Howes and Solomon, 1950).

One of the most common biases is social desirability bias frequently observed in responses to self-report questions in attitude and personality scales. The bias involves a tendency on the part of the subjects to represent themselves in terms that are flattering and to avoid derogatory attribution that could be derived from their answers. A method of overcoming social desirability and similar biases has been recently devised by Warner (1965). Subjects are given two forms of the same question (e.g., "I always cheat on exams" and "I never cheat on exams") and a randomizing device. By using the randomizing device which is concealed from the experimenter, they determine which question to answer. The interviewer never sees the question and receives only the answer, without the knowledge of the outcome of the randomizing device. Thus, it cannot be determined whether the response is flattering or derogatory. The method obtains only population parameters not individual scale values, however.

The other form of response bias in this connection was one that derived from word frequency. If recognition thresholds for words are assessed by the ascending method of limits, frequent words, because they are more accessible than infrequent ones, are used more often as guesses. Thus there will be a greater likelihood for those words to match the ones presented in the tachistoscope (Goldiamond and Hawkins, 1958), and the subject's recognition threshold will be lower for those words.

It is not clear whether the word frequency bias is in fact a bias, properly speaking. Even though the tendency has been labeled as response bias in the literature (Howes, 1954), it has heuristic elements. The subject simply does not remember the less frequent words as well as the frequent ones. So the subject offers the latter as guesses more often. Because the subject has little choice, the strategy of using as guesses the words remembered is

not unreasonable. Yet it is important to include the word frequency bias among the others because it parallels the availability bias in many respects. Note that there is no information about the subjects' conscious or unconscious intentions or rationale for their responses either in studies of word frequency bias or in studies of the availability heuristic.

Both the acquiescence and the general response bias are identified in signal detection theory (Green and Swets, 1966) as decision "strategies," and it is proper therefore to consider them also as heuristics. Given that there is a class of targets (say spies) that the subjects are seeking to detect, they can employ a reckless strategy that would ensure the capture of a maximum number of spies. The strategy would consist of maximum number of accusations. To the observer these inflated numbers of accusations would appear as a response bias. A lot of innocent people would have to prove that they are not spies. The strategy would guarantee a high proportion of hits. But these hits would be achieved only at the cost of a large number of false alarms. (Note that this "strategy" would be considered quite rational in probability learning.) To reduce the false alarm rate would require the number of wild accusations to be reduced. However, then the spy detector would be saving innocent people from accusations at the cost of missing some real spies.

Both strategies are defensible depending on one's goal, and both must be considered rational if they are congruent with their respective goals. Rewards and incentives can tilt the strategy in one direction or another, and they can change a conservative observer into a reckless one. But the observer's recklessness is meaningful only in the light of the false-alarm rate per se and may be entirely justifiable in the light of the observer's goals. Thus we have a clear participation of motivational factors in the general response bias. If accuracy (sensitivity) is sought, one needs to maximize hits without increasing false alarms. The perfect observer is one who can score 100 percent hits and 0 percent false alarms.

Ethnic Identification
A special case of general response bias that is apparently due to motivational and attitudinal factors is the result often obtained in *ethnic identification* studies. In this experimental paradigm, originally introduced by G. W. Allport and Kramer (1946), the subject is presented with photographs of faces with the instruction to identify members of a given ethnic group, usually Jews. Allport and Kramer originally thought that prejudiced individu-

als, because they feel threatened by the ethnic minority, would be more vigilant and thus better able to identify minority members than individuals without prejudice toward the given ethnic group.

These authors published data showing a higher level of ethnic identification of Jews on the part of anti-Semitic subjects. However, it was soon shown that the increased sensitivity of the anti-Semitic subjects was achieved at a cost of high false-alarm rates. Numerous subsequent studies have demonstrated that anti-Semitic subjects call out a much larger number of positive responses and thus have a greater chance of being correct when a Jewish photograph is shown (Lindzey and Rogolsky, 1950; Elliot and Wittenberg, 1955; Himmelfarb, 1966; Brand, Ruiz, and Padilla, 1974; Quanty, Keats, and Harkins, 1975; Kris, Kinchla, and Darley, 1977). In one careful study, however, that used a signal detection analysis (Dorfman, Keeve, and Saslow, 1971), a higher detection rate was shown for prejudiced subjects independent of their high response bias. But Quanty, Keats, and Harkins (1975) failed to replicate the effect.

While the Allport-Kramer hypothesis may have little promise for a solid confirmation, the ethnic identification literature has isolated an important phenomenon associated with prejudice, namely, a readiness to false alarms. Since only the prejudiced individual manifests such response bias, it should be assumed that the effect has some motivational origin. To be sure, one could interpret the bias as a strategy or a heuristic developed on the basis of prior cognitions associated with the person's attitude. But then the heuristic itself would have to be traced to a motivational antecedent. Thus again in the case of ethnic identification, we need to determine whether the response pattern represents a bias or whether there is a deliberate strategy making it a heuristic.

Functional Fixedness

Functional fixedness was first studied in America by Luchins (1942), who followed the earlier German work by Wertheimer (1945). It consists of an erroneous approach to a problem that results from an immediately preceding experience. Subjects are asked how they would bring, say, exactly 7 quarts of water, given that they have available a 43-quart pitcher, an 18-quart pitcher, and a 9-quart pitcher. The problem can be readily solved if the water is transferred from one pitcher to another a few times and the appropriate amounts are discarded. After a few such trials subjects are presented with the problem of bringing 22 quarts of water, and they are given a 48-quart

pitcher, an 18-quart pitcher, and a 4-quart pitcher. Instead of filling the 4-quart and the 18-quart containers and pouring both into the empty 48-quart pitcher, 81 percent of the subjects persist in the previous pattern, proposing that the 48-quart pitcher be filled and its contents poured into the 18-quart container once and into the 4-quart container twice, thus leaving 22 quarts in the 48-quart container. Apparently, the early method—much too complicated for the final problem—persisted, and the subjects followed the more convoluted route. More recently, the functional fixedness concept was applied in the context of priming social cognitions by Higgins and Chaires (1980).

Is the subjects' behavior irrational? Is the behavior of those who followed the old transfer method on the new problem wrong? If we define the task as requiring that collecting the given amount of water be collected in the least number of steps, then they are surely wrong. But if this requirement is not given, or if they had somehow forgotten it or disregarded it, then it is hardly fair to consider their behavior as irrational. For it may well be that a well-practiced solution is so automatized that even if it requires a greater number of steps, it is easier than a novel one that needs to be tried for the first time. Many people who have learned to type on an electric typewriter keep on using it in preference to a word processor because they imagine that the effort required to learn the new skill is not worth what they can gain in speed and convenience. One cannot evaluate the irrationality of these preferences without considering all the component preferences that may be involved in the subjective expected value of the change.

Positivity Bias

Matlin and Stang (1978) reviewed extensive evidence to show that much of verbal behavior—judgments, recall, associations, ratings, attitude statements—follows the Pollyanna principle. Positive judgments are generally more likely to be given than negative judgments; people remember positive terms better than negative terms; and in word associations they produce more words that are above the zero point of the evaluative dimension than negative words.

Marks (1951) had children pick a card from among ten. If the card contained a picture of a dog, the child was rewarded. He then asked the children to estimate how often they picked a dog (a pleasant outcome) and how often they picked a blank. The overestimation of positive events was quite substantial. Pollio and Gerow (1968) reported a greater likelihood of a pleasant free associate than an unpleasant associate given by subjects to both pleasant and unpleasant stimulus terms. And the selective recall effects that favor pleasant material over unpleasant are well substantiated in the literature (Koch, 1930; Meltzer, 1930; Thomson, 1930; Jersild, 1931; Stagner, 1931; O'Kelly and Steckle, 1940; Postman and Brown, 1952; Rychlak, 1975). Matlin and Stang (1978) reviewed ninty-nine studies on selective recall and found a majority showing selective effects favoring positive material.

Judgments of other people are also generally more favorable than one would expect by chance (DeSoto and Kuethe, 1959; Mettee, 1971; Sears and Whitney, 1972; Kleinke *et al.,* 1973; Frauenfelder, 1974). Zajonc and Burnstein (1965b) had subjects learn a social structure assumed to exist among four people (as in DeSoto, 1960). They found a *positivity bias* such that subjects tended to answer for any hypothetical pair that Jim liked Joe. Now it is possible that the positivity bias in this situation was simply another manifestation of the general yea-saying strategy. However, it is also possible that the subjects followed a rational base-rate strategy that reflected what they judged to be objective probabilities. Thus we would again atttribute heuristic properties to the positivity bias.

Given two hypothetical people, and given that there are only two alternatives, as is the case of these studies, a positive answer does seem more reasonable. In the learning of balanced structures, positivity bias (or heuristic) is evidenced in the fact that more errors are made on negative relations than on positive relations. It is interesting, therefore, in this respect that positive relations are over-called already on the very first anticipation—that is, before the subject received any feedback about a correct response. And it is also the case in other studies that when the subject is asked outright about the likelihood that Jim likes Joe, for a hypothetical Jim and a hypothetical Joe, the answers average to 59 percent (DeSoto and Kuethe, 1959). The subjective likelihood that a hypothetical Joe hates a hypothetical Jim, however, is only 35 percent. But, of course, *hating* is not the complement of *liking*.

It appears that there exists a special case of the positivity bias with respect to things human. According to recent research by Sears (1983), the more an object resembles a human being, the more positively it tends to be evaluated. Thus individual persons receive the most positive evaluations, while single attributes of individuals or groups of individuals receive much less favorable ratings.

Positivity bias is not contradictory to negativity bias in that the former refers to making guesses when virtually no information is available. The latter occurs under lesser uncertainty and is manifested in the differential weighting of information that is positive or negative with respect to a given target.

OPERATIONAL BIASES AND HEURISTICS

GENERAL INFERENCE HEURISTICS

Under some circumstances of making inferences, data are used inappropriately. This is true when conclusions are drawn from an inappropriate sample, or when they are drawn in the absence of *all* the data that such conclusions would normally require. Often these errors occur when the conclusions drawn are particularly desirable.

The prestige of the medical profession is a case in point. It is based on an inference made in the absence of some very important data base. The enormous financial success of this profession and its very high prestige are in large part based on estimates of their efficacy in addressing themselves to socially important problems. Yet this estimate is not justified by the data that are available. Many illnesses—the vast majority, in fact—have a course of their own, and the patient will eventually get better regardless of what is done. In most cases, also, the course of the illness will be affected negligibly by medication that is administered. When people recover after taking the medication or therapy prescribed, they attribute their recovery to the doctor's skill. But they really have no way of knowing the extent to which the physician contributed to the recovery. The control condition is not there. In the majority of cases the outcome could have been the same had we not gone to a doctor and not taken the medication.

The above example shows how judgments are sometimes made in the absence of a sufficient data base, and it illustrates one of the inference biases: illusory correlation (see pp. 190 ff.). This bias conspires to promote our illusion of the validity and success of medical judgment and practice. The cell—presence of illness *and* absence of medical treatment—that would allow us to assess the effectiveness of medical service accurately has no data. We need to know its frequency to evaluate the contribution of medical service to recovery.

In general, the biases and heuristics to be discussed in this section are characterized by a feature of the inference process that in principle should have no effect—the plausibility or the desirability of the conclusion that is reached with the data at hand. If the conclusion reached is plausible or acceptable, the inference process is terminated and the data that was used is considered sufficient. Often such a strategy may generate valid results, but certainly not always.

Representativeness

The *representativeness heuristic* (Kahneman and Tversky, 1972; Tversky and Kahneman, 1974) is invoked on the basis of the similarity between the specific attributes of a given instance and the defining attributes of a class of such instances. When using the representativeness heuristic, the person evaluates the probability of an uncertain event or sample of events "by the degree to which it: (*i*) is similar in essential characteristics to its parent population; and (*ii*) reflects the salient features of the process by which it is generated" (Kahneman and Tversky, 1972, p. 430). Thus "gambler's fallacy" is a representativeness heuristic because the gambler observing a long run of heads in a coin-tossing gamble tends more and more to predict tails. Since the tosses are independent, the gambler's predictions should ignore the previous history of outcomes. In the gambler's fallacy the long run is not representative of the random process assumed to underlie the toss outcome, and thus a change in the pattern is expected as the run becomes longer and longer. When subjects are asked about the relative likelihood of sequence of births in six-child families they believe that GBBGGB is considerably more likely than either BBBBBB or GGGBBB, even though they all have very similar probabilities. Sequence GBBGGB resembles a random process more than BBBBBB.

The classical demonstration of the representativeness heuristic, which illustrates an instance where sample membership is assigned by similarity of attributes rather than distribution likelihood, involved the following personality sketch (Kahneman and Tversky, 1973, p. 238):

> Tom W. is of high intelligence, although lacking in true creativity. He has a need for order and clarity, and for neat and tidy systems in which every detail finds its appropriate place. His writing is rather dull and mechanical, occasionally enlivened by somewhat corny puns and by flashes of imagination of the sci-fi type. He has a strong drive for competence. He seems to have little feel and little sympathy for

other people and does not enjoy interacting with others. Self-centered, he nevertheless has a deep moral sense.

When asked, "How similar is Tom W. to the typical graduate student in . . . nine fields of graduate specialization?" the subjects ranked computer science and engineering the highest and social science and social work the lowest, even though a comparable group of subjects judged the former types of students to be considerably less frequent in the university. Thus the subjects favor the individuating information over base rates, even when they estimate these base rates themselves.

Following these early experiments a great deal of effort has been devoted to revealing possible methodological artifacts in the representativeness research. Thus, for example, Ajzen (1977) argued that when the individuating information has strong causal implications for the judgment in question, it will be more likely to overwhelm base rates. Similarly, Ginosar and Trope (1980) were able to demonstrate that when individuating information is highly diagnostic, base rates are ignored; and where it is conflicting or irrelevant, base rates are much more likely to be taken into account.

Ajzen and Fishbein (1975) described the above differences in Bayesian terms, arguing that the subject assesses the probability of a given interpretation in the light of other possible interpretations, couching each one as the probability of the interpretation being true given that the action has taken place, divided by the probability of the interpretation being true at all. There is also some research that questions the meaning and the robustness of the results showing that subjects ignore base rates (C. L. Olson, 1976). In fact, Manis *et al.* (1980) found conditions under which subjects ignore individuating information and follow base rates. Other research has confirmed most of the earlier findings, however (Hammerton, 1973; Nisbett and Borgida, 1975; Lyon and Slovic, 1976; Tversky and Kahneman, 1978; Bar-Hillel, 1980).

In one study of the base-rate fallacy Kahneman and Tversky (1973) introduced the problem as follows (p. 241):

> A panel of psychologists have interviewed and administered personality tests to 30 engineers and 70 lawyers, all successful in their respective fields. On the basis of this information, thumbnail descriptions of the 30 engineers and 70 lawyers have been

written. You will find on your forms five descriptions, chosen at random from the 100 available descriptions. For each description, please indicate your probability that the person described is an engineer, on a scale from 0 to 100.

It is possible that given these instructions, a "personality schema" was primed in the subjects. Thus by conversational conventions (P. Grice, 1967), the subjects may have understood that it is important to pay attention to the personalities of the target persons because the *first* item of information that was given to them was the fact that "a panel of psychologists have interviewed and administered personality tests...." Why are the subjects given this item to start with if not to draw their attention to that fact? Suppose we rewrite the instructions to read as follows:

Consider 100 people successful in their fields. Thirty of them are engineers and 70 are lawyers. A panel of psychologists have interviewed and administered personality tests to these 100 people. On the basis of this information....

It is possible that the base rates would be ignored here as well and the individuating information become dominant.

One of the important applications of representativeness is in the area of stereotypes. It would seem at first that the existence of stereotypes and of stereotyping is contradictory to the representativeness heuristic. The hallmark of stereotyped perception involves attributing to an individual *all* of the traits that are attributed to the group. With prejudiced perception, individuating information is insufficient to overcome base rates implied by the stereotype. Yet the results of experiments on sex stereotypes (Locksley *et al.*, 1980) and other stereotypes (Locksley, Hepburn, and Ortiz, 1982) show just the opposite: Individuating information can overcome base rates associated with stereotypes. Locksley *et al.* take these results to argue against the motivational or affective basis of stereotypes, assuming that if these factors were critical in stereotyping, subjects should resist individuating information. These authors ran similar studies on desirable and undesirable stereotypes, obtaining an equivalent individuating effect.

While there is little doubt about the empirical validity of the phenomenon of representativeness for some situations, the significant question is the theoretical one. In probability learning, it has been shown that subjects often ignore probabilities and inappropriately make inferences on the basis of sheer frequency of events (Estes, 1976). What specific inference process is engaged when base rates are ignored and individuating information favored? One reasonable answer to this question is that people generally prefer a deterministic view of the world to a probabilistic view. When it comes to predictions—and especially when it comes to predictions about *single instances*—they shun base rates and invoke causal schemas. Such an explanation, however, goes only a little further beyond the actual data.

Another possibility, and one that applies to a variety of heuristics and biases, is that in day-to-day inference we avoid null hypotheses. If one is to guess whether an element is a member of a given set or of one of several other less specified sets, it might be useful under some circumstances to begin the solution with the preliminary hypothesis that the element is indeed a member of the given set. If I know that Joe likes people and that his sister had a psychotic breakdown, and if I am asked whether Joe is a psychologist, I risk little by entertaining the affirmative hypothesis, even though the population of people who, like others, have psychotic sisters but who are not psychologists must be vastly greater than the population of such people who are psychologists. Hogarth (1981) pointed out this functional utility of the representativeness heuristic. People shun the null hypothesis because it is an uninteresting and inconsequential way to proceed. The hypothesis, even when suggested by the experimenter, that a series of trials in probability learning is random is less interesting than one suggesting that it is not. What can one do with a random series? If we pretend that there is structure, we can at the very least amuse ourselves by trying to find a pattern.

On the whole, a statistical approach to a problem forces the person into categorical Aristotelean thinking: The item is viewed as a member of a category for which we can define a sample space. However, in doing so, we limit ourselves to thinking about the problem only in terms of those attributes that define the category membership and of those few that are correlated. Statistical inference thus obliterates the possibility of processing the information idiographically—that is, in a way that reflects the wealth of unique features, causes, dynamics, processes, and nuances that are typical of single cases.

Once I decide that Joe is *not* a psychologist, there is very little else to do. I might ask, of course, that if Joe is not a psychologist, what is he? What do people who like others and have psychotic sisters become? There is no clear answer. If I do entertain the hypothesis that Joe is a psychologist, I will be happy if the hypothesis is confirmed, of course. But even disconfirmation may be informative. In the process of fitting Joe in the "psychologist" category, I may find out more about psychologists and perhaps somewhat more about Joe. I may find out more about these matters, or I may think more specifically about these matters and thereby formulate the next step of the problem a bit more intelligently. I could find something out without the hypothesis, but my search for information would be unsystematic and undirected. The hypothesis constrains my information processing and imposes direction. In the study of concept learning Bruner, Goodnow, and Austin (1956) found that subjects forming such affirmative hypotheses were in fact quicker to attain the concepts. Further research on this problem by Reber (1967) suggests that processing without a hypothesis or rule may be useful in learning but only when the concept to be learned is quite easy or regular—features that rarely characterize social objects.

Conjunction Fallacy

The *conjunction fallacy* is a manifestation of representativeness bias, and it arises in interpreting compound events. Thus Kahneman and Tversky (1982) observe that when we consider conjunctive compound events, the probability of those events must not be greater than the probability of their components, and disjunctive events must not have smaller probability than their components. Thus the probability that a person is an Albanian *and* an entomologist cannot be greater than the probability that a person is an Albanian, nor can it be greater than the probability that the person is an entomologist. Yet this principle is shown to be readily violated under some circumstances that involve a strong representativeness bias. Thus, for example, individuals are presented with the following sketch (Tversky and Kahneman, 1982, p. 92):

> Linda is 31 years old, single, outspoken, and very bright. She majored in philosophy. As a student, she was deeply concerned with issues of discrimination and social justice, and also participated in anti-nuclear demonstrations.

Please rank the following statements by their probability:

- Linda is a teacher in elementary school.

- Linda works in a bookstore and takes Yoga classes.

- Linda is active in the feminist movement. (F)

- Linda is a psychiatric social worker.

- Linda is a member of the League of Women Voters.

- Linda is a bank teller. (T)

- Linda is an insurance salesperson.

- Linda is a bank teller and is active in the feminist movement. (T & F)

The striking result obtained by Tversky and Kahneman was that the probability of the compound item (T and F) was ranked above that of the component (T). Apparently, the "pull" of the representativeness of the sketch toward the feminist attribute was able to overwhelm the attribute "bank teller" in the compound case. These authors argue that their findings are not due to misinterpretation of linguistic conventions (P. Grice, 1967) because of the following result. Subjects are told that "John is 27 years old, with an outgoing personality. In college he was an outstanding athlete but did not show much ability or interest in intellectual matters" (Tversky and Kahneman, 1982, p. 95). Given this sketch, they guessed a greater probability for John being a "gym teacher" than John being simply a "teacher," again violating the compound-probability principle.

The effect in these instances obtains primarily for concrete cases. Apparently, when asked about the abstract principle, the Tversky-Kahneman subjects were quite able to verbalize and state the compound rule. These observations are contrary to those reported by Johnson-Laird and Wason (1977), who found the opposite. In both cases, however, there is some ambiguity in the way the problem is stated, and part of the effect may be due to the inability of the subjects to form a proper sample space.

Many homework problems in probability textbooks are stated in ways that steer the student away from forming a proper sample space. Thus, for example, we have the problem in Feller (1957, p. 107) about the probability of both children being boys in a family of two children, one of which is a boy. Because GG is excluded, the sample space consists of BB, GB, and BG, and hence the probability of both children being boys is not ½ as most people expect but ⅓. The error occurs because most people construe the question to be as follows: A boy is selected at random, and we discover that he comes from a two-child family. What is the probability that his sibling is also a boy? The confusion arises because the sample space in the first example consists of pairs of children, whereas the sample space in the second example consists of individual children. Maier (1970) noted that "we can make problems easy or difficult by requiring the correct response to occupy a high or a low position in the behavior repertoire.... [Most] tricky problems involve misleading the person so as to give the correct answers low probability" (p. 191). The horse-trading problem cited above (p. 178) is clearly such a problem. Trope and Bassok (1982) have found a proper use of prior probabilities by subjects judging handwriting samples, and Beyth-Marom and Fischhoff (1983) report that when available, relevant information is properly used, even though subjects have difficulties when they need to seek out such information or when they explain their information processing strategies.

It is not a foregone conclusion, however, that if the proper sample space were given, students without previous training would readily solve all homework problems. Often, however, the difficulty lies in the transition between the linguistic form and its formal representation, and it is in this transformation that the conjunction fallacy effect must enter.

Still one possibility needs to be eliminated from results such as those reported by Kahneman and Tversky (1982). Many subjects may have simply misunderstood the question and formed the wrong sample space *because* of their misunderstanding. Take, for example, the likelihood of finding both our neighbor Joe *and* our neighbor's wife Anne at home. This probability can be greater than the probability of finding Joe *alone* at home, and it can be greater than the probability of finding Anne *alone*. However, the probability of both being there cannot be greater than the probability of *at least* one of them being there, that is, Joe alone *or* Joe *and* Anne together. Nor can it be greater than the probability of *at least* Anne being home, that is, Anne alone *or* Anne *and* Joe together. The sample space for finding Joe is quite different from the sample space for finding Joe *alone*. Thus if we ask subjects, "What is the probability for finding Joe and Anne at home?" the subjects might think that the probability that both are at home is greater than the probability that just Joe is at home.

But this result may not be evidence of the conjunction fallacy because the problem was stated in a deliberately ambiguous form, leading the subject to assume that we were speaking of the comparison between $(P_{JOE}) < (P_{ANNE}$ and $P_{JOE}) < (1 - P_{ANNE})$ rather than

of the comparison between $(P_{JOE}) > (P_{ANNE}$ and $P_{JOE})$. Thus in the case of conjunction fallacy, very often individuating data are entered when they should have been ignored in the computation of joint probabilities. And the individuating information may lead the subject to select an inappropriate sample space. Recent work by Morier and Borgida (In press) confirms this conjecture. The structure of the response alternatives in the Linda problem invites false interpretation of the sample space. The subject sees the statements "Linda is active in the feminist movement" and "Linda is a bank teller" in a list containing also the statement "Linda is a bank teller and is active in the feminist movement." This context may well prompt the subject to interpret the statement "Linda is a bank teller" to mean "Linda is a bank teller *but not* a member of the feminist movement." In one experiment Tversky and Kahneman (1983) substituted for the T statement the alternative "Linda is a bank teller whether or not she is active in the feminist movement." Again a majority of subjects fell prey to the conjunction fallacy. However, this form is also ambiguous and it is increasingly apparent that a parametric study is needed to determine the linguistic conditions that invite the fallacy.

Illusory Correlation

Chapman (1967) noted that many clinicians believe that the draw-a-person test is very useful in diagnosis of their patients. Yet empirical studies evaluating the validity of the test showed it to be fairly worthless. Chapman and Chapman (1967, 1969) attributed the clinicians' attitude to their selecting out of the patients' drawings some features that seemed to them to be a priori associated with particular symptoms. Thus drawing a person with atypical eyes leads the clinician to believe that the patient is overly suspicious. In fact, when subjects are given actual covariation data and asked to estimate the correlation, there is a considerable overestimation of the relationship (Jennings, Amabile, and Ross, 1980).

Illusory correlation was first observed by Wells (1907), who had subjects rate authors for merit on ten dimensions. He found a much greater correlation among the ratings on these dimensions than would be expected by chance or by a reasonable conjecture. Thorndike (1920) christened the phenomenon the "halo error" when he found that the ratings of teachers by their superiors showed a correlation between rated intelligence and rated discipline of 0.8, whereas rated discipline correlated with *actual* intelligence at only 0.3. Hamilton and Rose (1980) and Hamilton and Gifford (1976) showed the role of illusory correlation in stereotyped judgments.

Illusory correlation may be explained by the joint influence of availability and representativeness bias. Illusory correlations are generally imputed to covariation for which many observations are lacking or ignored and because some pairs of observations especially stand out (Smedslund, 1963; Jenkins and Ward, 1965; Ward and Jenkins, 1965; Hamilton and Gifford, 1976.). Thus, for example, we may see swallows flying low and then shortly afterward witness a storm. Hence there is a tendency to impute a relationship between the altitude of swallows' flight and storm likelihood. The problem with these observations is that very often swallows do fly low and there isn't a storm, and, equally, there was a storm and there were no low-flying swallows about. (Or we were sick and didn't see a doctor.) But these events are less apt to come to mind. Thus the covariation may be particularly salient, and once mentioned and observed, it assumes an exaggerated validity, as Nisbett and L. Ross (1980) aptly pointed out.

McArthur and Friedman (1980) have shown that illusion of correlation is more likely to take place when the events are infrequent and thus stand out in contrast with the more common events. Of course, what is salient is not entirely "up to the environment." By deploying attention selectively, the perceiver and cognizer themselves "make" certain features salient and "make" others recede into the background. It is certainly the case that very intense stimuli become salient by virtue of the overwhelming pressure they exert at the point of sensory input. This, however, is seldom true of social stimuli. Persons and other social stimuli do not produce powerful sensory energy levels. Hence salience and vividness are very often "in the eye of the beholder."

This consideration raises the question of the role in heuristics of the cognizers and of the information-processing apparatus that they bring with them. If it is argued, for example, that availability represents the ease with which certain memories are brought to mind, and if illusory correlation or illusory causation are featured as biases that are produced by availability, then we need to ask if it is not possible that some independent determinants of the perceived contingency or correlation bring certain facts to mind and make them thus available. This argument would reverse the causal link assumed to exist for availability and illusory correlation. McArthur (1980) questions the availability basis of illusory correlation and suggests that there are environmental contingencies to which animals and people are especially attuned. She cites work by Lanzetta and Orr (1980) reporting that a correlation between a picture of a fearful face and an electric shock was learned more quickly than a correlation between a picture of a happy face and a shock. The seminal experiment on illusory correlation (Chapman and Chapman, 1967) involved very little memory. The subjects had all the information provided when making judgments.

The problem of illusory correlation is complicated by the following results: Oakes (1982) has shown that trained psychologists (lecturers, research fellows, and graduate students) are very poor at estimating correlation even when no data is missing at all. One group of these subjects was asked to produce a rank-order correlation equal to 0.5 for twelve ranks. That is, they were given twelve numbers from 1 to 12, representing a fictitious variable X, and they were asked to supply for each of the twelve scores a score from 1 to 12 for another variable Y, such that the resulting coefficient between X and Y would equal 0.5. Another group was given twelve pairs of ranks that did represent a 0.5 correlation, and they were asked to estimate its coefficient. In both cases accuracy was very low. There was an overestimation in the first group such that the mean rank correlation generated by the subjects was 0.68 (median = 0.76), whereas the mean estimated correlation coefficient in the second group was 0.24. Thus in the first group the subjects produced an average correlation that accounted for twice the required variance, and in the second group one-half the required variance. Note that these data contradict those of Jennings, Amabile, and L. Ross (1980). None of the above experiments shed much light on *how* estimates of correlation are made and what observations and rules people use in making such estimates. Such research is only beginning to appear (Arkes and Harkness, 1983). A part of this problem is the question of the criteria that are used to evaluate the subjects' estimates of correlation. We don't know a priori what type of correlation measure should the subjects' judgments be compared against. When these estimates are compared against Pearson Product Moment coefficients, then they appear to be quite inaccurate. But when more robust measures are employed as standards (e.g., Tukey, 1977), the subjects' performance appears quite respectable.

Hindsight

Events seem to acquire apparent inevitability as they recede into the past. What has already happened, happened because it was inevitable. Fischhoff (1975), who was first to explore this phenomenon, termed it *creeping determinism*. We attribute a firmer causal structure to past events and blame ourselves and others for not having foreseen these events. Given that a certain outcome has taken place, when subjects are asked what probabilities they would have assigned to that outcome if they were making the estimate beforehand, they overestimate the outcome probability. And when they are told what these outcomes actually were, they consider these outcomes to be much more likely than when they are given no information about what actually happened. Similarly, memory of past predictions is distorted so as to approximate postdiction (Fischhoff, 1975; Leary, 1982).

Hindsight may be considered from the point of view of representativeness. Since the event has taken place, whatever caused it must have been true. It is thus a heuristic because occurrence validates the presumed cases. If the event hasn't happened, our ideas about the causal structure of the event may or may not be correct; and if we had doubts about the causal structure, we should have more doubts about it occurring at all. Thus hindsight may well be an instance where individuating data—the fact that the event took place—dominates base rates. It is to be noted that hindsight may also be a reflection of an impression management strategy (Schlenker, 1980) and hence a product of a motivational process. "I knew it all along" is an assertion that increases our competence in the eyes of others. We would, therefore, expect that prediction and postdiction should differ more in public (anonymous) than in private and more for ego-involving material than for pallid material. However, Leary (1981) failed to find evidence in support of such a motivational interpretation of the hindsight bias.

Imputation of Regularity and Structure

In the experimental paradigm of probability learning (e.g., Estes, 1964), the individual is commonly presented with two events, say a green and a red light, that vary in probability of occurrence. For example, the green light goes on 70 percent of the time and the red light goes on 30 percent of the time. The individual's task is to predict on each of many trials which of the two lights will go on next. Incorrect responses are usually ignored, whereas correct predictions are rewarded. Thus the optimal strategy is always to guess the more frequent light.

This, however, is seldom the case. The phenomenon most commonly observed is probability matching. In fact, the typical subject goes slightly above 70 percent in guesses. In a study by R. A. Gardner (1957), for example, which went on for 450 trials, with reinforcement probabilities of 0.6 in one condition and 0.7 in another, subjects chose the more frequent stimulus on 0.62 and 0.72 of the trials respectively. Given that the distribution of the subjects' responses for the 0.6 condition are 62–38 for green and red lights, they would be expected to achieve only 53 percent accuracy (38 percent on the green light and 15 percent on the red light). If they guessed green all the time, they would be *sure* to attain 60 percent accuracy. In fact, the subject who matches his or her response frequencies to stimulus frequencies, if unlucky, could achieve as little as 24 percent correct performance.

While most of the theories of probability learning were concerned with discovering the reinforcement parameters that changed the individual's response tendencies from trial to trial, in some instances it was eventually recognized that the typical subject is actually searching for patterns and structure among the random series (Galanter and Smith, 1958). Thus subjects were imputing regularity and structure to a random sequence of trials. They developed schemas to deal with the random events. Is this rational?

Is probability matching a bias or a heuristic? How should a reasonable subject act in this situation? Subjects come to the laboratory to take part in an experiment in which they are required to guess whether one or another light will go on. There are a large number of trials and they are all the same. Subjects are told that the green light is more frequent (or they discover by themselves that it is, in fact, more frequent). The subjects are told that they will get 1¢ for each correct guess and will lose nothing for wrong guesses. The most reasonable thing to do would be to announce to the experimenter that it is one's intention always to press the green button, find out from the experimenter about the number of trials to be given, and ask to be paid off accordingly. But somehow, this might violate all kinds of expectations of what typically happens in experiments. So the subjects play along.

Now the subjects can certainly go ahead and guess the green light all the time. But given that there are hundreds of trials, this would be frightfully boring. So they might begin to explore. What can possibly be explored in a random sequence? Subjects might therefore impose structure and regularity on the sequences of events. Seeing a series of eight green lights in succession, one may fall for gambler's fallacy and guess a red light. Other imputations of structure are equally possible in which alternation and grouping are imagined. Thus again, depending on one's interpretation, probability matching may be a bias or a heuristic.

If the subject is allowed to interpret the experimental situation as one in which the events are sampled *without replacement,* the matching strategy can be shown to be quite rational. It has been demonstrated by von Briesen Raz (1983) that both an assumption that events are sampled without replacement and that there exists an association between the subject's prediction and the experimental outcome justify various forms of matching strategy.

It might be noted, incidentally, that all probability-learning models feature as their basic concept the incentive value of a correct guess. These incentive values are computed for each individual subject separately, and they reveal differences in how such subjects value being correct in predicting the next light. This approach to the problem, therefore, because it was a child of the fifties and sixties, stands in stark contrast with contemporary analysis of heuristics, which is shy of any "hot" concepts.

Note also the similarity of the ethnic identification paradigm to probability learning. Ironically, what is considered an error in one is a correct strategy in the other. Thus maximizing the frequency of the guesses for the frequent stimulus is a rational strategy in probability learning, a strategy that is seldom followed. Instead, a matching strategy is employed that guarantees a much lower percentage of correct responses. On the other hand, a matching strategy would seem desirable in ethnic identification, but maximizing seems more to be the case.

SOCIAL INFERENCE HEURISTICS

Representativeness, conjunction fallacy, and illusory correlation are shortcuts in the inference process. But they are not "fair" shortcuts because they are more readily acceptable when the conclusions reached are plausible or desirable. Imputation of structure is a heuristic of a somewhat different kind because it builds on the premise that the world is always orderly, or at least that there exists local order in some parts of the empirical world.

The biases and heuristics reviewed above apply to all kinds of inference, including inference about social entities. There are three heuristics that are uniquely social, however. Social inference heuristics imply premises about the social world. The fundamental attribution error implies the premise that people are more likely to be the cause of events than the circumstances surrounding these events. In false consensus the main premise holds that most people are like the individual in question. And the self-serving heuristic implies a premise that the self is more likely to be associated with things that are positive, good, or worthy than with their opposites.

The Fundamental Attribution Error

The *fundamental attribution error* (L. Ross, 1977a) was identified as a tendency in causal attribution to assign greater responsibility for outcomes to the person rather than to situations. Nisbett and L. Ross (1980) interpreted the fundamental attribution error as an instance of availability bias (not availability heuristic, however). They argued that the actor is more readily perceived as the origin of the outcome since he "is an easily available explanation of his action because of his perceptual proximity to his action." They also interpreted the fundamental attribution error as in part influenced by the vividness bias. "The actor...is dynamic and interesting, while situations more commonly are static and pallid....The actor and his action, in other words, are 'figural' against the 'ground' of the situation"(pp. 122–123).

The fundamental attribution error applies primarily to observers. Actors are more prone to explain events in terms of situational factors, as Jones and Nisbett (1971) noted, and a number of studies confirmed their hypothesis (Jones and Harris, 1967; Jones, 1979; Jones, Riggs, and Quattrone, 1979; A. G. Miller, Jones, and Hinkle, 1981; A. G. Miller and Rorer, 1982). Jones and Nisbett (1971) pointed out that dispositions for actors, unlike those for observers, are not figural—actors cannot easily see themselves act. It is the situation that is figural. The evidence about the actor-observer differences, however, does not show concretely that situations are indeed *figural* for actors and dispositions are in the background, whereas the opposite holds true for observers. It only demonstrates the presence of effects that are presumed to derive from the figural role of actors in our perception. Thus it may be that the actor-observer difference lies not in what is being attended to but in some other factor. In fact, the actor-observer difference is not always found (Taylor and Koivumaki, 1976).

One other possible feature of the fundamental attribution error is whether information about people is not more useful for observers than information about situations, and the other way around for actors. Nisbett and

L. Ross (1980) characterize person information as more interesting to observers. And person information may be indeed more interesting because persons' predispositions might be more predictive of their behavior than situations. If situations are less predictive of other people's behavior than personal dispositions, fundamental attribution is not an "error" but a defensible heuristic.

If personal dispositions are generally more informative and if it is this type of information we want to collect about other people, why is there an actor-observer difference? When another person's actions are observed and interpreted, we take them as instances of some general principle—dishonest people steal, careless people have accidents, poor students fail exams. The interpretation of one's own behavior is different. When offered to someone, it also includes a *justification* of this behavior. Moreover, individuals know that in cases of undesirable outcomes the observer will tend to interpret our behavior in dispositional terms. The hope is that the observer will pick out dispositions that are acceptable. But the observer may not. Thus the individual *offers* situational information to the observer in order to modulate and guide an unfavorable dispositional interpretation that the observer is ready to make. In private, the individual may interpret his or her own behavior quite differently, silently saying, "I should have been more careful," or "I really was too hasty in agreeing to write this chapter."

Thus on some occasions the fundamental attribution error is not an error. At the same time, however, much of the evidence provided in support of the fundamental attribution error (L. Ross, 1977b) may depend on the way the subjects interpret the attribution question (P. Grice, 1967). If the person is asked, "Why did Jim flunk calculus, geometry, and physics?" the answer will surely be something about Jim, and rightly so. It is unlikely that there were three situational conditions that conspired to prevent Jim from succeeding on each of the three courses. It is more likely, however, that a situational attribution would be given if the question was, "Why did Jim fail the *last* calculus quiz?" Here the conversational conventions imply that Jim did not flunk all the quizzes, and there must have been something about the conditions of the last quiz, or a temporary state in which Jim may have found himself, that led to his flunking the quiz. In fact, the vast majority of questions of the form "Why did X do Y?" imply "Why did X do Y *under*

the circumstances?"—implicitly instructing the information processor to hold situation factors constant (Kahneman and Miller, 1983). Hence as was the case with other inference phenomena, the fundamental attribution error includes both bias and heuristic elements.

False Consensus

Subjects are sometimes found to imagine that if they prefer an item, say some food, painting, or presidential candidate, other people prefer that item as well. For example, in a TV game show "Play the Percentages," the participants are asked to estimate the proportion of people who know an answer to a trivial question. If they themselves know the answer, the participants tend to overestimate the proportion of others who have that knowledge (Mullen, 1983). L. Ross, Green, and House (1977) described this bias as *false consensus*, a phenomenon that is the exact opposite of "pluralistic ignorance," first described by Schanck (1932), in which members of a community each believed that they were unique in violating a norm, whereas the violations were actually widespread. While false consensus has been interpreted as a form of wishful thinking, and hence a motivational phenomenon (Bramel, 1962; Edlow and Kiesler, 1966; Zuckerman, 1979; Brown, 1982), Carroll (1978) has argued for a purely cognitive explanation based on the availability heuristic. He suggested that if availability is implicated in the false consensus effect, then it would not matter if the events considered by the subjects were "imaginary or real, inferred or observed, true or later discredited" (p. 89). In fact, Zuckerman, Mann, and Bernieri (1982) found false consensus for actors and for observers as well. Moreover, these authors combined false consensus with a variety of other biases. Thus, for example, subjects were induced to make situational attributions or dispositional attributions, and the authors found a greater false consensus effect for the latter than for the former. They also found that behavior that is vivid or salient is perceived as more common among group members than pallid behavior. That is, given that a target person performs an action displayed to subjects in a vivid and attention-demanding manner, subjects tend to believe that many others would behave in a similiar manner—more so than when the target performs the action in a pallid manner. Also, the likelihood for false consensus increases when the behavior or attribute in question derives from external causes rather than from internal dispositions (Gilovich, Jennings, and Jennings, 1983). And finally, false consensus is augmented for representative targets.

Self-serving Bias

M. Ross and Sicoly (1979) have shown that people have a strong tendency to take more credit than they deserve. Each author of a joint project claims the greatest contribution and husbands say that they do more housework than their wives see them do. Actors seem to take more responsibility for their successes than for failures, which they may attribute to bad luck (Arkin, Appelman, and Burger, 1980; Arkin, Cooper, and Kolditz, 1980; Riess *et al.*, 1981). However, in at least one study the opposite was found (L. Ross, Bierbrauer, and Polly, 1974).

The clinical phenomenon of projection is a special case of a *self-serving bias.* Sherwood (1981) distinguished between *attributive projection,* in which a "self-ascribed undesirable trait is projected unto favorably perceived target persons," and *classical projection,* in which "an undesirable trait that is denied is projected onto unfavorably perceived persons" (p. 445). Sherwood's extensive review of the literature found evidence mainly for attributive projection, but clinical and theoretical considerations led him also to promote the potential validity and usefulness of the concept. Both types of projection seem to have self-serving functions, and the attributive form of projection was apparently found capable of helping patients reduce stress.

The earlier explanations of the phenomenon were couched in motivational terms (G. W. Allport, 1937; Murphy, 1947; Hastorf, Schneider, and Polefka, 1970). Especially rich in motivational content is the variant of the self-serving bias christened by Pettigrew (1979) as the *ultimate attribution error.* This tendency is related to the in-group–out-group bias (which we shall not review here because it is amply covered in Chapter 24 of the *Handbook*). The ultimate attribution error consists of attributing positive outcomes of the in-group and negative outcomes of the out-group to dispositional antecedents, and attributing negative outcomes of the in-group and positive outcomes of the out-group to situational factors.

D. Miller and M. Ross (1975) reviewed the literature on the self-serving bias and report evidence for self-enhancement in case of success but little support for self-protection in case of failure. They offer a cognitive explanation of the phenomenon, arguing that self-enhancement derives in part from the more frequent expectation that the person's behavior will produce success. Thus there seems to be an illusory correlation in that people see a greater covariation between behavior and increasing success than between behavior and constant failure (because in the typical experiment success involves improvement over time, while failure is constant over trials). Under some conditions the contingency between *desired* outcomes and *intended* behavior leads one to attribute the outcomes to *internal* dispositions.

D. Miller (1978) distinguished between the meaning of the self-serving bias that enhances and protects one's own self-perception and the meaning when the person is concerned with the perception by others. He points out that extending the term also to embrace the public image, as Bradley (1978) suggested, removes the important element of self-deception that is the core of the concept of the self-serving bias. Note, therefore, that it would be difficult to argue against a motivational interpretation of the phenomenon in the case of enhancement and protection of one's own image.

Greenberg, Pyszczynski, and Solomon (1982) found strong self-serving bias even in a private condition. They take these data as contradictory of the Miller-Ross hypothesis that the covariation between behavior and outcome is more probable for increasing success than for constant failure. They also offer their data against the Miller-Ross contingency argument, because their subjects had no norms of what their performance should be. They favor a return to a motivational view of the self-serving bias, also supported by Snyder, Stephan, and Rosenfield (1978), Weary (1979), Zuckerman (1979), and Burger (1981). The motivational correlates of the self-serving bias have been recently examined for hypochondriacs by T. W. Smith, C. R. Snyder, and Perkins (1983). It was found by these authors that in highly evaluative situations, hypochondriacal subjects report more recent and current physical illness to explain poor performance than similar individuals working in a nonevaluative situation.

Like D. Miller and M. Ross (1975), L. Ross (1977a) and Nisbett and L. Ross (1980) also argue against a motivational interpretation of the self-serving bias, and they believe that self-serving biases are so dysfunctional and maladaptive that individuals would soon learn not to indulge in such short-lived satisfactions. The "student who would treat all triumphs as reflective of his true abilities and all failures as irrelevant to those abilities must ultimately face more pain, disappointment, and embarrassment than if he acted on less flattering attributions'' (Nisbett and L. Ross, 1980, p. 234). In fact, Van der Pligt and Eiser (1983), in a study of differences between actors' and observers' attributions, found that positive outcomes are attributed to the dispositions of both actors and observers, while negative outcomes are attributed to situational factors of actors and observers.

Self-serving biases are not always dysfunctional and maladaptive, however. And a recent analysis of this bias in Bayesian terms suggests that it may not be illogical either (Wetzel, 1982). Under some circumstances self-serving bias is simply a reflection of self-confidence, which may be treated as an adaptive approach driven by achievement motivation. Taylor (1982) has suggested that the adjustment to threatening events is facilitated by self-serving evaluations. Einhorn and Hogarth (1978) developed an extensive theoretical analysis of overconfidence, which they called the "illusion of validity." They focus mainly on overconfidence as the result of persons' failure to appreciate properly the contingency between predictions and outcomes and in exposing oneself to disconfirming information. There is a tendency to formulate and reformulate judgmental problems in ways in which success becomes inevitable, thus generating an illusion of competence.

In research on self-serving bias the behavior in question is not always viewed in all its features. In particular, the subject's own perspective is not always fully explored. Thus often in these studies, subjects claim no responsibility for failure and are thereby said to exhibit a self-serving bias. Yet such an attribution only reveals a self-serving bias if the subjects claim responsibility for the behavior, that is, if they truly believe that they have failed and that the behavior was diagnostic of important abilities and characteristics. In studies where a failure condition is created by having the subject fail on some artificial task or problem of little consequence, it should not be surprising if the subjects do not see the failure as "my failure" and attribute it instead to some external or situational factors. The operation and consequences of the self-serving bias can only be meaningfully investigated within behavioral domains that the experimenter knows a priori are considered by the subject to be importantly self-revealing or diagnostic. Failing to solve a tremendously difficult puzzle or failing to reach a certain level in a ring-tossing game may not be considered

failures at all, and they differ considerably from a failure to land a sought-after job or failing an exam in the area of one's specialization.

BIASES AND HEURISTICS: SUMMARY AND RETROSPECT

The review of biases and heuristics shows that none of them necessarily reflect the irrationality of human cognition in general or social cognition in particular, although there are several examples of quite faulty human problem solving and inference. The review also shows that none of the biases or heuristics have been demonstrated to be free of extracognitive factors and that if the purposes, intentions, and particular circumstances of the cognizer are taken into account, the picture that emerges is not always that of a misguided creature but often of one who is willing to suffer a few misses and false alarms for the sake of overall greater cognitive efficiency and general adaptation to a capricious environment. As was noted with respect to schemas, a failure to consider the question of these biases and heuristics in the larger context—to ignore the goals of the perceiver and the nature of the problem and of the surrounding situation—can easily lead to unrealistic and unwarranted fears about the power of biases and heuristics to distort the inference process.

In a recent review of biases and errors Kruglanski and Ajzen (1983) have argued that human inference processes only appear deficient when set against conventional validity criteria. They point out that these conventional criteria can be defended only on arbitrary grounds. Thus Kruglanski and Ajzen propose that "one is never *objectively* justified in holding a given proposition as true" (p. 17) and that "any model of empirical reality is a conceptual construction whose degree of actual correspondence to objective reality is in principle inestimable" (p. 17). Verification that uses direct observation of "data" is also unreliable because "facts" are conceptual constructions and therefore also indeterminate. Thus Kruglanski and Ajzen argue that the presumed deficiency of the ordinary, everyday inference process can be demonstrated only if we assume the existence of strict validity criteria. And since the existence of such criteria is questioned by them, the conclusion that human inference is a process fraught with bias and error is not justified. Of course, if their position is taken literally, then we may well question the very argument they themselves developed. It is certainly the case that validity criteria are conventional and arbitrary. However, the students of biases and heuristics have never evaluated human inference against "absolute truth" (Nisbett and Ross, 1980). On the other hand, these same students of biases and heuristics are not always careful to verify whether their subjects observe the validity criteria that the experimental measures assume for their performance.

It is useful to contrast the contemporary view of cognitive processes with the view that was prevalent as social psychology was just beginning to take its first steps. The parallel to the contemporary analysis of inference processes and the biases attending them was the New Look in perception (Bruner, 1951). The central concept of the New Look was the "hypothesis." The individual was viewed as approaching the perceptual situation not empty-handed but with an expectation—a readiness for being confronted with certain types of things and events (Bruner, 1957b). The act of perception involved checking the "hypothesis" of the individual's making against the clues (evidence) that the environment provided. (Note the similarity to the later attributional concept of the "naive scientist.")

The outcome depended on the relative strengths of the "hypothesis" and of the "evidence." The stronger the hypothesis, the fewer were the cues necessary to confirm it. And the beauty of the theory was that one could now try to specify the factors that influenced the contribution made by the perceiver to the percept or to the product of his or her cognition. This could now be accomplished by learning what factors influenced hypothesis strength. Among these factors were the frequency of previous confirmation, the presence of competing hypotheses (monopoly), and the motivational, emotional, or social consequences associated with the confirmation or denial of the hypothesis. It was this theorizing that spawned perceptual defense, subception, selective memory, and set effects. It was a rich theory that accommodated both the stimulus information and the internal structures that processed that information.

To be sure, the methods of the New Look research were crude, and the ideas about cognitive structures were primitive, but much of this early thinking can be seen to be implicated in the experimental study of cognition today. Findings on "perception without awareness," which took the brunt of criticism from experimental psychology, have been replicated. The phenomenon is now regarded as respectable and reliable (Posner, 1982). The perceiver, as in the New Look conception, is again

viewed as vulnerable to selective biases, illusions, and self-deception. But curiously, one hardly sees in the modern work references to this early seminal research that laid ground for much of the sophistication that has developed over the past thirty years.

Finally, it needs to be stressed again that heuristics are a special case of cognitive biases. They represent problem-solving routines that are deliberately selected in the service of judgments, decisions, and inferences. The most pressing research question in the field of inference is to find methods that would discriminate between those effects that are produced by a general bias and those effects that derive from the deliberate utilization by the individual of a specifiable heuristic.

STRUCTURAL DYNAMICS

The concepts of schema, prototype, and category describe "cold" cognitive structures. They deal with the organization of knowledge in static terms. That is to say, these concepts refer to structures in which the cohesion of components or elements does not arise as a question. Why certain elements remain members of the same configuration—why, for example, a particular element does not abandon one structure and travel to another—is not a meaningful question for propositionally based cognitive theories. It is equally meaningless for these theories to inquire why Bach, Brahms, and Beethoven form a coherent structure that would not readily admit Nixon. The theories that employ the concepts of schema, prototype, or category—in fact, all propositional theories of cognition—would treat these phenomena in associative terms. The Bach-Brahms-Beethoven structure would not readily admit Nixon because of weak associative links between the main structure and Nixon and because of strong associative links of each of these to other stuctures that do not share components in common. Thus temporal and spatial proximity as well as similarity would be the properties of elements that would be used to explain the fact that a particular collection of cognitive units forms a cohesive structure.

This view is, of course, quite different from the approach taken by the cognitive precursors of contemporary social cognition, namely, balance and dissonance. Cognitive consistency theories that were advanced by social psychologists in the early forties invoked structures having important dynamic properties. The elements formed a structure *because* they were held together by gestaltlike cohesive forces. Inconsistency and imbalance produced tension within the structure, and the tension called for resolution. Tension impelled cognitive work to focus on certain elements, constraining the individual to modify either a particular cognitive element or his or her behavior.

In this sense these approaches parallel other perceptual phenomena that were conceptualized in terms of structural dynamics. For example, uncertainty, ambiguity, incongruity, and conflict were constructs treated by Berlyne (1960) as structures of information generating tension and having motivational consequences. In the case of uncertainty and ambiguity the individual sought to supply the missing information. In the case of incongruity and conflict the individual sought to resolve it. Like balance and dissonance, cognitive structures characterized by uncertainty, ambiguity, incongruity, and conflict were unstable and generated internal forces for their own change toward steady states. Thus the information-processing approach "cooled off" the conceptual representations of cognition in general and of social cognition in particular.

BALANCE THEORY

The principle of *structural balance* was first proposed in 1946 by Heider. It is a theory of social perception, but unlike many such theories, which are concerned with social determinants of perception, Heider's theory deals with the perception itself: the perception of social objects such as persons, ideas, and concepts. It implicitly assumes that social perception obeys gestaltlike structural principles and that it is subject to gestaltlike dynamics.

The principle of balance was derived from Heider's earlier work on the perception of causality (1944) and from a set of conditions underlying *unit formation,* which he identified in this earlier work. The basic assumptions of his approach are that steady and unsteady states can be specified for cognitive units and that these cognitive units tend to seek steady states. Fundamental to determining the state of a unit is the *dynamic character* (positive or negative) of its parts. For example, a unit might consist of a person p and of the person's action x. Each of these two parts might be evaluated either positively or negatively and hence have either positive or negative dynamic character. If the parts of a unit have the same dynamic character, a steady (*balanced*) state is said

to exist. When the parts of a unit are of different dynamic character, disequilibrium arises and the parts tend to become segregated from each other (Heider, 1946, p. 107).

These two tendencies inherent in balanced and imbalanced states correspond to what the Gestalt theory of perception understands by cohesive and restraining forces. Thus, for instance, a positive person p^+ and the person's virtuous act x^+ are perceived together without "cognitive strain." But the perception of a virtuous person p^+ who is seen or known to have commited a heinous crime x^- is an unbalanced perception. Since the two parts of this latter cognitive unit are of different dynamic character, cognitive work will be accomplished so that either the dynamic character of one of the parts changes or the parts become segregated.

In the analysis of interpersonal perception, the parts of cognitive units are considered to be *persons* (p, o $q, \ldots$) and *objects* or *events* ($x, y, z, \ldots$), as well as the relations of these to one another. The principle of balance begins by focusing analytical attention on the perceiver p. The relational or dynamic parts of the cognitive units in which p appears as a term are p's relationships to other persons, objects, and events. Thus the aspect of the cognitive unit that the balance principle analyzes is *attitude.*

The relations considered by balance theory are *sentiment relations* and *unit relations.* Sentiment relations are symbolized by L^+ and L^-, as in the following examples: Bill likes Jane ($pL + o$); Jane dislikes candy ($oL - x$); Bill feels neighborly toward Jane ($pL + o$); Jane can't stand Bill ($oL - p$); Bill is dissatisfied with a lecture ($pL - x$). Unit relations are symbolized by U, as in these examples: Bill owns a car (pUv); Bill does not own this house ($pU - w$); Jane built a bookcase (oUz); Jane told a lie (oUu). These latter unit relations, or U relations, are not to be confused with cohesive and restraining forces of unit formation.

When a set of relations or bonds is perceived as a unit, the bonds are assumed to be dynamically interdependent. In this respect structures of interpersonal and attitudinal bonds are assumed by Heider to have a gestaltlike or fieldlike property. As in field theory and Gestalt psychology, steady states and disequilibria are identified. Two such states, balance and disharmony (or imbalance), are said to characterize structures composed of sentiment and unit relations (Heider, 1958, p. 202):

If no balanced state exists, then forces towards this state will arise.

A dyad is balanced if the relations between the two entities are all positive or all negative. Disharmony results when relations of different sign character exist.

A triad is balanced when all three of the relations are positive or when two of the relations are negative and one is positive.

When only two relations of the triad are positive, imbalance is said to characterize the structure. Although Heider tends to define as imbalanced a triad which has three negative relations, he admits that such structures are ambiguous (p. 203).

When a structure is in a state of imbalance, a tendency exists to change it into a balanced one. The dynamic principle of change proposed by Heider does not involve psychological forces of overwhelming strength. They are more akin to preferences than to driving forces (Heider, 1958, pp. 204–205). There is no anxiety when structures are imbalanced; imbalanced states are not noxious; a compelling need to strive for balance is not assumed. Forces toward balance have the same character as gestalt forces toward "good figures" in the perception of forms.

However, they also involve another component. The dynamic effects in structures analyzed by Heider derive from juxtaposition of attitudes. However, in at least one publication Heider (1960) assumed that in addition to the "good figure" forces, these attitudes are themselves significant sources of dynamic effects: "What Köhler or Koffka called the ego-object forces enter in an important way, namely, the attitude toward the parts of the constellation—whether we like or dislike another person or whether we like or dislike what he has done" (p. 168). But it has never been theoretically clear how these attitudinal forces *interact* with the good-figure forces —whether the former are more or less important, or even whether they have the same dynamic properties as gestalt forces. The interaction between gestalt and attitudinal forces still remains an unsolved theoretical problem of the balance theory.

The bulk of the evidence bearing on Heider's assumption of an underlying preference for balanced states comes from studies in which hypothetical situations are rated for their pleasantness. For instance, using Heider's definition of balance, Jordan (1953) showed statements of the following kind to his subjects: I dislike *o*; I like *x*; *o* has no sort of bond or relationship with *x*. The subject was instructed to imagine himself in the situation playing the role of 'I' and then to rate it for experienced pleasantness or unpleasantness" on a ninety-point scale. Each statement consisted of information about the relation between the subject (*p*), a hypothetical person (*o*), and some undefined entity (*x*). *Unit* as well as *sentiment* relations were considered, and each statement gave information about three bonds. In all, sixty-four situations were rated by 288 subjects in a lattice square design. In general, Jordan's results supported Heider's hypothesis, but important discrepancies between predictions and data were also present. Other studies employing the same technique are in agreement with these results (Morrissette, 1958; Price, Harburg, and McLeod, 1965; Rodrigues, 1965, 1966, 1967; Price, Harburg, and Newcomb, 1966) and seem to show similar discrepancies.

In some experiments, instead of rating the pleasantness of hypothetical situations, subjects were asked to predict a missing bond (Morrissette, 1958; Shrader and Lewit, 1962) or to indicate which of the relations given they would most like to see changed (Rodrigues, 1966, 1967). These studies give general but not unequivocal support to Heider's hypothesis. Similiar evidence comes from experiments in which subjects learn hypothetical balanced and unbalanced structures (Zajonc and Burnstein, 1965a, 1965b). As in the studies on the learning of social structures carried out by DeSoto (1960), a paired-associates list is constructed. The items of the list correspond to the sentiment relations between *p*, *o*, and *x*. The stimulus terms of the list are the actors (*p*, *o*, and *x*) and issues (*x*), and the response terms are the bonds themselves. Thus, for instance, the stimulus term of one of the items in the list is ["Bill; Bob"], and the response term is ["likes"]. Errors in the learning of entire structures and in the learning of the components of structures (i.e., of individual bonds) are observed. These studies, too, give general support to the balance hypothesis.

Other experiments have exploited actual interpersonal attitudes to test the balance hypothesis. For instance, Horowitz, Lyons, and Perlmutter (1951) asked members of a discussion group to evaluate an event originated by one of the members. In agreement with the balance prediction the evaluation of this event was found to depend on the liking relation between the evaluator and the originator of the event; the event was judged positively to the extent that the evaluator liked the originator. Festinger and Hutte (1954), when they conducted their parallel experiments in the United States and the Netherlands, manipulated information given to subjects about how people whom these subjects liked or disliked felt about each other. Their results, too, were consistent with the balance hypothesis. Subjects reported feeling unstable about their relationships in the group when people they liked disliked each other.

Jaspers *et al.* (1965) measured Dutch children's attitudes toward six countries by means of Thurstone scales. The data were subsequently converted into distance matrices, and the analysis of these distances gave strong support to the balance model. Scott (1963) found that college students as well as noncollege adults show preference for balance in international alliances. But he also found that this preference for balanced international relations is more pronounced among individuals characterized by lesser cognitive complexity.

In a sociometric study of naval personnel Kogan and Tagiuri (1958) and Davol (1959) found that balanced units occur more frequently than one would expect on a chance basis. Recent work, however, suggests caution in calculating the presence of balanced relationships in an intact population. For example, Feld and Elmore (1982) have demonstrated that the presence of sociometric transitive triads depends on the distribution of popularity and cannot in itself be taken as evidence for balance theory. Sampson and Insko (1964) manipulated the liking between *p* and *o* as well as the initial agreement of *p* and *o* about apparent movement in an autokinetic situation. When there was liking and disagreement or disliking and agreement, subjects tended to feel nervous and change their own judgments in the direction consistent with the balance prediction. Gollob and Fischer (1973) found that balance relations apply to consistencies between perceived personal dispositions and their acts.

Tashakkori and Insko (1981) have carried out extensive tests of the major models of balance theory. One of those was Wiest's (1965) tetrahedron model (see Zajonc, 1968, pp. 349–350). Another was Feather and Simon's (1971) discrepancy model, which holds that for two relations of the same sign small discrepancies recruit a strong positive third relation, whereas for relations of opposite sign large discrepancies recruit a strong negative third relation. Wellens and Thistlethwaite (1971) employed the Wiest tetrahedron model but imposed equal weights on its boundaries. Tashakkori and Insko (1979, 1981) found good agreement between predictions from these models and their data.

The relative contributions of attraction and agreement to the balance effect are now better understood (C. E. Miller and Norman, 1976; Tyler and Sears, 1977;

Mower-White, 1979; Cacioppo and Petty, 1981; Insko, Sedlak, and Lipsitz, 1982). Insko and his associates attempted to reformulate attraction effects in terms of agreement. Thus if subjects view *p* and *o* to be similar to each other (e.g., there is agreement), a positive unit relation can be assumed to exist between them. Therefore, if the *p* − *x* and the *o* − *x* relations have the same sign (agree), balance would exist. But Insko and Adewole (1979) did not always find agreement effects when similarity between *p* and *o* was varied.

With the emergence of the information-processing approach, two important contributions were made to the understanding of how the sorts of social relations that Heider (1946) had in mind are represented in the subjects' minds. Picek, Sherman, and Shiffrin (1975) had subjects read stories about pairs of people selected from among four hypothetical individuals. They found better recall of stories of balanced groups than of imbalanced groups. Moreover, when stories that were incomplete descriptions of the relationships were given to subjects, they sometimes filled in missing pairwise relationships in their recall. These constructions by the subjects balanced groups that were capable of being balanced. Picek *et al.* treat these results as indicating that balance effects derive from particular ways of encoding and storing social information. A similar effect is reported by Spiro (1977).

Cottrell (1975) has also interpreted balance effects as consequences of information-processing strategy. In his study subjects were exposed to balance information as if it were concept learning. Cottrell demonstrated that in this "social concept" learning subjects used the "balance rule" quite readily. But interestingly, they also used other rules such as the "attraction rule" and the "agreement rule," both of which were more readily accessible to subjects than the "balance rule." Bear and Hodun (1975) argued in a similar vein, although their work derived from Abelson's (1968) psychologic, not from Heider's. Cacioppo and Petty (1981) allowed subjects different amounts of time to think about *p* − *o* − *x* triads and found that the attraction effect emerged after the shortest time. The agreement effect required longer time, and the balance effect the longest. Note that these configurations are ordered in increasing complexity (i.e., degrees of freedom) such that attraction requires only one sign, agreement two signs, and balance all three signs.

Sentis and Burnstein (1979) employed modern methods of cognitive chronometry to demonstrate that balanced triads are indeed stored as integral units—perhaps gestalten, as Heider suggested—and not as disjoint elements. Their findings revealed that balanced triads were processed with greater speed than imbalanced triads. However, many questions about balance remain unresolved (Gerbing and Hunter, 1979), and some are perhaps not resolvable (Insko, 1980). Thus, for example, Pichevin and Poitou (1974) regard experimentation on balance generally artificial and subject to powerful experimenter demands (Orne, 1962). They asked subjects to construct three-person structures involving liking relationships. When the hypothetical persons were identified simply by first names, the typical balance effect emerged. However, when status differences were introduced among the hypothetical members of the triads, subjects constructed structures in which there were liking bonds between equals and negative relationships between members who differed in status. Note that balance is a bias of sorts in that its elements are themselves biases. Thus, for example, balance can be represented as the interaction of positivity bias (p. 185), agreement bias (Zajonc and Burnstein, 1965b), and transitivity bias (Van Kreveld and Zajonc, 1966).

Gollob (1974) reformulated the balance principle in syntactic terms. The triad can be described in grammar-like constraints using the concepts of subject, verb, and object. Thus, Jerry likes Jane, Jerry dislikes Jim, and Jane dislikes Jim can be restated from Jerry's point of view to read Jane (whom I like) dislikes Jim (whom I dislike, too). Gollob's model calculates balance by considering the components of the subject-verb-object triad in an analysis-of-variance model such that a plus or a minus is assigned to the main terms subject, verb, and object and to the interactions subject-verb, subject-object, verb-object, and subject-verb-object. The outcomes are then summed. The sums thus generated rank the triads for positivity, and a degree of balance can be estimated from these ranks. Thus, for example, the triad $+ + +$, indicating that p likes o, o likes x, and p likes x, implies that the subject (p likes o), the verb (o likes x), and the object (p likes x) are all positive and would score 7, one for each of the seven components (S, V, O, SV, SO, VO, and SVO). When all the factors and all the interactions are examined, several ties result in the ranking of triads. Gollob therefore assigned differential weights to the various elements of the factors and was thereby able to describe a great deal of the literature.

Considerable research has been stimulated by Gollob's approach (Insko, Songer, and McGarvey, 1974; Wyer, 1974, 1975; Wyer, Henninger, and Wolfson,

1975; Rossman and Gollob, 1976; Thompson, Gard, and Phillips, 1980). However, Anderson (1977, 1979) has criticized the approach on methodological grounds, objecting that tests of goodness of fit were not carried out by these researchers in testing the S–V–O theory. While some elements of Anderson's critique are valid, the descriptive and explanatory power of Gollob's representation of balance theory, and its elegance, cannot be questioned.

THE THEORY OF COGNITIVE DISSONANCE

No theory in social psychology has stimulated more research during the sixties than the theory of *cognitive dissonance*. For an entire decade articles in this area constituted the modal category in journals publishing results of social psychological research. They dealt with topics and problems whose range extended well beyond the boundaries of social psychology, from delay of reward and intermittent reinforcement effects (Lawrence and Festinger, 1962) to the behavior of cultists (Festinger, Riecken, and Schachter, 1956). Part of the appeal of the cognitive dissonance theory was in the scope of phenomena it subsumed. It implicated perception, cognition, affect, motivation, and action.

The theory of cognitive dissonance is stated in less formal terms than the balance principle. The basic propositions are couched in broad and sweeping form, and there is some uncertainty about how one arrives at specific predictions. The balance principle generated direct experimental predictions. These predictions were quite precise and unambiguous. The data, unfortunately, did not always agree with the predicted values.

In contrast, the theory of cognitive dissonance, as originally stated, did not make specific predictions, and it required a set of extratheoretical assumptions for practically every experimental application. These assumptions were in themselves exciting and interesting, and they have opened up new fields of research for social psychologists. Some attempts have been directed toward the systematization of these extratheoretical assumptions, their verification, and their eventual incorporation within the framework of the theory (e.g., J. W. Brehm and Cohen, 1962; Festinger, 1964; Wicklund and J. W. Brehm, 1976). Yet it was especially the open character of dissonance theory that made it a viable and highly productive scientific instrument. The other feature of cognitive dissonance research, not necessarily derived from the theory but generated by the type of phenomena to which the theory turned, was the use of powerful experimental manipulations that engaged the subjects' nontrivial beliefs, motives, and emotions.

Although none of the basic definitions and assumptions of this theory has been carefully or precisely stated, an overwhelming number of hypotheses have been derived from them. The basic term *cognition* is undefined; it corresponds to what is ordinarily understood by *belief, opinion, knowledge, conviction,* etc. Since there are no specifications as to how cognitions are to be identified and measured, it is left to the experimenter's intuition to determine whether a given cognition exists and what its nature may be.

Cognitions can be in a relevant or an irrelevant relation to each other. They interact only if they are relevant to each other; they may support one another, act in concert, produce offshoots, form units, contradict one another, modify one another, conflict with one another. In short, relevant cognitions can be either consonant or dissonant with respect to one another. The state of consonance implies mutual consistency, while the state of dissonance implies inconsistency: *"Two elements are in dissonant relation if, considering these two alone, the obverse of one element would follow from the other. To state it a bit more formally, x and y are dissonant if not-x follows from not-y"* (Festinger, 1957, p. 13).

There has been some misunderstanding about the above definition and some criticism of it (Asch, 1958; Jordan, 1963; Lott, 1963; Mowrer, 1963; Chapanis and Chapanis, 1964; Elms and Janis, 1965; Rosenberg, 1965). Questions have been raised about the appropriateness of the term *obverse,* about how one knows that dissonance actually exists, about the meaning of *"follow from* and of *element*, about how one can consider two cognitive elements *alone,* etc. But such questions would be pertinent only if the definition were intended to serve strictly empirical and descriptive purposes.

Actually, the purpose of Festinger's definition was not to describe reality but to formulate a basic theoretical statement that would generate testable hypotheses. It is true, on the other hand, that these hypotheses do not derive from the basic statement in an absolutely compelling manner. The researcher needs some imagination, some ingenuity, and a good deal of outside knowledge to produce them. But once the pattern has been set, the process of generating specific hypotheses from dissonance theory is easy to master. Requiring that the theoretical definition of dissonance have at every point a specific empirical interpretation would probably destroy its heuristic usefulness.

The entire theory of cognitive dissonance can be stated in a few propositions:

1. Cognitive dissonance is a noxious state.

2. In the case of cognitive dissonance the individual attempts to reduce or eliminate it, and the individual acts so as to avoid events that will increase it.

3. In the case of consonance the individual acts so as to avoid dissonance-producing events.

4. The severity or the intensity of cognitive dissonance varies with (a) the importance of cognitions involved and (b) the relative number of cognitions standing in dissonant relation to one another.

5. The strength of the tendencies enumerated in Propositions 2 and 3 is a direct function of the severity of dissonance.

6. Cognitive dissonance can be reduced or eliminated only by (a) adding new cognitions or (b) changing existing ones.

7. Adding new cognitions reduces dissonance if (a) the new cognitions add weight to one side and thus decrease the proportion of cognitive elements that are dissonant, or (b) the new cognitions change the importance of the cognitive elements that are in dissonant relation with one another.

8. Changing existing cognitions reduces dissonance if (a) their new content makes them less contradictory with others or (b) their importance is reduced.

9. If new cognitions cannot be added or the existing ones changed by means of a passive process, behaviors that have cognitive consequences favoring consonance will be recruited. Seeking new information is an example of such behavior.

The dynamics of dissonance are attributed to two postulated tendencies. On the one hand, interaction of individuals with their "real" environment exerts pressure on their cognitions to come into correspondence with "reality." On the other hand, there is as well a tendency to maintain consistency among the cognitions themselves. However, both the environment and the cognitive process can be sources of inconsistency together.

The individual may experience inconsistency of *sensory* character with a visual, auditory, or other kind of illusion: The immediate sensory information is likely to conflict with another sensory event or with previous knowledge. Inconsistency of *social* origin is a commonplace experience, because the individual very often faces the pressures of conflicting role demands or of conflicting norms.

Individuals experience *informational inconsistency* if they receive a communication that contradicts what they already know. *Disconfirmed expectations* are clearly a source of dissonance, for individuals may have prepared themselves behaviorally and cognitively for an event that never occurs—or even worse, an event whose opposite occurs. Individuals who find themselves engaged in action for which there is *insufficient justification* (Aronson, 1966) are equally in a state of cognitive dissonance, for they fail to find adequate cognitive support for their behavior. Following every choice individuals experience some degree of *postdecision dissonance*: They experience it to the extent that the alternative they have selected has negative features and all those they have rejected have some positive features.

According to the early version of the theory of cognitive dissonance, every decision is followed by dissonance of greater or lesser magnitude. Since decision involves a selection among a set of alternatives, it necessarily entails forsaking the attractive features of rejected alternatives and reconciling oneself to the negative features of the selected alternative. If there are just two alternatives, x and y, the cognition that the chosen alternative x has negative features is dissonant with the cognition that it has been chosen. Also, the cognition that y has some attractive features is dissonant with the cognition that it has been rejected. Supporting the choice, however, and hence acting to reduce dissonance, is the knowledge that x has positive features and y negative features.

The situation may be represented in balance theory notation with choice coordinated to U-relations (Zajonc, 1968; Insko *et al.*, 1975). A reevaluation of alternatives may often involve self-deception and distortion, and the individuals may deliberately seek information that would allow them to maximize inequalities. Ehrlich *et al.* (1957), for instance, found that shortly after buying a car, the new owner is more likely to read ads for the car she actually bought than for cars she considered but did not buy. The former ads enhance $x+$, while the latter enhance $y+$.

The typical experiment on postdecision effects requires the subject to make a choice among a set of alternatives whose attractiveness is measured both before and after the decision. In the pioneering study of J. W. Brehm (1956), subjects rated eight products (each worth approximately $20), believing that they would receive one of them for taking part in the experiment. Following the initial preference rating the subject was given the opportunity to choose among two of the eight products. In all experimental conditions neither of these two products had received either an extremely high or an extremely low rating. But half the subjects were choosing between two alternatives to which they gave similar ratings (high dissonance), and half between two alternatives that had been rated farther apart (low dissonance). A control group was given no choice at all following the initial-rating task. These subjects, however, received a gift chosen by the experimenter and equal in desirability to those in the experimental groups.

Since the subjects' decisions could not be revoked or reversed, the only means of dissonance reduction was reevaluation of the alternatives. J. W. Brehm found rather clear support for the hypotheses derived from dissonance theory:

1. The chosen alternative increased in attractiveness following the choice.

2. The rejected alternative decreased in attractiveness following the choice.

3. Both these changes were more pronounced when the subjects chose between products closer together on the preference-rating scales than between products farther apart.

4. In the control group no changes in attractiveness of the received products occurred.

A thorough review of the earlier studies exploring dissonance theory and the controversies that ensued can be found in Zajonc (1968), and a more recent summary is given by Wicklund and J. W. Brehm (1976).

The Self and Dissonance

The major new development in dissonance theory since the publication of the last edition of the *Handbook* has been in the importation of the self as a critical intervening factor. The self entered dissonance theory in a variety of ways. D. Bem's self-perception theory was the first serious theoretical challenge to dissonance theory. It soon had to be stated in less extreme terms, however. The assumption that people know their internal states by observing their own behavior had to be restricted to ambiguous cases (Bem, 1972).

A number of studies sought to resolve the controversy that centered around the motivational components of counterattitudinal behavior research (Snyder and Ebbesen, 1972; M. Ross and Shulman, 1973; Green, 1974; Schaffer, 1975; Swann and Pittman, 1975). Dissonance theory postulated the presence of tension deriving from the opposition of the dissonant cognitions, whereas self-perception theory held that there were no motivational pressures that were necessary conditions for the effect. Following the earlier work that attempted to demonstrate drive properties of dissonance (Cottrell and Wack, 1967), other studies reported evidence showing the presence of motivational and tensionlike states that accompanied dissonance (Pallak and Pittman, 1972; Worchel and Arnold, 1974; Zanna and Cooper, 1974; Pittman, 1975; Kiesler and Pallak, 1976; Zanna, Higgins, and Taves, 1976; Higgins, Rhodewalt, and Zanna, 1979).

However, these studies did not show arousal to be a *necessary* condition for the production of the attitudinal effects of dissonance. Thus in a thorough theoretical analysis, Greenwald (1975) concluded that no empirical grounds existed for choosing one theory over the other. In a widely cited paper that is a benchmark in the dissonance versus self-perception research, Fazio, Zanna, and Cooper (1977) have shown that as is often the case with social psychological theories, they were both untenable. Moreover, they specified conditions under which the predictions of dissonance theory would be assumed to hold and conditions under which the self-perception theory could make valid predictions. These conditions were attitude-discrepant and attitude-congruent behavior. Cooper, Zanna, and Taves (1978) and Croyle and Cooper (1983) were also able to find evidence of arousal as importantly implicated in dissonance reduction. A review by Fazio and Cooper (1983) summarizes impressive evidence showing that physiological measures taken under conditions of dissonance reveal clear arousal effects.

Of particular interest was the use of the *overjustification* paradigm (Kiesler, Nisbett, and Zanna, 1969; Deci, 1971; Lepper, Greene, and Nisbett, 1973; Benware and Deci, 1975; M. Ross, 1976). The overjustification paradigm constitutes an ambiguous situation in which causal attribution is problematic. Since the subject is asked to argue in the direction of his or her own beliefs *and* is rewarded for it, there are two causes, each of which could be sufficient for the subject's action (Kelley, 1973). Hence misattribution is likely. Thus given external justification and attitude-congruent behavior, subjects can misattribute their proattitudinal behavior to the external demands.

Fazio, Zanna, and Cooper (1977) argued, following Zanna and Cooper (1974), that in the attitude-discrepant case arousal is misattributed to an internal state: The subjects attribute their tension to the counterattitudinal act, experience dissonance as a result, and attempt to reduce it by changing their attitudes. In the attitude-congruent case, however, especially when the subjects had freedom to engage in attitude-congruent behavior, they should perceive the act as actually reflecting their "true" beliefs. Thus dissonance theory applies to counterattitudinal situations and self-perception to proattitudinal cases. Similarly, Frey *et al.* (1979) asked secondary school students to carry out attitude-congruent and attitude-discrepant actions for monetary incentives. Attitude change in the various conditions revealed support for both self-perception theory in the attitude-congruent conditions and for dissonance theory in the counterattitudinal condition.

In an extensive and carefully designed series of studies, Nuttin (1975) also obtained similar attitude change both in counterattitudinal and in proattitudinal conditions. However, Nuttin takes his results as evidence against dissonance theory, because proattitudinal advocacy involves no dissonance. Nuttin considers the emerging attitude effects to be local and transitory. In fact, the title of his monograph is *The Illusion of Attitude Change*. Much other research has numerous contributions to make to either one or the other side of the controversy (Carlsmith, Collins, and Helmreich, 1966; Linder, Cooper, and Jones, 1967; Collins and Hoyt, 1972; Frey and Irle, 1972; Gerard, Connolley, and Wilhelmy, 1974).

Note that the overjustification paradigm that has been employed to resolve the self-perception versus dissonance controversy—a controversy whose core centers around the issue of presence of motivational factors—is itself subject to some controversy over the presence of these factors. One position (Lepper, Green, and Nisbett, 1973; Lepper, 1981) features the effect primarily in cognitive terms, implicating self-perception and misattribution as key concepts.

The view of the phenomenon from the perspective of intrinsic motivation (Deci, 1975; Shapira, 1976; Condry and Chambers, 1978; Harter, 1978; Boggiano, Ruble, and Pittman, 1982), however, implicates a confounding of motivational incentives. The person who has an intrinsic interest in the task is challenged by it and sets up internal standards of excellence and success. When external incentives are added, there is a confusion of purpose and goal, and the person's criteria of success are diluted. In the same vein, the arguments of self-perception theory, the Fazio, Zanna, and Cooper (1977) position, and the Nuttin monograph assume that since there is no dissonance in the proattitudinal case, there is no tension. Thus all accept a nonmotivational interpretation of the overjustification result.

However, the proattitudinal advocacy cannot be said to be entirely bereft of tension. As has been shown in research on cognitive tuning (Zajonc, 1960), having to transmit attitudinal information of *any* sort influences the individual to activate structures and schemas that are tightly organized and highly resistant to change. The assumption is that transmitters of their own beliefs may face challenge and must prepare themselves for a possible defense of these beliefs. It is not stretching the point to imagine that a subject may experience some dissonance-like state when asked by the experimenter to prepare a concise statement displaying and justifying her beliefs. "Why," she asks herself, "must I do this, and why am I offered a reward?" Such an experience is neither common nor trivial. Thus it should be noted that in the studies that attempted to resolve the dissonance versus self-perception controversy, no evidence was supplied that (1) the proattitudinal advocacy is free of motivational factors or (2) these factors do not contain dissonance elements.

Self entered dissonance theory first when Festinger (1957) pointed out that greater dissonance results from a conflict among important cognitions. But what are *important* cognitions? According to Eagly and Himmelfarb (1978) and Wicklund and Brehm (1976), dissonance effects emerge when the subject can anticipate the unwanted consequences of the counterattitudinal behavior and is willing to take responsibility for it. The perception and anticipation of the consequences of counterattitudinal behavior were found to be a significant variable, and dissonance effects were obtained when people could anticipate these consequences and also when they were shown, after having carried out the counterattitudinal behavior,

that they could have foreseen (Walker and Arrowood, 1977; M. H. Davis, 1979; Goethals, Cooper, and Naficy, 1979). Finally, because dissonance reduction can be conceived of as a form of ego-defensive action, Zanna and Aziza (1976) argued that it should be reflected in such individual differences as repression sensitization. Their experiment confirmed the expectation.

The second significant challenge to dissonance theory was made by the *impression management theory* (Tedeschi, Schlenker, and Bonoma, 1971; Schlenker, 1980). The main point of the impression management explanation of dissonance effects, especially those obtained in counterattitudinal advocacy, is that people are really much more interested in *looking* consistent than in being consistent. Considerable evidence has been collected to show that positive evaluations can be received by individuals who change their minds (Cialdini, Braver, and Lewis, 1974; Cialdini and Mirels, 1976; Braver *et al.*, 1977). Braver *et al.* showed the striking effect that individuals change most if they communicate only with the persuader, apparently to preserve and protect an amicable relationship with the persuader. They change least if they communicate only with a passive witness. And the change is intermediate when both the witness and the persuader are present. Steele and Lin (1983) have recently shown that when the subject has access to self-affirming cognitions, dissonance effects are absent.

The impression management position has been supported mainly by studies attempting to obtain measures of subjects' "true" attitudes and comparing them with attitude measures obtained by means of the typical questionnaire method. Thus, for example, Quigley-Fernandez and Tedeschi (1978) and Gaes, Kalle, and Tedeschi (1978) used the "bogus pipeline" technique to measure attitudes and found little dissonance effect in comparison with the case when standard methods were employed. Baumeister (1982) distinguished between two self-presentational concerns. On the one hand, he postulated an attempt on the part of the subject to construct a general public self. On the other hand, there is a more limited and temporally bound concern: pleasing the immediate audience. Baumeister's review of the literature revealed that these two concerns often stand in conflict with one another, as is the case in some experiments on counterattitudinal behavior, for example. The focus on the self in dissonance research has been so striking that Greenwald and Ronis (1978) and Ronis and Greenwald (1979) pointed out that recent experiments featured as being concerned with dissonance effects are in fact addressed to the study of cognitive changes that occur for ego-defensive and self-serving purposes.

Reactance Theory

One of the indirect products of dissonance theory was J. W. Brehm's (1966) *reactance theory,* which must have been kindled in the course of his earlier work on volition and choice. Reactance theory holds that when the individual's freedom of choice is restricted or threatened, the alternative that suffers the restriction will gain in attractiveness. The effect derives essentially from the individual's desire to restore freedom of choice.

Substantial evidence was collected in support of the reactance hypothesis (J. W. Brehm *et al.,* 1966; Linder and Crane, 1970; Wicklund, 1970, 1974; Worchel and J. W. Brehm, 1971; J. W. Brehm and Mann, 1975; M. L. Snyder and Wicklund, 1976; S. S. Brehm and J. W. Brehm, 1981; Wright and S. S. Brehm, 1982). As in the case of dissonance theory, there were several attempts to account for reactance effects in terms of impression management (Heilman and Toffler, 1976; Schlenker, 1980). This account assumes that the person is more interested in projecting an image of autonomy to others than in actually having autonomy. This is especially so if the perception by others of the person's autonomy is somehow necessary to protect and enhance the relationships of the person whose freedom is being threatened. However, Wright and S. S. Brehm (1982) argued cogently against the impression management view, showing that reactance effects were obtained even where observers could not perceive reactance-produced behavior as an expression of autonomy.

Motivational Consequences of Dissonance

To the extent that dissonant states have motivational properties, they should have motivational consequences for behavior other than attitude change and preference. Thus, for example, Tiller and Fazio (1982) have shown that subjects are more committed to a goal and perform at a higher level following a dissonance-produced attitude change. Specific effects on goal-directed behavior were predicted by dissonance theory in the area of *selective exposure* to information. It follows from the basic assumptions of dissonance theory that the individual will seek information that reduces dissonance and avoid information that increases or maintains it. However, earlier reviews found little confirmation for the hypothesis (Freedman and Sears, 1965). Later reviews (Wicklund

and J. W. Brehm, 1976; Frey and Wicklund, 1978), on the other hand, concluded that there is indeed good evidence for the selective exposure hypothesis (Lowin, 1967; Kleinhesselink and Edwards, 1975) provided appropriate experimental controls are introduced to eliminate such factors as curiosity, opportunity to counterargue (Frey, 1981), confidence, or such individual difference factors as repression sensitization (Olson and Zanna, 1979, 1982).

The premise of motivational consequences of dissonant states guided an important program of research by Zimbardo (1969) and his colleagues. A number of experiments carried out in his laboratory have produced results suggesting rather strong motivational consequences of dissonant states. For example, Zimbardo *et al.* (1966) used the insufficient-justification paradigm where the subjects were either given very little reason to take part in an experiment that involved verbal learning using electric shock or given very sufficient reasons. In the high-dissonance condition the subjects were told that their participation "may not add anything more to what Dr. Zimbardo's study has already found" (p. 108). Subjects in other conditions had either no choice in taking part in the experiment or moderate freedom of choice. All subjects were tested for their GSR reactions to shock, subjective judgments of shock, and learning efficiency (trials to learn). The shocks were not contingent on the subject's learning responses. The subjects in the high-dissonance group showed a clear decrease in GSR, whereas the subjects in the low-dissonance condition manifested a slight increase in GSR responsiveness. The subjective estimates of pain caused by shock paralleled the GSR results.

Most interesting, however, are results on trials to learn. Since the list was of some difficulty (serial anticipation), Zimbardo *et al.* expected that the subjective shock intensity would interfere with learning. In fact, control groups that received two different levels of shock behaved in just that way. The experimental groups in which dissonance was manipulated but in which the objective shock level was held constant behaved as if there were in fact differences in shock intensity. Thus the low-dissonance group showed no change in trials to criterion, whereas the high-dissonance groups showed a reduction in trials to learn. The learning data for the dissonance groups duplicated the data for the control group that received high and low shocks. The group receiving a high level of shock did not change, whereas the group whose shock level was reduced showed a reduction in trials to learn. Other experiments in this series are equally suggestive of strong motivational consequences associated with insufficient-justification effects. However, Furedy and Doob (1972) failed to find such evidence for cognitive control over aversive events.

POSTSCRIPT ON CONSISTENCY THEORIES

Consistency theories derive their name from the end states that individuals are presumably seeking to attain. When one looks at the antecedents of consistencies, however, then these theories are all conflict theories. By that we must mean that all consistency theories have one basic conceptual property in common—they must invoke *at least* two elements that stand in opposition to each other. This is true of dissonance in which there are two cognitions that are obverse to each other. It is true of the congruity principle, where the elements involved are a concept, a source, and an assertion about the source (Osgood and Tannenbaum, 1955). In balance theory the conflict is of a similar nature: It is in the structure of positive and negative bonds.

But there is also conflict in many other phenomena of social psychology that were studied under different labels. For example, the frustration/aggression hypothesis involves a conflict between a goal-directed behavior and a blocking of the path to that goal. Decision research involves a conflict between alternatives whose nature allows predictions about decision time (Cartwright, 1941). Level of aspiration involves a conflict between actual attainment and the ideal or the expected goal (Festinger, 1942). Social comparison is a form of conflict between one's own ability or opinion and some prevalent standard (Festinger, 1954). Conformity research involves a conflict between one's own perception and the judgments of others (Asch, 1951). And Milgram's (1965) obedience work involves a conflict between what one knows to be a right thing to do and the experimenter's instruction.

All these forms of conflict are useful conceptualizations because they postulate some tendency toward a resolution, and the nature of the opposing forces allows one to make predictions about probable outcomes. They give the system energy and they propel the individual from one state to another in a systematic way. In other words, all these theories focus on an instability, and they all attempt to make predictions about the steady state of the organism at a subsequent time. In each case there is some form of dynamic property that can produce a change in the organism, and because the constellation of the opposing vectors is specified, there is also a possibility of predicting direction of change. This is not to deny the fact that the individual can tolerate considerable cognitive inconsistency (e.g., Silverman, 1971).

Note that imbalance and dissonance are unsteady states and that all the above conflict theories try to capture the nature of this unsteady state, to distinguish the dynamic properties that specify the unsteady elements, and to predict the outcome.

The most compelling difference between the study of cognition in the 1960s and more recent studies is that today conflict or dynamic properties are absent. As social psychologists turned from "hot" cognition to "cold" information-processing approaches, they almost entirely eliminated any concern for the dynamics of social cognition and perception. Dissonance researchers had hardly any doubt that there was a rich participation of affect and motivation in the processing of social information. The agitated behavior of the subjects they observed made it obvious that not all behavior would be explained in cognitive terms.

However, there is little of affect or motivation to be seen in more recent, typical social cognition experiments. One cannot become very excited about combining three trait adjectives. Moreover, there is little in the way of overt behavior that can be observed in these studies. The information-processing approach to social behavior does not involve motivation and affect as explanatory factors, but it does not always try to predict overt behavioral outcomes—a defining feature of dissonance studies. In fact, the majority of investigations of cognitive structures end with a set of provisos and caveats that further research is necessary to determine if and under what conditions the cognitive structures studied will have an impact on overt behavior.

Because the social cognition researchers of the seventies and eighties have been primarily concerned with the description and explanation of *mental* events that intervene between the stimulus and the response and have not emphasized overt behavior, there also has been a dramatic change in the *methods* of social cognition research. Consider the subject in a counterattitudinal experiment required to utter a boldface lie to a stranger, with a person of some status (the experimenter) looking on and taking stock of the subject's behavior.

Compare this situation with one in which a person is given a questionnaire asking him to estimate the product of an eight-digit series or to say how much he might like a fictitious person about whom he knows nothing except that he is intelligent, generous, and honest. Clearly, given information-processing methods that are only a step removed from the earlier experimental predecessors of verbal learning, it is not surprising that there has been a controversy about the role of motivation in social cognition (D. Miller and M. Ross, 1975; Nisbett and L. Ross, 1980).

Further work on processes of social cognition may necessitate a return to some of the concerns of the dissonance theorists. It is likely that there are severe limitations to an understanding of the processes of social cognition if they are studied apart from affective and motivational constraints and without being linked to overt behavior. Some of the most important properties of cognitive structures or cognitive processes, in general, may only be evident when two cognitive structures are in conflict or when social information processing is serving a particular need or value of the individual.

ISSUES AND PROSPECTS

There have been significant advances in the understanding of processing of social information as a result of the application of cognitive science to social psychology (Hastorf, Schneider, and Polefka, 1970; Wyer, 1974; Carroll and Payne, 1976; Schneider, Hastorf, and Ellsworth, 1979; Wyer and Carlston, 1979; Hastie *et al.*, 1980; Cantor and Kihlstrom, 1981; Forgas, 1981; Higgins, Herman, and Zanna, 1981; Hastorf and Isen, 1982). The material reviewed in this chapter also highlights a number of important issues that emerge in the course of application of the theory and findings of cognitive psychology to such social psychological problems as stereotyping (Ebbesen and Allen, 1979; Hastie and Kumar, 1979; Wyer and Srull, 1980; Hamilton, 1981; Tajfel, 1981; Taylor, 1981), person perception (Cantor and Mischel, 1979), and the self (Markus, 1977).

The foremost issue that needs to be resolved is whether *social* cognition is a process formally identical to other perceptual and cognitive processes—and whether it can therefore be studied by a straightforward application, of cognitive science, or, alternatively, whether it is distinct and can be studied only if considerable adjustments and modifications are made in the concepts and methods of cognitive psychology that adapt it to the special needs and requirements of social cognition.

The view that social cognition does not differ in essential ways from cognition in general is best represented by Hastie and Carlston (1980). They assert that "the mind [is] an active information processing computer" (p. 2). They foresee "that eventually a proper theory of the mind will be in the form of a computational model expressed in abstract logical or Automata Theory terms and embodied in an operating computer program" (p. 2). On this basis they set down the requirements of a model that would serve for the analysis of social cognition. The model must specify the following features of the cognitive performance (Hastie and Carlston, 1980, p. 39):

1. Provide a vocabulary to describe the stimulus.

2. Characterize encoding transformations of stimulus information that occur during acquisition.

3. Describe the structure of the mental representation that is created and retained in memory.

4. Characterize the decoding function that operates during retrieval.

5. Provide a vocabulary to describe to-be-measured responses.

These features apply to *any* general model for cognition and have no unique specifications for the *social* aspects of cognition because the purpose of these authors in identifying these tasks was to outline and examine some critical "choice points" of cognitive psychology of which social psychologists working in person memory could and should become aware (p. 40). Hastie and Carlston (1980), however, do specify some lines of divergence between general memory research and person memory. They acknowledge that the stimuli in person memory research are generally richer and more complex in that the work implicates a greater number of dependent variables, that there is a greater between-subject variance, that evaluative responses are more pronounced in person memory than in ordinary verbal learning, that there is substantial self-reference, and that a great deal of causal inference takes place. Thus except for the fact that there is self-reference, Hastie and Carlston consider person memory to be merely a more complex special case of general memory research. And it is not clear that, as such, self-reference constitutes a substantively and qualitatively different case. In fact, Bower and Gilligan (1979) argue that it does not.

Perhaps the most critical issue raised by Hastie and Carlston (1980) is their assumption about two stores—event memory and conceptual memory. It is here that social psychologists may find concepts useful to their problems. Social event memory refers to the representation of information about specific social events that occur in particular temporal and spatial locations (p. 26). Social conceptual memory, on the other hand, contains information about procedures for making inferences and about the way some abstract items of social knowledge relate to each other. The prototype of event memory is "John did Rubic's Cube in 83 seconds." The prototype for social conceptual memory is the knowledge that "intelligent people are likely to solve puzzles rapidly." The latter is studied in implicit personality theory by attempts to describe the multidimensional space of personality traits as they are perceived by the members of a given linguistic community (e.g., Rosenberg and Sedlak, 1972). It is also conceptualized as schemas (Markus, 1977), prototypes (Cantor and Mischel, 1977), or scripts (Schank and Abelson, 1977). Hastie and Carlston do not insist on a strict and unequivocal distinction between event and conceptual memories and point out that "the two stores are inextricably bound together." All information according to Hastie and Carlston is processed by activating both stores (p. 26).

The flowchart of social information processing, according to the Hastie-Carlston (1980) general person memory model, is laid down explicitly (p. 12):

> Suppose that our observer has set the goal of evaluating the intelligence of one of the speakers. . . . This goal is registered in the Executive portion of the cognitive system, and the goal is explicated by consulting the inference procedure for impression formation in the Conceptual Memory store. This procedure is copied into Working Memory, and the Executive initiates attention routines that seek information relevant to the evaluation of intelligence in the ongoing interaction being observed. The Executive also initiates a search of Event Memory at the locus of the speaker's representation in that store. Information coming from the sense organs via Short-Term Memory and from Event Memory is evaluated with reference to the lexicon of social information in Conceptual Memory. For instance, a search of Event Memory might yield the fact that the speaker was an accomplished pianist. Reference to the lexicon of social attributes in Conceptual Memory would produce an evaluation of high intelligence based on the instantiation of the category of generic behaviors "skillful musician."

Evaluations of the speaker's personal characteristics and actions would be passed on to the impression formation procedure in Working Memory. The Executive monitors the perceptual and mnemonic search and terminates information seeking when sufficient evaluations have been received to yield a judgment of intelligence.

A closer scrutiny of the problems of social cognition, however, suggests that they differ from other cognitive problems more profoundly than one would at first expect. N. H. Anderson (1983) has recently pointed out that, unlike in traditional verbal learning, person memory is seldom a "verbatim" memory. Moreover, the goals of person perception are to be taken into account for they set up "valuation schemas that extract relevant memory from present and memorial information" (p. 4). Heider (1958) was quite clear on the distinction between perceiving persons and perceiving other nonsocial entities (p. 21):

> In . . . thing perception, we assume that there are real, solid objects with properties of shape and color, things placed in particular positions in real space, having functional properties making them fit or interfere with our purposes, and in general defining their place in the space of means-end relations. There is a chair on which one can sit; there is an object with which one can cut paper, tie a package, or write a note.

> In . . . person perception, we also assume that these "objects" have color and occupy certain positions in the environment. They are, however, rarely manipulanda; rather they are usually perceived as action centers and as such can do something to us. They can benefit or harm us intentionally, and we can benefit or harm them. Persons have abilities, wishes and sentiments; they can act purposefully, and can perceive and watch us. They are systems having an awareness of their surroundings and their conduct refers to this environment, an environment that sometimes includes ourselves.

Similarly, Asch (1952) noted the unique features of social perception (p. 142):

> We experience direct communication with others: emotion clashing with emotion, desire meeting desire, thought speaking to thought. Often there is virtually no lag between the psychological event in

one person and its grasp in the other. We may even anticipate the thought and feelings of those we know, and it would appear that we are as directly connected with others as with our own psychological processes.

The fact that cognitive processes as they are studied by experimental psychologists differ in a number of ways from those that are of interest to social psychologists should not be construed to infer that there are two "kinds" of cognitions—social and nonsocial. The features discussed below that characterize social cognition are also true largely of cognition in general. They are simply not attended to when cognition is examined by experimental psychologists, or at best held constant.

There are four features of social cognition that distinguish it from cognition as investigated by experimental psychologists: (1) the participation of "hot" factors, affect and motivation; (2) the social basis of categorization; (3) the consequences of our perceptions and cognitions for the target; and (4) the communicative context of cognition. The importance of all four of these features in distinguishing social cognition from other forms of cognition derives from the potentially reciprocal nature of the former. Many earlier authors, such as Mead (1934), Merleau-Ponty (1945), Asch (1952), and Heider (1958), have held the reciprocal nature of person perception to be an essentially unique feature of this process. Thus, for example, Asch (1952, p. 142) argued that in interacting with objects

> perceiving, thinking, and feeling take place on one side, whereas in relations between persons these processes take place on both sides. . . . We interact with each other . . . via emotions and thoughts that are capable of taking into account the emotions and thoughts of others.

Merleau-Ponty (1945) wrote in similar vein (p. 407):

> In the experience of a conversation . . . my thoughts and his make up a single tissue, my words and his are called out by the phase of the discussion, they insert themselves in a common operation of which neither of us is the sole creator. A double-being comes about, and neither is the other one for me a simple behavior . . . nor am I that for him, we are, one for the other, collaborators in a perfect reciprocity, our perspectives glide one into the other.

The importance of the intersubjectivity described by Merleau-Ponty is readily appreciated from the frustra-tion that is immediately felt when a conversational communion cannot be easily reached. More recently, Bandura (1978, 1982) has also written about this unique feature of social cognition.

PARTICIPATION OF AFFECT

Strictly speaking, nearly all cognition and perception is *evaluative.* It is a rare case when a perceptual event does not engage some affective, motivational, or evaluative reaction. At the minimum there must be interest and attention—processes that are accompanied by affect and motivation (Izard, 1977). Stimuli as primitive as patches of monochromatic light or pure tones evoke in the person not simply a discriminative reaction but a response that also varies on the approach-avoidance continuum. The evaluative factor was found by Osgood (1962) to account for more than half of the variance in the semantic analysis of various concepts in a variety of cultures. The impact of evaluation is sometimes so great that it will influence even the perception and cognition of purely objective features and qualities of a stimulus. The early work on the perceptual effects of context and of values (e.g., Bruner and Goodman, 1947; Bruner, Postman, and Rodrigues, 1951; Hendrick, Wallace, and Tappenbeck, 1968) has shown this influence quite pointedly.

When the targets are social objects—persons, their actions and their motives—evaluation dominates the perception to a much greater extent. Stereotyping, in fact, is quite typical of this phenomenon, as is self-deception. It is not possible to view a social object or a social act without at the same time making an assessment on dimensions closely corresponding to good/bad, pleasant/unpleasant, etc.

Evaluation and affect make many aspects of social cognition particularly vulnerable to idiosyncratic influences. Since persons are perceived in evaluative terms, it is to be expected that a great deal of variation will exist among a number of individuals viewing the same target persons. The individual differences in the evaluation of persons are especially great because persons relate to each other in a reciprocal way, whereas this is not true of person-object relationships. In the course of this reciprocation, Joe will receive a different treatment from Jim than from Joan. Note that Joe, too, will reciprocate Jim differently than Joan in his actions and implicit evaluations. Therefore, following each reciprocation he becomes a somewhat different perceptual object to Jim and to Joan. For example, in seeking a particular evaluation of himself (say, praise for his recent publication), Joe might evaluate Jim in a way that might induce Jim to make the desired evaluation (Joe may praise Jim's recent speech). This aspect of social cognition is especially salient in the case of interacting cognizers, and it is totally absent in nonsocial cognition.

Thus one of the consequences of affective involvement is the heightened encoding idiosyncrasy. To put it differently, if we were to compare the contributions to the product of a cognitive process made by the target and by the cognizer, then in the case of social cognition the cognizer would generally play a more significant role than in the case of nonsocial cognition. There is indeed greater between-subject variance in social cognition, and the sources of this variance are nontrivial. They are not caused by random error and need to be systematically explored. In seeking to describe the properties of perceptual objects, the social psychologist cannot rely exclusively on object features and must take into account the relation of the perceiver to these objects.

SOCIAL BASIS OF CATEGORIZATION

Social objects, when they are targets of perception and cognition, are distinct from natural objects in a number of important ways—ways that influence the processing of information about them. In many cases stimulus properties are so salient that they form an important basis of categorization (Rosch, 1973). For example, Berlin and Kay (1969) asked subjects from twenty different linguistic communities to point to the best examples of eleven basic color names from among 320 color chips. They found very high consensus. Generally, perception of physical properties is seldom characterized by high degree of encoding idiosyncrasy.

In the case of most social objects categorization is not based on stimulus properties of objects but on their function, effects, or origins. Forgas (1983), Moscovici (1983), and Tajfel (1980) argue cogently for a view of social cognition that includes the social basis of categorization and representation. The hammer, the chair, and the saw are categories that are based principally on the function and purpose these objects serve. To be sure, the function of the object most frequently determines its form. Yet it is not the form that figures as the most salient feature in object identification but the function (Wallach, 1949), because one cannot guess the object's function from its form alone. What imposes itself upon a person suddenly confronting a hammer is the purpose this object serves, and it is likely that if the encounter with that object is brief and the perceptual access

somewhat restricted, the person may well not have registered most of the physical properties of that object. Yet under these conditions the function of the object would be encoded quite readily.

This conjecture is suggested by Marcel's (1980) work on unconscious priming, which shows that the person has access to semantic properties of words before and without conscious access to their physical properties. Wallach (1949) observed that the function of the hammer is perceptually just as accessible as its shape, color, or orientation. Mostly, social objects are not categorized according to their directly observable, ostensive features but according to their function or some equivalent, such as role or status. *Leader, my mother, your guest* are such categories. The stimulus features needed to discriminate *us* from *them* are often quite subtle and minimal. The most significant fact to be considered in this connection is that very often the non-ostensive basis of this categorization takes on objective-like qualities (Moscovici, 1983). We end up believing that WE are different from THEM in objective ways, and fail to see that the very basis of this distinction lies uniquely and exclusively in our social experience.

Derived bases of categorization that implicate the perceiver in the defining attributes of the category are perhaps the most frequent and the most important for social objects in one's daily experience. They are important because they are likely to have direct consequences *for* the perceiver. Yet because they implicate perceiver attributes that are partly or completely independent of stimulus properties, they represent a difficult challenge for perceptual studies. Objects and experiences that are *mine* do not share any stimulus properties in common and cannot be objectively distinguished from those that are *his* or *hers*.

The strongly evaluative aspect of social perception and the requirement for the perceiver attributes to figure as defining features of social categories are, of course, closely related. If I define the world in terms related to me, I do so in order to be better able to have inferential access to the consequences of these objects and events *for me*. I know that I do not need to worry about familiar objects; I know how to react to them. I don't know unfamiliar objects, and it matters to me enormously whether you are one of us or one of them (Tajfel, 1980). The fact that social perception has consequences for the perceiver was the property that Jones and Davis (1965) referred to as the *hedonic relevance* of an action for a perceiver. Perceptual acts vary in their motivational significance for the perceiver; some promote one's values, others undermine them. Some perceptual acts fulfill particular purposes, and others obstruct them. According to their theory, self-relevance provides "a potent criterion for grouping and packaging the effects of action" (p. 239).

CONSEQUENCES FOR THE TARGET

The evaluative features of social perception and the participation of the perceiver attributes stress consequences of social perception for the perceiver. Thus social perception has another very important feature distinguishing it from nonsocial perception. It often has significant and nearly direct influence on the perceived target. It creates social reality (Moscovici, 1983). Social categories have a pronounced Aristotelean quality. Research on labeling (Schachter, 1964; D. Bem, 1972), on the Pygmalion effect (Rosenthal and Jacobson, 1968), on the self-fulfilling prophecy (Merton and Kitt, 1950; Snyder, Tanke, and Berscheid, 1977), and Zimbardo's prison study all demonstrate this quality.

Do these facts make social perception and cognition formally different from nonsocial perception? Does the fact that A's perception of B is capable of affecting B's behavior, have an impact on A's perception? Will A modulate or modify his or her perception, or be selective about features of B or about the categories he or she employs? Will A process information about B differently knowing that this information may affect B? Social perception is not unique in having consequences for the target. In nonsocial perception this is also sometimes the case. Perceiving a snake as poisonous has a clear consequence for the perceiver and for the target—the snake may be destroyed by the perceiver. However, the reciprocity of these perceptions is not involved in the above example, as it is in perception among people. The snake behaves quite the same regardless of whether it is perceived as poisonous or nonpoisonous. However, in social perception if person A perceives person B as untrustworthy, B will respond to this perception (or to A's subtle nonverbal cues deriving from A's perception) in a way that might create interpersonal difficulties between A and B. Knowing that this is the consequence of perceiving somebody as untrustworthy, A may refrain from this sort of category in processing information about B.

Again, it must be pointed out that it is the evaluative feature of social perception that dominates its consequential aspects for the target. There are two aspects of perceptual consequences that make social perception and

nonsocial cognition distinct. First, the fact that social cognition affects its targets is most obvious in the case of self-perception, since the person is simultaneously the perceiver and the target. Seeing oneself fail, for example, implicates a host of powerful psychological consequences. Such a condition exists in no other form of cognition, and in no cases of nonsocial cognition are the subject and object the same entity. In the case of self-perception and in many other forms of social perception, the perceiver can create the context, alter the stimulus, make some features salient for display, and distort or conceal others.

Second, the fact that the perceiver and the target are the same person creates another unique feature for this instance of social perception, namely, that the perceiver has a more complete *access to the process* of perceiving. The implications of this fact are quite complex and not yet clear. No theory of cognition or of social cognition has analyzed them, although the concepts of objective self-awareness (Duval and Wicklund, 1972) are concerned with situations that are tangentially similar. Bandura (1978, 1982) has also attacked the problem and has initiated a promising line of research.

THE COMMUNICATIVE ASPECT OF SOCIAL COGNITION

The reciprocal nature of social perception noted by Mead (1932), Merleau-Ponty (1945), Asch (1952), Heider (1958), and Bandura (1982) is especially evident when we consider it in the context of interpersonal communication. The products of social cognition are messages communicated among people, and messages communicated among people become incorporated as parts of their knowledge structures. Hence communication and social cognition are processes that are extensively implicated in one another (Zajonc, 1960; Higgins, McCann, and Fondacaro, 1982). The participation in social communication predisposes individuals to be differentially attentive to information from various sources, to interpret it differently depending on its content, import, and self-reference, to subject it to a self-serving bias under some circumstances, and to ignore it altogether under others. In fact, social cognition is much better understood if viewed in the context of social communication. Forgas (1981) considers the communicative aspect to be the very essence of social cognition. As such, it is not well served by the flowchart model of information processing that presents us only with a unilateral input/output paradigm that stops short of reciprocity. It is likely that in the near future the major new method of studying social cognition and of cognition in general will be the dialogue, supplementing the paradigm of recognition memory and reaction time. Individual subjects in interaction, each asking the other questions and responding, may disclose a great deal of content and structure of their own cognitions and help reveal the cognitions of the other.

CONCLUSION

Social perception and social cognition are concerned with social influences upon perceptual and cognitive processes and also with the perception and cognition of social objects. Because all perceptual and cognitive processes require the contribution of the perceiver, and because this contribution derives from the individual's past experience that contains a heavy social component, *all* cognitive and perceptual processes are subject to social influence in one form or another. However, the social influence upon perception and cognition is most significant when the target is a social object. Thus the hallmark of the cognitive perspective in social psychology is the constructive nature of social cognition. The product of a perceptual and cognitive process that is of interest to the social psychologist derives much more from the contribution of the perceiver than it does in the case of other forms of cognition and perception. And it is the nature of the perceiver's contribution that will reveal the fundamental elements of social cognition.

The past two decades have seen social psychology build upon the progress in cognitive psychology. And as a result, much had been learned, as this chapter has shown. However, the appropriation of theoretical and methodological sophistication from information-processing science by social psychologists enables them only to study those phenomena of social cognition that are basically and fundamentally the same as those that are studied by experimental psychologists. And for the most part, experimental psychologists study cognitive phenomena that from the social psychological perspective appear quite restricted. Moreover, they seek to explicate variation in encoding, memory, and higher cognitive processes by attending primarily to the properties of the information given. The contribution of the perceiver has been less actively studied, and as a result, there is little systematic knowledge about what aspects of the cognitive product are influenced by the perceiver, in what ways, and by virtue of what processes.

The contribution of the individual to the cognitive product is revealed in nearly all aspects of social cognition reviewed in this chapter. Some of the most important aspects of this contribution are self-referential. The richly evaluative nature of social cognition makes this self-referential aspect especially salient, as does the fact that the main context for social cognition is communication. Social cognitions are both the sources and the products of a social process in which communication is the main vehicle.

The constructive nature of social cognition is not limited to the mind of the perceivers, but it derives from their contact with the cognitions of those around them —cognitions that are transmitted to them via various communication channels. Thus the study of social cognition must reach beyond the simple experimental paradigms of information processing that are studied by cognitive psychologists. The properties of social perception and social cognition that make them distinct are reciprocity and intersubjectivity. Schutz (1970, p. 167) spoke of this property cogently in terms of two kinds of meanings: One was the

> objective meaning of your words, the meaning which they would have had, had they been spoken by you or anyone else. But second, there is a subjective meaning, namely what is going on in your mind while you speak. In order to get your subjective meaning, I must picture to myself your stream of consciousness as flowing side by side with my own. Within this picture, I must interpret and construct your intentional acts as you choose your words. To the extent that you and I can mutually experience this simultaneity, growing older together for a time, to the extent that we can live in it together, to that extent *we can live in each other's subjective contexts of meaning.* (Italics ours.)

This involvement of the communication matrix in social cognition and the heavy contribution of the perceiver to the cognitive product require an understanding of the role of motivational and emotional factors that have an influence on the perceivers' contribution and their construction and creation of social reality.

It is also clear from the above review that another unresolved issue that dominated social cognition of the seventies was the role of "hot" factors. In every area of research reviewed here, there was a concerted effort to see if one could parsimoniously explain all the variance in cognitive terms *without* invoking such concepts as motives, values, affect, emotions, goals, incentives, fears, or rewards. This was equally true of balance and of dissonance, as it was true of the self-serving bias, stereotypes, overjustification, hindsight, negativity, or other problem areas. Also ignored were the motivational dynamics that derived from the internal interaction of cognitive elements, such as were identified in the study of balance and dissonance, and those that arise in reactions to uncertainty, conflict, novelty, or incongruity.

The search for parsimony has generated a great deal of theoretical and empirical progress, as is evident from the literature reviewed here and in other chapters of this *Handbook,* and a great deal has been learned. But the approach is now beginning to wear. Experimental results seem to produce controversies that defy solutions without going beyond the bounds of information-processing concepts, and the participation of affective and motivational factors is more frequently being explored. The cyclical swings of dissonance research from the "hot" view of its initial formulation, to the "cool" view of the self-perception explanation, and then back again to the "warmer" conceptions of impression management give an example of these trends.

The parsimonious emphasis on cognitive functions as the exclusive source of knowledge about social influences on behavior has generated a concept of the *socius* as an information-processing machine of doubtful efficiency and reliability who must consult the output to determine whether he or she loves or hates and whose fears are default values or interrupt commands. The study of social cognition that seeks parsimony of a single process, unencumbered by motives and emotions or dynamic factors intrinsic to the internal structure of the cognitive content, will soon be replaced by a more complex and richer approach that makes room for the interplay of purely informational processes with those deriving from social factors. The swing toward "hot" cognition is already in progress.

REFERENCES

Abelson, R. P. (1968). Psychological implication. In R. P. Abelson, E. Aronson, W. J. McGuire, T. M. Newcomb, M. J. Rosenberg, and P. H. Tannenbaum (Eds.), *Theories of cognitive consistency: a source book.* Chicago: Rand McNally.

────── (1976). Script processing in attitude formation and decision making. In J. S. Carroll and J. W. Payne (Eds.), *Cognition and social behavior.* Hillsdale, N.J.: Erlbaum.

Adorno, T. W., E. Frenkel-Brunswik, D. Levinson, and R. N. Sanford (1950). *The authoritarian personality.* New York: Harper & Row.

Ajzen, I. (1977). Intuitive theories of events and the effects of base-rate information on prediction. *J. Pers. soc. Psychol., 35,* 303–314.

Ajzen, I., and M. Fishbein (1975). A Bayesian analysis of attribution processes. *Psychol. Bull., 82,* 262–277.

Allport, F. H. (1955). *Theories of perception and the concept of structure.* New York: Wiley.

Allport, G. W. (1937). *Personality: a psychological interpretation.* New York: Henry Holt.

────── (1954). *The nature of prejudice.* Reading, Mass.: Addison-Wesley.

────── (1968). The historical background of modern social psychology. In G. Lindzey and E. Aronson (Eds.), *The handbook of social psychology.* Vol. I. Reading, Mass.: Addison-Wesley.

Allport, G. W., and B. M. Kramer (1946). Some roots of prejudice. *J. Psychol., 22,* 9–39.

Amabile, T. M., and A. H. Glazebrook (1982). A negativity bias in interpersonal evaluation. *J. exp. soc. Psychol., 18,* 1–22.

Anderson, C. A., M. R. Lepper, and L. Ross (1980). Perseverance of social theories: the role of explanation in the persistence of discredited information. *J. Pers. soc. Psychol., 39,* 1037–1049.

Anderson, J. R. (1978). Arguments concerning representations for mental imagery. *Psychol. Rev., 85,* 249–277.

────── (1980). Concepts, propositions, and schemata: What are the cognitive units? *Nebraska Symposium on Motivation.* Lincoln, Neb.: Univ. of Nebraska Press.

Anderson, J. R., and G. H. Bower (1973). *Human associative memory.* Washington, D.C.: V. H. Winston.

Anderson, N. H. (1962). Application of an additive model to impression formation. *Science, 138,* 817–818.

────── (1965(a). Averaging versus adding as a stimulus-combination rule in impression formation. *J. Pers. soc. Psychol., 2,* 1–9.

────── (1965b). Primacy effects in personality formation using a generalized order effect paradigm. *J. Pers. soc. Psychol., 2,* 1–9.

────── (1967). Application of a weighted average model to a psychophysical averaging task. *Psychon. Sci., 8,* 227–228.

────── (1970a). Functional measurement and psychophysical judgment. *Psychol. Rev., 77,* 153–170.

────── (1970b). Averaging model applied to the size-weight illusion. *Perception and Psychophysics, 8,* 1–4.

────── (1976). Equity judgments as information integration. *J. Pers. soc. Psychol., 33,* 291–299.

────── (1974). Information integration theory: a brief survey. In D. H. Krantz, R. C. Atkinson, R. D. Luce, and P. Suppes (Eds.), *Contemporary developments in mathematical psychology.* Vol. 2. San Francisco: Freeman.

────── (1977). Some problems in using analysis of variance in balance theory. *J. Pers. soc. Psychol., 35,* 140–158.

────── (1979). Indeterminate theory: Reply to Gollob. *J. Pers. soc. Psychol., 37,* 950–952.

────── (1981). *Foundations of information integration theory.* New York: Academic Press.

────── (1983). Schemas in person cognition. CHIP Report 108. Center for Human Information Processing. LaJolla, Calif.

Anderson, N. H., and A. A. Barrios (1961). Primacy effects in personality impression formation. *J. abnorm. soc. Psychol., 63,* 346–350.

Anderson, N. H., and C. A. Butzin (1974). Performance = Motivation × Ability: an integration-theoretical analysis. *J. Pers. soc. Psychol., 30,* 598–604.

—— (1978). Integration theory applied to children's judgments of equity. *Developmental Psychology, 14,* 593–606.

Anderson, N. H., and D. O. Cuneo (1978). The height + width rule in children's judgments of quantity. *J. exp. Psychol.: General, 107,* 335–378.

Anderson, N. H., and A. J. Farkas (1975). Integration theory applied to models of inequity. *Pers. soc. Psychol. Bull., 1,* 588–591.

Anderson, N. H., and S. Hubert (1963). Effects of concomitant verbal recall on order effects in personality impression formation. *J. verbal Learn. verb. Behav., 2,* 379–391.

Anderson, N. H., and A. Jacobson (1965). Effect of stimulus inconsistency and discounting instructions in personality impression formation. *J. Pers. soc. Psychol., 2,* 531–539.

Anderson, N. H., and J. C. Shanteau (1970). Information integration in risky decision making. *J. exp. Psychol., 84,* 441–451.

Arkes, H. R., and A. R. Harkness (1983). Estimates of contingency between two dichotomous variables. *J. exp. Psychol.: General, 112,* 117–135.

Arkin, R. M., D. J. Appelman, and J. M. Burger (1980). Social anxiety, self-presentation, and the self-serving bias in causal attribution. *J. Pers. soc. Psychol., 38,* 23–35.

Arkin, R., H. Cooper, and T. Kolditz (1980). A statistical review of the literature concerning the self-serving bias in interpersonal inference situations. *J. Pers., 48,* 435–448.

Arkin, R. M., and S. Duval (1975). Focus of attention and causal attributions of actors and observers. *J. exp. soc. Psychol., 11,* 427–438.

Aronson, E. (1966). The psychology of insufficient justification: an analysis of some conflicting data. In S. Feldman (Ed.), *Cognitive consistency: motivational antecedents and behavioral consequents.* New York: Academic Press.

Aronson, E., and J. M. Carlsmith (1962). Performance expectancy as determinant of actual performance. *J. abnorm. soc. Psychol., 65,* 178–183.

Asch, S. E. (1946). Forming impressions of personality. *J. abnorm. soc. Psychol., 41,* 258–290.

—— (1951). Effects of group pressure upon the modification and distortion of judgment. In H. Getskow (Ed.), *Groups, leadership, and men.* Pittsburgh: Carnegie Press, 177–190.

—— (1952). *Social psychology.* Englewood Cliffs, N.J.: Prentice-Hall.

—— (1958). Review of a theory of cognitive dissonance by L. Festinger. *Contemporary Psychology, 3,* 194–195.

Bacon, F. T. (1979). Credibility of repeated statements: memory for trivia. *J. exp. Psychol.: hum. Learn. Memory, 5,* 241–252.

Bandura, A. (1977). *Social learning theory.* Englewood Cliffs, N.J.: Prentice-Hall.

—— (1978). The self-system in reciprocal determinism. *Amer. Psychologist, 33,* 344–358.

—— (1982). The self and mechanisms of agency. In J. Suls (Ed.), *Psychological perspectives on the self.* Vol. 1. Hillsdale, N.J.: Erlbaum.

Bargh, J. A. (1982). Attention and automaticity in the processing of self-relevant information. *J. Pers. soc. Psychol., 43,* 425–436.

Bargh, J. A., and P. Pietromonaco (1982). Automatic information processing and social perception: the influence of trait information presented outside of conscious awareness on impression formation. *J. Pers. soc. Psychol., 43,* 437–449.

Bar-Hillel, M. (1980). The base-rate fallacy in probability judgments. *Acta Psychologica, 44,* 211–233.

Bartlett, F. C. (1932). *Remembering: a study in experimental and social psychology.* Cambridge: Cambridge Univ. Press.

Baumeister, R. (1982). A self-presentational view of social phenomena. *Psychol. Bull., 91,* 3–26.

Bear, G., and A. Hodun (1975). Implicational principles and the cognition of confirmatory, contradictory, incomplete, and irrelevant information. *J. Pers. soc. Psychol., 32,* 594–604.

Belleza, F. S., and G. H. Bower (1981). Person stereotypes and memory for people. *J. Pers. soc. Psychol., 41,* 856–865.

Bem, D. J. (1965). An experimental analysis of self-persuasion. *J. exp. soc. Psychol., 1,* 199–218.

—— (1967). Self-perception: an alternative interpretation of cognitive dissonance phenomena. *Psychol. Rev., 74,* 183–200.

—— (1972). Self-perception theory. In L. Berkowitz (Ed.), *Advances in experimental social psychology.* Vol. 6. New York: Academic Press.

Bem, S. (1981). Gender schema theory: a cognitive account of sex-typing, *Psychol. Rev., 88,* 354–364.

Benware, C., and E. L. Deci (1975). Attitude change as a function of the inducement for espousing a proattitudinal communication. *J. exp. soc. Psychol., 11,* 271–278.

Berlin, B., and P. Kay (1969). *Basic color terms: their universality and evolution.* Berkeley: Univ. of California Press.

Berlyne, D. E. (1955). The arousal and satiation of perceptual curiosity in the rat. *J. compara. physiol. Psychol., 48,* 238–246.

—— (1957). Uncertainty and conflict: a point of contact between information-theory and behavior-theory concepts. *Psychol. Rev., 64,* 329–339.

—— (1960). *Conflict, arousal, and curiosity.* New York: McGraw-Hill.

Birnbaum, M. (1972). Morality judgments: tests of an averaging model. *J. exp. Psychol., 93,* 35–42.

Birnbaum, M. H., and B. A. Mellers (1983). Bayesian inference: combining base rates with opinions of sources who vary in credibility. *J. Pers. soc. Psychol., 45,* 792–804.

Blankenship, D. A., and N. H. Anderson (1976). Subjective duration: a functional measurement analysis. *Perception and Psychophysics, 20,* 168–172.

Boggiano, A. K., D. N. Ruble, and T. S. Pittman (1982). The mastery hypothesis and the overjustification effect. *Social Cognition, 1,* 38–49.

Bolster, B., and B. Springbett (1961). The reaction of interviewers to favorable and unfavorable information. *J. appl. Psychol., 45,* 97–103.

Borgida, E., and B. Howard-Pitney (1983). Personal involvement and the robustness of perceptual salience effects. *J. Pers. soc. Psychol., 45,* 560–570.

Borgida, E., and R. E. Nisbett (1977). The differential impact of abstract vs. concrete informations on decisions. *J. appl. soc. Psychol., 7,* 258–271.

Bower, G. H., J. B. Black, and T. J. Turner (1979). Scripts in memory for text. *Cognit. Psychol., 11,* 177–220.

Bower, G. H., and S. G. Gilligan (1979). Remembering information related to one's self. *J. Res. Pers., 13,* 42–432.

Bower, G. H., and M. Masling (1981). Causal explanations as mediators for remembering correlations. Unpublished manuscript.

Bradley, G. W. (1978). Self-serving biases in the attribution process: a reexamination of the fact or fiction question. *J. Pers. soc. Psychol., 36,* 56–71.

Bramel, D. (1962). A dissonance theory approach to defensive projection. *J. abnorm. soc. Psychol., 64,* 121–129.

Brand, E., R. A. Ruiz, and A. M. Padilla (1974). Ethnic identification and preference: a review. *Psychol. Bull., 81,* 860–890.

Bransford, J. D., and M. K. Johnson (1973). Considerations of some problems of comprehension. In W. G. Chase (Ed.), *Visual information processing.* New York: Academic Press.

Braver, S. L., D. E. Linder, T. T. Corwin, and R. B. Cialdini (1977). Some conditions that affect admissions of attitude change. *J. exp. soc. Psychol., 13,* 565–576.

Brehm, J. W. (1956). Post-decision changes in the desirability of alternatives. *J. abnorm. soc. Psychol., 52,* 384–389.

_____ (1966). *A theory of psychological reactance.* New York: Academic Press.

Brehm, J. W., and A. R. Cohen (1962). *Explorations in cognitive dissonance.* New York: Wiley.

Brehm, J. W., and M. Mann (1975). Effect of importance of freedom and attraction to group members on influence produced by group pressure. *J. Pers. soc. Psychol., 31,* 816–824.

Brehm, J. W., L. K. Stires, J. Sensenig, and J. Shaban (1966). The attractiveness of an eliminated choice alternative. *J. exp. soc. Psychol., 2,* 301–313.

Brehm, S. S., and J. W. Brehm (1981). *Psychological reactance: a theory of freedom and control.* New York: Academic Press.

Brock, T. C., and H. L. Fromkin (1968). Cognitive tuning set and behavioral receptivity to discrepant information. *J. Pers., 36,* 108–125.

Brown, C. E. (1982). A false consensus bias in 1980 presidential preferences. *J. soc. Psychol., 118,* 137–138.

Bruner, J. S. (1951). Personality dynamics and the process of perceiving. In R. R. Blake and G. V. Ramsey (Eds.), *Perception: an approach to personality.* New York: Ronald.

_____ (1957a). Going beyond the information given. In H. Gulber et al. (Eds.), *Contemporary approaches to cognition.* Cambridge, Mass.: Harvard Univ. Press.

_____ (1957b). On perceptual readiness. *Psychol. Rev., 64,* 123–152.

Bruner, J. S., and C. D. Goodman (1947). Value and need as organizing factors in perception. *J. Abnorm. soc. Psychol., 42,* 33–44.

Bruner, J. S., J. J. Goodnow, and J. G. Austin (1956). *A study of thinking.* New York: Wiley.

Bruner, J. S., and D. Krech (1950). *Perception and personality: a symposium.* Durham, N.C.: Duke Univ. Press.

Bruner, J. S., L. Postman, and J. Rodrigues (1951). Expectation and the perception of color. *Amer. J. Psychol., 64,* 216–227.

Burger, J. M. (1981). Motivational biases in the attribution of responsibility for an accident: a meta-analysis of the defensive-attribution hypothesis. *Psychol. Bull., 90,* 496–512.

Burnstein, E. (1962). Some effects of cognitive selection processes on learning and memory. *Psychol. Monogr., 76,* No. 35 (whole No. 554).

Burnstein, E., and Y. Schul (1983). The informational basis of social judgments: memory for integrated and nonintegrated trait descriptions. *J. exp. soc. Psychol., 19,* 49–57.

Cacioppo, J. T., and R. E. Petty (1981). Effects of extent of thought on the pleasantness ratings of P-O-X triads: evidence for three judgmental tendencies in evaluating social situations. *J. Pers. soc. Psychol., 40,* 1000–1009.

Cantor, N. (1978). Unpublished dissertation. *Prototypicality and personality judgments.* Stanford: Stanford Univ. Press.

_____ (1981). A cognitive-social approach to personality. In N. Cantor and J. F. Kihlstrom (Eds.), *Personality, cognition, and social interaction.* Hillsdale, N.J.: Erlbaum.

Cantor, N., and J. F. Kihlstrom, Eds. (1981). *Personality, cognition, and social interactions.* Hillsdale, N.J.: Erlbaum.

Cantor, N., and W. Mischel (1977). Traits as prototypes: effects on recognition memory. *J. Pers. soc. Psychol., 35,* 38–48.

_____ (1979). Prototypes in person perception. In L. Berkowitz (Ed.), *Advances in experimental social psychology.* Vol. 12. New York: Academic Press.

Cantor, N., W. Mischel, and J. Schwartz (1982). Social knowledge: structure, content, use, and abuse. In A. M. Isen and A. H. Hastorf (Eds.), *Cognit. soc. Psychol.* New York: Elsevier North-Holland.

Cantor, N., E. E. Smith, R. French, and J. Mezzich (1980). Psychiatric diagnosis as prototype categorization. *J. abnorm. Psychol., 89,* 181–193.

Carlsmith, J. M., B. E. Collins, and R. Helmreich (1966). Studies in forced compliance: I. Attitude change produced by face-to-face role playing and anonymous essay writing. *J. Pers. soc. Psychol., 4,* 1–13.

Carlston, D. E. (1980). Events, inferences, and impression formation. In R. Hastie et al. (Eds.), *Person memory: the cognitive basis of social perception.* Hillsdale, N.J.: Erlbaum.

Carroll, J. S. (1978). The effect of imagining an event on expectations for the event: an interpretation in terms of the availability heuristic. *J. exp. soc. Psychol., 14,* 88–96.

Carroll, J. S., and J. S. Payne (1976). The psychology of the parole decision process: A joint application of attribution theory and information-processing psychology. In J. S. Carroll and J. S. Payne (Eds.), *Cognition and social behavior.* Hillsdale, N.J.: Erlbaum.

Cartwright, D. (1941). Relation of decision-time to the categories of response. *Amer. J. Psychol., 54,* 174–196.

Carver, C. S., and M. F. Scheier (1981). *Attention and self-regulation: a control-theory approach to human behavior.* New York: Springer.

_____ (1982). Control theory: a useful conceptual framework for personality, social, clinical, and health psychology. *Psychol. Bull., 92,* 111–135.

Chapanis, N. P., and A. Chapanis (1964). Cognitive dissonance. *Psychol. Bull., 61,* 1–22.

Chapman, L. J. (1967). Illusory correlation in observational report. *J. verb. Learn. verb. Behav., 6,* 151–155.

Chapman, L. J., and J. P. Chapman (1967). Genesis of popular but erroneous psychodiagnostic observations. *J. abnorm. Psychol., 72,* 193–204.

_____ (1969). Illusory correlation as an obstacle to the use of valid psychodiagnostic signs. *J. abnorm. Psychol., 74,* 271–280.

Cialdini, R. B., and H. Mirels (1976). Sense of personal control and attributions about yielding and resisting persuasion targets. *J. Pers. soc. Psychol., 33,* 395–402.

Cialdini, R. B., and R. E. Petty (1981). Anticipatory opinion effects. In R. E. Petty, T. M. Ostrom, and T. C. Brock (Eds.), *Cognitive responses in persuasion.* Hillsdale, N.J.: Erlbaum..

Cialdini, R. B., S. L. Braver, and S. K. Lewis (1974). Attributional bias and the easily persuaded other. *J. Pers. soc. Psychol., 30,* 613–637.

Clark, L. F., and S. B. Woll (1981). Stereotype bias: a reconstructive analysis of their role in reconstructive memory. *J. Pers. soc. Psychol., 41,* 1064–1072.

Clary, E. G., A. Tesser, and L. L. Downing (1978). Influence of a salient schema on thought-induced cognitive change. *Pers. soc. Psychol. Bull., 4,* 39–43.

Cohen, A. R. (1961). Cognitive tuning as a factor affecting impression formation. *J. Pers., 29,* 235–245.

Cohen, C. E. (1977). *Cognitive basis of stereotyping.* Paper presented at the American Psychological Association Annual Meeting, San Francisco.

_____ (1981a). Goals and schemata in person perception: making sense from the stream of behavior. In N. Cantor and J. F. Kihlstrom (Eds.), *Personality, cognition, and social interaction.* Hillsdale, N.J.: Erlbaum.

_____ (1981b). Person categories and social perception: testing some boundaries of the processing effects of prior knowledge. *J. Pers. soc. Psychol., 40,* 441–452.

Cohen, C. E., and E. B. Ebbesen (1979). Observational goals and schema activation: a theoretical framework for behavior perception. *J. exp. soc. Psychol., 15,* 305–329.

Cohen, L. J. (1981). Can human irrationality be experimentally demonstrated? *Behav. brain Sci., 4,* 317–331.

Colby, K. M., S. Weber, and F. D. Hilf (1971). Artificial paranoia. *Artificial Intelligence, 2,* 1–25.

Collins, B. E., and M. F. Hoyt (1972). Personal responsibility-for-consequences: an integration and extension of the "forced compliance" literature. *J. exp. soc. Psychol., 8,* 558–593.

Combs, A., and D. Snygg (1959). *Individual behavior* (2nd ed.). New York: Harper.

Condry, J. C., and J. D. Chambers (1978). Intrinsic motivation and learning. In M. R. Lepper and D. Greene (Eds.), *The hidden costs of reward.* Hillsdale, N.J.: Erlbaum.

Cooper, J., M. P. Zanna, and P. A. Taves (1978). Arousal as a necessary condition for attitude change following induced compliance. *J. Pers. soc. Psychol., 36,* 1101–1106.

Cottrell, N. B. (1975). Heider's structural balance principle as a conceptual rule. *J. Pers. soc. Psychol., 31,* 713–720.

Cottrell, N. B., and D. L. Wack (1967). Energizing effects of cognitive dissonance upon dominant and subordinate responses. *J. Pers. soc. Psychol., 6,* 132–138.

Couch, A., and K. Keniston (1960). Yeasayers and naysayers: agreeing response set as a personality variable. *J. abnorm. soc. Psychol., 60,* 151–174.

Cox, S. D., and K. A. Wollen (1981). Bizarreness and recall. *Bull. psychon. Soc., 18,* 244–245.

Crespi, L. P. (1942). Quantitative variation of incentive and performance in the white rat. *Amer. J. Psychol., 55,* 467–517.

Cronbach, L. J. (1950). Further evidence on response sets and test design. *Educ. psychol. Measmt., 10,* 3–31.

Croyle, R. T., and J. Cooper (1983). Dissonance arousal: physiological evidence. *J. Pers. soc. Psychol., 45,* 782–791.

Darley, J. M., and R. H. Fazio (1980). Expectancy confirmation processes arising in the social interaction sequence. *Amer. Psychologist, 35,* 867–881.

Davis, M. H. (1979). Changes in evaluative beliefs as a function of behavioral commitment. *Pers. soc. Psychol. Bull., 5,* 177–187.

Davol, S. H. (1959). An empirical test of structural balance in sociometric triads. *J. abnorm. soc. Psychol., 59,* 393–398.

Deci, E. L. (1971). Effects of externally mediated rewards on intrinsic motivation. *J. Pers. soc. Psychol., 18,* 105–115.

_____ (1975). *Intrinsic motivation.* New York: Plenum.

DeSilva, A. M. (1983). Unpublished dissertation. Perceiving others: stereotyping as a process of social cognition. Univ. of Michigan.

DeSoto, C. B. (1960). Learning a social structure. *J. abnorm. soc. Psychol., 60,* 417–421.

DeSoto, C. B., and J. J. Bosley (1962). The cognitive structure of a social structure. *J. abnorm. soc. Psychol., 64,* 303–307.

DeSoto, C. B., and J. L. Kuethe (1958). Perception of mathematical properties of interpersonal relations. *Percept. motor Skills, 8,* 279–286.

_____ (1959). Subjective probabilities of interpersonal relations. *J. abnorm. soc. Psychol., 59,* 290–294.

Deutsch, M. (1968). Field theory in social psychology. In G. Lindzey and E. Aronson (Eds.), *Handbook of social psychology.* Vol. I. Reading, Mass.: Addison-Wesley.

Dooling, D. J., and R. L. Mullett (1973). Locus of thematic effects in retention of prose. *J. exp. Psychol., 97,* 404–406.

Dooling, D. J., and R. S. Lachman (1971). Effects of comprehension on retention of prose. *J. exp. Psychol., 88,* 216–222.

Dorfman, D. D., S. Keeve, and C. Saslow (1971). Ethnic identification: a signal detection analysis. *J. Pers. soc. Psychol., 18,* 373–379.

Dreben, E. K., S. T. Fiske, and R. Hastie (1979). The independence of evaluative and item formation: impression and recall order effects in behavior based impression formation. *J. Pers. soc. Psychol., 37,* 1758–1768.

Duncan, B. L. (1976). Differential social perception and attribution of intergroup violence: testing the lower limits of stereotyping of blacks. *J. Pers. soc. Psychol., 34,* 590–598.

Duval, S., and R. A. Wicklund (1972). *A theory of objective self-awareness.* New York: Academic Press.

Eagly, A. H., and S. Himmelfarb (1978). Attitudes and opinions. *Ann. Rev. Psychol., 29,* 517–554.

Ebbesen, E. B. (1980). Cognitive processes in understanding ongoing behavior. In R. Hastie et al. (Eds.), *Person-memory:*

the cognitive bases of social perception. Hillsdale, N.J.: Erlbaum.

———— (1981). Cognitive processes in inferences about a person's personality. In E. T. Higgins, C. P. Herman, and M. P. Zanna (Eds.), Social cognition: the Ontario symposium on personality and social psychology. Vol. 1. Hillsdale, N.J.: Erlbaum.

Ebbesen, E. B., and R. B. Allen (1979). Cognitive processes in implicit personality inferences. J. Pers. soc. Psychol., 37, 471–488.

Ebbesen, E. B., C. E. Cohen, and R. B. Allen (1979). Cognitive processes in person perception: behavior scanning and semantic memory. Unpublished manuscript. San Diego: Univ. of California.

Edlow, D. W., and C. A. Kiesler (1966). Ease of denial and defensive projection. J. exp. soc. Psychol., 2, 177–193.

Edwards, A. L. (1963). A factor analysis of experimental social desirability and response set scales. J. appl. Psychol., 47, 308–316.

Edwards, W., H. Lindman, and L. J. Savage (1963). Bayesian statistical inference for psychological research. Psychol. Rev., 70, 193–242.

Ehrlich, D., I. Guttman, P. Schoenbach, and J. Mills (1957). Post-decision exposure to relevant information. J. abnorm. soc. Psychol., 54, 98–102.

Einhorn, H. J., and R. M. Hogarth (1978). Confidence in judgment: persistence in the illusion of validity. Psychol. Rev., 85, 395–416.

Eisen, S. V., and L. Z. McArthur (1979). Evaluating and sentencing a defendant as a function of his salience and the perceiver's set. Pers. soc. Psychol. Bull., 5, 48–52.

Eiser, J. R., and C. J. M. White (1975). Categorization and congruity in attitudinal judgment. J. Pers. soc. Psychol., 31, 769–775.

Elliott, D. N., and B. H. Wittenberg (1955). Accuracy of identification of Jewish and non-Jewish photographs. J. abnorm. soc. Psychol., 51, 339–341.

Elms, A. C., and I. L. Janis (1965). Counter-norm attitudes induced by consonant versus dissonant conditions of role-playing. J. exp. Res. Pers., 1, 50–60.

Epstein, S. (1973). The self-concept revisited: or a theory of a theory. Amer. Psychologist, 28, 404–416.

Erdelyi, M. H. (1974). A new look at the new look: perceptual defense and vigilance. Psychol. Rev., 81, 1–25.

Estes, W. K. (1964). Probability learning. In A. W. Melton (Ed.), Categories of human learning. New York: Academic Press.

———— (1976). The cognitive side of probability learning. Psychol. Rev., 83, 37–64.

Evans, J. St. B. T. (1982). On statistical intuitions and inferential rules: a discussion of Kahneman and Tversky. Cognition, 12, 319–323.

Fazio, R. H., J. M. Chen, E. C. McDonel, and S. J. Sherman (1982). Attitude accessibility, attitude-behavior consistency and the strength of the object-evaluation association. J. exp. soc. Psychol., 18, 339–357.

Fazio, R. H., and J. Cooper (1983). Arousal in the dissonance process. In J. T. Cacioppo and R. E. Petty (Eds.), Social psychophysiology. New York: Guilford Press.

Fazio, R. H., M. P. Zanna, and J. Cooper (1977). Dissonance and self perception: an integrative view of each theory's proper domain of application. J. exp. soc. Psychol., 13, 464–479.

Feather, N. T., and L. G. Simon (1971). Attribution of responsibility and valence outcome in relation to initial confidence and success and failure of self and other. J. Pers. soc. Psychol., 18, 173–188.

Feld, S. L., and R. Elmore (1982). Patterns of sociometric choices: transitivity reconsidered. Soc. Psychol. Quart., 45, 77–85.

Feldman, R. S., and A. G. Bernstein (1978). Primacy effects in self-attribution of ability. J. Pers., 42, 732–742.

Feldman, S. (1966). Motivational aspects of attitudinal elements and their place in cognitive interaction. In S. Feldman (Ed.), Cognitive consistency. New York: Academic Press.

Feller, W. (1957). An introduction to probability theory. New York: Wiley.

Festinger, L. (1942). A theoretical interpretation of shifts in level of aspiration. Psychol. Rev., 49, 235–250.

———— (1950). Informal social communication. Psychol. Rev., 57, 271–282.

———— (1954). Theory of social comparison processes. Hum. Rel., 7, 117–140.

———— (1957). A theory of cognitive dissonance. Evanston, Ill.: Row, Peterson.

———— (1964). Conflict, decision, and dissonance. Stanford: Stanford Univ. Press.

Festinger, L., and H. A. Hutte (1954). An experimental investigation of the effect of unstable interpersonal relations in a group. J. abnorm. soc. Psychol., 49, 513–523.

Festinger, L., H. W. Riecken, and S. Schachter (1956). When prophecy fails: a social and psychological study of a modern group that predicted the destruction of the world. New York: Harper.

Fischer, C. T. (1968). Social schema: response sets or perceptual meanings? J. Pers. soc. Psychol., 10, 8–14.

Fischhoff, B. (1975). Hindsight ≠ foresight: the effect of outcome knowledge on judgment under uncertainty. J. exp. Psychol.: hum. Percept. Perform., 1, 288–299.

Fischhoff, B., and D. MacGregor (1980). Judged lethality. Decision Research Report 80-4. Eugene, Oregon: Decision Research.

Fishbein, M., and R. Hunter (1964). Summation versus balance in attitude organization and change. J. abnorm. soc. Psychol., 69, 505–510.

Fiske, S. T., and M. G. Cox (1979). The effect of target familiarity and descriptive purpose on the process of describing others. J. Pers., 47, 136–161.

Fiske, S. T., D. A. Kenny, and S. E. Taylor (1982). Structural models for the mediation of salience effects on attribution. J. exp. soc. Psychol., 18, 105–127.

Fiske, S. T., and D. R. Kinder (1981). Involvement, expertise, and schema use: evidence from political cognition. In N. Cantor and J. Kihlstrom (Eds.), Cognition, social interaction, and personality. Hillsdale, N.J.: Erlbaum.

Fiske, S. T., D. R. Kinder, and W. M. Larter (1983). The novice and the expert: knowledge based strategies in political cognition. J. exper. soc. Psychol., 19, 381–400.

Fiske, S. T., and P. W. Linville (1980). What does the schema concept buy us? Pers. soc. Psychol. Bull., 6, 543–557.

Fiske, S. T., S. E. Taylor, N. Etcoff, and J. Laufer (1979).

Imaging, empathy, and causal attributions. *J. exp. soc. Psychol., 15,* 356–377.

Flavell, J. H. (1963). *The developmental psychology of Jean Piaget.* Princeton, N.J.: Van Nostrand.

Fong, G. T., and H. Markus (1982). Self schemas and judgments about others. *Social Cognition, 1,* 191–204.

Forgas, J. P. (1981). *Social cognition: perceptives on everyday understanding.* London: Academic Press.

_____ (1983). What is social about social cognition? *Brit. J. soc. Psychol., 22,* 129–144.

Frauenfelder, K. (1974). A cognitive determinant of favorability of impression. *J. soc. Psychol., 94,* 71–81.

Freedman, J. L., and D. O. Sears (1965). Selective exposure. In L. Berkowitz (Ed.), *Advances in experimental social psychology* . Vol. 2. New York: Academic Press.

Frey, D. (1981). Postdecisional preferences for decision-relevant information as a function of the competence of its source and the degree of familiarity with this information. *J. exp. soc. Psychol., 17,* 51–67.

Frey, D., and M. Irle (1972). Some conditions to produce a dissonance and an incentive effect in a "forced-compliance" situation. *Europ. J. soc. Psychol., 2,* 45–54.

Frey, D., R. Ochsmann, M. Kumpf, C. Sauer, and M. Irle (1979). The effects of discrepant or congruent behavior and reward upon attitude and task attractiveness. *J. soc. Psychol., 108,* 63–73.

Frey, D., and R. A. Wicklund (1978). A clarification of selective exposure: the impact of choice. *J. exp. soc. Psychol., 14,* 132–139.

Furedy, J. J., and A. N. Doob (1972). Signaling unmodifiable shocks: limits on human informational cognitive control. *J. Pers. soc. Psychol., 21,* 111–115.

Gaes, G. G., R. J. Kalle, and J. T. Tedeschi (1978). Impression management in the forced compliance situation. *J. exp. soc. Psychol., 14,* 493–510.

Galanter, E. H., and W. A. Smith (1958). Some experiments on a simple thought-problem. *Amer. J. Psychol., 71,* 359–366.

Galper, R. E. (1976). Turning observers into actors: differential causal attributions as a function of "empathy." *J. Res. Pers., 10,* 328–335.

Gardner, R. A. (1957). Probability learning with two and three choices. *Amer. J. Psychol., 70,* 174–185.

Gerard, H. B., E. S. Conolley, and R. A. Wilhelmy (1974). Compliance, justification and cognitive change. In L. Berkowitz (Ed.), *Advances in experimental social psychology.* Vol. 1. New York: Academic Press.

Gerbing, D. W., and J. E. Hunter (1979). Phenomenological bases for the attribution of balance to social structure. *Pers. soc. Psychol. Bull., 5,* 299–302.

Gibson, J. J. (1941). A critical review of the concept of set on contemporary experimental psychology. *Psychol. Bull., 38,* 781–815.

Gibson, J. J., and E. J. Gibson (1955). Perceptual learning: differentiation of enrichment? *Psychol. Rev., 62,* 32–41.

Gillig, P. M. and A. G. Greenwald (1974). Is it time to lay the sleeper effect to rest? *J. Pers. and soc. Psychol., 29,* 132–139.

Gilovich, T., D. L. Jennings, and S. Jennings (1983). Causal factors and estimates of consensus: an examination of the false-consensus effect. *J. of Pers. and soc. Psychol., 45,* 550–559.

Ginosar, Z., and Y. Trope (1980). The effects of base rates and individuating information on judgments about another person. *J. exp. soc. Psychol., 16,* 228–242.

Goethals, G. R., J. Cooper, and A. Nafficy (1979). Role of foreseen, foreseeable and unforeseeable behavioral consequences in the arousal of cognitive dissonance. *J. Pers. soc. Psychol., 37,* 1179–1185.

Goldiamond, I., and W. F. Hawkins (1958). Vexierversuch: the log relationship between word-frequency and recognition obtained in the absence of stimulus words. *J. exp. Psychol., 56,* 457–463.

Gollob, H. F. (1974). The subject-verb-object approach to social cognition. *Psychol. Rev., 81,* 286–321.

Gollob, H. F., and G. W. Fischer (1973). Some relationships between social inference, cognitive balance, and change in impression. *J. Pers. soc. Psychol., 26,* 16–22.

Graesser, A. C., S. E. Gordon, and J. D. Sawyer (1979). Recognition memory for typical and atypical actions in scripted activities: test of a script pointer and tag hypothesis. *J. verb. Reas. verb. Behav., 18,* 319–332.

Graesser, A., S. B. Woll, D. J. Kowalski, and D. A. Smith (1980). Memory for typical and atypical actions in scripted activities. *J. exp. Psychol.: hum. Learn. Memory, 6,* 503–515.

Green, D. (1974). Dissonance and self-perception analyses of "forced-compliance": when two theories make competing predictions. *J. Pers. soc. Psychol., 29,* 819–828.

Green, D. M., and J. A. Swets (1966). *Signal detection theory and psychophysics.* New York: Wiley.

Greenberg, J., T. Pyszczynski, and S. Solomon (1982). The self-serving attributional bias: beyond self-presentation. *J. exp. soc. Psychol.*

Greenwald, A. G. (1968). Cognitive learning, cognitive response to persuasion, and attitude change. In A. G. Greenwald, T. C. Brock, and T. M. Ostrom (Eds.), *Psychological foundations of attitudes.* New York: Academic Press.

_____ (1975). On the inconclusiveness of "crucial" cognitive tests of dissonance vs. self-perception theories. *J. exp. soc. Psychol., 1,* 490–499.

_____ (1976). Within-subjects designs: to use or not to use? *Psychol. Bull., 83,* 314–320.

_____ (1982a). Self and memory. In G. H. Bower (Ed.), *Psychology of learning and motivation.* Vol. 15. New York: Academic Press.

_____ (1982b). Ego task analysis: an integration of research on ego-involvement and self-awareness. In A. H. Hastorf and A. M. Isen (Eds.), *Cognitive social psychology.* New York: Elsevier North-Holland.

Greenwald, A. G., and D. L. Ronis (1978). Twenty years of cognitive dissonance: a case study of the evolution of a theory, *Psychol. Rev., 85,* 53–57.

Grice, G. R. (1966). Dependence of empirical laws upon the source of experimental variation. *Psychol. Bull., 66,* 488–498.

Grice, P. (1967). Logic and communication. The William James Lecture.

Gurwitz, S. B., and K. A. Dodge (1977). Effects of confirmations and disconfirmations on stereotyped attributions. *J. Pers. soc. Psychol., 35,* 495–500.

Hamilton, D. L., Ed. (1981). *Cognitive processes in stereotyping and intergroup behavior.* Hillsdale, N.J.: Erlbaum.

Hamilton, D. L., and R. K. Gifford (1976). Illusory correlation in interpersonal perceptions: a cognitive basis of stereotypic judgments. *J. exp. soc. Psychol., 12,* 392–407.

Hamilton, D. L., and L. B. Katz (1975). *A process-oriented approach to the study of impressions.* Paper read at American Psychological Association Meeting, Chicago.

Hamilton, D. L., and T. R. Rose (unpublished). *Illusory correlation and the maintenance of stereotypic beliefs.* Santa Barbara: Univ. of California.

Hamilton, D. L., L. B. Katz, and V. O. Leirer (1980). Organizational processes in impression formation. In R. Hastie, T. Ostrom, E. Ebbesen, R. Wyer, D. Hamilton, and D. Carlston (Eds.), *Person memory: the cognitive basis of social perception.* Hillsdale, N.J.: Erlbaum.

Hamilton, D. L., and T. L. Rose (1980). Illusory correlation and the maintenance of stereotypic beliefs. *J. Pers. soc. Psychol., 39,* 832–845.

Hamilton, D., and M. Zanna (1972). Differential weighting of favorable and unfavorable attributes in impressions of personality. *J. exp. Res. in Pers., 6,* 204–212.

Hammerton, M. (1973). A case of radical probability estimation. *J. exp. Psychol., 101,* 252–254.

Hamill, R., T. D. Wilson, and R. E. Nisbett (1980). Insensitivity to sample bias: generalizing from atypical cases. *J. Pers. soc. Psychol., 39,* 578–589.

Harkins, S. G., J. H. Harvey, L. Keithly, and M. Rich (1977). Cognitive tuning, encoding, and the attribution of causality. *Memory and Cognition, 5,* 561–565.

Harter, S. (1978). Effectance motivation reconsidered: forward a development model. *Hum. Development, 21,* 34–64.

Harvey, J. H., S. G. Harkins, and D. K. Kagehiro (1976). Cognitive tuning and the attribution of causality. *J. Pers. soc. Psychol., 34,* 708–715.

Harvey, J. H., K. L. Yarkin, J. M. Lightner, and J. P. Town (1980). Unsolicited interpretation and recall of interpersonal events. *J. Pers. soc. Psychol., 38,* 551–568.

Hasher, L., D. Goldstein, and T. Toppino (1977). Frequency and the conference of referential validity. *J. verb. Learn. verb. Behav., 16,* 107–112.

Hasher, L., and M. Griffin (1978). Reconstructive and reproductive processes in memory. *J. exp. Psychol.: hum. Learn. Mem., 4,* 318–330.

Hastie, R. (1981). Schematic principles on human memory. In T. E. Higgins, C. Herman, and M. P. Zanna (Eds.), *Social cognition: the Ontario symposium on personality and social psychology* Vol. 1. Hillsdale, N.J.: Erlbaum.

—— (1983). Social inference. In M. Rosenzweig and L. W. Porter (Eds.), *Ann. Rev. Psychol.* Vol. 34, 511–542.

—— (1984). Causes and effects of causal attribution. *J. Pers. Soc. Psychol., 46,* 44–56.

Hastie, R., and D. E. Carlston (1980). Theoretical issues in person memory. In R. Hastie, T. M. Ostrom, E. B. Ebbesen, R. S. Wyer, Jr., D. L. Hamilton, and D. E. Carlston (Eds.), *Person memory: the cognitive basis of social perception.* Hillsdale, N.J.: Erlbaum.

Hastie, R., and P. A. Kumar (1979). Person memory: personality traits as organizing principles in memory for behaviors. *J. Pers. soc. Psychol., 37,* 25–38.

Hastie, R., T. M. Ostrom, E. B. Ebbesen, R. S. Wyer, D. L. Hamilton, and D. E. Carlston, Eds. (1981). *Person memory: the cognitive basis of social perception.* Hillsdale, N.J.: Erlbaum.

Hastorf, A. H., and A. M. Isen, Eds. (1982). *Cognitive social psychology.* New York: Elsevier North-Holland.

Hastorf, A. H., D. J. Schneider, and J. Polefka (1970). *Person perception.* Reading, Mass.: Addison-Wesley.

Head, H. (1920). *Studies in neurology.* London: Oxford Univ. Press.

Heider, F. (1944). Social perception and phenomenal causality. *Psychol. Rev., 51,* 358–374.

—— (1946). Attitude and cognitive organization. *J. Psychol., 21,* 107–112.

—— (1958). *The psychology of interpersonal relations.* New York: Wiley.

—— (1960). The Gestalt theory of motivation. In M. R. Jones (Ed.), *Nebraska symposium on motivation.* Lincoln: Univ. of Nebraska Press.

Heider, F., and M. Simmel (1944). An experimental study of apparent behavior. *Amer. J. Psychol., 57,* 243–259.

Heilman, M. E., and B. L. Toffler (1976). Reacting to reactance: an interpersonal interpretation of the need for freedom. *J. exp. soc. Psychol., 12,* 519–529.

Helson, H. (1949). Adaptation-level as a basis for a quantitative theory of frames of reference. *Psychol. Rev., 55,* 297–313.

Hendrick, C. (1968). Averaging vs. summation in impression formation. *Percept. motor skills, 27,* 1295–1302.

Hendrick, C., B. Wallace, and J. Tappenbeck (1968). Effect of cognitive set on color perception. *J. Pers. soc. Psychol., 10,* 487–494.

Henley, N. M., R. Horsfall, and C. B. DeSoto (1969). Goodness of figure and social structure. *Psychol. Rev., 76,* 194–204.

Higgins, E. T. (1981). Role-taking and social judgment: alternative developmental perspectives and processes. In V. H. Flavell and L. Ross (Eds.), *New directions in the study of social-cognitive development.* Cambridge: Cambridge Univ. Press.

Higgins, E. T., and W. M. Chaires (1980). Accessibility of interrelational constructs: implications for stimulus encoding and creativity. *J. exp. soc. Psychol., 16,* 348–361.

Higgins, E. T., R. Fondacaro, and D. McCann (1981). Rules and roles: the "communication game" and speaker-listener processes. In W. P. Dickson (Ed.), *Children's oral communication skills.* New York: Academic Press.

Higgins, E. T., G. A. King, and G. H. Mavin (1982). Individual construct accessibility and subjective impressions and recall. *J. Pers. soc. Psychol., 73,* 35–47.

Higgins, E. T., C. D. McCann, and R. Fondacaro (1982). The "communication game": goal-directed encoding and cognitive consequences. *Social Cognition, 1,* 21–37.

Higgins, E. T., F. Rhodewalt, and M. P. Zanna (1979). Dissonance motivation: its nature, persistence, and reinstatement. *J. exp. soc. Psychol., 15,* 16–34.

Higgins, E. T., and W. S. Rholes (1978). Saying is believing: effects of message modification on memory for the person described. *J. exp. soc. Psychol., 14,* 363–378.

Higgins, E. T., C. Herman, and M. P. Zanna, Eds. (1981). *Social cognition: the Ontario symposium on personality and social psychology.* Vol. 1. Hillsdale, N.J.: Erlbaum.

Higgins, E. T., W. S. Rholes, and C. R. Jones (1977). Category accessibility and impression formation. *J. exp. soc. Psychol., 13,* 141–154.

Himmelfarb, S. (1966). Studies in the perception of ethnic group members. I. Accuracy, response bias, and antisemitism. *J. Pers. soc. Psychol., 4,* 347–355.

Hodges, B. (1974). Effect of valence on relative weighting in impression formation. *J. Pers. soc. Psychol., 30,* 378–381.

Hoffman, L. R., and N. R. F. Maier (1961). Sex differences, sex composition, and group problem solving. *J. abnorm. soc. Psychol., 63,* 453–456.

_____ (1966). Social factors influencing problem solving in women. *J. Pers. soc. Psychol., 4,* 382–390.

Hogarth, R. M. (1981). Beyond discrete biases: functional and dysfunctional aspects of judgmental heuristics. *Psychol. Bull., 90,* 197–217.

Horowitz, M. W., J. Lyons, and H. V. Perlmutter (1951). Induction of forces in discussion groups. *Hum. Rel., 41,* 57–76.

Howard, J. W., and M. Rothbart (1980). Social categorization and memory for in-group and out-group behavior. *J. Pers. soc. Psychol., 38,* 301–310.

Howes, D. H. (1954). On the interpretation of word frequency as a variable affecting speed of recognition. *J. Exp. Psychol., 48,* 106–112.

Howes, D. H., and R. L. Solomon (1950). A note on McGinnes' emotionality and perceptual defense. *Psychol. Rev., 57,* 229–234.

Insko, C. A. (1980). Balance theory and phenomenology. In R. E. Petty, T. M. Ostrom, and T. C. Brock (Eds.), *Cognitive responses in persuasion.* Hillsdale, N.J.: Erlbaum.

Insko, C. A., and A. Adewol (1979). The role of assumed similarity in the production of attraction and agreement effects in P-O-X triads. *J. Pers. soc. Psychol., 37,* 790–808.

Insko, C. A., A. J. Sedlak, and A. A. Lipsitz (1982). A two-valued logic or two-valued balance resolution of the challenge of agreement and attraction in P-O-X triads, and a theoretical perspective on conformity and hedonism. *Europ. J. soc. Psychol., 12,* 143–167.

Insko, C. A., E. Songer, and W. McGarvey (1974). Balance, positivity, and agreement in the Jordan paradigm: a deference of balance theory. *J. exp. soc. Psychol., 10,* 53–83.

Isen, A. M., and A. H. Hastorf (1982). Some perspectives on cognitive social psychology. In A. M. Isen and A. H. Hastorf (Eds.), *Cognitive social psychology.* New York: Elsevier North-Holland.

Izard, C. E. (1977). *Human emotions.* New York: Plenum.

Jackson, D. N., and S. Messick (1958). Content and style in personality assessment. *Psychol. Bull., 55,* 243–252.

_____ (1961). Acquiescence and desirability as response determinants on the MMPI. *Educ. Psychol. Measmt., 21,* 771–790.

Jaspars, J. M. E., J. P. Van De Geer, H. Tajfel, and N. Johnson (1965). On the development of international attitudes. Psychological Institute, University of Leiden, Report ESP No. 001-65.

Jeffrey, K. M., and W. Mischel (1979). Effects of purpose on the organization and recall of information in person perception. *J. Pers., 47,* 397–419.

Jenkins, H. M., and H. D. Ward (1965). Judgments of contingency between responses and outcomes. *Psychol.*

Monogr., 79, No. 1 (whole No. 594).

Jennings, D., T. M. Amabile, and L. Ross (1980). Informal covariation assessment: data-based vs. theory-based judgments. In A. Tversky, D. Kahneman, and P. Slovic (Eds.), *Judgments under uncertainty: heuristics and biases.* New York: Cambridge Univ. Press.

Jersild, A. (1931). Memory for the pleasant as compared with the unpleasant. *J. exp. Psychol., 14,* 284–288.

Johnson, J. T., and C. M. Judd (1983). Overlooking the incongruent: categorization biases in the identification of political statements. *J. Pers. soc. Psychol., 45,* 978–996.

Johnson-Laird, P. N., and P. C. Wason (1977). A theoretical analysis of insight into a reasoning task. In P. N. Johnson-Laird and P. C. Wason (Eds.), *Thinking.* Cambridge: Cambridge Univ. Press.

Jones, E. E. (1979). The rocky road from acts to dispositions. *Amer. Psychol., 34,* 107–117.

Jones, E. E., and K. E. Davis (1965). From acts to dispositions: the attribution process in person perception. In L. Berkowitz (Ed.), *Advances in experimental social psychology.* Vol. 2. New York: Academic Press.

Jones, E. E., and V. A. Harris (1967). The attribution of attitudes. *J. exp. soc. Psychol., 3,* 1–24.

Jones, E. E., and D. McGillis (1976). Correspondent inferences and the attribution cube: a comparative reappraisal. In J. H. Harvey, W. J. Ickes, and R. F. Kidd (Eds.), *New directions in attribution research.* Vol. 1. Hillsdale, N.J.: Erlbaum.

Jones, E. E., and R. E. Nisbett (1971). *The actor and the observer: divergent perceptions of the causes of behavior.* Morristown, N.J.: General Learning Press.

Jones, E. E., and J. W. Thibaut (1958). Interaction goals as bases of inference in interpersonal perception. In R. Tagiuri and K. Petrullo (Eds.), *Person perception and interpersonal behavior.* Stanford: Stanford Univ. Press.

Jones, E. E., J. M. Riggs, and G. Quattrone (1979). Observer bias in the attitude-attribution paradigm: effect of time and information order. *J. Pers. soc. Psychol., 37,* 1230–1238.

Jordan, N. (1953). Behavioral forces that are a function of attitudes and of cognitive organization. *Hum. Relat., 6,* 273–287.

_____ (1963). Fallout shelters and social psychology—the "theory" of cognitive dissonance. Croton-on-Hudson: The Hudson Institute.

Judd, C. M., and J. A. Kulik (1980). Schematic effects of social attitudes on information processing and recall. *J. Pers. soc. Psychol., 38,* 569–578.

Kahneman, D., and A. Tversky (1972). Subjective probability: a judgment of representativeness. *Cognit. Psychol., 3,* 430–454.

_____ (1973). On the psychology of prediction. *Psychol. Rev., 80,* 237–251.

_____ (1982). On the study of statistical intuitions. *Cognition, 11,* 123–141.

Kahneman, D., P. Slovic, and A. Tversky (1982). *Judgment under uncertainty: heuristics and biases.* Cambridge: Cambridge Univ. Press.

Kanouse, D., and L. Hanson (1971). Negativity in evaluations. In E. Jones et al. (Eds.), *Attribution: perceiving the causes of behavior.* Morristown, N.J.: General Learning Press.

Kaplan, M. F. (1977). Discussion polarization effects in a modified jury decision paradigm: informational influences. *Sociometry, 40,* 262–271.

Katz, D. (1960). The functional approach to the study of attitudes. *Publ. Opin. Quart., 24,* 163–204.

Katz, L. (1964). Effects of differential monetary gain and loss on sequential two-choice behavior. *J. exp. Psychol., 68,* 245–249.

Kelley, H. H. (1950). The warm-cold variable in first impressions of persons. *J. Pers., 18,* 431–439.

——— (1967). Attribution theory in social psychology. *Neb. sympos. motivation, 14,* 192–241.

——— (1972a). Attribution in social interaction. In E. E. Jones et al. (Eds.), *Attribution: perceiving the causes of behavior.* Morristown, N.J.: General Learning Press.

——— (1972b). Causal schemata and the attribution process. In E. E. Jones, D. E. Kanouse, H. H. Kelley, R. E. Nisbett, S. Valins, and B. Weiner (Eds.), *Attribution: perceiving the causes of behavior.* Morristown, N.J.: General Learning Press.

——— (1973). The process of causal attribution. *Amer. Psychol., 28,* 107–128.

Kelley, H. H., and A. J. Stahelski (1970). The social interaction basis of cooperators' and competitors' beliefs about others. *J. Pers. soc. Psychol., 16,* 66–91.

Kellogg, R. T. (1982). When can we introspect accurately about mental processes? *Memory and Cognition, 10,* 141–144.

Kelly, G. A. (1955). *The psychology of personal constructs.* New York: Norton.

Kiesler, C. A., R. E. Nisbett, and M. P. Zanna (1969). On inferring one's beliefs from one's behavior. *J. Pers. soc. Psychol., 11,* 321–327.

Kiesler, C. A., and M. S. Pallak (1976). Arousal properties of dissonance manipulations. *Psychol. Bull., 83,* 1014–1025.

Kintsch, W., and T. A. van Dijk (1978). Toward a model of text comprehension and production. *Psychol. Rev., 85,* 363–394.

Kleinhesselink, R. R., and R. E. Edwards (1975). Seeking and avoiding belief-discrepant information as a function of its perceived refutability. *J. Pers. soc. Psychol., 31,* 787–790.

Kleinke, C., A. Bustos, F. Meeker, and R. Staneski (1973). Effects of self-attributed and other-attributed gaze on interpersonal evaluations between males and females. *J. exp. soc. Psychol., 9,* 154–163.

Koch, H. L. (1930). The influence of some affective factors upon recall. *J. gen. Psychol., 4,* 171–190.

Kogan, N., and R. Tagiuri (1958). Interpersonal preference and cognitive organization. *J. abnorm. soc. Psychol., 64,* 31–38.

Krech, D., and R. S. Crutchfield (1948). *Theory and problems of social psychology.* New York: McGraw-Hill.

Kris, M., R. A. Kinchla, and J. A. Darley (1977). A mathematical model for social influences on perceptual judgments. *J. exp. soc. Psychol., 13,* 403–420.

Kruglanski, A. W., and I. Ajzen (1983). Bias and error in human judgment. *Europ. J. soc. Psychol., 13,* 1–44.

Kuethe, J. L. (1962). social schemas. *J. abnorm. soc. Psychol., 64,* 31–38.

Kuethe, J. L., and G. Stricker (1963). Man and woman: social schemata for males and females. *Psychol. Reports, 13,* 655–661.

Kunst-Wilson, W. R., and R. B. Zajonc (1980). Affective discrimination of stimuli that cannot be recognized. *Science, 207,* 557–558.

Langer, E. (1978). Rethinking the role of thought in social interaction. In J. Harvey, W. Ickes, and R. Kidd (Eds.), *New directions in attribution research.* Hillsdale, N.J.: Erlbaum.

Langer, E. J., and R. P. Abelson (1972). The semantics of asking a favor: how to succeed in getting help without really dying. *J. Pers. soc. Psychol., 24,* 26–32.

Langer, E. J., S. E. Taylor, S. Fiske, and B. Chanowitz (1972). Stigma, staring, and discomfort: a novel-stimulus hypothesis. *J. exp. soc. Psychol., 12,* 451–463.

Lanzetta, J. T., and S. P. Orr (1980). Influence of facial expressions on the classical conditioning of fear. *J. Pers. soc. Psychol., 39,* 1081–1087.

Lawrence, D. H. and L. Festinger (1962). *Deterrents and reinforcement: the psychology of insufficient reward.* Stanford: Stanford Univ. Press.

Lazarus, R. S., and R. A. McCleary (1951). Autonomic discrimination without awareness: a study of subception. *Psychol. Rev., 58,* 113–122.

Leary, M. R. (1981). The distorted nature of hindsight. *J. soc. Psychol., 115,* 25–29.

——— (1982). Hindsight distortion and the 1980 presidential election. *Pers. soc. Psychol. Bull., 8,* 257–263.

Leon, M., G. C. Oden, and N. H. Anderson (1973). Functional measurement of social values. *J. Pers. soc. Psychol., 102,* 27–36.

Lepper, M. R. (1981). Social control processes, attribution of motivation, and the internalization of social values. In T. E. Higgins, D. N. Ruble, and W. W. Hartup (Eds.), *Social cognition and social behavior: a developmental perspective.* San Francisco: Jossey-Bass.

Lepper, M. R., D. Greene, and R. E. Nisbett (1973). Undermining children's intrinsic interest with extrinsic reward: a test of the "overjustification" hypothesis. *J. Pers. soc. Psychol., 28,* 129–137.

Leventhal, H. (1962). The effect of set and discrepancy on impression change. *J. Pers., 30,* 1–15.

Levin, I. P. (1975). Information integration in numerical judgments and decision processes. *J. exp. Psychol.: General, 104,* 39–53.

Lewicka, M. (1977). Evaluative and descriptive aspects of organization of cognitive structures. *Polish Psychol. Bull., 8,* 3–12.

——— (1979). Effect of cognitive set—to diagnose or to evaluate—upon impression formation and change. *Polish Psychol. Bull., 10,* 21–30.

Lewin, K. (1946). Behavior and development as a function of the total situation. In L. Carmichael (Ed.), *Manual of child psychology.* New York: Wiley.

——— (1951). *Field theory in social psychology.* New York: Harper.

Lewis, H. B. (1941). Studies in the principles of judgments and attitudes: IV. The operation of "prestige suggestion." *J. soc. Psychol., 14,* 229–256.

Linder, D. E., and K. A. Crane (1970). Reactance theory analysis of predecisional cognitive processes. *J. Pers. soc. Psychol., 15,* 258–264.

Linder, D. E., J. Cooper, and E. E. Jones (1967). Decision freedom as a determinant of the role of incentive magnitude in attitude change. *J. Pers. soc. Psychol., 6,* 245–254.

Lindzey, G., and S. Rogolsky (1950). Prejudice and identification of minority group membership. *J. abnorm. soc. Psychol., 45,* 37–53.

Lingle, J. H., and T. M. Ostrom (1979). Retrieval selectivity on memory-based judgments. *J. Pers. soc. Psychol., 37,* 180–194.

_____ (1981). Principles of memory and cognition in attitude formation. In R. Petty, T. M. Ostrom, and T. C. Brock (Eds.), *Cognitive responses in persuasion.* Hillsdale, N.J.: Erlbaum.

Lingle, J. H., N. Geva, T. M. Ostrom, M. R. Leippe, and M. H. Baumgardner (1971). Thematic effects of person judgments on impression organization. *J. Pers. soc. Psychol., 37,* 674–687.

Linville, P. W., and E. E. Jones (1980). Polarized appraisals of out-group members. *J. Pers. soc. Psychol., 38,* 689–703.

Little, K. B. (1968). Cultural variations in social schemata. *J. Pers. soc. Psychol., 10,* 1–7.

Locksley, A., E. Borgida, N. Brekke, and C. Hepburn (1980). Sex stereotypes and social judgment. *J. Pers. soc. Psychol., 39,* 821–831.

Locksley, A., C. Hepburn, and V. Ortiz (1982). Social stereotypes and judgments of individuals: an instance of the base-rate fallacy. *J. exp. soc. Psychol., 18,* 23–42.

Lord, C. G. (1980). Schemas and images as memory aids: two modes of processing social information. *J. Pers. soc. Psychol., 38,* 257–269.

Lorge, I. (1936). Prestige, suggestion, and attitudes. *J. soc. Psychol., 7,* 386–402.

Lott, B. E. (1963). Secondary reinforcement and effort: comment on Aronson's The effect of effort on the attractiveness of rewarded and unrewarded stimuli. *J. abnorm. soc. Psychol., 67,* 520–522.

Lowin, A. (1967). Approach and avoidance: alternative modes of selective exposure to information. *J. Pers. soc. Psychol., 6,* 1–9.

Luchins, A. S. (1942). Mechanization in problem-solving. The effect of Einstellung. *Psychol. Monogr., 6,* No. 54 (whole No. 248).

Lyon, D., and P. Slovic (1976). Dominance of accuracy information and neglect of base rates in probability estimation. *Acta Psychologica, 40,* 287–298.

McArthur, L. Z. (1980). Illusory causation and illusory correlations: two epistemological accounts. *Pers. soc. Psychol. Bull., 6,* 507–519.

_____ (1981). What grabs you: the role of attention in impression formation and causal attribution. In E. T. Higgins, C. P. Herman, and M. P. Zanna (Eds.), *Social cognition: the Ontario symposium.* Vol. 1. Hillsdale, N.J.: Erlbaum.

McArthur, L. Z., and S. Friedman (1980). Illusory correlations in impression formation: variations in the shared distinctiveness effect as a function of the distinctive person's age, race, and sex. *J. Pers. soc. Psychol., 39,* 615–624.

McArthur, L. Z., and E. Ginsberg (1981). Causal attribution to salient stimuli: an investigation of visual fixation mediators. *Pers. soc. Psychol. Bull., 7,* 547–553.

McGuire, W. J., and C. V. McGuire (1982). Significant others on self-space: sex differences and developmental trends in the social self. In J. Suls (Ed.), *Psychological perspectives on the self.* Vol. 1. Hillsdale, N.J.: Erlbaum.

Maier, N. R. F. (1970). *Problem solving and creativity.* Belmont, Calif.: Brooks/Cole.

Maier, N. R. F., and A. R. Solem (1952). The contribution of a discussion leader to the quality of group thinking: the effective use of minority opinions. *Hum. Relat., 5,* 277–288.

Mandler, J. M. (1978). A code in the node: the use of a story schema in retrieval. *Discourse Processes, 1,* 14–35.

Manis, M. (1960). The interpretation of opinion statements as a function of recipient attitudes. *J. abnorm. soc. Psychol., 60,* 340–344.

Manis, M., I. Dovalina, N. E. Avis, and S. Cardoze (1980). Base rates can affect individual predictions. *J. Pers. soc. Psychol., 38,* 231–248.

Marcel, A. (1980). Conscious and preconscious recognition of polysemous words: locating selective effects of prior verbal context. In J. Requin (Ed.), *Attention and performance Vol. VII.* Hillsdale, N.J.: Erlbaum.

Marks, R. (1951). The effect of probability, desirability, and privilege on the stated expectations of children. *J. Pers., 19,* 332–351.

Markus, H. (1977). Self-schemas and processing information about the self. *J. Pers. soc. Psychol., 35,* 63–78.

Markus, H., and K. Sentis (1982). The self in social information processing. In J. Suls (Ed.), *Social psychological perspectives on the self.* Hillsdale, N.J.: Erlbaum.

Markus, H., and J. Smith (1981). The influence of self-schemata on the perception of others. In N. Cantor and J. Kihlstrom (Eds.), *Personality, cognition, and social interaction.* Hillsdale, N.J.: Erlbaum.

Markus, H., J. Smith, and R. L. Moreland (1983). The role of the self in social perception: a cognitive analysis. Unpublished manuscript.

Markus, H., M. Crane, S. Bernstein, and M. Siladi (1982). Self-schemas and gender. *J. Pers. soc. Psychol., 42,* 38–50.

Massad, C. M., M. Hubbard, and D. Newtson (1979). Selective perception of events. *J. exp. soc. Psychol., 15,* 513–530.

Matlin, M., and D. Stang (1978). *The Pollyanna principle.* Cambridge, Mass.: Schenkman.

Mead, G. H. (1934). *Mind, self and society.* Chicago: Univ. of Chicago Press.

Meltzer, H. (1930). Individual differences in forgetting pleasant and unpleasant experiences. *J. educ. Psychol., 21,* 399–409.

Merleau-Ponty, M. (1945). *Phenomenologie de la perception.* Paris: Gallimard.

Merry, R. (1980). Image bizarreness in incidental learning. *Psychol. Reports, 46,* 427–430.

Merry, R., and N. C. Graham (1978). Imagery bizarreness in children's recall of sentences. *Brit. J. Psychol., 69,* 315–321.

Merton, R. K. (1948). The self-fulfilling prophecy. *Antioch Rev., 8,* 193–210.

Merton, R. K., and A. S. Kitt (1950). Contributions to the theory of reference group behavior. In R. K. Merton and P. F. Lazarsfeld (Eds.), *Continuities in social research.* Glencoe, Ill.: Free Press.

Messick, S. (1962). Response style and content measures from personality inventories. *Educ. psychol. Measmt., 22,* 41–56.

Mettee, D. R. (1971). The true discerner as a potent source of positive affect. *J. exp. soc. Psychol., 7,* 292–303.

Mika, S. Postawy a zapamietywanie (1966). Attitudes and remembering. *Studia Psychologiczne, 7.*

Milgram, S. (1965). Some conditions of obedience and disobedience to authority. *Hum. Relat., 8,* 57–76.

Miller, A. G., E. E. Jones, and S. Hinkle (1981). A robust attribution error in personality domain. *J. exp. soc. Psychol., 17,* 587–600.

Miller, A. G., and L. G. Rorer (1982). Toward an understanding of the fundamental attribution error. *J. Res. Pers., 16,* 41–59.

Miller, C. E., and R. M. Norman (1976). Balance, agreement, and attraction in hypothetical social situations. *J. exp. soc. Psychol., 12,* 109–119.

Miller, D. T. (1978). What constitutes a self-serving attributional bias? *J. Pers. soc. Psychol., 36,* 1221–1223.

Miller, D. T., and M. Ross (1975). Self-serving bias in the attribution of causality: fact or fiction? *Psychol. Bull., 82,* 213–225.

Miller, G. A., E. Galanter, and K. H. Pribram (1960). *Plans and the structure of behavior.* New York: Holt, Rinehart, and Winston.

Miller, N. E., and J. Dollard (1941). *Social learning and imitation.* New Haven: Yale Univ. Press.

Minsky, M. (1975). A framework for representing knowledge. In P. H. Winston (Ed.), *The psychology of computer vision.* New York: McGraw-Hill.

Montgomery, K. C. (1954). The role of the exploratory drive in learning. *J. compara. physiol. Psychol., 47,* 60–64.

Morier, D. M., and E. Borgida (In press). The conjunction fallacy: a task specific phenomenon? *Pers. soc. Psychol. Bull.*

Morrissette, J. (1958). An experimental study of the theory of structural balance. *Hum. Relat., 11,* 239–254.

Moscovici, S. (1983). Social representations and social explanations: from the "naive" to the "amateur" scientist. In M. Hewstone (Ed.), *Attribution theory: social and functional extentions.* Oxford: Blackwells.

Mower-White, C. J. (1979). Factors affecting balance, agreement, and positivity biases in PDQ and POX triads. *Europ. J. soc. Psychol., 9,* 129–148.

Mowrer, O. H. (1963). Cognitive dissonance or counter-conditioning? A reappraisal of certain behavior "paradoxes." *Psychol. Record, 13,* 197–211.

Mullen, B. (1983). Egocentric bias in estimates of consensus. *J. soc. Psychol., 121,* 31–38.

Murphy, G. (1947). *Personality: a bisocial approach to origins and structure.* New York: Harper.

Nappe, G. W., and K. A. Wollen (1973). Effects of instructions to form common and bizarre mental images on retention. *J. exp. Psychol., 100,* 6–8.

Neisser, U. (1976). *Cognition and reality: principles and implications of cognitive psychology.* San Francisco: Freeman.

Newtson, D. (1976). The foundations of attribution: the unit of perception of ongoing behavior. In J. H. Harvey, W. J. Ickes, and R. F. Kidd (Eds.), *New directions in attribution research.* Vol. 1. Hillsdale, N.J.: Erlbaum.

Nisbett, R. E., and E. Borgida (1975). Attribution and the psychology of prediction. *J. Pers. soc. Psychol., 32,* 932–943.

Nisbett, R. E., and L. Ross (1980). *Human inference: strategies and shortcomings in social judgment.* Englewood Cliffs, N.J.: Prentice-Hall.

Nisbett, R. E., and T. D. Wilson (1977). Telling more than we can know: verbal reports on mental processes. *Psychol. Rev., 84,* 231–259.

Nisbett, R. E., E. Borgida, R. Crandall, and H. Reed (1976). Popular induction: information is not always informative. In J. S. Carroll and J. W. Payne (Eds.), *Cognit. soc. Behav., 2,* 227–236.

Norman, D. A., and D. G. Bobrow (1975). On the role of active memory processes in perception and cognition. In C. Cofer (Ed.), *The structure of human memory.* San Francisco: Freeman.

Nottenburg, G., and E. J. Shoben (1980). Scripts as linear orders. *J. exp. soc. Psychol., 16,* 329–347.

Nuttin, J. M. (1975). *The illusion of attitude change: towards a response contagion theory of persuasion.* New York: Academic Press.

Oakes, M. (1982). Intuiting strength of association from a correlation coefficient. *Brit. J. Psychol., 73,* 51–56.

O'Kelly, L. J., and L. C. Steckle (1940). The forgetting of pleasant and unpleasant experiences. *Amer. J. Psychol., 53,* 432–434.

Oldfield, R. C., and O. L. Zangwill (1942). Head's concept of schema and its application in contemporary British psychology. *Brit. J. Psychol., 32,* 267–286.

Olson, C. L. (1976). Some apparent violations of the representativeness heuristic in human judgment. *J. exp. Psychol.: hum. Percept. Perform., 2,* 599–608.

Olson, J. M., and M. P. Zanna (1979). A new look at selective exposure. *J. exp. soc. Psychol., 15,* 1–15.

_____ (1982). Repression-sensitization differences in responses to a decision. *J. Pers., 50,* 46–57.

Orne, M. T. (1962). On the social psychology of the psychological experiment: with particular reference to demand characteristics and their implications. *Amer. Psychol., 17,* 776–783.

Osgood, C. E. (1962). Studies on the generality of affective meaning systems. *Amer. Psychol., 17,* 10–28.

Osgood, C. E., and P. H. Tannenbaum (1955). The principle of congruity in the prediction of attitude change. *Psychol. Rev., 62,* 42–55.

Ostrom, T. M. (1966). Perspective as an intervening construct in the judgment of attitude statements. *J. Pers. soc. Psychol., 3,* 235–244.

Ostrom, T. M., J. H. Lingle, J. Pryor, and N. Geva (1980). Cognitive organization of person impressions. In R. Hastie, T. M. Ostrom, D. L. Hamilton, R. S. Wyer, E. Ebbesen, and D. Carlston (Eds.), *Person-memory: the cognitive basis of social perception.* Hillsdale, N.J.: Erlbaum.

Ostrom, T. M., J. B. Pryor, and D. D. Simpson (1981). The organization of social information. In E.T. Higgins, C. Herman, and M. Zanna (Eds.), *Social cognition: the Ontario symposium.* Vol. 1. Hillsdale, N.J.: Erlbaum.

Ostrom, T. M., and H. S. Upshaw (1979). Race differences in the judgment of attitude statements over a thirty-five year period. *J. Pers., 38,* 235–248.

Ostrom, T. M., C. Werner, and M. J. Saks (1978). An integration theory analysis of jurors' presumptions of guilt or innocence. *J. Pers. soc. Psychol., 36,* 436–450.

Owens, J., G. H. Bower, and J. B. Black (1978). *The "soap opera" effect in story recall*. Unpublished manuscript. Stanford University.

Pagano, D. F. (1973). Information-processing differences in repressors and sensitizers. *J. Pers. soc. Psychol., 26,* 105–109.

Pallak, M. S., and T. S. Pittman (1972). General motivational effects of dissonance arousal. *J. Pers. soc. Psychol., 21,* 349–358.

Peterson, C. R., and L. R. Beach (1967). Man as an intuitive statistician. *Psychol. Bull., 68,* 29–46.

Pettigrew, T. (1979). The ultimate attribution error: extending Allport's cognitive analysis of prejudice. *Pers. soc. Psychol. Bull., 5,* 461–476.

Petty, R. E., and J. T. Cacioppo (1977). Forewarning, cognitive responding, and resistance to persuasion. *J. Pers. soc. Psychol., 35,* 645–655.

_____ (1981). *Attitudes and persuasion: classic and contemporary approaches*. Dubuque, Iowa: Wm. C. Brown.

Petty, R. E., T. M. Ostrom, and T. C. Brock (1981). Historical foundations of the cognitive response approach to attitudes and persuasion. In R. E. Petty, T. M. Ostrom, and T. C. Brock (Eds.), *Cognitive responses in persuasion*. Hillsdale, N.J.: Erlbaum.

Piaget, J. (1954). *The construction of reality in the child*. New York: Basic Books.

Picek, J. S., S. J. Sherman, and R. M. Shiffrin (1975). Cognitive organization and coding of social structures. *J. Pers. soc. Psychol., 31,* 758–768.

Pichevin, M., and J. Poitou (1974). Le "bias d'equilibre": un exemple de consigne implicite. *Cahiers de Psychologie, 17,* 111–118.

Pittman, T. S. (1975). Attribution of arousal as a mediator in dissonance reduction. *J. Exp. soc. Psychol., 11,* 53–63.

Pollio, H. R., and J. R. Gerow (1968). The role of congruent and incongruent evaluative contexts on word association. *J. verb. Learn. Verb. Behav., 7,* 122–127.

Posner, M. I. (1982). Cumulative development of attentional theory. *Amer. Psychol., 37,* 168–179.

Postman, L., and D. Brown (1952). The perceptual consequences of success and failure. *J. abnorm. soc. Psychol., 47,* 213–221.

Postman, L., J. S. Bruner, and E. McGinnies (1948). Personal values as selective factors in perception. *J. abnorm. soc. Psychol., 43,* 142–154.

Potts, G. R. (1974). Storing and retrieving information about ordered relationships. *J. exp. Psychol., 102,* 431–439.

Poulton, E. C. (1968). The new psychophysics: six models for magnitude estimation. *Psychol. Bull., 69,* 1–19.

_____ (1977). Qualitative subjective assessments are almost always biased, sometimes completely misleading. *Brit. J. Psychol., 68,* 409–425.

Price, K. O., E. Harburg, and J. M. McLeod (1965). Positive and negative affect as a function of perceived discrepancy in ABX situations. *Hum. Relat., 18,* 87–100.

Price, K. O., E. Harburg, and T. M. Newcomb (1966). Psychological balance in situations of negative interpersonal attitudes. *J. Pers. soc. Psychol., 3,* 265–270.

Pryor, J. B., and T. M. Ostrom (1981). The cognitive organization of social information: a converging-operations approach. *J. Pers. soc. Psychol., 41,* 628–691.

Quanty, M. B., J. A. Keats, and S. G. Harkins (1975). Prejudice and criteria for identification of ethnic photographs. *J. Pers. soc. Psychol., 32,* 449–454.

Quigley-Fernandez, B., and J. T. Tedeschi (1978). The bogus pipeline as lie detector: two validity studies, *J. Pers. soc. Psychol., 36,* 247–256.

Ray, J. J. (1983). Reviving the problem of acquiescent response bias. *J. soc. Psychol., 121,* 81–96.

Reber, A. S. (1967). Implicit learning of artificial grammars. *J. verb. Learn. verb. Behav., 5,* 855–863.

Reeder, G. D., and M. B. Brewer (1979). A schematic model of dispositional attribution in interpersonal perception. *Psychol. Rev., 86,* 61–79.

Regan, D. R., and J. Totten (1975). Empathy and attribution: turning observers into actors. *J. Pers. soc. Psychol., 32,* 850–856.

Rettig, S., and B. Pasamanick (1964). Differential judgment of ethical risk by cheaters and non-cheaters. *J. abnorm. soc. Psychol., 69,* 109–113.

Richey, M., L. McClelland, and A. Shimkunas (1967). Relative influence of positive and negative information in impression formation and persistence. *J. Pers. soc. Psychol., 6,* 322–327.

Riess, M., P. Rosenfeld, V. Melburg, and J. T. Tedeschi (1981). Self-serving attributions: biased private perceptions and distorted public descriptions. *J. Pers. soc. Psychol., 41,* 224–231.

Robinson, J., and L. Z. McArthur (1982). Impact of salient vocal qualities on causal attribution for a speaker's behavior. *J. Pers. soc. Psychol., 43,* 236–247.

Rodrigues, A. (1965). On the differential effects of some parameters of balance. *J. Psychol., 61,* 241–250.

_____ (1966). The psycho-logic of interpersonal relations. Ph.D. thesis. Ann Arbor, Mich.: University Microfilms.

_____ (1967). Effects of balance, positivity, and agreement in triadic social relations. *J. Pers. soc. Psychol., 5,* 472–476.

Rogers, C. R. (1951). *Client-centered therapy*. Boston: Houghton Mifflin.

Rogers, T. B., N. A. Kuiper, and W. S. Kirker (1977). Self-reference and the encoding of personal information. *J. Pers. soc. Psychol., 35,* 677–688.

Rokeach, M. (1960). *The open and closed mind*. New York: Basic Books.

_____ (1968). *Beliefs, attitudes and values*. San Francisco: Jossey-Bass.

Ronis, D. L., and A. G. Greenwald (1979). Dissonance theory revised again: comment on the paper by Fazio, Zanna, and Cooper. *J. exp. soc. Psychol., 15,* 62–69.

Rorer, L. G. (1965). The great response-style myth. *Psychol. Bull., 63,* 129–156.

Rosch, E. H. (1973). Natural categories. *Cognit. Psychol., 4,* 328–350.

_____ (1975). The nature of mental codes for color categories. *J. exp. Psychol.—Hum. Percept. Perform., 1,* 303–322.

Rosch, E., and C. B. Mervis (1975). Family resemblances: studies in the internal structure of categories. *Cognit. Psychol., 7,* 573–605.

Rosenberg, M., and H. B. Kaplan (Eds.) (1982). *Social psychology of the self-concept*. Arlington Heights, Ill.: Davidson.

Rosenberg, M. J. (1965). When dissonance fails: on eliminating evaluation apprehension from attitude measurement. *J. Pers. soc. Psychol., 1,* 28–42.

Rosenberg, S., and A. Sedlak (1972). Structural representations of implicit personality theory. In L. Berkowitz (Ed.), *Advances exp. soc. Psychol., 6,* 235–297.

Rosenthal, R. (1966). *Experimenter effects in behavioral research.* New York: Appleton-Century-Crofts.

Rosenthal, R., and L. Jacobson (1968). *Pygmalion in the classroom.* New York: Holt, Rinehart, and Winston.

Ross, B. M., and J. F. DeGroot (1982). How adolescents combine probabilities. *J. Psychol., 110,* 75–90.

Ross, L. (1977a). Problems in the interpretation of ''self-serving'' asymmetries in causal attribution: comments on the Stephen et al. paper. *Sociometry, 40,* 112–114.

—— (1977b). The intuitive psychologist and his shortcomings: distortions in the attribution process. In L. Berkowitz (Ed.), *Advances in experimental social psychology.* Vol. 10. New York: Academic Press.

Ross, L., T. M. Amabile, and J. L. Steinmetz (1977). Social roles, social control, and biases in social perception processes. *J. Pers. soc. Psychol., 35,* 485–494.

Ross, L., G. Bierbrauer, and S. Polly (1974). Attribution of educational outcomes by professional and non-professional instructors. *J. Pers. soc. Psychol., 29,* 609–618.

Ross, L., D. Greene, and P. House (1977). The false consensus phenomenon: an attributional bias in self perception and social perception processes. *J. exp. soc. Psychol., 13,* 279–301.

Ross, L., M. R. Lepper, and M. Hubbard (1975). Perseverance in self-perception and social perception: biased attributional processes in the debriefing paradigm. *J. Pers. soc. Psychol., 32,* 880–892.

Ross, M. (1976). The self-perception of intrinsic motivation. In J. H. Harvey, W. J. Ickes, and R. F. Kidd (Eds.), *New directions in attribution research.* Hillsdale, N.J.: Erlbaum.

Ross, M., and R. F. Shulman (1973). Increasing the salience of initial attitudes: dissonance versus self-perception theory. *J. Pers. soc. Psychol., 28,* 138–144.

Ross, M., and F. Sicoly (1979). Egocentric biases in availability and attribution. *J. Pers. soc. Psychol., 37,* 322–336.

Rossman, B. B., and H. F. Gollob (1976). Social inference and pleasantness judgments involving people and issues. *J. exp. soc. Psychol., 12,* 374–391.

Rothbart, M., M. Evans, and S. Fulero (1979). Recall for confirming events: memory processes and the maintenance of social stereotypes. *J. exp. soc. Psychol., 15,* 343–355.

Rugg, D., and H. Cantril (1944). The wording of questions. In H. Cantril (Ed.), *Gauging public opinion.* Princeton, N.J.: Princeton Univ. Press.

Rumelhart, D. E., and A. Ortony (1977). The representation of knowledge in memory. In R. C. Anderson, R. J. Spiro, and W. E. Montague (Eds.), *Schooling and the acquisition of knowledge.* Hillsdale, N.J.: Erlbaum.

Sampson, E. E., and C. A. Insko (1964). Cognitive consistency and performance in the autokinetic situation. *J. abnorm. soc. Psychol., 68,* 184–192.

Sarbin, T. R. (1962). A preface to a psychological analysis of the self. *Psychol. Rev., 59,* 11–22.

Schachter, S. (1964). The interaction of cognitive and physiological determinants of emotional state. In L. Berkowitz (Ed.), *Advances in experimental social psychology.* Vol. 1. New York: Academic Press.

Schachter, S., and J. Singer (1962). Cognitive, social, and physiological determinants of emotional state. *Psychol. Rev., 65,* 379–399.

Schaffer, D. R. (1975). Some effects of consonant and dissonant attitudinal advocacy on initial attitude salience and attitude change. *J. Pers. soc. Psychol., 32,* 160–168.

Schanck, R. L. (1932). A study of a community and its groups and institution conceived of as behavior of individuals. *Psychol. Monogr., 43*(2), 1–133.

Schank, R. C., and R. P. Abelson (1977). *Scripts, plans, goals, and understanding.* Hillsdale, N.J.: Erlbaum.

Scheier, M. F., A. Fenigstein, and A. H. Buss (1974). Self-awareness and physical aggression. *J. exp. soc. Psychol., 10,* 264–273.

Schlenker, B. R. (1980). *Impression management: the self-concept, social identity and interpersonal relations.* Belmont, Calif.: Brooks/Cole.

Schneider, D. J., A. H. Hastorf, and P. C. Ellsworth (1979). *Person perception.* Reading, Mass.: Addison-Wesley.

Schul, Y., E. Burnstein, and J. Martinez (1983). The informational basis of social judgments: under what conditions are inconsistent trait descriptions processed as easily as consistent ones? *Europ. J. soc. Psychol., 13,* 143–152.

Schuman, H., and M. P. Johnson (1976). Attitudes and behavior. *Ann. Rev. Sociol., 2,* 161–207.

Schutz, A. (1970). *On phenomenology and social relations.* Chicago: Chicago Univ. Press.

Schwartz, M. (1982). Repetition and rated truth value of statements. *Amer. J. Psychol., 95,* 393–407.

Schweder, R. A. (1975). How relevant is an individual difference theory of personality? *J. Pers., 43,* 455–484.

Schweder, R. A., and R. G. D'Andrade (1979). Accurate reflection or systematic distortion? A reply to Block, Weiss and Thorne. *J. Pers. soc. Psychol., 37,* 1075–1084.

Scott, W. A. (1963). Conceptualizing and measuring structural properties of cognition. In O. J. Harvey (Ed.), *Motivation and Social Interaction.* Ronald Press.

Sears, D. O. (1983). The person-positivity bias. *J. Pers. soc. Psychol., 44,* 233–250.

Sears, D. O., and R. Whitney (1972). Political persuasion. In I. Pool et al. (Eds.), *Handbook of communication.* Chicago: Rand McNally.

Secord, P. F. (1959). Stereotyping and favorableness in the perception of Negro faces. *J. abnorm. soc. Psychol., 59,* 309–315.

Sentis, K. P., and E. Burnstein (1979). Remembering schema-consistent information: effects of a balance schema on recognition memory. *J. Pers. soc. Psychol., 37,* 2200–2211.

Shanteau, J. C. (1970). An additive model for sequential decision making. *J. exp. Psychol., 85,* 181–191.

Shapira, Z., (1976). Expectancy determinants of intrinsically motivated behavior. *J. Pers. soc. Psychol., 34,* 1235–1244.

Sherif, M. (1935). An experimental study of stereotypes. *J. abnorm. soc. Psychol., 29,* 370–375.

—— (1936). *The psychology of social norms.* New York: Harper.

Sherwood, G. G. (1981). Self-serving biases in person perception: a reexamination of projection as a mechanism of defense. *Psychol. Bull., 90,* 445–459.

Shrader, Elizabeth G., and D. W. Lewit (1962). Structural factors in cognitive balancing behavior. *Hum. Relat., 15,* 265–276.

Silverman, I. (1971). On the resolution and tolerance of cognitive inconsistency in a natural-occurring event: attitudes and beliefs following the Senator Kennedy incident. *J. Pers. soc. Psychol., 17,* 171–178.

Slovic, P., and S. Lichtenstein (1968). Relative importance of probabilities and payoffs in risk taking. *J. Exp. Psychol., 78,* Part 2.

Smedslund, J. (1963). The concept of correlation in adults. *Scand. J. Psychol., 4,* 165–173.

Smith, E. E., and D. L. Medin (1981). Categories and concepts. Cambridge, Mass.: Harvard Univ. Press.

Smith, E. E., N. Adams, and D. Schorr (1978). Fact retrieval and the paradox of interference. *Cognit. Psychol., 10,* 438–464.

Smith, E. E., E. J. Shoben, and L. J. Rips (1974). Structure and process in semantic memory: a featural model for semantic decisions. *Psychol. Rev., 81,* 214–241.

Smith, T. W., C. R. Snyder, and S. C. Perkins (1983). The self-serving function of hypochondriacal complaints: physical symptoms as self-handicapping strategies. *J. Pers. soc. Psychol., 44,* 787–797.

Snyder, M. (1974). The self-monitoring of expressive behavior. *J. Pers. soc. Psychol., 30,* 526–537.

_____ (1981). On the self-perpetuating nature of social stereotypes. In D. L. Hamilton (Ed.), *Cognitive process in stereotyping and intergroup behavior.* Hillsdale, N.J.: Erlbaum.

Snyder, M., and B. H. Campbell (1980). Testing hypotheses about other people: the role of the hypotheses. *Pers. soc. Psychol. Bull., 6,* 421–426.

Snyder, M., and D. Kendzierski (1982). *J. exp. soc. Psychol., 18,* 165–183.

Snyder, M., and W. B. Swann (1978). Hypotheses-testing processes in social interaction. *J. Pers. soc. Psychol., 36,* 1202–1212.

Snyder, M., and W. B. Swann, Jr. (1976). When actions reflect attitudes: the politics of impression management. *J. Pers. soc. Psychol., 34,* 1034–1042.

Snyder, M., E. D. Tanke, and E. Berscheid (1977). Social perception and interpersonal behavior: on the self-fulfilling nature of social stereotypes. *J. Pers. soc. Psychol., 35,* 656–666.

Snyder, M., and E. Ebbesen (1972). Dissonance awareness: a test of dissonance theory versus self-perception theory. *J. exp. soc. Psychol., 8,* 502–507.

Snyder, M., and S. W. Uranowitz (1978). Reconstructing the past: some cognitive consequences of person perception. *J. Pers. soc. Psychol., 36,* 941–950.

Snyder, M. L., and R. A. Wicklund (1976). Prior exercise of freedom and reactance. *J. exp. soc. Psychol., 12,* 120–130.

Snyder, M. L., W. G. Stephan, and D. Rosenfield (1976). Egotism and attribution. *J. Pers. soc. Psychol., 33,* 435–441.

_____ (1978). Attributional egotism. In J. H. Harvery, W. J. Ickes, and R. F. Kidd (Eds.), *New directions in attribution research.* Vol. 2. Hillsdale, N.J.: Erlbaum.

Spence, J., and R. Helmreich (1978). *Masculinity and femininity.* Austin: Univ. of Texas Press.

Spiro, R. J. (1975). *Inferential reconstruction in memory for connected discourse* (Tech. Rep. No. 2). Urbana, Ill.: Univ. of Illinois. Laboratory for Cognitive Studies in Education.

_____ (1977). Remembering information from text: the "state of schema" approach. In R. C. Anderson, R. J. Spiro, and W. E. Montague (Eds.), *Schooling and the acquisition of knowledge.* Hillsdale, N.J.: Erlbaum.

Srull, T. K., and R. S. Wyer (1979). The role of category accessibility in the interpretation of information about persons: some determinants and implications. *J. Pers. soc. Psychol., 37,* 1660–1662.

Srull, T. K. (1981). Person memory: some tests of associative storage and retrieval models. *J. exp. Psychol.: human Learn. Memory, 7,* 440–463.

Stagner, R. (1931). The reintegration of pleasant and unpleasant experiences. *Amer. J. Psychol., 43,* 463–468.

Steele, C. M., and T. J. Liu (1983). Dissonance processes and self-affirmation. *J. Pers. soc. Psychol., 45,* 5–19.

Sternberg, S. (1969). Memory-scanning: memory processes revealed by reaction-time experiments. *Amer. Scient., 57,* 421–457.

Stotland, E., and L. K. Canon (1972). *Social psychology: a cognitive approach.* Philadelphia: Saunders.

Sulin, R. A., and D. J. Dooling (1974). Intrusion of thematic ideas in retention of prose. *J. Exp. Psychol., 103,* 255–262.

Suls, J. Ed. (1982). Vol. 1. *Psychological perspectives on the self.* Hillsdale, N.J.: Erlbaum.

Swann, W. B., and T. S. Pittman (1975). Salience of initial ratings and attitude in the J "forbidden toy" paradigm. *Pers. soc. Psychol. Bull., 1,* 493–496.

Swann, W. B., and S. J. Read (1981). Self-verification processes: how we sustain our self-conceptions. *J. exp. soc. Psychol., 17,* 351–372.

Sweeney, P., and R. L. Moreland (1980). Self-schemas and the perseverance of beliefs about the self. Paper presented at the Annual Meeting of the American Psychological Association, Montreal, Canada.

Tagiuri, R., and L. Petrullo (1958). *Person perception and interpersonal behavior.* Stanford: Stanford Univ. Press.

Tajfel, H. (1970). Experiments in intergroup discrimination. *Scientific Amer., 223,* 96–102.

_____ (1981). *Human groups and social categories: studies in social psychology.* Cambridge: Cambridge Univ. Press.

Tashakkori, A., and C. A. Insko (1979). Interpersonal attraction and the polarity of similar attitudes: a test of three balance models. *J. Pers. soc. Psychol., 37,* 2262–2277.

_____ (1981). Interpersonal attraction and person perception: two tests of three balance models. *J. exp. soc. Psychol., 17,* 266–285.

Taylor, S. E. (1981). A categorization approach to stereotyping. In D. L. Hamilton (Ed.), *Cognitive process in stereotyping and intergroup behavior.* Hillsdale, N.J.: Erlbaum.

_____ (1982). Adjustment to threatening events: a theory of cognitive adaptation. Tenth Katz-Newcomb Lecture, Ann Arbor, Michigan.

Taylor, S. E., and J. Crocker (1981). Schematic bases of social information processing. In E. T. Higgins, C. A. Harman, and M. P. Zanna (Eds.), *Social cognition: the Ontario symposium on personality and social psychology.* Hillsdale, N.J.: Erlbaum.

Taylor, S. E., and S. T. Fiske (1975). Point of view and perceptions of causality. *J. Pers. soc. Psychol., 32,* 439–445.

———— (1978). Salience attention and attribution: top of the head phenomena. In L. Berkowitz (Ed.), *Advances in experimental social psychology.* Vol. 11. New York: Academic Press.

———— (1981). Getting inside the head: methodologies for process analysis. In J. Harvey, W. Ickes, and K. Kidd (Eds.), *New directions in attribution research.* Vol. III. Hillsdale, N.J.: Erlbaum.

Taylor, S. E., and J. H. Koivumaki (1976). The perception of self and others: acquaintanceship, affect, and actor-observer differences. *J. Pers. soc. Psychol., 33,* 403–408.

Taylor, S. E., and S. C. Thompson (1982). Stalking the elusive "vividness" effect. *Psychol. Rev., 89,* 155–181.

Taylor, S. E., S. T. Fiske, M. Close, C. Anderson, and A. Ruderman (1977). *Solo status as a psychological variable: the power of being distinctive.* Unpublished manuscript.

Taylor, S. E., J. Crocker, and J. D'Agostino (1978). Schematic bases of social problem solving. *Pers. soc. Psychol. Bull., 4,* 447–451.

Taylor, S. E., J. Crocker, S. T. Fiske, M. Sprinzen, and J. D. Winkler (1979). The generalizability of salience effects. *J. Pers. soc. Psychol., 37,* 357–368.

Taylor, S. E., S. T. Fiske, N. Etcoff, and A. Ruderman (1978). The categorical and contextual bases of person memory and stereotyping. *J. Pers. soc. Psychol., 36,* 778–793.

Tedeschi, J. T. (Ed.) (1981). *Impression management theory and social psychological research.* New York: Academic Press.

Tedeschi, J. T., B. R. Schlenker, and T. V. Bonoma (1971). Cognitive dissonance: private ratiocination or public spectacle? *Amer. Psychologist, 26,* 685–695.

Tesser, A. (1978). Self-generated attitude change. *Advances in experimental social psychology.* Vol. 11. New York: Academic Press.

Tesser, A., and C. L. Cowan (1975). Some effects of thought and number of cognitions on attitude change. *Soc. Behav. Pers., 3,* 165–173.

———— (1977). Some attitudinal and cognitive consequences of thought. *J. Res. Pers., 11,* 216–226.

Tesser, A., and P. Danheiser (1978). Anticipated relationship, salience of partner and attitude change. *Pers. soc. Psychol. Bull., 4,* 35–38.

Tesser, A., and C. Leone (1977). Cognitive schemas and thought as determinants of attitude change. *J. exp. soc. Psychol., 13,* 340–356.

Tetlock, P. E. (1983). Accountability and perseverance of first impressions. *Soc. Psychol. Quart., 46,* 285–292.

Thomson, R. H. (1930). An experimental study of memory as influenced by feeling tone. *J. exp. Psychol., 13,* 462–468.

Thompson, E. G., J. W. Gard, and J. L. Phillips (1980). Trait dimensionality and "balance" in subject-verb-object judgments. *J. Pers. soc. Psychol., 38,* 57–66.

Thorndike, E. L. (1920). A constant error in psychological ratings. *J. appl. Psychol., 4,* 25–29.

Thorndyke, P. W. (1977). Cognitive structures in comprehension and memory of narrative discourse. *Cognit. Psychol., 9,* 77–110.

Thorndyke, P. W., and B. Hayes-Roth (1979). The use of schemata in the acquisition and transfer of knowledge. *Cognit. Psychol., 11,* 82–106.

Tiller, M. G., and R. H. Fazio (1982). The relation between attitudes and later behavior following dissonance-produced attitude change. *Pers. soc. Psychol. Bull., 8,* 280–285.

Trope, Y., and M. Bassok (1982). Confirmatory and diagnosing strategies in social information gathering. *J. Pers. soc. Psychol. 43,* 22–39.

Trzebinski, J. (In press). Action oriented representations of "implicit personality theories." *J. Pers. soc. Psychol.*

Tsujimoto, R. N., J. Wilde, and D. R. Robertson (1978). Distorted memory for exemplars of social structure: evidence for schematic memory processes. *J. Pers. soc. Psychol., 38,* 1402–1414.

Tukey, J. W. (1977). *Exploratory data analysis.* Reading, Mass.: Addison-Wesley.

Tversky, A. (1977). Features of similarity. *Psychol. Rev., 84,* 327–352.

Tversky, A., and I. Gati (1978). Studies of similarity. In E. Rosch and B. B. Lloyd (Eds.), *Cognition and categorization.* Hillsdale, N.J.: Erlbaum.

Tversky, A., and D. Kahneman (1973). Availability: a heuristic for judging frequency and probability. *Cognit. Psychol., 5,* 207–232.

———— (1974). Judgment under uncertainty: heuristics and biases. *Science, 185,* 1124–1131.

———— (1978). Causal schemata in judgments under uncertainty. In M. Fishbein (Ed.), *Progress in social psychology.* Hillsdale, N.J.: Erlbaum.

———— (1982). Judgments of and by representativeness. In D. Kahneman, P. Slovic, and A. Tversky (Eds.), *Judgment under uncertainty: heuristics and biases.* New York: Cambridge Univ. Press.

Ugwuegbu, D. C. E. (1979). Racial and evidential factors juror attribution of legal responsibility. *J. exp. soc. Psychol., 15,* 133–146.

Upshaw, H. S. (1962). Own attitude as an anchor in equal-appearing intervals. *J. abnorm. soc. Psychol., 64,* 85–96.

———— (1965). The effect of variable perspectives on judgments of opinion statements for Thurstone scales: equal-appearing intervals. *J. Pers. soc. Psychol., 2,* 60–69.

Van der Pligt, J., and J. R. Eiser (1983). Actors' and observers' attributions, self-serving bias and positivity bias. *Europ. J. soc. Psychol., 13,* 95–104.

Van Kreveld, D., and R. B. Zajonc (1966). The learning of influence structures. *J. Pers., 34,* 205–223.

Verplanck, W. S. (1957). A glossary of some terms used in the objective science of behavior. *Psychol. Rev., 64,* Supplement, Part 2.

Vinokur, A., and I. Ajzen (1982). Relative importance of prior and immediate events: a causal primacy effect. *J. Pers. soc. Psychol., 42,* 820–829.

Von Briesen Raz, J. (1983). Probability matching behavior, association and rational choice. *Behav. Sci., 28,* 35–52.

Walker, C. J. (1976). The employment of vertical and horizontal social schemata in the learning of a social structure. *J. Pers. soc. Psychol., 33,* 132–141.

Wallach, H. (1949). Some considerations concerning the relation between perception and cognition. *J. Pers., 18,* 6–12.

Walster, E. (1964). The temporal sequence of post-decision processes. In L. Festinger (Ed.), *Conflict, decision, and dissonance.* Stanford: Stanford Univ. Press.

Walster, E., E. Berscheid, D. Abrahams, and V. Aronson (1967). Effectiveness of debriefing following deception experiments. *J. Pers. soc. Psychol., 6,* 371–380.

Waly, P., and S. W. Cook (1966). Attitude as a determinant of learning and memory: a failure to confirm. *J. Pers. soc. Psychol., 4,* 280–288.

Ward, W. D., and H. M. Jenkins (1965). The display of information and the judgment of contingency. *Canadian J. Psychol., 19,* 231–241.

Warner, S. L. (1965). Randomized response: a survey technique for eliminating evasive answer bias. *J. Amer. Statist. Assoc., 60,* 63–69.

Watson, D. (1982). The actor and the observer: how are their perceptions of causality divergent? *Psychol. Bull., 92,* 682–700.

Weary, G. (1979). Self-serving attributional biases: perceptual or response distortions? *J. Pers. soc. Psychol., 37,* 1418–1420.

Wegner, D. M., and R. R. Vallacher, Eds. (1980). *The self in social psychology.* New York: Oxford Univ. Press.

Weldon, D. E., and R. S. Malpass (1981). Effects of attitudinal, cognitive, and situational variables on recall of biased communications. *J. Pers. soc. Psychol., 40,* 39–52.

Wellens, A. R., and D. L. Thistlethwaite (1971). An analysis of two quantitative theories of cognitive balance. *Psychol. Rev., 78,* 141–150.

Wells, F. L. (1907). A statistical study of literary merit. *Arch. Psychol., 16,* 7.

Wertheimer, M. (1945). *Productive thinking.* New York: Harper.

Wetzel, C. G. (1982). Self-serving biases in attribution: a Bayesian analysis. *J. Pers. soc. Psychol., 43,* 197–209.

Wicklund, R. A. (1970). Prechoice preference reversal as a result of threat to decisional freedom. *J. Pers. soc. Psychol., 14,* 8–17.

——— (1974). *Freedom and reactance.* Potomac, Md.: Erlbaum.

Wicklund, R. A., and J. W. Brehm (1976). *Perspectives on cognitive dissonance.* Hillsdale, N.J.: Erlbaum.

Wiest, W. M. (1965). A quantitative extension of Heider's theory of cognitive balance applied to interpersonal perception and self-esteem. *Psychol. Monogr., 79,* No. 1 (whole No. 607).

Wills, T. A. (1981). Downward comparison to principles in social psychology. *Psych. Bull., 90,* 245–271.

Wilson, D. T., J. G. Hull, and J. Johnson (1981). Awareness and self-perception: verbal reports on internal states. *J. Pers. soc. Psychol., 40,* 53–71.

Woll, S., and H. Yopp (1978). The role of context and inference in the comprehension of social action. *J. exp. soc. Psychol., 14,* 351–362.

Wollen, K. A., and S. D. Cox (1981). Sentence cueing and the effectiveness of bizarre imagery. *J. exp. Psychol.: hum. Learn. Memory, 7,* 386–392.

Wollen, K. A., A. Weber, and D. H. Lowry (1972). Bizarreness versus interaction of mental images as determinants of learning. *Cognit. Psychol., 3,* 518–523.

Woodworth, R. S. (1947). Reinforcement of perception. *Amer. J. Psychol., 60,* 119–124.

Worchel, S., and S. E. Arnold (1974). The effect of combined arousal states on attitude change. *J. exp. soc. Psychol., 10,* 549–560.

Worchel, S., and J. W. Brehm (1971). Direct and implied social restoration of freedom. *J. Pers. soc. Psychol., 18,* 294–304.

Wright, R. A., and S. S. Brehm (1982). Reactance as impression management: a critical review. *J. Pers. soc. Psychol., 42,* 608–618.

Wyer, R. S., Jr. (1970). Information redundancy, inconsistency, and novelty and their role in impression formation. *J. exp. soc. Psychol., 6,* 111–127.

Wyer, R. S., Jr., and D. E. Carlston (1979). *Social cognition, inference and attribution.* Hillsdale, N.J.: Erlbaum.

Wyer, R. S., Jr. (1974). *Cognitive organization and change: an information processing approach.* Potomac, Md.: Erlbaum.

——— (1975a). The role of probabilistic and syllogistic reasoning in cognitive organization and social change. In M. Kaplan and S. Schwartz (Eds.), *Human judgment and decision processes.* New York: Academic Press.

——— (1976). Effects of previously formed beliefs on syllogistic inference processes. *J. Pers. soc. Psychol., 33,* 307–316.

Wyer, R. S., Jr., and S. F. Gordon (1982). The recall of information about persons and groups. *J. exp. soc. Psychol., 18,* 128–169.

Wyer, R. S., Jr., M. Henninger, and M. Wolfson (1975). Informational determinants of females' self-attributions and observers' judgments of them in an achievement situation. *J. Pers. soc. Psychol., 32,* 556–570.

Wyer, R. S., Jr., and T. K. Srull (1980). The processing of social stimulus information: a conceptual integration. In R. Hastie, T. M. Ostrom, E. B. Ebbesen, R. S. Wyer, Jr., D. L. Hamilton, and D. E. Carlston (Eds.), *Person memory: the cognitive basis of social perception.* Hillsdale, N.J.: Erlbaum.

——— (1981). Category accessibility: some theoretical and empirical issues concerning the processing of social stimulus information. In E. T. Higgins, C. P. Herman, and M. P. Zanna (Eds.), *Soc. Cognit.* Hillsdale, N.J.: Erlbaum.

Zadny, J., and H. B. Gerard (1974). Attributed intentions and informational selectivity. *J. exp. soc. Psychol., 10,* 34–52.

Zajonc, R. B. (1960). The process of cognitive tuning in communication. *J. abnorm. soc. Psychol., 61,* 159–167.

——— (1968). Cognitive theories in social psychology. In G. Lindzey and E. Aronson (Eds.), *The handbook of social psychology. Vol. I.* Reading, Mass.: Addison-Wesley.

——— (1980a). Cognition and social cognition: a historical perspective. In L. Festinger (Ed.), *Four decades of social psychology.* New York: Oxford Univ. Press.

——— (1980b). Feeling and thinking. *Amer. Psychol., 35,* (2), 151–175.

Zajonc, R. B., and E. Burnstein (1965a). The learning of balanced and unbalanced social structures. *J. Pers., 33,* 153–163.

_____ (1965b). Structural balance, reciprocity, and positivity as sources of cognitive bias. *J. Pers., 33,* 570–583.

Zajonc, R. B., and H. Markus (1982). Affective and cognitive factors in preferences. *J. Consumer Research, 9,* 123–131.

_____ (1983). Affect and cognition: the hard interface. In C. E. Izard, J. Kagan, and R. B. Zajonc (Eds.), *Emotions, cognition, and behavior.* New York: Cambridge Univ. Press.

Zanna, M. P., and C. Aziza (1976). On the interaction of repression-sensitization and attention in resolving cognitive dissonance. *J. Pers., 44,* 577–593.

Zanna, M. P., and J. Cooper (1974). Dissonance and the pill: an attribution approach to studying the arousal properties of dissonance. *J. Pers. soc. Psychol., 29,* 703–709.

Zanna, M. P., E. T. Higgins, and P. A. Taves (1976). Is dissonance phenomenologically aversive? *J. exp. soc. Psychol., 12,* 530–538.

Zenker, S., R. C. Leslie, E. Port, and J. Kosloff (1982). The sequence of outcomes and ESP: more evidence for a primacy effect. *Pers. soc. Psychol. Bull., 8,* 233–238.

Zimbardo, P. G. (1969). *The cognitive control of motivation: the consequences of choice and dissonance.* Glenview, Ill.: Scott, Foresman.

Zimbardo, P. G., A. R. Cohen, M. Weisenberg, L. Dworkin, and I. Firestone (1966). Control of pain motivation by cognitive dissonance. *Science, 151,* 217–219.

Zuckerman, M. (1979). Attribution of success and failure revisited, or: the motivational bias is alive and well in attribution theory. *J. Pers., 47,* 245–287.

Zuckerman, M., R. W. Mann, and F. J. Bermieri (1982). Determinants of consensus estimates: attribution, salience, and representativeness. *J. Pers. soc. Psychol., 42*(5), 839–852.

CHAPTER 5

Decision Making and Decision Theory

Robert P. Abelson
Yale University

Ariel Levi
Teachers College, Columbia University

INTRODUCTION

It is difficult to begin this chapter without the obligatory cliche that the authors' reviewing task was monumental. It is estimated that over two hundred fifty relevant publications are appearing yearly, often in journals obscure to psychologists. The major reviews by Slovic, Fischhoff, and Lichtenstein (1977) and Einhorn and Hogarth (1981) coped with the glut of references by being extremely selective, and we shall follow suit.

One basis for selectivity is to concentrate on the individual as the decision-making entity rather than the group, the institution, or the polity. (Some aspects of group decision making, however, are considered in Chapter 22.) A related basis for selectivity is to focus on a descriptive psychology of how decisions are actually made rather than on a prescriptive analysis of how decisions might be made in the service of formal decision

criteria. Recent developments demonstrate that the psychology of decision making is substantively developing independently of prescriptive notions. This trend seems destined to continue, and it has the fortunate aspect that in a number of social policy areas involving public perception of risk (Fischhoff *et al.,* 1981; Fischhoff *et al.,* 1982; Johnson, 1982; Raiffa, 1982; Ravetz, 1977; Schwing and Albers, 1980; Slovic *et al.,* 1982), a realistic psychology has long been overdue.

A third selection criterion is that we will not cover experimental literature in which *decision making* refers to decisions about properties of a stimulus, say whether a tone was or was not present (e.g., Green and Swets, 1966; Shaw, 1982). Even though we may thereby miss the transfer of some useful ideas (Estes, 1980; Lockhead, 1980), we confine our definition of *decision* to cases in which individuals act in the service of preferences.

A final caveat is that for the most part we will treat decisions as though they were one-shot responses, albeit it would be much more ecologically valid to recognize that many decisions involve repeated interactions with a possibly changing environment, with feedback enabling the intelligent modification of previous decisions (Hogarth, 1981). A major experimental context in which decisions act so as to change the environment for future

The authors wish to thank Irving Janis, George Loewenstein, John Michela, and Amos Tversky for critical readings of section drafts, and Linda Rodman for the arduous preparation of the manuscript. Preparation of the chapter was facilitated by a grant from the System Development Foundation to the Yale Cognitive Science Program.

decisions is that of games and gaming (cf. Pruitt and Kimmel, 1977). This literature will not be covered here but is discussed elsewhere in the *Handbook*.

DISTINCTIONS AND DIMENSIONS

There are many distinctions to be drawn within the decision area. The major ones are outlined here and discussed in later sections.

Structure Versus Process

The investigator may be concerned either with *what* the decision maker chooses or with *how* choices are made. The former orientation leads to a study of input/output relationships, i.e., with the *structure* of sets of choices made under specified conditions. The latter promotes analysis of the intervening steps in the cognitive *processing* of choice situations. Of course, process could be studied along with the study of structure, as Simon (1976b) has urged, but in practice, both the inclinations of investigators and differences in methodological emphases have militated toward separate study of structure and process. We consider structure in the section "Structural Models" and process in the section "Process Models."

Riskless Versus Risky Choices

In some choice situations the decision maker is confronted with options among fixed, riskless outcomes. Preferences but not probabilities are involved, as when the chooser must decide which record to purchase or what meal to order. By contrast, many decisions involve probabilistic outcomes. Lotteries, insurance options, and gambling games are explicitly of this character. Implicitly, many personal decisions are also gambles in that the individual cannot anticipate all the consequences of the choice of a given option. Within the class of risky choices the distinction is sometimes made between cases of *risk*, where the relevant outcome probabilities are known (or readily ascertainable), and *uncertainty*, where the objective outcome probabilities are unknown and in practice unknowable.

In real decisions it is hard to think of a case that might not involve some minimum of uncertainty. Thus even in riskless choices such as what meal to order, there is always a chance that the chosen meal will be overcooked, etc. (even though the chooser may not necessarily consider this). Thus practical distinctions between riskless and risky choices are not absolute. In the laboratory, however, an idealized separation may be approximated by being highly explicit about whether probabilistic outcomes are or are not involved. Structural analysis of riskless choices is taken up in "Models of Riskless Decisions" and of risky choices in "Models of Risky Decisions." When process considerations are included, the distinction between risky and riskless blurs somewhat. The main division is between well-defined choice situations, whether risky or riskless, and ill-defined situations, which usually involve uncertainty, i.e., outcomes with unknown probabilities.

Normative Versus Descriptive Models

As already noted, decision models can be oriented toward either how people *should* choose (*normative models*) or how they *do* choose (*descriptive models*). When a disparity between the two exists, it raises issues of human rationality. We discuss rationality broadly below and return to concrete aspects in the section "Potential Constraints on Effective Decision Making."

VIEWS OF RATIONALITY

Discussions of decision making are ubiquitously laced with references to human rationality or irrationality, optimality or error, functionality or maladaptiveness. Einhorn and Hogarth (1981), noting that the question of rationality arises for purposive human behavior but not for the physical behavior of inanimate objects, observe that "if one grants that behavior is goal-directed, it seems reasonable to assume that some ways of getting to the goal are better, in the sense of taking less time, making fewer errors, and so on" (p.54). It is thereupon tempting to adopt a kind of engineering attitude toward improving human performance on these attributes, raising questions about discrepancies between actual and optimal performance.

For a perspective on why decision-making research is so concerned with rationality, however, the appropriate comparisons are not with the study of inanimate objects but with typical concerns in other psychological research areas. When social psychologists study affiliation, aggression, conformity, etc., they do not usually ask whether these tendencies are excercised rationally or optimally (goal-directed though they may be). Analysis is typically descriptive, specifying what conditions produce these tendencies in whom. One reason normative theories are not pursued in these areas may be that it is not clear how to formulate them, whereas it seems, on the face of it, easy to state normative models for decision making.

In any case issues of rationality and irrationality excite a great deal of debate, and it has become almost obligatory to deal with these issues in discussions of decision making. Of the large number of nuanced positions on human rationality (March, 1978), we cover the major ones. The human decision maker has been variously seen as a corrigible rationalist, a bounded rationalist, an error-prone intuitive scientist, a slave to motivational forces, or the butt of faulty normative models.

The Corrigible Rationalist

There are many human judgments that violate some model of optimum task performance, such as the proper use of Bayes' theorem for evaluating the likelihood of competing hypotheses (Edwards, 1968). One stance toward these violations is that subjects may be insufficiently trained in the appropriate probability calculations or other logical tools, and that task instruction can close the gap (Edwards, 1977a). If in the most optimistic view all violations of optimality are merely correctable slipups, then the problem is minimized or disappears entirely.

It is certainly important to investigate how judgments and decisions can be improved (by whatever standard). Indeed, major investigators varying greatly in how sanguine they are about the perfectability of human decision making all give considerable attention to the potential for learning (Einhorn and Hogarth, 1978; Hammond, 1978; Janis, 1972; Janis and Mann, 1977; Kahneman and Tversky, 1979a; Nisbett and Ross, 1980, Chap. 12; Nisbett, Krantz, Jepson, and Fong, 1982). If learning directly from experience (Brehmer, 1980; Einhorn, 1981) or from training in the use of unfamiliar decision strategies (Keeney and Raiffa, 1976) were a simple matter, all would be well. But, in fact, there are many serious issues involved, such as the degree of generalization from one newly mastered task to another and the cognitive, perceptual, and motivational variables that affect the degree to which learning from experience or instruction is possible in the first place.

The Bounded Rationalist

Since Herbert Simon (1955) formulated his position that what the decision maker does is not necessarily to optimize but to *satisfice*—i.e., to choose options that are good enough—it has been a popular view that people are indeed rational but only up to a point. The phrase *bounded rationality* has been applied to this as an alternative to the economist's demanding conception requiring a complete cost/benefit analysis for any decision.

The complete analysis is viewed as often impractical in terms of limitations of time and processing capacity.

It is hard to react unkindly to such a seemingly reasonable view of rationality. However, it suffers from the risk of being too glib. All departures from optimality, even severe ones, can be dismissed as being reasonable enough or perhaps as serving some secondary function when properly interpreted.

The Error-Prone Intuitive Scientist

Spurred in part by the seminal work of Tversky and Kahneman (1971, 1973, 1974; Kahneman and Tversky, 1972, 1973) on apparent biases in human probability judgments arising from the use of *heuristics* (simplifying shortcuts), it has become fashionable to probe for experimental situations in which human fallibility is manifest. Slovic *et al.* (1977) review a large number of such findings, and we discuss them further in the section "Potential Constraints on Effective Decision Making."

Nisbett and Ross (1980), in a major collection and discussion of heuristics and biases, conclude that people's "attempts to understand, predict and control events in the social sphere are seriously compromised by specific inferential shortcomings" (p. 3). The human is seen as trying vaguely to be rational but as often coming up short when the situation gets subtle. This view is thus related to that of bounded rationality, but the boundedness comes not from the impracticality of spending the time and effort to make truly optimal judgments but from genuine failure to appreciate normatively appropriate strategies. Some consideration is given to possible trainability and some to the potential underlying advantages (e.g., speed and simplicity) of seemingly imperfect strategies, but in general, the picture has a pessimistic tone.

Many have been quick to criticize or disbelieve this picture. Some have seen the Nisbett and Ross emphasis on laboratory findings as compromising the ecological validity of their thesis. Cohen (1981), a philosopher, says, "Nothing in the existing literature on cognitive reasoning, or in any possible future results of human experimental inquiry, could have bleak implications for human rationality....At best, experimenters...may hope to discover revealing patterns of illusion....At worst, they risk imputing fallacies where none exist" (p. 330).

In future research increasing attention will be given to what boundaries define domains in which apparently serious errors of judgment do or do not occur. There will also continue to be controversy over what constitutes genuine error and what can be excused as really rational after all. As Kahneman and Tversky (1982b) state, following a discussion of several nonnormative phenomena, "it is often far from clear whether [these] effects . . .should be treated as errors or biases or whether they should be accepted as valid elements of human experience" (p. 173).

The Slave to Motivational Forces

The commonsense view of the major cause of irrationality, when it occurs, is that people fall into the grip of emotional or motivational forces they cannot or will not control. Emotion is commonly regarded as a disorganizer of ongoing deliberative behavior; thus the irrationality produced by emotional arousal would on this view have a diffuse and impulsive character. Complementarily, general motives, such as the enhancement of self-esteem, the management of the impression one makes on others, and the avoidance of anxiety, might produce well-organized and systematic violations of normative standards.

These observations seem straightforward enough. It is not obvious, however, how one can tell that motivational, rather than cognitive, factors lie behind judgmental errors and biases. For example, consider the phenomenon of theory-driven biased scanning of evidence, whereby estimates of the degree of covariation of events are biased in the direction of preconceived hypotheses. Is this a motivational effect or a cognitive one?

Nisbett and Ross (1980) argue that there is no need to invoke motivational explanations when information-processing mechanisms are sufficient. Other psychologists (Brehmer, 1976; Hamilton, 1979; Hammond and Brehmer, 1973) have offered cognitive explanations for phenomena long thought to be motivational in character. It is so often difficult to decide between these types of explanations, in fact, that Tetlock and Levi (1982) have argued that in certain theoretical domains it is impossible to make a critical determination favoring one or the other.

Motivated irrationality is nevertheless an intuitively appealing category. The literature of clinical psychology is, of course, replete with examples. In the analysis of motivated defects in decision making, Janis and Mann (1977) give a systematic treatment emphasizing the phenomenon of *defensive avoidance,* wherein information that could improve a decision is ignored or downplayed.

Occasional motivated irrationality could be consistent with the bounded rationality view or with the con-

cepts of error-prone intuition. It could even be consistent with the corrigible rationalist position if one believes that individuals can learn to overcome maladaptive motives. But belief in widespread, uncontrollable motivational influence constitutes a separate viewpoint.

The Butt of Faulty Normative Models

Quite a different attitude is possible. One can argue that where people do not conform to normative models, the normative models are wrong. Cohen (1981) has advanced an indeterminacy thesis, maintaining that it is always possible to construe human competence as rational, albeit for various reasons performance may be flawed. He attempts to dismiss with epistemological furbelows the concern with error-prone intuitions: "Normative theory. . .is. . .acceptable. . .only so far as it accords. . . with the evidence of untutored intuition. . . .Ordinary human reasoning. . .cannot be held to be faultily programmed: it sets its own standards" (p. 317).

Cohen does not explain whose intuition should be definitive in cases of disagreement, nor is he very convincing when arguing that statistical tutoring interferes with rationality. A further problematic aspect of his view is its subtle encouragement of indifference to empirical results. Whether or not they constitute true violations of rationality, the judgmental phenomena uncovered by Tversky and Kahneman, Nisbett and Ross, and others are interesting and consequential for theories of human judgment and decision making. Nevertheless, provocations such as Cohen's serve to prevent the field from taking standard normative models and standard experimental procedures too much for granted.

Likelihood of Resolution

As we have seen, there is a variety of views on human rationality, and often considerable heat is generated in value-laden debates about these views. Data do not seem to resolve differences between protagonists but only to sharpen the cleverness of the defense of original positions.

The argument about whether humans are rational is reminiscent of arguments such as whether humans are basically selfish or whether human nature is intrinsically aggressive. Empirical psychologists generally have had the good sense to stay away from such diffusely stated, unanswerable questions. Indeed, it is generally the case that psychologists have been more interested in detailed research on judgments and decisions than on abstract positioning on human rationality. It is usually from economics and philosophy that pressure comes to argue a general position, and psychologists cannot totally resist being drawn in. But as Abelson (1976a) put it, "Rationality. . . preempts the way we organize our views of human thought and behavior. We tend to think always in terms of default from a standard—in such-and-such a situation, why do people *not* behave rationally? But searching for the idealization that isn't there is a less productive strategy than finding out what *is* there" (p. 61). In retrospect, this critique is perhaps too strong: Departures from rationality certainly provoke attention, which may spur the research effort to find what "is there."

Of course, if the accumulated evidence massively disposed toward one or another clear conclusion—that humans are (when tooled up) strict rationalists, or bounded by limited mental resources, or rife with natural misapprehensions, or vulnerable to self-defeating motives, or rational in a manner not previously anticipated by theorists—then we would certainly want to endorse that conclusion. It seems to us clear, however, that there is a bit of truth in each position and that no definitive resolution of the argument is likely. We postpone further confrontation with general rationality issues until the section "Potential Constraints on Effective Decision Making," when a reprise is useful in light of the accumulated content of the chapter.

STRUCTURAL MODELS

There are two major categories of decision models: structural and process. *Structural models* are concerned with describing the relationship between stimulus and response or between input and output. *Process models,* in contrast, focus on the transformation process that occurs between the stimulus and response.

Structural models can be partitioned into two main types, according to whether they deal explicitly with probabilistic outcomes. In the first type of model probability and risk are not a primary consideration in the judgment of alternatives (e.g., the interpretation of MMPI profiles or the judgment of nutritional benefits of breakfast cereals). The second type of model deals with choice among risky options, and there is an emphasis on explicit representation of individuals' subjective probabilities. The different research approaches and tasks that characterize these two types of models reflect the models' disparate origins. The investigation of decision making under risk has its roots in economics (e.g.,

von Neumann and Morgenstern, 1947), whereas the study of judgment has its ancestry in psychophysical measurement and the psychological theorizing of Egon Brunswik (1943, 1955; Hammond, 1966), which emphasizes issues of perceptual judgment and accuracy.

MODELS OF RISKLESS DECISIONS

Individuals are constantly faced with the need to make judgments—to combine information from a variety of sources into a global evaluation. Structural models attempt to describe mathematically how individuals make such judgments. The domain of structural models thus includes cognitive operations that fall under the rubric of "deliberative processes"—the integrating, weighing, balancing, and combining of information (Slovic and Lichtenstein, 1971).

There is a question, however, of whether such deliberative processes are synonymous with choice. Does knowing an individual's evaluation of an object necessarily enable us to predict whether he or she will choose that object when given the opportunity? Researchers have generally assumed the essential equivalence of judgment and choice. Slovic and Lichtenstein (1971), for example, in their comprehensive review of research on information processing in judgment, stated that the "distinction between judgments and decisions is a tenuous one [that] will not be maintained here; we shall use these terms interchangeably" (p. 652). Hammond, McClelland, and Mumpower (1980) also noted decision theorist Zeleny's (1976) assertion that it is misleading to maintain the distinction between judgment and decision making, since both represent a process of making a choice among several alternatives (Wallsten, 1980). In addition, normative decision models treat judgment and choice as equivalent: An individual will select an alternative if and only if it is evaluated more highly than other alternatives.

Nevertheless, the presumed equivalence between judgment and choice can be questioned. Not only does making a choice imply greater commitment and conflict than does making a judgment; it also tends to bring responsibility and regret strongly into consideration. These factors may cause the decision maker to ignore his or her previous judgment when the choice point arrives. Thus judgment is neither necessary nor sufficient for choice, a point highlighted by the common expression "choosing in spite of one's better judgment" (Einhorn and Hogarth, 1981).

The upshot is simply that structural models of judgment pertain to *judgment* and not necessarily to choice *behavior*. Though it is a plausible assumption that there will generally be a close connection between judgment and choice, in some situations the connection will be much looser. Thus we are dealing here less with descriptions of decision behavior than with descriptions of the cognitive operations that may underlie and precede behavior.

Approaches to the Study of Judgment

There are several approaches to the study of judgment, each with its own characteristic assumptions, concepts, and methods. Hammond *et al.* (1980) proposed a descriptive framework that includes six approaches: decision theory, behavioral decision theory, psychological decision theory, social judgment theory, information integration theory, and attribution theory. These approaches are listed in an order that corresponds roughly to their degree of economic, as opposed to psychological, orientation. The first three—decision theory, behavioral decision theory, and psychological decision theory—in their primary concern with the concepts of probability and utility, evince the influence and orientation of economics. Decision theory, as exemplified in the work of Keeney and Raiffa (1976), is largely normative; it formulates decision problems in terms of probabilities and utilities and prescribes how decision makers *should* make decisions. Behavioral decision theory (Edwards, 1954, 1961; Slovic *et al.*, 1977) is concerned primarily with describing the *departures* of individuals' judgments and choices from normative decision theory and with explaining how task and psychological conditions give rise to such departures. Psychological decision theory, exemplified in the work of Tversky and Kahneman (1974; Kahneman and Tversky, 1979), also aims to explain departures from normative decision theory, but in addition, it provides a cognitive account of judgment to replace the normative emphasis of behavioral decision theory. These three approaches are generally, though not always, applied to the domain of risky choice.

The other three approaches—social judgment theory, information integration theory, and attribution theory—differ from the previous three in a number of ways. First, they have their origins in psychology rather than in economics. Second, they do not consider probability and utility as the fundamental theoretical concepts in judgment or choice behavior. Third, they are less concerned with comparing individuals' judgments against those specified by normative models; instead, judgments are typically investigated and modeled on their own terms.

Of these three approaches, social judgment theory and information integration theory have provided the bulk of quantitative structural models most directly relevant to judgment and choice. Attribution theory, which has given rise to a largely autonomous strand of research, has been less closely integrated with research into decision making (Fischhoff, 1976). Accordingly, we shall briefly describe the distinguishing features only of social judgment theory and information integration theory.

Social judgment theory. Social judgment theory (Hammond *et al.*, 1975) is rooted in Brunswik's (1955) theory of *probabilistic functionalism,* which attempts to describe how organisms adjust to a probabilistic, ambiguous environment. In order to so adjust, the organism must draw correct inferences from observable data, or *cues.* In particular, the organism must correctly judge the relation between observable, or *proximal,* cues (e.g., the type of clouds in the sky) and unobservable, or *distal,* criteria (e.g., likelihood of rain). This can be a difficult task, since the relations between proximal cues and distal criteria may assume various forms (e.g., linear, curvilinear). In addition, proximal cues are related not only to criteria but to each other as well. Such interdependence among cues, or *cue redundancy,* may make it difficult for the organism to know which cues are in fact crucial for inferring or predicting the criterion of interest. Consequently, one important research area within social judgment theory, *multiple-cue probability learning* (Brehmer and Slovic, 1980), is concerned with the individual's use of feedback to learn the relationship among cues and criteria in the environment.

Brunswik viewed judgment in terms of the relationship between organismic and environmental systems. His *lens model* (see Brunswik, 1956; Dudycha and Naylor, 1966; Hammond, 1966; Hammond *et al.*, 1980; Hoffman, Slovic, and Rorer, 1968; Hursch, Hammond, and Hursch, 1964; Petrinovich, 1979; Slovic and Lichtenstein, 1971) represents these two systems symmetrically, the environmental or task system on one side and the organismic or subjective system on the other. Parallel concepts are applied to both. Thus *ecological validity,* the true relation of environmental cues to the criterion, parallels *cue utilization,* the relation of environmental cues to the subject's judgment or inference. *Ecological function forms,* whether the cues relate linearly or nonlinearly to the criterion, parallel *subjective function forms,* whether the cues relate linearly or nonlinearly to the subject's judgment. In addition, social judgment theory is concerned with *cognitive control,* the subject's ability to apply a judgment policy consistently and without error (Hammond and Summers, 1972). The key link between the two systems, and the key measure of interest to the researcher, is the subject's *achievement,* which represents the degree of match between the statistical properties of the environmental system and those of the subjective system. A variety of statistical measures have been developed to operationalize the concepts of ecological validity, cue utilization, cognitive control, and achievement (see Castellan, 1973; Dudycha and Naylor, 1966; Hammond, Hursch, and Todd, 1964; Hammond *et al.,* 1980; Hursch *et al.,* 1964; Petrinovich, 1979; Stenson, 1974; Tucker, 1964).

In keeping with Brunswikian tradition, social judgment theory emphasizes the strong influence of the environmental system on human judgment. Researchers working within this approach thus advocate what Brunswik called "representative design." Individuals are presented with tasks representative of those that occur in everyday experience. Most experimental tasks require the subject to respond to sets of schematic descriptions of objects on a variety of dimensions or cues. These descriptions are typically presented in numerical form, with cue properties such as means, ranges, and intercorrelations constructed or selected to reflect natural environmental variation (e.g., Hammond *et al.,* 1977). Multiple regression is then used to model subjects' "judgment policies" and measure their achievement or optimality in the task.

Information integration theory. Information integration theory (Anderson, 1970, 1974a, 1974b), like social judgment theory, aims to describe human judgment in mathematical terms. There are two aspects to this attempt: (1) identifying the combination rules that individuals use to make their judgments and (2) scaling the stimulus items and determining their subjective values. Algebraic models characterized by one or another operation (e.g., adding, subtracting, averaging, or multiplying) are tested for goodness of fit to subjects' judgments, generally within an analysis of variance framework. The presence or absence of interactions and the form of the interactions indicate which algebraic model is most appropriate.

The information integration theory approach differs from the social judgment theory approach in three major ways. First, whereas social judgment theory researchers typically analyze individuals' responses to the objective cue values presented in the task, informa-

tion integration theory researchers attempt to discover individuals' *subjective* scale values for the cues and determine combination rules based on these subjective values. Information integration theory does not assume a linear relation between objective and subjective scale values of cues. For example, in a judgment task requiring ratings of accident severity, it is likely that the subjective difference between $1 and $2 million in property damage will be greater than that between $11 and $12 million in damage. In this case dollar amount of property damage is perceived nonlinearly.

The second difference is that information integration theory lacks social judgment theory's emphasis on task realism and representative design. This is a consequence of information integration theory's primary goal, which is to test the goodness of fit of various algebraic models. To accomplish this, information integration theory relies almost exclusively on factorial designs, in which each subject or group of subjects judges each possible combination of cue levels. Because they force otherwise correlated dimensions to be orthogonal, factorial designs tend to produce rather artificial tasks. For example, in a study involving the judgment of graduate school applicants, subjects might be required to judge incongruous cue combinations such as low grade point average and low Graduate Record Examination scores in conjunction with enthusiastic letters of recommendation. This type of incongruous cue combination would probably not occur in a social judgment theory task, in which the naturally occurring cue interdependencies would be maintained.

The third main difference is in the relative importance attached to assessing the optimality of subjects' judgments. As the lens model notion of achievement suggests, social judgment theory emphasizes comparison between the environmental and the subjective systems. In social judgment theory both task characteristics (e.g., ecological validity of cues) and task outcomes (i.e., subjects' judgments) are known, enabling one to assess the accuracy or optimality of judgments. In information integration theory, however, task characteristics are of less concern. In fact, in most information integration theory research there is no environmental criterion or optimal judgment against which subjects' judgments can be assessed.

Linear Models

A tremendous amount of research has been devoted to the topic of *linear models* and human judgment. Linear models have been applied to extremely diverse types of judgment tasks, involving personality assessment (e.g., Hammond *et al.,* 1964), managerial decisions (e.g., Hamner and Carter, 1975; McCann, Miller, and Moskowitz, 1975; Moskowitz, 1974), MMPI profiles (e.g., Einhorn, Kleinmuntz, and Kleinmuntz, 1979; Goldberg, 1968, 1970; Wiggins and Hoffman, 1968), graduate school applicants (e.g., Dawes, 1971, 1979), auditing and accounting (e.g., Ashton, 1974), medical diagnosis (e.g., Elstein *et al.,* 1978; Hoffman *et al.,* 1968), stockbrokers' decisions (Slovic, 1969), judicial decisions (e.g., Kort, 1968), performance appraisal and promotion (e.g., Marques, Lane, and Dorfman, 1979; Naylor and Wherry, 1965; Zedeck and Kafry, 1977), livestock (Phelps and Shanteau, 1978), and poker hands (Lopes, 1976). In addition to the large amount of empirical work using linear models, a number of theoretical and methodological developments have attracted the attention of researchers.

One reason for the prominent role of linear models in judgment research is that they are simple. They consist of two types of elements, component variables and weights. A *component variable* is an informational item, or attribute, that is combined with other attributes to form a composite (e.g., a global judgment). A *weight* is a measure of the importance of a component variable. To obtain a composite, one merely multiplies each component by its appropriate weight and adds the products.

Linear models have been put to a variety of uses: to aid the decision maker to represent, or "capture," the decision maker's judgment policy, to serve as a point of comparison for the decision maker's judgments, and to "bootstrap," or replace, the decision maker with his or her own policy representation (Dawes and Corrigan, 1974).

Policy capturing. It is intuitively plausible that individuals rely more heavily on some attributes than on others when making judgments about an object. Linear models can be constructed to reflect the differential weights a judge attaches to various cues. Modeling a judge's policy of cue utilization is most often accomplished through multiple regression analysis.

In this approach the judge makes quantitative evaluations of a number of stimuli, each of which is defined by a different pattern of quantified component variables or cue dimensions (Slovic and Lichtenstein, 1971). For example, in a task involving the evaluation of graduate school applicants, one applicant might be described as having high values on the three cue dimensions of grade point average, Graduate Record Examination score, and quality of letters of recommendation. A second applicant might be described as moderate, moderate, and high on the same dimensions, respectively; and so on. Given a sufficient number of stimuli evaluated by an individual judge, a regression analysis can be performed in which the $k = 1$ to n cue dimensions are treated as predictor variables and the judge's evaluations are treated as the dependent, or criterion, variable Y. The resulting regression equation represents the policy of the judge:

$$Y = b_1X_1 + b_2X_2 + \ldots + b_nX_n,$$

where Y is the best prediction the equation can make of the judge's evaluation, given the values $X_1, X_2, \ldots, X_n$ on the respective cue dimensions; and $b_1, b_2, \ldots, b_n$ are the weights (i.e., the regression slopes) given to the cue dimensions in order to maximize the multiple correlation between the predicted and actual evaluations. These weights are assumed to reflect the relative influence of the cue dimensions on the judge's evaluations.

The regression approach to policy capturing is exemplified by a study of nurses' evaluations of effective job performance (Zedeck and Kafry, 1977). Judges evaluated each of forty hypothetical nurses on a seven-point scale of overall effectiveness. Each of the hypothetical nurses was behaviorally described in terms of nine specific skill and performance dimensions (e.g., ability to assess the client's physical and emotional problems; interviewing skills; ability to make appropriate recommendations).

Regression analyses were performed separately on each nurse's evaluations of the forty profiles. The results were fairly representative of policy-capturing studies in general. First, most of the predictable variance in evaluation was accounted for by four or fewer dimensions. Second, the squared multiple correlation R^2, indicating the consistency of evaluation across the forty descriptions, was statistically significant for all the judges but varied widely, from .90 to .20. Third, there were large individual differences in the weights accorded the nine dimensions.

Paramorphic representation. Can the results of policy-capturing studies such as that of Zedeck and Kafry (1977) be taken at face value? Are judgment policies actually "captured" by linear regression models? There are two issues here: Do judgment processes take place in a linear, additive fashion? And do the cue weights derived from regression analyses in fact represent the true importance of those cues in subjects' judgments?

With regard to the first issue, substantial individual R^2's (such as those obtained by Zedeck and Kafry, 1977) show that linear regressions can predict judgments to a reasonably high degree. Good predictive accuracy, however, does not necessarily imply that actual judgment processes have been captured. Hoffman (1960; cf. Einhorn, 1971; Yntema and Torgerson, 1961) suggested that linear models provide simulations, or *paramorphic representations,* of judgments; they do not mirror the actual psychological processes involved in judgment.

More recently, however, Einhorn *et al.* (1979) claimed that linear regression models may do more than merely simulate judgment. The widespread success of linear models in predicting judgments "suggests that some fundamental characteristic of judgment has been captured" (p. 468). They point out several ways in which linear models may do this. First, the linear model's additive combination function implies a fully compensatory system in which cues can be traded off against each other. Second, the degree to which trade-offs occur depends on the specific judgmental environment; the beta weights are determined by considering all of the cues and their particular levels in the situation. Third, cue redundancy—which commonly occurs in the natural environment—is incorporated in the model, since the beta weights depend on the correlational structure of the cues. Fourth, linear regression models explicitly define and measure the random error in judgment that comes from the inability of individuals to apply consistently their knowledge of strategy.

Einhorn *et al.* (1979) acknowledge that these apparent congruities between human judgment processes and linear-regression models do not establish that individuals use additive, compensatory processes all or even most of the time. There are situations in which judgment involves nonlinear, noncompensatory processes (e.g., Einhorn, 1971). In such situations, however, linear models may still provide excellent predictions of individuals' judgments. This robustness of linear models (discussed more fully later in this section) implies that in the absence of independent evidence concerning decision processing (e.g., "process tracing"), one cannot draw firm conclusions about psychological processes on the basis of regression analysis alone.

Whether the regression cue weights reflect the actual influence of those cues in the judgment process involves two statistical considerations: (1) the index that is used as a measure of cue weight and (2) the degree to which the cue dimensions in the task are correlated.

There are several statistical indexes of cue weight, including (1) the simple correlation between a cue and the judgment, (2) the semipartial correlation (removing the effects of all other cues), (3) the standardized regression coefficient associated with a cue, and (4) the raw-score regression weights (cf. Darlington, 1968; Lane, Murphy, and Marques, 1982). When cue dimensions are uncorrelated, these indexes are equivalent; they lead to the same conclusion regarding the absolute and relative importance of cues in producing the subject's judgment. However, when cue dimensions are correlated, the indexes can differ substantially from each other in the cue weights they indicate, and even in their rank ordering of cue importance (Schmitt and Levine, 1977; Ward, 1962). In addition, intercorrelations among cue dimensions can lead to indeterminacy in estimating cue weights (Darlington, 1968).

These considerations are troublesome because they challenge the ability of regression analysis to determine an objective, "correct" set of weights that captures an individual's cue utilization policy. Also, they undermine the validity of some of the practical applications of policy capturing, most notably the use of statistically derived cue weights as feedback to judges to enhance their learning of judgment tasks (e.g., Adelman, Stewart, and Hammond, 1975; Balke, Hammond, and Meyer, 1973; Brady and Rappoport, 1973; Hammond and Brehmer, 1973). If cue weights are indeterminate, or if different indexes of cue weights provide different rank orderings of cues, it becomes difficult to know which set of cue weights should be fed back to represent the judge's true policy.

One possible resolution to the problem of disagreement among different cue-importance indexes is to avoid using judgment tasks in which the cues are correlated (e.g., Phelps and Shanteau, 1978; Schenk and Naylor, 1968). The problem of deciding which index to use is thereby avoided, since all will produce equivalent results. The difficulty with this research strategy, however, is that it makes it difficult to investigate judgment in ecologically representative tasks, in which cue dimensions are typically correlated.

Another possible resolution is to determine which index best measures the actual causal influence of cues on subjects' judgments. This tack was taken by Lane *et al.* (1982). They argued that raw-score regression weights provide the most appropriate measure of cue importance, because by representing the average change in the criterion (i.e., the individual's judgment) per unit change in the predictor, they indicate directly the causal influence of the predictor on the judgment.

Lane *et al.* compared the stability of raw-score weights, standardized regression weights, simple correlations, and semipartial correlations across three cue structures. Raters evaluated the suitability of hypothetical job applicants on the basis of quantified measures of intelligence, motivation, and job experience. The applicant profiles were derived from three cue structures that differed in the magnitude and direction of cue intercorrelations. When raters' policies were captured and the different indexes of cue importance were compared across cue structures, only the raw-score regression weights remained constant; the other indexes changed dramatically. This stability of raw-score weights suggests that they may be superior to other available indexes as indicators of the relative importance of cues in determining judgments.

What can be concluded, then, about the relation between linear regression models of judgment and the actual psychological processes involved in judgment? With regard to the manner in which information is aggregated, linear regression models do appear to provide a good fit to the data whether or not the judge is literally processing information in an additive, linear fashion. With regard to cue weights, linear regression models appear capable of accurately mirroring the degree to which individuals are relying on various items of information to form their global judgments. Whether individuals' reports of their cue utilization policies match those determined by regression equations is another question.

Relation between objective and subjective weights. Researchers have investigated the relation between the objective cue weights determined by linear regression models and the subjective cue weights individuals state they are using in a judgment task. Correspondence between the two is generally interpreted as an indication of the judge's insight into his or her own cue utilization policy.

The most commonly used method for obtaining subjective weights is to ask the judge to distribute 100 points in proportion to the relative importance of each cue dimension (e.g., Cook and Stewart, 1975; Hoffman, 1960; Slovic, Fleissner, and Bauman, 1972; Summers, Taliaferro, and Fletcher, 1970; Wright, 1979; Zedeck and Kafry, 1977). The judge distributes the points after do-

ing the judgment task. A variety of methods are available for comparing objective and subjective weights. For example, one may calculate correlations between objective and subjective weights, multiple correlations with the judgment for both sets of weights, and the variability of weights across individuals within both sets.

In general, discrepancies between objective and subjective weights have been found. Judges tend to overestimate the importance they place on minor cues and underestimate their reliance on a few major cues (e.g., Feldman and Arnold, 1978; Slovic and Lichtenstein, 1971; Zedeck and Kafry, 1977). Judges also tend to overestimate the number of cues that affect their judgment relative to the number indicated by the objective weights. In addition, the correlations between objective and subjective weights are usually rather low. In a study of stockbrokers' judgments, for example, Slovic *et al.* (1972) reported a correlation of only .34. However, when compared with objective weights in terms of the amount of variance accounted for, subjective weights perform reasonably well. Cook and Stewart (1975) found subjective weights to account for 80 percent and 93 percent of the systematic linear variance in a financial aid and a graduate admissions judgment task, respectively.

These discrepancies have stimulated a number of psychological process explanations. The overweighting of minor cues and the underweighting of important ones may occur because the judge is relying on recall to estimate his or her cue weights. Recalling having attended to each of the cues, the judge may conclude that most or all of them influenced the global judgment to some extent. Einhorn *et al.* (1979) pointed out a similar possibility: An individual may attend closely to a cue and therefore feel that it is an important influence, when in fact the cue has little variance and thus does not receive a significant weight in the regression equation. Finally, it is possible that individuals' subjective weights are based more on "implicit theories" (Nisbett and Wilson, 1977b) of what cues should be influential than on introspective insight into actual cue use.

Clinical versus statistical judgment. In many judgment tasks (e.g., rating preference for different brands of a consumer good), there is no objective criterion against which to evaluate the subject's judgment. Other tasks, however, do have objective criteria. The task of rating the severity of a disease as indicated by patients' biopsies, for example, contains the criterion of patients' survival time. Judges' predictions can be tested against this criterion. In terms of Brunswik's lens model, criterionless judgment tasks involve only the subjective system, whereas tasks with a criterion involve both subjective and environmental systems.

When an objective criterion exists, one may investigate humans' accuracy at combining information to make evaluations, diagnoses, and predictions. How good are human judgments compared with those made on a statistical or actuarial basis? These questions are the central focus of the clinical versus statistical controversy, launched with the publication of Meehl's (1954) monograph. Meehl reviewed about twenty studies in which actuarial methods were pitted against judgments of the clinician. In all cases the actuarial method either won or tied the contest.

In a typical clinical versus statistical contest, the same coded input data are given to a human judge and to a computer program. The goal is to make accurate predictions concerning an objective criterion (Wiggins, 1973). In nearly all such studies the computer program uses multiple regression to weight the cues so that the correlation between prediction and criterion is maximized. The predictive accuracy of the linear regression model is then compared with that of the human judge.

A representative study of this type, involving interpretation of polygraph protocols obtained from thirty students, was conducted by Szucko and Kleinmuntz (1981). Fifteen of these students, at the researchers' prompting, had been involved in the "theft" of a $5 bill; the other fifteen were "clean." The former group was instructed to try to deceive the polygraph examiner, the latter group to be truthful. The physiological data from the examination were then submitted to six experienced polygraph judges, who were instructed to arrive at independent judgments of each protocol, ranging from "truthful" to "untruthful" on an eight-point scale. The judges knew that half of the subjects had stolen something.

Statistical analyses of the combined physiological cues (galvanic skin response, blood pressure, abdominal and thoracic respiration) indicated that significant discrimination between the truthful and untruthful groups was possible. Judges' ratings of the polygraph data were then analyzed according to a lens model equation (Tucker, 1964), which yields measures of judgment accuracy and consistency. Of the six judges four had validity coefficients (i.e., correlations between judgments and the criterion) that differed significantly from zero, indicating an ability to differentiate between the protocols of theft and no-theft subjects. Two judges, however, performed at no better than chance level in differentiating the two sets of protocols. A simple linear combination of cues outperformed all the judges without exception. The validity coefficient of this linear combination was .52, in comparison with that of the most accurate judge, .43.

One major reason for the judges' relatively poor performance is that their *cognitive control,* or ability to apply cue weights consistently, was poor. That is, judges were generally aware of which physiological cues were important but were unable to use this knowledge optimally. Interestingly, amount of previous experience with the judgment task was unrelated to cognitive control.

Results such as these are fairly typical. The superiority of statistical over clinical judgment has been upheld in a large number of studies (e.g., Dawes, 1971, 1979; Dawes and Corrigan, 1974; Einhorn, 1972; Goldberg, 1965; Kleinmuntz, 1967, 1975; Meehl, 1957; Sawyer, 1966; Wiggins, 1973) and across a wide range of judgment tasks, including success in academia, parole violation, medical diagnosis, and job satisfaction.

As Dawes (1971) pointed out, it should not be surprising that actuarial methods are superior to clinical judgment. Since it is always possible in principle to devise an actuarial method that simulates the clinician's judgment, there will necessarily be at least one method that performs as well as the clinician and possibly others that will perform even better. The important point, however, is that humans can be outperformed by very simple models with linear combinations of cues but no nonlinear terms such as powers and cross products.

There are a number of reasons for the strong performance of linear models (Dawes and Corrigan, 1974). First, linear models have been investigated in tasks in which each cue has a *conditionally monotone* relationship to the criterion such that higher values on each cue predict higher values on the criterion, regardless of the values of the other cues. For example, consider graduate student applicants' scores on grade point average, Graduate Record Examination, and quality of letters of recommendation. The higher the score on any one of these variables, the more likely it is that the student will be successful in graduate school. Linear models provide good approximations to all multivariate models that are conditionally monotone in each cue. Second, the relative weights determined by regression analysis are not affected by error in the criterion variable. Third, error in the measurement of the cues tends to make optimal functions more linear. The more error, the better "true" nonlinear relationships can be approximated by linear functions. Linear models perform well, then, because they are investigated in tasks with conditional monotonicity and in which there is much error.

Bootstrapping.   In a comparison of clinical with statistical judgment, individuals' predictions or evaluations are tested against the *best possible* linear model. Such models, in which the cue weights are chosen to optimize the relationship between the prediction and the criterion, are called *proper linear models* (Dawes, 1979). In order to construct a proper linear model through regression analysis, one must have a sample size large enough (a ratio of fifteen or twenty observations to each predictor variable) (Claudy, 1972; Einhorn and Hogarth, 1975; Goldberg, 1972) so that stable estimates of cue weights can be obtained. It is also necessary to have a measurable criterion variable. When these conditions are not met, proper linear models cannot be derived. It is possible, however, to construct *improper linear models,* in which weights are obtained by some nonoptimal method.

Bootstrapping is one often-used method of obtaining cue weights to construct an improper linear model. In bootstrapping, a judge's policy is captured and the obtained cue weights are then substituted for the judge (Goldberg, 1970). Because the weights are not derived from the relationship between the cues and the criterion variables themselves, the resulting linear model is improper.

A great deal of evidence indicates that bootstrapping models perform as well as or better than the individuals from whom they were derived (e.g., Ashton, 1975; Dawes, 1971; Goldberg, 1970; Kunreuther, 1969; Wiggins and Kohen, 1971). More specifically, the correlation between the model's output and the criterion exceeds the correlation between the individual's judgment and the criterion. Wiggins and Kohen (1971), for example, asked 98 psychology graduate students to predict first-year grade point average for 110 other graduate students on the basis of variables such as Graduate Record Examination scores, sex, and personality ratings. The linear model of every one of these judges was more accurate than were the judges themselves in predicting actual grade point average. Moreover, superior accuracy was maintained even when the model was based on a small subset of cases and cross-validated on the remaining cases.

Bowman (1963), Goldberg (1970), and Dawes (1971) all suggested that bootstrapping models work because

they capture the judge's weighting policy and apply it consistently. Assuming that the policy has some validity, filtering out the error by applying the model will increase accuracy. Thus linear models derived through bootstrapping "distill" underlying policy from variable, error-prone judgments. Bootstrapping models are thus most useful in judgment situations in which environmental cue structures are unknown or criterion information is vague (Camerer, 1981).

There are other cue-weighting methods for constructing improper linear models, however, that can be used when criterion information is vague. These methods exhibit some surprising characteristics.

Other weighting schemes.   Proper linear models and bootstrapping require the calculation of differential weights. It is plausible to assume that such weighting allows linear models to outperform human judges—in the case of proper linear models because the weights reflect the true relationship between cues and criterion; in the case of bootstrapping because they reflect the judge's valid expertise while eliminating error.

Dawes and Corrigan (1974) cast doubt on this assumption by demonstrating that the establishment of differential weights is unnecessary; linear models still perform quite well even when very simple weighting schemes are used. For instance, random linear models, with weights randomly chosen except for sign and then applied to standardized variables, performed about as well as bootstrapping models. Equal-weighting models performed even better. These results, which held true across five data sets, suggest that improper linear models are remarkably robust over deviations from optimal weighting. Provided the signs of the relationships between cues and criterion are known, Dawes and Corrigan (1974) concluded, "The whole trick is to decide what variables to look at and then to know how to add" (p. 105).

This provocative conclusion, and subsequent studies showing that the outputs of linear models are relatively insensitive to changes in cue weights (e.g., Wainer, 1976; Wainer and Thissen, 1976), stimulated much research attention. A number of studies focused on the conditions under which equal weights produce good predictive accuracy. Wainer (1976) stated that two conditions are necessary for equal weights to work well: All cues should be monotonically related to the criterion, and cues should be positively intercorrelated. Einhorn and Hogarth (1975) examined analytically the predictive ability of equal versus regression weights as a function of sample size, number of predictors, intercorrelations among cues, and definitional clarity of criterion. Across most of their experimental combinations equal weighting produced optimal or near-optimal predictions. Einhorn and Hogarth suggested that equal weights are especially appropriate to use when the sample size is small and the predictors are highly intercorrelated. Newman (1977) found that in situations having no well-defined criterion variable, equal weights performed as well as differential weights (cf. Cattin, 1978). Since these conditions are quite typical, equal weighting may be an efficient way of representing judgment.

There appear to be two conditions, however, under which equal weights will be inferior to differential weights: (1) when the cues are negatively intercorrelated (Newman, 1977; Stillwell, Seaver, and Edwards, 1981) and (2) when suppressor variables (i.e., variables that by their inclusion increase the predictive validity of other variables in a regression equation) (Conger, 1974) are present (Keren and Newman, 1978). The first of these conditions is likely to occur primarily in choice tasks in which all clearly inferior alternatives have been eliminated from consideration by an initial screening phase (Dawes, 1975a; Stillwell *et al.*, 1981). In contrast, most judgment or prediction tasks will exhibit positive cue intercorrelations.

Although researchers have focused mainly on equal weights, other weighting schemes have been proposed. Some of them differ from statistical approaches such as multiple regression in that they require subjects to rate the cue dimensions of a stimulus separately instead of responding to a holistic stimulus with a single judgment. For example, multiattribute utility measurement (MAUM) (Edwards, 1971, 1977b, 1980; Huber, 1974; Keeney and Raiffa, 1976) involves the decomposition of an object into its component attributes, the determination of the utility of each attribute, and the mechanical combination of the utilities into a composite or total utility. The MAUM system yields weights that have ratio properties. Rank-order weights (e.g., Einhorn and McCoach, 1977; Stillwell *et al.*, 1981), which have ordinal properties, also require decomposition of the stimulus.

A study by Schoemaker and Waid (1982) experimentally compared five different weighting schemes in a task involving evaluation of college applicants. These five methods were (1) MAUM, (2) pairwise comparison of attributes as developed in "analytic hierarchy theory" (Saaty, 1977), (3) multiple regression, (4) direct allocation of important points, and (5) equal weighting.

Predictive performance was assessed by examining how well the model predicted the subjects' ordinal and interval preferences in the task.

The five methods yielded significantly different weight estimates. Moreover, the differences in weights did matter statistically in predicting subjects' preferences. The MAUM, multiple regression, and direct allocation methods performed the best, and the analytic hierarchy theory and equal-weights methods performed the worst. As Schoemaker and Waid point out, however, these results are suggestive but not conclusive. More comparative tests are necessary to determine the predictive accuracy of different weighting schemes across types of subjects and tasks.

MODELS OF RISKY DECISIONS

Research on the structure of risky decisions has concentrated on the testing of particular formal models. Generally, subjects are presented with decisions between simple gambles with specified gains or losses and levels of risk. There has been a historical evolution of models, starting with the simplest, requiring sums of products of objective probabilities and values. However, the search for neat models for simple decisions has encountered a series of instructive difficulties, necessitating ever more refined models.

Expected-Value and Utility Models

The expected-value principle. Consider the option of buying a lottery ticket offering one chance in a thousand of winning a $5000 prize. What is the "fair" price to pay for such a ticket? A seemingly straightforward, objective answer to this question is provided by the mathematically expected value of the ticket: the probability that it will be a winner, multiplied by the prize to be won. In the simple case given the expected value would be $(1/1000) \times$ $5000, or $5. The sense in which $5 is a "fair" price requires a hypothetically unlimited repetition of offers of the same lottery. On the average the lottery would pay off once in every thousand offers, and each thousand outlays of the fair $5 would balance the $5000 prize for the win.

The simplest theory of decision making is based on the notion of expected monetary values. Imagine multiple possible prizes (or penalties), each with a particular probability of occurrence. Suppose that a risky option involves k possible monetary outcomes. If we denote the gain (loss) associated with the ith outcome by x_i and the probability of its occurrence by p_i, the expected value of the gamble is

$$V = \sum_i p_i \cdot x_i. \tag{1}$$

This formula, of course, covers the previous simple example, where 1 chance in 1000 (p_1) of winning $5000 ($x_1$) and 999 chances in 1000 (p_2) of winning nothing (x_2) yields

$$V = (.001)(5000) + (.999)(0) = 5.$$

Equation (1) allows the statement of a choice principle: Given a choice between an option with expected value V_1 and an option with expected value V_2, the individual will pick the option with the higher expected value. If $V_1 = V_2$, the individual will be indifferent between the options. This *expected-value principle* could be applied to our simple lottery example by posing the question "Which would you rather have: five dollars or a lottery ticket with one chance in a thousand of winning five thousand dollars?" The ticket has expected value of $5, and the $5 in hand also has "expected value" of $5. [The latter tautological statement is consistent with Eq. (1), defining a single outcome with $p = 1$ and $x = 5$.] Thus an individual following the expected-value principle would be indifferent between the ticket and the money in hand but would prefer the ticket to $4 in hand and would reject the ticket in favor of $6 in hand.

The expected-value principle has long been recognized as predictively inadequate. The history of this recognition goes back before Bernoulli (1738), who tried to resolve the "St. Petersburg paradox" (see the historical review by Samuelson, 1977). That paradox involves a game in which a true coin is tossed until it falls heads; if this occurs at the ith throw, the player receives 2^i dollars. The player thus has probability ½ of winning $2, probability ¼ of winning $4, probability ⅛ of winning $8, and so on. The sum of cross products of probabilities and rewards according to Eq. (1) is $1 + 1 + 1 + \ldots$, carrying on for an infinite number of terms, for an expected value of infinity. The "fair" price for the privilege of playing this game thus seems to be infinite; but this strikes one as a manifestly absurd conclusion, and it seems unthinkable that any human player would account infinity the fair price.

Two centuries after Bernoulli, probability theorists (e.g., Feller, 1950) have argued that expected value is an undefined quantity when variance of outcome is infinite, as it is in the St. Petersburg game. Others (e.g., Shapley, 1977) have noted that since, in practice, the house offer-

ing the game could not guarantee paying off beyond its total available assets, the game is unimaginable except in "truncated" form. In this form expectation (and variance) of outcome is finite, there is a reasonable fair price, and the paradox disappears. These arguments seem not to have been universally acknowledged, however, and the game continues to be cited as problematic (e.g., Lopes, 1981).

The expected-utility principle.   Bernoulli took another tack. He held that the psychological value of money does not increase proportionately as its objective amount increases. He suggested a logarithmic function relating the utility u of money to its amount x; such a function manifests *concavity,* or decreasing marginal utility—repeated constant additions to the monetary amount have less and less increased utility to the receiver. He then proposed that it is not the objectively expected value that matters in assessing a risky option but the *expected utility,* given by

$$V = \sum_i p_i \cdot u(x_i). \tag{2}$$

As before, p_i is the probability of outcome i, but $u(x_i)$ is now the utility of outcome i, some function (perhaps logarithmic) of the monetary value x_i.

The *expected-utility principle* says that preferences between options accord with their relative expected utilities. One does not need gambles as exotic as the St. Petersburg game to show that the expected-utility principle seems more plausible than the expected-value principle. A robust simple demonstration is the choice between a 50–50 chance to win $x or nothing and to win $y for sure, where y is half of x, or slightly less. There is a very common tendency to prefer the sure thing. Among the many studies yielding this result, Hershey and Schoemaker (1980b), for example, find that almost three-quarters of their subjects would opt for a guaranteed $5000 in preference to a 50–50 gamble on $10,000 or nothing. Indeed, this type of preference was intuited by Bernoulli (1738) himself, with the rhetorical parable of a pauper who happens to acquire a lottery ticket by which he may with equal probability win either nothing or 20,000 ducats. Will he have to evaluate the worth of the ticket as 10,000 ducats, asks Bernoulli, and would he be acting foolishly, if he sold it for 9,000 ducats?

Thus the expected-utility principle might seem better motivated than the expected-value principle, given a concave utility function. However, the expected-utility principle, in turn, has run into a variety of troubles. It is a problem for the expected-utility principle to explain why gambling should be popular. Bets with small probabilities to win big money (lotteries, roulette wheels, etc.) ought to be especially unattractive, given that a concave utility function drives the worth of a large prize considerably lower than the value warranting the very small probability of obtaining it.

In the laboratory it is difficult to try to construct an individual's utility function; thus searches for possible violations of the expected-utility formulation have been indirect, based on the way it implies certain consistencies between related bets. One set of consistencies involves the *sure-thing principle*: If option A is preferred to option C, then A should be preferred also to any lottery B, that offers some probability of A, but otherwise C. In turn, this lottery B should be preferred to C. This principle has been used along with other axioms to derive the presumed logical necessity of the expected-utility principle (von Neumann and Morgenstern, 1947) without reference to the long-run repetition of gambles (Coombs, Dawes, and Tversky, 1970, p. 126). Nevertheless, violations of the sure-thing or closely related principles have been found, thereby challenging the expected-utility formulation (Becker *et al.*, 1963; Coombs and Huang, 1974; the summary in Schoemaker, 1980, Ch. 2).

The most classic of these challenging examples stems from Allais (1953). The *Allais paradox* and its variants have been adapted and much extended by Kahneman and Tversky (1979b). A single, simple example from the latter authors is the following: One group of subjects was asked to choose between options A and B, where A was $4000 with probability .8, otherwise nothing; and B was $3000 for sure. Only a small minority (20 percent) chose to gamble on A, with the larger prize, over B for sure.

Meanwhile, another group of subjects was faced with options C and D, where C was $4000 with probability .20, otherwise nothing; and D was $3000 with probability .25, otherwise nothing. Here a clear majority (65 percent) chose to gamble on C, with the larger prize, over D, with a smaller but somewhat more likely prize. This violates the expected-utility principle, which requires consistency in the A versus B and C versus D choices. These two choice pairs are linked because C versus D is interpretable as a two-stage lottery in which the first stage provides a 25 percent chance of surviving to a second stage offering A versus B. When the ratio of two lottery prizes is fixed, the preference between their respective options should be completely determined by the *ratio* of the

probabilities of getting the prizes. In the A versus B and C versus D choices above, this ratio is the same: $(.8/1)$ = $(.20/.25)$. Yet the preference tends to reverse.

Evidently, the weight given a probability of .8 as a proportion of the weight given a sure thing is psychologically smaller than the weight given a probability of .20 as a proportion of the weight given a probability of .25. In this type of example the reduction of probability from certainty to some degree of uncertainty produces a more pronounced loss of attractiveness than does a corresponding reduction from one level of uncertainty to another. [Kahneman and Tversky (1979b) call this the *certainty effect*.] Psychological responses to probabilities, in other words, apparently do not have the ratio-scale properties corresponding to those of objective probabilities. Kahneman and Tversky (1979b, 1982) have articulated this idea in their *prospect theory,* discussed further below.

Subjectively expected utility. The idea that nonstandard probability interpretations might affect choice behavior is embodied in *subjectively expected utility,* a modification of the expected-utility principle. Ramsey (1926) was probably the first to propose this idea, which has since mushroomed in many varieties (Arrow, 1951; Lee, 1971). This modified principle can be expressed by Eq. (2), with the different interpretation of the p's as subjective rather than objective probabilities. A common application is to cases in which no objective probabilities are available but individuals must supply their own estimates. The term *personal probability* popularized by Savage (1954) refers to the degree of belief attached to uncertain outcomes, such as whether it will rain on a given day or whether a particular egg is rotten. There have been a variety of interpretations of the nature of such probabilities (DeFinetti, 1937; Edwards, 1954; Fisher, 1930; Jeffreys, 1948; Pratt *et al.,* 1965). Whether such subjective probabilities, like objective probabilities, sum to unity for mutually exclusive and exhaustive outcomes has been conjectural.

For the choice problems discussed in this section, however, objective probabilities are specified in the problem statement. Here models of the subjectivization of probability do well to avoid the semantic baggage accompanying the term *subjective probability* and to refer instead to a weighting function that transforms the objective probabilities. Edwards (1954) was apparently the first to suggest this now standard terminological clarification. With the *subjective weight w(p)* attaching to an event of probability *p,* the class of *subjectively weighted utility* models is given analogously to previous utility models (Eq. 2), with weighted probabilities replacing raw probabilities. One recent model in this class is due to Handa (1977) [but criticized by Fishburn (1978)] and another (with a modified equation for options with more than two outcomes) to Karmarkar (1978, 1979).

Prospect Theory

The most comprehensive attempt at meeting the various objections to other models is Kahneman and Tversky's (1979b) *prospect theory.* Like subjectively weighted utility theory, it assumes that the value *V* of an option is calculated as a sum of products over its specified outcomes *x,* each product consisting of a utility *v(x)* and a weight $\pi(p)$ attaching to the objective probability *p* of obtaining *x,* or

$$V = \sum_i \pi(p_i)v(x_i). \qquad (3)$$

Prospect theory is unique in the set of assumptions made about the functions *v* and π and about contextual effects surrounding the choice.

The probability-weighting function.   The function $\pi(p)$ is not given in closed mathematical form but, on the basis of inference from a number of choice problems, seems to have a shape something like that indicated in Fig. 1. One of the noteworthy features of this function is that it changes sharply near the endpoints, where $\pi(0) = 0$ and $\pi(1) = 1$, such that small probabilities are overweighted and large probabilities are underweighted. ["Objective" weighting would require $\pi(p) = p$.] It is interesting that evidence for these weighting biases was available more than thirty years ago (Attneave, 1953; Griffith, 1949; Preston and Baratta, 1948; Sprowls, 1953) and since then (Ali, 1977; Hershey and Schoemaker, 1980; Yaari, 1965); but only recently have specific weighting function forms been proposed in formal treatments such as that of prospect theory.

The sharp increase in π in moving from high probability to certainty contributes to the *certainty effect* underlying choice paradoxes such as the one discussed above. On the figure it will be seen that $\pi(.20)/\pi(.25) > \pi(.8)/\pi(1)$, for example.

The overweighting of small probabilities potentially explains the attractiveness of long-shot gambling (as in lotteries), as well as the tendency to insure against rare potential catastrophes (as in fire insurance). In both cases the rare events—the lottery success or the disastrous

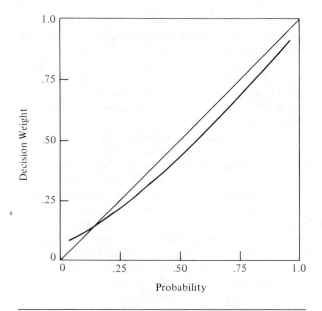

FIGURE 1
The Probability-Weighting Function of Prospect Theory

property loss—loom larger in the decisions (to gamble or to buy insurance) than the objective probabilities would seem to warrant. There are at least two other lines of explanation of the simultaneous attractiveness of lotteries and insurance, however. One suggestion, advanced variously by Friedman and Savage (1948), Markowitz (1952), and more recently by Machina (1982) with new supporting arguments, is that the utility function is inflected in such a way that large losses are especially aversive and large gains especially attractive. While Kahneman and Tversky acknowledge the occasional possibility of "kinks" in utility functions, this type of suggestion seems to lack general explanatory power for the complexities of insurance behavior. Laboratory studies of insurance preferences (Hershey and Schoemaker, 1980a; Schoemaker and Kunreuther, 1979) suggest a crucial role for subjective-probability weighting.

A second competing explanation argues that in lotteries and insurance the respective possibilities of loss are especially dramatic and capable of capturing the imagination. Thus the overweighting of these events might be a use of the *availability heuristic* (Tversky and Kahneman, 1973), wherein events are judged objectively more likely if they come readily to mind. This line of argument is appealing—and indeed probably correct in its own right—but misses the point of the prospect theory claim about small probabilities. That claim is that small probability *in itself* produces overweighting of the corresponding outcome event, whether it is dramatic or not. If you like, overweighting in prospect theory is a cold, cognitive "availability" effect having nothing to do with event vividness. The mere fact that an event is possible may give it a certain credence, of magnitude insufficiently sensitive to the size of the objective probability. The probability-weighting function π of prospect theory is "regressive with respect to p," as Kahneman and Tversky put it (1979b, p. 282). In other words, all uncertainty tends to have a common character, regardless of degree. A probability of .20 is not very different psychologically from a probability of .35 or even .50, at least not as different as it ought to be according to the expectation principles of choice. Even small-probability events partake of what we might call "possibilityhood," enhancing the extent to which they influence decision.

The effects on decision of possibilityhood can also be enhanced by factors such as dramatic salience. Thus TV images of tragic fire losses or of delirious jackpot winners could exaggerate the perceived probability of these rare events. An objective probability of 1 in 100,000 may seem subjectively to be 1 in 100—and once seen as 1 in 100, will be overweighted by the π-function relative to what would be normatively appropriate for an objective probability of .01. Thus *both* overexaggeration and overweighting may characterize some low-probability events.

However, it is also possible that extremely low probability events will be ignored entirely. This leads Kahneman and Tversky (1979b) to posit that "the π-function is not well-behaved near its end-points." This is so because "people are limited in their ability to comprehend and evaluate extreme probabilities, [thus] highly unlikely events are either ignored or overweighted, and the difference between high probability and certainty is either neglected or [amplified]" (p. 283). In ordinary firsthand experience very rare potential events do not provide people with the mammoth data sets necessary to give a relative-frequency interpretation to the probability. (What is the probability that a given can of mushrooms will produce botulism? That during an earthquake a nuclear power plant accident will occur?) Public estimates of the likelihood of various uncommon diseases and accidents are demonstrably inaccurate (Slovic,

Fischhoff, and Lichtenstein, 1976). In laboratory decision tasks as well, options containing extremely small probabilities produce uncertain response behavior (Which would you prefer: a one-in-a-billion chance to win $100 or a one-in-a-million chance to win $10?).

The probability-weighting function of prospect theory is not only regressive with respect to p (i.e., has a slope generally less than 1 when plotted against p) but is also depressed with respect to p throughout most of the range of p. Mere possibility is a relatively unpersuasive feature of posed outcomes. Note that the weight $\pi(.5)$ accorded to a probability of .5 in Fig. 1 is somewhat less than .5—somewhere between .35 and .40; a probability of about .65 is necessary to achieve a π of .5. In other words, half a chance is subjectively weighted not much better than a third of a chance, and two-thirds of a chance is necessary to produce a subjective impact halfway between impossibility and certainty. This latter assertion implies that in the pursuit of a risky venture with equally balanced potential gains and losses, an objective probability of success below two-thirds will tend to make the venture seem somewhat rash, and a probability above two-thirds will tend to make the venture seem generally sound. A psychological division between rashness and soundness at a probability around .65 has in fact been found by Myers and Lamm (1977) in an analysis of what used to be called the "risky shift" phenomenon.

The postulated behavior of the π-function has been controversial. If $\pi(.5) < .5$, then the sum of the weights associated with two events having probability of .5 is less than unity: $\pi(.5) + \pi(.5) < 1$. In fact, Kahneman and Tversky's π-function is such that $\pi(p) + \pi(1 - p) < 1$ for all p, a property they call *subcertainty*. Among other supports for this idea, they cite experimental evidence from MacCrimmon and Larsson (1979).

The value function.   The other major quantitative component of prospect theory is the *value function,* $v(x)$ in Eq. (3). The authors specify that v is defined in terms of gains and losses of wealth or welfare from some reference point or adaptation level. This idea plays a crucial psychological role in the theory, as we shall see. Figure 2 specifies the generic shape of the value function.

In the region of gains above the reference point, the function is concave. Each unit increase in gain of wealth has less and less value as gain increases—the classical assumption of utility theory. This type of function (as we noted previously) disposes toward risk aversion, as in the

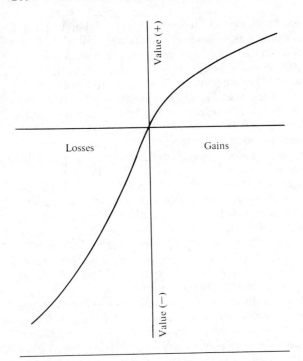

FIGURE 2
The Value Function of Prospect Theory

preference for a sure $500 over a 50–50 chance for $1000 or nothing.

Note that in choices of the form $y for sure versus equal chances of $x or nothing, both the subcertainty of the probability-weighting function and the concavity of the value function predict risk aversion. Thus risk aversion in such choices does not prove anything about either function without some assumption about the other. With long-shot prospects in which there is a small probability (say less than .10) of a large gain, the probability weights work in favor of the *seeking* of risk against the risk aversion due to the concave utility function. Prediction of which tendency will be dominant depends on the precise details of the two functions.

In the region of losses below the reference point, each unit increase in potential loss has less and less impact on overall (negative) value. This predicts risk seeking: A 50–50 chance of losing $1000 or losing nothing would be preferred to a sure loss of $500. Here, too, the effects of subcertainty work in the same direction as the effects of the shape of the value function, in this case the

direction of risk seeking. Again, the dominant tendency may be countervailed when small probabilities are involved. If a prospect contains a small-probability large loss, subjects may show risk aversion because the small probability is overweighted.

The value function postulated in prospect theory also predicts risk aversion when potential gains and losses are presented in the same prospect. Figure 2 shows *v* sloping more steeply below than above the reference point. As a consequence, a 50–50 chance to gain or lose $x is less attractive than the status quo.

Reference-point shifts.   The conjunction of risk aversion for gains and risk seeking for losses produces what Kahneman and Tversky (1979) call the *reflection effect*. Reflection of the signs of the outcomes in each of two prospects typically reverses the preference order between those prospects, and this phenomenon is capable of producing paradoxes in conjunctions of two decisions respectively involving gains and losses (Tversky and Kahneman, 1981). A related effect is that translation of the reference point downward (thereby adding a positive constant to all outcomes) typically produces some increase in the tendency toward risk aversion for the types of prospects we have been considering. We may refer to this as the *translation effect*.

Several factors can shift the reference point. One of these is the semantic "framing" of the choice options, according to Tversky and Kahneman (1981). They give the following example, contained in a questionnaire administered to university undergraduates. The total *N* and the percentage favoring each option are given in parentheses (p. 453):

Problem 1 (*N* = 152):   Imagine that the U.S. is preparing for the outbreak of an unusual Asian disease, which is expected to kill 600 people. Two alternative programs to combat the disease have been proposed. The accepted scientific estimate of the consequences of the programs are as follows:

If Program A is adopted, 200 people will be saved.   (72%)

If Program B is adopted, there is ⅓ probability that 600 people will be saved, and ⅔ probability that no people will be saved.   (28%)

Which of the two programs would you favor?

Problem 2 (*N* = 155 other subjects):   Imagine that the U.S. is preparing for the outbreak . . . [etc., identical to the introduction above].

If Program C is adopted, 400 people will
die.   (22%)

If Program D is adopted, there is ⅓
probability that nobody will die, and ⅔
probability that 600 people will die.   (78%)

Which of the two programs would you favor?

Majority choice is heavily in favor of the cautious alternative A in Problem 1, but a majority endorses the *risky* alternative D in Problem 2, despite the objective identity of the two problems. In Problem 1 the expected 600 deaths have been presupposed, whereas in Problem 2 they have not. That is, the reference point is 600 people lower in Problem 1 than in Problem 2 (so that the first program is described as 200 lives saved rather than 400 lives lost). From the translation effect it is correctly predicted that respondents would be more risk-averse in Problem 1.

The workings of the translation effect are not confined to semantic framing. Whenever an individual is faced with a succession of risky decisions, as in an evening of gambling or many months of stock management, there is ambiguity about the appropriate reference point. Gains or losses could be reckoned cumulatively with reference to the beginning of the decision series or with reference to assets or debit position at the time of each current decision. If, over time, the individual were sustaining increasing losses, the current reference point would be a downward translation of the original reference point. From the translation effect, therefore, one would predict relatively greater risk aversion when using the current reference point than when using the original reference point. The heavy loser still maintaining an original reference point is apt to try to win all losses back in devil-may-care gambles where further total losses don't seem much worse than the catastrophe already sustained. This frame of mind is common among poker players, horse players (McGlothin, 1956), and casino gamblers in the throes of losing streaks. The decision maker able to accommodate to losses—i.e., to forget the past and shift the reference point to the present—will by contrast tend toward more cautious decisions. Levi (1981) found a type of reference-point effect in an experimental war game situation involving the repeated unsuccessful commitment

of resources. The more favorable the historical past, the more the decision maker tried to recapture it by further commitments.

Both the presupposition of expected deaths in the framing example and the coming to terms with previous losses in sequential decision situations embody accommodation to loss by updating the psychological present. Accommodation to losses, then, induces risk aversion (relative to decisions without such accommodation). By similar reasoning, accommodation to gains disposes toward risk seeking. Imagine a poker player who has been winning throughout the evening. Focus on the beginning of the evening translates the reference point downward, further gains have relatively little marginal value, and behavior is risk-averse. When the reference point is financial status of the moment, there is less aversion to risk.

Editing operations.   An especially psychological aspect of prospect theory is the provision for an *editing phase* preceding the evaluation phase of choice. In Kahneman's and Tversky's (1979b) words, "The function of the editing phase is to organize and reformulate the options so as to simplify subsequent evaluation and choice"(p. 274). They list six major operations involved in editing (and there may well be more).

In *coding,* the individual sets the reference point for gains and losses in terms of current asset position modified by suppositions. In *simplification* the individual may round off probabilities or outcomes. Thus a .49 probability to win $101 might be seen as a .50 probability to win $100. An important simplification is the "rounding" of tiny probabilities to zero, i.e., ignoring highly unlikely outcomes entirely.

Combination entails grouping equivalent outcomes together; thus a prospect with a .1 chance on one outcome worth $100 and a .1 chance on another outcome also worth $100 might be reinterpreted in terms of a combined outcome with a .2 chance worth $100.

Segregation refers to the treatment of prospects in which all outcomes are positive (or all are negative). Kahneman and Tversky propose that the assured minimum gain (loss) is segregated from the rest of the prospect, which is then evaluated in terms of deviations from the assured minimum. Thus a .25 chance to win $300 and a .75 chance to win $100 is reinterpreted as a guaranteed $100 on top of a .25 chance to win $200 and a .75 chance to win nothing. This effect has been entered intrinsically into prospect theory. For these *must-win* (or must-lose) propositions, Eq. (3) is replaced by an equation adding the value of the guaranteed gain (loss) to the value of the prospect reckoned on additional gains (losses).

Cancellation is the operation by which the outcomes common to all prospects are discarded. Kahneman and Tversky (1979b) cite this illustration (p. 271):

> Consider the following two-stage game. In the first stage, there is a probability of .75 to end the game without winning anything, and a probability of .25 to move into the second stage. If you reach the second stage, you have a choice between
>
> A: 4000 with probability .8, otherwise nothing.
>
> B: 3000 for sure.
>
> Your choice must be made before the game starts, i.e., before the outcome of the first stage is known.

Of subjects answering this question, 78 percent chose option B. This proportion is extremely close to the 80 percent who chose B when the first stage was omitted entirely from the problem statement, but it is very different from the proportion (35 percent) choosing 3000 with probability .25 over 4000 with probability .20, the objectively equivalent choice if the probabilities in the two-stage problem are multiplied. Thus subjects act as though they ignore the first stage entirely, presumably because it is a feature common to prospects A and B. Within prospect theory (but not within expected-utility theory) the cancellation operation can produce preference reversals.

Dominance detection refers to the scanning of prospects to determine dominated alternatives, which are eliminated without further consideration.

Through appeal to editing operations, Kahneman and Tversky are able to sidestep what would otherwise be a bizarre consequence of the subcertainty property of the π-function. Consider the choice between $100 for sure and a coin flip offering $100 if heads and $100 if tails. Since $\pi(.5)$ is less than .5, Eq. (3), if used directly, would predict distinctly lower preference for the coin flip, even though it is conceptually identical to the sure thing. To give a role to editing is to allow theoretically for the fact (among others) that people would obviously notice such a conceptual identity. Application of the cancellation operation would merge the heads and tails outcomes, and the paradoxical preference would disappear.

It can be shown that *any* probability-weighting function will lead to paradox unless editing by cancellation is allowed. Consider the choice between ($x with

probability p; otherwise nothing) and ($x with probability $p/2$; $x with probability $p/2$; otherwise nothing). Without editing, Eq. (3) implies indifference between these two equivalent prospects only if $2\pi(p/2) = \pi(p)$. Given the boundary condition $\pi(1) = 1$, such a relation throughout the range of p could only hold if $\pi(p) = p$, that is, if weighting were unnecessary. Thus *editing is a requisite part of any risky-decision model postulating probability weighting*. This generalization applies to Karmarkar's (1978) slightly different decision model as well, by a variant of the argument in the text.

Editing is fundamental for psychological as well as for technical reasons. It concerns the set of strategies by which individuals reduce the confusion intrinsic to risky decisions. Thus how people edit choices might be at least as interesting as how they choose after editing. However, editing has been far less extensively investigated.

Criticisms of prospect theory. Prospect theory is appealing because its formal assumptions seem psychologically apt. It has not gone uncriticized, however. There are those (e.g., Machina, 1982) who still regard probability weighting as unnecessary. Others complain that the sub-

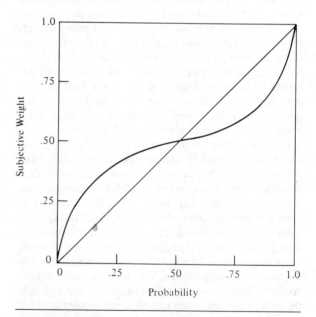

FIGURE 3
The Probability-Weighting Function of Karmarkar's Model

certainty property of the probability-weighting function is gratuitous. Karmarkar (1978), for example, agrees that a probability-weighting function is necessary to account for examples such as the one discussed earlier suggesting that $\pi(.2)/\pi(.25) > \pi(.8)/\pi(1)$. The function need not be subcertain, however, and he proposes the function shown in Fig. 3:

$$w(p) = \frac{p^{\alpha}}{p^{\alpha} + (1 - p)^{\alpha}}; \qquad 0 < \alpha < 1. \tag{4}$$

This function overweights small probabilities and underweights large probabilities, as required by the findings of most investigators, and it is not subcertain; that is, $w(p) + w(1 - p) = 1$. When there are three outcomes with respective probabilities p, q, r, in general it is not true that $w(p) + w(q) + w(r) = 1$. In order to re-create this property, Karmarkar resorts to normalized probability weights in the value of an option:

$$V = \frac{\sum_i w(p_i)u(x_i)}{\sum_i w(p_i)} \tag{5}$$

With only two outcomes Eq. (5) is of the same form as the usual Eq. (3) because the denominator equals 1. However, with three outcomes the denominator alters the weights so as to avoid subcertainty yet at the same time permit explanation of certain celebrated choice paradoxes such as the original Allais (1953) example.

Equation (5) is in the spirit of the Anderson and Shanteau (1970) information integration model of risky decision. Equation (4), however, has not been given any psychological justification, despite its mathematical nicety. Whether the Karmarkar model survives as a rival to prospect theory depends on evidence pertinent to the disparity between the functions $\pi(p)$ and $w(p)$ for $p < .5$. (Compare Figs. 1 and 3.) The Kahneman and Tversky function is (slightly) convex; the Karmarkar function is (considerably) concave. Experiments testing whether the probability-weighting function is concave or convex for $p < .5$ would therefore be diagnostic between the two models. At the time of this writing the evidence is not definitive, but it seems likely that the convex function from prospect theory will fit data better.

An important general criticism of prospect theory concerns its status in explaining individual choices. Kahneman and Tversky's examples are typically presented in terms of majority choice for particular configurations of options. For example, most subjects show risk aversion for gains and most subjects show risk seeking for losses, but these are not necessarily the same subjects. Some subjects may generally seek risk, and others may avoid it over both gain and loss domains (while some few may even show risk seeking for gains and risk aversion for losses).

Consider two choice problems such that a majority choose option A in an A versus B decision and a majority choose D in a C versus D pairing. The combination of A and D is said to constitute some paradoxical phenomenon or some effect such as the translation effect specified by prospect theory. What percentage of subjects choosing *both* A and D would one need in order to declare prospect theory supported? Fifty percent is the figure deemed sufficient by Kahneman and Tversky. Yet should not one also demand that the A–B choice and the C–D choice be statistically associated? That is, if there is a mix of prospect theory followers and nonfollowers in the population, the followers ought systematically to choose both A and D and the nonfollowers split their joint choices somehow otherwise among the four possibilities.

Hershey and Schoemaker (1980b) have tested for the *reflection effect* predicted by prospect theory, examining both aggregate and correlational data. Subjects were presented with a variety of "fair" choices between prospects, in both gain and mirror-image-loss form. One of these pairs of choices, for example, was the following:

- A: $9000 for sure;
- B: $10,000 with probability .9, otherwise nothing;

and

- C: −$9000 for sure;
- D: −$10,000 with probability .9, otherwise nothing.

The choices of a small sample of Wharton business school students showed risk aversion for gains and risk seeking for losses. Both of these main effects were significant, as was the association between the two choices (in the direction predicted by prospect theory).

Results were not generally as strongly supportive of reflectivity as in the one example cited. Of 28 pairs of prospects tested in three studies by the authors, the direction of the interpair association was in the dominant direction 23 times, but in only 6 of these cases was it significant, despite usually adequate sample sizes (as many as

200 in one nonsignificant pair). Meanwhile, in only 20 of the 28 pairs were there aggregate majorities favoring opposite tendencies *vis-à-vis* gains and losses (with both significant only 6 times). In situations of long-shot ($p < .01$) prospects of gains or losses above $1000, majorities were cautious each way. (Were these business school students trying to convey an impression of prudence?)

Failures of reflectivity sometimes occurred on the very pairs showing significant within-subject associations. For example, in the choice pitting $5000 with probability .001 against $5 for sure, the sure gain was preferred by more than half the subjects; also, a sure loss of $5 was a majority preference over a .001 risk of losing $5000. However, there was a highly significant tendency (gamma = .71) for those who were cautious on the gain side to be risky on the loss side and vice versa.

It is unclear what caused this curious pattern of results. This identical choice pair, given to Israeli university students by Kahneman and Tversky (1979b), produced different results, suggesting a difference in subject populations. Within a given subject population there is no guarantee, even if prospect theory is apt, that all subjects share the same forms of value and probability functions nor that they follow them assiduously. Hershey and Schoemaker (1980b), echoing Schoemaker (1979), assert that "statistically untrained subjects have difficulty focusing on several [choice quantities] simultaneously; ". . . The problem may . . . be . . . that subjects just do not follow expectation models" (p. 414). Kahneman and Tversky (1979b) are acutely aware of the fragility of prospect theory in predicting real behavior: "The evidence suggests that minor changes in the formulation of the decision problem can have marked effects," and "a comprehensive theory . . . should consider, in addition to pure attitudes toward uncertainty and money, such factors as the value of security, social norms of prudence, . . ." (p. 286).

However the scorecard eventually tallies pro and con prospect theory, it is clear that in initial intent it is a nomothetic rather than an idiographic theory. It poses broadly general effects in the psychology of choice, but its assumptions pertain to an idealized individual. Except for its failure to incorporate individual-difference parameters in its ken, it is a much more intrinsically psychological theory than its overly mechanical decision model forebears. It represents an excellent point of departure for further empirical and theoretical exploration.

Other Models

It is hard to escape from the fact that risky decisions depend, in one way or another, on the values attached to potential outcomes and on the chances of realizing those outcomes. However, decision models need not use sums of products of (objective or subjective) probabilities and (objective or subjective) values. There are several alternatives: a general product rule could be maintained, but strict summation over outcomes could be questioned; the product rule could be abandoned in favor, say, of a linear-combination rule for probability and value; a product rule could be supplemented by some other function of probability and value toward which individuals might be sensitive, such as risk. We consider each of these in turn.

Information integration models.   Information integration theory (Anderson, 1974a, 1974b) consists of a general set of techniques for testing the mathematical form of rating scale judgments on the basis of combinations of components. Multiplicative relationships are among the most commonly tested forms.

Anderson and Shanteau (1970) elicited judgments of the worth of "one-part" gambles such as 5/6 to win 25¢, to test the multiplicativity of probability and monetary amount. When judgments of all combinations from sets of probabilities and amounts were plotted, the characteristic fan of straight lines that implies a multiplicative model was obtained. Shanteau (1974) obtained similar results using verbal phrases such as *somewhat unlikely* and *toss-up,* and objects to be won such as *bicycle* and *sandals.* Shanteau (1975), summarizing a number of studies to similar effect, noted that these information integration results are consistent with the multiplicative postulate of subjectively expected utility theory (and though it did not exist at the time, presumably also prospect theory).

However, in separate analyses Shanteau (1974) found reason to question the additive property for separate products. He posed "two-part" offers, such as "highly probable to win a watch and toss-up to win a bicycle," and had subjects rate their worth. The set of outcome ratings suggested a *subadditivity effect,* by which the simultaneous offer of two valuable objects had less worth than would be predicted from their individual worths. In various comparisons involving one-part and two-part risky and riskless offers, Shanteau (1974) consistently found subadditivity. It can be interpreted as a generalization of the familiar idea of diminishing marginal utility, wherein each unit of increase in amount possessed is worth less and less to the possessor: In subadditivity what is possessed is a collection of differing items.

Methodological controversy attaches to the evidence for subadditivity. Indeed, part of Shanteau's (1974) claim comes from the reanalysis of earlier studies (e.g., Hicks and Campbell, 1965; Thurstone and Jones, 1957) that had claimed support for strict additivity. On the other hand, Shanteau's evidence is possibly vulnerable to the criticism that the meaning of the rating scale shifts for two-part offers.

If subadditivity cannot be explained away, it will have to be accommodated in choice models. One possible line of psychological explanation for subadditivity is that in offers of multiple potential objects there is some tendency toward averaging rather than adding the separate utilities. Averaging has been found by Anderson in many domains of information integration (e.g., Oden and Anderson, 1971). However, strict averaging does not fit Shanteau's (1974) data, so a partial rather than complete averaging tendency would need to be postulated. Another possible explanation is that when multiple objects are offered, there is a tendency to focus on the most valuable and to discount or underweight the least valuable. Such a discounting tendency would be broadly consistent with Tversky and Kahneman's (1974) anchoring-plus-adjustment heuristic, and it might be included in a portfolio of editing operations in prospect theory. Barring such editing, the presence of subadditivity in prospects with multiple outcomes would create trouble for prospect theory.

Linear combinations of probability and utility.   A radical departure from the product rule for probability p and utility u would occur if value V could be predicted from the rule

$$V = c_1 p + c_2 u, \tag{6}$$

with a summation over outcomes to yield the total value of a gamble. Equation (6), appropriately qualified, is not as bizarre as it might seem. For a positive outcome, value increases with both the utility and the probability of that outcome—so why not a linear combination of those two factors? Of course, with a negative outcome, value *decreases* as probability increases—but this could be handled by separating positive and negative outcome terms in any summation over outcomes.

Slovic and Lichtenstein (1968) used a model based on the rule in Eq. (6) to fit both ratings and bids for two-part bets such as .4 to win 20¢ and .8 to lose 10¢. However, although the fit to an additive rule was adequate, reanalyses and new data by Shanteau (1975) make fairly clear that the standard multiplicative rule is superior. Despite an optimistic review of the additive model by Payne (1973), it appears that unless convincing new data surface in some special context, a rule such as Eq. (6) will offer no serious competition to the multiplicative rule.

Portfolio theory.   People may be sensitive not only to the expected value (or expected utility) of an option but also to a global feature having to do with its riskiness (Fishburn, 1977; Lopes, 1981; Pruitt, 1962) for discussions of conditions under which risk models differ from expected-utility models (see Levy and Markowitz, 1979; Libby and Fishburn, 1977). As Coombs (1975) so eloquently puts the argument for considering riskiness, "With expected value fixed,...a gamble reflects a conflict between greed and fear....For each individual there is an optimum level at which greed and fear are in unstable balance—at a lower level of risk, greed drives him on, and at a higher level of risk, fear holds him back" (p. 71).

This statement claims not only that riskiness is an important feature of options but also that for any given individual, it has an optimum level. (In Coombs's terms there is a "single-peaked preference function" for risk.) These are central assumptions of *portfolio theory* (Coombs, 1975; Coombs and Meyer, 1969). The point of departure for the theory is the demonstration that the expected-utility principle is inadequate to account completely for preference orderings among options. As we noted earlier, a "probability mixture" of two options can never, under expected-utility theory, be systematically preferred (or dispreferred) to both of them. For example, consider the following three gambles:

- A: .5 to win $1, .5 to lose $1;
- B: .5 to win $5, .5 to lose $5;
- C: .25 to win $5, .25 to win $1, .25 to lose $1, .25 to lose $5.

Gamble C can be constructed by offering a 50–50 chance on playing A or playing B, and thus expected-utility theory requires that the value of C lie (halfway) between the value of A and the value of B.

Coombs and Huang (1974) tested this *betweenness property* of triples of gambles similar to the one above by soliciting preference orderings within several triples. In one experiment over 45 percent of the preference orderings violated the betweenness property; i.e., the mixture option C was either rated above both A and B or below both A and B. Conceivably, these violations could be attributed to random responding. However, in portfolio theory a probability mixture is intermediate in risk between its components; therefore a preference for C over both A and B could indicate that the individual's optimum risk level was intermediate in the range of risk spanned by the triple. Further, portfolio theory would not predict that C could be rated *below* both A and B, and indeed, this type of violation occurred with significantly lower frequency. This argues against the random-response interpretation.

Portfolio theory makes no commitment as to which particular optimum level of risk a given individual will prefer; in fact, individual differences are strongly expected. In the preference rankings of many subjects on several gambles matched in expected value but varying in risk, it is predicted that some preference rankings will not occur, and the ones that do can be "unfolded" to form a "J-scale" (Coombs, 1964).

A unique feature of portfolio theory is that it offers something coherent to say about individual differences. However, it makes no prediction about choices between gambles differing in both expected value and risk, and in that respect it is extremely limited. Furthermore, because it was played off against expected-value theory in particular, it is not clear how it relates to later developments, mainly prospect theory.

Prospect theory (and any other theory with subjective probability weights) does not in general make the betweenness prediction. Probability mixtures do not necessarily have values between the values of the components; low probabilities can have weights high enough to render a mixture extreme in preference. Thus the original Coombs demonstrations do not necessarily militate against prospect theory. However, with certain specific bet structures, portfolio theory allows preference rankings inadmissible under prospect theory.

Consider the set of prospects: p to win $\$x$, p to lose $\$x$, $(1 - 2p)$ for status quo, with p varying from near zero to .5. If the utility function is steeper for losses than for gains (as assumed in prospect theory), then for any fixed x such prospects should be ranked monotonically according to p, with greater aversion the larger the p. If the utility function is steeper for gains than for losses (unusual but conceivable for some individuals), then the preference ordering would again be monotonic in p but with preference increasing rather than decreasing. There is no way (barring a nonmonotonic π-function or some cagey editing operation) for prospect theory to predict anything but a monotonic relation between p and preference. Coombs (1975) collected data on preference rankings over four bets with the structure above and obtained nonmonotonic preference rankings 22 percent of the time. Half of these cases were interpretable by portfolio theory.

Isolated results can, of course, seem to advantage one or another simple choice theory. There are so many possibilities for task and situational variables, individual differences, and bet structures that no one theory seems destined to be infallible over all data tests. It would be splendid, however, if a general framework could be established that would not only prove to be rather robust against empirical violations but would speak to the mediating mechanisms of choices as well as to their structure.

PROCESS MODELS

Structural models describe the observable input/output relationships for decision behavior. In contrast, *process models* are concerned with the dynamic aspects of decision making, with the heuristics and algorithms that people use in dealing with decision problems. Structural models focus on the *what* of decision behavior, but process models focus on the *how*.

In recent years decision research has become increasingly process-oriented, for two reasons. First, decision researchers recognize that structural models do not necessarily provide insight into psychological processes. The fact that linear models (for example) provide excellent fits between predicted and observed decision behavior may be due more to the features of the task and to the insensitivity of the models than to the properties of the decision maker (Dawes, 1975b, 1979; cf. Simon, 1976b). Moreover, models of judgment or choice may be algebraically equivalent but may nevertheless suggest very different underlying processes (Graesser and Anderson, 1974; Green, 1968; Hoffman, 1960). Second, decision researchers have become increasingly familiar with concepts and methods drawn from cognitive psychology. This has facilitated attempts to construct and validate process models of decision making (Simon, 1976b; Taylor, 1976). The information-processing approach to human problem solving (Newell and Simon, 1972; Simon, 1978), in particular, has been viewed as highly applicable to decision behavior (Payne, 1980).

For these reasons process models have often been regarded as somehow superior to structural models. Less one-sided views have been proposed by Einhorn *et al.* (1979) and by Svenson (1979). The former suggested that structural models (specifically, linear regression models) and process-tracing models can provide complementary analyses of judgment and choice behavior.

Linear regression models can provide estimates of the amount of systematic and error variance, as well as various statistical tests. This can help compensate for the lack of explicit error theories in process models, which may tend to mistake irrelevant details or inconsistency in judgment for systematic rules. Moreover, as discussed in "Models of Riskless Decisions," linear models may provide information about the relative importance of cues in judgment or choice. Such information is difficult to obtain from process-tracing models. Process models, on the other hand, are useful in providing information about individuals' attentional processes during judgment or choice tasks. Information on which cues are attended to and when, and whether attention to cues shifts as the task is learned, can be provided by process-tracing methods but not by linear models.

Process models have been proposed to explain behavior both in well-defined and in ill-defined decision problems. In well-defined problems the decision maker has a clear idea of what objectives should be attained and is aware of the available alternatives and their associated outcome probabilities. Well-defined problems are exemplified by many judgment tasks (e.g., Einhorn, 1974; Phelps and Shanteau, 1978) and consumer choice tasks (e.g., Bettman, 1979a). In ill-defined decision problems, on the other hand, the decision maker does not have a clear idea of the objectives to be attained nor of alternative available choices. Group and organizational strategic decisions (e.g., Janis, 1972; MacCrimmon and Taylor, 1976; March and Olsen, 1976) are representative of ill-defined decision problems. Problems can, however, lie at intermediate points on a continuum representing varying degrees of structure (Conrath, 1967; Simon, 1965, 1976a).

Models of behavior in well-defined problems typically employ the concepts and methods of cognitive psychology, whereas models of behavior in ill-defined problems often incorporate social psychological and sociological concepts and methods as well as cognitive ones. The former type usually deals with individuals in relatively simple settings; the latter deals with individuals or groups in relatively complex settings.

WELL-DEFINED DECISION PROBLEMS

In well-defined problems the decision maker must gather and process information about fixed alternatives and make a preferential choice. This type of problem is faced, for example, by a shopper choosing among laundry detergents or by a student deciding which one of six college admissions offers to accept. Such decisions can be regarded as instances of problem solving. It is in the domain of problem solving that the information-processing approach has proved empirically and theoretically productive.

The information-processing approach highlights the concept of the *problem space,* the individual's cognitive representation of the problem. It is assumed to have a crucial influence on how a problem is solved (Simon, 1978; Simon and Hayes, 1976). This assumption is like one familiar to social psychologists: Behavior is in large part a function of the individual's perception or interpretation of the environment (Lewin, 1951).

Another important assumption is that individuals are limited in their information-processing capabilities (Dawes, 1976). This assumption, supported by a substantial amount of empirical evidence (e.g., Broadbent, 1975; Kahneman, 1973; Miller, 1956; Newell and Simon, 1972; Simon, 1974), has the important implication that people will generally rely on simple decision strategies, or heuristics, to keep the information-processing demands of the task within bounds. Heuristics, according to Braunstein (1976), are problem-solving methods which tend to produce efficient solutions to difficult problems by restricting the search through the space of possible solutions. The use of heuristics had been demonstrated in a variety of areas, including problem solving (Newell and Simon, 1972), pattern recognition and depth perception (Braunstein, 1976), probability estimation (Howell and Burnett, 1978; Kahneman and Tversky, 1972; Tversky and Kahneman, 1974), and decision making under risk

(Payne, 1975; Slovic *et al.,* 1977; Tversky, 1969). Later in this section we will review the substantial literature on how and under what conditions individuals use heuristics to deal with preferential choice problems.

Cognitive Representation of Alternatives

It has commonly been proposed that the individual's representation of each alternative in preferential choice problems can be characterized by values on a number of attributes or dimensions (e.g., Svenson, 1979; Wallsten, 1980). Moreover, researchers have generally assumed that when comparing alternatives, individuals refer their representations of attributes to scales of attractiveness (Montgomery and Svenson, 1976; Park, 1978a, 1978b; Payne, 1976a, 1976b; Svenson, 1979). For example, an automobile will be represented not simply by its miles per gallon but also by the degree of attractiveness of that many miles per gallon.

Only if attractiveness values on different attributes are *commensurable* can they be compared with, or traded off against, each other. If a consumer believes that the value of a new washing machine on the attribute of price may be combined with its value for length of warranty, for example, then commensurability across attributes (for that individual) obtains.

The notion that individuals represent decision alternatives as a set of attractiveness values corresponding to a set of attributes is, of course, a very general one. To generate decision predictions, however, one must postulate some rule by which the attractiveness values are combined. Before describing some possible rules, we discuss methods by which subjects' decision processing can be traced.

Process-Tracing Methods

Process-tracing methods have been used to determine what information individuals seek to acquire before making a choice, how this information is structured to form a cognitive representation of the problem, and how the representation is processed in order to make a choice.

Three major types of methods have been used to tap individuals' information acquisition and processing. Two of these methods—the recording of eye movements and the monitoring of explicit information search—have been useful primarily for examining information acquisition. The third method—the collection of verbal proto-cols—has been valuable for tracing both acquisition and processing phases of the choice process.

Recording eye movements. Eye movements can be measured on various characteristics (e.g., duration, fixation density, sequence of fixations) that presumably indicate how the individual was acquiring and processing information. Techniques for recording eye movements have been used to study decision behavior (e.g., Rosen and Rosenkoetter, 1976; Russo, 1978; Russo and Rosen, 1975) as well as other cognitive performances.

In spite of some technical problems (e.g., the necessity of keeping the items of information relatively few and spaced far enough apart to permit precise measurement), the recording of eye movements appears to be a useful technique for understanding information acquisition and processing (Payne, Braunstein, and Carroll, 1978). For example, Russo and Dosher (1980) used eye-fixation data to identify whether subjects were using intra- versus interdimensional forms of processing in a binary-choice task.

Monitoring explicit information search. The second major process-tracing method requires the decision maker to search explicitly for information about the available alternatives. The decision maker is typically presented with information arranged in a matrix containing the value of each alternative on each attribute. The matrix values are hidden, and the decision maker must specifically request to see them.

The usual method for eliciting explicit search strategies has employed cards covering the cells of the alternatives × attributes matrix (e.g., Bettman and Jacoby, 1976; Payne, 1976b; Schaninger and Sciglimpaglia, 1981; Thorngate and Maki, 1976). A technique with slides shown on request was employed by Carroll and Payne (1977), and a computer-controlled information retrieval system was used by Payne and Braunstein (1978).

Analyses and interpretations of information acquisition records rely on a number of assumptions (Jacoby *et al.,* 1976; Payne *et al.,* 1978; Svenson, 1979). First, when an individual looks at an item of information, it is assumed that this item is attended to, encoded, and processed. Second, an individual's attention to an item is assumed to indicate a purposeful search based on a particular strategy or decision rule. Third, longer periods of attention to items of information are assumed to indicate more complex cognitive processes than are shorter periods. These assumptions appear reasonable and are probably correct in most circumstances. However, it is difficult to determine when they are not correct, unless techniques for monitoring information search are used along with other process-tracing techniques.

Verbal protocols.   Verbal protocols are collected while the subject is working on the decision task. The subject is asked to "think aloud," to report every passing thought. The protocols are interpreted to indicate the subject's sequence of information-processing operations (Newell and Simon, 1972). Collection of verbal reports during performance of the decision task is a *concurrent verbalization method,* in Ericsson and Simon's (1980) terms. A *retrospective verbalization method* is one in which the individual is asked about cognitive processes occurring earlier in time.

Ericsson and Simon (1980) proposed cognitive process models to account both for individuals' concurrent and retrospective verbal responses. In general, concurrent verbal responses are considered the more likely to reflect accurately individuals' information processing during tasks (Payne *et al.,* 1978). This is because concurrent responses usually consist of direct reports of contents in short-term memory, whereas retrospective responses often involve interpretation and summary of previously occurring cognitive processes.

Transcribed protocols are broken down into short phrases, each assumed to represent the information being processed by the subject at a particular time (Newell and Simon, 1972). Thus the protocol from a subject choosing among gambles would be broken down into phrases such as "let's take a look at gamble A"; "probability to win is .35"; "not so good" (Payne and Braunstein, 1978). Some coding scheme is then applied to these phrases.

Among the numerous coding systems (e.g., Bettman and Park, 1980; Carroll and Payne, 1977; Payne, 1976b; Payne and Braunstein, 1978; Waterman and Newell, 1973), perhaps the most common, developed by Newell and Simon (1972), leads to the construction of a problem behavior graph (PBG). These PBGs, which resemble flowcharts, are composed of nodes (representing knowledge states) connected by arrows (representing the application of a process or operation).

Uses of protocol data.   Protocol data have been used for a variety of purposes in decision research (Payne *et al.,* 1978). First, such data may be useful for *exploratory research,* as a source of hypotheses during early phases of research on decision behavior.

Second, protocol data can be used to supplement data collected by other methods. For example, information acquisition behavior measured by the monitoring of eye movements or explicit information search methods can be compared with verbal responses. Payne (1976b) used such a convergent method to determine the effects of task complexity on the information-processing strategies used in a preferential choice task. Russo and Rosen (1975) used verbal protocols to confirm the interpretation suggested by subjects' sequences of eye fixations. While looking at a replay of their eye-fixation sequences superimposed on the original display of decision alternatives, subjects were asked to report retrospectively the thoughts they had had during the task just completed. Russo (1979) found that such prompted protocols yielded more information about search behavior than did concurrent or retrospective verbalization alone.

A third use for verbal protocol data is to test hypotheses about decision behavior. Bettman and Park (1980a, 1980b), for example, tested postulated effects of prior knowledge, experience, and phase of the choice process on consumer decision processes. Montgomery (1976) replicated previous findings by Tversky (1969) on intransitive preferences among gambles. Predictions concerning the use of choice rules were confirmed by the examination of subjects' statements about probabilities and amounts to win.

The fourth use for protocol data is to build detailed models of individuals' decision processes, formalized in computer algorithms. Examples are computer models by Clarkson (1962) on portfolio selection in trust investment, Kleinmuntz (1968) on clinical judgment of MMPI profiles, and Bettman (1970) on consumer choice in a supermarket.

Abelson (1968) and Einhorn *et al.* (1979) have suggested that such computer models have a number of attractive features. Computer models appear to capture ongoing problem solving, since they are based on decision makers' own reports in the natural environment or problem space. Also, computer models allow for configurality in judgment and choice, which fits our notions about human performance. As against such advantages, the drawbacks of computer models are that they are unparsimonious and difficult to validate (Abelson, 1968). The most stringent validation test is for the model not only to predict input/output behavior but also to match the process description of the human subject.

Most such matching tests have relied on informal comparisons between verbal protocol and process model. Payne *et al.* (1978) suggested a more formal procedure, involving construction of a PBG for both the verbal protocol and the trace of the model. The correspondence between the two PBGs could then be analyzed in terms of the sequential dependencies among the various types of operation statements found in the protocol and the trace. The correspondence between protocol and trace could also be measured in terms of the items of information being searched and evaluated at each point in time (cf. Bettman, 1974a, 1974b; Tuggle and Barron, 1980). Analyses such as these, though perhaps difficult to develop and apply, would enable researchers to make use of the attractive features of computer models developed from verbal protocols.

Reliability and validity. A number of important issues regarding verbal protocol methods remain. For one thing, how good is interjudge agreement on the interpretation of protocols according to coding schemes? With some exceptions (e.g., Haines, 1974), satisfactory levels of interjudge reliability (> .75) have been obtained (e.g., Bettman and Park, 1980b; Montgomery, 1976; Simon and Newell, 1974; Thorngate and Maki, 1976), but, of course, levels vary with the complexity of the coding scheme and the amount of training of the coders. Computerizing the coding process (e.g., Waterman and Newell, 1973) and comparing protocol data with other process measures of decision behavior (e.g., by monitoring information search) are ways to increase the reliability of protocol analysis.

Another issue concerns the validity of verbal protocol methods. There are three aspects to this issue. First, what is the relation between verbal protocol methods and the now-discredited introspective methods used many years ago by psychologists such as Titchener? Despite the superficial resemblance because both methods rely on verbal reports, there are some important differences (Hayes, 1968; Payne, 1980; and Payne *et al.,* 1978). The introspectionist school attempted to discover the elementary images and feelings, the fundamental contents of the mind. To this end, verbal reports were collected from observers trained to recognize the fundamental contents when they occurred in consciousness. These observers were thus generally knowledgeable about the theoretical concepts under investigation. In contrast, present-day process-tracing techniques are used primarily to determine the processes of thought rather than the contents of consciousness. Subjects are usually not knowledgeable about the theoretical constructs of interest to the researcher; they are asked simply to report their thoughts while they are performing the task. Thus the criticisms against introspective methods lose their force when directed against current methods for collecting and analyzing verbal protocols (cf. Lieberman, 1979).

A second aspect of validity concerns the reactivity of verbal protocol methods: Does verbalization of thoughts during task performance interfere with the cognitive processes such verbalization is supposed to reflect? Ericsson and Simon (1980) proposed that when the cognitive contents being verbalized are already encoded verbally, no interference will occur. When the cognitive contents must be recoded in order to be verbalized, task performance may be slowed but will still remain largely unchanged. Such slowing is likely, for example, when a subject is asked to think aloud while working on a spatial task such as mental object rotation. In contrast, protocol methods that require subjects to summarize or explain their thoughts rather than simply report them are likely to alter task processing.

Studies of decision tasks involving gambles (Montgomery, 1976), parole requests (Carroll and Payne, 1977), and consumer goods (Smead, Wilcox, and Wilkes, 1981) suggest that verbal protocol procedures are nonreactive. Verbalization of thoughts may slow the choice process but appears to leave it basically unaltered. Ericsson and Simon's (1980) analysis, however, suggests qualifications to such a conclusion.

A third aspect of the validity issue has gained prominence primarily because of the case presented by Nisbett and Wilson (1977b). These authors (see also Nisbett and Bellows, 1977; Nisbett and Wilson, 1977a), after reviewing a large number of studies in perception, problem solving, and social psychology, concluded that people often cannot report accurately on the effects of particular stimuli on responses. People's conscious awareness is limited to the *products* of mental processes; the processes themselves are unconscious and not directly retrievable from memory. Because individuals do not have access to their cognitive processes, they base their verbal reports on implicit, a priori theories about the causal connections between stimuli and responses. Individuals' explanations for their own mental processes are therefore either completely inaccurate or no more accurate than explanations made by observers with publicly observable information about the situation and the individual's behavior. When individuals do seem to report accurately about their cognitive processes, it is only because the a priori theory they are using just happens, in fact, to be correct.

If, indeed, people cannot report accurately on their cognitive processes, the rationale for using verbal protocols would seem to be undermined. However, several writers have defended the validity of verbal protocols by pointing out that they are usually collected during task performance, whereas Nisbett and Wilson focused on verbal reports collected afterward (Payne, 1980; Payne *et al.,* 1978). In concurrent verbal reports individuals are presumed able to describe the contents of short-term memory. Their reports will therefore generally reflect the actual sequence of cognitive operations as they occur. In contrast, when giving retrospective verbal reports, individuals are often unable to report the contents previously held in short-term memory. Such reports are therefore likely to be inaccurate with respect to the actual cognitive operations occurring earlier (Ericsson and Simon, 1980; cf. Kelley and Michela, 1980) and to rely heavily on the construction of explanatory rationalizations.

Another factor that weakens the force of Nisbett and Wilson's (1977b) argument here is the distinction between cognitive products and processes. Nisbett and Wilson make no claim that *products* are not accurately available, and much of the content of protocols concerns the products of processing. All in all, Nisbett and Wilson's conclusions seem not to pose a great threat to the validity of verbal protocol procedures (Ericsson and Simon, 1980; Rip, 1980; Wright and Rip, 1980).

Choice Rules

A large number of rules have been proposed as possible models for choices among well-defined alternatives (e.g., Bettman, 1979a; Coombs, 1964; Einhorn, 1970, 1971; Fishburn, 1974; Lee, 1971; Luce, 1956; Montgomery and Svenson, 1976; Payne, 1976a, 1976b; Rapoport and Wallsten, 1972; Svenson, 1979; Thorngate and Maki, 1976; Tversky, 1969, 1972a, 1972b; Wallsten, 1980). These rules can be characterized on metric level of attractiveness, commensurability across attributes, and *form of processing* (Bettman, 1979a). This last aspect can be of two general types: processing by alternative and processing by attribute. In the former case each alternative in the choice set is processed and evaluated as a whole, and then a choice is made on the basis of these evaluations. In the latter case all alternatives are compared on a single attribute, then on another, etc. These two forms of processing are generally referred to, respectively, as *interdimensional* versus *intradimensional* (Payne, 1976b); in the consumer choice literature (where much of the relevant research is reported) they are termed choice by processing brands versus choice by processing attributes (Bettman and Jacoby, 1976).

Since the numerous choice rules have been described in great detail elsewhere (e.g., Bettman, 1979a; Svenson, 1979), we will focus only on the most prominent ones. Our order of presenting these rules corresponds roughly to a ranking from the most simple to the most complex.

A hypothetical choice among automobiles will serve to illustrate these rules. For the sake of simplicity, we assume that only three attributes play a part in the decision: price, safety (i.e., crashworthiness), and economy (represented by miles per gallon, mpg). The values of the three automobiles in the choice set are displayed in Table 1.

Noncompensatory rules. Noncompensatory rules do not allow trade-offs between alternatives and thus are suitable when commensurability is absent. The noncompensatory category includes, among others, the conjunctive and disjunctive rules, both of which require only an ordinal ranking of attractiveness values.

The *conjunctive rule* assumes that the decision maker defines minimum cutoffs for each dimension. If an al-

TABLE 1
Choice Among Automobiles

AUTOMOBILE	PRICE	SAFETY (on 10-point scale; 10 = maximum)	ECONOMY (mpg)
A	$2500	2	14
B	$5000	6	27
C	$7000	7	23

ternative does not exceed all the cutoffs, it is rejected. The form of processing associated with this rule is usually interdimensional. Thus the individual using a conjunctive rule would consider each automobile separately and reject it if it failed to pass muster on cost, safety, and economy. If the decision maker's cutoffs are $6000, 5, and 25 for price, safety, and economy, respectively, then automobile B would be chosen. Automobile A fails to reach the cutoff for safety and economy, automobile C for price and economy.

The noncompensatory nature of the conjunctive rule becomes apparent when an automobile with the following hypothetical characteristics is added to the original choice set: price, $6005; safety, 6; economy, 50 mpg. Assuming that the decision maker retains the original cutoff points, this automobile would be rejected just as surely as one that is far below the cutoff points on all three dimensions; the tremendous value on the dimension of economy does not compensate for the very slight excess in price.

When more than one alternative exceeds the cutoffs on all dimensions, the conjunctive rule will yield more than one acceptable alternative. A decision maker may then proceed either by making the cutoffs more stringent and applying the conjunctive rule again or by using a different choice rule that will yield a single alternative. This situation will not arise, however, if the decision maker stops examining alternatives as soon as an acceptable alternative is found [Simon's (1955) satisficing principle].

The *disjunctive rule* also requires a set of cutoffs on the dimensions. An alternative is acceptable when it has at least one value greater than the corresponding cutoff. With regard to the automobile choice problem, a decision maker employing cutoffs of $4000 for price, 8 for safety, and 28 mpg for economy would select alternative A—the only alternative to exceed any of the cutoffs. With a different set of cutoffs it is possible that the disjunctive rule would select more than one alternative, ordinarily necessitating an additional choice process.

The preceding two rules do not specify any ranking or weighting of attribute dimensions by the decision maker. When dimensions are rank-ordered in importance, they are said to be in lexicographic order. The *lexicographic rule* assumes that alternatives are first compared with respect to the most important attribute. If one alternative has a higher value on this attribute than do the others, that alternative is chosen, regardless of the values the alternatives have on other attributes. If the al-

ternatives are equally attractive on the most important attribute, the decision will be based on the attribute next in order of importance. The lexicographic rule thus implies an intradimensional form of processing: The decision maker compares the alternatives on one attribute at a time rather than examining each alternative separately as a whole. To illustrate, suppose that a decision maker considers the attribute of price as first in importance, safety as second, and economy as third. In this case a lexicographic rule would dictate the choice of automobile A.

The *elimination-by-aspects rule,* proposed by Tversky (1972a, 1972b; see also Tversky and Sattath, 1979), states that attributes are weighted according to their importance. Then an attribute is selected with probability proportional to its weight. All alternatives not having satisfactory values for the selected attribute are eliminated. A second attribute is then selected with probability proportional to its weight, and the process continues until only one alternative remains. The elimination-by-aspects rule resembles the conjunctive rule in that alternatives failing to meet the decision maker's cutoff points are rejected. In the elimination-by-aspects rule, however, the form of processing is intradimensional: The decision maker need only consider the alternatives on one dimension at a time.

Compensatory rules. Compensatory choice rules require commensurability, wherein attractiveness values on different attributes can be traded off against one another. In choosing an automobile, for example, a decision maker may sacrifice some economy (mpg) for an increase in safety (selecting automobile C over B), or may accept an automobile that is unattractive on safety and economy if its price is sufficiently low (automobile A).

The precision with which the decision maker engages in such trade-offs may vary. Quick-and-dirty trade-off processes involve only ordinal attractiveness comparisons (e.g., "the low price of $2500 is more attractive than the high safety rating of 7"), whereas sophisticated processes require comparisons involving cognitive representations of attractiveness at interval levels (e.g., "for each additional mpg I am willing to spend an additional $100 on the price of the car"). This latter type of trade-off illustrates the translation of two disparate attributes or dimensions onto a common scale of *utility*. Compensatory choice rules generally require an interdimensional form of processing in which the decision maker gives an overall utility rating to each alternative in the choice set. For example, *the addition-of-utilities rule* states that the decision maker sums all the utilities for each alternative and then chooses the alternative with the greatest sum.

Use of Choice Rules

We now turn to research that has used process-tracing methods to investigate individuals' use of choice rules. It is generally assumed that individuals command a repertoire including most of the choice rules discussed above (e.g., Montgomery and Svenson, 1976; Thorngate and Maki, 1976; van Raaij, 1976). Research therefore has been concerned primarily with determining how a variety of task variables affect the way individuals encode and process task information, which in turn influences the choice rules they use and therefore the final choices they make.

The two types of task variables that have received the most attention are task complexity and information format.

Task complexity. The usual plausible assumption is that because individuals are limited in their information-processing capacity, they will tend to simplify the cognitive requirements of the decision process. This tendency will be more pronounced as the decision increases in complexity.

Information load. The most obvious component of task complexity—information load—has typically been defined as m (the number of alternatives) $\times$ n (the number of attributes). This operationalization, based on the objective number of informational items, has been criticized on the grounds that subjective experience of load does not necessarily correspond to objective task load (e.g., Russo, 1974; Summers, 1974). Milord and Perry (1977) recommended a self-report operationalization in which each decision maker individually defines "high," "medium," and "low" information loads. A disadvantage of the idiographic approach, however, is that self-reports of experienced information load may be influenced by extraneous factors such as experimental demand characteristics and social desirability concerns. It seems desirable both to manipulate information load objectively and to obtain self-reports of experienced load (e.g., Malhotra, 1982).

Process-tracing techniques have been used to reveal how individuals deal with the $m \times n$ informational items

in the choice task. For example, Payne's (1976b) protocols revealed that when choosing between two alternatives, individuals typically employed compensatory choice rules such as the addition-of-utilities rule. Such rules require that the same number of attributes be examined for both alternatives. The following protocol segment illustrates a subject's use of a type of compensatory rule in choosing between two apartments (Payne, 1976b, p. 378):

> OK, we have an A and a B. / First look at the rent for both of them. / The rent for A is \$170 and / the rent for B is \$140. / \$170 is a little steep, / but it might have a low noise level. / So we'll check A's noise level. / A's noise level is low. / We'll go to B's noise level. / It's high. / Gee, I can't really very well study with a lot of noise. / So I'll ask myself the question, is it worth spending that extra \$30 a month for, / to be able to study in my apartment.

As the protocol indicates, this subject used an intradimensional search procedure: Both apartments were examined first with respect to rent and second with respect to noise level. The subject then attempted to make a trade-off between rent and noise level.

In contrast, individuals faced with six or twelve alternatives were very unlikely to examine each alternative on all attributes. Rather, individuals tended to reduce quickly the number of alternatives by using a noncompensatory screening process. When the number of alternatives was reduced sufficiently (usually to two or three), a more intensive examination of each alternative was made. This protocol segment illustrates a typical screening procedure (Payne, 1976b, p. 375):

> Apartment E. / The rent for apartment E is \$140. / Which is a good note. / The noise level for this apartment is high. / That would deter me right there. / Ah, I don't like a lot of noise. / And, if it's high, it must be pretty bad. / Which means, you couldn't sleep. / I would just put that one aside right there. / I wouldn't look any further than that. / Even though, the rent is good.

In this case the subject used a conjunctive rule to screen out unsatisfactory alternatives. The search pattern was interdimensional.

In general, the more alternatives in the initial set, the smaller is the proportion of information searched and the greater is the tendency for choices to be based on simple rather than complex decision rules. This generalization appears to hold for both risky (e.g., Payne and Braunstein, 1978) and riskless (e.g., Lussier and Olshavsky, 1979; Mills, Meltzer, and Clark, 1977; Payne, 1976a, 1976b) choice problems.

Individuals tend also to reduce their information search as the number of attributes increases (e.g., Jacoby, Speller, and Berning, 1974, 1975; Jacoby, Speller, and Kohn, 1974). Svenson (1979), summarizing the results of a number of studies, noted that increasing the number of attributes has an even greater effect on the proportion of information searched than does an increase in the number of alternatives. That is, given a constant number of informational items ($m \times n$), an increase in the number of alternatives m, and a corresponding decrease in the number of attributes n, usually leads to a higher utilization of the available information. For example, individuals will tend to use more information when considering five alternatives with three attributes than when considering three alternatives with five attributes. This finding probably reflects individuals' predominant use of noncompensatory choice rules such as the conjunctive or lexicographic rules. Such rules necessitate that the decision maker consider at least some information for each alternative added to the choice set. In contrast, an increase in the number of attributes characterizing each alternative does not necessarily require the decision maker to process additional information. It is often possible for the decision maker using a noncompensatory rule to make a satisfactory choice on the basis of a few important attributes without even considering others (Olshavsky, 1979).

In addition to increasing the number of alternatives or attributes, one may increase information load by decreasing the time allowed for making the decision. Wright (1974) hypothesized that under conditions of time pressure or distraction, individuals will tend to simplify the decision task by disproportionately weighting unfavorable information. The conjunctive choice rule is apt for this purpose since it efficiently screens out unacceptable alternatives. Wright's prediction was supported: Time pressure did increase reliance on unfavorable information, and distraction showed a tendency toward the same effect. In a similar vein, Wright and Weitz (1977) found that subjects evaluated possible unfavorable outcomes more severely when these outcomes were expected sooner rather than later (Ainslee, 1975) and also when greater commitment to a chosen alternative

was required. Wright and Weitz suggested that under time pressure individuals tend to dichotomize dimensions into accept and reject regions, again implying a conjunctive rule. Additional evidence on the effect of time pressure on information use comes from Wallsten's (1980) study. Wallsten found that subjects under time pressure typically relied on a few salient attributes when making a choice. When not under time pressure subjects usually used most of the available information. The effect of increasing time pressure is thus similar to that of increasing the amount of data: The decision maker uses less of the available information and tends to rely on simple, noncompensatory choice rules.

As the Wright (1974) and Wright and Weitz (1977) studies suggest, however, time pressure appears to have the additional effect of making the decision maker more cautious. As time pressure increases, the decision maker attaches greater weight to unfavorable as compared with favorable information. This tendency toward caution was found by Hansson, Keating, and Terry (1974) in an investigation of student voting on pending state legislation. Students allowed two minutes to vote were significantly more conservative (i.e., status quo–oriented) in their voting than were students allowed unlimited time. Ben Zur and Breznitz (1981) found that subjects chose safer gambles (i.e., gambles characterized by lower variance or lower potential losses) under high (eight seconds) as compared with medium (sixteen seconds) or low (thirty-two seconds) time pressure. In addition, subjects paid more attention to the probability of losing and amount of possible loss than to the probability of winning and amount of possible gain as time pressure increased. Ben Zur and Breznitz suggested that under time pressure individuals' primary objective becomes that of reducing the threat of future negative consequences. To this end, subjects place heavy emphasis on unfavorable information about the available alternatives.

The shift toward caution appears not to occur, however, when there is an increase in the amount of data. A possible explanation is that an increase in the amount of data, in itself, does not increase the perceived threat of future negative consequences. Thus although decision makers confronted by a large amount of data may use simple choice rules, they will not necessarily accord greater weight to unfavorable than to favorable information. The divergence of effects of amount of information and time pressure on the decision process suggests that the concept of information load be treated in a more differentiated manner.

Information load and decision quality. Because noncompensatory rules such as the conjunctive rule are more likely than compensatory rules to produce suboptimal choices, increases in information load might be expected to decrease decision quality. In consumer choice research information load has typically been manipulated by varying the number of informational items (brands × attributes) in the task. Decision quality has typically been defined idiographically, by comparing the decision maker's actual choices against his or her criteria for what the "best" or "ideal" alternative would be.

Jacoby and his associates (Jacoby, Speller, and Berning, 1974; Jacoby, Speller, and Kohn, 1974) found, across a variety of products (laundry detergents, rice, and prepared dinners), a curvilinear relationship between decision quality and information load. Decision quality was lower at high levels (e.g., sixteen brands described on sixteen attributes) than at moderate levels (e.g., eight brands described on eight attributes) of information load.

The conclusion that consumers could be overloaded with information provoked a substantial amount of controversy. Jacoby's research was criticized for the definition of information load and the measure of decision quality (e.g., Russo, 1974; Summers, 1974; Wilkie, 1974; cf. Jacoby, 1977; Jacoby, Speller, and Berning, 1975). Moreover, according to Malhotra (1982; Malhotra, Jain, and Lagakos, 1982), a reanalysis of Jacoby's (Jacoby, Speller, and Berning, 1974; Jacoby, Speller, and Kohn, 1974) data revealed an *increase* rather than a decrease in decision quality as a function of information load (see also Staelin and Payne, 1976).

Following Wilkie's (1974) suggestion that overload may occur only at information levels higher than those manipulated by Jacoby, Malhotra (1982) investigated the effects of a very wide range of informational items on decision quality. Using a between-subjects design and a choice task involving hypothetical profiles of houses, Malhotra varied both the number of alternatives and the number of attributes from five through twenty-five. Information overload effects were examined with several types of measures, including a self-report on information overload, and two different correct-choice measures based on closeness to the decision maker's ideal alternative.

Subjects reported experiencing overload, and made significantly fewer correct choices, when the number of alternatives reached ten or when the number of attributes reached fifteen. The negative effects of information load remained relatively constant for more alternatives and attributes. These results suggest that sufficiently high information load can reduce decision quality. Since process-tracing techniques were not employed in the study, however, it is not clear what processing produced the results. Malhotra suggested that subjects faced with too many alternatives or attributes were cognitively unable to make the number of comparisons necessary to completely rank the alternatives and therefore resorted to simple choice rules to accomplish the task. This explanation, which is consistent with Payne's (1976a, 1976b) findings, assumes that simple choice rules are more likely than complex ones to result in low-quality decisions.

The effect of information load on decision quality, however, occurs even when the choice rule is held constant. Wright (1975) instructed subjects in the use of lexicographic, conjunctive, and averaging rules and required their use in choice problems containing two, six, and ten alternatives. Since the correct choices implied by each rule could be specified beforehand, it was possible to measure decision-making accuracy. Across all rules accuracy was fairly high for two alternatives but declined considerably for six and ten alternatives.

Information load, as defined by amount of data, thus appears to affect decision quality in two ways: First, individuals tend to use simpler and less optimal rules as information load increases. Second, the reliability with which individuals use choice rules tends to decrease as information load increases. The relative importance of these processes is unclear.

Dimensional commensurability. Information load, whether brought about by increases in data, time pressure, or distraction, is the most prominent aspect of task complexity. However, there is another important aspect—the degree to which alternatives share dimensions in common. In general, task complexity increases to the extent that decision alternatives have unique dimensions and lack common dimensions. The larger the number of unique relative to common dimensions, the greater is the necessity for the decision maker to make trade-offs and use compensatory choice rules. This increases cognitive strain (Bruner, Goodnow, and Austin, 1956; Kahneman, 1973) and may prod individuals to try to minimize their information acquisition and processing.

One way to do this is to rely heavily on dimensions common to all alternatives in the set and to ignore or give little weight to dimensions unique to particular alternatives. A set of experiments by Slovic and MacPhillamy (1974) supported such a *common-dimension effect* and demonstrated its robustness. Subjects compared pairs of students with respect to potential grade point average in college. In each pair both students had scores on one common dimension (e.g., English skills) and one unique dimension (e.g., quantitative aptitude for student A and need to achieve success for student B). In making their comparisons, subjects relied more heavily on common than unique dimensions, even after they had been warned not to yield to such a tendency. Reliance on common dimensions was also found by Russo and Rosen (1975). When selecting their most preferred of six alternatives, subjects tended to employ sequences of binary comparisons between alternatives that shared the same attributes (see also Russo and Dosher, 1980; Tversky and Russo, 1969). Interestingly, reliance on common dimensions affects the assessed worth of alternatives. Alternatives that are partially described (i.e., that have missing values on a dimension) tend to be devalued relative to fully described alternatives (Yates, Jagacinski, and Faber, 1978).

Information format.   The format of data presentation has been hypothesized to affect information search patterns (Slovic, 1972, p. 14). Tversky (1969) suggested that if alternatives are displayed sequentially (as in exposure to advertisements for competing brands), processing by alternative will be facilitated. If, in contrast, information on dimensions of several alternatives is available simultaneously, processing by attribute will be facilitated.

These ideas have been supported in several experiments. When presented with a complete matrix display (i.e., all $m \times n$ informational items available simultaneously), or when allowed to control information acquisition, individuals tend to process information by attribute (e.g., Capon and Burke, 1977; Olshavsky and Acito, 1980; Russo and Dosher, 1975; Russo and Rosen, 1975). When this is not convenient, however, individuals will readily adopt a processing strategy that fits the information format of the task. For example, Bettman and Kakkar (1977) presented subjects with information about eleven brands of breakfast cereal, each characterized by thirteen attributes. Comparing an alternative-centered condition, where each alternative was described in a separate booklet, with an attribute-centered condition, in which information about each attribute was given in a separate booklet, it was found that in the former case subjects processed in an intraalternative man-

ner and in the latter in an intraattribute way. Bettman and Zins (1979) investigated the effect of information format by prespecifying the rules subjects were to use in choice tasks in which information format was varied. Subjects required less time to make a choice when the information format was congruent rather than incongruent with the prespecified rule. For example, use of a lexicographic rule was facilitated when information was presented in a matrix format as compared with a format in which alternatives were presented separately.

The effect of information format is apparently mediated by the representation of information in short-term memory. Payne (1976b) suggested that information may be stored in one of the following forms: alternative (attribute, value) or attribute (alternative, value). For example, information about the rent of an apartment could be represented as apartment A (rent, $400) or rent (apartment A, $400). The former mode of representation would facilitate an interdimensional search and evaluation process, the latter an intradimensional one. Johnson and Russo (1978) demonstrated such effects of information format on storage in memory. Their analysis of recall response times indicated that if information was presented by alternative, it was stored by alternative; if presented by attribute, it was stored by attribute. Again, it appears that people will cognitively adapt to the characteristics of the decision problem.

Multistage models.   A general summary of the research on the effects of task complexity and information format is that subjects adapt by using the most convenient choice rule—one that results in a satisfactory choice without undue cognitive effort.

Sometimes, convenience is best served by using a sequence of different choice rules rather than just one rule. It is, in fact, rare to find individuals systematically using only a single choice rule. More often, individuals do some switching from intra- to interattribute processing and from one choice rule to another. Occasionally, individuals combine elements of different rules to construct new heuristics (e.g., Bettman and Park, 1980b; Bettman and Zins, 1977). In some models it is assumed that the decision process has a sequence of stages, with different rules applicable at each.

In a general model of this type, proposed by Montgomery and Svenson (1976), choice rules are ordered sequentially such that simpler rules will be used before complex ones. The individual is presumed to use first the dominance rule, i.e., to determine whether any one alternative is best on all attributes (allowing for some ties). If no such alternative is found, the individual will resort to the conjunctive or disjunctive rule. If these rules do not result in a unique choice, the decision maker will increase the criterion cutoff levels or the differentiation of attractiveness of attributes. Eventually, the decision maker may use a choice rule requiring the addition of utilities and trade-offs between attributes. These more demanding choice rules, however, will generally be used only when a fairly high level of confidence is desired.

In the same spirit, Wright and Barbour's (1977) model views the typical choice process as consisting of two stages. In the initial screening stage the decision maker attempts to reduce the set of alternatives as closely as possible to a desired target number (usually but not necessarily $n = 1$). In executing the screening stage, individuals employ a conjunctive choice rule. If the resulting number of eligible alternatives is the same as the target number, the decision process is terminated. If not, a secondary stage is initiated. In this stage the decision maker might use a variety of rules, including the conjunctive, lexicographic, and variations of additive-utility rules. If the conjunctive rule is reapplied, the decision maker redefines his or her initial cutoffs, appropriately making them more stringent or more lenient.

Such an iterative strategy can lead to a subtle bias: In starting a decision-making episode, the decision maker may consider only a small set of alternatives remembered as the output from earlier stages. If the initial screening process is based on convenience, it is likely that some attractive options will be excluded from entry into the secondary choice stage. Wright and Barbour found evidence that subjects occasionally made suboptimal choices because they failed to review alternatives rejected early in the initial screening stage.

Wright and Barbour's (1977) model suggests that decision makers apply screening rules in a rather rigid, all-or-none manner: Alternatives that are rejected in the initial stage are excluded from later consideration. However, it seems likely that for many choice problems individuals are more flexible in their use of choice rules. Alternatives rejected in initial screening may ultimately be reconsidered and reevaluated, depending on subsequent processing. Park (1978a, 1978b) proposed a multistage satisficing-plus choice model that allows for such reconsideration of alternatives. Individuals are assumed to distinguish attribute dimensions in the way they enter the decision. Dimensions on which the decision maker establishes a minimum acceptable threshold are referred to as *rejection-inducing dimensions*. Dimensions on which the decision maker's categories range only from good to excellent are called *relative-preference dimensions*.

In the initial choice stage decision makers are hypothesized to rely primarily on rejection-inducing dimensions. Alternatives are tentatively eliminated if they are below the minimum cutoff value on any rejection-inducing dimension *and* if they do not possess highly compensating values on other dimensions. This conditional elimination process resembles a conjunctive rule but is applied less rigidly.

Once the set of alternatives has been reduced to a manageable number, the decision maker enters a kind of lexicographic second stage in which dimensions are examined in order of their importance. Reliance is again placed primarily on rejection-inducing dimensions, taking relative-preference dimensions into consideration only to resolve ties. Park's model thus suggests a type of checks-and-balances system that efficiently prevents the selection of suboptimal alternatives.

The primary strength of these multistage models is that they are both specifiable in detail and testable by means of process-tracing techniques. This very strength, however, is often associated with the disadvantage of narrowness: Any highly detailed multistage model, however well grounded in a plausible assumption (e.g., that individuals attempt to reduce cognitive effort), is likely to hold only under certain conditions. Undoubtedly, a wide variety of multistage models can be demonstrated, under the appropriate circumstances, to adequately represent individuals' decision processes.

The contingency approach. It is undeniable that individuals are remarkably adaptable to decision task requirements and to variables such as information load and format (Carroll, 1980; Ebbesen and Konecni, 1980). It is unclear, however, to what degree individuals exercise conscious control over their choice of decision strategy or choice rule. Are choice rules simply triggered by environmental cues, or are they chosen by the individual on the basis of some "metastrategy"? Triggering by cues is evidenced, for example, by the effects of information format on choice rule selection (e.g., Bettman and Kakkar, 1977; Russo and Rosen, 1975), whereas the use of a metastrategy is implied by most multistage choice models.

A reasonable assumption is that different aspects of the choice process are under varying degrees of conscious control. The distinction made in cognitive psychology between structural and control processes is relevant here (e.g., Schneider and Shiffrin, 1977). Structural processes, being more "wired-in," are relatively inflexible, while control processes are modifiable and largely under conscious influence. Thus basic cognitive processes such as attention, which are likely to be driven primarily by characteristics of the task environment, will tend to admit of only limited control by the decision maker. In contrast, higher-level cognitive processes, such as deciding whether to give more weight to cost avoidance versus reward maximization, may be more under conscious control.

Given that individuals can exercise some control over selection of choice rule or rules, on what factors might a typical metastrategy be based? Multistage models (e.g., Montgomery and Svenson, 1976) often invoke a *cognitive least effort principle*. Individuals may also take account of other factors such as speed of execution, chance of making errors, and ease of justifiability. In fact, choice rules themselves can be conceptualized as multidimensional objects varying in a set of such attributes (Einhorn and Hogarth, 1981). A metastrategy, then, is a decision process or set of principles by which choice rules are evaluated and selected.

The relative importance of choice rule attributes, shifting according to the decision task, will, of course, influence the choice of a choice rule. For example, under certain conditions (e.g., a severe deadline) speed of execution may be of paramount importance, while under other conditions (e.g., high importance of the choice) minimizing errors may take precedence. A decision maker will tend to use a simple and quick rule in the former case and a complex but accurate rule in the latter.

Beach and Mitchell (1978) proposed a model of choice rule selection, applicable in both well- and ill-defined situations, which assumes that choice rule selection is contingent on a cost/benefit compromise between the desire to make an optimal decision and the perceived costs of investing time and effort in the decision-making process. The desire to make an optimal decision depends in turn upon the irreversibility and significance of the decision, the time and resource constraints, and the accountability of the decision maker for decision outcomes. The perceived costs of the decision process are influenced by the complexity of various choice rules and by the decision maker's abilities and style. More elaborate and costly decision rules will tend to be used only when the decision maker considers it "worth it."

Christensen-Szalanski (1978) extended Beach and Mitchell's (1978) model and formalized the functional relationships between the complexity of a strategy, the cost of using it, and the perceived probability that it will lead to an optimal outcome. In experimental tests the cost/benefit contingency model has fared well. Studies (Christensen-Szalanski, 1980; McAllister, Mitchell, and Beach, 1979) have found that as predicted, more complex—and therefore costly—decision strategies were chosen when (1) time constraints (i.e., deadlines) for finding solutions were lenient; (2) the decision problem was significant; (3) the decision outcomes were irreversible; and (4) the decision maker was personally accountable for the decision outcome.

The contingency model, moreover, is attractive because as a metastrategy, it is broader in scope than the multistage choice models described earlier. Whereas multistage models tend to treat cognitive effort minimization as the primary principle, the contingency model recognizes the role of other considerations also. When the decision problem warrants it, individuals will not hesitate to rely on a decision strategy requiring a substantial amount of cognitive effort. Another appealing aspect of the contingency model is its parsimony. The predicted effects of a large number of task, situational, and individual-difference variables can be specified once the cost/benefit implications of these variables have been determined. Finally, the model accords with the common-sense view that people generally take a pragmatic and adaptive approach to decision problems.

Criticisms of the contingency approach.   Nevertheless, the cost/benefit contingency model is vulnerable to a number of criticisms. The major criticism, relevant generally to cost/benefit approaches to psychological functioning, is that the model tends to become tautological. Unless one can obtain an assessment of the decision maker's cost and benefit functions independent of the decision actually made, the model will be unassailable.

In some experimental settings it is possible to solve this problem. In their tests of the model Christensen-Szalanski (1980) and McAllister *et al.* (1979) controlled subjects' perceptions of the decision tasks and the costs of using the various decision strategies. They used a cafeteria-style experimental setup, which offers subjects a set of clearly specified decision strategies from which to choose. It is unclear, however, whether a satisfactory test of the model is possible in less rigid situations.

A second criticism concerns the generality, or external validity, of the model's selection mechanism. In experimental settings such as those used by Christensen-Szalanski (1980) and McAllister *et al.* (1979), individuals may make the type of trade-offs the model predicts primarily because the task strongly suggests that they do so. In nonexperimental settings, however, the set of decision strategies is not prespecified, nor are the cost and benefit functions well defined. In such settings trade-offs between potential benefits and costs of various decision strategies are difficult to make. Since people find it difficult to make trade-offs, even under conditions that apparently favor doing so (e.g., Shapira, 1981; Slovic, 1975), it may be unlikely that the cost/benefit selection mechanism represents typical decision-making behavior.

A third criticism of the contingency model is that it underemphasizes the importance of previous learning and habit in choice behavior. The model assumes that individuals are free to choose, from a sizable repertoire of decision strategies, a strategy appropriate to the demands of the decision they confront. In any given decision domain, however, individuals may be familiar with and apply only the one or two strategies that have worked satisfactorily in previous experience, even if more efficient strategies are possible. The literature on *Einstellung* effects (e.g., Luchins, 1942; cf. Langer, 1978, on "mindless" behavior) supports this argument. The contingency model's range of applicability may thus be limited to those situations in which individuals are familiar with a variety of decision strategies and have some notion of the relative costs of using them.

Measuring the cost of thinking. Researchers have generally defined the cost of using a choice rule as the total amount of cognitive effort the rule requires of the decision maker, rather than the momentary cognitive strain, or peak load (Kahneman, 1973; Russo and Dosher, 1980). The cost of thinking is therefore closely tied to the number and type of cognitive operations. Huber (1980) demonstrated how choice rules could be broken down into sequences of *elementary information processes* (EIPs), or cognitive operations producing specific outputs in response to specific inputs (cf. Newell and Simon, 1972). Analysis of choice rules in terms of EIPs enabled Huber to investigate how the information-processing costs of different rules varied with type of information (verbal versus numerical), number of alternatives, and number of dimensions.

Similarly, Johnson (1979) developed a metric of cognitive effort, which he used to derive cost functions for different decision rules in choices involving two, six, and ten alternatives varying on from two to ten attri-

butes. Comparison of these cost functions revealed an interesting pattern. In the binary-choice situation the difference between the effort required by the various rules was small, even with as many as ten attributes. In the situations involving six and ten alternatives, however, even a modest number of attributes made some rules much more costly than others. In general, the cost of compensatory rules increased rapidly as a joint function of number of alternatives and number of attributes, while the cost of noncompensatory rules increased only slightly or leveled off. Johnson's analysis provides a basis for making very specific predictions about the effect of information load on rule selection.

Shugan (1980) has noted that current methods assume that thinking costs remain essentially constant over time. It is likely, however, that learning and memory have an important effect on the relative costs of using different choice rules (Bettman, 1979b). Thus as individuals gain increasing experience with a particular rule, it will tend to require less and less cognitive effort. Despite this difficulty and others, the development of a dynamic model of thinking costs is an important endeavor likely to attract research attention.

Perceptions of choice rules. Individuals' perceptions of the properties of choice rules do not necessarily match the actual characteristics of those rules. Individuals may under- or overestimate the thinking costs and decision benefits associated with different choice rules, thus influencing their selection. What little research there is in this area indeed suggests discrepancies between the actual and perceived characteristics of choice rules.

Wright (1975) studied subjects' perceptions of the difficulty and the usefulness of lexicographic, conjunctive, and two types of averaging rules in choice problems with two, six, and ten alternatives. According to objective measures of actual thinking costs, the compensatory averaging rules and the conjunctive rule should be more difficult to use than the lexicographic rule. Subjects' ratings mainly agreed with this ordering. Interestingly, subjects perceived the conjunctive rule, rather than the averaging rules, to be most efficient at detecting the ideal alternative in the choice set.

Adelbratt and Montgomery (1980) investigated perceptions of the merits of three noncompensatory and three compensatory rules. Subjects were instructed in the use of these six rules, after which they rated the rules' "applicability." Subjects also reported which rules they had used in making their choices, how difficult it was to make a decision, and how confident they were that their choices had been good ones. Overall, the compensatory rules were rated most applicable. Of the noncompensatory rules the conjunctive and lexicographic rules were rated moderately applicable, and the disjunctive rule was rated the least applicable. Subjects reported predominant use of the conjunctive and two of the compensatory rules. Perceived difficulty was fairly constant for all the rules, and confidence was highest [much as in the Wright (1975) study] when the conjunctive rule was used.

In the absence of further studies of the perception of choice rules, these findings should be seen as tentative. The Wright (1975) and Adelbratt and Montgomery (1980) studies lacked methods for verifying that subjects executed the choice rules exactly as task instructions specified. Moreover, these two studies investigated only a limited range of choice conditions.

Optimality of choice rules. Underlying research on choice rules is the assumption that certain rules are more likely to select the best alternative (as defined, for example, according to the decision maker's own criteria for the "ideal" alternative). In general, researchers have assumed that rules requiring the decision maker to consider all the relevant information are more likely to be optimal than are rules that ignore some of the relevant information. Thus most compensatory rules, which require that all relevant attributes be given some weight, are better optimizers than are noncompensatory rules, which permit some attributes to be ignored.

How much do choice rules differ in the likelihood with which they select optimal alternatives? Does it make much difference if not all available and relevant information is used? To answer such questions, one must use experimental settings in which one can unambiguously identify a priori the optimal alternative in a choice set. In such settings it has been shown that rules that make incomplete use of available information can lead to choices that are suboptimal or that violate principles of consistency, such as transitivity.

Rules characterized by intradimensional processing (i.e., comparison of alternatives on one dimension at a time) can produce inconsistent choices. For example, noncompensatory rules such as the lexicographic or elimination-by-aspects rules can lead to intransitivities, in which alternative A is preferred to alternative B, which is preferred to alternative C, which is (paradoxically) preferred to alternative A (Tversky, 1969).

Screening rules (e.g., the conjunctive rule) used to reduce a large set of alternatives to a more manageable number can also lead to suboptimal choices. Such rules may cause rejection of alternatives that fail a criterion on one dimension but whose overall value is higher than alternatives that are minimally acceptable on all dimensions (e.g., Wright and Barbour, 1977). Finally, sequential elimination rules, in which alternatives are accepted or rejected according to a hierarchical structure of attributes, can also lead to suboptimal choices. This will occur when the order of presented alternatives causes the early rejection of any alternative with an undesired attribute (Tversky and Sattath, 1979; see also Plott and Levine, 1978). The key characteristic of all the rules mentioned here is that they ignore information that is potentially useful for selecting the best alternative.

Thus there is ample evidence that several choice rules, especially simple noncompensatory ones, can lead to suboptimal choices. The *extent* to which such rules do so, however, is not clear, since much of the research has employed experimental tasks designed specifically to reveal the shortcomings of the choice rules.

Thorngate (1980) suggests that the shortcomings of many simple choice rules are not very consequential. Using Monte Carlo techniques, Thorngate tested the ability of ten different choice rules to select the best alternative from each of several sets of gambles. He found surprisingly high levels of accuracy for most of the rules, all of which chose the optimal alternative (defined according to the expected-value rule) beyond chance expectation. Several of the rules were remarkably robust, even though they ignored information critical to the calculation of expected value. For example, the *equiprobable rule,* which ignores all probability information, selected the better of two gambles 88 percent of the time and the best of eight gambles 73 percent of the time. Chance performance in these tasks would be 50 percent and 12.5 percent, respectively. Simple choice rules thus may often represent "bargains" in that they can often select optimal alternatives while imposing low cognitive costs upon the decision maker.

Thorngate's conclusions received support from a series of studies on binary choice by Russo and Dosher (1980), who investigated how individuals make the trade-off between accuracy and cognitive effort when selecting between two alternatives. They found a strong tendency for subjects to use choice rules requiring intradimensional information processing. Such rules minimized cognitive effort in comparison with more complex, interdimensional rules. Most importantly, however, the consequent decrease in accuracy was not severe. For example, in one experiment, a simple noncompensatory rule was found to increase the error rate over that of a pure expected-value rule only from 8 percent to 14 percent. But there was a substantial difference in the cognitive effort for these two rules: about two minutes for the expected value rule, but only fifteen seconds for the noncompensatory rule. It was reasonable, then, for subjects to resolve the accuracy-effort trade-off in favor of minimizing effort.

Thus individuals may rely upon suboptimal rules consistently without necessarily suffering in their decision making, as some "faulty" judgmental strategies are surprisingly robust. Nisbett and Ross (1980) calculated how one such strategy—reliance on small samples to estimate population characteristics—performed quite well in a situation representative of everyday experience. Their scenario had an individual relying on testimony from friends about whether a particular college course was worth taking. Small and normatively insufficient sample sizes (say, $n = 2$ or 3) were shown typically to accurately indicate the majority attitude toward the course, given the assumption that there was a high degree of attitudinal consensus (e.g., 80 percent) in the population. Only when the degree of consensus was low (e.g., 60 percent) did the small samples become clearly deficient in providing accurate estimates of the majority attitude. Thus in many circumstances the robustness and efficiency of simple heuristics and choice rules may enable individuals to make relatively accurate judgments with little cognitive effort.

This is not to say, however, that the lower decision accuracy associated with simple choice rules is always inconsequential. A slight increase in the probability of selecting the second-best rather than the best alternative may under some circumstances (e.g., a series of product-pricing decisions in a competitive market) entail substantial costs for the decision maker. Also, there may be real-world analogs of certain experimental settings (Slovic, 1975; Tversky, 1969; Wright and Barbour, 1977) in which simple choice rules *consistently* select suboptimal alternatives.

ILL-DEFINED DECISION PROBLEMS

With well-defined decision problems the decision alternatives and their outcomes are experimentally specified, and researchers have been able to develop detailed models of how the information available in the task is encoded and processed. Moreover, the methodological tools for investigating cognitive processes in preferential choice tasks are well established and generally uncontroversial.

In contrast, research on *ill-defined decision problems* is more diffuse. There is no one dominant research paradigm; the range of decision problems investigated is very wide; and methods and concepts are adopted from a variety of disciplines, including sociology, administrative science, and political science, as well as psychology. Because ill-defined decision problems often occur in group and organizational contexts, much of the research and many of the process models are concerned with macrolevel phenomena (e.g., the effects of organizational structure). In keeping with our emphasis in this chapter, we shall concentrate on the individual rather than the group or institution as the decision-making entity. We shall, however, draw upon group- and organizational-level research findings to the extent that they shed light on individual-level decision making.

Uncertainty

The key characteristic of ill-defined decision problems is uncertainty. Gifford, Bobbitt, and Slocum (1979) listed a dozen different definitions or measures of this term, drawn from psychological and organizational research on decision making. However, the classic definition of uncertainty as the inability to assign specific probabilities to outcomes (Luce and Raiffa, 1957) is the most prominent and widely accepted definition within psychological research on individual decision making (Hogarth, 1975; Howell and Burnett, 1978).

It is possible to distinguish various degrees of uncertainty. In some cases a decision maker may be unsure of the exact outcome probabilities but may nevertheless have sufficient information to assign ballpark estimates such as .7 to .9. In other cases the decision maker may have no basis whatsoever on which to estimate outcome probabilities. It is intuitively obvious that the latter state of affairs represents a greater degree of uncertainty. Thus uncertainty can be characterized by second-order, subjective probability distributions (i.e., subjective probabilities of probabilities). The greater the dispersion of the second-order distribution, the greater is the uncertainty. Though there is disagreement over some details (Lee, 1971; Toda and Shuford, 1965; cf. Yates and Zukowski, 1976), the definition of uncertainty as a second-order probability distribution appears to be a conceptually useful one.

It is nevertheless a rather restricted definition, since it assumes that the decision maker has structured the alternatives and outcomes. In many decision problems, however, even this assumption does not hold; the decision maker may be unaware of, or may not have identified, the alternatives and their associated outcomes (Steinbruner, 1974). A broader conception of uncertainty was proposed by Conrath (1967). In his scheme uncertainty can exist for *states of nature* (the outcomes and their probabilities), for alternative actions or choices, and for the payoffs or values attached to action/outcome pairs. Each of these three components can be bounded (a finite set defined by the decision maker) or unbounded (a psychologically undefined set).

Making further distinctions among levels of uncertainty regarding outcomes and payoffs, Conrath proposed a taxonomy of thirty-two possible types of decision situations. Aspects of Conrath's taxonomy received support in a psychometric scaling study by Gifford *et al.* (1979). It indicated that perceptions of uncertainty varied, as predicted, according to the status—bounded versus unbounded—of the three components (states of nature, choices, and payoffs). The effects of the components were essentially additive: Perceived uncertainty was lowest when all three were bounded, highest when all three were unbounded, and intermediate otherwise.

Conrath's scheme corresponds roughly to Mac-Crimmon and Taylor's (1976) analysis of decision problem structure. They represented decision problems as consisting of an initial state, a terminal or desired state, and a set of transformations required to move between them. If all three of these components are familiar to the decision maker, the decision is well defined, or programmed, and can be resolved by the use of standard operating procedures such as the choice rules described earlier. On the other hand, if all three components are unfamiliar, the decision is most ill defined, or unprogrammed (Reitman, 1964; Simon, 1965).

Both MacCrimmon and Taylor's (1976) view of decision problem structure and Conrath's (1967) conceptualization of uncertainty suggest a very general process model in which individuals deal with ill-defined decision problems by attempting to reduce their uncertainty regarding initial states, alternatives, outcomes, and the payoffs and probabilities associated with the outcomes. Moreover, these attempts at uncertainty reduction will be concentrated on the aspects of the decision problem with the greatest degree of uncertainty. Essentially, this process is an attempt to transform an ill-defined decision problem into a well-defined one.

Most of the research on responses to ill-defined decision problems takes some such uncertainty reduction model as a point of departure. Key questions derived from the model concern how individuals deal with the following phases: *problem recognition, identification of alternatives, evaluation of alternatives,* and *selection of an alternative* (Simon, 1966). These phases, in fact, correspond to those specified by normative models for dealing with ill-defined decision problems (e.g., Hogarth and Makridakis, 1981; von Winterfeldt, 1980). As we shall see, however, individuals are rarely as systematic, sequential, and thorough in their decision processes as normative models dictate.

Problem Recognition

The key characteristic of a decision problem is the perception of a discrepancy between the existing state and a desired state. Recognition of a decision problem could involve a discrepency that is perceived for the first time, one that has been perceived previously and becomes more salient, or one that is anticipated should no action be taken.

What causes individuals to realize that a discrepency exists between what *is* and what *should be*? Miller and Starr (1967) described several common ways in which problem recognition occurs in organizational settings. Two of these are most relevant at the individual level. First, a challenging event may prompt the person to notice that a problem exists; reality may be "so obstreperous that it literally hits [the individual] head-on with the problem" (Miller and Starr, 1967, p. 151). Second, individuals may become aware of a problem because they are monitoring certain diagnostic signs that indicate departures from normality or equilibrium (Steinbruner, 1974). A marketing manager, for example, may notice problems caused by rapid changes in consumer preferences for his division's products because he is keeping track of sales trends. In both of these processes the signal that a problem exists is relatively unambiguous—in the first process because the challenging event is so salient and powerful; in the second because the individual is "primed" to notice the problem indicator.

Often, however, potential indicators of problems are weak and must be distinguished from environmental "noise." In an analysis of administrative decision making in unstructured situations, Mintzberg *et al.* (1976) proposed that most decisions "do not present themselves in convenient ways; problems and opportunities...must be identified in the streams of ambiguous, largely verbal data that decision makers receive" (p.

253). The challenging event often consists of a set of stimuli rather than a single stimulus, and it is the cumulative amplitude of this set that elicits recognition of a decision problem.

Simply perceiving that there is a discrepancy between the existing and a desired state does not necessarily lead the individual to take action (Pounds, 1969). MacCrimmon and Taylor (1976) pointed out that the individual must also be motivated to resolve the problem and must perceive that there exist the necessary abilities and resources to do so. For example, although many individuals perceive poverty in developing countries to be a problem, they do not act upon this perception because they are not motivated or do not perceive the capability to affect the problem. Mintzberg *et al.* (1976) suggested that for the individual to take action, it is necessary that the cumulative amplitude of challenging stimuli reach or exceed the decision maker's *action threshold*. Action thresholds shift continuously according to information load and the number and type of decision problems already in progress. The more burdened an individual is with ongoing decisions, the higher his or her action threshold will be for a new decision.

Ideas similar to that of an action threshold have been implied by other theorists. Janis and Mann (1977) proposed that the decision maker will scan any challenging stimulus rapidly to determine if it can be dismissed as untrue or personally irrelevant. Only if the stimulus is judged to imply a genuine threat will the decision maker proceed to the next stage of the decision process, the surveying of alternatives. The challenging event or communication must be "powerful enough to induce in the decision maker an image of himself as headed for serious setbacks and as ultimately failing to attain one or more of his main objectives" (p. 173). Corbin (1980) suggested that individuals will refrain from responding to a decision problem until at least one alternative that exceeds an uncertainty cutoff is identified. The implication is that delay will be a common response to many decision problems.

The various hypothesized thresholds and cutoffs have received little research attention. In fact, there is a paucity of research altogether on the problem recognition phase of decision making, perhaps because it is often taken for granted. It is obvious that no (conscious) decision can occur unless problem recognition occurs. Yet problem recognition is rarely viewed as the "heart" of the decision process; it is viewed merely as a starting point that precedes the conflictful and more demanding alternative identification and evaluation phases.

Moreover, in laboratory studies of decision making the experimenter rather than the subject defines the decision problem, obscuring the possibility of interesting psychological processes occurring during the problem recognition phase.

Among the questions that might be addressed are these: Is it possible to obtain a valid measure of an action threshold independently of decision behavior? How strongly, and under what conditions, does decision problem recognition depend on whether the problem can be acted upon? Do individuals suppress or forget decision problems that are recognized but have not reached the action threshold? Or alternatively, are they kept in awareness because they represent "unfinished business"?

Identification of Alternatives

Once a problem has been recognized, the decision maker attempts to identify solution alternatives. Presumably, the general nature or domain of the decision problem itself will immediately suggest the type of alternatives likely to be feasible. As a first step, however, the decision maker usually has to structure, or diagnose, the decision problem.

Structuring the decision. There are two major ways for decision makers to formulate a decision problem. The first involves a matching process: The problem is assigned to a certain category, or type, on the basis of similarity to types of problems faced previously. This process can be characterized as *top-down,* or *theory-driven,* since the category to which the decision problem is matched is typically retrieved wholesale from memory and applied with little modification. The second involves a more inductive process: The decision maker constructs hypotheses and revises them on the basis of incoming information. This can be characterized as a *bottom-up process,* since it features "local" inferences responsive to the unique aspects of the problem. These two types of diagnostic processes are not mutually exclusive. In many situations, such as when reading fictional material, individuals will use both types in succession (see e.g., Schank and Abelson, 1977). But in many other situations one or the other will be used predominantly. We will now describe some of the salient features in each process.

Structuring by matching. Decision makers are likely to rely on a matching or categorizing process when they have a great deal of knowledge about the domain in question. This implies having not only a large cognitive store of patterns or prototypes but also the ability to extract efficiently the relevant features of a new situation to match it with a known pattern. Just as experienced chess players are very efficient at "homing in" on the essential features of novel chess positions and categorizing them by prototypical chessboard patterns (deGroot, 1965; Goldin, 1978), experienced decision makers are efficient at structuring novel decision problems by matching them to known types of decisions.

A pertinent and much-discussed example here is the ability of foreign policy specialists to employ detailed political belief systems, or *operational codes* (George, 1969; Walker and Murphy, 1981/1982), to interpret new international events (Fiske and Kinder, 1980; Jervis, 1976; Kinder and Weiss, 1978). Salient features of the event are extracted and matched against a set of patterned political *scripts,* events containing expected sequences of actions and outcomes, such as military moves and countermoves and the formation of alliances (Abelson, 1976b, 1981; Carbonell, 1978). The script with which the event is matched brings to the decision maker's mind a "package" of inferences. Thus, for example, the armed insurgency against the government of El Salvador tends to be viewed in terms of a "Communist guerilla movement" script, which entails outside Communist supplies, implacable hostility of the rebels toward the United States, a domino effect in case of a rebel victory, etc. Decisions on how to react are, of course, colored by this set of beliefs.

There is no guarantee that the efficiency of this matching process is equaled by its accuracy; in fact, there is substantial evidence that even experienced decision makers may retrieve and apply scripts or other cognitive schemata in ways that turn out to be inappropriate. Moreover, the matching process may lead the decision maker to ignore or misperceive information unique to the event in question (Gilovich, 1981; Jervis, 1976; May, 1973). For decision theory, however, the important point is that in familiar domains category- or theory-driven processes are efficient for structuring decision problems and thus reducing uncertainty.

Structuring by hypothesis generation.   When they lack knowledge of the decision domain, individuals are likely to generate hypotheses in an attempt to explain why and how the decision problem arose. There has been little research on this hypothesis generation process. However, Gettys and Fisher (1979) provided a start by proposing that hypotheses are generated by a recursive memory search. Memory searches are initiated if no hypotheses currently exist or if hypotheses already retrieved from memory do not meet a threshold of plausibility. Hypotheses that meet this threshold are added to a current hypothesis set.

The key question in the Gettys and Fisher (1979) model is how the plausibility threshold is determined. They examined subjects' responses in three hypothesis generation tasks and found that subjects tended to require a new hypothesis to be at least half as likely as their best one before adding it to their current hypothesis set. Thus the plausibility threshold is relative rather than absolute, and it shifts according to the plausibility of the best current hypothesis. In addition, as new data are processed, the relative standing of the hypotheses in the set may change.

Identification of alternative actions.   Decision problem diagnoses do not exist in a vacuum; they imply, or are associated with, particular courses of action. This close connection between diagnosis and identification of alternatives was noted by Witte (1972) in a study of 233 organizational decision processes dealing with the acquisition of data-processing equipment. Witte's decision makers generally did not separate the diagnosis from the alternative generation process. Rather, they typically developed or identified alternatives *while* diagnosing the decision problem. As information was gathered, both diagnoses and alternatives were developed, revised, rejected, or retained (McCall *et al.,* 1982). The connection between diagnosis and alternative identification is perhaps most clearly exemplified in the medical domain, where a given diagnosis typically implies a given treatment and where additional information relevant to the problem has a bearing on both the diagnosis and the treatment.

Even in less well defined domains, however, diagnoses channel, or constrain, the alternatives that are identified or generated. For example, a business manager's diagnosis of falling profits as due to a general decline in the nation's economy would suggest a different set of alternatives than would the diagnosis of increased competition from other companies. In this case, as in most, the diagnosis indicates a general *type* of alternative rather than a *particular* alternative.

The search-design continuum.   The process of developing particular alternatives can conveniently be viewed along a continuum, with one end representing the search for ready-made alternatives, the other representing the design or creation of custom-made alternatives (Alexander, 1979; Mintzberg *et al.,* 1976). Between these endpoints are various blends of search and design.

Four types of search processes for ready-made alternatives were identified by Mintzberg *et al.* (1976) in an empirical study of organizational decision making in unstructured situations. It is plausible that the same types occur in individual decision making as well. They are (1) memory search (scanning of long-term memory); (2) passive search (waiting for unsolicited alternatives to appear); (3) trap search (activating "search generators" that can signal or notify the decision maker of the availability of alternatives—e.g., letting personal contacts know that one is looking for a job); and (4) active search (directly seeking alternatives). Following a least effort principle, memory and passive search are likely to be used at first, followed by the more effortful trap and active search processes.

In contrast to these search processes is the design process, which requires combining elements into new alternatives rather than simply retrieving alternatives ready-made. The elements that are combined typically consist of flexible, general-purpose procedures. If the decision maker has a relatively clear idea of what objectives to obtain, design will resemble the problem-solving process described by Newell and Simon (1972). That is, the decision maker will mentally test various combinations of procedures (i.e., alternatives) against goal attainment, retaining them if successful and rejecting them if not. If the decision maker does not have specific objectives in mind, however, the design process will be less systematic because it will be difficult to know either what elements should be combined to form alternatives or how to test alternatives once formed.

The search-design continuum has important implications for decision quality. Other factors aside, alternatives developed through design will tend to fit the requirements of decision problems better than will alternatives obtained through search. The latter are more likely to overlook or distort aspects unique to the current decision problem. An important question, therefore, is what determines whether a decision maker will rely predominantly on search or on design when developing alternative actions. With little research to appeal to, a few generalities can be ventured. First, decision makers will follow the least effort principle. Other things being equal, they will initially employ a variety of search procedures in an attempt to find ready-made alternatives. If this fails, they will modify familiar alternatives in ways appropriate to the current decision problem. Decision

makers will attempt to design novel alternatives only as a last resort, when the less demanding strategies are felt to be ineffective.

Second, there will be a close association between the ease with which the decision problem is diagnosed and the process by which alternatives are developed. When diagnosis consists of the wholesale application of a script or operational code, alternatives are likely to be retrieved from memory rather than designed *de novo*. On the other hand, an inductive, hypothesis generation diagnostic process is more likely to be associated with the design of custom-made alternatives. For example, a political leader applying the Communist subversion schema to revolutionary activity is likely to retrieve readily from memory a set of alternative counteractions. In contrast, the same leader confronting a problem that cannot be so easily schematized (e.g., simultaneous high unemployment and inflation) is likely to design alternatives rather than simply retrieve them from memory. This generalization derives from the finding that well-developed schemata, in domains ranging from chess (e.g., deGroot, 1965; Goldin, 1978) to politics (e.g., Axelrod, 1976; George, 1969; May, 1973), often guide action as well as diagnosis.

A third generalization is in the spirit of the Beach and Mitchell (1978) contingency model for decision strategy selection. Presumably, those variables that heighten the decision maker's desire to obtain an optimal outcome will increase the likelihood that alternatives will be developed through design rather than obtained through search. Decisions that are significant and irreversible, and for which the decision maker is accountable, are likely to elicit the effort necessary to design custom-made alternatives. This prediction follows also from the more formal cost/benefit model proposed by Christensen-Szalanski (1978).

Finally, individuals may possess characteristic styles of information processing associated with differences in structuring ill-defined problems. McKenney and Keen (1974) proposed that styles of information gathering and of information evaluation would yield a useful taxonomy of managerial decision styles. At one end of the information-gathering dimension are *preceptive individuals,* who rely heavily on their preexisting precepts or schemata to interpret information and guide information acquisition. At the other end are *receptive individuals,* who are more sensitive to the stimulus itself. Given the tendency for schema-driven processing to be associated with search, it is reasonable to expect that preceptive individuals will tend to rely upon search processes to identify alternatives, whereas receptive individuals will tend to rely upon design.

Influences on the number of alternatives identified. Besides the question of *how* alternatives are identified, there is the question of *how many:* What determines when decision makers will terminate the development of alternatives? This issue is important in the evaluation of decision quality. According to Janis and Mann (1977), decisions of high quality are in general characterized by thorough canvassing of alternatives.

Several factors affect the number of alternatives decision makers will identify, including how the decision problem is structured. As noted previously, the schemata employed in diagnosing a decision problem restrict the number of options that come to mind or that are retained for consideration. For example, U.S. policymakers' application of the domino theory to Vietnam led them to overlook, or dismiss without consideration, nonescalation alternatives (Alexander, 1979). Such a restricting effect is most likely to occur when the decision maker applies only a single schema to the decision problem. The use of multiple schemata, however, may facilitate identification of a wide variety of alternatives, just as multiple advocacy groups (George, 1972) can enlarge the set of alternatives considered in organizational decisions.

Structuring a decision problem in terms of objectives also appears to facilitate the generation of alternatives. Pitz, Sachs, and Heerboth (1980) compared the effect of several methods of decision structuring on the number of alternatives generated by subjects in solving hypothetical but typical problems of personal choice. Subjects generated significantly more alternatives when they were presented with the decision maker's objectives one by one than when they were shown examples of possible alternatives either organized in categories or listed randomly. Interestingly, the one-by-one presentation of objectives also elicited significantly more alternatives than did a two-by-two or a simultaneous presentation of the same objectives. A possible interpretation is that only when processing objectives separately does the decision maker attend to the unique aspects of each objective. The number of alternatives generated probably depends, in turn, on the number of independent aspects perceived in the decision problem.

Other factors aside, information-processing limitations may constrain individuals to generate only a small number of alternatives. This is especially likely when the

decision maker designs rather than searches for alternatives, since the development of custom-made alternatives usually imposes a heavy cognitive burden (for evidence at the organizational level, see Alexander, 1979; Mintzberg *et al.,* 1976; Steinbruner, 1974). In very unstructured problems decision makers may concentrate effort on developing a single feasible alternative, which then serves as a psychological anchor, or point of reference, for other alternatives that may be developed subsequently.

Another way decision makers reduce cognitive effort is by sequential search: Alternatives are examined one at a time and rejected if they fall short on important goal attributes. Alternatives acceptable on these attributes are retained by the decision maker in an active roster for more intensive examination during a subsequent evaluation phase (Soelberg, 1967; Corbin, 1980). This is most likely to occur when alternatives are discrete, easily identified, and numerous.

A final factor affecting the number of alternatives identified is whether the decision problem requires an optimal or a very good solution rather than just an adequate one (Beach and Mitchell, 1978). The higher the level of motivation for making a good decision, the more alternatives may be sought. Nevertheless, limitations of time and other resources may prevent decision makers from identifying more than a few alternatives, even if their motivation to do so is high. Time pressure, for example, may necessitate curtailing the search for information relevant to the design of novel alternatives. Time pressure can induce caution and conservatism in decision makers (e.g., Ben Zur and Breznitz, 1981; Hansson *et al.,* 1974; Wright, 1974) or, on the other extreme, impulsive seizure of some salient but risky available alternative. The latter is the *hypervigilance reaction* discussed by Janis and Mann (1977). In either case creative alternatives will be overlooked or remain undeveloped.

Evaluation of Alternatives

In general, the identification of alternatives may also entail evaluative processing. Decision makers must necessarily use *some* criteria for deciding what constitutes an alternative. Moreover, in ill-defined decision problems there is rarely a clear separation between the identification phase and the evaluation phase. This lack of separation is clearly seen in studies of organizational decision making, which indicate that alternatives are often developed iteratively, during successive cycles of progressively more detailed evaluation (e.g., Alexander, 1979; McCall *et al.,* 1982; Mintzberg *et al.,* 1976).

Evaluation can be construed as a set of uncertainty-reducing processes. The decision maker must clarify the criteria by which to judge the alternatives, then identify the possible outcomes of the decision, and estimate the probabilities that the alternatives will produce these various outcomes.

Because evaluative criteria are clarified progressively over time, it is difficult for decision makers to establish stable utility functions, as normative decision theories would dictate. Individuals are often unsure of their preferences; they often hold inconsistent preferences; and they frequently change their preferences in response to firsthand experience (e.g., Dyckman, 1981; Fischhoff *et al.*, 1980; Koopmans, 1964; March, 1978). Consequently, decision makers generally do not cognitively represent criteria, or dimensions, at higher than ordinal levels. Moreover, decision makers generally treat evaluative dimensions as noncommensurable. Thus decision makers generally do not assign weights to the different dimensions to reflect their relative importance.

These generalizations appear consistent with the familiar theme that people are limited in their information-processing capacity. Studies of decision making at the organizational (e.g., Carter, 1971a, 1971b; Cyert, Simon, and Trow, 1956; Mintzberg *et al.*, 1976; Steinbruner, 1974) and the individual level, moreover, lend support to these generalizations. Soelberg (1967), for example, in a detailed longitudinal study of the career decisions of MIT graduates, concluded that "scalar utility theory is a poor way of representing the structure of human values." In addition, decision value attributes are "not compared or substituted for each other during choice," and stable utility-weighting functions "[do not] appear to enter into each person's decision processing" (p. 25). With the exception of the attributes the decision maker considers critical, the importance of attributes is determined iteratively, during successive cycles of investigation and evaluation of alternatives.

The second uncertainty reduction process involves attempts by the decision maker to identify the possible states of nature that may result from the decision. From the practically infinite set of possibilities, the decision maker must somehow selectively attend to those aspects that are consequential. This will to a great extent be relative to the decision maker's goals. Thus, in identifying the outcomes of a potential U.S. sale of wheat to the Soviet Union, a Kansas grain farmer would be likely to estimate the impact on his income for the year, whereas a State Department official would attend to the effect on balance of payments and degree of conflict between the two countries.

Goals are not the only influence, however, on the types of outcomes the decision maker attempts to identify. Often the states of nature that become salient to the decision maker are inherent in the alternative itself. Goals aside, the decision maker sometimes cannot help thinking of certain outcomes associated with an alternative. For example, in hiring decisions the presence of a racial minority candidate is likely to cause the decision maker to consider possible outcomes relevant to racial relations.

In the third process, reducing uncertainty about probabilities, decision makers typically try to define the upper and lower bounds of possible outcomes and to progressively "tighten the confidence intervals." Pitz (1975) suggested that this is occasionally achieved by mental rehearsal of different problem representations so that three different point estimates—a *best guess,* a smallest-possible case, and a largest-possible case—can be made. A business manager deciding whether to develop and introduce a new product, for example, may apply different models of the business environment in an attempt to estimate the range of possible effects the product will have on the company's market share. In estimates of this sort, the most probable, or best-guess, outcome is likely to be of most concern to the decision maker (Gettys, Kelly, and Peterson, 1973).

The three processes of uncertainty reduction just described typically take place simultaneously or during successive cycles rather than in any particular systematic sequence. Unless the decision maker's level of subjective uncertainty is sufficiently low with regard to both outcomes and probabilities, he or she is likely to postpone the decision (Corbin, 1980). As goals and evaluative criteria are clarified, and as more information about the alternatives is obtained, a "favorite" alternative typically emerges. Often this alternative is identified on the basis of very few criteria, rarely more than one or two (Soelberg, 1967).

As the decision maker begins to establish preferences among alternatives, information acquisition and processing may become directed toward *confirmation processing,* in which decision makers attempt to resolve problems connected with the preferred alternative (Soelberg, 1967). This attempt is reflected in the finding that decision makers obtain more information on the preferred alternative than on other alternatives (Englander and Tyszka, 1980). During this confirmation phase decision makers also try to arrive at a decision rule that shows unequivocally that the choice candidate dominates other strong candidates. To this end, goal attribute rankings or weights are arrived at or changed to become consistent with the desired decision outcome. This process contrasts clearly with normative decision theory, which dictates that attribute weights be decided upon independently of the evaluation of alternatives.

Selection and Commitment

A process of selection generally occurs throughout the evaluation phase, as the set of alternatives is first narrowed down to an active roster of perhaps three to six alternatives and then reduced further. The final commitment to a single alternative, however, occurs only when "a satisfactorily...dominant decision rule has been constructed, or when the decision maker runs up against an inescapable time deadline during confirmation processing" (Soelberg, 1967, p. 23).

When unable to construct a weighting scheme that would decisively establish the superior attractiveness of one alternative over the others, the decision maker will try to trade off the goal attributes against each other. Thus as in well-defined problems, decision makers will usually trade off attributes only after they have tried cognitively simpler processes.

In ill-defined problems one key trade-off the decision maker is likely to confront is that between uncertainty and other attributes. Typically, the value of an alternative will be psychologically "discounted" as a function of the uncertainty characterizing the alternative [Fellner, 1965; recall the study by Yates et al. (1978), in which partially described alternatives were devalued relative to fully described alternatives; see also the certainty effect in Kahneman and Tversky's (1979) prospect theory]. Thus an alternative with a higher (i.e., more attractive) best-guess value on an important attribute may be rejected in favor of an alternative with a lower best-guess value if the latter is less uncertain (i.e., has a tighter probability distribution of outcomes) than the former.

The trade-offs that the decision maker confronts are likely to make the final selection phase a difficult one, especially if the alternatives remaining in the choice set are close in overall value and if substantial uncertainty about outcomes and probabilities still remains. Thus in Soelberg's (1967) study of MIT graduates' decisions concerning job offers, the selection phase was found to be highly involved and affectively painful.

The selection phase also tends to be a stressful one because it makes salient the fundamental conflict inherent in decision making: To choose one alternative necessitates that the other alternatives and their unique attractive aspects must be forgone (Festinger, 1964; Gerard, 1968). As the point of commitment approaches, the decision maker becomes increasingly aware of costs the decision may entail. A period of *anticipatory regret* may occur, as decision makers mentally project themselves into the uncertain future in an attempt to determine whether the alternative to which they are about to commit themselves will turn out to be disappointing (Janis and Mann, 1977). Such preemptive worrying, according to Janis and Mann (1977), is most likely to occur when the alternatives are similar in attractiveness and the decision maker is therefore uncertain about whether the preferred alternative is really superior to the others; when potential negative aspects of the preferred alternative are likely to appear soon after the commitment is made; when new information about the alternatives can be obtained; and when the decision is important and irrevocable. Anticipatory regret can act as a "brake" on public commitment: If the decision maker becomes aware of the possibility that the preferred alternative has some previously unconsidered risks, he or she may delay commitment, begin an extensive reevaluation process, or even seek new alternatives.

When the decision maker does make the commitment to an alternative, his or her psychological orientation is likely to change. With the announcement of the decision the consequences of the chosen alternative become "actualized." As Walster and Walster (1970) state, "The positive and negative elements of the chosen alternative are bound to have a greater emotional impact after the decision, when they are definite consequences, than they did before the decision" (p. 1002). Phenomenologically, choice and commitment impart a greater sense of reality than do mere judgment or evaluation (Brickman, 1978; Hogarth, 1981).

A great deal of theorizing and empirical research has focused on cognitive and motivational reactions during the postdecisional phase. Cognitive dissonance theory has been the source for the prediction that decision makers will cognitively bolster (i.e., exaggerate the attractiveness of) the chosen alternative and derogate the rejected alternatives (e.g., Festinger, 1957, 1964; Festinger and Walster, 1964; Gerard, 1968; Walster, 1964). Another postdecisional reaction is regret, as evidenced in Walster's (1964) field experiment dealing with career decisions. She found a brief period of regret (indicated by a convergence in attractiveness ratings of chosen and rejected alternatives) sandwiched in between periods of bolstering. Brehm (1966, 1972) and Wicklund (1974) asserted that postdecisional regret is a manifestation of *psychological reactance,* a motivational state aroused whenever freedom is threatened or lost. Making a decision entails the loss of the freedom to reject the chosen alternative, to select the unchosen alternative, or to remain uncommitted. In response to these self-imposed losses of freedom, the decision maker reevaluates the attractiveness of the chosen and unchosen alternatives. As the decision maker becomes reconciled to the loss of freedom entailed by the decision, the effects of reactance will diminish, and bolstering effects will again become predominant (Wicklund, 1974).

The evidence on postdecisional reactions can best be characterized as mixed. Although it is clear that regret and bolstering effects are real psychological phenomena, it has not been easy to predict when they will occur. Soelberg (1967), for example, found a variety of reactions following commitment to a particular job choice. Out of twenty-six decision makers none showed a consistent, long-term spreading apart of attractiveness of chosen versus rejected alternatives; two showed the effect starting only two or more weeks after commitment; nine showed the effect initially after commitment but to a decreasing extent thereafter; ten showed no change in attractiveness ratings of the alternatives; and five exhibited regret, as indicated by a narrowing of attractiveness ratings between chosen and rejected alternatives. Janis and Mann (1977) found that after committing themselves to a difficult decision (e.g., to stop smoking), decision makers were less likely to show regret than an enthusiastic, raring-to-go reaction.

In view of these findings accurate predictions of postdecisional reactions seem possible only if many variables are taken into account. Specifically, the nature of the decision problem (e.g., importance, irreversibility, valence), social and self-presentational implications of the decision, and the nature of the decision maker's predecisional information processing are likely to influence the type of postdecisional reaction. As Janis and Mann (1977) have stated, "Neither regret nor bolstering will occur following commitment unless certain conditions are fulfilled that make for persisting decisional conflict" (p. 329).

Integrated Views of the Decision Process

We have presented the overall decision process as consisting of four basic phases: problem recognition, identification of alternatives, evaluation of alternatives, and selection and commitment. These phases correspond more or less to the modal pattern used by most decision theorists as a framework to organize research on ill-defined decision problems.

In a sense, though, the phases are a convenient fiction. Decision processing is frequently iterative and cyclical, and the cognitive processes described as characterizing one phase often occur in other phases as well. Thus, for example, the outcome and probability estimation processes that we have placed under the evaluation phase will almost certainly take place also in the alternative identification phase.

Because researchers have tended to investigate the phases and their particular processes separately, a great deal is known about different subparts of the decision process. It is a difficult task, though, to integrate the subprocesses to arrive at an overall realistic view of how people deal with ill-defined decision problems. In the next section we will describe some attempts at such integration.

Conflict models. Hogarth (1980) proposed, unsurprisingly, that decision processes are initiated in response to goals. Before the decision maker takes action, however, there is a predecision choice of whether to make the effort to analyze the problem or to preserve the status quo by choosing not to choose. This preliminary choice of whether or not to face the decision conflict is made by roughly estimating the benefits and costs of analyzing the problem.

The general *benefits* of thinking include increasing control of one's own behavior and therefore of the environment; clarifying goals and preferences; restructuring the decision problem so that creative alternatives can be discovered or generated; discovering new sources of information relevant to the decision problem; and minimizing psychological regret if a chosen alternative turns out unfavorably. The general *costs* of thinking include increasing the uncertainty in one's preferences and values; increasing one's confusion about how to structure the decision problem; and increasing the cognitive strain associated with acquiring, processing, and retrieving information. Note that in contrast to the Beach and Mitchell (1978) and Christensen-Szalanski (1978) contingency models, increases in thinking are not necessarily assumed to increase the perceived probability that a good alternative will be found. If more thought heightens the uncertainty regarding preferences or how to structure the problem, the perceived ease of finding a good alternative may decrease.

If the decision maker chooses to confront the decision conflict, he or she begins analysis of the decision proper. However, the no-choice option is possible at any point until an alternative is chosen and acted upon. The individual can go through several cycles of information search, delay, further search, problem structuring, and development and refinement of alternatives, before choosing an alternative and becoming committed to it through behavior. Hogarth's model thus conceptualizes decisions as dynamic series of conflicts that are resolved by intuitive cost/benefit comparisons.

Like Hogarth (1980), Janis and Mann (1977) view decisions as composed of a series of issues that lead the decision maker to adopt one or another mode of decision processing. Janis and Mann's highly detailed model places special emphasis on the stress and affective reactions engendered by decisional conflict. Each key issue arising during the decision process can be represented by a particular question. The first question occurs at the challenge phase: Are the potential risks serious if the current policy is not changed? If the answer is no, then the decision maker maintains the status quo. This condition of *unconflicted inertia* allows the decision maker to avoid the decision conflict and its attendant stress.

If the potential risks of maintaining the policy are considered serious, the decision maker asks whether a feasible ready-made alternative exists to meet the problem. To answer this, the decision maker quickly surveys possible alternative solutions. If a good solution is perceived, it is readily adopted, a response called *unconflicted change.*

If the decision maker perceives no satisfactory solution, he or she next confronts whether it is realistic to expect to find a solution. If this assessment is pessimistic, a condition of *defensive avoidance* occurs, which can take a number of forms: procrastinating, shifting decision responsibility to others, and bolstering (i.e., exaggerating the favorable consequences and minimizing the unfavorable consequences of the status quo). These are all modes of coping with stress.

If the decision maker is optimistic about finding a satisfactory solution, the next question arises: Is there sufficient time to find or construct a solution? A pessimistic answer will produce a state of hypervigilance, which can be likened to a state of panic. This typically occurs when the passage of time is perceived to result in the closing of escape routes or the removal of possible solutions to a dilemma.

The states of defensive avoidance and hypervigilance represent nonvigilant, or deficient, modes of information processing. Vigilance, or high-quality information processing, on the other hand, entails that a wide range of alternatives be thoroughly canvassed, that the costs and benefits of each alternative be carefully weighed, that relevant new information be sought and assimilated, and that the alternatives include contingency plans for dealing with likely changes in circumstances. Vigilance is likely to occur when the decision maker perceives a challenge to the present course of action; satisfactory alternatives are not immediately present; there is hope for finding a solution; and when the decision maker perceives that there is enough time to find it.

These general response and information-processing patterns—unconflicted inertia, unconflicted change, defensive avoidance, hypervigilance, and vigilance—are ways of dealing with decisional conflict and stress. Janis and Mann (1977) proposed an elaborate model that focuses on coping responses within five stages of decision making: appraising the challenge, surveying the alternatives, weighing the alternatives, deliberating about commitment, and adhering to the choice. This five-stage model contains feedback loops and other recursive processes.

In stage three (weighing the alternatives) the decision maker determines which alternative is the best, or least objectionable, of those available. If this alternative does not meet the decision maker's essential requirements for an acceptable solution, however, a reversion to stage two (a resurveying of alternatives) is likely, especially if one of the existing alternatives cannot be improved sufficiently through modification. The reversion from stage four (deliberating about commitment) to stage three, the cold-feet phenomenon, occurs when the decision maker realizes the negative implications of making a commitment to the chosen alternative. If persons within the decision maker's social network judge the alternative to be unacceptable, the decision maker is especially likely to shrink back from adopting the alternative in order to reexamine other alternatives. The decision maker may then cycle repeatedly through stages two, three, and four in a quest for a satisfactory alternative that can safely be implemented. Such cycles of vacillation, though fraught with conflict, may have potentially useful effects. They may stimulate the decision maker to acquire valuable new information, adopt new criteria for acceptability of alternatives, and develop contingency plans. On the other hand, vacillation may have the deleterious effects of making one or more reasonable alternatives unacceptable or of weakening the decision maker's decisiveness when an alternative is eventually implemented. Whether or not the cycling process gives rise primarily to constructive effects depends on whether the conditions for vigilance predominate throughout the course of the decision.

A key question in Janis and Mann's (1977) model—and in Hogarth's (1980)—concerns the decision maker's *stopping rule* (Miller *et al.,* 1960). What factors determine the point at which the decision maker exits from the decision cycle? Two general categories of factors come to mind: situational constraints, such as time and other resources, and psychological variables, such as fatigue, stress, and estimates of the likelihood of obtaining additional relevant information or devising a better alternative.

The conflict models are eclectic in derivation and ambitious in scope. They aim to capture both cognitive and affective influences within the decision process and thus provide a counterweight to the exclusive cognitive orientation of much decision theorizing. As Kinder and Weiss (1978) and Toda (1980) have pointed out, stress and other affective responses infuse decision making. Thus though it may be difficult to assess the validity of the more intricate aspects of the conflict models (e.g., the particular feedback loops and recursive processes), the major premise—that complex, extended decisions are composed of a series of conflictful choices—appears sound.

The cybernetic model. Conflict models represent one type of alternative to the normative, or analytic paradigm, in which the decision maker defines alternatives, calculates probabilities and utilities, and acts so as to maximize subjective expected utility. The cybernetic model explicated by Steinbruner (1974) is another type of alternative. Whereas conflict models emphasize conflict and stress reduction, the cybernetic model emphasizes "the business of eliminating the variety inherent in any significant decision problem" (Steinbruner, 1974, p. 56).

The essential premise of the cybernetic model is that in dealing with ill-defined decision problems, individuals

behave much like servomechanisms. That is, they monitor a small set of critical variables and respond with a set sequence of actions if these variables move outside tolerable ranges. Such cybernetic decision behavior is highly programmed; it works by standard operating procedures established by prior experience.

Since the cybernetic decision maker aims simply to keep a few feedback variables within a given range, there is no need to form a cognitive representation of the environment, as in other models. Further, whereas most models assume that decision makers reduce uncertainty by trying to specify goals, find alternatives, and estimate the likely outcomes of these alternatives, the cybernetic model assumes that decision makers reduce uncertainty largely by ignoring it. They simply avoid direct outcome calculations; moreover, they psychologically do not engage in the pursuit of an explicitly designed result. Cybernetic decision makers screen out information that the established set of responses is not programmed to accept. In short, the cybernetic model posits a very circumscribed decision process, involving highly focused sensitivity to a few critical variables, the avoidance of outcome calculations, and the reliance on well-learned action sequences established by prior experience.

It is clear that cybernetic processes are pervasive in everyday life. Routine activities such as walking down the street or fixing breakfast rely on the type of cybernetic processes that Steinbruner describes. In such activities action sequences are well established, and it is necessary only that the individual monitor a few cues to ensure that the behavior "runs off" smoothly. Much social behavior also seems to fit the cybernetic model. For example, in responding to a request for a routine favor, individuals may attend to a few criterion variables, such as the politeness and size of the request. If these variables are within an acceptable range, the scripted, or preprogrammed, action sequence is performed (Abelson, 1981). As Langer (1978) has shown, much everyday behavior is "mindless" in that it is triggered by the mere presence of an environmental cue rather than being driven by considered choices.

The important question, however, is whether consequential decisions can be understood in terms of the cybernetic model. Mindless behavior, after all, tends to become mindful when the stakes are high (Langer, 1978). Steinbruner (1974), however, asserts that the cybernetic model, with its central principle of controlling uncertainty and reducing variety, is applicable to important and complex decisions as well as to simple inconsequential ones, provided the model is supplemented with assumptions drawn from cognitive psychology. These assumptions are that in the service of uncertainty reduction, decision makers impose clear, coherent meaning on ill-defined decision problems; they use categorical rather than probabilistic judgments in doing so; they expect to anticipate outcomes exactly rather than assign probabilities to a range of outcomes; and they deal with trade-offs either by denying them or by transforming them into single-valued problems. These cognitive processes, according to Steinbruner, result in a simplified structure of the decision problem within which the usual cybernetic processes—monitoring of a small number of critical variables and the activation of a standard sequence of actions—can operate.

How is the cybernetic model to be evaluated? As a process model, it has not been specified in enough detail to be easily testable. The organizational and political decisions (e.g., Defense Department budgeting decisions; nuclear sharing within NATO) recruited by Steinbruner as evidence for cybernetic decision processes do seem to exhibit the central characteristics of the model. Even in these decisions, however, cybernetic processes do not appear in "pure" form; they are interwoven with other processes deriving, for example, from political forces and governmental structures (Allison, 1971). The same holds true for decision making at the individual level. The pure form of cybernetic processing, in which the individual monitors one or two key variables without cognitively diagnosing the decision problem, is probably confined to scripted or routine decisions.

Even when modified by cognitive processes, the cybernetic model nevertheless still views decision making in ill-defined situations as falling far short of normative standards. Little room is provided in this view for high-quality vigilant decision making characterized by openness to information and creative design of novel alternatives.

There is certainly a great deal of case study evidence that individual decisions in ill-defined situations sometimes show the deficiencies identified by the modified cybernetic model. Both Jervis (1976) and Axelrod (1976), for example, described numerous instances in which foreign policy decision makers ignored or distorted information inconsistent with their prior, well-established beliefs about the political environment; analyzed that environment superficially by relying on a few key attributes relevant to some salient historical analogy; and failed to confront trade-off relationships. Thus even in conse-

quential decisions the uncertainty reduction tendencies of the cybernetic model appear.

What the modified cybernetic model lacks, however, is a specification of the conditions under which its processes will be more or less powerful. As it stands now, the model would be challenged by evidence that decision makers do occasionally approach high normative standards. In fact, individuals are sometimes creative in designing decision alternatives; they are sometimes sensitive to a wide range of new information; they are sometimes capable of updating their beliefs in response to the new information; and they do sometimes confront trade-offs directly (e.g., Janis, 1972; Snyder and Diesing, 1977; Zeev, 1981). The absence of cyberneticlike processes within some decisions suggests that the cybernetic paradigm, as described by Steinbruner (1974), cannot claim to be the sole plausible alternative to the normative paradigm. Its value lies in painting a picture of decision making that differs substantially from other models.

POTENTIAL CONSTRAINTS ON EFFECTIVE DECISION MAKING

In this section we assemble a catalog of factors that in one way or another may exert a constraining influence on effective decision making. The decision maker may face up to three separate problems: defining what is relevant, assembling the relevant information, and integrating the information so as to make the decision.

Constraints arise in several ways: It may be costly or impossible to gather all the relevant information—indeed, it may not be clear what information is relevant. Important information may be overlooked by the individual or nonessential information overweighted for a variety of reasons. Information may have been gathered for other purposes and uncritically applied. Information from different sources or of different kinds may not be easy to combine. Reasoning about uncertain outcomes may involve misapprehensions attributable to lack of experience or insight. A number of motives may render decisions hasty or biased or based on irrelevancies.

Altogether, decision making is a complex performance. We have not in this section or chapter exhausted but a fraction of the possible complications. (For a sobering litany of decision nuances, see March, 1978.) As with other complex human performances, it would be a conceit to suppose that perfection is readily attainable. Thus it is neither a surprise nor a cause for lament that rationality is "bounded," to use Simon's (1956) famous phrase. As we list factors that could conceivably disturb good decision making, therefore, the reader should resist the conclusion that we are making a general indictment of human intelligence. Each listed factor points up a difficulty in the choice process, many of them of general psychological interest and necessary to take into account if decisions are to be improved in a variety of applied areas.

Much of the literature on cognitive limitations or biases concerns phenomena of *judgment* and not necessarily of behavioral *choice,* as such. We should be careful not simply to equate judgment and choice (Einhorn and Hogarth, 1981); nevertheless, certain judgments are necessary to choices, and thus we can learn much about decision constraints from judgment constraints.

It is not really easy to separate cognitive from motivational factors, but for convenience we divide our list of constraints in two, using that distinction. In a final section we discuss proposals for overcoming the various constraints on effective decision making.

INFORMATION GATHERING AND INTEGRATION

Information pertinent to a decision may be available prior to the posing of a decision, or it may be gathered in the service of a decision. In both cases the information could concern the probability of particular outcomes or the utility of those outcomes (or both).

Difficulties in Estimating Outcome Probabilities

How do people estimate the probabilities of particular outcomes? One obvious way is to use the relative frequency of comparable outcomes in the past. The football coach deciding whether to call a particular play, the diner wondering what to order, the faculty member screening candidates for graduate school—all may rely on past probabilities of success and failure. There are several problematic aspects of such probability estimates.

Positive versus negative instances. Even though the probability of an outcome can, in principle, be estimated by its relative frequency within a set of opportunities, there is an empirical question whether individuals can keep accurate track of the number of successes and failures of occurrence of a particular outcome over a long series of trials. Peterson and Beach (1967), in an early re-

view of the evidence, concluded that in general they could. Since then, questions have been raised.

One issue concerns the well-known finding in concept formation research that positive instances of a concept are more readily used by the learner than negative instances (cf. Hovland and Weiss, 1953; Wason, 1960, 1968). That is, the occurrence of an example belonging to a particular concept class seems more helpful in narrowing the possible rules defining the class than is the occurrence of an example that does not belong to the concept class. The latter type of event might often be more objectively informative by negating a number of potential rules, but subjects seem to have difficulty with the indirect reasoning involved. The strategy of seeking confirmations appears easier than the strategy of seeking disconfirmations; i.e., reasoning about sufficiency is easier than reasoning about necessity. Smedslund (1963) hypothesizes that confirmatory reasoning is based on an earlier Piagetian stage than that of disconfirmatory reasoning.

This proclivity may carry over from concept learning to probability estimation. Suppose that a person is scanning evidence relevant to the proposition "A tends to imply B." A positive instance containing both A and B may carry more weight toward confirmation than a negative instance containing A and not-B (or not-A and B) may weigh toward disconfirming (or undercutting) the proposition. Indeed, Jenkins and Ward (1965), Schustack and Sternberg (1981), and others have found such effects empirically. Beyond the biased use of positive instances is also the biased collection of potentially positive instances. In a detailed analysis of the *illusion of validity* (Kahneman and Tversky, 1973), Einhorn and Hogarth (1978) note that while attention is often given to the success rate of accepted options, data are often not even available on the potential success rate of rejected options. The upshot is that subjects may tend to overestimate the comparative frequency of success in hypothesized contexts. (We return to this tendency below.) The earlier review by Peterson and Beach (1967), claiming general accuracy of estimation, touched largely upon tasks lacking such focused hypotheses.

A curious experiment by Estes (1976) raises in a different way the failure of subjects' probability judgments to be relativized adequately. He pitted absolute frequently against relative frequency of occurrence, as follows: Subjects saw a series of simulated public opinion survey responses, most trials posing the choice between candidate A versus candidate B, the remaining few (randomly interspersed) trials pitting candidate C versus candidate D. In one version the data specified 50–50 preferences between A and B and also between C and D. When subjects were then asked to predict preference when A was pitted against C, they showed a strong tendency to predict choice of A more often than C, presumably because they had witnessed preference for A more often than preference for C. This illogically ignores the data that A's competition B was preferred more than C's competition D. It is as though a baseball team that had played .500 ball over a 100-game schedule were deemed stronger than another team in another league that had played .500 ball over a 20-game schedule, given no information about the relative strength of the two leagues! This phenomenon again demonstrates the tendency for positive instances to outweigh negative instances in using data to estimate future probabilities.

Availability effects.   For several reasons, beyond the positive versus negative instance distinction, different experiences may be differentially easy to retrieve from memory. The relative frequency of retrieved experiences may not correspond to their actual relative frequency.

The term *availability* was introduced by Tversky and Kahneman (1973) to refer to ease of retrieval when items are mentally sampled in order to estimate objective relative frequency. They asked their subjects, Which is more frequent in ordinary English, words with 'k' as the first letter, or words with 'k' as the third letter? Most people replied "first letter," even though that is objectively incorrect. The explanation is that it is easier to generate words given the starting letter than otherwise, and people take the relative mental availability as a sign of corresponding relative frequency. Other examples yielded comparable results.

The influence of availability has been identified or conjectured in a great many contexts. As Nisbett and Ross (1980) have pointed out, greater availability of a mental item could come about because of greater *attention* to the item when presented, more effective *coding* of the item, more stable *storage,* or more effective *retrieval.* Additionally, in the case of hypothetical future outcomes for which past data are scarce, availability may devolve on the *rehearsal of relevant event scenarios that have been provided to subjects.* Carroll (1978), for example, found that subjects told to mentally rehearse a plausible hypothetical victory scenario for Carter (Ford) in the 1976 presidential election later rated it more probable that Carter (Ford) would actually win, compared with a

no-rehearsal control group. Gregory *et al.* (1982) found that imagining oneself in plausible scenarios for getting falsely arrested, or for watching a new cable TV service, increased probability ratings for these events; the *actual* probability of later subscribing to cable TV was even increased by imaginative rehearsal.

Within social psychology most of the focus has been on attention and encoding effects, under the rubric of the general concept of *salience* (Taylor and Fiske, 1978) rather than availability. Perceptually salient events are more readily remembered than nonsalient events (Pryor and Kriss, 1977; Taylor and Fiske, 1975), and thus presumably the probability of their future occurrence would be overestimated. Salience has been manipulated by varying the seating placement of observers of a face-to-face interaction (Taylor and Fiske, 1975), the visual prominence of people being observed (McArthur and Post, 1977), the unexpected nature of presented information (Hastie and Kumar, 1979), and in several other ways.

In most such studies the main emphasis has been on person attributions as a dependent variable rather than on ease of memory and estimates of frequency or probability. Salience affects both, although there is controversy about the direction of causal mediation (Fiske, Kenny, and Taylor, 1982). There is also a good deal of uncertainty about the mixed bag of influences characterized by the term *salience.* Perceptual *vividness,* or dramatic impact, is an intuitively appealing characterization of the underlying operative variable in salience effects, but it has been reviewed with considerable skepticism (Taylor and Thompson, 1982). At any rate, more research is needed on the effects of salience on probability estimates.

Illusory conditionals and insensitivity to base rates. Judgments of the conditional probability of *B* given *A* can be seriously affected by subjects' hypotheses of a connection between *A* and *B.* Hypotheses can in fact override extensional evidence about the relationship between *A* and *B.* In one of their famous demonstrations of *illusory correlation,* Chapman and Chapman (1969) presented subjects with a large set of face drawings by putatively categorized mental patients and afterward asked for estimates of the frequency of certain features in drawings by members of particular patient categories. Although there was no objective correlation between categories and features, subjects grossly overestimated the occurrence of pairings well steeped in clinical lore, such as "shifty eyes" expressing paranoia. To the extent that this result generalizes, it can be said that evidence about co-occurrences tends to be misremembered (or misreconstructed) in the direction of stereotypic expectations.

Nisbett and Ross (1980) review additional evidence of this theory-driven distortion, concluding that it is widespread, especially in view of the difficulty people have in accurately keeping track of data-driven contingencies (i.e., instance-by-instance presentations) (Crocker, 1981; Jennings, Amabile, and Ross, 1982).

Another way to examine theory-driven versus data-driven strategies is to study the conditions under which subjects use relevant, prepared statistical summaries, or *base-rate data*. It has often been shown that base-rate data are underutilized or not even used at all. The seminal demonstration was by Kahneman and Tversky (1973). They presented subjects with descriptions said to have been drawn at random from a set containing seventy lawyers and thirty engineers, and they asked subjects to estimate the probability that each person described was an engineer. One of the descriptions gave biographic details about a man named Jack, whose hobbies (carpentry, sailing) and traits (conservative, careful) were suggestive of an engineer.

The striking feature of the results was that the base-rate data had no effect. Subjects told that the case was drawn at random from a set with seventy lawyers and thirty engineers gave an almost identical average estimate for the probability that Jack was an engineer as did subjects told that the set contained thirty lawyers and seventy engineers. In both groups the probability estimate was very high because Jack's case history seemed very prototypic of engineers. Normatively, it is incorrect to ignore the base rates unless the case information is completely definitive. Subjects understood the simple sampling consequence of random selection of a case from a set biased toward lawyers (engineers), since they responded appropriately to the base rates when no case information was given. But in the presence of the case vignettes, the base-rate information dropped out of consideration.

Kahneman and Tversky's (1973) explanation for this phenomenon is that probability judgments are sometimes made as a result of conformance of a stimulus to some prototype rather than of a count of relative frequencies. If the stimulus is "representative" or prototypic of the category, then it may be judged likely to have come from the category, even with statistical base-rate information to the contrary. There is a large research literature on the conditions under which base-rate information is or is not ignored (e.g., Ajzen, 1977; Bar-Hillel and Fischhoff, 1981; Ginosar and Trope, 1980; Manis *et al.,* 1980; Tversky and Kahneman, 1982a). It is not necessary to review this literature here—that is done elsewhere (Borgida and Brekke, 1981; and Chapter 4 of this *Handbook*). For our purposes it is sufficient to note that in some circumstances subjects set aside statistical information—the *extensional* basis for probability judgments—in favor of global intuition based on the characteristics of the stimulus—an *intensional* basis.

Kahneman and Tversky (1982a) have noted that extensional and intensional orientations toward probability (or, as they call them, the "distributional mode" versus the "singular mode") can produce quite different judgments in practical as well as laboratory situations. They report the true story of a high school curriculum-planning team that polled its members as to the likely time it would take to complete a textbook for a particular new course. The estimates clustered closely around two years. Then the leader asked an experienced member about the history of other teams trying to write textbooks in comparably new areas. Of the many relevant examples the shortest time to completion of a textbook was five years, and in the majority of cases the project was abandoned after extensive delays! The team was jarred to be confronted with this obviously relevant extensional evidence. Several other members had been aware of similar background data, but discussion revealed that everyone on the team had instead made their estimate by constructing an apparently plausible (but actually much too optimistic) scenario of the single textbook chore at hand.

Classical, formal models of probability have emphasized extensional reasoning instead of the intuitive, intensional mode, which seems often to be more psychologically congenial. The popularity of Bayesian statistics in the past thirty years, with its prominent role for "prior probabilities", signals some motion toward the intuitive mode. This trend has been accelerated by recent revisionist models of probability (Cohen, 1977; Shafer, 1976), which are even more subjectivist in orientation. Whatever direction future formal models take, the important psychological point is that under many circumstances people have difficulty with extensional reasoning; but more research is needed to delimit those circumstances.

Conjunctive probabilities. There may be a general tendency for people to overestimate the probability of conjunctions of events (Cohen *et al.,* 1971). The occurrence of two (or more) events resembles in imagination the occurrence of the most salient one of the events; the probability judgment of the pair tends thereby to resemble the probability judgment for that single event. In its mildest form this bias may be understood as an *anchoring effect* (Quattrone, 1982; Tversky and Kahneman, 1974), with a single event acting as an anchor and subjects failing to adjust their judgments adequately to consider the second event.

In the strongest form of a conjunction bias, the probability of events *A* and *B* together can actually be judged higher than the probability of event B alone. This violates the rules of all probability logics. Tversky and Kahneman (1982b, 1983), calling this phenomenon the *conjunction effect,* have given several demonstrations, including the following (1982b, p. 92):

> Linda is 31 years old, single, outspoken, and very bright. She majored in philosophy. As a student, she was deeply concerned with issues of discrimination and social justice, and also participated in antinuclear demonstrations.

Please rank the following statements by their probability, using 1 for the most probable and 8 for the least probable.

- Linda is active in the feminist movement.

- Linda is a bank teller.

- Linda is a bank teller and is active in the feminist movement.

- Linda is [five other filler items, interspersed with those above].

Mean estimates of the probability of the conjunction "bank teller and feminist" clearly and significantly exceeded estimates of the probability that Linda is a bank teller. This effect obtains for statistical designs with either within-subject or between-subject comparisons, with many different contents and with different ways to elicit probability judgments. The finding is very robust in situations where a highly representative element appears in conjunction with a highly unrepresentative element.

Tversky and Kahneman explain the conjunction effect by a version of the *representativeness* bias: Subjects find that the conjunction increases the similarity match with other information about the case. The probability judgment reflects a similarity judgment; it is not based on

an extensional analysis in which the logic of subsets would make obvious that a conjunction cannot be more likely than its components.

In sum, we have listed four factors that can degrade the accuracy of application of event-frequency data to the estimation of probability: the overweighting of positive instances, available instances, instances that conform to some preconceived hypothesis, and the shift away from statistical evidence to intuitive judgments of similarity to a prototype, as illustrated most starkly in the neglect of base rates and the lack of spontaneous appreciation of the proper application of compound probabilities. These factors can, of course, overlap, as when a positive, theory-consistent, vivid instance is especially highly weighted.

Many of these limiting factors seem to be general predilections across a wide range of stimulus materials. Others appear to depend on a combination of judgmental vulnerability and clever stimulus design playing up that vulnerability (e.g., compound events designed to take advantage of similarity relations). Not enough is presently known about the details of the latter type of case: Are the stimuli in demonstrations typical or exceptional? Neither is much known about whether people can be trained to avoid the probability biases. However, because of its great practical importance, the trainability issue is one of lively discussion and research (Fischhoff, 1982; Kahneman and Tversky, 1979; Nisbett and Ross, 1980, Chap. 12; Nisbett *et al.,* 1982).

Difficulties in Applying Values

Inasmuch as probabilities can often be objectively estimated, there is a standard against which to assess probability judgments. With questions of value, however, standards are typically subjective. Thus it doesn't seem that normally an individual could be misinformed about values or that there would be a list of distorting factors like those for probabilities. On closer inspection, however, there are at least five ways in which values might be inadequately considered by the decision maker: relevant values may be overlooked; the decision maker may not really know his or her own values; data by which to set value size may be misused; the context, or frame, of the decision problem may alter the accounting of values; or there may be too many values to permit easy, simultaneous comparison. The last of these factors will be discussed in the next section. Here we comment somewhat speculatively on the first four factors.

Failure to consider relevant values.   To ignore important positive or negative features associated with one or more choice options is to engage in defective decision making. As Janis and Mann (1977; see also Janis, 1972) have emphasized, the quality of decision making should be judged not by its outcome but by whether its processes are complete and unbiased. In their view the idealized decision maker keeps a "balance sheet" on which are listed all the conceivably important value considerations, pro and con, for each alternative. One function of this device is to guard against omissions.

Often negative features of favored choice objects tend to be overlooked. A decision maker already committed to a particular alternative is ordinarily not disposed to scan that course of action for hidden drawbacks. Both cognitive and motivational factors are involved. Cognitive processing is apt to be mindless (Langer, 1978) and/or scripted (Abelson, 1976b, 1981) when the individual has routinized or schematized a habitual solution to a particular decision problem.

Janis and Mann (1977) have analyzed in detail the conditions under which people ignore warning signals about smoking, overeating, natural disasters, and many other hazards. Great health problems arise from public inattentiveness to preventable health risks, and a considerable literature has developed in this area (Etzioni, 1978; Maccoby *et al.,* 1977; Richmond, 1979). To some extent, public diffidence about health risks is associated with difficulty in appreciating very small probabilities, resolved by treating the risk as zero. [The tendency to pooh-pooh seat belts, for example, could embody an estimated zero probability of an accident on each trip (Slovic *et al.,* 1978).] Heedlessness for warnings can also be motivated by defensive avoidance (Janis and Mann, 1977; Janis and Terwilliger, 1962), to be discussed later.

Janis's balance sheet procedure has turned up another type of value consideration that people often otherwise omit from conscious deliberation (Janis, 1968)—namely, anticipations of approval or disapproval from significant others for one's chosen course of action. There is probably in many individuals a general tendency, when trying hard to make decisions rationally, to screen out considerations of what other people may think. In deciding whether to buy, say, airplane flight insurance, is it "rational" to take into account that your spouse may be upset if you don't? Presumably, it is, especially if one is concerned with "practical rationality" rather than mere "epistemic rationality" (Mortimore,

1976). But such considerations may enter only as afterthoughts in a rational calculus, because the individual may be insufficiently aware of them (Abelson, 1976a).

There may also be uncertainty in the individual's balance sheet because of "irrational" feelings. Suppose the individual feels uncomfortable about an otherwise attractive option but doesn't know why. It is problematic how this feeling will enter the individual's decision accounting (Fiske and Taylor, 1984, p. 333).

Ignorance of own values.   Beyond cases of failure to include value considerations are those in which the decision maker isn't even sure what values are held. Fischhoff *et al.* (1980) point out that "people are most likely to have clear preferences regarding issues that are familiar, simple, and directly experienced." [This is a point confirmed in the attitude and behavior literature (Fazio and Zanna, 1978).] However, Fischhoff *et al.* (1980) continue (p. 119):

> Today [issues of] social policy and . . . new technologies . . . take us into situations for which we have never thought through the implications of the values and beliefs acquired in simpler settings. We may be unfamiliar with the terms in which issues are formulated. . . . We may not even know how to begin thinking about some issues (e.g., the appropriate tradeoff between the opportunity to dye one's hair and a vague, minute increase in the probability of cancer some twenty years from now). . . . We may see things differently in theory than in the flesh. We may lack the mental capacity to think things through reliably and therefore come up with different conclusions each time we consider an issue.

This provocative passage comes from a paper concerned with the hazards of trying to measure labile values, but the questions it raises are applicable to the psychology of decision making as well. Decision models presume that people have clear-cut representations of the personal desirability of potential events. To the extent that this is not the case—and unfortunately we know much too little about the conditions governing this—then decision models are to a degree gratuitous.

Naive estimates of value.   To assess the maximum warranted risk to try to achieve a good outcome (or the maximum warranted cost to avoid a bad outcome), the decision maker will want to know just how good (bad) the outcome will be. In ill-defined decision situations, the value considerations to be taken into account (e.g., money, effort, social costs) may be anticipated, but their outcome sizes may be unknown, and the decision maker may have to estimate them from data at hand. The most obvious such data are often the outcome values of previous similar decisions. Thus a potential buyer of a certain type of car may consider the road repair record of a previously owned car of that type as a good predictor of that attribute in the potential new one, and a book publisher considering whether to publish a children's story about chipmunks might well take into account the sales figures for a recent story by the same author about rabbits.

One pitfall of this seemingly reasonable strategy for estimating expected future values from past models or prototypes is that a connection between the past model and the case at hand might be irrelevantly triggered by some feature(s) without diagnostic significance. Abelson (1976b) illustrated such a tendency with the hypothetical faculty admissions committee member who finds in an application folder some clue(s) that the applicant is similar to an outstandingly successful (or unsuccessful) prior student and thereupon estimates a comparable outcome for the new applicant. The clue(s) could have been only gratuitously associated with academic ability (comes from Philadelphia, got a D in physical education), and the decision process therefore arbitrary. Evidence for the occurrence of such effects has been provided by Gilovich (1981). He found that football experts are influenced in judging the talent of rookies by irrelevant associative similarities with pro football stars of the past (winning a high school award named after the star, for example, rather than another equally prestigious award). Gilovich also found evidence for inappropriate use of historical analogies.

A second drawback to the use of familiar past models for estimating unknown value sizes is that individuals typically fail to take into account the unreliability of one-shot estimates: If the past datum was extremely good (bad), then the target datum will be naively estimated as comparably extremely good (bad). Research (Kahneman and Tversky, 1973; Nisbett and Ross, 1980) clearly establishes this tendency for prediction to be insufficiently regressive. The new car is unlikely to be as bad as the lemon it follows; the new book may not be as big a seller as last year's hit; etc.

Nonregressive prediction has been explained as a variant of the representativeness heuristic (Kahneman and Tversky, 1973) discussed above, in which a vivid case outweighs statistical base data. The case provides an underlying model ("this brand is a lemon"), and the target is predicted to represent that model ("here comes another lemon").

The effect of nonregressive prediction on decision making is to promote overoptimistic repetition of successful patterns of behavior and quick abandonment of unsuccessful ones. Success creates data (e.g., high sales figures) that become encouraging background facts for the next similar opportunity. With no discounting for the possibility of lucky success, there is a built-in tendency toward overoptimism. On the other hand, failure produces data that encourage overpessimism. The net strategy is the commonsense dictum: "win-stay, lose-change."

We do not claim that this strategy is maladaptive per se only that nonregressive prediction exaggerates the tendency to adopt it. Sometimes, other factors in the decision situation might objectively warrant a different strategy but might escape close scrutiny by the decision maker. For example, people may persist in overly dangerous activities partly because they can tell themselves "nothing bad has happened to me yet" (implying nonregressively that nothing bad ever will).

Framing effects on value accounting.   Sometimes, the size of the value attached to an outcome may depend on how the outcome is *framed*. Hershey and Schoemaker (1980a) have shown that people are generally more willing to pay premiums to avoid losses when the label "insurance" is used. Framing phenomena are found also in the reference-point shifts of Kahneman and Tversky's (1979) prospect theory.

Tversky and Kahneman (1981) advance further sets of examples and propose the idea of a *psychological account* of transactions (see also Kahneman and Tversky, 1984; Thaler, 1980). A psychological account is a frame specifying a set of elementary outcomes and how they are to be combined, along with a reference outcome considered neutral or normal. They propose that people usually employ an account that includes only the direct consequences of the choice act and directly related acts bearing some intrinsic relation to the choice act. Consequences of unrelated acts in the general situation are excluded from consideration. This is illustrated by the example below (Tversky and Kahneman, 1981, p. 457):

Imagine that you have decided to see a play and paid the admission price of $10 per ticket. As you enter the theater you discover that you have lost the ticket. The seat was not marked and the ticket cannot be recovered. Would you pay $10 for another ticket?

A majority (54 percent) of Tversky and Kahneman's (1981) subjects said no, in contrast to only 12 percent who declined the $10 ticket in the following dilemma (p. 457):

Imagine that you have decided to see a play where admission is $10 per ticket. As you enter the theater you discover that you have lost a $10 bill. Would you still pay $10 for a ticket for the play?

In the first statement many subjects apparently included the lost ticket in the same account as the new ticket and judged $20 as excessive for a theater ticket. In the second problem statement, however, the lost $10 was set aside as irrelevant, and subjects were willing to pay $10, a (formerly) normal price for a ticket. This difference in reactions might be considered capricious, since in both cases the final outcome states are $10 out of pocket with no ticket versus $20 out of pocket with a ticket.

It is difficult to make a general statement about the effects of psychological accounts on decision making. The concept seems an interesting one, deserving of much further investigation. As an aside, we note that when two interacting individuals or nations have *different* accounts for the same situation, so that one party but not the other includes past acts in the present situation, the potential for conflict and miscommunication is high. For example, when the Argentines invaded the Falklands in 1982, they cited British usurpation 150 years earlier. The British argued for present realities, discounting events of long ago. Variation in how a situation is accounted certainly increases the difficulty of stable normative analysis of the "true" interests of decision makers.

Problems in Combining Information

We have discussed several factors potentially distorting the estimation of probabilities and values. Typically, moreover, several values weighted by their probabilities must be combined by the decision maker for overall evaluation of each choice alternative. Such combination can involve the decision maker in a host of new difficulties.

Overload.   Virtually all investigators of human decision making agree that there are practical limits on the number of factors that can be simultaneously considered by a decision maker. There is less agreement on the extent and the type of decision degradation to expect and on the degree of *overload* necessary to exceed decision makers' tolerances. Weiss (1982), for example, has cautioned against underestimating the capacities of public policymakers.

Earlier, we discussed some of the variables moderating the relation between overload and decision quality. In the context of the present discussion, a good general principle might be this: Since overload provokes a need for decision simplification, existing informational biases that serve a simplifying function are likely to be amplified under overload conditions. This principle includes at least the following tendencies discussed in the two previous sections (along with others to be discussed in the next section): reliance on positive instances and available episodes; theory-driven estimates of conditional relationships; omission of hidden value considerations; and naive estimates of value via similarity to a familiar prototype. As plausible as this principle may be, we confess, however, that we know of no systematic laboratory evidence specifying whether or not these particular biases increase as a function of decision overload. Case studies of political decision makers (George, 1974), however, are broadly consistent with this overload principle.

Avoidance of value trade-offs.   It is characteristic of many realistic decisions that good and bad features covary over alternatives. For example, better quality is accompanied by higher cost, higher profit by greater risk, etc. Such trade-offs complicate the task of the decision maker. Beyond the cognitive strain of netting out the positive and negative features of alternatives, trade-offs also create a social problem: Whatever the decision maker chooses, he or she is always open to criticism based on disadvantages of the chosen alternative (and advantages of unchosen alternatives). The negotiator must yield concession B to obtain advantage A; the political leader may offend constituency X to please constituency Y. In anticipation of facing the music, the decision maker may try to deny that the potential disadvantage is as bad as it seems. The chosen policy doesn't really hurt the farmers; the apparent loss of wages is dwarfed by the fabulous fringe benefits; etc.

In the political realm there is both documentary evidence that national leaders tend to avoid confronting trade-offs (Axelrod, 1976; Jervis, 1975, 1982) and data from experimental gaming that naive subjects do so (Steinbruner, 1974). The form such avoidance takes is to focus on one salient value dimension on which choice alternatives vary and to screen out of consideration any countervailing differences on other value dimensions. As Hammond and Mumpower (1979, p. 247) put it, "We are not accustomed to presenting the rationale for the choice between values; we are not skilled in speaking to more than one value at a time [even though] that is precisely what social problems call upon us to do. When our . . . values compete, we . . . return to singular emphasis on our favorite value."

In Slovic's (1975) interesting laboratory demonstration of how trade-off problems are resolved, subjects were given choice problems pitting smaller differences on more important dimensions against larger differences on less important dimensions. Thus, for example, a subject might be asked for a preference between two secretaries: one who types twice as fast and the other who makes only a third as many errors. These numerical values would have been established from prior judgments by the subject as to what error ratio *exactly* compensated for what speed ratio. But a subject who had previously indicated speed as a more important dimension than accuracy would tend to prefer the faster secretary, even in the face of the exactly compensating disadvantage. The rule here is: If you can't decide, go with the single most important dimension dividing the alternatives. This rule was followed roughly 80 percent of the time.

The suppression of countervailing considerations may not be wise in the long run, but it does not imply that a given decision is defective. After all, in a delicately balanced decision some choice must be made, and it is functional to have some mechanism for avoiding decision paralysis. When alternatives are close, the decision maker must "spread apart the alternatives" (Brehm and Cohen, 1959) before a decision is made (Janis, 1959) and/or afterward to rationalize it (Festinger, 1964; Janis, 1959). The long-run cost is that the decision maker is likely to be more confident of the choice than the closeness of the choice warrants and be insufficiently sensitive to changing circumstances that might otherwise suggest a reversal of the decision (Janis and Mann, 1977; Jervis, 1976).

The difficulty in integrating positive and negative value considerations may be part of a more general difficulty in combining incommensurates. We have previously discussed the tendency not to combine case information with base information in estimates of probability. Subjects tend to rely on one (usually the former) and suppress the other. Partly, this may be due to discomfort with the forbidding task of calculating how to combine them. For further discussion of choice procedures that avoid the combining of incommensurate factors, see "Use of Choice Rules."

SOCIAL AND MOTIVATIONAL FACTORS

Beyond the cognitive factors that constrain the effectiveness of decision making are influences of a possibly motivational character, both individual and social.

Commitment

The most obvious candidate for a motivational variable constraining effective decision making is psychological commitment to a prior decision. By *commitment* is usually meant some public behavior on behalf of a position, making it more or less irrevocable because change is costly, socially awkward, damaging to self-esteem, or personally dangerous. It is possible to include *private commitment* in the definition as well, in which the individual privately resolves to stick by a particular position. However, as McGuire (1964) and Janis and Mann (1977) have noted, there is a continuum of degrees of commitment; private commitment is at the weakest end, and the evidence is that it has small effects, if any.

Evidence from the attitude change literature (e.g., Deutsch and Gerard, 1955; Hovland *et al.,* 1957) indicates that public announcement of a position exerts a significant restraining effect when pressure occurs to move away from the position. The dissonance theory tradition has given prominence to public commitment as a strengthener of dissonance-provoking choices such as agreeing to give a counterattitudinal speech (Helmreich and Collins, 1968). When the possibility of undoing the decision is blocked, the individual must do more cognitive work to justify the decision. A related argument can be made about the effects of public commitment to pro-attitudinal (i.e., initially congenial) choices when these are later attacked (Kiesler, 1971). Commitment followed by challenge forces individuals to justify why they have bound themselves to their decisions. This could lead to a repeated cycle of commitment, attack, self-justification, and further commitment, further attack, etc. [See Tomkins' (1965) biographical analysis of the deepening commitment to the abolition of slavery by leading northern abolitionists, who started out somewhat half-heartedly.]

The deepest forms of commitment are virtually irreversible behaviors with many entailments—for example, quitting one's job and selling one's house in order to join a doomsday cult (Festinger *et al.,* 1956), or ordering troops sent overseas to implement a national policy (discussed extensively in commitment terms by Jervis, 1976, 1982). The possibility of disadvantageous eventual outcomes arises sharply when extreme behavioral commitment to a decision is followed by new information or changed circumstances strongly suggesting that the decision was wrong. The individual may well persist in defending the original decision, while a neutral observer would regard such defense as foolish. This was the case with the doomsday cult studied by Festinger *et al.* (1956). Foreign policy fiascoes such as the Vietnam involvement illustrate on many levels the stubborn persistence of committed individuals, groups, and institutions.

The very property of commitment—that it insulates the individual from later pressures to renege—can sometimes be used by individuals to bind themselves to courses of action in the face of anticipated contrary temptations. In a famous literary example Ulysses orders his crew to lash him to the mast so that the next day he will not be lured away by the sirens' song. Economists have been fascinated by this example (Elster, 1979) and other similar examples (Schelling, 1978). If it is truly in Ulysses' best interests to resist being lured, it seems paradoxical that he lash himself. Psychologists may not see this action as paradoxical and may think of experimental analogs such as commitment to social supervision to prevent backsliding in a resolve to give up smoking (Janis, 1975).

A very detailed catalog of different types of behavioral commitment has been given by Kanter (1972) in her study of nineteenth-century utopian communities. She argues that such communities can survive and flourish only by exacting extraordinary instrumental, affective, and moral commitments from those who have decided to join, so various and insistent over time are the pressures to reverse that decision. Data on community practices and longevities support her argument, and her analysis is readily applicable to modern totalistic religious cults such as the Jonestown commune and the Unification Church.

Stress and Defensive Avoidance

Psychological *stress* has been identified as a source of defective scanning of alternative options in complex decisions. Janis and Mann (1977) provide the following analysis:

1. The more important the goals that will remain unfulfilled by a conflictful decision, the greater will be the stress.

2. The greater the commitment to a prior course of action challenged by new information, the greater will be the stress.

3. The greater the stress, the greater will be the tendency to lose hope of finding a better solution to the decision conflict, leading to greater *defensive avoidance* of information about risks associated with the chosen alternative (or of opportunities associated with the unchosen alternative).

In the postulated state of defensive avoidance, there is lack of vigilant search, distortion of the meaning of warning messages, selective inattention and forgetting, and construction of wishful rationalizations. A prototypic case of defensive avoidance is the confirmed smoker who denigrates the danger of lung cancer, as evidenced by protocols taken while the smoker listens to health warnings (Janis and Terwilliger, 1962), or by skeptical attitudes elicited afterward (Leventhal and Watts, 1966).

The hypothesized tendency toward defensive avoidance is possibly controversial. The evidence that people systematically ignore contrary information is mixed. A case in point is the general lack of support for the *selective exposure hypothesis* originally developed from dissonance theory (Freedman and Sears, 1965). Janis and Mann (1977) account for the discrepancy between the selective exposure literature and their analysis of defensive avoidance by accentuating the subtle role of stress: Only when stress is high does the decision maker avoid messages undermining his or her commitment to a prior decision. When stress is moderate, interest in information is more open-minded, leading to active inspection of messages emphasizing the potentially serious risks of the present course of action. Another factor contributing to open-mindedness is the perceived inevitability of the dangers accompanying a decision: Publicly resisting the draft during the Vietnam War certainly brought government prosecution, for example, whereas the grave consequence associated with continuing to smoke is "merely" statistical. Janis and Rausch (1970) indeed found that Vietnam War resisters processed all information quite openly; but as we have noted, many people are notoriously defensive about health risks.

Research on stress has emphasized its negative consequences for decision quality. At the other end of the affective spectrum is the question of whether good feelings might improve decisions, and indeed, preliminary evidence for such an effect has been found (Isen *et al.*, 1982). Preceding a decision task with an unrelated success experience leads to information search that is highly effective, being abbreviated by less repetitiveness and less use of unimportant dimensions.

Short-Term Gain Versus Long-Term Cost

Often overlapping with the defensive avoidance phenomenon is the decisional preference for short-term gain in the face of potentially higher long-term cost. The smoker who maintains the benefits of his or her habit even if it entails an increased chance of a premature death; the gourmand willing to eat now and pay with overweight later; the individual who postpones a needed health checkup because it is too anxiety arousing—all these examples and many others suggest a proclivity for future costs and benefits to be taken less seriously than present costs and benefits.

Many of these types of behavior, to be sure, are explainable in other ways besides a preference for short-term gain—chiefly by noting that the long-term risks may have low perceived probabilities, which would downweight them anyway. But in some instances (e.g., the overeater who knows full well what the consequences will be), probability is not a factor, and it would seem plausible to assume that the future typically looms less important to the decision maker than does the present. There are, however, examples to the contrary (e.g., Christmas clubs), and the interesting challenge for the psychologist is to specify the conditions under which future states are downweighted or discounted.

Although psychologists may not find the expositions highly penetrable, economists have devoted some attention to the psychology of discounting of the future (Hirshleifer, 1970, Chap. 2). As one might expect, the analysis centers mainly (though not exclusively) on money. Since present money is exchangeable for future money through investment, a dollar now might be considered worth more than a dollar a year from now (inflation aside), because the present dollar accrues interest in the meanwhile.

The concept of exchangeability is crucial to economic analyses. Once one gets away from salable commodities, however, it is hard to calibrate the present against the future. How much does one (or should one) value a state of improved health now versus the same health improvement a year from now? What is the relative value of a lobster dinner tonight versus a potential lobster dinner a year from tonight? (In this latter simple example one might intuit that there would be a strong impulse toward immediate consumption.)

There are many difficult questions in the psychology of discounting that invite study. One line of existing research is applicable to the discounting of consumables, and it supports our speculation in the lobster dinner example. When a young child is given a choice of (say) a pretzel now versus (say) a lollipop a half hour from now, the experiments by Mischel (1974) on delay of gratification make clear the child has trouble resisting the lesser but more immediate prize. A psychologically interesting economic analysis of the struggle for self-control over short-run gratifications has been attempted by Thaler and Shefrin (1981).

The phenomenon of *anticipated regret* is especially worthy of study. Anticipated regret (Janis and Mann, 1977) is enabled via the mental rehearsal of how the present decision situation would look when viewed from a future point in time. The ability to carefully examine the question "Will I regret this decision later?" seems to be an important mechanism to counteract a natural tendency to discount the future—and may indeed result in reversing an ill-considered, short-run decision.

Wishful-Thinking and Pollyanna Effects

It has been noted (McGuire, 1960) that more desirable events tend also to be seen as more likely. This tendency is sometimes called the *wishful-thinking effect,* implying that certain events are seen as likely *because* they are desirable, while others are seen as unlikely because undesirable. Such motivated exaggeration of probabilities would, of course, affect decision making—by overencouraging risk taking with the wishful notion that good outcomes will probably happen and bad ones won't.

The correlational nature of the data, however, does not warrant a causal conclusion. It is also possible that events are seen as desirable because they are likely, a *Pollyanna effect* (Matlin and Stang, 1978). Or the two variables could covary in an ecologically valid way without any distortion by the decision maker. Good outcomes may be likely and bad outcomes unlikely in the experience of many individuals because they seek out the good and avoid the bad. It is both bad and unlikely, for example, that a sensible person will be electrocuted by tampering with a wall socket, and both good and likely that a person will eat every day. What is needed to assess mutual distortions of probabilities and utilities is to present events outside the direct control of the individual, manipulating probability or desirability and observing the effect on the other variable.

Just such an experiment was carried out by Carlsmith (1962). He told three groups of subjects they might have to sustain mildly unpleasant electric shocks, with varying probabilities. Subjects' ratings of personally anticipated unpleasantness were lower the more likely the shocks. This supports the Pollyanna effect: If a bad thing will probably happen, regard it less unfavorably. Pyszczinski (1982) has found a complementary Pollyanna result for the pending pleasant event of winning a lottery prize. When told there was a 90 percent chance that they would win a gift certificate to a pizza parlor, subjects rated it more attractive than when there was a 20 percent chance.

Experimental results for wishful thinking are less clear (perhaps because there are more of them). Several studies (Carlsmith, 1962; Crandall *et al.,* 1955; Irwin, 1953; Marks, 1951) show that mildly unpleasant chance outcomes (losing coins or game points; experiencing mildly unpleasant shocks) are judged less likely than comparable mildly pleasant outcomes (winning coins or game points; experiencing shocks said to pleasantly tickle). However, at greater extremes of unpleasantness a protective, rather than wishful, tendency may set in. Carlsmith's (1962) subjects, faced with uncertainty about a rather painful shock, considered it more probable than those faced with uncertainty about a mildly unpleasant shock. The subjects may acknowledge more readily the possible occurrence of the more threatening experience in order to prepare for it. Pyszczinski (1982) hypothesizes that people rather generally employ strategies to cope with anticipated affective states. An instance he cites, with supporting data, is the downplaying of the likelihood of winning an attractive but unlikely lottery prize. This he attributes to the avoidance of disappointment.

What are the implications of this smattering of results? Most of what subjects do in these various contexts is not apt to be seriously maladaptive. To the extent that people take seriously a potential large loss, or are wary of banking too much on a large gain, they are behaving conservatively but functionally. The slight exaggeration of pleasantness as a direct function of probability has the opposite effect of leading the decision maker to take more risk, but the size of this effect is probably small. Thus present laboratory results on the interaction of probability and utility do not suggest the type of dysfunction that arises in defensive avoidance, where big losses are dismissed as having low probabilities. Defensive avoidance, however, requires special preconditions, namely, high stress and low hope of coping with the threat.

Any interaction of probability and utility, though, would create a theoretical challenge for decision models such as prospect theory, which assume independent definitions of probability and value-weighting functions. The conditions under which such interactions may occur need to be further clarified.

The Illusion of Control

One set of circumstances in which wishful thinking may prevail is when individuals incline toward belief that they can exert some sort of control over purely chance events. Langer (1975) calls this the *illusion of control,* hypothesizing that it occurs when cues from skill situations are present in chance situations. Some such cues are the availability of options, familiarity with the stimulus materials, involvement with the task, the presence of competition, and prior history of success.

In separate experiments testing this hypothesis, Langer (1975) found that tickets for lotteries were valued at vastly more than their purchase price when (1) subjects could choose the identity of their particular lottery ticket, (2) the tickets bore familiar identifying markings rather than unfamiliar nonsense symbols, or (3) the numbers on the tickets were revealed suspensefully one by one over three consecutive days. In another experiment subjects wagered more money on a card cut against a frumpily dressed, insecure opponent than against a dapper and confident one. Ayeroff and Abelson (1976) extended the illusion-of-control idea to a telepathy task involving the guessing of symbols on cards. Subjects' outcomes were actually at chance level, but their beliefs about how well they were performing depended very strongly on whether (1) they had been allowed to choose the set of symbols to be used in the card deck, and (2) the warm-up trials allowed them to talk to each other, thus ensuring apparent success.

The extent to which these and other related cues promoting overconfidence are serious impediments to effective real-life decision making is unclear. Superstition in casino- and street-corner-gambling behavior has often been reported (Goffman, 1967; Henslin, 1967; Oldman, 1974), and when people believe they can exert some control over purely chance events, they may overindulge in the risks of gambling. Even more insidious are decision situations with heavily disguised chance elements. In many spheres of human activity, such as closely contested sports events, military battles, and elections, the overall outcome can sometimes hinge critically on chance events. Dramatic success or failure, however, is likely to be attributed instead to the skills, deficiencies, or effort expenditures of the participants (Jervis, 1975). The resistance of decision makers to chance interpretation is highlighted in Amos Tversky's anecdote of the military officer who simultaneously believed that helicopter crashes were often a matter of chance, that whole battles could sometimes hinge on a few helicopter crashes, but that the outcomes of battles were always a matter of strategy, resources, and determination, never luck.

If skill attributions are made for chance outcomes, then behaviors arbitrarily connected with success are apt to be superstitiously repeated, and those connected with failure abandoned. There is considerable evidence for superstitious behavior in animals (Skinner, 1948; Staddon and Simmelhag, 1971) and humans (Einhorn, 1980), but the upshot is unclear. Obviously, there are many complex situations in which it is difficult to make the correct attribution for success (or failure). When one is in doubt, it may not be so dysfunctional to credit one's own behavior. The alternative of downplaying self-responsibility could be even worse, as in the phenomenon of learned helplessness (Maier and Seligman, 1976).

Groupthink

The prospect of social disapproval (or approval) can enter decision making as a value consideration, and there is nothing particularly irrational about this. A potential for dysfunction arises, however, when social pressures suffuse the entire decision context, at the expense of dispassionate consideration of the content of the choice alternatives. Such is the situation hypothesized by Janis (1972; 1982a) to occur in the *groupthink* phenomenon.

Groupthink is a strong psychological drive for consensus within insular, cohesive decision-making groups such that disagreement is suppressed and the decision process becomes defective. Janis developed his insights mainly from a study of elite decision-making groups that presided over military and political fiascoes such as the Bay of Pigs invasion or Watergate, but the analysis is pre-

sumably applicable to any small, cohesive decision-making group. Here we summarize the postulated bad effects on the decision process.

Under the appropriate antecedent conditions pertaining to the group, most or all of the following symptoms of groupthink are said to be manifest (Janis, 1972; Janis and Mann, 1977): the illusion of invulnerability and the belief in the inherent morality of the group; stereotyping of outgroups; collective rationalizations (for all of the above); the illusion of unanimity; self-censorship when dissenting thoughts arise; direct pressure if and when dissent appears; and the self-appointment of what Janis calls "mindguards," who vigilantly try to screen the group from exposure to dissent. As a result of these manifestations, many of the following defects in decision making may appear: the incomplete survey of values and of possible choice alternatives; poor information search; failure to examine the risks of the preferred choice; failure to reappraise rejected alternatives; and failure to work out contingency plans.

The bottom line is that these biased and careless decision practices raise the probability of gross policy blunders. Janis persuasively documents the antecedents and consequences of groupthink in such famous policy disasters as the Bay of Pigs invasion, the Watergate cover-up, and U.S. unpreparedness for Pearl Harbor. Particularly impressive in these historical cases is the penchant for the intelligent, often brilliant members of the decision-making groups to overlook or dismiss blatantly obvious signs of external danger or of flawed planning.

While there seems little doubt that these groupthink symptoms occur under the postulated conditions of group pressure (and can be mitigated by appropriate counternorms, as Janis also documents), the reader may have noted that the list of symptoms and defects covers much the same territory as our general list of factors distorting decisions. Stereotyping, rationalization, the failure to examine risks of preferred choices, etc., occur individually in many contexts not involving cohesive groups of decision makers. Furthermore, groupthink does not necessarily underlie every gross failure to heed obvious warning signs. In the famous case of the intruder in Queen Elizabeth's bedroom, for example, it appears that several isolated individuals at different status levels failed to raise an alarm at clear signs of a likely intrusion.

In short, the groupthink syndrome seems to be a sufficient but not a necessary condition for the elicitation of the panoply of decision defects listed by Janis. None of its manifestations—except the phenomena of mindguards and of self-censorship from dissenting thoughts

—are unique to the insular, cohesive, elite group. It can forcefully be argued, however, that in their tendency to co-occur and to be present in marked degree, tḥ ͇roup-think symptoms are not readily duplicated in oṫner contexts. What is needed to illuminate this issue is a study of comparably important decisions made by small face-to-face groups, by isolated individuals, and by relatively impersonal organizations.

OVERCOMING THE CONSTRAINTS

As it has gradually been recognized that in a variety of ways human decision making falls short of the effectiveness demanded by normative models, a literature has begun to develop on how the quality of human decisions might be improved. Approaches fall into three general categories: giving the decision maker relevant experience; providing training designed to overcome flaws in the decision process; and manipulating the context or manner in which decisions are made. The first two approaches presume that human decision flaws are corrigible, while the third admits a certain degree of defect whose impact one tries to minimize by structural arrangements. The approaches need not preclude one another, however.

Giving the Decision Maker Relevant Experience

At first blush it would seem that the most general curative measure for ineffective decision making is repeated experience with comparable decision problems. Feedback from past decision errors could serve as a natural corrective; in the interest of competitive survival the decision maker (supported by cultural traditions) could presumably avoid the repetition of previous mistakes. Fishers, farmers, and sailors seem to have an intuitive grasp of probabilism to assess the predicted behavior of fish or weather or tides. Otherwise, they might not survive.

Such a line of argument recruits a certain plausibility by invoking mundane realism rather than laboratory findings. Indeed, reservations have often been expressed about the applicability to the real world of laboratory findings on judgment and decision. Pointedly, Hogarth (1981) has complained that the laboratory orientation is usually toward one-shot decisions, whereas in life many (most?) decisions are of a recurrent nature, with opportunities for profiting from outcome feedback.

Close inspection of the nature of repeated decisions, however, raises a number of serious doubts about the automatic efficacy of decision repetition (Brehmer, 1980; Castellan, 1977; Einhorn, 1980; Einhorn and Hogarth,

1978, 1981; Hammond, 1978; Shweder, 1977). Among the drawbacks are that reinforcement may act upon irrelevant structures—i.e., the "wrong thing" may be learned—and that self-fulfilling prophecies may occur.

The wrong thing can be learned because the individual has an inappropriate formulation of the decision situation in mind when reinforcement occurs. Many lines of converging evidence suggest a general tendency for individuals to be highly sensitive to the contextual or framing (Kahneman and Tversky, 1984; Tversky and Kahneman, 1981) aspects of problems, apart from their structural aspects. Thus Simon and Hayes (1976) have shown that formally identical problems presented in different verbal housings are vastly different in the ease and manner of solution. Individuals tend to construct *mental models* (Johnson-Laird, 1980) of problem situations, metaphorical representations that may or may not be faithful to the logical relationships in the formal problem domain. Superstitious behavior (Staddon and Simmelhag, 1971), *Einstellung* effects (Luchins, 1942), and belief perseverance (Ross and Anderson, 1982) are three variants of the noncorrective effects of experience when the situation is misapprehended.

A systematic way in which the illusory efficacy of faulty decisions can be maintained is that the decision itself may alter the outcome in a compatible direction. Among other examples, Einhorn and Hogarth (1978) note that a foundation's decision to award a research grant to investigator X thereby provides X with funds to improve X's research capability, increasing the chances that X will merit having received the grant. But those turned down for grants may be forced to abandon their research plans. Another aspect of this example is that the foundation typically will not gather follow-up data on rejectees anyway (as is characteristic in many types of personnel decisions). This omission is a stark manifestation of the bias in favor of positive instances, which undercuts the evenhanded, corrective functioning of outcome feedback.

In fairness, we should add that de facto benefits may occur from self-fulfilling decisions, so there is some gain from the lessons of experience even though the problem structure be misunderstood. Imagine a witch doctor—or the modern equivalent—who prescribes a mysterious white power for a particular set of symptoms. Over time, the doctor observes that many more patients are cured with the powder than those treated by a rival doctor who advises patients to go to bed and rest. Even though the cures might be due to a placebo effect, it could be argued that the decision to prescribe the powder had proven successful. Experience can be a good teacher for the wrong reason.

It would be foolish to assert that experience never provides appropriate decisional correctives. The reinforcement properties of each case should be examined carefully. Our limited discussion suggests that experience is the most apt teacher when concrete actions with little generality, rather than abstract principles, are to be learned. Repetition of decisions with the same options helps, provided that outcome data are complete. Feedback is better when immediate (Lichtenstein *et al.,* 1982, p. 333). Self-fulfilling decisional successes are minimized if decisions operate *nonreactively,* i.e., if the outcome process is independent of the influence of the decision. For example, the behavior of the weather (Murphy's Law notwithstanding) is unaffected by the predictions of the forecaster.

In fact, rainfall predictions by weather forecasters have been shown to have excellent calibration with actual rainfall (Murphy and Winkler, 1977). (Calibration refers to the correspondence between judged probability and actual frequency: It rains about 40 percent of the time that forecasters state the probability as .4, etc.) Weather prediction satisfies the other favorable conditions listed above for learning from experience: It is concrete and repetitive, with clear and prompt feedback.

By contrast, medical diagnoses of pneumonia (Christensen-Szalanski and Bushyhead, 1981) and of skull fracture (DeSmet *et al.,* 1979) have been shown to be poorly calibrated. The physicians in these studies considerably overstated the probabilities that their diagnoses were correct, and the pattern of the bias could not be accounted for by the relative costs of false negatives and false positives. [The medical profession has been cited as vulnerable to other probability biases, particularly those that arise from ignoring base rates (Eddy, 1982).] Medical decisions in general do not partake of the most favorable conditions for learning from sheer experience: The typical physician makes a large variety of diagnoses, with a limited number of cases for each; feedback on the correctness of each diagnosis may be ambiguous, long-delayed, or sometimes not even made known to the physician. Moreover, medical decisions are reactive.

Laboratory studies of the improvement of decisions following untutored experience have been relatively specialized. A few discouraging results (e.g., Brown, 1973) occur in the literature on probability calibration (Lichtenstein *et al.,* 1982). There is a fairly sizable literature on trends over trials in the play of bargaining games. The fa-

cility with which players learn optimal behavior from outcome feedback alone is very critically dependent on the structure of the game. For example, while Siegal and Fouraker (1960) found near maximization of joint payoffs in a game simulating a bilateral economic monopoly, behavior in the Prisoner's Dilemma game (e.g., Rapoport and Chammah, 1965) and its variants and extensions (e.g., Dawes, 1975a) does not tend very strongly to converge on joint maximization, unless the participants can communicate with one another.

Another type of decision-learning task is provided by simulated simple economic or social systems that the subject tries to control from a computer console. For example, the subject tries to keep rates of inflation and unemployment as low as possible by setting the federal tax rate and budget deficit every "year." Or the subject tries to influence the "friendliness level" of a "computer person" through trial-by-trial variations in input friendliness. Some model, unknown to the subject, couples changes in the dependent variable(s) to present and/or past levels of the independent variable(s). The intriguing prototypical result (Berry and Broadbent, 1982; Broadbent *et al.,* 1982; Mackinnon and Wearing, 1982) is that if the model is reasonably stable, with short time-lag influences, subjects can often achieve rather good control of the variables in question—but they usually cannot characterize the underlying model at all well or articulate coherently how they achieve control.

This paradox comes about because subjects make small, probing changes in the variables they control. Good results prompt continued small changes in the same direction, while bad results lead to trying something else. Like a statistical ant climbing a hill, this procedure works reasonably well but is blind to the global features of the terrain. Such muddling through in sequential decisions seems related to the anchoring and adjustment heuristic identified by Tversky and Kahneman (1974), to the conservatism in information processing discussed by Edwards (1968), and to the "disjointed incrementalism" by which bureaucracies try to respond to pressures to change (Braybrooke and Lindblom, 1963). What is learned may be more or less functional without being very insightful or general.

Providing Conceptual Training to the Decision Maker

If, in addition to experience, the decision maker is provided with concepts for appropriately interpreting that experience, learning may be improved. Two types of conceptual equipment that may help are general sophistication with the class of relevant decision strategies and antidotes to specific common decision flaws.

General sophistication. A question frequently raised is whether experts are immune, or at least less vulnerable, to the fallacies that afflict naive decision makers. Several studies indicate that expertness is no guarantee of infallibility. In their many studies of misapprehensions in judgments of probability, Tversky and Kahneman (e.g., 1971, 1974, 1983) have often used judges highly trained in statistical reasoning and have still found fallacies. Alpert and Raiffa (1982) found large overconfidence effects among various graduate student groups taking courses in planning and decision making. Overconfidence effects, in fact, are rife among professional expert groups of many sorts (Slovic *et al.,* 1982). One phenomenon to which experts may be especially prone, if they are committed to a theoretical point of view, is the overendorsement of evidence consistent with it. In a well-controlled study of this tendency Mahoney (1977) found that editorial reviewers for a particular journal preferentially favored acceptance of a research article when the results favored their side of a controversy rather than the other side, despite equally strong statistical support in the two cases.

The weaker proposition that experts are less vulnerable than novices is often supported. However, there may be interactions with the difficulty of the judgment or decision task. Tversky and Kahneman (1983) studied intuitively compelling violations of the conjunction rule for probabilities, using both undergraduates naive about statistics and Ph.D. students who had taken advanced courses in statistics. When the structure of the stimulus task made the potential applicability of the conjunction rule obvious, sophisticated subjects did much better than naive subjects, who were typically still fooled. When the task structure was not obvious, sophisticated subjects went astray virtually as often as naive subjects.

Krantz *et al.* (1982) used open-ended survey responses to test appreciation of statistical regression in ordinary contexts, such as a decline in quality of meals from one visit to a restaurant to the next and the well-documented sophomore slump, in which star rookies perform less well their second season in a sport. Exposure to a single semester of a statistics course greatly enhanced the use of good statistical reasoning on these questions. In a separate study unselected undergraduates were

compared with Ph.D.-level scientists in their answers to the restaurant problem. Expertise made a large difference, but the difference was smaller when the restaurant anecdote was altered to have the customer deliberately picking items at random from the menu each time. This cue was intended to make the variability of meal quality salient, encouraging probabilistic reasoning—and indeed, the answers of the naive group improved.

These results illustrate what is probably a general set of phenomena for many cognitive operations in decison making. At issue is the competition between different modes of thought (Abelson, 1975; Hammond, 1981; Wason and Evans, 1975), where intuitive judgment (in the form, say, of the representativeness heuristic) disposes toward one conclusion and formal analytic reasoning (the conjunctive rule for probabilities, say) toward another. The competition between the two modes can be altered by various factors—for example, whether the problem statement makes salient the applicability of the formal rule. Expertise influences several such factors (Nisbett *et al.,* 1983): It provides formal rule systems, it gives facility in their use, and it enables recognition of when they might be applicable. The expert will not likely be infallible in applying formal analyses in the face of misleading intuitions but will find opportunities for their use sooner than will the novice who has only a sketchy grasp of formal principles. Of course, some formal principles are well diffused in the general culture and/or are readily available to intuitive inference. When these are at issue—for example, the superiority of large samples of behavior over small samples when making inferences about ability (Jepson *et al.,* 1984)—then the novice is not necessarily disadvantaged.

Briefings on specific flaws. Rather than rely on general expertise to prevail over impediments to effective judgment, one may train people to avoid flaws in specific situations. One way to do this is to give briefings on the responses of typical subjects, explain why they are flawed, and elicit new responses in the same situation. This makes subjects privy to the insights of the psychologist or decision analyst, in the hope that they will make appropriate corrections in their own behavior.

Research embodying this strategy has had moderate success. Alpert and Raiffa (1982), having found even fairly sophisticated subjects to be wildly overconfident in setting confidence boundaries on guesses about factual quantities, showed the subjects exactly how overnarrow were their group's boundaries. They then exhorted subjects to spread their boundaries, with the result that the overconfidence effect was reduced by about 50 percent.

Several other contexts also illustrate the strategy of making the subject aware of the behavior to be modified. Ross *et al.* (1975) applied it to experiments in which subjects were fooled by false feedback into thinking they were good (poor) at a highly novel task. Some subjects were debriefed by demonstrating to them how and why feedback was falsified (*outcome debriefing*), but this debriefing still did not eliminate the influence of the feedback on their self-evaluations. Other subjects were also given what Ross *et al.* called *process debriefing,* which gave an account of the paradoxical ineffectiveness of outcome debriefing. The effects of false feedback were then reduced virtually to nil.

In another variant, subjects may be informed of a phenomenon before they are in a position to be led astray by it. This might be dubbed *process prebriefing.* Lord *et al.* (1983) told subjects about the phenomenon of biased assimilation, in which very highly selective credence is accorded to evidence that confirms one's deeply held beliefs. Forewarned of this bias and urged to consider how they might evaluate the opposite of each result presented, the subjects did not show biased assimilation when given evidence on both sides of an involving issue.

One could argue that process-debriefing and -prebriefing effects are due to demand characteristics. Subjects told about the flawed performance of others are on the spot to avoid repeating the same mistakes, and naturally, they might not want to look foolish by doing so. That issues of self-presentation are implicated is indeed suggested by the fact that in the Ross *et al.* (1975) study observers did not profit as much from process debriefing as did actors. However, as in some other cases in psychology, the supposed artifact may shade over into the genuine phenomenon—perhaps process briefings do indeed work because subjects wish to avoid looking foolish, but they also internalize the lesson thus made prominent.

Two properties are necessary to the success of briefings: Subjects must agree that their flaws are indeed misguided, and they must know how to behave to correct them. Both of these factors are situationally highly variable, and the former factor, of course, may interact with formal training. When a subject commits an error and does not have the proper rule available, it is an *error of comprehension* (Kahneman and Tversky, 1982c). When the rule is known, but not applied, it is an *error of application.* The latter admits of immediate correction; the

former does not. Errors of comprehension have been noted in certain tasks (Kahneman and Tversky, 1982c; Wason and Johnson-Laird, 1970), and then the briefing method fails to improve performance unless supplemented by further training.

Manipulating the Decision Context
Instead of putting the burden for correcting flaws directly on the judge or decision maker, it may often be possible to provide operating aids and procedures that can be used during the decision process.

Systematic listing of relevant considerations. Janis (1968, 1972; Janis and Mann, 1977) has emphasized the possibly salutary effects of exhaustively listing all the advantages and disadvantages of each decision alternative before trying to make the decision. There is evidence (Janis, 1982b) that this helps to generate value considerations that may otherwise have been overlooked and create an analytic orientation disposing toward skepticism and caution. In a procedure related to the balance sheet, Koriat *et al.* (1980) asked subjects to write down reasons why they might be wrong about their judgments and then have an opportunity to correct them. This device considerably decreased the overconfidence effect discussed above.

While Janis's balance sheet procedures may make available considerations that might otherwise be ignored, there is no provision for how to weight and combine considerations that have already been listed. Other systematic listing procedures have addressed the problem of how to ensure that different value dimensions are carefully weighted relative each other. The *simple multiattribute-rating technique* (SMART) advocated by Gardiner and Edwards (1975) is one version of *multiattribute-utility measurement* (Edwards, 1971; Keeney, 1972; Raiffa, 1969) designed to help single or multiple decision makers clarify their thinking or resolve disagreements. The SMART involves numerical judgments of the relative weight of value dimensions and the location of decision alternatives on each.

Establishing protective norms of procedure. In his extended discussions of how to prevent groupthink, based on analysis of the conditions that promote it, Janis (1972, 1982a) emphasizes the importance of procedural norms surrounding the decision-making process. For example, if it is a well-established norm that someone in the group should play devil's advocate and air the disadvantages of any proposed action, then hasty and insufficiently considered decisions may be forestalled. Such a norm not only serves a cognitive function like the Koriat *et al.* (1980) procedure of calling disadvantages to mind, it also has the social aspect that it undercuts the illusion of immutable consensus endemic to groupthink.

Among other protective norms discussed by Janis (1982b) are habitually dividing the group for separate discussions under different leaders before coming back together; having the leader set a standard of genuinely welcoming criticism; and establishing a second-chance period following an apparently final decision, permitting a decision reversal. Each such suggestion entails some drawbacks, and the exploration of their relative advantages and disadvantages raises an important research challenge.

REFERENCES

Abelson, R. P. (1968). Simulation of social behavior. In G. Lindzey and E. Aronson (Eds.), *Handbook of social psychology*. Vol. I. Reading, Mass.: Addison-Wesley.

Abelson, R. P. (1975). The reasoner and the inferencer don't talk much to each other. In R. C. Schank and B. Nash-Webber (Eds.), *Theoretical issues in natural language processing*. Cambridge, Mass.: Bolt, Beranek & Newman.

_____ (1976a). Social psychology's rational man. In S. I. Benn and G. W. Mortimore (Eds.), *Rationality and the social sciences*. London: Routledge.

_____ (1976b). Script processing in attitude formation and decision making. In J. S. Carroll and J. W. Payne (Eds.), *Cognition and social behavior*. Hillsdale, N.J.: Erlbaum.

_____ (1981). Psychological status of the script concept. *Amer. Psychol., 36,* 715-729.

Adelbratt, T., and H. Montgomery (1980). Attractiveness of decision rules. *Acta Psychologica, 45,* 177-185.

Adelman, L., T. R. Stewart, and K. R. Hammond (1975). A case history of the application of social judgment theory to policy formulation. *Policy Sci., 6,* 134-157.

Ainslee, G. (1975). Specious reward: a behavioral theory of impulsiveness and impulse control. *Psychol. Bull., 82,* 463-496.

Ajzen, I. (1977). Intuitive theories of events and the effects of base-rate information on prediction. *J. Pers. soc. Psychol., 35,* 303-314.

Alexander, E. R. (1979). The design of alternatives in organizational contexts: a pilot study. *Admin. Sci. Quart., 24,* 382-404.

Ali, M. M. (1977). Probability and utility estimates for race-track bettors. *J. polit. Econ., 85,* 803-815.

Allais, M. (1953). Le comportement de l'homme rationnel devant le risque: critique des postulats et axiomes de l'Ecole Americaine. *Econometrica, 21,* 503-546.

Allison, G. T. (1971). *Essence of decision: explaining the Cuban missile crisis.* Boston: Little, Brown.

Alpert, M., and H. Raiffa (1982). A progress report on the training of probability assessors. In D. Kahneman, P. Slovic, and A. Tversky (Eds.), *Judgment under uncertainty: heuristics and biases.* Cambridge: Cambridge Univ. Press.

Anderson, N. H. (1970). Functional measurement and psychological judgment. *Psychol. Rev., 77,* 153-170.

_____ (1974a). Information integration theory: a brief survey. In D. H. Krantz, R. C. Atkinson, R. D. Luce, and P. Suppes (Eds.), *Contemporary developments in mathematical psychology.* Vol. 2. San Francisco: Freeman.

_____ (1974b). Cognitive algebra: integration theory applied to social attribution. In L. Berkowitz (Ed.), *Advances in experimental social psychology.* Vol. 7. New York: Academic Press.

Anderson, N. H., and J. C. Shanteau (1970). Information integration in risky decision making. *J. exp. Psychol., 84,* 441-451.

Arrow, K. (1951). Alternative approaches to the theory of choice in risk-taking situations. *Econometrica, 19,* 404-437.

Ashton, R. H. (1974). Cue utilization and expert judgments: a comparison of independent auditors with other judges. *J. appl. Psychol., 59,* 437-444.

_____ (1975). User prediction models in accounting: an alternative use. *Account. Rev., 50,* 710-722.

Attneave, F. (1953). Psychological probability as a function of experienced frequency. *J. exp. Psychol., 46,* 81-86.

Axelrod, R. (1976). *The structure of decision.* Princeton, N.J.: Princeton Univ. Press.

Ayeroff, F., and R. P. Abelson (1976). ESP and ESB: belief in personal success at mental telepathy. *J. Pers. soc. Psychol., 34,* 240-247.

Balke, W. M., K. R. Hammond, and G. D. Meyer (1973). An alternative approach to labor-management relations. *Admin. Sci. Quart., 18,* 311-327.

Bar-Hillel, M., and B. Fischhoff (1981). When do base rates affect predictions? *J. Pers. soc. Psychol., 41,* 671-680.

Beach, L. R., and T. R. Mitchell (1978). A contingency model for the selection of decision strategies. *Acad. management Rev., 3,* 439-449.

Becker, G. M., M. H. DeGroot, and J. Marschak (1963). An experimental study of some stochastic models for wagers. *Behav. Sci., 8,* 199-202.

Ben Zur, H., and S. J. Breznitz (1981). The effect of time pressure on risky choice behavior. *Acta Psychologica, 47,* 89-104.

Bernoulli, D. (1954). Specimen theoriae novae de mensura sortis. St. Petersburg, 1738. Translated in *Econometrica, 22,* 23-36.

Berry, D. C., and D. E. Broadbent (in press). On the relationship between task performance and verbal knowledge. *Quart. J. Exp. Psychol.*

Bettman, J. R. (1970). Information processing models of consumer behavior. *J. Marketng. Res., 7,* 370-376.

_____ (1974a). Decision-net models of buyer information processing and choice: findings, problems, and prospects. In G. D. Hughes and M. L. Ray (Eds.), *Buyer/consumer information processing.* Chapel Hill, N.C.: Univ. of North Carolina Press.

_____ (1974b). Toward a statistics for consumer decision net models. *J. Consumer Research, 1,* 71–80.

_____ (1979a). *An information processing theory of consumer choice.* Reading, Mass.: Addison-Wesley.

_____ (1979b). Memory factors in consumer choice: a review. *J. Marketng, 43,* 37–53.

Bettman, J. R., and J. Jacoby (1976). Patterns of processing in consumer information acquisition. In B. B. Anderson (Ed.), *Advances in consumer research.* Vol. 3. San Francisco: Assoc. for Consumer Research.

Bettman, J. R., and P. Kakkar (1977). Effects of information presentation format on consumer information acquisition strategies. *J. Consumer Research, 3,* 233–240.

Bettman, J. R., and C. W. Park (1979). *Description and examples of a protocol coding scheme for elements of choice processes.* Working paper No. 76, Center for Marketing Studies, University of California, Los Angeles.

_____ (1980a). Effects of prior knowledge and experience and phase of the choice process on consumer decision processes: a protocol analysis. *J. Consumer Research, 7,* 234–248.

_____ (1980b). Implications of a constructive view of choice for analysis of protocol data: a coding scheme for elements of choice processes. In J. C. Olson (Ed.), *Advances in Consumer Research.* Vol. 7. San Francisco: Assoc. for Consumer Research.

Bettman, J. R., and M. A. Zins (1977). Constructive processes in consumer choice. *J. Consumer Research, 4,* 75–85.

_____ (1979). Information format and choice task effects in decision making. *J. Consumer Research, 6,* 141–153.

Borgida, E., and N. Brekke (1981). The base-rate fallacy in attribution and prediction. In J. H. Harvey, W. J. Ickes, and R. F. Kidd (Eds.), *New directions in attribution research.* Vol. 3. Hillsdale, N.J.: Erlbaum.

Bowman, E. H. (1963). Consistency and optimality in managerial decision making. *Management Sci., 9,* 310–321.

Brady, D., and L. Rappoport (1973). Policy capturing in the field: the nuclear safeguards problem. *Organizat. Behav. hum. Perform., 9,* 253–266.

Braunstein, M. L. (1976). *Depth perception through motion.* New York: Academic Press.

Braybrooke, D., and C. Lindblom (1963). *A strategy of decision.* New York: Free Press.

Brehm, J. W. (1966). *A theory of psychological reactance.* New York: Academic Press.

_____ (1972). *Responses to loss of freedom: a theory of psychological reactance.* Morristown, N.J.: General Learning Press.

Brehm, J. W., and A. R. Cohen (1959). Reevaluation of choice alternatives as a function of their number and qualitative similarity. *J. abnorm. soc. Psychol., 58,* 373–378.

Brehmer, B. (1976). Social judgment theory and the analysis of interpersonal conflict. *Psychol. Bull., 83,* 985–1003.

_____ (1980). In one word: not from experience. *Acta Psychologica, 45,* 223–241.

Brehmer, B., and P. Slovic (1980). Information integration in multiple-cue judgments. *J. exp. Psychol.: hum. Percept. Perform., 6,* 302–308.

Brickman, P. (1978). Is it real? In J. Harvey, W. Ickes, and R. Kidd (Eds.), *New directions in attribution research.* Vol. 2. Hillsdale, N.J.: Erlbaum.

Broadbent, D. E. (1975). The magic number seven after fifteen years. In A. Kennedy and A. Wilkes (Eds.), *Studies in long term memory.* London: Wiley.

Broadbent, D. E., P. FitzGerald, and M. H. P. Broadbent (in press). Conscious and unconscious judgment in the control of complex systems. *Brit. J. Psychol.*

Brown, T. A. (1973). *An experiment in probabilistic forecasting* (Report R-944-ARPA). Santa Monica, Calif.: Rand Corp.

Bruner, J. S., J. J. Goodnow, and G. A. Austin (1956). *A study of thinking.* New York: Wiley.

Brunswik, E. (1943). Organismic achievement and environmental probability. *Psychol. Rev., 50,* 255–272.

_____ (1955). Representative design and probabilistic theory in a functional psychology. *Psychol. Rev., 62,* 193–217.

_____ (1956). *Perception and the representative design of psychological experiments* (2nd ed.). Berkeley: Univ. of California Press.

Camerer, C. (1981). General conditions for the success of bootstrapping models. *Organizat. Behav. hum. Perform., 27,* 411–422.

Capon, N., and M. Burke (1977). Information seeking in consumer durable purchases. In B. A. Greenberg and D. N. Bellenger (Eds.), *Contemporary marketing thought, 1977 educator's proceedings.* Chicago: American Marketing Assoc.

Carbonell, J. G. (1978). Politics: automated ideological reasoning. *Cognit. Sci., 2,* 27–51.

Carlsmith, J. M. (1962). *Strength of expectancy: its determinants and effects.* Unpublished doctoral dissertation, Harvard University.

Carroll, J. S. (1978). The effect of imagining an event on expectations for the event: an interpretation in terms of the availability heuristic. *J. exp. soc. Psychol., 14,* 88–96.

_____ (1980). Analyzing decision behavior: the magician's audience. In T. S. Wallsten (Ed.), *Cognitive processes in choice and decision behavior.* Hillsdale, N.J.: Erlbaum.

Carroll, J. S., and J. W. Payne (1977). Judgments about crime and the criminal: a model and a method for investigating parole decisions. In B. D. Sales (Ed.), *Perspectives in law and psychology.* Vol. 1. *The criminal justice system.* New York: Plenum.

Carter, E. E. (1971a). Project evaluations and firm decisions. *J. Managmnt. Studies, 8,* 253–279.

_____ (1971b). The behavioral theory of the firm and top level corporate decisions. *Admin. Sci. Quart., 16,* 413–428.

Castellan, N. J., Jr. (1973). Comments on the "lens model" equation and the analysis of multiple-cue judgment tasks. *Psychometrika, 38,* 87–100.

_____ (1977). Decision making with multiple probabilistic cues. In N. J. Castellan, D. B. Pisoni, and G. R. Potts, *Cognitive theory.* Hillsdale, N.J.: Erlbaum.

Cattin, P. (1978). A predictive-validity-base procedure for choosing between regression and equal weights. *Organizat. Behav. hum. Perform., 22,* 93–102.

Chapman, L. J., and J. P. Chapman (1969). Genesis of popular but erroneous psychodiagnostic observations. *J. abnorm. Psychol., 74,* 271–280.

Christensen-Szalanski, J. J. J. (1978). Problem-solving strategies: a selection mechanism, some implications, and some data. *Organizat. Behav. hum. Perform., 22,* 307–323.

_____ (1980). A further examination of the selection of problem-solving strategies: the effects of deadlines and analytic aptitudes. *Organizat. Behav. hum. Perform., 25,* 107–122.

Christensen-Szalanski, J. J. J., and J. B. Bushyhead (1981). Physicians' use of probabilistic information in a real clinical setting. *J. exp. Psychol.: hum. Percept. Perform., 7,* 928–935.

Clarkson, G. (1962). *Portfolio selection: a simulation of trust investment.* Englewood Cliffs, N.J.: Prentice-Hall.

Claudy, J. G. (1972). A comparison of five variable weighting procedures. *Educ. Psychol. Measmt., 32,* 311–322.

Cohen, J., E. I. Chesnick, and D. Haran (1971). Evaluation of compound probabilities in sequential choice. *Nature, 32,* 414–416.

Cohen, L. J. (1977). *The probable and the provable.* Oxford: Clarendon Press.

_____ (1981). Can human irrationality be experimentally demonstrated? *Behav. brain Sci., 4,* 317–331.

Conger, A. J. (1974). A revised definition for suppressor variables. A guide to their identification and interpretation. *Educ. psychol. Measmt., 34,* 35–46.

Conrath, D. W. (1967). Organizational decision making behavior under varying conditions of uncertainty. *Management Sci., 13,* 487–500.

Cook, R. L., and T. R. Stewart (1975). A comparison of seven methods for obtaining subjective descriptions of judgmental policy. *Organizat. Behav. hum. Perform., 13,* 31–45.

Coombs, C. H. (1964). *A theory of data.* New York: Wiley.

_____ (1975). Portfolio theory and the measurement of risk. In M. F. Kaplan and S. Schwartz (Eds.), *Human judgment and decision processes.* New York: Academic Press.

Coombs, C. H., R. M. Dawes, and A. Tversky (1970). *Mathematical psychology: an introduction.* Englewood Cliffs, N.J.: Prentice-Hall.

Coombs, C. H., and L. C. Huang (1974). Tests of the betweenness property of expected utility. MMPP Report 74–13. Ann Arbor: Univ. of Michigan.

Coombs, C. H., and D. E. Meyer (1969). Risk-preference in coin-toss games. *J. math. Psychol., 6,* 514–527.

Corbin, R. M. (1980). Decisions that might not get made. In T. S. Wallsten (Ed.), *Cognitive processes in choice and decision behavior.* Hillsdale, N.J.: Erlbaum.

Crandall, V. J., D. Solomon, and R. Kellaway (1955). Expectancy statements and decision times as a function of objective probabilities and reinforcement values. *J. Pers., 24,* 192–202.

Crocker, J. (1981). Judgment of covariation by social perceivers. *Psychol. Bull., 90,* 272–292.

Cyert, R., H. Simon, and D. Trow (1956). Observation of a business decision. *J. Business, 29,* 237–248.

Darlington, R. B. (1968). Multiple regression in psychological research and practice. *Psychol. Bull., 69,* 161–182.

Dawes, R. M. (1971). A case study of graduate admissions: application of three principles of human decision making. *Amer. Psychol., 26,* 180–188.

_____ (1975a). Formal models of dilemmas in social decision-making. In M. F. Kaplan and S. Schwartz (Eds.), *Human judgment and decision processes.* New York: Academic Press.

_____ (1975b). The mind, the model, and the task. In F. Restle, R. M. Shiffrin, N. J. Castellan, H. R. Lindman, and D. P. Pisoni (Eds.), *Cognitive theory.* Vol. 1. Hillsdale, N.J.: Erlbaum.

_____ (1975c). Graduate admission variables and future success. *Science, 187,* 721–723.

_____ (1976). Shallow psychology. In J. S. Carroll and J. W. Payne (Eds.), *Cognition and social behavior.* Hillsdale, N.J.: Erlbaum.

_____ (1979). The robust beauty of improper linear models in decision making. *Amer. Psychol., 34,* 571–582.

Dawes, R. M., and B. Corrigan (1974). Linear models in decision making. *Psychol. Bull., 81,* 95–106.

DeFinetti, B. (1937). La prevision: ses lois logiques, ses sources subjectives. *Annales de l'Institut Poincare, 7,* 1–68.

DeGroot, A. D. (1965). *Thought and choice in chess.* The Hague: Mouton.

DeSmet, A. A., D. G. Fryback, and J. R. Thornbury (1979). A second look at the utility of radiographic skull examination. *Amer. J. Radiology, 132,* 95–99.

Deutsch, M., and H. Gerard (1955). A study of normative and informational social influences upon individual judgment. *J. abnorm. soc. Psychol., 51,* 629–636.

Dudycha, A. L., and J. C. Naylor (1966). The effect of variations in the cue R matrix upon the obtained policy equations for judges. *Educ. Psychol. Measmt., 26,* 583–603.

Dyckman, T. R. (1981). The intelligence of ambiguity. *Account., Organ., Soc., 6,* 291–300.

Ebbesen, E. B., and V. J. Konecni (1980). On the external validity of decision-making research: what do we know about decisions in the real world? In T. S. Wallsten (Ed.), *Cognitive processes in choice and decision behavior.* Hillsdale, N.J.: Erlbaum.

Eddy, D. M. (1982). Probabilistic reasoning in clinical medicine: problems and opportunities. In D. Kahneman, P. Slovic, and A. Tversky, *Judgment under uncertainty: heuristics and biases.* Cambridge: Cambridge Univ. Press.

Edwards, W. (1954). The theory of decision making. *Psychol. Bull., 51,* 380–417.

_____ (1961). Behavioral decision theory. *Ann. rev. Psychol., 12,* 473–498.

_____ (1968). Conservatism in human information processing. In B. Kleinmuntz (Ed.), *Formal representation of human judgment.* New York: Wiley.

_____ (1971). Social utilities. *The engineering economist.* Summer Symposium Series, *6,* 119–129.

_____ (1977a). Use of multivariate utility measurement for social decision making. In D. E. Bell, R. L. Keeney, and H. Raiffa (Eds.), *Conflicting objectives in decisions.* New York: Wiley.

_____ (1977b). How to use multiattribute utility measurement for social decision making. *IEEE transactions on systems, man, and cybernetics,* SMC-7, 326–340.

_____ (1980). Reflections on and criticism of a highly political multiattribute utility analysis. In L. Cobb and R. M. Thrall (Eds.), *Mathematical frontiers of behavioral and policy science.* Boulder, Colorado: Westview Press.

Einhorn, H. J. (1970). The use of nonlinear, noncompensatory models in decision making. *Psychol. Bull., 73,* 211–230.

_____ (1971). The use of nonlinear, noncompensatory models as a function of task and amount of information. *Organizat. Behav. hum. Perform., 6,* 1–27.

_____ (1972). Expert measurement and mechanical combination. *Organizat. Behav. hum. Perform., 7,* 86–106.

_____ (1974). Expert judgment: some necessary conditions and an example. *J. appl. Psychol., 59,* 562–571.

_____ (1980). Learning from experience and suboptimal rules in decision making. In T. S. Wallsten (Ed.), *Cognitive processes in choice and decision behavior.* Hillsdale, N.J.: Erlbaum.

Einhorn, H. J., and R. M. Hogarth (1975). Unit weighting schemes for decision making. *Organizat. Behav. hum. Perform., 13,* 171–192.

_____ (1978). Confidence in judgment: persistence of the illusion of validity. *Psychol. Rev., 85,* 395–416.

_____ (1981). Behavioral decision theory: processes of judgment and choice. *Ann. rev. Psychol., 32,* 53–88.

Einhorn, H. J., D. N. Kleinmuntz, and B. Kleinmuntz (1979). Linear regression and process-tracing models of judgment. *Psychol. Rev., 86,* 465–485.

Einhorn, H. J., and W. P. McCoach (1977). A simple multiattribute utility procedure for evaluation. *Behav. Sci., 22,* 270–282.

Elstein, A. S., L. E. Shulman, and S. A. Sprafka (1978). *Medical problem solving: an analysis of clinical reasoning.* Cambridge, Mass.: Harvard Univ. Press.

Elster, J. (1979). *Ulysses and the sirens: studies in rationality and irrationality.* Cambridge: Cambridge Univ. Press.

Englander, T., and T. Tyszka (1980). Information seeking in open decision situations. *Acta Psychologica, 45,* 169–176.

Ericsson, K. A., and H. A. Simon (1980). Verbal reports as data. *Psychol. Rev., 87,* 215–251.

Estes, W. K. (1976). The cognitive side of probability learning. *Psychol. Rev., 83,* 37–64.

_____ (1980). Comments on directions and limitations of current efforts toward theories of decision making. In T. S. Wallsten (Ed.), *Cognitive processes in choice and decision behavior.* Hillsdale, N.J.: Erlbaum.

Etzioni, A. (1978). Caution: too many health warnings could be counterproductive. *Psychol. Today, 12* (7), 20–22.

Fazio, R. H., and M. P. Zanna (1978). Attitudinal qualities relating to the strength of the attitude-behavior relationship. *J. exp. soc. Psychol., 14,* 398–407.

Feldman, D. C., and H. J. Arnold (1978). Position choice: comparing the importance of organizational and job factors. *J. appl. Psychol., 63,* 706–710.

Feller, W. (1950). *Probability theory and its applications.* Vol. 1. New York: Wiley.

_____ (1965). *Probability and profit—a study of economic behavior along Bayesian lines.* Homewood, Ill.: Irwin.

Festinger, L. (1957). *A theory of cognitive dissonance.* Evanston, Ill.: Row, Peterson.

Festinger, L. (Ed.). (1964). *Conflict, decision, and dissonance.* Stanford: Stanford Univ. Press.

Festinger, L., H. Riecken, and S. Schachter (1956). *When prophecy fails.* Minneapolis: Univ. of Minnesota Press.

Festinger, L., and E. Walster (1964). Post-decision regret and decision reversal. In L. Festinger (Ed.), *Conflict, decision, and dissonance.* Stanford: Stanford Univ. Press.

Fischhoff, B. (1976). Attribution theory and judgment under uncertainty. In J. H. Harvey, W. J. Ickes, and R. F. Kidd (Eds.), *New directions in attribution theory.* Vol. 1. Hillsdale, N.J.: Erlbaum.

_____ (1982). Debiasing. In D. Kahneman, P. Slovic, and A. Tversky (Eds.), *Judgment under uncertainty: heuristics and biases.* Cambridge: Cambridge Univ. Press.

Fischhoff, B., S. Lichtenstein, P. Slovic, S. L. Derby, and R. L. Keeney (1981). *Acceptable risk.* Cambridge: Cambridge Univ. Press.

Fischhoff, B., P. Slovic, and S. Lichtenstein (1978). Fault trees: sensitivity of estimated failure probabilities to problem representation. *J. exp. Psychol.: hum. Percept. Perform., 4,* 330–344.

_____ (1980). Knowing what you want: measuring labile values. In T. S. Wallsten (Ed.), *Cognitive processes in choice and decision behavior.* Hillsdale, N.J.: Erlbaum.

_____ (1982). Lay foibles and expert fables in judgments about risk. *Amer. Statistician, 36,* 240–255.

Fishburn, P. C. (1974). Lexicographic order, utilities and decision rules: a survey. *Management Sci., 20,* 1442–1471.

_____ (1977). Mean-risk analysis with risk associated with below-target returns. *Amer. Economic Rev., 67,* 116–126.

_____ (1978). On Handa's "new theory of cardinal utility" and the maximization of expected return. *J. politic. Econ., 86* (2,1), 321–324.

Fisher, I. (1930). *The theory of interest.* New York: Macmillan.

Fiske, S. T., D. A. Kenny, and S. E. Taylor (1982). Structural models for the mediation of salience effects on attribution. *J. exp. soc. Psychol., 18,* 105–127.

Fiske, S. T., and D. R. Kinder (1980). Involvement, expertise, and schema use: evidence from political cognition. In N. Cantor and J. Kihlstrom (Eds.), *Personality, cognition, and social interaction.* Hillsdale, N.J.: Erlbaum.

Fiske, S. T., and S. E. Taylor (1984). *Social cognition.* Reading, Mass.: Addison-Wesley.

Freedman, J. L., and D. O. Sears (1965). Selective exposure. In L. Berkowitz (Ed.), *Advances in experimental social psychology.* Vol. 2. New York: Academic Press.

Friedman, M., and L. J. Savage (1948). The utility analysis of choices involving risk. *J. polit. Econ., 56,* 279–304.

Gardiner, P. C., and W. Edwards (1975). Public values: multiattribute utility measurement for social decision making. In M. F. Kaplan and S. Schwartz (Eds.), *Human judgment and decision processes.* New York: Academic Press.

George, A. L. (1969). The operational code: a neglected approach to the study of political leaders and decision-making. *Int. Stud. Quart., 13,* 190–222.

_____ (1972). The case for multiple advocacy in making foreign policy. *Amer. polit. Sci. Rev., 66,* 751–795.

_____ (1974). Adaptation to stress in political decision making: the individual, small group, and organizational contexts. In G. V. Coelho, D. A. Hamburg, and J. E. Adams (Eds.), *Coping and adaptation.* New York: Basic Books.

Gerard, H. B. (1968). Basic features of commitment. In R. P. Abelson et al. (Eds.), *Theories of cognitive consistency: a source book*. Chicago: Rand McNally.

Gettys, C. F., and S. D. Fisher (1979). Hypothesis plausibility and hypothesis generation. *Organizat. Behav. hum. Perform., 24*, 93–110.

Gettys, C. F., C. W. Kelly III, and C. F. Peterson (1973). The best guess hypothesis in multistage inference. *Organizat. Behav. hum. Perform., 10*, 364–373.

Gifford, W. E., H. R. Bobbitt, and J. W. Slocum, Jr. (1979). Message characteristics and perceptions of uncertainty by organizational decision makers. *Acad. Management J., 22*, 458–481.

Gilovich, T. (1981). Seeing the past in the present: the effect of associations to familiar events on judgments and decisions. *J. Pers. soc. Psychol., 40*, 797–808.

Ginosar, Z., and Y. Trope (1980). The effects of base rates and individuating information on judgments about another person. *J. exp. soc. Psychol., 16*, 228–242.

Goffman, E. (1967). *Interaction ritual*. New York: Anchor.

Goldberg, L. R. (1965). Diagnosticians vs. diagnostic signs: the diagnosis of psychosis vs. neurosis from the MMPI. *Psychol. Monog., 79*.

_____ (1968). Simple models or simple processes? Some research on clinical judgments. *Amer. Psychologist, 23*, 483–496.

_____ (1970). Man versus model of man: a rationale, plus some evidence, for a method of improving on clinical inferences. *Psychol. Bull., 73*, 422–432.

_____ (1972). Parameters of personality inventory construction and utilization: a comparison of prediction strategies and tactics. *Multivariate behav. Res. Monog.*, No. 72-2.

Goldin, S. E. (1978). Memory for the ordinary: typicality effects in chess memory. *J. exp. Psychol.: hum. Learn. Memory, 4*, 605–616.

Graesser, C. C., and N. H. Anderson (1974). Cognitive algebra of the equation: gift size = generosity × income. *J. exp. Psychol., 103*, 692–699.

Green B. F., Jr. (1968). Description and explanation: a comment on papers by Hoffman and Edwards. In B. Kleinmuntz (Ed.), *Formal representation of human judgment*. New York: Wiley.

Green, D. M., and J. A. Swets (1966). *Signal detection theory and psychophysics*. New York: Wiley.

Gregory, W. L., R. B. Cialdini, and K. M. Carpenter (1982). Self-relevant scenarios as mediators of likelihood estimates and compliance: does imagining make it so? *J. Pers. soc. Psychol., 43*, 89–99.

Griffith, R. M. (1949). Odds adjustments by American racehorse bettors. *Amer. J. Psychol., 62*, 290–294.

Haines, G. H. (1974). Process models of consumer decision making. In G. D. Hughes and M. L. Ray (Eds.), *Buyer/consumer information processing*. Chapel Hill: Univ. of North Carolina Press.

Hamilton, D. L. (1979). A cognitive-attributional analysis of stereotyping. In L. Berkowitz (Ed.), *Advances in experimental social psychology*. Vol. 12. New York: Academic Press.

Hammond, K. R. (1966). *The psychology of Egon Brunswik*. New York: Holt, Rinehart, and Winston.

_____ (1978). Toward increasing competence of thought in public policy formation. In K. R. Hammond (Ed.), *Judgment and decision in public policy formation*. Denver: Westview Press.

_____ (1981). Principles of organization in intuitive and analytical cognition. Center for Research on Judgment and Policy. Report No. 231. University of Colorado.

Hammond, K. R., and B. Brehmer (1973). Quasi-rationality and distrust: implications for international conflict. In L. Rappoport and D. A. Summers (Eds.), *Human judgment and social interaction*. New York: Holt, Rinehart, and Winston.

Hammond, K. R., C. J. Hursch, and F. J. Todd (1964). Analyzing the components of clinical inference. *Psychol. Rev., 71*, 438–456.

Hammond, K. R., G. H. McClelland, and J. Mumpower (1980). *Human judgment and decision making: theories, methods, and procedures*. New York: Praeger.

Hammond, K. R., and J. Mumpower (1979). Risks and safeguards in the formation of social policy. *Knowledge: Creation, Diffusion, Utilization, 1*, 245–258.

Hammond, K. R., J. Rohrbaugh, J. Mumpower, and L. Adelman (1977). Social judgment theory: applications in policy formation. In M. F. Kaplan and S. Schwartz (Eds.), *Human judgment and decision processes in applied settings*. New York: Academic Press.

Hammond, K. R., T. R. Stewart, B. Brehmer, and D. O. Steinmann (1975). Social judgment theory. In M. F. Kaplan and S. Schwartz (Eds.), *Human judgment and decision processes*. New York: Academic Press.

Hammond, K. R., and D. A. Summers (1972). Cognitive control. *Psychol. Rev., 79*, 58–67.

Hamner, W. C., and P. L. Carter (1975). A comparison of alternative production management coefficient decision rules. *Decision Sciences, 6*, 324–336.

Handa, J. (1977). Risk, probabilities and a new theory of cardinal utility. *J. politic. Econ., 85*, 97–122.

Hansson, R. O., J. P. Keating, and C. Terry (1974). The effects of mandatory time limits in the voting booth on liberal-conservative voting patterns. *J. appl. soc. Psychol., 4*, 336–342.

Hastie, R., and P. A. Kumar (1979). Person memory: personality traits as organizing principles in memory for behavior. *J. Pers. soc. Psychol., 37*, 25–38.

Hayes, J. R. (1968). Strategies in judgmental research. In B. Kleinmuntz (Ed.), *Formal representation of human judgment*. New York: Wiley.

Helmreich, R., and B. Collins (1968). Studies in forced compliance: commitment and magnitude of inducement to comply as determinants of opinion change. *J. Pers. soc. Psychol., 10*, 75–81.

Henslin, J. M. (1967). Craps and magic. *Amer. J. Sociol., 73*, 316–330.

Hershey, J. C., and P. J. H. Schoemaker (1980a). Risk taking and problem context in the domain of losses: an expected utility analysis. *J. Risk Insurance, 47*, 111–132.

_____ (1980b). Prospect theory's reflection hypothesis: a critical examination. *Organizat. Behav. hum. Perform., 25*, 398–418.

Hicks, J. M., and D. T. Campbell (1965). Zero-point scaling as affected by social object, scaling method, and context. *J. Pers. soc. Psychol., 2,* 793–808.

Hirshleifer, S. (1970). *Investment, interest and capital.* Englewood Cliffs, N.J.: Prentice-Hall.

Hoffman, P. J. (1960). The paramorphic representation of clinical judgment. *Psychol. Bull., 57,* 116–131.

Hoffman, P. J., P. Slovic, and L. G. Rorer (1968). An analysis of variance model for the assessment of configural cue utilization in clinical judgment. *Psychol. Bull., 69,* 338–349.

Hogarth, R. M. (1975). Cognitive processes and the assessment of subjective probability distributions. *J. Amer. Statist. Assoc., 70,* No. 350, 271–289.

_____ (1980). *Judgment and choice: the psychology of decision.* Chichester: Wiley.

_____ (1981). Beyond discrete biases: functional and dysfunctional aspects of judgmental heuristics. *Psychol. Bull., 90,* 197–217.

Hogarth, R. M., and S. Makridakis (1981). Forecasting and planning: an evaluation. *Management Sci., 27,* 115–138.

Hovland, C. I., E. Campbell, and T. Brock (1957). The effects of "commitment" on opinion change following communication. In C. I. Hovland (Ed.), *Order of presentation in persuasion.* New Haven: Yale Univ. Press.

Hovland, C. I., and W. Weiss (1953). Trasmission of information concerning concepts through positive and negative instances. *J. exp. Psychol., 45,* 175–182.

Howell, W. C., and S. A. Burnett (1978). Uncertainty measurement: a cognitive taxonomy. *Organizat. Behav. hum. Perform., 22,* 45–68.

Huber, G. P. (1974). Multiattribute utility models: a review of field and field-like studies. *Management Sci., 20,* 1393–1402.

Huber, O. (1980). The influence of some task variables on cognitive operations in an information-processing decision model. *Acta Psychologica, 45,* 187–196.

Hursch, C., K. R. Hammond, and J. Hursch (1964). Some methodological considerations in multiple-cue probability studies. *Psychol. Rev., 71,* 42–60.

Irwin, F. W. (1953). Stated expectancies as a function of probability and desirability of outcome. *J. Pers., 21,* 329–335.

Isen, A. M., B. Means, R. Patrick, and G. Nowicki (1982). Some factors influencing decision-making strategy and risk taking. In M. S. Clark and S. T. Fiske (Eds.), *Affect and cognition: The 17th Annual Carnegie Symposium on Cognition.* Hillsdale, N.J.: Erlbaum.

Jacoby, J. (1977). Information load and decision quality: some contested issues. *J. Marketng. Res., 14,* 569–573.

Jacoby, J., R. W. Chestnut, K. C. Weigl, and W. Fisher (1976). Pre-purchase information acquisition: description of a process methodology, research paradigm, and pilot investigation. In B. B. Anderson (Ed.), *Advan. consum. Res.* Vol. 3. San Francisco: Assoc. for Consumer Research.

Jacoby, J., D. E. Speller, and C. A. K. Berning (1974). Brand choice behavior as a function of information load: replication and extension. *J. consum. Res., 1,* 33–42.

_____ (1975). Constructive criticism and programmatic research: reply to Russo. *J. consum. Res., 2,* 154–156.

Jacoby, J., D. E. Speller, and C. A. Kohn (1974). Brand choice behavior as a function of information load. *J. Marketng. Res., 11,* 63–69.

Janis, I. L. (1959). Motivational factors in the resolution of decision conflicts. In M. R. Jones (Ed.), *Nebraska Symposium on Motivation.* Vol. 7. Lincoln: Univ. of Nebraska Press.

_____ (1968). Pilot studies on new procedures for improving the quality of decision making. Mimeographed research report. Yale Studies in Attitudes and Decisions.

_____ (1972). *Victims of groupthink: a psychological study of foreign policy decisions and fiascoes.* Boston: Houghton Mifflin.

_____ (1975). Effectiveness of social support for stressful decisions. In M. Deutsch and H. Hornstein (Eds.), *Applying social psychology: implications for research, practice, and training.* Hillsdale, N.J.: Erlbaum.

_____ (1982a). *Groupthink* (2nd. ed.). Boston: Houghton Mifflin.

_____ (Ed.) (1982b). *Counseling on personal decisions.* New Haven: Yale Univ. Press.

Janis, I. L., and L. Mann (1977). *Decision making: a psychological analysis of conflict, choice, and commitment.* New York: Free Press.

Janis, I. L., and C. N. Rausch (1970). Selective interest in communications that could arouse decisional conflict: a field study of participants in the draft-resistance movement. *J. Pers. soc. Psychol., 14,* 46–54.

Janis, I. L., and R. Terwilliger (1962). An experimental study of psychological resistance to fear-arousing communications. *J. abnorm. soc. Psychol., 65,* 403–410.

Jeffreys, H. (1948). *Theory of probability.* Oxford: Clarendon Press.

Jenkins, H. M., and W. C. Ward (1965). Judgments of contingency between responses and outcomes. *Psychol. Monogr., 79* No. 1, (Whole No. 594).

Jennings, D. L., M. Amabile, and L. Ross (1982). Informal covariation assessment: Data-based vs. theory-based judgments. In D. Kahneman, P. Slovic, and A. Tversky (Eds.), *Judgment under uncertainty: heuristics and biases.* Cambridge: Cambridge Univ. Press.

Jepson, D., D. H. Krantz, and R. E. Nisbett (1984). *Inductive reasoning: competence or skill? Behav. brain Sci.*

Jervis, R. (1976). *Perception and misperception in international relations.* Princeton, N.J.: Princeton Univ. Press.

_____ (1982). Update on perception and misperception. Talk delivered to the International Political Science Association.

Johnson, E. J. (1979). Deciding how to decide: the effort of making a decision. Technical Report, Center for Decision Research, Graduate School of Business, Univ. of Chicago.

Johnson, E. J., and J. E. Russo (1978). The organization of product information in memory identified by recall times. In H. K. Hunt (Ed.), *Advances in consumer research.* Vol. 5. Chicago: Assoc. for Consumer Research.

Johnson, E. L. (1982). Risk assessment in an administrative agency. *Amer. Statistician, 36,* 232–239.

Johnson-Laird, P. (1980). Mental models in cognitive science. *Cognit. Sci., 4,* 71–115.

Kahneman, D. (1973). *Attention and effort.* Englewood Cliffs, N.J.: Prentice-Hall.

Kahneman, D., and A. Tversky (1972). Subjective probability: a judgment of representativeness. *Cognit. Psychol., 3,* 430–454.

_____ (1973). On the psychology of prediction. *Psychol. Rev., 80,* 251–273.

_____ (1979a). Intuitive prediction: biases and corrective procedures. *TIMS studies Management Sci., 12,* 313–327.

_____ (1979b). Prospect theory: an analysis of decision under risk. *Econometrica, 47,* 263–291.

_____ (1982a). Variants of uncertainty. In D. Kahneman, P. Slovic, and A. Tversky (Eds.), *Judgment under uncertainty: heuristics and biases.* Cambridge: Cambridge Univ. Press.

_____ (1982b). The psychology of preferences. *Scientific Amer., 246,* 160–173.

_____ (1982c). On the study of statistical intuitions. In D. Kahneman, P. Slovic, and A. Tversky (Eds.), *Judgment under uncertainty: heuristics and biases.* Cambridge: Cambridge Univ. Press.

_____ (1984). Choices, values, and frames. *Amer. Psychol., 39,* 341–350.

Kanter, R. M. (1972). *Commitment and community: communes and utopias in sociological perspective.* Cambridge, Mass.: Harvard Univ. Press.

Karmarkar, U. S. (1978). Subjectively weighted utility: a descriptive extension of the expected utility model. *Organizat. Behav. hum. Perform., 21,* 61–72.

_____ (1979). Subjectively weighted utility and the Allais paradox. *Organizat. Behav. hum. Perform., 24,* 67–72.

Keeney, R. L. (1972). Utility functions for mulitattributed consequences. *Management Sci., 18,* 276–287.

Keeney, R. L., and H. Raiffa (1976). *Decisions with multiple objectives: preferences and value tradeoffs.* New York: Wiley.

Kelley, H. H., and J. L. Michela (1980). Attribution theory and research. *Ann. Rev. Psychol., 31,* 457–501.

Keren, G., and J. R. Newman (1978). Additional considerations with regard to multiple regression and equal weighting. *Organizat. Behav. hum. Perform., 22,* 143–164.

Kiesler, C. A. (Ed.) (1971). *The psychology of commitment.* New York: Academic Press.

Kinder, D. R., and J. A. Weiss (1978). In lieu of rationality: psychological perspectives on foreign policy decision making. *J. Conflict Resolution, 22,* 707–735.

Kleinmuntz, B. (1967). Sign and seer: another example. *J. abnorm. Psychol., 72,* 163–165.

_____ (1968). The processing of clinical information by man and machine. In B. Kleinmuntz (Ed.), *Formal representation of human judgment.* New York: Wiley.

_____ (1975). The computer as clinician. *Amer. Psychol., 30,* 379–387.

Koopmans, T. C. (1964). On flexibility of future preference. In M. W. Shelly, II, and G. L. Bryan (Eds.), *Human judgments and optimality.* New York: Wiley.

Koriat, A., S. Lichtenstein, and B. Fischhoff (1980). Reasons for confidence. *J. exp. Psychol.: hum. Learn. Memory, 6,* 107–118.

Kort, F. (1968). A nonlinear model for the analysis of judicial decisions. *Amer. polit. Sci. Rev., 62,* 546–555.

Krantz, D. H., G. T. Fong, and R. E. Nisbett (1982). *Formal training improves the application of statistical heuristics to everyday problems.* Unpublished manuscript. Bell Laboratories.

Kunreuther, H. (1969). Extensions of Bowman's theory on managerial decision-making. *Management Sci., 15,* 415–439.

Lane, D. M., K. R. Murphy, and T. E. Marques (1982). Measuring the importance of cues in policy capturing. *Organizat. Behav. hum. Perform., 30,* 231–240.

Langer, E. J. (1975). The illusion of control. *J. Pers. soc. Psychol., 32,* 311–328.

_____ (1978). Rethinking the role of thought in social interaction. In J. Harvey, W. Ickes, and R. Kidd (Eds.), *New directions in attribution research.* Vol. 2. Hillsdale, N.J.: Erlbaum.

Lee, W. (1971). *Decision theory and human behavior.* New York: Wiley.

Leventhal, H., and J. Watts (1966). Sources of resistance to fear-arousing communications on smoking and lung cancer. *J. Pers., 34,* 155–175.

Levi, A. S. (1981). *Escalating commitment and risk taking in dynamic decision behavior.* Ph.D. dissertation, Yale Univ. Press.

Levy, H., and H. M. Markowitz (1979). Approximating expected utility by a function of mean and variance. *Amer. econ. Rev., 69,* 308–317.

Lewin, K. (1951). *Field theory in social science.* New York: Harper.

Libby, R., and P. C. Fishburn (1977). Behavioral models of risk-taking in business decisions: a survey and evaluation. *J. Account. Res.*

Lichtenstein, S., B. Fischhoff, and L. D. Phillips (1982). Calibration of probabilities: the state of the art to 1980. In D. Kahneman, P. Slovic, and A. Tversky (Eds.), *Judgment under uncertainty: heuristics and biases.* Cambridge: Cambridge Univ. Press.

Lieberman, D. A. (1979). Behaviorism and the mind: a (limited) call for a return to introspection. *Amer. Psychol., 34,* 319–333.

Lockhead, G. R. (1980). Know, then decide. In T. S. Wallsten (Ed.), *Cognitive processes in choice and decision behavior.* Hillsdale, N.J.: Erlbaum.

Lopes, L. L. (1976). Model-based decision and inference in stud poker. *J. exp. Psychol.: General, 105,* 217–239.

_____ (1981). Decision making in the short run. *J. exp. Psychol.: hum. Learn. Memory, 7,* 377–385.

Lord, C., M. R. Lepper, and E. Preston (1983). Considering the opposite: a corrective strategy for social judgment. Unpublished manuscript, Princeton University.

Luce, R. D. (1956). Semi-orders and a theory of utility discrimination. *Econometrica, 24,* 178–191.

Luce, R. D., and H. Raiffa (1957). *Games and decisions.* New York: Wiley.

Luchins, A. S. (1942). Mechanization in problem solving: the effect of Einstellung. *Psychol. Monogr., 54,* 1–95.

Lussier, D. A., and R. W. Olshavsky (1979). Task complexity and contingent processing in branch choice. *J. Consumer Research, 6,* 154–165.

McAllister, D. W., T. R. Mitchell, and L. R. Beach (1979). The contingency model for the selection of decision strategies: an empirical test of the effects of significance, accountability, and reversibility. *Organizat. Behav. hum. Perform., 24,* 228–244.

McArthur, L. Z., and D. Post (1977). Figural emphasis and person perception. *J. exp. soc. Psychol., 13,* 520–535.

McCall, M. W., Jr., R. E. Kaplan, and M. L. Gerlach (1982). *Caught in the act: decision makers at work.* (Tech. Rep. 20). Greensboro, N.C.: Center for Creative Leadership.

McCann, J. M., J. G. Miller, and H. Moskowitz (1975). Modeling and testing dynamic multivariate decision processes. *Organizat. Behav. hum. Perform., 14,* 281–303.

Maccoby, N., J. W. Farquhar, P. D. Wood, and J. Alexander (1977). Reducing the risk of cardiovascular disease: effects of a community-based campaign on knowledge and behavior. *J. Community Health, 3,* (2), 100–114.

MacCrimmon, K. R., and S. Larsson (1979). Utility theory: axioms versus paradoxes. In M. Allais and O. Hagen (Ed.), *Expected utility hypothesis and the Allais paradox.* Dordrecht, Holland: Reidel.

MacCrimmon, K. R., and R. N. Taylor (1976). Decision making and problem solving. In M. D. Dunnette (Eds.), *Handbook of industrial and organizational psychology.* Chicago: Rand McNally.

McGlothin, W. H. (1956). Stability of choices among uncertain alternatives. *Amer. J. Psychol., 69,* 604–615.

McGuire, W. J. (1964). Inducing resistance to persuasion: some contemporary approaches. In L. Berkowitz (Ed.), *Advances in experimental social psychology.* Vol. 1. New York: Academic Press.

———— (1960). A syllogistic analysis of cognitive relationships. In M. J. Rosenberg et al. (Eds.), *Attitude organization and change.* New Haven: Yale Univ. Press.

Machina, M. J. (1982). Expected utility analysis without the independence axiom. *Econometrica, 2,* 277–332.

McKenney, J. L., and P. G. W. Keen (1974). How managers' minds work. *Harvard Bus. Rev., 52,* 79–90.

Mackinnon, A. J., and A. J. Wearing (1982). Decision making in dynamic environments. Paper delivered at the First International Conference on Foundations of Utility and Risk Theory, Oslo, Norway.

Mahoney, M. J. (1977). Publication prejudices: an experimental study of confirmatory bias in the peer review system. *Cognit. Therapy Res., 1,* 161–175.

Maier, S. F., and M. Seligman (1976). Learned helplessness: theory and evidence. *J. exp. Psychol.: General, 105,* 3–46.

Malhotra, N. K. (1982). Information load and consumer decision making. *J. Consumer Research, 8,* 419–430.

Malhotra, N. K., A. K. Jain, and S. W. Lagakos (1982). The information overload controversy: an alternative viewpoint. *J. Marketing, 46,* 27–37.

Manis, M., I. Dovalina, N. E. Avis, and S. Cardoze (1980). Base rates can affect individual predictions. *J. Pers. soc. Psychol., 38,* 231–248.

March, J. G. (1978). Bounded rationality, ambiguity, and the engineering of choice. *Bell J. Econ. management Sci., 9,* 587–608.

March, J. G., and J. P. Olsen (1976). *Ambiguity and choice in organizations.* Bergen, Norway: Universitetsforlaget.

Markowitz, H. (1952). The utility of wealth. *J. Polit. Econ., 60,* 151–158.

Marks, R. W. (1951). The effects of probability, desirability, and privilege on the stated expectations of children. *J. Pers., 19,* 332–351.

Marques, T. E., D. M. Lane, and P. W. Dorfman (1979). Toward the development of a system for instructional evaluation: is there consensus regarding what constitutes effective teaching? *J. educ. Psychol., 71,* 840–849.

Matlin, M., and D. Stang (1978). *The Pollyanna principle: selectivity in language, memory and thought.* Cambridge, Mass.: Schenkman.

May, E. R. (1973). *Lessons of the past.* New York: Oxford Univ. Press.

Meehl, P. E. (1954). *Clinical vs. statistical prediction: a theoretical analysis and a review of the evidence.* Minneapolis: Univ. of Minnesota Press.

———— (1957). When shall we use our heads instead of the formula? *J. Counsel. Psychol., 4,* 268–273.

Miller, D. W., and M. K. Starr (1967). *The structure of human decisions.* Englewood Cliffs, N.J.: Prentice-Hall.

Miller, G. A. (1956). The magical number seven, plus or minus two: some limits on our capacity for processing information. *Psychol. Rev., 63,* 81–97.

Miller, G. A., E. Galanter, and K. H. Pribram (1960). *Plans and the structure of behavior.* New York: Holt, Rinehart, and Winston.

Mills, J., R. Meltzer, and M. Clark (1977). Effect of number of options on recall of information supporting different decision strategies. *Pers. soc. Psychol. Bull., 3,* 213–218.

Milord, J. T., and R. R. Perry (1977). A methodological study of overload. *J. gen. Psychol., 97,* 131–137.

Mintzberg, H., D. Raisinghani, and A. Thoret (1976). The structure of unstructured decisions. *Admin. Sci. Quart., 21,* 246–275.

Mischel, W. (1974). Processes in delay of gratification. *Advances in experimental social psychology.* Vol. 7. New York: Academic Press.

Montgomery, H. (1976). A study of intransitive preferences using a think aloud procedure. In H. Jungerman and C. de Zeeuw (Eds.), *Proceedings of the fifth research conference on subjective probability, utility and decision making.*

Montgomery, H., and O. Svenson (1976). On decision rules and information processing strategies for choice among multiattribute alternatives. *Scand. J. Psychol., 17,* 283–291.

Mortimore, G. W. (1976). Rational action. In S. I. Benn and G. W. Mortimore (Eds.), *Rationality and the social sciences.* London: Routledge.

Moskowitz, H. (1974). Regression models of behavior for managerial decision making. *OMEGA, Int. J. Management Sci., 2,* 677–690.

Murphy, A. H., and R. L. Winkler (1977). Can weather forecasters formulate reliable probability forecasts of precipitation and temperature? *National Weather Digest, 2,* 2–9.

Myers, D. G., and H. Lamm (1977). The polarizing effect of group discussion. In I. L. Janis (Ed.), *Current trends in psychology: readings from the American Scientist.* Los Altos, Calif.: Kaufmann.

Naylor, J. C., and R. J. Wherry, Sr. (1965). The use of simulated stimuli and the JAN technique to capture and cluster the policies of raters. *Educ. Psychol. Measmt., 25,* 969–986.

Newell, A., and H. A. Simon (1972). *Human problem solving.* Englewood Cliffs, N.J.: Prentice-Hall.

Newman, J. R. (1977). Differential weighting in multiattribute utility measurement: when it should not and when it does make a difference. *Organizat. Behav. hum. Perform., 20,* 312–325.

Nisbett, R. E., and N. Bellows (1977). Verbal reports about causal influences on social judgments: private access versus public theories. *J. Pers. soc. Psychol., 35,* 613–624.

Nisbett, R. E., D. H. Krantz, C. Jepson, and G. T. Fong (1982). Improving inductive inference. In D. Kahneman, P. Slovic, and A. Tversky (Eds.), *Judgment under uncertainty: heuristics and biases.* Cambridge: Cambridge Univ. Press.

Nisbett, R. E., D. H. Krantz, C. Jepson, and Z. Kunda (1983). The use of statistical heuristics in everyday inductive reasoning. *Psychol. Rev., 90,* 339–363.

Nisbett, R. E., and L. Ross (1980). *Human inference: strategies and shortcomings of social judgment.* Englewood Cliffs, N.J.: Prentice-Hall.

Nisbett, R. E., and T. D. Wilson (1977a). The halo effect: evidence for unconscious alteration of judgments. *J. Pers. soc. Psychol., 35,* 250–256.

––––– (1977b). Telling more than we can know: verbal reports on mental processes. *Psychol. Rev., 84,* 231–259.

Oden, G. C., and N. H. Anderson (1971). Differential weighting in integration theory. *J. exp. Psychol., 89,* 152–161.

Oldman, D. (1974). Chance and skill: a study of roulette. *Sociology, 8,* 407–426.

Olshavsky, R. W. (1979). Task complexity and contingent processing in decision making: a replication and extension. *Organizat. Behav. hum. Perform., 24,* 300–316.

Olshavsky, R. W., and F. Acito (1980). The impact of data collection procedure on choice rule. In J. Olson (Ed.), *Advances in consumer research.* Vol. 7. San Francisco: Assoc. for Consumer Research.

Park, C. W. (1978a). A conflict resolution choice model. *J. Consumer Research, 5,* 124–137.

––––– (1978b). A seven-point scale and a decision maker's simplifying choice strategy: an operationalized satisficing-plus model. *Organizat. Behav. hum. Perform., 21,* 252–271.

Payne, J. W. (1973). Alternative approaches to decision making under risk: moments vs. risk dimensions. *Psychol. Bull., 80,* 439–453.

––––– (1975). Relation of perceived risk to preferences among gambles. *J. exp. Psychol.: hum. Percept. Perform., 104,* 86–94.

––––– (1976a). Heuristic search processes in decision making. In B. B. Anderson (Ed.), *Advances in consumer research.* Vol. 3. Ann Arbor: Assoc. for Consumer Research.

––––– (1976b). Task complexity and contingent processing in decision making: an information search and protocol analysis. *Organizat. Behav. hum. Perform., 16,* 366–387.

––––– (1980). Information processing theory: some concepts and methods applied to decision research. In T. S. Wallsten (Ed.), *Cognitive processes in choice and decision behavior.* Hillsdale, N.J.: Erlbaum.

Payne, J. W., and M. L. Braunstein (1978). Risky choice: an examination of information acquisition behavior. *Memory and Cognition, 6,* 554–561.

Payne, J. W., M. L. Braunstein, and J. S. Carroll (1978). Exploring predecisional behavior: an alternative approach to decision research. *Organizat. Behav. hum. Perform., 22,* 17–44.

Peterson, C. R., and L. R. Beach (1967). Man as an intuitive statistician. *Psychol. Bull., 68,* 29–46.

Petrinovich, L. (1979). Probabilistic functionalism: a conception of research method. *Amer. Psychol., 34,* 373–390.

Phelps, R. H., and J. Shanteau (1978). Livestock judges: how much information can an expert use? *Organizat. Behav. hum. Perform., 21,* 209–219.

Pitz, G. F. (1975). A structural theory of uncertain knowledge. In D. Wendt and C. Vlek (Eds.), *Utility, probability, and human decision making.* Dordrecht, Holland: Reidel.

Pitz, G. F., N. J. Sachs, and J. Heerboth (1980). Procedures for eliciting choices in the analysis of individual decisions. *Organizat. Behav. hum. Perform., 26,* 396–408.

Plott, C. R., and M. E. Levine (1978). A model of agenda influence on committee decisions. *Amer. Econ. Rev., 68,* 146–160.

Pounds, W. (1969). The process of problem finding. *Indust. Management Rev., 11,* 1–19.

Pratt, J. W., H. Raiffa, and R. Schlaifer (1965). *Introduction to statistical decision theory.* London: McGraw-Hill.

Preston, M. G., and P. Baratta (1948). An experimental study of the auction value of an uncertain outcome. *Amer. J. Psychol., 61,* 183–193.

Pruitt, D. G. (1962). Pattern and level of risk in gambling decisions. *Psychol. Rev., 69,* 187–201.

Pruitt, D. G., and M. J. Kimmel (1977). Twenty years of experimental gaming: critique, synthesis, and suggestions for the future. *Ann. Rev. Psychol., 28,* 363–392.

Pryor, J. B., and M. Kriss (1977). The cognitive dynamics of salience in the attribution process. *J. Pers. soc. Psychol., 35,* 49–55.

Pyszczinski, T. (1982). Cognitive strategies for coping with uncertain outcomes. *J. res. Pers., 16,* 386–399.

Quattrone, G. A. (1982). Overattribution and unit formation: when behavior engulfs the person. *J. Pers. soc. Psychol., 42,* 593–607.

Raiffa, H. (1969). Preferences for multiattribute alternatives. (Memorandum RM-5968-DOT/RC). Santa Monica, Calif.: Rand Corp. April.

––––– (1982). Science and policy: their separation and integration in risk analysis. *Amer. Statistician, 36,* 225–231.

Ramsey, F. P. (1931). Truth and probability (1926). In F. P. Ramsey, *The foundations of mathematics and other logical essays.* London: Kegan Paul.

Rapoport, A., and A. Chammah (1965). *Prisoner's dilemma.* Ann Arbor: Univ. of Michigan Press.

Rapoport, A., and T. S. Wallsten (1972). Individual choice behavior. *Ann. Rev. Psychol., 23,* 131–175.

Ravetz, J. (1977). The political economy of risk. *New scientist, 75,* 598–599.

Reitman, W. R. (1964). Heuristic decision procedures, open constraints, and the structure of ill-defined problems. In M. W. Shelly, II and G. L. Bryan (Eds.), *Human judgments and optimality.* New York: Wiley.

Richmond, J. B. (1979). *Healthy people: the surgeon general's report on health promotion and disease prevention* (DHEW PHS Publication No. 79-55071). Washington, D.C.: U.S. Government Printing Office.

Rip, P. (1980). The informational basis of self-reports: a preliminary report. In J. C. Olson (Ed.), *Advances in consumer research*. Vol. 7. San Francisco: Assoc. for Consumer Research.

Rosen, L. D., and P. Rosenkoetter (1976). An eye fixation analysis of choice and judgment with multiattribute stimuli. *Memory and Cognition, 4,* 747–752.

Ross, L., and C. A. Anderson (1982). Shortcomings in the attribution process: on the origins and maintenance of erroneous social assessments. In D. Kahneman, P. Slovic, and A. Tversky (Eds.), *Judgment under uncertainty: heuristics and biases.* Cambridge: Cambridge Univ. Press.

Ross, L., M. R. Lepper, and M. Hubbard (1975). Perseverance in self perception and social perception: biased attributional processes in the debriefing paradigm. *J. Pers. soc. Psychol., 32,* 880–892.

Russo, J. E. (1974). More information is better: a re-evaluation of Jacoby, Speller and Kohn. *J. Consumer Research, 1,* 68–72.

———— (1978). Eye fixations can save the world: a critical evaluation and a comparison between eye fixations and other information processing methodologies. In J. K. Hunt (Ed.), *Advances in consumer research*. Vol. 5. Chicago: Assoc. for Consumer Research, Univ. of Illinois.

———— (1979). A software system for the collection of retrospective protocols prompted by eye fixations. *Behav. res. Methods Instrumentation, 11,* 177–179.

Russo, J. E., and B. A. Dosher (1975). *Dimensional evaluation: a heuristic for binary choice.* Unpublished paper. Department of Psychology, University of California, San Diego.

———— (1976). An information processing analysis of binary choice. Working paper. Carnegie Mellon University.

———— (1980). Cognitive effort and strategy selection in binary choice. Technical Report, Center for Decision Research, Graduate School of Business, University of Chicago.

Russo, J. E., and L. D. Rosen (1975). An eye fixation analysis of multialternative choice. *Memory and Cognition, 3,* 267–276.

Saaty, T. L. (1977). A scaling method for priorities in hierarchical structures. *J. math. Psychol., 15,* 234–281.

Samuelson, P. H. (1977). St. Petersburg paradoxes: defanged, dissected, and historically described. *J. econ. Lit., 15,* 24–55.

Savage, L. J. (1954). *The foundations of statistics.* New York: Wiley.

Sawyer, J. (1966). Measurement and prediction, clinical and statistical. *Psychol. Bull., 66,* 178–200.

Schaninger, C. M., and D. Sciglimpaglia (1981). The influence of cognitive personality traits and demographics on consumer information acquisition. *J. Consumer Research, 8,* 208–216.

Schank, R. C., and R. P. Abelson (1977). *Scripts, plans, goals and understanding: an inquiry into human knowledge structures.* Hillsdale, N.J.: Erlbaum.

Schelling, T. (1978). Egonomics, or the art of self-management. *Amer. Econ. Rev., 68,* 290–294.

Schenk, E. A., and J. C. Naylor (1968). A cautionary note concerning the use of regression analysis for capturing the strategies of people. *Educ. Psychol. Measmt., 28,* 3–7.

Schmitt, N., and R. L. Levine (1977). Statistical and subjective weights: some problems and proposals. *Organizat. Behav. hum. Perform., 20,* 15–30.

Schneider, W., and R. M. Shiffrin (1977). Controlled and automatic human information processing: I. Detection, search, and attention. *Psychol. Rev., 84,* 1–66.

Schoemaker, P. J. H. (1979). The role of statistical knowledge in gambling decisions: moment versus risk-dimension approaches. *Organizat. Behav. hum. Perform., 24,* 1–17.

———— (1980). *Experiments on decisions under risk: the expected utility hypothesis.* Boston: Kluwer Nijhoff.

Schoemaker, P. J. H., and H. C. Kunreuther (1979). An experimental study of insurance decisions. *J. Risk Insurance, 46,* 603–618.

Schoemaker, P. J. H., and C. C. Waid (1982). An experimental comparison of different approaches to determining weights in additive utility models. *Management Sci., 28,* 182–196.

Schustack, M., and R. Sternberg (1981). Evaluation of evidence in causal inference. *J. exp. Psychol.: General, 110,* 101–120.

Schwing, R., and W. A. Albers, Jr. (Eds.) (1980). *Societal risk assessment: how safe is safe enough?* New York: Plenum.

Shafer, G. (1976). *A mathematical theory of evidence.* Princeton, N.J.: Princeton Univ. Press.

Shanteau, J. (1974). Component processes in risky decision making. *J. exp. Psychol., 103,* 680–691.

———— (1975). An information integration analysis of risky decision making. In M. F. Kaplan and S. Schwartz (Eds.), *Human judgment and decision processes.* New York: Academic Press.

Shapira, Z. (1981). Making trade-offs between job attributes. *Organizat. Behav. hum. Perform., 28,* 331–355.

Shapley, L. S. (1977). The St. Petersburg Paradox: a con game? *J. Econ. Theory, 14,* 439–442.

Shaw, M. L. (1982). Attending to multiple sources of information: I. The integration of information in decision making. *Cognit. Psychol., 14,* 353–409.

Shugan, S. M. (1980). The cost of thinking. *J. Consumer Research, 7,* 99–111.

Shweder, R. A. (1977). Likeness and likelihood in everyday thought: magical thinking in judgments about personality. *Current Anthropology, 18,* 637–658.

Siegel, S., and L. E. Fouraker (1960). *Bargaining and group decision-making: experiments in bilateral monopoly.* New York: McGraw-Hill.

Simon, H. A. (1955). A behavioral model of rational choice. *Quart. J. Econ., 69,* 99–118.

———— (1956). Rational choice and the structure of the environment. *Psychol. Rev., 63,* 129–138.

———— (1965). *The shape of automation for men and management.* New York: Harper & Row.

———— (1966). *New science of management decision.* New York: Harper.

———— (1974). How big is a chunk? *Science, 183,* 482–488.

———— (1976a). *Administrative behavior: a study of decision-making processes in administrative organization* (3rd ed.). New York: Free Press.

———— (1976b). Discussion: cognition and social behavior. In J. S. Carroll and J. W. Payne (Eds.), *Cognition and social behavior*. Hillsdale, N.J.: Erlbaum.

———— (1978). Information-processing theory of human problem solving. In W. K. Estes (Ed.), *Handbook of learning and cognitive processes*. Vol. 5. Hillsdale, N.J.: Erlbaum.

Simon, H. A., and J. R. Hayes (1976). The understanding process: problem isomorphs. *Cognit. Psychol., 8,* 165–190.

Simon, H. A., and A. Newell (1974). Thinking processes. In D. H. Krantz, R. C. Atkinson, R. D. Luce, and P. Suppes (Eds.), *Contemporary developments in mathematical psychology*. Vol. 1. San Francisco: Freeman.

Skinner, B. F. (1948). Superstition in the pigeon. *J. exp. Psychol., 38,* 168–172.

Slovic, P. (1969). Analyzing the expert judge: a descriptive study of a stockbroker's decision processes. *J. appl. Psychol., 53,* 255–263.

———— (1972). From Shakespeare to Simon: speculations—and some evidence—about man's ability to process information. *ORI research monograph, 12.* Eugene, Ore.: Oregon Research Institute.

———— (1975). Choice between equally-valued alternatives. *J. exp. Psychol.: hum. Percept. Perform., 1,* 280–287.

Slovic, P., B. Fischhoff, and S. Lichtenstein (1976). Cognitive processes and societal risk taking. In J. S. Carroll and J. W. Payne (Eds.), *Cognition and social behavior.* Hillsdale, N.J.: Erlbaum.

———— (1977). Behavioral decision theory. *Ann. rev. Psychol., 28,* 1–39.

———— (1978). Accident probabilities and seat belt usage: a psychological perspective. *Accident analysis Prevention, 10,* 281–285.

———— (1982). Facts versus fears: understanding perceived risk. In D. Kahneman, P. Slovic, and A. Tversky (Eds.), *Judgment under uncertainty: heuristics and biases.* Cambridge: Cambridge Univ. Press.

Slovic, P., D. Fleissner, and W. S. Bauman (1972). Analyzing the use of information in investment decision making: a methodological proposal. *J. Business, 45,* 283–301.

Slovic, P., and S. Lichtenstein (1968). Relative importance of probabilities and payoffs in risk taking. *J. exp. Psychol., 78,* (3, Part 2).

———— (1971). Comparison of Bayesian and regression approaches to the study of information processing in judgment. *Organizat. Behav. hum. Perform., 6,* 649–744.

Slovic, P., and D. J. MacPhillamy (1974). Dimensional commensurability and cue utilization in comparative judgment. *Organizat. Behav. hum. Perform., 11,* 172–194.

Smead, R. J., J. B. Wilcox, and R. E. Wilkes (1981). How valid are product descriptions and protocols in choice experiments? *J. Consumer Research, 8,* 37–42.

Smedslund, J. (1963). The concept of correlation in adults. *Scand. J. Psychol., 4,* 165–173.

Snyder, G. H., and P. Diesing (1977). *Conflict among nations.* Princeton: Princeton Univ. Press.

Soelberg, P. O. (1967). Unprogrammed decision making. *Indust. Management Rev., 8,* 19–29.

Sprowls, R. C. (1953). Psychological-mathematical probability in relationships of lottery gambles. *Amer. J. Psychol., 66,* 126–130.

Staddon, J. E. R., and V. L. Simmelhag (1971). The "superstitious" experiment: a reexamination of its implications for the principles of adaptive behavior. *Psychol. Rev., 78,* 3–43.

Staelin, R., and J. W. Payne (1976). Studies of the information seeking behavior of consumers. In J. S. Carroll and J. W. Payne (Eds.), *Cognition and social behavior.* Hillsdale, N.J.: Erlbaum.

Steinbruner, J. D. (1974). *The cybernetic theory of decision.* Princeton: Princeton Univ. Press.

Stenson, H. H. (1974). The lens model with unknown cue structure. *Psychol. Rev., 81,* 257–264.

Stillwell, W. G., D. A. Seaver, and W. Edwards (1981). A comparison of weight approximation techniques in multiattribute utility decision making. *Organizat. Behav. hum. Perform., 28,* 62–77.

Summers, D. A., J. D. Taliaferro, and D. J. Fletcher (1970). Subjective vs. objective description of judgment policy. *Psychon. Sci., 18,* 249–250.

Summers, J. O. (1974). Less information is better? *J. marketng. Res., 11,* 467–481.

Svenson, O. (1979). Process descriptions of decision making. *Organizat. Behav. hum. Perform., 23,* 86–112.

Szucko, J. J., and B. Kleinmuntz (1981). Statistical versus clinical lie detection. *Amer. Psychol., 36,* 488–496.

Taylor, S. E. (1976). Developing a cognitive social psychology. In J. S. Carroll and J. W. Payne (Eds.), *Cognition and social behavior.* Hillsdale, N.J.: Erlbaum.

Taylor, S. E., and S. T. Fiske (1975). Point of view and perceptions of causality. *J. Pers. soc. Psychol., 32,* 439–445.

———— (1978). Salience, attention and attribution: top of the head phenomena. In L. Berkowitz (Ed.), *Advances in experimental social psychology.* Vol. 11. New York: Academic Press.

Taylor, S. E., and S. C. Thompson (1982). Stalking the elusive vividness effect. *Psychol. Rev., 89,* 155–181.

Tetlock, R., and A. S. Levi (1982). Attribution bias: on the inconclusiveness of the cognition-motivation debate. *J. exp. soc. Psychol., 18,* 68–88.

Thaler, R. (1980). Toward a positive theory of consumer choice. *J. econ. Behav. Organizat., 1,* 39–60.

Thaler, R. H., and H. M. Shefrin (1981). An economic theory of self-control. *J. Politic. Econ., 89,* 392–406.

Thorngate, W. (1980). Efficient decision heuristics. *Behav. Sci., 25,* 219–225.

Thorngate, W., and J. Maki (1976). *Decision heuristics and the choice of political candidates.* Unpublished manuscript. Univ. of Alberta.

Thurstone, L. L., and L. V. Jones (1957). The rational origin for measuring subjective values. *J. Amer. Stat. Assoc., 52,* 458–471.

Toda, M. (1980). Emotion and decision making. *Acta Psychologica, 45,* 133–155.

Toda, M., and E. H. Shuford, Jr. (1965). Utility, induced utilities, and small worlds. *Behav. Sci., 10,* 238–254.

Tomkins, S. S. (1965). The psychology of commitment: I. The constructive role of violence and suffering for the individual and for his society. In S. S. Tomkins and C. Izard (Eds.), *Affect, cognition and personality*. New York: Springer.

Tucker, L. R. (1964). A suggestive alternative formulation in the developments by Hursch, Hammond and Hursch, and by Hammond, Hursch and Todd. *Psychol. Rev., 71,* 528–530.

Tuggle, F. D., and F. H. Barron (1980). On the validation of descriptive models of decision-making. *Acta Psychologica, 45,* 197–200.

Tversky, A. (1969). Intransitivity of preferences. *Psychol. Rev., 76,* 31–48.

—— (1972a). Choice by elimination. *J. math. Psychol., 9,* 341–367.

—— (1972b). Elimination by aspects: a theory of choice. *Psychol. Rev., 79,* 281–299.

Tversky, A., and D. Kahneman (1971). The belief in the law of small numbers. *Psychol. Bull., 76,* 105–110.

—— (1973). Availability: a heuristic for judging frequency and probability. *Cognit. Psychol., 5,* 207–232.

—— (1974). Judgment under uncertainty: heuristics and biases. *Science, 185,* 1124–1131.

—— (1981). The framing of decisions and the psychology of choice. *Science, 211,* 453–458.

—— (1982a). Evidential impact of base rates. In D. Kahneman, P. Slovic, and A. Tversky (Eds.), *Judgment under uncertainty: heuristics and biases.* Cambridge: Cambridge Univ. Press.

—— (1982b). Judgments of and by representativeness. In D. Kahneman, P. Slovic, and A. Tversky (Eds.), *Judgment under uncertainty: heuristics and biases.* Cambridge: Cambridge Univ. Press.

—— (1983). Extensional vs. intuitive reasoning: the conjunction fallacy in probability judgment. *Psychol. Rev., 90,* 293–315.

Tversky, A., and E. J. Russo (1969). Similarity and substitutability in binary choices. *J. Math. Psychol., 6,* 1–12.

Tversky, A., and S. Sattath (1979). Preference trees. *Psychol. Rev., 86,* 542–573.

van Raaij, W. F. (1976). *Consumer choice behavior: an information-processing approach.* Tilburg: Katholieke Hogeschool te Tilburg.

von Neumann, J., and O. Morgenstern (1947). *Theory of games and economic behavior* (2nd ed.). Princeton: Princeton Univ. Press.

von Winterfeldt, D. (1980). Structuring decision problems for decision analysis. *Acta Psychologica, 45,* 71–93.

Wainer, H. (1976). Estimating coefficients in linear models: it don't make no nevermind. *Psychol. Bull., 83,* 213–217.

Wainer, H., and D. Thissen (1976). Three steps towards robust regression. *Psychometrika, 41,* 9–33.

Walker, S. G., and T. G. Murphy (1981–1982). The utility of the operational code in political forecasting. *Politic. Psychol., 3,* 24–60.

Wallsten, T. S. (1980). Processes and models to describe choice and inference. In T. S. Wallsten (Ed.), *Cognitive processes in choice and decision behavior.* Hillsdale, N.J.: Erlbaum.

Walster, E. (1964). The temporal sequence of post-decision processes. In L. Festinger (Ed.), *Conflict, decision, and dissonance.* Stanford: Stanford Univ. Press.

Walster, E., and G. W. Walster (1970). Choice between negative alternatives: dissonance reduction or regret? *Psychol. Reports, 26,* 995–1005.

Ward, J. H. (1962). Comments on the paramorphic representation of clinical judgment. *Psychol. Bull., 52,* 74–76.

Wason, P. C. (1960). On the failure to eliminate hypotheses in a conceptual task. *Quart. J. exp. Psychol., 12,* 129–140.

—— (1968). Reasoning about a rule. *Quart. J. exp. Psychol., 20,* 273–281.

Wason, P. C., and J. St. B. T. Evans (1975). Dual processes in reasoning? *Cognition, 3,* 141–154.

Wason, P. C., and P. N. Johnson-Laird (1970). A conflict between selecting and evaluating information in an inferential task. *Brit. J. Psychol., 61,* 509–515.

Waterman, D., and A. Newell (1973). PAS-II: an interactive task-free version of an automatic protocol analysis system. *Proceed. int. joint conference artific. Intell.,* 431–445.

Weiss, J. (1982). Coping with complexity: an experimental study of public policy decision-making. *J. policy analy. Management, 2,* 66–87.

Wicklund, R. A. (1974). *Freedom and reactance.* Potomac, Md.: Erlbaum.

Wiggins, J. S. (1973). *Personality and prediction: principles of personality assessment.* Reading, Mass.: Addison-Wesley.

Wiggins, N., and P. J. Hoffman (1968). Three models of clincial judgment. *J. abnorm. Psychol., 73,* 70–77.

Wiggins, N., and E. Kohen (1971). Man versus model of man revisited. *J. Pers. soc. Psychol., 19,* 100–106.

Wilkie, W. L. (1974). Analysis of effects of information load. *J. Marketng. Res., 11,* 462–466.

Witte, E. (1972). Field research on complex decision making processes—the phase theorem. *Int. stud. Management Organizat., 2,* 156–182.

Wright, P. (1974). The harassed decision maker: time pressures, distractions, and the use of evidence. *J. appl. Psychol., 59,* 555–561.

—— (1975). Consumer choice strategies: simplifying vs. optimizing. *J. Marketng. Res., 12,* 60–67.

Wright, P., and F. Barbour (1977). Phased decision strategies: sequels to an initial screening. In M. K. Starr and M. Zeleny (Eds.), *Studies in the management sciences.* Vol. 6. Amsterdam: North Holland Publishing.

Wright, P., and P. Rip (1980). Retrospective reports on consumer decision processes: "I can remember if I want to, but why should I bother trying?" In J. C. Olson (Ed.), *Advances in consumer research.* Vol. 7. San Francisco: Assoc. for Consumer Research.

Wright, P., and B. Weitz (1977). Time horizon effects on product evaluation strategies. *J. Marketng. Res., 14,* 429–433.

Wright, W. F. (1979). Properties of judgment models in a financial setting. *Organizat. Behav. hum. Perform., 23,* 73–85.

Yaari, M. E. (1965). Convexity in the theory of choice under risk. *Quart. J. Econ., XX,* 278–290.

Yates, J. F., C. M. Jagacinski, and M. D. Faber (1978). Evaluation of partially described multiattribute options. *Organizat. Behav. hum. Perform., 21,* 240–251.

Yates, J. F., and L. G. Zukowski (1976). Characterization of ambiguity in decision making. *Behav. Sci., 21,* 19–25.

Yntema, D. B., and W. Torgerson (1961). Man-machine cooperation in decisions requiring common sense. *IRE trans. hum. Factors Electron., HFE-2*, 20–26.

Zedeck, S., and D. Kafry (1977). Capturing rater policies for processing evaluation data. *Organizat. Behav. hum. Perform., 18*, 269–294.

Zeev, M. (1981). The decision to raid Entebbe: decision analysis applied to crisis behavior. *J. Conflict Resolution, 25*, 677–708.

Zeleny, M. (1976). On the inadequacy of the regression paradigm used in the study of human judgment. *Theory Decision, 6*, 147–157.

CHAPTER 6

Symbolic Interaction and Role Theory

Sheldon Stryker
Indiana University

Anne Statham
University of Wisconsin at Parkside

INTRODUCTION

It is difficult for social psychologists to agree on a definition of their field of inquiry. This is true for the discipline as a whole, as it is for the somewhat more homogeneous, somewhat distinctive subtypes of social psychology, that is, those that emerge from the work of persons trained in departments of psychology, on the one hand, and those that result from the efforts of persons trained in departments of sociology, on the other (Stryker, 1971; 1977). If attention is limited to the latter, there is relatively strong agreement among sociologically trained social psychologists on the defining principle of their portion of the larger discipline; namely, social life is structured, and this structure is important to the development of the social person and to the production of social behavior.

Many sociologists would expand upon this uncontroversial definitional claim in elaborating on the intellectual tasks of a sociologically informed and oriented social psychology; they would specify their legitimating problematic by arguing the reciprocity of "society" and "individual," of social structure and social person (Hewitt, 1979; Heiss, 1981; McCall and Simmons, 1982). The proposition that social structure and person mutually constrain one another (if they do not indeed presup-

pose one another) has been called the fundamental insight motivating social psychology of this genre (Stryker, 1977) and at least some would argue that if sociologists did not capitalize on this insight, they could contribute little if anything distinctive to social psychology.

Whether expressed through Cooley's (1902) "two sides of the same coin" figure, or in terms of Mead's (1934) analysis of the necessarily joint emergence of society and self from the ongoing social process, then, sociologists doing social psychological work tend to begin with this fundamental insight; they take as their central task spelling out just what it is in society that impacts particular aspects of the person, just what it is in the person that makes a difference for particular aspects of society, and just how the mutually determinative process takes place.

Although this central task is simple to define, it is far from simple to accomplish. A theoretical framework is required that facilitates movement from the level of social structure to the level of the person, and vice versa, as well as explanatory principles articulating the two levels that reflect the inherent complexity of both. Ultimately, what is necessary is a well-developed theory that recognizes both the ways in which and the degree to which individual behavior, social interaction and the social person are constrained by social structure as well as how it is that persons can construct their behaviors, individually and collectively, even to the point of altering the structures within which they act. The needed theory does not exist although it may be evolving. If it evolves, it is likely to do so from the two theoretical frameworks that are the subject matter of this chapter: symbolic interaction theory and role theory.

Although the language is conventional, the terms "symbolic interaction theory" or "role theory" claim more than is warranted. Neither is a theory in the sense of "a set of assumptions or postulates with which one approaches some part of the empirical world, a set of concepts in terms of which this part of the world is described, and a set of propositions, emerging from the assumptions and relating the concepts, about the way this part of the world 'works' which are checked against observations of that world" (Stryker, 1959, p. 111). Both are theoretical approaches or, at best, frameworks: directives for examining certain features of the empirical world that are likely to be significant in the development of an eventual theory; and the assumptions that focus attention on these features. While theories have developed from these frameworks—an example is identity theory discussed later—they lack the scope required to answer all the needs previously noted.

This chapter reviews both symbolic interactionism and role theory, for neither alone possesses the intellectual and conceptual resources needed to construct an adequate social psychological theory. Each has characteristic and complementary strengths and weaknesses. Thus, each serves to "correct" the other; taken together they have the potential for adequate theorizing that separately they lack (Handel, 1979).

The preceding paragraph offers the basic theme of this chapter. We will present the rudiments of a reasonably general social psychological theoretical framework resulting from the integration of symbolic interactionist and role theoretic ideas, an integration not yet accomplished but well under way. We intend the present chapter to be a contribution to that integration as well as a review of what has been done to this point.

"Insiders" are sensitive to what distinguishes their own brand of ideas from related brands and recognize nuances that others find difficult to appreciate; "outsiders" are likely to be blind to those nuances and to gloss over distinctions. Both insiders and outsiders have confused the relationship of symbolic interactionism and role theory. Thus, Biddle and Thomas (1966) explicitly define role theory as excluding symbolic interactionist concepts and emphases. (Interestingly, a later work by

Biddle (1979) seems to assimilate the two.) Kuhn (1964) sees the two as coterminous; and others (e.g., Stryker, 1973) view them as somewhat different, overlapping theoretical traditions.

Symbolic interaction theory and role theory do share certain important elements. Both emphasize the need to analyze social phenomena from the perspectives of participants in social processes, that is, the need for the external observer to bring into explanatory models the subjective experiences and performances of those being observed (Martindale, 1960; Stryker, 1973). Both take the theater as a major metaphor of social life, making central use of the concept of "role" in their analyses (although some symbolic interactionists may not use the term). Indeed, if the two traditions did not share such elements, they could be integrated in the manner anticipated by this chapter.

Although there is no fundamental incompatibility between the two, there are differences in interests and emphases. To oversimplify, role theory developed through social anthropology, particularly the work of Linton (1936), and through German sociology, particularly the work of Simmel (1950) and Weber (1947) and came into prominence in the theoretical writings of Davis (1949), Parsons (1951), Merton (1957), Goode (1960b), and others. Social interaction is viewed as the behavior of actors playing out roles shaped through evolutionary adaptation. Primarily interested in problems of social organization, role theory uses the concept of role as a basic-building block in constructing its theoretical arguments about the structure and functioning of complex social organizations.

Symbolic interactionism developed from the writings of the Scottish Moral Philosophers (Smith, Ferguson, Hume, and others) and from American pragmatic philosophy (James, Dewey, Mead) and is exemplified in the sociological and social philosophical writings of Cooley, Thomas, Blumer, Kuhn, and others. Its theatrical metaphor differs from that of role theory in that the scripts are not detailed directives to be played as given but are constructed in the course of the play itself and are constrained only in outline form by the culture and social organization within which the play takes place. Interested primarily in personal organization and disorganization, socialization, and the analysis of interaction itself, symbolic interactionism has used role concept to build "down" to the level of the social person or to personality structure (Stryker, 1973).

These sketches of symbolic interactionism and role theory hint at their reciprocal strengths and weaknesses, and point to integrative strategies. Symbolic interactionism's strength is its ability to conceptualize social actors who can construct their lines of action individually and cooperatively and who can also alter the social structural conditions within which they act. Its weakness is its inadequate conceptualization and analyses of the social structural constraints—ranging from minimal to virtually total—within which social action is constructed and its inability to deal with stability in individual and social behavior. Role theory's strength is its sophisticated conceptualization of a differentiated social structure within which action takes place and of the ways in which structure organizes social behavior. Its weakness is its relative inability to capture the varying degree to which social behavior is constructed under different structural circumstance and the ways in which constructed behavior can alter social structure.

A strategy for integrating the two frameworks is suggested by their common dependence on the concept of role. That is, ''role'' articulates social structure as conceptualized by role theory and the social person as conceptualized by symbolic interactionism. Thus in our goal of integrating these two theories, it seems reasonable to begin with an elaboration of this concept.

As implied earlier, there is an evolving literature that has this goal and follows this strategy. We will preface our discussion of that literature with separate discussions of the historical roots, basic concepts, major theoretical emphases and contributions, and critical appraisals of symbolic interactionism and role theory in order to enable independent judgments of the strengths and weaknesses of these two theories and of the successes, problems and opportunities suggested by the current efforts to integrate them.

Following our separate treatments of the two frameworks, we turn to the integrative efforts and examine the ways in which symbolic interactionists have been modifying their perspective to deal with critiques leveled at it, in particular by building into their perspective a more adequate sense of social structure and its importance for social behavior. We also examine the ways in which role theorists are adapting their framework in response to criticisms of it so as to enable them to deal theoretically with negotiated and constructed aspects of social life.

We move in the next section of the chapter to an assessment of the current integrative efforts. This assessment serves as the basis for a concluding discussion of issues that remain in attempts to develop a theoretical framework integrating symbolic interactionism and role theory.

Our primary concern is with the development of an integrated conceptual framework, not with the statement of rigorous theory and certainly not with empirical tests of such theory. A strong theoretical framework is a necessary prologue to sound theories and empirical tests and the most significant work being done now is at the level of this conceptual framework. Given the practical necessity of circumscribing our efforts in some way, the decision was reached to concentrate on conceptual and theoretical issues.

SYMBOLIC INTERACTIONISM

Although the label is comparatively new, symbolic interactionism has strong roots in the eighteenth century, and its fundamentals have been important in U.S. sociological thought from early in the present century. For many, these fundamentals constitute a general framework for the anlaysis of society (Blumer, 1969), applicable to all sociological as well as social psychological problems. For others, they are the basis for a specialized social psychological enterprise (Stryker, 1964; 1980) whose strength lies in the analysis of socialization, personal organization and personal disorganization. The latter point of view underlies that of this chapter; indeed, symbolic interactionism's inadequacy in incorporating social structural concepts, and thus as a general sociological theory, is precisely what motivates attempts to bring into it elements of role theory.

Even as specialized social psychological theory, however, symbolic interactionism is not recently minted (in its fundamentals; modifications are continuous and important). Interestingly, the previous editions of this handbook contained chapters on role theory (Sarbin, 1954; Sarbin and Allen, 1968), but none on symbolic interactionism (although the original Sarbin chapter did incorporate aspects of it). The reasons why are a matter of conjecture as is the question why the editors chose to provide space for the symbolic interaction perspective in the current edition.

That there are ''two social psychologies'' tending to differ in what they do and how they do it (Stryker, 1971; 1977; 1983) and to proceed essentially independently of one another is hardly a secret. Symbolic interactionism's development and influence—at least until recently—has been within sociology in contrast to almost every other extant general and specific theoretical framework in social psychology. This fact alone, given the social organizational characteristics of the American academic enterprise, helps greatly in explaining the earlier absence of symbolic interactionism in a handbook purporting to represent the discipline as a whole.

What then has changed to make symbolic interactionism worthy of discussion in this edition of the *Handbook of Social Psychology?* Clearly, the rather remarkable shift to cognition-based social psychological theory and research among psychologists over recent decades makes more likely interest among psychologists in another framework with strong cognitive emphases. In addition, the resurgence of phenomenological thought in both sociology and psychology (Harré and Secord, 1972) makes more probable appreciation for a framework whose central theoretical concept is "self." Stryker (1971; 1977) remarks that the emergent "respectability" of subjective experience is a notable characteristic of recent social psychology; one can see this, for example, in the way the "self" is used to understand the results of dissonance studies (Aronson, 1969; Bem, 1972), and in the influence Heider's (1958) formulation of the problems of a naive psychology has had. Given that, the motivating problem of their work is the search for a theory that explains how people order their phenomenologies to provide meaning to their worlds, it is not surprising that students of attribution and related cognitive processes find relevant symbolic interactionist discussions of how social life is constructed. Indeed, there are considerable common elements (as well as some important differences) between symbolic interaction theory and attribution theory (Stryker and Gottlieb, 1981), and these common elements sustain mutual awareness. Moreover, the resurgence of humanistic orientations among psychologically trained social psychologists (Heider, 1958; Gergen, 1971; Gergen, 1982; Harré and Secord, 1972; Smith, 1974) make it possible to take more seriously a perspective that historically has been less oriented toward "hard" science than has the experimental social psychology centered in psychology. Finally, because symbolic interactionism places considerable emphasis on the openness of human action, the possibilities for creative rather than simply reactive responses, and the availability and the reality of choice and self-direction in human experience, it becomes appealing to the contemporary humanistic temper of many social psychologists trained in psychology.

We have been arguing that the topic of this chapter evidences a shift in the concerns of psychological social psychology and implicitly that symbolic interactionism has something to say about these concerns (for an explicit argument to this effect, see Stryker, 1983). We turn now to what that something is, beginning with a brief presentation of the broad imagery of the symbolic interactionist perspective to guide the more detailed discussion that follows.

THE UNDERLYING IMAGERY

Although there are significant differences among theorists of symbolic interaction, they all share an underlying imagery. This imagery addresses the nature of society and the human being, the relationship between the two, and the nature of human action and interaction.

The image of society held by symbolic interactionists is a web of communication. As the identifying label indicates, society is interaction: the reciprocal influence of persons who as they act take into account one another's characteristics. As the identifying label also indicates, interaction is "symbolic," conducted in terms of the meanings persons develop in the course of their conduct. From the standpoint of symbolic interactionism, the environment of human action and interaction is necessarily a symbolically defined environment. Persons act with reference to one another in terms of the symbols developed through their interaction, and they act through the communication of these symbols. Society is a summary name for such interaction.

Given this image of society, social life is visualized as a dynamic process. Society doesn't "exist"; it is continuously created and recreated as persons act with reference to one another. The fundamental image of social reality is a flow of events involving two or more interacting persons. Society and person are joined in the social process; indeed, both derive from the social process (Mead, 1934). Society and person take on their meanings as these meanings emerge in and through social interaction.

In this imagery, neither "society" nor "individual" is ontologically prior to the other, although this does not preclude recognizing that any historical person is born into an existing system of social interaction involving others who in turn interact with that person. Society, conceptualized as a web of symbolic interaction, creates the person; but it is persons who through interaction create society. Thus society and person are reciprocally related in a most fundamental way: They presuppose one another in that neither exists except in relation to the other. They are, in Cooley's (1902) terms, two sides of the same coin.

Implicit in this conception of society is a conception of the human being as "minded." Thought takes place as internal "conversation" utilizing the symbols that develop in the social process. Mind is viewed as arising in response to problems (i.e., to interruptions in the flow of activities) and as involving the formulation and selection of alternative courses of actions to resolve the problems. Thus, in this imagery, choice becomes a reality of the human condition, and the content of choices is contained in the subjective experience of the person as it is developed in and through the social process. It clearly follows from this imagery that to comprehend human behavior, a person must come to terms with that subjective experience and incorporate it into accounts of behavior.

It also follows that human beings, individually and collectively, are active and creative rather than merely responsive in relation to environmental forces impinging on them. If the environment of human action and interaction is symbolic, if the symbols that attach to things and people are the products of interaction and can be manipulated in the course of that interaction, if thought can be used to anticipate the effectiveness of alternative courses of action in the resolution of problems, and if choice among alternative courses is a feature of social conduct, we then emerge with an image of social interaction as literally constructed by participants in the course of interaction itself. We emerge with an image that insists on a degree of indeterminancy in human behavior, in the specific sense that the course and outcome of social interaction cannot (as a matter of principle) be totally predicted from the conditions and factors that exist previous to that interaction.

SYMBOLIC INTERACTIONISM
AND SCIENCE

Does this imagery commit symbolic interactionism to a nonscientific or even antiscientific position? The answer depends on what one means by science. Some symbolic interactionists (e.g., Blumer, 1969) have argued the fundamental incompatibility of symbolic interactionism with science, if one takes a view of science as a hypothesis generating and testing activity, using methods that maximize possible controlled observations to achieve its goal of developing empirically supported theoretical generalizations. Others (e.g. Gergen, 1973; 1982) have made the same argument with respect to social psychology and social science in general. All of the following—the absence of an assuredly deterministic universe, the possibil-

ity of choice in human behavior, the argument that persons create the meanings to which they respond and which guide and organize their behavior, and the reflexive and anticipatory thought these meanings make possible—have been cited to imply the inappropriate application of the causal imagery of science to human behavior and to argue that the aspiration for a defensible, evidence-based, predictive system of theoretical generalizations is illusory. The best we can aspire to, the argument concludes, is post hoc understanding based on the particulars of the historical circumstance in which the behavior we observe is imbedded.

Not all symbolic interactionists find the logic that places their perspective in opposition to conventional science compelling (Stryker, 1977; 1980; 1984; Gottlieb, 1977). They contend that the business of science can be conducted without assuming total determinism, that social life has some regularity and order, and that the task of social psychology as science is to describe and explain such regularity as exists. Some note that the choice, self-direction and self-control implied by their perspective are socially derived rather than created and operative outside of social interaction and that choice is not random. Some argue that the emphasis on meanings implies that meanings should be built into explanatory theories and not that the quest for explanatory theories should be abandoned. Some assert that science, properly understood, requires determinancy and causality in our theories about the world and not in the world. Finally some suggest, with the ethnomethodologist (Cicourel, 1973), that although the interpretations persons use to give meaning to their worlds are too variable and unstable to permit theoretical generalizations about the context of social interaction, there may be considerable stability or even invariance in the processes by which social interaction is constructed or accomplished; and that it is this stability or invariance to which our attention should be directed.

Having described the underlying imagery of symbolic interactionism, we turn now to a discussion of how this perspective developed.

SYMBOLIC INTERACTIONISM:
EARLY DEVELOPMENT

Bryson (1945) convincingly argues that the Scottish Moral Philosophers of the eighteenth century—in particular David Hume, Adam Smith, Adam Ferguson, and Frances Hutcheson—foreshadowed many fundamentals of the symbolic interactionist perspective through their attempts to provide an empirical basis for the study of society and of man. They legitimated a view of man as a natural object and rationalized the scientific as well as the pragmatic importance of considering everyday experience as the proper arena of observation in an attempt to develop principles of human behavior.

These Scotsmen approached human behavior from the standpoint of society, holding that achieving a science of man required taking into account the facts of human association. They emphasized habit relative to instinct, appreciated the relation of habit to custom, and understood custom as evolving through society's learned responses to its environmental problems. They viewed society as a network of interpersonal communication, connecting persons organically. And they saw mind as instrumental in human adaptation.

Although they differed on what was fundamental about the human mind, their emphasis on the importance of mind in human behavior and the importance of society for mind led them to examine communication, sympathy, imitation, habit, and custom as they formulated basic principles of behavior. Smith and Hume suggested "sympathy" as the principle through which humans find a sense of membership in society and the benefits derived from it as well as through which they come to be controlled by their fellows. Sympathy allows persons to put themselves in the place of others and to experience the world as these others do; it also makes possible the communication that shapes persons as they seek the approval of others. Sympathy and communication enable persons to learn from society who and what they are. In Smith's (1759) words: "Bring him into society, and he is immediately provided with a mirror which he wanted before. It is placed in the countenance and behavior of those he lives with. This is the only looking glass by which we can, in some measure, with the eyes of other people, scrutinize the propriety of our own conduct."

Linking the Scottish Moral Philosophers to symbolic interactionism proper are the American pragmatic philosophers, whose writings echo and elaborate the themes of their predecessors. James (1890) uses the concept of habit to argue the importance of society as a constraint on behavior. His discussions of the meaning and sources of self-esteem anticipate contemporary discussion of these topics that model the impact of society on the person. In addition, he develops a conception of the "self" as both multifaceted and the product of the person's relationships with others that is particularly relevant to current theoretical extensions of symbolic interactionism reviewed later in this chapter.

Dewey (1930) also insists on the intimate relation of person and society by analyzing personality organization primarily in terms of habit and social organization primarily in terms of custom defined as collective habit. Habit, he contends, necessarily reflects a previous social order, since every person is born into an existing association of human beings. Custom and habit are requisite bases for reflection or thinking, and thinking occurs as humans adjust to their environments. Thinking is instrumental; humans define objects in their worlds and rehearse possible lines of action, choosing those that facilitate adaptation. Anticipating a contemporary emphasis, he rejects a monolithic view of society by regarding it as a set of many differential associations.

Mead (1934) is clearly the single most important influence shaping symbolic interactionism, in part because his basic social psychological dictum was most compatible with the thinking of sociologists. That dictum, developing from evolutionary principles that viewed mental activity in, and symbolic communication among, human beings as making possible the cooperation essential for survival, asserted: Begin social psychological analysis with the social process. From the social process he derived mind, self, and society; and the subject matter of his social psychology was framed in terms of the interrelationships of these derivative phenomena.

The pivotal concept in Mead's thinking is the "self," defined as that which can be an object to itself. To understand the significance of this concept and its definition, one must go back to the social process and the communication that makes that process possible. With Dewey (1896), Mead asserts the active character of human behavior. Humans do not simply respond to external stimuli that exist independently of ongoing activity. Rather, a thing becomes an object—a stimulus—once it is defined as relevant to completing an act initiated by persons relating them to their environments. Things become objects by acquiring meaning, and they acquire meaning in activity. What holds for acts relating individuals to their physical environments also holds for social acts implicating other human beings. Social acts are the source of organized social behavior and of personality; they are developments from the social process made possible by communication through language.

This argument turns attention to communication, which involves a conversation of gestures: the use by participants in social acts of early stages of one another's behavior as indicators of later stages. Significant symbols, linguistic and otherwise, evolve from gestures when these come to have the same meaning to coparticipants in social acts in the sense of indicating the same future phases of the acts. Anticipation of responses, our own and those of others, and adjustment to those anticipated responses, are made possible by significant symbols. Through these, we "take the role of the other" and, through the role-taking process, engage in cooperative activity. Significant symbols allow the emergence of mind, of thinking, which symbolically represents alternative future courses our activity can take as we seek to complete our actions. The meanings of objects to which we are responsive are products of the social interaction in which significant symbols are formed and used. Since these meanings are social products, mind too is a social product.

The "self" develops via the same social process. It exists in the activity of viewing oneself reflexively, as an object, by using the standpoint of others to attach meaning to oneself. The self is a social structure, emergent from social interaction. To understand human behavior, according to Mead, one must understand the critical role played by the self. He specifies two parts to the self: the organized attitudes (expectations) of others and the responses of the person to these organized attitudes of others (Lewis, 1979). The former he labels the "me," the latter the "I". The "I" represents the spontaneous, creative aspect of human behavior, although creativity and spontaneity occur within the social process, not outside of it. Behavior is the outcome of an internal, dialectical conversation in which the attitudes of others (the "me") are responded to by the person (the "I") are responded to by the attitudes of others (the "me"), etc. Behavior is self-controlled; but social control is a necessary condition for self-control.

The self develops as does any other object, according to Mead. But the self develops in stages along with the child's language competence (Corsaro, 1979b). A "play" stage, in which a child takes the role of particular others, is first. Since social life is complexly organized, however, the person must learn to respond to an intricate pattern of related behaviors from multiple others. Mead uses the metaphor of the game to represent this second stage. To play an organized game, one takes the role of the "generalized other," anticipating the responses of all the other participants in a complex interaction pattern as the basis for adjusting one's own response.

The previous existence of organized groups is presupposed by the emergence of self. Mead holds that as society shapes the self, so the self shapes society through the I-me dialectic. Society is continuously recreated; social organization is not a final state but, in contemporary language, a continuous construction. Thus social order

and social change, and by implication personal order and personal change, are aspects of the larger social process.

Many of the ideas reviewed here were introduced to sociology by Cooley who added his own characteristic emphases, some of which (e.g., his more affective orientation relative to Mead's more cognitive emphasis) are currently receiving greater attention than in the past. His work (1902) builds on the arguments that there is no individuality outside of social order, that personality emerges from communication among those sharing extant social life, and that central to personality are the expectations of others. He insists on the importance of the mental and the subjective aspects in social life; this insistence is exemplified in his definition of society as a "relation among personal ideas" and in his assertion that "the imaginations which people have of one another are the solid facts of society." It is also exemplified in his call for "sympathetic introspection," that is, using sympathy to imagine things as others imagine them. This, Cooley states, is the prime method for discovering facts about not only these others but also society as well.

Also important to the early development of symbolic interactionism is the work of W. I. Thomas (1937). Sociological accounts of human behavior, Thomas holds, must incorporate both the subjective and the objective facts of human experience. The objective facts are in the form of situations, circumstances requiring some adjustive response on the part of persons or groups. Definitions of the situation, however, intervene between situations and response. Although Thomas never formulated precisely the meaning of this key term, the conception of definition of the situation provided a simple and powerful rationale for the significance of the subjective aspect in social life and thus provided symbolic interactionism with its prime methodological rule: "if men define situations as real, they are real in their consequences" (Thomas and Thomas, 1928).

When discussing its evolution beyond Mead, reviews of symbolic interactionism (e.g., Meltzer, Petras, and Reynolds, 1975) invariably introduce a contrast between a "Chicago School," identified with Blumer (1969) and an "Iowa School," identified with Kuhn (1964). In particular, characterizing a "Chicago School" of symbolic interactionism solely by reference to Blumer's work fails to recognize the influences of Park (1955) and Hughes (1945) on American sociology in general and on students at the University of Chicago in particular; these influences become more apparent as contemporary symbolic interactionists seek to remedy their approach to social psychology by incorporating social structural concepts. It is nevertheless convenient to use the work of Blumer and Kuhn as symbols for themes in the development of symbolic interactionism, since their ideas bridge the gap between those of the founding American fathers and those of the relatively recent past. Meltzer, *et al.* (1975, p. 123) summarize the contrast between the two: "The 'Chicago school' emphasizes process not structure, sympathetic introspection not attitude scales, indeterminacy and emergence not determinancy." While flawed, these assertions capture the flavor of the differences between Blumer and Kuhn.

Much of Blumer's writings are polemical, defining symbolic interactionism in contradistinction to conventional sociology. His starting point is the work of Mead; his claim, currently being debated (Blumer, 1980; Fallding, 1982; McPhail and Rexroat, 1979 and 1980), is that his work is a straightforward elaboration of that of Mead. Conventional sociology links social behavior to role requirements, expectations, norms, and values, etc.; Blumer (1969) sees this relation as inconsistent with the recognition that the human is a defining, interpreting, and indicating creature with a self through which his or her world is handled and action constructed. Social organization enters action only to the extent that it shapes situations and provides symbols used in interpreting situations and has little influence in modern society where situations for which there are no previous standardized actions abound. Even established and repetitive forms of action must be continuously renewed through interpretation and designation. Society is, from this point of view, not a structure or organization, but the actions of people taking place in situations and constructed by the persons' interpreting the situation, identifying and assessing things that have to be taken into account, and acting on the basis of this assessment (Blumer, 1962).

Thus, Blumer sees the person, organized action, and the environment as fluid, continuously constructed and reconstructed via definitional and interpretative processes. This vision leads him to enunciate methodological principles at odds with conventional science (Blumer, 1954; 1956). Rather than relying on "definitive concepts," he argues, we must rely on "sensitizing concepts" that suggest directions to look rather than (as "definitive concepts") prescriptions as to what to see. There is, he further argues, little point in measuring or seeking relationships among variables as part of scientific inquiry, since anything that is defined (and everything of consequence is) can be redefined and thus lacks the qualitative constancy required of variables. Effectively

ruling out experiments and surveys on these and similar grounds, Blumer calls for the direct examination of the empirical world of everyday experience as the means of attaining knowledge about human behavior.

Kuhn's (1964) symbolic interactionism is much more oriented toward and by conventional social science, seeking precisely stated theory and rigorous empirical test. Agreeing that social structure is created, maintained, and changed through symbolic interaction, he views it, once created, as constraining interaction. Adopting role theory's conception of social structure as networks of positions and associated roles and assimilating role theory (as well as reference group theory) to symbolic interactionism, he emphasizes role-taking and the self as mediating the relation between social structure and behavior. He accepts an indeterminancy in the relation of role expectations to behavior but tends to see determinancy in the relation of self to behavior.

Observing that for Mead objects are plans of action, or "attitudes," Kuhn conceptualizes the self in these terms. Knowing persons' subjective definitions of their own identity enables prediction of how they organize their behavior. Attitudes toward self are the best indicators of plans of action; consequently, the most significant object to be defined in any situation is the self. Stable sets of meaning attached to the self—the core self, in Kuhn's terms—are central to this theorizing for these give stability to personality and continuity and predictability to behavior. The core self constrains behavior: Stability of self results in stability in interaction. However, stability is relative. Kuhn sees creativity and novelty occurring through the self-control made possible by role taking. In addition, the self will have some volatility as a result of slippage between social structure and self-definitions.

Stability of self makes reliable measurement possible; Kuhn and his students developed the Twenty Statements Test (Kuhn and McPartland, 1954; Spitzer, Couch and Stratton, n.d.) in their attempt to be precise in formulating and testing theory. Kuhn sees no contradiction between exploring concepts referring to meanings, symbolic processes, and the internal and subjective aspects and meeting the requirements for precise concepts and sound measurement.

Blumer and Kuhn do not alone link Mead, Cooley, and Thomas to the present-day symbolic interactionist theorists and researchers. Many others applied a symbolic interactionist framework to particular forms or loci of interaction. Burgess (1926), Waller (1938), Cottrell

(1948), Hill (Waller and Hill, 1951), Cavan (1953), Kirkpatrick (1955), Stryker (1956; 1964), and Turner (1970) applied and extended this framework in analyses of husband-wife and parent-child relationships, stressing the dynamics of role relationships, the import of communicative and symbolic processes, and the significance of role-taking. Sutherland (1939) developed the implications of the framework in his differential association theory of criminality, as did Lindesmith (1947) in his theory of opiate addiction. Lemert (1951), Becker (1963), Goffman (1963b), and Scheff (1966), among others, applied the ideas more generally to deviance, viewing the shaping of self-concepts through society's application of stigmatizing labels as key to the production of deviants and deviance. Turner and Killian (1957) and Shibutani (1966) pursued another line of application, collective behavior, basing their treatments in part on earlier work by Blumer (1951).

Conceptual and theoretical issues were treated by various writers whose efforts have been assimilated into contemporary symbolic interactionism and that are discussed later in this chapter. Among those worthy of mention include Mills's (1940) classic statement on motivation from the perspective of symbolic interactionism that develops the concept of a vocabulary of motives, Foote's (1951) conceptualization of motivation in terms of identification and identity processes, Becker's (1960) use of the concept of commitment in analyses of the same issue, Coutu's (1951) clarification of the related concepts of role-taking and role-playing, Shibutani's (1955) interpretation of reference group concepts from the standpoint of symbolic interactionism, Becker and Strauss's (1956) use of the concept of career to analyze the time dimension incorporated into symbolic interactionism's view of social process, Goffman's (1961b) discussion of role distance and role embracement as means for understanding the consequences on behavior of variable commitment to identities, Stone's (1962) influential development of the concept of situated identity, Turner's (1962) introduction of the concept of role making in his effort to reinvigorate the sense of interaction as emergent and constructed, Weinstein and Deutschberger's (1963) attempt to specify self-presentational processes through the concept of altercasting, Glaser and Strauss's (1964) statement on awareness contexts, and Kinch's (1963) formalization of a theory of self-concept formation and behavioral impact.

Although varying significantly in rigor and systematic character, research on symbolic interactionist issues

has been considerable since the 1950s. The brief review that follows illustrates a concern with examining empirically fundamental premises of the perspective that has dominated the attention of symbolic interactionist researchers up to the present and illustrates the issues and varying research styles that have characterized this work. It limits itself by imposing an admittedly arbitrary quality standard.

A basic premise of Mead's thought is that the responses of others shape the self. The literature that verifies, sometimes conditions, and occasionally denies this premise utilizes both experimental and survey procedures; it includes studies by Miyamoto and Dornbusch (1956); Couch (1958); Reeder, Donahue, and Biblarz (1960); Videbeck (1960); Quarantelli and Cooper (1966); Sherwood (1965); Felson, (1981); Stager *et al.* (1983); Gecas and Schwalbe (1983). In this literature, the question of whether self-concepts affect behavior, the complementary premise on which symbolic interactionists' theorizing develops, is asked and answered, in general affirmatively, in various settings by using various research procedures. Lindesmith (1947) uses informal interviewing to develop, and an analytic induction procedure to refine, a theory of opiate addiction in which the self-concept of addicts is crucial. Cressey (1953), using essentially similar ideas and methods, portrays the process by which persons become embezzlers; and Becker (1953), again using these ideas and methods, traces the impact of self-definitions on marihuana use. Reckless, Dinitz, and Murray (1958) generate data through classroom questionnaires that focus on the ways self-concepts contribute to the making of delinquents, as do Schwartz and Stryker (1971). Stryker and Serpe (1982) use survey procedures and structural equation modeling to examine the link between role-linked self-concepts and role behavior, and Reitzes (1980), Burke and Reitzes (1981) and Mutran and Reitzes (1984) examine the same issue through the responses of university students and the elderly to questionnaires.

According to Mead, social interaction is made possible by taking the role of the other, a process by which one puts himself or herself in the place of the other and responds as that other does. O'Toole and Dubin (1968) provide behavioral demonstrations of this phenomenon through a systematic observational study of the physical movements of mothers while feeding their infant children and through an experimental study of body sway, and Cottrell (1971) finds evidence of role-taking in an experimental study of muscular tension in persons who observe the muscular tension of others. There has been some work showing consequences of variations in role-taking. Stryker (1956; 1957) examines both sources of and consequences of accuracy in role-taking in families, using structured interviews; Thomas, Franks, and Calconico (1972) investigate the relation between role-taking and power, again in families; Weinstein *et al.* (1972) inquire into the relation between empathy and communication efficiency, as do Goodman and Ofshe (1968).

From the standpoint of symbolic interactionism, socialization is largely a matter of shaping self-concepts. Thus, much of the research already cited on self as well as on role-taking is germaine to this topic. Studies treating socialization directly include those of Becker *et al.* (1961) on medical students and Olesen and Whitaker (1968) on nurses, both based on informal interviewing and direct observation, Denzin's (1972; 1975) observational studies of the emergence of self in early childhood, Thomas and Weigert's (1971) cross-national analysis of the conformity of adolescents to significant others' expectations, using data obtained through questionnaires administered in classrooms, and Brim's (1958) statistical analysis of sex-role learning by children in families with varying composition.

Qualitative analyses of interaction in diverse social settings have been taken by some to be *the* research style of symbolic interactionism (Lofland, 1970). Representative of the genre are Glaser and Strauss's (1964; 1968; 1971) studies of the interactions of hospital personnel, family members, and dying patients in hospital settings; Roth's (1963) study of the passage of patients through hospitals; Bittner's (1967) analysis of police dealings with the mentally ill; Goffman's (1963a; 1967; 1971) reports on strategies of interaction in diverse settings; and Lofland's (1973) study of the interaction of strangers.

Throughout this review of early symbolic interactionism and the work that followed initial formulations, there are occasional explicit references to, and frequently implicit use of, the basic conceptual apparatus of symbolic interactionism. We move now to a more systematic presentation of the more important concepts that make up the framework.

BASIC CONCEPTS

A set of concepts does not constitute a theory, and one is likely to weary quickly when faced with a procession of definitions and attempts to draw boundaries between and among aspects of social life that may be experientially confounded. Yet, such efforts are necessary to the construction of theory and so must be at least tolerated. The priorities and the limits of any theory are set by the concepts built into it, and no theory can incorporate phenomena it has not conceptualized as part of its domain. The concepts reviewed in this section, with exceptions to be noted, make up the framework common to symbolic interactionists. There are nuances that differentiate users of the framework; we pay little attention to these. There are also concepts, developed relatively recently, essential to current symbolic interactionist theorizing; these are introduced in a later discussion.

Meanings

The underlying premise of symbolic interactionism is that the subjective aspects of experience must be examined because the meanings people assign to things ultimately organize their behavior. Therefore, symbolic interactionists must examine both the emergence of meaning and the way meaning functions in the context of social interaction (Stryker and Gottlieb, 1981). The meaning of "meaning" is a question of critical importance in the framework.

The starting point in answering this question is with the *act,* behavior by an organism stemming from an impulse and requiring for its completion some adjustment to appropriate objects in the external world. Two implications of this definition are noteworthy: Acts occur over time and have a history; and acts are functional in that they occur to "satisfy" some impulse of the organism. Many acts are social: the appropriate objects—the objects to which adaptation or adjustment is necessary if the initiating impulse is to be satisfied—are other individuals (Stryker, 1964). The other individuals implicated in a social act are also actors; they do not "stand still" in the course of the social act. Rather, they also act with reference to the initial actor(s). Thus, by definition, every social act involves at least two individuals, each taking the other into account in the process of satisfying impulses. The meanings that enter experience as objects are necessarily social; they are anchored in and emergent from social interaction.

Since social acts occur over time, it becomes possible for *gestures* to appear. A gesture is any part of an act that comes to be an indication of parts of the act yet to occur. Persons responding to one another in the course of a social act may be involved in what Mead calls a "conversation of gestures"; they may come to use early stages of one anothers' acts as indicators of later stages. Vocal sounds, other physical movements, bodily expressions, and clothing may all serve as gestures. When they do, they have *meaning*: The meaning of a gesture (an early stage of an act) is the behavior that follows it (the later stages of an act). By definition, meaning is behavior rather than purely ideational, inherent in some thing, or residing in the sound, movement, or attire that may refer to that thing. And, almost by definition, meaning and social interaction are interdependent; meaning is shaped in and by interaction, and meaning shapes the course of interaction.

Significant Symbols

For symbolic interactionism, the core problem of social psychology is the analysis of interaction; concern with meaning derives from that core problem. Interaction proceeds on the basis of shared systems of meaning; thus, the achievement of a sufficient consensus with respect to things implicated in social acts is a necessary condition of interaction. The critical problem of the actor engaging in interaction occurs not in the observation of an event or thing nor in its representation per se, but when it becomes apparent that the meaning of relevant events or things is not shared, the solution to the problem lies in constructing and communicating meanings. Its solution lies, in brief, in the emergence of *significant symbols.*

For an individual actor an early stage of an act can come to represent a later stage of the act. Some gestures develop an additional and important property, that is, they come to mean the same thing (imply the same future behaviors) to both the individuals who produce and the individuals who perceive them. When this occurs, the gestures have become significant symbols.

Significant symbols emerge in social acts. They function by permitting these acts to move towards completion. Thus, symbols reflect the interests—the impulses whose satisfaction completes the act—from which acts stem. Persons respond to symbols in terms of the meaning they carry as predictors of their own and others' later behavior. Since significant symbols anticipate further behavior, they provide a basis for adjusting activity before that behavior has occurred. Significant symbols function in the context of social acts in the place of that which they represent, and they serve to organize behavior with reference to that which is symbolized. Rose (1962) refers to a significant symbol as an incipient or telescoped social act. An alternative phrasing is to say that a significant symbol entails a plan of action.

Social Interaction

The argument that the human is differentiated most importantly from other animals by its capacity for complex language is too well known to require either rehearsal or defense here. There is no need to argue this differentiation in absolute terms, and the absolute contention is likely invalid. The importance of language for social interaction is indicated by the fact that for many communication and social interaction are virtually synonymous terms and by the fact that language is typically seen as the primary vehicle for human communication. Language, to the degree that it is social, is a system of significant symbols. Given the preceding discussion, this statement asserts that language is a system of shared meaning and implies that language is a system of shared behavior. Not all words carry precisely the same meaning in a behavioral sense, and not all parties to a "conversation" understand words in precisely the same way. Yet meaning must be sufficiently shared for communication to take place; again, social interaction presupposes that linguistic as well as other symbols have this characteristic.

Since there is nothing in that which is symbolized or in the literal symbol itself that requires the attachment of the two, symbols are arbitrary representations. That they emerge in interaction implies that they potentially can take on any form or content. Nor are there limits on what can be symbolized: Things, ideas, relationships between and among things and ideas can all be symbolized and enter the experience of human actors as objects. Whatever their ontological status in the "natural" world, such objects constitute social reality.

From the standpoint of symbolic interactionism, social reality is a reality negotiated in the course of social interaction. Things take on meaning through a process initiated when a person is ready to act with reference to those things; this readiness requires that they be symbolized. When others are implicated, the symbols that convert things to objects are anchored in and emergent from social interaction. That meaning is derived from an interpersonal process implies that reality is defined through that process rather than independently of it. This social definition of reality implies that reality is negotiable. An important additional implication is that a totally determinant explanatory model of social interaction is not possible. A final implication is that neither interaction nor meaning can be taken as unilateral cause and effect. Since meaning both derives from social interaction and affects its future course, reciprocal rather than unidirectional causal models are essential (Stryker and Gottlieb, 1981).

Significant symbols emerge in the course of interaction. Meaning is neither inferred directly from things nor externally predetermined but is negotiated. If, in every interaction context, every aspect of social reality is assumed to be both negotiable and negotiated, the consequence is a completely indeterministic theoretical system. Some symbolic interactionists favor this extreme position. Most, however, take a more moderate stance, assuming that what may be open to negotiations varies as a function of specific contexts of interaction and that there are social structural constraints governing what can be negotiated and how negotiations proceed.

Definition of the Situation

What meanings evolve through interaction cannot be totally determined *a priori;* that meanings must emerge if interaction is not to break down is an assumption of symbolic interactionism. Meanings must be assigned to features of interactive situations in which people find themselves; if meanings organize behavior, it follows that without the assignment of meanings behavior will be disorganized and more or less random. When persons enter an interactive situation in which behavior is in any way problematic—when, in brief, pure habit will not suffice to order actions—meanings must be at least tentatively assigned. The situation must be symbolized, as must its constituent parts; the products of this symbolization process are termed *definitions of the situation.*

Symbolic interactionism assumes that persons symbolize things in order to simplify and to make manageable their complex worlds. The worlds in which people live are too complex and multifaceted to be conceptualized in detail. While some symbols represent relatively discrete phenomena, others represent generalizations of behavior toward objects; these latter are class terms, or categories. When one categorizes an object, one places it in a set of objects and signifies that it is to be responded to in the same way as other members of the set. Categories, or class terms, are symbols and so share the characteristics of symbols: They have meaning; they serve as cues to behavior; and they organize behavior.

Humans live in physical, biological and social worlds; and the characteristics of these worlds are relevant to them in a variety of ways. These worlds contain the ends of social actions and the means by which those ends are achieved. They represent conditions that actors must take into account in action, conditions that can impede or enhance, guarantee or deny the fruits of that action. Language as a symbolic system incorporates class terms referring to parts of these worlds, doing so by representing their meaning for human action.

Humans thus live in symbolic environments, environments whose features are named and placed in categories indicating their generalized meanings for behavior. When persons enter a situation in which behavior is problematic, in the sense that habit is insufficient to guide behavior, that situation must be represented in symbolic terms if behavior from the full repertoire of possible actions is not to be selected arbitrarily or randomly. In brief, the situation must be defined and the resultant definition of the situation serves to orient and to organize behavior.

A definition of the situation focuses attention on what is salient about an interactive setting and permits a preliminary organization of actions appropriate to that setting. From this perspective, culture specifies what is relevant to goal-oriented behavior and so significant for interaction, framing its specification in terms of language symbols. Implied is the fact that there sometimes exist culturally provided definitions to be applied when appropriate cues are perceived. To the degree that situations are novel, because not having been experienced by previous generations, so no cultural definitions are available, or because the actor has not yet experienced the situations or is not familiar with culturally provided definitions, definitions do not exist in fully articulated form. Then, persons sometimes self-consciously prepare to meet situations by constructing more or less elaborate definitions.

Regardless of whether a person constructs a definition before entering a situation, using whatever information or cues may be available as a basis for the construction and regardless of whether ready-made cultural definitions are available, the person typically revises or reconstructs definitions in the course of interaction with others. Tentatively held definitions are repeatedly tested and reformulated on the basis of this experience. A dialectic occurs in which putative definitions permit interaction to begin; reactions from others to the definitions implicit in one's actions serve to validate or invalidate these definitions wholly or in part, and revised definitions become the basis for additional interaction.

When a situation is defined, aspects of the nonhuman environment are named. However, since symbolic interactionism is concerned primarily with interaction and thus with the derivation of meaning in an interpersonal context, its emphasis is on the meaning of the persons who are involved. From the point of view of a given actor, the most important aspects of a situation to be resolved in the sense of discovering an appropriate definition is who (or what) the others are with whom one interacts in the situation and who (or what) one is in the situation. The first of these leads directly to the concept of role, the second to the concept of self.

Role

There are symbolic interactionists who do not use the concept of *role,* on the grounds that it denies that norms and behavior patterns are emergents from the course of interaction itself because it implies a fixed pattern of behavior or normative expectations for behavior existing before interaction in terms of which interaction is carried out. Clearly, those taking an extreme nondeterministic view of human behavior will find the concept of role unreasonable. Yet, the assumption on which this chapter is written is that the concept of role is essential if symbolic interactionism is to become a viable social psychological theory.

Most symbolic interactionists do use the concept of role. Some argue that there is no inconsistency among the ideas that persons enter interaction with existing conceptions about what other persons categorized in particular ways will be like and will do, that these existing conceptions will structure behavior at least in part, and that previous conceptions and behavior will likely be modified or even greatly changed in the course of interaction itself. Some do so by suggesting that for interaction to take place at all, the worlds of persons must be represented symbolically in parsimonious form, and that locating oneself and others in roles (whatever the "reality" of those roles) is the way people achieve the necessary parsimonious representations (Turner, n.d.a; n.d.b). Some do so avoiding the concept per se but nevertheless implicitly assume that what it refers to enters into social behavior (Strauss, 1978).

The symbolic interactionists' conception of role is somewhat different from that of role theorists. For the analyst of interaction, a particularly important kind of language category is *position.* For the role theorist, that term designates parts of organized groups. The symbolic interactionist uses the term more broadly to apply it to any social recognized category of actors. Thus, the symbolic interactionist usage will include "teacher," "daughter," and "sergeant," as well as "rebel," "divorcee," "intellectual," and "fat man." Positions refer to the kinds of people it is possible to be in a given society.

Like any category, a positional term can serve as a cue to or predictor of the behavior of persons to whom the term is attached. Doing so, the term organizes behavior with reference to these persons. When a positional label is attached to an actor, we expect behaviors from the actor, and we behave toward that actor on the premise of these expectations. It is these expectations that the term *role* designates.

This usage contains a number of implications. Roles are social in the same way any other significant symbol is social: The meaning of the positions to which expectations attach is shared behavior. Moreover, roles are social in the specific sense that it is not possible to talk sensibly about a position without at least implicit reference to other positions. To use the term role is necessarily to refer to interaction: There can be no "teacher" without "pupils," no "rebel" without "an establishment." Any position assumes a counterposition; any role assumes a counterrole.

Roles can vary on a number of dimensions potentially important to the analysis of interaction processes (Sarbin and Allen, 1968). Expectations can be general or specific in the behavior to which they refer; they can demand precise performances of particular actions, or they can simply suggest a script within which considerable ad-libbing is both possible and expected; they can refer to a minimal segment of one's range of interaction or cover a large part of that range; some are clear, while others are vague and uncertain; some may contain internal contradictions; some attach to positions in formally organized social structures and others relate to informal social relationships; some may be essentially statistical in nature, carrying no real normative freight, while others may be normatively laden; and some may carry heavy sanctions, others none. Such variations, and certainly others not mentioned, will almost certainly affect both social interaction and the person in ways that can be illustrated through anecdotes but have yet to be researched systematically.

Persons are, of course, typically categorized not in terms of a single position but rather in terms of multiple positions, including some sets that provide no clear means of organizing responses because they contain contradictory expectations. Some consequences of this state of affairs, a frequent possibility in a complex society, are discussed in a later section.

Self

Actors who enter or find themselves in situations deal with their interactional problems in part by defining the situation, which includes categorizing others in ways relevant to the interaction. So, too, towards the same end the actor will typically, although not necessarily, categorize himself or herself. People can respond to themselves by classifying, naming, and defining who and what they are. To engage in this reflexive behavior is to have a *self*.

The cautionary note in the preceding paragraph is not conventionally recognized in symbolic interactionists' treatment of self. That actors are not necessarily self-reflective implies that the self is variable in its occurrence in interaction. From the philosophic point of view from which symbolic interactionism derives, mental activity, that is, thinking, is a response to a problematic situation. The reflexive activity that defines the self is a form of thinking. The implication is straightforward: When situations are totally unproblematic—perhaps a very rare event in modern society—there may be no self. The point can also be stated in terms of degree.

The reality of the self is phenomenological; it has no physical or biological location. Mead's definition of self as that which is an object to itself is an elliptical assertion that humans can and sometimes do view themselves as objects in the same manner they view any other object. Given the way objects are created, this suggests that to have a self is to view oneself from the standpoint of others with whom one interacts. A root assumption of symbolic interactionism is that the reflexive activity which is the self is important in the process by which social interaction is produced.

Self-definitional activities proceed largely, although not exclusively, through socially recognized categories (again, the kinds of persons it is possible to be in a society) and their corresponding roles. Since roles imply relationships to others, so does the self: One's self is the way in which one describes to oneself relationships to others (Stryker, 1964).

Mead recognizes, with James, that the person has many selves, limited only by the number of different others (or categories of others) who respond to the person, thus implying that to speak of a unitary self is misleading. Apart from differentiating between the ''I'' and the "me" as phases of self, however, he goes no further with this implication. Traditional symbolic interactionism favored a conception of self as an undifferentiated unity.

Role-Taking

Expectations of others define roles and enter the structure of the self. Social interaction requires that situations be defined, and to do so entails recognizing physical and behavioral cues and locating self and others in situational settings. How do we learn, even very provisionally, what others' expectations are? How do we learn the meanings of environmental features? How do we learn the range of permissible variation built into roles?

The concept of *role-taking,* defined as the process of anticipating the responses of others with whom one is implicated in social interaction, is invoked in symbolic interactionism's answer to such questions. So defined, role-taking is conceptually distinct from concepts like empathy and sympathy in which some element of ''feeling with'' is typically incorporated. One takes the role of others by using language to put oneself in the place of others and to see the world as they do. Using previous experience, familiarity with comparable others, and symbolic cues available in the situation, one formulates a definition of others' attitudes that is then validated or reshaped in ongoing interaction. Actors take roles in order to anticipate the consequences of their own and others' projected patterns of action, and they take roles to monitor the results of actual patterns of action. They sustain, modify or redirect their own behavior, using the product of their role-taking.

Thus role-taking plays an important part in what Turner (1962) calls *role-making.* In his words (pp. 22–23):

> Roles 'exist' in varying degrees of concreteness and consistency, while the individual frames his behavior as if they had unequivocal existence and clarity. The result is that in attempting from time to time to make aspects of the role explicit he is creating and modifying roles as well as merely bringing them to light; the process is not only role-taking but *role-making.... The idea of role-making shifts emphasis from the simple process of enacting a prescribed role to devising a performance on the basis of an imputed other role.*

Role-taking may involve anticipating the responses of a particular other person. Mead uses the term *generalized other* to suggest that many social acts take place in the context of organized systems of action; therefore one is often put in the position of anticipating the responses of a differentiated yet interrelated set of others. (Mead's example invokes the image of a member of a baseball team anticipating the responses of other members of the team and of opponents in making a play.) To take the role of the generalized other is to see one's behavior as taking place in the context of a defined system of related roles. The concept of *significant other* implies that others' perspectives are differentially relevant to the actor, that some are to be given greater or lesser weight or priority when these perspectives differ or are incompatible.

The fact that organized social life exists is presumptive evidence that meanings are shared; no assumption is made, however, that meaning is universally or completely shared. Accuracy in role-taking is based at least in part on the common symbols that common experience creates. However, if meanings are not universally or completely shared, then the accuracy of role-taking will also vary. In addition, accuracy of role-taking is not necessarily followed by smooth and cooperative interpersonal relations (Stryker, 1957); conflict may sharpen the accuracy of interpersonal perceptions as well as result from such accuracy.

Socialization

Although role-taking is one way persons learn others' expectations, there is a larger process through which such learning takes place: *socialization.* Not peculiar to symbolic interactionism, this concept is nevertheless central to the framework. Socialization is the generic term used to refer to the processes by which the newcomer—the infant, rookie, and trainee, for example—becomes incorporated into organized patterns of interaction (Clausen, 1968; Goodman, forthcoming).

One is socialized in part by responding to others' expectations; since all interaction involves such responses, every interaction is a socializing experience. Many roles are learned through role play, often but not always before occupancy of a position to which a role attaches. Other roles are learned through *altercasting* (Weinstein and Deutschberger, 1963) by which others, deliberately or not, cast the person into a role and provide the symbolic cues that elicit appropriate behavior. Given the human's capacity for symbolic behavior, it is possible to learn vicariously how to behave in various situations, to imagine being another, and to try out roles. These and related processes have been labeled *anticipatory socialization;* clearly much education takes this form.

Whatever the mechanisms emphasized, symbolic interactionists are likely to conceptualize the key to socialization as the shaping of self images (Stryker and Serpe, 1983). From this perspective socialization is a continuous, life-long process (implied in the observation that every interaction is a socializing experience). However, early socialization takes on particular significance in these terms: Once a self is formed through the interaction process, it will modify subsequent experience.

ILLUSTRATIVE USES OF THE FRAMEWORK

Since all of the uses to which the symbolic interactionist framework has been put cannot be treated, this section is necessarily selective and illustrative. It is also generalized and does not rely on the specifics of particular analyses.

Symbolic interactionism is oriented to the abstract problem of the relationships among society, the person, and interaction. Its most general theoretical, explanatory proposition in elucidating this abstract problem is that society structures the self, and the self structures interaction. Thus, the major theoretical claim is that the self mediates the relationship between society and at least some important classes of social behavior.

Within this abstract problem, symbolic interactionists have concentrated on the more specific middle-range problems of personal organization, personal disorganization, early and adult socialization, social control, and personal control. In pursuing these middle-range problems, they ask: How does personal consistency and organization come about, and how are these maintained? How does personal disorganization arise? How are selves formed and changed? When will behavior comply with role expectations, when not? How can persons exercise choice in their own actions and interactions?

Analysis of personal organization begins with the observation that persons ordinarily interact in various social relationships, both at the same time and over time, and thus they are likely to be faced with a variety of role expectations. If persons responded in terms of role expectations unique to each relationship, their behavior would likely be discontinuous and disorganized. As a matter of empirical observation, there is considerable continuity and organization in the behavior of persons over both situations and time. However and equally as a matter of empirical observation, there is also discontinuity and disorganization in persons' behavior over situations and time. The theoretical challenge is to account for both continuity and discontinuity, organization and disorganization, through a common set of explanatory principles.

The concepts of self, role, and definition of the situation enter the basic account of personal organization. Characteristically, the initial analysis focuses on social organization; then, in keeping with the argument that individual processes mirror social processes, that analysis is transferred to the individual.

The person, entering an ongoing social situation, responds to that situation by defining it. This definition incorporates a number of social objects in some meaningful, that is, symbolized, pattern (McHugh, 1968; Hewitt, 1979). Among the social objects incorporated into the definition will be the others with whom one interacts in the situation and oneself. That is, the definition will include the assignment of positional designations to others in the situation and thus the setting up of a range of role expectations with respect to their behavior. The definition will also include an assignment of a positional designation and therefore a role to oneself. At the same time, others involved also define the situation. The interplay of behaviors that ensues is, critically, a function of this complex of defining activities. The important question with respect to the ordering of this interplay is consequently the congruence of definitions—of self, role, other social objects, and the situation itself—of the interacting persons. Congruence makes possible organized interpersonal behavior.

Intrapersonal processes echo interpersonal processes. The congruence of the definitions assigned to self and to others and thus the congruence of behavior expectations is fundamental to the continuity and the organization of that individual's behavior as he or she moves through a variety of interpersonal situations. Thus, personal organization cannot be considered a matter of what persons carry with them as they move from situation to situation, whether these are conceptualized as persistent behavioral traits or as self-concepts. Nor can personal organization be regarded simply a matter of the constancy of situational demands. Rather, it is a matter of what persons carry with them in the form of selves and the situations in which they interact as these are mediated symbolically.

If one pushes the question further by asking what are the social conditions that permit and even foster congruence of definitions, the generalized answer is those conditions under which meanings are widely shared within a society or within the segment of society represented by the persons with whom one actually interacts. And if one asks when is it likely that meanings are widely shared, the answers lead to the heart of social structure: when,

for example, the pace of social change is slow, when environments and experiences are widely shared, when communication flows are unimpeded by various kinds of social boundaries, and when interests are general.

The discussion has proceeded as though initial definitions produced upon entering situations held through the interaction in a situation. This is possible, at least for all practical purposes, and is the essence of habitual or routine interactions. It is also possible for definitions to change considerably in the process of interaction itself, as the concept of role-making asserts and as symbolic interactionism's view of the constructed nature of social reality (Berger and Luckmann, 1966) emphasizes. In Cohen's (1965, p. 6) words: "Human action . . . is something that develops in a tentative, groping, advancing, backtracking, sounding out process. People taste and feel their way along. They begin an act and do not complete it. They extricate themselves from progressive involvement or become further involved to the point of commitment." Inherent in this vision of the nature of human interaction is the idea that the definitions underlying social order are negotiated, albeit in varying degree and with varying constraints, in the course of social interaction itself (Strauss *et al.,* 1963; Lofland, 1969; Strauss, 1978; Stryker, 1972).

Regardless of whether definitions are stable or change through the course of interaction, the relevance of the congruence of meanings within and among definitions for continuity and organization in individuals' behavior remains the same. The same explanatory principle holds for personal disorganization. Reversing the process already discussed, symbolic interaction theory suggests that incongruities in definitions result in incongruities in role expectations and that personal disorganization is the likely outcome. There are many possible types of incongruity (Stryker and Macke, 1978): conflicts or lack of coordination between self-concepts and expectations of others, conflicts among self-concepts entering the same situations, conflicts in expectations deriving from significant others in the same set of social relationships, and conflicts in expectations deriving from significant others who do not themselves relate. Conflicts in expectations that do not touch, or that touch the self only minimally, should not be disorganizing; conversely, conflicting expectations heavily implicating the self should be maximally disorganizing unless resolved.

Since self-concepts are the products of relationships to others and since they require for their validation responses from others, symbolic interaction theory offers an explanation for changes in self-concepts and in the form personal organization takes. The behavior of others provides cues on the basis of which one builds and maintains a self; the behavior of others makes possible continued performance reflecting role expectations and the self that incorporates these expectations. Should cues from others become unavailable, the person in the short run can continue to play out a role. Over the longer run, however, the probability of continuing the performance drops considerably. Two mechanisms are involved; namely, (1) the failure to receive role-validating responses from others makes it difficult for the person to maintain a sense of self that depends on that role, and (2) the absence of appropriate counterrole responses from others makes the performance of a role difficult if not impossible and again jeopardizes a self that incorporates the role.

This point can be made in positive terms; doing so provides an analysis of how the self changes beyond the destruction of an extant self. A self is built through the responses of others. If others altercast (Weinstein and Deutschberger, 1963), if they impute a role to another and act on the basis of that imputation, they will cue responses in keeping with that role, whether or not the person's self at that moment reflects the role. If the person behaves in ways anticipated by the imputed role, the person is likely to adopt a self incorporating the role (Bem, 1972; Goffman, 1961a; Ball, 1967; Garfinkel, 1956).

Symbolic interactionism's analyses of socialization proceed similarly. An active, unorganized infant is born into ongoing relationships premised on shared meanings. Adults respond selectively to the infant's incipient gestures by supplying completions to acts (e.g., feeding the infant in response to his or her crying) and therefore the meaning of acts. The completions, or meanings, available to the adult are those in the repertoire of the society of which he or she is a part. Moreover, the adult will supply a definition of the situation that includes the positional relationship of adult and child and thus narrows the possibilities in the adult's response to the child. Whatever the precise completions selected, the adult as an already socialized participant in an ongoing society links the infant to the society by providing the social meanings of the child's gestures.

Among the incipient gestures of the child are random and imitated vocalizations. The noted process occurs; these vocalizations are responded to selectively by adults in ways reflecting the adult meanings of the sounds. Over time, a sound at first meaningless to the child comes to mean for the child what it means to adults and to the society of which they are a part.

The same is true for the self. Others name the infant and provide meaning to the name. The infant is categorized and expected to behave in ways anticipated by the categories. Others behave toward the infant on the basis of these expectations, and this behavior serves ultimately to produce a self. The child comes to categorize himself or herself as others categorize him or her and to act in ways implied by these categories that are thus appropriate to the expectations of others.

Adult socialization operates in similar fashion, except that it reflects prior selves developed through infancy, childhood, adolescence and other adult experiences. Thus, adult socialization may require resocialization in the form of altering existing self-concepts. The earlier discussion of personal organization and disorganization implies an important mechanism here: Changing self-concepts occurs through isolating persons from social relationships that validate and provide opportunities to cue behavior reflecting an "old" self in some manner incompatible with a different self (Dornbusch, 1955). Conversely, reinforcing that "old" self or structuring a new one compatible with the old is accomplished by integrating the person into relationships that validate and cue behavior reflecting them.

The way in which others' expectations give content to the self and through that process organize persons' behavior constitutes a theory of social control. However, persons are not simply controlled by others' definitions and expectations. The evolution of the self is, of course, gradual. At any time beyond the earliest infant stage, however, the person has a conception of self derived from past experience that interacts with present expectations in the production of behavior. Moreover, the self becomes increasingly complex as the person comes into contact with many others in a variety of self-relevant situations. The person is likely to come into contact with differing expectations and differing identifications on which these expectations are based. True for differing roles, this is likely in a complex society to be true for a single role as well. Given the possibility of role-taking, persons have available a variety of perspectives (Warshay, 1962) from which to view and evaluate their behavior, and they can act with reference to self as well as with reference to others. Socialization thus makes possible objectivity in the behavior of the individual. Since these processes can be internalized through symbolization and alternative courses of action can be projected symbolically and evaluated with respect to consequences for self and for interaction, there exists as well the possibility of choice and of self-control.

CRITICAL APPRAISALS OF SYMBOLIC INTERACTIONISM

The symbolic interactionism described has generated critical responses (Meltzer *et al.*, 1975; Stryker, 1980), that serve to motivate many of the more recent efforts to modify the framework.

Mead (1930) early commented critically on the solipsism inherent in Cooley's identification of society with the imaginations of individual actors and on the utopian elements in Cooley's thought. Mead's own ideas have been appraised negatively as well as positively, the negative evaluations focusing on the ambiguity of central ideas (Meltzer, 1959; Kuhn, 1964) or on the indeterminacy introduced into his theorizing through the concept of the ''I'' (Kolb, 1944; Lewis, 1979). The argument through the years between persons with visions of symbolic interactionism shaped by Blumer or by Kuhn represents the critique of one version of the framework by adherents of the other.

Summaries of more recent critical appraisals as well as pertinent citations are available in Meltzer *et al.* (1975) and Stryker (1980). These reduce to five fundamental criticisms of symbolic interactionism:

1. Key concepts are confused and imprecise and thus cannot provide the basis for sound theory development.

2. Concepts are difficult if not impossible to operationalize; the position generates few testable propositions and rejects scientific explanation in favor of intuitive understanding.

3. The pervasive importance of the emotions and of the unconscious in human behavior is overlooked.

4. The methodological demand that the point of view of the actor be incorporated into accounts of behavior and the focus on the immediate situation of interaction, on the definitional processes that organize ongoing interaction, and on the emergent character of that organization minimize the import of social structure and macro-organizational features of soci-

ety for behavior. Given this methodological demand and the consequent foci of attention, the perspective cannot deal adequately with large-scale social organizational features of societies or the relations among societies.

5. The neglect of social structure, hence of the facts of class and power inherent in that structure, constitute an ideological bias favoring liberal democracy and therefore the status quo in contemporary American society.

Given the internal variability of symbolic interactionism, whether these criticisms are telling or even appropriate depends on what version they are addressed to. The claims that key concepts are imprecise, difficult to operationalize, and do not lead to testable propositions and scientific explanations may be damning or regarded as irrelevant if it is Blumer's vision of the framework that is at issue. If one accepts Blumer's vision, one must conclude that the imprecision of concepts is advantageous, operationalization is a false procedure, and testable propositions and scientific explanations are not in accord with the empirical nature of human behavior. If one takes Blumer's vision as representing symbolic interactionism but opts for a conventional view of what science is about, the criticisms are damning. If, however, one takes our view of symbolic interactionism, the imprecision and operational difficulties that may characterize the position are not inherent in it and are likely to be progressively removed through the ''normal'' processes by which social science theories are devised, examined, and reformulated.

The framework's imputed failure to deal adequately with emotions and the unconscious is a well-taken criticism, relating closely to another that can be made: Symbolic interactionism neglects the socially routine and repetitive aspects of life. That it does so is interesting, since its intellectual sources from the Scottish Moral Philosophers through Dewey and Thomas placed considerable weight on habit and custom. That it does so is also understandable, given Mead's pre-eminence in influencing the framework. Mead modeled all life on the scientific method; problem-solving behavior was his paradigm for social interaction, and his evolutionary assumptions led him to see self-consciousness, reflexivity, and choice as the essence of the human condition. Symbolic interactionists, exploiting the pragmatic vein, begin human action in a problem; a problem, by definition, implies the absence of appropriate existing responses and calls into play the thought processes by which an appropriate pattern can be constructed. Thought, reflexivity, the construction of behavior connote—not necessarily—the more rational, deliberative aspects of human behavior, and lead away from the analysis of habit and custom and the use of these latter concepts in further analyses of social behavior.

They also lead the theorist away from emphasizing emotions and the unconscious. Had Cooley been more influential as symbolic interactionism established its intellectual direction, his emphases on sentiment and affect might well have led to greater attention to emotion in social life. It is certainly true that the self of the symbolic interactionist has been conceptualized largely if not exclusively in cognitive terms, and the framework accentuates a cognitive rather than emotive emphasis in its concerns with significant symbols, meanings, role-taking, and communication. Clearly, if the framework is to generate reasonably general social psychological theory, it must incorporate concepts dealing with affect and with habit and custom; whether a concept like the "unconscious" can be adequately incorporated into any social scientific theory without either radical redefinition or without foregoing the criterion that a satisfactory theory be amenable to negation via empirical test remains moot.

The criticisms that symbolic interactionism minimizes or denies the facts of social structure and the import of macro-organizational features of society for human behavior and social interaction and that the framework is ideologically biased are closely related and deserve more extended comment. Although some claim that symbolic interactionists willingly subserve their ideas to political ends (Smith, 1973), the more responsible ideological criticism asserts the social functions or implications of the idea structure of the framework. Insofar as the framework limits the reality studied to the subjective aspects of human experience and to definitions of the situation, it can be argued that the objective realities of stratification, of the differential distribution of wealth, status, and power in society, are neglected and taken as givens. This is the position taken by Gouldner (1970) and Kanter (1972). Huber (1973) also arrives at this conclusion, though her route is different. She argues that symbolic interactionism along with its parent pragmatism has an epistemology making it reflect the biases of the researcher and the persons whose behavior is observed. Pragmatism makes truth conditional on the outcome of

an event, rendering knowledge susceptible to social control, since the future is subject to manipulation by those currently holding power. Symbolic interactionism accords theory no clear place and formal logic an ambiguous status; consequently, theoretical expectations are not explicated. The social givens of researcher and subject serve as an (unidentified) theoretical framework, giving research a bias reflecting the unstated assumptions of the researcher, the climate of opinion in the discipline, and the distribution of power in the interaction setting being researched.

Huber's analysis applies to those versions of symbolic interactionism that eschew theory as a prelude to research. More generally, however, the validity of claims of symbolic interactionism's ideological bias depends on whether or not the framework is capable of dealing with the facts and the significance of social structure, particularly of social class and power. Judgments of capability will depend on answers to two questions. To what extent can social structural concepts be successfully incorporated into symbolic interactionism? To what extent is symbolic interactionism taken as a general framework for the analysis of society?

If one views the framework as limited in scope, the question becomes more complicated. Then, one must ask whether the framework can articulate with another that incorporates the "missing" structural concepts. In anticipation of the argument presented later in the chapter, as well as to restate the chapter's premise, symbolic interactionism can incorporate at least some structural concepts. Although it may be impossible to deal with the relations among broad social strata or nation-states using only the conceptual apparatus of symbolic interactionism augmented by role theory, one can recognize the facts of status, class, and power by conceptualizing these as variables constraining interaction and entering definitions of self and the situation, as resources utilized in interaction, and so on. Symbolic interactionism can incorporate macro-structural variables even if it provides little insight into the relations among such variables. Nothing in the framework necessitates denial of the facts of differentially distributed wealth, status, or power, or the import of such variables.

Implicit in what has just been said, however, is the argument that to be a viable social psychological framework, symbolic interactionism must be able to incorporate social structural variables into its theoretical accounts of the social person and social interaction. Admittedly, it in the past has not done this adequately. Before reviewing and appraising current efforts to accomplish this, we turn to the development of role theory; for, as we have stated, it is through the articulation of symbolic interactionism and role theory that we believe the promise of a sociologically informed social psychology can be met.

ROLE THEORY

There are two role theories: structural and interactional (Heiss, 1981). The former, rooted in classical sociological theory and structural-functionalism, is our concern now; it provides the conceptual and theoretical underpinnings for understanding stability in society and in persons. The latter blends into symbolic interactionism, emphasizing self-processes and interaction in creating and re-creating society and person as well as the constraining impact of social organization on these processes. Whether interactional role theory is seen in terms of modifications introduced into role theory via symbolic interactionism or into symbolic interactionism via role theory is largely arbitrary; as earlier noted, the separation of the two frameworks is a convenient, somewhat forced, didactic strategy. However perceived, interactional role theory represents the conceptual integration to which this chapter seeks to contribute.

Structural role theory is more than of historical interest. Without understanding its imagery, conceptualizations, propositions, and problematics, assertions and emphases in the emergent synthesis of role theory and symbolic interactionism are difficult to comprehend. Moreover, structural role theory is an active, viable sociological framework, dominant through the post-World War II period into the present. Although currently being challenged by Marxian macroperspectives used in analyses of the relationships among nation-states and the political economy of societies or by microsociological perspectives aimed at analyses of miniature interactive systems, it remains the principal framework available for analyses of intrasocietal organizational relationships. If a comprehensive social psychology includes transactions between persons and groups or organizations and the links of these to macroorganizational features of society, a reasonable appreciation of structural role theory is essential.

The overlap of role theory and symbolic interactionism in interactional role theory means that they share some history, concepts, and theoretical ideas. Reviewing them separately requires considerable redundancy or avoids redundancy by risking incomplete treatments. We have taken this risk but have been redundant when avoidance would mislead too much.

THE UNDERLYING IMAGERY

The major metaphor of structural role theory is the theater: Social interaction is visualized as actors playing assigned parts in a script written by a culture shaped in the course of evolutionary adaptation to environmental circumstance. These parts, played as given with minimal ad-libbing, are designed to restore the play to its original pattern should ad-libbing threaten its fundamental structure.

Role theory starts with interaction to be explained in terms of the larger systems into which it fits. The interaction may be of persons, groups, institutions, or total societies; whatever the focus, units are conceived as interdependent and functionally related parts of systems. The analysis of any part proceeds in terms of how it relates to other parts and how these relationships meet the needs of this larger system. Society is composed of institutions that collectively meet its survival needs (Aberle *et al.,* 1950). Thus, economic institutions, government, the family, and religion contribute to the maintenance of society by performing necessary functions: producing and distributing goods, enforcing norms, supplying personnel, and creating a sense of commonality or shared fate. However, just as society is a system with functional substructures, so these substructures have additional functional substructures.

The immediate structural context of most social interaction is the group, a system involving cooperating actors seeking a common goal, with recognized membership in an organized unit and recognized interdependency. These groups are composed of *parts* of persons. The parts are action systems of members, behaviors toward other persons in the group that are oriented by subjective meanings, definitions of the situation, anticipations of how interaction will unfold, evaluations using normative standards as referents, and the cognitive process of choice among means that have varying implications for goals sought by actors. Again, "whole" persons do not enter groups: a classroom consists of the actions of instructor and students vis-a-vis one another *as* instructor and students.

Interactions that repeat and are significant develop expectations with respect to proprieties, norms specifying the proper modes of relationships between and among persons involved in the interactions. Norms applying to a relationship (e.g., husband and wife) in a group need not apply to all relationships (e.g., parent and child) in that group. And norms governing a relationship typically are not the same for all parties to that relationship. The behaviors of interrelated pairs are likely to be reciprocal, mutually reinforcing and mutually satisfying. This image of complementary expected behaviors is partly a product of conceptualizing groups as cooperative, goal-seeking systems and partly a product of the assumption that the subparts of a social system are functional for that social system.

Social structures are thus visualized as differentiated units, with social actors expected to behave in varying, interrelated ways. Consequently, a language referring to these differentiated relationships is necessary. The language adopted by role theory is the familiar language of position and role. Concerned with social structure as it exists and functions, with institutionalized patterns of interaction, and with the consequences of interaction systems for the larger society, structural role theory uses the concept of position for the differentiated parts of organized groups rather than for the kinds of people it is possible to be in a society. Moreover, it roots the concept of role in moral norms whose violations are sanctioned and attaches a fixed or given rather than a negotiated quality to this concept.

Moral norms, originating in culture, are taken to underly roles, the expected patterns of behavior attached to positions. Roles exist before the interaction of particular occupants of positions in organized structures of relationships. They are residues from the experience of past occupants of these positions, molded slowly over time as successive generations adapt to the requirements of their environments. They are, in short, the products of culture.

Implicit in this conceptualization of groups as structures of positions and roles is the fact that usually persons are members of many groups. This means particular groups in society may be linked and that persons linking groups may carry the norms of one to the other in order to minimize conflict among groups. It also means that norms applying in one group to which persons belong may either conflict with or reinforce the norms applying in another.

In summary, role expectations are located in the culture of the larger society within which interaction takes place. Persons, in general, simply act out scripts written by the culture. Role expectations are grounded in societal values that tend to be shared widely throughout a society; they are givens of interaction, institutionalized prior to interaction. Persons learn through socialization, the process through which norms are transmitted, to hold expectations of themselves and others as a consequence of the positions they occupy in organized social structures. These expectations tend to become moral imperatives. If society is working properly, expectations dovetail; since expectations are complementary, conformity to them produces approval from persons in related positions playing related roles.

STRUCTURAL ROLE THEORY AND STRUCTURAL-FUNCTIONAL THEORY

As presented, structural role theory is closely linked to structural functionalism in sociology. The tie is empirical, not logical. Although the emphasis on social units as systems is inherent in any role theory (even then, the system quality of social units can be taken as working hypothesis in need of demonstration rather than as necessarily true), the functionality of parts vis-a-vis the system as a whole and the complementarity of role expectations are not necessary features of a role theoretical perspective.

Role theory developed at a time when much of social science was expressed in structural-functional terms; many influential role theorists (e.g., Davis, 1949; Parsons, 1951) took their metatheoretical cues from that perspective. Structural functionalism perceived society as an extensive blueprint for organization, with each unit of society clearly specified and connected directly or indirectly to all others. Roles located individuals in positions in one or more of these units and provided them with articulated sets of expectations specifying the rights and duties of occupants. The rights adhering to a position were taken to be the obligations adhering to other positions, and vice versa.

Clearly, this perspective is oriented toward order and stability (Dahrendorf, 1959). According to structural functionalism, social systems tend towards equilibrium, integration, and harmony of parts; disharmonies are regarded as temporary aberrations resolved through systematic responses moving the system back toward harmony. Given this image, a role theory with strong structural-functional roots provides accounts for the organization and continuity found in social life, for consensus among participants in that social life, and for the integration of various structural components of society. It should not be surprising then that this theory has been heavily criticized for failing to account for interpersonal and interorganizational conflict, power struggles, and other disharmonies that also are part of social existence. This particular criticism derives from the theory's ties to structural functionalism. Theorists who take conflict and change as normal, rather than aberrational, features of social life have tended to reject role theory because of this linkage.

Conflict and change are surely normal features of social life; so too are harmony and continuity. There are social structures in which persons fill positions carrying commonly understood and shared expectations, for example, families, work groups, and voluntary associations often have this character. Here persons play relatively clear roles that are defined in terms of norms widely shared in a society. We do feel some roles as obligations and as rights. In short, the image evoked by structural role theory as it developed through structural functionalism reasonably reflects aspects of social existence although it does not offer a comprehensive picture.

ROLE THEORY: EARLY DEVELOPMENT

The idea that persons in specific positions are systematically influenced to behave in certain ways by the social structure in which those positions are located is deeply embedded in sociological thought. It is present in the conceptions of exteriority (to individuals) and constraint through which Durkheim (1895) defines a social fact and is central to his classic accounts of anomie (1897) and moral behavior (1912). It is developed in Weber's (1947) treatments of bureaucratic structure, a continuing point of reference for organizational role theory, and in his (1946) use of the concept of calling, or vocation, as the point of articulation between social structure and social person. Weber is an especially significant forerunner of structural role theory; his argument that sociology must grasp the subjective motivation of the actor as part of its explanation of social behaviors has been adopted by role theory and helps to cement the bonding of role theory and symbolic interactionism.

The concept of vocation is also used by Simmel (1950), another of the intellectual resources on which role theory drew. Simmel raises the Hobbesian question of how society is possible and answers it in terms of *a prioris* of the minded association of persons: Society is possible because individuals are partly but not totally "general-

ized." That is, to be part of a group, persons must be both more and less than individual personalities. Persons enter society by exchanging part of their individuality for the generality of the parts to be played in society. Society appears to persons as a set of "vocations" that in principle can be filled by anyone. Individuals, moving into vocations in part as a consequence of an inner call, are motivated to accept the requirements of vocations they enter. The distance to the language of position and role and to the theoretical argument relating social structure and person in role theory is not great.

Summer (1906) elaborates on types of norms recognizing variability in the demands society places on its members. Simmel (1950) and Weber (1947) emphasize the differentiated character of the positions contained in social structures. Role theory had only to put together explicitly these two strains by recognizing that differentiated norms are organized into sets of expectations applicable to persons occupying particular positions. In essence, this is the meaning of the role concept from a structural perspective.

Although this conception of role had early and relatively wide currency as a consequence of its appearance in the works of Park (1926), Moreno (1934) and others and although the basic idea of group members' performances being structured by group norms had been exploited in small group contexts from a variety of theoretical contexts (Festinger *et al.,* 1950; Sherif, 1936; Bales, 1950; Milgram, 1964; Melbin, 1972), structural role theory developed largely through Linton (1936) and Parsons (1951), both of whom were concerned with society as a functional unit. Linton views societies as composed of individuals but requiring their adaptation and organization. Over time, a necessary division of labor is elaborated and stabilized, with individual conduct increasingly predictable and with cooperation among individuals increasingly complete and effective. The adaptations are perpetuated through constant training guided by ideal patterns originating in remembered and rationalized behavior and modified through adaptation to environmental conditions. Ideal patterns are positively valued ideas, transmitted across generations through instruction and imitation and guiding training and behavior in situations for which persons have not been specifically trained. Never completely realized in but strongly influencing behavior, ideal patterns shape relationships to approximations of their ideal form.

Every culture has ideal patterns for relationships between persons, the essence of which is reciprocity creating a circuit of rights and duties. Categories of persons may occupy polar positions in reciprocal ideal patterns, with particular persons participating in many such reciprocities. The totality of these patterns, being closely adjusted, constitutes a social system. Conflicting duties and obligations within the same or among different persons are rare; otherwise, society could not function. The polar positions in ideal patterns for reciprocal behavior, Linton calls "statuses." The dynamic aspect of statuses, the rights and duties in action, are called "roles." Every person plays a series of roles and has a general role—the summation of particular roles determining what a person does for society and what can be expected in return. Status and role reduce ideal patterns to individual form. Adjustment of persons to their statuses and roles implies a smoothly functioning society. General roles tend to be ascribed without reference to individual differences, since they are basic to the functioning of society; age and sex roles are prime examples of general roles. Other roles are open to achievement; most achieved roles are not central to societal existence but are baits for socially acceptable behavior and escapes for individuals.

Parsons (1951) began his analyses of interaction systems with the case of precisely mutual shared meanings, totally complementary expectations, and complete consensus on norms. Although this special case of perfect integration is (probably) impossible empirically, it is the context for an analysis of the ways in which conformity to expectations is induced: through actors gratifying one another's needs; through their performing actions useful to one another in attaining goals; through gratification produced by conforming to legitimate expectations and demands of others when values are shared and internalized; through approval and esteem, which are rewards from others for conformity induced by socialized sensitivity to others' attitudes.

Interactional systems relating individual actors comprise the structures of social systems. The most convenient analytic unit for the analysis of interactional systems is the status-role, the first term of which is equivalent to a position or social location of an actor. Roles are what actors in positions do, as constrained by normative expectations; they are institutionally defined and regulated parts of relationships; that is, they are shaped by shared values and norms internalized by actors and made parts of their personalities. Conformity to role expectations is a reward; failure to conform is met with sanctions; hence the equilibrium of interpersonal interactions is maintained. This miniature interpersonal system is a model for the larger systems of interaction developing in society.

Clearly, Parsons views social roles as complementary; and, as noted, there are a variety of inducements to bring persons to conform to their roles. However, persons choose courses of action with reference to one another in concrete situations of action. Choices, while in principle arrived at through freely expressed preference or through personality demands, are fundamentally understood as defined by the culture in which roles are embedded and institutionalized.

Both Parsons and Linton tended to apply their theoretical work to total societies, although their models of societies developed from analysis of the requirements of stable pair relationships. Many of the additional developments of role theory, to which we turn next, moved the level of analysis to the "middle range" (Merton, 1949), that is, to communities, organizations, associations, and groups that interface paired interaction and total societies. The principal themes of Linton's and Parson's work permeate these efforts: roles are the major mechanisms linking persons to social structure, and persons are under heavy pressure both outside and inside themselves to conform to expectations.

This sketch of early structural role theory has stressed the contributions of persons working from a functionalist framework. We began by noting that there is an alternative version of role theory. Some of the contributors to that alternative represent early bridges between a structural role theory and symbolic interactionism. Noteworthy in this respect are Hughes (1945), Park (1955), and Znaniecki (1965). According to Znaniecki persons through roles behave as though they were the kind of persons imagined by others, a significant idea in Turner's (n.d.c.) effort, reviewed below, to integrate role theory and symbolic interactionism. Hughes echoes and gives empirical substance to Park's (1955) comment that articulates the interactionist emphasis on self and the structuralist concern with status and role (pp. 285–286):

The conceptions which men form of themselves seem to depend on their vocations, and in general upon the role they seek to play in communities and social groups in which they live, as well as upon the recognition and status which society accords them in these roles. It is status, i.e., recognition by the community, that confers upon the individual the character of a person, since a person is an individual who has status, not necessarily legal, but social.

CONCEPTUAL DEVELOPMENTS AND ILLUSTRATIVE USES

Structural role theory develops in a variety of ways, most of which concern how roles are learned and how, once learned, they serve to organize and to simplify the lives of people. Much of the work done from this standpoint has an institutional flavor. Some of it, emphasizing the import and impact of social structures, invests considerable effort in examining behavior in complex organizational settings in which persons must deal with a wide variety of role demands, at least some of which are in conflict. Thus, over the years, structural role theory has paid particular attention to the causes, consequences, and resolution of institutionalized role conflict in the context of complex organizations. More recently, however, as the upsurge in women's labor force participation has lent theoretical and practical interest to the topic, role conflict in the less formally organized setting of the family has drawn widespread attention. For example, work on the family has increased awareness of the conflicting role demands persons frequently experience as a consequence of their positions in diverse and nominally "independent" units, especially those often impinging on mothers who work.

The following discussion reflects the emphasis of structural role theory on role conflict and its concomitants. Yet, role conflict is only one of a set of significant social psychological issues toward which structural role theory has oriented its conceptual and theoretical efforts. Socialization is, of course, a second. A third concerns the structure of role relationships. Here, interest is centered in the linkages that roles establish between persons, under the assumption that an understanding of these linkages will increase our appreciation of how roles constrain behaviors and lead to conformity. A fourth, not necessarily independent of the topic of role conflict, concerns role transitions, in particular, the problems of entering and leaving roles connected to stages in the life cycle.

Since processes of role acquisition are fundamental to all other issues, our discussion of conceptual developments in structural role theory and our effort to illustrate the use of that framework will begin with socialization.

Socialization into Roles

Conceptualizing socialization as the means through which persons acquire the knowledge, skills, dispositions and motivations making it possible for them to participate as effective members of society and of differentiated groups within society, structural role theory brings a particular perspective to the processes involved. Societies and groups are, from this point of view, structures of behavior patterns organized by norms, to which persons generally must conform for the continuing functioning of these social units. Being an "effective member" is, in the main, interpreted as implying the necessity of behaving in terms appropriate to social norms.

Thus, structural role theory is interested in socialization processes because they are viewed as central to the sociological answer to the question: How are persons made to conform to the normative requirements of society and of the groups to which they belong? Given this interest, the theory views socialization through the lens of collectivity, and it portrays the shaping of persons through social processes, ignoring or de-emphasizing potential reciprocal causal effects of the person on collectivity (as well as taking as minimal the possibilities of persons actively negotiating and restructuring their socialization outcomes). Too, given this interest, the theory takes as the most important aspect of socialization the extent to which cultural dictates are internalized by persons, for internalization is deemed the most efficient process available to a social unit in achieving necessary conformity from its members.

For structural role theory, internalization accounts for and links personal order and social order (Parsons, 1961). In particular, persons are seen as likely to internalize norms attached to roles they in fact play, an observation used by more recently formulated identity theory (e.g., Stryker, 1968; 1980) to integrate structural role theory and symbolic interactionism. While the perspective identifies a variety of socialization processes—direct instruction (Sears *et al.*, 1957), the transmission of moral imperatives (Kemper, 1968), imitation or modeling (Bandura, 1969), and altercasting (Weinstein and Deutschberger, 1963)—it tends to emphasize the direct internalization of communicated norms (Parsons, 1961) or the assimilation of norms indirectly through processes of identification with socialization agents who articulate or exemplify those norms (Sears *et al.*, 1965; Kagan, 1964).

Given the various elements in the perspective just reviewed, it is not surprising that the major socialization concern of structural role theory (although, interestingly, not of the empirical research undertaken in the name of the perspective) has been with children. This concern with childhood socialization follows in part from the assumption that all adult socialization builds upon the basic skills and values inculcated early in life. It is consistent with the view of socialization as an essentially one-way causal process flowing from social structure to person, with minimal negotiation entailed, since children are least likely to initiate restructuring of social relationships or the wider structures in which relationships are embedded. This concern leads to exploring the kinds of socialization processes involving imposition of an authority's desires on children and to identifying a variety of socialization agents who engage in such authoritative imposition as representatives of institutional complexes: parents (Kagan, 1964; Sears *et al.,* 1965; Hetherington, 1967), siblings (Rosenberg and Sutton-Smith, 1964; Kammeyer, 1967), peers (Gallagher and Aschner, 1963), and teachers (Rosenthal and Jacobsen, 1968; Burstyn, 1971). It also leads to a focus on impersonal socialization agents, again representing institutionalized norms, like television and magazines (Komarovsky, 1967; Weitzman *et al.,* 1972).

The structural role theory perspective on socialization underwrites a concern with phenomena to which the concept of anticipatory socialization (Merton and Kitt, 1950) calls attention. The key question from this perspective is the success of socialization practices, defined in terms of persons' conformity to norms. Clearly important to such success is the opportunity to practice roles—through play or through formal and informal education—and in so doing to take on not only the skills involved but also the attitudes and values that are part of the role. "Practice" implies that role learning can take place with minimal recrimination for inadequate performance (Mann and Mann, 1966; Goslin, 1969) and points to the general import of anticipatory socialization processes.

Other concerns that follow from the way structural role theory envisions socialization include the consequences of others' perceptions of adequate role performance (Borgatta, 1961) and the meaning of role performance for performers themselves (Cameron, 1950; Janis and King, 1954; Palmer and Humphrey, 1977; Blacher-Dixon and Simeonsson, 1978). With regard to the latter, the theory argues that motivation to meet role expectations is high, since the consequences of failure to do so are in some degree traumatic.

Pressures toward Conformity

That trauma results from failure to meet role expectations may be in part a function of internalized normative standards. In an important way, however, structural role theory assumes that trauma will result from the negative responses of others with a stake in the role performance. Persons are motivated to perform adequately, the perspective holds, largely because of the structure of role relationships and the ways in which relationships link to the wider social structure in which they are embedded.

Conceptualizations of the bonds between role partners are based largely on Linton's (1939) early observation that interdependency is inherent in the nature of role relationships. Roles exist in complementary pairs: There is no wife without a husband nor parent without a child. Minimally, the tacit cooperation of a role partner is requisite to adequate role performance. Partners come to rely on one another for rewards beyond the facilitation each provides for the other's performances: information, emotional support, and meeting of physical needs, for example. Consequently, partners exert heavy pressure on one another for conformity to what each has come to expect of the other. In Jackson's (1966) terms, interdependency leads predictions to become prescriptions.

Thibaut and Kelley (1959) offer additional clarification of the structure of role relationships that helps to account for the pressure toward conformity inherent in those relationships. Suggesting that complementary role definitions specify equitable exchanges of costs and rewards, they elaborate further that normative role expectations come, over time, to be seen as rewards each partner has a "right" to expect from the other. If those rights are not met, partners may threaten to withdraw from the relationship in order to seek a more favorable exchange of costs and rewards in other relationships; threat of withdrawal is a powerful source of securing conformity from a role partner; its power is based on the degree of interdependency. (See Waller's [1938] analysis of the principle of least interest for a comparable argument.)

The impact of role expectations on persons depends in part on whether expectations are integrated into the broader social structure, indicators which include the extent to which the expectations are clear and whether consensus with regard to them exists (Nye, 1976). Consensus and clarity are taken by role theory to be important determinants of the pressure persons feel toward conformity. If expectations are clear and consensus about them is high, then the pressure toward conformity will be considerable (Cottrell, 1942; Jackson, 1966; Sarbin and Allen, 1968). In contrast, low consensus resulting from the uncertainty of a population as a whole or from the concurrent existence of opposing subgroup expectations reduces the pressure toward conformity (Sarbin and Allen, 1968) as do double binds (Bateson *et al.,* 1956) of contradictory expectations deriving from the same source.

Consensus with respect to expectations not only is an indicator of the integration in structured social units but also is a consequent of social structure. Parsons (1951) implies that social systems evolve to increase clarity of expectations; others simply argue that structure affects clarity. Inkeles (1969), for example, suggests that a complex societal status structure induces confusion in expectations. Whatever may be true on this score, the role theoretic principle involved holds that persons are impacted by social structure through the clarity of role expectations.

Yet another, and perhaps the most powerful, source of pressure toward conformity noted by structural role theory is the existence of role expectations that are so totally taken for granted that they are assumed to contain immutable truths. It has been argued, for example, by Bem (1970) and Laws and Schwartz (1977) that some sex-role expectations attached to roles are so insidiously woven into the social fabric that they completely color perceptions of reality and thus prevent persons from viewing them as definitions subject to redefinition. Clearly, when this occurs, persons have minimal flexibility and the least possibility for deviating from role expectations: Where no conception of choice exists, there can be no choice of alternative patterns exercised.

Early structural role theorists tended to view a society as a coherent and unified system; thus the actors within society faced clear and consistent role expectations. Such a view is obviously so discrepant with experience in the world most of us know that it seems quaint, and theorists abandoned it for a vision of society that incorporated some conception of role conflict. Role conflict and the related idea of multiple-role involvement have generated the largest and perhaps most interesting theoretical and empirical work in the literature of structural role theory.

Multiple-Role Involvement and Role Conflict

The insight that multiple-role involvements and conflicting role expectations can result in social and personal disorder motivates much of structural role theory's interest in these phenomena, particularly in its attempts to conceptualize sources and types of role conflict and in its effort to discern their consequences and modes of resolution.

The source of much thinking about these matters is Merton's (1957) essay on status-sets and role-sets. Defining the former as the totality of positions a person occupies and the latter as the totality of expectations attached to a single position, Merton notes that status-conflict can involve conflicting demands from different statuses. Role-set conflict is seen as inherent in the structure of a single position, its source of inconsistency being the expectations of the subroles characteristic of most statuses. For example, a teacher may be required to be an instructor and a disciplinarian of a student and a confidant of a parent and a subordinate of the principal, and these requirements may not mesh.

Merton's conceptions have been exploited or expanded in various ways. Bates (1956) calls for recognizing the extent to which positions change as the person moves among particular others; the way in which the expectations a child meets change as she or he moves from father to mother is an illustration. Goode's (1960a) concept of role strain iterates sources of inconsistency but goes further by asserting that persons' role obligations are typically overdemanding, an idea exploited in work that considers the time demands made upon working mothers (Myrdal and Klein, 1968; Fogarty *et al.,* 1971; Holmstrom, 1972).

Others have further clarified types of role conflict or role strain, preparing the ground for understanding variable consequences. Gross *et al.* (1957) postulate two types of conflict experienced by persons in a single role: interperson and intraperson conflict. Later work distinguished types of the former. One is intraorganizational conflict, resulting from contradictory demands from members of the same organization. "Marginal" roles facing two reference groups—e.g., the plant foreman who must deal with both workers and management—are fertile ground for intraorganizational conflict; so are cases in which informal networks make demands contrary to formal organizational requirements (Crozier, 1964). Another type of interperson role conflict occurs when persons work in one organization but feel allegiance to extraorganizational reference groups. Such conflict is seen in scientists in industry (Roe, 1951; Kornhauser, 1962; Hagstrom, 1965; Perrow, 1970; Rothman and Perrucci, 1970), professionals in other types of bureaucratic settings (Blau and Scott, 1962; Hall, 1968; Daniels, 1969; D. T. Hall, 1972), and cosmopolites forced to consider local concerns (Gouldner, 1957). Such conflicts have detrimental individual effects in the form of job-related tensions and dissatisfactions

(Roe, 1951; Kahn *et al.,* 1964; Snoek, 1966; Coburn, 1975) as well as detrimental organizational effects in the form of low productivity, poor quality work, high employee turnover, and difficult company-worker relations (Kahn *et al.,* 1964; Aram *et al.,* 1971).

Recent research serves to clarify the determinants of such tension. For example, the nature of the task determines the amount of stress felt by individuals influenced by external groups. If the task permits adherence to these external norms, stress is minimal (Schuler, 1977). Too, the extent of bureaucratization is important. High levels of bureaucracy frequently produce stress for professionals in large organizations, but moderate amounts of bureaucracy may actually reduce the stress individuals feel (Engel, 1970; Haga *et al.,* 1974; Ritzer, 1975).

Miles (1977; 1976) has found that requirements of certain organizational positions may be especially tension producing: boundary spanners (persons forced to interact with others in different segments of the organization) and those with low authority suffer the greatest conflict. Less specific aspects of position requirements, such as general overload (Kahn *et al.,* 1964; Coburn, 1975) or ambiguous requirements (Merton and Barber, 1963; Miles, 1977) can also cause problems for persons involved.

Strategies for Role-Conflict Resolution

How do persons manage the overwhelming, simultaneous, inconsistent demands inherent in the totality of their status and role sets? This question generated a research response, still continuing, that locates the dominant factors in resolving role conflicts in social structure. Earlier research assumed that role demands were unalterable (Gerhardt, 1973) and that available alternatives were to abandon one role, effect a compromise, or withdraw from the situation in which conflict occurred; other possible reactions were labeled neurotic or maladaptive (Burchard, 1954). This assumption underlies studies of institutional norms conflicting with friendship norms (Stouffer, 1949; Stouffer and Toby, 1951), as well as studies of the role conflicts of business executives (Henry, 1948), military teachers (Getzels and Guba, 1954), chaplains (Burchard, 1954), insurance salesmen (Wispe, 1955), elected public officials (Mitchell, 1958), male nurses (Segal, 1962), sorority hashers (Zurcher *et al.,* 1966), and school superintendents (Gross *et al.,* 1957).

Although Merton (1957) postulates that conflicting expectations generate structural resolutions so that persons rarely face them directly, work on role conflict generally takes for granted that conflicting expectations must somehow be resolved. Given this assumption, it becomes important to discern the criteria persons use to decide which demands they will obey. Merton (1957) argues that choice depends on the importance of various roles or subroles for persons, the power of others in a role-set, the observability of behavior, and the clarity of others' expectations. Goode (1960a) catalogs structurally based strategies available for role conflict resolution: manipulation of role structures, compartmentalization, delegation, elimination of role relationships, expansion of these to justify neglect of other roles or to facilitate other role demands, and erection of barriers to intrusion. Implying that persons can not modify but may avoid role expectations, Goode envisions choice of avoidance strategy as functions of ascriptive statuses, being in positions with many institutional linkages, relationships with third parties, perceived norms of adequacy, and hierarchies of evaluation.

Gross and his associates (1957) confirm in their study of school superintendents Merton's assertion that relative power of others in a role set determines which of conflicting demands are and are not met, although an attempt at replication casts some doubt on this finding (Ehrlich *et al.,* 1962). The importance of power that persons ascribe to others, whatever the "reality" of the situation, may also be important, given that sex role traditionality appears to affect the work and family choices made by women (Waite and Stolzenberg, 1976; Scanzoni, 1978; Macke *et al.,* 1979).

Recent research has further explored the methods of reducing role conflict. Compartmentalization, as described by Goode (1960a), takes place in industry when individuals share certain experiences only with particular others (Pelz, 1966; Rothman and Perrucci, 1970), adhere to one of a pair of conflicting standards only in certain situations (Katz and Kahn, 1967; Kelly, 1971; Nelson *et al.,* 1973; Lally and Barber, 1974), avoid contact with others holding difficult expectations and privately discount particular others (Rothman and Perrucci, 1970), or seek contact with persons in a broader network and avoid the pressure from those in their immediate workplace (Rothman and Perrucci, 1970; Aram *et al.,* 1971; Smith, 1971). People reduce their perception of conflict by giving up one set of standards while rationalizing that they are not doing so (Katz and Kahn, 1967) or by attempting to co-opt a problematic aspect of their environment to bring it under the control of their own organization (Selznick, 1966).

Other strategies are seen in women who play both work and family roles, especially in mothers of young children, for whom the conflict seems to be the most acute (Nevill and Damico, 1977; Trocki, 1980). More and more women are encountering this dilemma, since married women who choose not to work at all—an increasingly infrequent choice—often feel unfulfilled, uncreative, and dull (Hoffman, 1974), suffering lower levels of self-esteem and self-rated capability (Burke and Weir, 1976; Scanzoni, 1978). The women establish priorities and separate roles, eliminate certain subroles, and rotate attention among roles (D. T. Hall, 1972). Women who do not use any of these coping strategies but attempt to meet all the demands appear to suffer high levels of strain (D. T. Hall, 1972).

Establishing priorities for roles is common among women who experience conflict between family and work. The problem is often solved by reducing involvement in one role or the other. Many career-successful women remain childless (Perrucci, 1970; Veevers, 1973; Houseknecht, 1977) or never marry (Havens, 1973), though few women prefer this option (Macke and Morgan, 1978). Those who do remain childless may be less satisfied with their marriages over the long run (Houseknecht and Macke, 1981).

Women who plan to work may limit the number of children they have or intend to have (Scanzoni and Murray, 1972; Waite and Stolzenberg, 1976; Scanzoni, 1976). Working women also renegotiate household responsibilities with children (Wallston, 1973) as well as with spouse (Blood and Wolfe, 1960; Scanzoni, 1970; Safilios-Rothschild, 1970). Husbands are more likely to share child-rearing responsibilities than housework (Beck, 1979); children share housework responsibilities.

Conversely, the woman may give more priority to her family roles and her family's needs than to her own work involvement (Mackie, 1983). Even highly dedicated professional women limit their career strivings in deference to their husbands' careers (Heckman *et al.*, 1977). And women, again even professional women, most often move for the sake of their husband's work rather than their own (Perrucci, 1970; Tatnall *et al.*, 1980). They may reduce work when their children are young or quit working altogether (Sweet, 1973), a pattern most young women plan to follow (Macke and Morgan, 1978). Women may choose flexible occupations like teaching, in part because they permit movement in and out of the labor force when rearing of children or the mobility of the husband require; they may choose specialities within

occupations for the same reason; women doctors and lawyers disproportionately work for the government (Kosa and Coker, 1965); women engineers teach (Perrucci, 1970); women dentists treat only children (Shuval, 1970); and women social workers approach their work as extensions of family roles. These strategies have implications for the woman's eventual success in the labor market, of course. Certainly, these work patterns are at least partly responsible for sex differences in earnings (Suter and Miller, 1973), the lower returns women receive for their education and occupational prestige (Treiman and Terrell, 1975; Hudis, 1976), and the professional woman's propensity to underutilize her training (Tatnall *et al.*, 1980).

Some of this research has prescribed solutions to the role conflict dilemma. Given the heavy structural bias of the perspective underlying the work, which tends to see organization members as passive objects manipulated by the organization itself, prescriptions typically take the form of enjoining those in power to provide the resolution of conflict through structural arrangements. Organizations are encouraged to delegate decision making (Blumberg, 1968; Dalton *et al.*, 1968), organize research and development groups so as to provide stimulation (Pelz, 1966), reward risk taking in their scientists (Aram *et al.*, 1971), facilitate informal structures among potentially marginal members (Raphael, 1965), give members more autonomy and flexibility in setting career paths (Roe, 1951; Argyris, 1962; Katz and Kahn, 1967), and arrange organizational components to facilitate needed contact among members (Katz and Kahn, 1967; Pelz, 1966; Blau and Scott, 1962).

The theoretical and empirical work we have been describing has generally seen the individual as helpless in the face of structural arrangements. The discovery of the no-win situations, for which no satisfactory resolution is available or even possible, both epitomizes the approach and provides some justification for it. Men seeking to participate in traditionally female activities illustrate the point: male professors in female-dominated university departments find they are resented by students for aggressive, "masculine" behavior and for any nurturing, "feminine" behavior they exhibit in the classroom (Macke *et al.*, 1980).

It is clear from the thesis of this chapter as well as from the tone of the occasional parenthetical remarks contained in this discussion that we view the structural emphasis of structural role theory as extreme. While certainly an advance over early work on persons in organizations that tended to attribute tensions in those persons to individual "illness" or weakness (Asumi and Hage, 1972), that emphasis needs tempering through the recognition that persons at least under some circumstances become active modifiers of the structures in which they are located.

Role Diversity as a Positive Experience

Some recent theorizing and research on the multiplicity of roles and on role conflict has begun to recognize that the individual is not completely helpless and passive in the fact of structural constraints. Miles (1977) does not find the levels of anxiety he expected in boundary spanners and argues that these persons possess resources used to relieve their personal strain and overload. Not strictly accountable to any superior, these people had flexibility in arranging work schedules, could innovate activities, and had unusually broad intraorganizational contacts that could be mobilized when they met difficulties. Sieber (1974) argues that role overload may actually have a positive rather than a disabling impact on the individual. Zurcher (1977) suggests that temporary or periodically recurring ephemeral roles may lessen rather than increase strain because ephemeral involvement makes it possible to ignore structural expectations that produce conflict. Sarbin and Allen (1968) suggest considering all of a person's roles in anticipating the strain engendered by any pair of conflicting roles. Adding a role to an existing set may also add important resources and flexibility, thus reducing rather than increasing strain. Thoits (1983) provides both theoretical underpinning and empirical evidence for this conjecture (see also Spreitzer *et al.*, 1979). Marks (1977) argues that it is not time and energy expenditures that occasions strain, but rather the level of commitment to roles. If persons can move readily from one role to the next, multiple roles can increase rather than decrease personal satisfaction; thus the commitment made to roles as well as the rigidity and clarity of role expectations should influence the conflict one experiences.

Role Change

Structural role theorists have also examined the problem of managing expectations when persons undergo role changes. Not surprisingly, the argument is that when individuals are required to change roles, problems often result. Persons may not occupy given positions and play given roles throughout their lives. Indeed, most roles have an entry and an exit point; family roles and occupa-

tional roles provide clear examples. Social structures can facilitate or hinder transitions, and important questions can be raised about what structures do so, how they do so, and with what consequences. Although few transitions are as highly structured as the rites of passage described by Benedict (1938), many are expected to occur at specific points in the life cycle. Persons making these transitions at atypical points or in unusual sequence have more difficulty than others with the changes, an observation that holds for early motherhood (Bacon, 1974), early grandparenthood (Neugarten, 1964) and unusual career sequences (Hogan, 1980). Difficulty appears to stem from the absence of social support for transitions that are either unanticipated or not valued by others and from the unavailability of peers sharing the experience.

Social support is a key factor easing transitions; conversely, social isolation is an important source of transition difficulties, in particular, to old age (Cavan, 1962; Lowenthal and Haven, 1968; Riley and Foner, 1968; Bock and Webber, 1972) and to motherhood (Rossi, 1968; Ryder, 1973; Bacon, 1974). Thus, if structural arrangements increase isolation during transitions, those transitions are likely to be stressful.

When support is lacking or other forms of structural control break down, the individual often experiences heightened distress (but see Hughes and Gove, 1981). Clarity of role expectations is one important type of structural control. Goode (1956) has noted the difficulty lack of clarity causes for divorced women; Cherlin (1978) and Duberman (1975) have noted similar difficulties for stepparents. Opportunity for anticipatory socialization can also be critical; its absence causes problems for new parents (Rossi, 1968) and for those continuously leaving and re-entering family role situations (Jones and Butler, 1980).

Structural factors not only are conceptualized as facilitators of role change but also are seen as the causes of such change. Lipman-Blumen (1973) notes that crises often cause role distinctions to de-differentiate. Under such conditions, behavior ordinarily seen as inappropriate for one partner in a role relationship may become temporarily acceptable. She uses this reasoning to account for the relaxation of role prescriptions that apply to the typically differentiated husband/wife roles—even when the woman works (Blood and Wolfe, 1960; Scanzoni, 1970; Berk, 1979)—during the Second World War. Lipman-Blumen argues that differentiation is re-established along traditional lines once the crisis has passed, but Bernard (1976) suggests that some permanent change remains for role innovators, enabling the process of change to move further during the next crisis.

This work being discussed has tended toward a system perspective, assuming that changes for one person typically imply change for those interacting with that person. Considerable early research explored the upheaval that typically occurs in families when a wage earner loses or resumes a job (Koos, 1946; Cavan and Ranck, 1938; Komarovsky, 1940) or returns to work after a long period of absence (Hill, 1949).

In summary, structural role theory, though limited in its perspective, has provided valuable insights into the ways role expectations affect behavior. It has shown how these expectations are communicated and instilled, how persons are pressured to conform to them, and how changes in them can cause difficulties. It has also demonstrated the impact structural influences can have on the content of role expectations. The picture presented is only partial, however. In particular, the process of role negotiation has been virtually ignored by structural role theorists. We will turn to this point after stating our criticism of structural role theory.

CRITICAL APPRAISAL

As noted, as a consequence of its link to structural functionalism, role theory has been criticized for neglecting both conflict and change in social life and thus for projecting a one-sided view of intrapersonal and interpersonal behavior. Role theory has also been charged with an ideological bias that favors the social status quo (Gouldner, 1970). The claim is, in part, that a role theory influenced by structural functionalism rationalizes the subservience of persons to the social order, whatever the principles on which that order may be built. Since capitalist principles underlay American society during the period when this form of role theory appeared, the argument of leftist critics is that structural role theory supports capitalist hegemony in the United States.

We have suggested that the link of role theory to structural functionalism is not necessary. The appropriateness, therefore, of this ideological criticism may be questioned. However, a related albeit more value-neutral critique of structural role theory is offered by Wrong (1961), and another related but perhaps even more basic critique appears in the work of ethnomethodologists and cognitive sociologists (Cicourel, 1964; 1973).

According to Wrong, structural role theory entails an oversocialized conception of man; it solves the Hobbesian problem of social order too simplistically by effectively denying or explaining away any impact or import of the characteristics of individual human organisms in social processes. Humans are seen as automatons, quietly acquiescent in reflecting the social norms they have been programmed through socialization to duplicate. The significance of biological imperatives, of impulse and instinct, and of the Freudian dynamics is ignored in favor of viewing individual motivation as one-sidedly social, the product of two basic processes: the internalization of social norms through socialization and conformity to social norms produced by a favorable self-image through positive feedback from others. The direction of influence in the society-person relationship is unilaterally from society to person. The social person is conceptualized as a pragmatic performer (Turner, 1974) without having essential impact on norms, roles, or society in general.

Although humanists find this view of persons insulting, its fundamental flaw lies in its inaccuracy (Bates, 1956): Behavior does not accord with norms as neatly as this model of human nature projects. Wrong (1961) advises sociologists and social psychologists not to forget the body in their theorizing; that is, that various biologically based urges and emotions intervene in the relationship between society and behavior. Other theoretical perspectives offer sources of possible nonconformity: Mead's "I" and individual differences in understandings of cultural imperatives, for example. All sociological theory, according to Wrong, could benefit by incorporating individually based determinants of social behavior.

Clearly, the impact of individual characteristics does not need to be treated as "unsystematic"; the person can be conceptualized as a social system (Jackson, 1966). Structural role theorists focused on the intra- and interpersonal integration and harmony facilitated by the force of structure on persons and generally ignored the conflicts and difficulties engendered by differences in goals, desires, and propensities across varying groups, both within and between persons. This criticism can be interpreted to mean that the social system of the self has been left out of role theory and thus the phenomenon and impact of possible disjuncts between role and self. Structural role theory largely ignores the issues engendered by self-role disjunctions.

The criticisms lodged by ethnomethodologists are broader. They argue for a different paradigm, positing that the interaction process itself *is* social life. Because structural role theorists do not recognize this, they contend, such theorists do not study the basic stuff of social life; their data are insignificant and their concepts mask, or gloss over, the important processes affecting individuals. From this perspective, role theory cannot simply add new "systems", that is, the self, to its present list of variables to become a viable framework. It must obtain information on entirely new phenomena in entirely new ways.

A basic tenet of this argument, however, could prove useful to structural role theory, even within its present paradigm. Structural role theory could consider the importance of the interaction process itself in modifying the more structured aspects of the social environment. According to Cicourel (1973), the interpretive procedures individuals use to construct consensus or shared agreement during interactions have as much, if not more, impact on how roles are played as do *a priori* structural arrangements. At the very least, all instances of role portrayal involve a dialectic between what is structurally or institutionally invariant and what depends upon the actor's perceptions and interpretations.

This point has been made by other theorists as well. Turner (1974) argues that role theory neglects the impact role enactment can have on social structure; hence, it can offer no systematic explanation for modification of role expectations without going outside itself by resorting to broad environmental causes, for example, wars, a cause of role change posited by Lipman-Blumen (1973). If the interaction process itself were conceptualized as a source of continual modification of social structure, such changes might be better accounted for—especially if the conditions under which changes most likely occur were specified (Jackson, 1966; Powers, 1980; Collins, 1981).

The incorporation of symbolic interactionist ideas into the role theoretic framework responds to these major criticisms: the neglect of individuals' characteristics and the neglect of the interaction process itself. From its inception, symbolic interactionism has stressed the significance of persons' perceptions (Cooley, 1902) and definitions of the situation (Thomas and Thomas, 1928) in structuring social behavior as well as the construction of shared meaning in the process of interaction (Mead, 1934). It is to the mutual interpenetration of the symbolic interactionist and role theoretic frameworks that we now turn.

SYMBOLIC INTERACTIONISM AND ROLE THEORY: MUTUAL INTERPENETRATION

Symbolic interactionism and role theory have been presented as more or less independent, historically separate lines of conceptual and theoretical development. Al-

though this characterization is an oversimplification (Handel, 1979; Heiss, 1981)—many (e.g., Sarbin, 1954; Turner, 1962; Kuhn, 1964; Stryker, 1964) have long blended the two—it is useful as a generalization. Many symbolic interactionists have rejected what they see as role theory's static, normatively deterministic view of social life, and many role theorists have rejected what they see as symbolic interactionism's nonstructured view of social life.

We have repeatedly asserted that elements of both frameworks are essential to an adequate social psychological theory, one that does justice to the reciprocity of society and person as its central problem. Our judgment is that symbolic interactionism requires a more adequate sense of social structure than it typically exhibits and that role theory can provide that more adequate sense. We also believe that role theory requires a more adequate sense of the processual, constructed aspects of social life than it generally shows and that symbolic interactionism offers that more adequate sense.

Others express these same judgments. Some begin with symbolic interactionism and introduce role theoretic ideas and concepts to accomplish their purposes; some start with role theory and modify it to accommodate symbolic interactionist principles and concepts. Our concern is to present an overview of this work and to contribute to it. Although the treatment of particular work is sometimes arbitrary, we will maintain our earlier organizational frame as a matter of convenience, first dealing with symbolic interactionism as informed by role theory and then treating role theory as influenced by symbolic interactionism. We will then abandon the fiction of separateness to appraise the success of the merged frameworks and to anticipate further developments of social psychological theory potential in the merger.

Our judgment that symbolic interactionism needs better ways of dealing with social structure is not universally shared. Some regard the framework as it exists in Mead or as elucidated by Blumer as sufficient in its sense of social structure. And some who share this judgment do not regard role theory as a reasonable corrective; they opt for an alternative framework as the means by which symbolic interactionism can be made more responsive to social organizational features of social life.

We believe that the first countercontention is incorrect. There can be no gainsaying that social structure is constructed by human beings through their interaction or that structure is continuously recreated in and by social interaction; neither can it be sensibly argued that structure exists only in interpretations by the concrete, interacting humans who are the focus of an analyst's attention at a given moment.

Class structure can constrain interaction or the development of selves in a variety of ways whether or not actors conceptualize their circumstances in class terms. Or, to paraphrase a point made by W. I. Thomas (1937), to stress definitions of the situation is not to deny the importance of the objective situation per se. There is no warrant in symbolic interactionism for the propensity of some adherents to dissolve objective social structure, that is, normatively influenced, stable patterns of interaction existing independently of particular human actors, in the universal solvent of those actors' definitions of the situation.

The second countercontention cannot be so easily dismissed. By and large, those holding this view focus on microstructure: the structure of some observed interaction and of the immediate context of that interaction. We regard that focus as disabling with respect to the full range of social psychological problems implied by a thorough concern with the reciprocities of society and person, and we believe role theory does better by this criterion. Nevertheless, their work merits attention before we discuss the interpenetration of symbolic interactionism and role theory.

Although many regard Blumer as exemplifying the propensity noted previously, Maines (1977) argues that critics who claim that symbolic interactionism neglects social structure overlook much in Blumer's work that references social organization and structure. Maines also argues that concern with structure is manifest in the work of many other symbolic interactionists, the critics notwithstanding. Defending Blumer's arguments, he cites the literature on situated interaction but makes his case primarily through work based on the concept of negotiations (Bucher and Strauss, 1961; Strauss *et al,* 1963; Friedson, 1967; Strauss, 1978). (He refers as well, albeit tangentially, to three works by symbolic interactionists frequently cited as evidencing the framework's capacity to deal with social structure: P. M. Hall [1972] on politics as symbolic interaction and Farberman [1975] and Denzin [1977] on economic constraints operative in the automobile and the liquor industries.)

The literature on situated interaction blends the symbolic interactionist concerns with self and definitions of the situation and a concern with social structure, bringing this blend to bear on focused interaction: interaction that "occurs when people effectively agree to sustain for a time a single focus of cognitive and visual atten-

tion, as in a conversation, a board game, or a joint task sustained by a close face-to-face circle of contributors" (Goffman, 1961b, p.7). Units of such focused interaction are variously called encounters, focused gatherings, or situated activity systems by Erving Goffman (1959; 1961b; 1963a), whose writings largely define this literature and can serve to characterize it.

The critical attribute of an encounter is "engrossment." Goffman (1961b) uses this attribute to distinguish what he is interested in from the social group as typically defined; encounters exist only in the occasions when members are physically together and continuously engrossed, while groups have continuity beyond the physical presence of the members and the single focus of attention. This distinction makes clear Goffman's interest in the situation of interaction itself rather than in the properties of interaction abstracted out of situations or in the properties of social persons who interact in situations. He thus takes for granted the previous existence both of selves and rules for interaction.

Engrossment may express commitment to the part being played in situated interaction. Goffman sees commitment as variable in interaction and relatively low commitment as consequential for both the person and the social organization. This observation initiates a critique of role theory, centering on the assumption that persons are committed to the roles they play, as presented in an essay on role distance (Goffman, 1961b). Role distance refers to the effective expression of pointed separateness between persons and their putative roles and is contained in any behavior saying to both person and others that the role is not really the person. The businessman in jeans and beads at a board meeting illustrates role distance. Expressions of role distance dissociate self from role as an ideal pattern; they can protect the self from implications of failures in role performance and frequently appear during high-risk performances. Role distance has significant organizational implications as well, permitting situated activity to go on when its disruption is threatened by the failure of participants to do their parts, by fears of disaster, or by tension; an example is provided by the surgeon who obscenely jokes in the midst of dangerous surgery.

Goffman's interest in what sustains situated activities is pursued in the context of "social establishments," that is, any "place" surrounded by barriers to perception in which some particular kind of activity regularly occurs (Goffman, 1959). Performances in social establishments involve presentations of self through expressions given (signs deliberately chosen to provide information) or given off (signs assumed to exist for reasons other than the ostensible information provided). Goffman assumes that presentation of self is an impression management technique; his question becomes: What permits an actor to carry off a performance? He finds his answers in contextual analyses of performances and performance settings. In general, however, sustained performances require cooperative activities of teams of performers and the cooperation of audiences in tacit agreements about who and what is involved in the performances. These tacit agreements, in turn, are supported by separation of back stage, where performances are prepared and characters released from parts they play, and front stage. When audiences intrude unexpectedly, they may witness behaviors contradicting the definitions cooperative performer-audience interactions are intended to maintain, and a performance may be discredited in the absence of repair work healing the breech. Performances, involving projections of definitions of the situation, involve presentations of self. If a presented self is discredited in interaction, possibilities for personal and social disorganization are rife. All interaction risks disruption: "Life may not be much of a gamble, but interaction is" (Goffman, 1959, p. 243).

Goffman's work is the pre-eminent example of a dramaturgical approach. Like the best theater, his writings give insight into the ironies and pathos of human existence; they are, in our opinion, the matter of art and not of science. With distinctions and illustrations drawn from observation, participation, novels, and newspapers, they catalog possibilities in situated activity systems and label these; they have not yet lead to systematic research or cumulative theory. Whatever the possibilities in these terms, the utility of Goffman's conceptual vision for the full range of social psychological tasks is limited; its attention is focused exclusively on situated activity itself, and it does not link that activity to the organized structure of the larger society.

This same limitation holds for the negotiation framework, Maines's (1977) primary referent in arguing that symbolic interactionism deals reasonably with social structure. The negotiation framework grows largely out of studies of interaction in hospital settings (Strauss *et al*, 1963; Glaser and Strauss, 1971) and is anchored in grounded theory methodology (Glaser and Strauss, 1967). Its most developed statement is by Strauss (1978).

From Strauss's point of view, all social orders are "negotiated orders." He assumes that all social structures are continuously constructed and that negotiation is central to any construction process. Negotiation, occurring when parties need to deal with one another to get things done, is perhaps best described by the key questions the framework raises: Who spoke to whom in what ways, in what sequences, and with what responses and results? What negotiation process occurred? What alternatives and options were considered? Attention is thus focused on ongoing interaction, the actors involved, the tactics and strategies used, subprocesses of negotiation (e.g., trading off), and consequences. The last are emergent, temporary, organized patterns of interaction, new or reconstituted orders that become context for continuing negotiations.

Negotiations occur in contexts, linking ongoing interaction to social structure. Two kinds of context are distinguished: structural and negotiation. Structural context refers to the general parameters within which negotiation occurs, illustrated by the division of labor in a hospital and the specializations in the health-care professions that are the context for negotiations observed in psychiatric wings of hospitals or by the market place and features of the judiciary system that are the context for covert negotiations of corrupt judges. Strauss gives greater attention, however, to negotiation contexts, illustrated by the number and skills of negotiators, whether negotiations are open to outsiders, whether negotiations are repetitive, the complexity and clarity of issues, and the relative power and resources of the negotiators.

Thus, attention is predominantly given to the microstructure of interaction, leaving relatively undeveloped and so unsatisfactory links to the larger social structures within which negotiations take place. The methodological stance typical of this work, which directs the researcher to eschew *a priori* conceptualization and theorizing and to ground concepts and theory in interactions being observed, tends also to impede empirical generalization and general theory by emphasizing the particularities of given cases.

Situated identity theory, formulated largely by C. Norman Alexander and various collaborators, draws inspiration from Goffman but develops differently. This theory proposes that the defining properties of social acts are situated identities, attributions made from salient perspectives about an actor's presence and performance in an immediate social context (Alexander and Wiley, 1981). As the reference to attributions suggests, Alexander argues that dispositional imputations provide stability, coherence, and predictability to interpersonal environments. The theory is concerned with situated activity: conduct in symbolically defined space and time within which actors presume that events are or might be monitored by others. Situated activity is conceived as a continuous process of affirming, modifying, and sometimes destroying situated identities.

The theory is to date limited for strategic reasons to normatively structured situated activities, that is, to situations in which the persons involved agree on relevant attributional dimensions and how the activity is to be characterized along each dimension. Inquiry focuses on expectations about decisions actors make, the expectations deriving from dispositional imputations others make from alternative possible choices. The attributional dimensions involved in these imputations are, in general, evaluative; thus the perception of an action is also an evaluation of that action. Normative expectations, other things being equal, should be a function of the social desirability of alternatives. The theory predicts that observers expect persons to choose from among a set of alternatives the most socially desirable option.

The prediction that behavior reflects situated identities has been examined in studies simulating or replicating classic social psychological experiments on forced compliance (Alexander and Knight, 1971), expectations states (Alexander and Lauderdale, 1977), choice behavior in Prisoner's Dilemma games (Alexander and Weil, 1969), the initiation severity-attraction (Alexander and Sagatun, 1973) and the similarity-attraction relationships (Touhey, 1974). The studies essentially reproduce initial results and find that these results can be explained relatively parsimoniously and precisely in situated identity terms. Some of these studies (e.g., Alexander and Sagatun, 1973) convert experimenter demand to a theoretical variable by manipulating the situated identity of the experimenter, thus providing a possible way out of the bind much current social psychological experimentation finds itself in.

However, situated identity theory, too, is limited as a general perspective for social psychology. It is (perhaps) temporarily limited by the tactical decision to avoid situations involving multiple and divergent normative judgments. Assuming that restriction is removed, its limitation is that of the situated interaction frame on which it draws: It does not provide for linking situated activity to the organized structure of the larger society.

To say that the dramaturgical, negotiations or situated identity frameworks do not adequately link person and larger social structure only finds them wanting by a specific criterion. Each offers its own insights into social behavior. Each, therefore, must find some place in a maximally useful, more general framework.

SYMBOLIC INTERACTIONISM AS INFORMED BY ROLE THEORY

Symbolic interactionism is a framework for the analysis of social interaction and the social person; it uses the concept of role to build "down" to the social person. Role theory is a framework for the analysis of social structure; it uses the concept of role to build "up" from interaction to larger units of organized social life. The point of articulation of the two frameworks is role; that concept serves to bridge social structure and social person, the essential task of a social psychology. The relation between the two frameworks has been long recognized; however, only comparatively recently have explicit attempts been made to work out the logic of this relationship and thus to exploit it thoroughly in developing social psychological theory.

Stryker (1980, pp. 53–55) has developed a generalized statement of symbolic interactionism reflecting importations from role theory that opens up possibilities for theorizing about the reciprocity of persons and society. The statement begins arbitrarily with the impact of the latter on the former. It asserts that:

1. Behavior depends on a named, classified physical and social environment. Names or class terms carry meaning in the form of shared behavioral expectations emergent through interaction. Through interaction with others, one learns to classify objects relevant to the interaction and in that process learns how to behave with respect to those objects.
2. Among the class terms learned through interaction are the symbols used to refer to positions, the relatively stable, morphological components of social structure. Shared behavioral expectations, or roles, attach to these positions.
3. Persons acting in the context of a social structure in part made up of positions and roles name one another in the sense of recognizing one another as occupants of positions. Doing so, they invoke expectations with regard to one another's behavior.
4. Persons acting in such contexts name themselves, in the same sense, as well. The reflexively applied positional designations become part of the self and create internal expectations with regard to the persons' own behavior.

5. Entering interactive situations, persons define the situation by applying class terms to it, themselves, other participants, and features of the situation relevant to the interaction. They use the resultant definitions to organize their own behavior in the situation.

6. Since interaction involves multiple persons defining situations and since early definitions may constrain emergent definitions, social behavior is not given by these definitions. Behavior is the outcome of role-making processes, initiated by expectations invoked by early definitions of the situation but developing through a tentative, sometimes subtle, probing interchange among interactants that can reshape the form and content of the interaction.

7. The larger social structures in which interactive situations are embedded will affect the degree to which roles are made rather than simply played as well as affecting the elements entering the roles constructed. Structures are variably open with respect to novelty in roles and role performances. All social structures impose limits on the kinds of definitions called into play and consequently on the possibilities for interaction.

8. Changes in definitions, in class terms used in definitions, and in possibilities for interaction can occur to the degree that roles are made rather than simply played. Such changes can in turn lead to changes in the larger social structures within which interaction takes place.

This framework leaves more room for the routine, habitual, and customary elements in social life than most versions of symbolic interactionism. It also gives greater importance to social structure in shaping selves and interaction, permitting the elaboration of structural concepts reflecting the complexities of the social worlds in which persons live. Whatever their potential for novelty, most interactions involve the same or slowly changing sets of others doing the same things repeatedly. Structural concepts like group, organization, and community, refer to patterns of social life that tie subsets of particular persons together and separate these persons from others. Structural concepts like age structure, power structure, class structure, and society refer to more abstract social boundaries that nevertheless bring some persons together and separate others. The generic concept of social structure implies that societies are differentiated entities, and consequently that only certain persons interact in certain ways with certain resources in certain settings. Persons do not come together randomly. Nor are the opportunities for, and the circumstances of, social relationships randomly distributed. The person is shaped by interaction, but social structures shape interaction.

Identity theory (Stryker, 1968; 1980) develops from this framework. The reciprocity of self and society is a root idea of symbolic interactionism. Introducing role theory into symbolic interactionism recognizes the complexities of contemporary society by imaging society as a multifaceted mosaic of interdependent but highly differentiated parts. If self reflects society and if society is highly differentiated, so must be the self. On purely theoretical grounds, then, a conception of society as complexly organized requires a parallel conception of the self. Empirically, there are issues of behavioral choices, of consistency and inconsistency across situations, and of persons' greater or lesser resistance to changes in the face of changing circumstances, that call for explication.

Identity theory introduces the concepts of identity (or role-identity; see Burke and Tulley, 1977; McCall and Simmons, 1978), identity salience, and commitment to meet these needs. Identities are internalized positional designations existing insofar as persons participate in structured role relationships, the consequence of being placed as a social object and appropriating the terms of placement for themselves (Stone, 1962). Persons have as many identities as they have different sets of structured relationships with others. Identities are conceived as organized in a salience hierarchy defined by the probability of various identities coming into play in a given situation or across situations; identity salience is the location of an identity in that hierarchy. Implied is the general proposition that the salience of an identity will affect its threshold of invocation, interacting with other defining characteristics of situations and other self-characteristics. Social clocks, calendars, and rosters can isolate situations structurally so that only a single identity is appropriate; conversely, they can guarantee that multiple identities are implicated. Identity salience becomes hypothetically important if multiple identities enter a situation.

Identity and identity salience are concepts intended to make more precise the concept of self. The concept of commitment, defined as the degree to which the individual's relationships to particular others depends on his or her being a given kind of person, is used to give greater precision to "society." One is committed to a social role to the degree that extensive and intensive social relationships are built upon that role. Conceived in this way, commitment affords a way of conceiving "society's" relevance for interaction, pointing to social networks: the number and importance of others to whom the person relates through a role, the multiplexity of linkages among those others, and so on. The most general theoretical proposition of identity theory, a specification of symbolic interactionism's basic formula, is that commitment affects identity salience which in turn affects behavioral choices. This general proposition in turn leads to a set of testable hypotheses (Stryker, 1980; 1981), which taken together approximate a theory in a technical sense. A number of these hypotheses are currently being tested with generally favorable results (Serpe, 1980; Hoelter, 1980; Stryker and Serpe, 1982; Hoelter, 1983).

Identity theory has a close counterpart in the role-identity model (McCall and Simmons, 1978). The central concept of that model, role-identity, emphasizes the intimate relation of social roles and the self; the framework from which the model evolves is a version of symbolic interactionism tempered by exchange theoretic ideas, and it is applied to the problem of why people spend their interactional resources as they do. The framework begins with Kuhn but moves to a more complex, differentiated vision of the self that is less tied to organizational roles and incorporates more of Mead's "I". The framework also contains a more fluid phenomenological as well as constructed sense of social structure and a corresponding emphasis on the unique and idiosyncratic in human behavior.

The core image underlying the role-identity model is of the human being as a planning animal. The imagery is also dramaturgical: the construction of social conduct involves roles and characters, props and supporting casts, and scenes and audiences. One's character is part of the self, a view of oneself as a person with a distinctive organization of statuses, motives, habits, traits and mannerisms. The self has a phenomenal aspect (the self as character performed), an active aspect (the self as performer), and a reactive aspect (the self as audience).

Persons plan to be particular kinds of people, the kinds deriving from systems of roles, statuses, social types, or social categories whose meanings are hammered out in social interaction. Persons appraise their intentions and monitor performances evidencing intentions through role-taking, anticipating the reactions of others to plans and performances. They identify others in terms of social positions, thus enabling a preliminary specification of the relevance of those others to plans of action and an assessment on which modifications of performances can be based. Role performance is improvised to

take into account the demands of a position and also to reflect one's character and self conceptions; positional demands are modified to blend with the latter.

Thus the model asserts the primacy of role-identities, the character and role persons devise as occupants of particular social positions. Role-identities are typically idealized self-conceptions. They are a primary source of plans; they provide criteria for appraising performances; they provide meaning by largely determining definitions of situations, events, and others encountered; they are important determinants of the objects of one's world. Social roles (conventional expectations) provide the structural framework for role-identities, each of which has a conventional and an idiosyncratic aspect. As idealized and partially idiosyncratic conceptions of self, role-identities often conflict with the realities of life. In this circumstance, people have the problem of legitimating their role-identities, of devising perspectives that enable them to maintain their views of self. They meet this problem through role performances as a consequence of which they can receive from both others and themselves necessary support for their idealized conceptions of self. They seek out others for whom and situations in which they can perform their roles, however imperfectly, thus earning support, however partial.

Complicating the picture are multiple role-identities mutually influencing one another. Role-identities are organized into a hierarchy of prominence, or relative importance. Their location in the hierarchy is a function of support received from others, how closely performances accord with them, and the degree to which self-esteem, resources, and gratifications depend on them. Performances depend in part on prominence; they also depend in part on a situationally specific hierarchical ordering McCall and Simmons (1978) term "salience," or the situational self. Salience is influenced by prominence and by the degree a role-identity needs support, that is, the kinds and amounts of gratifications available through performances in keeping with a role identity. The character and role persons try to express in any concrete performance will in part reflect the salience structure of the self and in part the audience. Behavior is a joint construction of performer and audience.

If conceptions of self like those reviewed are to result in research designed to test rather than simply to elaborate theoretically derived hypotheses, measurement procedures that tap the concept as theoretically understood are required. Schwartz and Stryker (1971) suggest that the semantic differential technique provides a measurement procedure consonant with symbolic interactionism's conception of meaning. Burke (1980) extends and refines this suggestion. The theoretical properties of the role-identity concept are that identities are meanings attributed to the person and by the person to the self as an object in a social situation or a social role, that identities are relational, that they are reflexive, that they operate indirectly, and that they are a source of motivation. The first property requires that a measure capture the multiple dimensions of meaning comprising the self. Burke conceptualizes the dimensions of meaning as a multidimensional space and uses discriminant analysis to map persons' responses to that space and to locate their role-identities in that space (Burke and Tully, 1977; Mutran and Burke, 1979a; Mutran and Burke, 1979b; Reitzes and Burke, 1980). The relational property of identities implies that they be measured relative to counteridentities; Burke meets this requirement by measuring identities in terms of commonalities among similarly situated persons and in terms of differences from persons in counterpositions.

Procedures for meeting the remaining requirements for a theoretically justified measure of identities are at this point more programmatic than realized. The reflexive property of the self implies the reciprocity of self and performance; that is, that although identities structure performances, performances are assessed for their identity implications. A control process (Powers, 1973; Heise, 1979) is thus implied. Burke proposes that we measure the strength of corrective responses when the meaning of a performance differs from the meaning of an initial identity and that we assess just what it is that is corrected to deal with this property.

Identities, Burke asserts, are relatively stable and insufficiently flexible to meet situational contingencies, operating only indirectly to structure performances. Operating directly are images, current working copies of identities, which have flexibility and can accommodate role-making as well as role-playing, and role construction as well as role enactment. Implied is a measurement procedure that includes both identity and image and that can deal with the dynamics of the relationships between the two.

Burke deals with the motivational property of identities by refining the idea that identities motivate through defining behavior and the action implications of meanings. Identities close to one another in meaning ought to be close to one in semantic space and ought to have similar action implications. Furthermore, since acts have meanings, acts in the same semantic locations as identities ought to be the action implications of those identities and ought to carry implications for those identities. A measurement procedure is implied that measures both identities and actions in common terms by locating these in the same semantic space (Burke and Reitzes, 1981).

Ralph Turner also seeks to integrate role theoretic elements and symbolic interactionism. He starts with a critique of role theory (Turner, 1962; n.d.c.) as overly structured and conformist, offers a corrective through the concept of role-taking, and then joins a modified conception of role and the concept of self to handle both stable, structured forms of social organization and less structured, more fluid forms.

The central contentions of the theory are that humans act as if others they meet are playing identifiable roles and they role-take in order to identify these roles. Since cultural cues to roles are often vague and contradictory, providing only a general outline within which lines of action can be constructed, actors make their roles and communicate to others what roles they are playing (Turner, n.d.a.; n.d.b.). Actors behave as though they and others are in particular roles as long as the assumption works to provide a stable, effective framework for interaction. They continually assess one another's behavior to check whether that behavior validates the occupancy of a position by corresponding to role expectations and by demonstrating consistency. Seeking to infer the roles of others, we inform others through gestures of our own roles and self conceptions, and we seek to inform them as to whether the roles being played are consistent with and invested with self (Turner, 1978).

There are two general explanatory principles in Turner's developing theory: (1) roles are used to achieve ends efficiently, and (2) the playing of roles is a means of achieving personal reward in the forms of validation of self, self-esteem, and reinforcement from others. These general principles are used to "account for" lower level principles that summarize and reflect variation in observed empirical regularities and that serve as the basis for new propositions subject to empirical verification.

An example of the theory-building strategy Turner advocates is illustrated in his (1978) discussion of role-person merger, that is, the degree to which roles are invested with self (the obverse of role-distance). Conceptualizing persons as a hierarchical ordering of all roles in their repertoire, he suggests that role and person are merged to the degree persons play roles in situations where the roles do not apply, when they resist abandoning a role in the face of advantageous alternatives, and when they acquire attitudes and behaviors appropriate to the roles. He notes that a conception of person in these terms serves a social control function, since effective control requires a more stable object than an actor who only plays a particular role.

Thus, role-person merger has an interactive function. Turner develops from this observation three interactive principles. The appearance principle asserts that people tend to accept others as they appear; the effect principle states that the disposition to see people in terms of their role behavior will vary with the potential effect of the role on interaction; the consistency principle suggests that people will accept the least complicated view of the person that facilitates interaction. Then, empirically testable propositions are derived from these principles: the greater the potential power invested in a role, the greater the tendency to see the person as revealed by the role; the more inflexible the allocation of actors to roles, the greater the tendency to see the person as revealed by the role.

Role-person merger also has individual functions: facilitating understanding, predicting, and controlling others by being more comprehensible and predictable to them; facilitating economy of effort when playing multiple roles; facilitating control and autonomy; and making possible playing of roles providing gratification. These functions underly guiding principles: A consensual frame of reference principle asserts that persons merge their persons into roles by which significant others identify them; an autonomy and favorable evaluation principle suggests that selective merger occurs to maximize autonomy and self-evaluation; an investment principle states that individuals will merge into their persons those roles in which greatest investment has been made or for which return on investment made is still to come.

The concept of role-person merger develops the link between self and social structure. So does Turner's (1976) concept of the "real self": the subjectively held sense people have of who and what they really are. People can locate their real selves in institutions; they can anchor their real selves in impulse. Institutionals recognize their real selves in acceptance of group obligations, and impulsives recognize their real selves through their noncomformity to institutional norms. Turner speculates that the last several decades in American society have seen a major shift from institution to impulse in the locus of self and that this shift has serious implications both for the empirical nature of social control and of societal order and for sociological theories of these phenomena.

Whatever the fate of the substantive theory developed in Turner's work, the theory illustrates the incorporation of social structure into social psychological theorizing. Turner utilizes the concepts of positions and role expectations, albeit cautiously. He views larger social structures as constraints on self and interaction and as products of self and interaction. That larger structure organizes social relationships, bringing some persons together and keeping others apart. A major factor in the functioning and change of societies is the articulation of self and social structure.

Weinstein and Tanur (1976) develop a complementary vision of the relation of person and social structure. They suggest that it is social structure, the aggregated outcome of many earlier episodes of interaction taking the form of shared meanings, codified rules, and material resources, that becomes the framework for interactions and links episodes of interaction. They argue that although the degree to which interactions exhibit "role-ness" is problematic and variable, norms and roles are part of the meanings available to persons in interaction and used as resources in that interaction. The extent, conditions, and means by which social structure enters interaction become subject to investigation rather than being assumed or ignored.

ROLE THEORY AS INFORMED BY SYMBOLIC INTERACTIONISM

The major contribution an interactionist perspective makes to role theory is the recognition that persons can have considerable latitude in constructing role portrayals. For interactionist role theorists, a major problem is not how persons fit their behavior to fixed sets of cultural expectations but how persons manage to interact with others in ways that are both meaningful and satisfying. Because the person is seen as capable of creating ongoing interaction, role-bargaining processes through which persons engaged in interaction work out suitable role arrangements come into focus. These processes are considered primarily as they occur during socialization and in the resolution of role conflicts. On the individual level, constructed role portrayals are seen as sources of personal satisfaction, and role bargaining is deemed basic to processes by which new roles emerge and social change occurs.

Satisfaction in Roles

Role relationships provide anchors for self-concepts, thus affecting feelings of general satisfaction with life. Since they also provide access to societal rewards, their impact on life satisfaction increases. It follows from such premises that persons with larger role repertoires are better prepared to meet life's exigencies (Sarbin and Allen, 1968) and thus are more satisfied with life in general (Orden and Bradburn, 1969; Spreitzer *et al.,* 1979). It also follows that persons playing roles restricting access to societal rewards, such as the housewife role (Macke *et al.,* 1979; also see Dohrenwend and Dohrenwend, 1976; Glenn and Weaver, 1978; Mechanic, 1980; Verbrugge, 1980), have lower self esteem.

The fact that roles provide anchors for self-definition and so life satisfaction becomes apparent when one considers those leaving or entering roles or those who temporarily have no roles. Work on aging perhaps demonstrates this observation most dramatically: Blau (1973) notes that loss of job and family roles severs connections with the most significant institutions of society, echoing Cavan's (1962) argument that in American society old age is more or less a role vacuum. Early theoretical approaches to role exits linked to aging posited a positive process of disengagement (Cumming and Henry, 1961); more recent work evidences the personal pain in these role losses. This literature on aging confirms the interactionist arguments that role occupancy is critical for self-definition and hence for positive feelings toward self and life in general and that interaction and social support are critical to satisfying role portrayals. Those who can create or turn to alternative role relationships, grandparenting for example, exhibit more life satisfaction (Neugarten and Weinstein, 1964; Robertson, 1977). The creation of strong peer networks reduces the negative impact of role loss (Petrowsky, 1976; Wood and Robertson, 1978), as does finding a close confidant (Lowenthal and Haven, 1968).

Satisfaction with interpersonal relationships in general depends on the extent to which interaction is consistent with existing dispositions (Ickes *et al.,* 1979). Persons' satisfaction in particular role relationships reflects, in part the extent to which personal preferences, value orientations, and self-images are integrated into these relationships. Job satisfaction depends to a large extent on the job rewards valued by persons (Kalleberg, 1975; Kalleberg and Loscocco, 1983), and satisfaction with the grandparent role depends on what components of the role are valued. Persons whose selves are only casually involved in a role differ in their performances from those whose involvement is extreme (Sarbin, 1954), and their performances have different consequences for satisfaction, as Goffman's (1961) discussion of role distance suggests. And variations in commitment to roles, conceptualized as the assessment of tradeoffs in costs and rewards (Schoenherr and Greeley, 1974) or in terms of side bets (Becker, 1960), affect the impact of role portrayals on satisfaction.

Early work by Mowrer (1935) on marital discord, Cottrell (1942) on age and sex roles, Hughes (1945) on inconsistent statuses, Cavan (1962) on aging, and Cressey (1962) and Deutscher (1962) on crime and delinquency recognizes that existing self-conceptions affect role performances; implied in this work is that persons are more satisfied in role relationships that accord with self-conceptions. Similarly, work on role conflict suggests that personality dispositions (Stouffer and Toby, 1951) and individual value orientations (Gross *et al.,* 1957) affect choice of resolution strategies. The implications here are that persons have some freedom in devising role portrayals to bring them into line with personal preferences and that achieving such consistency increases satisfaction in role relationships (Araji, 1977; Robertson, 1977).

The general principle is clear: the more persons have their preferences and needs met in role relationships, the more satisfied they are in those relationships. Another principle is also clear: the more others share a person's values, orientations, and preferences, the more readily role arrangements can be devised that meet the preferences and needs of those involved. From an interactionist perspective, the bargains struck with role partners constrain the extent to which role relationships satisfy. If role partners can agree on preferred role arrangements, their satisfaction is likely to be high. Given this supposition, role theorists influenced by interactionism emphasize role consensus in their treatment of roles.

In recognizing the role-bargaining process, researchers using a role theory approach have now become interested in the process whereby consensus is achieved between partners. Work on formal organizational roles is a case in point; it has been found, for example, that organizational distance and authority levels decrease the likelihood that role partners will achieve consensus (Alpender, 1975). Work on marital roles has also provided a great deal of information about how consensus is achieved between role partners and how it impacts personal satisfaction. Researchers have used a basic interactionist principle, namely, that consensus is not automatic but achieved. From this, they have postulated specific types of agreements that are important to satisfaction: fit between role partners with respect to norms for role performances, fit between their personality systems, and fit between role performance and personality systems and sustained ongoing interaction (Rapoport and Rosow, 1957). Interaction patterns can build an emotional climate that undermines satisfaction despite consensus on normative patterns and fit of personality systems.

Achieving fit between marital partners has a strong impact on marital satisfaction (Luckey, 1960; Komarovsky, 1967). If, for instance, the partners cannot achieve consensus concerning the amount of work involvement appropriate to both the husband and wife roles, marital disruption may result (Lewis and Spanier, 1979; Houseknecht and Macke, 1980). An alternative possibility is that one or both partners may change their occupational involvement (Jones and Butler, 1980). Again, this literature implies that role consensus is not automatic but must actually be achieved in individual role relationships.

Because of the impact of these and other interactionist principles, current research on marital roles argues that persons have flexibility in devising role arrangements acceptable to the role partners, even if these arrangements flagrantly violate standard cultural expectations. It was formerly assumed that marital roles rigidly prescribed that a husband must be more successful in the labor market than his wife, if the wife worked outside the home (Parsons and Bales, 1960). This assumption rests on the proposition, accepted by the vast majority of Americans (Mason *et al.,* 1976), that husbands ought to be the major family breadwinner. Now, however, many researchers assert that couples are capable of modifying these expectations so that the wife will have greater flexibility in seeking success in the labor market while still keeping the marriage intact. (See, for instance, Oppenheimer, 1977, and Richardson, 1979). Recent work on marital adjustment supports this argument; in general, it suggests that congruence between behavior and personal preference is much more important for marital satisfaction than conformity to pre-existing (traditional) role definitions.

Role Conflict and Its Resolution

Interactionist precepts have considerably broadened the structural approach to role conflict. Structural theorists traditionally conceived the individual as having little control over the content of role expectations to which he or she is pressured to adhere; consequently, these theorists tended to see role conflict as seriously undermining satisfaction with roles. Now, their perception has been broadened by the awareness that conflict may be reduced by bargaining strategies, an awareness that has generated a new area of role-conflict research. Much of this work has considered the power of self-definitions in using these bargaining strategies or in conditioning the actual experience of conflict. The literature on women's work and family role conflict, for instance, has explored the extent to which self-definitions guide the woman in fashioning suitable solutions to her own personal dilemma. Whether they play traditional or nontraditional roles, women are happiest when they are doing what they want to do rather than what they feel constrained to do (Orden and Bradburn, 1969; Hall and Gordon, 1973). Personal preferences can apparently condition the woman's entire experience of role conflict.

Self-definition is also a factor in men's resolution of similar conflicts. For instance, many men experience conflict in their family roles when the family's economic needs peak before their careers are in full swing, a structural discrepancy most men are unable to avoid if they marry when they are in their early twenties (Oppenheimer, 1977). Many men deal with this conflict by focusing on the role most likely to provide satisfaction, in this case, the family role. Deriving satisfaction from family roles when children are young and most demanding and when careers are still unstable (Harry, 1976), they may change their focus to career and obtain their satisfaction from it later when careers are more stable and family demands have declined.

Women have been found to use a similar strategy; if blocked in their occupational worlds, they may heighten the value placed on the family roles, thus increasing the probability of achieving satisfaction in what is taken to be a more important role (Peterson-Hardt and Burlin, 1979). A role theory informed by the interactionist's idea that self-definitions guide behavior helps to account for the individual's ability to handle effectively a situation that seems on the surface to be filled with frustration and structurally imposed conflict.

This research has also asked what individuals do when they are not able to define conflict away but experience it as a personal negative force. In these cases, it appears that a great deal of role bargaining occurs. For instance, working women frequently attempt to renegotiate family roles, especially with their husbands (Harrison and Minor, 1978). Their efforts may involve redesigning roles so that they can be performed together, eliminating some activities from roles, solving problems with others implicated in a role, or simply receiving support from role partners. Husbands' support and cooperation in redesigning family roles, in particular, are the single most important facilitators in reducing this conflict (Weill, 1961; Holahan and Gilbert, 1979). Role partners clearly can modify the structural sources of the conflict, often eliminating the conflict altogether. Some strategy to resolve conflict appears better than none; women who try to meet all expectations experience the greatest stress (Hall, D. T., 1972; Harrison and Minor, 1978). Some important general principles of the conflict resolution process, each reflecting the impact of symbolic interactionism on structural role theory, can be cited from the literature reviewed here: Persons differ in the extent they experience role conflict, and the personal experience of conflict determines whether reduction strategies are evoked; role bargaining, especially with intimates, is a preferred mode of resolving conflict; and persons can define what is important to them to achieve satisfaction in role relationships and can devalue what is unattainable.

Recent work on organizational role conflict argues that persons can avoid stressful aspects of role conflict by turning conflicts into positive experiences. Reconceptualizing role conflict as interactional overload and expanding Merton's (1957) account of difficulties developing from varying expectations from multiple others in role-sets, Snoek (1966) focuses on the confusion presumably inherent in dealing with role diversity resulting from interaction with large numbers of role partners. Snoek also notes, however, that the tension resulting from interactional overload can be resolved through bargaining. The implication that persons have some control over their situations is reinforced by findings that participating in diverse roles (Cummings and El Salmi, 1970), even troubled interaction (Miles, 1977), does not necessarily result in strain. The theoretical formulation incorporating this possibility reflects interactionism's insistence that persons playing roles do not simply comply to structural dictates but in part create their roles; thus they can derive positive experiences from what on the surface and from a structural perspective is a hopelessly negative situation.

Extending the idea that role diversity can increase satisfaction, Sieber (1974) invokes the concept of role accumulation, noting that expanded role privileges, status security, enhanced resources for status advancement and role performances, and enrichment of personality and ego gratification are all possibilities that inhere

in persons' playing multiple roles (see Thoits, 1983). Marks (1977) broadens this perspective in a theoretical approach encompassing both positive and negative outcomes of role diversity. His concern is with why some people have overload problems given multiple roles, while others do not. Noting that most theories of multiple roles assume scarce energy for social interaction, making involvement in many roles stressful, he argues that social energy can be boundless and that multiple-role involvement can create energy through increased stimulation; consequently, persons generally have sufficient energy for all role relationships to which they feel committed. For Marks, commitment, not energy, is the limiting variable in multiple-role involvement. Persons decide to devote more time and energy to certain relationships, less to others. The problem becomes pacifying those receiving less commitment, a source of stress associated with role diversity.

Marks emphasizes that both commitment and energy levels are socially constructed. Persons decide how much of each to devote to relationships on the basis of their preferences and role negotiations. Since their definitions of the situation vary, their psychological reaction to the same or similar sets of role relationships will vary; for one person, a given combination of roles will be stressful, for another invigorating. Reactions to multiple roles reflect definitions of the situation affecting commitment, not inherent limits on time and energy; reference to scarce time and energy serves to rationalize but does not explain lowered commitment. Marks's formulation represents perhaps the most thorough incorporation of individual propensities and interactional contingencies into role theory available to date. Although it lacks theoretical specification that can account for variations in energy expenditure and commitment levels, beginnings that might profitably be pursued are suggested.

Socialization

Structural role theory has adopted a variety of interactionist precepts with regard to socialization. Although interactionists treat childhood socialization, focusing on the interaction between children and socializing agents (Corsaro, 1977; 1979a), they concentrate on adult socialization, examining the negotiations that occur as adults acquire new roles or alter ongoing role relationships. They make two major points: Socialization is basically a role-bargaining process, and life is a continuous process of socialization. Again, much of the relevant work has been done on family roles, both those of husband and wife and parent and child.

That spouses socialize one another into marital roles has long been recognized. Many wives report their husbands "taught them all they know" about sex (Rainwater, 1964; Komarovsky, 1967); spouses influence one another's role portrayals (Hill and Aldous, 1969; Komarovsky, 1967); spouses' personality characteristics become more compatible over time (Vincent, 1965); and their family attitudes converge rapidly after marriage (Cronkite, 1977). Thus, each spouse serves as a strong socializing agent for the other (Cronkite, 1977). Berger and Kellner (1964) assert that married couples have the freedom to construct fully their private lives, infusing all their interactions and habits (and not only marital role portrayals) with personal meanings and slowly coming to agree with one another on what those meanings will be.

However, role bargaining involves persons beyond the immediate role partners. With respect to marital roles, friends influence both parties, often seeking to impose one spouse's view on the other (Bott, 1957; Komarovsky, 1967; Liebow, 1967; LeMasters, 1975). Friends' influence attempts can be strong, involving ridicule or sarcasm when the person fails to conform to expectations.

Work on childhood socialization (O'Toole and Dubin, 1968; Goslin, 1969; Rheingold, 1969; Zigler and Harter, 1969), viewing socialization as a role-bargaining process, finds that children shape parents' behavior to a degree that is surprising if one takes the structural perspective that socialization is fundamentally the imposition of culture on the person. Parents take cues from children in devising their own role strategies, and children have some veto power over their parents' behavior towards them. Too, parents' self and role conceptions are modified through interaction with children; for example, fathers' femininity scores vary by the sex of their children (Rosenberg, 1966; Sarbin and Allen, 1968). That children can socialize parents is especially evident in Weinstein's (1969) account of interpersonal competence, which characterizes childhood socialization as a child's learning to control others. From an interactionist perspective, all role partners can bargain over role definitions, and all role portrayals involve team efforts with participants fitting their behaviors to those of significant role partners (Elkin, 1958). This view impacts much of the current work on socialization.

Role theory informed by interactionism stresses that socialization occurs throughout the life cycle, a dramati-

cally new view of both socialization process and adulthood. Recent theorists (Lowenthal, *et al.,* 1975; Neugarten, 1979) argue that adults grow continuously, passing through development stages akin but not analogous to those of childhood. As Brim (1966) notes, this view is in keeping with the realities of modern society, which require constant adaptation to changing technology and social arrangements. Adult socialization differs from childhood socialization by its focus on teaching role-specific skills rather than general values or motives, on behavior synthesizing old materials rather than new, on transforming idealistic sentiments into realistic applications, and on resolving conflicts (Brim, 1966).

Although adults deal with such demands throughout their lives, specific issues may be more important at certain stages (Neugarten, 1979): for example, the issues facing retirees are not those facing young adults with small children (Parnes *et al.,* 1970; Lowenthal *et al.,* 1975; Neugarten, 1979). Especially in recent times, however, such life cycle stages are not as age-graded as are childhood developmental stages. Retirement, empty nest, and grandparenthood are entered by persons of varying age (Neugarten, 1979); there is, in brief, fluidity in the adult life cycle, a fluidity implying that persons may have fewer role definitions guiding transitions. As Turner (1962) notes, role creation and self-direction may become increasingly important skills as structural supports become less stable.

Role Emergence

Interactionism does more than argue the flexibility of persons in constructing unique role bargains within the broad confines of structural constraints; perhaps more importantly, this perspective argues that persons can affect those constraints directly. A basic premise of symbolic interactionism asserts the reciprocity of interaction, and emergent structural properties guide interaction. Alternative role bargains struck often and consistently can become part of more general social structure.

Recent work suggests how such change occurs. The concept of "aligning actions" (Stokes and Hewitt, 1976; Hewitt and Stokes, 1975) describes two continuous social processes: attempts by persons to align their actions with one another, and attempts by them to establish correspondence between their own behavior and cultural ideals and expectations. Alignment between persons is achieved through the testing, probing, negotiating process previously described, a process that can be complex in even "simple" interactions such as opening encounters (Schiffrin, 1977).

More significant to structural change, however, is the second type of aligning behavior for it facilitates widespread acceptance of newly negotiated role arrangements. Stokes and Hewitt observe that role innovations are often met with uneasiness because they conflict with cultural ideals. When discrepancies occur between behavior and cultural ideals or expectations, strategies like disclaimers, accounts, and quasi-theories are used to ease felt strain. With tension eased, interaction can proceed because ideals have been acknowledged, thus implying some attempt to conform (Stokes and Hewitt, 1976). These aligning strategies may facilitate change by permitting deviance from cultural expectations to occur over time without accompanying strain; they provide time for new role arrangements to stabilize through the interpersonal aligning process and to become accepted cultural standards. Without strategies for relaxing while still acknowledging standards, change would be rare, since sufficient numbers of persons would be unlikely to deviate significantly from cultural ideals.

Research on family and sex roles illustrates this process. Rationalization and denial occur in the face of widespread deviance from tradition. Even as women move into the occupational world, they deny their success (Horner, 1969; Kando, 1972), hide characteristics that facilitate such success (Rosen and Aneshensel, 1976) and fear resentment or other reprisals in response to such success (Parelius, 1975; Meeker and Weitzel-O'Neill, 1977). Young men cling to aspects of traditional roles even as they anticipate life styles that are in some respects nontraditional (Komarovsky, 1976). Thus, change is gradual and frequently denied, and traditional beliefs are retained and given credence as change occurs.

Change in the family roles of provider and housekeeper seem to be following the same model (Ross *et al.*, 1983). As married women increasingly work, provider and housekeeping roles come to be defined as properly shared rather than as uniquely either those of the husband or wife. At the same time, however, husbands who fail to meet provider responsibilities fully are severely sanctioned, although working wives are not (Nye, 1976; Slocum and Nye, 1976). This suggests that wives are not "truly" responsible and that older norms may continue to be held while role behavior undergoes change. Similarly with respect to the housekeeper role, spouses agree the role should be shared and more sharing occurs than prescribed by traditional role definitions, yet major re-

sponsibility belongs to the wife and the husband is viewed as "just helping."

Women adopt nontraditional family roles at a faster rate than do men (Parelius, 1975; Komarovsky, 1976; Araji, 1977; Albrecht *et al.,* 1979). Not identifying strongly with their traditional family role as housekeeper, they are more willing to modify it. Men's greater commitment to, and identification with, the provider role, on the other hand, indicates a heightened resistance to change. There are consequent alignment problems between husbands and wives, with the latter calling for more change than the former will concede. Fundamental changes in roles ultimately require relative alignment or consensus between role partners, since one cannot play a role except in relation to others. It may be that a period of ambiguity in which persons acknowledge cultural constraints while deviating from them permits realignment to occur and consensus to be reached.

As Laws and Schwartz (1977) note, for fundamental change in sex roles to occur, the scripts assigned to each sex must be modified. Such change requires that role partners arrive at a new construction of their realities. Some (e.g., Bem, 1970; Bernard, 1976; Laws and Schwartz, 1977) argue that this requires a preceding change in consciousness: Largely unconscious scripts assigned each role partner must be made conscious. The implication is that an aligning stage in which deviance is accompanied by denial and rationalization must be followed by a stage in which deviance is clearly recognized and in which altered definitions of roles are consciously accepted if new roles are to replace old as part of social structure. What may facilitate or impede that movement in stages is a question hardly asked, much less answered. A role theory informed by symbolic interactionism strongly suggests that the answers will be found in aspects of interaction itself.

There is some indication of how this process may occur in research dealing with the emergence of new components of roles. Nye's (1976) discussion of emerging dimensions in husband-wife roles, for instance, finds the ultimate source of change in structural contingencies. For example, the increasing expectations for companionship in marriage may arise from demographic changes that make the companionship perception feasible and reasonable: fewer children, longer life span, less harsh working and living conditions. The increasing expectation that spouses share leisure activities could also be linked to such altered life conditions. However, it is in the interaction itself that such changes are actually instituted. Nye finds that spouses quickly set about this task, establishing standards for who is to be responsible for the tasks, what sanctions will be invoked for performance failure, how competency will be evaluated, and what implications performance will have for general levels of satisfaction with the role relationship.

A general implication of the impact of symbolic interactionism on role theory and the impact of role theory on symbolic interactionism is that social behavior reflects both structural constraints and emergents from the interaction process itself and that interaction leads to changes in the structural constraints. We will return to this implication later.

FURTHER DEVELOPMENTS
OF SYMBOLIC INTERACTIONISM
AND ROLE THEORY

Symbolic interactionism's "new" interest in social structural concepts can be interpreted as a response to critics of the framework who argue its insensitivity to social structure as well as an ideological bias that follows from this failure. Role theory's "new" emphasis on the constructed character of social life can be interpreted as a response to critics of the framework who argue its lack of an adequate sense of social process and its oversocialized conception of man. The result of these criticisms has been the mutual movement of these frameworks toward one another through the adoption of theoretical and conceptual elements from the other.

There are, however, emphases in current work that are responsive to other issues and not accommodated neatly by our theme of an emerging general framework articulating elements of the two perspectives. If that wedding is successful, the emergent joined perspective will be affected by these other developments; thus there is reason to discuss them here.

Within symbolic interactionism, as might be expected, these other emphases focus attention on the concept of self. A common element in much of the work reviewed previously—that of Stryker, Burke, McCall and Simmons, Turner, and Weinstein and Tanur—is the attempt to create a viable social psychological framework adequate to the task of theorizing about the relationship of social structure and social person by bringing elements of role theory into symbolic interactionism. The concept depended upon in pursuing that aim is role; and the strategy used is to build this basic social structural unit into the self. Thus Turner (1978) defines the self as a hierarchi-

cal organization of roles. Stryker (1968) conceptualizes the self as comprised of identities reflecting the roles persons play. McCall and Simmons (1978) and Burke (1980) emphasize the interdependence of self and role. Roles, as normative expectations, attach to statuses or positions via a cognitive process. Whether one conceptualizes positions relatively narrowly with role theory as differentiated parts of organized social units (groups, formal associations, communities, and societies) or relatively broadly with symbolic interactionism as the kinds of people it is possible to be in a society (thus freeing the term from highly organized, publicly recognized social units), the concept carries three emphases vis-a-vis alternative possibilities:

1. It ties selves to the immediate social situation and so neglects the aspects of self that transcend localized structures.

2. It accentuates the organized and coercive character of social life rather than the "free" and creative.

3. It focuses primary attention on the rational, problem-solving dimensions of humans' responses to their environments as opposed to the cognitive and cathectic dimensions (Stryker, 1968).

Clearly, there is more to social life than can be comprehended by limiting consideration to aspects of self-reflecting immediate requirements of particular social situations; constraint is not the totality of social life; and there are other modalities of response to the environment than rationality ordinarily subsumes. We now turn to developments in symbolic interactionism and role theory that address such matters.

EMOTIONS AND THE SELF

The judgment of persons writing about the emotions from a symbolic interactionist standpoint is that the topic has been neglected but requires attention (Shibutani, 1961; Shott, 1979; Flaherty, 1980; Gordon, 1981; Denzin, 1983). The judgment is undoubtedly correct, despite the fact that attention to emotion has been manifest in the framework's literature from its inception. Both Frances Hutcheson (1742) and Adam Smith (1759) stressed the importance for effective social control of linking inner feelings to the fate of others, and Smith's (1759) doctrine of sympathy, more than simply a precursor of the role-taking concept, argues the social significance of both feeling with, and sharing the feelings of, another. Cooley's (1902) concept of the looking-glass self incorporated not only the person's imaginations of how others saw him or her but also that person's feelings about those imaginations. James's (1890) emphasis on self-esteem speaks to the significance of emotional as well as cognitive responses to the self. Discussions of emotions appear in symbolic interactionist textbooks, emphasizing the ways in which emotional arousal and behavior are responsive to situations and to definitions of the situation (Lindesmith and Strauss, 1966) or the transformation of emotional arousal into social sentiments through the development of sustained feelings in interpersonal relationships (Shibutani, 1961). These themes are elaborated in various substantive applications, from discussions of love and affection in intimate interpersonal relationships (Kirkpatrick, 1955; Turner, 1970) to discussions of the pain associated with identity loss (Weigert and Hastings, 1977) to discussions of failures in the social control of emotional responses in collective behavior (Blumer, 1951; Turner and Killian, 1957). Analyses of particular emotional states are also offered, for example, Goffman's (1967) and Gross and Stone's (1964) analyses of embarrassment as the discreditation of identities (see also Modigliani, 1968) and Reizler's (1943) analysis of shame as the consequence of inability to perform in accord with ideal self-conceptions.

Nevertheless, Mead's images of human behavior as instrumental problem-solving activity and of the human as a scientist seeking solutions to problems tend to dominate symbolic interactionism. The consequence is the priority given rational cognitive activity and the relative neglect of emotion. This appears to be changing. Kemper (1978) develops a complex argument relating physiological, psychological and sociological levels of analysis in a social interactional theory of emotions. His argument emphasizes the ways in which power and status relationships—extant or anticipated, real or imaginary—underlie variations in emotional expressions. Although not developing strictly from a symbolic interactionist perspective (this argument accepts the idea that there may be a one-to-one correspondence between specific physiological states and emotional expressions, an idea most symbolic interactionists do not find appealing) it nevertheless is informed by that perspective (see also Kemper, 1981). Hochschild (1975; 1979) examines the social structural patterning of affect, and Gordon (1981) analyzes the organization of emotion into sentiments and the manners in which sentiments are differentiated, socialized, and

managed. Both of these men work from a symbolic interactionist perspective.

Shott (1979) brings together a number of common elements in symbolic interactionists' treatment of the emotions. Beginning with a conception of emotions that combines physiological arousal and cognitive labeling of that arousal as affect (Schacter, 1971), she develops a theory of emotions addressed to the actor's construction of emotion, how role-taking emotions (feelings that cannot occur without putting oneself in another's place and taking that person's perspective—e.g., embarrassment, shame, guilt, pride, vanity, empathy, but not anger, fear, or joy) enter social control processes, and the socialization of affect. The theory is presented as a set of propositions (Shott, 1979, pp. 1330–1331).

1. Norms create pressures establishing the appropriateness of emotions in particular situations.

2. Different cultures emphasize or suppress different elements of attractive experience.

3. Persons usually express their emotions in ways prescribed by their cultures.

4. Within cultural limits, people construct emotions in a process that requires both internal cues indicative of physiological arousal and definition of these cues as emotionally induced.

5. Within the range bounded by the recognition of cues indicating some minimal arousal and intense arousal, the affective labeling of physiological states can be manipulated.

6. Particular emotions (see above) presuppose for their evocation role-taking with real, imaginary, or generalized other(s).

7. Embarrassment is the role-taking emotion most closely tied to the actual presence of others, shame less, and guilt least.

8. Embarrassment depends most on role-taking with specific others; guilt requires taking the role of the generalized other, and shame is intermediate in this respect.

9. Role-taking emotions make that part of social control that is self-control possible, since they can be felt in the absence of external sanctions.

10. Guilt, embarrassment, and shame motivate altruistic behavior; altruistic behavior repairs damaged self-conceptions and so reduces unpleasant affect.

11. Embarrassment or shame minimize role-taking that would exacerbate these emotions by avoiding witnesses of embarrassing or shameful behavior.

12. Guilt minimizes role-taking by avoidance of interaction with victims that would increase guilt.

13. Empathy links emotional states of persons with those of others and motivates altruistic behavior toward persons with whom they empathize.

This theory, for which some largely indirect evidence can be adduced, focuses on the construction and presentation of emotional responses; it does not meet directly critics' charges of neglect of the emotions since it does not deal with issues of how emotions enter and affect social interactions more generally. A very different theoretical use of affect is found in Heise's (1979) affect-control theory, however, and this does meet the issue more directly. Explicitly presented as a version of the symbolic interactionist framework, the theory argues that all common social actions have an underlying basis in the psychology of affect. Persons in social relationships are said to act to maintain established feelings. They react to events straining these feelings by anticipating and implementing new events to restore normal impressions. Events cause people to have affective responses, and people expect and construct new events to confirm established sentiments. Both the responses to, and anticipations of, events develop from feelings about aspects of events, in particular, actor, act and object.

Somewhat more formally, affect and behavior are linked in a feedback loop. Distinguishing between established affective associations (fundamentals) and situational feelings (transients), the theory draws on the concept of perceptual control systems (Powers, 1973) for its basic postulate: Acts are constructed to maintain congruency between transients and fundamentals. Because the former are typically too favorable or too unfavorable relative to the latter, they have an inverse affect on behavior. Persons are taken to be active forces in these affective dynamics, acting to change what they are experiencing to keep momentary feelings aligned with established sentiments. The affect-behavior dynamic, in accord with symbolic interactionist emphases, is viewed

as implicated in a hierarchical system and subordinate to definitions of the situation, that is, to the person's categorization of people and objects in a scene. Definitions of the situation provide a restricted set of cognitive elements used in recognizing and constructing events. Through specifying which cognitive categories are salient in a situation, definitions "retrieve" appropriate established sentiments to which immediate feelings are compared. Thus, the following model of the natural history of social action in a particular setting emerges:

1. The persons in the setting do cognitive work, defining the situation.

2. They recognize events comprehensible within this definition of the situation.

3. These recognitions generate transients about the participants in the events.

4. Discrepancies between these feelings and corresponding fundamentals lead to conceptualizations of new events that will bring feelings closer to established sentiments. If the self is the actor in a conceptualization, a behavioral intention or disposition results; if another is the actor, the result is an expectation for that other's behavior.

5. Behavior intentions are implemented when possible, and the new events loop the process back to the second step.

6. If fundamentals cannot be confirmed behaviorally, higher order feedback causes a redefinition of the situation on the basis of the most recent event and thus helps stabilize the process.

Heise's (1979) goal is the development of an interpretive sociology—one focusing on the meanings of events to actors—formulated with mathematical rigor, grounded in empirical analyses, and permitting subtle analyses of complex social relationships. His own empirical work (Heise, 1979; Smith-Lovin and Heise, forthcoming) concentrates on producing equations that generate culturally sensible actor-act-object combinations by using semantic differential ratings of evaluation, potency, and activity dimensions of these components as the raw materials for the equations. His work illustrates the potential of the affect-control model in the analysis of social behavior. In doing so, it indicates how affect can be accorded an important place in a theory developing from a symbolic interactionist framework.

One application of affect-control theory offered by Heise is in the study of social roles. It links Heise's work to other developments of symbolic interactionism discussed earlier and to the ongoing merging of symbolic interactionism and role theory. This application proceeds by examining the kinds of events constructed when a person has a particular social identity as actor or object. From the perspective of affect-control theory, a role exists in the process of constructing events confirming fundamental feelings about self and others. Settings defined as different bring together different identities and so different combinations of fundamental affects calling for confirmation; thus they generate different actions. However, since situations are frequently defined in terms of a set of identities relating to a single institution, variations in sentiment-confirming behavior can reflect institutional variations. Thus, another theoretical bridge is formed between social structure and social person.

THE SELF BEYOND
THE IMMEDIATE SITUATION

Strengths of theoretical frameworks are often also their weaknesses. A focus on identities associated with roles emphasizes the situational dependency of self and behavior and downplays the significance of situation-transcending elements in the structure of self. This alternative focus is not totally absent in symbolic interactionism. The concept of identity salience in Stryker's (1968; 1980) work, for example, is intended specifically to account for behavior that is consistent across situations. Role theory has long recognized some roles that do not require singular organizational settings in which they must be played (e.g., the sick role). There is nothing in the essentials of either framework that demands that self-concepts be limited to role-linked identities per se, in the sense of narrowly defined organizational roles. The processes by which roles are constructed could result in roles being defined that are independent of organizational membership; the honest woman, the shy person, the obnoxious man, the stuffed shirt, and the innovator are all potential products of that process, which could provide not only the expectations associated with those labels but also the cues that triggered recognition and application.

Possibly because the spectre of a trait psychology haunts them, symbolic interactionists have shied away from trans-situational conceptualizations. Early work on social types (e.g., Strong, 1943, Gerth and Mills, 1953) tended not to be further investigated and resulted largely in ethnographic inventories rather than systematic social psychological theorizing. The same may be said of work (e.g., Klapp, 1962) that defined symbolic types in terms of the values of a society or that abstracted the types from interactional relationships and discussed them as disembodied symbols.

This discussion carries no suggestion that situation-free, person-centered conceptualizations of the self are required. A symbolic interactionist conception of self is interactional to the core, and a theory that locates aspects of self solely in persons without reference to others violates fundamentals of the framework. Nor do cross-situational constancies in social behavior require situation-free concepts; what is necessary is that concepts are able, under specifiable conditions, to cross particular situations. Identity-salience is such a concept; so is "master status," used typically to refer to a position in a stratification system of society having relevance for social interaction within some set of subsystems of that society. By this usage, sex, age and social class are clearly master statuses in American society. There are few if any limits to what *may* qualify as a master status in a society. What *does* qualify will reflect values held generally through the society, and it is in this sense that a master status transcends particular local structures and interactions.

Master statuses are, by definition, relevant across interactional situations. How do they become so? What is the process by which expectations—both self and other—attached to age, sex, race, class, etc., enter interactions? This is the fundamental question to which expectations states theory (Berger, Conner and Fisek, 1974; Berger, Rosenholtz and Zelditch, 1980) is addressed. This theory, to our knowledge, has not been explicitly presented as a variant or as a derivative of symbolic interactionism (but see Zelditch, in Webster and Sobieczek, 1974), and the research program developed around the theory has been explicitly contrasted with symbolic interactionism's presumed antipathy to experimental methods (Webster and Sobieczek, 1974, p. 162). We have denied that symbolic interactionism requires the rejection of any method of conventional social science, and our reading of the expectation states literature convinces us that its fundamental idea structure is that of symbolic interactionism.

The theory initially evolved as an explanation of the finding that problem-solving groups of status-equal persons quickly evolve stable interrelated orderings of power and prestige. Through the interaction in these groups, persons develop high and low self-conceptions of their performance capabilities at the same time others develop high- and low-performance conceptions for these persons (Berger, Connor, and Fisek, 1974). Thus, expectations about future performances arise from task-related interactions and determine subsequent task-related interactions so that these expectations are confirmed and maintained by the interaction that depends on them. When problem-solving groups are composed of persons initially unequal on some status dimension, these inequalities significant outside the group are reproduced and maintained inside the group in the form of power and prestige orderings; this effect is virtually instantaneous and independent of the particulars of the status differentiation involved (Berger, Rosenholtz, and Zelditch, 1980). Expectation states theory adapted to these findings through the assumption that expectations arise not only out of interaction but also from existing beliefs about, and evaluations of, the characteristics of group members who are strangers but who differ in perceived external status.

Expectation states theory invokes the concept of status characteristic, that is, a characteristic of an actor having two or more states differentially evaluated in terms of honor, esteem, or desirability and each state associated with distinct moral and performance expectations. These expectation states are specific if they refer to how individuals will act in clearly defined and specifiable situations; they are general if they are not restricted to specifiable situations. Specific and general expectation states relate to specific and diffuse status characteristics, respectively (reading ability illustrates the former, sex the latter insofar as varying states of these are differentially evaluated and carry differing expectations).

As presently developed, the theory is limited to groups (two or more persons who see themselves as jointly responsible for an outcome and oriented toward a collective decision) engaged in tasks (actions having a goal, an idea of the difference between success and failure in achieving the goal, and an idea that members' contributions are relevant to success or failure) performing task-related activities (the power-prestige order of groups: performance opportunities accorded members, performance outputs, performance evaluations, and influence). The theory is general with respect to kind and number of status characteristics and number of interactants.

Status characteristics become salient—admitted as usable cues in a situation—by having a direct path or indirect path of task relevance or by providing a basis of discrimination among group members. The theory assumes that interactants must define situations to act and will use either of these types of cues in that defining activity. Where there is no path of task relevance, discriminating (and not equating) characteristics become salient, whether or not they are factually relevant to the immediate situation.

Indirect paths of relevance may provide only weak information on which to base expectations for self and other. Then, if discriminating status characteristics exist, the theory assumes that interactants will take these as relevant to the task, the burden of proof being on anyone who would show otherwise. (Note the similarity between this assumption and Turner's assumption to the effect that people will attribute roles to others and behave on that basis until proved wrong.) This burden of proof principle is one element in the theory's specification of how definitions of the situation are completed (Humphreys and Berger, 1981). Other elements include the lengths of paths of relevance whether created by the burden of proof process or not (the shorter the path, the stronger the actor's expectation state based on a given status element, since more information is provided by a shorter path), and sequencing. Definitions achieved through interaction in a pair relationship will operate when one of the pair is superceded by another person.

Actors have multiple-status characteristics of varying strength in their connection to the group task at hand and to the positive or negative significance of the task. The theory says that actors process information by combining all units of status to form aggregated expectation states for self and other. The process of aggregation is assumed to be governed by a principle of organized subsets (actors organize information first within like-signed subsets and then combine the subsets) and by an attenuation principle (a subset's strength is proportional to the strengths of the paths combined, but the incremental strength of an additional status item is a decreasing function of the strength of existing subset items).

Behaviors implicated in the prestige-power ordering in groups are seen by the theory to be a direct function of the expectation states of actors, and the relative position in this ordering of any two persons is seen as depending on the relative expectation advantage of these actors (expectation advantage is the difference between the aggregated expectation state an actor holds for self and that held for another).

As described, expectation states theory has relatively limited scope, deliberately designed to permit a step-by-step experimental program examining assumptions and defining the parameters of mathematical models implied by the theory. It is also important to note that the theory incorporates statements about how expectations attached to positions in a wider social structure come into play across specific situations (Pugh and Wahrman, 1983). In addition, a large variety of characteristics exist in terms of which persons can be labeled. These carry differential evaluation and performance expectations, and go far beyond the status characteristics currently defined in the theory. It is thus possible to broaden the current conception of tasks contained in the theory, and it may not be unreasonable to look to expectation states for a more general answer to the question of how cross-situational constancies are generated.

INDIVIDUALITY AND CREATIVITY

There is irony in dealing with the topic of individuality and creativity as a recent emphasis or development, since historically symbolic interactionism has treated these twin potentials as central to the human experience and since it is precisely this emphasis that role theory has borrowed as a corrective to its oversocialized and overconstrained perspective on social life. Yet, re-introducing the topic here not only permits discussion of relevant work but also serves to remind us that building a sound conception of social structure into social psychological theorizing must not be accomplished at the price of denying individuality and creativity.

Although Mead's "I" is ambiguous and open to a variety of interpretations (Lewis, 1979), its function within symbolic interactionist theorizing is to assert that social behavior is not merely responsive to others' expectations. It is not necessary to view the "I" as pure impulse to stake this claim; indeed, doing so may win a phyrric victory, thus foregoing the opportunity for a social psychological view of individuality and creativity. If the "I" is taken to be the observer of, or a participant in, an internal conversation of gestures (Lewis, 1979), there is the possibility of the person's entering into and redirecting the symbolic process so as to escape from or modify the impact of external constraints; to the degree this is possible (how possible it is will vary with the char-

acter of the constraints involved), behavior may be "free" and "creative."

The classic symbolic interactionist treatment of this issue, other than invoking the concept of the "I", argues that self-control is an outgrowth of social control. Persons build meanings through interaction and use these in role-taking. One role-takes with respect to a variety of others and can use the standpoint of one other in order to react to, evaluate, and resist the standpoint of a second. Dependence on multiple others makes possible independence from the expectations of any given other(s), freeing the person in an important degree and making choice possible.

Distinctions like that between conventional and personal roles (Shibutani, 1961) and conceptions like that of character (McCall and Simmons, 1978), long a part of symbolic interactionism's conceptual repertoire, are used to denote relative freedom from immediate expectations of others and to re-emphasize the degree to which the self-concepts guiding behaviors are the product of constructed rather than fully scripted interactions. Goffman (1961b), through the role-distance concept, argues that persons will use whatever means are available to introduce some freedom and maneuverability between their self and the self ascribed; even in a situation of maximal coerciveness, persons creatively seek and find means to assert their individuality.

That persons are constrained by being involved in social relationships is inherent in the very idea of a social psychology. This observation carries an important implication. There are two ways to deal with individuality and creativity in social life: (1) by placing these outside the framework of a social psychology (e.g., by invoking untamed biological instinct or some human "essence" independent of social life) or (2) by placing these inside such a framework. If the latter route is taken, it must be that creativity and individuality are the product of essentially the same social processes that produce constraint and conformity. This further implies that the study of conformity is at the same time the study of individuality, the study of creativity at the same time the study of constraint. This restatement of Cooley's two-sides-of-the-same-coin figure is nicely illustrated in Webster and Sobieczek's (1974) formal theory of significant others and social influence. As Zelditch (Webster and Sobieczek, 1974, p. viii) notes, the real subject of this theory is the symbolic interactionist conception of the self. Focusing on self-evaluation, the theory translates symbolic interactionist conceptions into the language and approach of expectation states theory (Berger, Connor, and Fisek, 1974) and applies the product to questions arising from the interactionist perspective: What are the determinants of self-concepts and of variations in self-concepts? What is the nature of self-structure, and what are the determinants of stability and changes in structure? What are the consequences of various possible types of self-concepts?

Webster and Sobieczek start with key ideas of symbolic interactionism, adding some slight modification: That persons' self-concepts are directly dependent on the opinions and actions of others, although persons may not correctly perceive the opinions of others and will give meaning to those opinions in the light of what they know of the others, and that persons do not change their self images to conform perfectly to the images of them held by others with whom they interact in particular situations but that their assessments of self enter into the meanings accorded to responses of others, and that not all others are equally important in determining persons' selves.

These theoretical premises, and the questions growing out of them, are given precision through expectation states theory. The self is defined in terms of the evaluation of attributes relevant to a task performance. Others are defined in terms of their capacities to evaluate. And consequences are defined as the formation of performance expectations for self and others, which, having been formed, permit persons to be independent of influence from others.

The central argument of the Webster-Sobieczek theory holds that persons in problem-solving groups motivated to do the best possible job must actively seek definitions of the situation that assign expectation states to self and others that tell them whose suggestions are likely to be helpful and whose not. Two basic sources of useful information are their own evaluations of performances of self and others and the evaluations that others make. When tasks are relatively difficult and evaluative standards unclear, the latter become increasingly important determinants of the actors' own evaluations of performances. At this point, differences in others become relevant to the theory, and the argument is that persons accept the evaluations of those they regard as competent to evaluate. Competence may be directly observed in group interaction with respect to the task; in the absence of such information, it may be inferred from the status characteristics of potential sources of influence.

A series of experiments both examines and underlies refinements and extensions of this argument. Competent sources are accepted; incompetent evaluators do not become negative sources in the sense of having an impact inversely related to the direction of the evaluations. Status characteristics do not have to be directly relevant to a task to be used as the basis for evaluating competency. When multiple competent sources exist whose evaluations differ, persons accept the evaluations of both, averaging them in their self-evaluations. When the competence of multiple sources differs, their evaluations have an impact relative to their competence. Persons do not selectively distort perceptions of evaluations to maximize self-evaluation.

The present discussion concerns individuality and creativity. The emphasis has been on the conditions specifying the impact of others on the person, that is, in terms of social conformity. Again, however, individuality is simply the other side of the conformity coin; the two emerge from the same basic social processes. The experimental paradigm used by Webster and Sobieczek involves ascertaining the expectation states of persons in a situation in which one of them can accept or reject a suggestion of the other(s). Their data indicate that if persons' expectation states for self with regard to task performance are lower than for the others, they tend to accept the opinions of those others. If, on the other hand, their self-expectations are higher with respect to the task than their expectations for others, they tend to reject the opinions of the others. Conformity and individuality are mirror images of one another.

SYMBOLIC INTERACTIONISM: A SOCIAL STRUCTURAL VERSION

We have been developing through the prior discussions what we believe to be a more satisfactory social psychological framework than either symbolic interactionism or role theory taken by itself. That more satisfactory framework is either a role theoretically informed symbolic interactionism or, alternatively, a role theory informed by symbolic interactionism. What it is labeled is arbitrary; we have adopted in the heading of this section the title of a work whose goal is the integration of symbolic interactionism and role theory and whose starting point is the former (Stryker, 1980).

However labeled, the emergent framework contains many of the assumptions, concepts, and general theoretical propositions of the two partial frames that contribute to it. Key to their integration is the concept of role, precisely because role is basic to the framework's image of society *and* to its image of the social person. Thus, the concept of role is strategic in the development of specific theories dealing with the transactions between society and person. In identity theory, affect control theory, and status expectancy theory, for example, the link between social structure and the person is justified theoretically by articulating their common referent in role.

Rather than offering a largely redundant discussion of the emergent framework, we will characterize it by elaborating its dual focus: an emphasis on the constructed character of that social life and an emphasis on culture and social structure as constraints on what, in fact, occurs in social interaction. Persons, the emergent framework asserts, reflect in their social behavior two often simultaneously operative, contrasting social forces; to use the terms offered by Powers (1980), persons manage opposing tendencies toward improvisation and imposition. Improvisation suggests that persons often ad-lib their social interactions, as symbolic interactionists have insisted. Imposition reasserts the role theoretic premise that much social behavior is constrained by the culture and social structure within which interactions take place. Improvisation and imposition reflect the symbolic interactionist and role theoretic concerns with self and society.

Given the assumed validity of both elements in the dual focus of the emergent framework, the theoretical challenge is to integrate them in specific theories building from the assumptions and concepts that make up the framework. Such theories must deal with questions concerning the relationships between the contrasting tendencies—between construction and constraint, between improvisation and imposition—as these influence persons' social behavior. What conditions whether improvisation or imposition or some mix of the two will occur? How does one tendency shape or limit the other? What features of culture and social structure limit improvisation in general, and in specific situations? How do these features constrain? And, under what circumstances does improvisation affect the system of constraints within which it occurs?

Integrative efforts have to this point stressed constraints on improvisation. Improvisation is seen as taking place within social structural impositions; persons are viewed as "free" to fill in specifics of behaviors whose general nature is given by structural role definitions. Powers (1980) treats role improvisation as necessarily occurring within the confines of pressures toward role imposition. Handel (1979) notes a variety of structurally

imposed limits on meanings negotiated in particular interaction contexts. Stokes and Hewitt (1976) assume that new alignments among persons' actions can be achieved only after cultural norms are recognized. Turner (n.d.c) posits that role-making behavior is limited by the positions persons occupy in organized social structures and by their accompanying role expectations, as does Stryker (1980).

This stress on the impact of imposition on improvisation exists despite the recognition that improvisation can alter constraints themselves. The elucidation of this recognition is a major part of the unfinished theoretical business of a social structural version of symbolic interactionism, a topic to which we will return in the final section of this chapter. Here, our discussion follows the extant literature in its concerns with how constraints limit the construction of social behavior and with the variables that condition the degree to which behavior patterns are imposed on persons. We deal here also with conditions that appear to affect whether imposition or improvisation predominate in the production of behavior through a discussion of factors increasing the likelihood of one or the other. Since improvisation must occur before it can impact on existing social structure, an understanding of factors conditioning its appearance is a necessary prelude to an understanding of how it alters structure.

CONSTRAINTS ON THE CONSTRUCTION OF BEHAVIOR IN INTERACTION

However redundant, no discussion of the constraints on the construction of behavior from the point of view of a social structural symbolic interactionism is possible without insisting that since roles enter the selves of persons engaged in interaction, social structure must strongly condition that interaction. Blumer (1969) is surely correct in insisting on the virtually unlimited behavior *possibilities* that follow from the importance of selves and symbolic processes in organizing human responses to situations. However, it is just as surely true that, whatever the possibilities, the *probabilities* that certain kinds of behaviors will ensue are considerably enhanced when the persons interacting are mother and child, employer and employee, or professor and student. Structural role theorists assumed that institutionalized role expectations are the major constraint on persons' behaviors and that internalization of those role expectations proceeded largely automatically and without problem in the course of socialization. While this approach to social control, so stated, is overly facile and somewhat naive in the conceptualizations of society and person implied, it contains an important insight: To the extent role expectations are built into persons, the probability that behavior will accord with those expectations is enlarged, and to the extent this probability is enlarged, the probability of behaviors being constructed that depart significantly from those role expectations is diminished.

The major mechanism by which social structure is imposed on behavior patterns operates in a context in which interpersonal processes, macrosocial structure, and microsocial structure also function to constrain the construction of behavior.

Interpersonal Constraints

Interaction itself both reinforces and supplements internalization in the process of limiting the construction of behavior—indeed, potentially imposing limits in the absence of internalization. The interpersonal pressure exerted by significant others—e.g., through ridicule and sarcasm (Komarovsky, 1967; Liebow, 1967)—are well documented. To the extent that significant others hold culturally standard role expectations, social structure is imposed on persons when various techniques of social control enter interaction itself. Work on role consensus (e.g., Cronkite, 1977) and role change (e.g., Slocum and Nye, 1976) suggests that role partners have greatest impact in this process, although expectations communicated from the entire range of significant others are effective (Komarovsky, 1967). Simmel (1950) noted the impact of a third party in increasing pressure toward conformity. Thus, day-to-day influence exerted by others, including role partners and audiences, is important in the imposition of structural constraints.

Influence is exerted by others, as suggested, through the overt actions of those others; it is also exerted independently of intentional or explicit influence attempts. Constraint is implied by the fact of mutual orientation of persons in social interaction. To the extent interacting persons role-take and adopt the standpoint of the other(s) implicated in the interaction, their individual behaviors will be relatively circumscribed. As Turner (1956, p. 323) observes, [adopting another's standpoint limits] "the kind of discretion . . . permitted the actor in shaping his behavior." In taking the role of the other, actors become more likely to acquiesce to the other's wishes independent of content. In general, both habit and the fact that persons' needs are met through the performance of institutionalized role expectations imply that such ac-

quiescence further limits the construction of behavior in interaction. Insofar as the emotional attachments of persons are high and there is empathy in the role-taking linking them, this limitation should be strengthened.

Interaction patterns appear to communicate powerfully and to reinforce structurally premised expectations, despite such improvisation as occurs. Perhaps, those expectations could not long endure were they not reinforced in the course of interaction. The principle that interaction patterns tend to reproduce the social structural bases that initially shape the patterns themselves is convincingly evidenced in status expectancy research (Berger *et al.,* 1980). It is also evident in work on sex-role definitions and resulting interaction patterns, which notes that expectations women hold on entering interaction affect interactions that serve to reinforce initial expectations. To illustrate: Since women in our culture are not expected to be assertive or aggressive, they are conflicted and inhibited in situations that require such behaviors (Horner, 1969; Kando, 1972; Gove and Herb, 1974; Parelius, 1975; Rosen and Aneshenshel, 1976; Warheit *et al.,* 1976). Asked to exhibit intelligence, instrumental competence, leadership, or aggressiveness, many women feel that to behave in these ways will deny their "desirability" as women. Women in high-status positions requiring these behaviors lose friends, respect, and access to information, indicating that the concern has some validity. To handle the resentment these consequences index, women placed in task-oriented groups tend to adopt "female" styles of accomplishing tasks. That strategy understates their instrumental abilities to the point that these remain unrecognized by others. In contributing to a group task, for example, women will not engage in obvious leadership behaviors (e.g., sitting at the head of the table) or assertively suggest solutions. They tend to allow others to lead, registering their opinions by agreeing with or expanding upon what someone else has said. Consequently, group members perceive women as making few instrumental contributions to the group, even though women seem to be as persuasive as men in affecting group decisions (Eskilson and Wiley, 1976; Nemeth *et al.,* 1976; Meeker and Weitzel-O'Neil, 1977; Wiley and Eskilson, 1983). Thus, original sex-role expectations structure the interaction process that reinforces the original expectations.

When women are in atypical situations, *a priori* sex-role definitions are reinforced through interaction in another manner. The most salient feature to others of women "tokens" in male-dominated professions is their sex; more attention is paid to their sex than is paid their performance in achieving difficult professional goals (Epstein, 1970; Kanter, 1977a; Kanter, 1977b; Macke, 1981). Prior expectations are thus reinforced through distracting attention from behavior that is not typical. Interaction structured by role expectations serves to confirm those expectations.

Macrosocial Structural Constraints

What persons come together for what purposes and at what time and at what place constrain the possiblities for innovation, improvisation, or construction of behavior. For example, if a parent and child interact in order to feed the child in a restaurant on a Saturday evening, the probabilities are that little innovative behavior will be produced. The range of probable alternative patterns will be equivalently but differently constricted if a professor and students interact in a social psychology class on a college campus on a weekday afternoon. Given kinds of people relating to one another for given purposes at given times in given settings will have a nonrandomly restricted set of identities, behavioral and symbolic repertoires, and other interactional resources to use in organizing and producing their behavior (McCall and Simmons, 1978).

The meaning of social structure is importantly contained in the observation that structure serves to bring certain persons together and keep others apart. Interaction shapes selves, but structure shapes interaction (Stryker, 1980). From this point of view, the meaning of social class is precisely that it affects the probability of particular interactions occurring. Insofar as class affects residential patterns, school attendance patterns, work place patterns, and so on, it will affect the probability of persons interacting at all or interacting in particular ways. For example, intimate relationships are more likely to form between same-class persons than between different-class individuals. Equivalent assertions can be made with regard to ecological aspects of social structure, that is, age, sex, and race, etc. (Feld, 1982). Clearly, features of social structure beyond institutionalized role expectations constrain the construction of behavior in interaction by placing limits on the raw materials available for such construction.

Similarly, broad macrosocial factors, such as economic and market conditions, constrain persons' behavior (Handel, 1979; Liker and Elder, 1983), as do broad cultural norms (Stokes and Hewitt, 1976). Cohen (1965), in an early integration of structural and interactionist perspectives, joined Merton's (1938) emphases on means-ends disjunctions, structured roles, and anticipatory socialization and also incorporated Mead's emphases on self and definitions of the situation in his treatment of deviant behavior. Cohen argues both that self and other definitions condition the impact of structural variables, in that the latter must be incorporated into a view of self as deviant (see also Schwartz and Stryker, 1971) and that the structural variables set limits for behaviors.

Microstructural Constraints

The most elemental social constraints on the behaviors constructed in interaction are the significant symbols emerging from earlier interactions (Mead, 1934). The common meanings that are those symbols act as cues to limit the range of responses acceptable to participants in interaction; these symbols specify expectations applicable to the interaction, expectations whose violations are likely to be met by a control mechanism functioning to "set things straight."

A current vision of how the structure of small-scale interactions restricts behavioral possibilities in those interactions is contained in Goffman's (1974) analysis of frames: the rules that operate in particular social encounters into which strips of the everyday life of persons can be analyzed. Rejecting for his purposes the utility of the contention that general rules or norms apply to all members of a society, Goffman seeks the ways in which persons frame their differentiated "worlds." That is, his search is for the prior rules persons use to specify what is going on when they enter the interactional settings encountered in the course of their daily lives. Distinguishing among primary frames (a framework or perceptual schema that renders some aspect of a scene meaningful that would be otherwise meaningless) as "natural" or "social," Goffman seeks the governing principles (e.g., rule of "keying" or transcription, rules of fabrication) by which alternative senses of interactional worlds can be organized. Once called into play, these frames heavily constrain interaction. The rules constituting a frame are not easily modified by any given instance of interaction (Gonos, 1977), although they are variably permissive with regard to the use of interaction of nuance and style peculiar to the persons involved.

Situated identity theory (Alexander and Wiley, 1981) assumes that behavior is structured by identities and that the identities actually invoked from among the range of those available to actors are determined by the structure of the situation in which they interact. Particularities of situations, then, serve to constrain behavioral possibilities by affecting attributions to others as well as to self (Santee and Jackson, 1982). Since self is an important source of improvisation or creativity, what specifies its definition in situational contexts limits in significant degree the improvisational possibilities. Identity theory (Stryker, 1980) argues that the aspect of self it stresses, identity salience, is a consequence of the location of persons in structured social relationships. It also hypothesizes that behavior in accord with role expectations follows in the degree that one is committed to the role and that the identity based on the role is salient. Expectation states theory posits that social structurally emphasized general statuses provide expectations for behavior and tend to produce behavior confirming the expectations and reaffirming the status distinctions on which they were based.

We have stressed the ways in which limits are imposed on the innovative construction of behavior in interaction. The implication of our framework is that, except under extreme circumstances, human social behavior will reflect improvisational and impositional tendencies operating conjointly. We turn now to a consideration of the conditions under which each of these tendencies is likely to be more strongly activated.

DETERMINANTS OF IMPOSITION OR IMPROVISATION

The philosophy of conduct underlying the social psychology developed in this chapter sees social life as adaptive. Patterns of interaction emerge as pesons collaborate in the development of significant symbols whose meanings relate the objects symbolized, including themselves, to the ends or goals of the interactants. The existing patterns worked out before any current interaction are fundamentally the referent of the concept of social structure. To the degree, then, that structure meets the ends or goals of those interacting, we can anticipate that behavior will conform relatively closely to the expectations built into the structure and that little consequential improvisation of behavior will occur. Obversely, when social structure fails to meet interactants' needs and goals, we can expect the construction of behavior that seeks to do so.

Actors, in general, cannot be expected to know when and how existing structure fails them; they can, however, be aware that interaction in which they are involved is in one or another sense troubling when the "working consensus" that underlies their interaction

with others has in some degree broken down and is no longer tenable. The improvisation of behavior aimed at producing new or altered interactive patterns occurs, as Mead (1934), Blumer (1969) and others insist, in problematic situations. Handel (1979 p. 873) notes in his discussion of the negotiations that frequently characterize interactions—negotiations over the identities of the persons interacting, the meaning of the situation of interaction, etc.—that "actors...continually renegotiate elements of order as the need arises—but only as the need arises." When situations are problematic, the need for order motivates the construction of lines of action, and deviations from standard, "normal" procedures are likely to be approved, or at least tolerated, by others, making these more probable.

When are situations problematic? The generalized answer is clear: when conditions draw attention to inadequacies of the existing patterns of social organization. That generalized response is insufficient in ways that cannot be pursued here, but it points to various determinants of improvisation or imposition.

Interactionists have long noted the personal and social disorganization that follows catastrophe-interrupted normal social process and the opportunities for change in behavior patterns afforded by such interruptions (Blumer, 1951). Catastrophes, natural or human-made, destroy the social definitions as well as the interactional resources and opportunities on the basis of which routine social life proceeds. Thus improvisation is required to deal with everyday practical exigencies whose major normal feature is routine.

Role theorists are likely to emphasize the significance of predictable events, such as life-cycle changes, in creating role confusion and opening up possibilities for novel solutions. For example, Coser (1966) argues that points of role transitions like adolescence are especially likely to produce improvisation. She contends that during transition periods identities are confused; the result is ambivalence toward behavior alternatives, with the confusion and ambivalence likely to be both recognized and tolerated by others.

Whether predictable or not, circumstances that disrupt role relationships may generate "exempting periods" in which the rejection of normative standards and relatively radical improvisation of behavior become temporarily acceptable (Shibutani, 1978; Powers, 1980). Exemptions can be provided persons in a wide variety of problematic situations, from illness to natural disasters to periodic disturbance in specific types of social relationships. Powers (1980) suggests that relationships characterized by transitory affect often are managed via an exempting period: When the emotional climate becomes confused or unbearable, participants may relax role requirements. Typically, role improvisation is not directly a goal of exempting periods; nor is improvisation undertaken to replace permanently previous understandings. Rather, it represents collective effort to restore behavioral alignments so that interactional objectives can be realized (Stokes and Hewitt, 1976). Improvisation becomes oriented not to structural change but to manipulating the situation so that, in the long run, conformity to earlier norms is more likely. Nevertheless, change may not be easy to control, and improvisation can have the longer term consequences of fundamental social structural change.

In a general sense, any role improvisation—except in the atypical case of evolving new roles without any institutionalized expectations attached to them—represents social deviance. Relatively permanent, subcultural deviance results from a situation of structural failure, in which dominant social structure appears incapable of permitting identifiable segments of a society's population to compete effectively for available rewards (Merton, 1938; Cohen, 1965). Powers (1980) postulates that system failure leads to improvisation, with the long-term consequence being renegotiated role arrangements incorporating the improvisation.

The principle involved operates in reverse fashion: When the structure in which roles are embedded meets the needs of those playing the roles, conformity demands are heightened; role requirements will be imposed in greater degree, and improvisation will be limited. When role partners have or negotiate interactional arrangements answering to needs, they will likely insist that those arrangements be maintained and will act to reinforce those arrangements. Should their power be imbalanced, this tendency is accentuated: Persons differing in power will have difficulty agreeing on new patterns that can threaten the power position of one or the other (Scheff, 1966). This phenomenon has been repeatedly noted in the literature on marital role change (Safilios-Rothschild, 1970). It speaks, in general terms, to the investments persons have in given social arrangements, and it is reasonable to suggest that the greater the investments, the less inclination persons will have to improvise with respect to those arrangements. Multiple mechanisms underlie this suggested linkage: the longer persons are interrelated, the more likely they will be mutually significant others whose

capacity to control one another is thus increased; the longer a relationship endures, the greater the investment in it and the more participants have to lose by risking innovation; pressures toward conformity with past arrangements build with the duration of a relationship; the more persons depend on one another for performances cueing or reinforcing their own role performances, the less tolerance for deviations from habitual patterns; and the greater the consensus between role partners, the less likely is improvisation (Goffman, 1961; Alexander and Wiley, 1981).

Role partners, of course, could agree to permit improvisation as part of their role agreement, but this possibility is difficult to sustain if initiated. Habitual patterns develop and become entrenched; the longer social arrangements exist, the more difficult it is to change them (Handel, 1979). Marital counselors testify to the inertia that builds over time in marriages, making any change threatening to spouses (Rapoport and Rosow, 1957). In general, the more routinized a situation, the stronger the conformity pressures.

Routinizing of interaction is related to, but not identical with, the institutionalization of role expectations; the latter implies the infusion of value into role expectations, their relative formalization, and their widespread acceptance. Goslin (1969) argues that the greater the institutionalization of role expectations, the less the tolerance for improvisation, an argument making sense on a variety of grounds including those relating to the impact of routinizing and duration of social relationships. Furthermore, institutionalization relates to the clarity with which role expectations are communicated by role partners and outsiders to particular relationships as well, and clearly communicated expectations are likely to increase pressures to conform (Sarbin and Allen, 1968). Institutionalization also may relate to the degree to which role relationships expose persons to public scrutiny of performances. The greater such exposure, the greater are the pressures toward conformity, an hypothesis anticipated by Simmel's (1950) early discussion of the effect of a third party on dyadic interaction. Public exposure implies the possibility of public accountability, again a factor likely to inhibit improvisation in roles (Powers, 1980). Goffman (1961) and Elkin (1958) have noted the effort often exerted to impede public scrutiny of relationships—the right to privacy claimed for familial relationships is a case in point—apparently in order to provide the opportunity for improvisation. On the other hand, Powers (1980) contends that certain kinds of institutionalization may increase tolerance for improvisation by narrowing the scope of behavior over which control is exerted and freeing some behavior for individual expression.

Additional variables affect the probability of imposition or improvisation. Imposition is enhanced when interaction networks are dense. A dense network, that is, a large set of persons related to a focal person who are related to one another, raises the probability that others to whom one relates share common standards and present the same "face" with respect to putative deviation from those standards. Other aspects of social networks function in an equivalent manner. Bott (1957) long ago suggested the importance of husbands and wives having overlapping networks in fostering adherence to traditional familial role expectations; if spouses share significant others, the feedback they receive will be relatively consistent, and more persons are involved in attempted renegotiations of role definitions.

The other side of the coin just described, in many ways, is contained in the observation that role diversity enhances the probability of improvisation. The more a given role provides persons with differentiated contacts and experiences, the more resources they will have to sustain improvized behavior and to protect themselves against interactional recrimination (Sieber, 1974; Marks, 1977). In addition, the more persons' entire role repertoires are diverse, the more likely they are to have nonoverlapping role sets, the less the influence exerted by the conformity demands of any given other or set of others, the greater the awareness of alternative behavior possibilities, and the more probable the improvisation in role behavior. This process is abetted by interactions across organizational boundaries, a circumstance characterizing persons with differentiated and nonoverlapping role-sets (Miles, 1977; Sieber, 1974): Interactions across social boundaries afford greater privacy for nonconforming behaviors as well as make enforcement of structural rules more difficult.

The discussion has emphasized interactional and structural variables. For Mead, as well as for later symbolic interactionists, the prime source of creativity in human behavior is the self itself, and that insight need not be lost to a structural symbolic interactionism. Apart from recognizing the possibility that not all of what people do in interactions with others is either determined or motivated and that Mead's "I" may appear in behavior in the form of pure impulse, this insight can recognize that the self serves variously as an impetus to improvisation. Goffman (1961a) documents attempts by inmates in total institutions to preserve their individuality through self-assertions breaking institutional rules in small ways. Perhaps more substantially, from the point of view of possible impact on the structure of rules themselves, when self is conceptualized as an organization of multiple identities, it becomes possible to visualize the differential salience of identities as a source of innovation (Stryker, 1968; McCall and Simmons, 1978; Burke and Tully, 1977). Given a highly salient identity, behavior in accord with that identity may be introduced into roles and situations in which the behavior represents a considerable alteration of culturally or situationally standard forms and denial of standard expectations. Indeed, the more the expectations applicable in a given interactional setting conflict with the imperatives of a highly salient identity, the more improvisation is to be expected. Stated generally, self-role disjuncts increase the probability of role improvisation.

We must recognize complicating possibilities that are only implicit in the discussion thus far. The behavioral expectations termed role may be relatively situation specific or may be relatively culturally standard. The logic connecting conditioning variables to imposition or improvisation may lead in opposite directions depending on whether roles are one or the other. For example, one can argue that personnel turnover decreases deviation from culturally standard expectations in social relationships because, presumably, turnover generates a felt need to control newcomers by reasserting these expectations (Powers, 1980). Alternatively, the argument can be made that turnover increases improvisation because it frees persons from long-standing obligations. Which logic applies may be linked to whether one is talking about relatively culturally standard or situation-specific expectations. Similarly, given the complexity inherent in the recognition of various levels of social structure—from the broadly societal to the narrowly situational—as well as the complexity involved in recognizing the very different worlds (Goffman, 1974) experienced by persons within the "same" society, it is entirely possible that variables encouraging imposition on one level encourage improvisation on another. It pays to keep in mind that abstract societal conditions must be activated in the experience of persons to impact their behavior (Stryker and Macke, 1978). Part of the challenge to a structural symbolic interactionism is precisely to address the question of how and when that activation occurs.

Another kind of complication inheres in the distinction between relatively culturally standard role expectations and more situation-specific expectations, specifically in the relation between the two. There is a normal range of variation in the behavior called for by most culture-level role expectations, a fact which our treatment of the concept of role throughout this chapter has slighted in the interests of avoiding continuous qualification but which is recognized in current efforts at conceptualization and measurement of role and indentity (Burke, 1980). Adaptational processes on the level of concrete interaction settings produce selection within the culturally approved range of variation; that is, behaviors from within the normal range of variation are selected as actors negotiate in the interests of achieving their interactional goals. Tensions between standard-role expectations and situational-specific expectations will exist to the degree that the latter represent or go beyond the extreme boundaries of the former. It is reasonable to suppose that a feedback system (Powers, 1973; Heise, 1979; Burke, 1980) develops relating the two that ordinarily keeps the former within reasonable bounds but that can work to produce change on the level of the cultural expectations.

CONCLUDING REMARKS

We have now reviewed symbolic interactionism and role theory as relatively distinctive theoretical frameworks in social psychology and as an emerging integrated framework taking as its defining problem the reciprocal relationships between society and person. As this language asserts, the integration is in process and not complete. Indeed, it may be misleading to suggest the possibility of completion when the task is the production of a theoretical framework; such intellectual heuristics continuously undergo change as shifts in the questions asked by persons using them occur. And, given that humans live in an historical social world, there is reason to think that these questions will change over time. Concepts that are the heart of a theoretical framework will undergo reformulation; distinctions within concepts will be offered; and new concepts will be introduced as problems emerge through time and are recognized.

These concluding remarks are oriented toward issues likely to concern social psychologists whose work is guided by a social structural version of symbolic interactionism over the next set of years. Some of these have been previously noted, some not.

A variety of issues related to the concept of self demand attention. Most general and important, perhaps, is how far the concept can be pushed to incorporate elements of human "freedom" and "spontaneity" without

undermining the social scientific search for empirically verifiable theory (Gergen, 1982; Stryker, 1984). This is not a new issue; it is reflected in a long-standing symbolic interactionist concern with the conceptualization of that aspect of self Mead termed the "I." The question of what Mead meant by the "I" is under contention (Kolb, 1944; Gillin, 1975; Lewis, 1979), but whatever Mead may have meant, the underlying problem is how to cope theoretically with what many see as a fundamental of human existence: the human's capacity for autonomy from social circumstance. Personality theorists, such as Maslow (1968), contemplate a self-development transcending role definitions and allowing for self-actualization. Some argue that a person's total motivation can transcend a role orientation (Lester, 1979) or that entire societies can move beyond role-based motivations and so permit persons to relate on the basis of the rewards of the immediate contact rather than on the basis of expectations engendered by role definitions (Itskhokin, 1980). If autonomy from social constraints can be understood in a disciplined rather than an adventitious way, it can perhaps be incorporated into a systematic social psychology and used in the explanation of creative behavior or improvisation.

Other issues relating to the concept of self are considerably more mundane. A wide number of facets of a comprehensive concept of self can be distinguished (Rosenberg, 1979). Which of these is necessary to and/or useful in linking self to social structure, especially as an antecedent of interactive behavior? It may be that some conceptually distinct aspects of self enter behavior minimally if at all, while others enter importantly. The strategic theoretical role given identity salience by the role-identity model (McCall and Simmons, 1978) or by identity theory (Stryker, 1980) represents a bet that this facet of self will prove important in the explanation of interaction. It may be that some aspects of self distinguished by various theorists are epiphenomenal. At the moment, strong assumptional and theoretical bases for focusing effort on particular aspects of self rather than others are lacking. The emphasis, as earlier noted, is currently on cognitive dimensions (and only certain of these). Although it is recognized that there are other dimensions of self than the cognitive, including the cathectic and conative (Stryker, 1968) and although some work on these has been done, widespread and systematic attention to these from the standpoint of a structural symbolic interactionism awaits the coming decades.

Even if we were to have available a reasonable listing of significant aspects of self, questions concerning the internal structure or organization of self would remain, since that structure as well as the elements entering into it can be presumed to influence behavior. How, other than in salience terms, are multiple identities related to one another? Does the existence of some identities preclude the appearance of others in the self? What is the impact among cognitive, cathectic and conative aspects of self, that is, how are these aspects organized? And what relationships exist among those parts of the self that have been referred to as extant, ideal, and presented (Rosenberg, 1979)? We can expect that over the next years these questions and others like them will be pursued by persons whose social psychology features the concept of self.

The foregoing asserts that the conceptualization of self remains an important and continuing task. So does the conceptualization of the mechanisms that link social structure to self, self to interaction, and interaction to social structure. If there are cues in social situations that activate particular identities, how do they do so? What focuses attention on particular cues and permits inattention to other objects in a situation that could have cued the selection of an appropriate in situ identity. Identity salience presumably helps account for such selective attention and inattention, but certainly other variables are at work. Expectation states theory argues that in the absence of available task-related information in a situation requiring definition, cues familiar to persons by virtue of their relevance in the wider status structure of a society will cue expectations and consequently behavior. What other mechanisms operate? Furthermore, precisely how do identities enter interaction? A theoretically pregnant response to this question has recently been offered by Burke and Reitzes (1981), who suggest that it is the commonality of meaning shared by identity and behavior that links the two; that is, persons behave in ways whose meanings are those built into an identity that has been invoked in a situation (see also Stryker and Craft, 1982). If the evidence sustains this theorizing, a critical theoretical problem of a structural symbolic interactionism will have been solved; we can predict that considerable effort will be expended to test and refine Burke's statement.

With the solution to this problem in hand, however, the promise of a structural symbolic interactionism will not be fulfilled until issues attached to a final link in the chain that leads from social structure to identities to interaction to social structure have been resolved. Our earlier discussion of this final link largely pointed to mechanisms by which interaction reinforced extant

structure. Presumably, however, the constructive potentialities in human social behavior that arise out of self and symbolic processes can also change the larger social organizational framework within which interaction occurs. The question is: precisely how? The idea that change processes require persons to align their actions (Stokes and Hewitt, 1976) addresses this question, largely by restating it, but leaves open questions of the principles that guide realignment and whether or not the realignments that occur reproduce or alter significantly existing structure. In the same vein, we should recognize that accounts (Scott and Lyman, 1968) or disclaimers (Hewitt and Stokes, 1975) may permit people to believe that no change has occurred when it has, thus permit change to stabilize, but we need to know a great deal more before we can believe we have an adequate theory of how interaction alters social structure.

Conceptual developments yet to occur will undoubtedly be critical to the resolution of the issues we have discussed. Equally critical, in our judgement, will be methodological—particularly measurement—developments. Few, if any, of the concepts of the theoretical framework of a structural symbolic interactionism have been adequately measured, even in that research motivated by the framework which is at the same time motivated by the ideal of a rigorous and quantitatively-expressed science. The argument that measurement must be principled—that is, that measurement procedures must be based as unequivocally on the assumptions and concepts of the theory being examined as the hypotheses that logically (and ideally) derive from the theory—has been made by Schwartz and Stryker (1971), Burke (1980), and others. As yet, however, the implementation of the argument's implications lags. Surely the next decades will see increasing attention to measurement issues attached to self and role concepts and, hopefully, the resolution of at least some of these.

Finally, and to return to a point made in the beginning pages of this chapter, structural symbolic interactionism is a theoretical framework that to this point has produced only a few reasonably rigorous theories. It largely consists of a set of assumptions and concepts, with relatively few sets of logically related assertions about how particular assumptions and concepts imply specifiable connections among its variables in relation to one of them taken as an object of explanation. We have, in brief, a considerable catalog of assertions about how various aspects of social life may work to affect other aspects of social life, but little by way of testable assertions that under specifiable conditions, a given outcome will occur. Converting framework to theory must be a central intellectual task of structural symbolic interactionists over the next years if the framework itself is to deserve continued respect.

REFERENCES

Aberle, D. F., A. K. Cohen, K. Davis, M. Levy, and F. X. Sutton (1950). The functional prerequisites of society. *Ethics, 9,* 100–111.

Albrecht, S. L., H. M. Bahr, and B. A. Chadwick (1979). Changing family roles: an assessment of age differences. *J. Marriage and Family, 41,* 41–50.

Alexander, C. N. and G. Knight (1971). Situated identities and social psychological experimentation. *Sociometry, 34,* 65–82.

Alexander, C. N., and P. Lauderdale (1977). Situated identities and social influence. *Sociometry, 40,* 225–233.

Alexander, C. N., and I. Sagatun (1973). An attributional analysis of experimental norms. *Sociometry, 36,* 127–142.

Alexander, C. N., and H. G. Weil (1969). Players, persons and purposes: situational meaning and the prisoners' dilemma game. *Sociometry, 32,* 121–144.

Alexander, C. N., and M. G. Wiley (1981). Situated activity and identity formation. In M. Rosenberg and R. H. Turner (Eds.), *Sociological perspectives on social psychology.* New York: Basic Books.

Alpander, G. G. (1975). Developing team effectiveness by eliminating supervisor/subordinate gap in role perception. *Hum. resource Management, 14,* 29–32.

Araji, S. (1977). Husbands' and wives' attitude-behavior congruence on family roles. *J. Marriage and Family, 39,* 309–321.

Aram, J. D., C. P. Morgan, and E. S. Esbeck (1971). Relation of collaborative interpersonal relationships to individual satisfaction and organizational performance. *Admin. Sci. Quart., 16,* 289–296.

Argyris, C. (1962). *Interpersonal competency and organizational effectiveness.* Homewood, Ill.: Dorsey.

Aronson, E. (1969). The theory of cognitive dissonance: a current perspective. In L. Berkowitz (Ed.), *Advances in experimental social psychology.* Vol. 4. New York: Academic Press. Pp. 2–34.

Azumi, K. and G. Hage (1972). *Organizational systems.* Lexington, Mass.: D. C. Heath.

Bacon, L. (1974). Early motherhood, accelerated role transition, and social pathologies. *Soc. Forces, 52,* 333–341.

Bales, R. (1950). *Interaction process analysis.* Reading, Mass.: Addison-Wesley.

Ball, D. W. (1967). An abortion clinic ethnography. *Soc. Problems, 14,* 293–301.

Bandura, A. (1969). Social-learning theory of identificatory processes. In D. A. Goslin (Ed.), *Handbook of socialization theory and research.* Chicago: Rand McNally. Pp. 213–262.

Bates, F. L. (1956). Position and role, and status: a reformulation of concepts. *Soc. Forces, 34,* 313–321.

Bateson, G., D. D. Jackson, J. Haley, and J. Weakland (1956). Toward a theory of schizophrenia. *Behav. Scient., 1,* 251–264.

Becker, H. S. (1953). Becoming a marihuana user. *Amer. J. Sociol., 59,* 235–242.

——— (1960). Notes on the concept of commitment. *Amer. J. Sociol., 66,* 32–40.

——— (1963). *Outsiders.* New York: Free Press.

Becker, H. S., B. Geer, E. C. Hughes, and A. Strauss (1961). *Boys in white.* Chicago: Aldine.

Becker, H. S., and A. Strauss (1956). Careers, personality and adult socialization. *Amer. J. Sociol., 62,* 253–263.

Bem, D. (1972). Self-perception theory. In L. Berkowitz (Ed.), *Advances in experimental social psychology.* Vol. 6. New York: Academic Press.

Bem, S. (1970). Case study of a non-conscious ideology: training the woman to know her place. In D. Bem (Ed.), *Beliefs, attitudes, and human affairs.* Belmont, Calif.: Brooks-Cole.

Benedict, R. (1938). *Continuities and discontinuities in cultural conditioning.* Reprint No. 5–18. Indianapolis: Bobbs-Merrill.

Berger, P., and H. Kellner (1964). Marriage and the construction of reality. *Diogenes, 45,* 1–25.

Berger, P. H., and T. Luckmann (1966). *The social construction of reality.* Garden City, N.Y.: Doubleday.

Berger, J., T. L. Connor, and M. H. Fisek (1974). *Expectation states theory.* Cambridge, Mass.: Winthrop.

Berger, J., S. J. Rosenholz, and M. Zelditch, Jr. (1980). Status organizing processes. *Ann. rev. Sociol., 6,* 21–40.

Berk, S. F. (1979). Husbands at home: organization of the husband's household day. In Karen W. Feinstein (Ed.), *Working women and families.* Beverly Hills, Calif.: Sage.

Bernard, J. (1976). Change and stability in sex-role norms and behavior. *J. soc. Issues.* Vol. 32. 3, 207–223.

Biddle, B. J., and E. J. Thomas (1966). *Role theory: concepts and research.* New York: Wiley.

Biddle, B. J. (1979). *Role theory: expectations, identities, and behaviors.* New York: Academic Press.

Bittner, E. (1967). Police discretion in emergency apprehension of mentally ill persons. *Soc. Problems, 14,* 285–290.

Blacher-Dixon, J., and J. J. Simeonsson (1978). Effect of shared experience on role-taking performance of retarded children. *Amer. J. ment. Defic., 83,* 21–28.

Blau, P. M., and W. R. Scott (1962). *Formal organizations.* San Francisco: Chandler.

Blau, Z. S. (1973). *Old age in changing society.* New York: New Viewpoints.

Blood, R. O., Jr., and D. W. Wolfe (1960). *Husbands and wives.* New York: Free Press.

Blumberg, P. (1968). *Industrial democracy: the sociology of participation.* London: Constable & Co., Ltd.

Blumer, H. (1951). Collective behavior. In A. M. Lee (Ed.), *Principles of sociology.* New York: Barnes and Noble. Pp. 167–222.

——— (1954). What is wrong with social theory? *Amer. sociol. Rev., 19,* 3–10.

——— (1956). Sociological analysis and the variable. *Amer. sociol. Rev., 22,* 683–690.

_____ (1962). Society as symbolic interaction. In A. M. Rose (Ed.), *Human behavior and social process.* Boston: Houghton-Mifflin. Pp. 179–192.

_____ (1969). *Symbolic interactionism: perspective and method.* Englewood Cliffs, N.J.: Prentice-Hall.

_____ (1980). Social behaviorism and symbolic interactionism. *Amer. Sociol. Rev., 45,* 409–419.

Bock, E. W., and I. L. Webber (1972). Suicide among the elderly: isolating widowhood and mitigating circumstances. *J. Marriage and Family, 34,* 24–31.

Borgatta, E. F. (1961). Role-playing specification, personality and performance. *Sociometry, 24,* 218–233.

Bott, E. (1957). *Family and social network: roles, norms, and external relationships in ordinary urban families.* London: Tavistock.

Brim, O. G., Jr. (1958). Family structure and sex role learning by children: a further analysis of Helen Koch's data. *Sociometry, 21,* 1–16.

_____ (1966). Socialization in later life. In O. G. Brim, Jr., and S. Wheeler (Eds.), *Socialization after childhood.* New York: Wiley. Pp. 18–33.

Brown, P. G. (1957). Masculinity-femininity development in children. *J. consult. Psychol., 21,* 197–202.

Bryson, G. (1945). *Man and society: the Scottish inquiry of the eighteenth century.* Princeton, N.J.: Princeton Univ. Press.

Bucher, R., and A. Strauss (1961). Professionals in process. *Amer. J. Sociol., 66,* 325–334.

Burchard, W. W. (1954). Role conflicts of military chaplains. *Amer. sociol. Rev., 19,* 528–535.

Burgess, E. W. (1926). The family as a unity of interacting personalities. *The Family, 7,* 3–9.

Burke, R. J., and T. Weir (1976). Some personality differences between members of one-career and two-career families. *J. Marriage and Family, 38,* 453–459.

Burke, P. J. (1980). The self: measurement requirements from an interactionist perspective. *Sociometry, 43,* 18–29.

Burke, P. J., and D. Reitzes (1981). The link between identity and role performance. *Soc. Psychol. Quart., 44,* 83–92.

Burke, P. J., and J. Tully (1977). The measurement of role/identity. *Social Forces, 55,* 881–897.

Burstyn, J. N. (1971). Sex-role stereotypes and the classroom teacher. *School and Community, 58,* 8–9.

Cameron, N. (1950). Role concepts in behavior pathology. *Amer. J. Sociol., 55,* 464–467.

Cavan, R. S. (1953). *The American family.* New York: Crowell.

_____ (1962). Self and roles in adjustment during old age. In A. M. Rose (Ed.), *Human behavior and social processes.* Boston: Houghton Mifflin.

Cavan, R. S., and K. H. Ranck (1938). *The family and the depression.* Chicago: Univ. of Chicago Press.

Cherlin, A. (1978). Remarriage as an incomplete institution. *Amer. J. Sociol., 84,* 634–650.

Cicourel, A. V. (1964). *Methods and measurement in sociology.* New York: Free Press.

_____ (1973). *Cognitive sociology.* Middlesex: Penguin.

Clausen, J. A., Ed. (1968). *Socialization and society.* Boston: Little, Brown.

Coburn, D. (1975). Job-worker incongruence: consequences for health. *J. Health soc. Behav., 16,* 198–212.

Cohen, A. K. (1965). The sociology of the deviant act: anomie theory and beyond. *Amer. Sociol. Rev., 30,* 5–13.

Collins, R. (1981). The microfoundations of macrosociology. *Amer. J. Sociol., 86,* 984–1011.

Cooley, C. H. (1902). *Human nature and the social order.* New York: Scribner's.

Corsaro, W. A. (1977). The clarification request as a feature of adult interactive styles with young children. *Lang. soc., 6,* 183–207.

_____ (1979a). Sociolinguistic patterns in adult-child interaction. In E. Ochs (Ed.), *Developmental pragmatics.* New York: Academic Press. Pp. 373–390.

_____ (1979b). Young children's conceptions of status and role. *Sociol. Educat., 52,* 46–59.

Coser, R. L. (1966). Role distance, sociological ambivalence, and transitional status systems. *Amer. J. Sociol., 72,* 173–181.

Cottrell, L. S. (1942). The adjustment of the individual to his age and sex roles. *Amer. Sociol. Rev., 7,* 617–620.

_____ (1948). Present status and future orientation of research in the family. *Amer. Sociol. Rev., 13,* 123–135.

_____ (1971). Covert behavior in interpersonal interaction. *Proceed. Amer. Philosoph. Assoc., 115,* 462–469.

Couch, C. (1958). Self-attitudes and degree of agreement with immediate others. *Amer. J. Sociol., 63,* 491–496.

Coutu, W. (1951). Role-playing vs. role-taking: an appeal for clarification. *Amer. Sociol. Rev., 16,* 180–187.

Cressey, D. R. (1962). Differential association and compulsive crimes. In A. M. Rose (Ed.), *Human behavior and social processes.* Boston: Houghton Mifflin. Pp. 443–467.

_____ (1953). *Other people's money.* Glencoe, Ill.: Free Press.

Cronkite, R. C. (1977). The determinants of spouses' normative preferences for family roles. *J. Marriage and Family, 39,* 575–585.

Crozier, M. (1964). *The bureaucratic phenomenon.* Chicago: Univ. of Chicago Press.

Cummings, L. L., and A. M. El Salmi (1970). The impact of role diversity, job level and organizational size on managerial satisfaction. *Admin. Sci. Quart., 15,* 1–10.

Cumming, E., and W. E. Henry (1961). *Growing old: the process of disengagement.* New York: Basic Books.

Dahrendorf, R. (1959). *Class and class conflict in industrial society.* Stanford: Stanford Univ. Press.

Dalton, G. K., L. Barnes, and A. Zalenik (1968). *The distribution of authority in formal organizations.* New York: Free Press.

Daniels, A. (1969). The captive professional: bureaucratic limitations in the practice of military psychiatry. *J. Health soc. Behav., 10,* 255–265.

Davis, K. (1949). *Human society.* New York: Macmillan.

Denzin, N. K. (1972). The genesis of self in early childhood. *Sociol. Quart., 13,* 291–314.

_____ (1975). Play, games, and interaction: the contexts of childhood socialization. *Sociol. Quart., 16,* 458–478.

_____ (1977). Notes on the criminogenic hypothesis: a case study of the American liquor industry. *Amer. Sociol. Rev., 42,* 905–920.

_____ (1983). A note on emotionality, self, and interaction. *Amer. J. Sociol., 89,* 402–409.

Deutscher, I. (1962). Socialization for post-parental life. In A. M. Rose (Ed.), *Human behavior and social processes.* Boston: Houghton Mifflin. Pp. 506–525.

Dewey, J. (1896). The reflex arc in psychology. *Psychol. Rev., 3*, 357–370.

_____ (1930). *Human nature and conduct.* New York: Modern Library.

Dohrenwend, B. P., and B. S. Dohrenwend (1976). Sex differences and psychiatric disorders. *Amer. J. Sociol., 81*, 1447–1454.

Dornbusch, S. M. (1955). The military academy as an assimilating institution. *Soc. forces, 33*, 316–321.

Duberman, L. (1975). *The reconstituted family: a study of remarried couples and their children.* Chicago: Nelson-Hall.

Durkheim, E. (1895). *Les règles de la méthode sociologique.* Paris: Alcan.

_____ (1897). *Le suicide.* Paris: Alcan.

_____ (1912). Les formes élémentaires de la vie religieuse. Paris: Alcan.

Ehrlich, H. J., J. W. Rinehart, and J. C. Howell (1962). The study of role conflict: explorations in methodology. *Sociometry, 25*, 85–97.

Elkin, F. (1958). Socialization and the presentation of self. *Marriage and family Living, 20*, 320–325.

Engel, G. V. (1970). Professional autonomy and bureaucratic organization. *Admin. Sci. Quart., 15*, 12–21.

Epstein, C. F. (1970). Encountering the male establishment: sex-status limits on women's careers in the professions. *Amer. J. Sociol., 75*, 965–982.

Eskilson, A., and M. G. Wiley (1976). Sex composition and leadership in small groups. *Sociometry, 39*, 183–193.

Fallding, H. G. H. Mead's orthodoxy (1982). *Social Forces, 60*, 723–737.

Farberman, H. A. (1975). A criminogenic market structure: the automobile industry. *Sociol. Quart., 16*, 438–457.

Feld, S. (1982). Social structural determinants of similarity among associates. *Amer. Sociol. Rev., 47*, 797–801.

Felson, R. B. Self- and reflected appraisals among football players: a test of the Meadian hypothesis (1981). *Soc. Psychol. Quart., 44*, 116–126.

Festinger, L., K. Back, S. Schacter, H. H. Kelly, and J. Thibaut (1950). *Theory and experiment in social communication,* Ann Arbor, Mich.: Research Center for Group Dynamics. Institute for Social Research.

Flaherty, M. G. (1980). Social construction of job grief. Unpublished paper presented to the Seventh Annual Symposium for the Study of Symbolic Interaction, SUNY-Stony Brook.

Fogarty, M., R. Rapoport, and R. Rapoport (1971). *Sex, career, and family.* Great Britain, London: Allen and Unwin, Ltd.

Foote, N. N. (1951). Identification as the basis for a theory of motivation. *Amer. Sociol. Rev., 16*, 14–21.

Freidson, E. (1967). Review essay: health factories, the new industrial sociology. *Sociol. Problems, 14*, 493–500.

Gallagher, J. J., and M. J. Aschner (1963). A preliminary report on analyses of classroom interaction. *Merrill-Palmer Quart., 9*, 183–193.

Garfinkel, H. (1956). Conditions of successful degradation ceremonies. *Amer. J. Sociol., 61*, 420–424.

Gergen, K. G. (1971). *The concept of self.* New York: Holt, Rinehart, and Winston.

_____ (1973). Social psychology as history. *J. Pers. soc. Psychol., 26*, 309–320.

_____ (1982). *Toward transformation in social knowledge.* New York: Springer-Verlag.

Gerhardt, U. (1973). Interpretive processes in role conflict situations. *Sociology, 7*, 225–240.

Gerth, H., and C. W. Mills (1953). *Character and social structure.* New York: Harcourt, Brace and World.

Gecas, V., and M. Schwalbe (1983). Beyond the looking glass: social structure and efficacy-based self esteem. *Soc. Psychol. Quart., 46*, 77–88.

Getzels, J. W., and E. G. Guba (1954). Role, role conflict, and effectiveness: an empirical study. *Amer. Sociol. Rev., 19*, 164–175.

Gillin, C. T. (1975). Freedom and the limits of social behaviorism: a comparison of selected themes from the works of G. H. Mead and Martin Buber. *Sociology, 9*, 29–47.

Glaser, B., and A. Strauss (1967a). Awareness contexts and social interaction. *Amer. Sociol. Rev., 29*, 669–679.

_____ (1967b). *The discovery of grounded theory.* Chicago: Aldine.

_____ (1968). *Time for dying.* Chicago: Aldine.

_____ (1971). *Status passage.* Chicago: Aldine.

Glenn, N. D., and C. N. Weaver (1978). A multivariate, multi-survey study of marital happiness. *J. Marriage and Family, 40*, 269–282.

Goffman, E. (1959). *The presentation of self in everyday life.* New York: Doubleday.

_____ (1961a). *Asylums,* New York: Anchor.

_____ (1961b). *Encounters.* Indianapolis: Bobbs-Merrill.

_____ (1963a). *Behavior in public places.* Glencoe, Ill.: Free Press.

_____ (1963b). *Stigma.* Englewood Cliffs, N.J.: Prentice-Hall.

_____ (1967). *Interaction ritual.* New York: Anchor.

_____ (1971). *Relations in public.* New York: Basic Books.

_____ (1974). *Frame analysis.* Cambridge: Harvard Univ. Press.

Gonos, G. (1977). Situation versus frame: the interactionist and the structuralist analyses of everyday life. *Amer. Sociol. Rev., 42*, 854–867.

Goode, W. J. (1956). *After divorce.* Glencoe, Ill.: Free Press.

_____ (1960a). Norm commitment and conformity to role-status obligations. *Amer. J. Sociol., 66*, 246–258.

_____ (1960b). A theory of role strain. *Amer. Sociol. Rev., 25*, 483–496.

Goodman, N. (forthcoming), Socialization. In H. A. Farberman (Ed.), *Social psychology,* New York: Harper & Row.

Goodman, N., and R. Ofshe (1968). Empathy, communication efficiency and marital status. *J. Marriage and Family, 30*, 597–603.

Gordon, S. L. (1981). The sociology of sentiments and emotion. In M. Rosenberg, and R. H. Turner (Eds.), *Sociological perspectives on social psychology.* New York: Basic Books.

Goslin, D. A., Ed. (1969). *Handbook of socialization theory and research.* Chicago: Rand McNally.

Gottlieb, A. (1977). Social psychology as history or science: an addendum. *Pers. soc. Psychol. Bull., 3,* 207–210.

Gouldner, A. W. (1957). Cosmopolitan and locals: toward an analysis of latent social roles. *Admin. Sci. Quart., 2,* 444–480.

——— (1970). *The coming crisis in western sociology.* New York: Basic Books.

Gove, W. R., and T. R. Herb (1974). Stress and mental illness among the young: a comparison of the sexes. *Soc. Forces, 53,* 256–265.

Gross, E., and G. P. Stone (1964). Embarrassment and the analysis of role requirements. *Amer. J. Sociol., 70,* 1–15.

Gross, N., A. W. McEachern, and W. S. Mason (1957). Role conflict and its resolution. In E. E. Maccoby, T. M. Newcomb, and E. L. Hartley (Eds.), *Readings in Social Psychology* (3rd ed.). New York: Holt. Pp. 447–459.

Haga, W. J., G. Graen, and F. Dansereau, Jr. (1974). Professionalism and role making in a service organization: a longitudinal investigation. *Amer. Sociol. Rev., 39,* 122–133.

Hagstrom, W. (1965). *The scientific community,* New York: Basic Books.

Hall, D. T. (1972). A model of coping with role conflicts: the role behavior of college educated women. *Admin. Sci. Quart., 17,* 471–486.

Hall, D. T., and F. E. Gordon (1973). Career choices of married women: effects on conflict, role behavior, and satisfaction. *J. appl. Psychol., 58,* 42–48.

Hall, P. M. (1972). A symbolic interactionist analysis of politics. *Sociol. Inquiry, 42,* 35–75.

Hall, R. (1968). Professionalization and bureaucratization. *Amer. Sociol. Rev., 33,* 92–104.

Handel, W. (1979). Normative expectations and the emergence of meaning as solutions to problems: congruence of structural and interactionist views. *Amer. J. Sociol., 84,* 855–881.

Harré, R., and P. F. Secord (1972). *The explanation of social behavior.* Totowa, N.J.: Rowman & Littlefield.

Harrison, A. O., and J. H. Minor (1978). Inter-role conflict, coping strategies, and satisfaction among black working wives. *J. Marriage and Family, 40,* 799–805.

Harry, J. (1976). Evolving sources of happiness for men over the life cycle: a structural analysis. *J. Marriage and Family, 38,* 289–296.

Havens, E. M. (1973). Women, work, and wedlock: a note on female marital patterns in the United States. In J. Huber (Ed.), *Changing women in a changing society.* Chicago: Univ. of Chicago Press.

Heckman, N. A., R. Bryson, and J. B. Bryson (1977). Problems of professional couples: a content analysis. *J. Marriage and Family, 39,* 323–330.

Heider, F. (1958). *The psychology of interpersonal relations.* New York: Wiley.

Heise, D. R. (1979). *Understanding events.* Cambridge: Cambridge Univ. Press.

Heiss, J. (1981). Social roles. In M. Rosenberg, and R. H. Turner (Eds.), *Sociological perspectives on social psychology.* New York: Basic Books.

Henry, W. E. (1948). The business executive: the psychodynamics of a social role. *Amer. J. Sociol., 54,* 286–291.

Hetherington, E. M. (1967). The effects of familial variables on sex role typing, parent-child similarity and imitation in children. In J. P. Hill (Ed.), *Minn. Symposia child Psychol.,* Vol. 1.

Hewitt, J. P. (1979). *Self and society,* (2nd Ed.), Boston: Allyn and Bacon.

Hewitt, J. P., and R. Stokes (1975). Disclaimers. *Amer. Sociol. Rev., 40,* 1–11.

Hill, R. (1949). *Families under stress.* New York: Harper.

Hill, R., and J. Aldous (1969). Socialization for marriage and parenthood. In D. A. Goslin (Ed.), *Handbook of socialization theory and research.* Chicago: Rand McNally. Pp. 885–950.

Hochschild, A. R. (1975). The sociology of feeling and emotion. In M. Millman, and R. M. Kanter (Eds.), *Another voice,* Garden City, N.Y.: Doubleday.

——— (1979). Emotion work, feeling rules and social structure. *Amer. J. Sociol., 85,* 551–575.

Hoelter, J. (1980). Worker alienation and the self: a structural symbolic interactionist approach. Paper presented at the annual meetings of the American Sociological Association, New York City.

——— (1983). The effects of role evaluation and commitment on identity salience. *Soc. Psychol. Quart., 46,* 140–147.

Hoffman, L. W. (1974). The employment of women, education, and fertility. *Merrill-Palmer Quart., 21,* 99–119.

Hogan, D. P. (1980). The transition to adulthood as a career contingency. *Amer. Sociol. Rev., 45,* 261–276.

Holahan, C. K., and L. A. Gilbert (1979). Interrole conflict for working women: careers versus jobs. *J. appl. Psychol., 64,* 86–90.

Holmstrom, L. (1972). *The two career family.* Cambridge, Mass.: Schenkman.

Horner, M. (1969). Fail: bright women. *Psychol. Today, 3,* 36, 38, 62.

Houseknecht, S. K. (1977). Reference group support for voluntary childlessness: evidence for conformity. *J. Marriage and Family, 39,* 285–292.

Houseknecht, S. K., and A. S. Macke (1981). Combining marriage and career: the marital adjustment of professional women. *J. Marriage and Family, 43,* 651–661.

Huber, J. (1973). Symbolic interactionism as a pragmatic perspective: the bias of emergent theory. *Amer. Sociol. Rev., 38,* 278–284.

Hudis, P. M. (1976). Commitment to work and to family: marital status differences in women's earnings. *J. Marriage and Family, 38,* 267–278.

Hughes, E. C. (1945). Dilemmas and contradictions of status. *Amer. J. Sociol., 50,* 353–359.

Hughes, M., and W. E. Gove (1981). Living alone, social integration, and mental health. *Amer. J. Sociol., 87,* 48–74.

Humphreys, P., and J. Berger (1981). Theoretical consequences of the status characteristics formulation. *Amer. J. Sociol., 86,* 953–983.

Hutcheson, F. (1742). An essay on the nature and conduct of the passions and affections, with illustrations on the moral sense (2nd ed.). London. Sold by J. Osborne and T. Longman.

Ickes, W., B. Schermer, and J. Stieno (1979). Sex and sex-role influences in same-sex dyads. *Soc. Psychol. Quart., 42,* 373–385.

Inkeles, A. (1969). Social structure and socialization. In D. A. Goslin (Ed.), *Handbook of socialization theory and research,* Chicago: Rand McNally. Pp. 615-632.

Itskhokin, A. (1980). The dual system. *Amer. J. Sociol., 85,* 1317-1336.

Jackson, J. (1966). A conceptual and measurement model for norms and roles. *Pacific Sociol. Rev., 9,* 35-47.

James, W. (1890). *The principles of psychology.* New York: Holt.

Janis, I. L., and B. T. King (1954). The influence of role playing on opinion change. *J. abnorm. soc. Psychol., 49,* 211-218.

Jones, A. P., and M. C. Butler (1980). A role transition approach to the stresses of organizationally induced family role disruption. *J. Marriage and Family, 42,* 367-376.

Kagan, J. (1964). Acquisition and significance of sex-typing and sex-role identity. In M. L. Hoffman and L. W. Hoffman (Eds.), *Review of child development research.* Vol. I. New York: Russell Sage.

Kagan, J., and H. A. Moss (1962). *Birth to maturity: a study in psychological development.* New York: Wiley.

Kahn, R. L., D. M. Wolfe, R. P. Quinn, J. Snoek, and R. H. Rosenthal (1964). *Organizational stress: studies in role conflict and ambiguity.* New York: Wiley.

Kalleberg, A. L. (1975). The fit of the individual and the job: a theory of job satisfaction. Paper presented at the annual American Sociological Association meetings.

Kalleberg, A. L., and K. A. Loscocco (1983). Aging, values, and rewards: explaining age differences in job satisfaction. *Amer. Sociol. Rev., 48,* 78-90.

Kammeyer, K. (1967). Sibling position and the feminine role. *J. Marriage and Family, 29,* 494-499.

Kando, T. (1972). Role strain: a comparison of males, females, and transsexuals. *J. Marriage and Family, 34,* 459-464.

Kanter, R. M. (1972). Symbolic interactionism and politics in systematic perspective. *Sociol. Inquiry, 42,* 77-92.

_____ (1977a). Some effects of proportions on group life: skewed ratios and responses to token women. *Amer. J. Sociol., 82,* 965-990.

_____ (1977b). *Men and women of the corporation.* New York: Basic Books.

Katz, D., and R. L. Kahn (1967). *The social psychology of organizations.* New York: Wiley.

Kelly, H. E. (1971). Role satisfaction of the Catholic priest. *Social Forces, 50,* 75-84.

Kemper, T. D. (1968). Reference groups, socialization, and achievement. *Amer. Sociol. Rev., 33,* 31-45.

_____ (1978). *A social interactional theory of emotions.* New York: Wiley-Interscience.

_____ (1981). Social constructionist and positivist approaches to the sociology of emotions. *Amer. J. Sociol., 87,* 336-362.

Kinch, J. W. (1963). A formalized theory of the self-concept. *Amer. J. Sociol., 68,* 481-486.

Kirkpatrick, C. (1955). *The family as process and institution.* New York: Ronald.

Klapp, O. E. (1962). *Heroes, villians, and fools.* Englewood Cliffs, N.J.: Prentice-Hall.

Kohlberg, L. (1966). A cognitive-developmental analysis of children's sex-role concepts and attitudes. In E. Maccoby (Ed.), *The development of sex differences.* Stanford: Stanford Univ. Press.

Kolb, W. L. (1944). A critical evaluation of Mead's "I" and "me" concepts. *Social Forces, 22,* 291-296.

Komarovsky, M. (1940). *The unemployed man and his family.* New York: Dryden.

_____ (1967). Learning conjugal roles. In M. Komarovsky with J. H. Phillips, *Blue collar marriage.* New York: Vintage. Pp. 33-48.

_____ (1976). *Dilemmas of masculinity: a study of college youth,* New York: Norton.

Koos, E. L. (1946). *Families in trouble.* New York: King's Crown Press.

Kornhouser, W. (1962). *Scientists in industry: conflict and accommodation.* Berkeley: Univ. of California Press.

Kosa, J., and R. E. Coker, Jr. (1965). The female physician in public health: conflict and reconciliation of the sex and professional roles. *Sociol. soc. Research, 49,* 294-305.

Kuhn, M. H. (1964). Major trends in symbolic interaction theory in the past twenty-five years. *Sociol. Quart., 5,* 61-84.

Kuhn, M. H., and T. S. McPartland (1954). An empirical investigation of self-attitudes. *Amer. sociol. Rev., 19,* 68-76.

Lally, J. J., and B. Barber (1974). The compassionate physician: frequency and social determinants of physician-investigator concern for human subjects. *Social Forces, 53,* 289-296.

Laws, J. L., and P. Schwartz (1977). *Sexual scripts: the social construction of female sexuality.* Hinsdale, Ill.: Dryden Press.

LeMasters, E. E. (1975). *Blue-collar aristocrats.* Madison: Univ. of Wisconsin Press.

Lemert, E. M. (1951). *Social Pathology.* New York: McGraw-Hill.

Lester, M. (1979). Making music together: a sociological formulation of intimate encounters between males and females. Paper presented to the Amer. Sociol. Assoc., Boston.

Lewis, J. D. (1979). A social behavioristic interpretation of the Meadian "I". *Amer. J. Sociol., 85,* 261-287.

Lewis, R. A., and G. B. Spanier (1979). Theorizing about the quality and stability of marriage. In W. R. Burr, R. Hill, F. I. Nye, and I. L. Reiss (Eds.), *Contemporary theories about the family,* Vol. I. New York: Free Press. Pp. 268-294.

Liebow, E. (1967). Why marriage does not work on Tally's Corner. In E. Liebow, *Tally's corner.* Boston: Little, Brown. Pp. 116-136.

Liker, J., and G. H. Elder (1983). Economic hardship and marital relations in the 1930s. *Amer. Sociol. Rev., 48,* 343-359.

Lindesmith, A. R. (1947). *Opiate addiction.* Bloomington, Ind.: Principia Press.

Lindesmith, A. R., and A. Strauss (1966). *Soc. Psychol.* (rev. ed.). New York: Holt, Rinehart, and Winston.

Linton, R. (1936). *The study of man.* New York: Appleton-Century.

_____ (1939). A neglected aspect of social organization. *Amer. J. Sociol., 45,* 870-886.

Lipman-Blumen, J. (1973). Role de-differentiation as a system response to crises: occupational and political roles of women. *Sociol. Inquiry, 43,* 105-129.

Lofland, J. (1969). *Deviance and identity,* Englewood Cliffs, N.J.: Prentice-Hall.

_____ (1970). Interactionist imagery and analytic interruptus. In T. Shibutani (Ed.), *Human nature and collective behavior: papers in honor of Herbert Blumer,* Englewood Cliffs, N.J.: Prentice-Hall.

Lofland, L. (1973). *A world of strangers.* New York: Basic Books.

Lowenthal, M. F., and C. Haven (1968). Interaction and adaptation: intimacy as a critical variable. *Amer. Sociol. Rev., 33,* 20–30.

Lowenthal, M. F., M. Turner, and D. Chiriboga (1975). *Four stages of life.* San Francisco: Jossey-Bass.

Luckey, E. B. (1960). Implications for marriage counseling of self-perceptions and spouse perceptions. *J. counsel. Psychol., 7,* 3–9.

McCall, G., and J. L. Simmons (1978). *Identities and interaction* (2nd ed.). New York: Free Press.

_____ (1982). *Soc. Psychol.* New York: Free Press.

McHugh, P. (1968). *Defining the situation.* Indianapolis: Bobbs-Merrill.

Macke, A. S. (1981). Token men and women: a note on the saliency of sex and occupation among professionals and semi-professionals. *Sociology of Work and Occupations, 8,* 25–38.

Macke, A. S., P. Hudis, and D. Larrick (1979). Sex role attitudes and employment among women: a dynamic model of continuity and change. In I. V. Sawhill (Ed.), *Women's changing roles at home and on the job.* National Commission on Manpower Policy. Special Report No. 26 (September).

Macke, A. S., L. W. Richardson, and J. Cook (1980). *Sex-typed teaching styles of university professors and student reactions.* Final report to the National Institute of Education. Grant No. NIE-G-78-0144. Washington, D.C.

Macke, A. S., and W. Morgan (1978). Maternal employment, race and work orientation of high school girls. *Social Forces, 57,* 187–204.

Mackie, M. (1983). The domestication of self: gender comparisons of self imagery and self esteem. *Soc. Psychol. Quart., 46,* 343–350.

McPhail, C. and C. Rexroat (1979). Mead vs. Blumer: the divergent methodological perspectives of social behaviorism and symbolic interactionism. *Amer. Sociol. Rev., 44,* 449–467.

_____ (1980). *Ex cathedra* Blumer or *ex libris* Mead. *Amer. Sociol. Rev., 45,* 420–430.

Maines, D. R. (1977). Social organization and social structure in symbolic interactionist thought. *Ann. Rev. Sociol., 3,* 235–239.

Mann, J. H., and C. H. Mann (1966). The effect of role-playing experience on role-playing ability. In B. J. Biddle and E. J. Thomas (Eds.). *Role theory: concepts and research.* Pp. 212–216.

Marks, S. R. (1977). Multiple roles and role strain: some notes on human energy, time and commitment. *Amer. Sociol. Rev., 42,* 921–936.

Martindale, D. (1960). *The nature and types of sociological theory.* Boston: Houghton Mifflin.

Maslow, A. H. (1968). *Toward a psychology of being* (2nd ed.) New York: Van Nostrand.

Mason, K. O., J. L. Czajba, and S. Arber (1976). Change in U.S. women's sex-role attitudes, 1964-1974. *Amer. Sociol. Rev., 41,* 573–596.

Mead, G. H. (1930). Cooley's contribution to American social thought. *Amer. J. Sociol., 35,* 693–706.

_____ (1934). *Mind, self and society.* Chicago: University of Chicago.

Mechanic, D. (1980). Comment on Gove and Hughes. *Amer. Sociol. Rev., 45,* 513–514.

Meeker, B. F., and P. A. Weitzel-O'Neill (1977). Sex roles and interpersonal behavior in task-oriented groups. *Amer. Sociol. Rev., 42,* 91–105.

Melbin, M. (1972). *Alone and with others: a grammar of interpersonal behavior.* New York: Harper & Row.

Meltzer, B. M. (1959). *The social psychology of George Herbert Mead.* Kalamazoo: Center for Sociological Research.

Meltzer, B. M., J. W. Petras, and L. T. Reynolds (1975). *Symbolic interactionism: genesis, varieties, and criticism.* London: Routledge.

Merton, R. K. (1938). Social structure and anomie. *Amer. Sociol. Rev., 3,* 677–682.

_____ (1949). *Social theory and social structure: toward the codification of theory and research.* Glencoe, Ill.: Free Press.

_____ (1957). The role-set: problems in sociological theory. *Brit. J. Sociol., 8,* 106–120.

Merton, R. K., and E. Barber (1963). Sociological ambivalence. In E. A. Teryakian (Ed.), *Sociological theory, values, and socio-cultural change,* New York: Free Press. Pp. 91–220.

Merton, R. K., and A. S. Kitt (1950). Contributions to the theory of reference group behavior. In R. K. Merton and P. R. Lazarsfeld (Eds.), *Continuities in social research: studies in the scope and method of "The American soldier."* Glencoe, Ill.: Free Press.

Miles, R. H. (1976). Role requirements as sources of organizational stress. *J. appl. Psychol., 1,* 172–179.

_____ (1977). Role-set configuration as a predictor of role conflict and ambiguity in complex organizations. *Sociometry, 40,* 21–34.

Milgram, S. (1964). Behavioral studies of obedience. *J. abnorm. soc. Psychol., 67,* 371–378.

Mills, C. W. (1940). Situated action and vocabularies of motives. *Amer. J. Sociol., 5,* 904–913.

Mitchell, W. C. (1958). Occupational role strains: the American elective public official. *Admin. Sci. Quart., 3,* 210–228.

Miyamoto, S. F., and S. M. Dornbusch (1956). A test of interactionist hypotheses of self-conception. *Amer. J. Sociol., 61,* 399–403.

Modigliani, A. (1968). Embarrassment and embarrassability. *Sociometry, 31,* 313–326.

Moreno, J. L. (1934). *Who shall survive?* Washington: Nervous and Mental Disease Publication.

Mowrer, H. (1935). *Personality adjustment and domestic discard.* New York: American Book.

Mutran, E., and P. J. Burke (1979a). Feeling "useless": a common component of young and old adults' identities. *J. Research Aging, 1,* 187–211.

_____ (1979b). Personalism as a component of young and old adults' identities. *J. Research Aging, 1,* 37–63.

Mutran, E., and D. C. Reitzes (1984). Intergenerational support activities and well-being among the elderly. *Amer. Sociol. Rev., 49,* 117–130.

Myrdal, A., and V. Klein (1968). *Women's two roles: home and work*. London: Routledge.

Nelson, H. M., R. Yabley, and T. Madron (1973). Ministerial roles and social actionist stance: protestant clergy and protest in the sixties. *Amer. Sociol. Rev., 38,* 375–386.

Nemeth, C., J. Endicott, and J. Wachtler (1976). From the '50's to the '70's: women in jury deliberations. *Sociometry, 39,* 293–304.

Neugarten, B. L. (1964). *Personality in middle and late life*. New York: Atherton.

———— (1979). Time, age, and the life cycle. *Amer. J. Psychiatry, 136,* 887–894.

Neugarten, B. L., and K. K. Weinstein (1964). The changing American grandparent. *J. Marriage and Family, 26,* 199–204.

Nevill, D., and S. Damico (1977). Developmental components of role conflict. *J. Psychol., 95,* 195–198.

Nye, F. I. (1976). *Role structure and analysis of the family*. Beverly Hills, Calif.: Sage.

Oleson, V. L., and E. W. Whitaker (1968). *The silent dialogue*. San Francisco: Jossey-Bass.

Oppenheimer, V. K. (1977). The sociology of women's economic roles in the family. *Amer. Sociol. Rev., 42,* 387–405.

Orden, S. R., and N. Bradburn (1969). Working wives and marriage happiness. *Amer. J. Sociol., 74,* 392–407.

O'Toole, R., and R. Dubin (1968). Baby feedings and body sway: an experiment in George Herbert Mead's "Taking the role of the other." *J. Pers. soc. Psychol., 10,* 59–65.

Palmer, S., and J. A. Humphrey (1977). Suicide and homicide: a test of a role theory of destructive behavior. *Omega, 8,* 45–58.

Parelius, A. (1975). Emerging sex-role attitudes, expectations, and strains among college women. *J. Marriage and Family, 37,* 146–153.

Park, R. E. (1926). Behind our masks. *Survey, 56,* 135–139.

———— (1955). *Society*. New York: Free Press.

Parnes, H. S., J. R. Shea, R. S. Spitz, and F. A. Zeller (1970). Dual careers: a longitudinal study of labor market experiences of women. Vol. 1. *Manpower research monograph,* No. 21, Washington, D.C.: U.S. Government Printing Office.

Parsons, T. (1951). *The social system,* Glencoe, Ill.: Free Press.

———— (1961). An outline of the social system. In T. Parsons et al., *Theories of society*. New York: Free Press.

Parsons, T., and R. Bales (1960). *Family socialization and interaction processes,* Glencoe, Ill.: Free Press.

Pelz, D. (1966). Some social factors related to performance in a research organization. *Admin. Sci. Quart., 1,* 310–325.

Perrow, C. (1970). *Organizational analysis: a sociological view,* Belmont, Calif.: Wadsworth Publishing.

Perrucci, C. C. (1970). Minority status and the pursuit of professional careers: women in science and engineering. *Social Forces, 49,* 245–259.

Peterson-Hardt, S., and F. D. Burlin (1979). Sex differences in perceptions of familial and occupational roles. *J. vocational Behav., 14,* 306–316.

Petrowsky, M. (1976). Marital status, sex, and the social networks of the elderly. *J. Marriage and Family, 38,* 749–756.

Poloma, M. M., and T. N. Garland (1971). The myth of the egalitarian family: familial roles and the professionally employed wife. In A. Theodore (Ed.), *The professional woman,* Cambridge, Mass.: Schenkman.

Porteus, B. D., and R. C. Johnson (1965). Children's responses to two measures of conscience development and their relation to sociometric nomination. *Child Development, 36,* 703–711.

Powers, C. (1980). Role-imposition or role-improvisation: some theoretical principles. Paper prepared for presentation at the annual meeting of the Pacific Sociological Association.

Powers, W. T. (1973). *Behavior: the control of perception*. Chicago: Aldine.

Pugh, M. D., and R. Wahrman (1983). Neutralizing sexism in mixed-sex groups: do women have to do better than men? *Amer. J. Sociol., 83,* 746–762.

Quarantelli, E. L., and J. Cooper (1966). Self-conceptions and others: a further test of Meadian hypotheses. *Sociol. Quart., 7,* 281–297.

Rabban, M. (1950). Sex role identification in young children: two diverse social groups. *Genetic Psychol. Monogr., 42,* 81–158.

Rainwater, L. (1964). Marital sexuality in four cultures of poverty. *J. Marriage and Family, 26,* 457–466.

Rapoport, R., and I. Rosow (1957). An approach to family relationships and role performance. *Hum. Relat., 10,* 209–221.

Raphael, E. E. (1965). Power structure and membership dispersion in unions. *Amer. J. Sociol., 71,* 274–283.

Reckless, W., S. Dinitz, and E. Murray (1958). Self-concept as an insulator against delinquency. *Amer. Sociol. Rev., 21,* 744–748.

Reeder, L. G., G. Donahue, and A. Biblarz (1960). Conceptions of self and others. *Amer. J. Sociol., 66,* 153–159.

Reitzes, D. C. (1980). College student identities and behaviors. *Sociological Focus, 13,* 113–124.

Reitzes, D. C., and P. J. Burke (1980). College student identity: measurement and implications. *Pacific Sociol. Rev., 23,* 45–66.

Reizler, K. (1943). Comment on the social psychology of shame. *Amer. J. Sociol., 48,* 457–465.

Rheingold, H. L. (1969). The social and socializing infant. In D. A. Goslin (Ed.), *Handbook of socialization theory and research*. Pp. 779–790.

Richardson, J. G. (1979). Wife occupational superiority and marital troubles: an examination of the hypothesis. *J. Marriage and Family, 41,* 63–72.

Riley, M. W., and A. Foner with M. E. Moore, B. Hess, and B. K. Roth (1968). *Aging and society,* Vol. 1. New York: Russell Sage.

Ritzer, G. (1975). Professionalism, bureaucratization and rationalization: the views of Max Weber. *Social Forces, 53,* 627–634.

Robertson, J. F. (1977). Grandmotherhood: a study of role conceptions. *J. Marriage and Family, 39,* 165–174.

Roe, A. (1951). A psychological study of eminent biologists. *Genetic Psychol. Monogr., 43,* 121–239.

Rose, A. M. (1962). A systematic summary of symbolic interaction theory. In A. M. Rose (Ed.), *Human behavior and social processes*. Boston: Houghton Mifflin. Pp. 3–19.

Rosen, C. B., and C. S. Aneshensel (1976). The chameleon syndrome: a social psychological dimension of the female sex role. *J. Marriage and Family, 38,* 605–617.

Rosenberg, B. G. (1966). Family interaction and sex role identification. *Amer. J. Orthopsychiatry, 36,* 355–356.

Rosenberg, B. G., and B. Sutton-Smith (1964). Ordinal position and sex role identification. *Genetic Psychol. Monogr., 70,* 297–328.

Rosenberg, M. (1979). Conceiving the self. New York: Basic Books.

Rosenthal, R., and L. Jacobsen (1968). *Pygmalion in the classroom.* New York: Holt, Rinehart, and Winston.

Ross, C. E., J. Mirowsky, and J. Huber (1983). Marital patterns and depression. *Amer. Sociol. Rev., 48,* 809–823.

Rossi, A. S. (1968). Transition to parenthood. *J. Marriage and Family, 30,* 26–39.

Roth, J. A. (1963). *Timetables.* Indianapolis: Bobbs-Merrill.

Rothman, R., and R. Perrucci (1970). Organizational careers and professional expertise. *Admin. Sci. Quart., 15,* 282–293.

Ryder, R. G. (1973). Longitudinal data relating marriage satisfaction and having a child. *J. Marriage and Family, 35,* 604–606.

Safilios-Rothschild, C. (1970). The influence of the wife's degree of work commitment upon some aspects of family organization and dynamics. *J. Marriage and Family, 32,* 671–691.

Santee, R. T., and S. E. Jackson (1982). Identity implications of conformity: sex differences in normative and attributional judgments. *Soc. Psychol. Quart., 45,* 121–125.

Sarbin, T. R. (1954). Role theory. In G. Lindzey (Ed.), *The handbook of social psychology,* Vol. I. Cambridge, Mass.: Addison-Wesley. Pp. 223–258.

Sarbin, T., and V. L. Allen (1968). Role theory. In G. Lindzey and E. Aronson (Eds.), *The handbook of social psychology,* Vol. I. (2nd ed.) Reading, Mass.: Addison-Wesley. Pp. 488–567.

Scanzoni, J. (1970). *Opportunity and the family.* New York: Free Press.

_____ (1976). Sex role change and influences on birth intentions. *J. Marriage and Family, 38,* 43–58.

_____ (1978). *Sex roles, women's work, and marital conflict.* Lexington, Mass.: Lexington Books.

Scanzoni, J., and M. McMurray (1972). Continuities in the explanation of fertility control. *J. Marriage and Family, 34,* 315–322.

Schachter, S. (1971). *Emotion, obesity, and crime.* New York: Academic Press.

Scheff, T. J. (1966). *Being mentally ill.* Chicago: Aldine.

Schiffrin, D. (1977). Opening encounters. *Amer. Sociol. Rev., 42,* 679–691.

Schoenherr, R. S., and A. M. Greeley (1974). Role commitment processes and the American priesthood. *Amer. sociol. Rev., 39,* 409–426.

Schuler, R. S. (1977). Role conflict and ambiguity as a function of the task-structure-technology interaction. *Organizat. Behav. hum. Perform., 20,* 66–74.

Schwartz, M., and S. Stryker (1971). *Deviance, selves and others.* Washington: American Sociological Association.

Scott, M. B., and S. M. Lyman (1968). Accounts. *Amer. Sociol. Rev., 33,* 46–62.

Sears, P. (1951). Doll aggression in normal young children: influence of sex, age, sibling status, father's absence. *Psychol. Monogr., 65,* 6.

Sears, R. R., E. Maccoby, and H. Levin (1957). *Patterns of child rearing.* Evanston, Ill.: Row, Peterson.

Sears, R. R., L. Rau, R. Alpert (1965). *Identification and child rearing.* Stanford: Stanford Univ. Press.

Segal, B. E. (1962). Male nurses: a case study in status contradiction and prestige loss. *Social Forces, 41,* 31–38.

Selznick, P. (1966). *TVA and the grass roots.* New York: Harper & Row.

Serpe, R. T. (1980). Placing social psychological analysis in a structural context: commitment, identity salience, and role behavior. Paper presented at the annual meeting of the American Sociological Association, New York City.

Sherif, M. (1936). *The psychology of social norms.* New York: Harper.

Sherwood, J. J. (1965). Self-identity and referent others. *Sociometry, 28,* 66–81.

Shibutani, T. (1955). Reference groups as perspectives. *Amer. J. Sociol., 60,* 562–596.

_____ (1961). *Society and personality.* Englewood Cliffs, N.J.: Prentice-Hall.

_____ (1966). *Improvised news,* Indianapolis: Bobbs-Merrill.

_____ (1978). *The derelicts of company K: a sociological study of demoralization.* Berkeley: Univ. of California Press.

Shott, S. (1979). Emotion and social life: a symbolic interactionist analysis. *Amer. J. Sociol., 84,* 1317–1334.

Shuval, J. T. (1970). Sex role differentiation in the professions: the case of Israeli dentists. *J. Health soc. Behav., 11,* 236–244.

Sieber, S. D. (1974). Toward a theory of role accumulation. *Amer. Sociol. Rev., 39,* 567–578.

Simmel, G. (1950). *The sociology of Georg Simmel.* Glencoe, Ill.: Free Press.

Slocum, W. L., and F. I. Nye (1976). Provider and housekeeper roles. In F. I. Nye *et al., Role structure and analysis of the family.* Beverly Hills, Calif.: Sage Publications. Pp. 81–100.

Smith, A. (1759). *A theory of moral sentiments.* London.

Smith, C. (1971). Scientific performance and the composition of research teams. *Admin. Sci. Quart., 16,* 485–495.

Smith, D. L. (1973). Symbolic interactionism: definitions of the situation from Becker and Lofland. *Catalyst, 7,* 62–75.

Smith, M. B. (1974). *Humanizing social psychology.* San Francisco: Jossey-Bass.

Smith-Lovin, L., and D. Heise (forthcoming). Impressions, expectations, behavior. New York: Academic Press.

Snoek, J. D. (1966). Role strain in diversified role sets. *Amer. J. Sociol., 71,* 363–372.

Spitzer, S., C. Couch, and J. Stratton (n.d.). *The assessment of self,* Iowa City: Escort-Serroll.

Spreitzer, E., E. Snyder, and D. Larson (1979). Multiple roles and psychological well-being. *Sociological Focus, 12,* 141–148.

Stager, S. F., L. Chassin, and R. D. Young (1983). Determinants of self esteem among labelled adolescents. *Soc. Psychol. Quart., 46,* 3–10.

Stokes, R., and J. P. Hewitt (1976). Aligning actions. *Amer. Sociol. Rev., 41,* 838–849.

Stone, G. P. (1962). Appearance and the self. In A. M. Rose (Ed.), *Human behavior and social process.* Boston: Houghton Mifflin. Pp. 86–118.

Stouffer, S. A. (1949). An analysis of conflicting social norms. *Amer. Sociol. Rev., 14*, 707–717.

Stouffer, S. A., and J. Toby (1951). Role conflict and personality. *Amer. J. Sociol., 56*, 395–406.

Strauss, A. (1978). *Negotiations*. San Francisco: Jossey-Bass.

Strauss, A., L. Schatzman, D. Ehrlich, R. Bucher, and M. Sabshin (1963). The hospital and its negotiated order. In E. Friedson (Ed.), *The hospital in modern society*. New York: Free Press. Pp. 147–169.

Strong, S. (1943). Social types in a minority group. *Amer. J. Sociol., 48*, 563–573.

Stryker, S. (1956). Relationships of married off-spring and parent: a test of Mead's theory. *Amer. J. Sociol., 52*, 308–319.

_____ (1957). Role-taking accuracy and adjustment. *Sociometry, 20*, 286–296.

_____ (1959). Symbolic interaction as an approach to family research. *Marriage and Family Living, 21*, 111–119.

_____ (1964). The interactional and situational approaches. In H. T. Christensen (Ed.), *Handbook of marriage and the family*, Chicago: Rand McNally. Pp. 125–170.

_____ (1968). Identity salience and role performance. *J. Marriage and Family, 30*, 558–564.

_____ (1971). Review symposium: the handbook of social psychology. *Amer. Sociol. Rev., 36*, 894–898.

_____ (1972). Coalition behavior. In C. G. McClintok (Ed.), *Experimental social psychology*. New York: Holt, Rinehart, and Winston. Pp. 338–380.

_____ (1973). Fundamental principles of social interaction. In N. J. Smelser (Ed.), *Sociology* (2nd ed.). New York: Wiley. Pp. 495–548.

_____ (1977). Developments in two social psychologies: toward an appreciation of mutual relevance. *Sociometry, 40*, 145–160.

_____ (1980). *Symbolic interactionism*. Menlo Park, Calif.: Benjamin/Cummings.

_____ (1981). Symbolic interactionism: themes and variations. In M. Rosenberg and R. H. Turner (Eds.), *Sociological perspectives on social psychology*. New York: Basic Books.

_____ (1983). Social psychology from the standpoint of a structural symbolic interactionism: toward an interdisciplinary social psychology. In L. Berkowitz (Ed.), *Advances in experimental social psychology*. Vol. 16. New York: Academic Press.

_____ (1984). Science as rhetoric: nothing to lose but our gains. *Contemporary Sociology, 13*. 251–254.

Stryker, S., and E. A. Craft (1982). Deviance, selves and others revisited. *Youth and Society, 14*, 159–183.

Stryker, S., and A. Gottlieb (1981). Attribution theory and symbolic interactionism: a comparison. In J. H. Harvey, W. Ickes, and R. Kidd (Eds.), *New directions in attribution research*. Vol. 3. Hillsdale, N.J.: Erlbaum.

Stryker, S., and A. S. Macke (1978). Status inconsistency and role conflict. *Ann. Rev. Sociol., 4*, 57–90.

Stryker, S., and R. T. Serpe (1982). Commitment, identity salience, and role behavior: theory and research example. In W. Ickes and E. Knowles (Eds.), *Personality, roles and social behavior*. New York: Springer-Verlag.

_____ (1983). Toward a theory of family influence in the socialization of children. In A. C. Kerckhoff (Ed.), *Research in sociology of education and socialization*. Vol. 4. *Personal change over the life course*. Greenwich, Conn.: JAI Press.

Sumner, W. G. (1906). *Folkways*. Boston: Ginn.

Suter, L., and H. Miller (1973). Income differences between men and career women. In J. Huber (Ed.), *Changing women in a changing society*. Chicago: Univ. of Chicago Press.

Sutherland, E. H. (1939). *Principles of criminology* (3rd ed.). Philadelphia: Lippincott.

Sweet, J. (1973). *Women in the labor force*. New York: Seminar Press.

Tatnall, P. A., A. S. Macke, and S. K. Houseknecht (1980). The underutilization of professional women's training among highly educated women: a role conflict perspective. Presented to the American Sociological Association. New York, August.

Thibaut, J. W., and H. H. Kelley (1959). *The social psychology of groups*. New York: Wiley.

Thoits, P. A. (1983). Multiple identities and psychological well being: a reformulation and test of the social isolation hypothesis. *Amer. Sociol. Rev., 48*, 174–187.

Thomas, D. L., D. D. Franks, and J. M. Calconico (1972). Role-taking and power in social psychology. *Amer. Sociol. Rev., 37*, 605–614.

Thomas, D. L., and A. J. Weigert (1971). Socialization and adolescent conformity to significant others: a cross-national analysis. *Amer. Sociol. Rev., 36*, 835–846.

Thomas, W. I. (1937). *Primitive Behavior*. New York: McGraw-Hill.

Thomas, W. I., and D. S. Thomas (1928). *The child in America*. New York: Knopf.

Touhey, J. C. (1974). Situated identities, attitude similarity and interpersonal attraction. *Sociometry, 37*, 363–374.

Treiman, P. J., and K. Terrell (1975). Sex and the process of status attainment: a comparison of working women and men. *Amer. Sociol. Rev., 40*, 174–200.

Trocki, K. (1980). Preliminary report on sex role changes, peer influence, and mental health. Institute for Scientific Analysis. Oakland, Calif.

Turner, J. H. (1974). *The structure of sociological theory*. Homewood, Ill.: Dorsey.

Turner, R. H. (1956). Role-taking, role standpoint, and reference group behavior. *Amer. J. Sociol., 61*, 316–328.

_____ (1962). Role-taking: process vs. conformity? In A. M. Rose (Ed.), *Human behavior and social processes*. Boston: Houghton Mifflin. Pp. 20–40.

_____ (1970). *Family Interaction*. New York: Wiley.

_____ (1976). The real self: from institution to impulse. *Amer. J. Sociol., 81*, 989–1016.

_____ (1978). The role and the person. *Amer. J. Sociol., 84*, 1–23.

_____ (n.d.a). Role-taking as process.

_____ (n.d.b). Role-playing and process.

_____ (n.d.c). A strategy for developing an integrated role theory.

Turner, R. H., and L. M. Killian (1957). *Collective behavior*. Englewood Cliffs, N.J.: Prentice-Hall.

Veevers, J. E. (1973). Voluntarily childless wives: an exploratory study. *Sociol. Soc. Research, 57*, 356–366.

Verbrugge, L. (1980). Possible causes of the apparent sex differences in physical health. *Amer. Sociol. Rev., 45,* 507–512.

Videbeck, R. (1960). Self conception and the reaction of others. *Sociometry, 23,* 351–359.

Vincent, C. E. (1965). Socialization data in research on young marrieds. *Acta Sociologica, 8,* 118–127.

Waite, L. J., and R. M. Stolzenberg (1976). Intended childbearing and labor force participation of young women: insights from nonrecursive models. *Amer. Sociol. Rev., 41,* 235–252.

Waller, W. (1938). *The Family.* New York: Dryden.

Waller, W., and R. Hill (1951). *The Family.* New York: Holt, Rinehart, and Winston.

Wallston, B. (1973). The effect of maternal employment on children. *J. child Psychol. Psychiatry allied Disciplines, 14,* 81–95.

Warheit, G. J., C. E. Holzer, III, R. A. Bell, and S. A. Arey (1976). Sex, marital status, and mental health: a reappraisal. *Social Forces, 55,* 459–470.

Warshay, L. (1962). Breadth of perspective. In A. M. Rose (Ed.), *Human behavior and social processes.* Boston: Houghton Mifflin. Pp. 148–176.

Weber, M. (1946). In H. Gerth and C. W. Mills (Eds.), *From Max Weber: essays in sociology,* New York: Oxford Univ. Press.

––––––– (1947). *The theory of social and economic organization.* New York: Free Press.

Webster, M., Jr., and B. Sobieczek (1974). *Sources of self-evaluation.* New York: Wiley-Interscience.

Weil, M. (1961). An analysis of the factors influencing married women: actual or planned work participation. *Amer. Sociol. Rev., 26,* 91–96.

Weigert, A. J., and R. Hastings (1977). Identity loss, family, and social change. *Amer. J. Sociol., 82,* 1171–1185.

Weinstein, E. A. (1969). The development of interpersonal competence. In D. A. Goslin (Ed.), *Handbook of socialization theory and research.* Chicago: Rand McNally. Pp. 753–775.

Weinstein, E., and P. Deutschberger (1963). Some dimensions of altercasting. *Sociometry, 26,* 454–466.

Weinstein, E. A., K. A. Feldman, N. Goodman, and M. Markowitz (1972). Empathy and communication efficiency. *J. soc. Psychol., 88,* 247–254.

Weinstein, E. A., and J. M. Tanur (1976). Meanings, purposes, and structural resources in social interaction. *Cornell J. soc. Relations, 11,* 105–110.

Weitzman, L., D. Eifler, E. Hokada, and C. Ross (1972). Sex role socialization in picture books for pre-school children. *Amer. J. Sociol., 77,* 1125–1150.

Wiley, M. G., and A. Eskilson (1983). Scaling the corporate ladder: sex differences in expectations for performance, power and mobility. *Soc. Psychol. Quart., 46,* 343–350.

Wispe, L. G. (1955). A sociometric analysis of conflicting role-expectations. *Amer. J. Sociol., 61,* 134–137.

Wood, V., and J. Robertson (1978). Friendship and kinship interaction: differential effect on the morale of the elderly. *J. Marriage and Family, 40,* 367–375.

Wrong, D. (1961). The oversocialized conception of man. *Amer. Sociol. Rev., 26,* 184–193.

Zigler, E. F., and S. Harter (1969). The socialization of the mentally retarded. In D. A. Goslin (Ed.), *Handbook of socialization theory and research,* Chicago: Rand McNally.

Znaniecki, F. (1965). *Social relations and social roles.* New York: Irvington Publishers.

Zurcher, L. A., Jr. (1977). The naval reservist: an empirical assessment of ephemeral role enactment. *Social Forces, 55,* 753–768.

Zurcher, L. A., Jr., D. W. Sonenschein, and E. L. Metzner (1966). The hasher: a study of role conflict. *Social Forces, 44,* 505–514.

CHAPTER 7

Organizations and Organization Theory

Jeffrey Pfeffer
Stanford University

INTRODUCTION

Organization theory encompasses the interdisciplinary study of all aspects of behavior in and by formal organizations. As such, it incorporates aspects of sociology, psychology, economics, political science, and anthropology. It treats as units of analysis everything from individuals acting, feeling, and thinking in an organizational context to groups, larger subunits such as departments or divisions, the organization as a whole, and, recently, even populations of organizations and the relationship of organizations to larger social structures such as the state and society. The study of organizations occurs in disciplinary departments such as departments of economics, political science, anthropology, sociology, and psychology, as well as in various professional schools, particularly schools of administration such as business administration, hospital and health administration, and public administration and public policy.

The author gratefully acknowledges the helpful comments of Charles O'Reilly, Gerald Salancik, W. Richard Scott, and Barry Staw.

Encapsulating such a large and diverse intellectual domain in a chapter—or for that matter a book—is obviously an impossible task. As a field that is both interdisciplinary and relatively young, organization theory can be described as being very much in a preparadigm stage of development, with new conceptual schemas and theoretical perspectives being introduced on a regular and frequent basis, but without there yet emerging the consensus on exemplars, styles of inquiry, and the major substantive issues that characterize a field at a more advanced stage of development (Kuhn, 1970).

At the same time many of the major themes and issues that underly the research activity in organization theory are shared with the other social sciences, including psychology. In particular, the organizing principle chosen for this chapter focuses on two such issues: (1) the appropriate level of analysis at which theory and empirical research is most productively couched, and (2) the perspective on action implied in the theories. Adopting such a focus provides one way of obtaining perspective on the field of organizations and of beginning to understand the various theories and how they interrelate. At the same time any particular framework serves to highlight some theoretical schemas and ignore others. The present chapter is no exception; not every body of literature in the field of organizations is covered. Indeed, it could not be, given the constraints of time and space. Rather, major schools of thought are selectively reviewed to compare and contrast them in order to explore the remaining conceptual and empirical issues that must be solved in order to organize, integrate, and develop knowledge of organizations. As such, our purpose is not just to outline the various theoretical perspectives but to critically evaluate and compare them to assess where they are similar, where they are different, and where the unanswered questions lay. The intent is not only to review the literature but also to stimulate at least some of the readers of this chapter to become involved in researching and resolving the myriad conceptual and empirical issues that make the study of organizations both exciting and difficult.

Two facts are important in understanding the field of organizational behavior. First, the field is, indeed, very young. Scott (1981) dates the emergence of the field within sociology to the translation into English of Weber (1947) and the studies of organizations launched by students and colleagues of Merton's, such as Selznick's (1949) study of the Tennessee Valley Authority, Gouldner's (1954) study of a gypsum mine and factory, Blau's (1955) study of an employment agency and government bureau, and the study of the typographical union (Lipset, Trow, and Coleman, 1956). Freeman (1982) reported that the first index in sociology with formal organizations or organizations as subject headings was the index of the *American Journal of Sociology* published in 1965, though the index of the *American Sociological Review* published in 1955 did have six entries under the heading "bureaucracy." The *Administrative Science Quarterly,* an interdisciplinary journal devoted to the study of organizations and administration, was founded in 1956, and the *Academy of Management Journal* began publication in that same year. The Carnegie group of March, Simon, and Cyert were active in the middle 1950s, and the study of business decision making (Cyert, Simon, and Trow, 1956; Cyert, Dill, and March, 1958) and the appearance of a review of psychological principles relevant to the study of organizations (March and Simon, 1958) appeared at about that time. One of the first textbooks, *Managerial Psychology* (Leavitt, 1958), also appeared during that period. Thus although there were clearly important analyses of organizations undertaken prior to that period (Barnard, 1938; Merton, 1940; Simon, 1947), the field of organizations can be said to have really become organized and defined only about twenty-five years ago. Moreover, much of the growth in terms of the num-

bers of programs, number of courses, number of articles and books, and number of active researchers identifying with the field has occurred in the past ten to fifteen years.

The age of the field is at least partly an explanation for the theoretical diversity and lack of a coherent paradigm. New ideas and new people are still being recruited into the study of organizations; a period of theoretical consolidation and the development of consensually agreed-upon exemplars, research methods, and perspectives is now only beginning to be visible. The relative youth of the field, coupled with its interdisciplinary, pre-paradigmatic nature, has led to a proliferation of theories of the middle range (Merton, 1968; Pinder and Moore, 1979), theories or conceptual schemas using a variety of perspectives to deal with a variety of different substantive issues. Comparative testing and theory rejection has not yet occurred to any great degree. It is likely, however, that the proliferation of variables, schemas, frameworks, and theories is reaching an upper bound and that the next ten years will witness much more of an effort at comparative testing and theory disconfirmation, moving toward the resolution of the numerous inconsistencies and substantively different predictions that now coexist in the various theories of organizations.

Because the study of organizations is housed in both disciplinary departments and schools of administration, there is also a tension between the theoretical and the administratively relevant and useful, which characterizes the development of knowledge and the politics of the field. On the one hand, there are those who maintain that to the extent an applied, practice-oriented focus comes to dominate the field, the selection of the research problems, the variables, and even, at times, the answers come to be under the control of the client organizations, the business firms or governmental agencies that employ or sponsor the work of the organization theorists. Baritz (1960) has argued that too close association with clients has hindered the development of industrial psychology. Important issues such as control structures and power were ignored because of the focus on employer-determined foci of selection, training, and worker motivation and control. He further maintained that the scientists' critical capacities were dulled by the close association and subordinate position that often accompanied working for or with a management to solve some pressing practical problem. Nehrbass (1979) has commented on the ideological content of much of organization theory and the resultant reluctance of the field to learn from data on issues, such as participative management and quality-of-working-life experiments, in which there is a strong ideological component. The implication of the Nehrbass argument is again that values and ideology have gotten in the way of the development of a science of organizations.

On the other side are those who argue either that description and understanding are inevitably value-laden and ideological or that attempts to develop a theory of organizations free of concerns of application and practice are inevitably unproductive even for the intended aim of the acquisition of scientific knowledge. The first position is that taken by Gergen (1978) in a critique of the methodology implicit in much of social psychology. He maintained that "understanding may also entail 'assigning a meaning' to something, thus creating its status through the employment of concepts" (Gergen, 1978, p. 1344). As Unger (1975, p. 32) has argued, what are preceived as facts, and what is distinguished from other phenomena, inevitably results from the particular theoretical position one has adopted before one begins the study. Gergen further maintained that the very methodology of the social psychological experiment tended to produce support for the hypotheses being tested. Inevitably, he maintained, one measured according to one's theoretical predispositions, analyzed the data accordingly, and thus tended to produce support for the initial conjectures. Gergen also argued that what was selected for study, as well as the theoretical concepts used to address the phenomenon, was a result of ideology and beliefs held by those doing the investigating. Thus to pretend scientific inquiry was value-free was to be intentionally misleading. The implication of Gergen's argument is that what one needs is passionately contested perspectives rather than the myth of dispassionate science. Gergen's model is more of an advocacy paradigm, such as that used in the law, in which each side has a position and attempts to prove it and to disconfirm the other within a code of established rules and procedures.

The second position is that taken by Argyris (1968, 1972). He maintained that the best way of overcoming problems arising from the use of static correlational analyses and contrived variables and situations with no external validity was to develop and test theory in clinical settings, as part of a consulting or change effort. He argued, "The applicability and utility of knowledge are criteria that should be integrated and given equal potency in the development of behavioral science theories and the execution of such empirical research" (Argyris, 1972, p. 83). It was only by testing theories in actual applications,

Argyris maintained, that valid knowledge could be developed. Argyris's prescription can be seen as one way out of the problem identified by Gergen (1978) of creating processes of hypothesis testing that are almost always self-fulfilling prophecies. By confronting real situations and the constraints of providing usable, practical knowledge to guide ongoing organizations, Argyris maintained that theory would be not only more useful but also more valid as a descriptive statement of the world as it exists apart from the world of the scientist's mind.

The possibility exists that much of organization theory is and serves the role of political language (Edelman, 1964) in that it diverts analysis and dulls the critical faculties through the use of evocative, affect-producing terminology and symbols (Pfeffer, 1981). The nature of the conduct of scientific research is a subject much beyond the scope of this chapter. However, the reader should be aware of the dual functions and multiple masters served by organizational theory and organization theorists and of the controversy concerning the presence and role of ideology in the discipline. Cartwright (1979) has indicated the effects of demography and the social context on the development of social psychology, noting, for instance, how the infusion of scholars from Europe at the time of World War II led to an interest in democratic versus authoritarian leadership styles and how the civil rights controversies of the early 1950s sparked interest in attitude research and in the relationship between attitudes and behaviors. He has noted that "the knowledge attained is the product of a social system and, as such, is basically influenced by the properties of that system and by its cultural, social and political environment" (Cartwright, 1979, p. 82).

One would expect, then, that there would be systematic variation both over time and over disciplines and departments in the extent to which practice versus theory was stressed, as well as in the particular forms and varieties of ideology that were expressed implicitly in the organizational science developed. It is not by chance that the sociologists with, in general, more radical political views (Ladd and Lipset, 1975) have adopted a somewhat more pure scientific orientation, while concern with application has been stronger in professional school, and particularly business school, contexts. The sociology of organizational science is a subject to be empirically explored. The importance of such issues for understanding the development of organization theory, particularly because the different perspectives on action and levels of analysis have different ideological implications and connotations, makes it imperative that the field be viewed with these underlying controversies in mind. It is important to understand the social context of organization theory in evaluating where it has been, where it is, and where it is going.

LEVELS OF ANALYSIS

There are two dimensions that are heuristically useful in characterizing the various theories of organizations. The first, the level of analysis at which activity is analyzed, distinguishes between those theories that treat the organization as an undifferentiated collectivity and those that deal with smaller social units within organizations, such as individuals, coalitions, and subunits. There is some controversy over the issue of whether or not it is permissible to reify the organization and treat it as a single unit, as well as how to define the appropriate level and unit of analysis. Argyris (1972), for instance, has argued that analyzing larger collectivities in terms of their structural properties has led to an unwarranted neglect of the processes that occur within such units that produce the observed results. Weick (1969) has similarly argued that "organizations" don't behave, people do. On the other hand, Perrow (1970a) has taken organizational psychology to task for attributing everything to the actions of people and couching the analysis solely in terms of people, their responses, and their idiosyncrasies and traits, thereby ignoring the enormous structural regularities that often have more prominent influences on organizational activity.

The issue of the appropriate unit of analysis (Freeman, 1978) has both theoretical and statistical aspects. The statistical issue arises because under certain conditions the process of aggregating to a larger social unit inflates the estimate of the true relationship among the variables (Hannan, 1971). An organizationally relevant example of this problem is Bidwell and Kasarda's (1975) attempt to examine the effect of some administrative properties of school districts on district effectiveness, defined in terms of the average achievement level of students in certain grade levels. They reported that district-level pupil/teacher ratios, administrative ratios, and measures of teacher qualifications all had effects on average pupil achievement. Hannan, Freeman, and Meyer (1976), using individual student data, demonstrated the impact of aggregation bias on estimates of administrative effects. In virtually every case a correctly specified model—including controls for input variation such as student ability and social background, estimated at the individual level of analysis—yielded smaller estimates of school administration effects.

The level of analysis should correspond to the level of the theoretical mechanisms that are presumed to be affecting the dependent variables. Hannan *et al.* (1976, p. 138) contrasted estimating the effects of school properties on student learning or achievement, an individual-level process, with estimating the effects of schooling on the rationalization of labor markets by a signaling function (Spence, 1975), a process that occurs on a society-wide basis and that would require analysis at the level of economic systems. Unfortunately, unit- and levels-of-analysis problems are quite common in organizational research and, as seen in the Bidwell and Kasarda (1975) example, can lead to incorrect conclusions.

Units-of-analysis problems have plagued motivation and task design research (Roberts and Glick, 1981), in which intraindividual predictions have been tested by using interindividual data. As Kopelman (1977) has noted, "There is wide agreement that expectancy theory is a model of individual choice behavior" (p. 651). The choice is made by an individual from among a set of possible actions, such as working harder or less hard. As Roberts and Glick noted, however, the empirical testing of such theories most often involves seeing whether or not a person with a given level of need strength or set of valences and expectancies works harder (or is absent more) than someone else with a different level. An intraindividual theory of choices among actions became transformed into an interindividual comparison of behavior on a single act. Roberts and Glick argued that this made it necessary to rethink and reformulate the theory. Kopelman (1977) reported that twice as much variation was explained when within-individual expectancy predictions were tested as contrasted with across-individual predictions.

The point is that the unit-of-analysis choice is more than a matter of empirical or theoretical convenience; it has theoretical and statistical implications that are often overlooked in the design of organizational research (Freeman, 1978). Pennings (1975) attempted to study the effects of environmental variations on structure by using a sample drawn from the stock brokerage industry. But as Freeman (1978, p. 347) noted, the sample consisted of forty local offices from a single company; most variations in environmental variables, such as the level of the market, trading volume, and regulations, would vary longitudinally, not cross-sectionally. Furthermore, it is likely that the local offices were not free to adjust internal structures at will. Consequently, the finding of no environmental effects on structure may speak more to the sample and choice of units than to the correctness of the underlying theory. Meyer's studies of state and municipal finance departments (1972a, 1975) also raise the question of whether the right hierarchical level is being investigated. One might wonder whether agency chiefs have the authority to change structures within the finance agency, and whether the structural changes accompanying changes in finance department leadership are peculiar just to the finance department or rather are reflective of larger political change. As Freeman (1978) has noted, "The answer to this question affects the locus of causation. If one's research is conducted at the local level, one may be missing the most important causal variables" (p. 338).

Organizations are, of course, hierarchical in the sense that they are comprised of smaller units (Simon, 1962), such as individuals and groups. This fact suggests that research spanning multiple levels of analysis may be both useful and necessary (Roberts, Hulin, and Rousseau, 1978). Lincoln and Zeitz (1980) have argued that it is necessary to separate individual from organizational effects in order to test theories that may operate at both levels. They further suggested that an analysis-of-covariance framework affords an appropriate mechanism for accomplishing this. Using Hauser's (1971) path-analytic conceptualization of covariance analysis, Lincoln and Zeitz demonstrated how effects operating at the individual level could be distinguished from those operating at the organizational level. Using data from twenty social service organizations, they estimated a model in which decentralization was the dependent variable, lateral communications and administrative intensity were intermediate dependent variables, and size, the amount of division of labor, professionalization, and change in the task environment were exogenous variables. The important finding was that estimates of total effects in some instances hid differences in processes that were operating at the individual as contrasted with the organizational level of analysis.

By far the majority of the studies contained in the domain of organizations and organization theory have proceeded by using the individual as the unit of analysis. Thus in a typical study of motivation employees in a single organization may be surveyed to assess their perceptions of job characteristics (Hackman and Oldham, 1975), their growth need strength, and their attitudes and motivational states. The analysis considers each individual observation as independent. The importance of this choice of both unit of observation and associated methodology derives from the fact that such choice virtually predetermines the type of theoretical variables employed. Because of the focus on the individual as the unit of analysis, attention is given to individual-level variables such as individual demographics, needs (Maslow, 1943; Alderfer, 1972), and attitudes. The effects of more inclusive variables—such as the normative context and interaction structures, as well as the technology, economic conditions, and so forth, that might affect individual reactions to work—are neglected. The critique of task design and job attitudes literatures as being too preoccupied with need theories and neglecting contextual effects on the assessment of job characteristics and the development of job attitudes (Salancik and Pfeffer, 1978b) reflects the fact that such a limited focus is an almost inevitable result of the choice of the unit of analysis. To take account of contextual effect requires moving to a more inclusive unit of analysis. Similarly, with only a few notable exceptions (e.g., Zucker, 1977), experimental studies have made no effort to incorporate elements of context into the design, thereby leaving Weick's (1965) promise of the potential for experimentation to enrich organizational analysis largely unfulfilled.

The unit problem in organizational research is an important one, not only because of issues of aggregation bias (Hannan, 1971) and the unwarranted supporting or disconfirmation of theories because of the choice of an inappropriate unit (Freeman, 1978), but also because the choice of the unit is bound up with the type of theoretical variables that will be used to investigate the process under study. Because of the focus on the individual in much of the literature treating organizations, it turns out there is very little organizational or even social content in many of the theories currently prominent in organizational behavior. The attention to the unit issue evidenced by Freeman (1978) and the multilevel analysis paradigm demonstrated by Lincoln and Zeitz (1980) provide promise that a more comprehensive and theoretically coherent treatment of organizational phenomena are possible.

PERSPECTIVES ON ACTION

The second dimension distinguishing among organization theories is the perspective on action adopted, either implicitly or explicitly, by each theory. Three perspectives on action are evident in the literature:

1. Action is seen as purposive, rational or boundedly rational, and prospective.

2. Action is seen as externally constrained or situationally determined.

3. Action is seen as being somewhat more random and dependent on an emergent, unfolding process, with rationality being constructed after the fact to make sense of behaviors that have already occurred.

In part because of its relationship to the world of practice and in part because of the ideology dominant in the United States, the first perspective on action is the more common one found in theories of organizations. This perspective has several critical elements. In the first place, behaviors are construed to be chosen. Second, such choice is presumed to occur from within a set of consistent preferences. As Allison (1971) has noted, rationality presumes that events are "purposive choices of consistent actors" (p. 11). Thus behavior is determined by and reflective of conscious, purposive action. Allison has stated that "behavior reflects purpose or intention" (p. 13). Third, as implied by the above, choice is presumed to occur prior to the action itself—rationality is prospective rather than retrospective in that actions are chosen in light of some anticipated consequences. Fourth, action is goal-directed. Friedland (1974) has argued that rationality cannot be defined apart from the existence of goals. Choice, then, is value maximizing.

The presumption that actions are consciously undertaken to attain some goal or set of goals means that preferences can be inferred from the choice. Allison (1971) has illustrated this inference process in the realm of foreign policy analysis in which the actions of nations are scrutinized to infer from them what the underlying goals and motives of the nations are. The problem, however, is that "an imaginative analyst can construct an account of value-maximizing choice for any action or set of actions performed" (Allison, 1971, p. 35). In a similar fashion, the choices and actions of individuals may be employed, after the fact, to construct statements about the needs and goals of the individuals that would be consistent with such actions. Indeed, the ability of observers to readily construct such statements concerning personal dispositions, after the fact, to account for any observed behavior may be a factor underlying the widespread acceptance of personal dispositional theories of organizational behavior (e.g., Salancik and Pfeffer, 1977b).

The maximizing model of rational choice employed in economics (Simon, 1978) has been criticized as being insensitive to the cognitive limitations possessed by individuals and organizations. Thus a subset of theories of

rational choice have emerged emphasizing the boundedly rational nature of decision making (Simon, 1957). Bounded rationality encompasses choice "theories which incorporate constraints on the information-processing capacities of the actor" (Simon, 1972, p. 162). Such theories incorporate the notion of satisficing (Simon, 1957) or the fact that search for alternatives stops when an option is available that is satisfactory, in the sense of meeting the actor's aspiration levels, rather than necessarily being the optimal decision. Furthermore, boundedly rational choice incorporates explicitly the fact that search is costly (Simon, 1978) and that heuristic procedures for decision making arise that are based on experience and that economize on information processing requirements. One such decision-making procedure is incrementalism (Lindblom and Braybrooke, 1970), defined by Padgett (1980) as "a pattern of marginal change in final allocation outcome relative to some base, which frequently is the previous year's allocation outcome" (p. 355). Incrementalism has been used to explain budget allocations, particularly in governmental organizations (Wildavsky, 1979). Boundedly rational choice also forms the foundation for behavioral theories of decision making (e.g., Cyert and March, 1963).

We treat bounded rationality as a slight modification of rational choice more generally and as consistent with rationality perspectives on action rather than with the other perspectives described below. The basic assumptions of the rational model are left largely untouched by the boundedly rational perspective: Decisions are still made prospectively, choice is value satisficing (if not maximizing), and preferences are still frequently presumed to be consistent. Furthermore, bounded rationality is a theory that is clearly time-bound—as new decision technologies are uncovered and new information-processing systems are developed, the boundaries of bounded rationality are pushed back. Indeed, the task implicitly set out by the bounded rationality perspective is the development of new decision technologies to increase the capacity of taking rational action.

The second perspective on action has been called situationism (Bowers, 1973) in psychology. Much like its psychological analogue, situationism in theories of organizational behavior or the external constraint perspective tends to ignore individual or organizational factors, including preferences, goals, and information processing, or to see them as less important than the primary impact of the external stimulus or effect (Harre and Secord, 1972). Action is seen not as the result of conscious choice but, rather, as the result of external constraints, demands, or forces that the social actor may have little control over or even cognizance of (Pfeffer and Salancik, 1978). Choice may have little to do with the values or preferences of the actor taking the action but, rather, may reflect the values and constraints of external elements. Some variants of theories in this second category do speak to the role of cognition, but cognition is viewed as a mechanism for legitimating or making sense of behavior that has already occurred. Cognition is used to provide meaning and a sense of control to the world, but this meaning is developed after the fact of the behavior, rather than guiding the behavior prospectively.

The third perspective on action is not as homogeneous as the first two. Basically, this view of behavior at times denies either an internally directed or externally determined rationality of behavior. Some variants of this perspective, such as decision process theories (e.g., Cohen, March, and Olsen, 1972; March and Olsen, 1976; Mackenzie, 1978), stress the sequential, unfolding nature of activity in organizations. Because participation in organizational decisions is both segmented and discontinuous, and because organizations are viewed as contexts in which people, problems, and solutions come together, the emphasis on process implies that the results cannot be predicted a priori either by the intention of individual actors or by the conditions of the environment. Rationality, goals, and preferences are viewed as emerging from the action rather than guiding the action. Indeed, March (1978) has argued that one of the purposes of behavior is to discover preferences through experiencing various outcomes.

Other variants of the third perspective emphasize the socially constructed nature of organizational realities. These cognitive perspectives on organizations (Weick, 1979) view the organization as a system of shared meaning, in which much of the organizational work consists of symbol manipulation and the development of a shared organizational paradigm (Brown, 1978). Action is governed by the systems of meaning that emerge within the social structure to provide understanding of the social world and, through the development of a shared perspective and negotiated order, to provide order and cohesion for those in the social system.

The three perspectives on action imply very different views about the fundamental nature of organizations and about the task of administration. The rational, goal-directed view presumes that administrative action impacts firm performance. The task of management is

viewed as figuring out what to do to enhance organizational goal attainment. Action is presumed to be planned and purposeful, and such a perspective is quite compatible with the various normative choice and planning procedures that have been developed in management science and economics. The second, externally constrained perspective views both organizational actions and the outcomes of such actions as being largely outside the control of administrators or others in the organization. The administrative task is viewed as being either a relatively unimportant task (Pfeffer, 1977) or, at best, one of registering the environmental constraints and demands and attempting to align the organization with these external pressures. The third perspective can potentially encompass a sophisticated integration of the first two points of view (Pfeffer, 1981, Chap. 6) in which organizations are viewed as externally constrained and administrative action is focused on creating the illusion of competence and control to maintain support both internally and externally for what the organization or other social unit is required to do to survive. However, this view of the social-construction-of-reality process is not one shared by all of those working in this third perspective. With its emphasis on the relativistic nature of social reality and the focus on randomness and unpredictability, the third perspective would appear to deny the possibility to proactively manage organizations as well as the capacity to even forecast the course of organizational behavior over time.

There are some methodological differences associated with the three perspectives on action that have made their comparative evaluation difficult. The third social-construction-of-reality view has been generally studied either through the use of case analysis and natural language (Daft and Wigginton, 1979) or through the use of computer simulations, as in the instance of some of the decision process theories (Cohen, March, and Olsen, 1972). In almost no instance has there been the kind of quantitative, comparative empirical work more commonly found in examining either of the other two perspectives, though such approaches are clearly possible (e.g., Axelrod, 1976; Bougon, Weick, and Binkhorst, 1977). This difference in methodology has led to some tendency for methodological preferences to drive perspectives on organizational action.

The research task remains to first sharpen the outlines of the three perspectives so that they are more precisely specified and differentiable and then to examine the various organizational circumstances that appear to

TABLE 1
Categorization of Theoretical Perspectives in Organization Theory

	PERSPECTIVES ON ACTION		
LEVEL OF ANALYSIS AT WHICH ACTIVITY OCCURS	*PURPOSIVE, INTENTIONAL, GOAL-DIRECTED*	*EXTERNALLY CONSTRAINED, DETERMINED*	*RANDOM, EMERGENT, RETROSPECTIVELY RATIONAL*
Individuals, coalitions, or subunits	Needs theories and job design Goal setting Expectancy theory Path-goal leadership theory Political theories	Operant conditioning Role theories Social influence and social information processing	Cognitive theories of organizations Institutionalization theory Language in organizations Ethnomethodology Symbolic interactionism
Total organization	Structural contingency theory Markets and hierarchies Marxist perspectives	Resource dependence Population ecology	Decision process theories (e.g., gargage can model)

be associated with the greater empirical validity of one rather than the others. Whether or not the perspectives are inherently incompatible, or whether they can be combined (as in thinking about taking rational action in the context of a socially constructed world), must await the development of the perspectives into more specific and refined models of action. This kind of empirical specification has begun in the more limited domain of decision models (Chaffee, 1980; Padgett, 1980), in which the dimensions that distinguish among decision-making theories, and the empirical outcroppings of such distinctions, have been formulated so that empirical disconfirmation is possible.

In Table 1 the two dimensions along which organization theories are to be compared and categorized, as well as the theories to be reviewed, are displayed. The remainder of the chapter provides some detail about these perspectives or theories.

THEORIES OF INDIVIDUAL OR SUBUNIT RATIONAL ACTION

Much of the research domain of organizational behavior—and most of that research that has emerged from the industrial psychology tradition within the field—adopts a focus on the individual as the unit of analysis and pro-

ceeds from the premise of conscious, foresightful, goal-directed action. To the extent that variables such as norms, organizational climate, shared cultures (Ouchi and Johnson, 1978), and shared organizational paradigms (Brown, 1978) condition individual responses, the unit of analysis may be inappropriate, and many of the results may be incomplete in terms of their assessment of causality for this reason. This argument will be developed in more detail as the specific theories are reviewed.

NEEDS THEORIES OF JOB DESIGN

According to the variants of needs theory, individuals are motivated to seek need fulfillment primarily from their job or task environment. Action is seen as goal-directed in that actions are calculated to bring the individual into a situation in which his or her needs are fulfilled or to avoid those situations in which important needs are frustrated. Presumably, motivation, positive job attitudes, and increased performance result from providing individuals settings in which their needs can be fulfilled through effective work performance. The needs postulated to reside in individuals range from the five needs of physical, safety, social, esteem and competence, and self-actualization offered by Maslow (1943, 1954), to the existence, relatedness, and growth needs postulated by Alderfer (1972), to the power, affiliation, and achievement needs advanced by McClelland (1961). Most of the needs theories argue that a satisfied need is not a motivator of behavior, which means that as more of the basic needs have been satisfied, it is incumbent on the organization to provide jobs that facilitate the satisfaction of higher-order needs.

Presumably, the higher-order needs for feelings of competence and self-actualization are best satisfied by the nature of the job itself (Herzberg, Mausner, and Snyderman, 1959). Thus needs theories are closely intwined with the large literature on job design and its effects on worker attitudes and behavior (Hackman and Oldham, 1980). The job design literature (e.g., Hackman and Oldham, 1976) has emphasized the importance of changing dimensions of the task to enhance worker satisfaction and effectiveness. But the early studies of the relationship between task attributes and task satisfaction found no simple, consistent linear relations (Turner and Lawrence, 1965; Hulin and Blood, 1968). Thus it was proposed that there were moderator variables that affected the job attribute–job attitude relationship, and one of the more important of such moderators was, presumably, higher-order need strength, sometimes called growth need strength. For instance, Hackman and Lawler (1971), Brief and Aldag (1975), Stone (1976), Stone, Mowday, and Porter (1977), and Steers and Spencer (1977) all investigated the extent to which individual need strengths moderated the job design–job attitude relationship, with the hypothesis being that enriched jobs, higher on variety, autonomy, task significance, and feedback, would be positively associated with favorable work outcomes primarily for those individuals who had stronger levels of the more growth- and competency-related needs.

The evidence for this prediction is weak, at best. White (1978) reviewed more than thirty articles investigating the relationship between personal characteristics, such as needs, urban-rural background, education, locus of control, and so forth, on the job scope–job attitude relationship. He concluded, "Nineteen years of theory building and empirical research have not provided much hope in finding generalizable individual difference moderators of the relationship between job quality and worker responses" (White, 1978, p. 278). In Hackman and Lawler's (1971, p. 279) comparision of the one-third of their subjects with the highest growth need strength with the one-third with lowest growth need strength, there were almost no significant differences in the correlations between job attributes and job attitudes for the two

subsamples. The difference in correlations between those with the higher growth need strength and those with lower growth need strength on the item measuring overall job satisfaction was only 0.08. The Brief and Aldag (1975) replication of this study was equally disconfirming. Only three of thirty-two correlations were statistically significantly different between the high- and low-growth need strength groups at the 0.05 level of probablity in the expected direction. The amount of explained variance in most of these studies has been small, typically under 10 percent for measures of absenteeism or other, more behavioral indicators of work activity.

Salancik and Pfeffer (1977b) criticized the basic structure of needs theory as well as how it has been tested. They argued that tests of the model have most frequently involved the use of questionnaires, which led to correlating perceptions with perceptions. Furthermore, the structure of the instruments themselves could easily produce priming and consistency response artifacts. Salancik and Pfeffer (1977b) noted that needs theory had been formulated in a way that made it almost impossible to refute, and that the conceptual status of needs, job characteristics, and job attitudes had been incompletely considered. As a trait approach to the explanation of work behavior, needs theory is inconsistent with the trend toward situationism in psychology (e.g., Bowers, 1973).

Roberts and Glick (1981) argued that many of the tests of task design theories have mixed within-person and person-situation relations. Job design theory argues that it is the objective nature of the job or task environment, interacting with personal characteristics, such as needs, that determines motivation and job attitudes. Yet few of the studies even measured task characteristics separately from how they were perceived by respondents, and those that did (e.g., Hackman and Lawler, 1971) tended to use such measurements only to provide evidence for the validity of the perceptual measures. Roberts and Glick (1981) argued, "Based on the observation of within-person relations between task perceptions and job responses, researchers often jumped to the conclusion that a person-situation relation also held and suggested objective job changes in order to change job responses" (p. 196). Not only are the concepts themselves, such as needs and job characteristics, open to a variety of theoretical interpretations, but many of the properties being investigated have not been assessed in a way compatible with the theoretical model being tested.

A further problem arises from the fact that most of the studies used data collected from only one or a very few locations or departments. Even when a quasi-experimental design was employed (e.g., Hackman, Pearce, and Wolfe, 1978), the individual was the unit of analysis. In Fig. 1(a), the causal model implicit in the task design and needs theory literature is diagrammed. However, suppose that the perceptions of job characteristics, need statements, and the attitudes toward the job were being shaped by informational social influence (Festinger, 1954) and conformity pressures (Kiesler and Kiesler, 1969), certainly not an unreasonable supposition given the interactions among people in work settings. This alternative model is diagrammed in Fig. 1(b). It suggests that any observed association between task characteristics and task attitudes may be a spurious result of the fact that both are consequences of the prevailing normative and informational structure of the work environment. With no attempt to identify or measure variables assessing context effects, there is no way for any analysis to discriminate between the two alternative models.

And there is evidence for the effect of just social influences on both task attitudes and task perceptions. Herman and Hulin (1972), Herman, Dunham, and Hulin (1975), and O'Reilly and Roberts (1975) all reported data indicating that job attitudes were more strongly related to organizational position, identified by department or divisional affiliation, than to various background and demographic characteristics. Pfeffer (1980) observed a structural or subunit effect on both attitude and needs statements. O'Reilly, Parlette, and Bloom (1980) examined differences in perceptions of task characteristics in a sample of nurses who were, by all available evidence including job analyses, doing the identical task. These authors found that perceptions of job characteristics were systematically related to the nurses' frame of reference, which included things such as education, tenure, orientation toward professionalism, and income. Most importantly, overall job satisfaction influenced perceptions of job dimensions. O'Reilly, Parlette, and Bloom (1980) concluded that "the results are...consistent with the social construction of task characteristics" (p. 129). The studies just cited indicate that Fig. 1(b) is consistent with some available data and offer an alternative explanation for the results that have been obtained thus far by people working in the need-theoretic tradition.

In addition to testing needs theories through task design studies, some more direct tests of needs theory have been made. First, there have been studies that have investigated the extent to which there is evidence for the hierarchical arrangement of needs (Blai, 1962;

Goodman, 1968). Then studies have investigated the extent to which unsatisfied needs motivate behavior. And finally, studies have looked at whether as some needs are satisfied, new needs emerge (Hall and Nougaim, 1968; Wofford, 1971). As summarized by Wahba and Bridwell (1976), these studies in general provide virtually no support for Maslow's hierarchy-of-needs theory. A more recent study using longitudinal data to test needs theory (Rauschenberger et al., 1980) also failed to find evidence consistent with the predictions of that theory.

The literature on needs theory and task design may be the archetypical example of theory being accepted regardless of the empirical evidence. For task design and the associated technology and ideology have flourished in the world of practice. The quality-of-working-life movement and the associated activities of job redesign and the assessment of job redesign brought needs theories to the field (Lawler, Hackman, and Kaufman, 1973; Hackman, Pearce, and Wolfe, 1978). Prescriptive works have been written arguing for the efficacy of job redesign as a solution to many motivational problems and providing guidelines on how to implement such task redesign to make the chances of success higher (Lawler, 1974; Hackman et al., 1975; Hackman and Oldham, 1980). Commenting on Maslow's need hierarchy theory more specifically, Wahba and Bridwell (1976) made a statement that is applicable to other theories of needs and task design as well: "Maslow's need hierarchy theory...presents the student of work motivation with

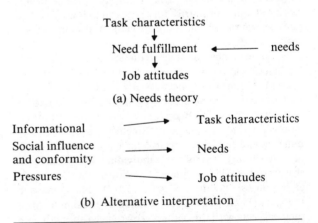

FIGURE 1
Causal Model of Needs Theory and an Alternative Interpretation

an interesting paradox: The theory is widely accepted but there is little research evidence to support it'' (p. 212).

The theoretical status of needs theories and the related theories of task design are mixed. Such theories offer a trait-based conception of human behavior that fits those attributional biases that emphasize personal as contrasted with situational explanations of behavior (Jones and Nisbett, 1971; Kelley, 1971). In addition, the perspective offers implementable prescriptions for solving motivational problems through work redesign. On the other hand, the theories imply a requirement for change that sometimes impacts the organization's basic power and governance system (Hackman, 1978), causing resistance on the part of managers who see their control eroded through worker participation in the task design process. Alternative perspectives to needs theory, addressing the same issue of the development of job attitudes, have arisen (e.g., Salancik and Pfeffer, 1978b). Given the overwhelming lack of support for many aspects of this theory in spite of the methodological artifacts that frequently favor finding support, one might question whether, indeed, further research is necessary. However, if such research is undertaken, the required focus would seem to be around the issues of the social construction of task perceptions and the possibilities for social influences on task and need statements versus the effect of individual predispositions and objective task characteristics on the development of motivation and job attitudes. The research of O'Reilly (O'Reilly and Caldwell, 1979; O'Reilly, Parlette, and Bloom, 1980) is an example of the type of analysis needed, though his research paradigm must be expanded to include measures of needs and other individual traits to really test the relative validity of the models diagrammed in Fig. 1.

GOAL SETTING

Locke (1968) proposed a model of rational, consciously chosen, motivated individual behavior emphasizing cognitive processes. Locke's model is an excellent example of the type of theory of individual-level rational action that characterizes research from this perspective. Locke suggested that it was an individual's conscious intentions that regulated actions. Goals were defined in terms of what the individual was consciously trying to accomplish. Two sets of predictions followed from Locke's analysis:

1. Specific goals were more effective in motivating higher performance than general goals, such as ''do your best.''

2. More difficult goals, if accepted, tended to produce higher levels of performance than easy goals.

Locke further argued that it was goal setting that mediated how individual performance was affected by monetary incentives, knowledge of results, and participation in decision making. In goal-setting theory, behavior is argued to be the result of conscious intention, or goals, chosen by the individual. Consequently, attempts to change behavior must proceed from attempts to change the individual's goals.

Since the setting of goals and the difficulty of those goals are both relatively controllable supervisory activities, Locke's theory has spawned a large number of empirical studies. Several studies were correlational in nature, making the assessment of causality difficult in this instance. Weick (1969) has argued that goals may be retrospective attempts to make sense of behavior, a position consistent with Bem's (1972) self-perception theory. In the goal-setting context what this means is that one cannot tell if hard goals were used to make sense of the higher levels of performance or whether the hard goals actually produced the higher performance. Thus, for instance, Carroll and Tosi (1970) reported that perceived goal difficulty was positively correlated with self-rated effort of managers, although this relationship was found only for managers who perceived rewards to be contingent on performance and for managers who were high in self-assurance and maturity. Dachler and Mobley (1973) found significant correlations between employee's stated goals and performance, though the strength of the relationship differed significantly between the two organizations studied. Steers (1975) observed no correlation between perceived goal difficulty and the rating made by the supervisor's bosses in a study of female first-line supervisors. Steer's results indicate that, as in much of the literature, one gets somewhat different and frequently weaker results when independently derived measures of the dependent variable, in this case performance, are used.

Many of the studies in this research tradition are experimental, and these avoid some of the causation and self-perception issues. Stedry and Kay (1966) assigned nineteen foremen in a nonrandom fashion to conditions that varied goal difficulty along two criterion dimensions. Performance improvement was measured as the difference between average performance during the thirteen weeks before the experimental treatment and the thirteen weeks afterward, and goal difficulty was defined by reference to the average level of performance achieved during the prior six-month period. Stedry and Kay found that total perceived difficulty for both goals was significantly associated with a composite index of performance improvement. Latham and Kinne (1974) randomly assigned pulpwood producers and their crews to either a one-day program on goal setting or to a control condition. Data on production, absenteeism, and turnover were then collected for a twelve-week period. The data indicated that those with training in goal setting experienced a decrease in absenteeism and an increase in production. Latham and Baldes (1975), using a sample of unionized truck drivers, implemented goals to increase the net weight of logs carried. A specific, difficult goal resulted in a substantial improvement in performance, which persisted over a nine-month period. Latham and Yukl (1975a), reviewing goal-setting studies, concluded that the evidence supported the importance of setting specific goals. Further evidence on the relative effectiveness of setting specific goals has been provided by Ivancevich (1976, 1977), Kim and Hamner (1976), Terborg (1976), and White, Mitchell, and Bell (1977).

Locke's emphasis on the primacy of goal setting led him to downplay the importance of monetary incentives. Locke (1968) argued, "Offering an individual money for output may motivate him to set his goals higher than he would otherwise, but this will depend on how much money he wishes to make and how much effort he wishes to expend to make it" (p. 185). In a series of experimental studies Locke (1968) reported that once goal level was controlled, incentives did not affect task performance. However, Pritchard and Curtis (1973) criticized the studies as not offering sufficiently large incentives to test their impact. On the basis of another experimental study Pritchard and Curtis concluded that incentives affected performance independently of the level of the goal and goal commitment. Dachler and Mobley (1973) found that tenure mediated the relationship between goals and performance but that this occurred primarily because employees with longer tenure in the organization perceived outcomes to be contingent on task performance. London and Oldham (1976), Latham, Mitchell, Dossett (1978), and Terborg and Miller (1978) also provided empirical data consistent with the position that subsequent performance is increased more in goal-setting treatments when rewards are contingent on perfor-

mance. Latham and Yukl (1975a, p. 835) concluded that the perceived contingency between goal attainment and positively valued outcomes moderated the effects of goal difficulty on performance. Their interpretation was that this contingency relationship affected goal acceptance. However, alternative explanations stressing the independent effects of incentives are also consistent with the data.

Because the effects of goal setting depend importantly on the acceptance of the goal (Steer, 1975), how to obtain goal acceptance has become a focus of the research. The customary prescription is for having goals set participatively rather than unilaterally. However, evidence on this point is inconsistent, with Latham and Yukl (1975b) and Arvey *et al.* (1976) finding positive effects for participation but other studies finding no difference between participatively or unilaterally set goals (Carroll and Tosi, 1970; Latham and Yukl, 1976; Ivancevich, 1977; Latham, *et al.*, 1978).

Just as needs theory and task design theories illustrated the importance of ideology in overcoming inconsistent data, goal-setting theory illustrates a different problem confronting research in the field, a tendency to be so concerned with application that the investigation of more precisely formulated aspects of the theory can get neglected. In the case of goal-setting the prescriptions are so relatively straightforward—participatively to set specific, difficult goals, with rewards contingent on goal attainment, and have feedback provided on performance—that there has been only limited effort to disentangle the relative effects of the various components of the process. This task is important because of Locke's (1968) explicit statements concerning the primacy of the goal-setting process itself over other aspects such as rewards and feedback. Most goal-setting treatments, for instance, also include feedback or knowledge of results. There is impressive evidence that feedback, even in the absence of goal setting, can impact behavior (Annett, 1969; Erez, 1977; Nadler, 1977; Seligman and Darley, 1977). Thus one would want to know, Is it the goal setting that produces the change in attitudes and behavior or the feedback? Some of the studies cited (Seligman and Darley, 1977) suggest that feedback by itself can have an important influence on behavior. Latham and Yukl (1975a, p. 836) reported that field studies that independently manipulated goal setting and feedback did not exist. In a similar fashion, there is concern over the extent to which goal-setting effects are mediated by contingent rewards. If goal setting works only through reward expectations, then alternative theoretical explanations ranging from expectancy theory to social learning theory (Bandura, 1977) and even variants of operant conditioning might account for the results. And those studies that have demonstrated moderating effects of individual-difference variables (Carroll and Tosi, 1970; Steers, 1975) have produced data not anticipated in Locke's formulation of the theory.

Yet another issue in goal-setting research has to do with the dependent variable. In some cases actual performance measures were used as the dependent variables (Stedry and Kay, 1966; Blumenfeld and Leidy, 1969; Latham and Kinne, 1974; Latham and Baldes, 1975). In other cases effort (sometimes self-rated) was used (Carroll and Tosi, 1970; Steers, 1975). In still other cases measures of attitudes such as satisfaction were used (Kim and Hamner, 1976; London and Oldham, 1976; Ivancevich, 1977), although these studies tended to also include measures of performance. Performance, however, is a function of both ability and effort (Vroom, 1964). Therefore studies that have emphasized performance may have used an inappropriate dependent variable, since without controls for ability the empirical findings are difficult to interpret.

Anderson and O'Reilly (1981) presented data that indicate the difficulties just enumerated. First, in a study containing both job satisfaction and performance (supervisors' ratings) data, the correlation between the two variables was only 0.11. Collecting separate measures of the various components of goal-setting theory, they used multiple-regression analysis to try to assess which of the variables had significant independent effects. They found that goal difficulty and feedback were both significantly associated with performance, though neither were associated with satisfaction; in their multiple-regression results only reward contingency significantly affected satisfaction. This result, however, may have been due to the collinearity among the various goal-setting dimensions. Furthermore, the possibility of an interactive or multiplicative formulation, which is what is implied by some variants of the theory, was not investigated. However, the study is notable in its explicit attempt to untangle the relative effects of the various components of the goal-setting process.

In addition to investigating the dimensions of the goal-setting process and their effects and interrelationships, the other area of further required work involves remedying the neglect of considerations of organizational context in the studies of goal setting. It is quite possible that the particular norms and values of the organization can account for both differences in the effects of goal setting and, perhaps, for the behavior and attitudes themselves without recourse to notions of goal setting. Dachler and Mobley (1973) found that the correlation of stated goal with performance across employees was 0.46 in one organization and only 0.16 in the second. One possibility is that differences in reward contingencies may be responsible for the different results. Another possibility is that the normative structure of the two organizations differed with respect to adequate performance and how performance at different levels was cognitively evaluated. The varying conditions under which goal setting and its more applied variant, management by objectives, have been implemented suggest the incorporation of variables assessing the shared beliefs and culture of the settings in which these interventions are applied. More information on the organizational conditions that affect the impact of goal setting is required, given the differences in results sometimes obtained by the various field studies.

EXPECTANCY THEORY

Closely related to goal setting as a theory of motivation and behavior in organizations is expectancy theory. Originally presented in detail by Vroom (1964), expectancy theory is a theory of rational choice based on the principle of expected value. The theory is based on two models, one predicting the valence of an outcome and the second predicting the force motivating an individual toward some behavior. According to Vroom, valence was the anticipated satisfaction with an outcome, or an individual's positive or negative affect toward it. "The valence model states that the valence of an outcome...is a monotonically increasing function of the algebraic sum of the products of the valences of all other outcomes and his conceptions of the specific outcome's instrumentality for the attainment of these other outcomes" (Mitchell and Biglan, 1971, p. 445). The force toward behavior was conceptualized by Vroom as "a monotonically increasing function of the algebraic sum of the products of the valences of all outcomes, and the strength of his expectancies that the act will be followed by the attainment of these outcomes" (Mitchell and Biglan, 1971, p. 445). This distinction between first-level outcomes, or the immediate result of the act, and the second-level outcomes, the value assigned to these first-level outcomes (e.g., promotion or a raise) in terms of more fundamental goals, has been further developed by Galbraith and Cummings (1967), Graen (1969), and Lawler (1973).

The testing of expectancy theory has developed over time. Prior to the mid 1970s, respondents were typically asked to rate the importance of a number of outcomes, sometimes from a list provided by the experimenter, sometimes from lists culled from earlier responses from the subjects. Lawler and Porter (1967), for instance, had respondents rate the importance of pay, promotion, prestige, security, autonomy, friendship, and opportunity to use skills. Then subjects would be asked to what extent job performance or effort might produce those outcomes. Ratings of effort and performance were obtained, sometimes from the subjects alone, sometimes from superiors or company records, and sometimes from multiple sources. The model was evaluated by seeing the extent to which the various links posited by expectancy theory actually were empirically valid. The correlations were computed across individuals within the same organization.

The results from these studies tended to find support for expectancy theory, but the strength of the results was not great. Lawler and Porter (1967) found support for the expectancy × importance ratings for their seven outcomes and correlations with superior, peer, and self-ratings of effort, but the amount of explained variance was small. Not surprisingly, given methodological considerations, the largest amount of explained variance was obtained for self-ratings of effort. Hackman and Porter (1968) found that the products of expectations and valences for a set of some fourteen outcomes correlated with a series of effectiveness measures, but again, the correlations were not high, with at most about 16 percent of the variation being explained.

Mitchell (1974) criticized much of this early expectancy theory research on two fundamental grounds. First, it is clear that the original Vroom (1964) formulation required a within-subjects rather than an across-subjects design. The model predicts the choice of an action from among those available to an individual, but unless one is willing to make claims for the comparability of the outcome valence and expectancy estimates across subjects, no across-person comparisons are possible. Second, Mitchell (1974) noted that there were problems with the dependent variable, much as in the case of goal-setting research. Some people were attempting to predict effort, the variable proposed in the orignial formulation. Many, however, used some indicator of job performance, and performance could be affected by numerous

factors besides the individual's level of effort. A third issue was raised by Schmidt (1973), who noted that the multiplicative model advanced in expectancy theory required ratio-scale measurement to be tested. Following Mitchell's (1974) criticism, several studies did employ a within-subjects design (Parker and Dyer, 1976; Matsui and Ohtsuka, 1978), with results generally supportive of the expectancy model. Arnold (1981) used a within-subjects design and a procedure to overcome scaling problems, finding support for a multiplicative formulation.

Peters (1977) has noted that in expectancy and other cognitive theories of motivation, there are, in fact, three links. First, there is the overall link from environmental conditions to the observed behavioral responses. Second, there is the perceptual link from environmental conditions to the individual's belief system, as in the link between the actual pay-performance contingencies to individual beliefs about the pay-performance relationship. And finally, there is the link from the belief system to the behavioral responses. Peters argued that expectancy theory, predicting the force to perform some act, explained only this latter link, from the belief system to the behavioral response. Given Lawler's (1967) findings, for instance, concerning employees' misperceptions of organizational pay policies, the reason there was only mixed support for the link between environmental conditions and behavioral responses could be because of misperceptions of environmental factors, not because of failings of the expectancy model itself. Using an experimental paradigm, Peters (1977) found support for all three links in the model.

The applications of expectancy theory have typically involved recommendations to clarify behavior-outcome linkages, as in making certain that employees know that effective performance will be rewarded, and to find out what outcomes have the highest valences and provide these outcomes as rewards. Thus there have been recommendations to use cafeteria-style compensation schemes, in which the employee is allowed the option of choosing particular pay, retirement, and other benefit trade-offs, subject to an overall budget constraint.

Expectancy theory research has evolved over time to use designs both more consistent with the theoretical formulation and less prone to priming and consistency response artifacts. However, two problems have continued to plague the research. First, in spite of Mitchell's (1974) criticism, across-subject designs still are used (e.g., Peters, 1977). Second, and more importantly, although

Dulany (1968) included motivation to comply in his theory of propositional control to reflect the effect of group norms and compliance pressures on the choice of behavior, this concept has almost never been incorporated in expectancy theory formulations. Expectancy theory, as a model of rational choice, has also been criticized for its assumptions about human information processing and rationality. However, these aspects of the theory are also its strengths, since the perspective provides a portrayal of individual motivation that is quite consistent with the individualistic, rational orientation found in other social sciences such as economics and that form the core of the prescriptive management literature.

PATH-GOAL THEORY OF LEADERSHIP

There are numerous theories and studies of leadership, many of which have been reviewed by Stogdill (1974). The path-goal theory is highlighted here because it is a direct extension of the type of instrumentality theory that expectancy theory represents. House (1971) argued that subordinate performance and job satisfaction could be improved if the leaders clarified the paths to various desired outcomes and provided valued outcomes when goals were achieved. In other words, House conceptualized the leader's task as one of working on the various links in the expectancy theory framework to enhance subordinate performance and satisfaction. House's approach suggested why the traditional leader behavior approaches, focusing on the dimensions of consideration and initiating structure (Fleishman and Peters, 1962), might not produce consistent research results. House predicted that the consideration behaviors would be more effective in situations with well-defined goals and technologies, or in unambiguous settings. Initiating structure behaviors, which organize and direct task activity, were more effective in situations evidencing high ambiguity and task complexity. In other words, when the task itself provided direction, the leader's role was one of providing social and emotional support. When the task was ambiguous, more leader direction was effective.

House (1971) further argued that the subordinate's preferences for various kinds of leader behavior would determine satisfaction. Subordinates who valued consideration behavior and support would respond well to those leaders who exhibited such behaviors, while those subordinates who preferred more direction would be more satisfied under leaders who exhibited more initiating structure behavior.

The evidence for the path-goal theory is more consistent with the predictions of satisfaction than with predictions of performance (Evans, 1970; House, 1971). Again, however, note that performance may be an inappropriate dependent variable, since effort may be the variable that is explained, given the structure of instrumentality theories from which the path-goal theory is derived.

POLITICAL PERSPECTIVES ON ORGANIZATIONS

The last theoretical perspective reviewed in this section, a political approach to organizational analysis, is different from the preceding in several respects. First, this perspective considers groups within organizations as well as individuals as the unit of analysis. More fundamentally, political theories have tended to be less managerial and less prescriptive in orientation, focusing more on the description of activities within organizations rather than on developing normative guidelines for management. Furthermore, in the sense that political perspectives on organizations neither assume nor prescribe goal homogeneity within the organization, they depart from assumptions of rationality as defined at the organizational level, because consistent preferences that guide action are fundamental elements in theories of rational choice (Allison, 1971; Friedland, 1974; March, 1976). Although they are not models of organizational rationality, political models belong in this section because they are models that presume intentional, rational action on the part of individuals or subunits within the organization. Such social actors are presumed to act in their own self-interest and to engage in strategic action in pursuing this interest. The final difference is that although other perspectives on behavior considered thus far have at times considered outcomes or actions, they have also focused heavily on attitudes as dependent variables (Bem, 1967). By contrast, political models have tended to focus on the decisions and allocations that result from the interaction of interdependent, competing political actors. Thus there have been studies of the allocation of budgets (Pfeffer and Salancik, 1974; Pfeffer, Salancik, and Leblebici, 1976; Pfeffer and Leong, 1977; Hills and Mahoney, 1978), changes in curricula and programs of study (Baldridge, 1971; Manns and March, 1978), succession to administrative positions (Zald, 1965), increases in university tuition (Baldridge, 1971), the choice of a particular computer (Pettigrew, 1973), and the organizational structure that results from the interplay of political interests (Pfeffer, 1978, 1981).

The various political theories view organizations as pluralistic, divided into interests, subunits, and subcultures. Action results "from games among players who perceive quite different faces of an issue and who differ markedly in the actions they prefer" (Allison, 1971, p. 175). Because decisions are the result of bargaining and compromise, the resultant choice does not perfectly represent the preferences of any single social actor. Political models further presume that it is power that determines whose interests are to prevail more in the conditions of conflict. Power "is an intervening variable between an initial condition, defined largely in terms of the individual components of the system, and a terminal state, defined largely in terms of the system as a whole" (March, 1966, pp. 168–169).

Thus the concept of power is fundamental in political theories. Power is defined most often in terms of the capacity of the particular social actor to overcome opposition (Dahl, 1957; Emerson, 1962; Blau, 1964; Salancik and Pfeffer, 1977a). Power is one of the more controversial of the social science concepts. March (1966) has argued that the inference of power in decision-making situations is extremely difficult, and that often power is used in a way conceptually similar to needs or personality to construct explanations for otherwise unexplained variance after the fact. March (1966) argued that to infer that power was a valid concept and was operating in a particular decision situation, one should observe consistency in patterns of outcomes over time, or else the outcome could have been produced by a chance process instead of by power. Furthermore, March argued that power would be more useful to the extent that it could be experimentally manipulated with predictable results and to the extent that power of social actors was itself explainable from a theory of the sources of power.

Most problematic to March (1976) in power models is the underlying assumption of conscious, rational, strategic action taken on the part of various social actors to obtain their preferences in situations of conflict. March (1978) has argued that preferences are not nearly that well formed or consistently held. This issue is indeed central to political models of organizations, for as Nagel (1975) has indicated, power can be virtually defined by the relationship between the preferences of an actor and the outcomes achieved. If preferences are themselves problematic, then the validity of the political model is open to doubt.

Power has been measured typically by interviews (Perrow, 1970b; Pfeffer and Salancik, 1974) in which actors are asked to rate the power of other units in the organization and, less frequently, by various unobtrusive indicators, such as departmental representation on important committees (Pfeffer and Salancik, 1974; Pfeffer and Moore, 1980). In those situations in which both types of measures were used, good convergence was observed. The use of archival or less obtrusive measures of power is important for studying power historically as well as avoiding some of the criticisms of reputational measures of power that have emerged in the community power research (Polsby, 1960).

Political theories of organizations address the issues of what determines the power of the various social actors, the conditions under which power is used, and what various strategies there are for the development and exercise of influence. The source of power is typically argued to be the ability of the social actor to provide some performance or resource to the organization that is valued and important, and the inability to obtain such performance or resource from alternate sources. Sometimes, this critical performance is the ability to cope with critical organizational problems or contingencies. Thus Crozier (1964) argued that the power of maintenance workers in a French factory was due to their control over the one remaining organizational contingency, the breakdown of machines. Hickson *et al.* (1971) also argued that power accrued to those units that could successfully cope with the most central, pervasive, and critical uncertainties. A study of seven organizations by Hinings *et al.* (1974) supported this formulation. Arguing that the power of academic departments came from their ability to provide important resources to the organization, Salancik and Pfeffer (1974) found that departmental power was strongly related to the amount of grants and contracts brought in. Pfeffer and Moore (1980), examining a different university, also found evidence for the importance of grants and contracts as well as student enrollment levels as sources of power. Emerson's (1962) conception that power derived from one's position of net dependence was tested in an interorganizational context by Pfeffer and Leong (1977). They found that the power of agencies in the United Fund, measured by their ability to obtain resources, was a result of the agency's dependence on the fund for budget and the fund's dependence on the agency for visibility and legitimacy. This finding was replicated by Provan *et al.* (1980), who also found that agency linkages to the local community enhanced its power in the budget allocation process.

Most of the studies have been cross-sectional in nature, but Pfeffer and Moore (1980) studied both power and budget allocations over time. Controlling for initial budget and changes in enrollment over the period, these authors found that power did account for budget allocations some ten years later. And controlling for the initial levels of departmental power, they found that grants, contracts, and enrollment levels predicted power. These results provide some answer to March's (1966) argument concerning the need to study power and political processes dynamically.

Power is not used equally in all situations, and thus what March (1966) termed force activation models have developed, specifying the conditions under which power is more or less likely to be employed. Salancik and Pfeffer (1974), examining allocations of four additional resources, found that subunit power was more strongly related to the allocation of the more critical and scarce resources. Hills and Mahoney (1978) found that power accounted for more of the allocation of incremental budgetary resources at the university in times when resources were more scarce. Thus scarcity seems to be one condition associated with the use of power. Another condition is uncertainty or disagreement about either goals or technology, the connections between actions and consequences. Conceptualizing the level of paradigm development as a measure of technological certainty in a scientific discipline (Lodahl and Gordon, 1972), evidence has been presented indicating that power is used more in paradigmatically less developed fields to allocate federal research funds (Pfeffer, Salancik, and Leblebici, 1976), positions on editorial boards (Yoels, 1974), jobs (Hargens, 1969), and journal publication access (Pfeffer, Leong, and Strehl, 1977). Therefore uncertainty and disagreement appear to be conditions associated with the use of power. Salancik and Pfeffer (1978a) presented experimental evidence suggesting that secrecy, both concerning the information used in decision making and concerning the identity of the decision makers, might be associated with the use of power. Although the range of conditions for power use has been far from fully explored, the existing empirical work does suggest that concepts of power activation are important in understanding organizations from a political perspective.

Research on strategies of power acquisition and use, including the determinants of the choice of strategies and the effectiveness of different strategies in different circumstances, is somewhat less developed. Pettigrew (1972), examining the decision to purchase a computer, found that control over the flow of information permitted the individual with such control to affect the decision outcome. This suggests that information control is one important political strategy. Salancik and Pfeffer (1974) found that department heads tended to favor basing allocations on criteria that favored their subunits, and Pfeffer and Salancik (1977a) found that after controlling for departmental power and objective bases of allocation, the selective advocacy of criteria favoring one's subunit was correlated with allocation outcomes. Plott and Levine (1978) have argued that the agenda, or the order in which decisions are considered, can affect the results, a point further developed by Pfeffer (1981). Since power is seldom concentrated enough to have one social actor make the decision without the support of others, the development of coalitions is another important element of political strategy (Bucher, 1970). And the obtaining of political support through strategies of co-optation (Selznick, 1949), such as appointing committees and having powerful interests represented on such committees, is a strategy used to obtain support within organizations as well as to obtain support from the organization's environment.

Two important issues confront political perspectives on organizations. First, Chaffee (1980) has argued that it is, in fact, quite difficult to distinguish among political, bureaucratic, chance, and rational models by using the procedures that have been typically employed—regressions in which indicators supposedly representing the various models are included in the equation. For instance, the fact that budgets tend to be incremental and stable over time (Wildavsky, 1979), which is sometimes taken as support for a model of bounded rationality and incrementalism, could reflect that the power distribution that determines the budget is stable over time or even could be consistent with a more rational, optimizing model (Williamson, 1966). Chaffee (1980) suggested that it would require attention to both process and outcome to diagnose the use of power and politics in organizations. The explication of procedures for testing and assessing the use of power as contrasted with alternative perspectives on decision making remains an important task.

The second issue is the extent to which organizational decision making can produce results that deviate from those predicted by rational choice procedures and survive over time. If the organization is tightly linked to an environment that is reasonably competitive, then over time, surviving organizations will come to act as if they were making rational choices, whether the actual decision-making procedure is incrementalism and bounded rationality (Padgett, 1980) or political power. Williamson (1981) has made the argument that efficiency drives out the effects of power, although this argument rests importantly on the extent to which there are binding external constraints. Even if these arguments were true, one might want to study political processes because the results predicted from rational models may be equilibrium models, and the time required to reach such equilibria may be long enough to make the dynamic process of interest in its own right. Thus the importance of political models depends both on the extent to which the environment is binding and on the interest in adjustment and adaptation processes as contrasted with equilibrium analyses.

EXTERNAL CONTROL OF INDIVIDUAL BEHAVIOR

If one assumes that individuals and organizations are adaptive to their environments, then in order for one to understand behavior, it is both necessary and largely sufficient to consider the characteristics and constraints of the environments in which they are embedded. This approach is the one taken by those who have focused on the external control and external constraint on behavior, de-emphasizing both individual traits and dispositions and cognitive processes.

Within psychology generally there is a continuing debate concerning the relative importance of personal versus situational explanations for behavior (Sarason, Smith, and Diener, 1975). To some extent this controversy has involved the concept of personality (Mischel, 1968) and the extent to which behavior is consistent across situations. However, cross-situational consistency is not a necessary or perhaps even the most appropriate test of the usefulness of a cognitive, individually based perspective (Bem and Funder, 1978). If one takes the rational model of choice seriously, then what are consistent are goals and values. Certainly, behavior would be expected to adjust as the situation warranted. Rational behavior is value-maximizing choice, but whether such choices are consistent over time depends importantly on the situational constraints. Indeed, Salancik (1977) has illustrated, in his review of commitment, that at times persistence in a course of action may be a nonrational response. Thus psychological theories illustrating informa-

tion-processing biases (Kahneman and Tversky, 1973; Ross, 1977) are equivalent to theories of bounded rationality in organizations—both are in the domain of a rational model of prospective action taken in the context of values, albeit subject to various kinds of cognitive and attributional limitations.

The perspectives reviewed in this section for the most part downplay the role of cognitive processes *or* individual traits such as personality in determining behavior; if cognitive processes have a role at all, it is to retrospectively make sense of behavior that has occurred (Salancik, 1977). Rather, these theories emphasize the understanding of behavior by considering solely the conditions and constraints of the contexts in which the individuals are embedded. The controversy over the extent to which behavior is externally controlled or individually chosen touches not only empirical and theoretical nerves but also basic assumptions about the nature of humans, embedded in religion and philosophy. Because the view of humans as active exercisers of choice fits somewhat more closely prevailing beliefs and ideologies, perspectives emphasizing external control and constraint have been somewhat less popular.

OPERANT CONDITIONING

Long after it was a major domain of psychology, learning theory—and more specifically, operant conditioning versions of learning theory—found its way into the literature on organizational behavior. Nord (1969) was one of the first to introduce the concepts to the field, followed shortly by Luthans (Luthans and White, 1971; Luthans and Kreitner, 1975). The basic premises of this perspective, as applied to organizational issues, were quite straightforward. First, since behavior was presumably a function of its consequences, it was incumbent on analysts of organizations to diagnose the behavior-consequence linkages and on managers to systematically manage the behavior-consequence contingencies. Indeed, the very phrase *contingency management* became a part of the language (Luthans and Kreitner, 1974, 1975), encapsulating these ideas.

Although there has been great attention in the experimental psychology literature with issues such as reinforcement schedules and whether ratio or interval scales were more effective (Ferster and Skinner, 1957), such abstract, more theoretcal concerns have not found their way as strongly into the organizations literature, in part because its more applied orientation looked to results rather than to the specific elements that produced the results. There has been some attempt to examine the effect of reinforcement schedules (e.g., Yukl, Wexley, and Seymore, 1972; Berger, Cummings, and Heneman, 1975; Pritchard *et al.,* 1976), because that is one of the ways of distinguishing between the predictions of operant conditioning and those of expectancy theories of motivation. According to expectancy theory, continuous reinforcement should presumably be more effective, because it strengthens the link between the behavior and the instrumental outcome to be received if such outcome is a certain consequence of engaging in the behavior. In contrast, learning theory argues for the greater effectiveness, particularly once the behavior has been learned, of intermittent reinforcement schedules (Luthans and Kreitner, 1975). The empirical results have been mixed, with some studies finding superior results for intermittent reinforcement (Yukl, Wexley, and Seymore, 1972), others finding no difference (Berger, Cummings, and Heneman, 1975; Deslauriers and Everett, 1977), and still others finding an advantage for continuous reinforcement (Zifferblatt, 1972; Copeland, Brown, and Hall, 1974). One problem is that there has been little attention to whether the activity was well or poorly learned in advance, and more importantly, the size of the reinforcers used has often times been so small as to call into question the generalizability of the results.

Most of the published work has merely demonstrated the effectiveness of treatments labeled as operant conditioning interventions, though on occasion there is some question as to whether that is an apt label. The issues and problems in this research can be illustrated by the case of Emery Air Freight, one of the most-cited examples of the effectiveness of operant conditioning interventions (At Emery Air Freight, 1973). Emery, a freight-forwarding concern, was worried about its container utilization rates, an important item affecting cost. The firm implemented a measurement program assessing container utilization and provided self-administered feedback to the employees involved in assembling the freight into the containers. In addition, supervisors were instructed in techniques of verbal reinforcement for improved container utilization performance. The program saved Emery millions of dollars; more surprisingly, the results were almost instantaneous. Locke (1977) has argued that the program was really one of goal setting rather than one of positive reinforcement. It is certainly the case that knowlege of results and feedback increased substantially. It is also the case that there was a now-explicit goal for container utilization. One might wonder whether the reinforcement provided by the supervisors really accounted for the dramatic improvement, particularly given the fact that the improvement occurred in one day.

Other interventions have focused on absenteeism (Pedalino and Gamboa, 1974; Stephens and Burroughs, 1978) and have used devices such as lotteries and card games that depend on attendance on the job. Again, the published results have been positive. Occupational safety has been another significant area for the application of positive reinforcement techniques (Komaki, Barwick, and Scott, 1978). The principle has been to reinforce compliance with safety regulations.

In addition to its emphasis on schedules and controlling behavior by controlling the consequences of that behavior, reinforcement perspectives on activity emphasize the relative efficacy of positive reinforcement coupled with extinction for the undesired behaviors over the more typically used punitive forms of control (e.g., Luthans and Kreitner, 1975). There are no field studies that have directly addressed this aspect of reinforcement theory. However, O'Reilly and Wietz (1980), studying the disciplinary practices of managers in a department store chain, have argued that punishment can have important symbolic value and can positively impact performance. They argued that punishment, when administered on a clearly deserved basis, conveys to the other employees the fact that the organization is concerned with performance; furthermore, it makes clear the contingency between inappropriate behavior and the response to that behavior. Much of the literature on punishment deals with its effective administration (Miner and Brewer, 1976). There is some evidence that indicates that discipline can be an effective performance-enhancing technique (Booker, 1969; McDermott and Newhams, 1971; Heizer, 1976). In order for one to directly test the propositions of reinforcement perspectives, however, it would be necessary to compare the effectiveness of punitive control strategies with others that rely on positive reinforcement coupled with extinction.

Hamner and Hamner (1976) detailed the generally favorable experience a number of firms have had implementing behavior modification principles. But to some extent the very success in practice has led to a lack of attention to some of the details and refinement of the theory. Locke (1977) has argued that many of the successes ascribed to behavior modification interventions can be understood from a cognitive, goal-setting perspective.

Bandura (1977) has similarly taken behaviorism to task for its neglect of cognition, arguing that while the reinforcement of certain simple forms of verbal and motor behavior might be possible without any necessary recognition on the part of the person being shaped, in general, the engagement of cognitive processes made the reinforcement process more effective. Bandura (1977) also introduced the intervening construct of perceptions of efficacy as explaining how social learning occurred. The extent to which cognitive concepts are necessary to understand behavior and the extent to which behavior modification can be successfully distinguished from goal setting and other cognitive approaches remain important theoretical and empirical concerns.

ROLE THEORY

Somewhat less controversial than behavior modification, but still emphasizing the externally determined basis of individual behavior, is role theory. As outlined by Kahn *et al.* (1964), role theory argues that individuals occupy positions in organizations, and associated with these positions (or jobs) are a set of activities, including required interactions, that constitute the individual's role. Because of the nature of organizations as systems of interdependent activity, the occupant of any given role is interdependent with others; these other roles constitute the role set (Merton, 1957) for that particular, or focal, role. Interdependence means that the performance of that individual's role depends importantly on the activities that others in the role set perform, and at the same time their performance is affected by what the role incumbent does also. Because of this interdependence, and particularly the dependence of others in the individual's role set on his or her performance, these others come to have role expectations for appropriate behavior. These expectations are communicated and constitute role pressures. Although the sent role pressures (as seen from the perspective of members of the role set) may not be necessarily experienced in exactly the same way by the focal-role incumbent, who may receive and perceive somewhat different demands, it is nevertheless the case that role demands form an important set of constraints on the behaviors of role occupants.

As seen by Kahn *et al.* (1964) and other role theorists (Gross *et al.,* 1958; Merton, 1975), organizations are systems of mutual social constraint in which the activities of any given position occupant are importantly determined by the demands and expectations of those others in his or her role set. From this perspective changing the focal-role occupant, either by sending the individual to some training or educational program or by actually replacing the person with someone else, would be expected to have limited impact on the behavior of the person occupying the role. The individual or the replacement would still presumably confront the same set of role pressures and role expectations from the same set of interdependent others and would, moreover, face the same information about what appropriate role activity was. Because the person was confronted with the same social demands and social information, behavior would quickly fall into the old pattern.

Roles and role pressures were viewed by Kahn *et al.* (1964) as important sources of tension and psychological stress in organizations. In particular, in a survey of a random sample of employees they identified the following forms of role conflict:

1. Intersender conflict, in which the demands of one member of the person's role set conflict or are incompatible with the demands of another person in the set.

2. Intrasender conflict, in which the demands from a single member of the role set are mutually contradictory.

3. Interrole conflict, in which the demands of one role occupied by an individual, such as employee, conflict with the demands of another role, such as family member.

4. Person-role conflict, in which the expectations associated with fulfilling a role conflict with the individual's moral or ethical beliefs or self-concept.

5. Role overload, in which the demands of the role are not contradictory per se but are so extensive and time-consuming that the individual can not cope with all the role expectations.

6. Role ambiguity, in which the individual faces stress because of uncertainty about what behaviors are, in fact, required in the role.

Kahn and his colleagues found that role conflict was faced by a large proportion of the work force surveyed and, furthermore, was an important cause of stress and tension on the job. Subsequent studies of role ambiguity and conflict (Rizzo, House, and Lirtzman, 1970; Hall, 1972) have provided further documentation on the effects of uncertainty and role-related stress in producing dissatisfaction, turnover, and tension. There is, then, good evidence that the external pressures one confronts because of the occupancy of a given position and role in the organization are both real and potent.

Perhaps the classic study of role effects is Lieberman's (1956) field study of the workers in a plant. Initial attitudes were measured, and then subsequently, some of the workers were promoted to foremen, others were made shop stewards, and others remained in their previous role. Lieberman (1956) demonstrated, first of all, that there was no difference in their attitudes (e.g., toward the company, the job, and the union) prior to the new positions being assumed. Thus although one could scarcely make the argument that there was random assignment of persons to roles, there was at least no correlation between the new positions and previous attitudes. Subsequent to assuming their new positions, Lieberman reexamined attitudes. He found that there was systematic attitude change in a direction predicted by the role assumed. Foremen had developed more procompany and other attitudes and beliefs consistent with their supervisory role; shop stewards had changed their attitudes in a pro-union direction. After these later measurements the company encountered some financial problems, and some of the foremen were demoted back to regular employees. Lieberman examined their attitudes once again and found that those back in their original role as regular employees had readopted their original attitudes. Lieberman's time-series design provides a nice demonstration of the extent to which attitudes are shaped by one's position and role occupancy.

Pfeffer and Salancik (1975) examined the effects of peer, subordinate, and supervisor expectations on the reported behavior of a set of leaders in a state university housing office. Behaviors were measured using the Leader Behavior Description Questionnaire (Stogdill and Coons, 1957). These authors found that both work-related and social behaviors could be accounted for by role set members' expectations, with work-related behavior being most heavily influenced by the expectations of the boss, and social behaviors being most influenced by the expectations of subordinates. In addition, Pfeffer and Salancik (1975, p. 152) reported:

Whether the supervisor attends more to the expectations of his boss or to those of his immediate subordinates appears to be a function of (a) the demands to produce coming from his boss, (b) the percent of the time the supervisor actually engages in supervision rather than in routine task activities, (c) the number of persons supervised, (d) the sex of the supervisor, and (e) whether task decisions are made primarily by the supervisor, by his boss, or by his subordinates.

Most of these factors were related to the social similarity between the supervisor and others in the role set and the amount of interaction (and, perhaps, interdependence) with them.

The investigation of role set determinants of behavior requires the collection of data on both behavior and expectations for that behavior from a large number of persons in the organization, as well as the application of some form of network analysis paradigm (e.g., Roistacher, 1974; Burt, 1977). The empirical investigation of this perspective must await additional research using such methodologies. For the moment role-type effects have been used to argue for the relative ineffectiveness of individually based change approaches (Campbell and Dunnette, 1968) and, by inference, for the need to have attempts at organizational change undertaken on a more systemwide basis. Clearly, interventions such as team building and other work focusing on group process (Dyer, 1977) implicitly accept the critical nature of roles and role pressures in the determination of both attitudes and behaviors in organizations.

The fact that people conform to the expectations of others is, of course, not news, given the extensive social psychological literature on conformity (e.g., Kiesler and Kiesler, 1969). What is somewhat different about the role effects perspective, however, is that it argues that the demands and expectations for the behavior of the occupant of a given focal role are not strictly exogenous but emerge from the technology and task interdependence inherent in the work itself. Thus role pressures and role demands are presumably amenable to the restructuring or reorganization of jobs and duties. Indeed, one might argue that successful occupants of roles in which previous occupants have been unsuccessful use their recruitment to the position to argue for and obtain just such restructuring, to prevent them from facing the same difficulties as their predecessors.

SOCIAL INFLUENCE AND SOCIAL INFORMATION PROCESSING

The effect of others in the individual's environment on both attitudes and behavior is one of the oldest and most prominent themes in the literature of both sociology and social psychology. Two different mechanisms are generally presumed to be responsible for these effects of the environment on behavior, and the two effects are not mutually exclusive. The first effect is one positing an explicit exchange of behavior in which, in order to achieve acceptance by one's social environment, the individual alters his or her behaviors, including the behavior of reporting attitudes and opinions, in a direction to be more consistent with the prevailing norms in the reference group in which acceptance is sought. This is an important mechanism posited in the literature on conformity (Kiesler and Kiesler, 1969). The second mechanism is one of informational social influence. Festinger (1954) argued that in the absence of an overwhelming physical reality, perceptions of the world become socially anchored. Confronted with uncertainty, people turn to informal social communication and resolve uncertainty through communication with others in a process in which shared social definitions of reality emerge. Smith (1973) has argued that uncertainty is a pervasive part of organizational life and that informational social influence comes to have a major impact on how people view their work environments. There is evidence that even the labeling and perception of one's emotions is under the influence of informational social influence, particularly when the situation is ambiguous (Schacter and Singer, 1962).

Blau (1960) and Davis, Spaeth, and Huson (1961) called the effects of group composition on individual attitudes and behavior structural effects. The general model of such effects is

$$Y = a_1 + b_1X_1 + b_2X_2 + b_3Z + u \quad \text{and}$$
$$Z = f(X_1 - kX_2)$$

(Blalock, 1967, p. 792). In the case of Blau's formulation X_1 can be viewed as an individual's score on some variable, for instance, an attitude toward clients (Blau and Scott, 1962), and X_2 represents the group mean on the variable. "The factor, Z, is...taken as a function of the difference between the individual score and that of the mean for his group, i.e., the degree of deviance or minority status" (Blalock, 1967, p. 792). As Blalock has pointed out, there are identification problems with the formulation that make estimation problematic. Hauser (1970) has recommended covariance analysis and multiple-regression analysis with dummy variables indexing group membership as a more appropriate way of assessing group or contextual effects than the methods used in the early research.

Methodological considerations aside, there are a large number of theories that take the form of the equation above, recognizing the effect of norms and context on the development of attitudes and behaviors by individuals embedded in these settings. Such a perspective is in sharp contrast to the dispositional view of attitudes (Calder and Schurr, 1981), which views attitudes as stable positive or negative dispositions acquired through experience and guiding behavior. It is this dispositional view that has guided research on individual attitudes and behaviors in the work setting for the most part. As Calder and Schurr (1981) have perceptively noted, the contextual argument, taken to its logical conclusion, does not even need individual cognitive concepts such as attitudes or needs. "Rather, it is sufficient simply to understand the parameters of the social context" (Calder and Schurr, 1981, p. 287).

One articulation of a contextual perspective on attitudes and other dispositional constructs that does retain cognitive elements is the social information-processing perspective advanced by Salancik and Pfeffer (1978b). This perspective argues (p. 226):

> Individuals...adapt attitudes, behavior, and beliefs to their present social context and to the reality of their own past and present behavior and situation. This premise leads inexorably to the conclusion that one can learn most about individual behavior by studying the informational and social environment within which that behavior occurs and to which it adapts.

The model has essentially two parts:

1. A focus on the use of social information in processes by which reality becomes socially constructed.

2. A focus on how behaviors are used to construct attitude and need statements through a process of attribution, a process that is itself affected by social elements such as definitions of legitimacy and external priming and cueing, which may cause the individual to attend to certain elements of behavior and to certain potential explanations for that behavior.

The first part of the process is the most clearly social and the one that departs the most significantly from dispositional or trait-based explanations for behavior. Salancik and Pfeffer asserted that there were two effects of social information or the social context:

1. An effect in which the attributes of the work environment become defined and evaluated by the perceptions of others.

2. An effect through which attitudes and needs become defined and determined by the information provided by others in the environment.

There is empirical evidence consistent with both social effects.

O'Reilly and Caldwell (1979) developed two versions of a task involving the processing of student application files, an enriched and an unenriched version. Using a group of control subjects, these authors found that the two tasks did significantly differ on the fundamental job description dimensions (Hackman and Oldham, 1975). Subjects were randomly assigned to either the enriched or the unenriched task condition. Simultaneously, subjects (students at UCLA) were also assigned to either a positive or a negative social-cueing condition. In the positive condition information was made available that implied that others who had done the task had found it meaningful, interesting, and worthwhile, while the reverse was implied by negative-cueing condition. O'Reilly and Caldwell (1979) reported that the social information had more effect on task perceptions and task attitudes than did the "objective" characteristics of the tasks. Although the study could be faulted for some of its demand characteristics, a replication by White and Mitchell (1979) provided substantially similar results using a somewhat different experimental methodology.

Indeed, the idea that job characteristics are, in part, perceptually filtered (Newman, 1975) is scarcely surprising once stated. It is only a slight step from that position to recognize that these perceptions are influenced in important ways by the views of others in the work environment (Weiss and Shaw, 1979) and, therefore, that perceptions of the environment of the job are, in large measure, socially constructed. The O'Reilly and Caldwell (1979) and White and Mitchell (1979) studies investigated the extent to which the assessment of job dimensions was socially mediated. But there are other forms of social effects on task environment perceptions. As Salancik and Pfeffer (1978b) noted, others in the social environment can cue workers to focus on some dimensions of work rather than others. If people talk about pay all the time, pay becomes an important dimension used in evaluating the job, and so forth. Ingham (1971) presented data that indicates that worker attitudes vary as the time for contract negotiations approaches. Not surprisingly, the approach of negotiations, accompanied by discussion of what the workers do not presently have on their job, results in focusing on those factors and a decline in worker attitudes.

In addition to providing information about what dimensions of the work environment are important and how a given job measures up on those dimensions, people in one's environment help in the interpretation of events that occur in that environment. "A supervisor who disciplines a worker who is not doing an adequate job may be seen as lacking concern for the employee, or alternatively, as concerned for the success of the firm. Which interpretation develops may be socially determined: the more equivocal events are, the more social definitions will prevail" (Salancik and Pfeffer, 1978b; p. 230). Peters (1978) and Pfeffer (1981, Chap. 6) have both suggested that the interpretation of events and the use of symbolic activity and political language as part of that process are critical parts of the administrative task. Clearly, such interpretations occur continuously in the work environment and provide information as to how that environment is to be viewed.

Others in the work environment tell us not only about that environment but also about what we should want from that environment (what our needs are) and how we should evaluate the environment (what our attitudes should be). This direct effect on attitude and need statements is also important and empirically demonstrable. Seashore (1954) was one of the first to find that the more cohesive work group, the more congruence there was in the job attitudes expressed by members of that group. In spite of the large literature on conformity, there have been almost no studies that have tested the relative effects of social influences on attitudes against the effects of individual traits, such as needs or personality dimensions. Seashore's (1954) data support a social explanation for attitudes only to the extent that the work groups did not differ in other ways and faced different amounts of variance in the actual work encountered.

Herman and Hulin (1972) attempted to account for individual job attitudes by using individual characteristics (which might be correlated with more basic individual traits) as well as the departmental and divisional affiliation of the employee. Herman and Hulin found that subunit membership accounted for attitudes better than did the various individual characteristics—age, sex, and time employed. Herman, Dunham, and Hulin (1975) and O'Reilly and Roberts (1975) conducted replications, coming to the same conclusion. O'Reilly and Roberts (1975) argued that "affective responses to work are predominately associated with organizational characteristics rather than individual ones" (pp. 148–149).

Examining the validity of the social information-processing perspective, particularly in contrast to older theories of task design and motivation, is not a simple task. For instance, the evidence just cited that job attitudes are more related to organizational location than to individual characteristics is consistent with a social information-processing approach, but the evidence is far from conclusive. Two possibilities are that the individual characteristics measured were not the right ones—for instance, more attention should have been paid to needs rather than to demographic variables—and that the reason the attitudes varied was that the jobs performed in the various subunits varied.

A second problem is that an individual's own view of what his or her needs are may result from behavior and from information provided by others about what needs are appropriate and what are being fulfilled (Salancik and Pfeffer, 1978b, p. 239). Thus needs and attitudes may be correlated even when both are derived socially. By randomly assigning persons with presumably different needs to jobs that are identical except for their social context and then seeing if individual attitudes can be predicted by that social information, one can partially overcome this problem. The work of White, Mitchell, and Bell (1977), O'Reilly and Caldwell (1979), and White and Mitchell (1979) comes close to accomplishing this experimentally. The existing evidence is supportive of the social information-processing perspective, but the evidence is not as extensive as one might like.

Pfeffer (1980) studied 113 engineers and collected information on their needs, their perceptions of task characteristics, their attitudes toward their job and the organization, and their subunit membership as well as which of two companies they were in. He also gathered data on their length of employment, which may be related to coming to terms with their work environment, and

how much choice they had and how difficult it was to get hired into their present organization. He found that there were effects of context (subunit membership) on the perceptions of task dimensions and on reported needs, and that there were subunit effects on satisfaction and intentions to leave the organization even when job dimensions and needs were statistically controlled. Although there was no random assignment of persons to subunits and one can assume that the jobs done in the various subunits differed, it is important that there were subunit effects on all of the predicted dependent variables and that there were subunit effects on attitudes even when job dimensions and needs were statistically controlled.

Although the three theories reviewed in this section differ in the extent to which they incorporate cognition and in their specific mechanisms, all emphasize the prediction and understanding of individual behavior through the analysis of the environment in which the individual is embedded. For behavior modification or operant conditioning approaches, the critical environmental variables have to do with the reinforcement contingencies, the form of reinforcement, and the schedule on which such reinforcement is administered. For role theories the critical variables are the system of role pressure and expectations that confront the occupant of the focal role. And for social information processing the critical variables are the informational environment and social norms concerning legitimacy that confront the individual as he or she comes to terms with the task environment. Each perspective offers an externally controlled view of individual behavior; it is likely that the three perspectives are more complementary than competing. With the exception of some limited research treating the social information-processing approach, however, there have been few attempts to explicitly test these external control perspectives against those theories stressing individual choice and individual traits and dispositions.

THEORIES OF ORGANIZATION-LEVEL RATIONALITY

Theories of rational action at the organizational level, designed to account for organization-level phenomena such as structures and vertical integration, share many of the problems of individual-level rational action as well as some unique to this level of analysis. The shared problems have to do with the information-processing and inference processes embedded in theories of rational choice (e.g., Ross, 1977). The cognitive limitations apparent at the individual level (Simon, 1957) are reproduced at the organization level in the use of standard operating procedures, limited search, and various heuristics to deal with ambiguous information and uncertainty (Cyert and March, 1963). The unique problems concern the extent to which one can presume homogeneity within the organization either in terms of the properties of its various units or in terms of the preferences and beliefs that guide the organization-level rational action. We will consider each of these problems, as well as the "as if" defense, to provide an overview of some issues of research in this domain.

As Scott (1981) has argued, "Efforts to relate technical and structural measures at the organizational level are extremely hazardous because organizations tend to employ a variety of technologies and to be structurally complex" (p. 226). There is often as much variation within an organization, as, for instance, among a personnel unit, a production unit, and a research and development unit, in goals, time horizon, structural measures, and so forth as there may be among organizations. To speak of structure, control systems, incentive systems, technology, or the environment as organization-level properties is suspect in many cases. Even within work groups there may be variety in the types of work and in the technologies and control employed. Comstock and Scott (1977) empirically illustrated the differences in results one would obtain by looking at different levels in a study of 142 patient care wards in 16 hospitals. They found (Scott, 1981, p. 288):

> The predictability of the tasks confronting individual nurses was more closely associated with the characteristics of the nursing personnel on that unit (for example, level of qualifications, professionalism) than with the characteristics of the control system of the ward itself (for instance, degree of formalization, centralization). The latter were more closely associated with measures of complexity and uncertainty at the *ward* level, for example, ward size, the extent of staff differentiation, and the level of workflow predictability.

Scott (1981) argued that rather than treating the organization as an average of the characteristics of its differentiated units, it would be more useful and appropriate to treat it "as an overarching framework of relations linking subunits of considerable diversity, and to devel-

op measures that capture the distinctive characteristics of this suprastructure" (p. 228).

If we aren't concerned with characteristics that can vary within organizations but only with overall organizational choices and decisions, such as the degree of vertical integration or merger behavior, there is still the issue of the consistency of preferences within the organization. In order to develop predictions based on organization-level rationality, one must have some degree of assurance that such a concept is reasonable. Why should the various managers in the organization be expected to act in the organization's as contrasted with their own, more parochial interests? The answer to this question is proposed in various perspectives on organizational control. There are, essentially, two perspectives on achieving control. One argues for the relative efficacy of achieving control through a process of socialization, in which the organization's culture, values, and preferences become internalized by the various participants [Ouchi and Jaeger, 1978). Once socialization is accomplished, persons act in the interests of the organization because they have been socialized to do so. The other perspective is based on the use of incentives, including both punishment and, more prominently, compensation schemes that attempt to develop a high correlation between the interests of the organization and the interests of its employees and, particularly, the managers. This is presumably accomplished by having compensation based importantly on overall organizational performance so that by acting in one's individual self-interest, one is automatically led to take actions that are rational from the perspective of the total organization.

The empirical evidence on both the extent of the use of socialization as a control strategy and its effectiveness in ensuring organization-level rationality has yet to be developed. The evidence on incentives, particularly the incentives confronted by high-level managers and executives, is equivocal. The problem arises at all because of the possible separation of ownership from control in the modern corporation (Berle and Means, 1968), leaving managers with the discretion to potentially pursue other goals such as growth (Baumol, 1959; Marris, 1967) or the various perquisites that make life more comfortable for the manager (Williamson, 1964). Presumably, the interest in growth and in firm size is because managerial compensation may be more proximately related to size than to profitability (Roberts, 1959).

Lewellen (1968, 1971), looking at the components of managerial compensation, found that ownership components (changes in stock price, capital gains, and dividends) were larger than the salary components and that, furthermore, the difference was increasing over time. Thus Lewellen concluded that there were finanical incentives for high-level managers to make decisions on the basis of considerations of organizational rationality. The evidence on the relationship of firm performance to compensation, however, is not clear-cut. Roberts (1959) and McGuire, Chiu, and Elbing (1962) found an effect of sales but not of profits on compensation, defined as salary plus bonus. Baker (1969) found an effect of both sales and profits. Ciscel (1974) has argued, however, that there is so much collinearity among the independent variables of sales and profits that it is virtually impossible to empirically assess what the determinants of managerial compensation are. Lewellen and Huntsman (1970) and Masson (1971) both used statistical techniques designed to overcome some of the specification and collinearity problems, and both found that executive compensation was strongly related to profits and was not significantly related to firm size, as measured by sales.

Both Larner (1970) and McEachern (1975) found that compensation and its relation to other variables was different depending on the control type or whether the firm was owner-controlled, management-controlled, or owner-managed. These findings suggest that to the extent that financial incentives are supposed to be designed to ensure the maintenance of organization-level rationality regardless of the issue of the separation of ownership and control, the incentives have not been fully successful in accomplishing this.

The position has been taken that forces of competition and natural selection make organizations (most often, just firms operating in competitive environments) operate as if they were behaving rationally. This is the position adopted by much of economic theory (e.g., Friedman, 1953; Machlup, 1967). The argument suggests that behavioral issues of the effects of various incentives or other control devices as well as issues of the convergence and homogeneity of goals and beliefs within the organization are irrelevant for understanding behavior. Firms behave "as if" they were acting rationally, and thus rational models of firm behavior at the organizational level of analysis are predictively useful even if not correct in all of their assumptions. The use of "as if" reasoning has been critiqued in economics by Nagel (1963) and Winter (1975), among others, and is embedded in philosophy of science issues. For the present the reader should be aware that "as if" logic is one rationale for the use of theories of organization-level rationality but that even this defense must confront the extent to which predictions are confirmed by empirical data. It is interesting to note that organization theory, which has frequently taken on economic theory for the unreasonableness of its behavioral assumptions and for the preference for the formal structure of theories rather than empirical validity, has been almost as guilty at times in using "as if" logic and in assuming rather than demonstrating organization-level rationality as a basis for predicting behavior.

A MARKET FAILURES PERSPECTIVE

The market failures or transactions cost approach (Williamson, 1975) addresses three issues:

1. Why are there organizations at all, as opposed to having transactions conducted solely through markets, and given that there are organizations, which transactions are more efficiently organized through markets as contrasted with hierarchies? This is sometimes called the efficient-boundary question (Williamson, 1981).

2. Given the fact of organizations, how can such entities be structured to economize on transactions costs within the firm?

3. What is the most efficient way of organizing the human assets in the firm, in the sense of structuring the exchange relations and incentives between the firm and its workers?

Because of the efficiency orientation, "Transaction cost reasoning probably has greater relevance for studying commercial than noncommercial enterprise—since natural selection forces operate with greater assurance in the former" (Williamson, 1981, p. 35). Carrying that argument one step further, the transactions cost approach probably is most applicable in the more competitive sectors of the economy.

Williamson (1975) argued that traditional economic theory emphasized production costs but neglected to consider transactions costs in evaluating the advantages of markets as contrasted with organizational arrangements. Transactions costs arise because of the occurrence of the following conditions in exchange relations:

1. Small numbers or noncompetitive markets.

2. Opportunism, which is self-interest seeking with guile.

3. Uncertainty concerning the future state of the environment and what will be required to cope with that world.

4. Bounded rationality, or cognitive limits on information processing.

Small-numbers problems occur not only because of initial market conditions of limited competition but also because, in an exchange relationship, transaction-specific investments in both knowledge and equipment may be built up (Williamson, 1979). Thus, for instance, a market may be competitive initially, but once a firm chooses a specific supplier for a part, that supplier may develop expertise in making the part, invest in specialized equipment, and develop idiosyncratic knowledge about the production process and exchange relationship that provides advantages in any subsequent competition with other potential suppliers. Uncertainty coupled with bounded rationality means that it is not possible to write complete, contingent claims contracts specifying every possible future eventuality and what the obligations of each party would be under those future conditions. The inability to write complete contingent claims contracts, coupled with potential opportunism and small-numbers problems, can potentially lead to haggling among the transaction participants concerning how future contingencies are to be resolved. Such haggling and transaction costs are reduced by organizing such transactions through hierarchical arrangements.

The market failures perspective has been used to analyze the employment relation (Williamson, Wachter, and Harris, 1975), and the issues can be seen clearly in that instance. One way of obtaining labor power is to contract for it, much as one might contract with a painter to paint some rooms. A specified price or wage per hour is set, and specified obligations for performance are offered in return. Such an arrangement will work, however, only to the extent that the unit purchasing the labor power can specify precisely the task to be accomplished, there is some competition among potential labor suppliers, and the technology of the production process is reasonably well understood. If the task is somewhat more complex and unpredictable than painting, the purchaser may not be able to specify completely what labor services will be desired or when. Furthermore, the laborer may learn in the course of doing the job, developing idiosyncratic knowledge of the task and enhanced skill. It may be difficult to write complete contracts specifying all eventualities in terms of the kind and amount of labor desired, and it may be difficult to specify a price deemed

to be fair to both parties that reflects the potential idiosyncratic investments in the exchange that both may acquire. In such a circumstance the employment relation offers an alternative. Labor of an unspecified kind, subject only to the constraints of the acceptance of the authority relation (Mechanic, 1962), is purchased. The future need not be perfectly foreseen; as contingencies arise, the tasks can be adjusted accordingly. And to a large degree, the enhanced skill and the benefits therefrom are captured by the employing organization.

The fact that both parties to an exchange may develop idiosyncratic capital unique to that exchange relationship makes it in the interests of both to organize transactions on a more permanent basis. In the employment context, Wachter and Williamson (1978) have noted, "When workers acquire imperfectly transferable skills, the firm and the worker have an interest in devising a governance structure to assure a continuing, cooperative relation between them" (p. 556). In exchanges among firms a similar problem can arise, which can lead to an efficiency incentive for vertical integration. Monteverde and Teece (1980) examined which parts and subassemblies were purchased through market mechanisms and which were produced internally by Ford and General Motors. Their argument was that parts that had a higher component of development engineering expense and time would tend to be produced in-house, because it was in just those cases that there was the type of knowledge and human capital development that made it costly for either party to the exchange to switch, thus creating a small-numbers situation. Their empirical results were consistent with this prediction, although the test of the argument is not without problems. First, the data on each part as to whether it was made internally or purchased was treated statistically as an independent observation. This is suspect in general and particularly given that the most significant variable in their probit equation was the identification of the company—there were large differences in the amount of integration between the two firms. Second, the fact of important differences between the firms was a result clearly not predicted by the theory. And third, the amount of explained variance was only about 20 percent, meaning that the analysis of make or buy decisions could potentially depend on a number of other factors outside the scope of the theory.

Williamson (1975) saw, then, organizations as alternate planning and control mechanisms, substituting for the price mechanisms of markets. However, he recognized that in this coordination and control process not all structural arrangements were likely to be equally effective. In particular, he argued for the benefits of the multidivisional, or M-form, structure. The M-form involves the separation of strategic and operating decision making. In the absence of such separation, accomplished through the development of a corporate office and self-contained divisions below that office, "operating decisions that require immediate attention displace management attention from less immediately critical strategic planning (capital allocation) decisions" (Armour and Teece, 1978, p. 107), with a consequent decrement in performance.

The multidivisional form represents an administrative innovation with presumably enhanced operating characteristics. Armour and Teece (1978) examined the effect of the M-form structure on profitability for a sample of firms in the petroleum industry. Controlling for other factors such as size, they found that the multidivisional form had a significant positive impact on performance but only until the innovation had been widely adopted within the industry. Once almost all firms had the same structure, structure per se no longer provided a competitive advantage, reflected in profitability. Teece (1980) demonstrated that a model of the diffusion of innovations, often used to study the spread of technological innovations, fit the data on the diffusion of this administrative innovation nicely. This suggested that "other insights from the study of the economics of technological innovation may be fruitfully applied to the domain of administrative and organizational innovation" (Teece, 1980, p. 470).

One difficulty with the market failures approach is the definition and measurement of the critical concept of transactions costs. Williamson (1979) recognized the problem himself when he wrote, "there are too many degrees of freedom; the concept wants for definition" (p. 233). The empirical tests of the market failures approach have tended to involve testing the relative efficiency advantages of the multidivisional form or testing diversification and integration (Teece, Armour, and Saloner, 1980) advantages. The theory, however, speaks to the issue of the conditions under which organizations will displace markets, and this kind of direct test has yet to be done.

STRUCTURAL CONTINGENCY THEORY

The M-form hypothesis advanced by Williamson (1975) and tested by Armour and Teece (1978) is noncontingent, in the sense that the M-form is argued to enhance effi-

ciency and therefore be preferred under all conditions. The only possible contingency factor considered by Williamson (1975) was organizational size, since the arguments concerning the advantages of the M-form proceeded from the premise of the need to overcome the loss of control that can accompany increasing organizational size. By contrast, the dominant approach to explaining organizational structures in the sociological literature has been structural contingency theory. This theory has two essential elements. First, it represents an explicit rejection of the one-best-way approach to administration and argues that the appropriate organizational design depends on the organization's context. Second, most versions have some variant of the consonance hypothesis embedded within them. The consonance hypothesis states that those organizations that have structures that more closely match the requirements of their contexts will perform better than those that do not. Tests of the structural contingency theory, then, have sometimes looked only for lawful relationships between dimensions of the organization's context and structure, and others have tested the effects of congruence on performance. However, the underlying mechanism of organizational decision making implied in these theories is one of rational adaptation. There is presumed to be an efficiency-seeking orientation that would cause the organization to align itself more closely with the requirements of the environment.

The structural contingency theory specifies an overall perspective of managerial adaptation to environmental constraints, but the specific structural dimensions so adapted, as well as the specific elements of context that affect structural choices, are left unspecified. In the research literature the three elements of context most frequently investigated have been size, technology, and the organization's environment. The structural variables presumably affected by these context variables are those emerging from a Weberian (1947) conception of organizational structure: the size of the administrative component, the degree of centralization and formalization of the structure, and the amount of differentiation, or the extent of task specialization and vertical elaboration.

Size is one of the most prominent characteristics of organizations, and the effects of size have been investigated in numerous studies (Kimberly, 1976). Weber's (1947) initial analysis argued that the elements of bureaucracy would emerge only in larger organizations, and Pugh *et al.* (1969) found size to be the most powerful predictor of a factor that measured specialization, use of procedures, and reliance on paperwork. Blau (1970) has been one of the principal contributors to the size literature, arguing that size generates structural differentiation within organizations, but that the differentiation increases at a decreasing rate as size increases. There are two causal arguments associated with the effects of size. One suggests that increasing size provides the opportunity to benefit from increased division of labor. This increased division of labor will be associated with the development of more subunits and also will require greater coordination by the managers because of the increasing division of labor and the coordination required by the interdependence created by that task specialization. The second argument proceeds by noting that with increasing numbers of employees personal control over the work process becomes increasingly difficult. Instead of personal, centralized control, impersonal mechanisms of control emerge, and these require a larger administrative component to operate. Thus the basic arguments from the size literature are the following:

1. Size leads to increasing structural differentiation.

2. Size is negatively related to centralization.

3. Size is positively related to formalization.

4. Size is related to the size of the administrative component, though whether there are decreasing or increasing administrative economies of scale is unclear.

Blau and Schoenherr (1971) found support for these hypotheses in a study of state employment service organizations, and Meyer (1972b) found support in a study of state and municipal finance departments. Meyer's analysis was longitudinal, adding support to the idea that it was size that caused structural differentiation rather than the other way around. However, as Meyer (1971) himself noted, if one assumes reasonably constant spans of control, the relationship between size and differentiation is mathematically true by definition. Thus there is some concern that the effects of size on differentiation are not of great theoretical interest or importance. Meyer (1972a) reported support also for the effects of size on formalization and centralization, support that has been found in other studies as well (Hall, Haas, and Johnson, 1967; Blau, 1973). The argument about size and centralization implies a trade-off between centralization and formalization as mechanisms of control. Child (1972b) has called specialization and standardization of activities

the bureaucratic strategy of control and has argued (Child, 1972b, 1973a, 1973b) that specialization, standardization and formalization of role activities, and centralization of decision making are all related, the first two positively and both negatively to the degree of centralization. Child (1973b) as well as Meyer (1972a) found that size was one of the principal factors causing variations in organizational control strategies.

The effect of size on the size of the administrative component is less clear, in large measure because of definitional dependency issues (Freeman and Kronenfeld, 1974) plaguing the research. Most studies in this genre (Anderson and Warkov, 1961, Raphael, 1967; Tosi and Platt, 1967) have correlated the proportion of administrative personnel $[A/(A + P)]$ with the total organizational employment $(A + P)$, where A is the number of administrators and P is the number of production or nonadministrative employees. It is clear that the term $(A + P)$ appears on both sides of the equation, and thus, the fact that there are statistically significant associations should not be surprising. Moreover, the research has tended to focus on the size of the administrative component in relationship to total size without worrying too much about the fact that the organizations being studied have varied from public organizations of different types to private firms.

Another issue in the size–size-of-the-administrative-component question is the fact that the administrative component itself has been conceptualized and measured differently in different studies and is probably not a homogeneous category. Rushing (1966) argued that a wide range of occupations had been included as administrative personnel but that, in fact, the various categories of administrative personnel may be affected differently by size. If this were the case and different organizations had different mixes of the personnel, that could account for the inconsistent results across studies. Using industry-level data (which may have problems because of aggregation bias), Rushing (1966) examined the intercorrelations among six administrative/production personnel ratios as well as the relationship of these ratios to size. He found that there were moderately high correlations among the ratios but that the correlations of the ratios with size were inconsistent. He concluded that the low overall correlation of the total administrative personnel ratio to firm size was the result of "firm size having negative effects on managerial and sales personnel, positive effects on professional and clerical personnel, and a weak and inconsistent effect on service personnel" (Rushing, 1966, p. 106).

A similar conclusion on the heterogeneity of the administrative personnel component emerged from a study by Kasarda (1974) of school districts in Colorado. He found that although the managerial component of administration declined with the size of the district, secretarial and clerical personnel and the professional component consisting of librarians, guidance counselors, and so forth, increased with size.

A further problem with this literature is that almost all of the studies have been cross-sectional in nature. Freeman and Hannan (1975), studying school districts in California, have found that the size of the administrative component and its relationship to total personnel depends on whether the school district is growing or declining. Using an essentially political argument, Freeman and Hannan maintained that in times of growth all the various personnel components (teacher, administrators, other support personnel) would grow about proportionately with enrollment. However, because of their protected political position, when enrollments declined, administrative personnel would be cut more slowly. Their data (Freeman and Hannan, 1975; Freeman, 1979) provided support for this position. What this means for the other literature is that it is impossible to estimate the size–administrative component effect without taking into account whether the organization is growing or shrinking, which requires analysis over time.

Although there are alternative ways of indexing size (Kimberly, 1976), it is nevertheless much more straightforward to assess than technology, another element of the organization's context that has been related to structure. Woodward (1965, 1970) conceptualized technology in terms of the time period at which the technology was introduced and the length of the production process, with the technical scale ranging from prototype production, through small-batch/large-batch, mass production, through process production. Woodward found support for the consonance hypothesis in her study and, indeed, introduced the term to the literature. She also observed that for many structural variables there was a curvilinear relationship, with batch and process production being more similar to each other than to mass, assembly line production. Hickson *et al.* (1969) failed to replicate Woodward's results for the importance of technology and argued that technology impacted structure only for those units most immediately associated with the work flow. In larger organizations, then, with a smaller proportion of the firm devoted to the actual production tasks, the effects of technology might be less observable.

Zwerman (1970), using Woodward's procedures on a sample of U.S. firms, did replicate her results.

Most conceptualizations of technology have not focused on the form of operations or production technology but instead have conceptualized technology in terms of its analyzability or routineness. Hage and Aiken (1969), for instance, found that organizations characterized by routine technology were more centralized and more formalized. Perrow (1967) argued that the extent to which procedures were analyzable and the extent to which there were few or many variations in the materials worked on by the organization were the critical dimensions defining technology. Thompson (1967) conceptualized technology in terms of its being long-linked, intensive, or mediating. In one other study attempting to test the technology argument, Mohr (1971) found no support for the consonance hypothesis and little support for Woodward's other arguments, either. Mohr studied health departments, however, and it might be argued that the consonance hypothesis would hold more strongly for organizations facing a higher degree of market pressure.

The definitional and measurement disagreements that have been associated with the concept of technology (Rushing, 1968; Meissner, 1969; Lynch, 1974) are found again in consideration of the effects of the environment on organizational structure. The basic argument is that "different environmental conditions and different types of relationship with outside parties will. . .require different types of organizational structural accommodation for a high level of performance to be achieved" (Child, 1972a, p. 3). The environmental dimension most often considered is uncertainty, sometimes measured merely as change and sometimes including a component of complexity. Burns and Stalker (1961) were among the first to notice the different environmental conditions made different organizational structures more or less appropriate. They found that a mechanistic or bureaucratic organizational structure was appropriate for more stable and certain environments, while an organic, less formalized, and centralized structure was found more frequently and was more successful in rapidly changing environments.

Even agreement on variability or uncertainty as an important environmental characteristic did not solve the issue of measurement and conceptualization. Duncan (1972), for instance, argued that environmental uncertainty was the result of two dimensions—complexity, or the number of elements dealt with, and variability, or the extent to which these elements changed over time. Duncan's scaling and methodological procedures, however, are open to a great deal of criticism (Downey, Hellriegel, and Slocum, 1975). In addition to the issue of how to best capture the dimensions of the environment, a second debate has centered on whether it is the objective characteristics of the environment or those characteristics as perceived by organizational decision makers that should be incorporated in studies of structure. Several studies have shown that the two are not the same thing (Tosi *et al.,* 1973; Downey *et al.,* 1975). This has led to further work to see whether perceptions of environmental uncertainty are more characteristic of the perceiver than of the environment (Downey and Slocum, 1975). The argument has been made, on the one hand, that the organizational structure is determined by decision makers who must ultimately base their decisions on their perceptions of the context in which they are operating. However, as Abell (1975) has noted, there are problems of tautology in arguing from the position that it is managerial perceptions that determine structural results, as well, it could be added, as problems of causality. In the latter case the argument could be made that the degree of uncertainty and differentiation in the structure conditions the extent to which a variable and complex environment is registered by the organization (Huber, O'Connell, and Cummings, 1975). In the former case the argument that managerial beliefs or perceptions govern the structure of the organization is a hypothesis only to the extent that the converse—managerial perceptions and beliefs are not related to the structure—is plausible. Given the implausibility of this position, the relationship is more true by definition than a scientific theory to be investigated.

Lawrence and Lorsch (1967) made a slightly different and more sophisticated argument concerning the relationship between structure and environment. They argued that different organizational units faced different subenvironments and that, for instance, the environment of a production department was very different from that faced by marketing or research and development. These authors then argued that each subunit would develop a structure matching its own subenvironment, therefore leading to a higher degree of differentiation within the organization. This higher degree of differentiation—in goal orientation, structures, and time horizons—would impose a more difficult task of integrating or coordinating the entire system. Lawrence and Lorsch (1967) argued and found, in a study of ten firms, that the most effective organizations were those that had the requisite level of internal differentiation for the different types of environments faced but that also were able to integrate the diverse departments effectively.

This study is one of the few that has avoided the problem of overaggregation to the total organization level of analysis. In addition, it introduced the concept of internal differentiation and integration. The basic environmental predictor of subunit structure was, however, again the concept of environmental uncertainty. As in the case of Duncan's research, the Lawrence and Lorsch empirical measures and procedures have been subjected to criticism (Tosi, Aldag, and Storey, 1973).

Although environmental uncertainty has been the primary variable employed in the environment-structure research, the extent of competition in the environment and the degree of resource munificence have also been considered. Pfeffer and Leblebici (1973b) argued that competition caused increased demands for control, producing direct effects for a more structured organization as well as causing product differentiation to lead to less decentralization and less structural elaboration than might otherwise be expected. Khandwalla (1973), in a study of ninety-six manufacturing firms, found that overall competition was associated with the use of management controls and selectivity in the use of controls. Of the three forms of competition investigated, price, marketing, and product competition, product competition had the greatest impact on top-management control structure. Staw and Szwajkowski (1975) found that firms facing less munificent environments committed a larger number of illegal acts, at least as reported by the Federal Trade Commission. One final environmental dimension that has been described as being important is the degree of interconnectedness of the system of organizations (Aldrich, 1979). Again, however, there is little empirical work investigating this dimension in terms of its effects on structure (Mindlin and Aldrich, 1975).

Pfeffer and Salancik (1978, Chap. 4) argued that the three basic dimensions of the environment were the degree of concentration of resources, the scarcity or munificence of the resources, and the degree of interconnectedness of the organizations. In Fig. 2, their diagram indicating the causal relationships among the elements of the environment, the relationships among social actors, and uncertainty is reproduced. They viewed uncertainty as the result of relationships among social actors, which in turn were governed by the conditions of the environment in which these actors operated. One implication of this argument is that uncertainty may be too global a concept to use in explaining structure, and that the more fun-

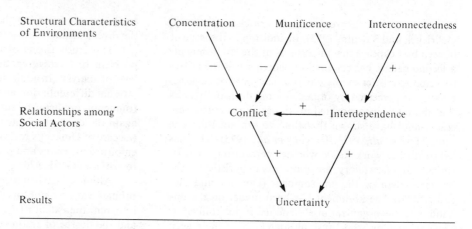

FIGURE 2
Relationships Among Dimensions of Organizational Environments
SOURCE: Pfeffer and Salancik, 1978, p. 68.

damental dimensions of either the environment itself or else relationships among the social actors should be used as the independent variables.

Child (1972a) has criticized the structural contingency theories for neglecting the importance of strategic choice. Child maintained that organizations were not as tightly coupled to environments as implied by the theory, and furthermore, profits and effectiveness were not the only outcomes of interest to those in the dominant coalition who determined the structure. Pfeffer (1978) elaborated this notion by arguing that organizational design was the result of a political process occurring within organizations, in which effectiveness or profitability was only an arguing point. Child's critique, although seductive, is inadequate by itself. To say that structures are chosen by those in the dominant coalition (with the power to choose them) is virtually tautological. The argument that structures are more coupled to internal political realities than to the environment (Pfeffer, 1978) may also be incomplete, as there is evidence (Hickson *et. al.,* 1971; Pfeffer, 1981) that this internal power is itself related to the environmental constraints and contingencies confronting the organization.

Structural contingency theory has received only mixed support over all. The consonance hypothesis has not always been tested and, when tested, has not always been supported. The concepts of technology and the environment are themselves complex and often poorly measured and dimensionalized. Scott (1975) has argued that the concept of technology is both complex and

multidimensional, including variability and complexity. Scott argued that this multidimensionality of the concepts, as well as inattention to the appropriate unit of analysis, had led to the disparities in research results. In addition, there has been little effort thus far to specify which of the elements of context, size, technology, or environment are more or less important under different conditions. The prescriptions for research in this area seem to be reasonably straightforward. More work is needed dimensionalizing and understanding the constructs, as in Pfeffer and Salancik's (1978) initial attempts to examine the concept of environment. Then attention must be paid to issues of the measurement of the concepts. Work is needed specifying more precisely the causal linkages and mechanisms between the variables presumably taken into account in designing organizations and the design outcomes. Finally, some attention to testing the concepts both against each other and against other perspectives can serve to sharpen the analysis and produce more precise understanding of the issues of organizational structure and design.

MARXIST ANALYSIS

If the market failures approach of Williamson is on one end of the continuum, with its emphasis on efficiency considerations, then Marxist approaches to organizations are at the other end, with an almost exclusive attention to power. Structural contingency theory fits somewhere in the middle, with some focus on effectiveness and efficiency but also attention to other managerial values and to the possibility that organizations and environments are not tightly coupled. Like the other two approaches, Marxist theory represents some blend of environmental determinism with strategic, rational choice. The decision to include it in this section is based on the judgment that, for the most part, Marxist analyses have proceeded from the premise of conscious, rational, strategic action taken on the part of the capitalist class and organizations controlled by that class. In this sense it is an analysis well in the domain of approaches presuming conscious, foresightful behavior.

The fundamentals of the Marxian approach to organizational analysis are quite simple and direct:

1. Employers seek a labor force that is both inexpensive and powerless.

2. To accomplish this goal, employers select means of production (technologies), along with accompanying administrative strategies, that have the effect of deskilling the workers and ensuring social control over them.

3. This attempt to deskill and control the work force has within it forces that produce resistance on the part of the labor force, including lack of motivation and effort as well as absenteeism, turnover, and collective action taken through labor unions.

4. Therefore a cycle of conflict and change is engendered by the struggle between capital and labor (Goldman, 1980).

Goldman (1980) has noted, ''The Marxian position sees a high degree of managerial consciousness and intentionality even omnipotence not only in technical decisions but also in ostensibly benign programs such as the welfare work in the early twentieth century or the democratization experiments of the 1970's'' (p. 12).

Marxist analysis focuses not only on the organization of work but also on the patterns of cooperation that develop among members of the capitalist class and the relationship of that class and its business interests to other social organizations in the society. The argument is that in order to maintain wealth and transmit that wealth intergenerationally and to defend itself from attempts by workers to redistribute income and to seize power, a firm must have cooperation and organized activity to preserve class interests and class position. This has led to Marxist approaches to interorganizational relations. The fundamental arguments of this approach are as follows:

1. There is not a separation of ownership and control to any great degree, and class interests in economic activity, as contrasted with managerial or technocratic interests, are still dominant.

2. Various kinds of social organizations, including business firms and their boards of directors, provide an arena in which class interests can be developed and articulated; rather than see people as linking interdependent organizations, Marxist analysis views organizations as contexts in which class relations can be renewed and developed.

3. The resultant patterns of organizational and interorganizational linkage and activity can be understood on the basis of class relations and class interests.

The various elements of the Marxist approach have not been subjected to equal amounts of research. The first issue, the structural conditions of labor markets and their relationship to worker power, has received by far the most attention. Concern with the structure of labor markets arose both from the importance of labor in the production of surplus capital and from the observation that women and ethnic minorities failed to attain the same level of wages and occupational status as white males even when their human capital characteristics were identical (Welch, 1973; Featherman and Hauser, 1976). Reich (1971) argued that employers' profits were enhanced by reducing the wages paid and that the mechanisms used to reduce wages was to segment the labor market and therefore prevent the development of solidarity within the working class. Presumably, differentiating and splitting the labor market into segments, for instance, along racial or sexual lines, hindered the development of powerful, collective organizations such as unions that could pose a threat to the power of employers. The thesis is essentially one of divide and conquer.

One issue central to this thesis has been the role of labor unions in this process of work force segmentation. One position (Beck, 1980) is that labor unions, through their policies of racial exclusion (Marshall, 1965; Jacobson, 1968), have served to facilitate the process of class fragmentation. By maintaining craft and occupationally based labor market segments with little movement across such segments and by excluding sectors of the population from those labor markets, unions have acted to hinder the development of solidarity among the working class. An alternative point of view argues from the following position:

1. The proportion of minority workers in unions is about the same as the proportion of the work force as a whole (Ashenfelter, 1972).

2. Unions have had the effect of reducing differentiation, or the return to individual characteristics, for workers covered by collective-bargaining agreements (Johnson and Youmans, 1971; Bloch and Kuskin, 1978; Pfeffer and Ross, 1980).

3. Unions have had some effect on reducing interrace income inequality (Ashenfelter, 1972; Leigh, 1980).

Both theoretical positions on labor unions have some evidence consistent with them. The point is that the role of labor unions is defined in both perspectives largely in terms of their impact on the distribution of income in society and, by inference, of their impact on the development of working class solidarity (Kahn, 1978). In the struggle between labor and capital postulated by the Marxists, the extent to which the working class can organize and unify becomes a critical variable.

Bonacich (1972, 1976) has critiqued the divide-and-conquer argument. She maintained that ethnic antagonism resulted from differentials in the price paid for labor identified along ethnic lines but that such differentials were the result of resources and motives within the groups themselves, not from the actions taken by capitalists. "Business. . . supports a liberal or laissez faire ideology that would permit all workers to compete freely in an open market. Such open competition would displace higher paid labor" (Bonacich, 1972, p. 557). Thus Bonacich saw the conflict as having three sides, business and two labor groups, one higher-paid, and with business seeking to displace the higher paid with the cheaper labor. She argued that, for instance, business was not able to benefit substantially from black unemployment. Rather, "large capitalists are unable to take advantage of ghetto labor and abandon it to marginal enterprises" (Bonacich, 1976, p. 49).

A variant of the split labor market thesis has been the extensive work on the dual economy (Bibb and Form, 1977; Beck, Horan, and Tolbert, 1978; Tolbert, Horan, and Beck, 1980). This work argues that there are two sectors in the economy—a core sector, characterized by large, capital-intensive, profitable firms with substantial market power, and a periphery sector, characterized by firms that have low profits, tend to be small, and have limited market power. Employment in the core tends to be more stable and higher-paid, with greater rewards earned for individual characteristics and human capital. More importantly, career ladders exist in the core sector in which there are chains of mobility across positions within organizations. Employment in the periphery, by contrast, is argued to be unstable and lower-paid. Additionally, there is little mobility across jobs in the periphery, and the concept of career ladders of increasingly responsible positions exists primarily in the core.

Although the evidence for the dual economy perspective is mixed (e.g., Baron and Bielby, 1980), the principal point of interest is that it posits a split both in the capitalist class and in the labor class. Given the descriptions of the sectors provided, a reasonable supposition is that there would be cleavage between those in the periphery sector—both owners and employees—and those who enjoyed the higher profits, higher wages, and more stable employment in the core sector of the economy. This apparent contradiction to Marxist theory, in which the cleavages cut across economic sectors rather than between labor and capital, has yet to be systematically treated.

In addition to using various forms of labor market segmentation and exclusion to maintain powerlessness on the part of the labor force, Marxist analyses place great emphasis on the role of technology in the struggle between labor and capital. Bonacich (1976) has argued that "technology should be seen as a resource which parties can use in a variety of ways to further their interests, or which they may choose not to use if their interests are harmed by its introduction" (p. 35). Edwards (1979) argued that the choice of technology might be based on considerations of profitability but that profitability included more than just technical efficiency. In particular, Edwards included considerations of the leverage the technology provided the managers to transform labor power into work actually done. Edwards argued that with the growth of larger enterprises the issue of control became more important. The solution was to embed the control process in the structure of work, either through technical control or through bureaucratic control. The assembly line and the consequent deskilling of work provided interchangeability of workers and meant that a reserve army of unemployed could, in fact, be readily substituted for the firm's present employees. This lack of development of person-specific human capital maintained the power of the capitalists over the employees.

Thus for Marxist analysis, deskilling of the work is an important part of the struggle between labor and capital, since it renders labor less powerful because it makes workers easier to replace as well as less necessary to the extent that production processes become even more automated. Noble (1978) has argued that the invention and expansion in the use of numerically controlled machine tools was motivated by the desire to reduce the power (and hence the wages) of the skilled and largely unionized machinists. The deskilling of labor is a theme also pursued by Braverman (1974) in his analysis of the evolution of jobs over time. Braverman argued that the transformation of jobs and the introduction of machine technologies have been undertaken not only for purposes of technical efficiency but also for the purpose of separating the working class into skilled and unskilled segments, thereby hindering the development of solidarity. Kraft (1977) has made similar arguments with respect to the introduction of computers and the work of programming and operating computers. Again, a deskilling process is evident in which attempts are being made to routinize the work, to reduce the wages, and to increase the substitutability of the computer personnel.

Marxist analysis introduces an element into the strategic choice of technology that provides an alternative to economic theories based on efficiency considerations concerning why certain technologies and arrangements for production are chosen. In contrast to many organizational theories of strategic choice, in Marxist analysis tastes for technology are not exogenous but are specified as deriving from the conflict between capital and labor. As Goldberg (1980) has noted, "An efficient institution is one that survives in a particular context. The efficacy of a particular arrangement will depend upon the ability of the parties to exert legal or extra-legal power" (p. 268).

The Marxist argument goes on to note that attempts at deskilling labor are ultimately counterproductive. Because workers are made more or less interchangeable, common fate is built that fosters the development of class consciousness and fosters collective action, as through the formation of labor unions. Furthermore, deskilling of work produces worker alienation, leading to strikes, absenteeism, turnover, and even vandalism. At this point Marxist perspectives are similar to the more traditional job and task design literatures in terms of the predictions of the effects of task characteristics on worker responses.

Marxist theory clearly predicts both a deskilling of work over time and a consequent cycle of conflict as workers become alienated and fight to have both a larger share of the resources and more meaningful tasks. Spenner (1979) has noted that there are two components to the deskilling process: (1) the actual change in the content of

jobs and (2) the distribution of the numbers of workers in jobs over time. Thus deskilling could proceed either by reducing the skill content somewhat in most jobs or by changing the structure of work so that the distribution between skilled and unskilled jobs changes. Spenner argued that in terms of the distribution of jobs, since 1900 there is evidence for some downgrading in average skill requirements. Using the *Dictionary of Occupational Titles* as a data source, he argued that in the recent past there have been few changes in skill requirements overall, and there has been some upgrading in skill requirements in several sectors of the labor force. If deskilling has occurred, it has not been a significant social process, at least according to the evidence presented by Spenner (1979).

It is significant that the evidence for the increasing alienation from the capitalist system is largely nonexistent (Strauss, 1974; Seeman, 1975). In an insightful study using fairly aggregated data, Flanagan, Strauss, and Ulman (1974) found that when factors such as general economic conditions were statistically controlled, there was no association between levels of job attitudes and work behavior outcomes such as quit rates (turnover) or strikes. Marxist theory seems to predict that in the struggle between labor and capital, workers will fight rather than exit (Hirschman, 1970) or accommodate psychologically to the realities of their work situations (Salancik, 1977; Salancik and Pfeffer, 1978b). Although there is certainly evidence consistent with differences in attitudes indexing alienation across workers in jobs with different technological characteristics (Blauner, 1964), survey data do not indicate increasing alienation over time (perhaps because, as Spenner has argued, there has not been that much net change in skill requirements), nor are there close relationships between measures of alienation and various types of conflict behavior. Seeman (1975) has argued that it is unlikely that "alienation alone, or alienation in the grand manner, can explain complex, collective, and historically situated events" (p. 100) such as strikes and other types of collective action and violence.

The final element in the Marxist analysis of organizations concerns the coordination of action across organizations and the development and implementation of capitalist interests in the society. The two issues are:

1. To what extent are there coordinated and consistent interests defined along class lines, and how is such coordination achieved?

2. To what extent and through what mechanisms are class interests maintained and transmitted through the various social institutions in society?

Both issues have begun to draw increasing empirical attention.

There is accumulating evidence that capitalists can organize themselves and use a variety of social institutions to provide the linking and socialization necessary for such organization. Whitt (1980) has distinguished between economic competition and political competition, arguing that although there is clearly economic competition within the capitalist class, there is not much political competition. Studying five referenda in California having to do with transportation issues, Whitt (1980) noted that even though there might have been reasons for some companies to favor and others to oppose the issue, "the money in every case is virtually *all on one side or the other of the issue*" (p. 106). Indeed, examining the campaign for the proposal to construct the Bay Area Rapid Transit System, Whitt (1979) observed a correlation of virtually 1.0 between corporate size and the amount of contribution to the campaign. He concluded that this evidenced a high degree of coordination on political issues among the business interests. Coordination of interests is achieved through association in social clubs (Domhoff, 1974), having common educational backgrounds (Mills, 1956), and the development and use of policy groups (Shoup, 1975), and coordination of interests within families is accomplished through the development of a family office (Dunn, 1980). Dunn's (1980) analysis of the Weyerhaeuser family office indicates how issues ranging from economic investments to political and charitable contributions were centrally coordinated.

Moore (1979) and Useem (1979) provide evidence both for the penetration of business elites into other social organizations as well as for the differentiation of the elite into an inner and outer group. Moore (1979) concluded that "no fragmentation of elites in different institutions or issue areas was found" (p. 689) on the basis of a network analysis of interview data from 545 leaders of major political, economic, and social institutions. Useem (1979) found that one of the differences between the inner and outer group in the business elite was that the inner group, persons who had multiple directorships and tended to be more prominently represented on the boards of other organizations as well, had a political perspective that took a broader, less parochial and strictly economic self-interest perspective. Thus this inner group was seen as being able to defend and promote the

more general interests of the class, rather than merely using their positions to argue for more proximate advantage to themselves or their firms. Ratcliff (1980) has presented data on loans made by banks in St. Louis indicating that banks more tightly connected into the capitalist structure through both economic and social positions tended to make a higher proportion of their loans to businesses, whereas banks less integrated into the capitalist class through the associations of their directors made a somewhat higher proportion of their loans for mortgages. These data are consistent with Useem's (1979) arguments concerning the differentiation of the capitalist class into a central and less central group and demonstrate the consequences of this differentiation for behavior.

The three approaches reviewed in this section each presume rational and conscious action, though each argues from a somewhat different motivational basis for describing the action, with Williamson emphasizing efficiency, the Marxists emphasizing economic and political power, and the structural contingency theorists implicitly posing efficiency arguments but not as strongly as the economists. All three approaches have used "as if" research procedures for the most part. Such procedures take an assumption (e.g., attempts to deskill the work force), trace the implications of such an assumption for various behaviors and outcomes, and then see to what extent such outcomes are, in fact, consistent with the empirical data. None of the three perspectives has yet to be really tested against the others; this kind of comparison against strong alternative arguments would be useful. Furthermore, particularly in the case of structural contingency theories, the processes by which the hypothesized outcomes are produced are often left quite implicit and unspecified. Elaboration of the process, as, for instance, in the description of the family office by the Marxists, is a major area for additional empirical and theoretical work. Otherwise, one tends to be left with static-equilibrium-type analyses (Williamson, 1975) with no concern for either time paths or processes that produce the predicted outcomes.

THE EXTERNAL CONTROL OF ORGANIZATIONAL BEHAVIOR

In a fashion analogous to that at the individual level, controversy continues concerning the extent to which organizational behavior, analyzed at a more macrolevel, is externally controlled or whether such outcomes are the result of planned, rational strategic actions. The theoretical consequence of this debate has implications primarily for whether one must attend to various choice and decision processes in understanding organizational behavior or if attention to the system of environmental constraints and contingencies is sufficient to enable prediction of organizational responses. It should be clear that there are really two issues involved in this debate. One is at some level a scientific question, asking the extent to which variance can be explained by attending to environmental characteristics and ignoring more microlevel processes or whether attention to such processes of choice and action are necessary. The second question revolves around a matter of research taste. Rather than argue what is necessary from a scientific standpoint, it revolves around the extent the researchers are willing to use "as if" reasoning and treat the organization, or at least some organizational processes, as a black box. Thus the questions of external control versus attention to more microlevel processes involves issues of reductionism and reification, issues that have been alive in the study of human behavior for some time. This chapter can certainly not resolve this debate; however, understanding its foundations can help provide some perspective on the various literatures reviewed.

Within the external-control-of-organizations perspective, there are two principal variants, corresponding, at some level, to the differences between behaviorism and social information processing at the individual level. The first, population ecology, treats the organization very much as a black box, while the second, resource dependence, is concerned somewhat more with internal adaptations and the politics that occur inside organizations.

POPULATION ECOLOGY

Most treatments of organizations have emphasized processes of adaptation; by contrast, population ecology argues that variations occur in part because of the operation of selection processes working on populations of organizations (Hannan and Freeman, 1977). The importance of selection derives from the fact that there are both internal and external constraints on the adaptability of organizations. Such constraints include the following (see Hannan and Freeman, 1977, pp. 931–932):

1. The organization's investment in specialized plant, equipment, personnel, and expertise, which makes changing product market domains difficult.

2. Limited and selected information received by organizational decision makers.

3. Political constraints, which make the change in strategy, with the accompanying change in power distributions, traumatic.

4. The constraints of precedent, custom, and the incorporation of standard operating procedures and decision rules that take on a life of their own.

5. Legal and fiscal barriers to the entry and exit of product markets, such as economies of scale and governmental rules.

6. Legitimacy of product or market abandonment.

7. The problems of obtaining information from the external environment to make adaptive strategic decisions.

If adaptation is constrained, then selection processes are important mechanisms through which the characteristics of populations of organizations evolve over time. It is this focus, the variety and evolution of organizational forms, that constitutes the core subject matter for the ecological perspective. According to Hannan and Freeman (1977, p. 936):

> We suggest that a population ecology of organizations must seek to understand the distributions of organizations across environmental conditions and the limitations on organizational structures in different environments, and more generally seek to answer the question, Why are there so many kinds of organizations?

As developed by Campbell (1969), the natural selection model has three stages: variation, selection, and retention. Variation is necessary to produce the variety on which differential selection processes operate. Variation can occur because of either planned actions or random, unplanned variations in organizations (Aldrich and Pfeffer, 1976). Hannan and Freeman (1977) and other strict ecologists have, for the most part, been uninterested in the sources of variation but only in their occurrence. More recently, Brittain and Freeman (1980), examining the development of the semiconductor industry, have noted how the movement of personnel from one organization to another, frequently a new organization, carries organizational forms and structures. Thus, for instance, semiconductor firms founded by persons from larger and older companies who came out of the manufacturing part of the operation have tended to have a production efficiency style of operation and structure, while those founded by persons from engineering and research and development are organized somewhat more organically and have a product strategy emphasizing technical innovation. Clearly, personnel movement across organizations can be one way in which variations in structures and decision-making procedures diffuse (Baty, Evan, and Rothermel, 1971; Pfeffer and Leblebici, 1973a). This effect can be clearly seen in academia, in which program innovations and styles of operating departments are carried by faculty as they move across institutions.

Once variation has occurred, for either planned or unplanned reasons, then these various organizational forms are selected according to how well they fit their environment. This suggests that there are as many kinds of organizational forms as there are kinds of organizational environments (Hawley, 1968). It is important to note that in this selection process, "it is the environment which optimizes" (Hannan and Freeman, 1977, p. 939). It is the environment that selects those combinations of organizational forms that are suited to the resource base of that environment. Selection occurs principally through the competition among forms (Hannan and Freeman, 1977), and thus population ecology comes to look, at points, very much like microeconomics (e.g., Winter, 1975). Both employ "as if" reasoning, and both imply that organizations are reasonably tightly linked to their environments, in the sense that suboptimal forms or decision procedures lead to organizational failure. Without failure, indeed, there can be no selection processes operating, unless failure is defined solely in terms of forms rather than in terms of individual organizations. For instance, one position on selection might argue that selection requires the failure of organizations in order to be operating. If the environment has shifted so that multidivisional firms are more suited than functionally organized firms, then one would expect to see more failures of firms organized functionally. Alternatively, firms may transform themselves from one structure to another (Chandler, 1966). In that case, although the functional form of organization may be selected against and diminish in number, the firms themselves may continue to exist, having changed their form. Since Hannan and Freeman (1977) base their arguments for the importance of selection largely on considerations of organizational inertia, one would expect to see at least some instances of organizational failure.

Indeed, it is around the issue of the extent to which selection processes operate that criticism of the ecological perspective tends to be focused. Although there are numerous instances of organizational failure, these tend to be concentrated primarily among relatively new and particularly small organizations (Aldrich, 1979), such as the firms one finds in the retail and service sectors of the economy. Failure of large organizations is often so politically and economically unpalatable that various interventions are taken to keep the organizations afloat, as in the case of Lockheed and, more recently, Chrysler. As Kaufman (1976) has documented, failures or the disappearance of public bureaucracies are even rarer events. On the other hand, the composition of lists such as the *Fortune* 500 have substantially changed over time as the result of mergers, and there is clearly an active merger market that accounts for the disappearance of thousands of firms each year. Given that the acquiring firm may, on occasion, pay enormous premiums for the acquisition, and furthermore, on occasion, the acquired firm may be operated as a largely autonomous division within the new parent organization, classifying merger as an example of a selection process at work may not be entirely consistent with the spirit of ecological arguments. Nevertheless, there is clearly evidence that firms at all size classes do disappear, although the form of competition that is implied in ecological reasoning occurs most strongly with smaller firms in a set of highly competitive sectors of the economy.

Retention involves the maintenance of the new organizational form into the future. Many of the mechanisms that Hannan and Freeman (1977) listed as impediments to adaptation are, in fact, mechanisms of retention. Certainly, standard operating procedures (Cyert and March, 1963) serve as a form of organizational memory and keep a degree of continuity in organizational operations. There is a clear tension between variation and retention, noted by a number of authors (Campbell, 1969; Weick, 1969; Pfeffer and Salancik, 1977b). The various factors that promote stability and retention of decision-making processes and structures in the organization delimit the organization's ability to innovate and change and, thus, its likelihood of coming up with new variations. One can argue, with some justification, that variation occurs most frequently around the founding of new organizations (Stinchcombe, 1965), which is why birth and death processes in organizations are critical for enabling the population of organizations to evolve and change over time.

Also critical to the ecological perspective is the identification of organizational forms, or what is being selected for or against. Hannan and Freeman (1977) maintained that "an organizational form is a blueprint for organizational action, for transforming inputs into outputs'' (p. 935). They went on to note that such a blueprint might be inferred from the organization's structure, the patterns of activity within the organization, or the normative order that characterized the particular organization. As it has been used empirically, form has been defined with respect to the particular subject population being investigated and has tended to focus on structural attributes of the organization. One of the more critical distinctions between organizational forms is the difference between specialists and generalists. Each can flourish in the appropriate environment or niche.

Niche, another term borrowed from biological ecology, is an important concept in the population ecology of organizations. Hannan and Freeman (1977) defined niche as ''that area in constraint space (the space whose dimensions are levels of resources, etc.) in which the population outcompetes all other local populations. The niche, then, consists of all those combinations of resource levels at which the population can survive and reproduce itself'' (p. 947). The empirical assessment of niches and niche widths has not progressed very far as yet, but the intuitive meaning of the concept is clear.

The relationship between niche characteristics and specialism and generalism is straightforward. Specialist organizations maximize their exploitation of the environment over a relatively narrow range of environmental conditions and have little slack or excess capacity. Generalist organizations can survive over a wider range of environmental conditions but are not optimally suited to any single condition. The trade-off is between security or risk reduction and efficiency or the exploitation of the particular environment in greater depth (Hannan and Freeman, 1977).

Environments in ecological theory are dimensionalized according to three criteria (Brittain and Freeman, 1980):

1. The uncertainty of the environment.

2. The compatibility of the different resource states, or whether changes between environmental states are large or small.

3. The grain of the environment, which is the frequency of changes in environmental state over time.

A fine-grained environment is one in which there are many changes in environment over time; a coarse-grained environment is one in which there are relatively few (but sometimes larger) changes in environmental condition.

Hannon and Freeman (1977) argued that specialist organizations are likely to dominate when uncertainty is low and also when uncertainty is high and the environment is fine-grained with large differences between environmental conditions. They explain (p. 953):

> When the environment changes rapidly among quite different states, the cost of generalism is high . . . since the environment changes rapidly, the organizations will spend most of their time and energies adjusting structure. It is apparently better under such conditions to adopt a specialized structure and ''ride out'' the adverse environment.

Because the optimal adaptation in the face of uncertainty is generalism, but generalism has its own costs in terms of slack or excess resources, another possibility is the development of polymorphism. Polymorphism is the development of population heterogeneity, some forms of which are adapted to one environmental state and others to the other possible environmental conditions. ''With such a combination at least a portion of the population will always flourish when the environment changes state'' (Hannan and Freeman, 1977, p. 953). Organizational equivalents of polymorphism are holding companies or confederations of organizations of different forms.

The empirical study of organizations from a population ecology perspective is only beginning, so an evaluation of the empirical evidence is impossible. It is clear, however, that ecological models are at times attempts to mathematically model changes in population components according to specified formula (e.g., Hannan and Freeman, 1978). Modeling an ecological process does not necessarily tell what the underlying causal mechanisms producing the change are. Furthermore, as Aldrich and Pfeffer (1976) noted, care must be taken in employing ecological analysis to avoid the tautological trap of saying that organizations survive because they are fit and, therefore, defining fitness in terms of survival and vice versa. The advantage of the ecological perspective is that it focuses explicitly on the importance of selection processes, largely neglected in previous organizational theorizing, and emphasizes the dynamics of change. Furthermore, ecological models can be used to understand the consequences of changing the variation or selection mechanisms for the diversity and prevalence of various types of organizational forms.

RESOURCE DEPENDENCE THEORY

Resource dependence theory (Pfeffer and Salancik, 1978) also holds that organizations are externally constrained, but "argues for greater attention to internal organizational political decision-making processes and also for the perspective that organizations seek to manage or strategically adapt to their environments" (Aldrich and Pfeffer, 1976, p. 79). Because organizations are not internally self-sufficient, requiring resources from the environment, they become interdependent with those elements of the environment with which they transact. This interdependence can lead to the imposition of external constraints, in a fashion analogous to that described by Kahn *et al*. (1964) for individuals. Indeed, Evan (1966) explicitly used the term *organization set* to describe the set of organizations with which a given focal organization transacted. Thus resource dependence theory suggests that organizational behavior becomes externally controlled because the focal organization must attend to the demands of those in its environment that provide resources necessary and important for its continued survival. As Pfeffer and Salancik (1978) summarized, "The underlying premise of the external perspective on organizations is that organizational activities and outcomes are accounted for by the context in which the organization is embedded" (p. 39).

Pfeffer and Salancik (1978, p. 44) specified ten conditions that affect the extent to which a given focal organization will comply with external control attempts. The basic mechanisms of the process have to do with power dependence relations among the organizations and the ability to use such interorganizational power to affect the behavior of the other organization. Power derives from dependence (Emerson, 1962), and dependence, in turn, is a function of the importance of the resource that is obtained and the extent to which an external social actor has discretion and control over access to that resource (Blau, 1964; Thompson, 1967; Jacobs, 1974; Pfeffer and Salancik, 1978). Dependence is also increased to the extent that control over the resource is concentrated in relatively few hands. When power asymmetric, and when the external organization has the legitimate right to use that power, and further, when the behavior of the focal organization is under its own control and is observable, exter-

nal control efforts will be more likely to be attempted and to be successful.

There have been relatively few empirical examinations of the correlates of interorganizational influence and control. Randall (1973) studied the implementation of human resource programs in offices of the Wisconsin employment service. Human resource efforts were in contradiction to the employment service's customary mode of operating as a free employment agency and thus were perceived as being undesirable by employers. Randall (1973) found that the extent to which offices implemented the program was a function of the power of employers over the employment service and the amount of competition the office faced. Employment service offices were more likely to engage in more of the activities specified by the human resource emphasis if they faced competition for the human resource program funds (measured by the presence of community action agencies in the area) and to the extent they had power over the local employers (employment was not concentrated in the hands of a few large organizations).

Pfeffer (1972a) examined the expressed willingness of Israeli managers to comply with various government requests, such as investing in development areas and forgoing local profits to engage in export activity. He found that dependence on the Israeli government, because of sales to the government, dependence on the government for financing, or dependence for legitimacy because of a high percentage of foreign ownership of the firm tended to be associated with compliance to governmental policies. Salancik (1979a) examined the response of U.S. defense contractors to affirmative action pressure, using a field stimulation research methodology (Salancik, 1979b). Firms were queried about their willingness and interest in hiring women MBA students. One measure of response was the length of time it took to get a reply, while another measure was how encouraging the response was in seeking applicants. Data on the percentage of the firm's sales to the government, the dollar amount of nongovernment sales (a measure of public visibility), and the firm's contributions to total defense expenditures (an indicator of the government's dependence on the firm), were obtained. Salancik (1979a) observed a complex relationship between the proportion of sales to the government, an indicator of the firm's dependence on the government, and the response to affirmative action pressure. Large visible firms not controlling the production of the items sold had a strong positive relationship between percentage of sales to the government and responsiveness to affirmative action pressure. For large visible firms with control of production, the relationship was significant but not as strong. For small less visible firms the relationship was either insignificant or, in the case of small firms with control of the production of some items, actually negative. Thus Salancik (1979a) concluded that the extent of external control was affected by both the net dependence position and also by the visibility of the target, which might presumably have indexed the amount of pressure exerted for compliance.

According to the resource dependence perspective, firms do not merely respond to external constraint and control through compliance to environmental demands. Rather, a variety of strategies may be undertaken to somehow alter the situation confronting the organization to make compliance less necessary. The argument is that the management of organizations seeks to maintain discretion over the organization's activities, in part to maintain its own power and discretion and in part to permit adaptation subsequently as new contingencies arise. An organization already tightly constrained by its environment has limited degrees of freedom left if and when new external demands arise. Thus, somewhat in contradiction to the ecological perspective, the resource dependence view argues that organizations are not only constrained by their environments but also undertake actions that alter those environments.

The empirical research has examined a number of organizational strategies for either establishing a negotiated environment or altering the pattern of interdependence confronted by the organization. In general, two types of interdependence have been considered: competitive or commensalistic interdependence and symbiotic interdependence, such as that found between buyers and sellers of some product or service. With respect to competitive interdependence the argument has been made (e.g., Pfeffer and Salancik, 1978) that interorganizational linkage activities among competitive firms will occur when industrial concentration is in an intermediate range or when there are a moderate number of organizations competing in the market. When there are very large numbers of organizations, and the market approaches perfect competition, it is impossible to coordinate the competitive interdependence through a series of interlocks, because the interlocking would be too great and too extensive to be readily accomplished. On the other hand, when there are only a very few firms in the market, stable conjectural variations (Cohen and Cyert, 1965a) can develop, much as in the minimal social situation in psycho-

logical experiments with interdependence (Rabinowitz, Kelley, and Rosenblatt, 1966), and tacit coordination can develop among interdependent actors even without communication. Thus interorganizational coordination, accomplished through interorganizational linkage, would occur when it is both necessary because of the larger number of firms and still possible to accomplish because concentration is intermediate.

Studying merger behavior, Pfeffer (1972c) found that the proportion of mergers undertaken within the same industry was negatively related to the difference in concentration from the median value, for the twenty two-digit Standard Industrial Classification manufacturing industries. Studying 166 joint ventures that took place between 1960 and 1971, Pfeffer and Nowak (1976) reported a similar finding for this form of interorganizational linkage activity, with the proportion of joint ventures made between firms in the same industry being lowest at both high and low levels of concentration and being greatest when industrial concentration was intermediate. Finally, Pfeffer and Salancik (1978, p. 166) reported that the number of officer and director interlocks among competitive firms was a function also of the level of concentration (positive) and the difference in concentration from an intermediate value (negative). Thus the evidence suggests that for three important form of interorganizational linkage activity, joint ventures, mergers, and board of director interlocks, competitive interlocking occurs relatively more frequently in intermediate ranges of market concentration.

Interfirm coordination can also be accomplished through the movement of executives across competitive firms within the same industry. The movement of personnel is an important mechanism for tying parts of a single organization together through the development of shared experiences (Edstrom and Galbraith, 1977) and, in an analogous fashion, can tie other organizations together by the transmission of a common culture and set of understandings (e.g., Baty, Evan, and Rothermel, 1971). Pfeffer and Leblebici (1973a), pursuing this argument, analyzed patterns of executive recruitment in twenty four-digit manufacturing industries. Consistent with the results reported previously, they found that there was evidence that executives in firms facing a competitive environment of intermediate concentration spent more years outside the company and had a larger number of job changes, spending correspondingly fewer years inside the company. These data are also consistent with the position that intermediate industrial concentration prompts the use of executive movement across firms as a way of establishing interorganizational networks.

With respect to symbiotic or buyer-seller interdependence, resource dependence theory suggests again that interorganizational linkage activities will be undertaken to manage such interdependence. This general proposition leads to the more specific prediction that the higher the level of transactions (purchase or sales) interdependence across economic sectors, the greater will be the extent of interorganizational linkage activity across those sectors. Pfeffer (1972c) found that large firm mergers conformed to this pattern of results, and Pfeffer and Nowak (1976) found that joint ventures could also be predicted from considerations of transactions interdependence. Pfeffer (1972b) found that the firm's capital structure predicted the proportion of bankers or others from financial institutions on its board, and in a study of the composition of electric utility boards of directors, Pfeffer (1974) again found support for the idea that the board of directors was used to link the organization to its environment in a way that would facilitate interdependence management. In a study of hospital boards of directors Pfeffer (1973) examined the function of the board, its size, composition, and the impact of board structure on organizational effectiveness. Explanatory variables included the hospital's ownership, the type of area it served (manufacturing, agricultural, etc.), its operating and capital budget structure, and the sources for its operating funds (private payments, government, insurers). The function of the board could be explained by its context including its source of funding, and in turn, the size and composition could be explained by the function of the board and the context in which the hospital operated. Finally, Pfeffer (1973) reported that hospitals that had boards that more closely fit their contextual requirements were better able to obtain resources and grow.

Recently, Burt (1980; Burt, Christman, and Kilburn, 1980) has employed a network methodology to investigate resource dependence notions with respect to both co-optation and merger activity. Burt found support for the idea that interorganizational activity across sectors matched transactions flows. And Burt also found support for the idea that such interorganizational linkage activity could affect the profitability of the firms so linked.

Resource dependence theory has been relatively broad in scope, treating both the external control and constraint of organizational behavior as well as attempting to develop predictions concerning interorganizational responses, including linkage activity, that might be undertaken to manage the constraining interdependicies. The existing evidence is largely consistent with the theory but not completely so. In addition, the theory has some problems of a more conceptual nature. In terms of evidence Palmer (1980) has reported that only a small fraction of corporate interlocks that are accidentally broken (as through the death or retirement of the person maintaining the interlock) are renewed, calling into question the importance of interfirm coordination as an explanation for board-of-director interlocking. Pennings (1980) has found no evidence for the effects of board interlocking on firm performance, although this result, in and of itself, may not be completely inconsistent with the theory. And Allen (1974), in a study of just manufacturing firms, failed to replicate Pfeffer's (1972b) findings, derived from a broader sample, of the relationship between firm financial structure and the proportion of bankers on the board.

The conceptual issues around resource dependence theory concern its potentially tautological character. To argue that firms act to manage resource interdependence or to comply with the demands of powerful external organizations requires the ability to specify in advance what the critical resources or the determinants of interorganizational power are. In the case of most of the empirical work cited, the proportion of transactions is used, along with the concentration of resource control, as a priori determinants of resource interdependence. However, it is possible to argue that small resources may be, in fact, more critical to the organization. Such an argument would need to be made on an a priori basis to avoid inferring resource criticality from the organization's response to external actors. Pfeffer and Salancik (1978) have illustrated how the basic concepts of resource interdependence and interorganizational power can be further developed to predict, for instance, when organizations will be more likely to attempt to manage sales rather than purchase interdependence and vice versa. Thus it appears to be possible to further refine the perspective to make more precise predictions about interorganizational behavior.

Both population ecology and resource dependence emphasize the importance of examining environmental characteristics and constraints to understand organizational forms and interorganizational behavior. However, there are a number of other differences between them. First, there is a level-of-analysis difference. As Freeman

(1982) has noted, natural selection presumes a population logic, while resource dependence is more concerned with adaptations and strategic responses of individual organizations. Second, there is a difference in the time frame, with population ecology taking a longer perspective. Third, there is a difference in the conceptualization of the environment in the two perspectives. From the ecological perspective the environment is strictly exogenous, although it can certainly change over time. In the resource dependence approach not only does the environment change, but there is a presumption that the environment itself reflects the actions taken by organizations to manage problems of interdependence. Perhaps most fundamentally, there is a distinction in terms of how much rationality is presumed. Resource dependence, although arguing for the external control of organizational behavior, has more elements of rational action and rational choice embedded in its argument than does population ecology. Freeman (1982) has suggested that political economy approaches such as that represented by resource dependence theory may provide a perspective on the functioning of individual organizations, which links with studies of organizational populations to give a more complete picture of organizational life cycles. The implication is that rather than being in some sense competing theories, by operating at different levels of analysis, the two perspectives are fairly complementary. Whether or not this is the case requires examining the predictions of each for some specific dimensions of structure or interorganizational behavior to see whether the predictions derived from each perspective are essentially similar.

SOCIAL CONSTRUCTIONIST VIEWS OF ORGANIZATIONS

Both purposive, goal-directed, rational theories and external control perspectives are, in some sense, stimulus-response (S–R) theories (Tuggle, 1978). Both take some conditions initially defined—in the first case preferences, expectancies, and alternative behaviors; in the second case external constraints and interdependencies—and predict the individual's or organization's response from these initial conditions. In other words, in each case there is some (internal or external) stimulus that elicits some organizational or individual response. By contrast, the theories to be considered in this final section are oriented to the consideration of process, or how action and interaction unfolds in organizations over time, and how meanings and interpretations are constructed around those events. Because of the very nature of these theories, they are almost all focused on the individual or subunit level of the organization. We have shown the decision process theories as being relevant in the total organizational level of analysis, but, in fact, all of these theories are more concerned with microlevel processes than with total organizational responses.

As noted in the introduction, these theories have tended to be developed by using methodologies that are more qualitative than quantitative. Daft and Wigginton (1979) have argued that such methodologies, employing the use of natural language rather than mathematical equations, are necessary to capture the full range and complexity of the phenomena being investigated. Their argument is that one must use relatively equivocal methodologies (natural language) to fully register the complexity of the phenomena being studied (complex organizations). Their argument can be turned around to maintain that there is no inherently real level of organizational complexity, that the level of equivocality seen is determined by the methods used, and that therefore the use of equivocal, uncertain methods such as natural language and case studies registers an uncertain and complex organization. Clearly, the implication of the social constructionist view is that there is, in some sense, no objective reality. Thus Daft and Wigginton's (1979) argument, which presumes that there is some actual level of uncertainty to be registered, is in many ways inconsistent with their own position.

Morgan and Smircich (1980, p. 492), following Burrell and Morgan (1979), describe six different assumptions about human nature and their corresponding research methods and epistemological assumptions. Their framework is reproduced in Table 2. The first two perspectives on the far-right hand side correspond to the external control and purposive, intentional actor views of action, respectively. The three on the left-hand side are all variations in what we would term a social constructionist or social definitionist perspective on organizational action. It is interesting to note that although these perspectives are all represented in both sociology and organization theory, there is almost no research at all in the discipline of psychology employing the social definitionist views of behavior. This may be because of psychology's almost exclusive reliance on the experimental method and other, similar objective methodologies (Morgan and Smircich, 1980). What Burrell and Morgan (1979) and Morgan and Smircich (1980) make clear is the link between views of human nature and political ideolo-

TABLE 2
Perspectives on Behavior in Organizations and Research Approaches

Core assumptions	Reality as a projection of human imagination	Reality as a social construction	Reality as a realm of symbolic discourse	Reality as a contextual field of information	Reality as a concrete process	Reality as a concrete structure
Assumptions about human nature	Man as a pure spirit, consciousness, being	Man as a social constructor	Man as a symbol user	Man as an information processor	Man as an adaptor	Man as a responder
Basic epistemological approach	To obtain phenomenological insight, revelation	To understand how social reality is created	To understand patterns of symbolic discourse	To map contexts	To study systems, process, change	To construct a positivist science
Research methods	Exploration of pure subjectivity	Hermeneutics	Symbolic analysis	Contextual analysis of Gestalts	Historical analysis	Lab experiments, surveys

SOURCE: Morgan and Smircich, 1980, p. 492.

gy, on the one hand, and between these conceptions of human nature and methodologies, on the other.

Pondy and Boje (1980), following Ritzer (1975), identified a social facts paradigm, a social behavior paradigm, and a social definition paradigm. The distinction between the first two was primarily level of analysis rather than conception of action, with social factists "treating collective characteristics as though they were real, material, objective entities capable of measurement and description" and social behaviorists taking "individual behavior as their primary explanandum" (Pondy and Boje, 1980, p. 85). Social definitionists treat the individual as a creator of his or her own reality, and thus social facts are not given the status of objective reality (Ritzer, 1975). Thus social definitionists, using the Pondy and Boje perspective, would include the ethnomethodologists and the phenomenologists as identified by Morgan and Smircich (1980).

Although all of the perspectives reviewed in this section are essentially cognitive and social definitionist in nature, particularly in the general sociological literature there are at least two important subgroups within the social constructionist perspective. Because of the more recent history of this perspective in organization theory, the divisions are not yet as sharply defined, yet the outlines of the different positions are in place. The two perspectives are as follows:

1. An interactionist approach, growing out of either the symbolic interactionist (Mead, 1938; Blumer, 1962) or ethnomethodological tradition (Cicourel, 1964, 1974; Garfinkel, 1967; Schutz, 1967).

2. A structuralist approach (Goffman, 1961, 1974; Berger and Luckman, 1966; Holtzner and Marx, 1979).

As Zucker (1980a) has noted, the interactionist approach focuses on the emergent properties of the interaction and on the processes which individuals create and attribute meanings to the events of the action and interaction occurring around them. The structural approach begins with the socially given "facts," the result of the consensus and social definition of the situation, and then treats how these social facts are imported and used in given social interactions (Gonos, 1977). In other words, the interactionists see all action as emergent and situationally defined and specific. The structuralists see patterns of meanings shaped by roles and shared paradigms (Brown, 1978), which structure and constrain the interpretations that are given to interaction patterns.

In Morgan and Smircich's (1980) typology, the interactionist view is represented at the far left of Table 2, while the structuralist view is the next column to the right. The interactionist position is one of extreme relativism, as each event is knowable only in the frame of the person experiencing the event. Structuralists, by contrast, see more shared understandings and social definitions in situations, even though these shared definitions are themselves clearly the result of cognitive processes.

Of the perspectives or theories reviewed below, the garbage can model and institutionalization theory are both readily classified as structuralist in their orientation, though some variants of institutionalization theory (Zucker, 1980a) attempt to bridge both perspectives. The cognitive approaches to organizational behavior tend to be more interactionist, though some of the perspectives are not well enough formulated to permit a clear classification.

COGNITIVE PERSPECTIVES ON ORGANIZATIONAL BEHAVIOR

Under the general rubric of the cognitive perspective on organizations, organizations have been conceptualized as systems of thought (Weick, 1979), systems of language (Pondy, 1978), shared paradigms or worldviews (Brown, 1978), systems of shared causal schemas (Bougon, Weick, and Binkhorst, 1977), contexts in which behavior is experienced subjectively (Gephart, 1978), and contexts in which political language is used to obfuscate the use of power and the allocation of actual benefits and costs (Edelman, 1964; Pfeffer, 1981, Chap. 6). Shared within these conceptualizations are the following common elements:

1. An emphasis on language as a mechanism for motivating and arousing organizational members.

2. A concern with the extent to which languages and interpretations are shared among participants.

3. A recognition of the subjective experiencing of reality and the possibility that subjective experience differs from what might be imputed or inferred by observers.

At the same time each differs somewhat in its emphases and conclusions.

Weick (1979) has argued that "an organization is a body of thought thought by thinking thinkers" (p. 42). Under this view the job of the manager is to manage myths, images and symbols. "Because managers traffic so often in images, the appropriate role for the manager may be evangelist rather than accountant" (Weick, 1979, p. 42). Weick specifically rejected the conceptualization of organizations as being dominated by routines, stan-

dard operating procedures, and uncertainty-reducing mechanisms, with a corresponding de-emphasis on thought and cognition. Organizations are bodies of thought, or causal schemas, and also embody specific types of thinking practices, or algorithms. Weick (1979) has suggested that the following issues are important for investigation:

1. What are such causal schemas, and how do they change in organizations?

2. What are some algorithms, and what are their functions and dysfunctions?

3. What is the relationship between thinking and action; particularly, what happens when action precedes thinking?

Bougon, Weick, and Binkhorst (1977) empirically studied a jazz orchestra and provided one of the few quantitative attempts to operationalize what is implied in a cognitive approach to organizations. The methodology used was to get orchestra members to enumerate a long list of activities and outcomes. Then each member was given the job of constructing a causal map from the variables. Thus some activities might lead to other activities, and still other activities might lead to various kinds of outcomes. For each member, then, a causal map can be created linking the variables to each other to the extent that relationships are perceived. Using techniques for measuring the similarity of matrices, then, one may assess the extent to which members of an organization (in this case a jazz orchestra) share causal schemas, as well as find those relationships in which causal perceptions vary. These causal schemas, in turn, reflect the members' understanding of the organization and represent the organization and its organizing process. It might be assumed that such causal schemas affect how members react to various situations and provide a guide to action in the organizational context. Axelrod (1976) has used archival sources for constructing causal maps of foreign policy decisions and has shown how these can be used to enhance decision making.

These studies are important because they illustrate that cognitive maps of organizations can be systematically collected, compared, and analyzed. They also, however, illustrate the difficulty of accomplishing that process, particularly on a large scale. Yet, Bougon *et al.* (1977) and Axelrod (1976) demonstrate that the presumed association between methodology and orientation (e.g., Burrell and Morgan, 1979), which suggests that cognitive approaches to understanding social systems require case study or other qualitative methodologies, may be untrue.

In a fashion similiar to that of Weick (1979), Brown (1978) conceptualized organizations in terms of the concept of paradigm. As used in science (Kuhn, 1970), *paradigm* refers to the shared understanding and, as importantly, the shared exemplars that emerge in scientific disciplines to guide research and instruction in the discipline. A paradigm is a way of doing things, a way of looking at the world. Brown (1978) maintained that the development of shared paradigms is what occurs in formal organizations. Standard operating procedures, shared definitions of the environment, and the agreed-upon system of authority and power represent the organization's worldview and paradigm. Kuhn (1970) has argued that in science, paradigms seldom evolve over time; rather, old paradigms are replaced almost in toto by new paradigms in a more revolutionary than evolutionary process. Sheldon (1980) has used precisely this imagery in describing problems organizations have in changing in some fundamental dimensions. Sheldon (1980) used the idea of paradigm as a diagnostic to help forecast when change would be relatively easy (when fundamental parts of the paradigm were not at issue) and when change would be more difficult and would need to be more comprehensive (when the basic paradigm was the object of change).

Pondy (1978) has emphasized the importance of language for understanding organizations. Analyzing leadership from the perspective of language, Pondy maintained "to practice, say, democratic leadership is to understand the set of meanings (values?) to be conveyed, to give them primitive expression, to translate them into stylistic representations, and ultimately, to choose sounds and actions that manifest them" (p. 89). Because language is one of the key tools of social influence, and organizations are contexts in which social influence is exercised, language is important in understanding organizations and how they are managed. Pondy (1978, p. 92), for instance, has hypothesized that to the extent that the language of the leader overlaps the language of his or her subordinates, the leader will be more effective. One of the important leadership functions, therefore, may be language development and language renewal.

Pondy (1978) defined leader or managerial effectiveness also in terms of language. He argued (p. 94):

> The effectiveness of a leader lies in his ability to make activity meaningful for those in his role set —not to change behavior but to give others a sense of understanding what they are doing and especially to articulate it so they can communicate about the meaning of their behavior.

Thus for Pondy, leadership, an important influence process in organizations, occurred through the development of evocative language that facilitated those in the organization to make sense of their activities by using language that was meaningful to all or most of them.

Pondy (1977) illustrated his point about the importance of language in his critique of strategic contingencies and resource dependence perspectives on power. He argued that what were the organization's most critical contingencies, or what were the resources most necessary for its functioning, were not predetermined but rather emerged through a process of social influence and social definition of the organization, its paradigm, and its mission. In order to understand power, Pondy maintained, one needed to understand how such definitions of critical problems or contingencies got created, and this was a process involving language and the social construction of reality.

Pfeffer (1981, Chap. 6), following Edelman (1964), viewed language and shared meanings as important in organizations but viewed the development of such meanings somewhat differently from Pondy or Weick. For Pfeffer activity could be analyzed on two levels: on the level of the actual activities, decisions, allocations, and other things with physical referents that occurred in organizations, and on the level of the beliefs, attitudes, sentiments, and values associated with those activities and choices. Pfeffer (1981, Chap. 6) argued that objective, external factors of the environment and the power and influence distribution that resulted within the organization affected the objective decisions and results; at the same time managerial language and symbolic activity had an effect on how organizational members felt about this set of decision outcomes. Management was seen, in this view, as helping to legitimate and quiet opposition to decisions that were made on the basis of power and influence. Just as Edelman (1964) had suggested that one side got the rhetoric and the other the substance in national politics, so Pfeffer argued that the purpose of language was to obfuscate and rationalize decisions made primarily for other reasons and serving other interests.

Pfeffer argued that such obfuscation was possible for the following reasons:

1. Participants occasionally had unclear or transitory preferences.

2. Participants frequently faced situations of information secrecy, which made the evaluation of what they were obtaining in the organization difficult.

3. The very fact of being in the organization made members susceptible to informational social influence.

4. The legitimacy of professionalism and the legitimacy of hierarchical authority gave some the right to define satisfaction and good decisions for others.

5. For persons with, perhaps, limited stakes in the organization, symbolic responses may have been sufficient, given their limited consequences regardless of what decisions were made.

The difference between Pfeffer's (1981) position and Pondy's (1978) is not that one emphasizes language and the other does not—for both, language and symbolic activity is an important component of administrative activity. Rather, Pondy (1977, 1978) has suggested that such language fundamentally affects the decisions taken in organizations, whereas Pfeffer (1981) argued that the effect of language was more on the sentiments and attitudes adopted toward the outcomes rather than on the outcomes themselves. Needless to say, this issue is far from being resolved.

Just as Pondy did for the issue of power, Gephart (1978) demonstrated the difference between a cognitive approach and the traditional approaches to the study of succession in organizations. Gephart (1978) argued that most traditional succession studies (e.g., Grusky, 1961, 1963; Helmich and Brown, 1972; Helmich, 1974, 1977) gave little attention to the departure of the predecessor and, more importantly, neglected the process by which members negotiated a common scheme that both facilitated the succession process and made sense of it in a way shared by those in the social system. Using his own replacement as an officer in a graduate student organization as the case under study, Gephart used Goffman-like (1959) terminology to note how the need for replacement was socially constructed, and then various gambits were employed to provide an opportunity for the succession issue to surface and for dissatisfaction of the members with his role to be articulated and used to force succession in a process of status degradation.

Gephart (1978, p. 578) concluded that succession through a process of status degradation occurred when an enforceable scheme is developed for interpreting the reality of organizational members; the behavior of the person being replaced becomes defined as problematic because it violates important organizational rules, it evi-

dences poor style or poor taste, and it is harmful to the integrity of the organization; and those who identify the problem specify the solution as the replacement of the position occupant. Gephart (1978) further argued that when succession occurred through a process of status degradation, the replacement would be "an actor whose words and deeds are 'the embodiment' (explicitly consistent with) the organizational scheme enforced in the accomplishment of the degradation" (p. 578). Gephart argued that the dramaturgy associated with forced replacement is probably different from the meanings and schemes associated with other types of succession, including retirement, voluntary resignation, promotion or transfer, and death of the position occupant. He argued for the development of similar ethnomethodological cases for these other types of succession events to see whether the cognitive processes and rituals differed, and how, among the different forms.

Gephart is probably at one end of the continuum in terms of emphasizing the emergent process and strategies embedded in that process. Clearly, the causal schemas implied in Weick's (1979) analysis of organizations and in Pondy's (1978) conceptualization of organization in terms of shared language emphasize more permanent, although still socially constructed, aspects of the situation. One source of the difference may be that Gephart was dealing with a student organization, which is undoubtedly less permanent and less stable in terms of membership rules and roles than those organizations dealt with by Weick and Pondy.

INSTITUTIONALIZATION THEORY

This dilemma between emergent meanings and structures and the idea of a consensually shared and therefore more stable social reality is addressed explicitly in institutionalization theory. As defined by Meyer and Rowan (1977), "institutionalization involves the processes by which social processes, obligations, or actualities come to take on a rulelike status in social thought and action" (p. 341). Institutionalization theory has been developed in two domains: First, it has been used to explain the decoupling of actions and of actions from structures and rules, as well as the decoupling of various parts of organizations from each other (Weick, 1976). Second, it has been treated as a variable and the determinants of the degree of institutionalization have been investigated.

In the first case various studies have indicated that there is little evidence for organizational properties of school districts (Meyer *et al.*, 1978). In particular, there is little evidence for agreement on the policies and practices between school district superintendents and their principals, between principals in the same district, between teachers and principals, and between teachers in the same school. Thus there is little evidence in school organizations for the existence of vertical coordination across levels or even for a common culture that unifies the organization at either the school or district level in terms of the technology of instruction. If this is the case, then why should it be, and what functions are being served by the district with its various administrative arrangements, forms, and bureaucratic trappings?

Meyer and Rowan (1977, pp. 340–341) argued:

> Organizations are driven to incorporate the practices and procedures defined by prevailing rationalized concepts of organizational work and institutionalized in society.... To maintain ceremonial conformity, organizations that reflect institutional rules tend to buffer their formal structures from the uncertainties of technical activities by becoming loosely coupled, building gaps between their formal structures and actual work activities.

Thus Meyer and Rowan argued that organizations are, indeed, linked to their environments but not in the way specified by either resource dependence or population ecology theory. Because there are shared, institutionalized views in the environment about what organizations should like and how organizational work should get performed, to maintain their legitimacy (Dowling and Pfeffer, 1975), organizations import the form, if not the substance, of these rules and incorporate them in their structure, rules, and reporting requirements. However, since such rules and structures may have little to do with how the work can or should get performed, in fact there is little impact on task performance and the behavior of those organizational members who actually do the work. This decoupling, Meyer and Rowan argued, is actually useful to the organization. It permits the work to get done according to the localized judgments of those doing the work while presenting to the outside world the appearance of legitimated, rational organization of work.

The decoupled nature of organizations is, it should be evident, the result of there being no shared, well-defined technology for, in fact, doing the work. In the presence of institutionalized social norms but in the absence of knowledge that would facilitate the work actually getting accomplished, institutionalized organizations develop in which ceremonies and symbols are used to en-

sure continued support and legitimacy from the social environment while not actually impacting the organization's operations. Meyer and Rowan (1977), for instance, argued that schools resist evaluation because in the absence of a known technology of instruction, all that evaluation could do would be to call into question their legitimacy and the legitimacy of the structures and procedures in place. The view of organizations described by Meyer and Rowan is one of a form of confidence game in which neither the organization nor those that it is fooling have any incentive to look more closely at what is going on.

Meyer and Rowan (1977) argued that societal modernization affected the presence of rationalized, institutional elements and, hence, the presence and elaboration of formal organizational structures and procedures. Thus these authors recognized that the degree of institutionalization varied within a society both over time and across settings and that organizations may vary in the extent to which norms and institutionalized expectations had developed.

Zucker (1977) examined some of the conditions affecting the degree of institutionalization in an insightful experimental study. For Zucker institutionalization was an important variable because "social knowledge once institutionalized exists as a fact, as part of objective reality, and can be transmitted directly on that basis" (p. 726). In contrast to those advancing perspectives that have emphasized the role of self-interest or necessity in the persistence of patterns of action or behavior, Zucker (1977, pp. 727–728) argued that institutionalization developed from shared, intersubjective reality. "To arrive at shared definitions of reality, individual actors transmit an exterior and objective reality; while at the same time this reality, through its qualities of exteriority and objectivity, defines what is real for these same actors" (Zucker, 1977, p. 728). Yet such realities are not continually being constructed and reconstructed, nor are they as fluid as implied by some ethnomethodologists. Zucker (1977) argued that "by being embedded in broader contexts where acts are viewed as institutionalized, acts in specific situations come to be viewed as institutionalized" (p. 728).

Zucker's experiment used the Jacobs and Campbell (1961) modification of Sherif's (1935) autokinetic experiment. Jacobs and Campbell established an artificial laboratory microculture concerning the distance a point of light appeared to move by using confederates, and then they watched the decay of this microculture as confederates were replaced by naive subjects over successive generations. Zucker replicated this condition and added two more. In the organization condition subjects were led to believe they were joining an experimental but still ongoing organization. In the office condition the organization instructions were further supplemented by giving the person who had been in the organization the longest the title of chief light operator. The basic transmission experiment was followed by a maintenance experiment in which one subject returned the following week and worked alone on the distance estimation task for thirty trials. There was also a resistance-to-change experiment in which, after the maintenance experiment was completed, a confederate was brought in and identified as another subject, who then attempted to establish a lower-baseline response by responding first with smaller distance estimates. Zucker's results were consistent across the three experiments. Subjects in the office condition demonstrated less decay in the distance estimates over time, evidenced greater maintenance, and were more resistant to change. Subjects in the organization condition were next, and subjects in the personal-influence condition, with no organization or position instructions, demonstrated the least resistance, the least maintenance, and the smallest transmission of the distance estimates (the microculture) over trials.

Zucker's study is a powerful demonstration of the effects of organizations and positions on behavior. The objectified, exterior nature of actions resulting from their association with the concepts of organization and office cause their persistence even in the face of contrary physical evidence and in the absence of any particular functional necessity.

Institutionalization ideas also have applicability to the analysis of social psychological experiments. Zucker (1980b) has argued that just as in other social situations, interaction in experimental situations varies in the extent to which it is determined by preexisting, structural elements or is emergent from the social reality that becomes defined in the situation. Meaning is situated in the experimental context (Alexander, Zucker, and Brody, 1970; Alexander and Knight, 1971) and can be used to predict the responses of subjects to that experiment. The argument is that the subjects are responding to meanings rather than to the experimental manipulations themselves. Zucker (1980b) has demonstrated that if one brings in normative elements that challenge the experimenter's authority, demand characteristic results (Orne, 1962) can be altered.

The work of those in the institutionalization theory tradition has provided evidence for the possibility of using experimentation to investigate cognitive, social definitionist processes, as well as evidence on the causes and effects of institutionalization on organizations. The importance of considering the degree of institutionalization as a variable is evident from this research.

PROCESS MODELS OF ORGANIZATIONAL DECISION MAKING

Decision process models of organizations and organizational decision making are at once similar and at the same time fundamentally different from the other cognitive models reviewed. They are similar in their rejection of stimulus-response logic and their emphasis on ongoing organizational processes. Most such models presume that outcomes can not be specified in advance by considering initial conditions but that such outcomes emerge from the complex interaction of elements of organizational processes over time. Most of the models, however, have not been as explicitly cognitive nor as radically social definitionist as many of the other cognitive theories. In fact, they are largely structural in orientation, with outcomes resulting from the structure of the decision situation and its constraints on decision processes.

Decision process models have been investigated by using both case studies and computer simulations, with some of the earliest work using simulation methodology. Thus Cyert and March (1963) showed how the use of a series of standard operating procedures concerning pricing and output levels produced certain joint results under conditions of duopoly, while Gerwin (1969) and Crecine (1967) examined process approaches to understanding school district and municipal budgeting, respectively. Clarkson (1962) used simulations employing simple information-processing rules to replicate the behavior of trust officers. And more recently, Cohen, March, and Olsen (1972) used a series of decision process routines to represent decision making in organized anarchies, a model they aptly refer to as a garbage can model of organizational choice.

Before considering the specifics and implications of the garbage can model in more detail, we must evaluate what can and cannot be learned from simulation techniques (Cohen and Cyert, 1965b). Some mathematical models (such as differential equations and linear programs) can be solved for unique or at least bounded solution sets. However, frequently the social process being modeled will be complex enough so that there are no mathematical procedures that enable one to diagnose what happens to the system under study. In such circumstances the use of computer simulations can enable the researcher to observe what happens as the various decision processes interact and play themselves out over time. Thus simulations enable the analysis of what will happen in the social system under study if the processes in question are operating over some time period. The fact that the simulation outcomes approximate what is empirically observed in the organization or other social system does not necessarily validate the input assumptions, nor is the converse the case. Rather, the use of simulation methodology permits the inference of nonintuitive results from sets of complex processes interacting over time. Whether or not such processes actually occur in organizations is another matter, and the issue of simulation validation is one that is both perplexing and controversial (Cohen and Cyert, 1961).

Distinct from how they are tested, decision process models are advocated under the assumption that the process itself is consequential for the outcome. March and Olsen (1976) have argued that process is important because of the ambiguity present in many choice situations. They identified four types of ambiguity (p. 12): the ambiguity of intention, or organizations characterized by inconsistent or ill-defined preferences; the ambiguity of understanding, which refers to the fact that technologies may be uncertain and that feedback from the environment may be misinterpreted; the ambiguity of history, which refers to the fact that what happened and why may be difficult to understand; and the ambiguity of organization, which refers to the varying degrees of involvement and participation of various organizational actors in choice situations. Thus March and Olsen (1976, p. 21) concluded:

> Individuals find themselves in a more complex, less stable, and less understood world than that described by standard theories of organizational choice.... Intention does not control behavior precisely. Participation is not a stable consequence of properties of the choice situation or individual preferences. Outcomes are not a direct consequence of process. Environmental response is not always attributable to organizational action. Belief is not always a result of experience.

Cohen, March, and Olsen (1972) conceptualized organizations as contexts into which there poured prob-lems, solutions, participants, and choice opportunities. The key structural variable considered was the right to participate in choice opportunities. This variable, specified in different forms, was used in a simulation with the other properties to develop implications of choice processes in organizations. Cohen, March, and Olsen concluded that problems were seldom resolved, the process was quite sensitive to variations in decision load, decision makers and problems tended to follow each other through choice situations, important problems were more likely to be resolved than unimportant ones, and important choices were somewhat less likely to actually resolve problems than were unimportant choices.

In chapters in the March and Olsen (1976) volume, individual contributors described choice processes using case study methodologies ranging from the selection of a dean (Olsen, 1976a), reorganization (Olsen, 1976b), the location of Norwegian university campuses (Stava, 1976), and the policies developed to deal with desegregation in San Francisco public schools (Weiner, 1976). In each case the garbage can analogy was employed to make sense of the choice process, and, in turn, elements of the choice process were used to illustrate the features of the garbage can model. Elsewhere, Cohen and March (1974) have argued that the garbage can, or organized anarchy, model is descriptive of many universities, and they have provided some prescriptions for presidents trying to manage such organizations.

The decision process approach, as exemplified by March and Olsen (1976), does incorporate some elements of the social definitionist perspective. They argued that "most of what we believe we know about events within organizational choice situations as well as the events themselves, reflects an interpretation of events by organizational actors and observers" (p. 19). For this reason the decision process approach and the other perspectives considered in this section pose the strongest challenge to the normal science paradigm that has tended to dominate organization theory over the past twenty years or so. Subjectively derived, shared realities pose both novel problems for methodology as well as important epistemological issues for the field of inquiry.

CONCLUSION

It is clear that organization theory is currently characterized by diversity in a number of fundamental dimensions, ranging from the unit of analysis considered to the perspective on behavior and action that is adopted. One issue this proliferation of perspectives raises is an appropriate strategy for the development of organizational science. Ritzer (1975, p. 164) has argued that paradigm conflict is fundamentally dysfunctional for the development of knowledge in a discipline. He argued that each paradigm needs insights from the others and that what is most useful is less conflict and more effort to integrate the various paradigms and perspectives. A contrary point of view has been posed by Mitroff and Pondy (1974), who argued that dialectic patterns of inquiry are very often productive. Furthermore, Maruyama (1974) has argued that communication across different paradigms is quite difficult, and thus the potential for paradigmatic integration is limited. As Pondy and Boje (1980) noted, Silverman's (1971) theory of action represents, to some extent, an attempt to bridge different paradigms. Silverman was sympathetic to the idea that reality was socially constructed, but he also recognized that structures of interaction constrained the interpretations that were placed on action, as well as the actions themselves. But Silverman's (1971) efforts are noteworthy because of their very rarity.

There are dangers in both the paradigm conflict and paradigm integration points of view. The danger in stressing conflict among competing perspectives on action is that complementarities and potential for integration may be overlooked. Thus, for example, Freeman (1982) has noted that rather than being competing theories, resource dependence and population ecology are actually complementary, differing primarily in their level of analysis and time perspective. However, it seems that this danger may be less than the danger of focusing too strongly on paradigm integration, because the primary way of accomplishing intergration is to incorporate theoretical diversity through contingency statements. For instance, research, instead of counterposing situational and need-theoretic perspectives on individual behavior, might seek a resolution by discovering situational contingencies that made one perspective more or less relevant, individual differences (e.g., in susceptibility to social influences or cross-situational behavior consistency) that would make one or the other perspective more relevant, or specific attitudes or behaviors that might be more or less under situational as contrasted with dispositional control.

There are several problems in this kind of contingency-building approach. First, once embarked upon, such contingency theories are virtually impossible to falsify. To say, for instance, that structure is contingent on technology and then to do a particular study and to find no result may only lead to arguing that the wrong measures of technology or structure were used or that the technology-structure relationship is itself contingent on other factors, such as the presence of competitive forces. The difficulty becomes that a possibly incorrect formulation is saved by continually developing new contingencies and then proceeding to test for their effects. Second, the resultant theory can become enormously complex, with numerous branches corresponding to the various contingency points. Such formulations violate the rule that theories should be parsimonious. Third, as Gergen (1978) has argued, since researchers tend to find what they look for anyway, the null hypothesis of no effect is a very weak alternative to the theory being examined. Rather, alternative theories provide a more stringent test. Indeed, the conflict among theoretical perspectives can force the advocates of each to sharpen their arguments and analytical procedures in a way that might not occur if attempts were made to accommodate all points of view. Bower (1965), in an experimental study of problem-solving groups, found that conflict was an important motivator of constructive thought and analysis. This constructive role of conflict may exist in the scientific arena as well, forcing a precision of thought and creativity that might be absent in more inclusive theoretical perspectives.

Kuhn's (1970) arguments concerning the development of other scientific disciplines would suggest that paradigm conflict and paradigm revolution represent the way science progresses, rather than expecting, or perhaps even desiring, paradigm integration. In this context the differentiation and fractionalization within the discipline of organization theory can be seen as a positive development for the advancement of knowledge, to the extent that these various theories are forced to confront each other.

The competition among different theoretical perspectives does not, however, extend to maintenance of distinctions among levels of analysis. As Roberts *et al.* (1978) have noted, a number of organizationally relevant phenomena could be more productively examined if a cross-level perspective were employed. For example, there is a large literature on turnover, which has emphasized the effects of individual-level variables, including both demographics such as age, sex, and level of education and attitudes (Mobley *et al.*, 1979). At the same time macroeconomic analyses have provided evidence for the strong effect of the unemployment rate and general economic activity level on the overall quit rate, defined at an economywide level. It does make sense that when jobs are scarcer, there will be less voluntary turnover. There are undoubtedly also organization-level policies, such as attempts to build long-tenured work forces (Ouchi and Jaeger, 1978), pension and benefit policies, and practices related to the quality of supervision and the amount of role stress that can also affect turnover. To understand turnover, then, as a complete process, one would want to incorporate individual-level, organization-level, and societywide predictors. Flanagan *et al.* (1974) moved in that direction in their study in which job attitudes were analyzed along with economic conditions. There is some question, however, as to whether the unit of analysis should be the individual, the unit that turns over, as contrasted with the more aggregated level of analysis those authors used.

Or as another example, consider the relationship between uncertainty and structure posited in the structural contingency literature. That literature is remarkably unclear about the more microlevel processes that would be expected to produce less bureaucratic and formalized structures in the presence of more environmental uncertainty. Indeed, one study has indicated that at the individual level uncertainty is perceived as stressful and threatening and produces, as a consequence, a tendency for more rigidity and control rather than less (Bourgeois, McAllister, and Mitchell, 1978). This may be one example of individual-level processes operating in a direction opposite to the effect of the same phenomena, uncertainty, at a higher level (Lincoln and Zeitz, 1980). Also, however, attention to the individual- or subunit-level processes may help to resolve the various inconsistencies in research results that have developed in the structural contingency literature.

Throughout the review of organization theory, we have tried to indicate the interconnections among the issues of the level of analysis, the perspectives on behavior, the methodology employed in the research, and the ideology or implicit political perspective underlying the research. Organization theory is very much a social science, affected by its social context and subject to the same social processes that have been outlined in this chapter. An emphasis on practice and the applicability of organization theory has tended to be associated with an emphasis on individual-level phenomena (Argyris, 1972) and a focus on action as rational and goal-directed. A more radical political orientation tends to be associated with the social definitionist, phenomenological treatment of organizations (e.g., Clegg, 1975; Clegg and Dunkerly,

1979) as well as with more macrolevel analyses and with an emphasis on external control and constraint. These interrelationships are consequential for both evaluating the development of organization theory as well as understanding the connections among the diverse perspectives and disciplines represented in the field of inquiry. Together, these factors—level of analysis, methodology, perspective on action, and ideology and politics—determine the unfolding pattern of development of the paradigms of organization theory.

REFERENCES

Abell, P. (1975). Organizations as technically constrained bargaining and influence systems. In Peter Abell, *Organizations as bargaining and influence systems*. London: Heinemann. Pp. 114–128.

Alderfer, C. P. (1972). *Human needs in organizational settings*. Glencoe: Free Press.

Aldrich, H. E. (1979). *Organizations and environments*. Englewood Cliffs, N.J.: Prentice-Hall.

Aldrich, H. E., and J. Pfeffer (1976). Environments of organizations. In Alex Inkeles, James Coleman, and Neil Smelser (Eds.), *Annual review of sociology*. Vol. 2. Palo Alto, Calif.: Annual Reviews. Pp. 79–105.

Alexander, C. N., and G. W. Knight (1971). Situated identities and social influence. *Sociometry, 40,* 225–233.

Alexander, C. N., L. G. Zucker, and C. Brody (1970). Experimental expectations and autokinetic experiences: consistency theories and judgmental convergence. *Sociometry, 33,* 108–122.

Allen, M. P. (1974). The structure of interorganizational elite cooptation: interlocking corporate directorates. *Amer. Sociol. Rev., 39,* 393–406.

Allison, G. T. (1971). *Essence of decision*. Boston: Little, Brown.

Anderson, J. C., and C. A. O'Reilly (1981). Effects of an organizational control system on managerial satisfaction and performance. *Hum. Relat., 34,* 491–501.

Anderson, T. R., and S. Warkov (1961). Organizational size and functional complexity: a study of differentiation in hospitals. *Amer. Sociol. Rev., 26,* 23–28.

Annett, J. (1969). *Feedback and human behavior: the effects of knowledge of results, incentives and reinforcement on learning and performance*. Baltimore: Penguin Books.

Argyris, C. (1968). Some unintended consequences of rigorous research. *Psychol. Bull., 70,* 185–197.

⸺ (1972). *The applicability of organizational sociology*. London: Cambridge Univ. Press.

Armour, H. O., and D. J. Teece (1978). Organizational structure and economic performance: a test of the multidivisional hypothesis. *Bell J. Econ., 9,* 106–122.

Arnold, H. J. (1981). A test of the validity of the multiplicative hypothesis of expectancy-valence theories of work motivation. *Acad. Management J., 24,* 128–141.

Arvey, R. D., H. D. Dewhirst, and J. C. Boling (1976). Relationships between goal clarity, participation in goal setting and personality characteristics on job satisfaction in a scientific organization. *J. appl. Psychol., 61,* 103–105.

Ashenfelter, O. (1972). Racial discrimination and trade unionism. *J. politic. Econ., 80,* 435–464.

——— At Emery Air Freight: positive reinforcement boosts performance (1973). *Organizational Dynamics, 1(3),* 41–50.

Axelrod, R. (1976). *Structure of decision: the cognitive maps of political elites.* Princeton, N.J.: Princeton Univ. Press.

Baker, S. H. (1969). Executive incomes, profits, and revenues: a comment on functional specification. *Southern Econ. J., 25,* 379–383.

Baldridge, J. V. (1971). *Power and conflict in the university.* New York: Wiley.

Bandura, A. (1977). *Social learning theory.* Englewood Cliffs, N.J.: Prentice-Hall.

Baritz, J. H. (1960). *The servants of power.* Middletown, Conn.: Wesleyan Univ. Press.

Baron, J. N., and W. T. Bielby (1980). Bringing the firm back in: stratification, segmentation, and the organization of work. *Amer. Sociol. Rev., 45,* 737–765.

Barnard, C. I. (1938). *Functions of the executive.* Cambridge, Mass.: Harvard Univ. Press.

Baty, G., W. Evan, and T. Rothermel (1971). Personnel flows as interorganizational relations. *Admin. Sci. Quart., 16,* 430–443.

Baumol, W. (1959). *Business behavior, value and growth.* New York: Macmillan.

Beck, E. M. (1980). Labor unionism and racial income inequality: a time-series analysis of the post-world war II period. *Amer. J. Sociol., 85,* 791–814.

Beck, E. M., P. M. Horan, and C. M. Tolbert, III (1978). Stratification in a dual economy: a sectoral model of earnings determination. *Amer. Sociol. Rev., 43,* 704–720.

Bem, D. J. (1967). Self-perception: the dependent variable of human performance. *Organizat. Behav. hum. Perform., 2,* 105–121.

——— (1972). Self-perception theory. In Leonard Berkowitz (Ed.), *Advances in experimental social psychology.* Vol. 6. New York: Academic Press. Pp. 1–62.

Bem, D. J., and D. C. Funder (1978). Predicting more of the people more of the time: assessing the personality of situations. *Psychol. Rev., 85,* 485–501.

Berger, C. J., L. L. Cummings, and H. G. Heneman (1975). Expectancy theory and operant conditioning predictions of performance under variable ratio and continuous schedules of reinforcement. *Organizat. Behav. hum. Perform., 14,* 227–243.

Berger, P. L., and T. Luckmann (1966). *The social construction of reality.* Garden City, N.Y.: Doubleday.

Berle, A. A., and G. C. Means (1968). *The modern corporation and private property* (rev. ed.). New York: Harcourt, Brace, and World.

Bibb, R., and W. H. Form (1977). The effects of industrial, occupational, and sex stratification on wages in blue-collar markets. *Social Forces, 55,* 974–996.

Bidwell, C. E., and J. D. Kasarda (1975). School district organization and student achievement. *Amer. Sociol. Rev., 40,* 55–70.

Blai, B., Jr. (1962). An occupational study of job satisfaction and need satisfaction. *J. exp. Education, 32,* 383–388.

Blalock, H. M., Jr. (1967). Status inconsistency, social mobility, status integration and structural effects. *Amer. Sociol. Rev., 32,* 790–801.

Blau, P. M. (1955). *The dynamics of bureaucracy.* Chicago: Univ. of Chicago Press.

——— (1960). Structural Effects. *Amer. Sociol. Rev., 25,* 178–193.

——— (1964). *Exchange and power in social life.* New York: Wiley.

——— (1970). A formal theory of differentiation in organizations. *Amer. Sociol. Rev., 35,* 201–218.

——— (1973). *The organization of academic work.* New York: Wiley.

Blau, P. M., and W. R. Scott (1962). *Formal organizations.* San Francisco: Chandler.

Blau, P. M., and R. Schoenherr (1971). *The structure of organizations.* New York: Basic Books.

Blauner, R. (1964). *Alienation and freedom: the factory worker and his industry.* Chicago: Univ. of Chicago Press.

Bloch, F. E., and M. S. Kuskin (1978). Wage determination in the union and nonunion sectors. *Indust. Labor Rel. Rev., 31,* 183–192.

Blumenfeld, W. E., and T. E. Leidy (1969). Effectiveness of goal setting as a management device: research note. *Psychol. Reports, 24,* 24.

Blumer, H. (1962). Society as social interaction. In Arnold M. Rose (Ed.), *Human behavior and social processes: an interactionist approach.* Boston: Houghton Mifflin. Pp. 179–192.

Bonacich, E. (1972). A theory of ethnic antagonism: the split labor market. *Amer. Sociol. Rev., 37,* 547–559.

——— (1976). Advanced capitalism and black/white race relations in the United States: a split labor market interpretation. *Amer. Sociol. Rev., 41,* 34–51.

Booker, G. (1969). Behavioral aspects of disciplinary action. *Personnel J., 48,* 525–529.

Bougon, M., K. Weick, and D. Binkhorst (1977). Cognition in organizations: an analysis of the Utrecht jazz orchestra. *Admin. Sci. Quart., 22,* 606–631.

Bourgeois, L. J., III, D. W. McAllister, and T. R. Mitchell (1978). The effects of different organizational environments upon decisions about organizational structure. *Acad. Management J., 21,* 508–514.

Bower, J. L. (1965). The role of conflict in economic decision-making groups: some empirical results. *Quart. J. Economics, 79,* 263–277.

Bowers, K. S. (1973). Situationism in psychology: an analysis and a critique. *Psychol. Rev., 80,* 307–336.

Braverman, H. (1974). *Labor and monopoly capital: the degradation of work in the twentieth century.* New York: Monthly Review.

Brief, A. P., and R. J. Aldag (1975). Employee reactions to job characteristics: a constructive replication. *J. appl. Psychol., 60,* 182–186.

Brittain, J. W., and J. H. Freeman (1980). Organizational proliferation and density-dependent selection. In J. Kimberly and R. Miles (Eds.), *Organizational life cycles.* San Francisco: Jossey-Bass. Pp. 291–338.

Brown, R. H. (1978). Bureaucracy as praxis: toward a political phenomenology of formal organizations. *Admin. Sci. Quart., 23,* 365–382.

Bucher, R. (1970). Social process and power in a medical school. In M. N. Zald (Ed.), *Power in organizations*. Nashville, Tenn.: Vanderbilt Univ. Press. Pp. 3–48.

Burns, T., and G. M. Stalker (1961). *The management of innovation*. London: Tavistock.

Burrell, G., and G. Morgan (1979). *Sociological paradigms and organisational analysis*. London: Heinemann.

Burt, R. S. (1977). Positions in multiple network systems, part one: a general conception of stratification and prestige in a system of actors cast as a social topology. *Social Forces, 56,* 106–131.

_____ (1980). Autonomy in a social topology. *Amer. J. Sociol., 85,* 892–925.

Burt, R. S., K. P. Christman, and H. C. Kilburn, Jr. (1980). Testing a structural theory of corporate cooptation: interorganizational directorate ties as a strategy for avoiding market constraints on profits. *Amer. Sociol. Rev., 45,* 821–841.

Calder, B. J., and P. H. Schurr (1981). Attitudinal processes in organizations. In L. L. Cummings and B. M. Staw (Eds.), *Research in organizational behavior*. Vol. 3. Greenwich, Conn.: JAI Press. Pp. 283–302.

Campbell, D. (1969). Variation and selective retention in sociocultural evolution. *General Systems, 16,* 69–85.

Campbell, J. P., and M. D. Dunnette (1968). Effectiveness of t-group experiences in managerial training and development. *Psychol. Bull., 70,* 73–104.

Carroll, S. J., and H. L. Tosi (1970). Goal characteristics and personality factors in a management by objectives program. *Admin. Sci. Quart., 15,* 295–305.

Cartwright, D. (1979). Contemporary social psychology in historical perspective. *Soc. Psychol. Quart., 42,* 82–93.

Chaffee, E. E. (1980). *Decision models in university budgeting*. Unpublished Ph.D. dissertation. Palo Alto, Calif.: Stanford Univ. Press.

Chandler, A. D., Jr. (1966). *Strategy and structure*. Garden City, N.Y.: Doubleday & Co., Anchor Books Edition.

Child, J. (1972a). Organizational structure, environment and performance: the role of strategic choice. *Sociology, 6,* 2–22.

_____ (1972b). Organization structure and strategies of control: a replication of the Aston study. *Admin. Sci. Quart., 17,* 163–177.

_____ (1973a). Strategies of control and organizational behavior. *Admin. Sci. Quart., 18,* 1–17.

_____ (1973b). Predicting and understanding organization structure. *Admin. Sci. Quart., 18,* 168–185.

Cicourel, A. V. (1964). *Method and measurement in sociology*. New York: Free Press.

_____ (1974). *Cognitive sociology*. New York: Free Press.

Ciscel, D. H. (1974). Determinants of executive compensation. *Southern Econ. J., 40,* 613–617.

Clarkson, G. P. E. (1962). *Portfolio selection: a simulation of trust investment*. Englewood Cliffs, N.J.: Prentice-Hall.

Clegg, S. (1975). *Power, rule and domination*. London: Routledge.

Clegg, S., and D. Dunkerly (1979). *Organization, class and control*. London: Routledge.

Cohen, K. J., and R. M. Cyert (1961). Computer models in dynamic economics. *Quart. J. Economics, 75,* 112–127.

_____ (1965a). *Theory of the firm: resource allocation in a market economy*. Englewood Cliffs, N.J.: Prentice-Hall.

_____ (1965b). Simulation of organizational behavior. In J. G. March (Ed.), *Handbook of organizations:* Chicago: Rand McNally. Pp. 305–334.

Cohen, M. D., and J. G. March (1974). *Leadership and ambiguity: the American college president*. New York: McGraw-Hill.

Cohen, M. D., J. G. March, and J. P. Olsen (1972). A garbage can model of organizational choice. *Admin. Sci. Quart., 17,* 1–25.

Comstock, D. E., and W. R. Scott (1977). Technology and the structure of subunits: distinguishing individual and work-group effects. *Admin. Sci. Quart., 22,* 177–202.

Copeland, R. E., R. E. Brown, and R. V. Hall (1974). The effects of principal-implemented techniques on the behavior of pupils. *J. appl. Behav. Analy., 7,* 77–86.

Crecine, J. P. (1967). A computer simulation model of municipal budgeting. *Management Sci., 13,* 786–815.

Crozier, M. (1964). *The bureaucratic phenomenon*. Chicago: Univ. of Chicago Press.

Cyert, R. M., W. R. Dili, and J. G. March (1958). The role of expectations in business decision making. *Admin. Sci. Quart., 3,* 307–340.

Cyert, R. M., and J. G. March (1963). *A behavioral theory of the firm*. Englewood Cliffs, N.J.: Prentice-Hall.

Cyert, R. M., H. A. Simon, and D. B. Trow (1956). Observation of a business decision. *J. Business, 29,* 237–248.

Dachler, H. P., and W. H. Mobley (1973). Construct validation of an instrumentality-expectancy-task-goal model of work motivation. *J. appl. Psychol., 58,* 397–418.

Daft, R. L., and J. C. Wiginton (1979). Language and organization. *Acad. Management Rev., 4,* 179–191.

Dahl, R. A. (1957). The concept of power. *Behav. Sci., 2,* 201–215.

Davis, J. A., J. L. Spaeth, and C. Huson (1961). A technique for analyzing the effects of group composition. *Amer. Sociol. Rev., 26,* 215–225.

Deslauriers, B. C., and P. B. Everett (1977). Effects of intermittent and continuous token reinforcement on bus ridership. *J. appl. Psychol., 62,* 369–375.

Domhoff, G. W. (1974). *The bohemian grove and other retreats: a study in ruling class cohesiveness*. New York: Harper & Row.

Dowling, J., and J. Pfeffer (1975). Organizational legitimacy: social values and organizational behavior. *Pacific Sociol. Rev., 18,* 122–136.

Downey, H. K., D. Hellriegel, and J. W. Slocum, Jr. (1975). Environmental uncertainty: the construct and its application. *Admin. Sci. Quart., 20,* 613–629.

Downey, H. K., and J. W. Slocum (1975). Uncertainty: measures, research, and sources of variation. *Acad. Management J., 18,* 562–578.

Dulany, D. E. (1968). Awareness, rules, and propositional control: a confrontation with s-r behavior theory. In D. Horton and T. Dixon (Eds.), *Verbal behavior and general behavior theory*. Englewood Cliffs, N.J.: Prentice-Hall.

Duncan, R. B. (1972). Characteristics of organizational environments and perceived environmental uncertainty. *Admin. Sci. Quart., 17,* 313–327.

Dunn, M. G. (1980). The family office: coordinating mechanism of the ruling class. In G. W. Domhoff (Ed.), *Power structure research*. Beverly Hills, Calif.: Sage. Pp. 17–45.

Dyer, W. G. (1977). *Team building: issues and alternatives*. Reading, Mass.: Addison-Wesley.

Edelman, M. (1964). *The symbolic uses of politics*. Urbana: Univ. of Illinois Press.

Edstrom, A., and J. R. Galbraith (1977). Transfer of managers as a coordination and control strategy in multinational organizations. *Admin. Sci. Quart., 22,* 248–263.

Edwards, R. C. (1979). *Contested terrain: the transformation of the workplace in the twentieth century*. New York: Basic Books.

Emerson, R. M. (1962). Power-dependence relations. *Amer. Sociol. Rev., 27,* 31–41.

Erez, M. (1977). Feedback: a necessary condition for the goal setting-performance relationship. *J. appl. Psychol., 62,* 624–627.

Evan, W. (1966). The organization-set: toward a theory of interorganizational relations. In J. D. Thompson (Ed.), *Approaches to organizational design*. Pittsburgh: Univ. of Pittsburgh Press. Pp. 175–190.

Evans, M. G. (1970). The effects of supervisory behavior on the path-goal relationship. *Organizat. Behav. and Hum. Perform., 5,* 277–298.

Featherman, D. L., and R. M. Hauser (1976). Sexual inequalities and socioeconomic achievement in the U.S., 1962–1973. *Amer. Sociol. Rev., 41,* 462–483.

Ferster, C. B., and B. F. Skinner (1957). *Schedules of reinforcement*. New York: Appleton-Century-Crofts.

Festinger, L. (1954). A theory of social comparison processes. *Hum. Relat., 7,* 117–140.

Flanagan, R. J., G. Strauss, and L. Ulman (1974). Worker discontent and work place behavior. *Indust. Relat., 13,* 101–123.

Fleishman, E. F., and D. R. Peters (1962). Interpersonal values, leadership attitudes, and managerial "success," *Personnel Psychol., 15,* 127–143.

Freeman, J. H. (1978). The unit of analysis in organizational research. In M. W. Meyer *et al.* (Eds.), *Environments and organizations*. San Francisco: Jossey-Bass. Pp. 335–351.

_____ (1979). Going to the well: school district administrative intensity and environmental constraint. *Admin. Sci. Quart., 24,* 119–133.

_____ (1982). Organizational life cycles and natural selection processes. In B. M. Staw and L. L. Cummings (Eds.), *Research in organizational behavior*. Vol. 4. Greenwich, Conn.: JAI Press.

Freeman, J. H., and M. T. Hannan (1975). Growth and decline processes in organizations. *Amer. Sociol. Rev., 40,* 215–228.

Freeman, J. H., and J. E. Kronenfeld (1974). Problems of definitional dependency: the case of administrative intensity. *Social Forces, 52,* 108–121.

Friedland, E. I. (1974). *Introduction to the concept of rationality in political science*. Morristown, N.J.: General Learning Press.

Friedman, M. (1953). The methodology of positive economics. In M. Friedman, *Essays in positive economics*. Chicago: Univ. of Chicago Press.

Galbraith, J., and L. L. Cummings (1967). An empirical investigation of the motivational determinants of task performance: interactive effects between instrumentality-valence and motivation-ability. *Organizat. Behav. hum. Perform., 2,* 237–257.

Garfinkel, H. (1967). *Studies in ethnomethodology*. Englewood Cliffs, N.J.: Prentice-Hall.

Gephart, R. P., Jr. (1978). Status degradation and organizational succession: an ethnomethodological approach. *Admin. Sci. Quart., 23,* 553–581.

Gergen, K. J. (1978). Toward generative theory. *J. Pers. soc. Psychol., 36,* 1344–1360.

Gerwin, D. (1969). A process model of budgeting in a public school system. *Management Sci., 15,* 338–361.

Goffman, E. (1959). *The presentation of self in everyday life*. Garden City, N.Y.: Doubleday.

_____ (1961). *Encounters: two studies in the sociology of interaction*. New York: Bobbs-Merrill.

_____ (1974). *Frame Analysis*. New York: Harper & Row.

Goldberg, V. P. (1980). Bridges over contested terrain: exploring the radical account of the employment relationship. *J. econ. Behav. Organizat., 1,* 249–274.

Goldman, P. (1980). The Marxist analysis of organizations: values, theories, and research. Unpublished manuscript. Department of Sociology. Univ. of Oregon.

Gonos, G. (1977). Situation versus frame: the interactionist and structuralist analyses of everyday life. *Amer. Sociol. Rev., 42,* 854–867.

Goodman, R. A. (1968). On the operationality of the Maslow need hierarchy. *British J. Indust. Relat., 6,* 51–57.

Gouldner, A. W. (1954). *Patterns of industrial bureaucracy*. Glencoe, Ill.: Free Press.

Graen, G. (1969). Instrumentality theory of work motivation: some empirical results and suggested modifications. *J. appl. Psychol. Monogr., 53,* 1–25.

Gross, N., W. S. Mason, and A. W. McEachern (1958). *Explorations in role analysis: studies of the school superintendency role*. New York: Wiley.

Grusky, O. (1961). Corporate size, bureaucratization, and managerial succession. *Amer. J. Sociol., 67,* 261–269.

_____ (1963). Managerial succession and organizational effectiveness. *Amer. J. Sociol., 69,* 21–31.

Hackman, J. R. (1978). The design of work in the 1980s. *Organizat. Dynamics, 7,* 3–17.

Hackman, J. R., and E. E. Lawler, III (1971). Employee reactions to job characteristics. *J. appl. Psychol., 55,* 259–286.

Hackman, J. R., and G. R. Oldham (1975). Development of the job diagnostic survey. *J. appl. Psychol., 60,* 159–170.

_____ (1976). Motivation through the design of work. *Organizat. Behav. hum. Perform., 16,* 250–279.

_____ (1980). *Work redesign*. Reading, Mass.: Addison-Wesley.

Hackman, J. R., G. R. Oldham, R. Janson, and K. Purdy (1975). A new strategy for job enrichment. *Calif. management Rev., 17,* 57–71.

Hackman, J. R., J. L. Pearce, and J. C. Wolfe (1978). Effects of changes in job characteristics on work attitudes and behaviors: a naturally occurring quasi-experiment. *Organizat. Behav. hum. Perform., 21,* 289–304.

Hackman, J. R., and L. W. Porter (1968). Expectancy theory predictions of work effectiveness. *Organizat. Behav. hum. Perform., 3,* 417–426.

Hage, J., and M. Aiken (1969). Routine technology, social structure and organizational goals. *Admin. Sci. Quart., 14,* 366–376.

Hall, D. T. (1972). A model of coping with role conflict: the role behavior of college educated women. *Admin. Sci. Quart., 17,* 471–486.

Hall, D. T., and K. E. Nougaim (1968). An examination of Maslow's need hierarchy in an organizational setting. *Organizat. Behav. hum. Perform., 3,* 12–35.

Hall, R. H., J. E. Haas, and N. J. Johnson (1967). Organizational size, complexity and formalization. *Amer. Sociol. Rev., 32,* 903–912.

Hamner, W. C., and E. P. Hamner (1976). Behavior modification on the bottom line. *Organizat. Dynamics, 4,* 3–21.

Hannan, M. T. (1971). *Aggregation and disaggregation in sociology.* Lexington, Mass.: D.C. Heath.

Hannan, M. T., and J. H. Freeman (1977). The population ecology of organizations. *Amer. J. Sociol., 82,* 929–964.

———— (1978). Internal politics of growth and decline. In M. W. Meyer et al. (Eds.), *Environments and organizations.* San Francisco: Jossey-Bass. Pp. 177–199.

Hannan, M. T., and J. H. Freeman, and J. W. Meyer (1976). Specification of models for organizational effectiveness. *Amer. Sociol. Rev., 41,* 136–143.

Hargens, L. L. (1969). Patterns of mobility of new Ph.D.'s among American academic institutions. *Sociol. Education, 42,* 18–37.

Harre, R., and P. F. Secord (1972). *The explanation of social behavior.* Oxford: Basil Blackwell and Mott.

Hauser, R. M. (1970). Context and consex: a cautionary tale. *Amer. J. Sociol., 75,* 645–664.

———— (1971). Socioeconomic background and educational performance. Washington, D.C.: Arnold and Caroline Rose Monograph Series of the American Sociological Association.

Hawley, A. H. (1968). Human ecology. In D. L. Sills (Ed.), *International encyclopedia of the social sciences.* New York: Macmillan. Pp. 328–337.

Heizer, J. (1976). Transfers and terminations as staffing options. *Acad. management J., 19,* 115–120.

Helmich, D. L. (1974). Organizational growth and succession patterns. *Acad. management J., 17,* 771–775.

———— (1977). Executive succession in the corporate organization: a current integration. *Acad. management Rev., 2,* 252–266.

Helmich, D., and W. Brown (1972). Successor type and organizational change in the corporate enterprise. *Admin. Sci. Quart., 17,* 371–381.

Herman, J. B., and C. L. Hulin (1972). Studying organizational attitudes from individual and organizational frames of reference. *Organizat. Behav. hum. Perform., 8,* 84–108.

Herman, J. B., R. B. Dunham, and C. L. Hulin (1975). Organizational structure, demographic characteristics, and employee responses. *Organizat. behav. hum. Perform., 13,* 206–232.

Herzberg, F., B. Mausner, and B. Snyderman (1959). *The motivation to work* (2nd ed.). New York: Wiley.

Hickson, D. J., C. R. Hinings, C. A. Lee, R. E. Schneck, and J. M. Pennings (1971). A strategic contingencies' theory of intraorganizational power. *Admin. Sci. Quart., 16,* 216–229.

Hickson, D. J., D. S. Pugh, and D. Pheysey (1969). Operations technology and organization structure: an empirical reappraisal. *Admin. Sci. Quart., 14,* 378–397.

Hills, F. S., and T. A. Mahoney (1978). University budgets and organizational decision making. *Admin. Sci. Quart., 23,* 454–465.

Hinings, C. R., D. J. Hickson, J. M. Pennings, and R. E. Schneck (1974). Structural conditions of intraorganizational power. *Admin. Sci. Quart., 19,* 22–44.

Hirschman, A. O. (1970). *Exit, voice, and loyalty.* Cambridge, Mass.: Harvard Univ. Press.

Holtzner, B., and J. H. Marx (1979). *Knowledge application: the knowledge system in society.* Boston: Allyn and Bacon.

House, R. J. (1971). A path goal theory of leadership effectiveness. *Admin. Sci. Quart., 16,* 321–338.

Huber, G. P., M. J. O'Connell, and L. L. Cummings (1975). Perceived environmental uncertainty: effects of information and structure. *Acad. management J., 18,* 725–740.

Hulin, C. L., and M. R. Blood (1968). Job enlargement, individual differences, and worker responses. *Psychol. Bull., 69,* 41–55.

Ilgen, D. R., C. D. Fisher, and M. S. Taylor (1979). Consequences of individual feedback on behavior in organizations. *J. appl. Psychol., 64,* 349–371.

Ingham, G. K. (1971). *Size of industrial organizations and working behavior.* Cambridge: Cambridge Univ. Press.

Ivancevich, J. (1976). Effects of goal setting on performance and job satisfaction. *J. appl. Psychol., 61,* 605–612.

———— (1977). Different goal setting treatments and their effects on performance and job satisfaction. *Acad. management J., 20,* 406–419.

Jacobs, D. (1974). Dependency and vulnerability: an exchange approach to the control of organizations. *Admin. Sci. Quart., 19,* 45–59.

Jacobs, R. C., and D. T. Campbell (1961). The perpetuation of an arbitrary tradition through successive generations of a laboratory microculture. *J. abnorm. soc. Psychol., 62,* 649–658.

Jacobson, J. (1968). Union conservatism: a barrier to racial equality. In J. Jacobson (Ed.), *The negro and the American labor movement.* Garden City, N.Y.: Anchor. Pp. 1–26.

Johnson, G. E., and K. C. Youmans (1971). Union relative wage effects by age and education. *Indust. labor Relat. Rev., 24,* 171–180.

Jones, E. E., and R. E. Nisbett (1971). *The actor and the observer: divergent perceptions of the causes of behavior.* Morristown, N.J.: General Learning Press.

Kahn, L. M. (1978). The effect of unions on the earnings of non-union workers. *Indust. labor relat. Rev., 31,* 205–216.

Kahn, R. L., D. M. Wolfe, R. P. Quinn, and J. D. Snoek (1964). *Organizational stress: studies in role conflict and ambiguity.* New York: Wiley.

Kahneman, D., and A. Tversky (1973). On the psychology of prediction. *Psychol. Rev., 80,* 237–251.

Kasarda, J. D. (1974). The structural implications of social system size: a three-level analysis. *Amer. Sociol. Rev., 39,* 19–28.

Kaufman, H. (1976). *Are government organizations immortal?* Washington, D.C.: Brookings.

Kelley, H. H. (1971). *Attribution in social interaction.* Morristown, N.J.: General Learning Press.

Khandwalla, P. (1973). Effect of competition on the structure of top management control. *Acad. management J., 16,* 285–295.

Kiesler, C. A., and S. B. Kiesler (1969). *Conformity.* Reading, Mass.: Addison-Wesley.

Kim, J., and W. Hamner (1976). The effect of performance feedback and goal setting on productivity and satisfaction in an organizational setting. *J. appl. Psychol., 61,* 48–57.

Kimberly, J. R. (1976). Organizational size and the structuralist perspective: a review, critique, and proposal. *Admin. Sci. Quart., 21,* 571–597.

Komaki, J., K. D. Barwick, and L. R. Scott (1978). A behavioral approach to occupational safety: pinpointing and reinforcing safe performance in a food manufacturing plant. *J. appl. Psychol., 63,* 434–445.

Kopelman, R. E. (1977). Across-individual, within-individual and return on effort versions of expectancy theory. *Decision Sciences, 8,* 651–662.

Kraft, P. (1977). *Programmers and managers: the routinization of computer programming in the United States.* New York: Heidleberg Science Library.

Kuhn, T. S. (1970). *The structure of scientific revolutions* (2nd ed.). Chicago: Univ. of Chicago Press.

Ladd, E. C., and S. M. Lipset (1975). *The divided academy: professors and politics.* New York: McGraw-Hill.

Larner, R. J. (1970). *Management control and the large corporation.* New York: Dunellen Publishing.

Latham, G. P., and J. J. Baldes (1975). The practical significance of Locke's theory of goal setting. *J. appl. Psychol., 60,* 122–124.

Latham, G. P., and S. B. Kinne, III (1974). Improving job performance through training in goal setting. *J. appl. Psychol., 59,* 187–191.

Latham, G. P., T. R. Mitchell, and D. L. Dossett (1978). Importance of participative goal setting and anticipated rewards on goal difficulty and job performance. *J. appl. Psychol., 63,* 163–171.

Latham, G. P., and G. A. Yukl (1975a). A review of research on the application of goal setting in organizations. *Acad. management J., 18,* 824–845.

———— (1975b). Assigned versus participative goal setting with educated and uneducated woods workers. *J. appl. Psychol., 60,* 299–302.

———— (1976). Effects of assigned and participative goal setting on performance and job satisfaction. *J. appl. Psychol., 61,* 166–171.

Lawler, E. E. (1967). Secrecy about management compensation: are there hidden costs? *Organizat. Behav. hum. Perform., 2,* 182–189.

———— (1973). *Motivation in work organizations.* Monterey, Calif.: Brooks/Cole.

———— (1974). For a more effective organization—match the job to the man. *Organizat. Dynam., 3,* 19–29.

Lawler, E. E., J. R. Hackman, and S. Kaufman (1973). Effects of job redesign: a field experiment. *J. appl. soc. Psychol., 3,* 49–62.

Lawler, E. E., and L. W. Porter (1967). Antecedent attitudes of effective managerial performance. *Organizat. Behav. hum. Perform., 2,* 122–142.

Lawrence, P. R., and J. W. Lorsch (1967). *Organization and environment.* Boston: Graduate School of Business Administration. Harvard University.

Leavitt, H. J. (1958). *Managerial psychology.* Chicago: Univ. of Chicago Press.

Leigh, D. E. (1980). Racial differentials in union relative wage effects—a simultaneous equations approach. *J. Labor Res., 1,* 95–114.

Lewellen, W. G. (1968). *Executive compensation in large industrial corporations.* New York: National Bureau of Economic Research.

———— (1971). *The ownership income of management.* New York: National Bureau of Economic Research.

Lewellen, W. G., and B. Huntsman (1970). Managerial pay and corporate performance. *Amer. Econ. Rev., 60,* 710–720.

Lieberman, S. (1956). The effects of changes in roles on the attitudes of role occupants. *Hum. Relat., 9,* 385–402.

Lincoln, J. R., and G. Zeitz (1980). Organizational properties from aggregate data: separating individual and structural effects. *Amer. Sociol. Rev., 45,* 391–408.

Lindblom, C. E., and D. Braybrooke (1970). *A strategy of decision.* New York: Free Press.

Lipset, S. M., M. A. Trow, and J. S. Coleman (1956). *Union Democracy.* Glencoe, Ill.: Free Press.

Locke, E. A. (1968). Toward a theory of task motivation and incentives. *Organizat. Behav. hum. Perform., 3,* 157–189.

Locke, E. A. (1977). The myths of behavior mod in organizations. *Acad. management Rev., 2,* 543–553.

Lodahl, J., and G. Gordon (1972). The structure of scientific fields and the functioning of university graduate departments. *Amer. Sociol. Rev., 37,* 57–72.

London, M., and G. Oldham (1976). Effects of varying goal types and incentive systems on performance and satisfaction. *Acad. management J., 19,* 537–546.

Luthans, F., and R. Kreitner (1974). The management of behavioral contingencies. *Personnel, 51,* 7–16.

———— (1975). *Organizational behavior modification.* Glenview, Ill.: Scott, Foresman.

Luthans, R., and D. White (1971). Behavior modification: application to manpower management. *Personnel Admin., 34,* 41–47.

Lynch, B. P. (1974). An empirical assessment of Perrow's technology construct. *Admin. Sci. Quart., 19,* 338–356.

McClelland, D. C. (1961). *The achieving society.* Princeton, N.J.: Van Nostrand.

McDermott, T., and T. Newhams (1971). Discharge-reinstatement: what happens thereafter. *Indust. labor Relat. Rev., 24,* 526–540.

McEachern, W. A. (1975). *Managerial control and performance.* Lexington, Mass.: D.C. Heath.

McGuire, J. W., J. S. Y. Chiu, and A. O. Elbing (1962). Executive incomes, sales, and profits. *Amer. Econ. Rev., 52,* 753–761.

Machlup, F. (1967). Theories of the firm: marginalist, behavioral, managerial. *Amer. Econ. Rev., 57,* 1–33.

Mackenzie, K. D. (1978). *Organizational structures.* Arlington Heights, Ill.: AHM Publishing.

Manns, C. L., and J. G. March (1978). Financial adversity, internal competition, and curriculum change in a university. *Admin. Sci. Quart., 23,* 541–552.

March, J. G. (1966). The power of power. In David Easton (Ed.). *Varieties of political theory.* Englewood Cliffs, N.J.: Prentice-Hall. Pp. 39–70.

_____ (1976). The technology of foolishness. In J. G. March and J. P. Olsen, *Ambiguity and choice in organizations.* Bergen, Norway: Universitetsforlaget. Pp. 69–81.

_____ (1978). Bounded rationality, Ambiguity, and the engineering of choice. *Bell J. Econ., 9,* 587–608.

March, J. G., and J. P. Olsen (1976). *Ambiguity and choice in organizations.* Bergen, Norway: Universitetsforlaget.

March, J. G., and H. A. Simon (1958). *Organizations.* New York: Wiley.

Marris, R. (1967). *The economic theory of "managerial" capitalism.* London: Macmillan.

Marshall, R. (1965). *The Negro and organized labor.* New York: Wiley.

Maruyama, M. (1974). Paradigms and communication. *Tech. Forecasting soc. Change, 6,* 3–32.

Maslow, A. H. (1943). A theory of human motivation. *Psychol. Rev., 50,* 370–396.

_____ (1954). *Motivation and personality.* New York: Harper.

Masson, R. T. (1971). Executive motivations, earnings, and consequent equity performance. *J. polit. Econ., 79,* 1278–1292.

Matsui, T., and Y. Ohtsuka (1978). Within-person expectancy theory predictions of supervisory consideration and structure behavior. *J. appl. Psychol., 63,* 128–131.

Mead, G. H. (1938). *The philosophy of the act.* Chicago: Univ. of Chicago Press.

Mechanic, D. (1962). Sources of power of lower participants in complex organizations. *Admin. Sci. Quart., 7,* 349–364.

Meissner, M. (1969). *Technology and the worker.* San Francisco: Chandler.

Merton, R. K. (1940). Bureaucratic structure and personality. *Social Forces, 18,* 560–568.

_____ (1957). The role-set: problems in sociological theory. *British J. Sociol., 8,* 106–120.

_____ (1968). *Social theory and social structure.* Glencoe, Ill.: Free Press.

_____ (1975). Structural analysis in sociology. In P. Blau (Ed.), *Approaches to the study of social structure.* New York: Free Press. Pp. 21–52.

Meyer, J. W., and B. Rowan (1977). Institutionalized organizations: formal structure as myth and ceremony. *Amer. J. Sociol., 83,* 340–363.

Meyer, J. W., W. R. Scott, S. Cole, and J. K. Intili (1978). Instructional dissensus and institutional consensus in schools. In M. W. Meyer *et al.* (Eds.). *Environments and organizations.* San Francisco: Jossey-Bass. Pp. 233–263.

Meyer, M. W. (1971). Some constraints in analyzing data on organizational structures. *Amer. Sociol. Rev., 36,* 294–297.

_____ (1972a). *Bureaucratic structure and authority.* New York: Harper & Row.

_____ (1972b). Size and structure of organizations: a causal analysis. *Amer. Sociol. Rev., 37,* 434–440.

_____ (1975). Leadership and organizational structure. *Amer. J. Sociol., 81,* 514–542.

Mills, C. W. (1956). *The power elite.* New York: Oxford Univ. Press.

Mindlin, S., and H. Aldrich (1975). Interorganizational dependence: a review of the concept and a reexamination of the findings of the Aston group. *Admin. Sci. Quart., 20,* 382–392.

Miner, J. B., and J. F. Brewer (1976). The management of ineffective performance. In M. D. Dunnette (Ed.). *Handbook of industrial and organizational psychology.* Chicago: Rand McNally. Pp. 995–1029.

Mischel, W. (1968). *Personality and assessment.* New York: Wiley.

Mitchell, T. R. (1974). Expectancy models of job satisfaction, occupational preference and effort: a theoretical, methodological and empirical appraisal. *Psychol. Bull., 81,* 1053–1077.

Mitchell, T. R., and A. Biglan (1971). Instrumentality theories: current uses in psychology. *Psychol. Bull., 76,* 432–454.

Mitroff, I. I., and L. R. Pondy (1974). On the organization of inquiry: a comparison of some radically different approaches to policy analysis. *Public Admin. Rev., 34,* 471–479.

Mobley, W. H., R. W. Griffeth, H. H. Hand, and B. M. Meglino (1979). Review and conceptual analysis of the employee turnover process. *Psychol. Bull., 86,* 493–522.

Mohr, L. (1971). Organizational technology and organizational structure. *Admin. Sci. Quart., 16,* 444–459.

Monteverde, K., and D. J. Teece (1980). Supplier switching costs and vertical integration in the U.S. automobile industry. Research Paper No. 575. Palo Alto: Graduate School of Business. Stanford University.

Moore, G. (1979). The structure of a national elite network. *Amer. Sociol. Rev., 44,* 673–692.

Morgan, G., and L. Smircich (1980). The case for qualitative research. *Acad. management Rev., 5,* 491–500.

Nadler, D. A. (1977). *Feedback and organization development: using data based methods.* Reading, Mass.: Addison-Wesley.

Nagel, E. (1963). Assumptions in economic theory. *Amer. Econ. Rev., 53,* 211–219.

Nagel, J. H. (1975). *The descriptive analysis of power.* New Haven, Conn.: Yale Univ. Press.

Nehrbass, R. G. (1979). Ideology and the decline of management theory. *Acad. management Rev., 4,* 427–431.

Newman, J. E. (1975). Understanding the organizational structure-job attitude relationship through perceptions of the work environment. *Organizat. Behav. hum. Perform., 14,* 371–397.

Noble, D. F. (1978). Social choice in machine design: the case of automatically controlled machine tools, and a challenge for labor. *Politics and Soc., 8,* 313–348.

Nord, W. (1969). Beyond the teaching machine: the neglected area of operant conditioning in the theory and practice of management. *Organizat. Behav. hum. Perform., 4,* 375–401.

Olsen, J. P. (1967a). Choice in an organized anarchy. In J. G. March and J. P. Olsen. *Ambiguity and choice in organizations*. Bergen, Norway: Universitetsforlaget. Pp. 82–139.

_____ (1976b). Reorganization as a garbage can. In J. G. March and J. P. Olsen. *Ambiguity and choice in organizations*. Bergen, Norway: Universitetsforlaget. Pp. 314–337.

O'Reilly, C. A., and D. Caldwell (1979). Informational influence as a determinant of perceived task characteristics and job satisfaction. *J. appl. Psychol., 64,* 157–165.

O'Reilly, C. A., G. N. Parlette, and J. R. Bloom (1980). Perceptual measures of task characteristics: the biasing effects of differing frames of reference and job attitudes. *Acad. management J., 23,* 118–131.

O'Reilly, C. A., and K. H. Roberts (1975). Individual differences in personality, position in the organization, and job satisfaction. *Organizat. Behav. hum. Perform., 14,* 144–150.

O'Reilly, C. A., and B. A. Weitz (1980). Managing marginal employees: the use of warnings and dismissals. *Admin. Sci. Quart., 25,* 467–484.

Orne, M. T. (1962). On the social psychology of the psychology of the psychological experiment: with particular reference to demand characteristics and their implications. *Amer. Psychol., 17,* 776–783.

Ouchi, W. G., and J. B. Johnson (1978). Types of organizational control and their relationship to emotional well being. *Admin. Sci. Quart., 23,* 293–317.

Ouchi, W. G., and A. M. Jaeger (1978). Type z organization: stability in the midst of mobility. *Acad. management Rev., 3,* 305–314.

Padgett, J. F. (1980). Bounded rationality in budgetary research. *Amer. polit. Sci. Rev., 74,* 354–372.

Palmer, D. A. (1980). Broken ties: some political and interorganizational determinants of interlocking directorates among large American corporations. Paper presented at the Annual Meeting of the American Sociological Association. New York.

Parker, D. F., and L. Dyer (1976). Expectancy theory as a within-person behavioral choice model: an empirical test of some conceptual and methodological refinements. *Organizat. Behav. hum. Perform., 17,* 97–117.

Pedalino, E., and V. U. Gamboa (1974). Behavior modification and absenteeism: intervention in one industrial setting. *J. appl. Psychol., 59,* 694–698.

Pennings, J. M. (1975). The relevance of the structural-contingency model for organizational effectiveness. *Admin. Sci. Quart., 20,* 393–410.

_____ (1980). *Interlocking directorates.* San Francisco: Jossey-Bass.

Perrow, C. (1967). A framework for comparative organizational analysis. *Amer. Sociol. Rev., 32,* 194–208.

_____ (1970a). *Organizational analysis: a sociological view.* Belmont, Calif.: Wadsworth Publishing.

_____ (1970b). Departmental power and perspectives in industrial firms. In M. N. Zald (Ed.). *Power in organizations.* Nashville, Tenn.: Vanderbilt Univ. Press. Pp. 59–89.

Peters, L. H. (1977). Cognitive models of motivation, expectancy theory and effort: an analysis and empirical test. *Organizat. Behav. hum. Perform., 20,* 129–148.

Peters, T. J. (1978). Symbols, patterns, and settings: an optimistic case for getting things done. *Organizat. Dynamics, 7,* 3–23.

Pettigrew, A. M. (1972). Information control as a power resource. *Sociology, 6,* 187–204.

_____ (1973). *The politics of organizational decision-making.* London: Tavistock.

Pfeffer, J. (1972a). Interorganizational influence and managerial attitudes. *Acad. management J., 15,* 317–330.

_____ (1972b). Size and composition of corporate boards of directors: the organization and its environment. *Admin. Sci. Quart., 17,* 218–228.

_____ (1972c). Merger as a response to organizational interdependence. *Admin. Sci. Quart., 17,* 382–394.

_____ (1973). Size, composition and function of hospital boards of directors: a study of organization-environment linkage. *Admin. Sci. Quart., 18,* 349–364.

_____ (1974). Cooptation and the composition of electric utility boards of directors. *Pacific Sociol. Rev., 17,* 333–363.

_____ (1977). The ambiguity of leadership. *Acad. management Rev., 2,* 104–112.

_____ (1978). The micropolitics of organizations. In M. W. Meyer (Eds.), *Environments and organizations.* San Francisco: Jossey-Bass. Pp. 29–50.

_____ (1980). A partial test of the social information processing model of job attitudes. *Hum. Relat., 33,* 457–476.

_____ (1981). *Power in organizations.* Marshfield, Mass.: Pitman.

Pfeffer, J., and H. Leblebici (1973a). Executive recruitment and the development of interfirm organizations. *Admin. Sci. Quart., 18,* 449–461.

_____ (1973b). The effect of competition on some dimensions of organizational structure. *Social Forces, 52,* 268–279.

Pfeffer, J., and A. Leong (1977). Resource allocations in united funds: examination of power and dependence. *Social Forces, 55,* 775–790.

Pfeffer, J., A. Leong, and K. Strehl (1977). Paradigm development and particularism: journal publication in three scientific disciplines. *Social Forces, 55,* 938–951.

Pfeffer, J., and W. L. Moore (1980). Power in university budgeting: a replication and extension. *Admin. Sci. Quart., 25,* 637–653.

Pfeffer, J., and P. Nowak (1976). Joint ventures and interorganizational interdependence. *Admin. Sci. Quart., 21,* 398–418.

Pfeffer, J., and J. Ross (1980). Union-nonunion effects on wage and status attainment. *Indust. Relat., 19,* 140–151.

Pfeffer, J., and G. R. Salancik (1974). Organizational decision making as a political process: the case of a university budget. *Admin. Sci. Quart., 19,* 135–151.

_____ (1975). Determinants of supervisory behavior: a role set analysis. *Hum. Relat., 28,* 139–154.

_____ (1977a). Administrator effectiveness: the effects of advocacy and information on resource allocations. *Hum. Relat., 30,* 641–656.

_____ (1977b). Organization design: the case for a coalition model of organizations. *Organizat. Dynam., 6,* 15–29.

_____ (1978). *The external control of organizations: a resource dependence perspective.* New York: Harper & Row.

Pfeffer, J., G. R. Salancik, and H. Leblebici (1976). The effect of uncertainty on the use of social influence in organizational decision making. *Admin. Sci. Quart., 21,* 227–245.

Pinder, C. C., and L. F. Moore, Eds. (1979). *Middle range theory and the study of organizations.* Leiden, The Netherlands: Martinus Nijhoff.

Plott, C. R., and M. E. Levine (1978). A model of agenda influence on committee decisions. *Amer. Econ. Rev., 68,* 146–160.

Polsby, N. W. (1960). How to study community power: the pluralist alternative. *J. Polit., 22,* 474–484.

Pondy, L. R. (1977). The other hand clapping: an information-processing approach to organizational power. In T. H. Hammer and S. B. Bacharach (Eds.), *Reward systems and power distribution.* Ithaca, N.Y.: Cornell University, School of Industrial and Labor Relations. Pp. 56–91.

_____ (1978). Leadership is a language game. In M. W. McCall, Jr., and M. M. Lombardo (Eds.), *Leadership: where else can we go?* Durham, N.C.: Duke Univ. Press. Pp. 87–99.

Pondy, L. R., and D. M. Boje (1980). Bringing mind back in. In W. M. Evan (Ed.), *Frontiers in organization and management.* New York: Praeger. Pp. 83–101.

Pritchard, R. D., and M. I. Curtis (1973). The influence of goal setting and financial incentives on task performance. *Organizat. Behav. hum. Perform., 10,* 175–183.

Pritchard, R. D., D. W. Leonard, C. W. Von Bergen, Jr., and R. J. Kirk (1976). The effects of varying schedules of reinforcement on human task performance. *Organizat. Behav. Hum. Perform., 16,* 205–230.

Provan, K. G., J. M. Beyer, and C. Kruytbosch (1980). Environmental linkages and power in resource-dependence relations between organizations. *Admin. Sci. Quart., 25,* 200–225.

Pugh, D. S., D. J. Hickson, C. R. Hinings, and C. Turner (1969). The context of organizational structures. *Admin. Sci. Quart., 14,* 91–114.

Rabinowitz, L., H. H. Kelley, and R. M. Rosenblatt (1966). Effects of different types of interdependence and response conditions in the minimal social situation. *J. exp. soc. Psychol., 2,* 169–197.

Randall, R. (1973). Influence of environmental support and policy space on organizational behavior. *Admin. Sci. Quart., 18,* 236–247.

Raphael, E. (1967). The Anderson-Warkov hypothesis in local unions: a comparative study. *Amer. Sociol. Rev., 32,* 768–776.

Ratcliff, R. E. (1980). Declining cities and capitalist class structure. In G. W. Domhoff (Ed.), *Power Structure Research.* Beverly Hills, Calif.: Sage. Pp. 115–138.

Rauschenberger, J., N. Schmitt, and J. E. Hunter (1980). A test of the need hierarchy concept by a markov model of change in need strength. *Admin. Sci. Quart., 25,* 654–670.

Reich, M. (1971). The economics of racism. In D. M. Gordon (Ed.), *Problems in political economy.* Lexington, Mass.: D.C. Heath. Pp. 107–113.

Ritzer, G. (1975). Sociology: a multiple paradigm science. *Amer. Sociol., 10,* 156–167.

Rizzo, J. R., R. J. House, and S. I. Lirtzman (1970). Role conflict and ambiguity in organizations. *Admin. Sci. Quart., 15,* 150–163.

Roberts, D. R. (1959). *Executive compensation.* Glencoe, Ill.: Free Press.

Roberts, K. H., and W. Glick (1981). The job characteristics approach to task design: a critical review. *J. appl. Psychol. 66,* 193–217.

Roberts, K. H., C. L. Hulin, and D. M. Rousseau (1978). *Developing an interdisciplinary science of organizations.* San Francisco: Jossey-Bass.

Roistacher, R. C. (1974). A review of mathematical methods in sociometry. *Sociol. Methods Res., 3,* 123–171.

Ross, L. (1977). The intuitive psychologist and his shortcomings: distortions in the attribution process. In L. Berkowitz (Ed.), *Advances in experimental social psychology.* Vol. 10. New York: Academic Press.

Rushing, W. A. (1966). Organizational size and administration: the problems of causal homogeneity and a heterogeneous category. *Pacific Sociol. Rev., 9,* 100–108.

_____ (1968). Hardness of material as related to division of labor in manufacturing industries. *Admin. Sci. Quart., 13,* 229–245.

Salancik, G. R. (1977). Commitment and the control of organizational behavior and belief. In B. M. Staw and G. R. Salancik (Eds.), *New directions in organizational behavior.* Chicago: St. Clair Press. Pp. 1–54.

_____ (1979a). Interorganizational dependence and responsiveness to affirmative action: the case of women and defense contractors. *Acad. management J., 22,* 375–394.

_____ (1979b). Field stimulations for organizational behavior research. *Admin. Sci. Quart., 24,* 638–649.

Salancik, G. R., and J. Pfeffer (1974). The bases and use of power in organizational decision making: the case of a university. *Admin. Sci. Quart., 19,* 453–473.

_____ (1977a). Who gets power—and how they hold on to it: a strategic-contingency model of power. *Organizat. Dynam., 5,* 3–21.

_____ (1977b). An examination of need-satisfaction models of job attitudes. *Admin. Sci. Quart., 22,* 427–456.

_____ (1978a). Uncertainty, secrecy, and the choice of similar others. *Soc. Psychol., 41,* 246–255.

_____ (1978b). A social information processing approach to job attitudes and task design. *Admin. Sci. Quart., 23,* 224–253.

Sarason, I. G., R. E. Smith, and E. Diener (1975). Personality research: components of variance attributable to the person and the situation. *J. Pers. soc. Psychol., 32,* 199–204.

Schacter, S., and J. Singer (1962). Cognitive, social, and physiological determinants of emotional state. *Psychol. Rev., 69,* 379–399.

Schmidt, F. L. (1973). Implications of a measurement problem for expectancy theory research. *Organizat. Behav. hum. Perform., 10,* 243–251.

Schutz, A. (1967). *The phenomenology of the social world.* Evanston, Ill.: Northwestern Univ. Press.

Scott, W. R. (1975). Organizational structure. In A. Inkeles, J. Coleman, and N. Smelser (Eds.), *Annual review of sociology.* Vol. 1. Palo Alto: Annual Reviews. Pp. 1–20.

_____ (1981). *Organizations: rational, natural, and open systems.* Englewood Cliffs, N.J.: Prentice-Hall.

Seashore, S. E. (1954). *Group cohesiveness in the industrial work group.* Ann Arbor, Mich.: Institute for Social Research. Univ. of Michigan.

Seeman, M. (1975). Alienation studies. In A. Inkeles, J. Coleman, and N. Smelser (Eds.), *Annual review of sociology.* Vol. 1. Palo Alto: Annual Reviews. Pp. 91–123.

Seligman, C., and J. Darley (1977). Feedback as means of decreasing residential energy consumption. *J. appl. Psychol., 62,* 363–368.

Selznick, P. (1949). *TVA and the grass roots.* Berkeley: Univ. of California Press.

Sheldon, A. (1980). Organizational paradigms: a theory of organizational change. *Organizat. Dynam., 8,* 61–80.

Sherif, M. (1935). A study of some social factors in perception. *Arch. Psychol.,* 187.

Shoup, L. H. (1975). Shaping the postwar world: the council on foreign relations and United States war aims during world war two. *Insurgent Sociol., 5,* 9–52.

Silverman, D. (1971) *The theory of organizations.* New York: Basic Books.

Simon H. A. (1947) *Administrative behavior.* New York: Macmillan.

_____ (1957). A behavioral model of rational choice. In H. A. Simon, *Models of man.* New York: Wiley.

_____ (1962). The architecture of complexity. *Proceedings of the American Philosophical Society, 106,* 467–482.

_____ (1972). Theories of bounded rationality. In C. B. McGuire and R. Radner (Eds.), *Decision and organization.* Amsterdam: North Holland Publishing.

_____ (1978). Rationality as process and as product of thought. *Amer. Econ. Rev., 68,* 1–16.

Smith, P. B. (1973). *Groups within organizations.* New York: Harper & Row.

Spence, M. A. (1975). *Market signalling.* Cambridge, Mass.: Harvard Univ. Press.

Spenner, K. (1979). Temporal changes in work content. *Amer. Sociol. Rev., 44,* 968–975.

Stava, P. (1976) Constraints on the politics of public choice. In J. G. March and J. P. Olsen, *Ambiguity and choice in organizations.* Bergen, Norway: Universitetsforlaget. Pp. 206–224.

Staw, B. M., and E. Szwajkowski (1975). The scarcity-munificence component of organizational environments and the commission of illegal acts. *Admin. Sci. Quart., 20,* 345–354.

Stedry, A. C., and E. Kay (1966). The effects of goal difficulty on performance. *Behav. Sci., 11,* 459–470.

Steers, R. M. (1975). Task-goal attributes, achievement, and supervisory performance. *Organizat. Behav. hum. Perform., 13,* 392–403.

Steers, R. M., and D. G. Spencer (1977). The role of achievement motivation in job design. *J. appl. Psychol., 62,* 472–479.

Stephens, T. A., and W. A. Burroughs (1978). An application of operant conditioning to absenteeism in a hospital setting. *J. appl. Psychol., 63,* 518–521.

Stinchcombe, A. L. (1965). Social structure and organizations. In J. G. March (Ed.), *Handbook of organizations.* Chicago: Rand McNally. Pp. 142–193.

Stogdill, R. M. (1974). *Handbook of leadership.* New York: Free Press.

Stogdill, R. M., and A. E. Coons (1957). Leader behavior: its description and measurement. Columbus, Ohio: Bureau of Business Research. College of Commerce and Administration. Ohio State University.

Stone, E. F. (1976). The moderating effect of work-related values on the job scope-job satisfaction relationship. *Organizat. Behav. hum. Perform., 15,* 147–167.

Stone, E. F., R. T. Mowday, and L. W. Porter (1977). Higher order need strengths as moderators of the job scope-job satisfaction relationship. *J. appl. Psychol., 62,* 466–471.

Strauss, G. (1974). Job satisfaction, motivation, and job redesign. In G. Strauss, R. E. Miles, C. C. Snow, and A. S. Tannenbaum (Eds.), *Organizational behavior: research and issues.* Belmont, Calif.: Wadsworth Publishing. Pp. 19–49.

Teece, D. J. (1980). The diffusion of an administrative innovation. *Management Sci., 26,* 464–470.

Teece, D. J., H. O. Armour, and G. Saloner (1980). Vertical integration and risk reduction. Unpublished manuscript. Graduate School of Business, Stanford University.

Terborg, J. (1976). The motivational components of goal setting. *J. appl. Psychol., 61,* 613–621.

Terborg, J., and H. Miller (1978). Motivation, behavior and performance: a closer examination of goal setting and monetary incentives. *J. appl. Psychol., 63,* 29–39.

Thompson, J. D. (1967). *Organizations in action.* New York: McGraw-Hill.

Tolbert, C., P. M. Horan, and E. M. Beck (1980). The structure of economic segmentation: a dual economy approach. *Amer. J. Sociol., 85,* 1095–1116.

Tosi, H., R. Aldag, and R. Storey (1973). On the measurement of the environment: an assessment of the Lawrence and Lorsch environmental uncertainty scale. *Admin. Sci. Quart. 18,* 27–36.

Tosi, H., and H. Platt (1967). Administrative ratios and organizational size. *Acad. management J., 10,* 161–168.

Tuggle, F. D. (1978). *Organizational processes.* Arlington Heights, Ill.: AHM Publishing.

Turner, A. N., and P. R. Lawrence (1965). *Industrial jobs and the worker: an investigation of response to task attributes.* Cambridge, Mass.: Harvard Univ. Press.

Unger, R. M. (1975). *Knowledge and politics.* New York: Free Press.

Useem, M. (1979). The social organization of the American business elite and participation of corporation directors in the governance of American institutions. *Amer. Sociol. Rev., 44,* 553–572.

Vroom, V. H. (1964). *Work and motivation.* New York: Wiley.

Wachter, M. L., and O. E. Williamson (1978). Obligational markets and the mechanics of inflation. *Bell J. Econ., 9,* 549–571.

Wahba, M. A., and L. G. Bridwell (1976). Maslow reconsidered: a review of research on the need hierarchy theory. *Organizat. Behav. hum. Perform., 15,* 212–240.

Weber, M. (1947). *The theory of social and economic organization.* New York: Free Press.

Weick, K. E. (1965). Laboratory experimentation with organizations. In J. G. March (Ed.), *Handbook of organizations.* Chicago: Rand McNally. Pp. 194–260.

_____ (1969). *The social psychology of organizing*. Reading, Mass.: Addison-Wesley.

_____ (1976). Educational organizations as loosely coupled systems. *Admin. Sci. Quart., 21,* 1–19.

_____ (1979). Cognitive processes in organizations. In B. M. Staw (Ed.) *Research in organizational behavior*. Vol. 1. Greenwich, Conn.: JAI Press. Pp. 41–74.

Weiner, S. S. (1976). Participation, deadlines, and choice. In J. G. March and J. P. Olsen, *Ambiguity and choice in organizations*. Bergen, Norway: Universitetsforlaget. Pp. 225–250.

Weiss, H. M., and J. B. Shaw (1979). Social influences on judgments about tasks. *Organizat. Behav. hum. Perform., 24,* 126–140.

Welch, F. (1973). Black-white differences in returns to schooling. *Amer. Econ. Rev., 63,* 893–907.

White, J. K. (1978). Individual differences and the job quality-worker response relationship: review, integration, and comments. *Acad. Management Rev., 3,* 267–280.

White, S. E., and T. R. Mitchell (1979). Job enrichment versus social cues: a comparison and competitive test. *J. appl. Psychol., 64,* 1–9.

White, S. E., T. R. Mitchell, and C. H. Bell, Jr. (1977). Goal setting, evaluation apprehension, and social cues as determinants of job performance and job satisfaction in a simulated organization. *J. appl. Psychol., 62,* 665–673.

Whitt, J. A. (1979). Toward a class-dialectic model of political power: an empirical assessment of three competing models of power. *Amer. Sociol. Rev., 44,* 81–100.

_____ (1980). Can capitalists organize themselves? In G. W. Domhoff (Ed.), *Power structure research*. Beverly Hills, Calif.: Sage. Pp. 97–113.

Wildavsky, A. (1979). *The politics of the budgetary process* (3rd ed.). Boston: Little, Brown.

Williamson, O. E. (1964). *Corporate control and business behavior: managerial objectives in a theory of the firm*. Englewood Cliffs, N.J.: Prentice-Hall.

_____ (1966). A rational theory of the federal budgetary process. In G. Tullock (Ed.), *Papers on non-market decision making*. Charlottesville, Va.: Thomas Jefferson Center for Political Economy.

_____ (1975). *Markets and hierarchies: analysis and antitrust implications*. New York: Free Press.

_____ (1979). Transaction-cost economics: the governance of contractual relations. *J. Law Econ., 22,* 233–261.

_____ (1981). The economics of organization: the transaction cost approach. Philadelphia: Center for the Study of Organizational Innovation. University of Pennsylvania. Working Paper No. 96.

Williamson, E. E., M. L. Wachter, and J. E. Harris (1975). Understanding the employment relation: the analysis of idiosyncratic exchange. *Bell J. Econ., 6,* 250–280.

Winter, S. G. (1975). Optimization and evolution in the theory of the firm. In R. H. Day and T. Groves (Eds.), *Adaptive economic models*. New York: Academic Press. Pp. 73–118.

Wofford, J. C. (1971). The motivational basis of job satisfaction and job performance. *Personnel Psychol., 24,* 501–518.

Woodward, J. (1965). *Industrial organization: theory and practice*. London: Oxford Univ. Press.

_____ (1970). *Industrial organization: behaviour and control*. London: Oxford Univ. Press.

Yoels, W. C. (1974). The structure of scientific fields and the allocation of editorships on scientific journals: some observations on the politics of knowledge. *Sociol. Quart., 15,* 264–276.

Yukl, G., K. N. Wexley, and J. D. Seymore (1972). Effectiveness of pay incentives under variable ratio and continuous reinforcement schedules. *J. appl. Psychol., 56,* 19–23.

Zald, M. N. (1965). Who shall rule? A political analysis of succession in a large welfare organization. *Pacific Sociol. Rev., 8,* 52–60.

Zifferblatt, S. M. (1972). The effectiveness of modes and schedules of reinforcement on work and social behavior in occupational therapy. *Behav. Therapy, 3,* 567–578.

Zucker, L. G. (1977). The role of institutionalization in cultural persistence. *Amer. Sociol. Rev., 42,* 726–743.

_____ (1980a). Typifying interaction: action, situation, and role. Unpublished manuscript. Los Angeles: Department of Sociology, UCLA.

_____ (1980b). Effect of sudden redefinition of institutional structure on "demand characteristics" in experiments. Paper presented at the West Coast Conference for Small Group Research. San Francisco, May, 1980.

Zwerman, W. L. (1970). *New perspectives on organization theory*. Westport, Conn.: Greenwood.

CHAPTER 8

Experimentation in Social Psychology

Elliot Aronson
University of California, Santa Cruz

Marilynn Brewer
University of California, Los Angeles

J. Merrill Carlsmith
Stanford University

INTRODUCTION

In social psychology, there are a great many ways of gathering information: We can simply observe behavior; we can interview people about their attitudes, beliefs, intentions, and motivation; we can obtain similar information by administering questionnaires and rating scales; through the use of the cross-cultural method, we can study the intercorrelations among a variety of social behaviors in different societies. The list of techniques and variations on these techniques is filled with interesting possibilities. These techniques have provided us with some of our richest and most fascinating data about social phenomena. In this chapter, we will limit our discussion to just one technique, the experiment.

In the mid 1960s, when two of us (Aronson and Carlsmith) began the initial (1968) version of this chapter, we attempted something that was original at the time. We tried to demystify the experimental process in social psychology by discussing in step-by-step fashion the concerns, problems, pitfalls, and excitements that the experimenter encounters from the moment he or she conceives an idea to the time when the data are collected from the final subject and the latter is debriefed and sent home happy and enlightened. Our aim was to write a cook-

book, that is, to make it possible for good experiments to be performed by almost anyone with a good idea who was willing to master the skills required.

In that chapter we described, in detail, how to translate a conceptualization into a set of research operations without losing too much in the translation. We discussed such issues as how to achieve maximum impact without sacrificing control and without violating the ethical standards current at the time. We explored problems concerning establishing realism in the laboratory, avoiding bias, and coping with demand characteristics. We also emphasized the importance of the post-experimental interview and the advantages and disadvantages of the use of deception and described the wide range of skills and interpersonal sensitivities required of an individual performing experiments in social psychology. Finally, we described the special joy, excitement, and feeling of accomplishment that develop from overcoming the myriad of problems uniquely posed by experimentation in this area and thereby extending the frontiers of knowledge somewhat.

In that chapter we discussed many styles of social psychological experimentation. The discussion focused, as did much of that chapter, on the phenomonological involvement of the subject in the experiment—the extent to which he or she was psychologically enmeshed in a set of events. We described paradigms ranging from the intense involvement characterized by the Milgram study, for example, to the less intense paper and pencil research that was the hallmark of the Yale research on communication. At the same time, we did not hesitate to reveal our own preferences. Specifically, we displayed a strong preference (some might say bias) for the high impact "scenario" model—the one that we ourselves practiced and taught our students. In this model of experimentation, the subjects become deeply involved in a set of events and perform actions that are usually somewhat different from what they originally thought they had volunteered to do. A good example of this kind of experiment is the classic study by Leon Festinger and J. Merrill Carlsmith (1959).

Here subjects who thought they were to perform a routine set of dull motor tasks suddenly found themselves telling a lie to an ostensibly naive subject. This experience was as engrossing as it was unexpected and had a dramatic impact on the subjects. Whatever the other strengths and weaknesses of that experiment (and they have been debated at length) there has never been debate about the fact that the scenario of the experiment was gripping for the subjects; they were responding to the immediate cues impinging upon them without theorizing about what they *might* have done in a hypothetical situation.

Our preference for this research style could not reasonably have been termed a weakness at the time the chapter was published. After all, the style of research we were emphasizing was the predominant emerging technique of the 1960s. Moreover, in delineating that style we were, in effect, codifying some three decades of the Lewinian tradition dating from the classic experiment in which Lewin and his collegues imposed either democratic, autocratic or *laissez faire* adult leadership styles on groups of boys (Lewin, Lippitt, and White, 1939).

Our bias became increasingly interesting and somewhat problematic, however, in the light of events following the publication of the chapter. Specifically, in the past decade there was a significant re-examination of experimental procedures and research strategies in social psychology. It is not our goal here to provide a definitive history of the development of the field during the past several years. Jones has done an admirable job of it else-

where in this volume (see Chapter 2). Nevertheless, because recent history has altered the way social psychologists view experimental methodology, it may be useful to discuss briefly some reasons for the major changes that have taken place.

One source of concern over the classical experimental paradigm was ethical. Critics both inside and outside the field began to question using deception (as in the Festinger and Carlsmith study described previously) and those generating extreme anxiety as in the well-known research of Milgram (1963, 1965, 1974), and Zimbardo and his students (Haney, Banks, and Zimbardo, 1973). The strength of this reaction was perhaps more influenced by societal events than by any clear evidence of gross insensitivity to the rights of experimental subjects or of harm having been done by experimenters (see Holmes, 1976a, 1976b). For example, in the late 1960s and early 1970s, most of us were strongly affected by the cynical, self-serving duplicity employed by our national leaders during the Vietnam War and during the Watergate investigation. In this atmosphere, many social psychologists grew alarmed lest we as a profession might lose the confidence of the public by behaving in a way that bore any resemblance to that exposed in Watergate investigations—no matter how superficial that resemblance might be. The rapid growth in government regulations on the protection of human subjects also reflected the same concerns.

At the same time, the epistemological basis for an experimental social psychology became the subject of widespread debate (see, for example, Gergen, 1973; Schlenker, 1974). To some extent, this debate was fueled by some general misconceptions about the role of single experiments in testing complex causal models of social behavior (see Henshel, 1980; Mook, 1983). Nevertheless, some fundamental issues were being raised concerning the basic premises of experimental design. How meaningful is it, critics were asking, to study causal processes "disembedded" from their real-world causal networks?

These concerns have contributed to a shift in the distribution of research efforts, away from the hegemony of a single experimental paradigm that marked the research of the 1950s and 1960s. At least three distinct modes of experimental research characterize the work of social psychologists today:

1. Although most researchers in the area have continued in the style of traditional experimental social psy-

chology, they have made some modifications. Primarily for ethical reasons, their experimental treatments tend to be weaker than they were in the earlier period. For example, although the use of deception was as common in the 1970s as in the 1960s (Gross and Fleming, 1982), the nature of the deception became far more trivial, and the operations, typically, became less stressful.

2. A common current research mode is the "judgment experiment," wherein the subject is asked to recognize, recall, classify, or evaluate stimulus materials presented by the experimenter. In such experiments, the focus is on controlled and systematic variations in the stimulus environment. Little direct impact on subjects is intended, except insofar as the stimulus materials capture their attention and elicit meaningful judgmental responses. In effect, the role of the subject in this type of research is that of an *observer*. Although there may still be considerable variation in how much subject involvement is engaged by the task, the defining characteristic of judgment experiments is that stimulus control is the primary concern.

3. An increasing number of researchers are turning away from laboratory research altogether in favor of experiments in field settings. By this strategy they are able to retain the advantages of direct impact on subjects in a highly involving setting. Although the impact and involvement usually exceed the laboratory, it is often achieved at the cost of full control over the stimulus environment or over the assignment of subjects to treatments (frequently regarded as the defining characteristics of the experiment). The focus of this research also tends to be more limited than the general theory-testing underlying most laboratory research, since it typically deals only with variables found in the particular applied setting under investigation.

In recognition of the increased diversity of styles of experimentation in social psychology, we have broadened the scope of this chapter accordingly. Nonetheless, our general purpose remains the same as it was the first time around, namely, to continue to demystify the experimental process by addressing the questions of how to and why in as straightforward and intelligible a manner as we can. Likewise, we will continue to draw on examples from our own research studies, not because we regard these as particularly exemplary but because our personal experience with them provides us with concrete details that cannot usually be captured from published

versions of others' research. By drawing on this experience, we hope to make the reader vividly aware of both the promise and the perils of designing and conducting experiments in social psychology.

THE LABORATORY EXPERIMENT

We consider the experiment to be the core research method in social psychology. In advocating the experimental method, we are taking it as axiomatic that the purpose for which this method is best suited is that of testing theory rather than describing the world as it is. Without doubt, for descriptive and exploratory purposes, there are alternative models of systematic observation and data collection that can better serve the needs of the researcher. However, for subjecting theory-inspired hypotheses about causal relationships to potential confirmation or disconfirmation, the experiment is unexcelled in its ability to provide unambiguous evidence about causation, to permit control over extraneous variables, and to allow for analytic exploration of the dimensions and parameters of a complex phenomenon.

The distinctions made earlier between field and laboratory research and between high impact and judgment experiments are useful and, at the extremes, clear and obvious. But the world is never that simple. Consider the distinction between the laboratory and the field. What could be more obvious? At first glance, most graduate students in social psychology can easily discern the difference and would articulate it something like this: A field experiment occurs in the real world; a laboratory experiment is more contrived, less natural, more deceptive, and less real. While such a distinction seems sensible, it is, in fact, a vast oversimplification. Consider the following variations on a typical "bystander intervention" experiment:

1. Suppose that you are a young man walking along a street in New York City and that a rather attractive young woman carrying an armload of books and papers approaches you. Just as you and she come to within ten steps of each other, she stumbles slightly, dropping her books and scattering her papers. Unknown to you, a social psychologist, sitting in a car parked at the curb, is observing whether or not you stop to help the woman retrieve her books and papers, how long you stay at the task, and so on, as a function of the physical attractiveness of the woman.

2. Suppose that you are walking along a street on the campus of Columbia University in New York City and that a rather attractive young woman carrying an armload of books and papers, is walking toward you. Just as you and she...

3. Suppose that you are a student at Columbia University and you have volunteered to participate in an experiment as part of a requirement for your course in introductory psychology. You enter the psychology building at the appointed time and as you are walking down the corridor, an attractive young woman is walking toward you carrying an armload...

4. Suppose, after signing up for an experiment in psychology, you arrive at the psychology department and are told to wait in a room for the experimenter until another student who will also be a subject in the experiment arrives. A few minutes later an attractive young woman enters; she is carrying an armload of books and papers. As she crosses in front of you, she stumbles...

5. Supose that you have just completed participating in a research project in psychology at Columbia University. The project consisted of your taking a written personality test and being interviewed about your political preferences, number of siblings, and so on. The researcher thanks you, gives you credit for your participation, and sends you on your way. Unknown to you, you are followed out of the building and off the campus by another student whose task it is to observe your behavior as you are approached by a rather attractive young woman carrying an armload...

6. Suppose that, as part of a research project, a psychologist hands you a sheet paper. On the sheet of paper are written the following words: "Suppose that you are walking along a street in New York City and that a rather attractive young woman carrying an armload of books and papers approaches you. Just as you and she come to within ten steps of each other, she stumbles slightly, dropping her books and scattering her papers. Do you think you would help her retrieve her books and papers? How long would you stay?"

As one can see, a simple distinction is wholly inadequate. Indeed, it is almost certainly the case that we are not talking about a dichotomy at all. But for the moment, let us pretend that experimentation in the laboratory and in the field does fit into a neat dichotomy. The advantage of this pretense is that, with a dichotomy in mind, one can list tentatively several dimensions in which experiments in these two arenas differ from one another.

One of the most important differences involves the actual phenomenology of the subjects—what the subjects think is going on. Are they aware that they are in an experiment, or does this event appear to be part of their normal life? *In general,* in field experiments, subjects are unaware that they are participants in an experiment. Another factor involves random assignment: *In general*, the laboratory makes it easier to accomplish the random assignment of subjects to conditions. In addition, a laboratory setting permits the researcher to be more precise in manipulating independent variables, in assessing outcomes, and in eliminating or minimizing the salience or intrusiveness of "extraneous" variables. Advocates of laboratory experiments believe that the world is a complex place consisting of a great many noisy variables, a condition that impedes the chances of obtaining a pure indication of the effect of one variable upon another. If the experimenter wants to discover the effects of an event on the behavior, attitudes, or feelings of subjects, the laboratory provides the sterility that enables observation of those effects unencumbered by extraneous variables that could confound interpretation. Conversely, the field is generally regarded as being more "real." In the real world the event in question always occurs in context; it is that very context that might have important but extraneous effects upon the behavior, feelings, or attitudes, of the individual. Critics of the laboratory setting have suggested that it is silly to eliminate contextual variables in the interest of precision if those variables are always present in the world.

We will elaborate on this discussion later in this chapter. For now, however, we must remind the reader that, for the sake of initial clarity, we intentionally oversimplified the laboratory-field distinction. In actuality, there is no clear dichotomy between the laboratory experiment and the field experiment. Rather, there is an array of possibilities with overlapping qualities or, to be more precise, there are several possible continua (depending upon which aspect of the definition one is looking at) that cut across one another in complex ways.

A PROTOTYPIC IMPACT EXPERIMENT

What constitutes an experiment in social psychology? Exactly when, where, and how would one use this technique in preference to some of the techniques listed earlier? Let us begin to answer this question by describing an experiment in some detail. We will then compare the procedures used in this experiment with some alternative techniques for investigating the same or similar questions. We have chosen for illustrative purposes a classic high-impact laboratory experiment designed and conducted by Aronson and Mills (1959). It was selected not for its purity as a model of experimental efficiency, but because it illustrates clearly both the advantages and the challenges of attempting to do experimental research in social psychology.

Aronson and Mills set out to test the hypothesis that individuals who undergo a severe initiation in order to be admitted to a group will find the group more attractive than they would if they were admitted to that group with little or no initiation. To test this hypothesis, they conducted the following experiment.

Sixty-three college women were recruited as volunteers to participate in a series of group discussions on the psychology of sex. This format was a ruse in order to provide a setting wherein subjects could be made to go through either mild or severe initiations in order to gain membership in a group.

Each subject was tested individually. When a subject arrived at the laboratory, ostensibly to meet with her group, the experimenter explained to her that he was interested in studying the "dynamics of the group discussion process," and that, accordingly, he had arranged these discussion groups for the purpose of investigating these dynamics, which included such phenomena as the flow of communications, who speaks to whom, and so forth. He explained that he had chosen as a topic "The Psychology of Sex" in order to attract many volunteers, since many college people were interested in sex. He then went on to say that this topic presented one great disadvantage to him; namely, that many volunteers, because of shyness, found it more difficult to participate in a discussion about sex than in a discussion about a more neutral topic. He explained that his study would be impaired if any group member failed to participate freely. He then asked the subject if she felt able to discuss this topic freely. The subjects invariably replied in the affirmative.

The instructions were used to set the stage for the initiation that followed. The subjects were randomly assigned to one of three experimental conditions: a severe-initiation condition, a mild-initiation condition, or a no-initiation condition. The subjects in the no-initiation condition were told, at this point, that they could now join a discussion group. It was not that easy for the subjects in the other two conditions, however. The experimenter told these subjects that he had to be ab-

solutely certain that they could discuss sex frankly before admitting them to a group. Accordingly, he said that he had recently developed a test that he would now use as a "screening device" to eliminate those students who would be unable to engage in such a discussion without excessive embarrassment. In the severe-initiation condition, the test consisted of having each subject read aloud (to the male experimenter) a list of 12 obscene words and two vivid descriptions of sexual activity from contemporary novels. In the mild-initiation condition, the women were merely required to read aloud words related to sex that were not obscene.

Each of the subjects was then allowed to "sit in" on a group discussion that she was told was being carried on by members of the group she had just joined. This group was described as one that had been meeting for several weeks; the subject was told that she would be replacing a group member who was leaving because of a scheduling conflict.

To provide all subjects with an identical stimulus, the experimenter had them listen to the same tape-recorded group discussion. At the same time, the investigators felt it would be more involving for the subjects if they were made to believe that this was a live-group discussion. In order to accomplish this and to justify the lack of visual contact necessitated by the tape recording, the experimenter explained that people found that they could talk more freely if they were not being looked at; therefore, each participant was in a separate cubicle, talking through a microphone and listening in on headphones. Since this explanation was consistent with the other aspects of the cover story, all the subjects found it convincing.

It was important to discourage the subject from trying to "talk back" to the tape, since by doing so she would soon discover that no one was responding to her comments. In order to accomplish this, the experimenter explained that it would be better if she did not try to participate in the first meeting, since she would not be as prepared as the other members who had done some preliminary readings on the topic. He then disconnected her microphone.

At the close of the taped discussion, the experimenter returned and explained that after each session all members were asked to rate the worth of that particular discussion and the performance of the other participants. He then presented each subject with a list of rating scales. The results confirmed the hypothesis. The women in the severe-initiation condition found the group much more attractive than did the women in the mild-initiation or the no-initiation conditions.

At first glance, this procedure has some serious problems. Most striking is the fact that the experimenters constructed an elaborate scenario bearing little relation to the "real life" situations in which they were interested. The "group" which the subject found attractive was, in fact, nothing more than a few voices coming in over a set of earphones. The subject was not allowed to see her fellow group members nor was she allowed to interact with them verbally. This situation is a far cry from group interaction as we know it outside the laboratory. In addition, reciting a list of obscene words is undoubtedly a much milder form of initiation to a group than an actual experience outside the laboratory. Moreover, the use of deception raises serious ethical problems as well as more pragmatic ones such as whether or not the deception was successful.

The hypothesis could have been investigated more directly and perhaps more simply by employing some of the nonexperimental methods we have mentioned. For example, one might try to study attraction to a group across cultures by using ratings of the severity of the initiation rites into manhood and then correlating these with some index of the extent to which adult males find their group attractive. A still more direct and perhaps simpler method would be to study existing fraternities. One might first observe whether or not initiations are required for membership. If initiations are required, one would rate them for severity. At a later time, one could return and interview the members of the various fraternities, assessing the degree to which they liked each other or found their particular fraternity attractive. If the result was that the men in fraternities requiring severe initiations liked their group better than did those in fraternities with no such requirement, then the results would seem to provide far greater support for the hypothesis, since the evidence was gathered in a real-life situation.

Unquestionably, this last procedure has certain obvious advantages over the laboratory experiment. First, it is simpler. There is no necessity for recruiting volunteers, tape recording a discussion, or providing an elaborate set of instructions designed to deceive college women. In addition, it is the real thing. Unlike a collection of individuals who do not know one another listening to a tape recording of disembodied voices for a short period of time, the actual fraternity situation involves real people living together in real groups over a relatively long period of time and developing strong positive or negative feelings toward one another. This environment would virtually guarantee more reliable ratings, since they would be based on a longer and more intense interaction among members. Moreover, there would be little question that the initiation we label as severe would, in fact, be a severe initiation. In the most extreme instances, the initiation would most certainly reach a level of magnitude that is not easily equaled in the laboratory.

On the other hand, there are some serious difficulties with this approach. First, the stimulus object, that is, the members of the fraternity, vary a great deal in their inherent attractiveness. The severity of initiation, although hypothesized to be a cause of attractiveness, is certainly not the only cause. Obviously, people have many characteristics that others find more or less attractive. Some people are attractive because they are friendly, perceptive, intelligent, athletic, warm, generous, handsome, and witty, for example. Others are unattractive because they are dull, stupid, cold, too loud, too quiet, too outgoing, or too inhibited, for example. In such a complex stimulus situation, the severity of initiation, although important, might be only one drop in a large bucket. Thus, because there is great variation among the fraternity members on these and other attributes, it might be very difficult to demonstrate differences between severe-initiation fraternities and mild-initiation fraternities even if initiation were the most important single determinant of attractiveness.

One of the great advantages of the experiment is that the experimenter can often exert a great deal of control over possible random variation and thus insure that the stimuli in the experimental conditions are similar. Thus, in the initiation experiment, the group whose attractiveness was to be judged was identical for all subjects. By doing this, Aronson and Mills succeeded in eliminating literally thousands of factors that may cause one group to be more attractive than another and, accordingly, increased markedly the possibility of attributing obtained differences to the experimental treatment. Thus, although some degree of realism was sacrificed, one of the great gains was the achievement of considerable control over possible random variation in all aspects of the situation.

This control, although highly desirable, is not in itself the major advantage of an experiment. There is one advantage that is far more important: the random assignment of experimental units to experimental conditions. Let us suppose that the random variation mentioned previously was not great enough to obscure the relationship between severity of initiation and attractiveness. That is, suppose we conducted a study of existing fraternities and discovered that the members of severe-initiation fraternities found one another more attractive than members of mild-initiation fraternities. If this occurred, we must still consider the possibility of other explanations,

The fundamental weakness of such a correlational study is its inability to specify causes and effects. We wish to assert as a conclusion to our study that severe initiation causes increased attractiveness of the group into which one is initiated. In our fraternity example there are a variety of other possible and, indeed, plausible explanations that involve different causal sequences. The simplest explanation for these results may involve a relationship that is the exact opposite of the one we have proposed. Rather than severe initiation causing high attractiveness, it may be that high attractiveness causes severe initiation. The more attractive groups may perceive that they are attractive and may attempt to maintain this pleasant situation. Since they perceive themselves as attractive, they may try to make it difficult for people to get into the group; perhaps out of a desire to prevent the group from becoming diluted, they try to discourage applicants by requiring a severe initiation. One could list many other reasons why the attractive groups might tend to have more severe initiations. The point is that any such reasons point to an explanation for the data that involves a causal sequence exactly opposite to the one hypothesized. Since this study necessitates the investigation of a group that was in existence before Aronson and Mills arrived on the scene, there is no clear way to determine from these data which of the two is correct.

The preceding analysis is nothing more than an elaboration of the old phrase "correlation does not prove causation." Whenever we observe that variable X (say severity of initiation) is correlated with variable Y (say attractiveness of a group), we cannot be sure whether X caused Y or whether Y caused X. In the experiment, of course, there is no ambiguity about the direction of effect. Thus, in their study Aronson and Mills could be certain, attractiveness of the group did not cause severity of initiation because *they* caused severity of initiation!

In some instances ambiguity may not be too serious a problem. Anyone who lacks faith in the possibility of developing a science through the exclusive use of correlational methods need only look to the history of astronomy. Admittedly, an understanding of the direction of causality is important. However, if we could really be

certain that there was a causal relation between X and Y, regardless of direction, there is no question that we would have made a great stride forward. A more distressing alternative is the possibility that neither X causes Y nor Y causes X; rather the observed correlation is simply produced by some third variable that affects both of them. A classic example of this problem was the observed correlation between the viscosity of asphalt and the incidence of polio in children during the 1940s and 1950s. We would not conclude from this correlation that asphalt of low viscosity was the cause of polio. Nor could we conclude that polio caused asphalt to become softer. We know that a third variable, a warm temperature, caused the asphalt to become softer and also tended to increase children's exposure and/or susceptibility to the polio-causing virus. Thus, even though there might be a perfect correlation between the viscosity of asphalt and the incidence of polio, the two phenomena are not causally related to each other. Let us return again to our fraternity example. It may well be that some constellation of personality traits produces people who are very attractive yet at the same time rather sadistic—the kind of people who like to administer severe initiations. If such were the case, we would certainly find that those fraternities with severe initiations also had members who liked the group a great deal. Yet there would be no direct causal connection between these two variables.

Again, the experiment circumvents this pitfall. It is extremely unlikely that there is some adventitious third variable that is correlated with the two variables under consideration. The reason for this is apparent when we look at the defining characteristic of the experiment. In the experiment the experimenter has control over what treatment a subject receives; that is, he or she determines that treatment by the principle of randomization, the simple device of assigning subjects to conditions in a random manner. The statistical niceties and elaborations of randomization have been ably discussed by others; here we merely wish to note that if the treatment a subject receives is truly determined at random, the chances are minimal for a third variable to be inadvertently associated with the treatment. Consequently, a third variable could not affect the dependent variable. In the real-life fraternity example, the demon of constant concern to the investigator is the possibility that the independent variable, severity of initiation, has not been randomly assigned to the various fraternities. Insofar as some unknown third variable affects how severely a given fraternity initiates its new members, that third variable might also affect how attractive the group will be to its new members.

A common example of the third-variable problem is the existence of possible differences in the initial motivation of the subjects. For example, it is reasonable to assume that some people will join *any* fraternity, while others will join only a specific fraternity, perhaps because they have reason to believe they will be happier with the members of that group. If a specific fraternity has a reputation for requiring severe initiations prior to admission, those people who have a strong desire to join that particular fraternity would be willing to go through the initiation in order to join. On the other hand, those people who simply want to belong to a fraternity—any fraternity—would be much more likely to choose a fraternity that requires little or no initiation. After all, if it makes no difference to a person which fraternity he joins, why would he bother to go through a severe initiation in order to get into a particular one? Consequently, a fraternity that requires little or no initiation will attract many people who initially have no great desire to be in that specific fraternity as well as some people who do have a great desire to be in that specific fraternity. On the other hand, a fraternity that requires a severe initiation will be joined primarily by those people who have a strong desire to be in that specific fraternity, strong enough to allow them to endure the initiation. Therefore, any relationship between attractiveness and severity of initiation may be strictly a function of a disproportionate number of highly motivated people joining the severe-initiation fraternity. This problem is averted by the experiment. Thus, random assignment not only guarantees that no other variable is causing one group to administer a more severe initiation than another but also prevents the possibility that systematic motivational differences among the potential joiners will cause the observed relationship.

Finally, in the laboratory experiment, one has the opportunity to vary the treatment in a systematic manner and thus to allow for the isolation and precise specification of the important differences. If one were to study fraternities with different initiations, the likelihood would be that the different initiations would differ both quantitatively and qualitatively on a large number of dimensions. Suppose that the fraternity requiring a severe initiation asked its pledges to do a large number of unpleasant jobs, wear funny clothes, submit to severe physical punishment, expose themselves to danger, and eat insects. In order to be sure which aspect of this complex treatment was causing the increased attractiveness, the ideal situation would be to have another fraternity ask pledges to do all of these things *except* submit to severe physical punishment. Instead, this second fraternity would ask pledges to submit to mild physical punishment. Unfortunately, such a fraternity does not exist. However, if we were experimentally creating initiation, we could produce the appropriate initiation, identical in all respects except for the severity of physical punishment.

PLANNING AND CONDUCTING A LABORATORY EXPERIMENT

Let us assume that you are a novice researcher with a terrific idea for an experiment. The first decision you would want to make is whether to design your experiment for the laboratory or the field. While this is an important individual decision for the novice, it is our position that all experiments should be conducted in a variety of settings. Thus, we advocate that, ideally, all experimentally researchable hypotheses, should be tested in both the laboratory and the field. We also believe that, for the most part, there is no logical reason for starting in one domain or the other nor is there any reason for assuming that particular hypotheses lend themselves more easily to the laboratory or the field. The decision is frequently dictated by such factors as the momentary availability of resources, idiosyncratic preferences of the experimenter, and so on.

Suppose you decide to bring the experiment into the laboratory. The next decision you must make is whether the experiment is to be a high-impact or a judgment type. The crucial distinction between an impact experiment and a judgment experiment is whether or not the event in question is happening to the subject. Thus, in the Aronson-Mills experiment, for example, the embarrassment produced by reciting obscene words was happening to the subjects themselves. It is the effect of that embarrassment that is the major interest of the experimenter. In a judgment study the event might be important and dramatic, but it is not happening to the subject. For example, I (the subject) might read about or witness (via film) an aggressive or violent act (which might sicken or outrage me), but the violent act is not happening to me.

Suppose you are interested in the effects of sexual arousal on persuasibility; you are in the domain of the impact study. It would be absurd to conduct an experiment on the effects of sexual arousal without doing something aimed at affecting the degree of sexual arousal among some of your subjects. On the other hand, some hypotheses are judgmental in nature. For example, suppose you are interested in determining the conditions under which the commission of clumsy blunders renders a person more or less attractive. Here you might present the subjects with a tape or film of a stimulus person committing a clumsy blunder and ask them to rate how much they like that person. There is little to be gained by creating a live situation in which the subject is directly affected by someone committing a clumsy blunder.

There *are* ideas that can be tested by either technique; for example, the investigation of equity. In some of these experiments, subjects are simply handed a description of the effort expended and product produced by individuals, given a distribution of the relative rewards or payments to the individual, and asked to evaluate the equity of the distribution. In other experiments, a person's *own* effort or output is rewarded in a more or less equitable way, and he or she is allowed to respond.

As you may have guessed by now, our position is: If you can do it either way, do it *both* ways!

THE FOUR STAGES OF LABORATORY EXPERIMENTATION

The process of planning a laboratory experiment consists of four basic stages: (1) setting the stage for the experiment, (2) constructing the independent variable, (3) measuring the dependent variable, and (4) planning the post-experimental followup. In this section we will suggest ways of developing a sensible and practical *modus operandi* for each of those stages. We will be looking at both the impact experiment and the judgment experiment. It should be mentioned at the outset that the four phases listed above apply to both types of laboratory experiment. Almost without exception, however, the impact experiment is much more complex and involves a wider scope of planning than does the judgment experiment. In effect, the judgment experiment is a "bare bones" operation. Although the design of both types requires attention to similar issues (e.g., random assignment, the order of presentation of the stimulus materials, and the context in which these materials are presented), the impact experiment entails a more elaborate scenario. Accordingly, much of our discussion will be devoted to the high-impact type of study, not because we consider such experiments as necessarily more important but because we consider them more complex.

Setting the Stage

In designing any laboratory experiment, a great deal of ingenuity and invention must be directed toward the context, or stage, for the manipulation of the independent variable. Because of the fact that our subjects tend to be intelligent, adult, curious humans, the setting must make sense to them. It not only must be consistent with the procedures for presenting the independent variables and measuring their impact but also can and should enhance that impact and help to justify the collection of the data.

Many experiments involve deception; if deception is used, the setting must include a sensible, internally consistent pretext or rationale for the research as well as a context that both supports and enhances the collection of the data *and* reduces the possibility of detection. This false rationale is often referred to as a *cover story*.

In a judgment experiment, the cover story is typically less elaborate and more straightforward than in an impact experiment. Although deception is frequently used in a judgment experiment, it is usually minimal and aimed primarily at increasing the interest of the subjects and providing a credible rationale for the data collection procedures and judgment task. As an example, recall the experiment on the blunder that we alluded to earlier. In this judgment experiment, Aronson, Willerman, and Floyd (1966) were testing the hypothesis that the attractiveness of a highly competent person would be *enhanced* if that person committed a clumsy blunder. To provide an adequate test of the hypothesis, it was necessary to expose subjects to one of four experimental conditions: (1) a highly competent person who commits a clumsy blunder, (2) a highly competent person who does not commit a clumsy blunder, (3) a relatively incompetent person who commits a clumsy blunder, and (4) a relatively incompetent person who does not. What would be a reasonable context that would justify exposing the subjects to one of these stimulus persons and inducing them to rate the attractiveness of that person? The experimenters simply informed the subjects (who were students at the University of Minnesota) that their help was needed in selecting students to represent the university on the *College Bowl,* a television program pitting college students from various universities against one another in a test of knowledge. They told the subjects that they could evaluate the general knowledge of the candidates objectively, but that this was only one criterion for selection. Another criterion was judgments from the subjects concerning how much they liked the candidates. The experimenter then presented the subject with a tape recording of a male stimulus person being interviewed. This stimulus person answered a number of questions either brilliantly or not so brilliantly and either did or did not clumsily spill a cup of coffee all over himself. The subject then rated the stimulus person on a series of scales. The cover story in this experiment was simple and straightforward and did succeed in providing a credible rationale for both the presentation of the stimulus and the collection of the data.

Providing a convincing rationale for the experiment is almost always essential, since subjects do attempt to make sense of the situation and to decipher the reasons for the experiment. A good cover story is one that embraces all the necessary aspects of the experiment in a plausible manner and thus eliminates speculation from a subject about what the experimenter really has in mind. It also should capture the attention of the subjects so that they remain alert and responsive to the experimental events. This is not meant facetiously; if a cover story strikes the subjects as being a trivial or silly reason for conducting an experiment, they may simply tune out. If the subjects are not attending to the independent variable, it will have little impact on them.

The setting may be a relatively simple one, or it may involve an elaborate scenario, depending on the demands of the situation. Obviously, the experimenter should set the stage as simply as possible. If a simple setting succeeds in providing a plausible cover story and in capturing the attention of the subjects, there is no need for greater elaboration. A more elaborate setting is sometimes necessary, especially in a high-impact experiment. For example, suppose one wants to make people fearful. One might achieve this goal by simply telling the subjects that they will receive a strong electric shock. Yet the chances of arousing strong fear are enhanced if one has set the stage with a trifle more embellishment. This can be done by providing a medical atmosphere, inventing a medical rationale for the experiment, having the experimenter appear in a white laboratory coat, and allowing the subject to view some formidable electrical apparatus as in Schachter's (1959) experiments on the effects of anxiety on the desire to affiliate with others. One might go even further by providing the subject with a mild sample shock and implying that the actual shocks will be much greater.

"Setting the stage" not only leads into the independent variable but also is often part of it. That is, in the preceding example, the electrical paraphernalia, the medical cover story, the white coat, and the electric shock constitute the manipulation as well as the setting. Indeed, in a well-constructed experiment it is often difficult to determine where the one leaves off and the other begins. Similarly, if the stage has been properly set, the measurement of the dependent variable follows naturally from the setting. The behavior asked for by the cover story may be, in fact, the actual dependent variable. For example, in Asch's (1951) classic experiment on conformity, subjects were told that the experiment concerned their judgments of the relative length of a set of lines. At the same time, their stated judgments of the lines were the crucial data; they were the dependent variable of the actual experiment. Similarly, in Milgram's (1963) study of obedience, the dependent variable was the point at which the subject ceased administering electric shocks, the same electric shocks that were an integral part of the cover experiment.

This technique is not always possible, however. More often, the dependent variable is not the behavior asked for by the cover story but some other behavior. For example, in Festinger and Carlsmith's (1959) experiment on induced compliance, the crucial datum was an evaluation of a boring task that the subject had performed. These data were not collected until after the cover experiment was completed, and they were collected not by the experimenter but by a different person for an apparently nonexperimental purpose. Still, in these kinds of experiments the behavior called for must make sense in the context of the created setting. If the experimenter simply says "Oh, by the way, I'd like you to fill out this questionnaire," this statement will almost certainly fail to engage the subject's full interest and attention, might arouse suspicion or annoyance, and will certainly weaken or invalidate the results.

The point we are making here is that a well-designed experiment consists of more than a reasonable set of procedures followed by a measuring instrument. Rather, it is an intricate and tightly woven tapestry. With this in mind, let us take another look at the Aronson-Mills (1959) experiment. Here we shall indicate how each aspect of the setting enhanced the impact and/or plausibility of the independent and dependent variables and contributed to the control of the experiment. The major challenge presented by the hypothesis was to justify an initiation for admission to a group. This was solved, first, by devising the format of a sex discussion, and second, by inventing the cover story that the experimenters were interested in studying the dynamics of the discussion process. Combining these two aspects of the setting, the experimenter could then, third, mention that because shyness about sex distorts the discussion process, it was, fourth, necessary to eliminate those people who were shy about sexual matters by, fifth, presenting the subjects with an embarrassment test.

All five aspects of the setting led directly to the manipulation of the independent variable in a manner that made good sense to the subjects, thereby allaying any suspicions. Moreover, this setting allowed the experimenter to use a tape-recorded group discussion (for the sake of control) and at the same time to maintain the fiction that it was an ongoing group discussion (for the sake of impact).

This fiction of an already formed group served another function in addition to that of enhancing the involvement of the subjects. It also allowed the experimenter to explain to the subject that all the other members had been recruited before the initiation was made a requirement for admission. This procedure eliminated a possible confounding variable, namely, that subjects might like the group better in the severe-initiation condition because of the feeling that they had shared a common harrowing experience.

Finally, because of the manner in which the stage had been set, the dependent variable (the evaluation of the group) seemed a very reasonable request. In many experimental contexts, obtaining a rating of attractiveness tends to arouse suspicion. In this context, however, it was not jarring to the subject to be told that each member stated her opinion of each discussion session, and therefore it did not surprise the subject when she was asked for her frank evaluation of the proceedings of the meeting. Ultimately, the success of a setting in integrating the various aspects of the experiment is an empirical question: Do the subjects find it plausible? In the Aronson-Mills experiment only one of sixty-four subjects expressed any suspicions.

The testing of some hypotheses is more difficult than others because of their very nature. But none is impossible; with sufficient patience and ingenuity a reasonable context can be constructed to integrate the independent and dependent variables regardless of the problems inherent in the hypothesis.

Constructing the Independent Variable

The independent variable is the experimental manipulation. It is, ideally, a variable that is independent of all sources of variation except those specifically under the control of the experimenter. Recall that the essence of an experiment is the random assignment of subjects to experimental conditions. For this reason, it should be obvious that any characteristics that the subjects bring to the experiment cannot be regarded as independent variables in the context of a true experiment. Although such characteristics as prejudice, intelligence, self-esteem, and socioeconomic class, for example, *can* be measured and taken into account or ignored, they should not be regarded as independent variables of an experiment. It is not infrequent to find an "experiment" purporting to assess the effects of a subject variable (like level of self-esteem, for example) on some behavior in a specific situation. It should be clear that although such a procedure may produce interesting results, it is not an experiment because the treatments were not randomly assigned.

Nonrandom assignment of subjects to experimental conditions is not confined to the use of personality measures in lieu of experimental treatments. It usually takes place in more subtle ways. One of the most common occurs when the experimenter is forced to perform an "internal analysis" in order to make sense out of his or her data.

The term "internal analysis" refers to the following situation. Suppose that an experimenter has carried out a true experiment, randomly assigning subjects to different treatment conditions. Unfortunately, the treatments do not produce any measurable differences on the dependent variable. In addition, suppose that the experimenter has had the foresight to include an independent measure of the effectiveness of the experimental treatment. Such "manipulation checks" are always useful in providing information about the extent to which the experimental treatment had its intended effect on each individual subject. Now, if the manipulation check shows no differences between experimental treatments, the experimenter may still hope to salvage his or her hypothesis. That is, the manipulation check shows that for some reason the treatments were unsuccessful in creating the internal states in the subjects that they were designed to produce. Since they were unsuccessful, one would not expect to see differences on the dependent variable. In this case, the experimenter may analyze the data on the basis of the responses of the subjects to the manipulation check, resorting subjects into "treatment" according to their responses to the manipulation check. This is an internal analysis.

For example, Schachter (1959) attempted to alter the amount of anxiety experienced by his subjects by varying the description of the task in which the subjects were to engage. However, in some of the studies, many subjects who had been given the treatment designed to produce low-anxiety actually reported higher anxiety levels than some who had been given the treatment designed to produce high anxiety. From the results of an internal analysis of these data, it does seem that anxiety is related to the dependent variable. Again, these data can be useful and provocative, but since the effect was not due to the manipulated variable, no causal statement can be made. Although many of the "highly anxious" subjects were made anxious by the "high-anxiety" manipulation, many were highly anxious on their own (so to speak). Since people who become anxious easily may be different from those who do not, we are dealing with an implicit personality variable. This means that we can no longer claim random assignment.

Another situation in which the treatments are assigned nonrandomly occurs when the subjects assign *themselves* to the experimental conditions. That is, in certain experimental situations the subject, in effect, is given a choice of two procedures in which to engage. The experimenter then compares the subsequent behavior of subjects who choose one alternative with those who choose the other. For example, in one study, Wallace and Sadalla (1966) placed subjects in a room with a complex machine and had a confederate tempt them to press a conspicuous button on the front of the machine. When a subject pressed the button, the machine exploded. Unfortunately, whether or not a particular subject chose to press the button was determined by the subject and not by the experimenter. Since there may be important differences between those who choose to press and those who do not, the experimenters in this kind of situation relinquish control to the subject and are left with a nonexperimental study.

The problem of free choice is a particularly sticky one because, if the hypothesis involves the effects of choice, it is obviously important to give the subject a perception of clear choice. Yet this perception must remain nothing more than a perception, for as soon as the subject takes advantage of it, we are beset with the problems of nonrandom assignment.

One solution to this problem is to conduct a pilot test of the variable until a level is found for it that is just sufficient enough to inhibit subjects from actually choosing the "wrong" behavior. For example, in an experiment by Aronson and Carlsmith (1963), children were given either a mild or severe threat to prevent them from playing with a desirable toy. In order for this experiment to work,

it was critical to make the mild threat strong enough to ensure compliance. On the other hand, it could not be too strong, for the experimental hypothesis hinged upon the child's not having a terribly good reason for declining to play with the toy. The situation had to be one in which the child was making a choice whether to play or not to play with the specific toy and was bothered by the lack of a good reason to avoid playing with that toy. It is sometimes possible to find such a level by elaborate pretesting. As an alternative, in some experimental situations a solution can be effected through the use of instructions that give a strong perception of choice, although little choice is actually present.

The judgment experiment presents the experimenter with a different agenda. Here the manipulation of the independent variable involves the systematic variation of the content of the stimulus material. Often (but not always), in judgment experiments, random assignment of subjects to treatment is not an issue because each subject receives all of the stimulus variations. This strategy has one great advantage: It reduces error variance due to individual differences among subjects; each subject serves as his or her own control. This is a major advantage and should be used wherever feasible. For instance, if a subject is asked to rate the attractiveness of one photograph of a person with particular facial characteristics, there is no obvious reason to suspect that doing this will interfere with the same subject's rating of a series of photographs that vary systematically. However, repeated measurements from the same person can contaminate one's findings if the order of presentation is not varied. Thus, it is essential for experimenters to alter the order of presentation across subjects in such a way as to preclude such systematic bias. This is where randomization enters into such experiments. Subjects are not randomly assigned to different treatments but are randomly assigned to different orderings of exposure to the stimulus materials that constitute the treatment variables.

There are many kinds of judgment experiments in which subjects cannot be used for more than one stimulus condition. For example, in the experiment by Aronson, Willerman, and Floyd, once a subject was exposed to a tape recording of a competent person spilling coffee, it would have been ludicrous to present that same subject with an otherwise identical tape of a competent person who *doesn't* spill coffee—to say nothing of an incompetent person spilling coffee.

By the same token, in the vast majority of *impact* experiments, the nature of the impactful manipulation precludes utilization of the same subjects in more than one condition. For example, in the Aronson-Mills experiment, once the experimenters put a subject through a severe initiation in order to join a group and then asked her to rate the attractiveness of that group, it would have been silly to ask her to start all over and go through a mild initiation!

In an impact experiment, the basic decision for the experimenter is whether the independent variable will be produced by some set of instructions to the subject or whether it will be generated by some event that happens to the subject. In practice, these two techniques are not always completely separable; the two usually blend into each other, at least slightly. Most "event" experiments contain some verbal instructions to the subject, at least as a means of setting the stage. In other experiments, some of the instructions consist of descriptions of things that might happen to the subject. Nevertheless, it is possible to separate the two conceptually. A good example of the manipulation of an independent variable primarily through the use of instructions is found in the well known "group cohesiveness" experiments conducted by Festinger and his colleagues (for example, Back, 1951; Festinger and Thibaut, 1951; Schachter, 1951). In these experiments the cohesiveness of a group was usually varied simply by informing the subject that the group members were specially selected so that they would like one another (high cohesiveness), or that, try as they might, the experimenters were unable to accomplish this feat (low cohesiveness). A different approach is to use a group-cohesiveness manipulation in which the confederates actually perform attractive acts. Similarly, in an experiment by Cohen (1959), effort was varied merely by informing subjects that a communication they were about to read would be difficult (or easy) to understand. This can be contrasted with an "event" manipulation of effort such as delaying auditory feedback (Zimbardo, 1965), reciting obscene words (Aronson and Mills, 1959), or applying electric shock (Gerard and Mathewson, 1966). Again, these "event" manipulations were preceded by an important set of verbal instructions.

Typically, when events happen to subjects, experimenters have much less control over them (and their interpretation) than a list of statements or instructions to the subjects. On the other hand, it is almost always the case that events that happen to a subject during the course of an experiment will have far more impact than a mere set of instructions. For example, being told that a group has values similar to yours or that you will find a group attractive is almost certain to have less impact on you than the experience of watching actual people doing "attractive" things. The problem, however, is that we cannot be completely certain that subjects will interpret these behaviors as "attractive."

It is often possible to increase the likelihood that an event will be interpreted by the subject in the same way that the experimenter interprets it. In some experimental situations, this can be accomplished through the skillful combination of events and instructions. An example is an experiment (Landy and Aronson, 1968) in which the investigators wished to test the hypothesis that if subjects were positively evaluated by a person who was highly "discerning," they would like that person better than an evaluator who was less discerning. On the other hand, if they were negatively evaluated by a discerning person, they would *dislike* that person more than if he or she was less discerning. How does one vary the subject's perception of the evaluator's ability to discern? One could do it by instruction; that is, one could simply say to the subject, "Say, by the way, this fellow has a great deal of discernment—I thought you might be interested." However, for reasons to be discussed in the next paragraph, the investigators felt it would be best to allow the subjects to discover this on their own. They therefore had the evaluator (a confederate) perform a task in the presence of the subject; the task was such that, by varying the confederate's behavior, the subject might easily regard the confederate as discerning or nondiscerning. The word "might" is a problem. The subject *might* interpret this behavior in a multitude of ways. In order to be certain that the subject would consider this behavior as being relevant to discernment and nothing else, the investigators did the following:

1. Asked the subject to observe the confederate's behavior on a task (in the context of an experiment on social judgment);

2. Told the subject that "degree of discernment" was an aspect of the confederate's behavior that was particularly interesting to the experimenter;

3. Asked the subject to rate the confederate's discernment;

4. Informed the subject exactly how the confederate's behavior might reflect high or low discernment;

5. Had the confederate behave either one way or the other;

6. Had (in the form of the subject's actual rating) a handy and meaningful check on the manipulation.

It can readily be seen that this technique is a compromise. Although it may lack the impact of obscene words or electric shock, it certainly has more potential impact than a set of verbal instructions and at the same time capitalizes on the easy interpretability of these instructions.

Avoiding subject awareness biases. As mentioned previously, one of the major problems with any laboratory experiment is that the subjects may become aware of the experimenter's hypothesis and allow this awareness to influence their behavior. One special form of subject awareness is closely related to the idea of "demand characteristics" as described by Orne (1962). Demand characteristics refer to features introduced into a research setting by virtue of the facts that it *is* a research study and that the subjects know that they are part of it. As aware participants, they are motivated to make sense of the experimental situation, to avoid negative evaluation from the experimenter, and perhaps even to cooperate in a way intended to help the experimenter confirm the research hypothesis (Sigall, Aronson and Van Hoose, 1970). Such motivational states are likely to make subjects highly responsive to any cues—intended or unintended—in the research situation that suggest what they are supposed to do to appear normal or "to make the study come out right." This problem can present itself in both impact and judgment experiments, particularly those in which each subject is exposed to more than one variation of the stimulus. Such a procedure, by its very nature, inceases the probability that the subject will begin to guess which aspects of the experiment are being systematically varied by the experimenter. This is less of a problem in most impact experiments where subjects are presented with only one variation of a given independent variable. But, of course, manipulations with high impact may also create problems of subject awareness. It is for this reason that experimenters frequently employ deception, elaborate cover stories, and the like.

Another aspect of the problem of demand characteristics and subject awareness is the possibility that the experimenter's own behavior provides inadvertent cues that influence the responses of the subjects (Rosenthal, 1963). This possibility caused a great deal of consternation among experimenters in the early 1960s. At that time, the major technique suggested for preventing such bias was to keep the person who conducts the experiment unaware of the hypothesis of the research. In our judgment, this technique is inadequate. One characteristic of good researchers is that they are hypothesis-forming organisms. Indeed, this is one characteristic of all intelligent humans. Thus, if not told the hypothesis, the research assistant, like a subject, attempts to discover one. Since most research assistants are more sophisticated than most subjects, it is more likely that they will arrive at the correct solution. Moreover, keeping the assistant in the dark reduces the value of the educational experience. Since most experimenters are graduate students, full participation in an experiment is the most effective way of learning experimentation. Any technique involving the experimenter's ignorance of the hypothesis or a reduction in contact with the supervisor is a disservice to him or her. A more reasonable solution involves allowing the experimenters to know the true hypothesis but somehow keeping them ignorant of the specific experimental condition of each subject. In theory, this is a simple and complete solution to the problem and should be employed whenever possible.

One way of implementing this "blind" technique is to keep the experimenter who carries out the entire experimental procedure in ignorance until the precise moment of crucial difference in manipulations. That is, in most studies, the experimenter need not know what condition the subject is in until the crucial manipulation occurs. When the choice point is reached, a randomizing device can be used, and the remainder of the experiment is, of course, not carried out in ignorance. For example, in the Aronson-Mills (1959) study, it would have been easy to delay assignment of subject to condition until the point of initiation; by reaching into a pocket and randomly pulling out one of three slips of paper, the experimenter could determine whether the subject would recite the obscene words, the mild words, or no words at all. Thus, all the premanipulation instructions would be unbiased. This is only a partial solution because the experimenter loses his or her ignorance midway through the experiment. However, if the experimenter left the room immediately after the recitation and assigned a different experimenter (ignorant of the subject's experimental condition) to collect the data, this solution would approach completeness. The use of multiple experimenters, each ignorant of some part of the experiment, offers a solution that is frequently viable.

An example of the partial blind technique aimed specifically at eliminating experimenter bias was an experiment performed by Aronson and Cope (1968), who were interested in testing the proposition (derived from Heider's balance theory) that "my enemy's enemy is my friend." In this experiment, subjects were treated either pleasantly or harshly by an experimenter. The subjects then "accidently" overheard the experimenter being either praised or berated by the latter's supervisor for the quality of a report the experimenter had written a few days earlier. Thus, there were four conditions: a pleasant or unpleasant experimenter who is either praised or berated by his supervisor.

In this study, the experimenter delivered all the instructions before becoming aware of the subject's experimental condition. The experimenter then reached for the slip of paper that indicated which of the two main conditions the subject was to be in; he behaved harshly if the slip of paper said "H," and pleasantly if it said "P." A few minutes later he casually leaned against the door. This action served as a signal to the "supervisor," who knocked, entered the room, and called the experimenter outside. The "supervisor", ignorant about whether the subject had been treated harshly or pleasantly, "inadvertently" left the door partially ajar, an action that enabled the subject to eavesdrop as the supervisor either praised or berated the experimenter. It should be mentioned that this variable was also randomized; the experimenter was unaware of whether the supervisor was going to praise or berate him at any particular session.

In summary, there were two experimenters (i.e., an experimenter and a supervisor) who, at the time of their own "crucial" behavior, were unaware of the other's behavior toward the subject. In this design, because an interaction was being predicted, systematic experimenter bias was effectively eliminated. If either experimenter had wittingly or unwittingly influenced the subject, this influencing factor would have interacted with the set of conditions being manipulated by the other experimenter. Since both experimenters were ignorant of which of the four conditions the subject was in at the time of their interaction with the subject, there is no way that their incidental behavior could have produced results consistent with the hypothesis. Finally, in this experiment, the dependent variable was collected by the department secretary who was totally ignorant of each subject's experimental condition. The results, as predicted, showed that the subjects liked the supervisor who berated the harsh experimenter or praised the pleasant experimenter; they disliked the supervisor who praised the harsh experimenter or berated the pleasant experimenter.

An interesting and effective variation on the blind technique can be performed by running subjects in all the experimental conditions simultaneously. For example, Cottrell (1965) varied whether a person developed an expectancy of high performance or of low performance on a task as well as whether this expectancy was confirmed or disconfirmed. He recited the general instructions to subjects in all the conditions simultaneously, creating the conditions by randomly assigning written scores to each subject. This technique makes it almost impossible for the experimenter to bias the results in a systematic manner.

Returning to the more general issue of demand characteristics, it should be clear that the most effective type of deception in an impact experiment involves the creation of an independent variable as an event that appears not to be part of the experiment at all. Creating such an independent variable not only guarantees that the subject will not try to interpret the researcher's intention but also that the manipulation has an impact on the subject. A subject, told that a particular communication was written by T. S. Eliot (Aronson, Turner, and Carlsmith, 1963) may yawn and ignore this fact or still more importantly may have the detachment necessary to sit back, relax, and begin to develop hypotheses that the experimenter is concerned with the effect of high-prestige communicators. For this reason, this kind of manipulation is a relatively weak one. However, consider subjects suddenly faced with the fact that a person, to whom they have been administering electric shocks, is now kicking, screaming, and asking to be let out of the room (Milgram, 1963), or consider subjects attached to electric shock generators who discover that the equipment in the experiment has short circuited and that they are in danger of being electrocuted (Ax, 1953). Or consider a young man who, to his dismay, discovers that a group of normal-looking people *all* judge the length of a line differently from his judgment (Asch, 1951). These subjects are unlikely to yawn or start playing the intellectual game of "being a subject." In a very real sense they are too busy to play such games; they have problems of their own (for example, whether or not to continue to administer electric shocks to someone who seems to be in great pain).

Several classes of techniques have been used successfully to present the independent variable as an event unrelated to the experiment, which accordingly has a maximum impact on the subject and is not perceived as something to hypothesize about. Many experiments have actually used a combination of several of these techniques. Perhaps the most effective, but one of the more difficult to set up, is the "accident," as employed in the experiment by Wallace and Sadalla (1966). Recall that in this experiment the subject was tempted (by a confederate) to touch a large button projecting from an apparatus. When touched, the apparatus exploded and was apparently destroyed. Festinger and Carlsmith (1959) used a variation on this technique when they asked the subject to play the role of the regular confederate who could not do so because of an unforseen event. Indeed, this general procedure has been used so frequently and so effectively that it might be said that part of being a good experimental social psychologist involves learning to say "whoops" convincingly.

A variation of the accident procedure is to have a confederate, apparently a fellow subject, introduce the manipulation of the independent variable. For example, Schachter and Singer (1962) attempted to manipulate euphoria by having a confederate waltz around the room shooting rubber bands, play with hula hoops, and practice hook shots into the wastebasket with wadded paper. Presumably, this behavior was interpreted by the subject as a spontaneous, unique event unrelated to the intentions of the experimenter. Similarly, Brehm and Cole (1966) attempted to produce feelings of "reactance" in the subject by having a confederate place the subject in the position of feeling obligated. The confederate bought himself a Coke from a vending machine and then "thoughtfully" bought another one to bring back to the subject. This (apparently) unique event, although it appeared to be unrelated to the experiment, succeeded in its purpose of making the subject somewhat uncomfortable in his or her feelings toward the confederate.

A third method of having the independent variable perceived as unrelated to the experiment is to use the whole experimental session as the independent variable and to measure the dependent variable at some later time. For example, Carlsmith and Gross (1969) performed an experiment aimed at investigating the effects of hurting someone on subsequent compliance. In their experiment, they induced their subjects to shock a confederate. The entire procedure was presented as a learning experiment, with subjects acting as teachers. After the subjects performed their chore, the experiment was explained and terminated. At a later time, the confederate made a request for help. The subjects responded to this request without awareness that it was part of the experiment. As a result they were unlikely to realize that the entire earlier experience was the independent variable of interest.

Of course, if one is primarily concerned with eliminating subject awareness, the ultimate strategy is to introduce the independent variable in such a manner that the subjects are oblivious to the fact that *any* experiment is taking place at all. This strategy is best implemented in a nonlaboratory setting. A good example is a field experiment by Abelson and Miller (1967) in which they pretended to conduct a "man-on-the-street" interview. The experimenter approached a person who was sitting on a park bench, obtained an expression of the person's views on an issue, and then queried a man sitting on the same bench, actually an accomplice. The accomplice expressed opposite views and in so doing mercilessly mocked the views of the subject. The experimenter then queried the subject again, who, as predicted, tended to take a more extreme position as a function of having been insulted. Since the subjects were approached by the "interviewer" while sitting on a park bench minding their own business, they were unaware of the fact that an experiment was being conducted. In another vein, Milgram (1966) devised a technique in which he distributed addressed envelopes with stamps on them where they could be found by subjects. Milgram was interested in whether or not the subjects dropped the envelopes in the mailbox. In these studies the addresses on the envelopes constituted the independent variable. Clearly, the subjects either mailed or did not mail the envelopes without any awareness that they were participating in an experiment.

Optimizing the impact of the independent variable. The question of how to present the independent variable so that it will have maximum impact and the intended impact is one that cannot be answered with a list of techniques. Yet some important general guidelines can be established. For example, one of the most common mistakes the novice experimenter makes is to present instructions too briefly; consequently, a large percentage of the subjects fail to understand some important aspects of the instructions. To ensure that all subjects understand what is going on in an experiment (especially one as complicated as most social psychological experiments), the instructions must be repeated in different ways.

More important than simple redundancy, however, is ensuring the instructions are expressed precisely so that each subject fully understands them and the events that occur in the experiment. This can be accomplished by a combination of clear instructions, questions, pauses, and probes, in which the experimenter must repeat or paraphrase key parts of the instructions until satisfied that the subject is completely clear about all of them. Although the point seems obvious, it has been our experience that many experiments fail precisely because the instructions were never made clear enough to become understandable to all the subjects.

The experimenter also must ensure that the subjects attend throughout the course of the experiment to the relevant stimulus conditions that constitute the independent variable. In judgment research this aspect of impact is particularly critical. All the care and effort devoted to careful and systematic stimulus control are wasted if the subject because of boredom or inattention fails to perceive the critical variations in the stimuli presented. It is in this area that microprocessing equipment with interactive capacities has some interesting applications for social judgment research. The use of microprocessors for stimulus presentation and response recording improves dramatically the precision and accuracy with which stimuli can be generated and sequenced. It has been our experience in using such devices that subjects find working at a computer console much more interesting and engaging than working with the usual paper-and-pencil instruments. Hence we may have a case in which the use of high-level technology for the sake of experimental control also has benefits for impact. However, it should be kept in mind that computerized experiments represent a highly artificial form of ''social exchange'' and their current interest value may be largely a function of novelty. As the use of microprocessors becomes more widespread and mundane, their proliferation in social psychological research should be carefully evaluated to assure that precision is not being gained at the cost of validity.

Although in the well-designed scenario type of experiment, there is less likely to be a question about whether the subject is paying attention to the relevant stimulus conditions, the experimenter should be as certain as possible that the complex bundle of stimuli constituting the independent variable produce the intended phenomenological experience in the subjects. For this purpose, there is no substitute for the thorough pretesting of the manipulation. During the pretesting, the experimenter can conduct long, probing interviews with the subject after the test run of the experiment is completed or, better yet, after the manipulation of the independent variable. Often the subject can provide valuable hints regarding where the weaknesses in the manipulation occurred and which one of these caused competing reactions to the one the experimenter wanted to effect. If deception is used, the subject is the best source of information concerning the effectiveness and credibility of the cover story. These interviews can, of course, be continued during the time the experiment is actually being run, but it is usually during pretesting that the most valuable information is obtained.

As implied in the preceding paragraph, it is often important to run pretest subjects, for whom the independent variable is manipulated, and then to interview them immediately. If one also attempts to interview subjects after they have been exposed to the dependent variable, they may no longer be able to describe how they were affected by the independent variable. This conjecture was confirmed by Nisbett and Wilson (1977) who conducted a series of experiments demonstrating that subjects are frequently unaware of the existence of a stimulus that had a profound influence on their response. The assessment of the dependent variable itself may serve as a means of working through, and thereby eliminating, the intervening effects of the independent variable. For example, in a dissonance study, the subjects might well report that the manipulation of the independent variable aroused no dissonance or discomfort whatever provided they had succeeded in reducing all of that dissonance via responses to the dependent variable. Thus, in the study by Festinger and Carlsmith (1959), subjects may report at the end of the experiment that they feel that one dollar is a perfectly sufficient reward for the behavior provided they had already changed their attitudes so as to reduce most of the dissonance that had been created.

This problem is the major difficulty with using introspective reports as a technique; too often subjects are unable or unwilling to explain just what the effects of some manipulation have been. After an experiment, it is not uncommon for subjects to deny any feelings of the kind the experimenter hoped to arouse, although their actual behavior implies strongly that they did experience precisely those feelings. By soliciting introspective reports immediately after the manipulation of the independent variable (in a pretest), one increases the likelihood of obtaining useful information, although it is still not certain that subjects will be able to describe their feelings adequately.

A more difficult but far better technique of checking whether the independent variable is having the desired effect is to run a number of pretest subjects and thus to collect data on whether some other behavior corresponds with the independent variable in an appropriate way. Let us look at the experiment by Aronson and Carlsmith (1963) in which children were asked not to play with an attractive toy. In one condition the admonition was in the form of a mild threat; in the other it was in the form of a severe threat. Although intuitively the two threats seemed to differ along a dimension of severity, it would have been desirable to obtain independent evidence of this difference. One way of doing this would have been to ask the children how severe the threat was; yet this was neither feasible nor valuable in the context of that experiment. As was previously mentioned, a better technique would have been to run other subjects in a pretest in which the toys were made more desirable so that many children would have disobeyed the admonition. In the experiment as run, even the mild threat was strong enough so that, with the toys actually used, no child deviated from instructions. If the toys were made more desirable and if more children disobeyed the admonition under the mild threat than under the severe threat, we could have been confident that the experimenters had manipulated severity of threat. This can best be done as a separate experiment. However, since the procedure is frequently tedious, it is not as common as it should be. It is sometimes possible to collect such data in the experiment itself. Typically, however, such checks are merely questionnaires given to the subject. For example, in an experiment designed to produce anxiety, one might ask subjects whether or not they felt anxious during the experiment. Although such questionnaires may sometimes be useful, they rarely provide a complete solution to the problem, for reasons discussed earlier. Certainly the best solution is to observe some other behavior that we expect to vary directly with our theoretical variable and see whether it does, as is the case when a GSR is used to monitor anxiety throughout the course of the experiment.

Finally, pretesting can provide an additional check on the independent variable by allowing us to find the precise intensity of the manipulation that will enable us to study its effects. For example, if we were conducting a study of obedience, it would be desirable for about half the subjects to obey and half to disobey so that we could see differences between different experimental treatments. Fairly elaborate pretesting may sometimes be necessary to set levels of the independent variable that are neither so high that virtually all subjects obey nor so low that virtually no one obeys.

Controlling the number of independent variables. We have been talking thus far of the independent variable in the social psychological experiment as if it were a simple two-level variation on a single dimension. Yet many, if not most, experiments conducted in the area involve procedures that simultaneously manipulate two or more variables. Once one has taken the time and trouble of setting up a laboratory experiment, recruiting subjects, and

training research assistants, it seems only efficient to use the occasion to assess the effects of more than one experimental treatment. Theoretically, there is no limit to the number of factors we can vary within one experiment, and there is a real temptation to "throw in" as many as possible. However, it is essential to realize that the more tests, measures, instructions, and events one hurls at one's research subjects, the more confused, bored, irritated, or resentful they are likely to become. Inclusion of too many independent variables can be self-defeating, potentially blunting the impact of the major variables under investigation.

There are no pat answers to the question of how many independent variables can or should be manipulated at one time, but our own rule of thumb is that any experiment should be only as complex as is required for the important relationships to emerge in an interpretable manner. Sometimes it is essential to vary more than one factor because the phenomenon of interest appears in the form of an interaction. Recall the experiment by Aronson, Willerman, and Floyd (1966) in which they predicted that a clumsy blunder would enhance the attractiveness of a highly competent young man because this action supposedly would make him appear more human and, hence, more approachable. In their experiment, a young man who had demonstrated that he was very bright committed a clumsy and embarrassing blunder, spilling a cup of coffee all over himself. As predicted, this action increased his attractiveness; he was rated more attractive than when he did *not* spill coffee. But these results could simply be a function of the fact that spilling coffee is not really so much a clumsy act as it is a charming act. That is, we may like people who spill coffee because it is an endearing, attractive thing to do. However, in this experiment, the authors also varied the competence of the stimulus person. In addition to a highly competent person, they exposed the subject to an incompetent person who either spilled or did not spill coffee. They found, as predicted, that the incompetent coffee spiller was *less* attractive than the incompetent nonspiller. Thus, the experiment demonstrated that spilling coffee, in and of itself, is no virtue; this action only enhances the attractiveness of particular kinds of people, not all people. In this situation, investigating a combination of variables added essential clarity to an experimental finding.

Measuring the Dependent Variable
In experimental social psychology, particularly in high-impact laboratory experiments, operationalization of the dependent variable has not always received the same

careful attention that is devoted to the construction of the independent variable. This imbalance in expenditure of thought and energy can be very unfortunate, since the power to detect the causal impact of experimental manipulations depends heavily on the reliability and validity of the outcome measures that are used and recorded. Thus, we recommend that dependent measures should be designed, pilot tested, and refined with the same concern that is given to the independent variable manipulations and with many of the same considerations in mind.

The basic decision facing the researcher in planning the measurement of dependent variables is whether to rely on subjective self-reports or observations by others as the means of assessing a particular subject's responses to the experimental situation. Actually, it is not that simple, for it is possible to imagine a continuum ranging from behaviors of great importance and consequence for the subject down to the most trivial paper-and-pencil measures about which the subject has no interest. At one extreme the experimenter could measure the extent to which subjects actually perform a great deal of tedious labor for a fellow student (as a reflection of, say, their liking for that student, which has been experimentally influenced). At the other extreme one could ask them to circle a number on a scale entitled "How much did you like that other person who participated in the experiment?" Close to the behavioral end of the continuum would be a measure of the subject's commitment to perform a particular action without actually performing it. We call this a "behavioroid" measure. An example of a behavioroid measure is supplied by Aronson and Cope (1968) who assessed the degree to which the subjects liked the experimenter by having the departmental secretary ask them to volunteer to make telephone calls (to prospective subjects) on behalf of the experimenter. This liking could be easily scaled since the number of phone calls the subjects agreed to make constituted the degree of their liking for the experimenter. The subjects did not actually make the phone calls, for the experimental session was terminated immediately after each of them volunteered.

Similarly, Marlowe, Frager, and Nuttall (1965) wanted to determine the extent to which subjects became *more* committed to their liberal beliefs as a function of their having lost a money-making opportunity because of these beliefs. The major dependent variable was a statement by each subject about whether or not he or she was willing to spend a great deal of time escorting some visiting blacks around campus. As in the Aronson-Cope experiment, the procedure did not actually require the subjects to perform the behavior, only to commit themselves to do so. Note that although the data in both of these studies were merely verbal statements, they were far different from a simple statement like "I like the experimenter" or "I think blacks are wonderful." The crucial difference between a simple questionnaire and a behavioroid measure is degree of commitment. Most subjects who volunteer to make phone calls or to escort blacks do so with the firm intention of following through. It is much easier and, therefore, much less meaningful to check an attitude questionnaire.

On our continuum, somewhere between a behavioroid measure and an attitude questionnaire is the interview. The great advantage of an interview over a questionnaire is that the interviewer, merely by being there, can succeed in inducing the subject to pay heed and therefore has a better chance of obtaining a serious, honest response. A frequent dilemma in this field is between impact and concealment. In order to conceal the hypothesis from the subject, the experimenter is tempted to administer the dependent variable in a casual manner, almost as an afterthought. A common device is the "Oh, by the way" technique. "Oh, by the way," the experimenter might say, "the psychology department is interested in how subjects feel about experiments." The experimenter then rummages around and finds a dog-eared questionnaire lying around, hands it to the subject, and leaves the room. By thus de-emphasizing his or her own interest in the questionnaire, the experimenter stands a good chance of masking its importance. The problem is that, unless we are careful, we may succeed too well; the subjects may treat the questionnaire as casually as the experimenter appeared to treat it and may thus check off their responses almost at random. The interview is an improvement over the questionnaire, and when used judiciously, can be more powerful than a questionnaire without arousing suspicion. In this regard, Aronson and Linder (1965) reported an experiment that failed when the dependent variable was measured by a questionnaire but succeeded when the subjects were interviewed. The interviewer, of course, must be kept unaware of experimental treatment of the subjects.

As implied previously, the questionnaire and the interview are often valuable. Moreover, behavioral measures are not always perfect. A specific segment of behavior can be determined by many different factors; thus, behavioral measures and questionnaire measures, even though they may appear parallel, occasionally tap different aspects of the subject's beliefs or feelings. For example, suppose in an experiment a confederate (posing as a fellow subject) either praises the subject, implying that he or she is brilliant, or insults the subject, implying that he or she is stupid. Suppose our dependent variable is how much the subject likes the confederate. We can measure it by handing subjects a rating scale and asking them to rate their liking for the confederate, from +5 to −5. Or, on a more behavioral level, we can observe the extent to which the subject makes an effort to join a group to which the confederate belongs. This latter behavior seems to be a reflection of liking, but it may reflect other things instead. For example, it may be that some subjects in the "insult" condition want to join the group in order to prove to the confederate that they are *not* stupid. Or it may be that some want an opportunity to see the insulting person again so that they can return the insult. Neither of these behaviors necessarily reflects "liking," and consequently, they may produce results different from those produced by the questionnaire measure.

At the same time, it should be clear that the greater the degree of commitment demanded of the subject by the dependent variable, the more confidence we can have in our experiment. For example, we would have a great deal of confidence that an experiment *really* involves antecedents of aggression if the experimenter reports that an experimental treatment induced more subjects to punch him in the nose than a control condition did. We would have far less confidence if the experimental treatment resulted in a higher rating of perceived feelings of aggression as measured by a questionnaire. In terms of the three goals mentioned previously: (1) a punch in the nose is probably a much closer approximation to the conceptual notion of aggression than " +3, I feel somewhat angry"; (2) a punch in the nose is a good indication that the subject is taking the situation seriously; (3) since a questionnaire, by its very nature, asks a question, there is clearly greater likelihood that some subjects will try to determine what they *should* answer in order to make themselves look good (Sigall, Aronson, and Van Hoose, 1970). An aspect of behavior, especially when not asked for (like the punch in the nose), is far less likely to reflect the subject's desire to look good.

Although these points seem fairly obvious, the use of behavioral or behavioroid measures is not as common as it might be. Occasionally, the situation makes it impossible to obtain anything more than a set of ratings. But, alas, all too often the questionnaire is chosen for no good reason other than the fact that it is easier to devise and administer. We regard this as a failure in the imagination of the researcher. With more effort and ingenuity,

many studies could be designed to include behavioral data. Thus, in the area of attraction, although most studies tend to rely on ratings of liking by the subjects, there are some interesting and laudable departures. For example, Snyder, Tanke, and Berscheid (1977) demonstrated that if a man believed that the woman he was talking to was physically attractive, then *her* verbal behavior became friendlier and more social as a consequence. Sometimes the change from a rating by the subject to a behavioral measure is a very simple one; for example, in his variation on Aronson and Carlsmith's (1963) experiment, Freedman (1965) instead of asking children to rate the attractiveness of several toys (as in the original experiment), observed the amount of time the children actually played with the toys. This strikes us as a more convincing measure of their liking for the toys.

It should be clear that we are not suggesting that questionnaires and rating scales are without value. Frequently, they are the only way to measure a particular phenomenon. When we must use questionnaires, we should use them in the most vivid and powerful manner possible. The key problem is the subject's lack of involvement with the task because it is impersonal and noncommitting. There is nothing more likely to produce error variance than a subject racing through pages of questions, checking without giving much thought, and not paying attention to the wording of the question. We have already discussed the structured interview as a way of minimizing this possibility. In an interview, the precise meaning of the question can be emphasized; the subject can be exhorted repeatedly to think carefully before answering; and the experimenter can repeat sections of the questions that are unclear. This procedure requires more time than a questionnaire, but it is time well spent. The interview is often shunned because of the fears of introducing bias; yet if the experimenter has been properly blinded to the condition the subject is in or if the interviewer is someone other than the experimenter and thus is blind to the condition, the interview can be a very effective method.

There are several more mundane problems to be considered in making concrete decisions about what the dependent variable should be. One constantly recurring question is the extent to which the behavior of the subject should be constrained. This takes several forms. First, should one attempt to block most possible alternative behaviors so as to maximize the likelihood of observing changes in the specific variable of interest? For example, in a dissonance study, should the experimenter attempt to rule out all possible methods of reducing dissonance except the one he or she has decided to study? Clearly doing this will maximize the likelihood of observing differences in the behavior studied. This is a perfectly sound and reasonable technique. Indeed, it is part of our definition of experimental control. However, we do this only when we ask a certain kind of question, namely: "Is there dissonance in this situation, and does it get reduced?" If this is the question, the experimenter should attempt to construct the experiment in order to be ready and able to measure the effects of the independent variable as powerfully as possible. For example, in a typical dissonance study in the area of communication and persuasion, hearing a very credible communicator state a position with which the subject does not agree produces dissonance. There are four major ways for the subject to reduce dissonance: (1) by changing his or her own opinion, (2) by trying to get the communicator to change, (3) by seeking social support, (4) by derogating the communicator. One *can* easily devise an experiment that makes it difficult for the subject to utilize all but the first of these techniques. The experimenter then stands a good chance of validating the hypothesis because most of the leaks have been sealed; most of the dissonance that is aroused will be channeled in the direction of attitude change —and that's where the experimenter has piled the measuring instruments.

But the investigator may have a different question in mind. He or she may want to find out how people typically reduce dissonance. If this is the question, the preceding technique will almost certainly obscure what the subject *really* is likely to do in a situation of this sort and present the experimenter with an artificial relationship.

The same concern arises when a researcher tries to decide whether to use open-ended questions or a rigidly constrained measure. Although the more quantitative measure may increase the likelihood of observing differences between experimental treatments, it also may obscure what the behavior of the subject would normally be. Any experimenter who has seen many subjects close at hand has experienced the feeling that a given subject is "really" showing many interesting effects, although the measures are too constrained to be sensitive to them.

The best answer to both of these concerns is to run a reasonably large number of pilot subjects with the dependent variable as unconstrained as possible. Thus, in pilot research it may be most effective to present subjects with the independent variable and then, in essence, ask them

to say or do what they feel like saying or doing. By this means we may obtain some ideas as to exactly what behaviors we can look at that are likely to reflect the processes we believe are taking place. As we observe what the subjects do and say in response to the manipulations, it becomes possible to select dependent measures that may accurately assess the responses of the subjects and thus rule out certain alternative behaviors so as to maximize the likelihood of change on an important variable. Once the pilot stage of an experiment is over, however, there are many obvious advantages to rigidly defined, quantitative measurement of the dependent variable.

Disguising the measure. For reasons that should be clear by this time, it is frequently important to disguise the fact that a particular collection of data is actually the measurement of the dependent variable. This presents problems very similar to those involved in attempting to disguise the independent variable, as discussed in the earlier section on guarding against demand characteristics. Again, there are several classes of solutions that can be applied to the problem of disguising the dependent variable.

Assessment of the dependent variable can be done in a setting totally removed from the remainder of the experiment. This is perhaps the most common solution. An excellent example of this technique is the Marlowe, Frager, and Nuttall (1965) study referred to earlier. In this case, the experimenter who asked the subjects whether they would be willing to escort some black people around campus was described as a professor who was in charge of a visiting program and who had nothing to do with the experiment. Similarly, Carlsmith, Collins, and Helmreich (1966) had the dependent variable assessed by a Madison Avenue consumer research analyst. Another common procedure here is to pretend that the dependent variable is being collected for some other and unrelated study. Festinger and Carlsmith (1959) presented the dependent variable as some information being collected for a study being conducted by other members of the psychology department. Let us repeat the caution that we issued earlier: if, as part of this "different context" technique, the experimenter finds it necessary to pretend to be uninterested in the data, he or she may succeed in making *the subject* uninterested. Our recommendation is merely that experimenters should be aware of this possibility and attempt to walk the fine line between appearing too interested and too uninterested. If they are too interested, the subject will become suspicious; if they are too uninterested, the subject may respond in a random or jocular fashion.

In attitude-change experiments, the most typical solution is to embed the key items in a lengthy questionnaire that is given to the subject. One may have some qualms about the extent to which this always disguises the measurement from the subject; yet it has been used effectively in some instances. An alternative technique involves actually *telling* the subject that you are interested in a particular measure but disguising the reasons for your interest. That is, instead of implying that it is the dependent variable, one may describe it as a covariate that must be measured because of its possible confounding effects. For example, Aronson (1961) hypothesized that if subjects expended effort to obtain objects of a particular color, that color would gain in attractiveness. In order to get subjects to rate the colors without telegraphing his hypothesis, Aronson told them that he wanted a rating of how attractive the colors were because he suspected that the attractiveness of the colors might have had an unpredictable effect on how hard they had worked.

One can dispense with the need for disguising the dependent variable by using experimental subjects who are, by nature, unsuspicious. For example, Aronson and Carlsmith (1963) were able to use a very simple and transparent method of collecting the dependent variable only because the subjects in that experiment were four-year-old children. These children were not suspicious of anything that was going on; they saw nothing peculiar about someone asking them to rate a number of toys on two occasions within a span of twenty minutes. The same procedure would not have been as effective with college sophomores as subjects.

There is a family of techniques for measuring a dependent variable that is parallel to the "whoops" procedure for manipulating an independent variable. The most common member of this family involves claiming that the pretest data were lost so that a second set of measures must be collected. A complicated variation on this theme was employed by Aronson and Carlsmith (1962) in their study of the effects of performance expectancy. Here, the experimenter timed the subject's performance on four successive tests and then pretended to neglect to time the final administration of the test. After some pacing, breast beating, and rumination, the experimenter asked the subject to retake the test so that his or her performance could be timed. The crucial purpose of this procedure was to provide the subjects with an opportunity to change their answers. The number of answers changed was the dependent measure; it was presumed to reflect the amount of discontent with the original score. As we pointed out in our discussion of the independent variable, this kind of procedure has the advantage of appearing to be an event that happens only once—to this particular subject—and thus is unlikely to be perceived as a situation that is of interest to the experimenter.

In many respects, the neatest technique for measuring the dependent variable involves the taking of physiological measures. Where they can be used, physiological measures are valuable because they are not under the subject's conscious control. The major difficulty is that not many physiological measures reflect the kinds of dependent variables in which social psychologists are interested. Recent research, however, such as Jemmott's (1980) use of chemical analysis of the subject's saliva as a measure of stress, suggests that such techniques may be practical and may indeed become increasingly common.

An interesting variation on the true physiological measure was devised by Jones and Sigall in 1971. Their technique, dubbed the "bogus pipeline," consists of convincing the subjects that the experimenter has an accurate physiological measure of their attitudes. This is accomplished by the use of an electrical apparatus rigged so that, before the experiment, the subjects receive a striking demonstration: the electrodes attached to their arm affect a needle on a dial in a manner consistent with their actual feelings on a number of issues. Actually, the dial is surreptitiously manipulated by the experimenter. Subsequently, the subjects are asked to state their true attitudes while attached to the electrodes (although they themselves cannot view the dial). Since the subjects believe that the experimenter *can* read the dial and that the dial reflects their real feelings, they are motivated to respond as accurately as possible. This device has proved particularly useful in measuring socially sensitive attitudes. For example, Sigall and Page (1971) found that white subjects connected to the "bogus pipeline" expressed attitudes toward blacks that were more stereotypically negative than did subjects in a "no pipeline" control condition.

Using indirect measures. In a sense, all measures of psychological variables are indirect in that we have no direct access to the thoughts or perceptions of another person, although some measures are conceptually more indirect than others. What we mean by indirect measures are those for which the link to the variable of interest involves a hypothetical intervening process. For example, in an interesting study of the "illusion of control" over chance events, Langer (1975) sold lottery tickets costing fifty cents each to subjects under one of two conditions—where buyers were arbitrarily handed a particular ticket by the salesperson or where the buyers were allowed to select their own tickets from the available set. What Langer was interested in was the effect of the illusory "control" implied in this latter condition on the confidence of the subjects that theirs might be a winning ticket. Rather than simply asking the subjects how confident they felt, however, Langer used a less direct measure of this variable. Each subject was approached after obtaining a ticket and was told that someone else wanted to purchase a ticket and the seller had run out. The subjects were then asked to state the amount of money for which they would be willing to sell their own tickets. The reasoning behind this procedure was that the subject's asking price for the ticket would reflect the *subjective* utility of the ticket for that subject, which in turn would reflect the probability that he or she attached to the ticket's winning a great deal of money. As predicted, subjects who had chosen their own ticket asked for significantly more money before they were willing to sell that ticket than subjects who had been given their ticket with no choice.

What is interesting about this use of an indirect measure is the likelihood that subjects would have been embarrassed to report on their differential confidence had they been asked directly whether they thought they had a winning ticket; after all, they would have known that the "objective" view was that the probability was quite low and might be influenced by purely chance factors. Assuming that the indirect measure used was closely related to true subjective confidence, it may have detected an effect that would not have appeared in the results of direct self-report.

The recent trend in social judgment research toward use of measures borrowed from cognitive psychology provides another example of indirect assessment techniques. Attitude researchers have long regarded differential or biased attention to, and memory for, pro versus con attitudinal statements as a measure of an individual's own attitudinal position. Recently, more sophisticated measures of recognition, reaction time, and accuracy of recall have been applied to other aspects of social perception as well. Again, assuming that subjects exercise less control over memory than they do over verbal self-reports, such measures may reveal biases that otherwise may be suppressed. For instance, it may no longer be so-

cially desirable for subjects to admit that they think that physicians should be men rather than women. Thus, a direct measure might fail to reveal such biased expectations even if they existed in the subjects' minds. Suppose instead that you present subjects with a picture of a man or woman dressed like a physician and surrounded by medical paraphernalia. You then ask them to identify the person's profession as quickly as possible. If it requires more time to correctly identify the female picture than the male picture, this differential recognition may be taken as an indication of a continuing propensity to think of the "ideal" doctor as a male. Similarly, suppose subjects are able to recall information about a person that fits social stereotypes to a greater extent than information that is unrelated to stereotype contents (e.g., Hamilton and Rose, 1980; Brewer, Dull, and Lui, 1981). This would provide indirect but reasonably conclusive evidence of the presence of stereotyping, where a direct trait-list measure may have revealed none. The use of all such measures presupposes some hypothetical mechanisms linking biases in information processing and recall with underlying cognitive structures or beliefs.

Planning the Postexperimental Follow Up

The experiment does not end when the data have been collected. Rather, the prudent experimenter will want to remain with the subjects to talk and listen in order to accomplish three important goals:

1. To ensure that the subjects are in a good and healthy frame of mind,

2. To be certain that the subjects understand the experimental procedures, the hypotheses, and their own performance so that they gain a valuable educational experience as a result of having participated;

3. To avail themselves of the subject's unique skill as a valuable consultant in the research enterprise; that is, only the subjects know for certain whether the instructions were clear, whether the independent variable had the intended impact on them, and so on.

In most situations all three of these goals can best be accomplished immediately after the data are collected. In addition, if the experimental procedures are especially stressful, the experimenter may want to follow up in a few days or a few weeks to make certain that there are no residual effects.

It is impossible to overstate the importance of the postexperimental follow up. The experimenter should never conduct it in a casual or cavalier manner. Rather, the experimenter should probe gently and sensitively to be certain that all of the above goals are accomplished. This is especially and most obviously true if any deception has been employed. In this case, the experimenter needs to learn if the deception was effective or if the subject was suspicious in a way that could invalidate the data based on his or her performance in the experiment. Even more important, where deception was used, the experimenter must reveal the true nature of the experiment and the reasons why deception was necessary. Again, this cannot be done lightly. People do not enjoy learning that they have behaved in a naive or gullible manner. The experimenter not only must be sensitive to the feelings and dignity of the subjects but also should communicate this care and concern to them. We have found that subjects are most receptive to experimenters who are open in describing their own discomfort with the deceptive aspects of the procedure. Then, in explaining why the deception was necessary, the experimenter not only is sharing his or her dilemma as an earnest researcher (who is seeking the truth through the use of deception) but also is contributing to the subjects' educational experience by exploring the process as well as the content of social psychological experimentation.

Although it is important to provide the subjects with a complete understanding of the experimental procedures, this is not the best way to begin the postexperimental session. In order to maximize the value of the subjects as consultants, it is first necessary to explore with each the impact of the experimental events. The value of this sequence should be obvious. If we tell the subjects what we expected to happen before finding out what the subjects experienced, they may have a tendency to protect us from the realization that our procedures were pallid, misguided, or worthless. Moreover, if deception was used, the experimenter before revealing the deception should ascertain whether or not the subject was suspicious and whether or not particular suspicions were of such a nature as to invalidate the results.

This should not be done abruptly. It is best to explore the feelings and experiences of the subjects in a gentle and gradual manner. Why the need for gradualness? Why not simply ask the subjects if they suspected that they were the victims of a hoax? Subjects may not be responsive to an abrupt procedure for a variety of reasons. First, if a given person *did* see through the experiment, he or she may be reluctant to admit it out of a misplaced desire to be helpful to the experimenter. Second, as mentioned previously, since most of us do not feel good about appearing gullible, some subjects may be reluctant to admit that they can be easily fooled. Consequently, if subjects are told pointedly about the deception, they might imply that they suspected it all along, in order to save face. Thus, such an abrupt procedure may falsely inflate the number of suspicious subjects and may, consequently, lead the experimenter to abandon a perfectly viable procedure. Moreover, as mentioned previously, abruptly telling subjects that they have been deceived is a harsh technique that can add unnecessarily to their discomfort and, therefore, should be avoided.

The best way to begin a postexperimental interview is to ask the subjects if they have any questions. If they do not, the experimenter should ask if the entire experiment was perfectly clear—the purpose of the experiment as well as each aspect of the procedure. The subjects should then be told that people react to things in different ways and it would be helpful if they would comment on how the experiment affected them, why they responded as they did, and how they felt at the time, for example. Then each subject should be asked specifically whether there was any aspect of the procedure that he or she found odd, confusing, or disturbing.

By this time, if deception has been used and any subjects have any suspicions, they are almost certain to have revealed them. Moreover, the experimenter should have discovered whether the subjects misunderstood the instructions or whether any responded erroneously. If no suspicions have been voiced, the experimenter should continue: "Do you think there may have been more to the experiment than meets the eye?" This question is virtually a giveaway. Even if the subjects had not previously suspected anything, some will probably begin to suspect that the experimenter was concealing something. In our experience, we have found that many subjects will take this opportunity to say that they did feel that the experiment, as described, appeared too simple (or something of that order). This is desirable; whether the subjects were deeply suspicious or not, the question allows them an opportunity to indicate that they are not the kind of person who is easily fooled. The experimenter should then explore the nature of the suspicion and how it may have affected the subject's behavior. From the subject's answers to this question, the experimenter can make a judgment as to how close a subject's suspicions were to the actual purpose of the experiment and, consequently, whether or not the data are admissible. Obviously, the criteria for inclusion should be both rigorous and rigid and should be set down before the experiment begins; the decision should be made without knowledge of the subject's responses on the dependent variable.

The experimenter should then continue with the debriefing process by saying something like this: "You are on the right track, we *were* interested in exploring some issues that we didn't discuss with you in advance. One of our major concerns in this study is. . ." The experimenter should then describe the problem under investigation, specifying why it is important and explaining clearly exactly how the deception took place and why it was necessary. Again, experimenters should be generous in sharing their own discomfort with the subject. They should make absolutely certain that the subject fully understands these factors before the postexperimental session is terminated.

It is often useful to enlist the subject's aid in improving the experiment. That is, before ending the interview, the experimenter should explain that researchers are forever searching for ways of improving experimental procedures to make them more powerful, more credible, and more pleasant for the subject. "I would be most appreciative if you would be good enough to point out any weakness, problems, or fuzziness in the instructions or procedure." This is the best way we know to find out any negative aspects of the experiment. As many investigators (e.g. Orne, 1962) have pointed out, experimental subjects tend to be pleasant and cooperative. Unfortunately, this cooperativeness may prevent them from admitting that the procedure caused them unnecessary anguish, that the procedure did not have any meaning for them, or that it did not mean what the experimenter thought it should mean. By specifically appealing to the subjects to help improve the experiment, the investigator can provide them with a beneficial outlet for cooperativeness. If this is done, the subjects will be only too pleased to criticize the experiment. Criticism often leads to improvement and is an indispensable aid to the experimenter, especially in the early stages of the research. In addition, this procedure often allows the subjects additional freedom to admit that they were (or still are) upset by the procedure or the deception; if this should occur, the experimenter knows that more must be done to help the subjects, that the experimental procedure must be modified, or both.

Finally, whether or not deception is used, the experimenter must attempt to convince the subjects not to discuss the experiment with other people until it is completed. This is a serious problem because even a few sophisticated subjects can invalidate an experiment. Moreover, it is not a simple matter to swear subjects to secrecy; some have friends who may subsequently volunteer for the experiment and who are almost certain to press them for information. Perhaps the best way to reduce intersubject communication is to describe graphically the colossal waste of effort that would result from experimenting with people who have foreknowledge about the procedure or hypothesis of the experiment and, who thus can rehearse their responses in advance. The experimenter should also explain the damage that can be done to the scientific enterprise by including data from such subjects. If we experimenters are sincere and honest in our dealings with the subjects during the postexperimental session, we can be reasonably confident that few will break faith. To check on the efficacy of this procedure, Aronson (1966) enlisted the aid of three undergraduates who each approached three acquaintances who had recently participated in one of his experiments. The confederates explained that they had signed up for that experiment, had noticed the friend's name on the sign-up sheet, and wondered what the experiment was all about. The experimenter had previously assured these confederates that their friends would remain anonymous. The results were encouraging. In spite of considerable urging and cajoling on the part of the confederates, none of the former subjects revealed the true purpose of the experiment; two of them went as far as providing the confederates with a replay of the cover story, but nothing else.

What if the subject *has* been forewarned before entering the experimental room? That is, suppose a subject does find out about the experiment from a friend who participated previously. Chances are, the subject will not volunteer this information to the experimenter before the experiment. Moreover, if not prodded, it is unlikely that he or she will confess this knowledge after the experiment, out of reluctance to implicate the friend who, after all, broke a promise to the experimenter. Yet, if the experimenter is unable to gain this information, the results of the experiment may be extremely misleading.

Once again, we as experimenters must appeal to the cooperativeness of the subject as well as to the good will that we hopefully built up during the postexperimental interview. First, as described above, we should carefully and vividly explain the disastrous problems presented to science and to ourselves personally if we unwittingly were to publish erroneous data. The experimenter should then explain to the subject that, although cautioned not to discuss the experiment, occasionally a former subject will accidentally slip. ''It would be of great help to me if you would let me know if you heard *anything* about the experiment before you came. It goes without saying that I don't care to know how or from whom—just *what*.'' In the face of such a plea, very few unnaive subjects will remain silent. We cannot overemphasize the importance of this procedure as a safeguard against the artifactual confirmation of an erroneous hypothesis because of the misplaced cooperativeness of the subject. If the subjects are indeed cooperative, they will undoubtedly cooperate with the experimenter in this regard also and will respond to a direct plea of the sort described.

We would like to close this section by emphasizing our recommendation that a thorough explanation of the experiment should be provided *whether or not deception or stressful procedures are involved.* The major reason for this recommendation is that we cannot always predict the impact of a procedure; occasionally, even procedures that appear to be completely benign can have a powerful impact on some subjects. An interesting example of such an unexpectedly powerful negative impact comes from a series of experiments on social dilemmas by Dawes and his students (Dawes, McTavish, and Shaklee, 1977). In these experiments, typically, the subject must make a decision between cooperating with several other people or ''defecting.'' The contingencies are such that if all subjects choose to cooperate, they all profit financially; however, if one or more defect, defection has a high payoff, and cooperation produces little payoff. Each person's response is anonymous and remains so. The nature of the decision and its consequences is fully explained to the subjects at the outset of the experiment. No deception is involved.

Twenty-four hours after one experimental session, an elderly man (who had been the sole defector in his group and had won nineteen dollars) telephoned the experimenter trying to return his winnings so that it could be divided among the other participants (who, because they chose to cooperate, had each earned only one dollar). In the course of the conversation, he revealed that he felt miserable about his greedy behavior and that he had not slept all night, etc. After a similar experiment, a woman who had cooperated while others defected revealed that she felt terribly gullible and had learned that people were not as trustworthy as she had thought. In order to alleviate this kind of stress, Dawes went on to develop an elaborate and sensitive follow-up procedure.

We repeat that these experiments were selected for discussion precisely because their important and power-ful impact *could not have been easily anticipated*. We are intentionally not focusing on experiments that present clear and obvious problems like the well-known obedience study (Milgram, 1963), or the Stanford prison study (Haney, Banks, and Zimbardo, 1973). We have purposely selected an experiment that involves no deception and is well within the bounds of ethical codes. Our point is simple but important. No code of ethics can anticipate all problems, especially those created through subjects discovering something unpleasant about themselves or others in the course of an experiment. However, we believe a sensitive postexperimental interview conducted by a sincere and caring experimenter not only instructs and informs, but also provides important insights and helps reduce feelings of guilt or discomfort generated by such self-discovery (see Holmes, 1976a, and Holmes, 1976b.)

ETHICAL CONCERNS IN LABORATORY EXPERIMENTS

In our discussion of the post-experimental follow-up, we have wandered on to the topic of ethics. Experimental social psychologists have been deeply concerned about the ethics of experimentation for a great many years precisely because our field is constructed on an ethical dilemma. Basically, the dilemma is formed by a conflict between two sets of values to which most social psychologists subscribe: a belief in the value of free scientific inquiry and a belief in the dignity of humans and their right to privacy. We will not dwell on the historical antecedents of these values or on the philosophical intricacies of the ethical dilemma posed by the conflict of these values. It suffices to say that the dilemma is a real one and cannot be dismissed either by making pious statements about the importance of not violating a person's feelings of dignity or by glibly pledging allegiance to the cause of science. It is a problem every social psychologist must face squarely, not just once, but each time he or she constructs and conducts an experiment, since it is impossible to delineate a specific set of rules and regulations governing all experiments. In each instance the researcher must decide on a course of action after giving careful consideration to the importance of the experiment and the extent of the potential injury to the dignity of the participants.

It should be emphasized, of course, that ethical problems arise even in the absence of either deception or extreme circumstances. We refer again to the experiment by Dawes *et al.* (1977) as one of many possible examples of a benign-appearing procedure that can profoundly affect a few subjects in ways that could not easily have been anticipated even by the most sensitive and caring of experimenters. Obviously, some experimental techniques present more problems than others. In general, experiments that employ deception cause concern because of the fact that lying, *in and of itself,* is problematical. Similarly, procedures that cause pain, embarrassment, guilt, or other intense feelings present obvious ethical problems.

In addition, any procedure that enables the subjects to confront some aspect of themselves that may not be pleasant or positive is of deep ethical concern. For example, many of Asch's (1951) subjects learned that they would conform in the face of implicit group pressure; many of Aronson and Mettee's (1968) subjects learned that they would cheat at a game of cards; and many of Milgram's (1963) subjects learned that they could be pressured to obey an authority even when such obedience involved (apparently) inflicting severe pain on another human being. Even more imposing are the findings of the Stanford prison experiment in which college students learned that, even in the absence of direct explicit commands, they would behave cruelly and even sadistically toward fellow students (Haney *et al.,* 1973).

It can be argued that such procedures are therapeutic or educational for the subjects. Indeed, many of the subjects in these experiments have made this point. But this does not, in and of itself, justify the procedure primarily because the experimenter could not possibly know in advance that it would be therapeutic for all subjects. Moreover, it is arrogant for the scientist to decide that he or she will provide people with a therapeutic experience without their explicit permission.

The use of deception, when combined with the possibility of "self-discovery", presents the experimenter with a special kind of ethical problem. In a deception experiment it is impossible, *by definition,* to attain informed consent from the subjects in advance of the experiment. For example, how could Milgram or Asch have attained informed consent from their subjects without revealing aspects of the procedure that would have invalidated any results they obtained? An experimenter cannot even reveal in advance that the purpose of an experiment is the study of conformity or obedience without influencing the subject to behave in ways that are no longer "pure." Moreover, we doubt that the experimenter can reveal that deception *might* be used without triggering vigilance and, therefore, adulterating the subject's response to the independent variable.

It could be argued that the results are good or useful for society even though the procedure may be harmful to some of the subjects. Again, this does not, in and of itself, justify the procedure unless the subjects themselves are in a position to weigh the societal benefits against the possibility of individual discomfort. It should also be clear that an *ex post facto* defense is not adequate. That is, suppose one finds *after* running the experiment that all subjects attest that they are glad they participated and would still have agreed to participate if they had been properly informed in advance. This is not adequate because many subjects who might *not* have agreed to participate in advance might attempt to justify their participation *after the fact* as an ego protective device or as a way of helping the experimenter save face. Once the experiment is over, an *ex post facto* endorsement is ambiguous at best.

During the past several years, moral philosophers have entered the controversy and have suggested some solutions to the problem of informed consent which, while creative enough, strike us as being impractical in the extreme. One example will suffice. Sable (1978) has suggested a technique called "Prior General Consent Plus Proxy Consent." In this technique, the experimenter first obtains the general consent of the subject to participate in an experiment that may involve extreme procedures. The subject then empowers a friend to serve as a proxy; that is, to examine the details of the specific procedure in advance and to make a judgment as to whether the subject would have consented to it if given the choice. If the proxy says yes, then the experimenter may proceed. While this technique may be ethical in the most technical sense, it has some obvious flaws both ethically and methodologically. First, the subjects are still agreeing to something that they cannot fully understand—the proxy can be wrong. Second, it is reasonable to assume that most proxies will probably make conservative errors; that is, they will try to protect the welfare of the subject by being more cautious than the subject would have been. If that is the case, and a substantial number of proxies say no, we may have a sample of extreme and unknown bias.

In recent years, a number of institutions have attempted to aid the experimenter and protect the welfare of the subject in a variety of ways. Universities, where most social psychological research is conducted, have instituted human subject committees (review boards) that must approve of the ethics of a specific procedure before an experiment may be conducted. In 1973 the

American Psychological Association (APA) published a set of guidelines for the conduct of research involving human subjects, which have since been revised and updated (APA, 1981, 1982). The APA ethical guidelines are based on the following ten principles (APA, 1981, pp. 637–638):

1. In planning a study, the investigator has the responsibility to make a careful evaluation of its ethical acceptability. To the extent that the weighing of scientific and human values suggests a compromise of any principle, the investigator incurs a correspondingly serious obligation to seek ethical advice and to observe stringent safeguards to protect the rights of human participants.

2. Considering whether a participant in a planned study will be a "subject at risk" or a "subject at minimal risk," according to recognized standards, is of primary ethical concern to the investigator.

3. The investigator always retains the responsibility for ensuring ethical practice in research. The investigator is also responsible for the ethical treatment of research participants by collaborators, assistants, students, and employees, all of whom, however, incur similar obligations.

4. Except in minimal-risk research, the investigator establishes a clear and fair agreement with research participants, before their participation, that clarifies the obligations and responsibilities of each. The investigator has the obligation to honor all promises and commitments included in that agreement. The investigator informs the participants of all aspects of the research that might reasonably be expected to influence willingness to participate and explains all other aspects of the research about which the participants inquire. Failure to make full disclosure before obtaining informed consent requires additional safeguards to protect the welfare and dignity of the research participants. Research with children or with participants who have impairments that would limit understanding and/or communication requires special safeguarding procedures.

5. Methodological requirements of a study may make the use of concealment or deception necessary. Before conducting such a study, the investigator has a special responsibility to (1) determine whether the use of such techniques is justified by the study's prospective scientific, educational, or applied value, (2) determine whether alternative procedures are available that do not use concealment or deception, and (3) ensure that the participants are provided with sufficient explanation as soon as possible.

6. The investigator respects the individual's freedom to decline to participate in, or to withdraw from, the research at any time. The obligation to protect this freedom requires careful thought and consideration when the investigator is in a position of authority or influence over the participant. Such positions of authority include, but are not limited to, situations in which research participation is required as part of employment or in which the participant is a student, client, or employee of the investigator.

7. The investigator protects the participant from physical and mental discomfort, harm, and danger that may arise from research procedures. If risks of such consequences exist, the investigator informs the participant of that fact. Research procedures likely to cause serious or lasting harm to a participant are not used unless the failure to use these procedures might expose the participant to risk of greater harm or unless the research has great potential benefit and fully informed and voluntary consent is obtained from each participant. The participant should be informed of procedures for contacting the investigator within a reasonable time period following participation in case stress, potential harm, or questions or concerns arise.

8. After the data are collected, the investigator provides the participant with information about the nature of the study and attempts to remove any misconceptions that may have arisen. Where scientific or human values justify delaying or withholding this information, the investigator incurs a special responsibility to monitor the research and to ensure that there are no damaging consequences for the participant.

9. Where research procedures result in undesirable consequences for the individual participant, the investigator has the responsibility to detect and remove or correct these consequences, including long-term effects.

10. Information obtained about a research participant during the course of an investigation is confidential unless otherwise agreed upon in advance. When the possibility exists that others may obtain access to such information, this possibility, together with the plans for protecting confidentiality, are explained to the participant as part of the procedure for obtaining informed consent.

These principles are of general value only. When specific decisions are to be made, such general guidelines, along with collegial review, can be helpful, but the ultimate responsibility rests with the individual investigator. The guidelines of the American Psychological Association (1982) clearly recognize the extent to which personal judgment is involved in making ethical decisions:

> The ethical problems associated with psychological research on human beings cannot be solved solely by enunciating principles that point to rights and wrongs. When an ethical question arises, the situation is usually one of weighing the advantages and disadvantages of conducting the research as planned. On one hand, there is the contribution that the research may ultimately make to knowledge and human welfare; on the other, there is the cost to the research participant. . . .

> Whether a proposed research project is ethically acceptable—taking into account the entire context of relevant considerations—is a matter on which the individual investigator is obliged to come to a considered judgment without abdicating this responsibility on the grounds of current practice, regulatory considerations, or judgment by others. In making this judgment, the investigator must take account of the potential benefits and possible costs likely to flow from the research, including those to the participants that the research procedures entail.

> Such an approach does not lend itself to any quantitative formula or decision rule. Further, there remain difficult questions as to how costs to the individual participant can be balanced against possible ultimate benefits to the participant, to science, and to society.

Thus acknowledging the complexity and subtlety of the ethical dilemma, the APA guidelines provide detailed and concrete analyses of the experimenter's decision making process, taking into account a variety of difficult and legitimate methodological concerns. Because these issues are treated at a level of specificity that cannot be duplicated here, we urge the reader to study this document fully before undertaking the difficult and often lonely task of ethical decision making.

One of the factors that makes such judgments difficult is that ethical decisions are not made in a vacuum. The *zeitgeist* surrounding scientific research changes continuously and sometimes profoundly. We, ourselves, have lived through a period of major changes in ethical standards and practices. Procedures that were commonplace and seemed benign in the late 1950s were disavowed a decade later. But changes in the *Zeitgeist* are not neces-

sarily linear. It is conceivable that what is generally considered to be unethical now may become acceptable or even commonplace in the 1990s. The major thrust of our argument here is that we are opposed to defining for the experimenter what *is* and *is not* a justifiable decision. Rather, it is to plead for care and concern for the welfare of subjects and at the same time to suggest that we not abandon totally the hope of testing interesting hypotheses in powerful ways simply because such tests do not come in packages that are ethically impeccable. The experimenter must exercise care, caution, and ingenuity every time he or she designs and conducts an experiment. There are no pat solutions in any era, much less for all time.

MOVING INTO THE FIELD

We have gone into considerable detail discussing the features and conduct of the high-impact laboratory experiment because we believe it provides the prototypic (if not necessarily modal) case of social psychological experimentation. Certainly the four stages of research associated with the lab experiment—setting the stage, constructing the independent variable, measuring the dependent variable, and debriefing—are in some form common to all experimental research endeavors. The alternative types of social psychological experiments we discussed can all be viewed as variants on these basic themes, with differences in emphasis on the various aspects of research procedure. For instance, the pure judgment experiment can be seen as a variant of the high-impact laboratory study, although, unlike the laboratory study it places less emphasis on staging and creating experimental realism and somewhat more emphasis on careful delineation of the stimulus materials that constitute the independent variable and on defining the task of the subjects in the lab setting.

Given the current popularity of field experimentation as an alternative to laboratory research, we should give some particular attention to the ways in which the conduct of field experiments is most likely to differ from that of the prototypic lab study.

CONTROL OVER THE INDEPENDENT VARIABLE

Although the essence of experimentation is systematic manipulation by the researcher of variations in treatment or conditions that constitute the independent variable of the study, the extent of experimenter-controlled manipulation in different research settings is a matter of degree. In some cases, the researcher constructs experimental situations from scratch, creating the background context as well as experimental variations. In other cases, the experimenter controls less of the setting but introduces some systematic variation into existing conditions, as in the field experiment by Piliavin, Rodin, and Piliavin (1969) where the behavior of an experimental accomplice was varied in the largely uncontrolled context of a New York subway train in order to study bystander helping in that setting.

In yet other cases, the experimenter does not manipulate any of the stimulus conditions directly but selectively directs the attention of subjects to particular aspects of the stimulus field as the experimental treatment. This type of manipulation is common in judgment studies in which some type of preliminary "sensitizing" experience is provided to make some aspect of the experimental materials particularly salient to subjects (e.g., Higgins, Rholes, and Jones, 1977) or when variations in seating arrangements are used to alter the visual perspective of subjects to a social situation (e.g., Taylor and Fiske, 1975) or when mirrors or cameras are used to focus attention on the self rather than the situation (e.g., Duval and Wicklund, 1973). Similar techniques have been used in a field setting. In a study by Kiesler, Nisbett, and Zanna (1969), subjects were induced to proselytize against air pollution; they then overheard another subject agreeing to do the same with slight variations in wording, a situation that served to make salient either belief-relevant or irrelevant reasons for the behavior.

In other field research, the experimenter neither manipulates the stimulus conditions directly nor controls subject attention but instead *selects* among naturally occurring stimulus situations those that embody representations of the conceptual variable of interest. Here the line between experimental and correlational research becomes thin indeed, and the distinction depends largely on how standardized the selected field conditions can be across subjects. One good illustration of the use of selected field sites in conjunction with laboratory research comes from the literature on mood and altruism. Mood-induction manipulations have been developed in laboratory settings. The inductions involve having subjects read affectively positive or negative passages (e.g., Aderman, 1972) or having them reminisce about happy

or sad experiences in their own past (e.g., Moore, Underwood, and Rosenhan, 1973). After the mood state induction, subjects are given an opportunity to exhibit generosity by donating money or helping an experimental accomplice. Results generally show that positive mood induction elevates helping behavior. Despite multiple replications of this effect in different laboratories with different investigators, the validity of these findings has been challenged both because of the artificiality of the setting in which altruism is assessed and because of the potential demand characteristics associated with the rather unusual mood-induction experience.

To counter these criticisms, researchers in the area took advantage of a natural mood-induction situation based on the emotional impact of selected motion pictures (Underwood, Froming, and Moore, 1977). After the pilot research in which ratings were obtained from movie goers, a double feature consisting of *Lady Sings the Blues* and *The Sterile Cuckoo* was selected for its negative affect-inducing qualities, and two other double features were selected to serve as neutral control conditions. A commonly occuring event—solicitation of donations to a nationally known charity with collection boxes set up outside the movie theater lobby—was chosen as the vehicle for a measure of the dependent variable of generosity.

Having located such naturally occurring variants of the laboratory mood-induction operation and altruism measure, the major design problem encountered by the researchers was that of subject self-selection to the alternative movie conditions. While random assignment of volunteer movie goers was a logical possibility, the procedures involved in utilizing that strategy would have recreated many of the elements of artificiality and reactivity that the field setting was selected to avoid. Therefore, the investigators decided to live with the phenomenon of self-selection and to alter the research design to take its effect into consideration. For this purpose, the timing of collection of donations to charity at the various movie theaters was randomly alternated across different nights so that it would occur either while most people were entering the theater (before seeing the movies) or while leaving (after seeing both features). The rate of donations given by arriving movie goers could then be used as a check on preexisting differences between the two populations apart from the mood induction. Fortunately, there proved to be no differences in initial donation rates as a function of type of movie, whereas post-movie donations differed significantly in the direction of lowered contribution rates following the sad movies. This pattern of results, then, preserved the logic of random assignment (initial equivalence between experimental conditions) despite the considerable deviation from ideal procedures for subject assignment.

Two points should be emphasized with respect to this illustration of field research. First of all, the field version of the basic research paradigm was not—and could not be—simply a "transplanted" replication of the laboratory operations. Significant alterations were necessary to take full advantage of the naturalistic setting. The researchers had considerably less control in the field setting. They could not control the implementation of the stimulus conditions or extraneous sources of variation. On any one night a host of irrelevant events may have occurred during the course of the movies (e.g., a breakdown of projectors or a disturbance in the audience) that could have interfered with the mood manipulation. The researcher was not only helpless to prevent such events but would not have been aware of them if they did take place. In addition, as already mentioned, in the field setting the experimenters were unable to assign subjects randomly to conditions and had to rely on luck to establish initial equivalence between groups.

The second point to be emphasized is that the results of the field experiment *as a single isolated study* would have been difficult to interpret without the context of conceptually related laboratory experiments. This difficulty is partly due to the ambiguities introduced by the alterations in design and partly to the constraints on measurement inherent in the field situation where manipulation checks, for example, are not possible. The convergence of results in the two settings greatly enhances our confidence in the findings from both sets of operations. Had the field experiment failed to replicate the laboratory results, however, numerous alternative explanations would have rendered interpretation very difficult.

RANDOM ASSIGNMENT IN FIELD SETTINGS

Subject self-selection problems plague field experimentation in multiple forms. In the field experiment on mood and helping behavior cited previously, random assignment to experimental conditions was not even attempted. Instead, the effects of potential selection factors were handled in other ways that involved an element of risk taking. The premovie data collection served as a check on the assumption that people who attend sad movies are not inherently different from people who attend other movies in their propensity to give to charities. But what if that assumption had proved false and there had been an initial difference in the rate of donations between attendants at the different types of movie? Such previous differences in behavior would have made interpretation of any differences in donations after exposure to the movies hazardous at best. In this case, the researchers were taking a gamble in counting on the absence of initial population differences. The logic of their experimental design required that the premovie data collection sessions be interspersed with postmovie data collection in order to control for timing effects. As a consequence, the investigators could not know until after the experiment had been completed whether the data supported their assumption of initial equivalence. Had they been wrong, the experimental design would have been undermined, and any effort expended would have been wasted. Presumably, the researchers would not have gone ahead with the study had they had strong reasons to doubt that no differences in premovie donation behavior would be found. Personal experience, or better yet, pilot research, could have led them to expect that the factors determining which type of movie most people saw on a particular night were irrelevant to their propensity to give to charity.

In other settings, too, the research may rely on the essentially haphazard distribution of naturally occurring events as equivalent to controlled experimental design. Parker, Brewer, and Spencer (1980), for instance, undertook a study on the outcomes of a natural disaster—a devastating brush fire in a southern California community—on the premise that the pattern of destruction of private homes in the fire constituted a "natural randomization" process. Among homes in close proximity at the height of the fire, only chance factors—shifts in wind direction and velocity, location of fire fighting equipment, and traffic congestion—determined which structures were burned to the ground and which remained standing when the fire was brought under control. Thus, homeowners who were victims of the fire and those who were not victimized could be regarded as essentially equivalent before the effects of the fire, and any differences in their attitudes and perceptions following the fire could be attributed to that particular differential experience. When comparisons are made between such naturally selected groupings, the burden of proof rests on the investigator to make a convincing case that the groups are not likely to differ systematically in any relevant dimensions other than the causal event of interest.

In other field research efforts, the researcher may be able to assign subjects randomly to experimental conditions. However, once assigned, some subjects may fail to participate or to experience the experimental manipulation. If such self-determined "de-selection" (also known as "subject mortality") occurs differentially across treatment conditions, the experimental design is seriously compromised. One way of preserving the advantages of randomization in such cases is to include subjects in their assigned experimental conditions for purposes of analysis regardless of whether they were exposed to the treatment or not (assuming, of course, that one is in a position to obtain measures on the dependent variable for these subjects). This was the solution applied in the two field experiments conducted by Freedman and Fraser (1966) to test the effectiveness of the "foot-in-the-door" technique for enhancing compliance.

In these studies the dependent variable was whether individuals contacted in their homes would agree to a rather large, intrusive request from the researcher (e.g., to permit a five-person market survey team to come into the home for two hours to classify household products). Of primary interest was the rate of compliance to this large request by subjects who had been contacted previously with a small request (e.g., to respond to a very brief market survey over the telephone), in comparison to that of the control subjects who were contacted for the first time at the time of the large request.

The purpose of the manipulation in the Freedman and Fraser studies was to test the effect of actual *compliance* to the initial small request on response to the later request. However, the operational experimental treatment to which potential subjects could be randomly assigned was exposure to the request itself. Approximately one-third of those who were given the initial small request refused to comply; hence they failed to complete the experimental manipulation. If these subjects had been excluded from the study, the comparability between the remaining experimental subjects and those randomly assigned to the no-initial-contact condition would have been seriously suspect. To avoid this selection problem, the researchers decided to include measures from all subjects in the originally assigned treatment groups, regardless of their response to the initial request. With respect to testing treatment effects, this was a conservative decision, since the full treatment was significantly diluted among those classified in the experimental group. As it

turned out, the initial compliance effect was powerful enough to generate a significant difference between treatment groups (of the order of 50 percent versus 20 percent compliance rates) despite the dilution of the experimental condition. Had the results been more equivocal, however, we would have been uncertain whether to attribute the absence of significant differences to lack of treatment effects or to failure to achieve the experimental manipulation. When the experimental treatment condition is diluted even more seriously than in the present illustration, comparisons between intact treatment groups become meaningless, and more sophisticated techniques for correcting for subject self-selection must be adopted (Brewer, 1976).

When full random assignment cannot be implemented in field settings, various forms of "quasi experiments" (cf. Cook and Campbell, 1979) can be creatively employed to preserve the logic of experimental design and control without rigid adherence to specific procedures. It should be kept in mind, however, that loss of control over stimulus conditions or subject assignment inevitably carries with it some measure of risk. Assumptions upon which the quasi-experimental design rests (such as initial equivalence of different groups) may prove untenable, or uncontrolled environmental inputs may "swamp" the stimulus conditions of interest to the researcher. In such cases, the costs in terms of wasted effort are high; thus decisions to take risks in undertaking field studies must be made sensibly. It would be foolish not to adjust the features of one's research design to the practical realities of a given field setting. But it is even more foolish to proceed with an expensive study that, from the start, has a high probability of resulting in uninterpretable outcomes.

ASSESSMENT OF DEPENDENT VARIABLES IN FIELD SETTINGS

In many field contexts, the design and evaluation of dependent measures is parallel to that of laboratory experiments. In the guise of a person-on-the-street interview or a market research survey, for example, the field researcher may elicit self-reports of relevant attitudes, perceptions, or preferences. Or behavioroid measures may be designed that assess the willingness of the subjects to engage in relevant acts such as signing a petition or committing themselves to some future effort. Finally, situations may be constructed so as to elicit the type of behavior of interest to the experimenter, such as providing subjects with opportunities to donate to charity (Underwood *et al.*, 1977), to help a stranger who has collapsed (Piliavin *et al.*, 1969), or to trade in a lottery ticket (Langer, 1975). One advantage of experimentation in field settings is the potential for assessing behaviors that are, in and of themselves, of some significance to the subject. Instead of asking subjects to report on perceptions or intentions, we may observe them engaging in behaviors with real consequences. In such cases, our dependent measures are much less likely to be influenced by experimental "demand characteristics" or social desirability response biases. In laboratory settings subjects may check a particular point on a liking scale in order to please the experimenter or to look good; however very few people would choose someone as a roommate for the entire year unless there were more powerful reasons.

In some field settings, the kinds of dependent measures typically employed in laboratory studies would be excessively intrusive in ways that would destroy the natural flow of events characteristic of the setting. Field experimenters have to be particularly sensitive to the issue of "reactivity" discussed by Campbell and Stanley (1963). This concept refers to the possibility that the measurement of the dependent variable reacts with the independent variable or related events in such a way that effects are found that would not have been present otherwise. For example, suppose some people have seen a movie designed to reduce prejudice. They may be completely unaffected by this movie *until* they are asked to fill out a questionnaire that clearly deals with prejudice. As a result of seeing this questionnaire, the movie goers may realize for the first time that the movie was about prejudice and may reflect on the movie in a new way that now has an influence. In effect, the introduction of the dependent measure has served as a kind of independent variable in combination with the originally intended treatment variable. Note that this kind of effect is conceptually different from experimental artifacts generated by demand characteristics or experimenter bias effects. We are not postulating that the respondent changes the expression of prejudicial attitudes in order to please the experimenter but only that no change would have taken place without the intrusion of a very obvious measurement.

In order to prevent or minimize the occurrence of reactivity, field researchers may devise a variety of techniques to make *unobtrusive* measurements of the dependent variable of interest (see Webb *et al.*, 1966; 1981).

Some unobtrusive measures are based on observations of ongoing behavior, utilizing methods of observation that interfere minimally or not at all with the occurrence of the behavior. For instance, voluntary seating aggregation patterns have been used as an index of racial attitudes under varied conditions of classroom desegregation; observational studies of conformity have recorded public behaviors such as pedestrians crossing against traffic lights or turn signaling by automobile drivers, and studies of natural language often resort to eavesdropping on conversations in public places. Cialdini *et al.* (1976) used naturalistic observation of clothing and accessories to study what they call the "Basking in Reflected Glory" phenomenon. They recorded the wearing of t-shirts and other apparel bearing the school name or insignia by students in introductory psychology classes at seven universities each Monday during football season. The proportion of students wearing such apparel at each school proved to be significantly greater on Mondays following a victory by that school's team than on Mondays following defeat. A simple monitoring of public displays provided quantitative confirmation of the hypothesized tendency to identify with success.

Other observational techniques may rely on the use of hidden hardware for audio or video recording of events that are later coded and analyzed. Finally, some techniques make use of the *natural* recording of events outside the experimenter's control, such as physical traces left after an event has occurred or archival records that are kept for administrative or economic purposes (police files, school absenteeism records, and sales figures). One interesting illustration of the use of unobtrusive physical trace measures is provided in Langer and Rodin's (1976) field experiment testing the effects of responsibility inductions on the well-being of residents of a nursing home. The major outcome of interest in that study was the general alertness and activity level of the residents following introduction of the experimental treatment. This level was assessed not only by the traditional methods of self-report and the ratings of nurses but also by various specially designed behavioral measures. One of these measures involved covering the right wheels of patients' wheelchairs with two inches of white adhesive tape, which was removed after twenty-four hours and analyzed for the amount of discoloration as an index of patient-activity level. Alas, clever ideas do not always work; the amount of dirt picked up by the tape turned out to be negligible for patients in all conditions.

The results of the Langer and Rodin nursing home study serve to illustrate some of the problems of reliance on unobtrusive measures in field settings. The adhesive-tape index did not produce any detectable treatment effect; other, more direct and experimenter-controlled, self-report, and behavioral measures demonstrated significant impact of the experimental treatment. Had the researchers been forced to limit their assessment of effects to the least intrusive measure, they would have missed a great deal. The validity of dependent variable measures—the extent to which they measure what they are supposed to measure—is of concern in any research endeavor. However, the farther removed the actual measure is from the variable of interest, the more reason there is for concern. For instance, consider the number of steps involved in going from the dependent variable of patient-activity level to the measurement of discoloration of white adhesive tape in the nursing home study. First patient activity had to be translated into distance traveled in the wheelchair, which in turn had to be related to the amount of dirt picked up by different sections of the tape, which in turn had to produce measurable differences in discoloration. In such a chain, many intervening processes can reduce the correspondence between the intial variable (activity) and the measured outcome—the speed with which the wheelchair traveled, how often the floors were cleaned, whether the patient's movement was self-propelled or passive, and so on. Reliance on a single measure affected by so many irrelevant factors would have been treacherous indeed.

Sometimes indirect, unobtrusive measures do prove sensitive to experimental treatments but still turn out to be measuring the wrong thing. For example, recently the residents of Portland, Oregon, participated in an experimental attempt to decrease automobile use by lowering bus fares for a trial period (Katzev and Backman, 1982). Bus-rider records provided evidence that the goals of the study were being met; during the experimental period, bus ridership was way up. Unfortunately, however, the use of bus-rider records as an indirect (and unobtrusive) measure of reduction in automobile use proved to be misleading. The researchers kept careful odometer records of cars before and during the study and found there was no decrease in average miles driven. One possible explanation is that people felt so virtuous riding to work on the bus every day that they treated themselves to long recreational car trips on weekends! Reliance on bus ridership alone as a measure of the program's success would have led to an inappropriate conclusion.

ETHICAL ISSUES IN FIELD RESEARCH

In our discussion of the ethics of laboratory experimentation we emphasized the researcher's judgment and sensitivity as deciding factors in whether or not ethical standards are followed in research practice. In many ways the nature of field research places even more responsibility on the researcher to weigh research needs against ethical principles. Whatever the ethical compromises of laboratory experiments may be, at least the laboratory setting assures that subjects are aware in some sense that they are participating in research. Even if the consent to participate is not fully informed (or is actively *mis*informed), there is the presence of an "implicit contract" between subject and experimenter that reflects their mutual expectations about the conduct of research. The researcher's contractual obligation is partially fulfilled at the time of the debriefing and postexperimental interview, where any deceptions are unveiled, subjects are informed about the goals and purposes of the research, and subject responses to the research procedures are assessed. Thus, even if the subjects enter the experimental session ignorant of the researcher's intent, they do so in the expectation of being fully informed by the time it is all over. The postexperimental session also provides an opportunity for subject feedback to correct errors of judgment on the part of the experimenter. If the researcher has misjudged the amount of distress or embarrassment the experimental procedure will cause subjects, information from the first few subjects can provide a basis for altering those procedures before the research has gone too far.

When experiments are conducted in field settings where subjects are *unaware* at the time that they are participating in research, the basic ethical dilemma is magnified. In such cases, there is not even an "implicit contract" to be adhered to, and decisions regarding ethical considerations rest solely with the experimenter. There are two different versions of participation without awareness—cases in which subjects are not informed until *after* their data have been collected that they have been involved in a research study, and cases in which subjects are not informed at all. When subjects are contacted and debriefed at the end of the field research, the goals and conduct of the postexperimental interview are essentially the same as those in a laboratory study, although there is one important difference, namely, the fact that the subjects had no previous opportunity to decline participation. Hence not even an implicit obligation to cooperate can be assumed. Special sensitivity on the part of the researcher is required to avoid embarrassing the subject and to ensure that mechanisms are available for refusal to be included in the study after the fact. Again, however, postexperimental contact allows for subject feedback and participation in judgments about the legitimacy and appropriateness of the research procedures.

When subjects are never told about the research, the opportunity for corrective feedback is greatly reduced. Under such circumstances, the researcher has the full obligation and responsibility of ensuring that the privacy of subjects has not been violated, that they have been protected from undue embarrassment or distress, and that their lives have not been altered in any significant way by the nature of the research procedures. This obligation places the researcher in an essentially paternalistic role that many find uncomfortable. To avoid this stance, some have suggested that ethical principles should proscribe the observation or recording of behavior for research purposes unless every person included in the study can be fully informed. This position strikes us as misguided. There are clearly cases of innocuous observation in public places (or the use of public records for research purposes) where the necessity to contact individual subjects would destroy the anonymity that makes the procedures innocuous in the first place. Where data are recorded with no possibility of identifying information being available on the persons observed, postexperimental debriefing could produce more subject embarrassment than any effects associated with the observation itself. In such cases it is probably better that the research is conducted in ways that maximize anonymity rather than informed consent.

Of course, the mere fact that the subjects (or the experimenter) may be embarrassed by disclosure of the research purpose does not by itself justify a decision to forego informing subjects of their research participation. Such decisions should be closely restricted to situations involving high frequency behaviors in public places where only aggregate data are needed for research purposes. The decision becomes especially delicate when the researcher has intervened in the setting in any direct way that alters the situation beyond the normal range of events. In such cases, the experimenter must be sensitive to any possibility that subjects may have been affected by the intervention in ways that warrant disclosure of the experimental setup. Finally the conscientious researcher should not rely on his or her judgment alone to make such determinations but should consult widely among people who may bring different perspectives to bear on the decisions to be made.

PROGRAMMATIC RESEARCH: THE INTERPLAY BETWEEN LABORATORY AND FIELD EXPERIMENTATION

In extolling the advantages of experimentation in this chapter, we do not mean to ignore some very serious difficulties with the use of the experimental method in an area as complex as social psychology. There are severe limitations on the kinds of control that can be achieved in social psychological experimentation; some of these may be overcome by new approaches; others may be inherent in the nature of our subject matter.

One of the major limitations on control is the extent to which unmeasured individual differences may obscure the results of an experiment. The ideal of an experiment is to take two identical units (corn plants, rocks, rats, children, or fraternities) and to apply different experimental treatments to them. Although it is a philosophical truism that no two units are ever precisely identical, the experimenter must strive to make them as close to identical as possible. One, can approximate this ideal much more satisfactorily in most sciences, and even in most of psychology, than is possible in social psychology. Our subjects differ from each other genetically, in learned personality characteristics, in values and attitudes, in abilities, and in immediate past experiences. Any and all of these differences may have a large impact on the way in which subjects respond to our experimental treatments.

Such sources of variability in our data are accentuated by the relatively narrow limitations imposed on the kinds of experimental treatment a social psychologist can use. Ethical considerations, restrictions of time, and the mere fact that the subjects usually know they are in an experiment limit or dilute the impact the experimenter can have on the subject. Typically, we see our subjects for only an hour or two. In that short period of time we attempt to expose them to a complex social stimulus. The range of possible stimuli to which we expose them is sharply restricted by ethical considerations; there are many interesting questions that we cannot study simply because they involve doing things to people that we are not willing to do. As a consequence, the treatment used is a compromise between the experimenter's desire to maximize the effectiveness of the experiment and a genuine concern with the welfare of research subjects.

In an experiment on animal learning, it is usually fairly easy to have impact on the animal, to force it, if you will, to take the situation seriously. For a pigeon at 75 percent of free-feeding body weight, the learning of a food-producing response is important. It is possible to set up a social psychological experiment in which the subject is as concerned about performance as our hypothetical pigeon. In order to do this, however, the situation must be a very realistic one for the subject; and this realism always leads to great difficulty in understanding precisely what actually constitutes the experimental treatment. Social experiences that are realistic and meaningful tend to be complex, and any two such experiences (treatments) tend to differ on a large number of dimensions. For this reason, as we increase realism in an attempt to have greater impact on the subject, we frequently sacrifice precision and control.

We see this as the basic dilemma of the experimental social psychologist. On the one hand we want maximal control over the independent variable. We want as few extraneous differences as possible between our treatments. We want a precise specification of the treatment we have administered and of its effect on the subject. These desires lead us to try to develop manipulations that are highly specifiable, in which the differences between treatments are extraordinarily simple and clear and in which all manipulations are standardized—in short, to an approximation of something like a verbal learning experiment. On the other hand, if the experiment is controlled to the point of being sterile, it may fail to involve subjects, have little impact on them, and therefore may not affect their behavior to any great extent.

As an example of this dilemma, let us consider a typical experiment on attitude change, such as the classic Hovland and Weiss (1951) experiment on communicator credibility. The standard design for such an experiment would be to have two identical communications, one attributed to a source of high credibility and the other to a source of low credibility. For maximal control, the communication is written out in both cases, with the content and presentation absolutely identical except for the attribution of source. Frequently experiments done in this manner show weak effects, often too weak to be statistically significant; or when statistical significance is achieved, the actual magnitude of the differences between conditions is not great. It is a reasonable conjecture that these weak effects are due to the fact that the impact of such a manipulation is very small. It is generally dull and uninvolving for subjects to be asked to read a printed communication on an issue of little direct consequence to them.

To show a strong effect, it would be much more desirable to have the communicator present, delivering a dramatic speech articulately and with great passion and perhaps even interacting and arguing with the members of the audience. An example of such a technique brilliantly used can be seen in some of H. A. Murray's (1963) studies on stressful interpersonal disputations in which each subject's philosophy of life was attacked by a talented lawyer. It is reasonably clear from Murray's report that impact was achieved. But at what price in control? In these studies it is difficult to be certain exactly what was going on. The point we are trying to make is not that one method is uniformly better than the other but that the two goals of a social psychological experiment, impact and control, are in constant tension; as one becomes reasonably great, the other tends to be sacrificed.

Attaining impact may result not only in a diminution of experimental control but may also lead to an increase in the number of possible conceptual constructs associated with the independent variable. We shall call this "multiple meaning" because, quite literally, certain experimental manipulations contain a multitude of possible interpretations. The problem of multiple meaning is pervasive in social psychological experimentation primarily because the manipulations that make most sense to the subjects and produce the most impact tend to involve a complex bundle of stimuli; consequently these operations can be understood in more than one way. For most such research it is relatively easy to generate at least one possible interpretation that differs from the one proposed by the investigator. It is much more difficult to redesign the experiment so that it is free of alternative interpretations. In a few cases the most plausible alternative explanations can be eliminated by a slight change in the design or manipulations, but these are rare.

In examining a completed experiment, one asks the following question: What is the defining difference between our two (or ten) experimental conditions? What is happening in Condition A that makes the subjects behave differently (on some dependent variable) from the subjects in Condition B? Although it is usually possible to list several differences, this is not what the investigator originally had in mind. The investigator wanted to conceptualize some variable assumed to be theoretically important and that apparently caused the observed difference in the subject's behavior. We shall refer to this as the *conceptual variable*. The difficulty occurs because in building the experiment we do not deal directly with conceptual variables; we must deal with imperfect translations of conceptual variables.

Let us restate the problem in general terms. In any given experiment, the experimental treatments differ in many ways. We wish to isolate some conceptual variable that "explains" or "is the reason for" our observed differences. Actually, in the design (or planning stage) of experiments, the problem usually arises in the reverse order. We have a conceptual variable (e.g., unpleasant effort) whose effects we wish to study. There are many ways to translate this abstract conceptual variable into a concrete experimental operation. If we have our subjects recite a list of obscene words, how can we be sure that this operation is, in fact, an empirical realization of our conceptual variable? Or, conversely, how can we abstract a conceptual variable from our procedure?

The same dilemma holds for the dependent-variable. When we devise an elaborate rationale for inducing our subjects to express their attitudes toward the experiment or toward some social object in the form of ratings on a structured questionnaire, how can we be sure that these responses reflect the effect variable of conceptual interest rather than (or in addition to) the myriad of other complex decision rules our subjects may bring to bear in making such ratings? And how do we know that the functional relationships observed between treatment and effect, under a particular set of operations, represent the conceptual processes of interest?

TYPES OF VALIDITY

Basically, what we are talking about here is the *construct validity* of our experimental procedures and measures. To understand fully what is meant by construct validity, it is necessary to refer to the distinction made by Campbell and his colleagues (Campbell, 1957; Campbell and Stanley, 1963; Cook and Campbell, 1979) among different types of validity issues. In Campbell's taxonomy, the interpretation of research results may be assessed with respect to at least three different kinds of validity concerns—internal validity, external validity, and construct validity.

The meaningfulness of experimental research rests first of all on *internal validity*. Basically, internal validity refers to the confidence with which we can draw cause and effect conclusions from our research results. To what extent are we certain that the independent variable, or treatment, manipulated by the experimenter is the sole source or cause of systematic variation in the dependent variable? Threats to the internal validity of research re-

sults arise when the conditions under which an experiment is conducted produce systematic sources of variance that are irrelevant to the treatment variable and not under control of the researcher. The internal validity of a study is questioned, for instance, if groups of subjects exposed to different experimental conditions are not assigned randomly and are different from each other in some important ways before the research operations. In the field study of mood and altruism cited earlier, had it happened that the movie goers who attend sad films differed from attendees at other movies in their propensity to contribute to charities even before exposure to the movies themselves, that difference would have constituted a threat to the internal validity of the study. In that case, any differences obtained between groups in donations following the movies could be interpreted *either* as an effect of the movie mood induction *or* of personality differences unrelated to the treatment. Other factors that can undermine internal validity include the occurrence of events during the course of the research that are unrelated to the treatment variable and that produce different effects in the various experimental groups.

Internal validity is the *sine qua non* of good experimental research. The procedures for standardizing treatments, avoiding bias, and assuring comparability of subject groups discussed in our earlier section on planning and conducting laboratory experiments are all addressed to internal validity concerns. The essence of good experimental design is to control the assignment of subjects to treatment groups and the conditions of treatment delivery in such a way as to rule out or minimize threats to the internal validity of the study. Thus any differences obtained on outcome measures can be traced directly to the variations in treatment introduced by the experimenter.

Even when internal validity is high, however, there may be questions about the validity of interpretations of causal effects obtained in any given study. It is here that the distinction between external validity and construct validity becomes relevant. *External validity* refers to the robustness of a phenomenon—the extent to which a causal relationship, once identified in a particular setting with particular research subjects, can safely be generalized to other times, places, and people. Threats to external validity arise from potential interaction effects between the treatment variable of interest and the context in which it is delivered or the type of subject population involved. When laboratory experimentation in social psychology is criticized as being "the study of the psychology of the college sophomore," what is being called into question is the external validity of social psychological findings. Because so many laboratory experiments are conducted with college students as subjects, the truth of the causal relationships we observe may be limited to that particular population. If it happens that college students—with their youth, above-average intelligence, and nonrepresentative socioeconomic backgrounds—respond differently to our experimental treatment conditions than other types of people, then the external (but not internal) validity of our findings would be low.

The issue is actually a little more subtle. No one would seriously deny that Princeton students will respond differently to a particular experimental treatment than would a sample of fifty-year-old working-class immigrants. External validity refers to the extent to which a particular causal relationship is robust across populations or settings. Thus, if we were interested in the effects of lowered self-esteem on aggression, we might have to use different *techniques* to lower self-esteem in the two populations. Being informed that one had failed a test of creative problem-solving might lower self-esteem for Princeton sophomores, but would have little effect on our working-class immigrants. But if we can find another technique of lowering self-esteem among that second sample, we still must ask whether this lowered self-esteem will have the same effects on aggression in both samples.

External validity is related to settings as well as to subject populations. The external validity of a finding is challenged if the relationship between independent and dependent variables is altered if essentially the same research procedures were conducted in a different laboratory or field setting or under the influence of different experimenter characteristics. The program of research on obedience conducted by Milgram (1963; 1965) provides some good illustrations of various types of external validity concerns.

In order to reduce the challenge to external validity associated with using college students as subjects, Milgram recruited research participants from the local community. As a result, the subjects in his studies represented a considerably wider range of personal characteristics (age, occupation, intelligence, and so on) than the subjects in the majority of research studies at that time. Still, all of his subjects did share some common characteristics: They were all *males* who *volunteered* to participate in a psychology experiment; either or both of these may have been important factors in the amount of obedience Milgram obtained in his studies.

Above and beyond the potential effects of subject

characteristics, the external validity of Milgram's initial experiment may have been influenced by the distinctive setting in which it occurred. Because subjects were drawn from outside the university and because many had no previous experience with college, the prestige and respect associated with a research laboratory at Yale may have made the subjects more susceptible to the demands for compliance that the experiment entailed than they would have been in other settings. Since Milgram wanted to demonstrate that the obedience elicited by his experimental procedures was not limited to experiments located in high-prestige institutions, he undertook a replication of his experiment in a very different physical setting. Moving the research operation to a "seedy" office in the industrial town of Bridgeport, Connecticut, adopting a fictitious identity as a psychological research firm, Milgram hoped to minimize the reputational factors inherent in the Yale setting. In comparison with data obtained in the original study, the Bridgeport replication resulted in slightly lower but still dramatic rates of compliance to the experimenter. Thus, setting could be identified as a contributing but not crucial factor to the basic findings of the research.

The replication across different settings provided a valuable test of the external validity of Milgram's research conclusions. Because the research procedures were too costly and time-consuming to permit repeated replication in a wide variety of different settings, he tried to maximize in one replication the difference between settings on those factors judged most likely to be critical. The reasoning was that, if such a large difference had no significant influence on outcomes, other minor variations in setting could not be expected to alter the findings of the research. It should be kept in mind, however, that in varying some features of the research setting, many details of experimental procedures were left unchanged. In both settings, for instance, the experimenter who interacted with subjects was a male in a white laboratory coat. The number of such details of setting and context in any study is virtually infinite. Decisions regarding what details to alter in a systematic replication inevitably reflect the researcher's judgment as to which factors can be considered plausible threats to external validity and which can be ignored as trivial.

To question the external validity of a particular finding is not to deny that a cause and effect relationship has been demonstrated in the given research study but only to express doubt that the same effect could be demonstrated under different circumstances or with different subjects. Similarly, concerns with *construct validity* do not challenge the fact of an empirical relationship between an experimentally manipulated variable and the dependent measure but rather questions how that fact is to be interpreted in conceptual terms. Construct validity refers to the correct identification of the nature of the independent and dependent variables and the underlying relationship between them. To what extent do the operations and measures embodied in the experimental procedures of a particular study reflect the theoretical concepts that gave rise to the research in the first place? Threats to construct validity derive from errors of measurement, misspecification of research operations, and, in general, the complexity of experimental treatments with numerous stimulus features (the "multiple meanings" discussed earlier).

Controversy over the correct interpretation of the results obtained in the Aronson and Mills initiation experiment discussed earlier provides an example of construct validity issues. The complex social situation used by Aronson and Mills has many potential interpretations, including the possibility that reading obscene materials generated a state of sexual arousal that carried over to reactions to the group discussion. If that were the case, it could be that transfer of arousal, rather than effort justification, accounted for the higher attraction to the group.

A replication of the initiation experiment by Gerard and Mathewson (1966) ruled out this interpretation. Their experiment was constructed so as to differ from the Aronson and Mills study in many respects. For example, Gerard and Mathewson used electric shocks instead of the reading of obscene words as their empirical realization of severe initiation; the shocks were justified as a test of "emotionality" rather than as a test of embarrassment; the tape recording concerned a group discussion of cheating rather than of sex; and the measure of attractiveness of the group differed slightly. Thus sexual arousal was eliminated as a concomitant of the experimental procedures. The results confirmed the original findings: people who underwent painful electric shocks in order to become members of a dull group found that group to be more attractive than did people who underwent mild shocks. Such a confirmation of the basic initiation effect under quite different experimental operations supports, at least indirectly, the construct validity of the Aronson-Mills interpretation. A considerable amount of research in social psychology has been motivated by similar controversies over the valid interpretation of results obtained with complex experimental procedures.

VALIDITY AND DEMAND CHARACTERISTICS

The distinctions among the different types of validity can perhaps be better clarified with reference to the concept of "demand characteristics" discussed earlier. Demand characteristics have been cited as threats to research conclusions in ways that correspond to all three types of validity issues. In some cases, demand characteristics are interpreted as irrelevant instructional cues that are inadvertently tacked on to different experimental conditions but are not inherent in the experimental manipulation itself. In this guise, demand characteristics constitute a threat to the internal validity of an experiment. Results attributed to "experimenter-expectancy effects" (Rosenthal, 1966) are often of this sort, referring to inadvertent nonverbal cues communicated from experimenter to subject that vary with different experimental conditions but are not part of the intended treatment.

In other research contexts, demand characteristics are cues that are inherent in the experimental manipulation and associated with different experimental conditions in such a way as to affect the construct validity of the independent variable. In other words, variations in demand characteristics and variations in the experimental treatment are inextricably confounded. Milgram's (1963; 1965) experiments on obedience again serve as an example here. Milgram was interested in rates of compliance to legitimate *authority,* but in all variations of his experiments the authority figure was the scientist-researcher who was conducting the experiment. One cannot be certain, then, whether it was the implicit authority of the scientist-researcher that was responsible for the degree of obedience from subjects or other aspects inextricably associated with his role in the experimental situation (e.g., the normative value of science, the potential for negative personal evaluation of the subject, etc.). In variations of the experiment where the salience or presence of the scientist-authority were reduced, so were these other features. Thus, one cannot determine which one (or combination) was the operative independent variable. Such ambiguities make us hesitate to assume that the processes underlying obedience in this experimental setting are the same as those operating in other authority situations, such as those of Nazi Germany.

Finally, the concept of demand characteristics is frequently utilized to refer to the presumed artificiality of laboratory settings in which many experiments take place. In this sense, demand characteristics are equated with threats to external validity; they are not confounded with experimental treatment variations, since the laboratory setting is constant across experimental conditions. Instead, they constitute a limiting factor within which the treatment effect is expected to hold. In other words, situational cues inherent in the laboratory setting are assumed to interact with the treatment variable to produce an effect that may not occur in other settings.

Internal validity may be considered a property of a single experimental study. Our confidence in the validity of cause and effect results from a particular experiment may be enhanced if the finding is repeated on other occasions. However, the degree to which a study has internal validity is determined by characteristics intrinsic to the study itself. With sufficient knowledge of the conditions under which an experiment has been conducted, of the procedures associated with assignment of subjects, and of experimenter behavior, we should be able to assess whether the results of that study are internally valid. Issues involving construct validity and external validity, on the other hand, can seldom be resolved within the context of a single experiment but require multiple *conceptual replications* of research procedures. Here, again, an understanding of the distinction between the two types of validity is important to clarify the nature and purpose of replication. To demonstrate the external validity of a causal relationship, we must demonstrate that a particular treatment produces similar results in different contexts and with different types of subjects. Construct validity, however, is enhanced if a given relationship can be demonstrated to hold when *different* experimental operations are used to represent the same theoretical concepts. Of course, variations in context and research operations are neither independent nor mutually exclusive, and both are intimately related to alterations in the setting in which an experiment is conducted.

PROGRAMMATIC RESEARCH

The foregoing discussion of validity suggests that the solution to problems of conceptual ambiguity in social psychological research lies in programmatic research efforts in which *different* experimental procedures are used to explore the same conceptual relationship. Essentially, there are two properties that we demand of a series of experiments before we are convinced that we understand what the conceptual interpretation should be.

First, we ask for a number of empirical techniques that differ in as many ways as possible, having in common only our basic conceptual variable. If all these techniques yield the same result, then we become more and more convinced that the underlying variable that all techniques have in common is, in fact, the variable that is producing the results. Miller (1957) lists one example dealing with hunger in which this was done. Several different procedures that might be thought to influence hunger were manipulated in different experiments. These procedures included bilateral lesion in the region of the ventromedial nuclei of the hypothalamus, injection of enriched milk directly into the stomach, injection of isotonic saline directly into the stomach, and normal intake of milk via the mouth. (Interestingly enough, the different effects observed led to changes in the conception of hunger as a variable.) In the domain of social psychology, the Gerard and Mathewson (1966) conceptual replication of the Aronson and Mills initiation experiment addresses the same concern.

Second, we must show that a particular empirical realization of our independent variable produces a large number of different outcomes, all theoretically tied to the independent variable. Again, we point to Miller's (1957) examples of research on hunger. In one study he compared volume of food consumed, stomach contractions, rate of bar pressing to obtain food, and amount of quinine tolerated in the food. Some of the similar results obtained here with the various different measures of hunger lend support to an idea of hunger as a single unitary variable. Similarly, if it can be shown that asking subjects to read a list of obscene words not only makes them like the group they join as a result but also enhances the attractiveness of *any* outcome gained as a result of reading the words, we are more convinced it is effort that is important in this experiment. We might ask for effects that are even more removed but still theoretically follow from our ideas of unpleasant effort. If theory predicts that exerting unpleasant effort to attain an ambiguous goal should lead to seeking social support for the behavior, our confidence would be increased by an experiment which showed that subjects who had read a list of obscene words were more likely to seek social support for the behavior.

The logic of conceptual replication as a solution to the problems of construct validity is both clear and compelling, and variations on this theme have been discussed at length (e.g., Brunswik, 1956; Campbell, 1957). Yet techniques of conceptual replication have not been used consistently in social psychological experimentation; in fact, they are rarely seen. Far more frequent are single, isolated studies that stand in the literature as the only evidence for some process, with no evidence indicating that the leap from the conceptual variable to its supposed empirical realization was justified. Conceptual replications are not easy to design and are often difficult to interpret when they are carried out.

When it comes to interpretation, there is a fundamental asymmetry between positive and negative results of replications. If proper techniques have been employed to preclude bias, successful replications speak for themselves; failures to replicate are ambiguous and therefore require supplementary information. For these reasons, good programmatic research involves replication with systematic differences *and* similarities in procedures and operations so that differences in results are potentially interpretable. In many cases, including exact replication along with conceptual variations are useful. Suppose, for example, that Jones, a hypothetical psychologist at the University of Illinois, produces a specific experimental result using Illinois undergraduates as subjects. In addition, suppose that Smith, at Yale University, feels that these results were not a function of the conceptual variable proposed by Jones but rather were a function of some artifact in the procedure. Smith then repeats Jones's procedure in all respects save one: He changes the operations in order to eliminate this artifact. He fails to replicate and concludes that this demonstrates that Jones's results were artifactual. This is only one of many possible conclusions. Smith's failure to replicate has several possible causes and is therefore uninterpretable. It may be a function of a change in experimenter, a different subject population (Yale students may be different on many dimensions from Illinois students), or countless minor variations in the procedure such as tone of voice. Most of this ambiguity could be eliminated by a balanced design that includes an "exact" replication of the conditions run by the original experimenter. That is, suppose Smith's design had included a repeat of Jones's conditions with the suspected artifact left in, and his results approximated those of Jones's experiment. If, as part of the design, Smith changed the experiment slightly and produced no differences, or differences in the opposite direction, one could then be sure that this result was not merely a function of incidental differences like the experimenter or the subject population but must be a function of the change in the procedure. If he failed even to replicate Jones's basic experiment, we would have to conclude that there was some important factor in the variables used in the original experiment, that the results are limited to a particular population, that either Jones or Smith (or both) had unconsciously biased their data, that Smith was simply incompetent, and so on.

In many situations it is difficult to modify the particular operational definition of the independent variable without changing the entire experimental setting. This is most dramatically true when conceptual replication involves a shift from laboratory setting to field setting. The potential complementary aspects of different research paradigms is best exemplified when operations of independent and dependent variables in laboratory procedures are significantly modified to take advantage of field settings so as to embed them appropriately in this altered context. Such modifications often involve fundamental rethinking about the conceptual variables; it is "back to square one," with attendant costs in time and effort. If the result is a successful conceptual replication, the effort has paid off handsomely in enhanced validity for our theoretical constructs. But what if the replication fails to confirm our original findings? In this case, the multitude of procedural differences that could have *increased* our confidence (with a successful replication) now contributes to the ambiguity.

In an overview of classic research on attitude change, Hovland (1959) pointed out that results from research in experimental laboratory settings tend to differ considerably from results obtained in quasi experiments in field settings. The most striking differences are in the degree of attitude change created by the persuasive communications. Research conducted in the two settings also tends to differ systematically along a number of dimensions of potential relevance to the impact of communications. Laboratory studies differ from field studies in the type of populations utilized, the time interval between exposure to communications and measures of attitude change, the type of attitude issue being discussed, and whether or not exposure to the persuasive communication was voluntary or involuntary. Any or all of these factors could operate to alter the relationships obtained between characteristics of the persuasive communication and amount of attitude change. Controlled variations in both research settings are needed in order to determine which interaction effects are critical.

EXPERIMENTAL REALISM VERSUS MUNDANE REALISM

Many social psychologists believe that the primary virtue of doing research in field settings lies in its realism. Our discussion of the need for conceptual replication and programmatic research suggests that the value of field experimentation rests not on its being more "real" than laboratory research but on its being "more different."

This is not to imply that realism is an unimportant feature of experimental research; rather, we contend that realism is not simply a matter of field versus lab settings. Aronson and Carlsmith (1968) distinguished broadly between two ways in which an experiment can be said to be realistic. In one sense, an experiment is realistic if the situation is involving to the subjects, if they are forced to take it seriously, if it has impact on them. This kind of realism they called *experimental realism*. In another sense, the term "realism" can refer to the extent to which events occurring in the research setting are likely to occur in the normal course of the subjects' lives, that is, in the "real world." They called this type of realism *mundane realism*. The fact that an event is similar to events that occur in the real world does not endow it with importance. Many events that occur in the real world are boring and unimportant in the lives of the actors or observers. Thus, it is possible to put a subject to sleep if an experimental event is high on mundane realism but remains low on experimental realism.

Mundane realism and experimental realism are not polar concepts; a particular technique may be high on both mundane realism and experimental realism, low on both, or high on one and low on the other. Perhaps the difference between experimental and mundane realism can be clarified by citing a couple of examples. Let us first consider Asch's (1951) experiment on perceptual judgment. Here the subjects were asked to judge the length of lines and then were confronted with unanimous judgments by a group of peers that contradicted their own perceptions. For most subjects this experiment seems to have contained a good deal of experimental realism. Whether subjects yielded to group pressure or stood firm, the vast majority underwent a rather difficult experience that caused them to squirm, sweat, and exhibit other signs of tension and discomfort. They were involved, upset, and deeply concerned about the evidence being presented to them. We may assume that they were reacting to a situation that was as "real" for them as any of their ordinary experiences. However, the experiment was hardly realistic in the mundane sense. Recall that the subjects were judging a very clear physical event. In everyday life it is rare to find oneself in a situation where the direct and unambiguous evidence of one's senses is contradicted by the unanimous judgments of one's peers. Although the judging of lines is perhaps not important or realistic in the mundane sense, one cannot deny the impact of having one's sensory input contradicted by a unanimous majority.

On the other hand, consider an experiment by Walster, Aronson, and Abrahams (1966) that, although high on mundane realism, was low indeed on experimental realism. In this experiment, subjects read a newspaper article about the prosecution of criminal suspects in Portugal. In the article, various statements were attributed to a prosecuting attorney or to a convicted criminal. The article was embedded in a real newspaper and, hence, the subjects were doing something they frequently do—reading facts in a newspaper. Thus the experiment had a great deal of mundane realism. However nothing was happening to the subject. Very few U.S. college students are seriously affected by reading a rather pallid article about a remote situation in a foreign country. The procedure did not have a high degree of experimental realism.

Murray's (1963) procedure, cited earlier, would appear to be high on both mundane and experimental realism. Recall that in this study the general philosophy of a subject was attacked by a skillful confederate. There is no doubt that this procedure had a good deal of impact on the subject (experimental realism). At the same time, it is the kind of situation which can and does occur in dormitory bull sessions (mundane realism).

It is frequently argued (by students as well as by some professionals) that experiments in social psychology are artificial and therefore worthless: The fact that a subject enters a laboratory lends an unreal atmosphere to the proceedings, thus making the data invalid. Although there may be some merit to this argument, we feel it rests on a confusion between experimental and mundane realism. There are some experiments that are so deficient in experimental realism that they do not even capture the attention of the subjects, let alone influence their behavior. It is the major objective of an experiment—lab or field —to have the greatest possible impact on a subject within the limits of ethical considerations and requirements of control. In effect, the experimental situation and operations must hit the subject squarely between the eyes; that is, they must have experimental realism. It is difficult to argue that the Asch experiment or the Milgram experiment had no impact on the subjects.

Although a laboratory experiment may be a precise analogue of some process occurring in the outside world, we still cannot be sure that the same variables will operate in a new situation. It should be obvious by this time that one cannot guarantee external validity simply by injecting mundane realism into an experiment. This factor does not increase our confidence in our ability to generalize from the results, for in the final analysis the question is an empirical one. In certain situations, increasing mundane realism will also increase impact to some extent. However, if an experimental procedure already has a good deal of impact, it is unnecessary to make it occur in a real-world setting.

On the other hand, occasionally the requirements of an experiment are such that adding mundane realism is the only way that impact can be achieved. For example, the experienced experimental social psychologist knows that in the laboratory it is difficult either to convince subjects that someone is angry at them or to provoke subjects into expressing aggressive behavior. That is, most subjects believe that such behavior is inappropriate within the confines of an experimental situation. Consequently, if one is performing an experiment in which the manipulation or expression of hostility is essential, it may be helpful to use an approach that has mundane realism. The experiment by Abelson and Miller (1967) provides an example of the creative employment of mundane realism. Recall that in this experiment a confederate, who appeared to be an ordinary person sitting on a park bench, disagreed with the subject and even ridiculed the person. As predicted, this experience had the effect of strengthening the initial attitudes of the subject.

In our opinion, concern over the artificiality of an experiment is not idle concern; it is simply misplaced. In part, it is a reflection of the fact that in social psychology we lack confidence in our operational variables because they have not been purified through systematic conceptual replication. All experimental procedures are "contrived" in the sense that they are invented. Indeed, it can be said that the art of experimentation rests primarily on the skill of the investigator in creating the procedure that is the most accurate realization of his or her conceptual variable and that has the greatest impact and the most credibility for the subject.

It is in this realm of conceptual replication with different scenarios that the interplay between lab and field experimentation is most clear. However, in considering these interrelationships, the tradeoff mentioned earlier between control and impact in different experimental settings becomes especially salient. In order to be defensible, weaknesses in one aspect of experimental design must be offset by strengths or advantages in other features, or the whole research effort is called into question. This dictum is particularly applicable to field experiments in which inevitable increases in cost and effort are frequently accompanied by decreases in precision and

control that can be justified only if there are corresponding gains in construct validity, impact, or the generalizability of findings.

FIELD EXPERIMENTATION AND APPLICATION

Conceptual replication highlights the advantages of combining laboratory and field experimentation for purposes of theory-building. In addition, the interplay between laboratory and field research is also critical to the development of an effective *applied* social psychology. Basic experimental research may isolate important causal processes; however, convincing demonstrations that those processes operate in applied settings are essential before theory can be converted into practice.

The research literature on psychological responsibility and control provides a particularly good example of how a synthesis between field and laboratory experiments can work at its best. It began with animal research in the laboratory (Brady, 1958), extended to field studies of stress in humans (e.g., Janis, 1958; Egbert, Battit, Tundorf, and Becker, 1963), then moved to laboratory analogues (e.g., Glass and Singer, 1972; Kanfer and Seidner, 1973), and returned to the field (e.g., Johnson and Leventhal, 1974; Langer and Rodin, 1976; Mills and Krantz, 1979). Results from both settings repeatedly demonstrated the potent effect of the perception of control or responsibility on an individual's ability to cope with stressful events. Even the *illusion* that one has control over the onset or the consequences of potential stressors is apparently sufficient to increase tolerance for stress and reduce adverse effects. As a result of these findings, procedures developed for inducing actual or perceived personal control are applicable in medical practice and in the administration of health-care institutions. At the same time, the fact that field applications permit testing research hypotheses in the presence of severe, noxious, or potentially life-threatening situations has contributed substantially to our theoretical understanding of the role of psychological factors in physiological processes.

Another good example of the creative interplay between laboratory and field experimentation is the work of Aronson and his colleagues on the effects of cooperative learning (Aronson *et al.,* 1978; Aronson and Bridgeman, 1979; Aronson and Osherow, 1980). The research began as an experimental intervention in response to a crisis in the Austin (Texas) school system following its desegregation. Aronson and his colleagues observed the dynamics of the classroom and diagnosed that a major cause of the existing tension was the competitive atmosphere that exacerbated the usual problems brought about by desegregation. They then changed the atmosphere of existing classrooms by restructuring the learning environment so that some students were teaching one another in small, interdependent "jigsaw" groups, while others continued to study in more traditional classrooms.

The results of this and subsequent field experiments showed that the cooperative classroom atmosphere decreased negative stereotyping, increased cross-ethnic liking, increased self-esteem, improved classroom performance, and increased empathic role taking. At the same time, Aronson and his colleagues were able to enhance their understanding of the underlying dynamic of this cooperative behavior by closer scrutiny under controlled laboratory conditions. For example, in one such laboratory experiment, they showed that, in a competitive situation, individuals make situational self-attributions for failure and dispositional self-attributions for success, while making the reverse attributions to their opponent. However, in a cooperative structure, individuals gave their partners the same benefit of the doubt that they gave to themselves, that is, dispositional attributions for success and situational attributions for failure (Stephan *et al.,* 1977, 1978).

Field experimentation in applied settings often provides an opportunity for impact and involvement of research subjects that vastly exceeds any ever achieved in the laboratory. However, the focus of such research also tends to be more limited than the general tests of theory underlying most laboratory research efforts, because they are forced to deal only with variables found in the particular applied context under study. If the distinctive contribution of experimental social psychology to the general body of knowledge is ever to be realized, an optimal integration of theory-oriented laboratory research with applied field experimentation will be required.

At present we are concerned because the alternative research modes in social psychology seem, for the most part, to be functioning in isolation from each other. What is needed now is a new attempt at synthesis, that is to construct a more limited (and perhaps closer to the original) version of the Lewinian model of the interplay between laboratory and field research. Such a synthesis will require a concern with discovering more specifiable relationships rather than with attempts to find sweeping general theories of human social behavior. It will require an emphasis on assessing the relative importance of several variables, which all influence an aspect of multiply-determined behavior, rather than on testing to see if a particular variable has a "significant" impact. It will require a sensitivity to the interaction between research design and research setting and the benefits of multiple methodologies. And it will require a continued deep concern with ethical behavior and, at the same time, a real attempt to ensure that those concerns do not strangle creativity and do not prevent the addressing of serious and important social psychological questions in unique ways that necessitate our engaging in equally serious and important experimental interventions both inside and outside the laboratory.

REFERENCES

Abelson, R. P., and J. C. Miller (1967). Negative persuasion via personal insult. *J. exp. soc. Psychol., 3,* 321–333.

APA Ad hoc Committee on Ethical Standards (1982). Ethical principles in the conduct of research with human participants. Washington, D.C.: American Psychological Association. See also, *American Psychologist* (1981) *36,* 637–638.

Aderman, D. (1972). Elation, depression, and helping behavior. *J. Pers. soc. Psychol., 24,* 91–101.

Aronson, E. (1961). The effect of effort on the attractiveness of rewarded and unrewarded stimuli. *J. abnorm. soc. Psychol., 63,* 375–380.

——— (1963). Effect of the severity of threat on the devaluation of forbidden behavior. *J. abnorm. soc. Psychol., 66,* 584–588.

——— (1966). Avoidance of inter-subject communication. *Psychol. Reports, 19,* 238.

Aronson, E., and D. Bridgeman (1979). Jigsaw groups and the desegregated classroom: in pursuit of common goals. *Pers. soc. Psychol. Bull., 5,* 438–446.

Aronson, E., and J. M. Carlsmith (1962). Performance expectancy as a determinant of actual performance. *J. abnorm. soc. Psychol., 65,* 178–182.

——— (1963). Effect of the severity of threat on the devaluation of forbidden behavior. *J. abnorm. soc. Psychol., 66,* 583–588.

——— (1968). Experimentation in social psychology. In G. Lindzey and E. Aronson (Eds.), *The handbook of social psychology.* Vol. 2. Reading, Mass.: Addison-Wesley. Pp. 1–79.

Aronson, E., and V. M. Cope (1968). My enemy's enemy is my friend. *J. Pers. soc. Psychol., 8,* 8–12.

Aronson, E., and D. Linder (1965). Gain and loss of esteem as determinants of interpersonal attractiveness. *J. exp. soc. Psychol., 1,* 156–171.

Aronson, E., and D. Mettee (1968). Dishonest behavior as a function of differential levels of induced self-esteem. *J. Pers. soc. Psychol., 9,* 121–127.

Aronson, E., and J. Mills (1959). The effect of severity of initiation on liking for a group. *J. abnorm. soc. Psychol., 59,* 177–181.

Aronson, E., and N. Osherow (1980). Cooperation, prosocial behavior, and academic performance: experiments in the desegregated classroom. *App. soc. Psychol. Ann., 1*, 163–196.

Aronson, E., C. Stephan, J. Sikes, N. Blaney, and M. Snapp (1978). *The jigsaw classroom*. Beverly Hills: Sage Publications.

Aronson, E., J. Turner, and J. M. Carlsmith (1963). Communicator credibility and communication discrepancy as determinants of opinion change. *J. abnorm. soc. Psychol., 67*, 31–36.

Aronson, E., B. Willerman, and J. Floyd (1966). The effect of a pratfall on increasing interpersonal attractiveness. *Psychon. Sci., 4*, 227–228.

Asch, S. (1951). Effects of group pressure upon the modification and distortion of judgment. In H. Guetzkow (Ed.), *Groups, leadership, and men*. Pittsburgh: Carnegie Press. Pp. 177–190.

Ax, A. F. (1953). The physiological differentiation between fear and anger in humans. *Psychosom. Med., 15*, 433–442.

Back, K. W. (1951). Influences through social communication. *J. abnorm. soc. Psychol., 46*, 9–23.

Brady, J. (1958). Ulcers in "executive monkeys." *Scientific Amer., 199*, 95–100.

Brehm, J. W., and A. H. Cole (1966). Effect of a favor which reduces freedom. *J. Pers. soc. Psychol., 3*, 420–426.

Brewer, M. B. (1976). Randomized invitations: one solution to the problem of voluntary treatment selection in program evaluation research. *Soc. Sci. Research, 5*, 315–323.

Brewer, M. B., V. Dull, and L. Lui. (1981). Perceptions of the elderly: stereotypes as prototypes. *J. Pers. soc. Psychol., 41*, 656–670.

Brunswik, E. (1956). *Perception and the representative design of psychological experiments* (2nd ed.). Berkeley: Univ. of California Press.

Campbell, D. T. (1957). Factors relevant to validity of experiments in social settings. *Psychol. Bull., 54*, 297–312.

_____ (1963). From description to experimentation: interpreting trends as quasi-experiments. In C. W. Harris (Ed.), *Problems in measuring change*. Madison: Univ. of Wisconsin Press. Pp. 212–242.

Campbell, D. T., and J. C. Stanley (1963). Experimental and quasi-experimental designs for research. In N. L. Gage (Ed.), *Handbook of research on teaching*. Chicago: Rand McNally. Pp. 171–246.

Carlsmith, J. M., B. E. Collins, and R. L. Helmreich (1966). Studies in forced compliance: I. The effect of pressure for compliance on attitude change produced by face-to-face role playing and anonymous essay writing. *J. Pers. soc. Psychol., 4*, 1–3.

Carlsmith, J. M., and A. E. Gross (1969). Some effects of guilt on compliance. *J. Pers. soc. Psychol., 11*, 232–239.

Cialdini, R. B., R. J. Borden, A. Thorne, M. R. Walker, S. Freeman, and L. R. Sloan (1976). Basking in reflected glory: three (football) field studies. *J. Pers. soc. Psychol., 34*, 366–375.

Cohen, A. R. (1959). Communication discrepancy and attitude change. *J. Pers., 27*, 386–396.

Cook, T. D., and D. T. Campbell (1979). *Quasi-experiments: design and analysis issues for field settings*. Shokie, Ill.: Rand McNally.

Cottrell, N. B. (1965). Performance expectancy as a determinant of actual performance: a replication with a new design. *J. Pers. soc. Psychol., 2*, 685–691.

Dawes, R. B., J. McTavish, and H. Shaklee (1977). Behavior, communication, and assumptions about other people's behavior in a common dilemmas situation. *J. Pers. soc. Psychol., 35*, 1–11.

Duval, S., and R. Wicklund (1973). Effects of objective self-awareness on attribution of causality. *J. exp. soc. Psychol., 9*, 17–31.

Egbert, L. D., G. E. Battit, H. Tundorf, and H. K. Becker (1963). The value of the preoperative visit by an anesthetist. *J. Ameri. medical Assoc., 185*, 553–555.

Festinger, L., and J. M. Carlsmith (1959). Cognitive consequences of forced compliance. *J. abnorm. soc. Psychol., 58*, 203–210.

Festinger, L., and J. Thibaut (1951). Interpersonal communication in small groups. *J. abnorm. soc. Psychol., 46*, 92–99.

Freedman, J. L. (1965). Long-term behavioral effects of cognitive dissonance. *J. exp. soc. Psychol., 1*, 145–155.

Freedman, J. L., and S. C. Fraser (1966). Compliance without pressure: the foot-in-the-door technique. *J. Pers. soc. Psychol., 4*, 195–202.

Gerard, H. B., and G. C. Mathewson (1966). The effects of severity of initiation on liking for a group: a replication. *J. exp. soc. Psychol. 2*, 278–287.

Gergen, K. J. (1973). Social psychology as history. *J. Pers. soc. Psychol. 26*, 309–320.

Glass, D., and J. Singer (1972). *Urban stress*. New York: Academic Press.

Gross, A. E., and I. Fleming (1982). 20 years of deception in social psychology. *Pers. soc. Psychol. Bull. 8*, 402–408.

Hamilton, D. L., and T. L. Rose (1980). Illusory correlation and the maintenance of stereotypic beliefs. *J. Pers. soc. Psychol., 39*, 832–845.

Haney, C., C. Banks, and P. Zimbardo (1973). Interpersonal dynamics in a simulated prison. *Int. J. Criminology Penology, 1*, 69–97.

Henshel, R. L. (1980). The purpose of laboratory experimentation and the virtues of deliberate artificiality. *J. exp. soc. Psychol., 16*, 466–478.

Higgins, E. T., W. S. Rholes, and C. R. Jones (1977). Category accessibility and impression formation. *J. exper. soc. Psychol., 13*, 141–154.

Holmes, D. S. (1976a). Debriefing after psychological experiments: I effectiveness of postdeception dehoaxing. *Amer. Psychologist, 31*, 858–867.

_____ (1976b). Debriefing after psychological experiments: II effectiveness of postexperimental desensitizing. *Amer. Psychologist, 31*, 868–875.

Hovland, C. I. (1959). Reconciling conflicting results derived from experimental and survey studies of attitude change. *Amer. Psychologist, 14*, 8–17.

Hovland, C. I., and W. Weiss (1951). The influence of source credibility on communication effectiveness. *Publ. Opin. Quart., 15*, 635–650.

Janis, I. L. (1958). *Psychological stress*. New York: Wiley.

Jemmott, J. B. III (1982). Mediation in stress and illness research: the inhibited power motivation hypothesis. Colloquium. Department of Psychology, University of California, Santa Cruz.

Jemmott, J. B. III, and S. E. Locke (1984). Psychosocial factors, immunologic mediation and human susceptibility to infectious diseases: how much do we know? *Psychol. Bull., 95,* 78–108.

Johnson, J. E., and H. Leventhal (1974). Effects of accurate expectations and behavioral instructions on reactions during a noxious medical examination. *J. Pers. soc. Psychol., 29,* 710–718.

Jones, E., and H. Sigall (1971). The bogus pipeline: a new paradigm for measuring affect and attitude. *Psychol. Bull., 76,* 349–364.

Kanfer, F. H., and M. L. Seidner (1973). Self control: factors enhancing tolerance of noxious stimulation. *J. Pers. soc. Psychol., 25,* 281–389.

Katzev, R., and W. Bachman (1982). Effects of deferred payment and fare rate manipulations on urban bus ridership. *J. Applied Psychol., 67,* 83–88.

Kiesler, C., R. E. Nisbett, and M. Zanna (1969). On inferring one's beliefs from one's behavior. *J. Pers. soc. Psychol., 11,* 321–327.

Landy, D., and E. Aronson (1968). Liking for an evaluator as a function of his discernment. *J. Pers. soc. Psychol., 9,* 133–141.

Langer, E. J. (1975). The illusion of control. *J. Pers. soc. Psychol., 32,* 311–328.

Langer, E. J., and J. Rodin (1976). The effects of choice and enhanced personal responsibility for the aged: a field experiment in an institutional setting. *J. Pers. soc. Psychol., 34,* 191–198.

Lewin, K., R. Lippitt, and R. K. White (1939). Patterns of aggressive behavior in experimentally created "social climates." *J. soc. Psychol., 10,* 271–299.

Marlowe, D., R. Frager, and R. L. Nuttall (1965). Commitment to action taking as a consequence of cognitive dissonance. *J. Pers. soc. Psychol., 2,* 864–868.

Milgram, S. (1963). Behavioral study of obedience. *J. abnorm. soc. Psychol., 67,* 371–378.

_____ (1965). Some conditions of obedience and disobedience to authority. *Hum. Relat., 18,* 57–76.

_____ (1966). Four studies using the lost letter technique. Address given at American Psychological Association, New York, September

_____ (1974). *Obedience to authority: an experimental view.* New York: Harper & Row.

Miller, N. E. (1957). Experiments on motivation. *Science, 126,* 1271–1278.

Mills, R. T., and D. S. Krantz (1979). Information, choice, and reactions to stress: a field experiment in a blood bank with laboratory analogue. *J. Pers. soc. Psychol., 37,* 608–620.

Mook, D. G. (1980). In defense of external invalidity. *Amer. Psychologist, 38,* 379–388.

Moore, B. S., B. Underwood, and D. L. Rosenhan (1973). Affect and altruism. *Develop. Psychol., 8,* 99–104.

Murray, H. A. (1963). Studies of stressful interpersonal disputations. *Amer. Psychologist, 18,* 28–36.

Nisbett, R. E., and T. D. Wilson (1977). Telling more than we can know: verbal reports on mental processes. *Psychol. Review, 84,* 231–259.

Orne, M. (1962). On the social psychology of the psychological experiment. *Amer. Psychologist, 17,* 776–783.

Parker, S. D., M. B. Brewer, and J. R. Spencer (1980). Natural disaster, perceived control, and attributions to fate. *Pers. soc. Psychol. Bull., 6,* 454–459.

Piliavin, I. M., J. Rodin, and J. A. Piliavin (1969). Good samaritanism: an underground phenomenon? *J. Pers. soc. Psychol., 13,* 289–299.

Rosenthal, R. (1963). On the social psychology of the psychological experiment: the experimenter's hypothesis as unintended determinant of the experimental results. *Amer. Scientist, 51,* 268–283.

Rosenthal, R. (1966). *Experimenter effects in behavioral research.* New York: Appleton-Century-Crofts.

Sable, A. (1978). Deception in social science research: is informed consent possible? *Hastings Center Report, 8,* 40–46.

Schachter, S. (1951). Deviation, rejection, and communication. *J. abnorm. soc. Psychol., 46,* 190–207.

_____ (1959). *The psychology of affiliation: experimental studies of the sources of gregariousness.* Stanford: Stanford Univ. Press.

Schachter, S., and J. E. Singer (1962). Cognitive, social and physiological determinants of emotional state. *Psychol. Rev., 69,* 379–399.

Schlenker, B. R. (1974). Social psychology as science. *J. Pers. soc. Psychol., 29,* 1–15.

Sigall, H., E. Aronson, and T. Van Hoose (1970). The cooperative subject: myth or reality? *J. exp. soc. Psychol., 6,* 1–10.

Sigall, H., and R. Page (1971). Current stereotypes: a little fading, a little faking. *J. Pers. soc. Psychol., 18,* 247–255.

Snyder, M., E. D. Tanke, and E. Berscheid (1977). Social perception and interpersonal behavior: on the self-fulfilling nature of social stereotypes. *J. Pers. soc. Psychol., 35,* 656–666.

Stephan, C., J. Kennedy, and E. Aronson (1977). The effects of friendship and outcome on task attribution. *Sociometry, 40,* 107–112.

Stephan, C., N. R. Presser, J. C. Kennedy, and E. Aronson (1978). Attributions to success and failure after cooperative or competitive interaction. *Europ. J. soc. Psychol., 8,* 269–274.

Taylor, S. E., and S. T. Fiske (1975). Point of view and perceptions of causality. *J. Pers. soc. Psychol., 32,* 439–445.

Underwood, B., W. J. Froming, and B. S. Moore (1977). Mood, attention, and altruism: a search for mediating variables. *Dev. Psychol., 13,* 541–542.

Wallace, J., and E. Sadalla (1966). Behavioral consequences of transgression: I. The effects of social recognition. *J. exp. Res. Pers., I,* 187–194.

Walster, E., E. Aronson, and D. Abrahams (1966). On increasing the persuasiveness of a low prestige communicator. *J. exp. soc. Psychol., 2,* 325–342.

Webb, E. J., D. T. Campbell, R. D. Schwartz, and L. Sechrest (1966). *Unobtrusive measures: nonreactive research in the social sciences.* Chicago: Rand McNally.

Webb, E. S., D. T. Campbell, R. D. Schwartz, L. Sechrest, and J. Grove (1981). *Nonreactive measures in the social sciences.* Boston: Houghton Mifflin.

Zimbardo, P. G. (1965). The effect of effort and improvisation on self-persuasion produced by role playing. *J. exp. soc. Psychol., 1,* 103–120.

CHAPTER 9

Quantitative Methods for Social Psychology

David A. Kenny
The University of Connecticut

During the 1970s and early 1980s we witnessed major developments in data analysis, many of which are described in this chapter. These developments were facilitated by the use of high-speed computers that relieved researchers of the burden of tedious computation. We no longer need to devote most of our efforts to learning computational formulas and algorithms. We need now to focus our attention on *statistical models* and *modeling* in particular.

Issues in the analysis of models can be divided into four types: specification, identification, estimation, and testing. *Specification* refers to the process of translating theory into a statistical model. *Identification* refers to whether there is sufficient information available to esti-

Supported in part by National Science Foundation Grants BNS–7913820 and BNS–8210137 and by the MacArthur Foundation during my stay at the Center for Advanced Study in the Behavioral Sciences, 1982–1983. I would like to thank Mark Appelbaum, Jeffrey S. Berman, Marilynn Brewer, Steven H. Cohen, Dennis Deal, Susan Fiske, Paul Gondek, Judith Harackiewicz, Charles Judd, Lawrence La Voie, Michael Milburn, Lincoln Moses, Steven Needel, and Robert Rosenthal, who provided me with comments on an earlier version of this chapter. Lauren Hafner assisted me in the survey of 1978 journals. I would like to dedicate this chapter to Donald T. Campbell.

mate the model's parameters. *Estimation* refers to the use of statistical procedures to obtain the best guess of the value of the model's parameters. *Testing* refers to the ability of a model to reproduce the data. Let us consider each in more detail.

Very often arguments seemingly about statistics are really arguments about theory. For instance, the choice between oblique and orthogonal rotations in factor analysis should be based on whether or not theory tells us the constructs are correlated and not based on some statistical principle. The process of translating theory, ideas, and even hunches into a model is called specification. Specification is made very difficult in social psychology because our theories are rarely elaborated well enough to tell us how to set up the research. Even when theoretical notions are vague, it is still possible to make theory-consistent choices in research. Research in general and data analysis in particular are theory-laden. The fundamental questions in data analysis are not statistical but theoretical.

Identification is a technical but crucial part of modeling. Before researchers gather and analyze their data, they must determine whether there is sufficient information to estimate the parameters of interest. A simple example might best illustrate this abstract concept. If an investigator is to estimate a treatment effect, a control group is absolutely necessary. Thus to measure or identify a treatment effect, the researcher needs both an experimental and a control group. The theory of identification tells what type of design, how many measurements, and what type of restrictions are needed for a given model. For instance, the classical multiple-factor analysis model is not identified even with 100 measures. The fact that the solution can be rotated implies that there are many equally good estimates of the model's parameters, and hence the model is not identified. Perfect multicollinearity in multiple regression is another example of a failure to identify a model. If two variables are perfectly correlated, we cannot simultaneously measure the effects of each.

Given that there is a unique mathematical solution for a model's parameters, the principles of statistics can be brought to bear to derive the "best" solution. Least squares or the method of maximum likelihood can be used to estimate parameters. Most of us think that estimation (i.e., formulas and computations) is the main part of data analysis. However, since the advent of high-speed computers we can, for the most part, delegate estimation problems to the computer scientist and statistician. The essential aspect of data analysis is the examination of the parameter estimates. Perhaps the most common mistake that researchers make is that they fail to study carefully the estimates of the model's parameters. Means and regression coefficients are ignored while F- and t-values are carefully scrutinized.

The researcher can evaluate how consistent the model is with the data, i.e., whether the data support the model. Measures such as R^2 for multiple regression and χ^2 for log-linear and structural models are measures of model fit. A high R^2 and a low χ^2 mean good fit. The researcher can evaluate the extent to which simpler models are just as adequate in reproducing the data. For instance, the researcher may wish to evaluate whether certain parameters of the model are different from zero. This can be done by estimating a model that includes those parameters (model I) and a second model (model II) in which those parameters are set to zero. Since model I is more complex than model II, it will reproduce the data at least as well as model II. At issue is whether poorer fit of model II is only due to chance. Thus is the R^2 of model I significantly larger than the R^2 of model II? With χ^2 as a measure of fit, the interest is whether the χ^2 of model I is significantly smaller than the χ^2 of model II.

Tukey (1969) has proposed two different approaches to model specification: confirmatory and exploratory. In confirmatory data analysis the researcher has strong notions concerning (1) how to measure the variables, (2) what interactions or complex terms are in the data, (3) what observations are correlated, and (4) what the general pattern of results is. The experimenter may be dead wrong about the answers to these questions, but he or she is willing to bet on the pattern of results.

With exploratory data analysis the researcher has only hunches. The theoretical ideas of a research area are not rich enough to specify fully the design, the measures, and the statistical model. In such cases the researcher cannot and should not impose much structure on the data gathering and analysis. Data must be collected, arranged, and analyzed to allow the data "to speak for themselves." Exploratory data analysis is primarily descriptive and makes few assumptions. Data are used not to test hypotheses but to generate hypotheses. The methods of exploratory data analysis are extensively detailed in Tukey (1977) and Mosteller and Tukey (1977).

In practice, research is and ought to be a mixture of both the confirmatory and the exploratory modes. When possible, the researcher should set up explicit hypotheses and test their validity. But the researcher should be willing to learn from the data and use the data to generate hypotheses for future research. Generally, in social psychology, exploratory data analysis is not undertaken, and if it is, the researcher does not admit that what was learned was *post hoc*. Thus what little exploratory analysis is done is usually sold as confirmatory.

The basic organization of this chapter is topical. My choice of topics is guided first by current practice. Thus the largest section of the chapter is devoted to analysis of variance even though I feel it is overused in social psychology. Second, I chose to discuss methods that are underutilized but are important in social psychology. Here I include multiple regression, structural equation modeling, log-linear analysis, and designs for social interaction. Throughout, I have tried when possible to discuss issues in terms of model specification, identification, estimation, and testing. Certain topics are not reviewed in this chapter. Multidimensional scaling (Kruskal and Wish, 1978) and the analysis of quasi-experimental designs in general (Cook and Campbell, 1979; Judd and Kenny, 1981a) and the time-series designs in particular (Gottman, 1981; McCleary and Hay, 1980) have not been covered in this chapter because there are comprehensive treatments elsewhere.

Before considering specific analysis techniques, a very troubling matter must be discussed. Errors are frequently made in reporting means, degrees of freedom, correlations, and inferential statistics. These errors in computation and reporting can be reduced—but not by pious statements about being careful and suggestions of taking one's time. Rather, a number of concrete strategies can make the results more accurate.

First, when using computers for complex analyses, one should always print, for each analysis, the means and variances of each variable in the analysis. One should then compare these means and variances to prior runs to ensure that the variables used are the correct ones. This is especially important when new variables are being created. Errors are one of the prices that we pay for using computers.

Second, special care is required in reporting *negative* correlations, regression coefficients, and the like. Too often investigators or their typists forget to include a negative sign, and this omission obviously has serious consequences. For hand computations the ingredients that have negative signs should be carefully noted.

Third, it is wise to probe the analysis by computing some results by hand, trying a different computer program, studying carefully *all* the output, and being on the lookout for anomalous results. We should at times have others redo our analysis. It is also helpful to look at descriptive results and to examine residuals. (A careful examination of the data not only tells us if the correct analysis was done, but it also may give us new hints about how the model might be changed.) Other equivalent procedures that should give the same results should be tried. The data should be probed not only when we are dissatisfied with the results but also when we feel comfortable about the results. Remember that an intelligent researcher knows how easy it is to make mistakes and guards against them.

ANALYSIS OF VARIANCE

The analysis of variance is still the most common analysis strategy in social psychology. In a survey of 1978 articles in the *Journal of Personality and Social Psychology, Journal of Experimental Social Psychology,* and *Social Psychology Quarterly* (nee *Sociometry*), 84 percent of the articles that employed statistical analysis used analysis of variance as one method of analysis. Its role in social psychology far transcends that of an analysis tool, and it has now become the framework in which we think

about theoretical and research issues. Dorwin Cartwright (1979) has wondered aloud if our journals would have anything to print if it were prohibited. It was only a matter of time before someone proposed that the naive social psychologist uses analysis of variance to make sense out of social reality (Kelley, 1967). Although most of us can set up higher-order factorial designs with great ease, there are a number of finer issues that present certain difficulties. Let us consider them one by one.

PRESENTATION OF RESULTS

A serious problem in the use of analysis of variance can be easily remedied. All too often the results are incompletely presented, and the reader is then unable to understand and interpret them. For instance, only the inferential F-statistic or the p-value might be reported. By itself, neither of these provide the reader with information about the magnitude, pattern, or uncertainty of the effect. *Magnitude* answers the question of how big the effect is, *pattern* shows which mean is larger than which mean, and *uncertainty* assesses how replicable the result is. The magnitude of the effect is given by measures like d (Cohen, 1977), the pattern of means by the means themselves, and uncertainty by the mean square error. Ideally, in equal-n conditions (the problem is much more complex in the unequal-n case, as is discussed later) for a given effect, the researcher should report all the means, the cell size, the F-statistics, and the mean square error. For cases in which journal space precludes printing of a complete set of results, the researcher need report only the means and the F-statistic. A careful reading of the method section should indicate the cell n, and mean square error can be derived from the means and the F-statistic. One should prefer to state the inferential statistic over the p-value since the latter is derived from the former. Moreover, one should *ordinarily* prefer to report a table of means rather than a graph since the reader can more accurately compute further results from means.

A problem with analysis-of-variance routines of many computer packages is that either the means are not outputted or if they are, the researcher must use great ingenuity to obtain them. A good example is the analysis of covariance. Many computer packages do not print adjusted means. All too often researchers report the unadjusted means, but since these means are *not* the ones employed in the hypothesis-testing stage of research, the adjusted means should be reported instead, or at least in addition to the unadjusted means.

DEPENDENCE ON FACTORIAL DESIGN

The second issue is the overreliance upon strict factorial design. Although the notion of factorially combining independent variables and randomly assigning subjects to the various cells of the design is the key idea behind analysis-of-variance experiments, it represents only a starting point. Consider a large hypothetical design with 8 factors, each with 2 levels and 12 subjects in each cell of the design. The number of subjects required for such an experiment is 3072! One of my teachers, the sociologist Howard Becker, often remarked that to fill out the cells of *the complete experiment* in an area of study would require the participation of every person, living, dead, and yet to be born. Actually, thousands of subjects are not required to study 8 independent variables if one is willing both to lose some information and to confound partially certain terms. In the following sections are discussed two related strategies that vary in the way in which higher-order interactions are confounded.

Design in Which Interactions Are Confounded with Error

Let us return to our hypothetical design with 8 factors, each with 2 levels. The total number of cells is 256, which results in a source table with 255 terms besides the within-cell term (256 if the mean is included). If there is only one subject per cell of the design, all 255 terms of the model can be estimated, but what cannot be estimated is a mean square within cell, the error term. Of the 255 terms only 92 are main effects and first- and second-order interactions. If all third-order and higher interactions were zero, one might simply pool these terms and treat them as error. Such an error term would have a healthy 163 degrees of freedom. The strategy of one observation per cell results in a loss of information and a possible risk. The loss of information is that the higher-order interactions cannot be tested. However, since such higher-order interactions are never estimated by smaller designs, there is no loss compared with what is commonly done. The risk is that the error term estimates not only true error variance but also the effects of the ignored higher-order interactions. Thus the *F*-ratios would have a downward bias, making the tests conservative. In practice, the amount of bias is minimal. (To verify this claim, readers might find their biggest between-subject analysis of variance. If they pool the higher-order interactions into error, they should see that the pooled interaction is probably only slightly

larger than the mean square subjects within cells. Moreover, if it is larger, one should not be too uncomfortable in using it as error, because it is too large for a very good reason: When one tests the main effects, their significance is evaluated to the degree to which there is random error and to the degree to which effects in the study vary as a function of other variables.)

Design in Which Higher-Order Interactions Are Confounded with Main Effects

A response to the previous discussion is that the design still requires 256 subjects to be implemented. Could one do the study with the 8 factors with 128 subjects? Yes, if one confounds the main effects with higher-order interactions. These designs are called *fractional replications* (Winer, 1971, pp. 240–260). First, a little notation is needed. The 8 factors of the design are designated as *A* through *H*, and the usual χ symbol to denote interaction is omitted. The design is set up by confounding the factor *H* with the *ABCDEFG* interaction. (How to do this is explained later.) Such a setup would, in turn, confound *AH* with *BCDEFG* and *ABH* with *CDEFG*. In general, each main effect would be confounded with a sixth-order interaction, each first-order interaction with a fifth-order interaction, each second-order interaction with a fourth-order interaction, and each third-order interaction with another third-order interaction. Information about the seventh-order interaction (*ABCDEFGH*) would be lost. There are only 128 cells of the design, with the other 128 cells empty, and so one would cut the number of subjects in half with the cost that every term in the source table is confounded with some other term. However, such confounding may well be worth price of running half as many subjects.

One would execute the confounding as follows: If the levels of *A* are designated as a_1 and a_2, *B* as b_1 and b_2, etc., then the *ABCDEFG* interaction compares cells whose sum of subscripts is odd (e.g., cell $a_1b_2c_1d_1e_1f_2g_1$) with cells whose sum is even. Thus to confound *H* with *ABCDEFG*, the researcher would assign all h_1 subjects to *ABCDEFG* cells with an odd sum and all h_2 subjects to cells with an even sum, or vice versa.

Counterbalancing

Many times, a study contains a series of factors that are thought to be devoid of any theoretical meaning but must be included for methodological purposes. Examples of such factors are order of response, order of presentation, stimulus form, experimenter, room, time of day, etc. Let us consider an attribution study with two conditions, each requiring a story. Two stories are written, one about an accident victim and the other about a polio victim. What all too often occurs is that the researcher realizes that he or she cannot fill out the complete factorial design with all possible cells and, unfortunately, decides not to counterbalance. Either things are left to chance (e.g., no attempt is made to ensure that conditions have equal numbers of accident or polio victims), only one level of the variable is studied (only the accident victim story is used), or worst of all, the variable ends up being confounded (e.g., all subjects in one condition receive a story about an accident victim, while the subjects in the other condition receive a story about a polio victim). None of these three strategies are optimal, and the latter is disastrous but very common. Researchers adopt this last strategy because the factorial design requires too many cells and, therefore, too many subjects. But such a design is not necessary if one is no longer wedded to factorial design.

If one counterbalances to control only for the main effect of the variable, a simple analysis strategy can be adopted. One simply treats the counterbalancing factor as a covariate. (There is no need to worry about the covariate being a dichotomy since the dependent variable, not the covariate, needs to be measured at the interval level.) The variance due to the covariate is subtracted out, and the interactions of the covariate with other factors are pooled with error. With this strategy it is possible to control for main effects of many factors by counterbalancing, without appreciably increasing the size of the experiment or decreasing the precision.

Although not commonly done, counterbalancing can be executed by yoking pairs of subjects together. For instance, if we wish to compare the ratings by subjects of friends with their ratings of strangers, we first randomly create pairs of strangers and designate persons as A and B. We then use person A's friend as a stranger for person B and person B's friend as stranger for A. The same persons are then used as both friends and strangers, and person is not confounded with the friend-stranger variable. Storms (1973) employed this type of counterbalancing. Persons A and B interacted, but only A was videotaped. They then viewed a videotape of that interaction and made various attributions. By showing both A and B the same videotape, Storms held the stimulus constant (and

so A and B are yoked), but he was able to vary whether the person viewed self or other on the videotape.

HETEROGENEITY OF CORRELATION

The previous discussion is primarily relevant to between-subject designs. However, many studies use a repeated-measures format in which subjects are not in a single condition but in many. For repeated-measures designs there is an important exception to the general rule that analysis of variance is robust: the existence of *heterogeneity of correlation*. Imagine a simple experiment with no between-subject factors and a single repeated measure of trials. The experimenter estimates a mean square for trials, subjects, and the interaction between trials and subjects. To create the *F*-ratio for the main effect of trials, the experimenter divides its mean square by the mean square for interaction. In most cases such a test is too liberal (i.e., the obtained *p*-value is too small). This problem increases as the degrees of freedom of the repeated measure increase, but for repeated-measure variables with a single degree of freedom, the problem evaporates.

What is heterogeneity of correlation? Let us consider the correlation matrix between trials. Given homogeneity of covariance and variance, all the correlations should equal the same value once sampling error is taken into account. A moment's reflection will indicate that such an assumption is totally implausible. The most likely structure is that the more nearly adjacent trials (e.g., trials 1 and 2, trials 3 and 4) are more highly correlated than trials farther away in time (e.g., trials 1 and 4). A correlation matrix with such a structure is called a *simplex*. Such a structure violates the homogeneity-of-correlation assumption. [Equal correlations are only a sufficient condition for the homogeneity assumption (Harris, 1975, pp. 125–127).]

One solution to the problem of heterogeneity of correlation is to perform a multivariate analysis of variance (Harris, 1975). An alternative strategy is to create contrasts, e.g., orthogonal polynomials. Since these tests have one degree of freedom for the numerator, the tests are not affected by heterogeneity of covariance. However, if one partitions the sum of squares of a repeated-measures effect into orthogonal contrasts, one should also partition the error term (Winer, 1971). While such a partitioning is incredibly awkward when computed by hand and most computer packages are not set up for such a partitioning, the following computational strategy is fairly simple. For each contrast one multiplies each subject's score by the appropriate contrast value and sums these products within each subject. One now computes a *between-subject* analysis of variance on this single score for each subject. The test that the mean is zero evaluates the significance of the contrast, and each between-subject effect now indicates whether the contrast interacts with that between-subject effect. To scale the subjects' score to fit in with the overall analysis, one should divide each score by $(\Sigma q_i^2/n)^{1/2}$, where q_i is a contrast value and n is the total number of observations that each score is based on.

For instance, imagine a design with six repeated measurements. The researcher wishes to test the following contrast on the six measures: 1, 1, −2, 2, −1, and −1. The researcher then computes the following score for each subject:

$$(1)Y_1 + (1)Y_2 + (-2)Y_3 + (2)Y_4 + (-1)Y_5 + (-1)Y_6,$$

where Y is the repeated measure. To scale these sums so that the results can be incorporated into the unpartitioned analysis, the researcher should divide each score by $(1 + 1 + 4 + 4 + 1 + 1)^{1/2} = (12)^{1/2}$. If the scores ($Y_1$ and through Y_6) are means, then the sum should be multiplied by $(n/12)^{1/2}$, where n is the number of observations that each mean is based on. The researcher performs a between-subject analysis of variance on these sums. Suppose, for instance, that the test of a zero mean and the test of the sex effect are both significant. The nonzero mean would indicate the contrast is significant overall, and the main effect would indicate that the contrast interacts with sex.

TREATING STIMULI AS RANDOM

The standard lore in social psychology is that results fail to replicate. Although this claim is somewhat exaggerated, one reason is that we do not treat stimuli as random factors. Consider a hypothetical line of research that investigates the effect of a given manipulation on attitude change. One experiment shows that the manipulation significantly affects attitude change for a given topic. A second experiment replicates the study, using a different topic, but the effect reverses. One reasonable explanation for this failure to replicate is that the size of the effect varies as a function of the topic. It may be that for most topics the effect is positive but that for a few topics the ef-

fect is negative. We seem to be able to understand that experimental results vary across subjects, but we fail to realize that results may also vary across stimuli. For instance, Goldberg (1978) has shown that the actor-observer attribution effect varies across different traits as well as subjects.

One can generalize across stimuli by replicating the study across different stimuli within a single experiment. One must then treat stimuli as a random factor in the analysis. For such studies in a test of the effect of fixed factors and their interactions, quasi-F-ratios must typically be formed (Clark, 1973). The numerator and the denominator of a quasi-F-ratio are formed by taking linear combinations of mean squares. Given the null hypothesis, the expected value of the numerator and the denominator is the same. The distribution of the ratio under the null hypothesis is only approximately distributed as F—hence the name *quasi-F*. The formation of quasi-F-ratios is discussed in the standard analysis-of-variance texts as well as in Kenny and Smith (1980).

The use of quasi-F-ratios to control for stimulus generalizability is a controversial practice. At least three arguments have been made against their use. Some have claimed that since they are not true F-statistics, they are dubious statistically. Others have pointed out that since it is difficult to sample randomly such stimuli, one should not treat stimuli as truly random. The final argument, which is usually unstated, is that quasi-F-ratios would mean much larger and more costly experiments with less power. Although all three of these arguments have a kernel of truth, a careful consideration of each shows that they should not deter us from using quasi-F-ratios since such statistics allow us to generalize across stimuli.

First, the fact that the distribution of the quasi-F-ratio under the null hypothesis is only approximately F is usually the first argument made. Its proponents seem to forget that in *every* experiment the data are not continuous, not normal, and not homoscedastic, making the F-ratios only approximate. The key question is how good the approximations are. The answer appears to be that quasi-F-ratio are very good even under severe violation of assumptions (Santa, Miller, and Shaw, 1979).

Second, many have pointed out that it is virtually impossible to sample stimuli. However, random sampling is not required to treat a factor as random. What is not commonly recognized is that we hardly ever sample even subjects randomly; if we took seriously the objection of nonrandom sampling, we should never use signif-

TABLE 1
Design to Illustrate Erlebacher's Rule

—	C	D	$C \times D$	I/CD
A	$A \times C$	$A \times D$	$A \times C \times D$	$A \times I/CD$
B	$B \times C$	$B \times D$	$B \times C \times D$	$B \times I/CD$
$A \times B$	$A \times B \times C$	$A \times B \times D$	$A \times B \times C \times D$	$A \times B \times I/CD$
S/AB	$S/AB \times C$	$S/AB \times D$	$S/AB \times C \times D$	$S/AB \times I/CD$

icance tests since we do not randomly sample subjects. Indeed, except for survey research, we never even pretend to!

If we are to employ quasi-*F*-ratios, experiments will have to become larger and more costly. Because results must generalize across both subjects and stimuli, it is also more difficult to obtain significant results. It should not be surprising that to buy broader generalizations, researchers must pay through larger designs.

There is a simple rule for forming quasi-*F*-ratios. It is based on an elegant rule for choosing the error term, developed by Albert Erlebacher and reviewed by Keppel (1973). To apply the rule, one denotes all factors in an experiment, including subjects, by capital letters. To symbolize nesting, one uses a slash sign as follows: S/AB means that subjects are nested within the AB cells. The proposed error term for a given line of the analysis-of-variance table must include all the terms of that line plus one and only one random variable. Terms of the proposed error term to the right of the slash sign can be ignored unless those terms are random. (Thus S/AB is an error term for A if S is random and B is fixed, but it is not if both S and B are random.) If two or more terms satisfy Erlebacher's rule (i.e., include all the relevant variables plus one random variable), then there is no simple appropriate error term.

As an example, consider the design in Table 1. Factors A and B are between-subject factors, while factors C and D are within-subject factors within which items I are nested. Table 1 presents the various main effects and their interactions. If we treat only subject S as random, then S/AB is the error term for A, B, and $A \times B$ since S/AB contains each term plus one and only one random variable. For C, D, and $C \times D$, their error terms are $S/AB \times C$, $S/AB \times D$, and $S/AB \times C \times D$, respectively. Error terms for the within/between-subject factor interactions can be similarly derived.

The rule can be adapted for quasi-*F*-ratios where more than one factor in the design is random. If there are two and only two lines that satisfy Erlebacher's rule, they can be summed to form the denominator of the quasi-ratio F″. For the numerator one sums the effect to be tested, with the common error term for the two terms in the denominator. So given the design in Table 1, if both S and I are random, for the term A both S/AB and $A \times I/CD$ satisfy Erlebacher's rule, since they include A plus a random variable. We can ignore B and CD since they are to the right of the slash and are fixed. The error term for each is $S/AB \times I/CD$. The quasi-*F*-ratio F″ is then

$$\frac{\text{MS}_A + \text{MS}_{S/AB \times I/CD}}{\text{MS}_{S/AB} + \text{MS}_{A \times I/CD}}.$$

This quasi-*F*-ratio evaluates the A–main effect.

UNEQUAL CELL SIZES

No other issue has created more debate and less resolution than the issue of how to handle unequal cell sizes. Much of the confusion results when researchers fail to be clear about what it is they are doing. In data analysis there are four stages: model specification, identification, estimation, and hypothesis testing. I will discuss the issue of unequal cell sizes relative to each of the four stages. To be discussed is the simple two-way design with fixed factors. The generalization to higher-order designs is straightforward, while the analysis of designs in which other factors besides subjects are random generally requires an equal number of subjects in each cell of the design.

Model Specification

The usual specification for two-way analysis of variance is given by model I in Table 2. The term m is the grand

TABLE 2
Analysis of Variance Model Specifications

I	$X_{ijk} = m + a_i + b_j + g_{ij} + e_{ijk}$
II	$X_{ijk} = m + a_i + b_j + e_{ijk}$
III	$X_{ijk} = m + a_i + e_{ijk}$
IV	$X_{ijk} = m + b_j + e_{ijk}$
V	$X_{ijk} = m + e_{ijk}$
VI	$X_{ijk} = m + a_i + g_{ij} + e_{ijk}$
VII	$X_{ijk} = m + b_j + g_{ij} + e_{ijk}$
VIII	$X_{ijk} = m + g_{ij} + e_{ijk}$

mean, a is the row effect, b is the column effect, g is the interaction, and e is random error. (For ease of presentation the usual specification with Greek letters is not used.) We assume that there are A levels of the row effect and B levels of the column effect. Model I, which is sometimes called the full-rank model, is the most general model, and its seven special cases are in Table 2. Although many of us usually only consider model I, the seven other models need to be considered both to test hypotheses and improve efficiency. To some researchers, models VI, VII, and VIII may seem to be anomalous since they include the interaction term without both of the main effects. Although it may be difficult to make sense out of these models, models VI, VII, and VIII are perfectly permissible.

Identification

There is a problem with the models as they are formulated in Table 2. One is unable to obtain *unique* estimates for the model parameters. The technical term for this condition is *underidentification*. The problem cannot be remedied by increasing the cell size. Rather, it is *mathematically* impossible to uniquely solve for the parameters even if the population means (m_{ij}) were known. To see the problem, note that there are, for model I, a total of AB cell means but a total of $AB + A + B + 1$ unknown parameters. Since there are more unknown parameters (m, a_i, b_j, g_{ij}) than known statistics (cell means), it is impossible to uniquely solve for the unknown values.

The common solution to the preceding problem is to respecify or reparameterize the model. The simplest approach is to make the following constraints on the model:

$$\sum_i a_i = \sum_j b_j = \sum_i g_{ij} = \sum_j g_{ij} = 0. \qquad (1)$$

With the above constraints there are now unique estimates for the model parameters if the cell n's are all nonzero.

These very simple constraints are not the only ones possible. For instance others have been proposed:

$$\sum_i n_i a_i = \sum_j n_j b_j = \sum_i n_{ij} g_{ij} = \sum_j n_{ij} g_{ij} = 0,$$

and

$$\sum_i w_i a_i = \sum_j w_j b_j = \sum_i w_{ij} g_{ij} = \sum_j w_{ij} g_{ij} = 0,$$

where n_{ij} is the cell size for the cell in row i, column j. The term w_{ij} is the population weight for cell ij (Keren and Lewis, 1976). These different side conditions lead to different effect estimates and also alter some significance test results. Keren and Lewis (1976) have argued for unequal weights when theory or sampling considerations may place greater emphasis on certain cells of the design.

Generally, equal weights are most sensible for the following three reasons:

1. It is difficult to conceive of a method that would weight the cells of an experiment in a way acceptable to all researchers.

2. Since the choice of weights affects certain significance tests, we might worry that an investigator would judiciously choose the weights to obtain a solution that was more satisfying.

3. Standard analysis-of-variance programs assume equal weights.

Given the side condition of Eq. (1), all eight models in Table 2 are identified if the cell sizes are nonzero. The following discussion assumes the side conditions of Eq. (1).

Estimation

The standard estimation method is least squares. Given identification, parameter estimates are chosen to minimize $\Sigma \hat{e}^2$, the sum of squared residuals. What is not commonly recognized is that the parameter estimates vary depending on which of the eight models in Table 1 is estimated. There is not *one* estimate of the grand mean; rather, there is an estimate for a particular model. For instance, for model I the estimate is the unweighted average of cell means. For model V it is the weighted (by cell size) mean of cell means. In fact, for unequal-n designs the estimate of the grand mean is ordinarily different for each of the eight models. The row, column, and interaction effects also vary for the eight models.

This creates a nontrivial problem that has gone unrecognized by many researchers. If a researcher wishes to report means of an effect for an unbalanced design, what should be reported, the weighted means, the unweighted means, or some other set of values? When means are published in our journals, it is not clear exactly what is reported. Ideally, what should be presented as the estimate of the row mean is

$$\hat{m} + \hat{a}_i,$$

which would equal the unweighted row means for model I, the weighted means for model III, and for model II a complicated weighted mean given by Herr and Gaebelein (1978, pp. 209–210). These alternative values almost certainly differ when the cell sizes are unequal.

The choice of which to report depends on the tradeoff between inefficiency and bias. The estimates of the row means are generally the most efficient for model III, since model III has fewer parameters than models I and II. However, the estimates of model III are biased when there are either column or interaction effects. (Similarly, the column-effect estimates of model IV are more efficient than those of models I and II but are subject to bias when interaction or row effects are present.) The estimates of model I are always unbiased but are less efficient than those of models II and III. Thus to avoid presenting estimates that are biased, we must be reasonably certain that terms omitted from the model are zero or nearly zero. To do so, we must have tested such hypotheses.

Testing

A major concern of most researchers is testing the presence of main effects and interactions. Consider the test of the hypothesis of no row main effect. To test such a hypothesis, we compare the fit of the model that includes the row effect with an identical model save row effect. If the former model fits significantly better than the latter, then we judge that a row effect is needed. Testing hypotheses about determining whether model parameters equal zero, then, always requires the measuring of the relative fit of two models: one in which the parameters are included and a second just like the first but with the relevant parameters dropped.

A problem immediately presents itself. To test for row effects one might compare model I with model VII, model II with model IV, or model III with model V. In each case one model contains the row effect and the second model is identical in every respect but the row effect is omitted. As there is not a general estimate of row effects, there is no general test of row effects.

Numerous strategies of hypothesis testing have been proposed to resolve this choice (see Herr and Gaebelein, 1978, for a review). One reasonable strategy is to test for row effects by comparing model I with model VII, to test for column effects by comparing model I with model VI, and to test for interaction effects by comparing model I with model II. Such tests evaluate each of the parameter sets controlling for the effects of the other parameters. Herr and Gaebelein (1978) call this the *standard parametric procedure.*

Appelbaum and Cramer (1974; Cramer & Appelbaum, 1980) argue that to test the row effect, one should compare the fit of model II with model III; and to test the column effect, one should compare the fit of model II with model IV. They argue that tests of main effects are only meaningful when interaction effects are not present. The presence of an interaction indicates that the main effect of one variable depends on the other variable.

Neither the standard parametric procedure nor the Appelbaum and Cramer procedure is the one and true approach to model testing. The researcher must decide which to employ. There are two considerations that the reseacher should be aware of. First, for designs that are slightly unbalanced (cell sizes differing by one or two), the use of any testing procedure normally produces essentially the same parameter estimates and significance-test results. One might as well use the full-rank estimates and the standard parametric procedure, since the costs in terms of efficiency and power would be small. Second, for cases in which interaction effects are unlikely and the design is unbalanced, the Appelbaum and Cramer approach would seem to be sensible.

A Note on Unweighted-Means Analysis

Unweighted-means analysis of variance has the advantage of being almost as easy to compute as a balanced (equal-*n*) analysis of variance. It provides model parameter estimates that are equivalent to the full-rank model. However, its significance test results are generally not equivalent to any procedure since the principle of least squares is not used to estimate parameters. The resulting

F-tests are then only approximate. Other things being equal, an unweighted-means analysis should not be employed when a least-squares solution is possible. (Also, the discarding of data to obtain equal cell sizes is not to be recommended either.)

MULTIPLE REGRESSION

The survey of the articles in our journals for 1978 showed that 10 percent employed multiple-regression analysis. No doubt the use of this procedure will increase as the recent cohort of Ph.D.'s who know this technique begin to publish. Numerous articles have documented that the analysis of variance is only a special case of multiple regression. Various problems that arise in an analysis-of-variance context (e.g., unequal cell sizes or *post hoc* tests in analysis of covariance) are relatively easily handled within a multiple-regression framework. Multiple regression is almost certainly the most important statistical method in the social sciences.

Fortunately, there is a set of classic review articles that summarize various issues in multiple-regression analysis. The papers are by Darlington (1968) and Cohen (1968). There are now a number of readable textbooks entirely devoted to the topic of multiple regression, such as Cohen and Cohen (1975) and Achen (1982). Here I will discuss three problems that require clarification: standardization, stepwise regression, and interaction testing.

The most common practice in social psychology is to report results of multiple regression in terms of beta coefficients and the multiple correlation. Although these statistics are often useful and informative, their counterparts, the unstandardized regression coefficients (or *b*-weights) and error variance, are often to be preferred, for two reasons. [The unstandardized regression coefficient equals the beta weight times the ratio of the criterion's standard deviation to the predictor's standard deviation, and error variance equals the sum of squares of the predictor variable times $(1 - R^2)/(N - k - 1)$, where R^2 is the squared multiple correlation, k is the number of predictor variables, and N is the sample size. Both are routinely printed by computer programs.] First, since beta weights and the R^2 refer to the solution in which all the variables are standardized, they are not as interpretable as the unstandardized coefficients and the error variance when the units of measurement are meaningful. The unstandardized coefficient measures the change

in the criterion that results from a change of one unit in the predictor variable. For instance, in a study of attitude change a coefficient of 2 for sex of communicator (female = 1, male = 0) would indicate a two-point advantage for female communicators over males. The beta weight would not be nearly as interpretable.

Second, there is hardly any reason to expect the standardized solution to replicate across populations or occasions since differences in standard deviations of the variable affect the solution. Rarely, then, should one compare the beta weights or R^2 across different populations. Rather, one should compare the unstandardized coefficients and the error variance. (When one is comparing the *fit* of alternative models within the same data set, R^2 may be informative.) In sum, social psychology researchers should get out of the habit of looking only at beta and R^2.

Many of us feel uncomfortable in interpreting unstandardized regression coefficients. We would be much more comfortable if we had the means. Imagine a 2×2 experiment with means as in Table 3. The means very clearly show two main effects such that the A_2 subjects score higher than the A_1 subjects and the B_2 subjects higher than the B_1 subjects. A regression analysis was also done by using two dummy variables ($X_1 = 1$ for A_1 and $X_1 = -1$ for A_2; $X_2 = 1$ for B_1 and $X_2 = -1$ for B_2). The resulting equation (given equal cell *n*'s) is

$$Y = 14.315 - 0.695X_1 - 1.185X_2 + E,$$

where Y is the dependent variable.

Only by knowing the definitions of X_1 and X_2 can we interpret the equation. Very often it is easier to interpret not the equation itself but rather the predicted values of the equation. We can estimate what the predicted values are for the four cells of the design. To find each, we must substitute into the equation the appropriate values of X_1 and X_2. For cell A_1B_1, X_1 and X_2, both equal -1:

$$14.315 - 0.695 - 1.185 = 12.435.$$

For cell A_1B_2, X_1 is 1 and X_2 is -1:

$$14.315 - 0.695 + 1.185 = 14.805.$$

For cell A_1B_2, X_1 is -1 and X_2 is 1:

$$14.315 + 0.695 - 1.185 = 13.825.$$

And for cell A_2B_2, both X_1 and X_2 are 1:

$$14.315 + 0.695 + 1.185 = 16.195.$$

TABLE 3
Hypothetical Means from a Two-by-Two Design

	FACTOR *B*	
FACTOR *A*	B_1	B_2
A_1	12.31	14.93
A_2	13.95	16.07

Thus we can and often should obtain a table of predicted values from the regression equation. Such a table may be more interpretable than the equation itself. Thus if one is having difficulty interpreting a regression equation, it is wise to substitute into the equation hypothetical values for each predictor variable. These predicted "means" can be tabled or graphed and interpreted in the same way as a table or graph from analysis of variance. (The predicted means in the example do not exactly equal the cell means. Since the equation does not include interaction between *A* and *B*, the predicted cell "means" do not exhibit any interaction.)

Determining which values of X_1 and X_2 to substitute into the equation is fairly obvious when X_1 and X_2 are nominal variables. We use dummy codes for the various levels of the nominal variable. However, if X is continuous, the choice is not so clear. One strategy might be to use the mean of X, the mean plus one standard deviation of X, and the mean less one standard deviation.

Normally, a series of multiple-regression equations are estimated. For instance, stepwise regression is used to select a subset of predictor variables in a prediction equation. Stepwise regression is a widely applied, but often misused, explanatory tool. There are two problems with stepwise regression. First, stepwise regression is often needlessly applied. For various computational reasons stepwise regression is the default way to perform multiple regression for various computer packages. If the ratio of the number of predictors to sample size is small and multicollinearity is not high, little is gained by a stepwise analysis. What the researcher should do is to perform only one step by simultaneously entering all the variables into one equation. Second, in stepwise regression the standard tests of the coefficients and R^2 are inflated (Wilkinson, 1979) since the predictor variables are selected to explain maximally the criterion. Such capitalization on chance can be avoided in a nonstepwise analysis.

Earlier in this chapter we suggested that researchers employing analysis of variance should ignore the higher-order interactions in certain cases. Researchers employing multiple regression have just the opposite problem. They tend to ignore all interactions. The reasons for this neglect are that, first, interactions are not usually estimated; second, they are typically not statistically significant; and third, the inclusion of interaction terms often radically changes the coefficients of the components. The first reason is no reason at all. The second reason simply states that interactions rarely increase the R^2 significantly. However, the low power of a test should not preclude its use but should only create cautious interpretation when the test yields no significant results.

The third reason is important. The estimate of main effects in the analysis of variance does not differ much depending on whether or not the interaction is present. However, for the following regression equation,

$$Y = a + bX_1 + cX_2 + dX_1X_2 + E, \qquad (2)$$

the presence of the product term X_1X_2 as a predictor dramatically affects the coefficients for the components X_1 and X_2 even if the coefficent for X_1X_2 is very small. To understand this, note that the coefficient for X_1 measures the effect of X_1 when X_1X_2 is held constant. However, X_1X_2 can only be constant as X_1 varies when the variable X_2 is zero. Thus the effect of X_1 is measured for the case of $X_2 = 0$. But if X_2 is zero only in extreme cases or never, the main effect for X_1 is measured for an extreme case. In fact, the estimate of the regression coefficient for X_1 in Eq. (2) can ordinarily be set to *any value* by strategically choosing the value of g and h and forming the interaction by $(X_1 - g)(X_2 - h)$. To make the estimates of the components more interpretable and more comparable to the effect estimates when the interaction term is dropped from the equation, we should form the product term as follows: $(X_1 - g)(X_2 - h)$, where g and h are "typical" values of the variables X_1 and X_2, respectively. A typical value can be chosen by using a measure of central tendency such as mean, median, or mode. The estimate of the main effect then measures the effect of X_1 when X_2 equals h and the effect of X_2 when X_1 equals g. [The significance-test results of the coefficient for the product term are invariant of g and h (Cohen, 1978).]

If we fail to subtract the typical value of the components, anomalous results are likely. Imagine a study that evaluated the effects of the height and the sex of a stimulus person on judgments of intelligence. If a sex and height product term were entered into the equation, the sex effect in that equation would refer to a person who is zero centimeters tall!

Some researchers are reluctant to form product terms to estimate the effect of an interaction since they do not think they can interpret the interaction. With analysis of variance the researcher can examine the means, but what can be looked at in the regression equation? We can employ the strategy of computing predicted means. However, the regression coefficients by themselves may be interpretable. For example, imagine

$$A = 0.5S - 0.5IS,$$

where A is attraction, S is similarity, and I is the future interaction expected (1 = impossible, 0 = possible). At first glance the -0.5 coefficient for the product term seems impossible to interpret, but it is fairly simple if one first rewrites the equation as

$$A = (0.5 - 0.5I)S. \tag{3}$$

The equation is now written so that attraction is only a multiplicative function of similarity but the similarity effect on attraction is a function of future interaction. To interpret Eq. (3), we substitute into it the possible values of I. The coefficient for S is zero when there is no future interaction, or $I = 1$ ($= 0.5 - 0.5$), and 0.5 [$= 0.5 - (0.5 \times 0)$] when interaction is possible, or $I = 0$. The seemingly complex equation makes perfect sense when values of I are substituted and two equations are set up.

STRUCTURAL EQUATION MODELING

Perhaps the most exciting development in data analysis in the social sciences during the 1970s was the development of *structural equation modeling,* or, more simply, *structural analysis.* It subsumes the techniques of path analysis, causal modeling, and covariance structure analysis.

Path analysis can be viewed as a structural analysis in which the variables have been standardized. Path analysis has also been more narrowly defined to limit it to models that can be estimated by multiple regression. Multiple regression is only one of many multivariate methods that can be employed in structural analysis in general or path analysis in particular. Factor analysis, partial correlation, and canonical correlation can also be used, depending on the structural model.

PRINCIPLES

I will only briefly introduce structural analysis. An excellent introduction to the topic is given by Bentler (1980), and a good introduction for social psychologists is given by Reis (1982). For a more detailed discussion the reader should consult various textbooks: Duncan (1975), Heise (1975), Kenny (1979), and Namboodiri, Carter, and Blalock (1975).

Although the terms *causal analysis* or *causal modeling* are still in use, one should be careful in using the adjective *causal.* No statistical method by itself provides estimates of causal effects. Causal inferences are products of human thought and not products of statistical techniques. Moreover, the term *causal* carries certain philosophical connotations to which some object.

Structural analysis can estimate the parameters of a researcher's stated model, and in certain cases it can be used to test whether the data are consistent with the model. But structural analysis cannot prove that a causal model is true. It can only disconfirm. A quote from Duncan (1975, p. 20) restates this point:

> One can *never* infer the causal ordering of two or more variables knowing only the values of the correlations (or even the partial correlations). We can reason in the other direction, however. Knowing the causal ordering, or, more precisely, the causal model linking the variables, we can sometimes infer something about the correlations, or, assuming a model for sake of argument, we can express its properties in terms of the correlations and (sometimes) find one or more conditions that must hold if the model is true but that are subject to refutation by empirical evidence.

The terms of structural modeling often confuse the researcher. What follows is a brief glossary. The variables in a causal or structural equation can be divided into two types: causes and effects. Most causal modelers prefer to use the terms of econometricians: endogenous variables for effects (or dependent variables) and exogenous variables for causes or independent variables. Each exogenous variable is multiplied by a causal or structural coefficient. These coefficients measure the causal impact of the exogenous variables on the endogenous variable. Normally, the structural equation contains a residual or disturbance term, which represents a weighted sum of all causes of the endogenous variable that the researcher does not specify. Thus in words a structural equation is

endogenous variable
> = sum of each exogenous variable
> × its structural coefficient
> + disturbance.

Variables in structural models may be standardized (zero mean and variance of one) or left in their original metric. If all the variables in the model are standardized, the structural coefficients are called *path coefficients*. As is discussed later, the variables of the model may be unmeasured. Structural equations can be conveniently summarized by a path diagram that has arrows leading from causes to effects. Curved lines are used to represent possible association between uncaused variables in the model.

It is the task of theory to state which variables are the causes for each endogenous variable. The specification of the structural equations is the most difficult part of modeling since our theories are usually not clear about which variables are causes and effects. The earlier quotation from Duncan emphasizes that the causes must first be specified by the researcher; the causes are not gleaned from structural modeling.

Once the equations are specified, it must be determined whether one can solve for the unknown parameters, the structural coefficients, from the known correlations. This task is called identification. If a model is identified, then one must find an analysis strategy to estimate and, if possible, test the model. The fit of the model is judged by its ability to successfully reproduce the correlation matrix.

There are three major advantages of causal modeling. First, it forces researchers to be up-front about what assumptions they are making. Without structural modeling it is possible to hide implausible assumptions or to make even contradictory ones, but with structural models the equations clearly state researchers' assumptions. Structural modeling does not prevent implausible assumptions; rather, it only makes them more visible.

Second, it encourages the estimation of multiequation models that elaborate a process. Perhaps the major disadvantage of analysis-of-variance thinking is that it encourages examining a single dependent variable. With causal modeling, researchers are encouraged to be explicit about the causal sequence in the same way that our theories are.

Third, researchers must choose an analysis strategy that is consistent with their theoretical assumptions. The theory comes first; then comes the statistical approach.

In sum, the promise of structural modeling is data analysis guided by theory.

While structural analysis is virtually required in the analysis of correlational data, it can be very useful in analysis of data with experimentally manipulated independent variables. Experimentation actually makes the specification of the model easier since certain causal paths are known to be zero given the logic of experimentation (Kenny, 1979). By employing structural modeling, we can learn even more from the data that we worked so hard to collect. Let us consider two advantages: testing of mediational models and construct validation of the dependent variable.

Perhaps one of the most exciting tasks in social psychology is locating the mediational process that explains a given social psychological effect. Illusory correlation, mere exposure, overjustification, and perceptual salience are all examples of effects that social psychologists are currently attempting to explain. One type of explanation focuses on the internal processes of persons—for example, memory, cognitions, and the like. Thus the mediational model postulates that the experimental manipulation causes some internal-state variable, which in turn causes the dependent variable. Such a model can and should be tested by structural modeling, but it can only be crudely tested by conventional analysis-of-variance models. Judd and Kenny (1981b) and Smith (1982) show that mediational hypotheses can be tested through structural modeling. The work by Smith is especially relevant to social psychology since he discusses methods to test feedback between dependent variables in experimental settings.

Structural modeling also can help experimenters validate their dependent variables. Researchers are told by methodologists to have multiple measures of the dependent variable, yet it is not clear how to use these measures to demonstrate construct validity, i.e., the extent to which the measures are valid indicators of one construct. Structural-modeling procedures can evaluate, simultaneously, the following:

1. Whether the measures cohere (internal consistency).

2. The extent to which covariation between the measures and the independent variables can be explained by one postulated construct.

3. Whether the more reliable indicators of the construct share more variance with the independent variables than less reliable indicators do.

All three of these conditions point to strong construct validity (Kenny, 1979, Chap. 8). What is even more remarkable is that with structural modeling the analysis of variance can in a sense be done on the construct itself and not the measures. Such causal modeling with latent variables is the topic we turn our attention to now.

LATENT VARIABLES

Virtually no measure perfectly operationalizes the construct it purports to measure. Consider a measure of cognitive skill that is known to be highly reliable if not valid: the Graduate Record Examination. Those of us who have handled admissions to graduate school have all come across cases of students who have retaken the examination. Usually, the scores are close, varying by about fifty points, but they are rarely identical. An honest theory of measurement must recognize that instruments tap both the construct and the noise we usually call error of measurement.

Let us consider the example of subjects who read a story and then rate the responsibility of a stimulus person for an accident. No doubt the subjects' ratings will be influenced by a whole host of such irrelevant factors such as unimportant details in the story and details in the previous story. Although we pay lip service to the notion that our measures are errorful, we fail to realize its implications. Considered here are three different problems created by ignoring measurement error: low multiple correlations, bias in regression coefficients, and failures of discriminant validity.

First, if our measures contain noise, then the total amount of potentially explainable variance is smaller than the total variance. For instance, if 50 percent of variance of attitude scales is noise, then there is a theoretical limit in the multiple correlation of attitude scales of 0.7. Stated more technically, the multiple correlation is attenuated due to measurement error. Many of the low correlations or low percentages of variance explained in social psychology are no doubt partially attributable to the large amounts of error variance in our measures. Both Weigel and Newman (1976) and Fishbein and Ajzen (1975) have taken just such a tack in explaining the low attitude-behavior correlations. We might be doing a much better job explaining variance than we realize after we adjust for unreliability in our measures.

Second, the presence of measurement error in variables may actually lead to the overestimation of effects. Even though the multiple correlation is underestimated, a b-weight can be overestimated. This is because the other b-weights are underestimated. We might mistakenly conclude that a given variable is causally relevant when it is not. This is particularly the case for a test of a mediational hypothesis. Suppose a researcher believes that the negative effects of high density on performance are mediated through perceived crowding. The simple model is that density causes perceived crowding, which in turn causes performance. Such a microtheory would imply that the partial correlation of density with performance should be zero, after we have controlled for perceived crowding. However, when perceived crowding is measured with error, the partial correlation is *not* zero even if the mediational model is true. Given measurement error in perceived crowding, the causal effect of density is typically overestimated. This is an unfortunate state of affairs for social psychology. For models in which we attempt to show that internal psychological variables mediate the effect of the objective variables on outcomes, we often tend to *overestimate* the effect of the objective variables and *underestimate* the effect of the psychological variables, which are measured with error.

Third, it can happen that a structural analysis may reveal that two constructs correlate too highly. That is, once measurement error is controlled, the two constructs may be perfectly correlated. Very high correlations between constructs would be indicative of a failure of discriminant validity. At least for the sample studied, the measures of two supposedly distinct constructs actually tap only one construct. As an example, Kenny and Berman (1980) show that ratings of responsibility for planning and responsibility for organization have little discriminant validity.

How can we control for the biasing effects of measurement error? One approach is to disattenuate correlations for measurement error (Cohen and Cohen, 1975). A more elegant but complicated approach is to simultaneously integrate the factor analysis (which measures load on which construct) and the causal model (which construct causes which construct). Such an approach performs a regression analysis (or an analysis of variance) on the *constructs themselves,* not the measures. The idea is simple. First, the measures are factor-analyzed. Second, the correlations among the constructs serve as input for the path analysis. The actual computations require complex computer programs.

It should be emphasized that the type of factor analysis done in structural analysis is very different from the exploratory-factor-analysis procedures that dominate the field. The factor analysis employed is called confirmatory because the factors and the measures that load on them are specified in advance by the researcher. The usual arbitrary choices in factor analysis of communality values and of rotational scheme vanish in a confirmatory analysis because the model is identified.

In these models there are many parameters that must be estimated:

1. The correlations and variances of the exogenous variables.

2. The loadings of the measured variables on the constructs of latent variables.

3. The causal paths between causes and effects.

4. The variance of the disturbance and its correlation with any other disturbance.

5. The amount of measurement error in each measured variable and the degree of correlated measurement error.

Many of these parameters are fixed to zero or in some cases to one. For instance, many of the factor loadings are set to zero. The remainder of the parameters are said to be free and must be estimated.

Five major programs have been developed for the estimation of structural-equation models. Since only one of the programs has been widely distributed (LISREL), my comments about the other programs are only preliminary. Moreover, in the next few years some or all of these programs will be replaced by a new generation of computer programs.

The program LISREL (Jöreskog and Sörbom, 1982) is the most commonly used program for structural analysis. It is rather complicated to set up, it can be expensive to use, and it is quite expensive to acquire. Despite these drawbacks it is the program that is most commonly used in latent-variable structural modeling.

The program COSAN (Fraser, 1982), which embodies the conceptual work of McDonald (1978), is the most general of the computer programs that are available. It appears to be cheaper to run than LISREL, but it requires rather extensive knowledge of matrix algebra to set up. Its acquisition cost is quite cheap.

The program EQS (Bentler, 1982) is in the process of development. It appears to be similar to LISREL in its internal workings, but it is much easier for the user to set up. Its acquisition cost, while not fixed yet, should not be quite as high as LISREL's.

The program RAM (McArdle, 1980) is also in development. It essentially uses COSAN to estimate the parameters, but RAM's setup is simpler than COSAN while retaining COSAN's flexibility.

Finally, Hunter *et al.* (1983) have developed a program called PACKAGE. This program uses a traditional factor-analytic estimation procedure called multiple groups. While probably the simplest and cheapest of the programs, PACKAGE is the least general. Its most important limitation is that no significance tests are performed.

All of these programs, with the exception of PACKAGE, have the option to estimate the parameters of the model by maximum-likelihood estimation, and most applications of latent-variable structural modeling use these maximum-likelihood estimates. The advantages of maximum-likelihood estimation is that it provides an overall test of the fit of the model. This test is a χ^2-test whose degrees of freedom equal the number of correlations and variances for the measured variables minus the number of unconstrained parameters in the model. Moreover, for each parameter of the model a standard error can be estimated.

There are some important drawbacks to maximum-likelihood estimation. First, it assumes that the variables have a multivariate normal distribution. The consequences of violating this assumption are not well understood. Second, significance tests are based on the assumption that the sample size is large. Tests with moderate and small sample sizes are quite approximate. Standard errors generally seem much too small (Rubin and Thayer, 1982). Third, maximum likelihood is prone to giving impossible values. For instance, an embarrassing number of times one obtains correlations greater than one and negative variances (Jackson and Chan, 1980). Fourth, the algorithm for maximum likelihood is iterative for most models. This is a major reason for the high cost in using these programs.

All too often, the overall χ^2-test of fit is reported with the incorrect degrees of freedom. This happens whenever a researcher mistakenly fixes a parameter that should be free. There are two major situations when this happens. First, for a variable like sex with no measurement error, it may be necessary to create a latent variable. What one should do is fix the loading of sex at one on the sex factor and free the variance of the sex factor, instead of fixing the variance to one, as is often mistakenly done. Second, in experiments we typically have equal-*n* designs. We do this to uncorrelate the independent variables. In the parlance of causal modeling, the exogenous variables are uncorrelated. We should still free these correlations and not fix them to zero.

Researchers are often quite confused about issues in scaling of the latent variables. Traditionally, in factor analysis, latent variables are standardized. However, for all the computer programs but PACKAGE, this does not seem to be generally possible. What is done is to fix the loading of one variable to one and to free the factor's variance if it is exogenous or the factor's disturbance variance if it is endogenous. The variable whose loading is fixed is called the *marker variable,* and the factor is now in its metric.

A related confusion concerns the use of a correlation versus a covariance matrix. Either can be used as input. Regardless of what is input, either can be analyzed if the variances are entered with the correlation matrix. The covariance matrix should be analyzed if the metric is interpretable, if equality constraints are made, or if coefficients are to be compared across time or populations. Even if the correlation matrix is analyzed, the solution is not necessarily standardized because the latent endogenous variables are not necessarily standardized. If standardized coefficients are designed, the solution must then be rescaled to derive a standardized solution.

The test of overall fit of the model is a χ^2-test. Many researchers are confused about this test (and the use of χ^2 in log-linear models). A nonsignificant χ^2 means that the observed correlations agree within the limits of sampling error with the correlations predicted by the model. A significant χ^2 indicates that the model is some way in error. Since most researchers believe in the model that they are testing, a nonsignificant χ^2 is what they desire. Thus they seek to retain the null hypothesis. The ability to reject the null hypothesis in this case depends on sample size and the size of the correlations. As they both get larger, so does power. As Bentler and Bonett (1980) point out, with large samples sizes ($N > 100$) it is difficult to obtain a nonsignificant χ^2, and with small sample sizes ($N < 50$) χ^2 is usually nonsignificant for almost every model.

The χ^2-values for two different models can be compared when one model is a special case of the other. Thus if we delete some paths between constructs, we have a simpler model that is a special case of the model without the deleted paths. We can then statistically evaluate the significance of deleting the paths by comparing the χ^2-values of the two models. (This type of comparison of χ^2 is also done in log-linear analysis.)

The unification of path analysis and factor analysis is called structural modeling. It promises to usher into social psychology a new era in data analysis. However, like any method, it is subject to abuse. First, it does not justify the analysis of sloppily collected data. Only data collected carefully and with thought to theoretical issues will be aided by a structural analysis. Although they may be more difficult to recognize, poorly designed studies are poor studies even when dressed up by a structural analysis. Second, models can and should be altered after one has examined the results. Such altered models will fit relatively well since they were chosen opportunistically to improve fit. The analysis then becomes an exploratory one and not confirmatory, and the researcher should say as much by recognizing that the good fit of the model is due to the fact that the data were examined and the model was altered. Third, given the complexity of the analysis and the model, the descriptions of the results of structural-equation modeling can be uninterpretable to the uninitiated. If the results are presented in matrices with Greek notation, the results are unintelligible to most of the audience. The complexity becomes manageable if one discards complex notation and relies on previously understood methods like factor analysis and multiple-regression analysis. Fourth, these programs, while allowing researchers to overcome problems of measurement error, in no way solve the question of causal priority. The earlier-cited quotation by Duncan is just as true of structural-equation models as it is of path-analytic models.

LOG-LINEAR MODELS

It is not uncommon in social psychological research for the dependent variable to be nominally measured. In particular, field experiments often have dichotomous dependent variables: help or do not help, conform or not, or respond yes or no. We still analyze such data by old-fashioned χ^2-statistics instead of by the modern methods of log-linear analysis, GSK analysis, and probit analysis. About 19 percent of the articles in our 1978 survey have nominal data, but only 8 percent of those articles employed one of these modern methods. For log-linear analysis there is no longer any excuse for this ignorance, since there are now a number of introductory texts available on the technique: Reynolds (1977), Fienberg (1977), and Upton (1978). Moreover, Duncan and Duncan (1978) describe the technique and give many examples. Two more-advanced texts are also available: Bishop,

TABLE 4
Proportions

	B	
A	1	2
1	0.80	0.90
2	0.95	?

Fienberg, and Holland (1975) and Magidson (1978). Below, only log-linear analysis is discussed. However, the same points could have been made by using GSK or probit analysis. Moreover, for ease of presentation only dichotomous dependent variables are discussed.

It is surprising that social psychologists have not adopted log-linear analysis since the model specification is very similar to *n*-way analysis of variance with a dichotomous dependent variable. We typically summarize tables of counts by computing the proportion of subjects at one level of the dependent variable within each cell of the experimental design. For instance, we compute the proportion who helped, conformed, agreed, etc. One problem with proportions is that they have a floor of zero and a ceiling of one. Consider the proportions in Table 4. What value must be inserted into the lower right-hand cell so that there is no interaction? The answer is 1.05, which is an impossible value. One result of the ceiling in proportions is spurious interactions. The log-linear model employs *logits* rather than proportions. A logit is a logarithm of odds. In a helping-behavior study odds are defined as the number of helpers over the number of nonhelpers. For instance, if for one cell 28 helped and 7 did not, the odds of helping are 28/7, or 4.00; that is, a person is four times more likely to help than not. Since odds have a floor of zero, the logarithm (usually natural) of the odds is taken, and the log (odds) is called a logit. A logit has no floor or ceiling. Most of us are not very familiar with logits, but their interpretation is very simple. A logit of zero is equal to a proportion of 0.50. Positive logits indicate a proportion greater than 0.50, and negative logits indicate proportions less than 0.50.

These logits can be treated as means, and from them one can compute parameter estimates of a full-rank model, i.e., a model with main effects, first-order interactions, and all higher-order interactions. The full-rank model is called a *saturated model* in log-linear analysis. For models that are not fully saturated the expected cell

frequencies can be estimated only by an iterative procedure that is discussed in texts on log-linear models. From the expected values one can compute maximum-likelihood parameter estimates and χ^2 to evaluate the fit of the model.

Log-linear models are useful for other reasons besides not being subject to floor and ceiling effects. First, tests of interactions are possible. The usual, simple χ^2-test cannot evaluate a test of an interaction controlling for main effects. Second, tests of complex hypotheses are possible. For instance, Vidmar (1972) investigated the effect of decision alternatives on the verdicts of juries. Some juries were given four alternatives, varying from first-degree murder to not guilty. The appropriate way to evaluate the effect of removing options from a jury is a test of quasi independence (Larntz, 1975), which can be done within a log-linear framework. Third, the log-linear model and its estimation statistical procedures are based on a theory of sampling. Other methods (e.g., chi-squared partitioning) do not have such a grounding and are then less likely to replicate across different populations.

DESIGNS FOR SOCIAL INTERACTION

Surprisingly, perhaps, social interaction has proved to be an embarrassment for social psychologists. We all too often have prevented it from occurring in the laboratory and ignored it in the field. Since social psychology is in part the study of social interaction, it seems ironic that we have, to a large extent, ignored this most important topic.

In the laboratory we are taught to standardize the interaction between subject and experimenter. If there are confederates, we spend considerable time training them to act in exactly the same manner across subjects and within conditions. We use videotapes and one-way mirrors to ensure uniformity of behavior. Only the confederate is supposed to influence the subjects and not vice versa. Sadly, even this impoverished form of social interaction is decreasing with increasing use of written materials, slides, and videotapes as stimulus materials.

We also tend to isolate subjects from each other (Argyle, 1969, p. 18):

In order to eliminate interfering, subjects may be placed in separate cubicles and have to communicate by pressing buttons or passing notes. A visitor to a new laboratory which consisted of such cubicles said "but I thought this was supposed to be a *social* psychology laboratory."

Small-group research illustrates how unsocial social psychological research has become. Early research had face-to-face, interacting subjects. Experimenters then used confederates to fill in for subjects who failed to show up. It was only a matter of time before a confederate was inserted into all groups and his or her behavior was experimentally varied. In an effort to reduce variation, subjects were isolated into cubicles. Since information within cubicles was communicated by lights and written notes, it could be experimentally manipulated. Subjects no longer needed to interact with each other. The group had vanished from this line of small-group research.

In the field we cannot isolate subjects from one another. They interact and compare their reactions with the treatment; they may also compete to receive the treatment. Typically, we ignore these interactions and become embarrassed when questions are raised about them. However, such social interaction almost certainly mediates the effectiveness of social interventions. For instance, Katz and Lazarsfeld's two-stage model (1955) proposes that the effects of mass media are mediated through social interaction.

Although social interaction is a major area of study in social psychology, it is not easily amenable to investigation by the methods previously discussed in this chapter. All these methods require that the error or residual terms be uncorrelated across observations. This assumption, called independence, is the one assumption of analysis of variance that is not robust. Independence of experimental units may be plausible in agricultural experimentation, but in social psychology the give and take of social interaction guarantees nonindependent interacting persons. The nonindependence of social interaction data should not be treated as a statistical deficiency but rather as a challenge to develop new statistical methods.

Consider the difficulty in applying the standard methods to study dyadic social interaction. Assume, for example, that two variables are measured from each member of a dyad: attraction toward the partner and number of positive or favorable statements. The hypothesis is that the number of positive statements made by person A should lead to the attraction of person B toward A. A moment's reflection reveals that there is no simple way to compute this correlation and test its significance. For instance, if we use each dyad's data twice (correlate A's statements with B's attraction and correlate A's attraction with B's statements), the data are not indepen-

dent, and so we cannot employ a standard test of a correlation since observations are correlated. Second, if we used only one pair of scores from each dyad, we would be ignoring half the data. Third, if we *arbitrarily* designate dyad members A and B and compute two correlations (A's statements with B's attraction and A's attraction with B's statements), the results would be based on an arbitrary designation. These three practices of ignoring nonindependence, discarding data, and making an arbitrary designation pervade the literature. The fault does not rest with the researchers who employ these methods but with the methodologists who have failed to provide the discipline with the appropriate methods of analysis. Standard analysis strategies are just not well adapted to the ecology of social interaction.

Related to the nonindependence issue is the unit-of-analysis issue. With social interaction data the unit of analysis is not clear. Should the data be averaged across the dyad and then analyzed? Such an averaging would solve the nonindependence problem, but we may end up as victims of the ecological fallacy.

We are currently witnessing the development of a set of new techniques that are better adapted to the problems of social interaction. At present only a sketch of these techniques is possible, but in the future they and their offspring will become standard methods to complement today's standard methods. Below are discussed design and analysis strategies for the study of small groups and dyads.

SMALL GROUPS

Most of the research on small groups has employed the hierarchically nested design. In this design each subject is a member of one group and subjects are said to be nested within groups. The testing of effects in this design is discussed by Anderson and Ager (1978). Kenny and La Voie (1984) present methods for measuring group- and individual-level effects simultaneously.

Much less frequently employed in small-group research are two other designs. They are the generations design and the rotation design. In the generations design a group begins with n members ordered 1, 2, and so on, to n. In the second generation, person 1 is replaced by person $n + 1$. In the third generation, person 2 is replaced by person $n + 2$. In the kth generation, person $k - 1$ is replaced by person $n + k - 1$. The design was developed by Jacobs and Campbell (1961) to test hypotheses about conformity in groups and was most recently employed by

Insko *et al.* (1980). The generations design is quite useful in studying the stability of groups across different persons.

The rotation design is one in which each person is in a group with everyone else once and only once. In this design with a group size n, the set of persons must be n^2 and the number of groups in which each person is a member is $n + 1$. This design has been used by Cherkoff and Branden (1974) in bargaining research and by a number of researchers in the area of leadership (e.g., Barnlund, 1962). The rotation design is quite useful in studying the stability of persons across different groups. Little or no formal statistical work has been done on either the generations or the rotation design.

DYADS

The study of dyads can be divided into two types. One type replicates the dyad by using different pairs of persons or in some cases different partners: Replications are across persons. The other type examines one dyad in detail and obtains replications by repeatedly observing the same dyad over time: Replications are across time. Let us consider first replications across persons.

Kraemer and Jacklin (1979) present a procedure for analyzing the effect of variables such as a person's sex in dyadic interaction. Consider, for example, a study of sex differences in dominance. One could create three different types of dyads: male-male, male-female, and female-female. For each member of the dyad one would have observers rate the degree of dominance. Kraemer and Jacklin's model has each person's dominance being a function of his or her sex, the sex of the partner, and the interaction of these two variables. They provide methods to measure these effects and evaluate their statistical significance. Their work represents a significant advance over traditional analysis-of-variance procedures because those procedures either ignore the fact that the data are nonindependent, discard data, or confound the sex of a person and the sex-of-partner factors.

Kenny and La Voie (1985) have proposed a very general model for dyadic interaction. The model, which is called the social relations model, has three major components: an actor effect, a partner effect, and a relationship effect. For instance, for the measure of how much A likes B, the actor effect would be A's tendency to like others in general, the partner effect would be B's popularity, and the relationship effect would be the residual attraction of A toward B after controlling for the actor and partner effect. Kenny and La Voie (1984) discuss the usefulness

of the model for the areas of interpersonal attraction, nonverbal communication, peer ratings, and self-other studies. Use of the social relations model requires each actor to interact with two or more partners. The estimation of variances and correlations is similar to that in structural-modeling methods.

The second type of design focuses on a single dyad over time. A growing number of researchers are beginning to study quantitatively the "natural" interaction between mother and child, patient and therapist, and husband and wife. Methods for such a data collection are currently being developed and extended. For instance, Bakeman and Dabbs (1976) review the analysis of behavior streams, and Gottman (1979) suggests a procedure for detecting the presence of reoccurring cycles in such data. Thomas and Malone (1979) elaborate various specialized models of dyadic interaction for discretely measured variables.

If we can learn to view social interaction and the resulting nonindependence in data as a domain of study and not as a statistical problem, we can make significant methodological advances in social psychology. We must learn to live with nonindependence instead of preventing or ignoring it. But if we are to live with it, data must not be gathered haphazardly but in controlled ways and must be analyzed by new statistical methods that are currently being developed.

CONCLUSION

There is a growing recognition that cumulative growth in social psychology does not occur just by piling up study after study. Growth can occur when a host of studies are organized and summarized in a coherent fashion, a process Glass (1978) has called meta-analysis. Literature reviews are common in social psychology, but only recently have we developed the tools for a quantitative analysis of a series of studies. The basic methods are described by Rosenthal (1978) for combining probabilities, by Smith and Glass (1977) for combining effect sizes, and by Light and Smith (1971) for combining raw data. Glass, McGaw, and Smith (1981) present an excellent overview of the topic of metanalysis.

In qualitative reviews of the literature we often face the difficulty that a treatment effect fails to replicate across studies. We should not, however, expect the results to replicate if power is low, just as we do not expect every subject to show a difference favoring the treatment.

A quantitative analysis of research studies seems sacrilegious to some. Considering an experiment with all of its complexity as reducible to a single number seems a gross oversimplification. But recall that in our research we treat persons in the same way. We ignore many of the complexities of how individuals differ and we let one number summarize the individual. We can do exactly the same across studies. If the studies are thought to vary in systematic ways, this can also be investigated in the metanalysis. Although not commonly recognized, metanalysis was employed ago over twenty years by Fiedler (1964) in his contingency model of leadership effectiveness. He found a curvilinear relationship between the situation's conduciveness to leadership and correlation between style of leadership and productivity.

One trend within metanalysis is to prefer the effect-size estimate over the *p*-value. As a rule, social psychologists focus too much on the significance test and not enough on the estimate of the effect itself. We spend too much time looking at the *F*-ratios and not enough time looking at the means. Granted, statistically significant results are desirable, since they tell us that the result is not due to chance. But the pattern of results is the true sign of social reality, not the *F*-ratios. Because significance tests vary owing to many factors, their *relative* size is usually totally irrelevant to the scientific inquiry. We should spend more time asking ourselves, "What is it?" instead of "Is it significant?"

Tukey (1969) has stated that the main function of data analysis in psychology seems to be to sanctify the conclusions of researchers. Too often data analysis in social psychology is only a rite of "anovizing" the numbers for the purpose of obtaining the predicted significant *F*-ratio; extensive analysis of data is undertaken only to "salvage" an experiment that has failed to produce the desired significant results. It is a shame that we invest so much of our energy in data collection but spend so little time learning from that data. We should learn not to fear data analysis but to view it as method of helping us understand what the numbers really mean.

At times we seem to have forgotten that data analysis is intended to help us shed light on social reality. Actually, data analysis is inextricably tied to our ideas and theories. For without data analysis, theories could not be tested, and without theories we would not know how to analyze data. Theoretical or conceptual knowledge, either explicit or implicit, ought to guide us in the choice of the design, measurements, and statistical analysis. Most debates that appear to be statistical in nature (random versus fixed effects, raw gain versus residualized gain,

and within- versus between-subject designs) are fundamentally answerable only within the context of a theoretical model of social behavior. The principal question is, How well does the theoretical model match the chosen design, measurements, and statistical analysis?

One recommendation that runs through this chapter is that social psychological experiments should be larger, more elaborate projects. If stimuli are to be treated as random factors, if we are to have multiple indicators of constructs, if we are to have a causal model of the dependent variables, and if we are to allow our subjects to interact, experiments will become more costly and time-consuming. Although there are some personal costs to each of us in running fewer studies (fewer publications), it seems clear that the field as a whole will almost certainly benefit.

The study of data analysis within social psychology is endless because social psychology knows no bounds. A preparadigmatic science should not be expected to be paradigmatic in method. I have tried to explore some of the standard methods and to give extensions of them. Moreover, I have included a sampling of methods that approach data in what are new and exciting ways. If the field is to grow and prosper, it is necessary but not sufficient for both of these lines to be pursued.

REFERENCES

Achen, C. (1982). *Interpreting and using multiple regression.* Beverly Hills, Calif.: Sage.

Anderson, L. R., and J. W. Ager (1978). Analysis of variance in small group research. *Pers. soc. Psychol. Bull., 4,* 341–345.

Appelbaum, M. I., and E. M. Cramer (1974). Some problems in the nonorthogonal analysis of variance. *Psychol. Bull., 81,* 335–343.

Arygle M. (1969). *Social interaction.* London: Tavistock.

Bakeman, R., and J. M. Dabbs, Jr., (1976). Social interaction observed: some approaches to the analysis of behavior streams. *Pers. soc. Psychol. Bull., 2,* 335–345.

Barnlund, D. C. (1962). Consistency of emergent leadership in groups with changing tasks and members. *Speech Monogr., 29,* 45–52.

Bentler, P. M. (1980). Multivariate analysis with latent variables: causal modeling. In M. R. Rosenzweig, and L. W. Porter (Eds.), *Annual review of psychology.* Vol. 31. Palo Alto: Annual Reviews.

———— (1982). Theory and implementation of EQS: (1982). a structural equations program. Unpublished paper. University of California, Los Angeles.

Bentler, P. M., and D. G. Bonnett (1980). Significance tests and goodness fit in the analysis of covariance structures. *Psychol. Bull., 88,* 588–606.

Bishop, Y. M. M., S. E. Fienberg, and P. W. Holland (1975). *Discrete multivariate analysis*. Cambridge, Mass.: M.I.T. Press.

Cartwright, D. P. (1979). Contemporary social psychology in historical perspective. *Soc. Psychol. Quart., 42*, 82–93.

Chertkoff, J. M., and J. L. Braden (1974). Effects of experience and bargaining restrictions on coalition formation. *J. Pers. soc. Psychol., 30*, 169–177.

Clark, H. H. (1973). The language-as-fixed-effect fallacy: a critique of language statistics in psychological research. *J. verb. Learn. verb. Behav., 12*, 335–359.

Cohen, J. (1968). Multiple regression as a general data-analytic system. *Psychol. Bull., 70*, 426–443.

_____ (1978). Partialed products are interactions; partialed powers are curve components. *Psychol. Bull., 85*, 858–866.

Cohen, J., and P. Cohen (1975). *Applied multiple regression/correlation analysis for the behavioral sciences*. Hillsdale, N.J.: Erlbaum.

Cook, T. D., and D. T. Campbell (1979). *Quasi-experimentation: design and analysis issues for field settings*. Chicago: Rand McNally.

Cramer, E. M., and M. I. Appelbaum (1980). Nonorthogonal analysis of variance—once again. *Pscyhol. Bull., 87*, 51–57.

Darlington, R. B. (1968). Multiple regression is psychological research and practice. *Psychol. Bull., 69*, 161–182.

Duncan, O. D. (1975). *Introduction to structural equation models*. New York: Academic Press.

Duncan, B., and O. D. Duncan (1978). *Sex typing and social roles*. New York: Academic Press.

Fiedler, F. E. (1964). A contingency model of leadership effectiveness. In L. Berkowitz (Ed.), *Advances in experimental social psychology*. Vol. 1. New York: Academic Press.

Fienberg, S. E. (1977). *The analysis of cross-classified categorical data*. Cambridge, Mass.: M.I.T. Press.

Fishbein, M., and I. Ajzen (1975). *Belief, attitude, intention and behavior: an introduction to theory and research*. Reading, Mass.: Addison-Wesley.

Fraser, C. D. (1982). COSAN: a user's guide. C.B.S.E. University of New England.

Glass, G. V. (1978). Integrating findings: the meta-analysis of research. *Rev. Res. Educ., 5*, 351–379.

Glass, G. V., B. McGaw, and M. L. Smith (1981). *Meta-analysis in social research*. Beverly Hills, Calif.: Sage.

Goldberg, L. R. (1978). Differential attribution of trait descriptive terms to oneself as compared to well-liked, neutral, and disliked others: a psychometric analysis. *J. Pers. soc. Psychol., 36*, 1012–1028.

Gottman, J. M. (1979). Detecting cyclicity in social interaction. *Psychol. Bull., 86*, 338–348.

_____ (1981). *Time series analysis for behavioral scientists*. New York: Cambridge Univ. Press.

Harris, R. J. (1975). *A primer of multivariate statistics*. New York: Academic Press.

Heise, D. R. (1975). *Causal analysis*. New York: Wiley-Interscience.

Herr, D. G., and J. Gaebelein (1978). Nonorthogonal two-way analysis of variance. *Psychol. Bull., 85*, 207–216.

Hunter, J. E., D. W. Gerbing, S. H. Cohen, and T. S. Nicol (1983). *Package 1980: a friendly statistical package for the analysis of correlational data*. Academic Computing Services. Baylor University, Waco, Texas.

Insko, C. A., J. W. Thibaut, D. Moehle, M. Wilson, W. D. Diamond, R. Gilmore, M. R. Solomon, and A. Lipsitz (1980). Social evolution and the emergence of leadership. *J. Pers. soc. Psychol., 39*, 431–448.

Jackson, D. N., and D. W. Chan (1980). Maximum-likelihood estimation in common factor analysis: a cautionary note. *Psychol. Bull., 88*, 502–508.

Jacobs, R. C., and D. T. Campbell. The perception of an arbitrary tradition through several generations of laboratory micro culture. *J. abnorm. soc. Psychol., 62*, 649–658.

Jöreskog, K. G., and D. Sörbom (1982). LISREL V: *analysis of linear structural relationships by the method of maximum likelihood*. Chicago National Educational Resources.

Judd, C. M. and D. A. Kenney (1981a). *Estimating the effects of social interventions*. New York: Cambridge Univ. Press.

_____ (1981b). Process analysis: estimating mediation in treatment evaluations. *Evaluation Research, 5*, 602–619.

Katz, E., and P. F. Lazarsfeld (1955). *Personal influence*. New York: Free Press.

Kelley, H. H. (1967). Attribution theory in social psychology. In D. Levine (Ed.), *Nebraska symposium on motivation*. Vol. 15. Lincoln: Univ. of Nebraska Press.

Kenny, D. A. (1979). *Correlation and causality*. New York: Wiley-Interscience.

Kenny, D. A., and J. S. Berman (1980). Statistical approaches to the correction of correlational bias. *Psychol. Bull., 88*, 288–295.

Kenny, D. A., and L. La Voie (1984). Separating individual and group effects. *J. Pers. soc. Psychol.*

_____ (1985). The social relations model. In L. Berkowitz (Ed.), *Advances in experimental social psychology*. Vol. XVIII. New York: Academic Press.

Kenny, D. A., and E. R. Smith (1980). A note on the analysis of designs in which subjects receive each stimulus only once. *J. exp. soc. Psychol., 16*, 497–507.

Keppel, G. (1973). *Design and analysis: a researcher's handbook*. Englewood Cliffs, N.J.: Prentice-Hall.

Keren, G., and C. Lewis (1976). Nonorthogonal designs: sample versus population. *Psychol. Bull., 83*, 817–826.

Kraemer, H. C., and C. N. Jacklin (1979). Statistical analysis of dyadic social behavior. *Psychol. Bull., 86*, 217–224.

Kruskal, J. B., and M. Wish (1978). *Multidimensional scaling*. Beverly Hills, Calif.: Sage.

Larntz, K. (1975). Reanalysis of Vidmar's data on the effects of decision alternatives on verdicts of simulated jurors. *J. Pers. soc. Psychol., 31*, 123–125.

Light, R. J., and P. V. Smith (1971). Accumulating evidence: procedures for resolving contradictions among different research studies. *Harvard educat. Rev., 41*, 429–471.

McArdle, J. J. (1980). Causal modeling applied to psychonomic systems simulation. *Behav. res. Methods Instrumentation, 12*, 193–209.

McCleary, R., and R. A. Hay (1980). *Applied time series analysis*. Beverly Hills, Calif.: Sage.

McDonald, R. P. (1978). A simple comprehensive model for the analysis of covariance structures. *Brit. J. Math. Statist. Psychol., 31*, 59–72.

Magidson, J. (1978). *Analyzing qualitative/categorical data: log-linear models and latent structure analysis.* Cambridge, Mass.: ABT Books.

Mosteller, F., and J. W. Tukey (1977). *Data analysis and regression: a second course in statistics.* Reading, Mass.: Addison-Wesley.

Namboodiri, N. K., L. F. Carter and H. M. Blalock (1975). *Applied multivariate analysis and experimental designs.* New York: McGraw-Hill.

Reis, H. T. (1982). An introduction to the use of structural equations. Prospects and problems. In L. Wheeler (Ed.), *Rev. Pers. soc. Psychol.* Vol. III. Beverly Hills, Calif.: Sage.

Reynolds, H. T. (1977). *The analysis of cross-classifications.* New York: Free Press.

Rosenthal, R. (1978). Combining results of independent studies. *Psychol. Bull., 85,* 185–193.

Rubin, D. M. and D. T. Thayer (1982). EM algorithms for ML factor analysis. *Psychometrika, 47,* 69–76.

Santa, J. L., J. J. Miller, and M. L. Shaw (1979). Using quasi F to prevent alpha inflation due to stimulus variation. *Psychol. Bull., 86,* 37–46.

Smith, E. R. (1982). Beliefs, attributions, and evaluations: nonhierarchical models of mediation in social cognition. *J. Pers. soc. Psychol., 43,* 248–259.

Smith, M. L., and G. V. Glass (1977). Meta-analysis of psychotherapy outcome studies. *Amer. Psychol., 32,* 752–760.

Storms, M. (1973). Videotape and the attribution process: reversing actors' and observers' points of view. *J. Pers. soc. Psychol., 27,* 165–175.

Thomas, E. A. C., and T. W. Malone (1979). On the dynamics of two-person interactions. *Psychol. Rev., 86,* 331–360.

Tukey, J. W. (1969). Analyzing data: sanctification or detective work? *Amer. Psychol., 24,* 83–91.

_____ (1977). *Exploratory data analysis.* Reading, Mass.: Addison-Wesley.

Upton, G. J. G. *The analysis of cross-tabulated data.* New York: Wiley.

Vidmar, N. (1972). Effects of decision alternatives on the verdicts and social perceptions of simulated jurors. *J. Pers. soc. Psychol., 22,* 211–218.

Weigel, R. H., and L. S. Newman. (1976). Increasing attitude-behavior correspondence by broadening the scope of the behavioral measure. *J. Pers. soc. Psychol., 33,* 793–802.

Wilkinson, L. (1979). Tests of significance in stepwise regression. *Psychol. Bull., 86,* 168–174.

Winer, B. J. (1971). *Statistical principles in experimental design* (2nd ed.). New York: McGraw-Hill.

CHAPTER 10

Attitude and Opinion Measurement

Robyn M. Dawes
University of Oregon

Tom L. Smith
Research and Education Institute of Denver (REID)

This chapter consists of twelve sections. After a brief introduction, we have attempted an orderly progression from representational measurement techniques, through nonrepresentational ones, to specialized topics. While we make occasional back references, we have tried to make the sections as self-contained as possible, so they might be read separately by knowledgeable people desiring fresh information or perspective. One exception is a conclusion stated in the first section that we attempt to substantiate in the last.

Finally, we have presented critical analysis freely, but—with that one exception—we have tried to avoid prescriptions about what techniques and approaches should or should not be used.

We would like to thank Colleen Snyder, of the Psychology Department of the University of Oregon, and Deanna Dejan, of the Center for Advanced Study in the Behavorial Sciences, for their superb typing of this manuscript. We would also like to thank Professors Sheldon Cohen, Clyde Coombs, Constance Dalenberg, Robert Fagot, Lewis Goldberg, Myron Rothbert, Amos Tversky, and Allan Wicker for their valuable comment on parts or all of this manuscript. We also thank Virginia Parr for making the computer search and count of the number of attitude articles.

ATTITUDE

It is not uncommon for psychologists and other social scientists to investigate a phenomenon at great length without knowing what they're talking about. So it is with *attitude*. While 20,209 articles and books are listed under the rubric "attitude" in the *Psychological Abstracts* from 1970 through 1979, there is little agreement about the definition of *attitude* and hence what aspects of attitudes are worth measuring. In fact, the typical article on attitude contains a discussion of various classical definitions of *attitude,* which then concludes with a statement of what the author himself or herself will mean by the term. How cumulative science can survive this Humpty Dumpty operationalism is not entirely clear.

But why not? The philosophy of precise operational definitions of scientific terms—definitions agreed upon by all who use them—was expounded by the physicist P. W. Bridgman (1927). But his book was written after the great success of Newtonian physics, the general acceptance of special relativity theory, and the support of general relativity found by the bending of light rays during the 1919 solar eclipse. Thus precise operational definitions—or precise definition at all—may be the result of prior scientific progress rather than its precursor. For the purposes of this chapter we will regard it as such and attempt no precise definition of *attitude* or *opinion*. Instead, we will present oft-cited definitions of attitude to show how they can be roughly dichotomized into those that are tripartite (affective, cognitive, and conative) versus affective alone, and we note how few use purely behavioral terms—which may be why some behaviorists make a circular argument that the concept of attitude is unnecessary or even that attitudes don't exist. (In the tradition of Dr. Johnson's rock this latter assertion may be disproved by the attitude of the attitude theorist toward it.)

In the first *Handbook of Social Psychology* Allport (1935) considered a variety of definitions of attitude. Three are listed below:

1. *Attitudes* are individual mental processes which determine both the actual and potential responses of each person in a social world. Since an attitude is always directed toward some object it may be defined as "a state of mind of the individual toward a value" (p. 6).

2. *Attitude* is a mental and neural state of readiness organized through experience exerting a directive or dynamic influence upon the individual's response to all objects and situations with which it is related (p. 8).

3. *Attitude* is a "degree of affect" for or against an object or a value (p. 10).

Later, Krech and Crutchfield (1948) defined attitude as "an enduring organizational, motivational, emotional, perceptual, and cognitive process with respect to some aspect of an individual's world" (p. 152).

Campbell (1950) attempted a behavioral definition: "An individual's social attitude is a syndrome of response consistency with regard to social objects" (p. 31).

Following Allport, a totally nonbehavioral definition was proposed fifteen years later by Newcomb, Turner, and Converse (1965): Attitude is "a state of readiness for motive arousal" (p. 40).

The two definitions from which most researchers have proceeded—at least for the next twenty years—occurred in 1960. Katz (1960) writes: "*Attitude* is the predisposition of the individual to evaluate some symbol or object or aspect of his world in a favorable or unfavorable manner. . . . Attitudes include the affective, or feeling core of liking or disliking, and the cognitive, or belief, elements which describe the effect of the attitude, its characteristics, and its relation to other objects" (p. 168).

His definition does not include behavioral intention—or predisposition. Other authors have—and the concept of attitude as consisting of three components has provided a framework for investigating it ever since. Thus Rosenberg and Hovland (1960) write: "Considerable research and theorizing has been devoted toward the analysis of each of the three attitude components of interest to us—cognitive, affective, and behavioral" (p. 4). "For a majority of researchers, however, evaluation of the affective component has been central" (p. 5). For example, Fishbein (1967) defines attitude solely in terms of the affective component—"learned predispositions to respond to an object or class of objects in a consistently favorable or unfavorable way" (p. 257). We don't understand the insistence of attitude theorists that all attitudes are learned. There is no evidence mandating learning as a mechanism.

Is a tripartite definition viable? In general, those who accepted it cite "high intercorrelations" between the three components (e.g., Ostrom, 1969; Bagozzi, 1978). Those who do not accept it, or who emphasize affect (e.g., Fishbein), again investigate correlations between one component—usually affective—and the others, now referred to without the rubric "attitude." *As we will argue in the last section of this chapter, however, correlations are inappropriate measures of how highly related the three components are or of how attitudinal affect is related to belief and behavior.* That argument cannot be summarized in a single sentence or two here, but it leaves us (and the readers who accept our argument) in a quandry about the definition of *attitude*. If the correlations between attitude components cannot be accepted as a measure of the unity of the concept, how can a tripartite definition be acceptable? If the correlations between affective attitude and behaviors cannot be used as a measure of how they're related, how can the attitude concept be accepted for its heuristic value? But the need for the concept is clear.

In 1935 Gordon Allport observed that "attitudes are measured more successfully than they are defined" (p. 9).

MEASUREMENT

In an influential article S. S. Stevens (1951) defined *measurement* as "the assignment of numbers to objects or events according to rules" (p. 1). This definition is inadequate in two respects; first, not all measurement involves numbers; second, not all rules of assignment involve measurement. For example, the Mohs scale of hardness of minerals simply ranks them. And there are many rules for assigning numbers to a set of objects or events without measuring anything. Consider, for example, the number of rules that could be used to assign numbers to beauty contestants or politicians (e.g., cube the distance between the candidate's chin and left forefinger when he or she is standing at attention; then divide by the time of his or her birth). Few of these rules would tell us anything worth knowing (e.g., who will win). The assignment of numbers not only must be orderly if it is to yield measurement but must also represent meaningful attributes and yield meaningful predictions.

To understand the concept of measurement, consider the measurement of weight. It is an attribute of objects, and it is assigned according to the simplest of rules: The number of standard weights (e.g., pounds, grams) an object balances in a pan balance is its weight. (Fractional units are easily obtained by subdividing standard units.) Moreover, once the weights of several objects are determined, it is possible to make predictions about how objects will behave in a pan balance and predict which set will outbalance which. For example, if we know that object *a* balances 3 standard grams, object *b* balances 4, and object *c* balances 6, then we can predict that *a* and *b* placed together will outbalance *c*. (In fact, the original measurement involved a subtle form of concatenation, because it is necessary to place the standards together in order to obtain the original weight.) Technically, the behavior of the objects in the pan balance is said to constitute an *empirical relational system,* the mathematical system of numbers, addition, and subtraction is said to constitute a *formal representational system,* and the latter system is said to *represent* the former (see Krantz *et al.,* 1971, Chap. 2). Hence weight is termed *representational measurement.*

Such measurement contains an automatic consistency check to determine whether the representation is indeed valid; whatever inferences can be made in the numerical relational system apply to the empirical one. Thus in our example of weight the fact that three plus five equals eight implies that an object balancing three standards concatenated (placed together) with an object balancing five standards will together balance an object balancing eight standards. Of course, consistency does not *prove* validity—for it is always possible that some future check will yield inconsistent findings; if we do find these, however, we would be more likely to conclude that there is something wrong with our apparatus than that the

world was influenced by resurrection of John Stuart Mills's demon, who adds an invisible object weighing 1 gram whenever two other objects are concatenated together. [For a fascinating account of the potential scientific value of such a "dust in apparatus" explanation of inconsistent results, see Holton (1978).]

As mentioned above, not all representational measurement involves numbers. The Mohs scale of hardness orders minerals from diamonds to talc on the basis of which scratches which. Here scratching is the empirical relationship and order the formal one. When mineral a scratches mineral b, then a is represented above b in the order. Since order is transitive, it follows that scratching must be also. In fact, it is.

While the consistency check for the Mohs scale may at first appear trivial compared with the consistency check for weight, an order that represents behavior is just as valid a representational measure as is a number. In fact, the most successful types of representational measurement found in the attitude domain involve orders. Moreover, orders are not trivial, because what seems like an order often isn't—i.e., fails the consistency check. For example, we might assume that preferences among gambles is transitive. A gambler who prefers gamble a to gamble b and gamble b to gamble c should certainly prefer a to c. But Tversky (1969) has shown that such transitivity is not necessarily satisfied. Noting that subjects may ignore small probability differences in seeking larger payoffs, he constructed a set of gambles in which payoffs increased as probabilities of winning decreased by small degrees, and in fact, most subjects he studied consistently preferred—when presented with two such gambles—the one with the higher payoff. When subjects were presented with gambles with quite discrepant probabilities, however, over half preferred the one with the larger probability of winning but lower payoff.

Specifically, Tversky used the following gambles in his study:

- A: probability $\frac{7}{24}$ of winning $5.00
- B: probability $\frac{8}{24}$ of winning $4.75
- C: probability $\frac{9}{24}$ of winning $4.50
- D: probability $\frac{10}{24}$ of winning $4.25
- E: probability $\frac{11}{24}$ of winning $4.00

Over half the subjects preferred A to B, B to C, C to D, D to E, yet E to A.

Representational measurement is rare in the field of attitude; instead, this field is permeated by questionnaires and rating scales. While these devices attempt to assess important aspects or attributes of people's attitudes, they do not constitute representational measurement, because there are no specific behaviors they represent. That is, there are no internal consistency checks on subjects' rating scales or questionnaire responses that can be examined to see if they correspond to the numbers or orders derived from such responses. A man marks, for example, plus three, meaning "I agree strongly with the statement that taxes should be cut one-third without a simultaneous cutback in governmental services." We may wish to make many inferences on the basis of this behavior—e.g., that he will probably vote for someone advocating such a position, that he is an idiot, or that he believes in paying government workers by manufacturing money. But we cannot make a firm prediction about some other response to this or another rating scale. There is no consistency check, hence no representational measurement.

Measurement that predicts in the absence of such consistency checks has been termed *index measurement* by Dawes (1972a). That term is abandoned here for the simple reason that it didn't catch on. Instead, we'll use the term *nonrepresentational measurement,* even though purists who regard measurement as necessarily representational may be offended by the term. But as long as the distinction is clear, it seems preferable to "defining away" well over 90 percent of the work both social psychologists and others refer to as involving "attitude measurement." (Besides, as we argued in the previous section, purity of definition is often the result, rather than the precursor, of scientific progress.)

Nonrepresentational measurement is useful if it predicts. For example, pollsters use rating scales almost exclusively in their predictions about election outcomes and about voter trends; the pollsters are quite accurate; even when they are wrong, they are wrong only by a slight margin, as in the Truman-Dewey election in 1948. Of course, these predictions are statistical in nature, and there's nothing to prevent specific predictions from being quite wide of the mark on occasion. (For example, there's nothing to prevent a person who rates the president's performance as excellent one day from trying to impeach the president the next.)

The usefulness of nonrepresentational measurement is based on statistical predictability of two types: internal predictability and external predictability. *Internal predictability* refers to the ability of responses to predict other similar responses (e.g., from one rating scale to a highly similar one). *External predictability* refers to the ability to predict dissimilar behaviors (e.g., from rating scale responses to voting). Most good nonrepresentational measures can be shown to have both types of predictability. Representational measurement, in contrast, yields predictability through the consistency check. *Hence the basis of all measurement is empirical prediction.*

The relations found in formal relational systems used to establish representational measurement are typically those of order or distance (or some combination of the two). For example, the real numbers—which represent weight—are well ordered, and the distance (difference) between any two yields a third; thus the resulting additive structure represents concatenation. [We have deliberately chosen not to discuss—or even identify by name—the different types of formal algebraic systems that can be involved in measurement; the interested reader is referred to Krantz *et al.,* (1971) or Roberts (1979).] Thus in the four sections that follow about representational measurement, we will dichotomize techniques into those in which the basic empirical observation is represented by order (*order techniques*) and those in which it is represented by distance (*proximity techniques*).

The second dichotomy on which the next four sections are based concerns whether the representation is made about a single set of objects or events or about the relationship between two or more sets. For example, we may wish to represent the attitudinal similarity of two different people (one set—people); or we may wish to represent simultaneously the degree of liberality of people and opinion statements, depending on how people respond to the statements (two sets—people and statements).

Thus the following sections will be organized according to Dawes's (1972a) simplification of Coombs's (1964) classification system. This organization is illustrated in Table 1.

Before proceeding, however, we wish to point out that there is a great deal of choice involved in measure-

TABLE 1
Section Organization

	ONE SET	MULTISET
Order	Magnitude Techniques	Interlocking Techniques
Proximity	Proximity Techniques	Unfolding Techniques

ment. This point has been made especially strongly by Coombs (1964). First, we decide what to observe. Second, we decide which empirical relations among the things or phenomena we observe are worth trying to measure. Third, we decide which formal relational system to use to represent these relations.

Familiarity with the end product of all these choices may obscure their existence. How else, for example, would we measure weight except on the pan balance? Or by more sophisticated techniques developed later? Pan balance measurement is, however, a fairly recent development in the history of the human race, and in primitive barter and commerce there was a great deal of concern with weight prior to measuring it as is now done.

The degree of choice in attitude measurement should be appreciated by the reader. While some types of observations are clearly more interesting or important than others, and while some data are clearly more valuable, there is, at this point in time, no consensus that "if we are interested in this aspect of attitude, we should measure it thusly." Consider, for example, responses to the following two attitude statements: "The draft is a necessary evil." "The good points of the draft outweigh the bad points."

A yes answer to either item appears to indicate favorability toward the draft—but how is that response to be interpreted and represented? Our advice is that an affirmative response to the former item should be interpreted in terms of proximity between the item and the responder, which would then be represented by distance. The person who answers yes has a mildly positive attitude. Those with either a strongly positive or a strongly negative attitude would answer no. In contrast, an affirmative response to the latter item should be interpreted as meaning that the responder's favorability surpasses neutrality—but how far we do not know.

Our recommendations are, we trust, not at all unique—in fact, obvious. But the point is that they involve *choice* based on semantic knowledge, our *semantic knowledge*. There is nothing in the observation of affirmative answers themselves that dictates how they are to be interpreted and represented.

MAGNITUDE TECHNIQUES

PAIRED COMPARISONS

In 1928 L. L. Thurstone published an article in the *American Journal of Sociology* entitled "Attitudes Can Be Measured." In it he described a general method for obtaining a representational measurement of attitudinal intensity, or magnitude; the example he presented was that of judged seriousness of crimes.

The revolutionary aspect of Thurstone's study was that he borrowed methods from psychophysics without simultaneously assuming the existence of a physical attribute to which to relate psychological judgments. Specifically, he used the method of *paired comparisons*. Psychophysicists for years had been asking subjects to judge which of two lights was brighter, and so on, in an effort to relate the results of such judgments to light intensity or other dimensions measured in standard physical units. This paired-comparison method was based on the finding that subjects do not always discriminate brightness and other such psychological dimensions correctly and that therefore the relative frequency with which one stimulus is ordered above another could—given additional statistical assumptions—be related to the psychological distance between the two. The less consistent the discrimination, the smaller is the distance. This distance, in turn, could be related to the physical difference between the two stimuli, and the resulting plot of psychological against physical distance would form the much-sought *psychophysical function*.

The paired-comparison technique is based on two assumptions: (1) The paired-comparison judgments can be regarded as independent, and (2) the mapping from the probability that *a* is judged more intense than *b* into a distance between *a* and *b* is appropriate. The latter assumption may be evaluated by the type of consistency check mentioned in the previous section. Suppose that the probability that *a* is judged to be more intense than *b* can be mapped into a distance between *a* and *b*, and the probability that *b* is judged to be more intense than *c* can be mapped into a distance between *b* and *c*. Since the distance from *a* to *c* is simply the sum of the two former distances, the probability that *a* is judged more intense than *c* can be predicted prior to collecting the data. (The question of how much of a resulting discrepancy can be attributed to "error," rather than to an inappropriate mapping, is a difficult one that cannot be answered here. It arises in the application of *all* representative measurements in social psychology, where perfect fit is rare.) The assumption of independence is much more difficult to evaluate, and it really is crucial, for relative frequencies based on nonindependent observation may *not* provide unbiased estimates of population probabilities.

What Thurstone did, simply, was to assume that the *proportion of people in a sample* who judged crime *a* to be more serious than crime *b* could be mapped into a psychological distance between *a* and *b*. Specifically, he assumed that each crime had a distribution of judged seriousness, termed a *discriminable dispersion,* on the psychological dimension of "seriousness." These distributions were assumed to be normal, and their variances were assumed equal. (This latter assumption, termed case V, is not necessary for the technique to work.) It is, then, possible to map the probability with which *a* is judged more serious than *b* into a distance between the mean of the discriminable dispersion of *a* and that of *b*. All that must be done is to consider the distribution of $a - b$; it is also normal, has a mean equal to the difference between the means, and a variance equal to twice the variance of the two distributions, which are assumed to be equal. Setting this variance of $a - b$ equal to 1, the mean of $a - b$ can be determined by the proportion of times $a - b > 0$—i.e., the proportion of times *a* is ordered above *b*; the *z*-score corresponding to this proportion is (minus) the mean of *a* minus the mean of *b*. The technique is illustrated in Fig. 1.

Once a distance between every pair of points is obtained, it is possible to check for consistency by adding these differences and then converting back to probabili-

ties—although the usual check is made by combining all the distances first to get the best possible locations on a scale and then evaluating the results for goodness of fit.

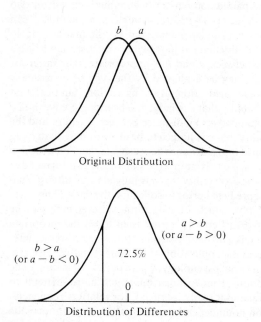

FIGURE 1
Mapping Psychological Distance
SOURCE: Dawes, 1972a, p. 6.

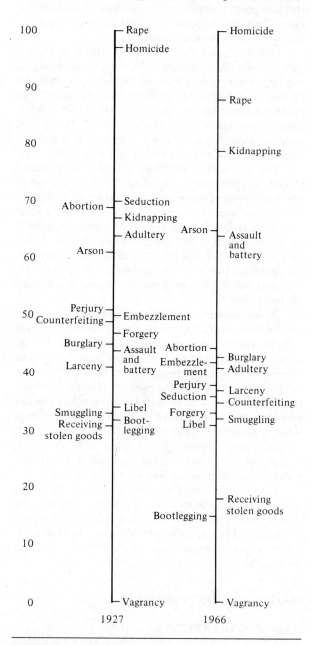

FIGURE 2
Scales of Judged Seriousness of Crimes
SOURCE: Dawes, 1972a, p. 7.

Scales obtained from Thurstone's 1927 University of Chicago students and obtained from Coombs's (1967) 1966 University of Michigan students are presented in Fig. 2. The differences in results add face validity to the procedure, although there are still some puzzles (e.g., adultery in 1966 being considered more serious than perjury, forgery, and libel).

There is one minor problem with the technique: dealing with relative frequencies of 0 or 1.00. Since any two normal distributions will overlap somewhat, such frequencies can't yield a true estimate of the population probability. Generally, 0 or 1 frequency is ignored, and the differences between the means of the two distributions are estimated by appropriate addition or subtraction of the distances from a common third mean. What Thurstone did, in contrast, was to take quite seriously the fact that none of the papers handed in to him gave rise to 0 or 1 frequency—e.g., that 3 of his 266 students checked that vagrancy was more serious than homicide. That procedure is not recommended here.

What have Thurstone and Coombs obtained? While in a psychophysical context it is possible to test a single subject repeatedly—and hope that the experimental situation is arranged in such a way that the repetitions will yield independent results—Thurstone and Coombs are obtaining what might best be called *group attitude scales*. And it is not clear exactly what a group attitude is. Group scales do, however, appear to have intrinsic interest; the question is whether developing the scale itself in this particular form yields any greater understanding of the paired-comparison judgments than would be obtained by *any* other coherent transformation of probability into distance. It might, however, be interesting to repeat the survey done by Thurstone and Coombs at some later date. (For example, the 1980 Republican National Convention adopted a plank urging a constitutional amendment to outlaw abortion, and it would have been interesting to compare the 1980 location of this noncrime to its location in 1927 and 1966.)

Aside from paired comparisons, other psychophysical techniques that can be applied to attitude measurement are *magnitude* and *ratio estimation*. These can be applied intraindividually, i.e., without pooling across subjects. Briefly, people make subjective estimates of the difference between two stimuli, or the ratio of two stimuli, and these judgments can then be checked for consistency. While these types of judgments were originally used to assess such characteristics as the brightness of lights or the heaviness of weights, they can equally well be used to assess political conservatism, occupational

prestige, beauty, or even degree of affect for or against a particular object or value. The consistency checks for such judgments are structurally straightforward; e.g., the sum of the differences between a and b and between b and c must equal that between a and c, or the ratio of a to b multiplied by the ratio of b to c must equal the ratio of a to c. There are, however, many ways of eliciting such judgments (e.g., simple matching, or adjusting one stimulus relative to a second to match the ratio of a third relative to a fourth). The particular form of the consistency check varies with the elicitation method.

Another psychophysical method that can be used in attitude measurement is that of cross-modality matching (Stevens, 1959; Krantz, 1972; Roberts, 1979, pp. 182–189). Basically, the technique requires subjects to compare the distances or magnitudes of stimuli varying in one modality with those varying in another. Usually, subjects are asked to select a stimulus whose ratio relative to a standard stimulus on one dimension is equal to the ratio between two stimuli on another dimension. For example, subjects could be presented with two statements expressing a conservative political philosophy, one more conservative than the other. They might also be presented with a moderately bright light and then be asked to manipulate a second light so that the brightness of it relative to the first light is equal to the intensity of the more conservative statement relative to the less conservative one. There are clearly many consistency checks available in such matching, especially when more than two modalities are used. Thus in the hypothetical example when three statements are evaluated by three lights, the brightness of the lights in matching the conservatism of the first statement to the third can be predicted from the brightness in matching the conservatism of the first and second, and the second and third. Standard numerical estimation procedures can be interpreted as cross-modality matching in which one modality consists of an internalized continuum of the real-number system.

SIMULTANEOUS CONJOINT MEASUREMENT

While the measurement of weight involves the concatenation of objects in balances, it is clearly impossible to concatenate sensations or attitudes. This impossibility—and subsequent lack of an addition operation in the representation—led the British Association for the Advancement of Science to question in 1940 whether psychology and other social sciences could ever measure the phenomena they studied. Hence could they be sciences at all (final report of the British Association for the Advancement of Sciences, 1940)?

Building on the work of Adams and Fagot (1959), Luce and Tukey (1964) proposed a measurement technique based on concatenation *across* rather than *within* attributes. This method, which they termed *simultaneous conjoint measurement,* begins with the ordering of stimuli that vary on two or more dimensions simultaneously, and it yields an intervally scaled numerical representation of the stimuli's location on each of these dimensions.

The basic assumption of the method is that the effects of the dimensions are additive. Thus a two-dimensional stimulus A defined by components a_1 and a_2 will be ordered above a stimulus B defined by components b_1 and b_2 if and only if $f_1(a_1) + f_2(a_2) > f_1(b_1) + f_2(b_2)$, where the f's are real numbers assigned to the components (real-valued functions). These f's are the representational measures of the components on the dimensions—directly analogous to pounds or ounces in the measurement of weight. For example, if an individual prefers a gamble A consisting of probability p_1 of winning an amount a_1 to a gamble B consisting of probability p_2 of winning an amount b_2, the representation demands that real-valued functions exist such that $f_1(p_1) + f_2(a_1) > f_1(p_2) + f_2(b_2)$. (If the bets have positive payoffs and the individual chooses according to expected value, then both f_1 and f_2 are logarithmic functions with the same base.)

For such a representation to be valid, two basic consistency conditions must be met. (We shall limit our discussion to the two-dimensional application of the technique.)

Independence

The ordering of stimuli that have the same component on a particular dimension should be the same no matter what that component is. Consider, for example, stimuli A and B with an identical component x on the first dimension. Then if A and B consist of x and a_2 and x and b_2, respectively, the representation requires that if $A > B$, then real-valued functions exist such that $f_1(x) + f_2(a_2) > f_1(x) + f_2(b_2)$, which means that $f_2(a_2) > f_2(b_2)$. But now consider A' consisting of y and a_2 and B' consisting of y and b_2. Since $f_2(a_2) > f_2(b_2)$ implies that $f_1(y) + f_2(a_2) > f_1(y) + f_2(b_2)$, it follows that A' is ordered above B'. Note that it must be possible to *find* or *construct* such stimuli, or the consistency check is valueless.

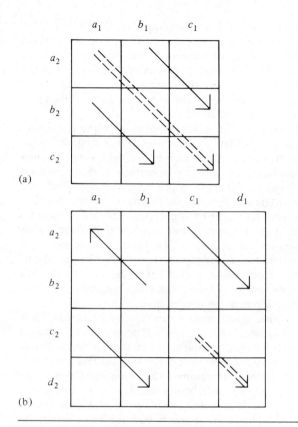

FIGURE 3
Cancellation Types

Cancellation

Two different types of cancellation are illustrated in Fig. 3. These conditions rely on the fact that when certain inequalities are combined, terms can be canceled to yield implications about meaningful combinations of components.

For example, in part (a) of the figure the stimulus consisting of components b_1 and a_2 is preferred to one consisting of component c_1 and b_2; thus the representation requires real-valued functions such that $f_1(b_1) + f_2(a_2) > f_1(c_1) + f_2(b_2)$. Similarly, the stimulus consisting of components a_1 and b_2 is ordered above that consisting of components b_1 and c_2; therefore $f_1(a_1) + f_2(b_2) > f_1(b_1) + f_2(c_2)$. Adding the two inequalities and canceling the $f_1(b_1)$ and $f_2(b_2)$ from both sides yields $f_1(a_1) + f_2(a_2) > f_1(c_1) + f_2(c_2)$. Hence, the combination of a_1 and a_2 is preferred to that of c_1 and c_2. In the figure the solid arrows indicate the premises and the double dotted arrows conclusions of the cancellation implications. The second cancellation condition, which is taken from Coombs, Bezimbinder, and Goode (1967), follows from the same algebraic reasoning, which will not be worked out in detail here.

Of course, addition is not the only simple algebraic operation that might be used to represent the joint effects of multiple dimension, and Tversky (1967) has extended the conjoint measurement technique to representations including all simple polynomial functions. (Consider, for example, the probability of winning a payoff, as mentioned earlier. If some of the payoff values are negative, the expected-value ordering cannot be represented by the addition of logarithms. It can, however, be represented by products; in fact, products define expected value.)

Thus simultaneous conjoint measurement provides (simultaneously) the combination rule and the scale values. In practice, the latter are often approximate—precise values depending upon extensive data collection—but the combination rules can be assessed with some rigor.

Conjoint measurement techniques have been used in a wide variety of contexts, ranging from psychophysics to consumer research (e.g., see Green and Srinivasan, 1978). No example will be presented here, but one of great social interest combining conjoint measurement with unfolding will be presented in a later section.

Finally, the developers of the conjoint measurement technique did not just specify consistency checks but also other conditions that imply, together with these consistency checks, that the representation is indeed possible and unique up to a permissible transformation. These conditions concern continuity and an Archimedean axiom (actually due to Eudoxus) that states, roughly, that no effect is greater than a sufficiently large number of repetitions of any given smaller effect.

The specification of the minimal conditions—both necessary and sufficient—to establish a measurement scale was first presented by Holder (1901) in the context of measuring weight. When these conditions are met, *fundamental measurement* is said to have been achieved. In this chapter we are limiting ourselves to the necessary conditions (i.e., the consistency checks), because most of the sufficient conditions are difficult, if not impossible, to evaluate in the domain of attitude measurement. These necessary conditions are, in fact, the ones first specified by Adams and Fagot (1959).

Functional measurement (Anderson, 1970) is closely related to conjoint measurement. Again, the ordering of multicomponent stimuli serves as a basis for determining the algebraic rule by which component combinations can be represented. Again, numerical values representing the position of the components on the relative dimensions may be determined or approximated. Functional measurement is, however, different from simultaneous conjoint measurement in two respects.

First, subjects are usually required to make a numerical evaluation of the multicomponent stimuli rather than simply to order them.

Second, these numerical evaluations are subjected to standard analyses of variance, whose factors are defined by dimensions of interest. The analysis of variance and the fit to obtained scale values are used as the primary consistency check. For example, if there are no interaction effects, the data support a strictly additive model. But the converse is not true. There can be interaction effects even though a strictly additive model fits, as demonstrated by Krantz *et al.* (1971, pp. 445–447). (Interaction effects are usually identified with *significant* interaction effects—an ambiguity, because for any departure whatsoever from linearity in the population, a sufficiently large sample yields significance.)

As stated above, simultaneous conjoint measurement and functional measurement are clearly distinct. When, however, Anderson—the chief proponent of functional measurement—states that he is willing to make any monotone transformation on subjects' numerical ratings in order to achieve a good fit with a hypothesized combination rule, the distinction blurs (Anderson, 1971; Kratz and Tversky, 1971) because the resulting implications appear to be simply ordinal, as in simultaneous conjoint measurement. In our opinion much of the debate between the conjoint measurement theorists and the functional measurement ones has arisen over the term *any* in "any monotone transformation." When Anderson uses this term, he is using it in the sense of a man who states he will pay any price to preserve the health of his children. He is not indifferent between all possible bills; he would prefer small ones to large ones. On the other hand, the purely ordinal data of simultaneous conjoint measurement is equally compatible with *all* numerical assignments preserving that order.

Anderson and his students have provided an unusually large number of examples of the use of functional measurement to study people's attitudes and preferences. No attempt will be made to survey empirical applications here. A prototypical study is one in which an individual's attitude toward a meal is viewed as a function of his or her attitude toward the hors d'oeuvre, the salad, the main dish, the side dish, the beverage, and the dessert (if any). By using the technique of functional measurement, one may construct meals from all component combinations of these six variables and determine, for example, whether one's attitude toward one's food as a whole is an additive function of one's attitude toward the component foods, or whether there are interactions—as would occur if white wine were preferred to red with a main course of fish, and red preferred to white with a main course of meat (violating the independence assumption).

If there were three possibilities for each type of component (courses plus beverage), there would be 729 possible meals; hence such a study would probably be done with hypothetical rather than real dinners (and even then, perhaps, with some fractional design). In point of fact, almost all the studies using the functional measurement approach have been done with hypothetical stimuli (which is, some critics have claimed, a major reason they work out so nicely).

INTERLOCKING TECHNIQUES

In the previous section the stimuli compared and ordered—whether crimes, occupations, or meals—were from the same set; any two stimuli could be compared. The present section presents techniques for representing orders from different sets—i.e., where an element from one set may be ordered with respect to another but where two elements from the same set cannot be ordered directly. For example, the individual who endorses the item "the good points of the draft outweigh the bad points" may be inferred to have an attitude that should be ordered above that of the item on a continuum of favorability toward the draft. But the favorability of one individual cannot be compared with the favorability of another, except with respect to which items they accept or reject; similarly, the favorability of two items cannot be compared directly but only in terms of the endorsement patterns of individuals accepting or rejecting them.

The basic interlocking technique is *Guttman scaling*. To explain it, we will begin with a common example.

Consider a set of arithmetic items that can be ordered perfectly in terms of difficulty and a set of people who can be ordered perfectly in terms of their arithmetic ability. Then each person who passes a given arithmetic item would pass all the easier ones, and each person who

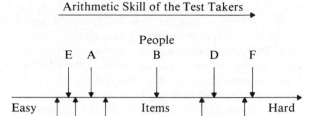

FIGURE 4
Guttman Scaling-Interlocking Technique

fails the given item would fail all those more difficult. The result would be an interlocking order of people and items, people being ordered with respect to items and items being ordered with respect to people. Each person could be represented as lying between the hardest item he or she passes and the easiest one failed; correspondingly, each item can be represented as lying between two people, as illustrated in Fig. 4.

Guttman scaling consists of the construction of such interlocking scales; the success or failure of constructing these scales tests the hypothesis that an interlocking order exists. Usually, as in the arithmetic example, people are interlocked with stimuli. Abstractly, the scaling technique can be used to construct, or test for, such interlocking orders between the elements of any two sets (Coombs, 1964). For simplicity of exposition, however, the method will be explicated in terms of stimuli and people.

Observations must be interpreted as meaning that each individual should be ordered above or below each stimulus. While passing or failing an arithmetic item is an obvious observation to be so ordered, there are others—e.g., the votes of Supreme Court justices (Spaeth, 1965)—that are not as obvious. The perfect Guttman Scale exists given the condition that if there are people that should be ordered above the stimulus j but not stimulus k, then there is no one who should be ordered above k but not j (Ducamp and Flamange, 1969). When this condition is met, it follows that stimulus k can unequivocably be represented above stimulus j in the resulting interlocking order.

STIMULI

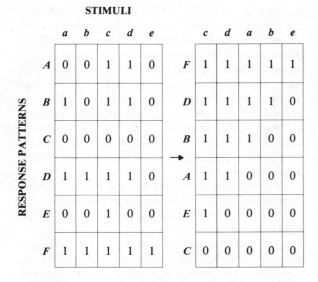

	a	*b*	*c*	*d*	*e*		*c*	*d*	*a*	*b*	*e*
A	0	0	1	1	0	*F*	1	1	1	1	1
B	1	0	1	1	0	*D*	1	1	1	1	0
C	0	0	0	0	0	*B*	1	1	1	0	0
D	1	1	1	1	0	*A*	1	1	0	0	0
E	0	0	1	0	0	*E*	1	0	0	0	0
F	1	1	1	1	1	*C*	0	0	0	0	0

RESPONSE PATTERNS

FIGURE 5
Algorithm for Constructing a Guttman Scale

A simple algorithm for constructing a Guttman Scale is to form a matrix whose rows represent people and whose columns represent stimuli. (All people with the same response pattern are treated as identical, as are all stimuli that elicit identical response patterns.) A 1 is put in each cell if and only if the row person surpasses the column stimulus; a 0 otherwise. Then a perfect Guttman Scale exists if and only if it is possible to rearrange the rows and columns of this matrix in such a way that a triangular pattern of ones is obtained. The person farthest on the order should surpass all the stimuli (those surpassed by no one are irrelevant); the person next should surpass all but the most extreme stimulus; the person next should surpass all but the two most extreme; etc. The most extreme person is represented in the top row of the matrix, the second most extreme in the second row, etc.; the result is a triangular pattern of ones. This algorithm is illustrated in Fig. 5.

Successful Guttman Scales have been constructed in a number of contexts. For example, feelings about social distance can be ordered from a desire to exclude group members from close kinship to desire to exclude them from the country (Borgadus, 1925). (This result may explain the potency of "Would you want one to marry your sister?" as a rallying point for racists, despite the fact that intermarriage is a very rare event. People who have any negative ethnic feeling at all have a very strong tendency to oppose that.) Fear systems in combat range from pounding heart to frequent involuntary urination and being scared stiff (Stouffer *et al.,* 1959); thus, for example, soldiers who lose control of their bowels have a very high possibility of having previously vomited, and those who do not vomit have a very low probability of losing control of their bowels; some vomit without losing control of their bowels, but very few have the reverse pattern of fear. Sexual behaviors progress from touching to cunnilingus (Podell and Perkins, 1957; Bentler, 1968). Coercive behaviors of young children range from disapproval to humiliating others (Patterson and Dawes, 1975). Voting behaviors of Supreme Court justices can be ordered on the basis of their economic liberalism and favorability toward civil rights (Spaeth, 1965).

Moreover, items for attitude scales are often *selected* on the basis of satisfying the crucial Guttman condition of Ducamp and Flamange.

A recent study of a topic of recurring interest is one done by Koslowski, Pratt, and Wintrob (1976) regarding physicians' approval of abortion under varying circumstances. In this study the physicians constitute one set in the interlocking order and the *conditions* under which they approve of performing abortions is the second. The authors asked whether the conditions can be ordered from "easy" (pregnancy would be a threat to life) to "hard" (pregnancy would disrupt the woman's education or career), and whether the physicians' approval or disapproval of performing abortions under these circumstances could be interlocked with this order. That is, could a physician's approval of performing an abortion under a certain circumstance be represented by his or her being ordered above that circumstance in the interlocking order of physicians and circumstances? In addition to discovering if such Guttman scaling were possible, the authors were interested in determining how the physicians were distributed on that interlocking order.

The subjects who participated in 1973 (Koslowski, Pratt, and Wintrob, 1976, p. 301) were

drawn from two medical specialties: (a) obstetrics and gynecology, and (b) family medicine. All subjects were randomly selected from the Connecticut Health Department listing of licensed physicians by specialty. Of the physicians contacted, 96% of the obstetricians/gynecologists and 85% of the family physicians consented to participate in the study. Data were eventually collected through personal interviews of 40 obstetricians/gynecologists (of 353 in the state) and 25 family physicians (of 817 in the state).

The eleven circumstances studied and the percentage of the doctors who would accept or reject each as a reason for performing an abortion is presented in Table 2.

Of course, the Guttman Scale is not perfect, which presents a problem that will be discussed in the next subsection. Using a standard statistic termed the *coefficient of reproducibility,* the authors concluded from its 0.96 value that there was a very good approximation to a perfect Guttman Scale. While that coefficient can be seriously misleading, the other statistics they cite in favor of that conclusion generally do, in fact, support it.

The approval ratings may be distressingly low, or high, to some readers, but it should be kept in mind that

TABLE 2
Percentage Rejection for Each Circumstance in Guttman Scale

CIRCUMSTANCE	RESPONSE (%), REJECT
1. Career or education would be disrupted	60
2. Too young to have the child	57
3. Financially unable to support the child	55
4. Too old to have the child	55
5. Does not want the child	54
6. Being unmarried would be a problem	48
7. Pregnancy or childbirth is a threat to mental health	32
8. Pregnancy or childbirth is a threat to physical health	28
9. Pregnancy is a result of rape or incest	28
10. Risk of congenital abnormality	25
11. Pregnancy or childbirth is a threat to life	23

SOURCE: Koslowski, Pratt, and Wintrob, 1976, p. 302.

NOTE: For the response category, $n = 715$.

the physicians were not asked whether they would actually perform the abortion, which is the question of most interest to a woman seeking one. The relationship between approval or disapproval and the actual performance of the operation could be the topic of another study, because the degree to which any of us engage in legal profit-making behavior of which we "personally disapprove" (e.g., deducting the expenses of vacationing at an APA convention) is, to our knowledge, unknown. Such a study would have to take account of all the qualifications and problems discussed in the last section of this chapter.

The basic test of the consistency of Guttman scaling is the success of actually constructing the scale. It can be constructed if and only if the basic condition of Ducamp and Flamange is satisfied.

But most Guttman Scales are not perfect. Thus some assessment must be made of the *degree* to which the actual pattern of responses approximates a perfect Guttman Scale.

An ideal method would be to obtain some measure of the consistency of subjects' responses (e.g., through repeated administration of the stimuli) and then to see whether the deviations from a perfect scale could be explained by the degree of "error" evaluated by such inconsistency. If the deviation is greater, the hypothesis of a perfect Guttman Scale obscured by unreliability could be abandoned. But that approach has the same problem as abandoning additivity in a large analysis-of-variance design simply because there is one interaction that can be demonstrated to be statistically significant (reliable). Also, there is the problem of evaluating error; to begin, it is necessary to assume it is independent of "true" response, which is dubious.

The opposite extreme is to determine whether the hypothesis of a *random*-response pattern can be rejected in favor of that of one corresponding to the Guttman Scale. That hypothesis will surely be rejected in any context in which the results look anything like a Guttman Scale.

One statistical technique lying between these extremes is to test the "marginals" null hypothesis: that the probability that individual i is ordered above stimulus j is equal to the probability that individual i dominates stimuli in general multiplied by the probability that stimulus j is dominated by individuals in general. Then we would reject this null hypothesis in favor of hypotheses of greater Guttman structure. Such a test can be found in Green (1956).

In lieu of testing null hypotheses (of perfect fit, random fit, or marginal fit), many investigators compute coefficients meant to assess the *degree to which* the observed data fit a Guttman pattern. The most popular of these coefficients is Guttman's *coefficient of reproducibility,* which is simply 1 minus the proportion of responses that must be changed in order to obtain a perfect fit. The problem with this coefficient is that by a judicious choice of changes it is possible to make almost any pattern yield a high value. Coefficients of around 0.90 are not at all uncommon for *randomly* generated data. The following hypothetical example from Dawes (1972a) illustrates the problem (pp. 52–53):

> Consider, for example, sampling 20 observations of domination of two stimuli *a* and *b* from a population in which there is *no* interlocking pattern of people and stimuli. Consider, also, that all four responses to these stimuli are equally likely in the population [sampled]; that is, 25% of the people dominate both *a* and *b*, 25% dominate *a* but not *b*, 25% dominate *b* but not *a*, and 25% dominate neither. It would not be at all unlikely to obtain a sample in which seven people dominate both *a* and *b*, two people dominate *a* alone, six people dominate *b* alone, and five people fail to dominate either. Then 90% (18 of 20) of the the response patterns conform to a Guttman Scale in which *a* is ordered above *b*. Moreover, it is necessary to regard only 2 of the 40 actual responses to be in error in order to have a perfect Guttman Scale. (The people who dominated *a* should have dominated *b* also.) The resulting coefficient is .95!

To remedy these misleading values of the coefficient of reproducibility, Green (1956) has proposed that the actual value be compared with one that would be predicted on a marginal basis alone—i.e., one obtained from the marginal proportions of individuals dominating stimuli in general multiplied by the marginal proportions of items being dominated by individuals in general. These products are not zeros or ones. When the items and individuals are ordered according to domination, however, these proportions yield the expected number of changes that must be made in order to have a perfect Guttman pattern, which in turn yields the chance coefficient of reproducibility for these particular items and individuals. Green proposes that a corrected reproducibility coefficient be computed by subtracting the chance repro-

ducibility from the obtained one and then dividing by 1 minus the expected reproducibility. That is:

$$R_{\text{corrected}} = \frac{R - R_{\text{chance}}}{1 - R_{\text{chance}}}.$$

It is for this coefficient that Green has devised the significance test mentioned earlier.

Another approach, closely related to Green's, can be found in Kenny and Rubin (1977). The main difference is that Kenny and Rubin do not allow for judicious choice of response changes to define the coefficient of reproducibility and the chance coefficient, but instead demand that a *cutline* between dominations and failures to dominate be determined strictly on the basis of how many stimuli each individual surpasses. To understand this difference, consider the following two individual response patterns to ten items arranged in order of difficulty (the +'s refer to domination of an item, the −'s to failure to dominate):

$$+ \ + \ + \ - \ - \ - \ + \ - \ + \ -$$

$$+ \ + \ + \ - \ + \ - \ + \ - \ - \ -$$

Either of these patterns may be made to conform perfectly to a Guttman Scale by changing two +'s to −'s, i.e., by a change of 20 percent of the responses. But clearly, the first pattern is more aberrant than the second. What Kenny and Rubin propose is that since both patterns contain five dominations, the expected pattern should be five +'s followed by five −'s. That yields four errors in the first pattern but only two in the second. (The major problem we see with this procedure is that it treats individuals and stimuli differentially, and the identity of the two sets in interlocking techniques should not be germane to the evaluation of how well they interlock.)

Cliff (1977) has developed an approach to consistency based on the number of pairs of stimuli ordered compatibly or incompatibly by pairs of people, or the number of pairs of people ordered compatibly or incompatibly by pairs of stimuli. For example, if individual 1 passes stimulus *j* and fails stimulus *k* while individual 2 fails stimulus *j* and passes stimulus *k*, then these individuals have ordered stimuli *j* and *k* incompatibly; if both pass *j* and fail *k* or vice versa, then items have been ordered compatibly. If either of them passes both *j* and *k*, or fails both, then no inference may be made about compatibility or incompatibility. The Goodman and Kurskel (1954) *gamma statistic* is defined as the number of compatible orderings minus the number of incompatible ones, divided by the number of compatible ones plus the number of incompatible ones. (It is basically a generalization of Kendall's *tau*.) Cliff has shown how variants of that statistic can be used to evaluate fit in a Guttman Scale. Still, there is the problem that different statistics must be computed for people and for stimuli, and there is the problem that when applied to Guttman Scales, the variants of the gamma statistic require an ordering of the stimuli and people that is determined *post hoc*.

PROXIMITY TECHNIQUES

When using the methods described in the section on magnitude techniques, investigators supply the subject with the attitudinal dimension to be assessed (e.g., seriousness). In contrast, when investigators use proximity techniques, they ask the subject to assess the psychological proximity (similarity) of stimuli, and then they *infer* the dimensions used by the subject. The problem with the former approach is that subjects may be quite compliant in supplying dimensional judgment—perhaps highly consistent ones that yield clear representational measurement—even though the dimensions are of little or no import to them. When using proximity techniques, in contrast, investigators assume only that certain primitive (simple) judgments of psychological similarity or proximity are meaningful to the subjects. Then these judgments are represented by distance, and the space of the lowest dimensionality and greatest meaningfulness in which these distances can be embedded is sought. These dimensions are not supplied a priori by the experimenter; hence they may be more valuable than those that are. On the other hand, they are often indeterminate, because most techniques allow the construction of many possible coordinate systems (dimensions) to describe a set of distances (e.g., in Euclidean space any rotation of axes may be made without altering the distances between points).

The problem with magnitude scaling was emphasized by the philosopher Nelson Goodman in his book *The Structure of Appearance* (1951). Although he was concerned with more classic problems in psychophysical judgment, his basic argument is equally applicable to attitude measurement. It is that these other techniques beg the basic question of perception, which is, *What are* the basic dimensions that best describe our perception of reality? When an individual is asked to judge the brightness of lights, it is assumed, not demonstrated, that brightness is an important dimension in his or her visual perception. Similarly, when an individual is asked to judge how liber-

al or conservative a statement of opinion is, it is assumed, not demonstrated, that the liberal-conservative dimension is important in his or her perception of opinion statements. Goodman suggested that in several contexts these assumptions may be premature and that it would be better to ask subjects to behave in ways in which the investigator could *discover* important dimensions.

Goodman further proposes (1951, Chap. IX, Sec. 2) that rather than ask subjects for magnitude judgments, investigators should ask them for matching judgments; that is, instead of eliciting some behavior that allows the placements of stimuli, or stimuli and people, on a dimension determined a priori, the investigator should ask which stimuli match which other stimuli—and then *infer* what dimension or dimensions underlie such matching judgments. If, for example, the liberal-conservative dimension were important for a particular individual's judgments about opinion statements, then this individual would match statements later determined to be alike in liberalness or conservatism.

With the exception of Galanter (1956), few investigators have used judgments of matching in the manner suggested by Goodman. Instead, they have used judgment of similarity or dissimilarity or the degree to which stimuli are confused. Because confusion is not found in the attitude measurement domain (i.e., confusion between stimuli), most attitude investigators using proximity techniques have asked for judgments of attitudinal similarity or have inferred it from similarity of response.

Some critics of proximity techniques have asked: "Similarity with respect to what?" For example, G. A. Kelly (1955) writes: "We do not see merely that some things are similar to each other: we see them only with respect to something! Similarity does not exist, except as it has a reference axis" (p. 305).

The answer to such objections is that people profess no difficulty in assessing "similarity"; for example, most of us readily agree that the color orange is more similar to red than to blue, even though we are not requested to judge similarity with respect to wavelength. Moreover, most of us with a knowledge of American politics in the 1980s would agree that the political philosophy of President Ronald Reagan is more similar to that of North Carolina Senator Jesse Helms than to that of North Dakota Senator George McGovern. Again, we would make this assertion without being asked to judge political philosophy with respect to a liberal-conservative dimension. (In the following section data will be presented that indicate that this liberal-conservative dimension is indeed an important determinant of political preferences.) In fact, such judgments can be expected from people who do not even know about light frequency or about left-right political orientation.

Proximity techniques are all variations on a single theme: Subjects make judgments of similarity between stimuli, and then the data analyst (measurement theorist) constructs a space in such a way that the distances between the points in the space represent the judged similarities between the stimuli. Finally, the goodness of fit between the interpoint distances and the similarity judgments is assessed by some statistic. The consistency check for the representation is that the triangular inequality must be satisfied (i.e., the similarity judgments together with the means of representing them *cannot* lead to the conclusion that the distance between stimuli *a* and *c* must be greater than the distance between *a* and *b* plus that between *b* and *c*). As with the Thurstone technique discussed earlier, this representation is usually not tested directly for each triple but is tested for all simultaneously by whatever goodness-of-fit statistic is deemed appropriate. (The situation is further complicated by the fact that increasing the dimensionality of the space cannot logically *decrease* the goodness of fit, because the worst that can happen is to get a previous configuration by collapsing on the new dimension; in most applied cases the fit will undoubtedly improve. Thus people who perform proximity analyses evaluate goodness of fit relative to the number of dimensions in the representation; they are in the same position as factor analysts who must evaluate the ever-increasing proportion of variance accounted for with respect to the number of factors extracted, or multiple-regression analysts who must evaluate an ever-increasing R^2 with reference to the number of predictor variables included in their equation.)

The major variations on the proximity analysis concern how the similarity judgments are made and which aspects of these judgments are to be represented in the space. Other variations—which, in our view, are not as crucial—are what computer programs should be used to construct the space and what goodness-of-fit statistics should be considered. (This field is huge; many authors present their own computer program with their own criterion of fit; there are undoubtedly papers comparing different programs on different data sets using different statistics, but we know of none involving stimuli of *substantive* interest in the field of attitude measurement. That does not mean that none exist.)

Similarity judgments may be collected in a variety of ways. For example, subjects may be presented with pairs of stimuli and asked to make a numerical rating about

how similar they are; or subjects may be presented with three stimuli and asked to judge which of the latter two is more similar to the first; or people may be presented with three stimuli and asked to judge which two are the most similar and which two are the least similar; or people may be presented with two pairs of stimuli and asked to judge which pair is the most similar; or people may even be asked to make a numerical rating about the difference between the similarity between two pairs; etc. Rather than attempt to enumerate all the possibilities here, we refer the reader to the 1980 *Annual Review of Psychology* paper by Carroll and Arabie (1980). We do, however, note that there is an essential difference between a *symmetric* similarity judgment (e.g., Which two of these three stimuli are most alike and which two are least alike?) and a *conditional* judgment (e.g., Which of these two stimuli is most like a third?). A judgment is symmetric if the similarity of stimulus *a* to stimulus *b* is automatically determined at the time that the similarity of *b* to *a* is elicited; otherwise, the judgment is conditional.

When numerical (termed *metric*) judgments are collected, the spatial representation may be constructed so that the distances represent these numbers as closely as possible—i.e., are approximate multiples of these numbers or multiples plus a positive constant (cf. Torgerson, 1958, p. 268). It is far more common, however, to construct a space in which the *order* of the interpoint distances represents the order of the similarity judgments. Thus, for example, if stimulus *b* is judged to be more similar to stimulus *a* than is stimulus *c*, all that is required in the representation is that the distance between *b* and *a* is less than that between *c* and *a*. Such *nonmetric* representations have become increasingly popular in the past twenty years, especially with the proliferation of computer programs designed to achieve them. This "nonmetric breakthrough" is not, however, without its disadvantages. As Torgerson (1965, p. 381) writes:

> The new procedures [nonmetric proximity techniques] would seem to offer advantages over the old; they require very little and yield very much. Yet there are many problems connected with these which . . . have not been at all obvious . . . ; it's like doing a factor analysis. And, like factor analyses, the methods always yield an answer. But it can be even more difficult to fully comprehend the meaning of that answer.

In the development thus far we have discussed distance without defining it. The general meaning of this term is *Euclidean distance.* The distance d_{jk} between two points j and k is given by the formula

$$d_{jk} = \left(\sum_{i=1}^{n} (x_{ij} - x_{ik})^2 \right)^{1/2},$$

where i refers to the coordinates of the space, x_{kj} refers to the projection of the jth point in the ith coordinate, and x_{ik} refers to the projection of the ith point of the kth co-ordinate. This distance is simply the Pythagorean theorem applied to n dimensions. Most representations found in the literature involve Euclidean distance.

It is, however, possible to consider other definitions of distance; in particular, the *Minkowski distance* is quite common. It is defined by the following formula:

$$d_{jk} = \left(\sum_{i=1}^{n} |x_{kj} - x_{ik}|^p \right)^{1/p}, \qquad p \geq 1.$$

Just as the Euclidean distance is the generalization of a Pythagorean distance in two dimensions, the Minkowski distance is a generalization of the Euclidean. When $p = 2$, it is Euclidean. Otherwise, the smaller and larger discrepancies on the dimensions are combined in different ways as p goes from 1 to ∞. For example, when $p = 1$, the Minkowski distance is just the sum of the differences on the dimensions (a "city block" distance). When p approaches ∞, its distance approaches the largest single discrepancy on the n dimensions. (To obtain this latter result, raise the distance to p power, and then divide both the distance and each term in the summation by the maximum discrepancy raised to the pth power; the summation consists of a single 1 plus a number of fractions; as p approaches ∞, all these fractions disappear, and the conclusion follows that the distance raised to the pth power divided by the maximum discrepancy raised to the pth power approaches 1, i.e., that the distance approaches the maximum discrepancy.) Programs that use the Minkowski distance, i.e., that allow p to vary, yield a "maximum fit" p-value, which can then be interpreted in terms of the similarities collected.

A great many programs are available for proximity analysis. We do not have the expertise to attempt a comparative analysis of different programs here; instead, we'll mention a few of the more common ones used (as referenced in Carroll and Arabie, 1980). Ramsey's (1975, 1977) program named MULTI-SCALE yields maximum-likelihood results for a metric representation. The work of Shepard (1962a, 1962b) and Kruskal (1964a, 1964b) has led to a general program named KYST

(Kruskal, Young, and Seery, 1973, 1977) that performs nonmetric proximity analyses with varying values of p. Working independently, Guttman and Lingoes (Lingoes, 1973) have developed the SSA (smallest space analysis) programs for nonmetric Euclidean analysis. All of these programs yield a goodness-of-fit coefficient based on the discrepancy between the distances between the points that would be found if the representation were perfect and the actual discrepancy; the definition of discrepancies varies from program to program.

Funk *et al.'s* (1976) investigation of the stereotype similarity of different American ethnic groups can be used as an example here. Their extensive study included attributional judgments as well as conditional and symmetric similarity judgments. Analysis of only the last type will be summarized here.

Subjects were required to make judgments about how different two ethnic subgroups were from one another on a scale ranging from 1 (very similar) to 9 (very different). The questions read: "How different are _____-Americans and _____-Americans?" (e.g., black-Americans and Mexican-Americans). These subjects were "49 female and male university students...; 46 of the subjects were white, and most were Southern-born. The data were gathered in the fall of 1971" (Funk *et al.,* 1976, p. 119). Both metric and nonmetric data analyses were applied to the data with virtually identical results. The ethnic groups formed three clusters that could be represented in two dimensions at the corners of the nearly equilateral triangle. The first cluster consisted of black-Americans, Indian-Americans, Mexican-Americans, and Puerto Ricans; the second cluster consisted of Italian-Americans, Irish-Americans, Jewish-Americans, Polish-Americans, German-Americans, and Anglo-Americans; the final cluster consisted of Chinese-Americans and Japanese-Americans. The similarity judgments were clearly made on the basis of skin color or on some cultural characteristics perceived to be highly correlated with skin color. Moreover, additional analyses involving dimensional attributions indicated that the same characteristics tended to be attributed to the groups in each cluster. For example, the Chinese and Japanese were judged to be nonaggressive and unemotional but intelligent and moderately affluent, whereas the dark-skinned groups, with the exception of Indian-Americans, were viewed as activist, aggressive, emotional, nonindustrious, and poor. Interestingly, the subjects judged their own group (Anglo) to be high on most of the attributes assessed. The authors did not, however, have judges from another ethnic group rate similarity, so it is not possible to assess any in-group/out-group effects. (We speculate, for example, that black-American judges and Puerto Rican ones would *not* judge similarity in such a way that the two groups would be represented by points at the same corner of a triangle.)

This study illustrates both the attractions and drawbacks of proximity analysis. First, the spatial representations derived invariably "make sense." (They're usually even more compelling when the analysis is done to illustrate a new technique for obtaining a representation.) Second, the choice of program is often not very crucial; even though two programs may start with different types of data (e.g., metric versus nonmetric), may attend to different aspects of the data in constructing the representation, and may use a different criterion for evaluating goodness of fit, at the end they must both yield similar configurations of points in the space—if, indeed, these configurations represent proximity. Third, each result suggests a plethora of additional studies that may be of interest. One main drawback, in contrast, is that no hypothesis is tested—or at least tested more efficiently than it could be if it were stated directly. Another is that the results will not be "surprising." The reason is quite simple. The investigator himself or herself has some idea of the psychological similarities and dissimilarities in the domain of study. If not, there would be no investigation—just a "fishing expedition." Moreover, the investigator chooses the particular stimuli sampled. The spatial representation, then, can serve simply as a legitimizing device for presenting or refining the investigator's insights, with the trappings of such things as a Minkowski distance, a computer program involving numerical approximation techniques (understood only by experts in the field), and a goodness-of-fit coefficient, whose origin, algebraic structure, and statistical distribution will be a mystery to most readers. But the crucial question is, "Do we now understand our observations better?"

When Shepard (1962) published the first computer program for proximity analyses, he presented a striking example based on confusion of Morse code symbols by novices and experts. (The representation rule is that the less any two symbols are confused, the greater the distance between them in the spatial representation.) *Our* interpretation of that configuration is that novices confuse similar patterns (e.g., dot dash dash dot with dash dot dot dash), whereas experts' confusions are based on mistaking a single component (e.g., dot dash dash dot with dot dash dash dash). (Shepard interpreted these differ-ences in terms of response confusions versus stimulus confusions.) This finding does lead to some compelling hypotheses about how Morse code is learned (although new technology may be making this a question of diminishing interest), i.e., "from the top down." In contrast, our survey of the literature has not revealed unexpected findings in the attitude domain that resulted from a proximity analysis. (Again, that doesn't mean that there are no such findings, but that their number—if they exist at all—is probably quite small.) Why?

If our search were adequate, the answer may lie in a reexamination of Goodman's initial argument. Proximity techniques do not impose the dimensions of the investigator upon the subject. But the social psychologist who is an investigator is usually a *member* of the society he or she is investigating. Would there be any investigation at all if the social psychologists did not have a prior idea about the dimensions along which the subjects judge similarity and provided stimuli that vary along these dimensions? In short, is the process really one of discovery? If not, then the whole rationale for refraining from the imposition of dimensionality wilts. Of course, every investigation contains elements of hypothesis testing and of discovery, but the question we wish to raise here is whether the social psychologist really wishes to *discover* the dimensions underlying judgments of social psychological or attitudinal similarity. No definitive answer is proposed, but the paucity of findings generated by proximity analyses in this domain suggests that the importance of such discovery is not great, even though the particular virtue of proximity techniques is to allow it.

Finally, even if the investigator did *not* have a valid prior idea of the proximity of the stimuli analyzed, these techniques automatically provide a representation. How? Consider only three points and a metric proximity model that requires an exact representation of the three proximities between them. If the triangular inequality is satisfied, these distances correspond to the three sides of a triangle in a plane—or the points may even fall on a line if the sum of the two distances is equal to the third. Now introduce a fourth point. From each of the original three points, form spheres where radii correspond to the distances from the fourth point. If the triangular inequality is satisfied, these spheres will intersect on two common points, with the result that the four points can be represented in three-dimensional space; etc. That is, when the proximities between n stimuli are to be represented, there is always a solution in at most $(n - 1)$-dimensional space, provided the triangular inequality is satisfied. In practice, the dimensionality will be less, and then the investigator is left with a problem of evaluating how much less and how good the fit (via some coefficient) in order to determine whether the proximities have a meaningful structure.

One new development, however, shows some promise of providing more stringent consistency checks. Schwarz and Tversky (1980) point out that if points are distributed in a reasonably uniformly manner in a space, there are severe constraints on the characteristics of "nearness" relationships between them. For example, in a space of two dimensions it is *impossible* that a single point be the closest (nearest neighbor) to more than six other points; if the points are more uniformly distributed (i.e., do not form a perfect hexagon with the single point as its center), the number of points to which a single point is nearest is considerably less, on the average. Moreover, the probability that the nearest-neighbor relationship is reciprocated—i.e., that when x is the point closest to y, then y is the point closest to x—ranges from $\frac{2}{3}$ (for one dimension) to $\frac{1}{2}$ (for an indefinitely large number of dimensions) for roughly uniform distributions. If the actual number of reciprocal closest points in the observations to be represented are reliably above $\frac{2}{3}$ or reliably below $\frac{1}{2}$, then the spatial representation must be rejected. Such "nearness" results also hold if the distribution of points is independent and "smooth," even though not uniform.

UNFOLDING TECHNIQUES

In 1932 Likert proposed the following criterion for choosing statements to form an attitude scale: "Each statement should be of such a nature that persons with different points of view, so far as a particular attitude is concerned, will respond to it differently" (p. 5).

This advice may appear circular. For it is first necessary to determine which people have different points of view and which have similar ones. How is this determination made? Usually by observing people's responses to attitude statements—for example, their endorsement or rejection of such statements. Thus the appropriateness of an attitude statement, according to Likert, is determined by observing the attitudes of people responding to it, but their attitudes are assessed by observing their responses to attitude statements.

The procedure is, however, no more circular than is Guttman scaling, in which the representation of individuals in an interlocking order is determined by which

stimuli they dominate, and the location of the stimuli is determined by which individuals dominate them. One interpretation of Likert's advice is that techniques must be used that *simultaneously* represent individuals in terms of the attitude statements endorsed or rejected and attitude statements in terms of the individuals who endorse or reject them. That is precisely the goal of *unfolding techniques*. Such techniques begin with observations interpreted as conditional similarities between one set of entities (e.g., people) and another (e.g., attitude items), and they end with a spatial representation of the two sets in which interpoint distances represent these similarities. For example, the statement by individual i that he or she prefers statement j to k is interpreted as meaning that statement j is more similar to individual i's preferred attitude ("ideal point") than is stimulus k; in the final spatial representation the point representing j will be closer to that representing i than is that representing k.

That is, when individual i prefers j to k, a spatial representation is sought in which i is closer to j than to k (which is equivalent to saying that j is closer to i than is k). Representing preferences is the most common application of interlocking techniques. Thus interlocking techniques are often referred to as *preference methods,* and the resulting representations are often referred to as *preference spaces* or *preference scales* (if unidimensional). The techniques, however, have a scope broader than individual preference. They apply to any two sets with measures of conditional proximity only from one to the other. In a preference context we may know how much individuals prefer one candidate as opposed to another, but we have no *direct* observations indicating how similar individuals are in their preferences, how similar candidates are, or how much one individual prefers one candidate compared with how much another individual prefers that candidate. In an example to be presented later in this section, an interlocking technique will be used to represent U.S. senators in terms of the "approval ratings" of various interest groups. While such ratings may be considered to be a type of preference, they are based purely on voting records.

UNIDIMENSIONAL UNFOLDING

The original unfolding technique was developed by Coombs (1950) and it has come to be known as *the* unfolding technique. It is designed to construct a *single dimension* representing conditional proximity—most often of a set of stimuli to a set of individuals (or to the individuals' ideals). For example, the observation might consist of students' rank orders of expected grades in a course, of respondents' rank orders of preference for a set of nonmonotone attitude statements expressing a political philosophy, or of people's rank-order preference for the number of children they want in their families. It is natural in these examples to conceptualize the stimuli as lying on a single dimension—A through F, left wing through right wing, one through many—and to conceptualize people's expectations or preferences as corresponding to the proximity of the stimuli on the dimension to an ideal preference or expectation. The technique therefore begins with such observations of psychological proximity and constructs a unidimensional representation such that simulus j is closer on the dimension to individual i than is stimulus k if and only if it is more proximal psychologically; conversely, the technique may demonstrate that such a representation is impossible.

Coombs has developed his own terminology for discussing the technique, and we will use it here. On the basis of the psychological proximity judgments, the rank order of the proximity of all stimuli to the ideal of a single subject i is routinely obtained. (In fact, the investigator often begins by requesting such a rank.) This rank order for subject i is termed his or her *I-scale* (where I refers to "individual"). If the technique is successfully applied, the stimuli can be ranked on the common dimension,

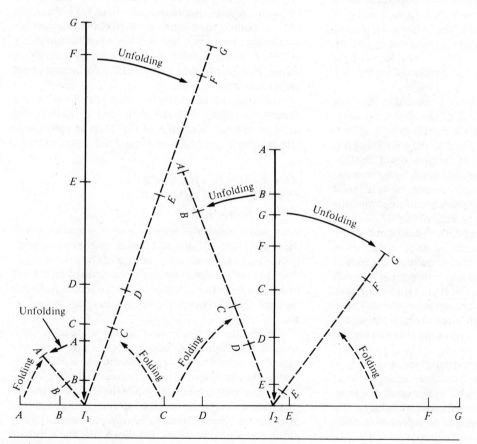

FIGURE 6
Illustration of Unidimensional Unfolding and Folding
SOURCE: Dawes, 1972a, p. 63.

termed *J-scale* (where *J* stands for "joint"). The purpose of the technique is to determine whether a set of *I*-scales can or cannot be represented on a single *J*-scale.

The basis of the technique is illustrated in Fig. 6. The letters on the horizontal line in the figure indicate the representation of certain hypothetical stimuli. The two vertical arrows pointing downward indicate places where hypothetical people might be represented. Given the representation of the person, it is possible to determine the rank order of the distances of the stimuli from that point; if the representation is perfect, this rank should correspond to the individual's *I*-scale. The distances from such points can be obtained by "folding" the *J*-scale about them; the *I*-scales correspond to the *J*-scale "folded" about the point representing the individual, and these *I*-scales must be *unfolded* into the common *J*-scale (hence the term *unfolding*). Figure 6 illustrates both folding and unfolding. The distance of the stimuli from I_1 and I_2 is represented on the lines above the arrows; the dotted lines indicate how these distances are obtained by folding the underlying scale about I_1 and I_2; the problem is to unfold these distances in order to obtain the underlying dimension.

The *I*-scale of the individual represented by the point labeled I_1 in the figure is *BACDEFG;* this *I*-scale corresponds to the distances of those stimuli from I_1. The *I*-scale of the individual represented by the point labeled I_2 is *EDCFGBA*, the rank order of the distances of the stimuli from I_2. The dotted arrows indicate how these distances are obtained by folding the *J*-scale, while the solid arrows indicate how the *I*-scale may be unfolded onto the *J*-scale. How is such unfolding accomplished?

If the representation is valid, there can be only two *I*-scales that are mirror images of each other, those corresponding to preference or ideal points at the ends of the dimension. (For example, the only people who will disagree completely about political philosophy are those at the two extremes of the conservative-liberal dimension.) These *I*-scales then define the order of the stimuli on the dimension, although it turns out that more information can be obtained.

For once order has been determined, unfolding is accomplished by constructing a Guttman Scale interlocking individuals and *midpoints* between stimuli. Suppose, for example, stimulus *k* is ordered above stimulus *j* on the *J*-scale; then if individual *i* should be represented closer to *j* than to *k* (i.e., *i* prefers *j* to *k*), individual *i* should be represented *below* the midpoint between *j* and *k*; conversely, if *i* should be closer to *k* than *j*, individual *i*

should be represented *above* the midpoint between *j* and *k*. The *I*-scale of each individual indicates which midpoint he or she should be represented above and which he or she should be represented below. Hence *the unidimensional representation required by Coombs's unfolding technique is obtained by constructing a Guttman Scale of individuals and midpoints.*

Moreover, the order of midpoints often yields some information about relative distances on the *J*-scale. For example, suppose four stimuli lie on the *J*-scale in the order *ABCD*. The first midpoint of these stimuli is of necessity the *AB* midpoint. The second must of necessity be the *AC* midpoint. The third, however, may be either the *BC* midpoint or the *AD* midpoint. In the former situation there will be an *I*-scale *CBAD;* in the latter there will be one *BCDA*. *But there will not be both.*

Suppose now that the *AD* midpoint precedes the *BC* midpoint. A little algebra indicates that *AD* will precede *BC* if and only if the distance between *C* and *D* is less than the distance between *A* and *B*. Thus when the unfolding technique yields a valid representation of underlying choice, individuals' rank orders yield information about orders between distances.

Because the unfolding technique is identical to a Guttman's scaling of individuals and midpoints, the basic consistency condition of DuCamp and Flamange (1969) yields a test of the validity of the representation.

AN EXAMPLE: THE LIBERAL-CONSERVATIVE DIMENSION IN THE U.S. SENATE

Each year a number of interest groups rate members of the United States House and Senate on their voting records. These approval ratings consist of the percentage of time that the individual legislators have voted on the side of a bill or issue that is approved by the group. Such ratings can range from 0 to 100 percent, and they, in fact, do so.

While the groups have a variety of specific goals ranging from opposing federal taxes to preserving and extending individual liberty, most endorse a philosophy that can be characterized by the degree to which it is liberal or conservative. Similarly, while the individual legislators have a number of specific interests and goals, they also can be characterized as having philosophies lying along the same dimension. It follows that the approval ratings might be analyzed by an unfolding technique. Specifically, the closer the legislator's philosophy is to that of the interest group, the higher is the approval rating he or she should get from that group. Moreover, if the important dimension underlying such voting and approval is the liberal-conservative one, the unfolding representation should be unidimensional.

It is important to note exactly how many inferential steps are made in hypothesizing a unidimensional unfolding representation for these ratings. First, there is no a priori reason to believe that legislators do not vote for or against bills and proposals for very specific reasons—or that the interest groups, which have quite specific charters, would have a coherent pattern of approving or disapproving votes outside their area of local concern. Second, even if coherent patterns exist (which may be spatially represented), there is no reason to believe that a *single* dimension would provide an adequate representation. Finally, even if the single dimension were obtained, there is no reason to believe that it should correspond to what is loosely termed "liberal" or "conservative" (especially since there is no clear definition of these terms!). The success of an unfolding analysis would, then, yield new information, even though political intuition suggests that jumping these inferential gaps may, in fact, be legitimate and that unfolding might be moderately successful.

Poole (1981) has shown that such approval ratings may be unfolded onto one dimension. He analyzed data from twenty-six different interest groups' ratings of all members of the U.S. Congress each year from 1969 through 1978. Using both metric and nonmetric techniques (the results of which were "indistinguishable"), he discovered a single liberal-conservative dimension that accounted for approximately 77 percent of the variance in these ratings.

Interest groups ranged from the Americans for Democratic Action (ADA), the Consumer Confederation of America (CFA), and the Citizens for a Sane World (SANE) on the left to the American Conservative Union (ACU), the Americans for Constitutional Action (ACA), and the National Taxpayers' Union (NTU) on the right. The ordering of senators ranges from Muskie of Maine, Kennedy of Massachusetts, and Nelson of Wisconsin on the left in 1972 to Fannin of Arizona, Hansen of Wyoming, and Goldwater of Arizona on the right. Six years later Metzenbaum of Ohio and Clark of Iowa had replaced Muskie and Nelson on the far left, while Scott of Virginia, Curtis of Nevada, and Garn of Utah had replaced Fannin, Hansen, and Goldwater on the far right (there being then seven senators to the right

of Goldwater). Nevertheless, the shift in Congress as a whole was to the left in 1974, and the average position was stable thereafter. In general, the Senate Democrats are the most liberal, and the House Democrats are the next most liberal; then after a considerable gap come the Senate Republicans, followed by the House Republicans. This pattern of averages was the same across the ten-year period. Finally, votes on such crucial issues as impeachment, the first Strategic Arms Limitations Treaty, and the Panama Canal Treaty could be very well predicted from the order of the senators, better than from party affiliations. For example, ninety-two of the Panama Canal votes were predicted from this order, whereas only eighty-eight could be predicted from party membership (keeping in mind that six Republicans would have had to vote for it in order to yield the final total of sixty-seven pro votes). Poole's results are striking. Not only does the unfolding technique yield a single dimension that fits the data well, but in addition, the results are in accord with intuitions about which congressional members are conservative or liberal—and can be used to predict crucial votes.

The question of what the dimension *means,* however, is not answered by the technique. Like the proximity techniques of the previous section, the unfolding techniques begin with an assessment of psychological proximity (of stimuli to people) and end with a spatial representation. If the representation is a familiar one, it is because the investigator has some prior understanding of, or at least hunches about, the social psychological dimensions underlying such judgments. But these dimensions need not be easily defined or interpreted, and the present example of the liberal-conservative dimension is not.

ANOTHER EXAMPLE: PREFERENCES FOR FAMILY COMPOSITION

Adults in many cultures can state firm preferences for the number of children they wish to raise. Moreover, as effective means of contraception become more available and acceptable, such preferences play an increasingly important role in determining actual fertility (Beckman, 1978).

But people's preferences are not just for number of children alone; instead, these preferences involve both number and *sex* of children (Coombs, Coombs, and McClelland, 1975; McClelland, Coombs, and Coombs, 1976). For example, in many cultures (especially in India and Southeast Asia) boys are preferred to girls—with the result that while an individual may prefer three children to two in general, he or she may simultaneously prefer two boys to three girls. This example involves the simultaneous use of unfolding and conjoint measurement techniques to study such preferences and to compare them across cultures.

Coombs, Coombs, and McClelland (1975) began their investigation by hypothesizing two models of preferences among possible families (i.e., two ways of representing these preferences).

Model 1

Because a family consists of a certain number of boys plus a certain number of girls, the value of each set of children to an individual can be represented as the sum of the value associated with that number of boys plus the value associated with that number of girls. Thus the number of boys and the number of girls can be characterized by two numerical dimensions and a family as a combination of each. The value of the family is that associated with a combination of these two dimensions, and hence the technique of simultaneous conjoint measurement can be applied to each individual who ranks his or her preferences between families. Moreover, if this application is successful, it yields a numerical estimate not only of the value of each family but also of the values for the number of boys and for the number of girls separately. These values, in turn, can be subjected to an unfolding analysis to determine whether each individual can be represented as having an ideal number of boys on the male dimension and an ideal number of girls on the female dimension.

Model 2

Because a family consists of a certain number of children plus a certain difference between the number of boys and the number of girls, the value of each to an individual can be represented as the sum of the value associated with that number of children plus the value associated with that difference. Thus the number of boys and the number of girls can be characterized by two numerical dimensions (number and difference) and a family as a combination of each. The value of the family is that associated with a combination of these two dimensions, and hence the technique of simultaneous conjoint measurement can be applied to each individual who ranks his or her preferences between families. Moreover, if this application is successful, it yields a numerical estimate not only of the value of each family but also of the values for number

and for boy-minus-girl preference separately. These values, in turn, can be subjected to an unfolding analysis to determine whether each individual can be represented as having an ideal number of children and an ideal difference between the number of boys and the number of girls.

The investigators asked student subjects at the University of Michigan and 437 women in Taiwan "from a range of educational and urbanization level" (Coombs, Coombs, and McClelland, 1975, p. 188) to state preferences between sixteen families consisting of zero to three girls and zero to three boys. (Not all possible preferences were collected, because both models made the same inferences about how some follow from others; for example, a subject who preferred two boys to two boys and a girl could be assumed to prefer two boys to two boys and two girls.) Simultaneous conjoint measurement techniques were applied to the preferences to differentiate between the models.

Model 2 was overwhelmingly superior—and in both cultures (and in other cultures subsequently). The main difference between the cultures was a preference for greater difference between number of boys and number of girls in Taiwan than in Michigan. There nevertheless was a slight sex preference for boys in the Michigan sample. While the model ideal was for a completely balanced family (one boy and one girl), differences in favor of boys were generally preferred to those in favor of girls (e.g., two boys and one girl preferred to one boy and two girls).

To understand the superiority of model 2, consider an individual whose ideal family consists of two boys and one girl. According to model 1, he or she must prefer one girl and zero boys to two girls and zero boys (because one is the ideal number of girls *irrespective* of the number of boys). Also, he or she must prefer two boys and four girls to one boy and four girls (because two is the ideal number of boys irrespective of the number of girls). That this independence property (basic to simultaneous conjoint measurement) would be met is dubious on a priori grounds, because we know that people have preferences for sheer number of children.

Can the same objections be made to unfolding analyses that were made to proximity analyses at the end of the previous section? Yes, but they must be greatly ameliorated. While it is true, for example, that the investigator may merely be refining a previous idea, it is also true that the data may lead to the *rejection* of that idea, as it led to the rejection of the value-for-boy and value-for-girl model in our second example. Unfolding on a single dimension places severe constraints on the possible observations. When there are *n* stimuli, there are $n(n-1)/2$ midpoints between stimuli and hence only $n(n-1)/2 + 1$ possible *I*-scales, rather than $n!$, the number of possible ways to order *n* stimuli. (If $n = 8$, this is a difference between 29 and 40,320.) Moreover, *sets* of these *I*-scales must be compatible (combinatorics omitted). In contrast, the only structural constraint placed on observations represented by proximity techniques is that the triangular inequality be satisfied.

Multidimensional unfolding—i.e., constructing a multidimensional representation of the relationships between stimuli and ideals—is subject to the same criticisms directed toward proximity analysis. In fact, it is simply a form of proximity analysis in which all that is represented are the ranked distances of some points (e.g., stimuli) from other points (e.g., ideals). Such an "impoverished" set of observations is not difficult—in fact, in our view much too easy—to represent. The distressing ease of satisfying the triangular inequality and of fitting distances under such circumstances is what makes the approach of Schwarz and Tversky (1980) so promising.

Finally, one problem with unfolding analysis must be mentioned. It is peculiarly sensitive to the stimuli ranked *last* in the *I*-scales. Yet in a number of contexts (e.g., people expressing preference for objects) it is precisely these stimuli that are of least importance psychologically and that may be most prone to misplacement.

REPRESENTATIONAL AND NONREPRESENTATIONAL MEASUREMENT: GENERAL CONSIDERATIONS

SCALE TYPES

Weight can be measured in pounds, ounces, or grams; height in feet, inches, or centimeters. Guttman Scales and joint scales may be expressed in any way that illustrates relative distances implied by the interlocking order. All these measurement scales may, then, be transformed in some way (e.g., multiplying number of pounds by 16 to obtain the number of ounces). The way in which a scale may be transformed defines the *type* of scale it is. Some scales may be transformed only by multiplying or dividing by a constant (e.g., weight), while others (e.g., ordinal scales) may be stretched or contracted like rubber bands.

The principle for determining how a measurement scale may be transformed is really quite simple (Adams, Fagot, and Robinson, 1965): A scale can be transformed in any way that does not change implications about the empirical system it represents; it may *not* be transformed in such a way that the implications are changed. For example, an object weighing 5 pounds must perfectly balance an object weighing 3 pounds concatenated with an object weighing 2 pounds; this implication follows from the numerical fact that $5 = 3 + 2$. If the scale of weight is transformed by multiplying the weight of all objects by 16 (or by 7.5, by the square root of 2, or by pi), this implication is unchanged because the weight of the first object still equals the weight of the second two. If, however, the scale were transformed by adding 10 to the number of pounds, the implication would be changed—because the first object would now be said to weigh 15 units, the second 13 units, and the third 12 units; such weights would imply that the first should no longer balance the other two. Transformations that do not affect empirical implications are termed *permissible transformations,* and those that do are not permissible transformations.

The type of transformation that is permissible defines the *scale type* of the measurement procedure. To quote Stevens (1968): "The permissible transformations defining a scale type are those that keep intact the empirical information depicted by this scale. If the empirical information has been preserved, the scale form is said to remain invariant. The critical isomorphism [sic, homeomorphism] is maintained" (p. 850).

RATIO SCALES

Weight is a ratio scale. If all the weights of a particular set are transformed by multiplying them by a constant greater than zero, the implications about which would balance or outweigh in a pan balance are unchanged; hence multiplication by a constant is a permissible transformation. Measurement scales in which multiplication by a constant is the only permissible transformation are termed *ratio scales;* the term comes from the fact that if two numbers are multiplied by a constant, the ratio between them remains unaltered.

Ratio scales are not very common in the domain of attitude measurement, since most of the implications about the empirical relations such measurement is meant to represent are unchanged by transformations more drastic than multiplication by a constant.

INTERVAL SCALES

Temperatures are interval scales. Equal intervals of temperature correspond to equal volumes of expansion of mercury. Such intervals may, however, be measured either in Fahrenheit or Celsius units. The temperature in Fahrenheit units equals $\frac{9}{5}$ times the temperature in Celsius units plus 32. This relationship is of a form $x' = ax + b$ (a greater than 0). In the example x' is temperature in Fahrenheit, x is temperature in Celsius, a is $\frac{9}{5}$, and b is 32. Transformations of this form are termed *linear* because the graph representing x' as a function of x is a straight line. Mathematicians call them *affine*.

Whenever such linear transformations are the only permissible ones, the resulting scale is termed an *interval scale*. Notice that multiplication by a constant may be accomplished by the linear transformation in which $b = 0$; i.e., ratio scales are special types of interval scales.

The term *interval scale* derives from the fact that linear transformations leave the ratio of intervals unaffected. Consider, for example, the ratio of $(x_1 - x_2)/(x_3 - x_4)$. If a linear transformation of the form $x' = ax + b$ is applied to this ratio, the result is $[(ax_1 - b) - (ax_2 - b)]/[(ax_3 - b) - (ax_4 - b)]$ which equals $(ax_1 - ax_2)/(ax_3 - ax_4)$ because the b's cancel out, which equals $(x_1 - x_2)/(x_3 - x_4)$ because the a's cancel out. Of course, a ratio transformation—being a special type of linear one—also leaves the ratio of intervals unaffected.

ORDINAL SCALES

The Mohs scale of hardness is an ordinal scale. (One mineral is ordered above another on this scale if and only if the first scratches the second but not vice versa; moreover, observations indicate that scratching is transitive: If mineral a scratches mineral b, and mineral b scratches mineral c, then mineral a scratches mineral c; thus the order of minerals on the scale leads to correct implications about which scratches which.) If minerals are assigned numbers to indicate their position on this scale, then any transformation that preserves the order of the numbers is permissible. The scales for which only such order-preserving transformations are permissible are termed *ordinal scales;* order-preserving transformations are termed *monotone* ones. Note that just as the multiplication by a constant is a special type of linear transformation, the linear transformation is a special type of monotone transformation.

The bulk of representational measurement found in the field of attitude is measurement in which the empirical relations are interpreted in terms of dominance and the representation is based on order. Thus most scales are ordinal scales—even if numbers are used for reasons of convenience.

SCALE TYPES AND STATISTICS

Several common statistics are invariant under permissible transformations associated with certain scale types. For example, a linear transformation on all the numbers involved will not affect the value of a *t*-test or of a correlation coefficient; monotone transformations will not affect the values of Kendall's tau or Spearman's rho. Other transformations, of course, will; for example, a nonlinear monotone transformation will affect the value of a correlation coefficient—but not much (see Abelson and Tukey, 1963).

Some measurement theorists have proposed a term *empirically meaningful* to refer to statistical statements that are invariant under transformations permitted by a certain scale type. For example, weight is a ratio scale that is unchanged by multiplication by a positive constant. A *t*-test comparing two sets of numbers is also unchanged if all are multiplied by a constant. Thus a *t*-test comparing the weights of two groups of objects is said to be empirically meaningful, while the same test based on arbitrarily numbered ranks is not. This definition is quite precise and circumspect. It does not correspond to the use of the two words in ordinary discourse; for example, most of us would conclude that it was empirically meaningful that nonrepresentational ratings of attitudes toward making abortion illegal were different for two groups of people according to the standard *t*-test—even though these numbers were obtained by standard rating scale techniques and did not represent a specific empirical relational system of behavior concerning abortion. The fact that the *t*-value would not remain *invariant* under any transformation of the numbers that appear at all reasonable to us would not be that distressing. As long as it remained "large" and "significant," we would probably have only slight concerns about its meaningfulness.

Some measurement theorists maintained about twenty years ago that measures that were not intervally scaled should be analyzed only by ordinal statistics, but mathematical and simulation demonstrations that almost any assignment of number in such situations leads to roughly the same conclusions have blunted such purist zeal.

While it may be important to know which statistics are invariant under which transformations (and which conclusions are therefore "empirically meaningful" in the technical sense of that term), the conclusion that statistics should be computed and interpreted *only* when they are invariant under permissible transformations does not follow. Nevertheless, this inference appears to have implicitly permeated a great deal of thinking in the area. One result is a widespread misunderstanding of what constitutes an interval scale. Apparently believing that numerical (parametric) statistics can be computed only from interval scales, researchers often justify the use of statistics by providing incorrect and convoluted justifications of why their scales are "interval." The most common of these is that there are some physical intervals in the data collected (e.g., dashes of the same length on a piece of paper) or that subjects are asked to use "equal intervals" in filling out a questionnaire. But in such context there are no scale types, because there is no representational measurement.

Ironically, there is nothing wrong with translating the intervals (physical or psychological) into numbers and then treating the numbers as numbers in order to compute statistics. In the first place, any statistic computed on a set of numbers correctly is, in fact, correct as a description of those numbers. For example, a correlation coefficient precisely indicates reduction in mean square error of prediction when one set of numbers is predicted from another (paired) set. When the numbers are transformed into standard scores, that percentage reduction is r^2. It doesn't matter where the numbers came from. They could be pounds, ranks, codes for signs of the zodiac, or anything. Second, when one makes a statistical inference about a population on the basis of a statistic, what is necessary is an assumption of random sampling and further parametric assumptions about this population. The latter are hypotheses about *numerical distributions*. It doesn't matter what these numbers do or do not represent. For example, an (invariant) *t*-test on intervally scaled data that happens to be sampled from a population in which the distribution of measures is highly skewed and has large kurtosis may well yield an incorrect inference about this population. On the other hand, a *t*-test based on rating scale numbers sampled from a normal population of such numbers will be accu-rate, even though the numbers just happened to be normally distributed because that's the way rated opinions fall on that particular topic.

You *can* average rank orders (we do it all the time in swimming and track meets), and the result will be a meaningful average. Further, inferences based on the average rank will be valid or invalid depending on the accuracy of the assumptions about distribution of averages in the population from which you sampled. If you use a numerical statistical test, the result will *not* be invariant under all conceivable monotone transformations of numbers assigned to the ranks you average—nor will your statistical inference. But that's life. That doesn't mean that you can't do it.

One rather unusual assertion related to the belief that only intervally scaled data should be subjected to numerical statistical analysis is that if we *do* perform numerical statistical analyses, then the data *must* be intervally scaled. For example, Jensen (1969) uses this rationale for the contention that IQ scores form an interval scale: "In brief, IQ's behave just about as much like an interval scale as do measurements of height, which we know for sure is an interval scale. Therefore, it is not unreasonable to treat IQ as an interval scale" (p. 23). The "behavior" to which Jensen refers concerns the computation of correlation coefficients, proportion of variance, etc.

As Hays (1963) writes: "If statistical methods involve the procedures of arithmetic used in numerical scales then the numerical answer is formally correct" (p. 74). Further, as Anderson (1961) writes: "The statistical test can hardly be cognizant of the empirical meaning of the numbers with which it deals. Consequently, the validity of the statistical inference cannot depend on the type of measurement scale used" (p. 309). Stevens (1968) responds to the "sequitur": "However much we may agree that the statistical test cannot be cognizant of the empirical meaning of the numbers, the same privilege of ignorance can scarcely be extended to experimenters" (p. 849). So, as Hays states (1963): "If nonsense is put into the mathematical system, nonsense is sure to come out" (p. 74).

The point is that if numbers have been manipulated to some purpose, they must have some empirical meaning—either as representations or predictors. But the validity of statistical assumptions is another matter, because assumptions concern the *distribution* of numbers in the population, not their empirical meaning.

SCALE TYPES OF NONREPRESENTATIONAL MEASURES

There aren't any scale types of nonrepresentational measures. It is, nevertheless, as we have emphasized in the previous subsection, possible to compute and interpret statistics gathered from nonrepresentational measures. But if there is no representation, there are no permissible transformations, hence no scale types, hence no invariants. The lack of invariance, however, need not make the researcher impotent.

Unfortunately, the scale types of nonrepresentational measures are "studied." For example, one of us (RMD) was recently asked to review a paper whose authors proclaimed that "ordinal scales can be treated as interval ones." Using the standard format, these authors collected semantic differential ratings from one group of subjects; this standard format contains colons between blanks that indicate categories between bipolar adjectives. The existence of these colons meant, according to the authors, that the ratings were "ordinally scaled," because they separated the categories. Another group of subjects performed the identical task, except that the lines were not separated by colons. These data were said to be "intervally scaled," because the lack of colons meant that there were no category boundaries. The data from the two groups were subjected to separate factor analyses, with virtually identical results (which is not surprising given that the stimuli were identical except for the existence of the colons). Their conclusion: Ordinal scales can be treated as interval ones. Our conclusion: Omitting colons changes very little.

THE UBIQUITOUS RATING SCALE

Rating scales are nonrepresentational measurement techniques that attempt to assess an individual's attitudes by asking him or her to express them in terms of a categorical or numerical rating. These scales are ubiquitous in social psychology, particularly in attitude measurement. They usually consist of categories (often ordered), numbers, or lines; sometimes, they consist of combinations of categories, numbers, and lines. The individual whose attitude is being assessed is usually asked to select a single category, to pick a single number, or to place a check mark at a single point on a line; sometimes, individuals are asked to do something more complicated—for instance, to indicate on a line a range of positions that are acceptable to them.

Six examples of rating scales are presented in Fig. 7. In the example in Fig. 7(a), the subject is presented with statements that express authoritarian attitudes, and he or she is asked to indicate agreement with each statement by selecting a number from +3 to −3. Notice that the subject responding must select an integer value and that verbal categories are paired with each such integer. Notice also that subjects cannot express complete indifference toward a statement; there is no zero on the rating scale. (The first statement in this example is taken directly from the original scale of authoritarianism; the second is an adaptation that is used more frequently than is the original from which it was adapted.)

The example in Fig. 7(b) is that of the semantic differential rating scale. Here also the subject is to make a rating between two extreme positions; this rating is to indicate his or her feelings about the concept presented above the scale. The extremes of this scale are defined in terms of bipolar semantic adjectives instead of in terms of agreement or disagreement; furthermore, the positions between the extremes are not paired with verbal labels—although the midpoint is clearly meant to be used when the rater associates the concept with neither pole of the adjective pair.

The example in Fig. 7(c) is taken from a study in which police and community members engaged in a program of face-to-face interaction meant to alleviate tensions. After the program was over, each participant was asked to rate its success by choosing one of the four evaluative labels "excellent," "very good," "good," and "poor." Notice that although these labels are generally regarded as being on a continuum from poor to excellent, individuals responding are unable to indicate varying degrees of unfavorableness, yet they are able to indicate varying degrees of favorability.

The example in Fig. 7(d) is taken from a study that attempted to manipulate male subjects' attitudes toward *Playboy* playmate pictures by giving the subjects false information about their heart rates while they were looking at these pictures. Here the subject is able to choose any number between 0 and 100 to indicate his feelings about the attractiveness of the woman pictured; he is not constrained to choose among only a few alternatives. Another difference between this scale and the previous scale is that verbal categories are associated with the range of numerical values rather than with a single response.

The next example, Fig. 7(e), is taken from a study in which the attitude (favorability) of inductees toward military jobs was assessed at varying times after they had

The following statements refer to opinions regarding a number of social groups and issues, about which some people agree and others disagree. Please mark each statement in the left-hand margin according to your agreement or disagreement, as follows:

+1: slight support, agreement   −1: slight opposition, disagreement

+2: moderate support, agreement   −2: moderate opposition, disagreement

+3: strong support, agreement   −3: strong opposition, disagreement

Sciences like chemistry, physics, and medicine have carried men very far, but there are many important things that can never possibly be understood by the human mind.

Most people don't realize the extent to which their lives are governed by secret plots hatched in hidden places.

(a)

MY FATHER

active :_____:_____:_____:_____:_____:_____:_____: passive

soft :_____:_____:_____:_____:_____:_____:_____: hard

(b)

Please rate this program by circling your choice:

Excellent

Very good

Good

Poor

(c)

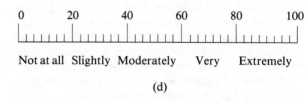

HOW ATTRACTIVE IS THIS PLAYMATE?

0   20   40   60   80   100

Not at all   Slightly   Moderately   Very   Extremely

(d)

HOW MUCH WOULD YOU LIKE TO WORK AT THIS JOB IN THE ARMY FOR THE NEXT TWO YEARS?

Would like extremely much

Would like very much

Would like fairly much

Would like and dislike equally

Would dislike fairly much

Would dislike very much

Would dislike extremely much

(e)

The blind adult is not quite as mature or "grown up" as the sighted adult.   (Circle one)

    strongly agree, mildly agree, mildly disagree, strongly disagree

(f)

FIGURE 7
Six Examples of Rating Scales

SOURCE: (a) Adorno *et al.,* 1950, p. 110; (b) Osgood, Suci, and Tannenbaum, 1957, p. 26; (c) Sykes and Cleveland, 1968, p. 767; (d) Valens, 1966, p. 403 (e) Festinger *et al.,* 1964, p. 116; (f) Cowen, Underber, and Verillo, 1958, p. 298.

chosen between two of them. The attitude scale is similar to that presented in Fig. 7(d), with the exception that the verbal labels are associated with single points on the scale, and the subjects may, therefore, make a response between two labels.

Finally, Fig. 7(f) is an example of a *Likert Scale* (as was Fig. 7a); such scales consist of a declarative statement and a number of categories on which the subjects are to rate their agreement or disagreement with the statement. There may be any number of categories, but the most common number is seven; there need not be a neutral category, but there usually is (and contra Sykes and Cleveland, it is usually placed in the middle).

There are many types of rating scales in addition to those presented in Fig. 7; they range from simple types that require subjects to respond only yes or no to those as complex as the one presented in Fig. 7(e). Rating scales are found throughout social and educational psychology, especially in research concerned with people's attitudes. While it is certainly possible to invent new rating scale techniques (e.g., involving choice of color rather than position on a line), those presented in Fig. 7—chosen from ten to twenty years ago—are still most representative (perhaps for reasons to be explained in a later topic in this section). The bipolar scale (Fig. 7b) and the Likert Scale (Figs. 7a and 7e) are the most common.

The investigator usually assigns numbers to the categories or positions on such scales and then adds, averages, or computes some other statistic that suits his or her purpose. As pointed out in the previous section, such statistics are valid descriptors of the data (provided they are accurately computed). They may also be used for making statistical inferences, provided the numerical assumptions about the population sampled are (at least approximately) met—even though these numbers are not representational ones.

THE SEMANTIC DIFFERENTIAL

Of all rating scales the *semantic differential* (Osgood, Suci, and Tannenbaum, 1957) is the most ubiquitous. This differential consists of a set of bipolar semantic scales such as those illustrated in Fig. 7(b); the scales are anchored at each pole by an adjective describing one side of a semantic continuum. Subjects are asked to rate a concept by placing a check mark at the point on this continuum where they feel that the concept lies. For example, consider a man asked to rate the concept "father" on the active-passive scale as in Fig. 7(b). If he thinks of his

father as a very active person, he should place his mark in the most extreme category, i.e., next to the word *active*. If he thinks of him as only a slightly active person, he should place his check mark in the category just on the *active* side of the middle category; if he thinks of his father as neither active nor passive, he should place his check mark in the middle category; etc.

The semantic differential is meant to assess the semantic connotations of the concept being rated. It is termed a *differential* because it is meant to assess the differential connotations of the people rating the concepts.

An impressive number of factor-analytic studies —using people from twenty-six different cultures around the world—have demonstrated that the major semantic dimensions used to evaluate such concepts are evaluation (i.e., good-bad), potency (i.e, strong-weak), and activity (i.e., active-passive). That is, if we know how an individual from these cultures rates a concept on these factors, we can fairly well predict how he or she will rate that concept on a wide variety of bipolar semantic scales. Thus the semantic differential has high internal predictive validity.

These factors in the context of factor-analytic studies are hypothetical variables; they correspond closely, however, to the semantic scales defined by the adjectives good-bad, strong-weak, and active-passive. Because this correspondence is not perfect, and because the reliability of single scales is low, additional scales are used to evaluate each of these three factors (dimensions). Three or four scales are used to assess each; for example, the scales good-bad, tasty-distasteful, and valuable-worthless may be used to assess the evaluative dimension.

Usually, the location of the concept on each of the three dimensions is determined by averaging the ratings assigned to it on the three or four bipolar scales meant to evaluate it. These averages are obtained by assigning values from 1 to 7 to correspond to each category. Once these values on each dimension are obtained, it is possible to represent the concept in a three-dimensional space and to evaluate the distance between concepts in that space. Osgood and Luria (1954, p. 580) believe that such distance represents "differences in meaning." They further propose that it is possible to study changes in meaning by observing changes in location in this space.

In the early 1950s, Osgood and Luria (1954) engaged in an extensive investigation of psychotherapeutic changes as evidenced by changes in semantic differential ratings. The concepts they asked patients to rate and the scales they used are presented in Table 3. The coefficients

TABLE 3
Concepts and Scales Used in This Analysis

CONCEPTS		
Love	Mental sickness	Self-control
Child	My mother	Hatred
My doctor	Peace of mind	My father
Me	Fraud	Confusion
My job	My spouse	Sex

SCALES AND THEIR FACTOR LOADINGS

SCALES	EVALUATION	ACTIVITY	POTENCY
Valuable-worthless	0.79	0.13	0.04
Clean-dirty	0.82	0.03	−0.05
Tasty-distasteful	0.77	−0.11	0.05
Fast-slow	0.01	0.70	0.00
Active-passive	0.14	0.59	0.04
Hot-cold	−0.04	0.46	−0.06
Large-small	0.06	0.34	0.62
Strong-weak	0.19	0.20	0.62
Deep-shallow	0.27	0.14	0.46
Tense-relaxed	−0.55	0.37	−0.12

SOURCE: Osgood and Luria, 1954, p. 580.

at the bottom of this table are the *factor loadings,* which are the correlations between the scales actually used and the three hypothetical variables (factors) of evaluation, activity, and potency.

In 1953 the editor of the *Journal of Abnormal and Social Psychology,* J. McVicar Hunt, received a manuscript from Thigpen and Cleckley describing a case history of a woman with multiple personalities. This manuscript was later expanded into a best-selling book entitled *The Three Faces of Eve* (Thigpen and Cleckley, 1957), which, in turn, was adapted into a movie with the same title. (Joanne Woodward won the best actress award for her portrayal of the woman with the multiple personalities.) This movie is still shown periodically on television.

Hunt, aware of the work of Osgood and Luria when he received the Thigpen and Cleckley manuscript, thought that it would be interesting to have semantic differential data from each of the "personalities" in the patient; thus he contacted Thigpen and Cleckley and suggested that they administer the semantic differential, which they did—twice to each of the three personalities. Hunt thought it would be "rather intriguing" to test the external validity of the semantic differential, asking Osgood and Luria to describe each of the three personalities on the basis of the semantic differential data—knowing little else about the patient. They agreed, and they further agreed to publish the results of their blind analysis. In the ensuing publication Osgood and Luria (1954) described what they knew about the patient (p. 580):

> We know that we are dealing with a case of triple personality, and these have been labeled for us (presumably by the therapists who collected the semantic data) "Eve White," "Eve Black," and "Jane." We suppose that the "White" and "Black" have some quantitative significance—certainly, as will be seen, the quantitative semantic data distinguish sharply between them. We also know, of course, that the patient is a woman, presumably participating in some kind of therapy; we do not know the stage of the therapy or whether or not she is hospitalized. We consider it also fair to ask (from J. McV. Hunt) about the following items of sociological status, because they contribute to the meaningful interpretation of certain concepts: CONCEPT CHILD—does this woman have a child? Yes, she does. CONCEPT SPOUSE—is this woman married? Yes, she is. CONCEPTS FATHER and MOTHER—are her parents alive? The mother is, but Hunt doesn't know about the father. CONCEPT MY JOB—has this woman had a job outside of homekeeping? Yes, she has. This is the sum total of our external information about the case.

The locations of the concepts of Eve White late in therapy are presented in Fig. 8. The evaluative dimensions are represented vertically (with good up and bad down), the activity dimension is represented from left to right (with active left and passive right), and the potency dimension is represented by depth (with weak near toward the viewer, strong away from the viewer).

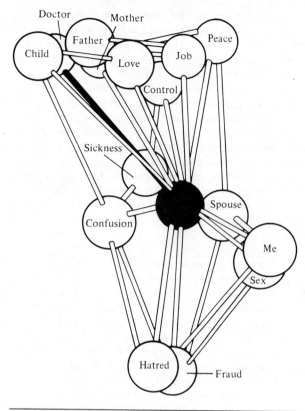

FIGURE 8
Eve White II
SOURCE: Osgood and Luria, 1954, p. 584.

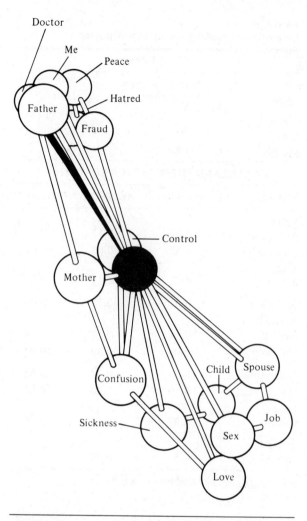

FIGURE 9
Eve Black I
SOURCE: Osgood and Luria, 1954, p. 585.

Osgood and Luria (1954) describe Eve White as follows (pp. 581–582):

> The most general characterization would be that *Eve White perceives "the world" in essentially normal fashion, is well socialized, but has an unsatisfactory attitude toward herself.* Here the usual societal "goods" are seen favorably—MY DOCTOR, MY FATHER, LOVE, SELF-CONTROL, PEACE OF MIND, and MY MOTHER are all *good* and *strong* whereas FRAUD, HATRED, and to some extent, CONFUSION are *bad.* Chief evidence of disturbance in the personality is the fact that ME (the self-concept) is considered a little *bad,* a little *passive,*

and definitely *weak.* Substantiating evidence is the *weakness* of her CHILD as she sees him (or her), and the essential meaninglessness to her of MY SPOUSE and SEX. Note also the wide evaluative separation between LOVE and SEX.

The location of the concepts for Eve Black are illustrated in Fig. 9. Again, the evaluative dimensions are represented vertically (with good up and bad down), the activity dimension from left to right (with active left and passive right), and the potency dimension by depth (with weak toward and strong away from the viewer).

Osgood and Luria (1954) describe Eve Black as follows (pp. 584–585):

> The most general characterization here would be that *Eve Black has achieved a violent kind of adjustment in which she perceives herself as literally perfect, but, to accomplish this break her way of perceiving "the world" becomes completely disoriented from the norm*. The only exceptions to this dictum are MY DOCTOR and PEACE OF MIND, which maintain their *good* and *strong* characteristics, the latter, interestingly enough, also becoming *active* [later]. But if Eve Black perceives herself as being *good,* then she also has to accept HATRED and FRAUD as positive values, since (we assume) she has strong hatreds and is socially fraudulent. So we find a tight, but very un-normal, favorable cluster of ME, MY DOCTOR, PEACE OF MIND, HATRED, and FRAUD. What are positive values for most people—CHILD, MY SPOUSE, MY JOB, LOVE, and SEX— are completely rejected as *bad* and *passive,* and all these except CHILD are also *weak* (this may be because child was weak in Eve White and much of the change here is a simple "flipflop" of meanings). Note that it is MOTHER in this personality that becomes relatively meaningless; FATHER, on the other hand, stays *good* but shifts completely from *strong* (in Eve White) to *weak*—possible implications of these familial identifications will be considered later. Note also that in this personality LOVE, SEX are closely identified, both as *bad, weak, passive* things.

The descriptions are remarkably accurate. Osgood and Luria continued to test Eve White and Eve Black as she progressed through therapy and continued to obtain semantic differential results reflecting personality change. Late in therapy a third personality, Jane, appeared, and while both she and her semantic differential results were "normal," Osgood and Luria speculated that her semantic differential ratings were so stereotypic of normality that she well might be unstable (an "as if" personality). In fact, she disappeared. It turned out years later that she was a fabrication of Eve Black (Osgood and Luria, 1976, p. 286).

At least in this striking example, the semantic differential appears to possess external, as well as internal, validity.

THE LITERAL INTERPRETATION FALLACY

Even when a rating scale technique has strong internal or external validity, subjects' responses to it cannot be interpreted literally. (Consider, for example, the rating of one's doctor on the tasty-distasteful scale.) When the validity of a rating scale technique is primarily based on prima facie considerations, the problems with literal interpretation mount.

For example, consider a policeman who has taken part in the Sykes and Cleveland (1968) program meant to ease police-community tensions. He is asked to evaluate it by choosing one of the four categories on the rating scale: "poor," "good," "very good," "excellent." He chooses "good." Does this choice really mean that he regards the program as, literally, "good"?

Suppose he thought that the program could best be described as "fair." Faced with the rating scale that Sykes and Cleveland used, he is unable to express this verbal judgment. He may, then, choose "good" in preference to "poor."

Suppose he has a tendency to avoid saying pejorative things about other people or their efforts. No matter how bad he thinks a program to be, he must now at least say that it is "good"—if he is to avoid the label "poor."

Suppose that he does not have a very strong opinion about the program; it would then be natural for him to try to avoid using an extreme category to characterize it. Such avoidance leaves him with the choice between saying the program is "good" or "very good."

In short, an individual's response to a rating scale may be determined by many factors other than his or her attitude. Responses cannot be interpreted literally. Sykes and Cleveland themselves are aware of this ambiguity and therefore worked out other, more sophisticated techniques for evaluating police and community attitude (Cleveland, 1970, personal communication).

To interpret rating scale responses literally is a fallacy. The Sykes and Cleveland scale has been used to illustrate this fallacy because the problems in interpreting responses to it in a literal manner are obvious. All scales are subject to the same problem. For example, respondents may tell pollsters that they "approve" of a particular presidential policy not because they like the policy at all but because they feel it is somehow unpatriotic to "disapprove" of the president—especially once he or she has blundered into war or served as a catalyst to an economic catastrophe. Or subgroups of neurotic people who are unable to express anger in their personal lives may likewise be unable to choose negative categories in rating scales.

EMPIRICAL JUSTIFICATION FOR RATING SCALES

It is clear that rating scales sometimes work—for instance, in the prediction of electoral outcomes and voter sentiment.

One method for demonstrating that they work is to show that rating scale responses can correlate very highly with representational measures. (Here both responses and measures are used to assess the same specific attribute, so the criticisms of correlational techniques found in the last section of this chapter do not apply.) Dawes (1977) asked whether rating scales of the sort used in social psychological attitude assessment could be used to obtain values predictive of people's height, measured in inches (a representational measure).

He investigated five of the six scales found in Fig. 7 (all but 7f). Each of the scales was modified so that it referred to height. For example, the scale in Fig. 7(a) was changed to read +3 very tall; +2 moderately tall; +1 tall; −1 short; −2 moderately short; −3 very short. The bipolar adjective pair on the scale in Fig. 7(b) was short-tall. The scale in Fig. 7(c) was changed to read extremely tall, very tall, tall, and very short. The scale in Fig. 7(d) was unmodified, except that the question read "How tall was this person?" Finally, the verbal labels on the scale in Fig. 7(e) were changed to extremely tall, very tall, fairly tall, neither tall nor short, fairly short, very short, and extremely short.

Each of the twenty-six male staff members of the Psychology Department at the University of Oregon was asked to rate the height of all twenty-five on the modified scales in the spring of 1970. These twenty-six staff members had all known each other for at least two years and were at the university at the time they made the ratings. Each staff member rated five members on each scale, each rating being made individually on a separate page.

The choice of which members were rated on which scale was made in such a way that no pair of subjects was rated on a given scale by more than two raters. The order in which the twenty-five staff members appeared on each rater's form was entirely random. No subject rated himself.

The design produced five ratings of each staff member on each scale. These ratings were averaged. (Numerical assignment was obvious in all but one scale, Fig. 7c; in it the number −2 was assigned to the category "very short," the number +1 to the category "tall," the number +2 to the category "very tall," and the number +3 to the category "extremely tall.") The correlations between these average ratings and (self-reported) physical height ranged from 0.88 (for the scale in Fig. 7d) to 0.94 (for scales in Figs. 7a, 7b, and 7e). The scale in Fig. 7(c), despite its peculiar characteristics, had a correlation of 0.90.

The data were further averaged by performing a principal-component analysis on the intercorrelations between the five scales and then using the first principal component (which accounted for 89 percent of the variance) as the final rating scale estimate of height. It correlated 0.98 with self-reported physical height.

Thus the rating scale assessment of height produced scale values very highly correlated with height (in inches). It follows that there is nothing intrinsic about rating scales per se that precludes their use in estimating scale values obtainable by representational techniques. It does not, of course, follow that these scales will do a good job of estimating some representational measure of *attitude* that they purport to evaluate. Thus all the study indicates is that rating scales can work; it does not indicate why they can work, and it certainly does not imply that they necessarily will work.

PSYCHOLOGICAL JUSTIFICATIONS FOR RATING SCALES

Certain rating scales may be compatible with the ways in which people using them think. For example, people often spontaneously characterize political attitudes in terms of a right-left continuum—with, as demonstrated earlier, some justification. A rating scale consisting of a line with the labels "left wing" and "right wing" at the extreme left and right may be compatible with such people's thinking; they can place attitudes on such a line because they think of others' (and perhaps their own) attitudes as falling on such a continuum. Clearly, not all rating scales are compatible with intuitive thought—nor does compatibility imply that rating scales are isomorphic with such thought.

There is some evidence that some people do, in fact, think about social phenomena in spatial terms (deSoto, London, and Handel, 1965); such thinking has been termed *spatial paralogic*. For example, the notion that the person A is "better than" (smarter than, healthier than, more ethical than, etc.) person B may be represented spatially by imagining A to be placed above B on a vertical axis. Such representation is *not* generally made by imagining A below B (or on the left or right of B on a horizontal axis.) Assuming such placement, deSoto, London, and Handel hypothesized that certain implications among social relationships should be easier to understand than others; thus the syllogism with premises "A is better than B" and "B is better than C" is solved with much greater accuracy than is the one with premises "B is worse than A" and "B is better than C"—according to the hypothesis, because it is easier to scan a mental line downward than from the middle toward both ends. Of course, there are a number of logical steps from the theorizing to the empirically confirmed conclusion: that people think in spatial terms, that the representation used by the subjects will be similar to that used by the experimenters, and that the ease of moving within these representations is the same for subjects and experimenters.

Another common assumption about the psychology of rating scale use is that the subjects responding are so used to dealing with numbers and spatial continua that comparisons *within an individual rater* must be valid. That is, the order in which an individual places items on rating scales corresponds to the order in which he or she views them on the dimension the scales are meant to assess; no *inter*individual comparison is assumed. For example, if an individual checks +3 to indicate his or her agreement with one statement and +2 to indicate agreement with a second, it is assumed that he or she agrees *more* with the first than with the second. No comparison is made between one individual who checks +2 and another who checks +3. (Note that this latter assumption abounds in the attitude-behavior literature, which is reviewed in the last section of this chapter.) People limiting themselves to this intraindividual assumption (see Dawes-Saraga, 1968; Anderson, 1970) often attempt to phrase their hypothesis—and devise their experiments—in such a way that the crucial aspect of the subjects' rating response is the order in which they place check marks on the scale—and only that order.

CONVERGENT VALIDITY: THE MULTICONCEPT-MULTIMETHOD APPROACH

One method for determining the validity of rating scales is to use a number of different ones and see if the same result is obtained—i.e., to see if they converge. This method was first proposed by Campbell and Fiske (1959) in the area of assessing personality traits; hence it has been termed the *multitrait-multimethod method*. But it is clearly applicable to constructs in the area of attitude measurement, such as conservatism and unfavorability toward the military draft.

Briefly, the validity of a number of measures purported to be of the same thing (trait, attitude) is assessed by the degree to which the measures agree. This agreement is assessed by the correlation coefficient across individuals (or, on a more abstract basis, across the entities being evaluated). These correlations are not in and of themselves, however, sufficient to establish convergent validity; they may be high or low depending on such factors as the measurement error in the ratings or the range of talent or the people (or entities) sampled. Rather, the correlation coefficients are compared with those between diverse constructs—assessed either by the same or by different measurement techniques. If the correlations between the measures of the same constructs using different techniques are higher than those between different constructs using either the same or different techniques, then the measurement is said to have *convergent validity*.

Before proceeding, we emphasize the generality of the approach. First, just as it is unnecessary to limit it to a study of personality traits, it is not necessary to limit it to the study of rating scales; the measurement techniques may be anything (including those discussed in the next section). Second, the approach may be seen as a criterion for establishing either internal or external validity, depending upon the topographical similarity of the techniques used. Third, since convergent validity is established on the basis of a comparison of correlation coefficients, rather than on their absolute magnitudes, the problems raised in the study of the attitude-behavior relationships are ameliorated (although they do not vanish).

In order to understand this "multi-multi" approach, it may be instructive to consider a study in which the investigators found no convergent validity whatsoever (Goldberg and Werts, 1966, p. 199):

> Four clinical psychologists independently ranked each of four equated samples of ten patients on one of four traits (social adjustment, ego strength, intelligence, and dependency), using one of four data sources (MMPI, Rorschach, Wechsler, and vocational history). A 4 × 4 squared design insured that the usual sources of judgmental confounding were absent from this study.

The experimental design did not include judges rating the same trait from the same data source, but the correlation between such ratings is *not* part of the convergent validity approach—unless it is used to assess error of measurement. The average correlation between the patients assessed on the *same trait* by different clinicians using *different data sources* was 0.10(!). The values ranged from 0.64 (social adjustment, judged by one clinician using the MMPI and by another using the Rorschach) to −0.31 (ego strength judged by one clinician using the Rorschach and another using vocational history).

In contrast, the average correlation between the patients ranked on *different traits* by different clinicians using the *same data source* was 0.37. These values ranged from 0.80 (for one clinician rating social adjustment from the MMPI and another rating ego strength from the MMPI) to −0.03 (from one clinician rating social adjustment from the Rorschach and another rating dependency from the Rorschach). Even if it is maintained that the psychological traits should be themselves correlated within the patient population studied, the correlations between the same traits assessed by different methods should *still* be higher than those between different traits using the same method—if the traits have any meaning other than "global adjustment" (or "global cosmetics" in a test-taking situation).

Finally, the average correlation between different judges ranking patients on different traits from different data sources is, as expected, quite low: 0.08.

While, in fact, all correlations are low, the consistent superiority of the correlations using the same method for different traits indicates that what convergent validity there is exists for methods, not traits. (In 77 percent of the comparisons between the same-method/different-trait correlations and the different-method/same-trait correlations, the former were higher.) It is as if—and here we are less kind than the authors of the study—each method yields an implicit ranking of the subjects on a "good-bad" dimension that has little to do with either the trait being evaluated or rankings based on other methods. But the traits themselves also have an implicit good-bad connotation, so irrespective of what trait is evaluated, a particular method will yield positively correlated ratings across clinicians. The clincher for such an interpretation would be to find an average correlation of 0.37 between different clinicians rating the *same* trait from the *same* data source, but they were not asked to make such ratings.

As illustrated in the prior example, the convergent validity "approach" is really just that. It is not a technique but rather a guideline for assessing the internal or external validity of *any* set of measures meant to assess a smaller number of constructs. A systematic method for comparing correlation coefficients exists (Hubert and Baker, 1978), and the substitution of path-analytic methods (Werts and Linn, 1970) or confirmatory factor analysis (Kenney, 1976) has been proposed as superior to direct comparison of correlation coefficients (for a review and critique, see Schmitt, Coyle, and Sarri, 1977). But all discussions of the approach have (to our knowledge) begged the question that is most important to the user, which is, Which measure should be included?

Clearly, a particular measure will have greater or lesser convergent or differential validity depending upon the other measures used in the analysis. That's true of all multivariate approaches, but in this particular approach the *meaning* of a variable is assessed *in terms of* its correlations with others. (That's also true in factor analysis, which we have omitted in this chapter.) Of the techniques described thus far, that dependency of meaning can be found only in the semantic differential, and there the authors systematically investigated a wide variety of connotative scales over a wide variety of cultures. They ended up with the dimensions of evaluation, potency, and activity; they did not begin with them and others in hopes of demonstrating convergent validity.

The validity of a representational technique, in contrast, is not evaluated by its relation to others, and the purpose of correlating most rating scale responses with other rating scale responses or external criteria is to establish their validity as they are, *not as part of a set*.

The problem is one of degree. Our evaluation of a technique will depend in part upon the stimuli sampled, the population of subjects sampled, and the other techniques with which it is compared. Correlation coefficients are particularly subject to instability as a result of such factors, and an approach that depends upon a context of correlation coefficients will be doubly vulnerable. Nevertheless, the logic of the convergent validity approach is compelling.

INDIRECT MEASURES

When people respond to most of the attitude and opinion questions discussed thus far, they are aware that their attitudes are being evaluated. Questions of the form "Do you prefer . . ." or "Rate your attitude toward. . ." usually leave little doubt about which attitudes are being assessed. And this knowledge may affect subjects' responses. For example, people may wish to appear unprejudiced, socially responsible, loyal to a confused president, ecologically aware, etc.

That is, subjects may *react to* knowledge that their attitudes are being evaluated—and consequently shade or color their responses (even if their judgments about what the questioner is aiming at are wrong). Responses that are determined partially or wholly by knowledge of being an object of study have therefore been termed *reactive* by Campbell and Stanley (1963), and the term is still in common use. Clearly, such reactive responses pose a problem for psychologists or other social scientists interested in subjects' responses to the questions per se.

Thirty years ago Campbell (1950) urged the development of attitude assessment techniques that would not elicit reactive responses. He wrote (p. 15):

> In the problem of assessing social attitudes, there is a very real need for instruments which do not destroy the natural form of the attitude in the process of describing it. There are also situations in which one would like to assess "prejudice" without making the respondent self-conscious or aware of the intent of the study.

Thus Campbell expressed the need for techniques that would not be affected by subjects' understanding that they were being assessed. That need has been amply met in the subsequent thirty years with a plethora of techniques that have come to be termed *indirect*. They may involve the following techniques:

1. Observing subjects without their awareness of being observed.

2. Observing aspects of subjects' behavior (usually physiological reactions) over which they presumably have no control.

3. Successfully duping subjects—either into believing that the questioner is observing something that has nothing to do with their attitudes or into believing that they have no control over their responses.

What has not been established is the *extent* of the need for such techniques. (And given that many are ethically dubious to begin with, many social psychologists decry their use.) The typical "validation" study for such techniques shows that they yield results compatible with those of more direct measures. In order to show the *need* for such techniques, however, researchers must show results that are incompatible. But then how would we know that they were valid? (As illustrated in the studies selected for report in this section, the resort is usually made to face validity—i.e., to showing that the indirect technique has greater face validity than does a corresponding direct one.)

Approximately fifteen years after Campbell made his plea, Webb *et. al.,* (1966) published a widely read book entitled *Unobtrusive Measures: Non-Reactive Research in the Social Sciences.* The book consisted in large part of a highly readable presentation of many indirect techniques. Perhaps more important for the growth of the field, it demonstrated that devising such techniques can be a great deal of fun.

The current section is divided into four parts. The first three will concern techniques in which subjects are unaware, in which they have no control, and in which they are duped. The fourth section is a brief discussion of the ethics of indirect assessment.

UNAWARE SUBJECTS

One of the most popular indirect techniques is Milgram's *lost-letter procedure* (Milgram, Mann, and Harter, 1965) for assessing political and social attitudes of people in a given location. In the "address" version of this technique a post office box is hired to receive mail for various bogus political organizations. Each of these organizations has a title indicating a certain political or social group or philosophy (e.g., Young Communist League, Citizens Against Gun Control, Citizens to Save Aquatic Mammals). Stamped letters addressed to these organizations are then "dropped" in various places within the community, such as telephone booths or department stores. In a more recent version of the technique envelopes are placed on the windshield of a car with a penciled note, "Found near your car" (thereby avoiding litter). The relative frequency with which the letters are picked up and mailed is used as an indicator of the positive or negative feelings in the location toward the philosophy or goal of the bogus organization.

The "return address" version of the technique differs only in that the organizational name is on the return part of the envelope, which is then addressed to one of the experimenters personally.

Recent applications of the technique have involved assessing attitudes toward a Metro-Atlanta Rapid Transit Authority (Baskett *et al.,* 1973), toward busing (Baskett *et al.,* 1973; Bolton, 1974) and toward permitting pharmacists to do physical exams (!) (Zoleno and Gagnon, 1977). All the studies mentioned showed a common problem with the technique. Return rate for pro and con organizations was much closer to 50–50 than were the attitudes as indicated by more direct measures, such as careful surveys or actual voting percentages. Thus the technique will *appear* to do well when community opinion on an issue is fairly evenly split but be quite misleading when opinion is more polarized. In fact, it is not clear from these and other studies that it is even possible to predict the direction of community opinion. (One study, which we will not reference, concluded that the lost-letter technique was valid because a chi-square computed on the *proportion* of pro-con letters returned versus the proportion of the pro-con vote was not significantly different from zero, even though the lost-letter technique led to the wrong prediction of the election outcome.) The reason for this bias toward an even split in return of the letters is probably that some people mail them anyway (out of politeness?), some throw them away anyway, and only the remaining subpopulation provides a differential response rate.

RESPONSES OVER WHICH SUBJECTS HAVE NO CONTROL

When people look at something that interests them, their pupils have a tendency to dilate. (The mechanism need not concern us.) That has been known for years by jewel salespeople, by able seducers, and by magicians.

Hess and his co-workers (Hess, 1965; Hess, Seltzer, and Shlien, 1965) first popularized pupil dilation as an indirect indicator of interest in 1965. Subjects cannot easily control the dilation (although it is possible to try to by attending to a nonpresent image), with the consequence

that if they are observed either informally or in the most sophisticated pupil dilation laboratory, pupil dilation is generally a nonreactive measure.

Hess originally studied dilation to sexual stimuli —pictures of unclothed or partially clothed men or women. Typically, subjects would be male heterosexuals or homosexuals. (Although females were also used, their response to visual stimuli was found to be less predictable on the basis of sexual interest.) The weight of the evidence is that pupil dilation is a good indicator of sexual interest (which comes as no surprise). Specific studies suffer from problems of equating the light value of various pictures (Janisse, 1973), although those finding an interaction effect between type of subject (e.g., heterosexual versus homosexual) and type of stimulus (e.g., unclothed women versus unclothed men) are not subject to this criticism (except that people may look at different *parts* of the pictures).

Perhaps the most striking of such studies was one conducted by Atwood and Howell (1971), who investigated the pupil dilation of ten normal males and ten male pedophiliacs (child molesters) when viewing pictures of nude or partially nude adult females and young girls. (All the subjects were prisoners; the pedophiliacs had all molested young girls, but none had been guilty of causing physical injury.) The results are presented in Table 4.

All but one of the pedophiliacs dilated more to pictures of young girls, and all but one of the normals dilated more to pictures of adult females. Concerning the single deviant pedophiliac, Atwood and Howell (1971, p. 116) write:

> This S reported that he molested girls only after drinking large amounts of alcohol. Possibly his choice of young girls as a sexual target was due to lack of discrimination rather than a preference.
> . . . He was the only S who blamed alcohol for his deviant act.

TABLE 4
Mean Pupil Change as a Function of Slide Content

SUBJECTS	STIMULI	
	ADULT FEMALES	*YOUNG FEMALES*
Pedophiliacs	−2.6	+21.0
Normals	+18.9	+2.3

SOURCE: Atwood and Howell, 1971, p. 116.

Hess also hypothesized that stimuli arousing distaste would result in pupil constriction, as opposed to dilation. The evidence does not support this contention, although it does not directly contradict it either (see Janisse, 1973, for a thorough review at that time). One of the more plausible explanations for the occasional finding of constriction has been that of Woodmansee (1970), who suggested that it may really be "de-dilation." The anticipation of a negative stimulus may cause pupillary dilation (due to interest), but when the stimulus is actually presented, the relief from anticipation may cause relaxation of the dilator muscle and hence a decrease in pupil size. If this hypothesis is correct, then the evidence in the literature for "constriction" would be sparse and scattered—which is exactly what it is. For the purposes of the present chapter, however, it is enough to note that pupillary constriction is *not* a good indirect measure of dislike or disinterest.

Another physiological response over which subjects have no control is their *galvanic skin response* (GSR). The GSR tends to occur when a person is anxious or aroused. The response itself is a change in the electrical conduction of the skin, which can be brought about by sweating, increased or decreased capillary flow, etc.; generally, the response itself consists of a drop in skin resistance, as measured by standard electrical measures. Cooper and Pollack (1959) had discovered that such responses occurred in prejudiced individuals when *favorable* remarks were made about the objects of their prejudice. Subsequent studies have shown that in fact the response will indicate arousal brought about by strong attitudinal responses, but—as with pupil dilation—attempts to use the GSR to indicate directionality of response have not succeeded (see Tognacci and Cook, 1975).

DUPING THE SUBJECT

Perhaps the mildest form of duplicity in the indirect assessment of attitude is that in which the subjects know that their attitudes are being assessed but do not know the *characteristic* of their attitudes that is being evaluated. For example, in the *own categories technique* (Sherif and Sherif, 1969; Sherif *et al.,* 1973) subjects are asked to place attitude or opinion statements into as many categories as they desire; than they are asked to pick the categories containing statements they accept, those containing statements they reject, and those containing statements about which they feel neutral or uncommitted. *In general*, greater involvement in the attitudinal is-

sues is characterized by (1) sorting into fewer categories, (2) rejecting more statements, and (3) feeling neutral about fewer. While research evidence has shown these characteristics to be related to involvement assessed on other bases, they themselves may be used as a basis for an indirect assessment of involvement. Note that subjects are not asked how involved they are; rather involvement is inferred from their sorting and their statements of acceptance, neutrality, and rejection. To quote Sherif *et al.,* (1973), the own categories technique is a method "for inferring degree of involvement from structural properties of behavior while the person engages in tasks that do not confront him directly with the issue of how salient the attitude object is for him personally"(p. 312).

While the own categories technique infers involvement from individuals' construction of categories and endorsement of them, a number of investigators have discovered that the position of an individual may be determined from his or her placement of statements in *predetermined* categories. Sherif and Hovland (1953) present evidence of assimilation and contrast in their famous 1953 article concerned with racial attitudes and civil rights. The assimilation finding in this article may have been due to an end effect on their rating scale, but what is quite clear is that the contrast effect holds up in a number of attitudinal domains (as well as psychophysical ones). When asked to place an attitude item on a typical bipolar rating scale (e.g., pro civil rights versus con civil rights, liberal versus conservative, etc.), people who disagree with the item tend to place it in a more extreme category than do those who agree with it.

Selltiz, Edrich, and Cook (1965) showed that such placement could be used as an indirect measure of subjects' attitudes. They showed that subjects who belonged to groups that generally entertained prejudiced or nonprejudiced attitudes toward blacks rated statements about blacks and about civil rights differently; consistent with the contrast findings, the subjects belonging to the prejudiced groups tended to rate statements that were pro black or pro civil rights as more extreme than did the subjects who belonged to the nonprejudiced groups and vice versa.

While the contrast finding is simple, its interpretation is not. What is involved is an interpersonal comparison of statements placed in categories; the naive interpretation of the difference found is that subjects judged the statements differently but used the categories the same way; the dual interpretation is equally supported from the data—that subjects view the statements the same way but use the categories differently. Thus, for example, the prochoice subject may be as aware as the antichoice subject of the difference between a right-to-life constitutional amendment and a prohibition against using welfare money for abortion but may choose to categorize both as falling in the extreme "anti" category of a pro-con–abortion rating scale, thereby creating a contrast effect because the antiabortion subjects tend to put these in different categories. The question of whether the contrast effect is due to differential judgment about statements or use of categories (or even whether it makes any sense at all to talk about how one "judges" or "perceives" social statements independent of social categories) has been investigated by Dawes, Singer, and Lemons (1971). By asking people to make comparative as opposed to categorical judgments, and by asking people to *create* items characteristic of those who support or oppose certain social actions (e.g., the war in Vietnam), these authors concluded that the contrast effect was due to differential judgment, not categorization. It occurred when people were asked to make comparative judgments (no categories involved) and also when people were asked to construct stimuli characterizing "typical" supporters of pro and con positions (e.g., doves and hawks).

One interesting by-product of this study was that when people were asked to write statements characterizing the beliefs of people with whom they disagree, these statements tended to be (1) more extreme than the statements written to characterize the typical people with whom they were in agreement and (2) so extreme that samples of people with whom they disagreed *in fact rejected* them overwhelmingly as being too extreme to characterize their position. Thus this item-writing technique was quite a strong indirect measure of the subjects' known attitudes. Table 5 presents statements written by a University of Oregon student who supported Wallace in 1968 and one who supported the Gregory write-in protest. [Incidentally, length of the statements was not as good an indicator as judged extremity in categorizing the writer; for the success of such categorization, see Dawes, Singer, and Lemons (1972), experiments 4, 5, 6.]

One astute graduate student at the University of California at San Diego (whose name we are sorry we do not remember) suggested that these studies were concerned with the meaning of the word *typical*. We are appreciative of her suggestion and might have been persuaded to withdraw the article from its in-press status had not all the other operations we used supported our final interpretation. For the purposes of an indirect mea-

TABLE 5
Student Statements

STATEMENTS WRITTEN BY A WALLACE SUPPORTER

WALLACE STATEMENTS	WRITE-IN PROTEST STATEMENTS
Executive orders and bureau directives should not be permitted to control areas of operation granted the state by the Constitution of the U.S.	Writing in McCarthy will give public declaration that all other candidates fail to embody American ideals.
Judicial "rewriting" of the U.S. should be curtailed—legislative lawmaking should prevail.	No ideology is worthy of war.
Peaceful resistance and demonstrations should not remove or restrict freedoms of any other persons—including freedom of HEARING at public gatherings.	Gregory is the only candidate who represents the Afro-American interest in the election.
Discrimination should be illegal—integration should occur on a voluntary basis so as to limit hostilities.	McCarthy is a candidate who has not sold himself to the Hawks as have Humphrey, Nixon, and Wallace.

STATEMENTS WRITTEN BY A WRITE-IN PROTEST SUPPORTER

WALLACE STATEMENTS	WRITE-IN PROTEST STATEMENTS
More law and order.	Provide the American public with leaders chosen by the public instead of by political party machinery.
Win militarily in Vietnam.	Withdraw from Vietnam as quickly as possible.
Prosecute all dissidents and revolutionists.	Defend American freedom to dissent and disagree.
Return power to the states.	Provide for equal opportunity for all Americans regardless of race, creed, color, or economic state.

SOURCE: Dawes, 1972a, p. 127.

sure, however, the fact that people have this tendency to write extreme and somewhat bizarre statements to characterize the belief of the "typical" person with whom they disagree results in a good indirect measure of attitude, whatever the explanation.

At the other extreme of duplicitousness from statement sorting, categorization, and writing is the *bogus pipeline* (Jones and Sigall, 1971). The subject is placed in front of an impressive (phony) electronic device and is asked to hold a steering wheel that is attached to it. The steering wheel purportedly controls a pointer that indicates position on an attitude scale. (For reasons to be clear soon the pointer is in fact obsured from the subject's view.) The subject is supposed to move the steering wheel to indicate (on the pointer) his or her attitudes about particular topics or answers to questions. Electrodes are attached to the subject's hands or arms. The whole device, termed an *electromyograph* (EMG), is said to analyze tiny involuntary muscle responses that will indicate the subject's truthful answers to the question asked, irrespective of any conscious attempt to dissimulate or control the wheel in an untruthful manner. Since there are, of course, no tiny muscular responses, no current, no movement of the needle, etc., the supposed rating on the EMG must be removed from the subject's view in order to maintain the ruse. (In one variant the subject moves a dial, and electrodes attached to the subject's fingers are said to assess the tiny muscle movements.)

Once the view of the true dial or pointer is obscured, subjects are asked to guess their readings in response to the experimenter's questions—to discover, for example, how in touch they are with their feelings. The hypothesis is that their guesses will give accurate indicators of their feelings, because they will believe that any lying or shading would be given away by their tiny muscle responses assessed by the EMG. Typical studies show that subjects on the EMG are more apt than are those using statement responses to admit to negative feelings about an obnoxious handicapped confederate (Sigall and Page, 1972), less apt to show cognitive dissonance effects (Gaes, Kalle, and Tedeschi, 1978), and more apt to admit having been told correct test answers by a confederate (Quigley-Fernandez and Tedeschi, 1978). (This last study may have set somewhat of a record for duping subjects; the EMG was a lie, the confederate was a lie, the information given by the confederate was a lie, and the test said to be the Mednick Remote Associates Test consisted instead of items taken from the Graduate Record Examination Study Manual.)

Judgmental errors may be another indirect indicator of attitude. Once again, subjects are duped in that they believe that the investigator is assessing their acuity rather than noting the direction and magnitude of their errors in hopes of relating these to their atttitudes.

That error should be related to attitude is an idea with a great deal of face validity. For example, the person who after reading the statistics on cigarette smoking and health concludes that smoking lowers life expectancy by five years may be more favorably disposed toward smoking than is the person who believes it lowers life expectancy by fifteen years (the correct answer is ten). Or the man who judges an ordinary-looking woman to be quite beautiful may be assumed to be more in love with her than is some other man who judges her to be quite ordinary looking. Whether or not such judgmental biases may influence "pure" perceptual judgments (e.g., about the size of a coin) was once a matter of some debate among psychologists. But the question does not matter from the point of view of using biases to assess attitude, because—as emphasized in this chapter—the issue of whether a particular technique can or cannot be used to assess a particular dimension of attitude is an empirical one, to be determined on the merits of the evidence.

MacNeil, Davis, and Pace (1975) investigated whether teenaged boys' errors in evaluating each other's physical skills could be used as an indirect measure of the social status of the boy being evaluated. The boys studied were from three cliques in a male boarding school located in the southeastern United States. Direct measures of each boy's status in each clique were evaluated by asking all the boys to respond to *scalogram* questions. A direct scalogram consisted of questions asking whom each boy would most like to spend time with or who decided during free time periods what to do and how to do it. A disguised scalogram asked questions about whom each boy would trust and put in a position of power during a civil defense emergency. The disguised scalogram was administered approximately one month prior to the evaluation of judgmental errors, the direct scalogram immediately afterwards.

The errors were evaluated by asking each boy in turn to pitch baseballs and asking the other boys to score the pitch. The boys were to score 5 for pitches on the corners of the strike zone, 3 for pitches directly over the center of the plate, 1 for pitches on the outer margins but outside the strike zone, and 0 for balls hitting wide outside the strike zone. While the boys made these judgments standing behind the pitcher, experimental assistants standing by the plate could make much more "objective" scores, aided by faint lines visible only to them. The average of the boy's scores minus the average of the objective scores was proposed as an indirect assessment of status within each group.

Three cliques were studied: the Covingtons, the Kickers, and the Stressed. For the Covingtons and the Kickers, the status ranks based on the direct scalogram, based on the disguised scalogram, and based on the error scores were identical. The stressed group was the most interesting.

The reason it was stressed was that one of its members had died a few hours before the baseball contest; he had downed a fifth of vodka after being dared to do so by the group leader. The incident, and the subsequent decision to continue with the investigation, are described in a footnote by MacNeil *et al.*, (1975, p. 294) as follows:

> Despite state laws and boarding school rules, alcohol was frequently smuggled onto the school grounds by a group member "whiskey runner." Group parties were held after dark in the school ground woods. At one such party, the death of a group member occurred as a result of his being challenged by the leader to chug-a-lug a fifth of vodka. The party broke up and the boys returned unobtrusively to their dormitories leaving the body. About an hour later at bed check school authorities missed the dead student, aroused the group members, asked where they had been, and found the boy's body. Police took statements from each boy.
>
> When the second author arrived, the police had finished taking initial statements. Alone in the dormitory with the boys, the observer listened to their story and then asked them if they still wanted to participate in the experiment. . . . After discussion among themselves they replied that they would "really rather do that than just sit around here waiting for the police—and anyway we don't want to miss the steak feed." (The steak feed was payment for all groups participating in the experiments since the boys were not allowed to have cash.) The experimenter telephoned the senior author and discussed the consequences of proceeding. The decision was that it would be better to follow the group's wishes. It was felt that denying participation would be interpreted as punitive. We were concerned with not letting the boys down since our relationship was that of nonauthoritarian, older friends.

What happened in the Stressed group was that the direct-scalogram status rank obtained immediately after the baseball throw agreed with the disguised-scalogram status rank obtained a month earlier: Martin, Rabb, Alky, Leaper, Kent, Lucky (all, of course, pseudonyms). The status rank obtained from the error scores was, however, quite different—and easily interpretable in terms of the role each boy had had in the activities leading to the death. MacNeil, *et al.* (1975, pp. 303–305) write:

> According to previous measures and the situational sociogram, Martin was the leader of the stressed group. In the highly unobtrusive judgmental index, however, Martin was "put down" to fifth place. He was one of the two members who received negative net error scores. Later investigation revealed that Martin personally conceived and planned the illegal party and had used the coercion available to him as group leader to encourage participation by some reluctant group members. He had been a direct contributor to the death of the low status group member by urging him to "chug-a-lug" a bottle of vodka. His actions in the entire situation resulting in the death were, as they usually were in group activities, those of the initiator. The sociogame, as a highly covert measurement made a few hours after the incident, showed a clear depreciation of Martin's value by the group members, although his long time effectiveness in group matters prevailed in the relatively more overt situational sociogram given immediately following the sociogame.
>
> Leaper's displacement from fourth to sixth (and last) status position is of interest because he was the only member excepting Martin to receive a negative score on the sociogame judgmental index. One of his functions in the party was that of liquor runner. In preparation for the party, he had collected assessments from other members and had bought and smuggled in the liquor. In general, Leaper had strongly supported Martin.
>
> Alky and Kent were displaced due to other position shifts. Rabb, who was the lieutenant, was ranked number one by an overwhelmingly high positive error score in the baseball throw judgment situation. Although he attended the party, he had attempted to prevent its occurrence, and during the party, he tried to terminate the activities at an early hour.

Lucky, the lowest status member of the group, was displaced upward to the next to highest rank as measured by the sociogame. Later investigation of the illegal party and death revealed that Lucky had had no part in it. He was not even there. Before the party began he had slipped out of the school without permission, defying the school regulations, Martin, and the group. Though he was in trouble officially for being absent from school without permission, his trouble did not involve the group. The sociogame, because of its ability to provide a convert [sic] measure of the group members' appraisal of each other, indicated tacit group approval of a member who had done what would have normally been considered as a deviation well outside of group norms (not attending the party).

This example of the error technique is striking, at least to us. It is important, however, to remember the caution that no matter how plausible a technique may sound for assessing attitude, it is necessary to demonstrate empirically that it actually works. (We have had, for example, a distressing history in psychology of widespread use of the Rorschach Ink Blot Test because it is plausible; the idea that people will structure an unstructured ink blot the same way they structure their psyches and social worlds is so compelling that literally thousands of research studies showing that ink blot responses don't predict what they're supposed to predict have been ignored.)

ETHICAL PROBLEMS OF INDIRECT ASSESSMENT

The attempt to obtain indirectly what we cannot find directly involves an inherent invasion of privacy. That invasion may be slight (as when we ask an individual to sort items in order to assess the intensity of his or her involvement), or it may be severe (as when we observe whether a male subject's pupils dilate more when observing a nude woman or a nude man). Under what conditions is such invasion ethical? Or necessary?

First, it should be noted that people are observing each other all the time ("I noted that his ears tend to get red when he lies")—sometimes even surreptitiously ("You looked depressed when I saw you walking down the street yesterday afternoon"). Second, we even use cues over which subjects have no awareness or control (e.g., pupil dilation on the part of those in whom we are

sexually interested). The question is, At what point are we inappropriately or unethically invading privacy? (A red ear, a dilated pupil, or a depressed gait are, after all, public—but so, it could be argued, is a change in skin resistance, except that it is just not noticeable to people who don't have a GSR machine handy.) It cannot be maintained that what we wish to conceal must remain private, because even that can become public—as in a Freudian slip, stammering, sweating, shaking, etc. Clearly, there seems to be no qualitative distinction between private and public behavior—although we would all generally agree that tapping an individual's telephone is a reprehensible invasion of privacy, whereas noting a sweaty handshake is not.

Questions about the ethics of indirect techniques have not, then, focused so much on privacy as on informed consent and on deception. How, for example, is it possible to inform subjects of what an assessment technique involves when the point of the technique is to evaluate something over which they have no control? Or which they would rather conceal? Or which they do not know is being evaluated? Because informed consent has become the major issue among university human subjects committees, it is difficult to justify some indirect techniques.

Deception is a more complicated problem. We deceive people all the time ("How are you?" "I am fine." "I'm pleased to meet you."), and in fact an absence of the ability to deceive at all would be boorish ("I couldn't care less about how you feel." "That's nice, because I feel awful." "I am sorry I was forced into talking with you, because I wish to hell I were somewhere else."). At what point does lack of boorishness slip into prevarication? Similarly, at what point in our assessments do our techniques slip into social fraud: When we ask people to write attitude statements because we are interested in assessing their own attitudes and not because we are constructing a scale? When we hook up somebody to an "electromyograph"?

For over fifteen years Baumrind (1964, 1979) has been advocating the position that while it is perfectly appropriate to engage in minor deceptions in everyday life, it is not appropriate to do so as a psychologist. Thus any deception at all is unethical. Her reasoning stems from the belief that psychologists are perceived as authorities and that people should not be encouraged to believe that authority figures would lie to them or deceive them. Not surprisingly, her initial attacks were on the Milgram (1963) experiments on destructive obedience, which involved deceiving subjects into thinking they were giving extremely painful shocks to confederates. Because Milgram believes that automatic obedience to authority figures can be destructive and wrong (1963), it is not surprising that he disagrees both with Baumrind's criticisms of his experiments per se and with the stance from which she makes these criticisms. In contrast to Baumrind, Dawes (1972b) argues that what is considered ethical or unethical *outside* the laboratory should be the cardinal criterion for deciding upon what is ethical inside. (A certain procedure should neither be justified nor excluded on the grounds that it is part of an experiment.)

The ethical standards of psychological research endorsed by the American Psychological Association (1973) did not concur with Baumrind's position. What is required (Article 8) is *debriefing*—i.e., explaining at the end of the study any deceptions involved and attempting to remove any "temporary harm" that they may have created. In fact, potential harm (and here the Department of Health, Education, and Welfare agrees) is the primary criterion for judging a study or an assessment to be unethical. Otherwise, deception—with debriefing—is acceptable, provided the potential knowledge gained from the experiment outweighs any temporary lying or discomfort involved in the deception.

We resonate, however, to a suggestion made by Silverman (1965). He compared deception and debriefing in psychological experiments to adultery and confession in marriage. In both cases, he suggests, the debriefing session may do more harm than the act itself. Besides, it doesn't undo the act. And even those holding that confession can absolve sin believe that the procedure works only when the confession is made to a proper authority. Briefly, if you think it's wrong in the first place, don't do it, and if you don't think it is, shut up about it. So Silverman recommends no debriefing at all and deception only in those situations where we feel that debriefing would not be necessary. If we feel that we must undo something, then we feel that it is wrong—so we shouldn't do it. Silverman's position appeals to us not only because of its moral persuasiveness (largely from an intuitionist ethics point of view) but also because the debriefing sessions can create many problems for subsequent experimenters. After a few, these subjects may cease to believe what experimenters tell them—and with good reason! In fact, Silverman *et al.* (1970) have shown that such skepticism does occur as the result of being in deceptive experiments.

RANDOMIZED RESPONDING

People are often loath to answer embarrassing questions (e.g., Have you ever had a venereal disease?), even when they are assured of anonymity. First, they may feel a sense of embarrassment at responding affirmatively because *someone* (the psychologist running the study, the coder, the assistant) may know of the response prior to the time it becomes anonymous. Second, people may have suspicions about the promise of anonymity. Occasionally, such suspicions are well based; for example, Rokeach (1960, p. 87) writes:

> The dogmatism and opinionation scales are typically administered to persons meeting in groups. They take the test without putting their names to it in order to encourage frank and honest answers.... We ask them to write down their birth date, city and state of birth, sex, and religion. When this information is matched with class rosters and registrar's records it enables us to identify each of the subjects by name.

An alternative technique to the assurances of anonymity is *randomized responding*. As it was originally proposed by Warner (1965), the technique requires the responder to reply yes or no to one of two statements concerning a sensitive behavior. The statements are "I have engaged in that behavior" and "I have not engaged in that behavior." One of these statements is chosen by a random device, and the interviewer does not know which statement is used. All the interviewer hears is a yes or a no. Yet the underlying probability of privately admitting to the behavior may be estimated from the observed proportion of yes responses and the probability with which each of the two questions is chosen. The probability λ of saying yes is equal to the probability π of privately admitting to the behavior times the probability P that the affirmative question is asked, plus the probability $(1 - \pi)$ of privately denying the behavior times the probability $(1 - P)$ that the negative question is asked. That is,

$$\lambda = \pi P + (1 - \pi)(1 - P), \tag{1}$$

or

$$\pi = \frac{(\lambda + P - 1)}{2P - 1} \quad \left(P \neq \frac{1}{2} \right). \tag{2}$$

A second version of the technique has been developed by Greenberg *et al.* (1969). It involves an *unrelated question.* Briefly, a random device is used to determine whether subjects answer the embarrassing or damning question (e.g., "In my heart of hearts I really do believe that women never will become outstanding mathematicians or composers") or an unrelated one ("My mother was born in April"). If the probability of a yes response to the unrelated question is already known, then the probability of a yes response to the sensitive one is given by

$$\pi = \frac{\lambda - (1 - P)p}{P}, \tag{3}$$

where λ is once more the probability of an overt yes response, P is the probability with which the sensitive question is asked, and p is the known probability of a yes response to the insensitive (unrelated) question.

Finally, the desired probability may be obtained by asking the sensitive question with two different probabilitites: P and P'. Then

$$\pi = \frac{\lambda(1 - P') - \lambda'(1 - P)}{P(1 - P') - P'(1 - P)} \tag{4}$$

where λ is the probability of an overt yes given the sensitive questions asked with probability P, and λ' is the probability of an overt yes response given that the sensitive question is asked with probability P'. These equations are identical to those proposed by Dawes and Meehl (1966) in the psychometric model that they termed *mixed-group validation;* in fact, they—or similar ones—can be found in *any* model in which different probability mixtures from two or more populations can be used to estimate the *assumed constant* parameters of those populations (e.g., see Golden and Meehl, 1978).

A third variant of randomized responding [possibly first proposed by Morton and referred to in Greenberg *et al.* (1969)] is that in which a random device determines whether the subject will answer the sensitive question, will automatically answer yes, or will automatically answer no. For example (Fiddler and Kleinknecht, 1977), some beads in a jar may be blank (instructing the subject to answer the question), some may be marked yes, and some marked no. The subject—after being convinced that the choice of beads is indeed random rather than controlled by the questioner—chooses a bead in private and either answers the sensitive question or follows the instructions on it.

A simple description of many forms of randomized responding can be found in Campbell and Joiner (1973).

One particular version of this technique—developed by Dawes and Moore (1979)—involves asking subjects to flip a coin of their own choosing. If the coin falls heads, subjects are to respond yes no matter what the question is; if it falls tails, they are to answer it. Then if the coin is fair and the probability of an affirmative response to the question is λ,

$$\pi = 2\lambda - 1 \tag{5}$$

For example, if $\lambda = 0.7$, then $\pi = 0.4$. Fifty percent of the time subjects answer yes because the coin has landed heads, 20 percent because it has landed tails, and they answer the sensitive question yes. Thus answering the question yes is 40 percent of that 50 percent.

The coin flip technique is different from others in two respects: First, a negative response can be interpreted directly as no to the sensitive question (and hence the technique cannot be used where there is some ambiguity about what would embarrass people—e.g., about having engaged or not having engaged in certain forms of recreational sex and drug use). Second, it is possible to Guttman-scale responses—again, because no means no.

Equations (1) through (5) all express simple probabilistic relationships that are analytically correct (which is not to say that subjects may not lie to themselves). Then π is the probability of answering yes to the sensitive question, irrespective of the interpretation made of that probability. When these techniques are used, of course, it is important to know the relationship between these probabilities and their estimates based on observed relative frequencies. Fortunately, when proportions are used in these equations, the resulting estimates of π are all maximum-likelihood, unbiased estimates—provided they are truncated at zero when a negative number is obtained. The variance of these estimators may be found in Greenberg *et al.* (1969) (if it is remembered that a random device requiring a yes or no answer is equivalent to an unrelated question in which the probability of an affirmative response is determined a priori).

Most empirical investigations of randomized responding have dealt with actual past behaviors, but the technique is equally applicable to studying sensitive attitudes and opinions. In fact, it might be more applicable than certain indirect techniques that raise ethical problems. In the randomized-responding technique subjects know exactly what the questioner is investigating, they understand the basis on which the confidentiality is protected (if they don't, these techniques won't work), and they are partners in the investigation—rather than unaware or duped objects of study whose attitudes are being drawn from them whether or not they wish to conceal them. Given the potential of randomized responding, and its fairly recent development, we have emphasized it here.

Empirical studies have shown—with strong but not perfect consistency—that people are more apt to admit to having engaged in questionable behaviors when some form of the randomized-responding technique is used than when they are assured anonymity in a standard questionnaire (Greenberg *et al.,* 1969; Goodstadt and Gruson, 1975; Fiddler and Kleinknecht, 1977; Dawes and Moore, 1979). Behaviors include use of illegal or hallucinogenic drugs, small larcenies, and private behaviors having to do with sex (e.g., group orgies, abortions). Typically, the epidemiologist and survey researchers using the technique have concentrated on a few questions asked to a broad sample of the general public, while psychologists have concentrated on many questions asked of a few hundred university students. Problems arise when a nontrivial proportion of the subjects do not believe that the randomizing device is really random (Weisman, Moriarity, and Schafer, 1975) or when the behavior is a recent one involving legal problems (e.g., drunk driving) (Locander, Sudman, and Bradburn, 1976). One investigation (Schimizu and Bonhan, 1978) found an inexplicable difference in estimates based on two halves of a large survey sample.

As well as yielding estimates of response probabilities to single questions, randomized responding can be used to construct Guttman Scales (Dawes and Moore, 1979). The coin flip version is used. The reason is that *no* has an unequivocal meaning. A subject who responds no to a given item has a probability of 0.50 of responding yes to any item more extreme on the scale (only when the coin falls heads). Thus the pattern of each subject's responses ordered along the scale from the least to the most extreme stimulus should consist of a series of yeses, followed by the first no, followed by yes or no, with probability 0.50.

The response patterns can be ordered according to the number of yeses they contain and the stimuli according to the number of yeses they elicit. The result will not, however, form a triangular Guttman pattern, because there will be many yes responses resulting from a coin toss of heads.

While the probability of a yes response to a stimulus more extreme than one eliciting a no response should be 0.50, the probability of yes responses prior to any no should be greater than 0.50, if in fact the less extreme behaviors are engaged in with greater frequency than are the more extreme ones. The Guttman pattern can, therefore, be assessed by estimating probabilities of yes responses following and preceding the first no. The former probability should not be significantly greater than 0.50, while the latter should be. Both assessments may be made by a simple chi-square test of a null hypothesis that these probabilities are 0.50. (Admittedly, the fit to the model for responses following the first no involves *acceptance* of the null hypothesis.) This *forward-stationarity condition* can also be assessed by standard techniques for evaluating backward stationarity on all-or-none learning.

To test the feasibility of Guttman-scaling randomized responses, Dawes and Moore (1979) asked 270 college students taking the introductory social psychology course at the University of Oregon in the winter of 1974 to give randomized responses to the twenty-one questions listed in Table 6.

They expected to find two Guttman Scales on the basis of wording alone (e.g., stealing something worth more than $100, stealing something worth more than $25, stealing something worth more than $1)—thereby providing a test of the technique per se. Other scales (e.g., those of sexual behavior) were hypothesized on the basis of past researchers' general knowledge of the population study.

All students placed their names on the papers. After that, the randomized response technique was explained, and the subjects were asked the twenty-one questions. In general, subjects appeared amused by the procedure; there was much laughter (e.g., after "Have you ever thrown litter from your car?"), sometimes of an embarrassed variety (e.g., after "Have you ever engaged in group sex?"). The explanation of the procedure and the twenty-one questions took approximately twenty minutes of class time.

The proportion of overt yes responses and the estimated underlying probabilities are presented in Table 6.

The Guttman pattern of stealing could not be assessed, because there was no evidence that anybody had stolen anything more than $25. Further, three of the five items concerning sex could not be assessed, again because

TABLE 6
Randomized Responses (*N* = 269)

QUESTION	$\hat{\lambda}$	$\hat{\pi}$
1. Have you ever thrown litter from your car?	0.91	0.82
2. Have you ever lied to a teacher to avoid taking an exam or handing in a term paper on time?	0.76	0.53
3. Have you ever tried LSD?	0.55	0.10
4. Have you ever stolen anything worth more than $1?	0.77	0.55
5. Do you smoke dope at parties?	0.83	0.66
6. Have you ever engaged in oral sex?	0.84	0.69
7. Have you ever engaged in group sex?	NS	
8. Have you ever cheated on an exam?	0.70	0.40
9. Have you ever lied to your parents?	0.96	0.93
10. Have you ever sold dope to someone other than a friend or relative?	0.62	0.23
11. Have you ever stolen anything worth more than $100?	NS	
12. Have you ever cheated on a term paper?	0.57	0.14
13. Have you ever smoked marijuana?	0.89	0.78
14. Have you ever had anal sex?	NS	
15. Have you ever stolen anything worth more than $25?	NS	
16. Have you ever tried heroin?	NS	
17. Have you ever cheated on your income tax?	NS	
18. Have you ever sold dope to a friend or relative?	0.74	0.49
19. Do you smoke dope regularly, even when you are alone?	0.56	0.12
20. Have you had a homosexual experience?	NS	
21. Have you ever engaged in rear entry heterosexual intercourse?	0.66	0.32

SOURCE: Dawes and Moore, 1979, p. 129.

the overt proportion of yes was not significantly greater than 0.50.

There were, however, some very clear Guttman patterns of responses; one involving two behaviors and one involving four behaviors will be examined here.

Table 7 presents a simple Guttman pattern concerning cheating on term papers and cheating on exams. The proportion of overt yes responses to the more extreme question (cheating on a term paper) given a no response to the less extreme one is 0.49. In contrast, the proportion of yes responses to the less extreme item given a no response to the more extreme one is 0.63. Thus we can conclude that roughly 40 percent of our population would admit to privately cheating on an exam, roughly 12 per-

TABLE 7
A Simple Guttman Pattern for Two Questions

HAVE YOU EVER CHEATED ON AN EXAM?	HAVE YOU EVER CHEATED ON A TERM PAPER?	FREQUENCY
Y	Y	119
Y	N	70
N	Y	39
N	N	41
0.40	0.12	(269)

SOURCE: Dawes and Moore, 1979, p. 130.

TABLE 8
A More Complicated Guttman Pattern: Four Questions

ROW	HAVE YOU EVER SMOKED MARIJUANA?	DO YOU SMOKE DOPE AT PARTIES?	DO YOU SMOKE DOPE REGULARLY EVEN WHEN ALONE?	HAVE YOU TRIED LSD?	FREQUENCY
1	Y	Y	Y	Y	79
2	Y	Y	Y	N	42
3	Y	Y	N	Y	46
4	Y	Y	N	N	42
5	Y	N	Y	Y	5
6	Y	N	Y	N	9
7	Y	N	N	Y	9
8	Y	N	N	N	7
9	N	Y	Y	Y	3
10	N	Y	Y	N	4
11	N	Y	N	Y	3
12	N	Y	N	N	3
13	N	N	Y	Y	2
14	N	N	Y	N	5
15	N	N	N	Y	1
16	N	N	N	N	8
	0.78	0.66	0.12	0.10	(268)

SOURCE: Dawes and Moore, 1979, p. 131.

cent to having cheated on a term paper, and that only those that cheat on exams cheat on term papers.

Table 8 presents a somewhat more complicated Guttman pattern consisting of four items: "Have you ever smoked marijuana?" "Do you smoke dope at parties?" "Do you smoke dope regularly, even when alone?" and "Have you tried LSD?"

As shown on rows 9 through 16, the proportion of yes responses to questions farther out on the scale given a no response to the question "Have you ever smoked marijuana?" is 0.41, which is not significantly different from the 0.50 hypothesized. (The split is 36–51.) As shown on rows 5 through 8 and 13 through 16, the proportion of yes responses to questions farther out on the dimension given a no response to the question about smoking at parties is 0.41, which again is not significantly different from 0.50 (the split is 38–54). As shown on rows 3, 4, 7, 8, 11, 12, 15, and 16, the proportion of yes re-

sponses to the questions concerning LSD given a no response to the question concerning regularly smoking is 0.50 (the split is 50–50). All these proportions support the Guttman pattern.

The conditional proportions in the other direction do so as well. As shown on rows 2, 4, 6, 8, 10, 12, 14, and 16, the proportion of overt yes responses to the questions less extreme given a no response to the LSD question is 0.70 (the split is 251–109). As shown on rows 3, 4, 7, 8, 11, 12, 15, and 16, the proportion of overt yes responses to the less extreme item given a no response to the item asking about regular smoking is 0.83, which is again significantly greater than 0.50 (the split is 194–40). As shown on rows 5 through 8 and 13 through 16, the proportion of yes responses to the "Have you ever smoked marijuana?" question given a no response to the question about smoking at parties is 0.65, which is significantly greater than 0.50 (the split is 30–16). Hence

TABLE 9
An Example of Unscalable Questions

ROW	HAVE YOU EVER LIED TO YOUR PARENTS?	HAVE YOU EVER LIED TO A TEACHER IN ORDER TO AVOID TAKING AN EXAM OR HANDING IN A TERM PAPER ON TIME?	HAVE YOU EVER CHEATED ON AN EXAM?	HAVE YOU EVER CHEATED ON A TERM PAPER?	FREQUENCY
1	Y	Y	Y	Y	84
2	Y	Y	Y	N	52
3	Y	Y	N	Y	31
4	Y	Y	N	N	29
5	Y	N	Y	Y	25
6	Y	N	Y	N	17
7	Y	N	N	Y	7
8	Y	N	N	N	11
9	N	Y	Y	Y	5
10	N	Y	Y	N	0
11	N	Y	N	Y	1
12	N	Y	N	N	1
13	N	N	Y	Y	1
14	N	N	Y	N	1
15	N	N	N	Y	0
16	N	N	N	N	0
	0.93	0.53	0.40	0.16	(265)

SOURCE: Dawes and Moore, 1979, p. 132.

the proportion of overt yes responses on either side of the no responses supports the hypothesis of a Guttman pattern.

In contrast, Table 9 presents response patterns that are incompatible with the hypothesized Guttman Scale. It is apparently *not* true that people who cheat also necessarily lie.

ATTITUDE MEASURES AND BEHAVIOR

Most social psychologists require one type of external validity for attitude and opinion measurements: the ability to predict behavior. In fact, those who include a conative component in their definition of attitude require such prediction—or by definition, the measure would not be of an attitude.

Whether, how, and under what circumstances which attitudes predict which behaviors has become a research topic of burgeoning interest, particularly since the middle 1960s. We cannot reference all the work done, nor do we wish to. (We studied over one hundred fifty papers published between 1970 and 1979 in this area alone.) Rather, we will present a logical overview of the question of how measured attitude (opinion) is related to behavior, and we will cover the most important general findings in this overview. Our presentation will be critical—not of the competence of the particular studies or researchers themselves but rather of the entire conceptualization (or lack of it) that led to the investigations.

The attitude-behavior question has been most prominent in the area of race relations and prejudice. Gunnar Myrdal's book *The American Dilemma* (1944) presented the thesis that there is a marked discrepancy between white Americans' expressed endorsement of equitable treatment of blacks and their actual treatment of blacks. Myrdal made his observations before World War II. [As late as 1962, however, Bill Russell, star center of the champion Boston Celtics and the most valuable player in the National Basketball Association, drove to his native Louisiana with his two sons and was turned away from "restaurant after restaurant." He had to sleep in the car because "I couldn't find a decent hotel that would let us spend the night" (Russell and Branch, 1979, p. 44).] Thus as Witz (1972) states, "Myrdal's *American Dilemma* is largely the societal discrepancy between attitudes and behavior, with a tolerant value system conflicting with discriminatory normative patterns" (p. 15). To put it more succinctly: Talk good, act bad. [While we agree that this discrepancy exists, we interpret Myrdal's thesis to concern instead a discrepancy between *general* (liberal) attitudes and *specific* (racist) ones.]

LaPiere (1934) conducted the most famous observational study on behavioral discrepancy in race relations (although it did not attract widespread attention until years after its publication). He traveled around the country in the early 1930s with a young Chinese couple. He kept track of the places they stopped (67 lodging places and 184 restaurants), and six months after the trio had finished traveling together, he wrote a letter to these 251 establishments asking, "Will you accept members of the Chinese race as guests in your establishment?" He received 128 responses, over 90 percent of which were no. In point of fact, unlike Russell, LaPiere and the Chinese couple had been refused service only once, and that was when they were shabbily dressed and driving an old car. (The difference between LaPiere's and Russell's experiences is most readily accounted for by greater behavioral prejudice of white Americans against blacks than against members of other racial minorities—certainly not by an increase in prejudice between 1932 and 1962.)

LaPiere's results are striking—not only because there was a contradiction between what the establishment proprietors said and what they did, but also because this discrepancy itself appeared to be in direct contradiction to the Myrdal dilemma. At least, it is a discrepancy between the *general policy* (racist) and the *specific prac-*

TABLE 10
LaPiere's Results

ATTITUDE	BEHAVIOR	
	PRO	*CON*
Pro	0	0
Con	X	0

tice (nonracist) that appears counter to Myrdal's discrepancy between general liberal attitudes and specific racist ones.

Whatever the sources (and they will be discussed later) of these attitude-behavior discrepancies, it is crucial to note for the purposes of this section that they are defined structurally. Myrdal observed a sample of people who talked good and acted bad, whereas LaPiere observed a sample (of proprietors) who talked bad and acted good. Neither investigator defined discrepancy by a *statistical* inconsistency in individual differences—i.e., by finding that people who expressed more favorable attitudes than others toward civil rights and equity were not necessarily those who behaved more equitably. This structural versus statistical distinction is important because it is one thing to hypothesize a discrepancy based on (main effects) population patterns and quite another to hypothesize one based on inconsistencies (lack of correlation) among individual differences within a population.

The findings of LaPiere are illustrated in Table 10.

Given the pattern of results found in Table 10, statistical contingency is *wholly undefined*. Discrepancy is defined purely in terms of the particular cell (singular) in which the observations are found, *not* in terms of contingency between row and column. We belabor this point because virtually all subsequent authors defined discrepancy (or rather lack of correspondence) in terms of statistical contingency between individuals—while nevertheless referencing LaPiere and indicating that they were studying the same attitude-behavior congruence problem. The words are the same, but the meaning is quite different.

Before examining statistical contingency studies of discrepancy, we would like to mention a few criticisms of the LaPiere study. He himself concluded (1934, p. 237):

The questionnaire is cheap, easy and mechanical.
The study of human behavior is time consuming,

intellectually fatiguing, and depends for its success upon the ability of the investigator. The former method gives quantitative results, the latter mainly qualitative. Quantitative measures are quantitatively accurate; qualitative evaluations are always subject to the errors of human judgment. Yet it should seem far more worthwhile to make a shrewd guess regarding that which is essential than to accurately measure that which is likely to prove irrelevant.

He earlier wrote (1934) that "all measurements of the questionnaire technique proceed on the assumption that there is a mechanical and simple relationship between symbolic and non-symbolic behaviors" (p. 231).

First, the impact of LaPiere's study has not been on the question of quantitative versus qualitative psychology. (As is argued in this chapter, measurement is defined by the existence of consistency or predictability, questions of whether the resulting measures are numbers or orders being secondary.)

Second, his assumption of a "mechanical and simple" relationship between attitude and behavior is quite untrue. He is postulating that the relationship is one-to-one; a given attitude corresponds to a given behavior and vice versa. Consider, however, the situation of the proprietors in the LaPiere study. Presumably, they not only had prejudiced attitudes against Chinese, but they also undoubtedly had attitudes about embarrassing people, creating a scene, etc. In fact, if they were particularly concerned about not offending their (presumably racist) regular clientele—and if they were most concerned with avoiding an unpleasant social scene—what better strategy could they have than advertising their prejudice in hopes that it would keep minority people away—and then quietly serving the very few such people who were unresponsive to their public presentation? (And for all they knew, LaPiere asked his question in preparation for descending upon them with hordes of unwanted guests.)

Thus the relationship between attitudes and behavior is *many-to-one;* i.e., many different attitudes—including especially favorable attitudes toward complying with social norms and pressures—may be associated with a particular behavior. For example, Schuman (1972) found that while only 13 percent of Detroit area heads of households and their wives agreed to discrimination in principle, 41 percent agreed if "it were necessary for the harmony of the firm," and 53 percent agreed if a majority of whites in the firm favored it. Schuman writes (1972, p. 332):

> But only to a true believer will any of these values win out in all situations regardless of the other values with which it competes. A few people go to the stake for a single value, but history and common sense tell us that most people work out compromises depending on the exact balance of positions.

Campbell (1963) has proposed that the many-to-one aspect of the attitude-behavior relationship is due to differing *behavioral thresholds*. To quote Calder and Ross (1973), "It is presumably easier to refuse anonymous, faceless Chinese in a letter (low threshold) than it is to refuse, in person, a well-dressed young couple (high threshold). In short, LaPiere's results were not at all inconsistent" (p. 18). Thus other attitudes—e.g., about anonymous or face-to-face refusal—determine the threshold levels. An ordering of thresholds implies a Guttman Scale; i.e., people who would express that attitude in a situation do so in all "easier" ones, and people who do not express that attitude in easy situations should not do so in more difficult ones. Raden (1977) has checked a number of empirical results to see if they correspond to Guttman Scales (albeit with only two thresholds), and he has discovered that they do not. Thus while the threshold notion is intuitively appealing, we do not emphasize it here.

The fact that a single behavior may be associated with many attitudes is illustrated in Fig. 10b. Figure 10(a) illustrates a one-to-one relationship. But the relationship is also one-to-many, as illustrated in Fig. 10(c). An attitude may be associated with a multitude of behaviors; for example, a positive attitude toward belief in God may be associated with going to church, giving money to religious charities, praying, etc. Fishbein and Ajzen (1974) have illustrated this relationship in the context of statistical contingency across individuals.

Because the relationship is both many-to-one and one-to-many, the overall relationship is many-to-many, as illustrated in Fig. 10(d); a single behavior is associated with many attitudes, and a single attitude is associated with many behaviors. Is it then any wonder that structural discrepancy may be found between what is said and what is done? Moreover, it is very difficult to analyze the antecedents of such discrepancies—because behavior that may appear to be disarrayed or hypocritical in considering some attitudes may make perfect sense when

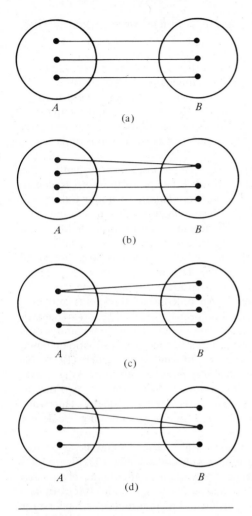

FIGURE 10
Possible Attitude-Behavior Relationships

considering other attitudes involved. (For example, a favorable attitude toward obedience to authority judged as legitimate may explain the compliance to Nazi commands of people who simultaneously purported to hold unprejudiced racial attitudes.) Moreover, differing judgments of fact also complicate the attitude-behavior relationship, as do social norms, fear, bravery, unconscious needs, inertia, etc. It is somewhat remarkable that there is so often a *lack* of structural discrepancy between attitude and behavior. We find this congruence because peo-

ple do in fact have coherent value systems that are related to their behaviors.

In some areas, structural discrepancy for groups of people may be found; in others, not. Where these areas are found, they may have intrinsic substantive interest. But the mere discovery of a discrepancy, or lack thereof, in a particular area does not, in our opinion, have much *theoretical* import for the general questions of how attitudes are related to behaviors, beyond demonstrating that the relationship is many-to-many and that people do not necessarily do what they say.

Before proceeding, we should mention two important criticisms of the LaPiere study that are quite specific. First (Dillehay, 1973), the people responding to the questionnaire may not have been the same people who served the couple. Second, it is quite possible that the stereotype of Chinese the proprietors had in mind when answering LaPiere's letter consisted of non-English-speaking people with pigtails, oriental dress, and incomprehensible manners—not the well-dressed "charming" couple with whom LaPiere actually traveled. While it is true that this particular couple was logically an element of the set "Chinese couples," it might not have been so psychologically. In fact, Schuman and Johnson suggest (1976, pp. 201–202) that some proprietors holding such stereotypes might not have even known that the couple was Chinese!

Before discussing the statistical contingency approach to the attitude-behavior relationship, we will once again stress its difference from the structural approach. A hypothetical example will demonstrate not only that there is a difference but that the same data analyzed in accord with these two different approaches may yield opposite conclusions.

Suppose, for example, Myrdal had systematically interviewed 100 Americans and had discovered that 60 professed positive attitudes toward equality for blacks while engaging in discriminatory behavior, 20 expressed

TABLE 11
Some Hypothetical Results

ATTITUDE	BEHAVIOR	
	PRO	*CON*
Pro	20	60
Con	0	20

positive attitudes while not engaging in discriminatory behavior, and 20 expressed negative attitudes while engaging in discriminatory behavior. These hypothetical results are illustrated in Table 11.

There is a structural discrepancy for 60 percent of those sampled. But the phi coefficient for assessing contingency yields a *positive* value of 0.25. Consider now that half the people in the pro (attitude)–con (behavior) cell were moved to the con-pro cell. There would *still* be an a priori discrepancy for 60 percent of the subjects, yet the phi value would have jumped from +0.25 to −0.20.

Phi coefficients are a special type of *Pearson product-moment correlation coefficient* (that in which each variable is a dichotomy). Since dichotomization is a crude way of measuring either attitude or behavior, most investigators use measures with gradations, and they compute the Pearson coefficient on these measures. Before discussing the results, we wish to discuss the meaning and the properties of this coefficient, because we believe that the major findings referenced in the contingency literature follow directly from its statistical properties.

Given two numerical variables (however obtained or devised), the Pearson product-moment correlation coefficient (r) indexes the reduction in mean square error when the *best-fitting* linear prediction is made of either variable from the other. The r^2 is the proportional reduction in mean square error. Because most monotone relationships can be well approximated by linear ones, the correlation coefficient is a good measure of monotone fit—provided, of course, the relationships are monotone to begin with (Abelson and Tukey, 1963; Dawes and Corrigan, 1974).

The first property of the correlation coefficient to be emphasized is that it can be interpreted meaningfully only in terms of the population sampled. That's true of any statistic, of course, but this restriction is usually more obvious from the verbal descriptions of means, standard deviations, etc. than from those of correlation coefficients; for example, we speak of the mean score for men or the standard deviation for graduate students, but we often talk about *the* correlation between two variables—e.g., between religious attitude and religious behavior—without making it clear that we are talking about a particular, specifiable population. (In fact, the variables themselves are often not specified, as when people assert that "attitude is uncorrelated with behavior" or "behavior is uncorrelated across situations.")

A second, related property is that if two variables have a monotone relationship, then *in general* the greater the range sampled, the higher is the correlation. This statement is true whether the sampling is done on the basis of one variable or of both simultaneously. In classical mental-testing theory this property is referred to as the *range-of-talent problem,* because it implies that the validity of the test computed on a sample of people with a low range (actually standard deviation) of scores will be less than that computed on a sample from a broad range.

Third, if two variables have a positive correlation because they share common aspects, then the more aspects of each not shared by the other, the lower is the correlation. (The converse is not true; variables need not have common aspects in order to be correlated. For example, the time an object takes to fall in a vacuum is a perfect linear function of the square root of the distance it must fall, although time and distance are entirely separate conceptual entities.)

Fourth, if one variable has a consistent (positive or negative) monotone relationship to a number of others, then—except under extraordinary circumstances—this variable will have a higher correlation with their sum than with each singly.

In our view the major substantive findings presented in the literature concerning statistical contingency between attitude and behavior follow directly from the four properties we have specified.

For example, Wicker (1971) has conducted a widely cited study on the relationship between religious attitudes and religious behaviors of 152 members of United Methodist churches in Milwaukee, Wisconsin. He used four nonrepresentational measures of religious attitudes; they correlated on the average 0.27 with frequency of church attendance, 0.16 with amount of contributions, and 0.11 with holding responsible positions. He concluded (p. 27) that the attitude measures had "relatively low behavioral validity" for predicting behavior. He further investigated the range-of-talent problem by noting that "behavioral validity does not directly co-vary with the standard deviations of the attitude measures" (p. 22).

But range of talent is not evaluated by the *relative* standard deviations of diverse attitude measures *within* the population sampled but by the range of the population itself. (For example, changing from feet to inches does not increase the range of length of a set of logs.) These people were all churchgoers. Suppose Wicker had sampled the general population and included a sizable proportion of people who never go to church. If many of these had negative attitudes (which is admittedly assuming attitude-behavior coherence), the correlation coefficient would have increased substantially, if not dramatically. Moreover, even with his sample the *unshared-aspect property* of correlation coefficients would militate against large values. Church attendance is clearly determined to large extent by conflicting demands on one's time, contributions by money, and holding responsible positions by energy and intelligence.

We can conclude, as does Wicker, that within a highly restricted range of people, religious behaviors dependent upon many things other than religious attitude do not correlate well with that attitude. But the absolute *magnitude* of the correlations in this particular context cannot be interpreted as meaning anything in particular—other than that individual differences in religious attitude are in fact monotonically related to individual differences in religious behavior. In fact, making a negative conclusion on the basis of a low correlation in a real-life setting is highly suspect (Dawes, 1979), because it is generally unclear just how predictable the behavior is from the psychological and social variables we study, if predictable at all.

That the correlation coefficient between attitude and behavior is also attenuated by behavioral factors having nothing to do with attitude has been noted by a number of authors (Warner and DeFleur, 1969; Kelman, 1974; Schuman and Johnson, 1976). Situational factors are those most often cited. In addition, attitudes other than those under consideration may be important as well. What was said earlier in this section about the many-to-one nature of attitude with respect to understanding structural discrepancies applies equally well to understanding low correlation coefficients across people between a single attitude and the corresponding behavior.

A slightly more subtle result of the unshared-aspect property may be found in the work of Fishbein and Ajzen (1977), who showed that attitudinal specificity increases the correlation between attitude and behavior (Abelson 1968; Crespi, 1971; Heberlein and Black, 1976; Ajzen and Fishbein, 1977). In fact, Ajzen and Fishbein concluded that strong attitude-behavior relationships are obtained only when there is high correspondence between the target and action elements of the attitude and behavior—or as Crespi (1971) states: "Improving behavioral prediction requires test items having stimulus properties very similiar to those present in the actual situation" (p. 333).

Thus the best behavioral prediction found in the literature is that of voting (Abelson, 1968). People are asked about their attitudes toward particular candidates; not only are behavioral intentions highly predictive of voting outcomes, but other attitudinal factors such as "softness" of support may also be used in hypothesizing possible shifts in electoral preference.

Here the situation is the converse of that where behavior is partially a function of factors other than a single attitude. When the attitude is *general* and the behavior *specific,* there are many aspects of the attitude unrelated to the behavior. For example, a person with a positive attitude toward behaving altruistically has in mind a wide variety of behaviors when he or she expresses this attitude. Donating bone marrow is only one. It naturally follows that we can predict individual differences in donating bone marrow less well from individual differences in general altruistic attitude than from individual differences in attitude toward donating bone marrow. Or individual differences in purchase of lead-free gasoline are better predicted from individual differences in attitude toward using lead-free gasoline than from individual differences in attitude about ecology (Heberlein and Black, 1976). The reductio ad absurdum occurs when the attitude question targets the behavior of interest with such specificity that the response to the former is tantamount to a behavioral intention concerning the latter.

In 1931 L. L. Thurstone, the researcher who virtually began the field of attitude measurement, wrote that while two individuals may hold exactly the same attitude, "their overt actions may take quite different forms which have one thing in common, namely that they are not equally favorable toward the object" (p. 262). Thus we could expect relatively low correlations between individual differences in a given attitude and individual differences in a particular "form" of behavior. It follows from the fourth property of correlation coefficients that if we were to sum across each separate behavior associated with a given attitude and correlate this sum with a related attitude measure, we would expect much higher correlations. The correlation between individual differences in attitude and individual differences in a composite of relevant behaviors generally *must* be higher than that between attitude and a single relevant behavior. For the reader most comfortable thinking in terms of multiple correlation, we point out that the prediction of a linear composite of behaviors from a single attitude measurement is precisely equivalent to the prediction of that attitude measure from that linear composite of behaviors, since both multiple *R*'s are nothing more than the simple Pearson product-moment correlation between predicted and actual scores. Hence the fact that many predictors all correlated with a criterion will outperform any single predictor is applicable here—as is the fact that except under extraordinary circumstances involving suppressor variables (which are easy to hypothesize but hard to find), unit weights will predict almost as well as will optimal weight (see Ghiselli, 1964; Dawes and Corrigan, 1974; Einhorn, 1975, 1976; Wainer, 1976).

For example, Fishbein and Ajzen (1974) sampled sixty college student subjects, assessed their attitudes toward religion with standard scales, and then asked them to recall the frequency with which they engaged in 100 behaviors such as praying before meals. Ajzen and Fishbein found that the correlations between single behaviors and attitudes were quite low; the average correlation for the five attitude scales ranged from 0.12 to 0.15. In contrast, the correlations with the behavior indices (i.e., the additive composites) were high and significant, ranging from 0.45 to 0.75, with an average of 0.63. Weigel and Newman (1976) reported a similiar finding about attitudes toward ecology.

In this section and the preceding ones dealing with the properties of the correlation coefficient, we have been discussing relative magnitude. It is possible in the present context to go one step farther and (on the basis of certain simplifying assumptions) to predict exact values of an attitude measure's correlation with a single behavior and with multiple behaviors, given the intercorrelations between the behaviors themselves. Assume that the correlations between the attitude measure and each single behavior are equal, as are the intercorrelations among the behaviors. [Departures from this assumption will not have much effect on the calculations as long as all intercorrelations are positive; see Green (1977).] Then it can be determined from Eq. (5) in Gullikson (1950, p. 89) that if the average correlation between an attitude measure and a single item is, for example, 0.13, and the average intercorrelation among the behaviors is 0.03, then the correlation between that single attitude and an additive composite of 100 such behaviors is 0.65. Moreover, any two of these numbers yield the third.

SUMMING UP

Errors, temporally unstable influences, and differential sensitivity in the assessment of attitude and behavior all yield components in one of these assessed variables not found in the other. The result is a lowered correlation between the two. Just as it is not a *finding* that test unreliability tends to lower test validity, it is not a finding that attitudes and behaviors assessed at different levels of specificity correlate less well than do those assessed at the same level. The only finding is of what affects specificity in a particular context. Nor is it a finding that multiple measures (of attitude or behavior or both) tend to yield higher correlations than do single measures.

Have the myriad studies of attitude-behavior contingency across individuals yielded no substantive information? No, they have not, but what they have presented are results quite consistent with four rather simple assumptions:

1. The relationship is monotone.

2. There are factors in behavior not related to particular attitudes.

3. There are factors in broad attitudes not related to particular behaviors.

4. There do not seem to be any suppressor variables involved in the contingency between attitude and behavior.

It is of interest to note that since the role of attitude and behavior in correlational studies is symmetric, the composite "findings" could be easily reversed. An experimenter can show that a single behavior is more highly correlated with an additive composite of many relevant attitudes better than with a single one. All that is necessary is to have a rough equivalence of prediction for each. (It's been done!)

There is no support in the literature for broad claims that individual differences in attitude measures do or do not predict individual differences in behavior well or poorly, or that attitude is paramount in importance in predicting behavior or that it is inconsequential. There can't be.

Much the same argument made here could be applied to the question of whether or how much behavior is situation-specific. The question, as that above, may be argued in terms of structural discrepancy or congruence ("He behaved much differently there"), or in terms of how correlation coefficients across individuals vary from situation to situation. To the degree to which the situations sampled are similiar and the subjects sampled are dissimilar, these correlations will be high—and people will be seen as consistent in their behavior. To the degree to which situations sampled are dissimilar and the people are similar, the correlations will be low (ω^2 is just another form of correlation coefficient). In fact, since there is no a priori definition of similarity of people or situations, it might make sense to *define* situational similarity and subject similarity in terms of the degree to which consistent behavior is elicited.

ALTERNATIVE APPROACHES

We have found one study that appears to go beyond showing that simple characteristics of attitude-behavior relationships, and elementary properties of correlation coefficients, yield predictable results. Kahle and Berman (1979) studied how individual differences in attitude *predict* later individual differences in behavior and compared this prediction with that from prior behavior to later attitude. (Once again, correlation coefficients are symmetric, but the temporal difference allows us to infer asymmetry of predictability; it would, for example, make little sense to talk about how well later behavior can predict prior attitude, except in a statistical sense.) Kahle and Berman computed cross-lag correlations predicting college student alcohol consumption (or at least self-reports of having one or two drinks a day), voting, and religious behavior from prior attitude. They also predicted subsequent attitude from prior behavior. Following all the precautions in interpretation suggested by Kenny (1975), they found greater predictability from attitude to behavior than vice versa. No simple characteristics of the attitude-behavior relationship nor elementary properties of correlation coefficients would suggest whether the attitude-to-behavior or the behavior-to-attitude correlation should be greater.

In fact, the most important test of the utility of attitude measures may lie not in the concurrent correlations with behavior (involving all the vicissitudes discussed above) but rather in the prediction of behavior change from attitude measures—or better yet, the prediction of behavioral change from change in attitude measures. If, for example, such prediction were possible from measures involving attitudes toward the self and toward social relationships, then these measures would be of extreme value in such contexts as psychotherapy. If it were to turn out, on the other hand, that changes in attitude only followed behavioral change, then attitude measures would be of much less value. In fact, such a finding would support those therapists who concentrate on behavioral change in their clients and note in passing that spirit and self-regard may improve. Those therapists at the other extreme who insist that "the transference must

be worked through" before attempting behavioral change are clearly assuming the primacy of attitude.

In fact, we know that both types of changes can take place (e.g., see Calder and Ross, 1973, pp. 19–25). The typical attitude change study often includes a behavioral dependent variable as well as standard attitude measures. Moreover, the cognitive dissonance studies and the self-observations studies indicate that behavioral change will lead to attitudinal change. But as Bem, the founder of the self-observation approach, himself notes (1972), change will occur "only to the extent that internal cues are weak, ambiguous, or uninterpretable" (p. 2). Most students of attitude change, on the other hand, are concerned primarily with attitudes whose "internal cues" are strong, unambiguous, and interpretable.

Finally, we would like to suggest another apparently neglected way in which attitude may be predictive of behavior—or at least correlated with it: in the *choice of behavioral situations,* as opposed to the choice of behavior within situations. One's attitude toward drinking and religion may be only weakly related to one's behavior at a tavern or at a church supper on a Sunday evening, but it may be strongly related to which place one is at. Or to take an example with which one of us (RMD) is familiar, the Democrats who worked for John Anderson in the 1980 campaign before he left the Republican party behaved indistinguishably from regular Republicans at Republican party headquarters—but it took a great deal to get some of them there (e.g., five steps backward for every ten forward as they approached).

On the one hand, people tend to underestimate the strength of situational influences once there (e.g., "I will just take care of things while my friends drop a little acid"); on the other hand, choice of situation is so natural and often so automatic that introspectively it does not appear to involve strong attitudes. Thus people may be surprised by low correlations within situations ("attitude doesn't predict behavior") and high correlation with situation choice ("but everyone comes here Saturday nights").

Were we writing a journal article, we could point out that most (though certainly not all) attitude-behavior studies involve behaviors within a situation and we could decry the fact that such work obviously overlooks the crucial role of situation choice. We could then pick a topic that would surely show that situation choice is more highly correlated with attitude than is behavior within situations. But what would it mean? It would mean that we had removed the situational pressures from the behavior, so that those homogenizing factors would be absent from our behavioral measure, predictably increasing the correlation with attitude (provided, of course, we have not done anything stupid in our attitude scale construction that would reintroduce them on that side). A new plethora of studies might result.

REFERENCES

Abelson, R. P. (1968). Computers, polls, and public opinion—some puzzles and paradoxes. *Transaction, 5,* 20–27.

Abelson, R. P., and J. Tukey (1963). Effective integration of numerical information on quantitative analysis: general theory and the case of simple order. *Ann. math. Statist., 34,* 1347–1369.

Adams, E. W., and R. F. Fagot (1959). A model of riskless choice. *Behav. Sci., 4,* 1–10.

Adams, E. W., R. F. Fagot, and R. E. Robinson (1965). The theory of appropriate statistics. *Psychometric, 30,* 99–127.

Adorno, T. W., E. Frankel-Brunswik, D. J. Levinson, and R. N. Sanford (1950). *The authoritarian personality.* New York: Harper.

Ajzen, I., and M. Fishbein (1977). Attitude-behavior relations: a theoretical analysis and review of empirical research. *Psychol. Bull., 84,* 888–918.

Allport, G. W. (1935). Attitudes. In C. Murchison (Ed.), *Handbook of social psychology.* Worcester, Mass.: Clark Univ. Press.

Anderson, N. H. (1961). Scales and statistics: parametric and nonparametric. *Psychol. Bull., 58,* 305–316.

_____ (1970). Functional measurement and psychophysical judgment. *Psychol. Rev., 77,* 153–170.

_____ (1971). Integration theory and attitude change. *Psychol. Rev., 78,* 171–206.

Atwood, R. W., and R. J. Howell (1971). Pupillometric and personality test score differences of female aggressing pedophiliacs and normals. *Psychon. Sci., 22,* 115–116.

Bagozzi, R. P. (1978). The construct validity of the affective, behavioral, and cognitive components of attitude by analyzing covariance structures. *Multivariate behav. Res., 13,* 9–31.

Baskett, G. A., J. G. Peet, D. A. Bradford, and S. A. Muliak (1973). The examination of the lost letter technique. *J. appl. Psychol., 3,* 165–173.

Baumrind, D. (1964). Some thoughts on ethics of research: after reading Milgram's "behavioral study of obedience." *Amer. Psychol., 19,* 421–423.

_____ (1979). IRBs and social science research: the costs of deception. *IRB: a review of human subjects research.* Vol. 1. *6,* 1–4.

Beckman, L. J. (1978). Couples' decision making processes regarding fertility. In K. E. Taubert, L. L. Bumpass, and J. A. Sweet (Eds.), *Social demography: studies in population.* New York: Academic Press.

Bem, D. J. (1972). Self-perception theory. In L. Berkowitz (Ed.), *Advances in experimental social psychology.* Vol. 6. New York: Academic Press.

Bentler, P. M. (1968). Heterosexual behavior assessment. *Behav. research Therapy, 6,* 21–30.

Bolton, G. M. (1974). The lost letter technique as a measure of community attitudes toward a major social issue. *Sociol. Quart., 15,* 567–570.

Borgadus, E. S. (1925). Measuring social distances. *J. appl. Sociol., 9,* 299–308.

Bridgman, P. W. (1927). *The logic of modern physics.* New York: Macmillan.

Calder, B. J., and M. Ross (1973). *Attitudes and behavior.* Morristown, N.J.: General Learning Press.

Campbell, C., and B. L. Joiner (1973). How to get the answer without being sure you've asked the question. *Amer. Statistician, 27,* 229–231.

Campbell, D. T. (1950). The indirect assessment of social attitudes. *Psychol. Bull., 47,* 15–38.

_____ (1963). Social attitudes and other acquired behavioral dispositions. In S. Koch (Ed.), *Psychology: a study of a science.* Vol. 6. New York: McGraw-Hill.

Campbell, D. T., and D. W. Fiske (1959). Convergent and discriminate validation of the multitrait-multimethod matrix. *Psychol. Bull., 56,* 81–105.

Campbell, D. T., and J. C. Stanley (1963). Experimental and quasi-experimental designs for research on teaching. In N. L. Gage (Ed.), *Handbook of research on teaching.* Chicago: Rand McNally.

Carroll, J. B., and P. Arabie (1980). Multi-dimensional scaling. *Ann. rev. Psychol., 31,* 607–649.

Cliff, N. (1977). A theory of consistency of ordering generalizable to tailored testing. *Psychometrika, 42,* 375–399.

Coombs, C. H. (1950). Psychological scaling without a unit of measurement. *Psychol. Rev., 57,* 145–158.

_____ (1964). *A theory of data.* New York: Wiley.

_____ (1967). Thurstone's measurement of social values revisited 40 years later. *J. Pers. soc. Psychol., 6,* 85–90.

Coombs, C. H., T. C. Bezimbinder, and F. Goode (1967). Testing expectation theories of decision making without measuring utility or subjective probability. *J. math. Psychol., 4,* 72–103.

Coombs, C. H., L. C. Coombs, and G. H. McClelland (1975). Preference scales for number and sex of children. *Population studies, 29,* 273–298.

Cooper, J. B., and D. Pollack (1959). The identification of prejudicial attitudes by the galvanic skin response. *J. soc. Psychol., 50,* 241–245.

Cowen, E. L., R. P. Underber, and R. T. Verillo (1958). Development and testing of an attitude to blindness scale. *J. soc. Psychol., 48,* 297–304.

Crespi, I. (1971). What kinds of attitude measures are predictive of behavior? *Publ. Opin. Quart., 35,* 327–334.

Dawes, R. M. (1968). Algebraic models of cognition, summarized by E. Sarago. In *Algebraic models in psychology: proceedings of the NUFFIC international summer session in science at "Het Oude Hof,"* The Hague, August 5–7.

_____ (1972a). *Fundamentals of attitude measurement.* New York: Wiley.

_____ (1972b). Doing evil to others vs. seducing others to do evil. Paper presented at Western Psychological Association meeting, Portland, Ore., April.

_____ (1977). Suppose we measured height with rating scales instead of rulers. *Appl. Psychol. Meas., 1,* 267–273.

_____ (1979). The robust beauty of improper linear models. *Amer. Psychol., 34,* 571–582.

Dawes, R. M., and B. Corrigan (1974). Linear models in decision making. *Psychol. Bull., 81,* 95–106.

Dawes, R. M., and P. E. Meehl (1966). Mixed group validation: a method for determining the validity of diagnostic signs without using criterion groups. *Psychol. Bull., 66,* 2, 63–67.

Dawes, R. M., and M. Moore (1979). Guttman scaling orthodox and randomized responses. In F. Peterman (Ed.), *Attitude measurement.* Gottinger: Verlag für psychologie. Pp. 117–133.

Dawes, R. M., D. Singer, and F. Lemons (1971). An experimental analysis of the contrast effect and its implications for intergroup communication and the indirect assessment of attitude. *J. Pers. soc. Psychol., 21,* 281–295.

deSoto, C. D., M. London, and S. Handel (1965). Social reasoning and spatial paralogic. *J. Pers. soc. Psychol., 2,* 513–521.

Dillehay, R. C. (1973). On the irrelevance of the classical negative evidence concerning the effect of attitudes on behavior. *Amer. Psychol., 28,* 887–891.

Ducamp, A., and J. C. Flamange (1969). Composite measurement. *J. math. Psychol., 6,* 359–380.

Einhorn, H. J. (1975). Unit weighting schemes for decision making. *Organizat. Behav. hum. Perform., 13,* 171–192.

_____ (1976). Equal weighting in multi-attribute models: a rationale, example, and some extension. In N. Schiff and G. Sorter (Eds.), *Proceedings of the conference on topical research in accounting.* New York: New York Univ. Press.

Festinger, L. (1964). In collaboration with D. Allen, N. Braden, L. K. Cannon, J. R. Davidson, J. D. Decker, S. B. Kisler, and E. Walster. *Conflict, decision, and dissonance.* Stanford: Stanford Univ. Press.

Fiddler, D. S., and R. E. Kleinknecht (1977). Randomized response versus direct questioning: two data-collection methods for sensitive information. *Psychol. Bull., 84,* 1045–1049.

Fishbein, M. (1967). A consideration of beliefs and their role in attitude measurement. In M. Fishbein (Ed.), *Readings in attitude theory and measurement.* New York: Wiley. Pp. 389–400.

Fishbein, M., and I. Ajzen (1974). Attitude toward objects as predictors of single and multiple behavioral criteria. *Psychol. Rev., 81,* 59–74.

Funk, S. G., A. D. Horowitz, R. Lipschitz, and F. W. Young (1976). The perceived structure of American ethnic groups: the use of multi-dimensional scaling in stereotype research. *Sociometry, 39,* 116–130.

Gaes, G. G., R. J. Kalle, and J. T. Tedeschi (1978). Impression management in the forced compliance situation. *J. exp. soc. Psychol., 14,* 493–510.

Galanter, E. H. (1956). An axiomatic and experimental study of sensory order and measure. *Psychol. Rev., 63,* 16–28.

Ghiselli, E. E. (1964). *Psychological measurement.* New York: McGraw-Hill.

Goldberg, L. R., and C. E. Werts (1966). The reliability of clinicians' judgments: a multitrait-multimethod approach. *J. consult. Psychol., 30,* 199–206.

Golden, R. R., and P. E. Meehl (1978). Testing a single dominant gene theory without an accepted criterion variable. *Ann. hum. Genetics, 41.* London, 507–514.

Goodman, L. A., and W. H. Kruskal (1954). Measures of association for cross-classification. *J. Amer. statist. Assoc., 49,* 732–764.

Goodman, N. (1951). *The structure of appearance.* Cambridge, Mass.: Harvard Univ. Press.

Goodstadt, M. S., and V. Gruson (1975). The randomized response technique: a test on drug use. *J. Amer. statist. Assoc., 70,* 814–818.

Green, B. F., Jr. (1954). Attitude measurement. In G. Lindzey (Ed.), *The handbook of social psychology.* Vol. I Cambridge, Mass.: Addison-Wesley.

_____ (1956). A method of scaleogram analyses using summary statistics. *Psychometric, 21,* 79–88.

_____ (1977). Parameter sensitivity and multivariate methods. *Multivariate behav. Res., 3,* 263.

Green, V. E., and V. Srinivasan (1978). Conjoint analysis in consumer research: research and outlook. *J. Consumer Research, 5,* 103–123.

Greenberg, B. C., A. L. Abdula, W. R. Simmons, and D. G. Horvitz (1969). The unrelated question in randomized response model, theoretical framework. *J. Amer. Statist. Assoc., 64,* 520–539.

Gulliksen, H. (1950). *Theory of mental tests.* New York: Wiley.

Hays, W. L. (1963). *Statistics for psychologists.* New York: Holt, Rinehart, and Winston.

Heberlein, T. A., and J. S. Black (1976). Attitudinal specificity and the prediction of behavior in a field setting. *J. Pers. soc. Psychol., 33,* 474–479.

Hess, E. H. (1965). Attitude and pupil size. *Scientific American, 212,* 46–54.

Hess, E. H., A. L. Seltzer, and J. M. Shlien (1965). Pupil responses of hetero- and homosexual males to pictures of men and women: a pilot study. *J. abnorm. Psychol., 70,* 165–168.

Holder, O. (1901). Die axiome der quantitat und die lebre von mass. *Berichte* über die verhandlugen der koniglich saclisischen gesellschaften der wissenschaften zu Leipsig. Mathematisch-Physische Classe, *53,* 1–64.

Holton, G. (1978). *The scientific imagination.* New York: Cambridge Univ. Press. Pp. 25–83.

Hovland, C. I., and M. Sherif (1952). Judgmental phenomenon on the scale of attitude measurement: item displacement on the thurstone scales. *J. abnorm. soc. Psychol., 47,* 822–832.

Hubert, L. J., and F. B. Baker (1978). Analyzing the multitrait-multimethod matrix. *Multivariate behav. Res., 13,* 163–179.

Janisse, M. P. (1973). Pupil size and affect: a critical review of the literature since 1960. *Canadian Psychol., 14,* 311–329.

Jensen, A. R. (1969). How much can we boost IQ and scholastic achievement? *Harvard educat. Rev., 39,* 1–123.

Jones, E. E., and H. Sigall (1971). The bogus pipeline: a new paradigm for measuring affect and attitude. *Psychol. Bull., 76,* 349–364.

Kahle, L. R., and J. J. Berman (1979). Attitudes cause behaviors: a cross-lagged panel analysis. *J. Pers. soc. Psychol., 37,* 315–321.

Katz, D. (1960). The functional approach to the study of attitudes. *Publ. Opin. Quart., 24,* 163–204.

Kelly, G. A. (1955). *The psychology of personal constructs.* Vol. I. *A theory of personality.* New York: Norton.

Kelman, H. C. (1974). Attitudes are alive and well and gainfully employed in the sphere of action. *Amer. Psychol., 29,* 310–324.

Kenny, D. A. (1975). Cross-lagged panel correlation: a test for spuriousness. *Psychol. Bull., 82,* 887–903.

—— (1976). An empirical application of confirmatory factor analysis to the multitrait-multimethod matrix. *J. exp. soc. Psychol., 12,* 247–252.

Kenny, D. A., and D. C. Rubin (1977). Estimating chance reproducibility in Guttman scaling. *Soc. sci. Res., 6,* 188–196.

Koslowski, M., G. L. Pratt, and R. N. Wintrob (1976). The application of Guttman scale analysis to physicians' attitudes regarding abortion. *J. appl. Psychol., 61,* 301–304.

Krantz, D. H. (1972). A theory of magnitude estimation and cross-modality matching. *J. math. Psychol., 9,* 168–199.

Krantz, D. H., R. D. Luce, P. Suppes, and A. Tversky (1971). *Foundations of measurement.* New York: Academic Press.

Krantz, D. H., and A. Tversky (1971). Conjoint-measurement analysis of composition rules in psychology. *Psychol. Rev., 78,* 151–169.

Krech, D., and R. S. Crutchfield (1948). *Theories and problems in social psychology.* New York: McGraw-Hill.

Kruskal, J. B. (1964a). Multi-dimensional scaling by optimizing goodness-of-fit to a non-metric hypothesis. *Psychometrika, 29,* 1–27.

—— (1964b). Non-metric multi-dimensional scaling: a numerical method. *Psychometrika, 29,* 115–129.

Kruskal, J. B., F. W. Young, and J. B. Seery (1973). How to use KYST: a very flexible program to do multi-dimensional scaling and unfolding. Murray Hill, N.J.: Bell Telephone Labs.

—— (1977). How to use KYST 2: a very flexible program to do multi-dimensional scaling and unfolding. Murray Hill, N.J.: Bell Telephone Labs.

LaPiere, R. T. (1934). Attitudes versus action. *Social Forces, 13,* 230–237.,

Likert, R. (1932). A technique for the measurement of attitudes. *Arch. Psychol., 140,* 5–53.

Lingoes, J. C. (1973). The Guttman-Lingoes non-metric program series. Mathesis.

Locander, W., S. Sudman, and N. Bradburn (1976). An investigation of interview method, threat and response distortion. *J. Amer. Statist. Assoc., 71,* 269–275.

Luce, R. D. D., and D. W. Tukey (1964). Simultaneous conjoint measurement: a new type of fundamental measurement. *J. math. Psychol., 1,* 1–27.

McClelland, G. H., C. H. Coombs, and L. C. Coombs (1976). Measurement and analysis of family composition preferences. In S.H. Newman and V. D. Thompson (Eds.), *Population psychology, research, and educational issues.* Washington, D.C.: Government Printing Office. DHEW Publication # IVIH-76-574. Pp. 105–112.

MacNeil, M. K., L. E. Davis, and D. J. Pace (1975). Group status displacement under stress: a serendipidous finding. *Sociometry, 38,* 293–307.

Milgram, S. (1963). Behavioral study of obedience. *J. abnorm. soc. Psychol., 67,* 371–378.

Milgram, S., L. Mann, and S. Harter (1965). The lost-letter technique of social research. *Publ. Opin. Quart., 29,* 437–438.

Myrdal, G. (1944). *An American dilemma.* New York: Harper.

Newcomb, T. N., R. H. Turner, and P. E. Convers (1965). *Social psychology.* New York: Holt, Rinehart, and Winston.

Osgood, C. E., and Z. Luria (1954). Applied analysis of a case of multiple personality using the semantic differential. *J. abnorm. soc. Psychol., 49,* 579–591.

—— (1976). A postscript to "The three faces of Eve." *J. abnorm. Psychol., 85,* 276–286.

Osgood, C. E., D. J. Suci, and P. H. Tannenbaum (1957). *The measurement of meaning.* Urbana: Univ. of Illinois Press.

Ostrom, T. M. (1969). The relationship between the affective, behavioral, and cognitive components of attitude. *J. exp. soc. Psychol., 5,* 12–30.

Patterson, G. R., and R. M. Dawes (1975). A Guttman scale of childrens' coersive behaviors. *J. consult. clinical Psychol., 43,* 594.

Podell, L., and J. Perkins (1957). A Guttman scale for sexual experience. *J. abnorm. soc. Psychol., 54,* 420–422.

Poole, K. T. (1981). Dimensions of interest group evaluation of the U.S. Senate, 1969–1978. *Amer. J. polit. Sci., 25,* 41–54.

Quigley-Fernandez, B., and J. T. Tedeschi (1978). The bogus pipeline as lie detector: two validity studies. *J. pers. soc. Psychol., 36,* 247–256.

Raden, D. (1977). Situational thresholds and attitude-behavior consistency. *Sociometry, 40,* 123–129.

Ramsey, J. O. (1975). Solving implicit equations in psychometric data analysis. *Psychometrika, 40,* 337–360.

—— (1977). Maximum likelihood estimation in multidimensional scaling. *Psychometrika, 42,* 241–266.

Roberts, F. S. (1979). Measurement theory with applications to decision-making and utility in the social sciences. In G. C. Rota (Ed.), *Encyclopedia of mathematics and its applications.* Vol. 7. London: Addison-Wesley.

Rokeach, M. (1960). *The open and closed mind.* New York: Basic Books.

Rosenberg, M. J., and C. I. Hovland (1960). Cognitive, affective, and behavioral components of attitudes. In M. J. Rosenberg (Ed.), *Attitude organization and change.* New Haven, Conn.: Yale Univ. Press. Pp. 1–14.

Russell, B., and T. Branch (1979). *Second wind: the memoirs of an opinionated man.* New York: Random House.

Schimizu, I. M., and G. S. Bonham (1978). Randomized response technique in a national survey. *J. Amer. Statist. Assoc., 73,* 35–39.

Schmitt, N., B. W. Coyle, and B. B. Sarri (1977). A review and critique of analyses of multitrait-multimethod matrices. *Multivariate behav. Res., 12,* 447–478.

Schuman, H. (1972). Attitudes vs. action *versus* attitudes vs. action. *Publ. Opin. Quart., 36,* 347–354.

Schuman, H. and M. P. Johnson (1976). Attitudes and behaviors. *Ann. rev. Sociol., 2,* 161–207.

Schwarz, G., and A. Tversky (1980). On the reciprocity of proximity relations. *J. math. Psychol., 22,* 157–175.

Selltiz, C., H. Edrich, and S. W. Cook (1965). Ratings of favorableness of statements about a social group as an indicator of attitude toward the group. *J. Pers. soc. Psychol., 2,* 408–415.

Shepard, R. N. (1962a). Analysis of proximities: multi-dimensional scaling with an unknown distance function. I. *Psychometrika, 27,* 125–140.

_____ (1962b). Analysis of proximities: multi-dimensional scaling with an unknown distance function. II. *Psychometrika, 27,* 219–249.

Sherif, C. W., M. Kelly, H. L. Rogers, Jr., G. Sarup, and B. I. Titler (1973). Personal involvement, social judgment, and action. *J. Pers. soc. Psychol., 27,* 311–328.

Sherif, M., and C. I. Hovland (1953). Judgmental phenomena and scales of attitude measurement: placement of items with individual choice of number of categories. *J. abnorm. soc. Psychol., 48,* 135–141.

Sherif, M., and C. W. Sherif (1969). *Social Psychology.* New York: Harper & Row.

Sigall, H., and R. Page (1972). Reducing attenuation of the expression of interpersonal effect via the bogus pipeline. *Sociometry, 35,* 629–642.

Silverman, I. (1965). Motives underlying the behavior of the subject in the psychological experiment. Paper presented at the Convention of the American Psychological Association. Chicago, Ill.: September.

Silverman, I., A. D. Shulman, and D. L. Wysenthal (1970). Effects of deceiving and debriefing psychological subjects on performance in later experiments. *J. Pers. soc. Psychol., 14,* 203–212.

Spaeth, H. J. (1965). Interdimensionality and item invariance in judicial scaling. *Behav. Sci., 10,* 290–304.

Stevens, S. S. (1951). Mathematics, measurement, and psychophysics. In S. S. Stevens (Ed.), *Handbook of experimental psychology.* New York: Wiley.

_____ (1959). Cross-modality validation of subjective scales. *J. exp. Psychol., 57,* 201–209.

_____ (1968). Measurement, statistics, and the schemapiric view. *A Science, 161,* 849–856.

Stouffer, S. A., L. Guttman, E. A. Schuman, D. Lazarsfield, A. Starr, and J. A. Clausen (1950). *Measurement and prediction.* Princeton, N.J.: Princeton Univ. Press.

Sykes, M. P., and S. E. Cleveland (1968). Human relations training for police and community. *Amer. Psychol., 23,* 766–769.

Thigpen, C. H., and H. M. Cleckley (1957). *The three faces of Eve.* New York: McGraw-Hill.

Thurstone, L. L. (1928). Attitudes can be measured. *Amer. J. Sociol., 33,* 529–554.

_____ (1931). The measurement of attitudes. *J. abnorm. soc. Psychol., 26,* 249–269.

Thurstone, L. L., and E. L. Chave (1929). *The measurement of attitude.* Chicago: Univ. of Chicago Press.

Tognacci, L. N., and S. W. Cook (1975). Conditioned autonomic responses as bidirectional indicators of racial attitude. *J. Pers. soc. Psychol., 31,* 137–144.

Torgeson, W. S. (1958). *Theory and methods of scaling.* New York: Wiley.

_____ (1965). Multi-dimensional scaling of similarity. *Psychometrika, 30,* 379–393.

Tversky, A. (1967). A general theory of polynomial conjoint measurement. *J. math. Psychol., 4,* 1–20.

_____ (1969). Intransitivity of preferences. *Psychol. Rev., 76,* 31–48.

Valens, S. (1966). Cognitive effects of false heart-rate feedback. *J. Pers. soc. Psychol., 4,* 400–408.

Wainer, H. (1976). Estimating coefficients in linear models: it don't make no never mind. *Psychol. Bull., 83,* 312–317.

Warner, L. G., and M. L. DeFleur (1969). Attitude as an interactional concept: social constraint and social distance as intervening variables between attitudes and action. *Amer. Sociol. Rev., 34,* 153–169.

Warner, S. L. (1965). Randomized response: a survey technique for eliminating evasive answer bias. *J. Amer. statist. Assoc., 60,* 63–69.

Webb, E. J., D. T. Campbell, R. D. Schwartz, and L. Sechrest (1966). *Unobtrusive measures: non-reactive research in the social sciences.* Chicago: Rand McNally.

Weigel, R. H., and L. S. Newman (1976). Increasing attitude-behavior correspondence by broadening the scope of the behavioral measure. *J. Pers. soc. Psychol., 33,* 793–802.

Weisman, F., M. Moriarity, and M. Schafer (1975). Estimating public opinion with a randomized response model. *Publ. Opin. Quart., 39,* 507–513.

Werts, C. E., and R. L. Linn (1970). Path analysis: psychological examples. *Psychol. Bull., 74,* 197–212.

Wicker, A. W. (1969). Attitudes versus actions: the relationship of verbal and overt behavioral responses to attitude objects. *J. soc. Issues, 25,* 41–78.

_____ (1971). An examination of the "other variables" explanation of attitude-behavior inconsistency. *J. Pers. soc. Psychol., 19,* 18–30.

Witz, S. (1972). Attitude, voice and behavior: a repressed affect model of interracial interaction. *J. Pers. soc. Psychol., 24,* 14–21.

Woodmansee, J. J. (1970). The pupil response as a measure of social attitudes. In G. F. Summers (Ed.), *Attitude measurement.* Chicago: Rand McNally. Pp. 514–533.

Zoleno, R. N., and J. P. Gagnon (1977). The viability of the lost letter technique. *J. Psychol., 95,* 51–53.

CHAPTER 11

Systematic Observational Methods

Karl E. Weick
University of Texas, Austin

"Now she's a nice person."
"Yep—fibs a little, I reckon."
"How do you know?"
"There ain't that much truth."
  —(Berry, 1975 p. 2)

To be ignorant of many things is expected.
To know you are ignorant of many things is the beginning of wisdom.
To know a category of things of which you are ignorant is the beginning of learning.
To know the details of that category of things of which you were ignorant is to no longer be ignorant.
  —(Phenella cited in Lacey, Weber, and Pruit, 1977, p. 220)

INTRODUCTION

If social scientists want to understand the human condition more fully, they'll have to find better ways to deal with bias than by the classical procedure of avoiding the object. They'll have to learn more about how to be objective in close. That's what this chapter is about.

Distance encourages fabrication. According to Lofland (1976, p. 10):

> The more ambiguous an object—the further one is from a thing and the less one knows about it—the greater is the freedom of the observer and the need of the observer to supply features of the object, to construct greater definition in the optical sense of that term.

In preparing this chapter, I oversampled both work that has appeared since 1968 (the publication date of the second edition of the Handbook*) and work that is not routinely skimmed by social psychologists. This chapter complements rather than replaces Weick (1968). I am grateful to the following people for their help with this review: R. Freed Bales, James Dabbs, Bill Dougan, Robert Faulkner, Susan Krieger, Lynn Sorenson, Linda Steele, John Van Maanen, Eugene Webb, Karen Weick, Nancy Wick, and Ed Willems.*

Distance also encourages fiction. As Skinner (1980, p. 77) notes:

> The less precise my verbal behavior, the more easily my listeners read something into it. Last night at the Academy of Arts and Sciences, I gave a few hurried excerpts from a paper to be published in *Daedalus*. A friend later told me he liked what I said but paraphrased it in terms I could not understand. Another friend commented at length with sentences which did not seem to bear any conceivable connection with my own. Is universality anything more than ambiguity?

To see firsthand the difference that closeness makes, compare the following: Giving bad news can be examined in the context of a subject who has to inform her laboratory partner that she is going to receive shock (Tesser and Rosen, 1972) or in the context of a coroner announcing death to next of kin (Charmaz, 1975). Interpersonal attraction can be examined in the context of anticipated interaction with a stranger whose traits are listed as more or less similar (Byrne, 1961) or in the context of the fear and loathing that may well up at a college mixer (Schwartz and Lever, 1976). Behavior in a subway can be described in a response to a rare implanted crisis

567

(Piliavin, Rodin, and Piliavin, 1969) or in response to a less rare defense of territory (Fried and DeFazio, 1974). Reactions to fear can be examined in the context of anticipating electric shock (Folkins, 1970) or in the context of learning firsthand how to work on high steel in a twenty-one-story building (Haas, 1977). Superstition can be examined in the context of predicting the sequence in which bulbs will light (Wright, 1960) or in the context of urban poker parlors in Gardena, California (Hayano, 1980). The loosening of internal controls in response to anonymity can be examined when college students decide how much shock to deliver when clothed in ill-fitting laboratory gowns with hoods (Zimbardo, 1969) or when tenants in high-rise housing complexes are exposed to danger and requests for help (Zito, 1974). Impression formation can be examined in the context of college students reading lists of adjectives (Anderson, 1965) or in the context of folk singers trying to "psych out" a new audience (Sanders, 1974).

Systematic observational methods do not guarantee objectivity in close. They do, however, contain tactics, strategies, and rationales that can be disaggregated and reassembled to create diverse trade-offs between closeness and objectivity. This diversification of trade-offs is what holds the potential to improve understanding.

A staggering variety of procedures and assumptions for inquiry can be assembled loosely under the category of systematic observational methods: participant observation, systematic observational surveys, field research, naturalistic methods, qualitative investigations, ethnography, case study, ecological psychology, professional social inquiry (Lindblom and Cohen, 1979), qualitative evaluation, unobtrusive measures, behavioral ecology, subjective inquiry, Verstehen tradition, ethnomethodology, field experiments, precision journalism, ethology, and behavioral assessment.

In portraying systematic observation, I will intentionally blur distinctions, will regroup techniques into categories that seem to uncover different qualities they may contribute to inquiry (Dolby, 1979), and in general will harangue people to be more reflective about how they construct their inquiries. The only way I can see to manage a literature of this heterogeneity is to impose a consistent idiosyncratic voice to sort through it.

The material to be presented in this chapter might best be termed a *soft technology of systematic observation*. By *soft* I mean that observers are equipped with algorithms, rules of thumb, exemplars, and guidelines for invoking common sense. Soft technologies preserve de-

grees of freedom, which is important both for getting in close and for improvising once the close look suggests that things are not as expected (e.g., Swidler, 1979). This chapter can be read as an incomplete list of things that can be systematized. An observer might systematize preconceptions *or* categories *or* settings. Having frozen one thing, however, the rest are left untouched and free to vary in the interest of maximizing authenticity. This trade-off between structure and freedom is standard in social science, but it has been managed in systematic observation by trade-offs among a limited set of elements such as category specificity and definition of reliability and sampling frame.

I assume that some people may find themselves temperamentally more suited to systematic observation than others. But I also assume that anybody can be trained to be a better questioner, a more careful methodologist, a more nuanced paraphraser, a more patient observer, a more subtle student of everyday life, a more complicated person capable of registering more of the complications in the world.

The remainder of this chapter will consist of an extended gloss on the seven elements in our proposed definition of observational work: (1) observing, (2) paraphrasing, (3) sustained work, (4) explicit work, (5) methodical work, (6) social situations, and (7) context.

DEFINITION

Systematic observation is defined as *sustained, explicit, methodical observing and paraphrasing of social situations in relation to their naturally occurring contexts*.

For comparison, systematic observation was defined in the first edition of the *Handbook* as the use of the trained human observer as a measuring instrument, both to define the stimulus situation and to record the responses (Heyns and Lippitt, 1954, p. 370) and in the second edition as "the selection, provocation, recording, and encoding of that set of behaviors and settings concerning organisms 'in situ' which is consistent with empirical aims" (Weick, 1968, p. 360). A representative definition from a source other than the *Handbook* is the following (Sykes, 1978, p. 155, ftn. 1):

> Systematic field observation is a scientific method for identifying and characterizing specific human behaviors occurring in natural field settings. The scientist uses a special observational language (e.g., IPA) with which he describes the events which are of

interest to him. It is the prior development of acquired skill in applying, and technique for subsequently analyzing the data collected with an observational language which distinguish systematic from other forms of observation.

The elements in the present definition are explicated as follows:

1. *Sustained:* Systematic observation is prolonged, continuous watching (Sanday, 1979). To sustain observing is to understand settings more deeply and to see more of a setting, which means in turn that more patterns may be detected and fewer instances of disconnectedness recorded (Glassman, 1973).

2. *Explicit:* To be explicit about procedures used for observing and recording is to make possible meaningful replications and return trips (Agar, 1980; Reiss, 1971, p. 4). Explicit procedures are self-conscious, public, open and contestable, fully and clearly expressed, and capable of reconstruction.

3. *Methodical:* Inquiry that is methodical is inquiry that adheres to an order of activities that has been carefully worked out. Methodical is often contrasted with the related word *systematic,* and examination of this contrast is instructive. *Systematic* is preferable to *methodical* when the emphasis is upon the integrity and completeness of a finished product, not upon the order followed to produce the product. Thus *methodical* training suggests training that follows its course according to a predefined sequence or schedule, whereas *systematic* training usually implies training long enough and intensive enough to gain specified ends in view (*Webster's Dictionary of Synonyms,* 1951, p. 592). Methodical inquiry, however, is *not* improvisation-free inquiry. The coupling of methodical with improvisation is one conspicuous place where a different set of elements for trade-offs is posited and different sequences of planning and improvisation are examined for the information they yield.

4. *Observing:* To observe is to notice and punctuate events that are of interest. Observing by social scientists differs from layperson observing in the sense that efforts are made to standardize the act of recognizing in accessible ways. But observing by social scientists also resembles lay observing in the sense that "truth" rests ultimately on direct individual experience. The essence of observing is described by Barton and Lazarsfeld (1969, p. 188):

> A careful observer who is aware of the need to sample all groups in the population with which he is concerned, who is aware of the "visibility bias" of the spectacular as opposed to the unspectacular case, who becomes intimately familiar with his material over a long period of time through direct observation, will be able to approximate the results of statistical investigation.

5. *Paraphrasing:* To paraphrase an observation is to restate, embed, or translate it so that a more limited and explicit set of meanings become attached to it. The act of paraphrasing commonly involves amplification and interpretation by the observer and can range from the literal translation of a specimen record through a much freer translation such as in free intuitive writing (Rainer, 1978, pp. 180–181).

All products of observation involve simplification, editing, imposed meaning, and omission. Because of this selectivity, all observers essentially gloss what they observe (Rabinow and Sullivan, 1979; Weick, 1981). They figuratively write interpretations and comments in the margins alongside the text of the overdetermined events that are observed to flow by them.

Systematic observation has traditionally meant the use of preformed categories to systematize an observer. In many ways the goal of observation, understood as paraphrase, is to *destroy* the a priori categories of the observer and to suggest more valid replacements.

6. *Social situations:* A social situation consists of three interacting elements: a place (any physical setting, e.g., a bank window), actors (people who are present in the setting doing something, e.g., newcomers), and activities (individual acts that fall into recognizable patterns, e.g., making small talk with the bank teller). The interdependence of these three elements underscores Bandura's (1977) argument that our tendency to view behavior as an outcome of a person-situation interaction is less accurate than to view behavior (activities), personal factors (actors), and environmental factors (place) as interlocking determinants capable of reciprocal determinism.

7. *In relation to their naturally occurring contexts:* A context is a differentiated rendering of one or more elements in a social situation. If, for example, actors (e.g., newcomers) and activities (e.g., making small talk), are held constant, and places are differentiated such that we sample and examine various places where newcomers engage in small talk, then we have begun to specify contexts where people do and do not perform this activity.

The phrase *in relation to* natural contexts is used to allow for the inclusion of free simulations (Fromkin and Streufert, 1976), ethnographic interviews (Spradley,

TABLE 1
Two Dimensions of Observational Methods

DEGREE TO WHICH RESTRICTIONS ARE IMPOSED ON RESPONSE MEASURE	DEGREE TO WHICH ANTECEDENT CONDITIONS ARE MANIPULATED	
	HI	LO
HI	(1) Anderson, 1965: person rates attractiveness of another who is presented as a list of both positive and negative traits	(2) Dabbs *et al.,* 1980: pairs converse normally while looking at each other through peephole
LO	(3) Piliavin, Rodin, Piliavin, 1969: simulated victim evokes varying kinds of attention	(4) Haas, 1977: apprentice high-iron worker learns to control fear of heights

SOURCE: After Willems, 1969, p. 47.

1979), tempered naturalness (Weick, 1968), and use of documents and archives as substitutes for familiarity that still allow for actor instigation of events and observer paraphrase in the natural language.

The seven-part definition just described partially specifies those tactics that we will treat as systematic observational methods. Taxonomies proposed by Willems and Douglas further specify the relevant elements.

WILLEMS

Willems (1969) suggested that observational methods can be arrayed along two dimensions (see Table 1):

1. Degree of investigator's influence over or manipulation of the antecedent conditions of the behavior studied.

2. Degree to which units are imposed by the investigator on the behavior studied (i.e., does she restrict the range or spectrum of the behavior itself?).

Consistent with the argument that to be methodical is to build both structure and freedom into inquiry, cell 2 (behavior is instigated spontaneously but only restricted

portions of the response are preserved) and cell 3 (behavioral instigation is less spontaneous but the complete response is paraphrased) are of central interest. Cell 4 is treated as an unstable situation because no order is imposed on the rapidly accumulating observations. To manage the situation of cell 4 in which everything seems relevant (Piaget, 1929, p. 9), the observer starts either to neglect specific acts (cell 2) or to evoke specific acts (cell 3). Cell one, the laboratory, is also treated as an unstable situation because there is an absence of meaningful variation. To reintroduce some variety, the observer either notices more facets of the acts emitted (cell 3) or specifies less of what the actor is to do (cell 2). Trade-offs between structure and freedom are commonplace in inquiry, but they need not be produced by alternation between completely structured laboratory studies and completely free naturalistic description. Instead, trade-offs can be managed simultaneously by partial structuring of response measures and antecedent conditions.

DOUGLAS

Douglas (1976) has suggested that social research information can be gathered at least twenty-seven different ways, ranging from total immersion in natural experi-

TABLE 2
The Continuum of Free-Flowing Existence to Controlled Observations

Everyday life social experience and thought	1. Unconscious experience
	2. Subconscious experience
	3. Dreams
	4. Conscious experience
	5. Practical thought and action
	6. Diaries and memories
	7. Travelogues
	8. On-site field visits and reports
	9. Systematic reflection
	10. Philosophical thought
Field research	11. Depth-probe field research
Participant field research	12. Investigative reporting, detective work
	13. Covert field research
	14. Overt journalism and police work
	15. Overt field research
Non-participant field research	16. Discussion (free-flowing), in-depth interviews
	17. In-depth interviews with flexible checklists of questions
Controlled experimental research	18. Natural experiments
	19. Preprogrammed interviews (statistical)
	20. Official data and business analysis reports
	21. Judicial investigations (operating under rules of evidence)
	22. Business studies (statistical)
	23. Panel (test and retest) studies
	24. Laboratory experiments
	25. Questionnaires and polls
	26. Computer simulation studies
	27. Mathematical models

SOURCE: Douglas, 1976, p. 15.

ence to totally controlled observations and analyses (Table 2). As one moves down Douglas's list, observation involves more control and more preconceived categories and is less inductive and holistic (Weiss, 1966). By "field research," Douglas (1976, p. 16) means

> all forms of study of society in natural situations by means of natural (relatively uncontrolled) social interaction. Field research might better be called naturalistic social research, since the crucial point is that it is done in natural settings by natural forms of interaction, and since some forms of controlled research (such as polls or questionnaires) are often done in the field.

This chapter will range somewhat outside the boundaries Douglas has drawn around field techniques

(categories 11–17). The chapter tacitly incorporates the lesser controlled techniques between categories 4 and 10, this being most evident in the argument that observers may lean increasingly to more self-observation (see pp. 577–579 of this chapter). Discussions in this chapter also flood out of the lower bound of field research (category 17) toward higher degrees of control in observation, tacitly incorporating procedures up through category 21, judicial investigations (e.g., Carter, 1979). These additional controlled procedures are included because they involve only partial structuring, they allow for paraphrase in natural language (I assume that category 19, preprogrammed interviews, is out of place and should be placed either between 22 and 23 or between 24 and 25), and they incorporate all three elements of a social situation. Furthermore, in none of these more controlled cases are the data instigated by the observer. Finally, categories 4 through 21 can be accommodated to the definition we have proposed. Category 2, subconscious experience, is excluded as being insufficiently explicit, methodical, or social situational. Category 22, Business studies (statistical), is excluded as being insufficiently social situational or naturally occurring.

OBSERVING

The model for an observational statement is not "If a person is confronted with stimulus X, he will do Y," but rather "If a person is in situation X, performance Y will be judged appropriate by native actors." The perspective of the actor is crucial.

The generic activity of *observing* will be illustrated by examining two sets of activities presumed to magnify some of its properties. First, observation as less animated watching will be portrayed by assuming that it closely resembles the design and collection of unobtrusive measures (Webb *et al.,* 1966). Second, observation as more animated watching will be portrayed by assuming that observing also resembles the strategy of field stimulation.

Having illustrated observing and ways in which it can be systematized, we will then focus on the actor's perspective. We will discuss the danger of presuming too much importance for the actor's view (observing and solipsism), the argument that observing is useful only at the initial stages of inquiry (observing and discovery), the contrast between observing and analysis (observing and thought), the use of conflict as a means to deepen inquiry (observing and suspicion), and the use of self as the phenomenon to be observed (observing of self).

LESS ANIMATED OBSERVING: UNOBTRUSIVE MEASURES

Traces of social activity, left indelibly in nonrandom patterns, provide the occasion for indirect understanding by observers of an actor's perspective (Bouchard, 1976; Gross and Doob, 1976; Kazdin, 1979; Sechrest, 1976, 1979). Examples of patterned traces and possible inferences are the following (Webb and Weick, 1979, p. 650):

1. The quality of food in a restaurant is in inverse proportion to the number of semicolons and exclamation marks on the menu.

2. You can tell how bad the musical is by how many times the chorus yells hooray.

3. The number of agency people required to shoot a commercial on location is in direct proportion to the mean temperature of the location.

4. The more sophisticated the equipment, the bigger is the adjustment department needed.

5. The quality of food and service is inversely proportional to the captivity of the clientele.

6. The length of a country's national anthem is inversely proportional to the importance of the country.

7. In war, victory goes to those armies whose leaders' uniforms are least impressive.

Some assumptions associated with this style of observing have been identified and include the following (Webb and Weick, 1979, pp. 652–653):

1. Investigators assume that noise is rare. People who use unobtrusive measures think in terms of a signal-to-noise ratio but tend to be generous in their definition of signal. The image of a signal-to-noise ratio reminds people that they reject much information that is available, that the definition of what is signal and what is noise is variable, and that there will be dross in any observational setting.

2. Investigators believe in amortization. Unobtrusive measures are sometimes viewed as flawed because they are generated outside the investigator's direct control. If an investigator manufactures data by the means of an experiment or an interview, then those data are thought to be more scientific than if the data were manufactured by someone else and were picked up opportunistically by the investigator. The way to preserve this point is to argue that "hard scientists don't believe in amortization." Hard science seems to be based on the premise that there can be only a single purpose for data and that the investigator should be the one who designs and defines that purpose and creates the universe so that it is ideal for scientific purposes. Data created for other purposes are seen as neither scientific nor hard. People who favor unobtrusive measures find that stance counterproductive and naive.

3. Investigators find foolishness functional. Unobtrusive measures have come to be associated with a playful stance toward the world in data collection. This stance furthers science in several ways. If the same event is regarded as both absurd and serious, then more of it is likely to be seen because, in fact, it contains both qualities. Foolish interludes generate novel inputs and

permit people to recognize and break the singular focus toward a problem in which they had persisted. Foolish interludes disconfirm assumptions, thereby creating interest (Davis, 1971), put distance between the observer and the phenomenon, sustain morale, recruit interest in the topic, aid retention, facilitate the content and process of free association, expose assumptions, forestall criticism that degenerates into cynicism, and offset the preoccupation with rational models that is characteristic of inquiry.

4. Investigators ponder the variance rather than the mean. People who use unobtrusive measures presume that the variance is at least as interesting as the mean and typically more so. The key question is, How do you get low variation? If individual differences are so abundant, then how can it be that for some populations in some settings, there is so little difference visible? For example, many theories of power are conspiratorial (e.g., Pfeffer, 1977), and one of the best indicators of conspiratorial power is a lack of variance. Governance of the District of Columbia, often said to be insensitive, can be indexed by the fact that much of the district's governance is done by people who have zip codes clustered in areas outside the district (Washburn, 1967). The unobtrusive measure of similarity of zip code, low variance when the expectation is for higher variance, suggests the presence of organizing and pattern where none was suspected.

5. Investigators use expectancy as a control. Expectancies are the controls of both common sense and science; surprise is an indicator of the abuse of expectancies. What people don't do, who isn't in a network, practices that weren't made—all become data because of the a priori expectations that existed. Everyone, for example, appoints a chairman for meetings, especially when those meetings are consequential. However, given this expectancy as a control, the fact that Kennedy didn't appoint a chairman of the deliberations on the Cuban missile crisis becomes an indicator of added interest.

Examples of unobtrusive measures are plentiful. If one monitors talk on a CB radio while driving from Atlanta to New York City, there is a steady increase in the amount of anger expressed the farther north one goes, with the most noticeable increase occurring just after entering the New Jersey Turnpike (John DeCastro, private communication). [For background on the CB fad and the functions it serves, see Kerbo, Marshall, and Holley, (1978).]

McGee and Snyder (1975) observed whether restaurant patrons salted their food before or after tasting it and coordinated this behavior with the tendency to make situational or dispositional attributions of action. Ettlie (1977) measured amount of dust on machines as an indicator of the frequency with which they were used. Squyres (1979) found that unaccompanied people did not look at themselves in reflective store windows more than did accompanied people. Levine, West, and Reis (1980) observed differential accuracy of clocks and of responses to requests for time in Brazil and Fresno, California. And Deaux, White, and Farris (1975) assessed the effect of gender on risk taking by observing which games (dime in the dish, Bingo) were played by what people for how long at county and state fairs in Indiana.

To "read" a setting for variation in its trappings and activities, to infer tendencies that make the variation meaningful, and to find evidence supporting the credibility of the inferences are all crucial features of the generic art of observing that are magnified in the design of data collection procedures around unobtrusive measures.

MORE ANIMATED OBSERVING: FIELD STIMULATION

The prototypic activity for the observer who is more active, though not necessarily more obtrusive or reactive, is *field stimulation* (Salancik, 1979a). Field stimulation (p. 638)

> belongs to the class of qualitative methodologies in which the respondent determines the character of the response. It differs from some qualitative methodologies by encouraging the investigator to determine the occasion for a response which is, in turn, a measure of the organization's nature and capacity. It has been called by Webb and his associates "contrived observation," to distinguish it from observational studies in which the investigator acts as a passive recorder who avoids provoking or interrupting responses.... Although contrived is an apt description, I prefer the emphasis which stimulation places on method.

There are several examples of occasions where people have stimulated a class of social situations and received differential responses. Salancik (1979b) asked firms to fill out a very short questionnaire with information that was publicly available, namely, the name, size, sales, and average return on common stock of the firm. The cover letter said that this was part of a study either of why organizations fail or of why they succeed. Twenty percent of the fail questionnaires were returned, 60 percent of the succeed questionnaires were returned. Phillip R. Kunz mailed 600 Christmas cards from Utah to midwestern addresses picked at random from a telephone book. In reply 117 families sent cards of their own containing pictures of families and reminiscences of "shared" friends. Ondrack (1975) studied socialization in nursing schools by comparing participation rates in his survey for teachers, graduating students, and entering students. Participation rate of the graduating students was predicted by participation rate of the teachers, but this was not so for the entering students.

Salancik (1979b) wrote to firms that varied in their dependency on federal funds requesting information about "management opportunities for women MBAs." The speed and quality of responses were used to assess how affirmative was their attempt to attract women job candidates. The more affirmative firms were those that were more dependent on the government funding, which is consistent with resource dependence theories of power. Finally, in an effort to learn how different firms partition their environment, Salancik (1979a) performed the following experiment (p. 646):

> Marketing firms were asked to send information about their services. The requests were made either by a potential job candidate, a potential client, or university researcher. The point of analysis was to examine if the agencies differentiate these three publics in their replies. About half did: most importantly, firms with longer histories were more likely to differentiate the audiences. The longevity of a firm was estimated from the presence of its name for over fifteen years in the telephone book.

The crucial point made by field stimulation studies is that response rates are not just methodological footnotes from which one can decide issues of internal and external validity. They are analogous to protracted reaction times from which can be inferred internal processes, sensitivities, priorities, and routines. Response rates, in stimulation studies, are signals rather than noise. They index contexts that are more or less mindless, more or less sensitive to status, resources, and contacts, more or less attuned to environments, and more or less penetrable.

OBSERVING AND SOLIPSISM

When observers examine the perspective of native actors, they run the risk of *solipsism*. It is this risk that must be managed actively throughout the observing. (Manning (1979, p. 660) states:

Observers create a domain of interest through concepts and perspectives, affirm it by selective and selected measures and, in a sense, construct that social world through these actions. [These people] raise the spector [sic] of solipsism by considering all analyses of the social world to be problematic accounts rather than objective descriptions subject to confirmation or disconfirmation through scientific investigation.

To dampen solipsism is to encourage multiple replications, discourage the view that a single study should be self-contained, look for commonalities in accounts, and to remind oneself that environmental determinism is part of the actor's reality (Baron, 1980).

This last reminder cannot be emphasized too heavily. Fascination with the view that reality is socially constructed (see Denzin and Keller, 1981; Goffman, 1981; Van Maanen, 1979, pp. 13–42) has sometimes resulted in investigators asserting that real things are an illusion. Erving Goffman's well-known introduction to "Frame Analysis" still provides the most eloquent argument against excess. Goffman begins with the W. I. Thomas dictum, "If men define situations as real, they are real in their consequences." Goffman (1974) says of that dictum (pp. 1–2):

> This statement is true as it reads but false as it is taken. Defining situations as real certainly has consequences, but these may contribute very marginally to the events in progress, in some cases only a slight embarrassment flits across the scene in mild concern for those who tried to define the situation wrongly. All the world is not a stage—certainly the theater isn't entirely (Whether you organize a theater or an aircraft factory, you need to find places for cars to park and coats to be checked, and these had better be real places, which incidentally, had better carry real insurance against theft). Presumably, a "definition of the situation" is almost always to be found but those who are in the situation ordinarily do not *create* this definition, even though their society often can be said to do so; ordinarily, all they do is to assess correctly what the situation ought to be for them and then act accordingly. True, we personally negotiate aspects of all the arrangements under which we live, but often once these are negotiated, we continue on mechanically as though the matter had always been settled. So, too, there are occasions when we must wait until things are almost over before discovering what has been occurring and occasions of

our own activity when we can considerably put off deciding what to claim we have been doing. But surely these are not the only principles of organization. Social life is dubious enough and ludicrous enough without having to wish it further into unreality.

This quotation is relevant to the study of topics such as negotiated order (Glaser and Strauss, 1971). Some investigators treat negotiating and reality construction as more basic social processes than others do. The point is, social situations are place-dependent. And theorists who prefer to talk about the construction of place rather than the constriction by place are overrepresented among those who do field observation. There is a delicate trade-off. With intimate familiarity goes greater understanding of the actor's perspective and a possible shift from situational to personal explanations for that actor's actions (Jones and Nisbett, 1971). There is a corresponding temptation to downplay situational constraints just as the actor does. In one sense to downplay such situational constraints is to render more accurately the actor's view of the world.

But the trade-off comes because while the data the actor acts upon *are* cryptic, the settings against which he or she acts are not. To say the world of everyday life is organized relative to the perceiving subject is not to say that its meaning structure is freely determined by that person. An example of taking Goffman seriously in naturalistic observation is Gonos's (1976) study of go-go dancing done within the guidelines of frame analysis. Throughout this analysis there is a noticeable tension between conduct as a social construction and conduct as outcome of rule determination. By maintaining that tension, Gonos avoids both solipsism and taking W. I. Thomas too seriously.

OBSERVING AND DISCOVERY

Observing is viewed by many as synonymous with discovery. Barton and Lazarsfeld (1969) provide a representative description (p. 182):

> Research which has neither statistical weight nor experimental design, research based only on qualitative descriptions of a small number of cases, can nonetheless play the important role of suggesting possible relationship [sic], causes, effects, and even dynamic processes. Indeed, it can be argued that only research which provides a wealth of miscellaneous, unplanned impressions and observations can play this role. Those who try to get suggestions for

possible explanatory factors for statistical results solely from looking at tabulations of the few variables which were deliberately included in the study in advance often can make no progress; sometimes even a single write-in comment by a respondent will provide a clue to additional factors.

There are several problems buried in the stereotype that observing is appropriate for discovery but not for verification. First, a discovered topic *is* an empirical finding. When an investigator produces evidence that something is in need of explanation, this is a conclusion as well as a prelude. Second, the laboratory is a site for discovery almost as frequently as is the field (Henshel, 1980; Weick, 1977). Third, the view that the laboratory is a site for verification is misleading when it fails to take account of the reality that "facts" are usually socially constructed rather than objectively discovered in these sites (e.g., Latour and Woolgar, 1979; Pepinsky and Patton, 1971). Fourth, to say that field studies are preliminary is to assume that social psychology is cumulative, an assumption that many reject. Fifth, to verify hypotheses generated by high-variety methods of discovery, investigators need verification methods of equally high variety that can detect hypothesized subtleties (Pondy and Mitroff, 1979). Thus if observational methods are treated as preamble, then investigators still face the problem of moving a discovery into verification without mutilating it. A shift from a high-variety method to a low-variety method usually defeats this objective. Sixth, discoveries often are known only late in a process of inquiry. Whyte, for example, did not discover that bowling success recapitulated group status until the last night he bowled in Cornerville (see p. 609 of this chapter). Seventh, and finally, both data tables and qualitative descriptions are preliminary. To understand the ways in which a data table is nuanced, what the data mean, and how people generated the activities summarized in the numbers, one must treat the table as a preliminary display that triggers serious descriptive analysis (Bogdan and Ksander, 1980; Gephart, 1979; Gubrium and Buckholdt, 1979). Thus we come full circle. Quantitative studies produce discoveries, the meaning of which is known only after they are verified qualitatively.

OBSERVING AND THOUGHT

Human knowledge can increase when people either observe something or think about something. Different disciplines tend to emphasize one or the other of these sources of knowing, but the social science practiced by social psychologists tends to emphasize thought. Successful careers can occur without people ever watching social life directly, for any length of time, in any detail. Methodology books emphasize accurate abstractions through proper thinking. They give advice on how to tell if, when, where, and why something is happening rather than *what* is happening. Knowledge that is obtained is not knowledge for clients but knowledge for writing lectures, books, and articles. Thus to understand something is to be able to write or talk about it. Schwartz and Jacobs (1979) pose the issue this way (p. 307):

> It is not possible to be a sociologist without knowing how to construct verbal representations of society and its parts, quite independent of how good or bad they are. This is also why observational skills, in and of themselves, are not central to the discipline. Although it is necessary that *somebody* have these skills and use them, it is not necessary that *everybody* have them and use them. The observing can be done by the census, graduate students, or other sociologists while you do the analyzing. In contrast, other disciplines such as microbiology, radiology, archeology, and psychotherapy, require almost every practitioner to learn how to observe and recognize things in detail.

Research that is grounded in thought downplays replication (do it once and do it right), presumes that one direct observation is enough (indirect information through data sets is sufficient for follow-up), and encourages a division of labor (the analyst need not be the observer). A high premium is placed on avoiding error within the confines of a single study.

Research that is grounded in sight translates into a different set of practices (Schwartz and Jacobs, 1979):

1. Know what you're talking about:
   a. Seek firsthand observation, avoid secondary sources of data.
   b. Combine analysis and observing in the same person.
   c. Interpret only what you've observed firsthand.

2. Detect errors by replication across studies (Epstein, 1980), not by precision within a single study.

3. Organize inquiry around themes, not studies. Single, self-contained studies count for less than do multiple, diverse studies focused on a common theme.

Neither sight nor thought suffice by themselves as modes of knowing. That's part of the reason why paraphrasing, with its emphasis on reciprocity between sight and thought, is so crucial to observational methodology. To say that, however, is not to assert blandly that we need both sight and thought. It's not that simple. Need both in what sense? Ever since social psychology became separated from abnormal psychology with its roots in psychotherapy and pragmatic, direct observation, it has focused on phenomena that can be grasped largely through abstract thinking (e.g., prisoner's dilemma "is" competition and cooperation). Social psychological knowledge is a way of talking and writing about social situations, not a way of observing them. To give more primacy to observational methods is to unlearn more of social psychology than people may realize.

OBSERVING AND SUSPICION

Intimate familiarity has a connotation of cooperation, and this needs to be made explicit so that it can be altered. Observers traditionally have presumed society to be basically homogeneous, nonconflictual, and capable of resolving conflict through normal operations. These assumptions have colored the way observers approach and describe participants in that society. The researcher expected to rely on the cooperation of the subjects and expected they would react naturally during the study. According to Douglas (1976, pp. 46–47), the observer

> would just "fit in naturally," adopt their (the group's) point of view, get along with them, be moral from their point of view (which would, of course, be the same as any other point of view in a homogeneous world), and report the findings with no great misgivings about their effects on the group studied—maybe they have some enemies, but that's aberrant and unimportant in a basically cooperative world.

Examples of work grounded in this classical cooperative paradigm include Barker and Wright (1955), Festinger, Schachter, and Back (1950), Lawrence (1958), Newcomb (1961, and Whyte (1955).

Rather than assume that cooperation is indigenous, one can assume that conflict is the rule (Riegel, 1976), that cooperation is feigned rather than granted, and that data collection requires hardball naturalistic inquiry. This alternative, called *investigative social research* (Douglas, 1976), follows a journalistic model rather than an anthropological model. In the anthropological model the observer is an outsider who gathers information by gaining cooperation from marginal members whose interests are defended. In a journalistic model (Levine, 1980) the observer tries to get behind fronts, looks for internal contradictions, and assumes conflict between the observer and the observed. Observers seek to expose those they study.

The investigative observer makes very different assumptions from those made by a cooperative observer. The investigative observer presumes that people hide and lie, suspect and are suspected, and that those who cannot stand to lie and conspire tend to lose the competitive struggle in our society. Suspicion is the guiding principle and translates into two attitudes: (1) Where there's smoke, there's fire; (2) there's always far more immoral or shady stuff going on than meets the eye. The stance may provide, by its self-fulfilling nature, an inexhaustible supply of clues that it is necessary. Having assumed that people have things to hide and are competitive, the investigator may provoke those behaviors that spuriously confirm the prediction and solidify the resolve to probe (Kelley and Stahelski, 1970).

To presume that what distinguishes investigative research is its heavy-handedness and paranoia is to miss the more crucial qualities of patience, persistence, cross-checking, and triangulation that also occur. Examples of investigative research include Dalton (1959), Ditton (1977), Douglas, Rasmussen, and Flanagan (1977), Humphreys (1970), Rasmussen and Kuhn (1976), and Manning (1974).

The issues that are crystallized by a consideration of suspicious intimacy are complicated. Naturalistic observers, by definition, are reluctant to meddle and prone to believe what they see and hear. They trust time, triangulation, and tact to transgress temporary fronts. The investigative observer differs from this in degree, not in kind. His or her suspicion occurs earlier and is sustained longer (Dean and Whyte, 1969).

The lengthened period of suspicion leads the investigative observer to bring in more informants (while fully believing none of them), to chronicle whose interests are best served by which definitions of the situation, and to assume that there are more rather than fewer distinct alliances and points of view in any setting. The imagery of cohesion and cooperation is suspect. Instead, observers presume the existence of fragments, weak ties, and units that function like systems only sporadically. Ethnocentrism is the rule, but it is thought to characterize significantly smaller units than anyone had realized.

To invoke these assumptions is not necessarily to moralize about mankind. Rather, it is to recognize that ambivalence may be the optimal compromise in a world where individuals are complicated, capable of generating psychological opposites (e.g., love-hate, warmth-coldness), closely attuned to situational nuance, and vastly different in their skills at marshaling and using power (Siu, 1979). To take situations and contexts seriously is to recognize that conflicting interests are woven into them.

OBSERVING OF SELF

So far, we have described intimate familiarity with other people. That focus is misleading because what we really want is intimate familiarity with phenomena. People happen to be the medium for phenomena, and that's why we try to get close to them. But when phenomena are mediated by other people, observation remains indirect because thoughts, strategies, and other subjective events are difficult to know, it is difficult to be around all the time to observe relevant happenings, and it is difficult to get others to report details that they usually do not remember, describe, or talk about.

One way to bypass these problems is to *become the phenomenon*. According to Mehan and Wood (1975, pp. 227–228):

> To become the phenomenon means to do a reality as its members do. Membership cannot be simulated. The researcher must not hold back. The researcher who holds back in the name of objectivity never comes to respect that reality or be respected by its practitioners. Traditional field work techniques counsel researchers to withhold a part of themselves to remain "objective." . . . While this methodological aloofness protects researchers from becoming "merely one of them," it also effectively prohibits knowing any of them. . . . In becoming the phenomenon, the researcher does not enter a reality for the purpose of describing it. Rather than analyze an activity for its truth value, the researcher learns to do it. This implies a social science methodology where "the notion of success replaces truth as criteria for validity."

There are various ways to become the phenomenon. One means is to perform ordinary activities while robbing oneself of the usual resources for getting things done. One might, for example, make all decisions for a period of time by rolling dice, flipping coins, or invoking randomly selected advice (Eno and Schmidt, 1978). People who use dice religiously to make decisions become the phenomenon in the sense that they discover what they take for granted in their normal activities. "In carrying out the 'advice' of the dice, they use many of the interpretive abilities which are employed in ordinary decision making. The advantage of the dice is that they provide a more recent, novel, and unusual way to make decisions and thus make the details of decision making more noticeable" (Schwartz and Jacobs, 1979, p. 286).

Another way to become the phenomenon is to turn one's academic discipline on oneself, whether that discipline be ethnomethodology (Mehan and Wood, 1975) or operant conditioning (Ulrich, 1975).

Perhaps the most direct means to initiate first-person inquiry is to ask, "Of what groups am I an insider, a person who knows what she is talking about?" Many contemporary investigators are not outsiders looking in. They are committed natives who are inside and need to estrange themselves from the inside view. To become the phenomenon is often to use at-hand knowledge and expertise (Riemer, 1977a). It is, for example, to treat one's own experience on a guided tour (Gorman, 1979; Schmidt, 1979), in a poker game (Zurcher, 1970), at an auction (Clark and Halford, 1978), as a hospital volunteer (Deegan and Nutt, 1975), as a daily bus rider (Nash, 1975) or in listening to talk radio (Ellis, Hawes, and Avery, 1979) as the phenomenon to be understood. One can also turn adversity to account by analyzing recovery from an illness (Roth, 1974), stress during combat (Glavis, Jr., 1946) or fear while learning to work high steel (Haas, 1977).

To become the phenomenon is also to turn the technology of self-monitoring on oneself, not necessarily to change the monitored behaviors—although that is a clear topic of inquiry, as in the cases of smoking reduction, weight loss, self-control of anger—but to detect situated patterns in monitored behavior. The literature on self-monitoring (e.g., Haynes and Wilson, 1979, Chap. 5; Nelson, 1977, pp. 217-254; Winett, Neale, and Williams, 1979) can be tapped both for leads as to phenomena to be observed and for conditions that affect the accuracy and reactivity of self-observation.

First-person-singular methods of inquiry are evident in discussions of self-observing (Torbert, 1972), self-management (Stuart, 1977), a science of self (Schwartz and Jacobs, 1979), experiential analysis (Reinharz, 1979), and self-generated attitude change (Tesser, 1978). To this can be added the increasingly sophisticated discussions of journals and diaries as systematic observational methods (e.g., Dougherty, 1977; Progoff, 1975; Rainer, 1978; Zimmerman and Wieder, 1977) and of self-report inventories (Bellack and Herson, 1977) and autobiographies (DeWaele and Harre, 1979).

Self-observation is not necessarily less objective than observation of another, because those practices used to objectify observation of others can be used just as readily to objectify observations of oneself (e.g., Nelson, 1977, pp. 230-239; Stephens and Norris-Baker, 1979). Nor is self-observation necessarily less generalizable if one assumes that people are pretty much alike. The beauty of self-monitoring is that the time lapse between the event and the recording is small. Furthermore, informed consent, subject dissembling, the privacy of cognition, the inability to know another person, and the hubris of speaking on behalf of others are removed as deterrents to understanding.

The prospect that the literature will contain endless documents of individual living is not necessarily exhilarating. But neither may it be particularly accurate. To become a phenomenon is to spend time doing, not writing. It is also to refine the writing until one gets it right. To become the phenomenon may be to display, present, and demonstrate it rather than write about it or describe it.

A science of self is clearly played for higher stakes. Having become a phenomenon, one cannot easily undo what one has become. The changes are permanent. Furthermore, true moments of innocence are extraordinarily rare. One can only become a specific phenomenon, ingenuously, once. If the phenomenon doesn't "take" or if one realizes after the fact that a different route of becoming is more provocative, it's too late.

My intent is not to deal in melodrama. Rather, it is to anticipate some costs and excitements of the ultimate commitment to an idea, an experiment on self. Observing viewed as intimate familiarity certainly should include the ultimate intimacy. The elements for it are already in place, elements such as ethnomethodology, phenomenology, self-management, self-monitoring, and diary studies. The vision for it is also already in place. As Schwartz and Jacobs (1979, p. 363) state:

> It is awesome to conceive of the entire history of civilization as having been crystallized in one's own being—in the way one thinks about the world in one's desires, emotions, activities. This leads us to take our own life experiences, and those of others

close to us, extremely seriously in trying to understand ordinary conversation, social stratification, or, for that matter, the nature of human beings. There are many in our profession who have been doing this for a long time, informally, and dressing up their hunches with experiments, data, and other rituals of the times. Phenomenology has given us perhaps its greatest gift by providing a warrant for doing this formally and without apology.

PARAPHRASING

The essence of observational work consists of fine-grained analysis of behavior so that particulars can be connected to philosophical systems. Kant foreshadowed this when he remarked, "Perception without conception is blind; conception without perception is empty."

The act of connecting particulars to concepts is literally an act of rewording the particular. The particular is comprehended through paraphrase, which means paraphrasing is the core linguistic activity in systematic observation. Lofland (1976) updates Kant and describes paraphase as "disciplined abstraction." Disciplined abstractions are "generic and generalized types and aspects of situations and strategies that emerge from personal immersion in concrete, qualitative data and remain adequately grounded in such data in written reports"(p. 62). Abstractions (presupposed patterns), are disciplined by continual reference to concrete qualitative data (documents).

There is a continuous alternation between episodes and abstractions, certainty (deduction) and authenticity (induction), deductive rigor and inductive relevance. The actual work of paraphrase is illustrated by attempts of police and indignant citizens to build *a* version of an explosive confrontation in Berkeley (Darrough, 1978), by reporters attempting to generate newsworthy stories (Lester, 1980), or by two people trying to reconcile incompatible versions of the same event (Pollner, 1975).

Paraphrasing will be described in the context of three topics. First, an analogue of paraphrase, the documentary method, will be described to provide an overview of the process. Second, the structure of paraphrase will be described as natural language assembled in the interest of requisite variety. Third, the content of paraphrase will be described as natural language assembled to contain affirmations rather than negations.

AN ANALOGUE OF PARAPHRASE: THE DOCUMENTARY METHOD

In experimental research, data collection and data analysis are isolatable steps. In naturalistic observation this is less true. The essence of ethnography is that the initial questions (and answers) may change during inquiry. It is this change that makes indexicality and the documentary method key metaphors for observational research [see Leiter (1980, Chaps. 5 and 6) for a lucid, extended discussion of these concepts].

Indexicality refers to the fact that practical actions are dependent on the natural habitat of their occurrence for recognizable meaning. People use ongoing contexts, commonsense knowledge, and biographically determined purposes to discover meaning. Utterances, such as "it," can stand for two or more things, and it is the work of the observer to remedy this basic ambiguity. Remedies lie in close attention to context, which is why the word *indexical* is often treated as synonymous with *context dependence* (e.g., Mishler, 1979, p. 14).

Indexical expressions become joined to the documentary method because the latter is the prototypic act to remedy the former.

The nature of the documentary method is defined by Garfinkel (1967, p. 78):

> The method consists of treating an actual appearance as "the document of," as "pointing to," as "standing on behalf of" a presupposed underlying pattern. Not only is the underlying pattern derived from its individual documentary evidence, but the individual documentary evidences, in their turn, are interpreted on the basis of "what is known" about the underlying pattern. Each is used to elaborate the other.

Garfinkel designed a demonstration to exaggerate the features of the method and to show how "facts" are produced (see also McHugh, 1968). Subjects were told that the department of psychiatry was exploring an alternative means of counseling. Each subject met a person who was portrayed as a trainee counselor and then was escorted to a room and told to formulate a series of yes and no questions about a personal problem. Subjects were told to ask a question and, after hearing the counselor's answer, comment privately into a tape recorder about what they had learned. Once they had commented on the counselor's answer, they were to ask another question; etc. The answers the subjects heard were predetermined and random.

An example of what happened (McHugh, 1968, p. 101) follows:

Background

I am hoping to go on to graduate school, to a good department of English. I have a scattered record. A's and C's. I believe my record is what it is because I do not apply myself. Oh, sometimes I study, but not consistently, not to the point where I always do my best. The C's show that, I think. They are C's in my major. My problem is whether I should go on to graduate school, and if I should, what I should do about it now.

Q1: I have a scattered record so far, but I would like to go on to graduate school. Should I?

A1: No.

C1: Well, yes I suppose not. Though it does seem a bit too certain to flatly ignore the possibility that I have the ability, even if not the personality, to do the kind of work that graduate school requires. The A's are evidence that I could do the work.

Q2: I have several A's on my record, and shouldn't that recommend my ability to do graduate work?

A2: Yes.

C2: I have the ability, but I do not study. It is too soon to discount the possibility of graduate school. I am only a junior, so there is quite enough time to improve my study habits this year and next. Then, if I do so, my prospects would be quite good. At least one would have to say they would be quite good.

Q3: If I improve my study habits to the point where I bring up my grades, should I then go on to graduate school?

A3: No.

C3: My. Let's see. Scattered record, I shouldn't go on. No, wait a minute. Good grades, I have the ability to go on. There, that takes care of it. Not that I should go on—that I have the ability. Then I shouldn't go on anyway, even with the ability. I guess he's against graduate school. It is a long haul, and often leads to eunuchism.

Q4: I gather you are not for graduate school? Just a minute. Rather, are you in favor of graduate school?

A4: Yes.

C4: My. That's strange. I am being put on notice here. It is hardly clear.

Students seemed to search for a pattern that would enable them to comprehend a meaning for each yes or no. As Wooton (1975, p. 63) puts it:

In cases where "incongruous" or "contradictory" replies were given, for example, students were able to interpret the incongruities as being the result of the adviser having learnt more about them between the two replies, or as having a "deeper" and unifying meaning behind them associated with the kind of advice the adviser was trying to give. In looking for the pattern behind the yes/no answers, students also employed cultural knowledge about counselors, the sort of things counselors might be expected to do, and so on.

Meaning is made possible because the particular is *tied to* a more generic supposition.

The research observer is obviously sitting in the counselee's chair trying to figure out what the cryptic comments mean that are being uttered by participants seated in the counselor's chair.

To initiate paraphrase, the observer asks questions such as these (Lofland, 1976, p. 32):

■ "Of what abstract, sociologically concerned class of situation is this particular situation an instance?"

■ "What generic features of this situation are most clear, exaggerated, sharp?"

■ "Of what is this the best example that one could conceivably find?"

To illustrate the extraction of generic issues from particular events, Lofland (1976, 1978) suggests that the specific situation of student may be viewed as the generic situation of an *open-ended and never-ending task* (Bernstein, 1972), the specific situation of milkman may be viewed as the generic situation of *power asymmetry* (Bigus, 1972), and the specific situation of baseball fielding and batting may be viewed as the generic situations of *certainty* and *uncertainty* (Gmelch, 1971).

The alternation between particulars and generalities can occur *at the time* of observation and be either modest, as when action is paraphrased into intentions and common sense (specimen records), or substantial, as in field notes that intersperse the generic with the particular. The alternation can also occur *after* initial observations have been recorded and can be disciplined either weakly by rereading original field notes or strongly by returning to the field to ask informants more specific questions. In either case the essence of the activity is paraphrase (Wilson, 1970).

THE STRUCTURE OF PARAPHRASE: REQUISITE VARIETY

To understand the structure of paraphrase is to understand the concept of requisite variety (Conant and Ashby, 1970) and the concept of affirmation.

The law of *requisite variety* "states that the variety within a system must be at least as great as the environmental variety against which it is attempting to regulate itself. Put more succinctly, only variety can regulate variety" (Buckley, 1968, p. 495).

If a photographer has to photograph twenty subjects, each of which is at a different distance from the camera, then the camera has to have at least twenty distinct settings if all of the negatives are to be brought to a uniform density and sharpness. If the camera has fewer than twenty settings, it lacks requisite variety and will not register the subjects accurately.

The transition to observational methodology is provided by Allport and Heider. Allport (1961) implies the idea of requisite variety when he says (p. 508):

> As a rule, people cannot comprehend others who are more complex and subtle than they. The single track mind has little feeling for the conflicts of the versatile mind. . . . Would it not follow, therefore, that the psychiatrist, since he deals with intricate mental tangles, should benefit by the possession of a complex personality? If he has neurotic difficulties of his own and manages them well, might they not add to his qualifications?

Allport states the general requirement for accurate paraphrase—complicate yourself—and Heider (1959)

suggests one way to do this. Heider argues that the world contains both things and media. People never know tangible items directly; their impressions are always mediated. This means that people will know those distant objects with greater or lesser clarity depending on the goodness of the medium (medium = observer).

At least three variables determine the quality of a medium:

1. The number of elements in the medium.

2. The degree to which each element is independent of other elements.

3. The degree to which the elements are externally rather than internally constrained.

Sand is a better medium than rock to represent wind currents because there are more independent elements in sand that can represent subtleties of wind speed and direction. To increase requisite variety is to increase the number, independence, and external constraint in those elements involved in observation. Those elements most susceptible to such modification are language elements, and that's why natural language is crucial to both observing and paraphrasing.

The specific link between requisite variety and observing occurs through a twist on epistemology. Rather than assume that seeing is believing, we assume that believing is seeing. This inversion suggests that beliefs are the medium through which the world is examined. Therefore we want to know the size, connectedness, and external orientation of an observer's belief system.

An observer who knows many theories, metaphors, images, and beliefs and who has had varied experiences (e.g., Douglas, 1976, p. ix) has more elements than an individual who has less content.

The crucial feature of an observer's belief system may lie in the second characteristic, the degree of independence among the elements. The observer with high requisite variety would have a loosely connected set of beliefs. The ideal circumstance for accurate observing would seem to be one in which use of one metaphor has *no* effect on adoption of another metaphor. Limited associations increase accuracy.

The final variable, external constraint, means that images are activated by events outside the individual, not by internally constrained reasons such as commitment, need satisfaction, or psychological defense. An observer who is pushing a certain view of the world not only reduces the independence among elements but makes those elements more internally constrained.

Individuals with large vocabularies should be better observers than those with small vocabularies. They have more independent elements that can be put into a greater variety of combinations. Notice that the requirement for independence of elements may preclude the development of a distinctive, singular voice (Brooks and Warren, 1972, Chap. 13) in write-ups of social science. To have a distinctive voice is to use selected words in a consistent, individual, internally patterned, and constrained manner, which may reduce the variety available to register nuance. Those with the most distinct voice may sense the least and invent the most.

Requisite variety may also vary directly with degree of self-acceptance. When people deny personal tendencies and experience, this works against requisite variety in two ways. First, denial produces a more simplistic view of the self, which means that the images available to be imposed on the world are less complex. This means that less complexity can be apprehended and understood. Second, denial takes vigilance to avoid contradiction. This means that sensory channels normally available for external perception are occupied with internal business. It also means that beliefs have additional dependencies imposed on them and are less available for independent registering.

To increase requisite variety is not just to loosen media, it is also to tighten the things that are observed. This additional approach to requisite variety has been called *tempered naturalness* (see p. 591, where this strategy is illustrated in more detail). The relevance of tempered naturalness to requisite variety is that "things" have a smaller number of dependent, internally constrained elements. When an event is made more thinglike, it should register more vividly on a medium, even if that medium is flawed.

The argument that natural language affects requisite variety has numerous implications for methodology.

First, narrative records, which can be criticized when they are not tied to abstractions, can also be supported because their reliance on natural language means that a complex sensing system is used to register a complex world (Daft and Wiginton, 1979; see Beebe, 1980, for a critique of this argument).

Second, the best observers may be those individuals who have a varied stock of images accumulated *either* through direct experience *or* fantasy. If beliefs control seeing, the origin of these sensing elements may be less crucial than their abundance and variety. To talk about an armchair observer is not a non sequitur, since time in the armchair can be time spent imagining scenes and explaining these imaginings in preparation for periods of on-site observation.

Third, to enhance requisite variety is to paraphrase with feeling, about feelings (Johnson, 1977). The realities of society and culture are a function of passion as well as judgment, and without both passion and judgment, realities cannot be apprehended (Bittner, 1973, p. 115). Observer feelings are identified and are available to register the feelings of others, and the resulting reports are valued as data (e.g., Johnson, 1975, pp. 152–159; Light, 1980, p. 368).

Fourth, to cultivate requisite variety is to value nonobvious media including poetry (Hugo, 1979), metaphors (Brown, 1977, Chap. 4) and professional jargon (McLeod, 1975). The merit in valuing these language resources is that they increase both the number of elements available for sensing and the independence of these elements. Professional jargon may be criticized (Steinbeck, 1941) for its pomposity and use to mystify the layperson, but that same language preserves distinctions that may improve seeing. To write clearly for laypeople may require the laundering of professional vocabularies cultivated in the interest of seeing more, but the resulting simplifications should *not* then be turned back onto the field as the sole observational categories used. To do so is to vulgarize natural contexts quite as fully as is done by attempts to fabricate them in the laboratory.

And fifth, the more tribelike (Campbell, 1979) and cohesive schools of thought become, the poorer mediums they become and the poorer is the quality of their data. Spence's students were more cohesive and loyal than were Tolman's, yet Tolman had a better explanation of learning and more persuasive data than did Spence. The best-quality observing is often associated with the most independence and least loyalty. This means that the best explanations will least often be disseminated, since there will be no group of mutually supportive people to preserve and perpetuate them.

THE CONTENT OF PARAPHRASE: AFFIRMATION

The *content* of meaningful paraphrase can be understood as the use of affirmation rather than negation to uncover subtleties. Traditional scientific preoccupation with falsification, doubt, disconfirmation, type I errors, and negative cases is of secondary importance in systematic observation and is replaced by a preoccupation with affirmation, conceptual laws, type II errors, and socio-rationalizing perspectives (Gergen, 1979), all of which operate to disclose dimensions that had previously gone unnoticed. The way affirmation works is suggested by the following description of *conceptual laws* (Schwartz and Jacobs, 1979, p. 327):

> Ordinarily one has a hypothesis, knows pretty well what it means, and wants to know if it is true. Here one has a hypothesis, is pretty sure it is true, and wants to know what it means (wants to know *what* is true). In order to answer this question, he treats his hypothesis as a conceptual law and puts a bit of knowledge beyond question for a while in order to "see where it leads."

A conceptual law serves as a scheme of interpretation rather than an empirical law. The reason it is so crucial is that many patterns can't be found *unless* one believes or knows that they are already there (see Riskin, 1970, for development of this point). A conceptual law sustains knowing long enough for observers to find what they know.

Conceptual laws are ways to search the world. They are laws believed in for reasons not obvious to the observer (I'm right about something but I don't know what it is), and they are laws whose outcroppings are discovered rather than predicted. They are attempts by the observer to impose distinct, strong images onto the world that affect seeing, attempts that are dismissed by people preoccupied with falsification and negation [see Armstrong (1980) for an example of such preoccupation].

Even though investigators seem to be preoccupied with criticism (Lumsden, 1973), most actually use *belief* rather than doubt to understand an event. One form that doubt takes is a concern with paradigms—who has them and who doesn't, who should have them and doesn't, and how best to get rid of the ones we have (e.g., Eckberg and Hill, 1979; Hirschman, 1979; Morgan, 1980). What gets lost in these discussions is the subtlety that if people want to break a paradigm, they are more likely to do so if they affirm it than if they deny it. The people who have been most successful at questioning the paradigm of rational man (Elster, 1979) are those who have applied that paradigm completely and, in doing so, have portrayed people in terms that are a caricature.

There are several reasons why affirmation makes sense for observers.

First, to treat field settings as sites capable of generating and testing multiple, theoretic degrees of freedom (Campbell, 1975), we must first affirm theories to see the subtlety with which they should be exhibited. If, for example, researchers believe that the more visible an act is, the more the actor will be committed to that act (Salancik, 1977), then they need to discover where people do visible things, when people suspect they're being watched, etc. Researchers have to believe that visibility and commitment *are* played out everywhere and that it is simply their oversights that keep them from seeing obvious examples. That's an act of affirmation.

Second, most observers agree that most events are overdetermined. If events are overdetermined, then multiple affirmations should capture more of the variables in those overdetermined events. Doubt should shrink the number of variables examined and the amount of variance explained.

Third, affirmation also makes sense because it seems that every hypothesis that people dream of is true for someone, somewhere, at some time. Part of the trick is to find those obscure places where confirmation occurs. If one person can view events in a particular way, it is probable that other people can too. To affirm is to uncover improbable realities.

Fourth, current enthusiasm for the use of metaphors (Ortony, 1975) can be understood as enthusiasm for acts of affirmation. Metaphors are affirmations in the sense that they suggest similarities that people should take seriously (e.g., Bryant, 1979). A metaphor simply says, A this is a that. It is the *is* in the *that* statement that is the act of affirmation. Because of our socialization into the doubting game, we are tempted to laugh at similarities too quickly and too intensely. As a result, we lack strong images of what social conduct is.

SUSTAINING

Whyte (1955, p. 303) gives this example:

> One has to learn when to question and when not to question as well as what questions to ask. I learned this lesson one night in the early months when I was with Doc in Chichi's gambling joint. A man from another part of the city was regaling us with a tale of the organization of gambling activity. I had been told that he had once been a very big gambling operator, and he talked knowingly about many interesting matters. He did most of the talking, but the oth-

ers asked questions and threw in comments, so at length I began to feel that I must say something in order to be part of the group. I said: "I suppose the cops were all paid off?"

The gambler's jaw dropped. He glared at me. Then he denied vehemently that any policemen had been paid off and immediately switched the conversation to another subject. For the rest of that evening I felt very uncomfortable.

The next day Doc explained the lesson on the previous evening 'Go easy on that 'who,' 'what,' 'why,' 'when,' 'where' stuff, Bill. You ask those questions and people will clam up on you. If people accept you, you can just hang around, and you'll learn the answers in the long run without even having to ask the questions.

The importance of *sustained familiarity* has been discussed by several investigators (e.g., Colson, *et al.,* 1976; Scott, 1965). Everett Hughes's (1960) definition of field work is representative: "Field work refers . . . to observation of people in situ; finding them where they are, staying with them in some role which, while acceptable to them, will allow both intimate observation of certain parts of their behavior, and reporting it in ways useful to social science but not harmful to those observed" (p. v). While sustained contact may be less crucial when phenomena are short-lived (e.g., Morehead, 1978), recapitulated in their beginnings (e.g., the first five minutes of therapy; see p. 609 of this chapter), preserved in records based on sustained past observation (e.g., self-rating) or ego involving such that all of the event is visible immediately (e.g., anxiety in sport parachuting), sustained contact is more crucial when observers want to discover recurrent events (the hallmark of culture), specify the order of events for purposes of causal modeling, and trace implications of seemingly brief events for a wider network of actors.

Social psychologists frequently have been impatient observers. As Willems (1976a, p. 243) observed, we have a psychology of short-term effects. The reason we know so little about adaptation, accommodation, functional achievement, and survival is that they demand longer periods to unfold than we have been willing to commit. Patient observers such as Barker and Schoggen (1973), Bateson (1958), Fox (1959), Hatch (1979), Manning (1980), Rappaport (1968), and Speck (1977) are in the minority.

Sustained contact will be explored first as a complex outcome of social competence, liking, and trust and second as complex input to any setting in the form of observer reactivity.

SUSTAINED INQUIRY AS AN ACCOMPLISHMENT

First impressions of the observer by the observed are crucial determinants of data quality (Van Maanen, in press, p. 2):

> The success of most research ventures depends inherently upon the success of the study the observed undertake of the observer. In other words, it is one thing for a researcher to believe he is acting in, for example, a warm, impartial, and confidential manner, it is another matter entirely to be seen as acting in such a fashion by the subjects of the research. One is not granted scientific or empathic status simply by staking out a claim, there must be both personal and impersonal evidence available to the observed such that any claims made by the researcher can be warranted.

To create favorable impressions is to have more social skill than most social scientists have, to cultivate the role of "nice guy," and to understand that trust is a necessary condition for valid findings. These points will be elaborated briefly.

The Socially Competent Observer

To be a sensitive observer of social life, one ought to be able to do social life. Therein lies the rub. Social scientists are a peculiarly asocial, abrasive, retiring lot (Wispe, 1963). Lofland (1976) states "The traditional bookish role of the academician and the reclusive nature of scholarship seem likely to exert a tendency toward selective recruitment of those who lack certain social graces; and the solitude characteristic of important portions of academic work does nothing to increase opportunities to learn to deal easily with situations involving unfamiliar people" p. 13).

Interestingly, those who manage socially competent familiarity are often the young. Whyte did Streetcorner Society when he was twenty-two years old. Van Maanen did his police study at age twenty-six. Lofland's (1976) hypothesis for this regularity is that people early in their professional careers are willing to admit they are ignorant, not yet experts, and have much to learn. As they age and become treated with too much respect by too many people over too many years, they are unable to wade back into the world, make mistakes, and admit candidly that this is what is happening. Confounded in most examples of better observation by the young is the fact that they were observing other people of roughly their own age. A crucial test case may be gerontological research (e.g., Mathews, 1975; Smithers, 1977). If the young are less status conscious than the old, and if their relaxation over status leads them to be more sociable and less threatening, then naturalistic studies of the elderly by the young should be at least as informative as those conducted by older investigators. However, if things like seasoning and similarity are crucial, then the supposed advantage of the young may vanish.

There are times when "playing" the harebrained academic can facilitate entree. A theoretical study conducted by a seemingly reclusive, naive individual looks harmless enough. In general, however, cultivation of skill is to be preferred to temporary exploitation of a weakness. Boobs may be given entree and tolerated, but boobs cannot be expected to know what to do with serious information, so they are given none.

It should be added that many observers have academic jobs that are notorious for their irregular, chopped-up days. Interruption is the rule (Pondy, 1977). That being the case, substitutes for familiarity such as survey data, census data, the fifty-minute laboratory hour, and library materials are less affected by interruptions than are sustained contacts. The fact that quantitative work, which *can* be factored more readily than sustained contact, is itself valued encourages the withdrawal from contact and restricts the very learning that could make those contacts more rewarding. There are few incentives in academia to remedy what probably only a handful of people view as a problem, namely, the relative shortage of socially competent observers.

This shortage deserves closer attention since it may affect not only the quality of data and the sites we examine but also the view of people we espouse. It is often asserted that people "normalize" trouble, concur that nothing unusual is happening, and avoid deeper questions (e.g., Emerson, 1970). These appearances may represent responses by informants in the presence of observers whose attractiveness for sustained interaction is nil. Informants don't grapple visibly with trouble or raise serious questions in front of these observers, which leads the observers to conclude, mistakenly, that informants never grapple with them.

Ways to counteract social incompetence and improve data quality are suggested in the next two sections.

The Role of Liking

"Good guys get better data. No sense leaving your humanness at home" (Guba, 1980, p. 21). That statement by Terry Denny shows why interpersonal attractiveness is not a luxury in observational research. To be trusted is first to be liked.

Douglas (1976) specifies the following prescription for an observer to be liked (p. 136):

> It is almost always important to be egalitarian, unthreatening, nonassertive (it's better to be somewhat submissive in most groups, except in tough lower class groups), easy-going, supportive, possess a sense of humor, and be emotionally labile, even to the point of being hearty and openly emotional, something which seems to help people "get out of themselves." Sharing things with people, doing things for them, builds up over time.

Van Maanen (in press), faced with being the nice guy among police, *tried* to act as "one who is rarely angry, never hostile, concerned for everyone's welfare, does little favors for others, and, generally, expresses humility and kindness in his everyday encounters" (p. 68). Some police made it easier to sustain this role than others.

Whyte (1955), in his effort to be a nice guy and fit into the Norton gang, presumed that one way to do this was to sound like them (p. 304):

> Trying to enter into the spirit of the small talk, I cut loose with a string of obscenities and profanity. The talk came to a momentary halt as they all stopped to look at me in surprise. Doc shook his head and said: "Bill, you're not supposed to talk like that. That doesn't sound like you." I tried to explain that I was only using terms that were common on the street corner. Doc insisted, however, that I was different and that they wanted me to be that way. This lesson went far beyond the use of obscenity and profanity. I learned that people did not expect me to be just like them; in fact, they were interested and pleased to find me different, just so long as I took a friendly interest in them. Therefore, I abandoned my efforts at complete immersion.

Whyte's discovery that his *differences* interested his informants and helped him to sustain contact is important to note because it is a side benefit associated with the normally problematic issue of observer reactivity. Part of the observer's charm is that he or she is not bound to routines in the setting being observed and is seldom bored. That's diverting and attractive to those who *are* bound to such routines (Johnson, 1975, p. 110). If the observer becomes vulnerable in the same way informants are through appropriate disclosure of real concerns and fallibilities, then the liking that converts into trust and validity should be initiated.

One way for observers to ensure their own sociability is to enter settings when the people in the setting are nice guys too. Light (1980, p. 363) argues that his greatest coup in observing psychiatric training was to start in June when the old-timers were relaxed, undefensive, and expansive (they graduated the following month) and the uptight newcomers were not yet on the scene. Corsaro (1980), who videotaped day-care centers, argued that intrusive observing should not be done at the beginning of the school year when parents, teaching assistants, and children are especially tense.

The Role of Trust

Trust is important for valid observation. There are at least four theories of trust, and they suggest that trust develops as an exchange for favors done, as a result of seeing that the observer is a moral person, as a result of observers adopting group morality and protecting the integrity of group members, or as a result of observers helping people gain something they want, such as a hearing for their views.

Trust that develops in field settings is a composite of these four and considerably more complicated. Johnson (1975) notes that relations of trust that developed between himself and welfare workers "were more fluid, emergent, and situational than any definitive set of procedural rules could possibly articulate" (p. 133). By this he means that relations of trust between informants and the observer recapitulate the relations among the informants themselves. "Individuals [at the Child Welfare Agency] trust some more than others, trusted some not at all, and trusted some for some purposes but not for others" (p. 132).

Given this complexity, trust building is not an all-or-none activity. The goal is to build "sufficient trust," which means "a personal common-sense judgment about what is accomplishable with a given person"

(Johnson, 1975, p. 142). Johnson identifies at least six practical procedures for developing trust, all of which are variations on the theme that the observer becomes a human capable of trust through a process of "identity spoilage." The tactics include the following:

1. Use reconstructions of one's own biography to minimize distance ("I too used to live on a farm").

2. Normalize the research you're doing ("It's a job").

3. Do practical activities needed by informants, such as serve as a driver, note taker, phone answerer.

4. Use plural pronouns to construct the appearance of membership ("I am one of us, not one of them. We....") (see Spiegelberg, 1973).

5. Use plural pronouns to construct the appearance of knowing what you're doing ("We scientists believe....").

6. Use charm.

As a final point, there are substitutes for trust. One is sequencing of procedures. Those procedures most threatening to the informants (e.g., tape recording) are withheld until trust has been established or entree granted. Most groups have members whose inputs can short-circuit the lengthy processes of building trust with everyone. These people include sociability gadflies (they'll talk to anyone at great length about quite private things), everyday-life historians, everyday-life philosophers, and marginal people and enemies (Douglas, 1976, p. 213). All of these people have unique perspectives and are not a representative sample, but neither are they irrelevant. They are mentioned simply because trust is not necessarily the central organizing principle in their lives.

REACTIVITY AND SUSTAINED INQUIRY

How the observer's sustained participation and presence change statements made by the participants is a central question related to the objectivity of field data. The behavioral effects of being observed are not well known, although investigators doing behavioral assessment are beginning to examine them (e.g., Baum, Forehand and Zegiob, 1979; Johnson and Bolstad, 1975; Johnson, Christensen, and Bellamy, 1976; Kent and Foster, 1977; Mash and Hedley, 1975; Nelson, 1977, pp. 218–230; Zegiob, Arnold, and Forehand, 1975). As an initial set of cautions, observers should not assume that stable behavior means typical behavior, that the stimulus array present when one is being observed is equivalent to the stimulus array when people are unobserved, or that the statement "People soon adapt to it" is equivalent to the statement "People would act as they do were it not even present" (Cone and Hawkins, 1977, p. 271).

People have strong needs not to examine their lives, and observers threaten this avoidance. Polansky *et al.* (1949), for example, found that during the first week of observation in a summer camp, campers ignored observers; but during the second week campers blew up at them. Delayed resistance, while not common, does suggest that once participants have resolved their own issues of inclusion, they move to issues of control and the question of who's in charge here. Observers, who are new to the scene, may become appropriate targets for this conflict.

One of the more prominent effects of being observed is that people emit more positive behaviors, whether these be more favorable self-reference (Roberts and Renzaglia, 1965), more positive play with children (Zegiob, Arnold, and Forehand, 1975), or more altruistic acts when being videotaped (Samph, 1969).

In many cases of apparent reactivity the problem may be that the observer is a nonresponsive stranger, an unusual role in an otherwise sociable society (Sykes, 1978). Barker and Wright's (1955) stipulation that observers *could* interact with informants in a friendly, nondirective manner has, however, been attacked as reactive. Johnson and Bolstad (1973) remark that this must certainly have increased the intrusiveness of the observer and provided the opportunity for the observer to influence the child's behavior. It seems most likely that intrusiveness is minimized, not maximized, when interaction is allowed, because interaction enables observers to close issues that remain open questions if one is unresponsive.

The general issue involved with reactivity seems to be the question "What is it possible to know for sure on the basis of a single observation?" The parallel between this question and the more general formulation known as the Heisenberg principle is apparent. "The principle says that knowing one thing about an object changes another thing about it. Therefore one cannot know both things about the same object at the *exact same time*. But neither thing is thereby rendered 'unknowable' in general" (Schwartz and Jacobs, 1979, p. 128). Reiss (1971, p. 21) ran into this limitation in his police research when he found it impossible to assess the differences between one and two officers working together because the presence of an observer made every situation a two-man or three-man situation.

A pragmatic position on the issue of reactivity begins with the stipulation that whenever possible, observers should design the observation so that its effect on people are relatively constant and noninteractive. If we know that observers reliably reduce deviant behavior by 30 percent, this systematic effect can be managed in reporting and analysis. In addition, either by means of a thought experiment or by intentional design, the observer can address the issue of reactivity in one of at least six ways:

1. Behavioral changes can be examined over time for evidence of habituation.

2. The conspicuousness of the observer can be varied and the results compared.

3. The subject's awareness of being observed can be manipulated with effects being compared.

4. People can be instructed to produce a specific behavior while they are being observed (e.g., "make your child look good") and the question is, *Can* this behavior be changed if people try? This fourth thought experiment does not assess whether people do change behavior when observed, but obviously that question becomes less compelling if it is demonstrated that they *can't* change it.

5. People can be asked about the effects of being observed.

6. The observer can monitor, simultaneously, behaviors about which the person has been made self-aware *and* behaviors that have not been singled out for attention to see differential effects of observation on their rate, frequency, content, and duration.

EXPLICITNESS

Explicit observing is self-conscious, public, contestable, fully and clearly expressed, and capable of reconstruction. Explicitness is both a means, in the sense that it facilitates evaluation and replication, and an end, in the sense that certain techniques of observation are designed to make tacit understandings of informants more evident.

If believing can influence seeing, then explicitness about observer preconceptions is crucial in establishing the validity of observational work. The relevant questions are the following:

1. What were your preconceived notions?

2. If you went in as a "blank slate," what did you do to keep it that way?

3. If you went in with preconceptions, what did you do to manage or decouple believing and seeing?

Explicitness about preconceptions is crucial, because in Gouldner's chilling phrase, "honesty is an independent variable in social research" (cited in Douglas, 1976, p.115). One of the newer trends in observational work is for investigators to be more candid about how research is *actually* done (e.g., Golden, 1976; Johnson, 1975; Malinowski, 1967; Reinharz, 1979; Styles, 1979; Zigarmi and Zigarmi, 1978; also see evaluations of Malinowski by Hsu, 1979; Wax, 1972). While full disclosure of actual research conduct has become a moral position for many, the issues are not cut and dried.

In the first place, inclusion of an appendix in which methodological sins are confessed all too often is preceded by a "factual" account written as if no sins had been committed. This borders on a dishonest use of honesty. Second, those sins that are confessed are usually "the second worst things that happened." Lofland (1971, pp. 132–133) states:

> One of my mentors has commented that what typically goes into "how the study was done" are "the second worst things that happened." I am inclined to believe that his generalization is correct. What person with an eye to his future, and who wishes others to think positively of him, is going to relate anything about himself that is morally or professionally discrediting in any important way? This is especially the case since field work tends to be performed by youngish persons who have longer futures to think about and less security about the shape of those futures. We delude ourselves if we expect very many field workers actually to tell all in print.

The third, and perhaps most troubling, aspect of honesty is that all these disclaimers may carry the actual message that the methods of observation we use simply do not work. The ironic twist to this troubling possibility is that if people are explicit about what they actually do, then these displays may provide the elements from which alternative patterns of more credible inquiry can be induced.

Explicitness is necessary for purposes of evaluation and replication. But it can be costly. The specific cost I have in mind is that those items one can specify most clearly are usually those items most limited in scope. To be self-conscious and explicit about what one is doing is to scale down the range and number of events that can be studied. If explicitness reduces scope, then the observer may need to manage this trade-off either by including a greater number and variety of explicit items to preserve variety in the sensing instrument or by becoming resigned to knowing more about less. To compound problems, Herbert and Attridge (1975, p. 10) argue that there may be no such thing as a low-inference, explicit item, category, or description. A completely specified and bounded item may violate the stream of behavior, which means you still have to resort to inference to see when and for how much behavior the item fits.

Observers cannot retreat into mystification in the name of scope and requisite variety, or if they do, they cannot be surprised when they are not taken seriously. What observers can do is ensure that explicit elements are plentiful, *non*redundant, and backed up by elements capable of more scope and more sensitivity to continuity, even if these backup elements are harder to replicate and more controversial.

Explicitness around four issues will be discussed in this section. We will discuss explicit preconceptions, the construction of explicit settings by means of tempered naturalness, explicit roles, explicit records.

EXPLICIT PRECONCEPTIONS

While preconceptions can affect seeing, they do not necessarily dominate it. People can be surprised and field notes can change. The crucial factor is that people be aware of potential personal influences on what they report. To manage preconceptions means, for example, intentionally to hold contradictory beliefs. If believing is seeing, then contradictory beliefs will either cancel one another or double the range of what is seen. Social psychological observers may see little because they go into situations either with too few beliefs or with beliefs that are not sufficiently varied. Observers don't want to do away with beliefs altogether because they have to look for something. What they want to avoid is prefiguring everything they'll find.

Preconceptions exist in various forms, including preferred styles of inquiring, prior questions, concurrent personal activities, and images of humankind.

Preferred styles of inquiring affect what is singled out for attention and what is ignored. To be explicit

TABLE 3
Composite Mitroff-Kilmann Table

		ANALYTIC SCIENTIST (ST)	CONCEPTUAL THEORIST (NT)	PARTICULAR HUMANIST (SF)	CONCEPTUAL HUMANIST (NF)
1.	Guarantors of scientific knowledge	Consensus, agreement, reliability, external validity, rigor, controlled nature of inquiry, maintenance of distance between scientist and objects studied	Conflict between antithetical imaginative theories, comprehensive holistic theories, ever-expanding research programs	Intense personal knowledge and experience	Human conflict between knowing agent (E) and subject known (S); inquiry fosters human growth and development
2.	Aims of science	Precise, unambiguous, theoretical and empirical knowledge for their own (disinterested) sake	To construct the broadest possible conceptual schemes; multiple production of conflicting schemas	To help *this* person know himself or herself uniquely and to achieve his or her own self-determination	To promote human development on the widest possible scale
3.	Preferred modes of inquiry	Controlled inquiry as embodied in the classic concept of the experiment	Conceptual inquiry; treatment of innovative concepts from multiple perspectives; invention of new schemas	The case study; the in-depth, detailed study of a particular individual	Conceptual inquiry; treatment of innovative concepts; maximal cooperation between E and S so that both may better know themselves and one another
4.	Personal dispositions expressed while in scientist role	Disinterested, unbiased, impersonal, precise, expert, specialist, skeptical, exact, methodical	Disinterested, unbiased, impersonal, imaginative, speculative, generalist, holistic	Interested, "all-too-human," biased, poetic, committed to the postulates of an action-oriented science	Interested; free to admit and know his biases; highly personal; imaginative, speculative, generalist; holistic

SOURCE: Adapted from Mitroff and Kilmann, 1978.

about styles of inquiry is to identify those assumptions necessary for a precise replication and to suggest areas of selective inattention and embellishment. A useful typology to catalogue styles of inquiring is Jung's distinction between two ways of taking in data (sensation S or intuition N) and two ways of coming to conclusions about these data (thinking T or feeling F). Since these two dimensions are independent, they can be combined into four personality types: (1) sensation-thinking (*ST*), (2) intuition-thinking (NT), (3) sensation-feeling (SF), and (4) intuition-feeling (NF). Mitroff and Kilmann (1978)

have coordinated these types with four styles of inquiring, labeled as the analytic scientist (ST), conceptual theorist (NT), particular humanist (SF), and conceptual humanist (NF). Ways in which these four styles vary in their views of the bases for scientific knowledge, the aims of science, preferred modes of inquiry, and personal dispositions expressed while in the scientist role, are displayed in Table 3.

Viewed as one means of organizing an inquiry into preconceptions, this fourfold table suggests the following:

1. One possible rule to compose an observational team is, Select one of each type.

2. Opposite styles should be imposed when evaluating the product of a specific style or recruiting a collaborator (the extreme opposite of ST is NF, of SF is NT).

3. Steps should occur in sustained observation. The scientific ideal would follow roughly the sequence NT/NF, pose significant questions; ST, model and answer questions; SF, implement the outcome. However, I emphasize my admonition that investigators *scramble* prescribed sequences in the interest of seeing new things.

4. Observers should be explicit, at least to themselves, about their actual location and work against this bias in whatever ways make sense (on the Myers-Briggs, this author is NT).

5. Evaluators, critics, replicators, and gatekeepers should be sensitive to their own preferred styles since these will color their appraisals.

Preconceptions, however, are not just an issue of inquiring style. They are also an issue of the questions one takes to a setting. Malinowski (cited in Smith and Geoffrey, 1968, p. 5) counseled observers to enter novel settings, not with preconceived ideas but with "foreshadowed problems":

> Good training in theory, and acquaintance with its latest results, is not identical with being burdened with "preconceived ideas." If a man sets out on an expedition, determined to prove certain hypotheses, if he is incapable of changing his views constantly and casting them off ungrudgingly under the pressure of evidence, needless to say his work will be worthless. But the more problems he brings with him into the field, the more he is in the habit of molding his theories according to facts, and of seeing facts in their bearing upon theory, the better he is equipped for the work. Preconceived ideas are pernicious in any scientific work, but foreshadowed problems are the main endowment of a scientific thinker, and these problems are first revealed to the observer by his theoretical studies.

To foreshadow, a person can write a short proposal, review a literature, skim a category system, read an account written by a good observer, copy verbatim the field notes of an accomplished ethnographer, read a graphic description into a tape recorder, page through a source with diverse images such as the *Whole Earth Catalog,* or ask people what they would like to know about a setting.

Preconceptions that influence data collection also come from whatever concurrent professional and personal activities are taking place for the observer. To be explicit is to deal consciously with these sources of input, even if only to list them privately so that one can later recall just what personal circumstances were unfolding that might have influenced the credibility of data. Observers under the pressure of tenure review, divorce, alcoholism, births, deaths, discrimination, envy, or boredom are not interchangeable. Furthermore, to triangulate a finding is not just to remove method variance but also to remove variance due to personal projections. To manage the effect of personal circumstances on data collection is either to minimize concurrent inputs (lead as bland a life as possible) or to ensure that concurrent inputs are diverse so that no systematic bias is introduced into the data.

A final source of preconceptions about which explicitness is important is images of people (Buff, 1977). Images are neither theories nor problems but coherent ideologies about mankind (Schafer, 1970).

Marceil (1977), for example, presents a useful clarification of the idiographic-nomothetic debate that helps observers specify images that make a difference in data collection. Two issues are involved. The first is an issue of method: Does the most fruitful mode of research involve selective examination of many subjects or intensive examination of a few? The second is an issue of theory: Are people basically alike or basically unique? These issues yield the combinations presented in Table 4.

TABLE 4
A Theory Versus Method Matrix

METHOD ASSUMPTIONS	THEORY ASSUMPTIONS	
	A. MAN IS MORE ALIKE	**B. MAN IS MORE UNIQUE**
A. Selective examination of many subjects	AA	AB
B. Intense examination of few subjects	BA	BB

The AA combination is exemplified by factor-analytic approaches; the peculiar AB combination by the Edwards Personal Preference Scale, which assumes that each individual is a unique configuration of needs evaluated in terms of *group* norms; the BB combination by case studies such as "Letters from Jenny"; and the BA combination by Ebbinghaus's classic work on memory. All four positions will be represented throughout this chapter with column A and row B tending to dominate, column A because of the heavy representation of sociologists, row B because of the heavy representation of ethnographers, qualitative researchers, and naturalistic observers. (The author regards himself as primarily BA.)

EXPLICIT SETTINGS THROUGH TEMPERED NATURALNESS

Greater deliberateness in the choice and arrangement of an observational setting can lead to sizable improvements in the precision and validity of observational studies. Any setting has properties that detract from clear observation, but these distractions are more prominent in some situations than in others. Furthermore, some properties of naturalistic settings can be eliminated or modified, and new properties can be added without necessarily destroying the naturalness that is valued. In short, naturalistic settings do not require passivity from the observer. Settings are also more flexible and permit more latitude for manipulation, intervention, and rearrangement than has often been realized.

Earlier (see p. 582 of this chapter) I noted that requisite variety improves when settings are consolidated, made more explicit, and more thinglike. When settings are consolidated, they are seen more clearly, even if the sensing medium is flawed. It may seem that consolidation of a natural setting defeats the purpose of systematic observation, namely, to study social situations in their naturally occurring contexts. Clearly, massive consolidations do render the familiar strange and do make participants aware they are being watched. This is not the type of intervention being suggested. *Subtle* modifications are the key. That's why the tactic is called *tempered naturalness*. The natural setting is adjusted, tailored, fine-tuned, trimmed, stabilized, and steadied, *not* converted, transformed, replaced, done over, disturbed, upset, or rebuilt.

The trappings of the natural situation are preserved, and it unfolds in a conventional manner, but some of its peripheral properties are tailored in the interest of visibility. The most common means to accomplish this adjustment is to put boundaries around some portion of the ongoing events. This means essentially that participants are exposed to an input that has a beginning and an end, an input that fits into the setting in the sense that it is plausible and expected, an input that is nonreactive and does not arouse suspicion, and an input that permits greater precision in measurement (e.g., Pearce, 1980). The input is modeled after a laboratory task that has been altered so that it fits into the setting. It is the task that elicits the behavior that the observer records. A directed setting consistent with this model can be created either when an intact task is plausibly "dropped into" the behavior stream or when the stream of activities is altered so that it contains the essential properties of a task.

Examples of tempered naturalness include dropping pennies in an elevator after the doors have closed to see if anyone will volunteer help (Latane and Dabbs, 1975), phrasing initial contacts of a waitress with a customer differently to increase the size of the purchase (Butler and Snizek, 1976), or soliciting contributions from a table in an area where students must make a visible response to avoid the solicitation (Pancer *et al.,* 1979).

In each of these examples a localized, bounded event is implanted without appearing absurd. Though the event may be improbable in the setting, it is not implausible. It becomes assimilated as normal, natural trouble.

EXPLICIT ROLES

There are numerous discussions of the roles observers can assume, and we will not rehash these adequate reviews (e.g., Adams and Preiss, 1960; Junker, 1960). Instead, we will focus on three roles specifically designed to make explicit some tacit understandings routinely invoked by participants. The nature of such understandings is illustrated by the phenomenon of following a set of instructions literally. According to Mehan and Wood (1975, p. 234):

> Researchers are instructed to learn a new activity from a set of written rules. Hoyle's book of games, cookbooks, and sewing manuals provide a large set of possible activities. Researchers are directed to do only what the instructions say. They are neither to improvise nor to make allowances. They are to approach the document as "strict constructionists."

> Researchers discover that the activities cannot be done. In following a recipe, for example, instruc-

tions are given for preparing the food, and for preheating the oven. There are seldom explicit instructions to put the food in the oven. Sometimes the instructions indicate that eggs still in their shells are to be placed in mixing bowls, or beaten with a stick, or whipped with a belt. Cookies sometimes must be dropped on the floor, not on cookie sheets. Researchers search in vain for behavioral representations of "cook until tender," "saute," "blanche," "fold."

Observers and participants both have a good deal of independent knowledge about situations that affects how they interpret what they observe. The necessity for observers to make their own tacit preconceptions explicit has already been argued. The necessity for participants to be explicit, interestingly, is driven by the same argument. Tacit understandings inform explicit conduct and determine meaning. Unless the observer or participant makes these tacit understandings explicit, meanings and conduct will be misunderstood.

To learn more about nonexplicit understandings, observers can become or use strangers, novices, and misfits.

To maximize the effectiveness of the *stranger* role, three conditions must be met (Schwartz and Jacobs, 1979, p. 251):

1. There will be a consistent stream of things the researcher *has to do* which can only be accomplished through members' knowledge.

2. These things have to be done quickly, "right now." Real practical misfortunes and mistakes are possible if not probable.

3. He can't talk his way out of failure, explaining "I am a sociologist." This means that the practical tasks are so designed that verbal accounts cannot excuse or mitigate the practical and emotional consequences of failure or misinterpretation.

Since people are so skillful at imposing some kind of sense on any puzzle, the attitude created by being a stranger decays very rapidly. This means that the preceding three steps should be followed closely. Furthermore, the more successfully those three conditions are met, the greater is the necessity for either a second person who can do a meaningful debriefing of the experience or for some kind of record that can stimulate recall later.

Examples of using the stranger role to discover tacit understandings include being a John for the first time (Stewart, 1972), observing gay baths, first as a nonparticipant and then as a participant (Styles, 1979), milling among inmates in a prison (Carroll, 1977; Jacobs, 1974), going through the initial stages of conversion to a religious sect (Gordon, 1974; Harrison, 1974; Robbins, Anthony, and Curtis, 1973), wearing eyeglasses with inverted lenses that turn the visual field upside down, wearing earphones connected to an apparatus with a side-tone delay that slows down the occurrence of sounds, or wearing a blindfold or negotiating during a day by using only mechanical devices constructed for the handicapped (Mehan and Wood, 1975, pp. 232–233).

A potential problem with the stranger role is that it is not for the timid, hesitant, or fearful. Confident, brash, and assertive observers should be overrepresented among those who use this strategy, which means that constructions of these same circumstances by the terrified will never be known.

To learn what is implicit, the observer can also become a *novice* to a group of skilled persons or try to teach a novice some skill that the observer has already taken for granted (e.g., teach another person to drive a car).

One of the better-known, recent examples of the novice strategy is David Sudnow's (1978, 1979) account of learning to improvise jazz piano. Not only did he learn about learning, but he also learned about improvisation as a key metaphor for understanding talk. Other examples of the novice role used to discover tacit understandings are studies by Davis (1974) while learning to become a cabdriver, Gladwin (1970) while learning navigation algorithms in Puluwat from Hipour, Riemer (1976, 1977b) while becoming a journeyman electrician, Haas (1970) while becoming a high-steel worker, and Feigelman (1974) while serving as an electrician's apprentice.

If an observer finds it difficult to become estranged from everyday life, another tactic is to find someone who can, a *misfit*. Such a person would find it difficult to do activities that everyone else does as a matter of course. A misfit frequently is someone who tries to pass as someone else. The best-known example is Agnes, a woman with well-developed breasts and a functioning penis, who was not practiced at being a woman since she had been raised as a male (Garfinkel, 1967). For Agnes, being a female was not something she automatically now is, always was, and always will be. Instead, what for most other people is an object, fact, or social thing was for Agnes an event, process, accomplishment, account, and interpretation.

EXPLICIT RECORDS

To be explicit is to be preoccupied with detail. Normally, in social science, a concern with the particular is incidental to an understanding of the general. But the bulk of observational work reverses this emphasis: "In writing an ethnography, as a translation in the full sense, the concern with the general is incidental to an understanding of the particular. In order for a reader to see the lives of the people we study, we must *show them through particulars,* not merely talk about them in generalities" (Spradley, 1980, p. 162). Specific tactics used by researchers to enhance explicitness and preserve detail include narratives, checklists, and visual records.

Narratives

There are at least three forms of narrative: ancedotes, specimen records, and ethnographic notes.

Anecdotes are descriptions of behavioral episodes and are most commonly associated with Piaget's work (1929). Anecdotes are detailed, objective statements of settings and actions that can be classified, quantified, and organized to test hypotheses. Here is an example from Brown (1892, p. 263):

> 34. (11 years). In my Sunday school class, we were taking about Christmas. One girl said, "Three wise men from the East brought the Lord gold, frankincense and myrrh." One of the children said, "What is myrrh and frankincense?" M. said, "Oh I know what frankincense is; it's the money they use in France; but when they talk in French, they say it backward." Then quite unconsciously she said to herself, "Cents in France."

Anecdotes are accessible, compact, and manageable, and they lend themselves to categorization and reshuffling of categories. They are not, however, easy to record, and they are subject to the errors of sampling and inference identified by Nisbett and Ross (1980).

Brandt (1972, pp. 84–85) has identified several guidelines for writing anecdotes:

1. Write an anecdote as soon after viewing the incident as possible.

2. Include the basic action or statements of the chief person in the episode, that is, what he did or said.

3. Include enough setting details to indicate where and when the behavior occurred, under what conditions, and who was involved.

4. Responses or reactions of others to the chief person's behavior should also be included (example: "Jim nodded affirmatively"; "I don't think so," Tom replied). Even no response when one might well be expected should be recorded (example: "Nothing else was said at the time").

5. Use direct quotations wherever possible in order to preserve the flavor of how things were stated.

6. Generally, ancedotes should preserve the sequence of actions and responses of the original behavior incident. [In other words, there is a *beginning,* a *middle,* and an *end.*]

7. Anecdotes should describe the major units of molar behavior (example: "Bill went to the grocery store with his mother") with sufficient subordinate molar units (example: "Bill *ran out of the house* as his mother was warming the car up, *slamming the door* behind him, and *rode off* to the grocery with his mother") and molecular activity (example: "panting and waving his arms") included to indicate something about how the main action was carried out.

8. Anecdotes should be objective, accurate, and complete as far as important details are concerned. Recording errors should be of commission, which can be disregarded in the analysis, rather than omission, which can never be corrected.

A *specimen record* is perhaps the best-known nonselective record used in observational research. It is defined as "a sequential, unselective, plain, narrative description of behavior with some of its conditions" (Wright, 1960, p. 86). The following excerpt is taken from a specimen record describing the actions of Ben, a six-year-old boy with cerebral palsy (Barker, 1964, p. 272):

> 1:33 Olivia walked in from the occupational therapy room and made a few gay, happy, cheerful remarks about the fact that Ben was going to be six very soon.
>
> Ben looked up at her but made no other response.
>
> Then Tom said somewhat seriously, "Well, any little boy who's going to be six is going to have to learn to crawl."
>
> With this Olivia and Tom walked to the far end of the room a distance of nine or ten feet, which was established as the goal for Ben's crawling.

Specimen records are assumed to have several advantages: face validity, permanence (see Barker *et al.,* 1961, for an example of a specimen record archive), theoretically neutral data, extensive detail, isomorphism with behavior, behavior recorded *in situ,* breadth due to lay language, and continuity. Furthermore, specimen records can be quantified (Wright, 1960, p. 89), and they can be collected by unsophisticated observers (Heyns and Lippitt, 1954, p. 389).

Good examples of research grounded in specimen records include Crowley (1976), Scott, (1977), Willems's studies of rehabilitation (1976b), and Barker *et al.*'s (1978) remarkably compact (48 pages) description *and analysis* of a complete day (May 12, 1949) in the life of eight-year-old Mary Ennis.

The best source on the technique of doing specimen records is Chapter 3 in Wright (1967). The emphasis in specimen records is on detailed, comprehended particulars.

The set given the observer is as follows (Wright, 1967, p. 38):

> The observer is not asked to theorize; he is asked to suspend biases from formal psychological training, and to fall back upon the elementary, garden variety, spur-of-the-moment notions and hunches about behavior that are common to man as a socialized being, that could never be abolished or appreciably suppressed if this should seem desirable, and that cannot help but astonish anyone who stops to reflect upon them with their high ratio of accuracy to error.

Wright (1967, pp. 48–53) has suggested nine rules of reporting that seem to make the difference between a good narrative record and a bad one, and these bear a close resemblance to Brandt's guidelines for anecdotes.

Ethnographic records are field notes that document a social situation. These notes resemble anecdotes but differ by including both interpretation and specialized jargon. Field notes often emphasize features that seem central to the interests of the observer. The notes often preserve generalizations rather than separate descriptions of each episode.

Fields notes are highly personalistic. Their reinterpretation is difficult because abstractions and descriptions are woven together so tightly and because observers overlook much of what is going on in pursuit of data relevant to their emerging hunches. Field notes document idea generation more than native actions.

Spradley (1980, pp. 65–69) suggests that observers should be sure to identify the different languages used in each field note entry, make a verbatim record of what people say, and use concrete language. This last point is crucial (Spradley, 1980, p. 68):

> Writing in concrete language is difficult because most people have had years of training to condense, summarize, abbreviate, and generalize. We have learned to avoid writing that is "too wordy." In writing up fieldnotes we must reverse this deeply ingrained habit of generalization and *expand, fillout, enlarge,* and give as much *specific detail* as possible.

> One way to help expand the concrete language of description in taking fieldnotes is to make lists of verbs and nouns which can be expanded later. For example, let's say you made observations of people standing in line and listed these verbs: standing, shifting, looking up, looking down, searching pockets, wagging head, nodding head, scratching, glaring, raising eyebrows, backing up, reclining, walking. This would enhance a concrete description in your fieldnotes. If you observed people walking their dogs in a park, you could list nouns like chain leash, leather leash, dirt path, sidewalk, curb, asphalt path, leaves, grass, fire plug, tree, stick, purse, coats.

Informative discussions and examples of ethnographic records can be found in Bogdan (1972, pp. 39–58), Bogdan and Taylor (1975, pp. 60–78), Erickson (1979), Patton (1980, pp. 160–168), Spradley (1980, pp. 63–84), and Schatzman and Strauss (1973, pp. 94–104). The latter authors' distinction among observational, theoretical, and methodological notes is typical of those who have discussed field notes. Observational notes are the hard evidence, contain as little interpretation as possible, and specify who said or did what under stated circumstances. Each observational note is constructed to stand alone as a datum. When the observer wants to go beyond the facts and make inferences, a theoretical note is prepared. This represents a self-conscious, controlled attempt to derive meaning from observational notes. And a methodological note is basically "an instruction to oneself, a reminder, a critique of one's own tactics. It notes timing, sequencing, stationing, stage setting or maneuvering. Methodological notes might be thought of as observational notes on the researcher himself" (Schatzman and Strauss, 1973, p. 101).

Checklists

The most thorough presentation of checklists is found in Brandt (1972), and my discussion draws heavily on this source. To be explicit about settings, observers can use static descriptors, action checklists, activity logs, discrete-event records, standardized situation responses, work measurement, performance records, trait indicator checklists, and ratings.

A *static descriptor* "is a set of descriptive items pertaining to highly stable characteristics of research subjects or settings that are to be checked or filled out, thus ensuring systematic notation of data" (Brandt, 1972, p. 94). Age, sex, occupation, homeownership, weather conditions and time of day are examples (e.g., Snel, 1978).

Action checklists describe behavior rather than settings and are appropriate when the behavior alternatives in a situation are visible, mutually exclusive, and limited (e.g., Farina, Arenberg, and Guskin, 1957; Puckett, 1928). Possible combinations of behavior and alternatives are listed in Table 5.

Activity logs provide a permanent performance record of an activity and can indicate how days and hours are divided into activities and events (Stewart, 1976, p. 140). The major task in developing logs is to select molar activity categories that have little overlap but, when taken together, account for an entire block of time. Brandt (1972, p. 105) says:

> Activity logs share a number of qualities with other, more traditional logs. First, the time when events start and stop is almost always a routine entry. Content is usually limited to major happenings and regularly taken performance or activity measures. Such logs serve to direct observations to certain important features of a performance at frequent intervals, thereby minimizing chances of important changes in activities going unnoticed.

Discrete-event records describe events that happen irregularly (e.g., Dawe, 1934). No attempt is made to account for time between the events, as is the case in an activity log. An adolescent dance diary indicating date, time, place, and name of the person with whom one attended the event is an example. "Construction of discrete-event records is simply a matter of identifying the class of event that is to be recorded and the specific features that are to be noted, and then systematically recording each event as it happens" (Brandt, 1972, p. 108).

Standardized situation responses involve the recording of behaviors that occur in specific, regular, natural, nonstressful, standardized situations, such as door holding (e.g., Walum, 1974), asking for directions (Pearce, 1980), or purchasing stamps.

Work measurement, as represented in time-motion studies, represents a specialized, precise attempt to measure human work behavior in natural settings. McCormick (1979) is a lucid introduction to the topic. Job analysts are without peer in their mastery of verbs to capture nuance in action.

Performance records are produced when people perform specific tasks under relatively standardized conditions and with rather precise, objective scoring measures (e.g., Lau and Russel, 1980; Lord and Hohenfeld, 1979). Records from golf, tennis, and duplicate bridge—given sufficient standardization (e.g., matching and rotating opponents)—as well as records from task performance such as pages typed per hour, merchandise sold in a week, and fish caught per voyage, are all objective measures.

The single most stunning display of performance records is Shapiro's (1978) 265-item story of what actually happened in New York City on one day, June 15, 1977 (e.g., fourteen women were raped, a comedy called

TABLE 5
Behaviors and Alternatives

BEHAVIOR CATEGORY	ALTERNATIVES
Contributes to Salvation Army bucket	Passerby contributes _____; doesn't _____
Drinks at lunch	Coffee _____; tea _____; milk _____; other _____
Uses seat belt	Yes _____; no _____
Uses magazine stand	Browses only _____; browses, then buys _____; buys only _____

SOURCE: Adapted from Brandt, 1972.

Love! Love! Love! opened off Broadway, eleven New Yorkers claimed prizes totaling $18,500 from offices of the State Lottery Division, etc).

Trait indicator checklists consist of observable behavioral indicators that are used to clarify the meaning of rating scales. "A teacher attempting to rate her pupils on visual deficiencies would be assisted by a list of observable indicators such as the following: book held close to face, rubbing eyes, loses place in reading, tilting head, and tense body during visual work" (Brandt, 1972, pp. 117–118). A general trait is broken down into a list of behavioral indicators, and a methodical procedure is then used to look for such behaviors.

Ratings are judgments made about the degree or extent of some human characteristic (e.g., McCord, 1979). Brandt (1972, p. 118) explains:

> A psychological continuum is defined in which the characteristic(s) to be rated is indicated and "a judge is asked to evaluate and allocate samples along this continuum at a sequential array of waypoints."... No assumption should be made of psychological equality of the intervals between these waypoints, but they must be in correct rank order. Although there are several varieties of rating scales, almost all are based on the concept of continuum and are merely different ways of describing the waypoints to the rater.

The literature on ratings is extensive and those observers who choose this as a tactic for explicitness should consult sources such as Carlsmith, Ellsworth, and Aronson (1976, pp. 178–191), McLemore and Bonjean (1977, pp. 400–435), Saal, Downey, and Lahey (1980), and Sommer and Sommer (1980, pp. 135–153).

Visual Records.
Visual social science in the form of still and motion pictures is an obvious means to be explicit about what has been observed.

The use of still photography in social science is best introduced by Wagner (1979). Examples include Ruesch and Kees's (1972) illustrated essay on nonverbal communication, Amerikaner, Schauble, and Ziller's (1980) illustration of the use of photographs in personal counseling, and the related essays by Ziller, Corbin, and Smith (1980) on autobiographical photography and by Michael Lesey (1980) on family photographs, the two earlier essays on rural Wisconsin (1973) and Louisville (1976) by Lesey

(see Gass, 1979, for an analysis of the Wisconsin essay), Grusky and Bonacich's (1980) related effort to build a manual by which to score phenomena such as intimacy and power from family photographs, Becker's (1979) statement of an initial set of threats to validity in photographs (Was it faked? Is it dominated by artistic conventions? Were events adequately sampled? Were some photos censored?), and Clore *et al.*'s (1978) heroic effort to use photographs taken by campers at an interracial camp to determine if cross-race persons were portrayed. The adjective *heroic* is used because, as the authors remark, "placing a $1.29 plastic camera in the hands of 8–12 year old children produced a curious photographic record of the camp. Often it was difficult to tell if the forms appearing in the photograph were human, let alone whether they were black or white" (p. 112).

The use of motion picture photography is illustrated in thoughtful work by Bateson and Mead (1976), Gottdiener (1979), Hass (1970), Heider (1976), Kendon (1979), McDowell (1978), Whyte (1980), and Wolfenstein (1953).

The interest in filming is understandable because motion picture records have several advantages. Michaelis (1955) noted that films have permanency, there is no limit to the size and complexity of the event that can be recorded, their range of time and velocity is greater than the human eye—if actions occur too slowly, the filmmaker can use time-lapse photos (e.g., Lewis, 1951); if events occur too rapidly, the filmmaker can resort to slow motion (e.g., Landis and Hunt, 1937)—films permit time sampling, film emulsions are more sensitive than the eye, and cameras can be concealed. Films also have the advantage that they provide a means whereby independent records can be made to improve validity and provide reliability checks. If two cameras are used to film an event, or if one camera films an event from two angles or with lenses of two different focal lengths, this is the equivalent of two independent observers watching from two different angles (Michaelis, 1955, p. 172).

Film records, however, also have disadvantages, and at times these drawbacks can be sizable. For example, the choice of camera angle is subjective and at the discretion of the filmmaker, film output is not immediately available because of time delays for processing, films and film equipment are expensive, and the analysis of film records is time-consuming and complicated because of the variety of information that is available. Unless a camera is equipped with a zoom lens, the filmmaker is confined to recording only those data that come onto the field of the lens. The filmmaker cannot, without moving the camera, get close-ups of the subject.

Of especial interest is time-lapse filming (Whyte, 1980, pp. 102–111). The technique is illustrated by Carey's (1978) finding, partially inferred from film shot at two frames per second, that civil inattention in the form of mutual gaze aversion on a sidewalk does not occur even though Goffman had predicted it would. The finding is not conclusive because the film was shot on the campus of Indiana University, a setting with low threat, low overload, and norms at least as likely to favor openness as privacy and inattention.

Memo-motion or time-lapse photography, in which the camera operates at speeds such as 1 foot per second instead of the usual 24 feet per second, produces films with a jerky "Keystone cop" quality but films that are invaluable to detect patterns of movement. The principle advantages of time-lapse are, first, that the viewer can get more of an event in mind to make sense of. For example, if an event lasts 180 seconds, when the event finally ends, it is difficult to remember how it started. If, however, the event is filmed with one frame exposed every 10 seconds, then it will take 18 seconds to view the event and all portions of it will be vivid when an attempt is made to interpret it. A second advantage is that the jerky event does not look like normal behavior, so all associations made to normal behavior disappear and the viewer becomes a stranger to the segment being examined. Jerky reproductions break gestalts. Nothing looks right. This means that all viewers examine the scene equally handicapped and equally naive. Other advantages of time-lapse techniques are that they reduce the costs of film (gross details are preserved at about 6 percent of the normal cost of film), they permit time sampling, and they facilitate analysis.

Considering the difficulty of making useful motion pictures and videotapes, it is well to review Hutt and Hutt's (1970) list of five kinds of studies for which such records are particularly suitable (pp. 97–98):

1. Where the action proceeds so swiftly that it is not possible to record all the required elements by any other method (the prey-killing of the cat).

2. Where the action is so complex that attention is focused on certain components at the expense of others (responses of human newborns to sound).

3. Where changes in the behavior are so subtle that satisfactory morphological delineation between one act and another is difficult (gaze behavior).

4. Where sequential changes in fairly complex behaviors are being considered (transition from investigation to play).

5. Where it is required to measure precisely specific parameters of certain brief or complex behavioral events (gait).

METHODICAL WORK

To be methodical is to design and follow an orderly sequence of data collection procedures (Alexander, 1979).

An example of one such sequence is provided by the flowchart (Fig. 1) and accompanying explanation (Table 6) developed by Alevizos and Berck (1974; reprinted in Mash and Terdal, 1976). The alternatives reviewed are thin on ethnography, participant observation, and traditional fieldwork, but they illustrate the form and content of methodical work.

In this section we will examine methodical comparisons, methodical multiples including both multiple methods and multiple-response modes, methodical category systems including category selection, reliability, and validity, and methodical analysis.

METHODICAL COMPARISONS

To be methodical is to design observing so that meaningful public comparisons are possible. Every datum becomes meaningful only as there is a relatum (Boring, 1954). The use of postcard reproductions to examine original art is a good example of this technique and an appropriate metaphor for all efforts to build comparisons. Parmenter (1968, Chap. 14) argued that the best way to understand a painting in a museum is to purchase a postcard reproduction of that same painting and hold it alongside the original to control what you see and look for in the original. For example, you will notice hues, color values, shadows, gestalts, and other features precisely because they are rendered less accurately in the postcard. By comparing the card with the original, you discover parts that were reproduced poorly, and in doing so, you gain an increased appreciation of what actually is going on in the original. Ideal types have served the same purpose for scholars (e.g., Kalberg, 1979). An ideal group is an affirmation, the compulsive, unqualified, and pure application of which reveals its faults when compared with an "original" actual group.

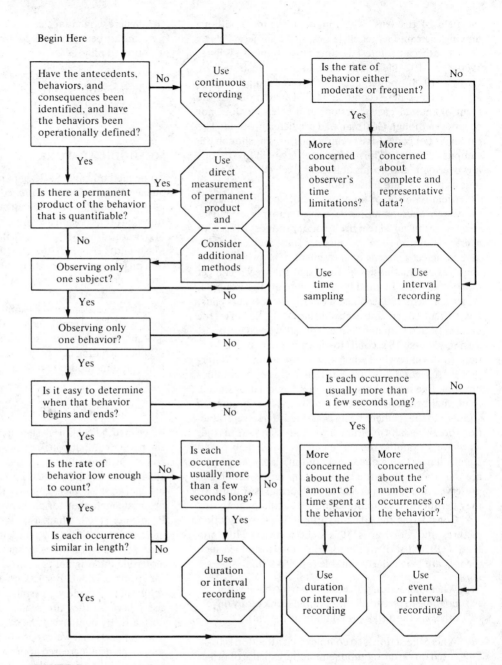

FIGURE 1
Flowchart for Selecting Recording Techniques

SOURCE: Reprinted, by permission, from Alevizos, P. N., and Berck, P. L. Communication: an instructional aid for staff training in behavioral assessment. *Journal of Applied Behavior Analysis. 7,* 1975, 472 and 660.

TABLE 6
Behavior Recording Techniques

METHOD AND DEFINITION	PURPOSE	APPLICATION
Continuous recording (running narrative)		
The observer writes a narrative describing in sequence all behaviors observed. These observations can be organized into a 3-column chart ("ABC" chart) consisting of the events occurring prior to the behavior (Antecedents), the subject's responses (Behaviors) following these antecedents, and the events that follow the behavior (Consequences)	1. Allows further specification of conditions in which the behavior occurs, including cues, verbal prompts, and the possible reinforcers that maintain behavior 2. Provides general information necessary for choosing an efficient recording method (e.g., is frequency, duration, or intensity the critical variable?)	1. Prior to assessment and modification, when unfamiliar with the subject 2. When the behaviors need to be more precisely defined (e.g., when two observers cannot agree on what is an instance of the behavior)
Direct measurement of permanent behavioral product		
A simple observation of a "physical" product of the behavior (e.g., the weight of an obese person, the test scores of an underachieving student, or the number of tokens spent): usually measured at the end of a predetermined time period	1. When available, it can provide a very direct measure of an effect of the behavior 2. Provides a means of measuring behavior which tends not to influence its occurrence or rate 3. Provides a standard of comparison or rough validity check on other measures	1. When other methods may interfere with the behavior under observation 2. When too difficult or too time-consuming to observe behavior directly 3. Since the product is quantifiable, use with another method whenever possible
Event recording		
The observer simply counts each occurrence of the behavior during a predefined time period, often extended over a whole day if the behavior is of low frequency	Gives an accurate record of frequency within a designated time period, thus estimating the rate at which the behavior occurs	1. When behavior is of moderate to low frequency, and occurrences are similar in length 2. Can be used by a trained observer to record more than one behavior or more than one subject when the behavior is very easy to observe [e.g., one can record different subjects engaging in the same simple behavior (such as patients entering the nurses' station), or one can record more than one simple behavior for a single subject (such as a child crying or calling out in class)]

SOURCE: Reprinted, by permission, from Alevizos, P. N., and Berck, P. L. Communication: An instructional aid for staff training in behavioral assessment. *Journal of Applied Behavior Analysis, 7,* 1975, 472 and 660.

continued

TABLE 6
Continued

METHOD AND DEFINITION	PURPOSE	APPLICATION
Duration recording The observer measures the total length of time that the behavior occurs during a predefined observation period	1. Provides a record of how long the behavior occurs within a given time period 2. Can provide a more accurate measure, especially when frequency alone is unrepresentative (see 4th application in adjacent box)	1. Only when behavior has an easily determined beginning and end 2. Ordinarily used with one subject 3. For behaviors with variable durations [e.g., a behavioral deficit of low frequency (poor eye contact)] 4. For a behavioral excess of long duration and moderate to low frequency (e.g., when a child is out of his seat for long periods at a time)
Interval recording The observer divides the observation period (e.g., $\frac{1}{2}$ hour) into a number of equal time intervals, usually ranging from 5 seconds to 1 or 2 minutes. He then notes whether or not the defined behavior(s) occurs in each interval. Interval length should be such that a behavior typically occurs only once in each interval	Gives a rough estimate of the frequency of the responses and the latency between responses	1. By establishing a code for the behaviors, multiple behaviors may be recorded for multiple subjects (e.g., observe 1–5 behaviors for a different subject for each interval. Repeat process after each subject is observed) 2. When event and duration recording do not work 3. For behaviors with highly variable frequencies 4. Behavior need not have easily determined beginning and end
Time sampling Brief observations are made at specified times throughout the subjects' active daily hours. These times can be evenly spaced or randomly selected	1. Very brief, providing staff with additional time for other duties or other observations 2. Provides a schedule for use of other recording methods (e.g., counting the frequency of prompted verbalizations at randomly sampled times throughout the day)	1. For multiple subjects and/or multiple behaviors 2. When behaviors have moderate to high frequency 3. When behavior can be prompted by staff (e.g., delusional speech of patient when questioned)

Glaser (1969) has described the heart of grounded theory as the method of constant comparisons. Williams (1980) has used Plutarch's device of "parallel lives" to suggest properties of leadership. Two figures in similar situations at similar times, one of whom is successful and the other not, are compared to see what might account for their differential success. In Williams's case, he compared three pairs of leaders, Erasmus and Luther, Lavoisier and Lamarck, Robespierre and Washington. Observers who do intensive studies of a single culture (e.g., Geertz and Bateson on Bali) clearly have these comprehended particulars available as comparisons to inform whatever additional topics they examine later.

There are other examples of methodical comparison. A written ethnography is the comparison by which an ethnographic film on the same group can be examined more closely and evaluated (Heider, 1976). The quality of life currently being experienced by a person undergoing rehabilitation for spinal cord injuries can be assessed by using, as a measure of predisease functioning, the observed activity of a healthy person closely matched in age, sex, marital status, location, and occupation (Lawson, Widmer, and Edens, 1979)

Prior experience, if consolidated and articulated, can serve as a comparison when a person undergoes a change, such as when a former heterosexual becomes gay (Lee, 1979), an orthodox Jew becomes momentarily distanced from his congregation (Heilman, 1980), or a male becomes a female (Garfinkel, 1967). Earlier discussions of strangers, novices, and misfits can be reread as strategies to establish a baseline, after which the meaning and particulars of a second experience can be seen more clearly.

METHODICAL MULTIPLES

Multiple Methods

To be methodical is to use multiple sources of evidence to triangulate a phenomenon and cancel method variance (Jick, 1979; Nay, 1979). The options available to the investigator for combining are limited only by imagination, although the conventional array available involves the assessment of one or more of three response systems, cognitive, motor, and physiological, by one or more of eight methods, interviews, self-reports, ratings by others, self-observation, direct observation by others in controlled or analogue environments, direct observation by others in natural environments, with the number of alternatives being expanded if participants are instructed to role-play rather than to behave as they normally would (Cone and Hawkins, 1977, p. 385). Instructive examples of work with multiple methods include Carey (1978), Krieger (1979), Plant, Kreitman, Miller, and Duffey (1977), Smith (1979), and Snow, Zurcher, and Ekland-Olson (1980).

A portfolio of methods represents an attempt to sidestep Thorngate's (1976) postulate of commensurate complexity. This postulate states that it is impossible for an explanation of social behavior to be simultaneously general, accurate, and simple. The more general a simple theory is, for example, the less accurate it will be in predicting specifics. To visualize this postulate, imagine the face of a clock. At twelve o'clock is inscribed the word *general,* at four o'clock is the word *accurate,* and at eight o'clock is the word *simple.* If an observer tries to secure any two of these virtues (e.g., two o'clock is a combination of generality and accuracy), the third virtue is impossible to achieve.

These trade-offs are inevitable because of the constraint of being "simultaneously" all three and because the visual device of a clock face is two-dimensional and precludes anything but pairs of elements being joined. What triangulation does is relax these constraints. Generality, accuracy, and simplicity are achieved sequentially in triangulation. Furthermore, methods, not just explanations, "specialize" in one of these three faces. In earlier sections (e.g., discussion of disciplined abstraction) it has been argued that the value of systematic observation lies in preservation of detail (accuracy), and that generality and simplicity are of secondary importance, a set of trade-offs that is different for sample surveys where generality dominates, simplicity is sometimes present, and accuracy is usually suspect. Simplicity dominates both accuracy and generality when projective exercises such as telling stories, taking pictures, or other unstructured activities are performed by informants. The specialization of methods means that by a combination of methods a third dimension is added to the clock face (it is covered by a domelike cover), and the *combination* accomplishes generality, accuracy, and simplicity of inquiry.

Multiple-Response Modes

To be methodical is to address the three major response systems—verbal, overt motor, physiological—and to anticipate their unequal representation in any phenomenon (e.g., Johnson and Lubin, 1972; Lang, Melamed, and Hart, 1974; Lang, Rice, and Sternbach, 1972; Schachter, 1980). This unequal representation can be depicted by simple binary coding of presence-absence, which yields eight combinations (YYY, YNN, . . ., etc.), or by notation analogous to Sheldon's somatotypes (Lang, 1977, p. 183). A person who expresses social anxiety verbally, but not motorically or physiologically (7-1-1), is presumed to be quite different from one showing the opposite pattern (1-1-7). In the case of verbally expressed anxiety without sympathetic activation (7-1-1), cognitive-restructuring therapy is predicted to be more effective than biofeedback.

Triple-response mode assessment has become common among those doing behavioral assessment, although the evidence for the independence of the systems remains sparse and difficult to interpret (Cone, 1979). According to Cone and Hawkins (1977, pp. 383–384):

> Comparisons of the three systems have confounded *method* of assessment with behavioral *content*. For example, self-report measures of cognitive activities are frequently compared with direct observation measures of motor or physiological ones, as when a man with an erection reports that he does not feel aroused. Resulting low correlations may be due to content differences, method differences, or both.

The issue of measuring responses in three different systems has several implications for observers. First, the bulk of social psychological theorizing presumes interdependence rather than loose coupling among these three systems. Evidence of independence is treated as measurement error rather than as a stable finding. To counteract this, one should initially treat triangulation that results in "contradictory" findings as an indication that different response systems are being measured. Second, vocal verbal behavior is both cognitive and motoric. This gives vocal behavior flexibility, high requisite variety, and complexity, though it also overdetermines its use as an indicator. Third, observation studies usually do not include assessment of physiological measures, which may be one reason why findings seem to cohere (fewer contradictions are possible). There are examples where the triple-response mode *is* assessed (e.g., Lowe and Mc-Grath, 1971), and these seemingly more complex measurements do retain interpretability. When physiological measures are excluded, findings should be qualified as specific to those systems assessed. Intentional handling of physiological measures is important now that psychology is becoming more actively involved in psychophysiology, neurobiology and behavior, biofeedback, behavioral medicine, and stress. Fourth, methodicalness should address both multimethod inquiry and multiresponse inquiry. Fifth, assessment of multiple-response systems means that observers must be much more resourceful if they wish to remain nonreactive. They must develop less obtrusive physiological measures of responses, such as palmar sweat [see Strahan, Hill, and Mount, (1977), and Strahan, Todd, and Inglis (1974) on the sweat bottle technique], and more novel measures that can be coordinated to social psychological variables such as arous-

al, social facilitation, and reaction time [see the program measuring cerebral blood flow by means of temperatures taken at the bridge of the nose (Dabbs and Choo, 1980) and in the external auditory canal (Dabbs, 1979, 1980)], and observers must develop more portable measures of variables such as human cerebral temperature (Dabbs and Neuman, 1978) or heart rate (Hanson, 1967). Sixth, research teams may work most effectively when composed of people who specialize in different response systems for a common problem. Seventh, interviewing and direct observation are not alternative methods for data collection since each taps a different response system. All studies need both.

METHODICAL CATEGORY SYSTEMS

Category Selection

Eventually, most observations are summarized in categories. Methodical construction and selection of category systems can strengthen interpretations. Methodical categories exhaust the type of behavior that is recorded, derive from theory, are recorded rapidly with little observer strain (the observer records an act and then forgets it), and focus on selected behaviors. Category systems differ in such ways as literal objectivity, psychological specificity, theoretical integration (Wright, 1960, p. 125), exhaustiveness, amount of inference required, scope, discreteness of units, size of unit, frame of reference for observation, and training required of coders.

Since categories are selective, they have sometimes been criticized because they violate the continuity and complexity of behavior. Campbell (1961, p. 346) suggested that it is impossible to decide a priori whether or not this fragmentation is consequential. Much of the debate concerning the values and drawbacks of categories is confused with the issue of when the categories are applied. Categorizing can occur when the behavior takes place or sometime later. If behavior is categorized as it occurs, there are such disadvantages as fewer reliability checks, more time pressure and therefore more errors, omission of descriptive detail, fewer chances to rework the data later, and a more fragmented impression of the event. As prominent as these limitations are, they may be offset by the fact that an observer who watches an event unfold is often in the best position to make accurate judgments about the behavior. Postcategorization seldom benefits from intelligent editing because too little context is preserved for the coder to judge which details are minor. The chief advantage of postcategorization is that a greater variety of categories can be applied in a more leisurely fashion by more coders. Furthermore, postcategorization may itself suggest new categories. Needless to say, postcategorization is only as good as the record on which it is based. Whether precoding is interchangeable with postcategorization depends largely on the variety of cues that are required to label behavior accurately. Postcategorization is often done from typescripts, with the result that facial expressions, postural changes, etc., are not available as cues. If such data would not change the categorization, even if they were known, then the systems are interchangeable.

The most thorough set of criteria available for choosing and constructing categories has been assembled by Herbert and Attridge (1975). They specify thirty-three criteria sorted into three main types. First, there are six identifying criteria to assist in the selection of the correct instrument (e.g., "Situations in which the instrument should not be used should be specified"). Second, there are fifteen validity criteria (e.g., "Instrumental items must be as low in the degree of observer inference required as the complexity of behavior under study will permit"). Third, there are twelve criteria of practicality (e.g., "Recommended data transmission and display techniques for an instrument should be described").

The Herbert and Attridge criteria contain no surprises, and much of what they specify is self-evident [e.g., "The instrument must be accompanied by a statement of purpose"]. The value of these criteria is in their extent (all observers all of the time overlook some of these criteria), their institutionalization of methodicalness in a methodology where improvisation is often equated with preserving natural events unobtrusively, their thorough grounding in actual practice, and their compact presentation (twenty-one pages).

Reliability

Traditionally, much discussion of observational methods has centered on questions of reliability because of the large number of judgmental measures that are used (e.g., Kent and Foster, 1977; Mitchell, 1979; Nay, 1979, pp. 219–251). A general rule of thumb concerning reliability of categories is summarized by Gellert (1955): "The fewer the categories, the more precise their definition, and the less inference required in making classifications, the greater will be the reliability of the data" (p. 194). Questions of reliability, however, are not confined to judgmental techniques. They are also relevant when the observer attempts to gain explicitness through tempered

naturalness. "The greater the direct accessibility of the stimuli to sense receptors, the greater the intersubjective verifiability of the observation. The weaker or the more intangible, indirect, or abstract the stimulus attribute, the more the observations are subject to distortion" (Campbell, 1961, p. 340).

The most common reliability measure in observational studies is observer agreement (different observers at the same time). However, as a predictive measure of the reliability of scores, this agreement is usually meaningless. Reliability is a property of measures, not instruments. "Reliability, in the measurement-theoretic sense, is a property of *measures* obtained through the application of a system, not a property of an instrument, nor of a system, nor of a record, nor of observers, though qualities of each of these constrain the reliability of measures obtained" (Herbert and Attridge, 1975, p. 14). Only when an instrument has been used to collect data, and the data manipulated to produce scores, is it appropriate to talk about reliability.

Interobserver agreement is not irrelevant to observation, however. It is simply not synonymous with reliability. "Coefficients or percentages of observer agreement should be described and discussed for system developers and users as indicators of the clarity of the structure, focus, and procedures of the system, and as measures of observer bias or the ambiguity of observed events" (Herbert and Attridge, 1975, p. 14).

Perhaps the best-documented aspect of interobserver agreement is the finding that observers change their recording when they are aware they're being observed. "Estimates of observer agreement obtained with the awareness of the observer are likely to overestimate true agreement level which would be obtained if the observer were not aware of such calibration" (Johnson and Bolstad, 1973, p. 19).

Interobserver agreement drops when observers are led to believe that accuracy is no longer being assessed or is being assessed by a stranger (Romanczyk *et al.,* 1973). To generate stable levels of observer agreement, researchers should overtly monitor their observers frequently and covertly monitor them at random intervals ("We randomly spot-check your performance, but we'll tell you when the check is being made"). The importance of continuous checking cannot be overestimated.

If we step back and look at reliability in a broader sense, a useful way to organize this thinking is Dunnette's (1966) proposal that four sources of error can occur in observations. The first, inadequate sampling of content, occurs when different observers sample only some elements of a complex behavior and these samples consist of different elements. The error of chance-response tendencies stems from imprecise category definitions or inadequate understanding of the category by the observer. When these sources of imprecision are present, observers often fall back on informal, intuitive definitions that are more variable. Two types of change over time also hinder reliability: subtle changes in the environment from observation period to observation period and changes in the person being observed. The latter source of error is especially tricky. If a person is viewed at two different times, he may behave differently the second time because some real change has occurred in him or simply because he is more accustomed to having an observer watching his actions. In either case the correlations between the two observations will be low.

Given these several sources of error, it is desirable to assess reliability in several ways to ensure that the investigator has a substantial phenomenon in hand. In the ideal observational study four comparisons would be made. Wicker (1975) demonstrates how the appropriate comparisons are made. First, the ratings of two persons observing the same event would be correlated, a measure that would rule out the errors of change in the person and the environment. Next, the ratings of the same observer watching a similar event at two different times would be compared (this would rule out error of content sampling). Then the agreement of two observers observing an event at two different times would be correlated. This measure is vulnerable to all four sources of error and would be expected to yield the lowest reliability of the four comparisons. Finally, the observations of a single observer watching a single event would be compared in a manner similar to odd-even item correlations in a test. This is a check on internal consistency or the extent to which the observer agrees with himself. If the category system is explicit and well defined, this measure of reliability would be expected to yield the highest correlation. Admittedly, it is possible only to approximate this ideal, but if investigators must assign priorities to these four comparisons, they should try hardest to secure satisfactory interobserver agreement of a single event, because unless this is achieved, there is no assurance that any distinct phenomenon is being preserved in the record. Probably the lowest priority would be assigned to the reliability of two observers who record events at two different times. This measure assumes the lowest priority because in many studies real changes are predicted and the investigator may wish to detect these changes as well as have stable measures.

Validity

Validity, formally defined as the agreement between two attempts to measure the same trait through maximally different methods, boils down to a question of credibility. And since credibility is audience-specific, different methods applied in different methodical sequences are needed if results are to be judged valid by different audiences. Validity is seldom discussed in observational work (see Haynes, 1978, Chap. 6, for an important exception) in the belief that to be in the field is to guarantee validity. That's one reason why observers are so concerned about reactivity. Reactivity hits at the very strength of the observational method, since people presumably go into the field to improve validity. If, while in the field, their mere presence deflects phenomena, then they might just as well have stayed in the laboratory where there are fewer distractions.

To deal methodically with validity is to make explicit one's status on those dimensions that are central to the assessment of credibility as defined by different audiences. In the case of an audience of scientists, observers provide evidence that displays their reasoning process including summary statements, supporting and nonsupporting anecdotes, and information on the range of variation in the phenomena observed (Agar, 1980). "An anthropologist is responsible for assessing the plausibility of patterns, especially inferential ones; for doubting his own construction, particularly the more important generalizations; and for being prepared if called upon to support patterns by providing evidence" (Honigman, 1976, p. 248). Validity in the eyes of colleagues is an outcome of tough-minded suspicion about lay reports, extensive checking out, and responsiveness to colleague criticisms.

Credibility in the eyes of informants stems less from explicit logic and suspicion and more from "getting it right," including the sense of necessity, obviousness, and facticity that attaches to informant perspectives. Valid understanding is indicated by skill at interpreting *and* expressing oneself *within* the world of informants.

Validity can be assessed in at least five ways (Diesing, 1972). Having constructed a tentative interpretation, the observer can (1) see if expected things happen, (2) search for negative or unexpected instances, (3) ask people about the interpretations ("Is this what you are doing?"), (4) act according to the interpretation to see how people respond (the member test), and (5) stir things up to see if people respond in expected ways.

Wiseman (1974, pp. 325–326) has summarized rules of thumb she uses to make valid reconstructions of people's views. These guidelines include the following:

1. "Assume, at least at first, that no one is lying."

2. If you must choose between an official's story and an individual's story, assume that the institution is being less honest.

3. "There is nothing that happens or that people tell you about that 'doesn't make any sense.' It is part of their lives. They think it makes sense. It is up to you to make sociological sense of it."

4. "Assume that human beings may not be very smart in the decisions they make, but that they do the very best they can."

5. "There is usually nothing that people tell you or that you will see (if it is within the research topic) that is truly irrelevant to your study. It probably belongs under another code heading, and is either background or foreground."

6. "There is no such thing as absolute truth. No one has the final word."

METHODICAL ANALYSIS

The product of most observation is an organized account of similarities and differences among the episodes that have been recorded, which participants recognize and ratify. While there are numerous ways to do methodical analysis, a common strand among these ways is their resemblance to the activity of concept attainment described by Bruner, Goodnow, and Austin (1956). An actual set of analytic procedures that closely approximates concept attainment is Spradley's (1980) use of domain analysis. We will describe his procedures in some detail because they incorporate steps imposed methodically by most analysts.

The starting point involves semantic relationships, nine of which are listed in Table 7. These nine relationships summarize the majority of ways in which items recorded in field notes can go together in the minds of informants. For example, the relationship of strict inclusion (X is a kind of Y) can be imposed meaningfully between most nouns in field notes (e.g., writing is a kind of

TABLE 7
Semantic Relationships

RELATIONSHIP	FORM	EXAMPLE
1. Strict inclusion	X is a kind of Y	An expert witness (is a kind of) witness
2. Spatial	X is a place in Y	The grand jury room (is a place in) the county courthouse
	X is a part of Y	The jury box (is a part of) the criminal courtroom
3. Cause-effect	X is a result of Y	Serving on the grand jury (is a result of) being selected
4. Rationale	X is a reason for doing Y	A large number of cases (is a reason for) going rapidly
5. Location-for-action	X is a place for doing Y	The grand jury room (is a place for) hearing cases
6. Function	X is used for Y	Witnesses (are used for) bringing evidence
7. Means-end	X is a way to do Y	Taking an oath (is a way to) symbolize the sacredness of jury duty
8. Sequence	X is a step (stage) in Y	Making jail visits (is a stage in) grand jury activities
9. Attribution	X is an attribution (characteristic) of Y	Authority (is an attribute of) the attorney

SOURCE: Spradley, 1980, p. 93.

malingering, fronting out is a kind of protective practice).

Using a specific semantic relationship such as inclusion, the observer scans nouns in the field notes, looking for those that can be grouped. The observer also scans verbs and sorts them into means-ends relationships (X is a way to do Y). The question being asked systematically is, Which words fit with which other words?

This form of analysis is called *domain analysis* and derives its name from the idea that cultural meaning is preserved by categories (domains) that include smaller categories. A domain contains three elements: a *cover term,* which is the name of the domain; *included terms,* which are the names for all the smaller categories included in a domain; and the *semantic relationship,* which links the two categories of cover term and included terms. A domain of terms used by glider pilots illustrates how the elements are assembled (Fig. 2).

The intent of a domain analysis is to identify cultural categories (e.g., X is a kind of space, a part of an object, a result of an act, a reason for doing an activity, a place for doing an event, a use for time, a way to become an actor, a step in achieving goals, and a characteristic of feeling).

An initial overview of field notes should produce from 50 to 200 distinct labeled domains with included terms. These labeled domains represent a superficial understanding that needs to be deepened back at the site. The observer goes back to the field to discover all elements that informants routinely group under selected cover terms (e.g., what are *all* ways to maneuver a glider). This return to the field could conceivably mean a return

MANEUVER		
	Is a kind of	
Take off	Land	Glide
Turn	Skid	Slip
Crab	Spiral	Chandelle
Sideslip	Stall	Basic 8

FIGURE 2
Domain of Terms Used by Glider Pilots
SOURCE: Spradley, 1980, p. 90.

TABLE 8
Paradigm for Kinds of Inmates

CONTRAST SET	DIMENSIONS OF CONTRAST					
	WORKS	DOING TIME	LIVING LOCATION	DIFFICULTY OF TIME	ABILITY TO HUSTLE	TYPE OF HUSTLING*
Drunk	No	Does drunk time	Drunk tank	Dead time = hard time	Limited	1, 2, 3, 7
Lockup	No	Does lockup time	Lockup cells	Usually does hard time	Limited	1, 2, 3, 5, 6, 7, 8, 9, 10
Trusty	Yes	Does trusty time	Trusty tank/ outside	Usually does easy time	Unlimited	All: 1–11
Kickout	No	Is doing short time	N/A†	Is doing easy time	Limited	2, 3, 7, 10, 11
Rabbit	No	Isn't doing time	Outside the jail	N/A	N/A	N/A

SOURCE: Spradley, 1979, p. 178.

*Inmates recognize eleven kinds of hustling that can be carried out in jail to gain needed goods and services. These are (1) conning, (2) peddling, (3) kissing ass, (4) making a run, (5) taking a rake-off, (6) playing cards, (7) bumming, (8) running a game, (9) making a payoff, (10) beating, (11) making a phone call.

†N/A indicates a dimension of contrast is not applicable.

to field notes, but it seems unlikely that *all* relevant instances of a domain would have been recorded since the observer had no idea such a domain existed. Domains are *post hoc* constructions.

Focused observation the second time around is done to produce the raw materials from which the observer then builds a taxonomy. A taxonomy resembles a cultural domain in the sense that it is a set of categories organized on the basis of a single semantic relationship, but it differs in that it shows more of the relationships *inside* a single domain. Close inspection of selected domains typically leads to the discovery of additional included terms. Once one has accumulated a fuller set of included terms, the question becomes, How are those included terms related to one another? Answering this question involves basically looking for similarities to collapse levels ("Are any of these terms similar because they can go together as a single larger stage?") and looking for differences to expand levels.

Having built detailed categories, the observer now shifts from similarities to differences. And the mode of observation now shifts to more structured interviewing of the informants. The basic question now asked is, In what ways are these two things (domains) different? Those differences that are mentioned suggest attributes that are associated with cultural categories. These attributes are basic dimensions in terms of which informants organize their world. This means that each cultural category can then be assigned a specific value on each dimension.

The end product of an analysis of differences is illustrated in Table 8. These data, taken from a study of the Seattle City Jail, describe five kinds of inmates, the descriptions being folk terms. All five labels are included terms in the domain "tramps" and are *similar* in this way. These five groups differ, however, on the six dimensions listed at the top of the table. These dimensions emerged from final intensive interviewing of the type "What is the difference between a 'drunk' and a 'lockup'?"

On the basis of this analysis we now have some idea of what different terms mean and we know a small part of the cognitive map of tramps. A person's cultural knowledge is made up of hundreds of maps such as this.

When these several analyses have been assembled, the observer is then ready to write a final report.

An overview of domain analysis is presented in Fig. 3. "Descriptive observation" is domain identification, "Focused observation" involves discovering all included

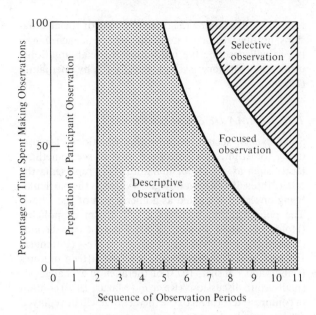

FIGURE 3
The Relationship of Observation Time to the Three Kinds of Observation
SOURCE: Spradley, 1980, p. 108.

terms in selected domains, and "Selective observation" involves discovering dimensions along which important domains can be contrasted. The diagram makes clear that these forms of paraphrasing are blended as well as sequenced.

SOCIAL SITUATIONS

Social situations, consisting of brief, local, and coherent clusters of activities, places, and actors, recapitulate larger, longer social events and provide resources that can themselves become enlarged into these larger events by means of amplifying feedback processes. Bounded social situations comprise the bulk of everyday life. Observers are not misled by the brevity, small scope, and mundane character of social situations, and most category systems are designed to represent one or more of the three elements found in situations.

In the following discussion we will look first at the ways in which social situations serve as representative anecdotes of larger events and also become expanded into larger events by processes of deviation amplification.

Next, we will examine the three elements of social situations, noting category systems that represent each. Finally, we will describe the unfolding of social situations, using the category system developed by Benjamin (1979a).

THE DRAMA OF SMALL EVENTS

Small events, such as momentary collections of actors doing something in a place, are ways to see something larger such as society or mankind. One represents the other. Intensive observation gains value as the particular being observed is treated as a microcosm of the whole. The police station becomes a microcosm of policing (Holdaway, 1980; Punch, 1978). The first five seconds (Schegloff, 1968), the first five minutes (Pittenger, Hockett, and Danehy, 1960), the first fifteen minutes (Labov and Fanshel, 1977) of therapeutic exchanges or small-group discussions (Rosa and Mazur, 1979) contain in compressed form all of the themes that will be replayed for however long those exchanges continue.

The credibility of treating specific situations as representative of larger events is dependent on the homogeneity of the culture within which the situation is embedded. "When one is dealing with primitive groups within a nearly homogeneous culture, in which one set of prescribed roles is just about universally carried out by the population, it may require only the observation and interviewing of relatively few cases to establish the whole pattern" (Barton and Lazarsfeld, 1969, p. 188). Situations may lose their representativeness in cultures that are competitive, conflictful, balkanized (Phillips, 1978), fragmented, cliquish. More specifically, social situations will be representative of those occasions, issues, and times when actors are most homogeneous (e.g., high ambiguity tends to accentuate differences and lower homogeneity; low ambiguity tends to have the opposite effect).

So far, we have been talking about intact situations that simulate larger, longer gatherings. Figuratively, we are looking for the social situation that is the mean, median, or mode of a distribution of situations with low variance. Part of the drama in small events is their capability to recapitulate large events. Part of their drama also lies in their capability to *become* large events. This is the process of deviation amplification.

Assume that the triad of elements composing a social situation is tied together by causal relationships, each of which can be either positive (a change in one element induces a change in the same direction in the related element) or negative (a change in one element induces a change in the opposite direction in the related element):

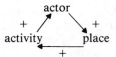

If there are an even number of negative signs in a closed causal loop (zero, two, four, etc.), then the loop is amplifying, and any disturbance of any variable in the loop will persist and grow unchecked. If there are an odd number of negative signs in a closed loop, the loop is self-correcting, and any disturbance will disappear.

Consider the situation of a socially inept actor in a crowd of strangers who stays at the edge of the crowd and seldom converses, thereby becoming more inept. This situation becomes enlarged through deviation amplification:

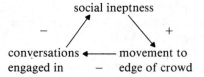

Ineptness leads to more movement toward edges, less conversation, more ineptness (even less to talk about), more edging away, until the person leaves, breaks down in tears, is noticed by all in the gathering, or some other discontinuous change occurs.

To see the counteraction of deviation, imagine this same socially inept person moving to the edge of a crowd but now finding other similarly inept people and striking up a conversation with these similar others:

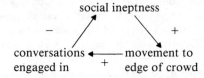

Now as the person moves to the edge, conversation increases, ineptness decreases, there is *less* movement to the edge where similar others congregate, which now *lessens* conversations, which *increases* ineptness, which drives the person back to the edge where *more* conversation occurs, and there is orderly oscillation between more and less conversing, more and less ineptness, more and less edging away from the heart of the action.

Short segments and small incidents that become enlarged have been discussed by several people (Ashton, 1976; Axelrod, 1976; Hoffman, 1971; London, 1977; Maruyama, 1963; Schelling, 1978; Weick, 1979, Chap. 3; Wender, 1968). Self-fulfilling prophecies (Bateson, 1951; Jones, 1977) gain their identity from amplifying causal loops.

The specification of loops and amplification is crucial for several reasons. First, it legitimates intensive study of small N's, not because the situation is representative of other situations but because it can enlarge and determine what happens in other situations. Wallflowers can ruin sociable gatherings. Second, seemingly minor cognitions such as member definition of situation (e.g., Stebbins, 1969) may not remain minor if they are coupled causally to other minor events. Third, social psychologists preoccupied with causal chains (e.g., similarity → attraction) have neglected how those chains can become closed and gain the potential either to enlarge or oscillate. Fourth, beginnings are of vital importance in social situations. In an amplifying loop, whatever the direction of an *initial* deviation (i.e., increase/decrease) for *any* variable, that direction will persist and be magnified. There is nothing in the loop to prevent that occurrence. Reexamine the situation where ineptness breeds ineptness. If in that situation the person had accidentally emitted a skillful response, been plunged into the center of a group, or been paired with someone who carried the conversation, then the other coupled variables would have changed and amplified that localized increase. In that case competence would have bred further competence. The source of either outcome, at least hypothetically, is a small, immediate incident lasting a matter of seconds, after which all else is mere embellishment and justification. Fifth, the amplification of small beginnings means that rarely will it be the case that causes are proportional in size to their effects. Fanaticism, hatred, greed, fury, and rage as intense outcomes may well have had innocuous beginnings that became less innocent through the working of deviation amplification. The likelihood that these small origins can be retrieved, given the disproportions involved, is remote. Futhermore, the importance of retrieval is not obvious since it is the presence of a loop, not the initial random deflection, that is crucial to change.

The main point to be retained about social situations viewed as small events is that intensive study of singular small events is justified if events are pretty much alike in a homogeneous world or if events themselves are embedded in amplifying loops and have the potential to induce amplifying loops in adjacent situations. Furthermore, singular small events can be studied intensively with warrant if they are widely distributed or occur with frequency in the everyday lives of members (Jehenson, 1973).

THE ELEMENTS OF SMALL EVENTS

Activity

Activity, though visible and abundant, is often overlooked by observers. Omission of such information from observational records seriously weakens them.

Whyte's (1955) discovery that bowling performance mirrored group structure in Doc's gang illustrates both the neglect and importance of activity (pp. 318–319):

> Then in April, 1938, one Saturday night I stumbled upon one of my most exciting research experiences in Cornerville. It was the night when the Nortons were to bowl for the prize money. . . . I listened to Doc, Mike, and Danny making their predictions as to the order in which the men would finish. At first, this made no particular impression upon me, as my own unexpressed predictions were exactly along the same lines. . . . I was convinced that Doc, Mike, and Danny were basically correct in their predictions, and yet why should the scores approximate the structure of the gang? Were these top men simply better natural athletes than the rest? That made no sense. . . . I went down to the alleys that night fascinated and just a bit awed by what I was about to witness. Here was the social structure in action right on the bowling alleys. It held the individual members in their places—and I along with them. I did not stop to reason then that, as a close friend of Doc, Danny, and Mike, I held a position close to the top of the gang and therefore should be expected to excel on this great occasion. I simply felt myself buoyed up by the situation. I felt my friends were for me, had confidence in me, wanted me to bowl well. As my turn came and I stepped up to bowl, I felt supremely confident that I was going to hit the pins that I was aiming at. I have never felt quite that way before—or since. Here at the bowling alley, I was experiencing subjectively the impact of the group structure upon the individual.

The point, concerning the observation of activity, is that Whyte recorded the scores of people on their final night of bowling, but he had been bowling with them every Saturday night for months and could have collected those scores too (Whyte, 1955, p. 320):

> I kept no record of these scores because at the time I saw no point to it. . . . I was bowling with the men in order to establish a social position that would enable me to interview them and observe important things. But what were those things? Only after I passed up this statistical gold mine did I suddenly realize that the behavior of the men in the regular bowling-alley sessions was the perfect example of what I should be observing. Instead of bowling in order to observe something else, I should have been bowling in order to understand bowling. I learned then that the day-to-day routine activities of these men constituted the basic data of my study.

The last sentence is the key point. Routine activity is the rule, but it seldom gets recorded and analyzed (Schwartz and Jacobs, 1979, p. 185). Observers say little about work but seem instead to see it as a staging ground for existential crises, extramarital affairs, or power grabs. Bertrand Russell (1930), in a marvelous essay on boredom, makes it clear that great people are great for only very short periods of time and the rest of the time (most of the time) their days are inconsequential. Robert Anderson (1965) has analyzed this theme in his drama, appropriately titled, *The Days Between.*

Activity is not synonymous with trivia, but activity often is neglected because it is continuous and taken for granted. It is ground for fleeting (and inconsequential) figures. It is the dross that observers suffer until something interesting happens. Perhaps the most striking feature of Barker's (e.g. Barker and Schoggen, 1973) research is his documentation of the way in which that which is ubiquitous both constrains *and* provides opportunities. Barker has developed a vocabulary that preserves the mundane and, in doing so, has provided a means for observers to account for more variance.

Willems (1976a) argues that the adaptive, coping function of behavior becomes clear only in free-ranging situations where the advantages of different activities can be seen. Behavior is viewed as the principal means by which the person accommodates to the environment and cognition is viewed as having questionable ties to this process. Willems (1976) puts it this way (pp. 225–226):

> To the ecologist, overt behavior simply is more important than many other psychological phenomena. For the ecologist, it is more important to know how parents *treat* their children than how they feel about being parents; more important to observe whether or not passersby *help* someone in need than what their beliefs are about altruism and kindness; more important to note that a person *harms* someone else when given an opportunity than to know whether his self-concept is that of a considerate person. . . . Behavior, in the sense of *doing* things overtly, is the principal means by which persons make long-range adaptations to the environment and it is the means by which they modify the environment. It is not readily apparent to me how all of the data on how-it-looks, how-it-feels, and what-people-think-they-want will become translated into understanding these problems of long-term environmental adaptation and adjustment.

Activity category systems are not plentiful, but Barker's listing of the varieties of social action is representative (see also Caldwell, 1969).

Barker and Barker (1963) measured the occurrence of forty varieties of social action in the behavior streams of children in 141 American and 141 English behavior settings. Examples of the actions recorded were adult dominates child, child is polite to adult, child plays with child. In each sentence the verb designates the variety of the action, and the subject and object of the sentence give its social context. The forty varieties of social action, listed below, follow the convention that X stands for the actor and Y for the object of the action (complete definitions and examples of each category are found in Barker, 1963, pp. 338–346):

1. X accommodates his behavior to Y.

2. X is affectionate to Y.

3. X is antagonistic to Y.

4. X is baffled by Y.

5. X comforts Y.

6. X competes with Y.

7. X complies with Y.

8. X accepts Y's control.

9. X cooperates with Y.

10. X defends Y.

11. X deprives Y.

12. X devalues Y.

13. X disagrees with Y.

14. X disciplines Y.

15. X is distant from Y.

16. X is distressed by Y.

17. X dominates Y.

18. X enjoys Y.

19. X exploits Y.

20. X asks favor of Y.

21. X forgives Y.

22. X is friendly with Y.

23. X gratifies Y.

24. X hates Y.

25. X helps Y.

26. X hinders Y.

27. X is impatient with Y.

28. X influences Y.

29. X manages Y.

30. X provides opportunity for Y.

31. X plays with Y.

32. X is polite to Y.

33. X punishes Y.

34. X resists Y.

35. X surrenders to Y.

36. X teases Y.

37. X understands Y.

38. X is unfriendly to Y.

39. X values Y.

40. X works with Y.

The social actions can be ordered along dimensions such as harmony-disharmony, social power, reaction to social power, expression of feelings, and benefit-harm.

The harmony-disharmony scale illustrates this use. The scale is ordered consistent with Heider's (1958) notions of interpersonal balance. "On the harmony end of the scale we have placed social actions which promote the closeness and interpersonal stability of the persons involved in an action, and on the disharmony end we have placed actions which increase stress, interpersonal instability and distance between the parties to an action" (Barker and Barker, 1963, p. 138). The social action varieties are listed below from most to least harmonious, with the identification number of each action given in parentheses (Barker and Barker, 1963, pp. 138–139).

1. gratifies (23)

2. affectionate (2)

3. comforts (5)

4. defends (10)

5. friendly (22)

6. enjoys (18)

7. helps (25)

8. values (39)

9. cooperates (9)

10. plays (31)

11. works (40)

12. accepts control (8)

13. accommodates (1)

14. provides opportunity (30)

15. forgives (21)

16. understands (37)

17. polite (32)

18. influences (28)

19. complies (7)

20. asks favor (20)

21. manages (29)

22. exploits (19)

23. baffled (4)

24. surrenders (35)

25. distant (15)

26. competes (6)

27. disagrees (13)

28. deprives (11)

29. hinders (26)

30. devalues (12)

31. distressed (16)

32. dominates (17)

33. resists (34)

34. teases (36)

35. impatient (27)

36. unfriendly (38)

37. disciplines (14)

38. punishes (33)

39. antagonistic (3)

40. hates (24)

Place

Behavior always occurs someplace. As Barker said (Willems, 1977, p. 50):

> The best way to predict the behavior of a human being is to know where he is: In a post office he behaves post office, at church he behaves church. In the conduct of everyday affairs, not only do we depend on location specificity in behavior for predictability and social order, but we often use departures from such correlations to label and diagnose persons as being sick, crazy, deviant, hyperactive, depressed, etc., and in need of help or control.

Neglect and mutilation of the environment during psychological inquiry has unwittingly led psychologists to become more and more impressed by the black box as the determinant of behavior.

Willems (1969) has described the development of this neglect of the environment (p. 32):

> Psychology has fallen into a self-validating roundabout here. Its prevailing methods of research shatter whatever pattern and organization may exist within the natural environment, and the conclusion

is reached on the basis of the resulting evidence that the environment is not a source of the order and organization observed in the behavior. This leads to further study of the mysterious mechanism of the black box that appears to bring order out of chaos; and this is done via ever more theory-determined, and less setting-determined environmental variables.

Preoccupation with cognitions of place has been the result partly of dismantling the place, partly of a preoccupation with the extraordinary to the exclusion of the mundane, partly of watching only one setting such that the amount of variance attributable to different settings could never be noticed or established, and partly of a lack of vocabulary and concepts that preserve place and introduce dynamics into it. Not only does behavior vary among settings, but this effect is more pronounced in normals than in the disturbed (Rausch, Dittman, and Taylor, 1959). It is plausible to argue that responsiveness to setting is selected in an evolutionary sense since location-appropriate behaviors are more crucial for adaptation in various settings.

Category systems designed specifically to represent general aspects of place are not common and usually are developed *ad hoc* to portray idiosyncracies of interest to the investigator. Perhaps the best example of careful attention to place is the work by Korte, Ypma, and Toppen (1975) to find adjacent locations in Holland where environmental input load varied so that its effects on helpfulness could be assessed. Other relevant work with place is found in Love (1973), Moos (1976), Reed (1974), Schoggen and Schoggen (1980), Stephens and Willems (1979); Stokols (1980), and Wicker (1981). The most sustained program of research on place is the work of Barker and his associates involving behavior settings. A behavior setting is "a bounded. self-regulated and ordered system composed of replaceable human and nonhuman components that interact in a synchronized fashion to carry out an ordered sequence of events called the setting program" (Wicker, 1979, p. 12). Barker and Schoggen's (1973, pp. 9–11) discussion of restaurants as behavior settings illustrates features listed in Wicker's definition that are common to all other behavior settings.

An introductory set of exercises and procedures to locate and describe behavior settings is found in Wicker (1979, pp. 19–25, 204–216). More technical discussions of ways to identify behavior settings are found in Barker and Wright (1955, pp. 50–83, 488–495) and Barker (1968, pp. 35–46). Listings of behavior settings, from which categories of place can be extracted, are found in Barker and Schoggen's comparison of the communities of Yoredale and Midwest (1973, pp. 448–540)—this listing is of genotypes that group highly similiar settings—Barker and Gump's comparison of behavior settings in Midwest and Capital City high schools (1964, pp. 205–218), and Barker and Wright's catalogue of community behavior settings in Midwest between 1951 and 1952 (1955, pp. 154–176).

Actor

Perhaps the best current example of assessment of sociable actors by means of systematic observation are the extensions of the Bales (1970) interaction process analysis (Bales and Cohen, 1979; Bales and Isenberg, 1980).

The extension to inferences about personality is guided by a taxonomy of twenty-six types embedded in the three-dimensional space illustrated in Fig. 4. The three dimensions are dominant versus submissive (up, down), friendly versus unfriendly (right, left), and instrumentally controlled versus emotionally expressive (forward, backward).

During interaction the acts initiated and received by specific individuals may be coded in the traditional manner, using a modified set of the IPA categories listed in Fig. 5 [categories 1, 2, 6, 7, 12 are altered slightly from the original 1950 version; see pp. 471–491 in Bales (1970) for the rationale behind the revision], or may be directly coded into the twenty-six combinations of the three-dimensional space (Bales and Cohen, 1979, pp. 161–238).

Once the frequency of acts initiated and acts received for each of the twelve IPA categories is recorded, they are converted into percentages and compared with the data in Tables 9 and 10, which coordinate interaction

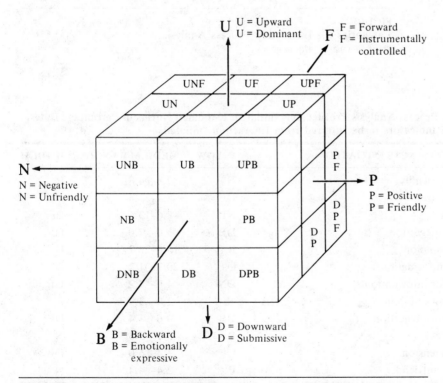

FIGURE 4
The SYMLOG Three-Dimensional Space
SOURCE: Bales and Cohen, 1979, p. 23.

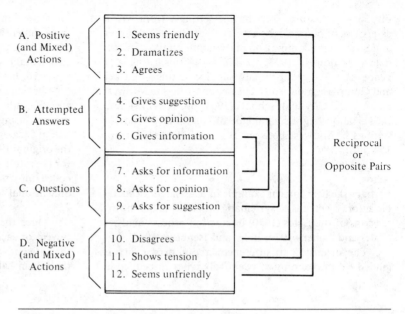

FIGURE 5
Categories for Interaction Process Analysis
SOURCE: Bales, 1970, p. 92.

TABLE 9
Interaction Process Analysis Profile: Acts Initiated, Estimated Norms in Percentage Rates.
Directional Indicators to be Inferred from Interaction Initiated

CATEGORY OF ACTS INITIATED	IF LOW	MEDIUM RANGE*	IF HIGH
1. Seems friendly	N	2.6– 4.8	P
2. Dramatizes	DF	5.4– 7.4	UB
3. Agrees	NB	8.0–13.6	PF
4. Gives suggestion	DB	3.0– 7.0	UF
5. Gives opinion	B	15.0–22.7	F
6. Gives information	U	20.7–31.2	D
7. Asks for information	DN	4.0– 7.2	UP
8. Asks for opinion	N	2.0– 3.9	P
9. Asks for suggestion	UB	0.6– 1.4	DF
10. Disagrees	P	3.1– 5.3	N
11. Shows tension	UF	3.4– 6.0	DB
12. Seems unfriendly	P	2.4– 4.4	N

SOURCE: Bales, 1970, p. 96.

NOTE: *Rates lower than the medium range shown are classed low; rates higher than the medium range shown are classed high.

TABLE 10
Interaction Process Analysis Profile: Acts Received, Estimated Norms in Percentage Rates.
Directional Indicators to be Inferred from Interaction Received

CATEGORY OF ACTS RECEIVED	IF LOW	MEDIUM RANGE*	IF HIGH
1. Seems friendly	N	2.6– 4.8	P
2. Dramatizes	NF	7.5–12.2	PB
3. Agrees	B	12.7–19.4	F
4. Gives suggestion	DN	2.9– 5.2	UP
5. Gives opinion	NB	15.0–22.7	PF
6. Gives information	N	15.0–22.8	P
7. Asks for information	UF	4.0– 7.2	DB
8. Asks for opinion	UP	1.4– 2.8	DN
9. Asks for suggestion	B	0.5– 1.2	F
10. Disagrees	DPB	3.6– 6.3	UNF
11. Shows tension	DPF	4.4– 7.5	UNB
12. Seems unfriendly	DPB	2.4– 4.4	UNF

SOURCE: Bales, 1970, p. 97.

NOTE: *Rates lower than the medium range shown are classed low; rates higher than the medium range shown are classed high.

behavior with the tendencies displayed in the three-dimensional space.

The specific rate observed is compared with the range of rates in the appropriate table. If the observed rate falls within the medium range (e.g., the rate for category 1 is between 2.6 and 4.8), then *no* diagnostic inference is made. If the rate is higher than the medium range, then the appropriate directional indicator is recorded (e.g., P); and if the rate is lower, the appropriate indicator for that range is indicated (e.g., N). A final tally is made of how many times each dimension is mentioned (e.g., DB counts two times, as a D and as a B). The two profiles are merged, and a final summary assessment is determined by following the steps summarized in Fig. 6.

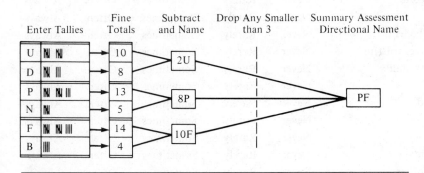

FIGURE 6
Scoring Procedure for Interpersonal Ratings
SOURCE: Bales, 1970, p. 9.

The characteristics associated with each of the twenty-six types comprise a substantial portion of Bales's 1970 book (pp. 189–386) and are rewritten in the 1979 book with more emphasis on nonverbal behavior associated with each direction as well as elaboration of content images used by and evaluations preferred by peo-

ple associated with each direction (Bales and Cohen, 1979, pp. 355–386).

Observers who wish to observe interaction in the field have several options. They can do traditional IPA recording, but now they can also debrief observation by using either a list of 123 variables coordinated with 26 in-

TABLE 11
The SYMLOG Adjective-Rating Form

Your Name_____Group_____

Name of person described_____Circle the best choice for each item

		(0)	(1)	(2)	(3)	(4)
U	Active, dominant, talks a lot	Never	Rarely	Sometimes	Often	Always
UP	Extroverted, outgoing, positive	Never	Rarely	Sometimes	Often	Always
UPF	A purposeful democratic task leader	Never	Rarely	Sometimes	Often	Always
UF	An assertive businesslike manager	Never	Rarely	Sometimes	Often	Always
UNF	Authoritarian, controlling, disapproving	Never	Rarely	Sometimes	Often	Always
UN	Domineering, tough-minded, powerful	Never	Rarely	Sometimes	Often	Always
UNB	Provocative, egocentric, shows off	Never	Rarely	Sometimes	Often	Always
UB	Jokes around, expressive, dramatic	Never	Rarely	Sometimes	Often	Always
UPB	Entertaining, sociable, smiling, warm	Never	Rarely	Sometimes	Often	Always
P	Friendly, equalitarian	Never	Rarely	Sometimes	Often	Always
PF	Works cooperatively with others	Never	Rarely	Sometimes	Often	Always
F	Analytical, task-oriented, problem-solving	Never	Rarely	Sometimes	Often	Always
NF	Legalistic, has to be right	Never	Rarely	Sometimes	Often	Always
N	Unfriendly, negativistic	Never	Rarely	Sometimes	Often	Always
NB	Irritable, cynical, won't cooperate	Never	Rarely	Sometimes	Often	Always
B	Shows feelings and emotions	Never	Rarely	Sometimes	Often	Always
PB	Affectionate, likeable, fun to be with	Never	Rarely	Sometimes	Often	Always
DP	Looks up to others, appreciative, trustful	Never	Rarely	Sometimes	Often	Always
DPF	Gentle, willing to accept responsibility	Never	Rarely	Sometimes	Often	Always
DF	Obedient, works submissively	Never	Rarely	Sometimes	Often	Always
DNF	Self-punishing, works too hard	Never	Rarely	Sometimes	Often	Always
DN	Depressed, sad, resentful	Never	Rarely	Sometimes	Often	Always
DNB	Alienated, quits, withdraws	Never	Rarely	Sometimes	Often	Always
DB	Afraid to try, doubts own ability	Never	Rarely	Sometimes	Often	Always
DPB	Quietly happy just to be with others	Never	Rarely	Sometimes	Often	Always
D	Passive, introverted, says little	Never	Rarely	Sometimes	Often	Always

SOURCE: Bales and Cohen, 1979, p. 393.

dicators [e.g., acceptance of authority, optimistic idealism, spontaneity, sophistication; these are reproduced on pp. 389–457 in Bales (1970)] or the adjective-rating form (Bales and Cohen, 1979, p. 393) that is reproduced in Table 11.

The list of 123 variables in Bales's 1970 book may be the single richest source of hypotheses about actor behavior available to social psychologists. One can enter the list of variables either with 1 of the 26 directions or with a tentative personality assessment, and converge on expected interaction behavior.

The adjective rating form is a refinement of Bales's classroom exercise used in 1970 to introduce the three-dimensional typology (pp. 5–8). Development and validation of the form are reported in the 1979 book (pp. 241–299). The attractiveness of this form is that it is unobtrusive; it is a powerful jog to memory when recalling group incidents and individual behaviors; it can be completed by members as well as observers; it is coordinated with the extended theory that underlies this program; it is not time consuming; it requires modest training; it has high requisite variety due to the inclusion of multiple adjectives for each rating; it has higher reliability than the IPA interaction scoring; and it provides tangible useable feedback so that observers can give something back to the people they watch (scores can be converted into graphic patterns showing coalitions and polarization within the group).

THE UNFOLDING OF SMALL EVENTS

Social situations are hypothesized to unfold in predictable sequences and some category systems are sensitive to this possibility. An especially powerful example of a system that is theoretically grounded, nuanced, detailed, and predictive of process is Lorna Smith Benjamin's (1979a, 1979b; McLemore and Benjamin, 1979) extension of Leary's (1957) dimensionalization of social behavior along the axis of love-hate, dominance-submission. Benjamin has retained love-hate as the horizontal axis but has altered the vertical axis to portray maximum independence–maximum interdependence [these dimensions correspond most closely to UD and PN in Bales (1970)]. The advantage of this alteration is that behaviors categorized somewhere in the independence region are not saturated with control, either in the sense of dominance (controlling the other) or submission (being controlled by the other). The system also departs from Leary in that it contains three planes: (1) other (behavior of an-

other person focusing on self, akin to parent), (2) self (responses of self to other; akin to child), and (3) introject (the effect when the self turns the behaviors of other inward onto the self).

The system is portrayed in Fig. 7, which will be used to illustrate features of the system.

The notation in all subsequent examples contains three numerals. The first numeral (range 1–3) indicates which plane is being discussed (1 = other, 2 = self, 3 = introject). The second numeral (range 1–4) indicates which quadrant is being discussed (1 = blends of independence-love, 2 = blends of independence-hate, 3 = blends of interdependence-hate, 4 = blends of interdependence-love). The third numeral (range 0–8) specifies content and topic with 0 = primitive basic, (which defines the poles of categories), 1 = approach-avoidance, 2 = need-fulfillment, 3 = attachment, 4 = logic communications, 5 = attention to self-development, 6 = balance in relationship, 7 = intimacy-distance, 8 = identity).

Consider some examples:

136: put down, act superior.

This is an act by other (1) that blends interdependence and hate (3) and deals with balancing a relationship (6).

242: accept, caretaking.

This is a response by self to some act of other that blends interdependence and love and that is about need-fulfillment.

333: vengeful, self-punish.

This is an introjection and turning against oneself of an action by other, and the result is a mixture of hate and interdependence that is about the topic of attachment.

Four principles guide predictions made from this system.

1. *Opposites:* Opposite behaviors are found at angles of 180 degrees and are located by tracing a diagonal line from any charted point to the point with the *same last digit* in the opposite quadrant. The opposite quadrant for 1 is 3 (and vice versa). The opposite quadrant for 2 is 4 (and vice versa). Thus the opposite of 115 (friendly, listen) is 135 (accuse, blame), of 114 (shows empathic understanding) is 134 (delude, divert, mislead). Opposites are crucial for breaking sequences of behavior, as

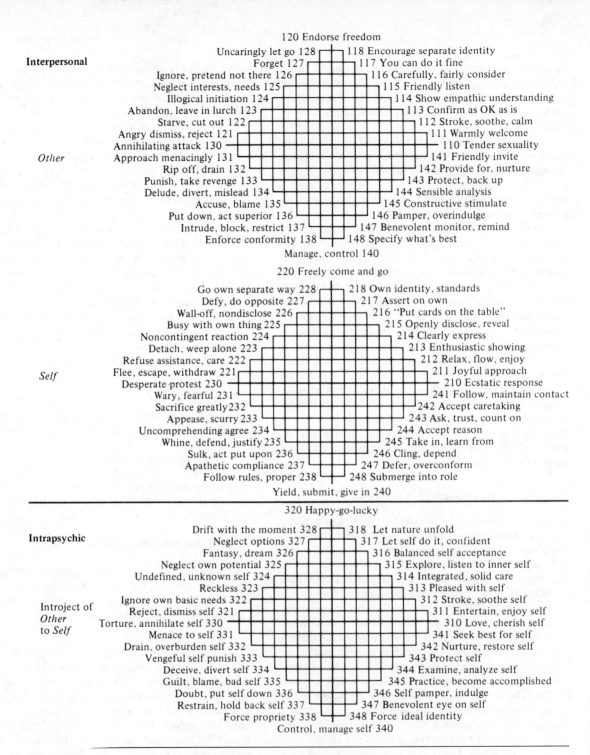

FIGURE 7
Categories for Structural Analysis of Social Behavior (SASB)
SOURCE: Benjamin, 1979a, p. 6.

will become clear in the subsequent discussion of antitheses.

2. *Complements:* Complements specify which behaviors tend to draw each other. Complements are located by identifying the same position on the self and other surfaces. Thus the complement of 146 (pamper, overindulge) is 246 (cling, depend). Pampering tends to elicit clinging, is the prediction thus generated.

3. *Antitheses:* An antithesis is the specification of a behavior whose enactment tends to draw out the opposite of what is at hand. An antithesis is the opposite of a complement. If other is misleading (134), this tends to draw the complement, which is uncomprehending agreement (234). This tendency of other to mislead often can be broken only if *self* produces the opposite behavior of clear expression (214), which in turn should force other to demonstrate empathic understanding (114). Notice that the principle of antithesis also suggests how one could change something that has been internalized by the self. If the person produces feelings of guilt (335), presumably this was the result of significant others blaming (135), which produced whining, defending, and justifying (235), which was eventually internalized in the form of guilt (335). If a therapist or other concerned person wishes to modify the guilt, then the antithetical opposite action (315) must be located on the introject plane and the complement located on the other plane (115) and initiated. These maneuvers predict that with more friendly listening (115) there should be a shift on the part of self away from whining and blame toward open disclosure (215), which then in turn is internalized as exploration of self (315). The predictions could be wrong, but they do generate a hypothetical sequence against which actual interaction behavior can be compared.

4. *Introject:* The third surface, labeled "introject," specifies how interpersonal experiences affect one's own treatment of self. Possible introjects are located by tracing a complement through all three surfaces. For example, when other neglects my needs and interests (125), I cope with that person by becoming absorbed in my own thing (225), the net result of which is that I wind up neglecting my own potential (325), which presumably requires the presence of others to be fully realized. Notice that in terms of content this sequence concerns the issue of self-development (track 5) and predicts that neglect by other stunts self-development. To reverse this continuing neglect of my own potential, I either need to locate a significant other who emits the opposite behavior to 125 (145, constructive, stimulate) or I need to start doing the opposite of my own thing (225), which is taking in and

learning (245). Taking in should put pressure on my current significant other to move from neglect (125) to stimulation (145).

The uses of the model are several. First, the categories can be used to debrief, formalize, and order episodes of observation. The 108 distinctions have been phrased into questionnaires (Benjamin, 1979a, pp. 20–23) that could either be given to participants or answered by the observer on behalf of the participants.

Second, the categories suggest the consequences of specific interventions such as might be attempted in field experiments. For example, if actors are observed to do what looks like reactance (227, do opposite) then interventions consisting of 147 (benevolent monitor) should decrease reactance, interventions consisting of 127 should intensify it, and interventions of 117 and 137 should decrease it slightly due to their irrelevance, unless doing the opposite is under the control of a periodic reinforcement, in which case the behavior should be maintained.

Third, the system can be entered at *any* position and a full array of hypotheses generated about what sequences should occur and what actions should produce change.

Fourth, the categories can capture phenomena such as double binds and paradoxical injunctions (1979a, p. 15–16).

Fifth, the system *does* take time to learn, although the symmetries involved in the system, the questionnaire items, and the content tracks aid comprehension and classification. Benjamin recommends that transactions be classified by first specifying the surface (self, other), second the affective tone (friendly, quadrants 1 and 4, unfriendly, quadrants 2 and 3), and third the degree of interdependence (power, quadrants 3 and 4; autonomy, quadrants 1 and 2). Once the appropriate section is located, then the observers can look for which of nine topics was discussed. These steps are diagrammed in Fig. 8.

Sixth, the observer need not invoke the fine grain of the 108 distinctions to use the system for classification and prediction. It is possible to use only the four quadrants. For example, if I exercise hostile power over students (quadrant 3, other), this provokes hostile compliance (quandrant 3, self), which students internalize as oppression of self (quadrant 3, introject). This sequence can be broken either when they start to enjoy and accept themselves or enact friendly autonomy or when I encourage their friendly autonomy or model this behavior myself. The nine specific behaviors in each quadrant are

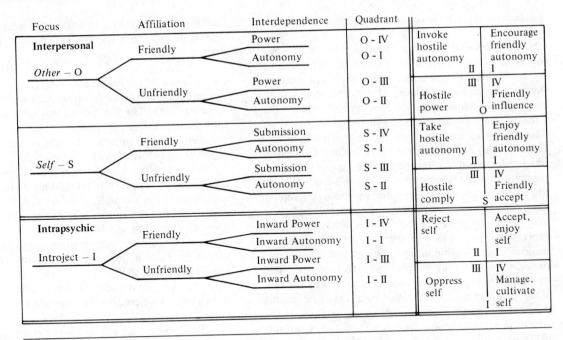

Focus	Affiliation	Interdependence	Quadrant		
Interpersonal	Friendly	Power	O - IV	Invoke hostile autonomy	Encourage friendly autonomy
		Autonomy	O - I		
Other – O	Unfriendly	Power	O - III		II I
		Autonomy	O - II	III	IV
				Hostile power	Friendly influence
					O
	Friendly	Submission	S - IV	Take hostile autonomy	Enjoy friendly autonomy
		Autonomy	S - I		
Self – S	Unfriendly	Submission	S - III		II I
		Autonomy	S - II	III	IV
				Hostile comply	Friendly accept
					S
Intrapsychic	Friendly	Inward Power	I - IV	Reject self	Accept, enjoy self
		Inward Autonomy	I - I		
Introject – I	Unfriendly	Inward Power	I - III		II I
		Inward Autonomy	I - II	III	IV
				Oppress self	Manage, cultivate self
					I

FIGURE 8
Flowchart for Choosing SASB Categories
SOURCE: Benjamin, 1979a, p. 13.

organized such that they grade away from a midpoint and become more pure examples of the pole toward which they are grading. For example, 115 (friendly, listen) is a midpoint blend of friendliness and autonomy. Lower numbers such as 114, 113, and 112 become progressively warmer, while higher numbers such as 116, 117, and 118 become progressively more reflective of autonomy. Systematic reductions of the full system of 108 categories in the interest of manageability could involve use of quadrants only (4 quadrants × 3 surfaces = 12 categories, with category content being the midpoint of each quadrant, 115, 125, 135,..., 315, 325, etc.). Reductions could also include pairs of mild extremity (e.g., 113, 116; 213, 216) or considerable extremity (e.g., 117, 112) within each quadrant, which would generate 24 categories (2 items × 4 quadrants × 3 surfaces). Observers might also use only odd- or even-numbered items (odd have more intensity for love-hate themes; even have more intensity for power themes), which reduces the number of categories to 54. The point is, observers can use gross features of the SASB system to encode rapid natural in-

teractions and retain the orderliness and prediction built into the system.

Seventh, the system can be applied to protocols, text, tape recordings, and video records.

Eighth, it can be used to triangulate findings since a questionnaire version exists to supplement the categories.

The SASB system is valuable for the refined distinctions it incorporates, refinements that improve requisite variety. But the system is also valuable because it generates sequences that can be used as a relatum to be compared with any observed sequence so that more can be seen in that observation.

CONTEXT

Each element in a social situation constrains the expression of and gives meaning to every other element in that situation. Each element thus is both context and element, underlying meaning and document, ground and figure (e.g., Smith-Lovin, 1979). Particulars do not have fixed meanings. The configuration of place and actor and activity is the underlying pattern from which the meaning of an element derives. "Even so innocuous a query as 'What time is it?' may be understood as constituting more than a request for information. As a consequence, one may find that the time is unobtainable from a whole population of opposite sex persons at certain public places" (Schwartz and Jacobs, 1979, p. 51).

Context can be described as a nuanced social situation and can be portrayed graphically by differentiating one of the three components of a social situation. A playground may seem to be a singular place until it is observed that different portions of the place are used for different activities by different people. Different locations within the place are linked by their physical proximity, but activities that occur within each place mean something different (Fig. 9). The activity of teenage smoking means something different if done on the embankment (guilt over engaging in forbidden activity), playground bench (mild flaunting of authority), swings (strong flaunting of authority), or sidewalk (a casual accompaniment of some other activity).

Social situations can be linked and differentiated because the same people are actors in different situations (Fig. 10). Spradley (1980, pp. 43–44) cites the example of a religious movement called "The Jesus People" who share a variety of settings.

Finally, similar activities can be differentiated on the basis of the different locations in which they take place (Fig. 11).

In each of these three examples the element in the center of the diagram potentially means something different when it is associated with different contexts created by the remaining two elements located at the periphery of the diagram. The central element is the document or specific detail that is referred to the other two elements on the periphery for meaning. The periphery is the relatum in terms of which the central element becomes a datum. The portrayal of context as the differentiation of situational elements suggests the informal observational rule that to identify context, the observer must hold at least one element constant and inspect, systematically, variations in the other elements. To discover contexts for double binding, the observer records actors and places present when double binds do and do not occur.

The content of context can be articulated and differentiated by using categories developed by anthropologists to describe social life and culture, higher-order

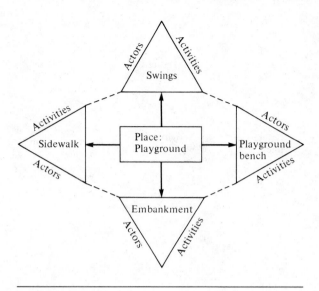

FIGURE 9
A Differentiation of Place
SOURCE: Spradley, 1980, p. 43.

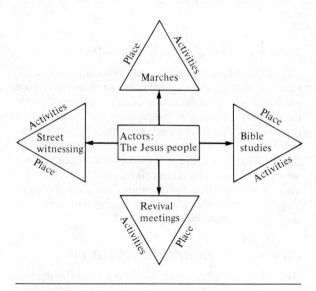

FIGURE 10
A Differentiation of Actors
SOURCE: Spradley, 1980, p. 44.

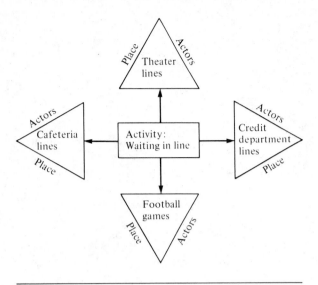

FIGURE 11
A Differentiation of Activities
SOURCE: Spradley, 1980, p. 44.

themes that transcend particulars, and locations such as edges where the components of context are unusually visible.

CONTEXT AS CULTURAL CATEGORIES

Cavan's (1974) eight-month study of hippie rural social structure in Northern California included, as part of the methodology, systematic use of contextual categories culled from the anthropological literature. Cavan would review each day's notes by using the checklist, assign specific episodes recorded to topics on the checklist, and use the checklist as a reminder of details that occurred but were not recorded. The categories she used are an invaluable reminder of the detail of context and a sharp prod to sluggish memories and lazy note taking. For these reasons they are reproduced in Table 12.

CONTEXT AS HIGHER-ORDER THEMES

Any taxonomy of universal themes is a potential starting point to examine the content of context. Combinations of place, actor, and activity usually converge on a small number of themes. To impose a universal theme is to pro-

vide a first abstraction in terms of which scattered detail can be organized. The coordinates in the Benjamin system—love/hate, independence/interdependence—are an example of universal themes in terms of which situations can be ordered.

A different set of six themes has been proposed by Spradley (1980, pp. 152–153). I paraphrase them here:

1. *Social conflict:* Cultural meanings are often organized around groups (e.g., police) with whom one is in frequent conflict. Ethnocentrism and intergroup relations are sites for conflict. As observers locate more perspectives on a specific issue, they should find more of these perspectives in conflict. Any evidence of risk taking is a potential symptom of conflict, since risk often means detection by or embarrassment in the eyes of some other group.

2. *Cultural contradictions:* Social psychologists interested in cognitive consistency have made a living watching how people manage inconsistency among assertions, beliefs, and ideas. Most social situations contain outcroppings of contradictions, and these can provide a starting point for inquiry. Spradley (1980, p. 152) says:

> One cultural contradiction that occurs in many cultural scenes has to do with the official "image" people seek to project of themselves, and the "insiders view" of what really goes on. Cultural contradictions are often resolved by *mediating themes.* Every ethnographer is well advised to search for inherent contradictions that people have learned to live with and then ask, "How can they live with them?"

3. *Informal techniques of social control:* Informal techniques by which people such as waitresses control what other people do are commonly played out in social situations. Ingratiation is an example familiar to social psychologists.

4. *Managing impersonal relationships:* People have developed strategies to deal with people they don't know, especially in urban settings, and an anchor for observing naturalistic settings is to look for just such devices.

5. *Acquiring and maintaining status:* In most settings there are symbols, often subtle, toward which one strives and, having attained them, strives to maintain. Appearing more cool, more religiously devoted, less agitated, more visible, more silent, more vocal than anyone else may comprise the bulk of what is being observed.

6. *Solving problems:* Given the pervasiveness of the problem-solving metaphor as well as the probability that

TABLE 12
Topic Categories from *Notes and Queries in Anthropology*

Life cycle
Death
Conception
Contraception
Pregnancy
Abortion
(Puberty)
Birth
Naming
Suckling and feeding
Tending
Weaning

Marriage (stable sexual
 union)
Betrothal
Marriage prohibitions
Marriage injunctions
Dowries
Rituals and ceremonies
 of marriage
Marital status
Offspring
Adultery ("affairs")
Dissolution of marriage

Household habits
Food
Sleep
Elimination

Personal hygiene
Clothing
(Cleaning)

Everyday round
Division of social labor
Language
Method of ordering,
 organizing

Method of counting,
 reckoning
Method of assessing,
 evaluating
Method of accounting,
 explaining

**Everyday etiquette
(practices)**
Signification of age
Signification of
 relationships
Signification of
 personages
Salutations
Leave taking

Forms of address
Introductions
Forms of request
Rules of hospitality;
 taboos
Standards of decency and
 propriety

Instructions to children
Food and bodily habits
Danger
Taboos
Customs

Rituals
Beliefs
Fears

**Social debts and
obligations**
Favors
Loans
Gifts

Illness and disease
Diagnosis
Treatment
Preventive Practices

Leisure forms
Pastimes
Decorative Art
Architectural Art
Music

Games and amusements
Sociable talk
Ceremonies and
 occasions
Jokes and laughter

Material culture
Styles of dress, ornamen-
 tation, grooming
Kind of dwelling unit
Cultivation, hunting,
 fishing, gathering,
 preserving

Manufacture,
 construction
Livestock, pets

Travel and transportation
Paths and roads
Halting places
Mode of travel

Politics
Type of collectivity
Method of governance
Figurehead, chieftain,
 leader

Councils and officials
Military and defense
Warfare

Economics
Sources of income
Method of production
Division of economic
 labor

Organization of work
Method of distribution
Method of exchange

Property
Concepts of ownership
Ritual of sacred objects

Property rights
Property obligations

The Supernatural
Fate of the dead
Spirits
Destiny
Prophets

Divine personages
Sacred places
Shrines
Sacred objects

SOURCE: Cavan, 1974, pp. 334–335.

people *are* trying to solve problems almost as often as we say they are, one can ask of any situation, "What problem is this knowledge and practice designed to solve?"

Other sources of themes that inform particulars include the literature on world views (Kearney, 1975), Wiseman's (1974) suggestion that notes can be analyzed in terms of careers, cycles, social types, social actions, and settings, and Davis's (1974) suggestion that notes can be analyzed as if written by Wirth, Hughes, Malinowski, or Simmel.

CONTEXT AT EDGES

Some of the best clues to context occur at edges, areas where one situation grades into another. Edges can occur at points of transition (Miller and Friesen, 1980), during turn taking in conversation (Beattie, 1980), at geographical edges such as fishing holes cut in ice or lines between gang territories in neighborhoods, at locations where the ecology suddenly changes, etc. An edge can be a halfway house, a portal to a mine (Vaught and Smith, 1980, pp. 164–165), a mixed bar catering to a homosexual and heterosexual clientele, which is described in guidebooks as AYOR ("at your own risk") (Lee, 1979), a children's play area in a hospital where the issue, "If you're sick enough to be in a hospital, you're too sick to play" arises (Hall, 1977).

The key property of edges is variety. Areas of transition between ecological communities, areas biologists call ectones, show just such variety. According to Raphael (1976, p. 5):

> Many of the most interesting things, say the biologists, happen on the Edges — on the interface between the woods and the fields, the land and the sea. There, living organisms encounter dynamic conditions that give rise to untold variety. Scientific studies of bird populations reveal that "forest edge" species are generally more abundant than those which confine their territory to the interior of the forest. The intertidal zone, meanwhile, that thin ribbon which separates the land from the sea, supports a plurality of life uniquely adapted to both air and water. When the tide is high, the flora and fauna of the beaches and tide pools may provide nourishment for fish; when the tide is low, land-bound mammals such as raccoons will claim the zone as their own by feasting on the intertidal creatures. . . . As a rule, the ectone contains more species and often a denser population than either of the neighboring communities, and this generality is known as the *principle of edges*. The greater variety of plants in the ectone provides more cover and food, and thus a greater number of animals can be supported.

Edges are diagnostic of contexts in the following ways. An edge is a built-in relation or comparison by which an adjacent "pure" context can be seen more clearly. A pond is seen more clearly to be a setting free of cattails because its edge is full of them. A factory is seen to be a noisy, distracting environment because of the large number of heavy doors needed to separate the reception area from machinery (the edge is wider and thicker to prevent one context from contaminating another one). Edges, since they contain portions of more than one context, reveal the elements that are available for assembly into a context. Edges are reductionist and show the larger pool from which a smaller selection has been made.

CONCLUSION

One way to operationalize the guidelines presented in this chapter is to list some observational studies that best illustrate their application. For both inspiration and information a reader cannot do better than Bennett (1980), Bernard and Killworth (1973), Bosk (1979), Dawe (1934), Geertz (1972), Homans (1950), Lofland (1975), Lowe and McGrath (1971), McNeil (1980), Melbin (1978), Millman (1977), Roberts, Golder, and Chick (1980), Rubinstein (1973), Van Maanen (1980), and Zurcher (1977).

A second way to operationalize the guidelines is to specify exemplary treatments of observational methodology. Again, the reader cannot do better than Barzun and Graff (1977), Becker (1958), Bogdan and Taylor (1975), Diesing (1971), Irwin and Bushnell (1980), Jarvie (1967), Manning (in press), Schwartz and Jacobs (1979), Spradley (1979, 1980), Truzzi (1974), Van Maanen (1979), and Willems and Rausch (1969).

A third way to operationalize the guidelines is in terms of an admonishment. The current reexamination of psychological inquiry shows an occasional, if ambivalent, tilt in the direction of naturalistic observation, (e.g., Koch, 1965). If social psychologists move toward naturalistic observation, they will have to be careful lest they commit again the same arrogant act they committed in the laboratory when they presumed to know what their subjects were thinking. The arrogance occurs in three steps.

1. The observer treats the observer's version of a participant's life *as* that person's real life.

2. The participant's version of that same life is treated as the subjective view of what "actually" happened.

3. The observer accommodates these two versions by explaining the processes that caused the participant to experience the life (version 2) other than the way it *actually* happened (version 1).

Perpetuation of these distortions will get us no closer to accounts that matter and say something.

Observational methods are no more forgiving of researcher arrogance than other methods if people forget they are not ends. As Emerson put it, "the necessity of nomenclature, of minute physiological research, of the retort, the scalpel, and the scales is incontestable. But there is no danger of its being underestimated. We only wish to insist on their being considered as means" (Robinson, 1980, p. 87).

REFERENCES

Adams, R. N., and J. J. Preiss, Eds. (1960). *Human organization research: field relations and techniques*. Homewood, Ill.: Dorsey.

Agar, M. (1980). Getting better quality stuff: methodological competition in an interdisciplinary niche. *Urban life, 9,*(1), 34–50.

Alevizos, P. N., and P. L. Berck, (1974). *An instructional aid for staff training in behavioral assessment*. Unpublished manuscript. Camarillo Neuropsychiatric Institute Research Program.

Alexander, J. L. (1979). Selecting the best behavioral measures of health status. In E. P. Willems (Chair), *Issues in monitoring health related behaviors*. Symposium presented at the meeting of the American Psychological Association. New York, September.

Allport, G. W. (1961). *Pattern and growth in personality*. New York: Holt, Rinehart, and Winston.

Amerikaner, M., P. Schauble, and R. Ziller (1980). Images: the use of photographs in personal counseling. *Personnel Guid. J.,* 68–73.

Anderson, N. (1965). Averaging versus adding as a stimulus—combination rule in impression formation. *J. exp. Psychol., 70,* 394–400.

Anderson, R. (1965). *The days between*. New York: Random House.

Armstrong, J. S. (1980). Advocacy as a scientific strategy: the Mitroff myth. *Acad. management Rev., 5,* 509–511.

Ashton, R. H. (1976). Deviation-amplifying feedback and unintended consequences of management accounting systems. *Account., Organizat. Soc., 1,* 289–300.

Axelrod, R., Ed. (1976). *Structure of decision: the cognitive maps of political elites*. Princeton, N.J.: Princeton Univ. Press.

Bales, R. F. (1970). *Personality and interpersonal behavior*. New York: Holt, Rinehart, and Winston.

Bales, R. F., and S. P. Cohen (1979). *SYMLOG: a system for multiple level observation of groups*. New York: Free Press.

Bales, R. F., and D. J. Isenberg. *SYMLOG and leadership theory*. Paper presented at the Sixth Biennial Leadership Symposium, Carbondale, Ill.

Bandura, A. (1977). *Social learning theory*. Englewood Cliffs, N.J.: Prentice-Hall.

Barker, R. G., Ed. (1963). *The stream of behavior*. New York: Appleton-Century-Crofts.

———— (1964). Observation of behavior: ecological approaches. *J. Mt. Sinai Hosp., 31,* 268–284.

———— (1968). *Ecological psychology: concepts and methods for studying the environment of human behavior*. Stanford: Stanford Univ. Press.

Barker, R. G., and L. S. Barker (1963). Social actions in the behavior streams of American and English children. In R. G. Barker (Ed.), *The stream of behavior*. New York: Appleton-Century-Crofts. Pp. 127–159.

Barker, R. G., and P. V. Gump (1964). *Big school, small school: high school size and student behavior*. Stanford: Stanford Univ. Press.

Barker, R. G., and P. Schoggen (1973). *Qualities of community life*. San Francisco: Jossey-Bass.

Barker, R. G., and H. F. Wright (1955). *Midwest and its children*. Evanston, Ill.: Row, Peterson.

Barker, R. G., H. F. Wright, L. S. Barker, and M. Schoggen (1961). *Specimen records of American and English children*. Lawrence: Univ. of Kansas Publications, Social Science Studies.

Barker, R. G., H. F. Wright, N. F. Schoggen, and L. S. Barker (1978). Day in the life of Mary Ennis. In R. Barker, *Habitats, environments, and human behavior*. San Francisco: Jossey-Bass. Pp. 51–98.

Baron, R. M. (1980). Social knowing from an ecological event perspective: a consideration of the relative domains of power from cognitive and perceptual modes of knowing. In J. Harvey (Ed.), *Cognition, social behavior and the environment*. Hillsdale, N.J.: Erlbaum.

Barton, A. H., and P. H. Lazarsfeld (1969). Some functions of qualitative analysis in social research. In G. J. McCall and

J. L. Simmons (Eds.), *Issues in participant observation.* Reading, Mass.: Addison-Wesley. Pp. 163–196.

Barzun, J., and H. F. Graff (1977). *The modern researcher* (3rd ed.). New York: Harcourt, Brace, Jovanovich.

Bateson, G. (1951). Conventions of communications: where validity depends on belief. In J. Reusch and G. Bateson (Eds.), *Communication, the social matrix of society.* New York: Norton. Pp. 212–227.

――― (1958). *Naven: a survey of the problems suggested by a composite picture of the culture of a New Guinea tribe drawn from three points of view* (2nd ed.). Stanford: Stanford Univ. Press.

Bateson, G., and M. Mead (1976). For God's Sake, Margaret. *Coevolution Quart.,* Summer, 32–44.

Baum, C. G., R. Forehand, and L. E. Zegiob (1979). A review of observer reactivity in adult-child interactions. *J. Behav. Assess., 1,*(2), 167–177.

Beattie, G. W. (1980). The skilled art of conversational interaction: verbal and nonverbal signals in its regulation and management. In W. T. Singleton, P. Spurgeon, and R. B. Stammers (Eds.), *The analysis of social skill.* New York: Plenum. Pp. 193–211.

Becker, H. S. (1958). Problems of inference and proof in participant observation. *Amer. Sociol. Rev., 23,* 652–659.

――― (1979). Do photographs tell the truth? In T. D. Cook and C. S. Reichardt (Eds.), *Qualitative and quantitative methods in evaluation research.* Beverly Hills, Calif.: Sage. Pp. 99–117.

Beebe, M. (1980). *Daft and Wiginton on language and organization.* Unpublished manuscript. University of British Columbia.

Bellack, A. S., and M. Herson (1977). Self-report inventories in behavioral assessment. In J. D. Cone and R. P. Hawkins (Eds.), *Behavioral assessment: new directions in clinical psychology.* New York: Brunner Mazel. Pp. 52–76.

Benjamin, L. S. (1979a). Structural analysis of differentiation failure. *Psychiatry, 42,* 1–23.

――― (1979b). Use of structural analysis of social behavior (SASB) and Markov chains to study dyadic interactions. *J. abnorm. psychol., 88,* 303–319.

Bennett, H. S. (1980). *On becoming a rock musician.* Amherst: Univ. of Massachusetts Press.

Bernard, H. R., and P. D. Killworth (1973). On the social structure of an ocean-going research vessel and other important things. *Soc. Sci. Res., 2,* 145–184.

Bernstein, S. (1972). Getting it done: notes on student fritters. *Urban life culture, 1,* 275–292.

Berry, W. (1975). *Sayings and doings.* Lexington, Ky.: Gnomon Press.

Bigus, O. E. (1972). The milkman and his customers: a cultivated relationship. *Urban Life Culture, 1,* 131–165.

Bittner, E. (1973). Objectivity and realism in sociology. In G. Psathas (Ed.), *Phenomenological sociology.* New York: Wiley. Pp. 109–125.

Bogdan, R. (1972). *Participant observation in organizational settings.* Syracuse, N.Y.: Syracuse Univ. Press.

Bogdan, R., and M. Ksander (1980). Policy data as a social process: a qualitative approach to quantitative data. *Hum. organization, 39,* 302–309.

Bogdan, R., and S. J. Taylor (1975). *Introduction to qualitative research methods: a phenomenological approach to the social sciences.* New York: Wiley.

Boring, E. G. (1954). The nature and history of experimental control. *Amer. J. Psychol., 67,* 573–589.

Bosk, C. L. (1979). *Forgive and remember: managing medical failure.* Chicago: Univ. of Chicago.

Bouchard, T. J. (1976). Unobtrusive measures: an inventory of findings. *Sociol. meth. Res., 4,* 267–300.

Brandt, R. M. (1972). *Studying behavior in natural settings.* New York: Holt, Rinehart, and Winston.

Brooks, C., and R. P. Warren (1972). *Modern rhetoric* (3rd ed.). New York: Harcourt, Brace, Jovanovich.

Brown, H. W. (1892). Some records of the thoughts and reasonings of children. *The pedagogical seminary, 2,* 358–396.

Brown, R. H. (1977). *A poetic for sociology.* Cambridge: Cambridge Univ. Press.

Bruner, J. S., J. J. Goodnow, and G. A. Austin (1956). *A study of thinking.* New York: Wiley.

Bryant, C. D. (1979). The zoological connection: animal-related human behavior. *Social Forces, 58,* 399–421.

Buckley, W. (1968). Society as a complex adaptive system. In W. Buckley (Ed.), *Modern systems research for the behavioral scientist.* Chicago: Aldine. Pp. 490–513.

Buff, S. A. (1977). Problems in the study of the stigmatized majority. Review of Blue collar aristocrats by E. E. LeMasters. *Urban Life, 6,* 97–105.

Butler, S. R., and W. E. Snizek (1976). The waitress-diner relationship: a multi-method approach to the study of subordinate influence. *Sociol. Work Occupations 3,* 209–222.

Byrne, D. (1961). Anxiety and the experimental arousal of affiliation need. *J. abnorm. soc. Psychol., 63,* 660–662.

Caldwell, B. M. (1969). A new "approach" to behavioral ecology. In J. P. Hill (Ed.), *Minnesota symposium on child psychology.* Vol. 2. Minneapolis: Univ. of Minnesota Press. Pp. 74–109.

Campbell, D. T. (1961). The mutual methodological relevance of anthropology and psychology. In F. L. K. Hsu (Ed.), *Psychological anthropology.* Homewood, Ill.: Dorsey. Pp. 333–352.

――― (1975). Degrees of freedom and the case study. *Comparative Polit. Stud., 8,* 178–193.

――― (1979). A tribal model of the social system vehicle carrying scientific knowledge. *Knowledge: creation, diffusion, utilization, 1,* 181–201.

Carey, M. S. (1978). Does civil inattention exist in pedestrian passing? *J. Pers. soc. Psychol., 36,* 1185–1193.

Carlsmith, J. M., P. C. Ellsworth, and E. Aronson (1976). *Methods of research in social psychology.* Reading, Mass.: Addison-Wesley.

Carroll, L. (1977). Humanitarian reform and biracial sexual assault in a maximum security prison. *Urban Life, 5,* 417–437.

Carter, L. H. (1979). *Reason in law.* Boston: Little, Brown.

Cavan, S. (1974). Seeing social structure in a rural setting. *Urban Life Culture, 3,* 329–346.

Charmaz, K. C. (1975). The coroner's strategies for announcing death. *Urban Life, 4,* 296–316.

Clark, R. E., and L. J. Halford (1978). Going... going... gone: some preliminary observations on "deals" at auctions. *Urban Life, 7,* 285–307.

Clore, G. L., R. M. Bray, S. M. Itkin, and P. Murphy (1978). Interracial attitudes and behavior at a summer camp. *J. Pers. soc. Psychol., 36,* 107–116.

Colson, E., G. M. Foster, T. Scudder, and R. V. Kemper (1976). Long-term field research in social anthropology. *Current Anthropology, 17,* 494–496.

Conant, R. C., and R. W. Ashby (1970). Every good regulator of a system must be a model of that system. *Int. J. Systems Sci., 1,*(2), 89–97.

Cone, J. D. (1979). Confounded comparisons in triple response mode assessment research. *Behav. Assessment, 1,* 85–95.

Cone, J. D., R. P. Hawkins, Eds. (1977a). *Behavioral assessment: new directions in clinical psychology.* New York: Brunner Mazel.

————— (1977b). Current status and future directions in behavior assessment. In J. D. Cone and R. P. Hawkins (Eds.), *Behavioral assessment: new directions in clinical psychology.* New York: Brunner Mazel. Pp. 381–392.

Corsaro, W. A. (1980). *Something old and something new: the importance of prior ethnography in the collection and analysis of audiovisual data.* Unpublished manuscript. Available from the Dept. of Sociology, Indiana University, Bloomington.

Crowley, L. R. (1976). *Development and assessment of an alternative to the narrative observation.* Unpublished Master of Arts thesis. University of Houston.

Dabbs, J. M., Jr., (1979). *Core temperature, chronometric processes, and social arousal: a preliminary proposal.* Unpublished manuscript. Available from the Dept. of Psychology, Georgia State University, Atlanta.

————— (1980). Left-right differences in cerebral flow and cognition. *Psychophysiology, 17,* 548–551.

Dabbs, J. M., Jr. and G. Choo, (1980). Left-right carotid blood flow predicts specialized mental ability. *Neuropsychologia, 18,* 711–713.

Dabbs, J. M., Jr., M. S. Evans, C. H. Hopper, and J. A. Purvis (1980). Self-monitors in conversation: what do they monitor? *J. Pers. soc. Psychol., 39,* 278–284.

Dabbs, J. M., Jr., and M. R. Newman (1978). Telemetry of human cerebral temperature. *Psychophysiology, 15,* 599–603.

Daft, R. L., and J. C. Wiginton (1979). Language and organization. *Acad. management Rev., 4,* 179–191.

Dalton, M. (1959). *Men who manage.* New York: Wiley.

Darrough, W. D. (1978). When versions collide: police and the dialectics of accountability. *Urban Life, 7,* 379–403.

Davis, F. (1974). Stories and sociology. *Urban Life Culture, 3,* 310–316.

Davis, M. S. (1971). That's interesting: towards a phenomenology of sociology and a sociology of phenomenology. *Philosophy soc. Sci., 1,* 309–344.

Dawe, H. C. (1934). An analysis of two hundred quarrels of preschool children. *Child Development, 5,* 139–157.

Dean, J. P., and W. F. Whyte (1969). How do you know if the informant is telling the truth? In G. J. McCall and J. L. Simmons (Eds.), *Issues in participant observation.* Reading, Mass.: Addison-Wesley. Pp. 61–141.

Deaux, K., L. White, and E. Farris (1975). Skill versus luck: field and laboratory studies of male and female preferences. *J. Pers. soc. Psychol., 32,* 629–636.

Deegan, M. J., and L. E. Nutt (1975). The hospital volunteer: lay person in a bureaucratic setting. *Sociol. Work Occupations, 2,* 338–353.

Denzin, N. K., and C. M. Keller (1981). Frame analysis reconsidered. *Contemporary Sociol., 10,* 52–60.

DeWaele, J. P., and R. Harre (1979). Autobiography as a psychological method. In G. P. Ginsburg (Ed.), *Emerging strategies in social psychological research.* New York: Wiley. Pp. 177–209.

Diesing, P. (1971). *Patterns of discovery in the social sciences.* Chicago: Aldine.

————— (1972). Subjectivity and objectivity in the social sciences. *Philosophy soc. Sci., 2,* 147–165.

Ditton, J. (1977). Learning to "fiddle" customers: an essay on the organized production of part-time theft. *Sociol. Work Occupations, 4,* 427–450.

Dolby, R. G. A. (1979). Reflections on deviant science. *Sociological rev. Monogr., 27,* 9–47.

Dougherty, T. W. (1977). *Development and evaluation of a self-recording diary for measuring job behavior.* Unpublished Master of Arts thesis, University of Houston.

Douglas, J. D. (1976). *Investigative social research.* Beverly Hills, Calif: Sage.

Douglas, J. D., P. K. Rasmussen, and C. A. Flanagan (1977). *The nude beach.* Beverly Hills, Calif.: Sage.

Dunnette, M. D. (1966). *Personnel selection and placement.* Belmont, Calif.: Wadsworth Publishing.

Eckberg, D. L., and L. Hill, Jr. (1979). The paradigm concept and sociology: a critical review. *Amer. Sociological Rev., 44,* 925–937.

Ellis, D. G., L. C. Hawes, and R. K. Avery (1979). *Some pragmatics of talking on talk radio.* Unpublished manuscript. Available from D. G. Ellis, Dept. of Communication, Purdue University, West Lafayette, Ind.

Elster, J. (1979). *Ulysses and the sirens: studies in rationality and irrationality.* Cambridge: Cambridge Univ. Press.

Emerson, J. P. (1970). Nothing unusual is happening. In T. Shibutani (Ed.), *Human nature and collective behavior.* Englewood Cliffs, N.J.: Prentice-Hall. Pp. 208–222.

Eno, B., and P. Schmidt (1978). *Oblique strategies.* Privately published.

Epstein, S. (1980). The stability of behavior: implications for psychological research. *Amer. Psychol., 35,* 790–806.

Erickson, F. (1979). Mere ethnography: some problems in its use in educational practice. *Anthropology Educ. Quart., 10,*(3), 182–188.

Ettlie, J. E. (1977). Validation of an unobtrusive measure of technological utilization. *Psychol. Reports, 40,* 123–128.

Farina, A., D. Arenberg, and S. Guskin (1957). A scale for measuring minimal social behavior. *J. consult. Psychol., 21,* 265–268.

Feigelman, W. (1974). Peeping: the pattern of voyeurism among construction workers. *Urban Life Culture, 3,* 35–49.

Festinger, L., S. Schachter, and K. Back (1950). *Social pressures in informal groups: a study of a housing project*. New York: Harper.

Folkins, C. H. (1970). Temporal factors and the cognitive mediators of stress reaction. *J. Pers. soc. Psychol., 14,* 173–184.

Fox, R. C. (1959). *Experiment perilous*. Philadelphia: Univ. of Pennsylvania Press.

Fried, M. L., and V. J. DeFazio (1974). Territoriality and boundary conflicts in the subway. *Psychiatry, 37,* 47–59.

Fromkin, H. L., and S. Streufert (1976). Laboratory experimentation. In M. D. Dunnette (Ed.), *Handbook of industrial and organizational psychology*. Chicago: Rand McNally. Pp. 415–465.

Garfinkel, H. (1967). *Studies of ethnomethodology*. Englewood Cliffs, N.J.: Prentice-Hall.

Gass, W. H. (1979). Wisconsin death trip. In W. H. Gass, *The world within the word*. Boston: Nonpareil Books. Pp. 39–44.

Geertz, C. (1972). Deep play: notes on the Balinese cockfight. *Daedalus, 101,*(1), 1–37.

Gellert, E. (1955). Systematic observation: a method in child study. *Harvard Educ. Rev., 25,* 179–195.

Gephart, R. P., Jr. (1979). *Doing statistical analysis: essential vagueness and taken-for-granted assumptions in the rules of quantitative social science*. Working paper 79–12 Unpublished manuscript. Available from Business Administration and Commerce, University of Alberta, Edmonton, Alberta T6G 2G1.

Gergen, K. J. (1979). *Social psychology and the phoenix of unreality*. Paper presented at the meeting of the American Psychological Association. New York.

Gladwin, T. (1970). *East is a big bird*. Cambridge, Mass.: Harvard Univ. Press.

Glaser, B. G. (1969). The constant comparative method of qualitative analysis. In G. J. McCall and J. L. Simmons (Eds.), *Issues in participant observation*. Reading, Mass.: Addison-Wesley. Pp. 216–228.

Glaser, B. G., and A. L. Strauss (1971). *Status passage: a formal theory*. Chicago: Aldine.

Glassman, R. B. (1973). Persistence and loose coupling in living systems. *Behav. Sci., 18,* 83–98.

Glavis, L. R., Jr. (1946). Bombing mission number fifteen. *J. abnorm. soc. Psychol., 41,* 189–198.

Gmelch, G. (1971). Baseball magic. *Trans-Action, 54,* 39–41.

Goffman, E. (1974). *Frame analysis*. New York: Harper & Row.

——— (1981). A reply to Denzin and Keller. *Contemporary Sociol., 10,* 60–68.

Golden, M. P., Ed. (1976). *The research experience*. Itasca, Ill.: F. E. Peacock.

Gonos, G. (1976). Go-go dancing: a comparative frame analysis. *Urban Life, 5,* 189–220.

Gordon, D. F. (1974). The Jesus people: an identity synthesis. *Urban Life Culture, 3,* 159–178.

Gorman, B. (1979). Seven days, five countries: the making of a group. *Urban Life, 7,* 469–491.

Gottdiener, M. (1979). Field research and video tape. *Sociological Inquiry, 49,*(4), 59–65.

Gross, A. E., and A. N. Doob (1976). Status of frustrator as an inhibitor of horn-honking responses: how we did it. In M.

P. Golden (Ed.), *The research experience*. Itasca, Ill.: F. E. Peacock. Pp. 487–494.

Grusky, O., and P. Bonacich (1980). *Manual for coding family photographs*. Unpublished manuscript. Available from Oscar Grusky, UCLA Sociology Dept.

Guba, E. (1980). *The evaluator as instrument*. Unpublished manuscript. Indiana University.

Gubrium, J. F., and D. R. Buckholdt (1979). Production of hard data in human service institutions. *Pacific Sociol. Rev., 22,* 115–136.

Haas, J. (1977). Learning real feelings: a study of high steel ironworkers' reactions to fear and danger. *Sociol. Work Occupations, 4,* 147–170.

Hall, D. J. (1977). Problems of innovation in a hospital setting: the example of playleaders. *Sociol. Work Occupations, 4,* 63–86.

Hanson, D. L. (1967). Cardiac response to participation in little league baseball competition as determined by telemetry. *Res. Quart., 38,* 384–388.

Harrison, M. L. (1974). Preparations for life in the spirit: the process of initial commitment to a religious movement. *Urban Life Culture, 2,* 387–474.

Hass, H. (1970). *The human animal*. New York: Putnam.

Hatch, E. (1979). *Biography of a small town*. New York: Columbia Univ. Press.

Hayano, D. M. (1980). Communicative competency among poker players. *J. Communication, 30,* 113–120.

Haynes, S. N. (1978). *Principles of behavioral assessment*. New York: Halstead Press.

Haynes, S. N., and C. C. Wilson (1979). *Behavioral assessment: recent advances in methods, concepts, and applications*. San Francisco: Jossey-Bass.

Heider, F. (1958). *The psychology of interpersonal relations*. New York: Wiley.

——— (1959). Thing and medium. *Psychol. Issues, 1,*(3), 1–34.

Heider, K. G. (1976). *Ethnographic film*. Austin: Univ. of Texas Press.

Heilman, S. C. (1980). Jewish sociologist: native-as-stranger. *Amer. Sociol., 15,* 100–108.

Henshel, R. L. (1980). The purposes of laboratory experimentation and the virtues of deliberate artificiality. *J. exp. Soc. Psychol., 16,* 466–478.

Herbert, J., and C. Attridge (1975). A guide for developers and users of observation systems and manuals. *Amer. educ. Res. J., 12,*(1), 1–20.

Heyns, R. W., and R. Lippitt (1954). Systematic observational techniques. In G. Lindzey (Ed.), *Handbook of social psychology*. Vol. 1. Reading, Mass.: Addison-Wesley. Pp. 370–404.

Hirschman, A. O. (1979). The search for paradigms as a hindrance to understanding. In P. Rabinow and W. M. Sullivan (Eds.), *Interpretive social science: a reader*. Berkeley: Univ. of California Press. Pp. 163–179.

Hoffman, L. (1971). Deviation-amplifying processes in natural groups. In J. Haley (Ed.), *Changing families: a family therapy reader*. New York: Grune and Stratton. Pp. 285–311.

Holdaway, S. (1980). The police station. *Urban Life, 9,* 79–100.

Homans, G. C. (1950). *The human group*. New York: Harcourt, Brace.

Honigman, J. J. (1976). The personal approach in cultural anthropological research. *Current Anthropology, 17,*(2), 243–261.

Hsu, F. L. K. (1979). The cultural problem of the cultural anthropologist. *Amer. Anthropologist, 81,* 517–532.

Hughes, E. C. (1960). Introduction: the place of field work in social science. In B. H. Junker, *Field work: an introduction to the social sciences.* Chicago: Univ. of Chicago Press. Pp. v–xv.

Hugo, R. (1979). *The triggering town: lectures and essays on poetry and writing.* New York: Norton.

Humphreys, L. (1970). *Tearoom trade.* Chicago: Aldine.

Hutt, S. J., and C. Hutt (1970). *Direct observation and measurement of behavior.* Springfield, Ill.: Charles C. Thomas.

Irwin, D. M., and M. M. Bushnell (1980). *Observational strategies for child study.* New York: Holt, Rinehart, and Winston.

Jacobs, J. B. (1974). Participant observation in prison. *Urban Life Culture, 3,* 221–240.

Jarvie, I. C. (1967). On theories of fieldwork and the scientific character of social anthropology. *Philosophy Sci., 34,* 223–242.

Jehenson, R. (1973). A phenomenological approach to the study of the formal organization. In G. Psathas (Ed.), *Phenomenological sociology: issues and applications.* New York: Wiley. Pp. 219–247.

Jick, T. D. (1979). Mixing qualitative and quantitative methods: triangulation in action. *Admin. Sci. Quart., 24,* 602–611.

Johnson, J. M. (1975). *Doing field research.* New York: Free Press.

———— (1977). Behind the rational appearances: fusion of thinking and feeling in sociological research. In J. D. Douglas, and J. M. Johnson (Eds.), *Existential sociology.* Cambridge: Cambridge Univ. Press. Pp. 201–228.

Johnson, L. C., and A. Lubin (1972). On planning psychophysiological experiments: design, measurement, and analysis. In N. S. Greenfield and R. A. Sternback (Eds.), *Handbook of psychophysiology.* New York: Holt, Rinehart, and Winston. Pp. 125–158.

Johnson, S. M., and O. D. Bolstad (1973). Methodological issues in naturalistic observation: some problems and solutions for field research. In L. A. Hamerlynck, L. C. Handy and E. J. Mash (Eds.), *Behavior change: methodology, concepts, and practice.* Champaign, Ill.: Research Press. Pp. 7–67.

———— (1975). Reactivity to home observation: a comparison of audio recorded behavior with observers present or absent. *J. appl. Behav. Analy., 8,* 181–185.

Johnson, S. M., A. Christensen, and G. T. Bellamy (1976). Evaluation of family intervention through unobtrusive audio recordings: experiences in "bugging" children. *J. appl. Behav. Analy., 9,* 213–219.

Jones, E. E., and R. E. Nisbett (1971). *The actor and the observer: divergent perceptions of the causes of behavior.* Morristown, N.J.: General Learning Press.

Jones, R. A. (1977). *Self-fulfilling prophecies.* Hillsdale, N.J.: Erlbaum.

Junker, B. H. (1960). *Field work: an introduction to the social sciences.* Chicago: Univ. of Chicago Press.

Kalberg, S. (1979). Max Weber's types of rationality: cornerstones for the analysis of rationalization processes in history. *Amer. J. Sociol., 85,* 1145–1179.

Kazdin, A. E. (1979). Unobtrusive measures in behavioral assessment. *J. appl. Behav. Analy., 12,* 713–724.

Kearney, M. (1975). World view theory and study. In B. J. Siegel (Ed.), *Annual review of anthropology.* Vol. 4. Palo Alto, Calif.: Annual Reviews. Pp. 247–270.

Kelley, H. H., and A. J. Stahelski (1970). Social interaction basis of cooperators and competitors' beliefs about others. *J. Pers. soc. Psychol., 16,* 66–91.

Kendon, A. (1979). Some theoretical and methodological aspects of the use of film in the study of social interaction. In G. P. Ginsburg (Ed.), *Emerging strategies in social psychological research.* New York: Wiley. Pp. 67–91.

Kent, R. N., and S. L. Foster (1977). Direct observational procedures: methodological issues in naturalistic settings. In A. R. Ciminero, K. S. Calhoun, and H. E. Adams (Eds.), *Handbook of behavioral assessment.* New York: Wiley. Pp. 279–328.

Kerbo, H. R., K. Marshall, and R. Holley (1978). Reestablishing "gemeinschaft"? an examination of the CB radio fad. *Urban Life, 7,* 334–358.

Koch, S. (1965). The allures of ameaning in modern psychology. In R. E. Farson (Ed.), *Science and human affairs.* Palo Alto, Calif.: Science and behavior books. Pp. 55–82.

Korte, C., I. Ypma, and A. Toppen (1975). Helpfulness in Dutch society as a function of urbanization and environmental input level. *J. Pers. soc. Psychol., 32,* 996–1003.

Krieger, S. (1979). *Hip capitalism.* Beverly Hills, Calif.: Sage.

Labov, W., and D. Fanshel (1977). *Therapeutic discourse.* New York: Academic Press.

Lacey, J. C., Jr., A. L. Weber, and K. M. Pruitt (1977). The edge of evolution: a molecular historical perspective. In R. D. Duncan and M. Weston-Smith (Eds.), *The encyclopaedia of ignorance.* New York: Pergamon Press. Pp. 219–225.

Landis, C., and W. A. Hunt (1937). Magnification of time as a research technique in the study of behavior. *Science, 85,* 384.

Lang, P. J. (1977). Physiological assessment of anxiety and fear. In J. D. Cone and R. P. Hawkins (Eds.), *Behavioral assessment: new directions in clinical assessment.* New York: Brunner Mazel. Pp. 178–195.

Lang, P. J., B. G. Melamed, and J. D. Hart (1974). Automating the desensitization procedures: a psychophysiological analysis of fear modification. In M. L. Kietzman (Ed.), *Experimental approaches to psychopathology.* New York: Academic Press. Pp. 289–323.

Lang, P. J., D. G. Rice, and R. A. Sternback (1972). The psychophysiology of emotion. In N. S. Greenfield and R. A. Sternback (Eds.), *Handbook of psychophysiology.* New York: Holt, Rinehart, and Winston. Pp. 623–643.

Latane, B., and J. M. Dabbs, Jr. (1975). Sex, group size and helping in three cities. *Sociometry, 38,* 180–194.

Latour, B., and S. Woolgar (1979). *Laboratory life: the social construction of scientific facts.* Beverly Hills, Calif.: Sage.

Lau, R. R., and D. Russell (1980). Attributions in sports pages. *J. Pers. soc. Psychol., 39,* 28–38.

Lawrence, P. R. (1958). *The changing of organizational behavior patterns*. Cambridge, Mass.: Harvard Univ. Press.

Lawson, N. C., M. L. Widmer, and R. Edens (1979). Quality of life in cancer and spinal cord injured patients. In E. P. Willems (Chair), *Issues in monitoring health related behaviors*. Symposium presented at the meeting of the American Psychological Association. New York.

Leary, T. (1957). *Interpersonal dimensions of personality*. New York: Ronald.

Lee, J. A. (1979). The gay connection. *Urban Life, 8,* 175–198.

Leiter, K. (1980). *A primer on ethnomethodology*. New York: Oxford Univ. Press.

Lester, M. (1980). Generating newsworthiness. *Amer. Sociol. Rev., 45,* 984–994.

Lesey, M. (1973). *Wisconsin death trip*. New York: Pantheon, 1973.

———— (1976). *Real life: Louisville in the twenties*. New York: Pantheon.

———— (1980). *Time frames: the meaning of family pictures*. New York: Pantheon.

Levine, M. (1980). Investigative reporting as a research method: an analysis of Bernstein and Woodward's *All the president's men*. *Amer. Psychol., 35,* 626–638.

Levine, R. V., H. T. Reis, and L. J. West (1980). Perceptions of time and punctuality in the United States and Brazil. *J. Pers. soc. Psychol., 38,* 541–550.

Lewis, R. E. F. (1951). *The objective measurement of driver behavior: a preliminary report on "test-retest consistency without traffic"*. A.P.U. 149/51 Cambridge, Eng.: Medical Research Council, Psychological Laboratory.

Light, D. (1980). *Becoming psychiatrists*. New York: Norton.

Lindblom, C. E., and D. K. Cohen (1979). *Usable knowledge*. New Haven: Yale Univ. Press.

Lofland, J. (1971). *Analyzing social settings*. Belmont, Calif.: Wadsworth Publishing.

———— (1975). Open and concealed dramaturgic strategies: the case of the state execution. *Urban Life, 4,* 272–295.

Lofland, J. (1976). *Doing social life*. New York: Wiley.

Lofland, J., Ed. (1978). *Interaction in everyday life: social strategies*. Beverly Hills, Calif.: Sage.

London, I. D. (1977). Convergent and divergent amplification and its meaning for social science. *Psychol. Reports, 41,* 111–123.

Lord, R. G., and J. A. Hohenfeld (1979). Longitudinal field assessment of equity effects on the performance of major league baseball players. *J. appl. Psychol., 64,* 19–26.

Love, R. L. (1973). The fountains of urban life. *Urban Life Culture, 2,* 161–209.

Lowe, R. C., and J. E. McGrath (1971). *Stress, arousal, and performance: some findings calling for a new theory*. Project report AF 1161–67, AFOSR.

Lumsden, J. (1973). On criticism. *Australian Psychol., 3,* 186–192.

McCord, J. (1979). Some child-rearing antecedents of criminal behavior in adult men. *J. Pers. soc. Psychol., 37,* 1477–1486.

McCormick, E. J. (1979). *Job analysis: methods and applications*. New York: AMACOM.

McDowall, J. J. (1978). Interactional synchrony: a reappraisal. *J. Pers. soc. Psychol., 36,* 963–975.

McGee, M. G., and M. Snyder (1975). Attribution and behavior: two field studies. *J. Pers. soc. Psychol., 32,* 185–190.

McHugh, P. (1968). *Defining the situation: the organization of meaning in social interaction*. New York: Bobbs-Merrill.

McLemore, C. W., and L. S. Benjamin (1979). Whatever happened to interpersonal diagnosis? *Amer. Psychol., 34,* 17–34.

McLemore, S. D., and C. M. Bonjean (1977). Some principles and techniques of scale construction. In D. M. Freeman (Ed.), *Foundation of political science*. New York: Free Press. Pp. 400–435.

McLeod, R. (1975). Doing snogging. *Urban Life Culture, 3,* 442–445.

McNeil, L. M. (1980). *Knowledge forms and knowledge content*. Paper presented at the meeting of the American Educational Research Association, Boston.

Malinowski, B. (1967). *A diary in the strict sense of the term*. New York: Harcourt, Brace, and World.

Manning, P. K. (1974). Police lying. *Urban Life Culture, 3,* 283–306.

———— (1979). Metaphors of the field: varieties of organizational discourse. *Administrative Science Quarterly, 24,* 660–671.

———— (1980). *The narc's game: organizational and informational limits on drug law enforcement*. Cambridge, Mass.: M.I.T. Press.

———— (In press). Making sense of field data. In T. J. Cottle and R. Weiss (Eds.), *The narrative voice*. New York: Basic Books.

Marceil, J. C. (1977). Implicit dimensions of idiography and nomothesis: a reformulation. *Amer. Psychol., 32,* 1046–1055.

Maruyama, M. (1963). The second cybernetics: deviation-amplifying mutual causal processes. *Amer. Scient., 51,* 164–179.

Mash, E. J., and J. Hedley (1975). Effect of observer as a function of prior history of social interaction. *Percept. motor Skills, 40,* 659–669.

Mash, E. J., and L. G. Terdal, Eds. (1976). *Behavior-therapy assessment*. New York: Springer.

Matthews, S. (1975). Old women and identity maintenance: outwitting the grim reaper. *Urban Life, 4,* 339–348.

Mehan, H., and H. Wood (1975). *The reality of ethnomethodology*. New York: Wiley.

Melbin, M. (1978). Night as frontier. *Amer. Sociol. Rev., 43,* 3–22.

Michaelis, A. R. (1955). *Research films in biology, anthropology, psychology, and medicine*. New York: Academic Press.

Miller, D., and P. Friesen (1980). Archetypes of organizational transition. *Admin. Sci. Quart., 25,* 268–299.

Millman, M. (1977). *The unkindest cut*. New York: Morrow.

Mishler, E. G. (1979). Meaning in context: is there any other kind? *Harvard Educ. Rev., 49,* 1–19.

Mitchell, S. K. (1979). Interobserver agreement, reliability, and generalizability of data collected in observational studies. *Psychol. Bull., 86,* 376–390.

Mitroff, I. I., and R. H. Kilmann (1978). *Methodological approaches to social science*. San Francisco: Jossey-Bass.

Moos, R. H. (1976). *The human context: environmental determinants of behavior.* New York: Wiley,

Morehead, J. (1978). Close encounters of another kind: the center for short-lived phenomena. *The serials Librarian, 3,*(2), 119–128.

Morgan, G. (1980). Paradigms, metaphors, and puzzle solving in organizational theory. *Admin. Sci. Quart., 25,* 605–622.

Nash, J. (1975). Bus riding: community on wheels. *Urban Life, 4,* 99–124.

Nay, W. R. (1979). *Multimethod clinical assessment.* New York: Gardner Press.

Nelson, R. O. (1977). Methodological issues in assessment via self-monitoring. In J. D. Cone and R. P. Hawkins (Eds.), *Behavioral assessment: new directions in clinical psychology.* New York: Brunner Mazel. Pp. 217–240.

Newcomb, T. M. (1961). *The acquaintance process.* New York: Holt, Rinehart, and Winston.

Nisbett, R., and L. Ross (1980). *Human inference: strategies and shortcomings of social judgement.* Englewood Cliffs, N.J.: Prentice-Hall.

Ondrack, D. A. (1975). Socialization in professional schools: a comparative study. *Admin. Sci. Quart. 20,* 97–103.

Ortony, A. (1975). Why metaphors are necessary and not just nice. *Educ. Theory, 25,* 45–53.

Pancer, S. M., L. M. McMullen, and R. A. Kabatoff (1979). Conflict and avoidance in the helping situation. *J. Per. soc. Psychol., 37,* 1406–1411.

Parmenter, R. (1968). *The awakened eye.* Middletown, Conn.: Wesleyan Univ. Press.

Patton, M. Q. (1980). *Qualitative evaluation methods.* Beverly Hills, Calif.: Sage.

Pearce, P. L. (1980). Strangers, travelers, and Greyhound terminals: a study of small-scale helping behaviors. *J. Pers. soc. Psychol., 38,* 935–940.

Pepinsky, H. B., and M. B. Patton (1971). Informative display and the psychological experiment. In H. B. Pepinsky and M. J. Patton (Eds.), *The psychological experiment: a practical accomplishment.* New York: Pergamon Press. Pp. 1–30.

Pfeffer, J. (1977). Power and resource allocation in organizations. In B. Staw and G. Salancik (Eds.), *New directions in organizational behavior.* Chicago: St. Clair Press. Pp. 235–265.

Phillips, K. (1978). The balkanization of America. *Harpers, 256,*(1536), 37–47.

Piaget, J. (1929). *The child's conception of the world.* London: Kegan, Paul.

Piliavin, I. M., J. Rodin, and J. A. Piliavin (1969). Good samaritanism: an underground phenomenon? *J. Pers. soc. Psychol., 13,* 289–299.

Pittenger, R. E., C. F. Hockett, and J. J. Danehy (1960). *The first five minutes: a sample of microscopic interview analysis.* Ithaca, N.Y.: Paul Martineau.

Plant, M. A., N. Kreitman, T. I. Miller, and J. Duffey (1977). Observing public drinking. *J. studies Alcohol, 38,* 867–880.

Polansky, N., W. Freeman, M. Horowitz, L. Irwin, M. Papanis, D. Rappaport, and F. Whaley (1949). Problems of interpersonal relations in research on groups. *Hum. Relat., 2,* 281–291.

Pollner, M. (1975). The very coinage of your brain: the anatomy of reality disjunctures. *Philosophy soc. Sci., 5,* 411–430.

Pondy, L. R. (1977). The other hand clapping: an information processing approach to organizational power. In T. H. Hammer and S. B. Bacharach (Eds.), *Reward systems and power distribution.* Ithaca, N.Y.: NYSSILR, Cornell Univ. Press. Pp. 56–91.

Pondy, L. R., and I. I. Mitroff (1979). Beyond open system models of organization. In B. M. Staw (Ed.), *Research in organizational behavior.* Vol. 1. Greenwich, Conn.: JAI Press. Pp. 3–39.

Progoff, I. (1975). *At a journal workshop: the basic text and guide for using the intensive journal.* New York: Dialogue House Library.

Puckett, R. C. (1928). Making supervision objective. *School Rev., 36,* 209–212.

Punch, M. (1978). Backstage: observing police work in Amsterdam. *Urban Life, 7,* 309–335.

Rabinow, P., and W. M. Sullivan, Eds. (1979). *Interpretive social system: a reader.* Berkeley: Univ. of California Press.

Rainer, T. (1978). *The new diary.* Los Angeles: J. P. Tarcher.

Raphael, R. (1976). *Edges: backcountry lives in America today on the borderlands between the old ways and the new.* New York: Knopf.

Rappaport, R. A. (1968). *Pigs for the ancestors: ritual in the ecology of a New Guinea people.* New Haven: Yale Univ. Press.

Rasmussen, P. K., and L. L. Kuhn (1976). The new masseuse: play for pay. *Urban Life, 5,* 271–292.

Raush, H. L., A. T. Dittmann, and T. J. Taylor (1959). The interpersonal behavior of children in residential treatment. *J. abnorm. soc. Psychol., 58,* 9–26.

Reed, P. (1974). Situated interaction: normative and non-normative bases of social behavior in two urban residential settings. *Urban Life Culture, 2,* 460–487.

Reinharz, S. (1979). *On becoming a social scientist.* San Francisco: Jossey-Bass.

Reiss, A. J., Jr. (1971). Systematic observation of natural social phenomena. In H. L. Costner (Ed.), *Sociological methodology.* San Francisco: Jossey-Bass. Pp. 3–32.

Riegel, K. F. (1976). The dialectics of human development. *Amer. Psychol., 31,* 689–700.

Riemer, J. W. (1976). Mistakes at work: the social organization of error in building construction work. *Soc. Problems, 23,* 255–267.

_____ (1977a). Becoming a journeyman electrician: some implicit indicators in the apprenticeship process. *Sociol. work occupations, 4,* 87–98.

_____ (1977b). Varieties of opportunistic research. *Urban Life, 5,* 467–477.

Riskin, S. R. (1971). Reasonable accounts in sociology: some problems in the logic of explanation. Doctoral dissertation, University of California, 1970. *Dissertation abstracts international.* University Microfilms, No. 71-9249.

Robbins, T., D. Anthony, and T. E. Curtis (1973). The limits of symbolic realism: problems of empathic field observation in a sectarian context. *J. scientific Study Religion, 12,* 259–271.

Roberts, J. M., T. V. Golder, and G. E. Chick (1980). Judgement, oversight, and skill: a cultural analysis of P-3 pilot error. *Hum. Organizat., 39,* 5–21.

Roberts, R. R., Jr, and G. A. Renzaglia (1965). The influence of tape recording on counseling. *J. counsel. Psychol., 12,* 10–16.

Robinson, D. (1980). Emerson's natural theology and the Paris naturalists: toward a theory of animated nature. *J. hist. Ideas, 41,* 69–88.

Romanczyk, R. G., R. N. Kent, C. Diament, and K. D. O'Leary (1973). Measuring the reliability of observational data: a reactive process. *J. appl. Behav. Analy., 6,* 175–186.

Rosa, E., and A. Mazur (1979). Incipient status in small groups. *Social Forces, 58,* 18–37.

Roth, J. A. (1974). Turning adversity to account. *Urban Life Culture, 3,* 347–359.

Rubinstein, J. (1973). *City police.* New York: Farrar, Straus & Giroux.

Ruesch, J., and W. Kees (1972). *Nonverbal communication: notes on the visual perception of human relations.* Los Angeles: Univ. of California Press.

Russell, B. (1930). *The conquest of happiness.* New York: Horace Liveright.

Saal, T. E., R. G. Downey, and M. A. Lahey (1980). Rating the ratings: assessing the psychometric quality of rating data. *Psychol. Bull., 88,* 413–428.

Salancik, G. R. (1977). Commitment and the control of organizational behavior and belief. In B. M. Staw and G. R. Salancik (Eds.), *New directions in organizational behavior.* Chicago: St. Clair Press. Pp. 1–54.

—— (1979a). Field stimulation for organizational behavior research. *Admin. Sci. Quart., 24,* 638–649.

—— (1979b). Interorganizational dependence and responsiveness to affirmative action: the case of women and defense contractors. *Acad. management J., 22,* 375–394.

Samph, T. (1969). The role of the observer and his effects on teacher classroom behavior. *Occasional Papers, 2,* Pontiac, Michigan: Oakland Schools.

Sanday, P. R. (1979). The ethnographic paradigm. *Admin. Sci. Quart., 24,* 527–538.

Sanders, C. R. (1974). Psyching out the crowd: folk performers and their audiences. *Urban Life Culture, 3,* 264–282.

Schachter, S. (1980). Non-psychological explanations of behavior. In L. Festinger (Ed.), *Retrospections on social psychology.* New York: Oxford Univ. Press. Pp. 131–157.

Schafer, R. (1970). The psychoanalytic vision of reality. *Int. J. Psycho-Analysis, 51,* 279–297.

Schatzman, L., and A. L. Strauss (1973). *Field research: strategies for a natural sociology.* Englewood Cliffs, N.J.: Prentice-Hall.

Schegloff, E. (1968). Sequencing in conversational openings. *Amer. Anthropologist, 70,* 1075–1095.

Schelling, T. C. (1978). *Micromotives and macrobehavior.* New York: Norton.

Schmidt, C. J. (1979). The guided tour: insulated adventure. *Urban Life, 7,* 441–467.

Schoggen, P., and M. Schoggen (1980). *Some emerging common themes in behavior-environment research.* Paper presented at the meeting of the American Psychological Association, Montreal.

Schwartz, H., and J. Jacobs (1979). *Qualitative sociology: a method to the madness.* New York: Free Press.

Schwartz, P., and J. Lever (1976). Fear and loathing at a college mixer. *Urban Life, 4,* 314–431.

Scott, M. (1977). Some parameters of teacher effectiveness as assessed by an ecological approach. *J. educ. Psychol., 69,* 217–226.

Scott, W. R. (1965). Field methods in the study of organizations. In J. G. March (Ed.), *Handbook of organizations.* Chicago: Rand McNally. Pp. 261–304.

Sechrest, L. (1976). Another look at unobtrusive measures. In H. W. Sinaiko and L.A. Broedling (Eds.), *Perspectives on attitude assessment: surveys and their alternatives.* Champaign, Ill.: Pendleton. Pp. 94–107.

Sechrest, L., Ed. (1979). *Unobtrusive measurement today: new directions for methodology of behavioral science.* San Francisco: Jossey-Bass.

Shapiro, T. C. (1978). Our local correspondents: a calm, pleasant day. *New Yorker,* June 12. Pp. 72–80.

Siu, R. G. H. *The craft of power.* New York: Wiley.

Skinner, B. F. (1980). *Notebooks.* Englewood Cliffs, N.J.: Prentice-Hall.

Smith, L. M., and W. Geoffrey (1968). *The complexities of an urban classroom: an analysis toward a general theory of teaching.* New York: Holt, Rinehart, and Winston.

Smith, M. D. (1979). Towards an explanation of hockey violence: a reference other approach. *Canadian J. Sociol., 4,* 105–123.

Smith-Lovin, L. (1979). Behavior settings and impressions formed from social scenarios. *Soc. Psychol. Quart., 42,* 31–43.

Smithers, J. A. (1977). Institutional dimensions of senility. *Urban Life, 6,* 251–276.

Snel, B. (1978). Observation in the courtroom. *Netherlands J. Sociol., 14,* 173–190.

Snow, D. A., L. A. Zurcher, Jr., and S. Ekland-Olson (1980). Social networks and social movements: a microstructural approach to differential recruitment. *Amer. Sociol. Rev., 45,* 787–801.

Sommer, R., and B. B. Sommer (1980). *A practical guide to behavioral research: tools and techniques.* New York: Oxford Univ. Press.

Speck, F. G. (1977). *Naskapi: the savage hunters of the Labrador peninsula.* Norman: Univ. of Oklahoma Press.

Spiegelberg, H. (1973). On the right to say "we": a linguistic and phenomenological analysis. In G. Psathas (Ed.), *Phenomenological sociology: issues and applications.* New York: Wiley. Pp. 129–156.

Spradley, J. P. (1979). *The ethnographic interview.* New York: Holt, Rinehart, and Winston.

—— (1980). *Participant observation.* New York: Holt, Rinehart, and Winston.

Squyres, E. M. (1979). Self-observation of one's own reflected image: a report. *Psychol. Reports, 45,* 760–762.

Stebbins, R. A. (1969). Studying the definition of the situation: theory and field research strategies. *Canadian rev. Sociol. Anthropology, 6*(4), 193–211.

Steinbeck, J. (1941). *The log from the sea of Cortez.* New York: Viking.

Stephens, M. A. P., and C. Norris-Baker (1979). Monitoring patient behavior by means of self-reports of patients. In E. P. Willems (Chair), *Issues in monitoring health related behaviors*. Symposium presented at the meeting of the American Psychological Association. New York.

Stephens, M. A. P., and E. P. Willems (1979). Everyday behavior of older persons in institutional housing: some implications for design. In A. D. Seidel and S. Danford (Eds.), *Environmental design: research theory and application*. Washington, D.C.: Environmental Design Research Association. Pp. 344–348.

Stewart, G. L. (1972). On first being a John. *Urban Life Culture, 1,* 255–274.

Stewart, R. (1976). *Contrasts in management*. Maidenhead, U.K.: McGraw Hill Book Company Limited.

Stokols, D. (1980). Group × place transactions: some neglected issues in psychological research on settings. In D. Magnusson (Ed.), *The situation in psychological theory and research*. Hillsdale, N.J.: Erlbaum.

Strahan, R. F., M. K. Hill, and M. K. Mount (1977). Site differences in electrolyte concentration assessed by the water bottle sweat measure. *Psychophysiology, 14,* 609–612.

Strahan, R. F., J. B. Todd, and G. B. Inglis (1974). Instrumentation: a palmar sweat measure particularly suited for naturalistic research. *Psychophysiology, 11,* 715–720.

Stuart, R. B., Ed. (1977). *Behavioral self-management: strategies, techniques, and outcome*. New York: Brunner Mazel.

Styles, J. (1979). Outsider/insider: researching gay baths. *Urban Life, 8,* 135–152.

Sudnow, D. (1978). *Ways of the hand: the organization of improvised conduct*. Cambridge, Mass.: Harvard Univ. Press.

_____ (1979). *Talk's body: a meditation between two keyboards*. New York: Knopf.

Swidler, A. (1979). *Organization without authority: dilemmas of social control in free schools*. Cambridge, Mass.: Harvard Univ. Press.

Sykes, R. E. (1978). Toward a theory of observer effect in systematic field observation. *Hum. Organ., 37,* 148–156.

Tesser, A. (1978). Self-generated attitude change. In L. Berkowitz (Ed.), *Advances in experimental social psychology*. Vol. 11. New York: Academic Press. Pp. 289–338.

Tesser, A., and S. Rosen (1972). On understanding the reluctance to transmit negative information, the MUM effect: the effects of similarity of objective fate. *J. Pers. soc. Psychol., 23,* 46–54.

Thorngate, W. (1976). In general versus it depends: some comments on the Gergen-Schlenker debate. *Pers. soc. Psychol. Bull., 2,* 404–410.

Torbert, W. R. (1972). *Learning from experience: toward consciousness*. New York: Columbia Univ. Press.

Truzzi, M., Ed. (1974). *Verstehen: subjective understanding in the social sciences*. Reading, Mass.: Addison-Wesley.

Ulrich, R. (1975). Toward experimental living, Phase II: "Have you ever heard of a man named Frazier, Sir". In E. Ramp and G. Semb (Eds.), *Behavior analysis*. Englewood Cliffs, N.J.: Prentice-Hall. Pp. 45–61.

Van Maanen, J. (1979). The fact of fiction in organizational ethnography. *Admin. Sci. Quart., 24,* 539–550.

_____ (1979). On the understanding of interpersonal relations. In W. Bennis, J. Van Maanen, E. H. Schein, and F. I. Steele, *Essays in interpersonal dynamics*. Homewood, Ill.: Dorsey. Pp. 13–42.

_____ (1980). Beyond account: the personal impact of police shootings. *Ann. Amer. Polit. Soc. Sci., 452,* 145–156.

_____ (In press). Notes on the production of ethnographic data in an American police agency. In R. Luckham (Ed.), *Anthropological methods in the study of legal systems*. New York: Academic Press.

Vaught, C., and D. L. Smith (1980). Incorporation and mechanical solidarity in an underground coal mine. *Sociol. Work Occupations, 7,* 159–187.

Wagner, J., Ed. (1979). *Images of information*. Beverly Hills, Calif.: Sage.

Walum, L. R. (1974). The changing door ceremony: notes on the operation of sex roles in everyday life. *Urban Life Culture, 2,* 506–515.

Washburn, W. E. (1967). Power in Washington: a zip-coded directory. *The Washington Post, Potomac Magazine,* April 16. Pp. 48–54.

Wax, M. L. (1972). Tenting with Malinowski. *Amer. Sociol. Rev., 37,* 1–13.

Webb, E. J., D. T. Campbell, R. D. Schwartz, and L. Sechrest (1966). *Unobtrusive measures*. Chicago: Rand McNally.

Webb, E., and K. E. Weick (1979). Unobtrusive measures in organizational theory: a reminder. *Admin. Sci. Quart., 24,* 650–659.

Webster's dictionary of synonyms (1st ed.) (1951). Springfield, Mass.: G. & C. Merriam.

Weick, K. E. (1968). Systematic observational methods. In G. Lindzey and E. Aronson (Eds.), *The handbook of social psychology* (2nd ed.). Reading, Mass.: Addison-Wesley. Pp. 357–451.

_____ (1977). Laboratory experimentation with organizations: a reappraisal. *Acad. Management Rev., 2,* 123–128.

_____ (1979). *The social psychology of organizing* (2nd ed). Reading, Mass.: Addison-Wesley.

_____ (1981). Psychology as gloss. In R. Kasschau and C. N. Cofer (Eds.), *Psychology's Second Century*. New York: Praeger. Pp. 110–132.

Weiss, R. S. (1966). Alternative approaches in the study of complex situations. *Hum. Organ., 25,* 198–206.

Wender, P. H. (1968). Vicious and virtuous circles: the role of deviation amplifying feedback in the origin and perpetuation of behavior. *Psychiatry, 31,* 309–324.

Whyte, W. F. (1955). *Street corner society*. Chicago: Univ. of Chicago Press.

Whyte, W. H. (1980). *The social life of small urban spaces*. Washington, D.C.: The Conservation Foundation.

Wicker, A. W. (1975). An application of the multitrait-multimethod logic to the reliability of observational records. *Pers. soc. Psychol. Bull., 4,* 575–579.

_____ (1979). *An introduction to ecological psychology*. Monterey, Calif.: Brooks/Cole.

_____ (1981). Nature and assessment of behavior settings: recent contributions from the ecological perspective. In P. McReynolds (Ed.), *Advances in psychological assessment*. Vol. 5. San Francisco: Jossey-Bass. Pp. 22–61.

Willems, E. P. (1969). Planning a rationale for naturalistic research. In E. P. Willems and H. L. Raush (Eds.), *Naturalistic viewpoints in psychological research*. New York: Holt, Rinehart, and Winston. Pp. 44–71.

―――― (1976a). Behavioral ecology, health, status, and health care: applications to the rehabilitation setting. In I. Altman and J. F. Wohlwill (Eds.), *Human behavior and environment*. New York: Plenum. Pp. 211–263.

―――― (1976b). *Longitudinal analysis of patient behavior*. Project No.: R–136. Waco, Texas: Research and Training Center No. 4. Texas Institute for Rehabilitation and Research, Baylor College of Medicine.

―――― (1977). Behavioral ecology. In D. Stokols (Ed.), *Perspectives on environment and behavior*. New York: Plenum. Pp. 39–68.

Willems, E. P., and H. L. Raush (1969). *Naturalistic viewpoints in psychological research*. New York: Holt, Rinehart, and Winston.

Williams, L. P. (1980). Parallel lives. *Executive, 6*(3), 8–12.

Wilson, T. P. (1970). Conceptions of interaction and forms of sociological explanation. *Amer. Sociol. Rev., 35,* 697–710.

Winett, R. A., M. S. Neale, and K. R. Williams (1979). Effective field research procedures: recruitment of participants and acquisition of reliable, useful data. *Behav. Assessment, 1,* 139–155.

Wiseman, J. P. (1974). The research web. *Urban Life Culture, 3,* 317–328.

Wispe, L. G. (1963). Traits of eminent American psychologists. *Science, 141,* 1256–1261.

Wolfenstein, M. (1953). Movie analyses in the study of culture. In M. Mead and R. Metraux (Eds.), *The study of culture at a distance*. Chicago: Univ. of Chicago Press. Pp. 267–280.

Wooton, A. (1975). *Dilemmas of discourse*. London: Allen & Unwin.

Wright, H. F. (1960). Observational child study. In P. H. Mussen (Ed.), *Handbook of research methods in child development*. New York: Wiley. Pp. 71–139.

―――― (1967). *Recording and analyzing child behavior*. New York: Harper & Row.

Wright, J. C. (1960). *Problem solving and search behavior under noncontingent reward*. Unpublished doctoral dissertation, Stanford University.

Zegiob, L. E., S. Arnold, and R. Forehand (1975). An examination of observer effects in parent-child interactions. *Child Development, 46,* 509–512.

Zigarmi, D., and P. Zigarmi (1978). *The psychological stresses of ethnographic research*. Paper presented at the meeting of the American Educational Research Association, Toronto.

Ziller, R. C., D. Corbin, and D. Smith (1980). *Children's self, social and environment percepts through autophotography*. Unpublished manuscript. Available from University of Florida.

Zimbardo, P. G. (1969). The human choice: individuation, reasons, and order versus deindividuation, impulse, and chaos. In W. J. Arnold and D. Levine (Eds.), *Nebraska symposium on motivation*. Vol. 17. Lincoln: Univ. of Nebraska Press. Pp. 237–307.

Zimmerman, D. H., and D. L. Weder (1977). The diary: diary-interview method. *Urban Life, 5,* 479–498.

Zito, J. M. (1974). Anonymity and neighboring in an urban, high-rise complex. *Urban Life Culture, 3,* 243–263.

Zurcher, L. A., Jr. (1970). The "friendly" poker game: a study of an ephemeral role. *Social Forces, 49,* 173–186.

―――― (1977). The many faces of Don Quixote—at a social science convention. *J. appl. Behav. Sci., 13,* 225–236.

CHAPTER 12

Survey Methods

Howard Schuman
University of Michigan

Graham Kalton
University of Michigan

This chapter identifies key features of the survey method—especially questioning, sampling, and interviewing—and indicates why they are important, what associated problems loom large for both survey users and survey methodologists, and where recent thought and research on these problems seem to be heading. The attempt is not to provide a comprehensive manual on how to carry out a survey; although practical advice is offered at a number of points, we do not hesitate to discuss problems for which we are unable to offer definite solutions. We should also note that our orientation in this chapter is to the use of survey methods by and for social psychology; a treatment of survey research in economics, political science, or sociology would require a somewhat different, though perhaps not radically different, emphasis.

We wish to thank the following individuals for reading parts of this chapter in draft and offering helpful suggestions: Marie Crane, Robert Groves, Steven Heeringa, Irene Hess, James House, Peter Miller, Stanley Presser, Eleanor Singer, and Seymour Sudman. Several paragraphs in the present chapter have been adapted from a section on response effects prepared by Schuman for a National Academy of Sciences report (Turner and Martin, 1984). The chapter also draws on research carried out by the author with the support of a National Science Foundation (SES–8016136).

We begin the chapter with a brief discussion of the development of the survey method, the uses and limitations of surveys for social psychology, and the applications of social psychology in survey research. The chapter then proceeds with discussions of the various stages of a survey, starting with issues of question formation, followed by techniques of survey sampling, methods of data collection (face-to-face, telephone, and mail surveys), interviewing, and editing and data processing. The chapter concludes with some brief comments on survey analysis, ethical problems, and various elaborations of the survey method.

THE NATURE AND DEVELOPMENT OF SURVEY RESEARCH

The development of survey research is based on several simple discoveries. The first, presumably dating back to the beginning of language, is that asking questions is a remarkably efficient way to obtain information from and about people. Whether the information desired is factual or consists of expressions of attitude, beliefs, judgments, or whatever, one can obtain an enormous amount of it in a relatively brief time, provided only that the person answering is able and willing to respond. We will later need to examine carefully what *able* and *willing* entail, but it is useful to start from the commonsense experience that replies are often adequate for the purpose one posed a question.

Questioning, of course, occurs in all spheres of life. When strangers are getting acquainted, questions like the following are commonplace:

- Where are you from?

- What line of work are you in?

- What kind of movies do you like best?

- How do you feel about President _____?

Surveys modify such normal inquiries in two ways. One is to define the process as nonreciprocal: The interviewer is entitled to ask the respondent's age, income, or political opinions but is not expected to reveal her own age, income, or political opinions. The other modification is that there are fewer limits on what can be asked about in a survey interview than in all but the most intimate encounters in ordinary life. In the early days of surveys there was indeed much uncertainty about what could and could not be inquired into—even a person's educational attainment was regarded as too sensitive to be asked directly (Converse, in press)—but in recent years the bounds have been extended so far that, rightly or wrongly, few topics are considered too personal or threatening to be included in an interview, though, of course, this does not guarantee that the answers are equally candid.

Furthermore, it is not necessary that respondents know precisely why they are being asked a question. They may be presented with items that on their face mean one thing but are later used by an investigator to mean something else. The classic F-scale items are a good example (Adorno *et al.*, 1950), but even a simple factual question about age may be turned into a measure of cohort experience that the average person is only dimly aware of. This makes survey interviews of unique value to social psychologists, who often want to conduct studies of people without the people concerned knowing exactly what is being studied, though it also raises ethical problems that we will need to consider at a later point.

The second discovery that makes survey research possible is much more recent. It is the fact that a relatively small sample, if properly drawn, allows inferences to a much larger population and, further, that the degree of error in these inferences due to sampling can be estimated with a fair degree of precision from the sample itself. This statement will seem obvious enough to anyone who has had an elementary statistics course, but what is not always equally obvious is that when one is sampling large populations, the precision of the sample estimates depends upon the size of the sample and not, for most practical purposes, on the size of the population. Thus a sample of 1000 cases can represent the United States (with an adult population of about 165 million) with virtually the same precision as it can represent New York City (with an adult population of about 5 million). It is this strongly counterintuitive fact, plus the development of such techniques as stratification and clustering to be discussed below, that allows surveys to be such a powerful tool for studying large populations, even whole societies like the United States or, potentially, the world.

The attempt to make rigorous inferences to large natural populations through probability or quasi-probability sampling was the major factor that distinguished survey research from somewhat similar developments in attitude measurement occurring in academic psychology over about the same period—roughly the second quarter of this century. (Bowley and Burnett-Hurst, [1915] are usually credited with the first use of survey sampling, but more recently the earlier contributions of A. N. Kiaer have been emphasized; see Kruskal and Mosteller (1980) for an account of the origins of survey sampling.) Most psychologists interested in attitudes were, and still are, content to use samples of college students, since they are so convenient and costless. This led to a further difference in development: the creation for surveys (but not for classroom samples) of an intermediate role between investigators and respondents, namely, the interviewer. Whereas psychologists ordinarily use captive groups of students to whom questionnaires can be self-administered, surveys need to locate people throughout a large area, persuade them to take part, and pose questions and record answers from persons who in many cases either would not or could not fill out a questionnaire themselves. Personal contact between real persons is probably essential to complex social psychological surveys, and it is doubtful that such contact can be supplanted entirely by mail questionnaires, television voting, or other more impersonal types of inquiry, at least not without loss of a large part of the population and of much of the richness of the survey interview. But having interviewers as intermediaries also raises a variety of problems, which we will have to consider at a later point.

Using interviewers to ask questions of probability samples from well-defined populations produces sets of answers. But simple aggregations of answers to attitude questions do not have much meaning, especially since they are usually influenced greatly by the exact wording of the particular questions. Construction of a multi-item index can reduce the effect of nuances in wording, but total scale scores also lack absolute or intuitive meaning considered alone. Such responses take on meaning only in the course of comparison, and the most obvious comparisons are between the responses produced by two or more important categories of the population. Hence we have the bivariate tables still common in poll reports (e.g., responses of men compared with those of women) and, equally useful once survey questions are repeated, comparisons of response distributions across time. But by the 1940s academic surveys were moving well beyond the two-variable table and generating a logic intended to reveal complex patterns that were quite invisible without careful analysis (Kendall and Lazarsfeld, 1950; Hyman, 1955). For example, Table 1, which is based on the famous *American Soldier* studies (Stouffer *et al.,* 1949) presents sample frequencies of World War II soldiers preferring army camps in the North or the South United States, categorized by soldier's race, region of origin, and present camp location.

This table provides the data for testing a large number of associations, partial associations, and interaction; see Goodman (1972) for conclusions based on log-linear analysis of these data. The direction of analysis is fairly typical of social psychological surveys, involving an attitude or belief as the focal dependent variable and several background, demographic, or social classifications as independent variables. On the assumption that causal direction ordinarily flows from rather than to the background variables, the analysis allows inferences about the determinants of the attitude, albeit without the rigor provided by true experimentation. (But experimentation is not possible with variables such as race and region in this context, at least not without shifting to a laboratory simulation that frequently loses vital connection with the original problem.) Moreover, interesting interactions or specifications can be explored, limited only by what is included in the survey. *Only* is an important word, of course, and since it is always possible to discover relevant variables that interact with an existing set, analysis of survey data can almost always be extended further. This is not basically different, however, from any other form of social psychological research.

Up until the midsixties, intuition and eyeballing were the major guides to analysis of most survey data, with simple significance testing the only formal aid and even that usually restricted to bivariate relations. Beginning in the 1960s with Blalock's (1961) treatment of causality and Duncan's (1966) adaptation of path analysis to sociological problems, increased concern for explicitly specifying causal connections developed, along with more routine use of multiple regression in analysis. This worked well with dependent variables that could be treated as approximately interval in character and with other variables assumed to have relatively little measure-

TABLE 1
Soldiers' Preferences for Camps in the North and South United States by Race, Region of Origin, and Location of Present Camp

RACE	REGION OF ORIGIN	LOCATION OF PRESENT CAMP	NUMBER OF SOLDIERS PREFERRING CAMP	
			In North	In South
Black	North	North	387	36
Black	North	South	876	250
Black	South	North	383	270
Black	South	South	381	1712
White	North	North	995	162
White	North	South	874	510
White	South	North	104	176
White	South	South	91	869

SOURCE: Adapted from Goodman, 1972, p. 290

ment error, but some important social psychological variables are nominal for most purposes, and most show large amounts of unreliability. The first of these problems has become more tractable with the development of systematic methods for the analysis of sets of categorical variables (e.g., Bishop *et al.,* 1975). The second has been approached by the application of structural equation models to problems of measurement error (Jöreskog and Sörbom, 1979). There is still a considerable way to go before the variety of analytic problems common to survey data can be handled without making unrealistic assumptions—and both the problems and the possibilities increase with the complexity of multiwave and multilevel surveys—but it is certainly possible today to discover a great deal more in survey data and with fewer errors of inference than was true only two decades ago. As Duncan (1978) has noted, reanalysis of older data with present statistical methods can show many previous conclusions to be untenable while also discovering much that was missed in the same data.

Technological developments have also greatly affected our capacity to carry out complex surveys. The spread of telephones to most households in the United States has allowed a shift to telephone surveys, which not only decreases costs and increases speed of completion but also makes possible centralization and tighter control of interviewing. Moreover, use of the telephone facilitates the integration of interviewing and coding within a single computer-assisted operation, which is now under way in a number of survey organizations, and this in turn affects the design of questionnaires and expedites the production of data. The computer also, of course, permits rapid processing and complex calculations with large masses of data, substantially changing the nature of survey analysis. We are no doubt far from the end of the line of progress on all these matters, and it is probable that procedures for gathering and analyzing data will look very different in another decade or two.

LIMITATIONS OF SURVEYS

In this account of advances in survey research, we have ignored a series of problems that have not been solved or in some cases may even have become more serious. Respondents do not always agree to take part in surveys, and in the United States the proportion of such nonrespondents has increased noticeably over the past two decades, threatening the assumption that we are indeed dealing with adequate samples of the general population that is usually our target (Steeh, 1981). Even where peo-

ple do take part, they are not necessarily able or willing to answer questions in the way we assume, nor are we very knowledgeable about how to ask questions most usefully or what to do with the answers once we have them. Old debates about the relationship between the kinds of attitudinal data obtained by surveys and the kinds obtained by other forms of research—including observation of "real" behavior—are far from resolved. Even technological progress is not an unalloyed good, for the telephone does not seem to raise response rates (in fact, the reverse) and may increase bias by losing more lower-socioeconomic-status households (Groves and Kahn, 1979), while pressures to computerize interviewing and coding may sometimes result in decisions that maximize efficiency at the cost of richness. In unskilled hands technical advances in analysis also have their drawbacks, for their complexities and sometimes poorly understood assumptions can lead to elegant looking but misleading results.

In the following pages we will attempt to deal with both the strengths and the limitations of surveys. But first, it is useful to consider what survey research offers to social psychologists and what social psychology can offer to survey research.

SURVEY RESEARCH FOR SOCIAL PSYCHOLOGISTS

Sample surveys are not needed if there is such a thing as human nature, which works in the same way in all important respects regardless of time or place. In that case we do not need to define populations and make inferences to them, since study of at most a few individuals can suffice to tell us about all the others. But this assumption clearly does not hold for the content of attitudes and beliefs, and it may not hold for some of the more interesting psychological processes (e.g., the need for logical consistency) nor for interactions of these processes with experimental manipulations. Variations due to cultural norms, to educational level, and to life experiences themselves must be assumed to affect most of mental life, except as proved otherwise. It is possible to build such variations purposively into experiments, and psychologists occasionally do so by attempting to obtain heterogeneity along some single dimension such as education. (Less advertently, one background variable used almost routinely by social psychologists is sex, but this is not in most cases because of a decision as to its importance but simply because college students ordinarily come in both sexes.) However, by sampling a natural population, one can usually obtain the needed variation across a range of variables, with the added advantage of relating one's generalizations to a definable and socially important set of people.

An additional, very valuable consequence is that repeated samples over time allow investigators to trace shifts in the phenomena being studied. As survey data accumulate from earlier points in time, the possibilities increase greatly for exploring the nature of change in social psychological content and processes. In this sense the survey method is consistent with a view of social reality as inherently historical (Gergen, 1973), and generalizations about change itself become a major goal of research. This does not mean that there are not formidable problems in studying change, including the fact that the words we use in questions are themselves shifting in meaning over time, but still the orientation to a specified population encourages a recognition of social psychological change that is precluded by the disregard of sampling characteristic of most laboratory experiments.

A second reason why surveys may *not* be used by social psychologists is if interest is limited to observing actual behavior. Except in the obvious sense that any verbalization is itself an instance of behavior, interview and questionnaire surveys are by nature not well suited to providing direct access to behavior. (However, sample surveys of behavior are certainly possible, and one example is noted at the end of the chapter.) It is also not clear that reports of past behavior are always adequately obtained by surveys, though there are seldom better methods. But if a social psychologist is interested in the rich world of attitudes, beliefs, judgments, preferences, personal values, and intentions, then a survey is about the only method of investigation geared to large populations. And there are a number of social classifications of people that are of high importance and that are usually obtained quite readily in the course of survey interviews.

A third reason often given for not using surveys is a concern for causality. This reason is not altogether compelling, since it is perfectly easy to divide a probability sample into two or more random subsamples and administer a different stimulus to each. Such a between-subjects design, traditionally known in survey research as a split ballot, is underutilized by both psychologists and survey researchers, but a number of examples, mainly of methodological relevance, will be given at later points in this chapter. It is also possible, of course, to employ within-subjects designs over two or more surveys (commonly called panel studies in survey jargon). To be sure, some of the more complex experiments possible in the laboratory could not be carried out in households or

over the telephone, but the difference is one of degree, not principle. Furthermore, for variables that cannot be manipulated experimentally, such as race or sex, causal connections can only be made on a logical basis, and this can be done about as well with survey data as with experimental data.

There are other large differences of a more practical character between experiments and surveys having to do with costs and related factors. Even the most straightforward survey of a major population costs thousands, usually tens of thousands and often hundreds of thousands, of dollars. Much of this money goes to the interviewing and coding staffs and to their supervision. Experiments on students in classes can frequently be done at virtually no cost, and even where some equipment is needed and subjects are paid, it is often possible for an experiment to be done for under a thousand dollars. (Lest this financial difference seem overwhelming, we should note that it is possible for an investigator to purchase, at relatively low cost, several minutes of data collection in an omnibus national survey.)

Part of this cost difference, of course, has to do with the number of respondents/subjects needed. A typical national survey has about 1500 cases, and whenever possible, this N is increased. Experiments are typically done with fewer than a hundred subjects. Since both types of investigation rely on basically similar inferential statistical techniques, it is not immediately obvious why so many more cases are needed in the one than in the other. Surveys, to be sure, include many more variables, and analysis (including analysis based only on subgroups) can therefore be much more extensive, but this does not seem to be the whole story. Several other possible reasons can be noted, although we are unsure of their relative weights. One factor is the tight control exercised in experiments: Extraneous variance is eliminated to a much greater degree when one or two experimenters work in a closed laboratory setting than when a large set of transient interviewers carry out a survey in widely varying and poorly controlled household settings. A second and similar factor is the greater homogeneity of student samples in experiments, which decreases the error variance with which created variance is compared. A third and quite different factor has to do with measurment: Surveys often use single items as dependent variables, since many different variables are being studied at once, while experiments more often employ multi-item scales having relatively high reliability. A fourth and less explicit factor is that published experiments are almost always preceded by rehearsals that allow an investigator to determine whether a significant effect will be obtained and then to adjust one of the above factors—or the strength of the stimulus itself—to ensure sufficient power. Pretests for surveys are normally too small and crude to serve this purpose and are used instead to assess respondent understanding of questions. Furthermore, surveys almost always have multiple purposes, and thus adjustments for the benefit of one or two dependent variables may not be practical.

There are other, less tangible differences between surveys and experiments. For example, experiments usually call for staging a production and often acting in it; running a survey is more like administering a complex organization. Differences in temperament, training, and experience lead some social psychologists to prefer one of these modes of gathering data to the other, and it can be very difficult to switch once one leaves graduate school. Thus most of us are bound more closely to a single method than may be desirable, and despite lip service to multimethod research, the investigator who departs from his or her familiar way is almost as rare as a white peacock.

This comparison with surveys has been restricted to experiments for the simple reason that experiments and surveys (including nonprobability surveys) are probably the two most frequent methods of creating data in social psychology (Katz, 1967). [This is not to claim that the survey method approaches experimentation in frequency of use by social psychologists, since the latter method is clearly the dominant one in the major journals (Presser, 1982), though *some* use of questionnaires is probably almost as common.] Other comparisons and contrasts are needed if content analysis, systematic social observation, or some other technique is considered. Of course, here again there are areas of overlap, so that surveys should not be thought of as an entirely self-contained methodological approach. Indeed, it is obvious that each of the two main features of surveys—sampling populations and asking questions—is detachable and can be linked fruitfully to methods considered in other chapters in this volume.

THE SOCIAL PSYCHOLOGY OF SURVEY RESEARCH

To this point surveys have been presented as an alternative method for social psychologists, and the limitations of surveys have been noted as pitfalls that the intelligent user will want to avoid. However, it is equally important to see the survey as a challenging and highly useful *ob-*ject of social psychological research. Most of the limitations of surveys result from our lack of adequate understanding of the question-answer process, of the effects of different modes of administration, of interviewer-respondent interaction, and of the characteristics and motivations of those who do or do not take part in a survey. Social psychologists should be able to contribute to the solution of these general problems and to the improvement of the survey method, and much of the research that we will discuss below is basically social psychological in character.

Moreover, such research should feed back into more general social psychological knowledge, for it means confronting real problems of social interaction in an extremely important type of realistic setting. Only such direct confrontation is likely to be fruitful in both directions, for the idea that there is an existing body of social psychological theory (or of cognitive, linguistic, or any other type of theory) that can simply be applied to surveys seems unrealistic. Sampling does derive from probability theory, but none of the social sciences at this point offers much in the way of basic theory that has clear implications for surveys going much beyond common sense. If there are connections and contributions to be made, social psychologists will have to become directly involved in studying the survey process, as indeed some have in the past.

THE MAJOR COMPONENTS OF SURVEYS

One way of conceptualizing the main stages of a survey is shown in Fig. 1. Ideally, sampling design and question construction should proceed hand in hand, both guided by the problem to be investigated. When these stages are not well integrated—a rather common failing—one ends up with questions that do not fit parts of the sample or with a sample that provides too few cases for a key analysis. An example of the first is a study of attitudes toward work that fails to anticipate the substantial adaptations needed for the large number of retired, unemployed, and other nonworking persons in the general population. An example of the second is a study of ethnicity that ends up with too few cases for most ethnic identities because so many people are "mixed" or do not have clear ethnic identifications.

We have pictured the relation between questions and concept as analogous to that between samples and population. In each case investigators use the one (sample, questions) to make inferences about the other (popula-

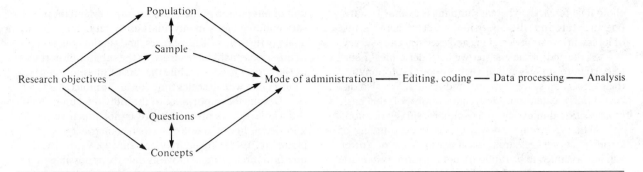

FIGURE 1
The Main Stages of a Survey

tion, concepts), with the latter being what one is primarily interested in. Sampling populations and operationalizing concepts are each intended to allow us to go from the observed to the unobserved. The analogy is only that, an analogy, since the precision with which inference can be made is quite rigorous in the one case and much less so in the other.

Mode of administration covers the decision as to whether to use face-to-face interviewing, telephone interviewing, self-administered questionnaires, or some combination of these. It also covers decisions concerning the setting for administration (e.g., home, school, workplace, etc.) and, if interviewing is to be used, the composition, organization, training, and supervision of the interviewing staff. Of course, here as with other parts of the diagram, the flow of decisions may actually be reversed, so the initial decision to use the telephone for purposes of economy affects decisions about the population (e.g., eliminating nonphone households) and about possible types of questions (eliminating any that would require show cards or other visual cues).

Coding and data processing are usually regarded as the more mechanical steps in the process. But if open questions are used, code construction and coding become more critical, and if the analytic goals are complicated (e.g., both individual respondents and their households to be treated as units for analysis), data processing may involve complex programming considerations. In any case both coding and data processing (which includes "cleaning" data by removing errors and inconsistencies) are usually more time-consuming than inexperienced investigators realize. Of course, researchers can avoid be-

coming involved in these or other stages by obtaining the services of an established survey organization, but it is unwise to remain too far from the many decisions that need to be made along the way or to remain unaware of the practical problems that come up in the course of actual interviewing, coding, and data processing.

In the balance of this chapter we will concentrate on three stages: formulation of questions, design of samples, and interviewing and related modes of gathering data. Analysis is treated elsewhere in the *Handbook* and will be discussed as such only briefly at the end of this chapter. (Attitude scaling, which can be considered as an important elaboration of the question-concept relation, is also treated in a separate chapter and not considered in detail here.) Our goal throughout will be to draw as far as possible on systematic theory and empirical research about surveys, but there is also a substantial body of lore, rule of thumb, and general experience that is an important part of the survey tradition and needs to be noted, though not at length nor uncritically.

The different sections of the chapter vary in style and purpose. Sampling procedures, which have an underlying mathematical basis, are presented in a fairly systematic and expository way. Question construction lacks such an overall theory but raises methodological problems that can usefully be brought to the attention of readers who would otherwise proceed on a purely commonsense basis. Mode of administration falls somewhere between these two extremes, though closer to the question end, and calls for an intermediate treatment. Moreover, questioning and interviewing both have important social psychological content and invite further social psychological research, whereas sampling is primarily statistical in nature and is discussed in some detail here because of its essential role in designing and executing any survey.

At the end of the chapter we consider ethical issues important to surveys and discuss proposed solutions and their effects on survey practice and results. We also discuss briefly extensions and elaborations of the basic cross-sectional interview/questionnaire survey method.

A theme throughout will be the understanding of error in survey research, both variable error (often vaguely assumed to be random) and the more systematic type of effect usually labeled bias. Variable error is relatively simple to conceptualize in most stages of survey research, since it involves only the deviations of the results of conceptually identical repetitions of a procedure from their overall average. Bias, however, requires that we conceptualize not merely an average value but also a "true value." This is easiest to do in the case of sampling, where bias represents deviation of the mean of a sampling distribution from the population value. Bias can also be conceptualized in the question-answer process when certain factual responses (such as age) are sought. However, when we consider attitudes, it becomes difficult to conceptualize a true value that is independent of the wording of the question, and the problem becomes even more difficult when attitude responses vary by type of interviewer or setting, since it may be impossible to contend that one response has greater claim on validity than another (cf. Mosteller, 1968). Semifactual inquiries such as "race" have much the same difficulties. For these reasons it seems best to refer to these types of differences as systematic effects, eschewing the term *bias* except where it is clearly applicable. For the same reason, it is difficult to apply the concept of "total survey error"—all forms of variable error plus all forms of bias—in most social psychological surveys, despite its heuristic value in some other types of surveys (Anderson *et al.,* 1979).

SURVEY QUESTIONS

The fundamental unit of meaning in a survey is the single question. There are smaller units to be sure, individual words being the most obvious, and we will be at some pains to show how their variation can affect meaning. There are also larger units, primarily scales and indices that may be desirable to employ in actual analysis. But the discrete question plays a role in survey research analogous to that of atoms in chemistry—it is the distinctive

unit of interaction in the course of a survey and the necessary building block in any analysis of data. To carry the analogy further, words, phrases, and similar constituents of questions might be regarded as the subatomic particles of the survey process, while the sets of questions and responses that we call scales function at the molecular level.

Despite the importance of the individual question to the whole survey process, there is not much scientific knowledge about questions. Psychometric texts (e.g., Nunnally, 1978) skip entirely or treat awkwardly the unit question, preferring to move as quickly as possible to the technically more tractable process of combining units. Survey texts (e.g., Babbie, 1973) are apt to spend some time on how to write good questions and identify bad ones but with primary emphasis on common sense and practical experience. The latter two ingredients, the importance of which should certainly not be underrated, will be found in abundance in a lively and still relevant little book devoted to *The Art of Asking Questions* by Payne (1951). A more recent systematic discussion of practical problems of questionnaire construction has been published by Sudman and Bradburn (1982), and relevant chapters also appear in Rossi *et al.* (1983) and in Dijkstra and van der Zouwen (1982).

The practical advice on question construction comes down to such rules as these: Stay away from difficult words; avoid double-barreled questions (e.g., "Do you like traveling on trains and buses?" is an impossible question for those who like one but not the other); keep questions short. Most of the rules are not controversial, though we will see below that the desirable length of a question is in fact subject to dispute. Yet it is also not always obvious ahead of time what is a difficult word or even what is a double-barreled item, and there is no substitute for pretesting questions to make as certain as possible that they are understandable and without serious ambiguity for most of the population.

A good example of the need to pretest *every* question comes from a study in which one of the present authors included the following agree/disagree item from Srole's (1956) Anomia scale: "In spite of what some people say, the lot of the average man is getting worse, not better." Because the item had been used many times before by others, it was assumed to be unproblematic and placed in the final interview schedule without pretesting. But when interviewers were routinely asked on completing each questionnaire to indicate which items caused the most difficulty, their answers pointed to the "lot of the average man" question as far and away the most problematic in the entire hour-long interview, mainly because this usage of *lot* is not familiar to many Americans. The question was variously interpreted to refer to a lot of average men, to the size of housing lots, and even in one case to cemetery lots! The fact that the original statement had seemed simple enough to many past investigators proved no guarantee that it was meaningful for the general population. For the same reason expert advice on questions is no substitute for pretest experience. Moreover, for such pretesting to be useful, it is necessary that investigators find ways to listen to their interviewers—and, ideally, do some pretest interviewing themselves. In addition, it is sometimes useful to build into a final questionnaire a random system of probing in order to determine whether respondents interpret a question in the way investigators assumed (Schuman, 1966) or to carry out a detailed postsurvey inquiry into respondent interpretations of question meaning (Belson, 1981).

A REVISION OF THE FACT VERSUS OPINION DISTINCTION

A long-standing distinction for survey researchers is that between objective and subjective questions—the former referring to phenomena that are "in principle, directly accessible to the external observer," the latter to phenomena "that, in principle, can be directly known, if at all, only by persons themselves" (i.e., through introspection) (Turner and Martin, 1981, p. 2). At a practical level the distinction is a useful one, since questions about age, sex, or education could conceivably be replaced or verified by use of records or observations, while food preferences, political attitudes, and personal values seem to depend ultimately on respondent self-reports.

On closer examination the distinction between objective and subjective questions becomes slippery. On the one hand, there are a number of external phenomena such as race that have a large subjective element in definition. Further, some basic economic indexes widely regarded as representing objective fact—the unemployment index, for example—depend in part on subjective judgments by respondents (Bailar and Rothwell, in press). On the other hand, concepts such as "love" that we ordinarily think of as highly subjective can be operationalized in terms of acts as well as in terms of self-reports: There can be instances where we give more weight to the former than to the latter, as when a man who frequently beats and abandons his wife is not believed when he protests his deep love for her; he may convince his psy-

chiatrist, but others are apt to think that he is either lying or using the word *love* differently from most English speakers.

At a more practical level the fact/opinion distinction obscures some large differences within each category with regard to the possibilities and difficulties of obtaining survey data of particular kinds. For this reason we shall use a somewhat more differentiated classification, one that facilitates discussion of certain issues appropriate to this chapter, though it is not intended to be exhaustive or to provide altogether mutually exclusive classes. The types of survey data to be discussed are obtained by questions dealing with:

1. social categories;

2. reports of past behavior;

3. attitudes, beliefs, and values;

4. behavioral intentions;

5. sensitive information—past, present, or future.

Social Categories

Surveys are especially efficient and useful in obtaining most of the broad categories into which the total population is divided by both common sense and social science formulation. Ask persons in the United States their age, sex (seldom necessary in personal interviews, of course), educational attainment, region of origin, present residence, or a number of similar questions, and for most purposes the answers are quick, easily given, and probably fairly accurate. To be sure, there is some evidence of both random and systematic error (e.g., Weaver and Swanson, 1974), but these are usually minor perturbations as compared with most other types of social science measurement.

In passing, we note that a check of age against birth certificates would seem to be the prototype of verification of answers to an objective question, and it is therefore unfortunate that we have not been able to locate such a systematic check for adults in the United States and must rely instead on an intuitive sense that age is reported with considerable accuracy provided the question is precisely phrased (e.g., "date of birth" rather than simply "age"). Checks of survey data on age against other self-report records (e.g., driver's license reports and voting registration records in Parry and Crossley, 1950) are of some value and show substantial but not perfect consistency (92 percent and 83 percent, respectively), but of course these sources are not independent of the respondent. Some direct comparisons of survey responses with birth certificates are available for several African countries and point to some systematic reporting errors involving both under- and overstatement of age, as well as heaping at certain digits (Ewbank, 1981).

Indicators of income and occupation are somewhat trickier to obtain, though for quite different reasons. Questions on total family income usually produce a noticeable number of refusals to respond (in NORC's General Social Survey, about 7 percent), and there is also reason to think that the answers carry a fair amount of distortion, both because of memory problems for incidental forms of income (e.g., interest) and because of some understatement especially on the part of the wealthy. Questions on occupation are difficult because of the wide range of occupational titles and the difficulties of classifying many reports; those with a need for careful occupational classification often make use of the U.S. Census *Alphabetical Index of Industries and Occupations.* Increasing use is also made of a parallel system of prestige ratings of occupations originally developed by North and Hatt (National Opinion Research Center, 1947) and later extended by Hodge, Siegel, and Rossi (1964). Occupations can also be classified in terms of the extent to which they involve work with people, data, or things (equipment), using the *Directory of Occupational Titles* (Cain and Treiman, 1981). It should be noted that the early practice of combining occupation, income, and education into some overall measure of socioeconomic status or social class (e.g., Hollingshead, 1949) has largely disappeared from the sociological literature, partly because of an interest in how the separate socioeconomic variables function and partly because of avoidance of identifying any one such measure with the broader theoretical concept of class.

From some standpoints ethnicity (including race) constitutes a background category similar to those already discussed. But since there is much less consensus as to both the nature of the categories and who fits into them, no single or successful system exists. The present (1980) census classification is a hodgepodge of different types of classification, but even where the investigator is not subject to the political pressures that the government agencies experience, it is difficult to come up with any satisfactory solution. An effort to treat ethnicity as "objective" by asking about country of origin quickly discovers that a large part of the American population comes from a very mixed background, not to mention the fact that there is a fair degree of ignorance as to one's own ethnic origins. A more subjective approach through questions about self-identity avoids some of these problems but ends by treating ethnicity as a kind of attitude, with attendant problems as discussed below. Smith (1980a) provides a useful consideration of the different approaches to measuring ethnicity and the relations among them. Respondent religion is simpler to assess than ethnicity but has some of the same problems.

There has been some interest in standardizing the measurement of these and other background questions, since most of them appear in almost every large-scale survey. A useful compendium of standard measures, with accompanying discussion, has been prepared by the Social Science Research Council (Van Dusen and Zill, 1975).

Reports of Past Behavior

Surveys are often the only practical way to learn about past actions and events in the general population. Although some events (birth) and behaviors (registration to vote) are recorded for administrative or legal purposes, the records are expensive and difficult to obtain access to, and even if accessible, they do not allow efficient analysis in relation to other variables. Other past events and behaviors may not leave systematic traces of any kind—for example, personal experience with racial or sexual discrimination, important friendships and romantic attachments, purchases of illegal drugs, and so forth. In both cases—those with recorded traces and those without—our only practical way of obtaining information is usually through self-report.

Some examples of questions about past behavior are these:

- Did you vote in the 1984 presidential election?

- What magazines did you read during the past month?

- Have you ever traveled outside the United States?

- Did you buy a car during the past twelve months?

- How many cigarettes have you smoked during the past twenty-four hours?

- Have there been any burglaries in your house in the past two years?

- In the past year how often did you become intoxicated while drinking any kind of beverage?

A major problem with each of these questions is that the respondent may not remember accurately the past action(s) or event(s) referred to. A second problem is that respondents may be unwilling to report, with frankness, certain sensitive behaviors; this complication is considered in a later section. Here we focus on problems of memory.

The main factors that determine a person's ability to supply information about such past behaviors and events have to do with the questions asked and with limitations of memory that are a function of both the interval of time covered and the degree of subjective importance of the event to be remembered:

1. *The adequacy of the questions:* It is a common experience for investigators to discover that a question elicits a different response than intended; it is probably even more common for this to happen and not be noticed. Reports of discrimination may be over- or underreported because the term *discrimination* means something different to some respondents than to investigators. "Crimes" as experienced by victims do not always fit questions about crimes posed in the National Crime Survey (Skogan, 1981). Similar discrepancies or uncertainties occur with concepts like friendships, drugs, etc. Even the word *you* is ambiguous in the car-buying question, since it is not clear whether it refers to all members of a family or only to the person who made the purchase. Furthermore, there is evidence that subtle presuppositions contained in questions can influence reported memories (Loftus, 1982). The problems here are ones of both conceptualization and communication, and perhaps the best advice that can be given is for investigators to do plenty of preliminary work and to put themselves in a position that maximizes awareness of the interpretations of others.

2. *Memory:* Whatever the true nature of long-term memory, much of our past life is not easily recalled when we are confronted with questions about it. Two fairly obvious variables play a large role here: interval of time since the past event or behavior and subjective importance of the past event or behavior. [Sudman (1980) breaks importance further into three components: the uniqueness of the event; economic and social costs and benefits—e.g., winning a $1000 lottery is more memorable than is winning a $10 lottery; and continuing consequences—a continuing disability is a reminder of a past accident.] Events that are unimportant are usually forgotten quickest and most completely, and events that happened longer ago are likewise harder to remember.

Whether this is due to memory decay, interference, or some other process would be difficult to test with survey data, but at an applied level length of time and importance correlate fairly regularly with inaccuracy of reporting. For example, Cannell and Fowler (1963) used hospital records to assess reports of hospitalization and found that 3 percent of hospitalizations in the first ten weeks were not reported, 6 percent in the next ten, and then 9, 11, 16, and 42 percent for succeeding ten-week periods up to a year. They also found that the number of days of hospitalization, which they took to be a measure of its importance, showed a positive association with accuracy of reports. As a second example, the Census Bureau chose respondents on the basis of records of victimization in San Jose, California, and found decreasing recall of the occurrence or of the period of occurrence, as shown in Table 2. However, there is conflicting evidence as to whether seriousness of crimes interacts with forgetting in such studies (Skogan, 1981). Still another interesting, though more speculative, example is reported by Mahalanobis and Das Gupta (1954): Sex ratios (male/female) of children for different marriage cohorts in India were higher for older than younger respondents in a survey. The authors assume the lower ratios (approaching 1.0) to be more accurate and interpret the inaccuracy of the older persons as a function of both the greater time since their children were born and the fact that in Indian culture the birth of a male child represents a more important event than the birth of a female child, especially when the child is stillborn or dies very young. [This example and several others from non-Western countries are discussed by Zarkovich (1966).]

The fact that respondent reports differ from those in records does not in itself indicate the source or nature of the error. Even if the possibility of error in the records is

TABLE 2
Record Check of Recall by Months of Recall Demanded

MONTHS BETWEEN INTERVIEW AND INCIDENT	PERCENT RECALLED	(*N*)
1–3	69	(101)
4–6	50	(100)
7–9	46	(103)
10–12	30	(90)

SOURCE: Turner, 1972, p. 8.

put aside—as doubtless occurring but unmeasurable and likely to be small—there remains the difference between random measurement error and systematic measurement bias. Since studies that begin with records regularly find respondents to underreport events in the records, it is often assumed that a bias toward underreporting is involved. However, Marquis (1978) has argued that retrospective record check designs—which start from recorded events and attempt to determine if such events are reported in interviews—are bound to confuse random reporting error with systematic underreporting. Likewise, prospective designs—which start from respondent reports and search for relevant records—will confuse random reporting error with overreporting. Since in each type of design only random error in one direction can be observed, it is classified as directional bias. In addition, Marquis summarizes a small number of "full design studies" as suggesting that little or no net bias occurs and that most inaccuracy in reporting past events is due to random error. Since the issue remains open at this point, we concentrate here on departures from accuracy, without attempting to determine whether they are inherently directional.

A related problem has to do with the incorrect dating of remembered events. A number of studies, of which Neter and Waksberg's (1964) is perhaps the most frequently cited, report that respondents tend to recall incidents as occurring more recently than in fact was the case—a process usually termed forward telescoping. Some backward telescoping—displacing recent events to an earlier time—also occurs but is usually thought to be a less serious problem. The term *telescoping* suggests a basic psychological process, but the existence of such a process has not been demonstrated. Some investigators believe that the evidence that has led to the concept of telescoping is better seen as a result of random dating errors in both directions, plus demand effects that lead respondents to include more prior and subsequent events within the assigned time interval, plus artifactual constraints resulting from the relation of the beginning and ending time boundaries to the time of actual interview (Sparks, in press). Perhaps the term *end effects* (Zarkovich, 1966) is a better one to use at this point, since it allows for a range of explanations as researchers attempt to clarify both the phenomenon and the contributing factors.

In studying reports of past events, Cannell *et al.* (1981) emphasize the extent to which effort on the part of respondents is needed in searching memory. This in turn is believed to require that investigators communicate to respondents the importance of their answers and motivate them to do the necessary mental work. Several techniques have been developed by Cannell and his associates:

1. *Instruction:* Respondents often have only a hazy idea as to the purpose of a survey and may not regard precise answers as particularly important. Clear instructions that emphasize the degree of completeness and accuracy that the investigator is after appear to increase the number of past events reported. (In most of their studies Cannell *et al.* do not have validating records and must assume that the more reports, the more accurate is the reporting. While there is reason to think that this is true of most health reports, it obviously may not be true in other areas.)

2. *Commitment:* Cannell *et al.* (1981) have experimented with having respondents read and sign a form such as the following:

> *AGREEMENT*
>
> I understand that the information from this interview must be very accurate in order to be useful. This means that I must do my best to give accurate and complete answers. I agree to do this.
>
> ———————————————
> Signature of Respondent

(An accompanying form pledging confidentiality is signed simultaneously by the interviewer.) The investigators find that about 95 percent of their respondents agree to sign such a form and that the agreement increases the number of health events reported, much as early work on commitment by Lewin (1951) would suggest.

3. *Question length:* There is some evidence that longer questions elicit more reports of past health events than do short questions, with the lengthening intended to be merely a matter of adding redundancy. For example:

- *Short question:* What health problems have you had in the past year?

- *Long question:* The next question asks about health problems during the last year. This is something we are asking everyone in the survey. What health problems have you had in the past year?

The reason for the effect is not altogether clear, but it may simply be that length and redundancy are taken as signs of the importance of the inquiry and serve both instructional and motivational purposes. In any case not only did respondents give more reports of relevant health events to long than to short questions, but the increase in reporting appeared to carry over to questions that were not lengthened (Cannell *et al.,* 1977).

4. *Reinforcement or Feedback:* Responses assumed to be more adequate by the investigators were positively reinforced (e.g., "Uh-huh, I see. This is the kind of information we want"). Since this refers more to interviewer style than to question construction, we defer consideration of the reinforcement technique to a later section. (Although the terms reinforcement and feedback are sometimes used interchangeably, Cannell appears to regard feedback as including instructional content as well as verbal reward.)

Cannell *et al.* (1981) report that all four of the above techniques are effective in increasing reports of health events such as doctor visits and illnesses. The extent to which the techniques are additive varies somewhat in their several studies, and there are other problems that caution against uncritical adoption of these approaches without further research (see Miller and Cannell, 1982). But the techniques do seem promising, and in particular they point toward a more analytic view of the survey interview as an instrument for obtaining reports of past events.

One other issue with regard to attempts to obtain reports of past events concerns the degree to which respondents should be provided with aids to memory. For example, asked to report magazines read in the last month, respondents can be given a list of all conceivable magazines (a form of recognition termed *aided recall* in the survey literature) rather than simply asked to recall without any assistance. Apart from the problem of providing a genuinely complete list, there is often concern that respondents may be tempted to report incorrectly having read magazines on the list that sound attractive (*Foreign Affairs, Scientific American,* etc.) regardless of their actual behavior. However, Belson and Duncan (1962) show not only that a list of television programs seen "yesterday" yielded more mentions than comparable open-ended questions but also that several nonexistent programs included on the list were rarely picked, though they did not test the "attractiveness" concern directly. The greater problems with using such lists are probably the difficulty of making them exhaustive and the further difficulty of using a very long list, especially in a telephone interview. There is also evidence for a primacy effect in choices from a long list (Becker, 1954), presumably due to loss of respondent interest or motivation. It might seem as though a useful compromise could be obtained by listing the main items apt to be chosen and then including an explicit category called "Others"; however, there is clear evidence that such a strategy leads to appreciable underreporting of events not included as separate substantive categories (Lindzey and Guest, 1951; Belson and Duncan, 1962).

Where more than a single interviewing contact is possible, respondents can be asked to keep diaries or other records rather than to rely on memory (Sudman and Ferber, 1971). This also avoids recalling events as having occurred within a focal time interval when in fact they fell outside it—the phenomenon discussed above as telescoping or end effects. An earlier interview can also be used to correct for forward telescoping by identifying events that occurred prior to the new recall period—a procedure known as bounded recall (Neter and Waksberg, 1964).

Attitudes, Beliefs, and Values

Surveys are the major means by which social psychologists and others attempt to assess the attitudes, beliefs, and values of the general public. Although for some purposes it is useful to distinguish among these terms—Fishbein and Ajzen, 1975—we shall refer to all of them under the rubric of "attitude," since the distinctions do not seem to be directly relevant to the points discussed below. Two fundamental problems that must be confronted with all survey questions are taken up here because they are especially salient with attitude questions. One is the problem of question constraint, the other of question specificity.

Question constraint refers to the fact that respondents ordinarily accept the framework provided by a question and try to answer within it. If the question presents two alternatives to choose from, most respondents will try to select one of them, even though they might prefer a third that is equally relevant but not offered. There are many examples of this phenomenon, an especially interesting one being "don't know" (DK) or "no opinion" responses. Standard survey questions ordinarily omit "no opinion" as an explicit option, though accepting it when offered spontaneously. However, there are some surveys that include "no opinion" as an explicit alternative in questions, and we will label these DK filter questions. Schuman and Presser (1981) used split-ballot experiments to compare the two approaches for nine different attitude items and found in every case a significant and substantial rise in "don't know" responses when the option was made explicit. The mean increase due to the filter for samples from the general population was 22 percent over and above the percentage saying "don't know" spontaneously to the more standard form. Moreover, the increment was fairly constant and seemed to bear little or no relation to the difficulty of the item: On a question about whether a Communist book should be removed from a public library, 3 percent volunteered DK to the standard form, but the percentage rose to 26 percent when "no opinion" was included as an explicit option; on a question about the government of Portugal, 63 percent volunteered DK to the standard form, but the percentage rose to 88 percent when "no opinion" was explicitly offered. Thus regardless of the rate of spontaneously admitted ignorance, a sizable jump occurred when DK was clearly legitimized. Later experiments by Bishop *et al.* (1983) do point to some positive association between the DK base rate on the standard form and the amount of DK increment, but the overall relation is not likely to be a strong one.

Similar findings occur with the omission or inclusion of a "middle alternative" between two extreme positions (Kalton *et al.,* 1980) and with omission or inclusion of an alternative from a checklist of nominal categories to choose from. In all these cases most respondents seem to assume that the rules of the game call for working within the categories offered, even though the desire to answer otherwise is demonstrated when greater freedom is allowed.

An important implication of this finding is that investigators need to remind themselves that it is they, not respondents, who are determining the frame of reference within which survey answers are given. To say that X percent of the population prefers alternative A to alternatives B, C, D, and E may be quite correct, but one needs to keep in mind that the percentage might have changed drastically had alternative F been included (or substituted for E). This is one reason—and there are others to be noted below—for distrusting absolute percentages, a distrust urged by McNemar (1946) many years ago. It is extraordinarily easy to forget that the proportion obtained, and even the ranking of several proportions, may be largely a function of the alternatives that were offered.

The traditional way to escape from this problem is to avoid offering any alternatives at all—i.e., to keep questions "open." Presumably, this allows respondents to give whatever answers they wish. In the early days of survey research there was a considerable argument over the virtues of open as against closed questions, with Rensis Likert and his colleagues being proponents of the more open form and Elmo Roper and other pollsters defenders

of closed questions (Converse, in press). The best-known remnant of this controversy is an essay "offer to negotiate" by Lazarsfeld (1944), a more recent and more fully developed version of which appears in McKennell (1974). The proposal is that open questions be used in the early stages of research to determine the substance and wording of alternatives, and that these findings then be converted into a set of choices in final closed questions. One worry about this approach is that although it may lead to inclusion of all important options, the final array presented to respondents may distract them from their own spontaneous preference, for example, by presenting a socially desirable alternative that they might never have thought of themselves.

Considering the importance of the issues caught up in the open-closed controversy, the absence of research in this area is unfortunate. However, there are some limited experimental data to show that a more qualified version of the Lazarsfeld strategy may be successful. Using a succession of open versus closed split-ballot experiments on a single item about work values, Schuman and Presser (1981) show that it is possible by pilot work to expand closed alternatives to embrace all major ones offered by respondents, and furthermore there is little evidence that variations among the alternatives in social desirability influence respondents to depart from their more spontaneous choices. The investigators also show that the gain in precision from using the closed form of a question is considerable, since by having respondents code themselves into categories, one eliminates a large number of errors due to ambiguous or incomplete recording of the open answer or misinterpretation by a third-party coder. These advantages all assume that the attitudes under investigation are not changing rapidly over time, for if they are, the closed alternatives may cease to provide appropriate choices.

The Schuman and Presser experiments must be regarded as merely a first effort to deal with these issues, since a single item is hardly a sufficient basis for generalization. Moreover, there are puzzling aspects of their data that cannot be detailed here but that leave the final conclusions in some doubt. Finally, they themselves note that their results do not show that the Lazarsfeld strategy provides a completely respondent-determined frame of reference, for the open question itself may serve unintentionally to discourage a particular type of response. Evidence is produced from an analysis of answers to an open question about "the most important problem facing the United States": "Crime" seems to be understated because many respondents apparently believe that it does not qualify as a "national" problem, even though this was not the investigator's intention. Thus the open question does not specify the frame of reference clearly enough. For all these reasons further research involving open-closed comparisons is much needed. [For an interesting parallel involving factual questions, see Loftus's (1982) discussion of narrative versus interrogative techniques in obtaining testimony from witnesses.]

The fact that a substantial number of respondents will shift their answer depending upon the choices available to them raises the further issues of exactly who these people are and how their shifts affect other results. The issue has been most thoroughly investigated for the "don't know" response, i.e., for people who choose "don't know" when it is offered but select a more substantive response when "don't know" is not an explicit option. Such respondents have been termed "floaters" by Schuman and Presser (1981). The fact that the proportion of floaters usually does not vary greatly from one item to another suggested initially that they might constitute a specific subset of the national population—in other words, that about a fifth of the American population would consistently give a "no opinion" response when it is offered but choose a substantive alternative when "don't know" is not offered (even though it is allowed). Further investigation, however, has indicated that the people who float on one item are generally not the same as the people who float on another, and that a process model rather than a simple trait model is needed. Such a process model conceives of the "don't know" response as one that may be given by anyone in the population depending upon the difficulty of the question content for that person and the degree to which the question form allows such a response.

Regardless of who floaters are, an important issue is whether when all "don't know" responses are excluded from calculations, attitude items relate differently to one another depending upon whether or not "no opinion" filters had been employed. The concept of nonattitudes developed by Converse (1970) suggests that a substantial number of people answer survey questions despite having no real opinion on the issue—in fact, knowing nothing about the issue. Respondents are said to do this because they interpret the survey questionnaire as a kind of test and consider it better to guess randomly at one of the alternatives offered than to answer "I don't know." But if this is the case, then legitimizing "don't know" by emphasizing it as an option should remove from the ef-

fective sample a set of people who are contributing random error to the data and therefore reducing correlations with other variables. (The reduction could be substantial since we have seen that the proportion of floaters averages around 22 percent of the national population.) The attenuation of correlations is not, however, the only hypothesis that can be derived from the nonattitude premise: such uninformed and unopinionated people might be easy prey to nonsubstantive cues, such as acquiescence bias when questions are in agree-disagree form. The effect on correlations of this type of bias would depend on the existence and direction of the underlying true correlation, but at least in some cases the failure to filter out "don't knows" might create an apparent positive association (due, say, to acquiescence on both items) where in reality there was none at all.

For the nine experimental items noted earlier, Schuman and Presser (1981) examined a variety of interitem correlations. In most of these cases filtering or not filtering "don't know" responses had no reliable effect on the substantive association of one item with another, despite the movement of large numbers of respondents into and out of the "don't know" category. In just two cases (each replicated sufficiently to be not dismissible as the result of sampling error) did filtering have effects: once raising a correlation as the simple version of the nonattitude theory suggests, but once lowering it. Close examination of the data, however, suggested that neither an interpretation in terms of random error nor one in terms of obvious response bias would explain the results. Instead, it appeared that those affected by DK filters—i.e., floaters—tended to define the attitude items in a more diffuse and general way than other respondents. Apparently, they handled their lack of knowledge of particular attitude objects by responding to a broader class to which they consigned the particular objects. This can be regarded as a "set," not in the sense of an agreeing response set but rather in the sense that any attitude can be called a set (Allport, 1954).

The phenomenon of nonattitudes can be examined further and in a purer form by presenting all respondents with a fictional object, or with an object so esoteric that they are unlikely to have ever heard of it. The former was tried by Bishop *et al.* (1980) using a fictional Public Affairs Act, the latter by Schuman and Presser (1981) using the real but virtually unknown Agricultural Trade Act of 1978. Results were very similar. On standard question forms, which allowed but did not encourage "no opinion," about one-third of the population gave an opinion, while about two-thirds volunteered that they had none. When a DK filter was added to legitimize "don't know," the proportions changed to 10:90. The results point to three important conclusions. First, a substantial proportion of the population will, when questioned, offer an opinion about an object they have never heard about, though the proportion does not reach the majority levels sometimes suggested. Second, the proportion can be radically reduced, though not eliminated entirely, by routinely including an explicit "don't know" option. Such an option can precede the question by asking respondents whether they have an opinion on the following issue (a full filter), or it can be included as one of the several alternatives to the question ("...or don't you have an opinion?"). Schuman and Presser show that the former removes more respondents than the latter, and Bishop *et al.* show that the exact wording of the filter ("no interest in the issue" versus "no opinion") also affects the proportion of "don't know's." Presumably, investigators interested in "informed opinion" may wish to make the legitimacy of the "don't know" option quite clear.

The third conclusion from these investigations of fictional and quasi-fictional issues is of special interest from the standpoint of attitude theory. Apparently, many of the responses about the Public Affairs Act and the Agricultural Trade Act are not merely guesses, as the concept of nonattitudes usually implies, but represent serious attempts by respondents to figure out what the object is and then to respond in terms of those individual definitions. This is shown by the facts that such responses sometimes depart significantly from 50:50 distributions, that they show some stability over time, and that they exhibit meaningful associations with answers to other attitude items of a nonfictional type. Thus although responses about fictional objects fit Converse's notion of nonattitudes in the sense that there was no thought about the specific attitude object prior to the interview, this does not mean that the attitudes evoked are themselves unreal. On the contrary, a fair number of the responses seem to represent deep-seated attitudes, such as trust or distrust of the government, which are expressed in a purer form because of the respondents' need to define the object themselves. Indeed, whereas Converse (1964, 1970) showed that real objects could elicit nonattitudes, the results discussed here indicate that what are essentially nonobjects can elicit real attitudes.

Moreover, there is probably no sharp line between

fictional or deliberately obscure objects, on the one hand, and the more ordinary objects in surveys of public opinion, on the other hand, since the latter (e.g., the SALT negotiations, Cambodia, nuclear power) are only barely understood, if that, by large segments of the public. The meaningfulness of attitude objects—as of other objects—must be considered to be a product of both knowledge about the specific object and the more general dispositions evoked by various aspects of the question. Whether filtered or standard questions should be used in a survey therefore depends on whether an investigator is interested mainly in informed opinion on an issue or mainly in underlying dispositions. Since both goals are pursued by social psychologists who employ survey research, there may be no general solution to the problem of which form of question is better.

Question specificity refers to the fact that respondents are normally affected by the exact wording of a question to a greater degree than naive investigators realize. This is often summarized in the dictum that "a small change in wording can have large effects on answers." Turned around, it also leads to the cynical belief that by manipulating question wording, clever survey practitioners can obtain almost any distribution of answers they wish.

The assertion that a small change in wording can have large effects on answers deserves closer examination. Two kinds of wording changes should be distinguished: substantive and nonsubstantive. Substantive changes occur because almost all social issues and internal feeling states are complex, yet individual survey questions must necessarily be kept simple. Thus a single question can usually tap only one facet of an issue. For example, the following two questions both deal with gun control, yet they would yield very different distributions of responses because they pose the issue in very different terms:

- Would you favor or oppose a law that would require a person to obtain a police permit before he or she could buy a gun?

- Would you favor or oppose a law that would ban possession of guns, except by police and military authorities?

Just as legislators might vote differently on these two questions if posed as possible laws, so respondents also "vote" differently when they are asked one or the other in a survey. Yet either of the questions might be cited by someone concerned to find a result bearing on the general issue of gun control. From past data (see Smith, 1980b) we can be reasonably sure that the first would yield a clear majority supporting gun control, the second a clear majority opposed.

Moreover, it should also be evident that the "smallness" of a change is a matter of judgment about shifts in meaning, not a matter of the number of letters, words, or phrases altered. If the first question above were revised by changing the word *buy* to *fire,* the original and the new question would differ in only one word, yet we might again expect a large difference in results if the two versions were administered to comparable samples of the American population. Indeed, the proposition that "a nose by any other name would smell as sweet" is altered in only one letter from Juliet's original declaration, yet the change in wording is hardly trivial.

In many cases, therefore, a small change in wording involves an unmistakable substantive shift in meaning and points to the sensitivity, rather than to the lability, of survey questions. Put in other terms, the problem is not one rightly attributable to either survey questions or survey respondents but rather to a strong tendency by survey users to be tempted by overly simple summaries of public attitudes and beliefs. What is called an issue is often really a constellation of issues, and the real issues (e.g., gun permits versus banning of guns) may be of more interest than the overall rubric.

Most so-called small changes in question wording are probably of a substantive nature. However, there is also compelling evidence that what appear to be nonsubstantive alterations in questions can lead to important shifts in response distributions. One of the most striking examples was reported by Rugg (1941), using split-ballot data collected by Elmo Roper in 1940. Only 25 percent of a national cross section of respondents were willing to allow "speeches against democracy," but 46 percent were against forbidding such speeches. It is no doubt true that the connotations of the terms [*not*] *allow* and *forbid* differ somewhat, but their operational consequences for holding or not holding speeches appear to be the same in the two versions—hence the response distributions should not differ. Furthermore, this particular response effect has been replicated experimentally quite recently, indicating that it was not limited to the 1940 Roper Poll in which it was first discovered (Schuman and Presser, 1981). Its exact cause and scope are not fully under-

stood—the forbid-allow effect occurs with some but not all other issues—but the findings suggest that apparently nonsubstantive changes in question wording can influence responses appreciably.

There is also strong evidence that response distributions are sometimes influenced by the order in which alternatives are read, the effect usually but not always being a recency one (Payne, 1951; Kalton *et al.,* 1978; Schuman and Presser, 1981). These well-documented examples of changes in marginals due merely to variations in response order show even more decisively the danger of treating response distributions as having absolute meaning.

However, three qualifications to these conclusions are required. First, it is not the case that *any* change in wording will alter survey response distributions. For example, an antiabortion advertisement in the *New York Times* in 1974 claimed that support for legalized abortion was lower when the word *abortion* was used in a question than when the term *end pregnancy* was substituted. An experimental test of this proposition in 1980, however, failed to show any evidence for such an effect (Schuman and Presser, 1981), though it is conceivable that the effect had once existed but subsequently disappeared. There are a number of other instances discussed by the same authors where rather noticeable changes in wording (or in response order) do not seem to change response distributions. Thus the problem is not that *any* change in wording will affect responses but that many do and that it is often impossible to predict in advance which changes will have effects and which will not.

A second qualification is that while the size of effects due to *substantive* modifications is probably unlimited—one could vary percentages by nearly 100 with appropriate modifications—most nonsubstantive effects are less than 20 percent and often less than 10 percent. (The forbid-allow difference seems to be the largest nonsubstantive wording effect ever discovered.) Thus if X percent endorse a particular position, it is extremely unlikely that the response will vary by more than $\pm$ 20 percent because of a nonsubstantive variation in form or wording. This hardly allows for much precision when stating a result in percentage terms, but it does tell us that, say, 75 percent pro is almost certainly not going to become 75 percent anti as a result of a nonsubstantive change in wording or response order.

An important qualification is also needed to our distinction between substantive and nonsubstantive alterations in wording. Although the distinction is usually clear, there are instances where it is not. Consider the following question asked by Gallup during the Vietnam War period (*Gallup Opinion Index,* No, 29, p. 6):

> If a situation like Vietnam were to develop in another part of the world, do you think the United States should or should not send troops?

Mueller (1973) noted that when the "same" question was asked with the addition of five words ("to stop a Communist takeover?"), the percentage agreeing to American intervention rose by some 15 percent, a difference later replicated several times experimentally (Schuman and Presser, 1981). It is not clear whether this effect on responses should be regarded as a substantive one, where mention of a Communist takeover specifies the situation more precisely, or is simply an emotional coloring to the question that is best considered nonsubstantive. It is possible that some of both occurs, and in any case the example cautions us against assuming that alterations in questions can always be neatly classified as substantive or nonsubstantive.

Finally, a general conclusion that flows from findings on both question specificity and question constraint is the important degree to which all survey responses are shaped by the questions we ask. It is easy on occasion to forget this obvious fact and to treat survey answers as entirely representative of dispositions or beliefs internal to the respondent. The tendency to forget this can be regarded as simply another form of what Ross (1977) has called the fundamental attribution error: the tendency "to overestimate the importance of personal and dispositional factors relative to environmental influences" (p. 184). Survey responses, like virtually all other behavior, are a joint product of internal and external forces, and an important goal of any analysis is to understand the interplay between the two, not least between answers and the questions that have evoked them.

Behavioral Intentions

Questions about behavioral intentions might be included in surveys as a way of measuring attitudes (in the sense of dispositions to respond) or perhaps as a way of assessing the outcome of an individual's attempt to combine his or her underlying attitudes with perceived situational exigencies. However, the main purpose of asking questions about intentions in surveys is often quite different: It lies in the hope that intentions can provide valid predictions of future behavior. Just as questions about the past are used to recover acts and events that would otherwise be unavailable, so questions about intentions seem to offer a means to study behavior that is unavailable because it has not yet occurred (e.g., voting in the next election). Moreover, in some cases intentions are used to try to predict behavior unlikely to happen at all except in the form of a hypothetical situation described to a respondent (e.g., how would you behave if a close relative married a person of another race?). Intentions are thus very attractive objects for measurement, since the ability to foretell the future is always much in demand.

Such exercises at prophesy are bound to be hazardous, however, for even when present intentions are obtained accurately, circumstances can always change in a way that upsets the best-laid plans. One might expect this to be most likely to happen as the distance into the future becomes greater, and there is evidence to support this expectation (Kelley and Mirer, 1974; Schwartz, 1978). There is a parallel here to our earlier conclusion that reports of past behavior decrease in validity as the time interval lengthens, although the explanations are no doubt different for the two types of inquiry. There is also an analogue for intentions to our earlier conclusion that the validity of reports of past behavior varies directly with the personal importance of an act or event: Predictions of future behavior are more successful when the respondent has had direct experience with the kind of act being asked about rather than encountering it only in the form of a survey question (Fazio and Zanna, 1981). This suggests that purely hypothetical questions about intentions are less likely to be useful for prediction than are questions about intentions concerning recurrent events.

A number of other variables also affect the success with which intentions can successfully predict future behavior. Most have been a concern of the attitude-behavior literature, extensive review of which lies outside the scope of this chapter. [A review of the attitude-behavior problem through the mid-seventies appears in Schuman and Johnson (1976), and a synthesis of more recent research is provided by Abelson (1982).] Perhaps the main conclusion to be drawn from the many empirical studies that have been carried out over the nearly fifty years since LaPiere's (1934) original and classic investigation is that the strength of the attitude-behavior relation varies greatly depending upon the topic covered, the time involved, the nature of the measurement of both the attitudes and the behaviors, and a wide variety of other factors. It is naive to expect to be able to substitute intentions for actual behavior in any one-to-one sense, but it is also incorrect to assume that good prediction is impossible. In some areas, such as voting, intentions have usually been rather successful predictors, but these tend to be areas where the choices are simple and clear-cut, the time interval relatively short, and the correspondence quite close between measures of intention and measures of behavior (cf. Ajzen and Fishbein, 1977).

Sensitive Questions

Crosscutting all the distinctions made thus far is that between questions on more and less sensitive topics. By *sensitive topics* we refer to those that are apt to be regarded as embarrassing or threatening to respondents because revealing accurate information might, at the very least, lower their image in the eyes of interviewers or, at the extreme, subject them to legal penalties. For example, because there is not good official information available on frequency of recent drug use or on willingness to discriminate on racial or sexual grounds, the survey becomes a possible instrument for obtaining such estimates, but by the same token one must worry that the data so obtained may be biased by systematic distortion. Moreover, it is not only survey reports of criminal acts that could be compromised in this way but even seemingly minor facts such as having voted or not voted in a recent election, since failure to vote may be seen by some as a source of embarrassment.

It can hardly be doubted that such distortions can occur, but the specification of sensitive topics is not as simple as may at first appear. One approach is to ask respondents whether particular questions are too personal either for themselves or for other people. For example, Bradburn *et al.* (1979) report that 56 percent of their national sample said that a question on masturbation would make most people "very uneasy," as against only one percent who said that this would be true for questions on sports activities. This tells us about the potential for distortion in answers but not about actual distortion nor, indeed, even with certainty the direction of distortion.

A common type of research with sensitive questions starts from the assumption that we know the direction in which answers will be distorted and then compares the results obtained by different survey methods. Thus we assume that people will tend to overstate behaviors generally regarded as "good" in our society, such as voting in an election, and when validity data are available, the larger part of error in such cases does appear to be in the direction of overstatement (Parry and Crossley, 1950). We assume that actions generally regarded as "bad," such as drunken driving, will be understated; there are also some data to support this commonsense assumption (Bradburn *et al.,* 1979), although a recent review of a large number of validation studies reports little or no evidence of systematic denial of undesirable behaviors (Marquis *et al.,* 1981). It should, however, be recognized that some sensitive subjects may well lead to distortion in both directions; for example, it is easy to imagine that reports of sexual behavior could be under- or overstated depending upon the respondent and, further, that such differences could vary across time and subculture. It is conceivable that such effects may tend to cancel out so that little or no net distortion occurs at the aggregate level, despite gross misreporting that affects correlations.

On the assumption that we usually know the predominant direction of response distortion, the interviewing and questioning techniques developed by Cannell and his colleagues (1981) show some success in encouraging frank responses to sensitive questions. Commitment and feedback additions to the interview appear to have been especially successful in increasing reports of health conditions involving the pelvic region, which the investigators assumed to represent more embarrassing conditions. Moreover, in a related study Miller and Cannell (1977) provide evidence that the several combined techniques can reduce *both* underreporting and overreporting of media contact. For example, the experimental group (which received a combination of instruction, commitment, and feedback) reported having watched significantly *more* television the previous day but also reported having read significantly *fewer* books in the last three months than the control group. If one assumes that both changes are in the direction of greater validity, then altering questionnaire and interviewing approaches in fairly small ways can apparently improve accuracy of reporting to a detectable extent, though in the absence of validating information we remain uncertain as to the amount of systematic error remaining.

A more radical change in questioning procedure is the random-response technique. Originally developed by Warner (1965), in its simplest form the technique provides two questions to a respondent, one of them innocuous (e.g., Is your birthday in June?) and one sensitive (e.g., Have you ever been arrested for a crime?). The choice of which question to answer is determined by a chance procedure, such as the draw of a card from a carefully shuffled deck of blue and red cards, with, say, the selection of a blue card indicating the choice of the innocuous question, a red card the choice of the sensitive question. The outcome of the chance procedure is known only to the respondent, and hence the confidentiality of his or her answer is protected. However, the investigator's knowledge of the probabilities of choice of each of the questions and of the expected distribution of responses to the innocuous question allows estimation of the overall distribution of responses for the sensitive question. Suppose in the example given that the deck consists of 20 blue cards and 40 red ones; that as a simplified approximation, 30 out of 365, or 8.2%, of the answers to the innocuous question are expected to be yes; and that 6.2% of the respondents answer yes to whichever question they chose by chance. Then the percentage of yes responses to the arrest question X can be estimated from the equation

$$6.2\% = \left(\frac{20}{60}\right)8.2\% + \left(\frac{40}{60}\right)X.$$

This gives an estimate of $X = 5.2\%$ answering yes to the arrest question. Many variants in procedure and in this simple model have been developed along several different lines. [Zdep and Rhodes (1976–1977), include a brief review; see also Chapter 10 of this *Handbook*].

A number of experimental comparisons between randomized-response techniques and traditional questioning have found the former to yield higher rates in reports of sensitive information that would be expected to be underreported, for instance, in responses to questions about abortions (Abernathy *et al.,* 1970) and school students' drug use (Goodstadt and Gruson, 1975). Such findings are further supported by a validation study by Tracy and Fox (1981) concerning reports of the number of times a respondent had been arrested (validated against police arrest files); however, even the randomized-response technique yielded rather substantial underreporting here, as it has also in other studies (cf. Bradburn *et al.,* 1979). In addition, the technique produces an appreciable increase in sampling error, which has to be set against its gains in bias reduction.

The complexity of the randomized response technique is likely to result in it being misunderstood by some respondents and mistrusted by others. This complexity is avoided in another form of indirect questioning technique in which respondents are asked to report only the

totals of their responses to a set of questions, with different respondents answering different sets (Smith *et al.,* 1974; Raghavarao and Federer, 1979; Miller, 1984). In the simplest form of the technique, the sample is divided randomly into two parts: One part is presented with a list of behaviors including the sensitive one under study, and the other part is presented with the same list except that the sensitive behavior is excluded. Respondents are simply asked to report how many of the behaviors *in toto* they have engaged in during the specified period. The proportion of the population engaging in the sensitive behavior is then estimated by the difference between the mean numbers of behaviors reported by the first and second parts of the sample. The technique provides protection to respondents since reporting the number of behaviors engaged in does not disclose which behaviors are involved (unless all or none are reported), and it is hoped that this protection reduces response bias. As with the randomized-response technique, however, a price to be paid for the use of this technique is a sizable increase in the sampling error of the estimate as compared with that of the estimate obtained from the direct approach. (With both techniques, estimates may even turn out to be negative.) The technique has notable advantages over the randomized-response technique in terms of simplicity and unobtrusiveness, and consequently seems to hold promise as a means of measuring the prevalence of highly sensitive behaviors (e.g., heroin use). However, further research is needed before the usefulness of this relatively new technique can be firmly established.

A variety of other approaches to asking sensitive questions are reported by Bradburn *et al.* (1979) in a book that deals entirely with such issues. For their samples no single method is without serious problems when a threatening question on drunken driving is employed. Moreover, in one chapter Stocking (1979) questions the usefulness of the Crowne-Marlowe Social Desirability Scale for identifying persons likely to distort answers to sensitive questions; she provides evidence that variance in scale scores reflects real differences in general behavior rather than merely differences in self-presentation relevant to distortion of other responses. A similar problem may occur with other attempts to obtain general measures of social desirability (see the careful work by Schuessler *et al.,* 1978): They all hinge on assuming that high scores represent false answers.

The examples of sensitive questions dealt with thus far have been mainly concerned with behavior, but disclosure of attitudes or beliefs might also be threatening if they are contrary to the views of others. There is some research suggesting deliberate distortions of attitudinal responses in survey situations (e.g., Silverman, 1974), and our discussion below of race-of-interviewer effects can be interpreted to provide further evidence. Yet it is probably a mistake to assume that distortion is large or pervasive in attitude surveys, even in areas (such as racial issues) where it seems most likely to occur. For example, self-reported racial attitudes by white Americans are much less liberal than they *could* be if only lip service were involved: A quarter of a sample of Detroit whites in 1976 said they would be "uncomfortable" in a neighborhood with just one black family, but the figure rose to 72 percent when a 50:50 black:white neighborhood ratio was described (Farley *et al.,* 1978). But why should responses change at all if only pretense is at stake, for it is as easy to avoid a prejudiced response to the second question as to the first? Evidently, those answering are greatly affected by the exact question posed, regardless of their concern for appearance.

There is also a strong theoretical reason to doubt that surveys are as open to social desirability bias of attitudes to the extent often feared. A large and growing number of studies indicate that a high degree of attitude projection occurs in ordinary life, so the majority of respondents assume that their own attitudes are widely shared by others. For example, Fields and Schuman (1976–1977) found that only a small number of Detroit whites (2 percent) believed in keeping white and black children from playing with one another even at school but that this tiny minority, when asked about the attitudes of other Detroiters, believed overwhelmingly that their own attitudes on the issue were shared by the majority. Thus rather than feeling like isolated defenders of unpopular opinions, these respondents perceived a world quite friendly to their own views. (The investigators also present evidence that these perceptions were *not* accurate.) Since survey interviewers are trained to be accepting and nondirective, they certainly do not discourage this kind of simple projection and are probably often believed to share the respondent's point of view. Thus what has been variously described as the false consensus effect (Ross *et al.,* 1977) or looking-glass perceptions (Fields and Schuman, 1976–1977) may well serve to protect the candor of respondents in expressing their opinions. Moreover, the protection may be greater for attitudes than for behaviors such as drunken driving,

since the latter are illegal as well as clearly counternormative.

All this is not to say that caution is not needed in both questioning and analysis when surveys deal with attitudes where there is reason to think that social desirability may be an important factor. A common approach that makes sense is to provide hypothetical support for both sides of a sensitive issue—for example, "Some people feel.... Other people feel...."—though one empirical test reported on this stratagem does not show a difference in results from a more straightforward question (Schuman and Presser, 1981). Several other techniques for wording sensitive questions about behaviors are illustrated in a brief and amusing note by Barton (1958). But the concern of social psychologists for misreporting of attitudes is probably exaggerated and, indeed, may represent their own projection of how *they* would feel expressing illiberal views.

QUESTION ORDER

Thus far we have considered survey questions as though each exists in isolation. Yet a survey always consists of a stream of questions, usually with items of a similar content grouped together to make for a smooth flow. Although it has been recognized from at least Cantril's (1944) volume on *Gauging Public Opinion* that question order might affect responses, the evidence that this actually occurs has been sparse, consisting of a handful of scattered reports that were unreplicated, atypical in question content, and occasionally negative in outcome. Certainly, there was nothing dramatic in the case of order effects to provide the publicity that occurred in 1936 when the *Literary Digest's* complete inattention to proper sampling requirements led to a widely advertised prediction of a Landon landslide (Parten, 1950).

The situation has changed in the past several years with the appearance of a number of experimental and quasi-experimental results suggesting that question order effects can be substantial and are especially dangerous when investigators attempt to use replication to study social change. In the latter situation it is often impossible and almost always inefficient to repeat an entire questionnaire; yet omission of even a few questions (because they are irrelevant to the purpose of the replication) may conceivably change results for those questions that are repeated. Turner and Krauss (1978) were among the first to emphasize that data showing important trends at the national level might contain serious artifacts because of changes in question order.

The clearest type of question order effect is one where some form of pressure toward consistency in response is created between two closely related items included in the same survey. For example, Hyman and Sheatsley (1950) asked a question about allowing Communist reporters to report freely from the United States and a parallel question about allowing American reporters to report freely from the Soviet Union. Using a split-ballot experiment, the authors found that if the American item (which elicited much more assent) came first, assent to the Communist item was higher than if *it* came first; in the latter case assent to the American item dropped below the level obtained when *it* came first. The differences were large and highly significant, and they could readily be interpreted as due to the fact that a norm of reciprocity is created or heightened when the items are asked together. (This important experiment was mentioned only in passing by the original authors and was overlooked for many years until recently replicated.) Other order effects that also seem to be based on a norm of reciprocal or evenhanded treatment have been drawn together by Schuman and Ludwig (1983), and a somewhat different form of consistency due to question order appears in an NORC experiment first reported by Turner and Krauss (1978).

There are three further important points to note about such consistency effects. First, it is far from obvious that results from one order of questions are inherently more valid than results from another. In real life the need for reciprocity is indeed sometimes made quite clear by the situation, and there is no reason why this should not be simulated in a questionnaire. Second, a traditional assumption of survey investigators that order effects can be eliminated by interposing other items between a contextually related pair has recently been shown to be incorrect in at least one case by Schuman *et al.* (1983a). Finally, the Hyman and Sheatsley (1950) effect was replicated in 1980 by Schuman and Presser (1981) and produced a further interaction with time: When the Communist reporter item was asked first at both points in time, willingness to allow Communist reporting from this country increased by 18 percent over 1948, but when the item came second, there was no reliable change (i.e., no shift in the strength of the norm of reciprocity). Thus *even with context held constant,* one drew different conclusions about change over time depending upon which

context was replicated. Looked at negatively, this finding indicates that response effects due to context cannot always be controlled simply by keeping context constant. But looked at positively, it indicates that split-ballot survey experiments on context can illuminate patterns of attitude change and stability that are not visible when only a single context is employed.

Two other types of context effects deserve mention both because they are well documented and of theoretical interest. One is probably a close cousin to consistency effects but involves increasing the salience of an item when it follows others that may raise the consciousness of the respondent. The most interesting example of an apparent salience effect is reported both by Gibson *et al.* (1978) and Cowan *et al.* (1978). From 1972 through 1975 the National Crime Survey Cities Sample obtained respondent reports of victimization experiences during the preceding twelve months. On a random half of the interviews these reports followed sixteen attitude questions about crime; on the other half the attitude questions were omitted. Victimization reports, especially of less serious crimes, increased significantly and appreciably for the subsample asked the attitude questions. The most plausible interpretation is that the attitude questions stimulated memory for and willingness to report more experiences, although some degree of misreporting cannot be ruled out. It is important to note that this order effect involved survey questions of a factual nature. Indeed, the attitude questions had been placed first in the survey on the common assumption that they, not the factual questions, would be sensitive to context.

The example just given concerned reports of past experiences. There are also instances with attitude items that may involve an increase in salience, especially where a general or summary type of question follows a set of more specific items. For example, self-reported interest in politics and religion increased in an experiment when the general-interest questions were asked after specific items on politics and religion, although responses to the latter were not affected when they were placed after the general items (McFarland, 1981). What is not clear at present is whether this involves a genuine arousal of interest, a clarification of what the general assessment is based on, some sort of behavioral self-report ("having answered all these specific questions, I must be interested in the more general issue"), or perhaps only a self-presentational strategy. Further controlled experiments are needed here.

The salience experiment just discussed reports effects on a general item but not on more specific or concrete items. Several other experiments involving items at different levels of generality provide similar reports (Kalton *et al.*, 1978; Smith, 1979; Schuman and Presser, 1981; Sigelman, 1981). Perhaps when an investigator tries to summarize a complex issue with a single general item, it takes on different meanings in different contexts as respondents attempt to interpret the general question. Sensible as such summary questions may seem to the investigator, they may not allow for either the ambivalence or the specific qualifications that are in the minds of respondents.

The Kalton *et al.* (1978) and Schuman and Presser (1981) experiments, one on driving standards and the other on legalization of abortion, point also to another and theoretically quite interesting type of order effect: that due to contrast rather than consistency. In the abortion experiment, for example, respondents were less apt to support abortion essentially on demand after hearing a question about abortion in the case of a defective fetus (which most people favor). One possible interpretation is that the compelling argument for abortion in the question about a defective fetus makes the abortion-on-demand rationale seem less justified (compare Pepitone and DiNubile, 1976).

We should not like to leave the subject of question order effects with the idea that they are pervasive in survey questioning. Although the examples we have given (and some not given) are important, they do not reflect the prevalence of such effects. Not only are there clear cases where the investigators attempted to create such effects and failed (Bradburn and Mason, 1964), but in addition a thorough search of a large questionnaire that contained many opportunities for order effects turned up only 8 significant effects out of 113 possibilities—just 2 more than might have been expected by chance (Schuman and Presser, 1981). It is likely that order effects occur in practice only under very special circumstances, and it may be possible, through careful experimentation, to identify what these are. Pressures toward consistency seem to underlie most question order effects discovered thus far, but *consistency* itself is a vague term and needs to be specified more clearly through systematic experimentation. In addition, we have also seen examples where contrast rather than consistency appears to be involved. Given the long-standing concern with order effects by experimental psychologists, this whole area is one where laboratory and survey approaches might usefully be brought into closer contact.

SYSTEMATIC AND RANDOM RESPONSE EFFECTS

It is often assumed that the kinds of systematic response effects we have been discussing occur primarily when attitudes or beliefs are not well crystallized on a subject. Rugg and Cantril (1944; pp. 48–49) operated on this assumption in their pioneering studies of question wording:

> The extent to which the wording of questions affects the answers obtained depends almost entirely on the degree to which the respondent's mental context is solidly structured. Where people have standards of judgment resulting in stable frames of reference, the same answer is likely to be obtained irrespective of the way questions are asked. On the other hand, where people lack reliable standards of judgment and consistent frames of reference, they are highly suggestible to the implications of the phrases, statements, innuendoes or symbols of any kind that may serve as clues to help them make up their minds.

It is interesting that much the same assumption has also been made about random response error, for example, in Converse's (1970) argument that much unreliability over time in survey results is due to respondents who lack attitudes on an issue but who nevertheless give answers. Thus although the connection is seldom made explicitly, both types of effects are being attributed to the same source, namely, the absence of crystallized attitudes by some people on some issues that are asked about in surveys. Moreover, following this reasoning, by omitting either certain questions or certain respondents or both, we should be able to reduce substantially the occurrence of both systematic and random response effects in attitude surveys.

Unfortunately, Rugg and Cantril did not operationalize crystallization independently, and therefore all their examples are circular. Where response effects appear, the absence of opinion crystallization provides the explanation. But the only indicators of lack of crystallization are response effects themselves. Thus although their emphasis on opinion crystallization is intuitively appealing, it cannot constitute a useful approach in its original form. Converse (1970) provides a more convincing model that points to evidence of lack of crystallization (nonattitudes), but he also does not identify individual respondents directly in these terms.

A possible approach to providing a separate indicator of attitude crystallization is to use measures of self-reported attitude strength. Respondents who say that they do not think an issue is important, or who do not feel strongly about it, might be expected to be especially susceptible to both random and systematic response effects when questions are asked about the issue. However, despite the intuitive appeal of this argument, supportive evidence is at best mixed. Schuman and Presser (1981) failed to find significant interactions between measures of attitude strength and a number of response effects due to question form. They do report interactions between attitude strength and over-time response reliability for individual attitude items, but Judd and Krosnick (1981), using a different approach with different data, present results that seem to contradict such an interpretation. Furthermore, in a recent analysis of panel data, Krosnick (1984) provides evidence indicating that attitude strength is not associated with reliability in the form of measurement error, though his results leave open the possibility that attitude strength may be related to random effects in the sense of attitude instability. (The distinction here is between precision of measurement at any given point in time and degree of attitude stability from one point in time to the next.) In sum, at present the psychological sources of and similarities between random and systematic effects in surveys remain largely a matter of speculation. The issues are important and challenging and are therefore well worth further attempts at clarification and solution.

STRATEGIES FOR OVERCOMING SYSTEMATIC RESPONSE EFFECTS

The problems of question form, wording, and context that we have been discussing appear formidable and may seem to raise doubts about the usefulness of surveys for any purpose beyond gathering the simplest information about a population. But there are two strategies that mitigate the difficulties to a considerable degree when used judiciously. One involves the assumption of form-resistant correlations, the other the use of multiple indicators.

Form-Resistant Correlations

Most of the systematic response effects we have illustrated occur at the level of marginals: A question produces different response distributions depending upon nonsubstantive variations in its form, wording, or context. But since substantive variations in wording are also possible for almost any issue and these usually create even larger univariate effects, the marginals to a question can seldom bear great weight anyway. In consequence, it is the associations and interactions among questions (or indexes constructed from questions) that provide the main results of survey analysis. The investigator asks whether, for example, men and women differ in their answers, not what the distribution is for the entire sample or for either category of sex considered alone. A long-standing assumption of survey analysts—though rarely an explicit one—has been that associations are not susceptible to systematic effects in the same way that marginals are. If the assumption is generally correct, then the examples we have presented recede in importance, provided that analysts confine their concerns to associations.

Schuman and Presser (1981) termed this assumption one of form-resistant correlations and investigated it extensively with respect to the association of attitude items to respondent education. Such investigations involve, at a minimum, three-way interactions: variation in response by experimental variation in question form by education. On the whole, the assumption held up quite well, despite an occasional interesting exception. With regard to variables other than education, conclusions were much more tentative, especially where "time" was the third variable, as in the case of the reporter example discussed earlier where the form effect differed at two points in time. But it does seem to be the case that the results of multivariate attitude survey analysis are much less apt to be seriously affected by variations in question form, wording, and context than are response marginals. Moreover, some similar evidence has been reported for retrospective factual data (Powers *et al.*, 1978) and also for data affected by social desirability bias (Gove and Geerken, 1977): in both cases the effects are noticeable at the univariate level, but they are weak or nonexistent when associations are the focus.

The assumption of form-resistant correlations should never be taken wholly for granted but, rather, continuously reexamined and tested as part of survey studies. To the extent that it receives further support across a range of attitude items and other variables, correlational analysis can proceed with less fear of having conclusions hinge on what may appear to be artifacts in the question-answer process.

Multiple Indicators

A second strategy for avoiding or at least discovering unwanted response effects is the use of more than one indicator (question) for a construct. The rule might be that if a concept or construct is worth measuring at all, it is worth measuring in more than one way within a survey, quite apart from advice going back to Campbell and Fiske (1959) about the advantages of multimethod investigations more generally. The problem with the single question or item is that it is always a unique combination of a number of substantive and nonsubstantive features, any one of which can influence the response of an individual or set of individuals. By considering combinations of items together, users can hope to better separate those features in which they are particularly interested.

The advantages of multiple items are most apparent in the case of examples such as the forbid versus allow experiment discussed earlier. The problem in that specific case involves the unusual wording or syntax of the item. Other questions constructed to operationalize the original concept (whatever that might have been) are unlikely to be similarly affected. However, the gain from multiple items is less apparent when what is at issue is a systematic feature of question form, such as including or omitting "don't know" filters, since unless deliberately varied, all the items will invite the same effect and therefore cumulate it. In principle, construction of a set of items to operationalize a single construct should vary formal features of question structure (e.g., see Andrews and Withey, 1976), but in practice, the opposite strategy is often followed and a stereotyped set of indicators created.

Multiple items are frequently administered as a step toward the construction of scales, as described in Chapter 10. But survey items usually differ in substantive as well as in formal features, so that several survey questions on "racial prejudice" each operationalize a somewhat different facet of the main construct. Often these separate facets are of interest in themselves, as well as because they tap a single construct of interest. The situation is further complicated in sample surveys by our strong interest in tracing change over time. Even where items forma seemingly meaningful scale at one point in time,

social change may lead to trends that not only differ among items but do so in a way that is of considerable importance to understand (Converse, 1972; Piazza, 1980). If individual items are buried within an index, this crucial information will be missed.

Perhaps the main difficulty here lies in the assumption that a set of attitude items is like a set of words in a spelling or vocabulary test. The latter can be thought of as a sample of more or less interchangeable elements from a population, even if the population cannot readily be enumerated. But attitude questions, especially those dealing with public issues, are much less interchangeable. Each one is apt to have unique meaning, so its distinctive determinants are of importance in themselves and not merely because they point to a single concept of interest to the social scientist. Theoretically, one might like to multiply items around each single issue, but in practice, a survey can seldom do this because of high costs in time and limited patience by respondents.

For all these reasons survey investigators are apt to work with sets of individual items, as well as sometimes combining them into a single scale or small set of scales. At the most elementary level comparison of the percentage distributions for two related items (e.g., gun permits versus banning guns) is frequently useful. Likewise, comparisons of the correlates (including time) of separate items is generally illuminating, pointing to differences in meaning and implication that may not be apparent from wording or marginal differences. For most purposes analysis of separate items, of their relations to one another, and of summary combinations should probably go together in survey work, with judgments made as to the best mix given a set of items and a set of analytic aims. After all, the ultimate goal of analyzing survey data is to discover their meaning, and for this purpose an investigator would be foolish to throw away any source of information. It is also likely that methods will be developed that allow analysis of the structure of items to be pursued in a more regular and rigorous fashion than at present, as advocated and illustrated by Duncan (1984).

CONSTRUCTING SURVEY QUESTIONS

Although we have touched on many aspects of question construction, we have not tried to tell readers how to write questions for surveys. Evidence has been noted on such issues as open versus closed questions, but on this issue, and even more so on a number of other issues, firm advice is hard to give with confidence. For example, the extent to and way in which acquiescence plays an important role when agree-disagree statements are used are still unresolved, despite a long history of research in both psychology and sociology. Yet some major controversies in substantive interpretations of attitude survey data turn on just this point (Bishop *et al.,* 1978; Sullivan *et al.,* 1978), and more generally, it would be helpful to know whether it is a good or a bad idea to employ agree-disagree statements in survey questionnaires. Our inclination is to avoid such statements, but the evidence for this inclination is not clear-cut (Schuman and Presser, 1981).

More systematic research on the question-answer process is certainly needed, but at the same time it should be recognized that question construction is not likely ever to become a matter of applied science in the same sense as sampling. One reason is that the construction of questions is closely tied to the operationalizing of concepts and therefore is—or should be—so interwoven with the development of ideas that it cannot be treated as a matter of separate instrumentation. Another reason is that language is so multifaceted that the difficulties of disentangling the effects of specific question forms and wordings are enormous. We can hope for increasing sophistication in our understanding of the implications of constructing questions in one way rather than another, but we are very far from being able to say, Do thus and so.

Some readers may wish to have recourse to questions already asked in well-established surveys. NORC's General Social Survey and ISR's American National Election Studies both regularly publish codebooks with response distributions, and each also provides volumes of trend data (Smith, 1979; Converse *et al.,* 1980). There are also useful collections of survey question sets and scales (Robinson *et al.,* 1968; Robinson and Shaver, 1973). All these sources provide helpful information on the variation obtained for specific questions at past points in time and in many cases analyses involving the questions offer evidence bearing on their construct validity. Some skepticism is always in order when using past questions, however, for often information on their origin and development is lacking, and their repeated use may testify more to the value of maintaining constancy in assessing change than to any inherent virtues of the questions themselves.

On the larger issue of the relation of questions to concepts and theory, it is well to avoid either of two extremes. One is the "interesting question" approach, whereby a questionnaire is constructed bit by bit without clear theoretical purpose. Because adding questions is relatively easy in surveys, there is a great temptation to pose them simply because they seem interesting and vaguely relevant to one's purpose. The temptation should usually be resisted. Yet the opposite extreme seems not to work well either in survey research. Although a narrowly focused deductive style may be appropriate for highly controlled laboratory experiments, a more expansive approach usually works better in survey research. A broad perspective on a survey problem can be accommodated at marginal cost by the addition of pertinent questions in the questionnaire; these allow construction of alternative measures of focal variables, as well as of other variables that may be needed as controls and for exploring possible interactions. Moreover, the basic cost of even a moderate-size survey is so great that it is often useful to pursue several only loosely related problems within the same questionnaire; these sometimes turn out to be connected in unexpected but valuable ways when analysis is carried out.

This recommendation to retain breadth in questionnaire construction is not meant to preclude sustained attempts to develop general-purpose scales for use in the general population. There have been a few such large-scale efforts in recent years, for example, in the area of quality of life or well-being indicators (see Andrews and Withey, 1976; Campbell *et al.,* 1976).

SURVEY SAMPLING

Most social psychological surveys are conducted to collect data from which inferences can be made about some defined group of persons, such as all adults in the United States, all the schoolchildren in a city, all the patients in a hospital, or all the workers in a factory. The element, or unit of analysis, for a survey need not, however, be restricted to persons, and in other subject areas other types of elements are common; economic surveys, for instance, often seek data for households, businesses, or farms. The totality of the elements for which the inferences are required is termed the *population,* and the subject of survey sampling is concerned with the selection of a suitable subset of the population to serve the survey's objectives. Since the way in which the sample is drawn has implications for the way in which estimates of population parameters are made, the subject is also concerned with estimation.

Survey sampling is a highly specialized and developed component of the total survey process. In this chapter we aim to provide only an introduction to the commonly used varieties of sample design. Expanded treatments at about the same level are provided by Moser and Kalton (1971) and Kalton (1983a). The text by Stuart (1976) illustrates the principles of sample design through a small classroom example, and Sudman (1976) provides a nonmathematical discussion of applied sampling procedures. For a detailed coverage the reader is referred to the books by Kish (1965), Hansen *et al.* (1953), and Yates (1981), which combine practical and theoretical treatments of sampling.

THE SAMPLING PROCESS

The starting point for sample design is a precise definition of the population to which inferences are to be made. While this may appear a simple matter, it is usually not so straightforward. For example, in a survey of workers in a factory, are all levels of workers to be included? Are only full-time workers to be included? If not, does a part-time worker have to work for more than a minimum number of hours per week to be included? A date needs to be specified for the population because a work force changes over time. The decisions on these and a variety of other such questions may have a noticeable effect on the survey results, and they should be made to conform to the survey's objectives. Once the step of defining what may be termed the *target population* has been carried out, a number of practical constraints may arise. Thus, for example, some workers may be on vacation at the time the survey is conducted, so no data could be collected from them if they were included in the sample. Constraints such as these may make it sensible to restrict the population covered by the survey to those potentially accessible or accessible at reasonable cost. The sample is then selected from this restricted *survey population,* and the inferences apply only to this population. Although ultimately the survey results relate only to the survey population, the process of starting by defining the target population and then removing some elements to give the survey population is an informative one, for it draws attention to the magnitude of the gap between the ideal and the operational definitions.

Once the population has been defined, researchers can turn their attention to the form of sampling to employ. One alternative, of course, is to conduct a complete enumeration of the population, but this is seldom a realistic possibility for the large populations studied in most surveys. In such cases a complete enumeration would be expensive and time-consuming, and the quality of the data may in fact be inferior to that of a sample survey: The lower nonsampling errors arising from the better data collection procedures possible with a sample survey—better supervisors, interviewers, etc.—may well outweigh the sampling errors arising from taking a sample. A complete enumeration is likely to be appropriate only when the survey population is small; this might apply, for instance, in the factory survey if the factory contained only, say, 200–300 workers. We return to the determination of sample size at a later point.

The choice of a suitable sample design for a survey depends on a number of practical and theoretical considerations. In the first place, the design needs to be tailored to the survey objectives. As will be shown later, different objectives can require different designs. Most surveys have multiple objectives, however, and sometimes these may require different designs; in such cases a compromise design may serve the conflicting objectives adequately. Second, the sample design has to be fashioned for economic data collection, taking into account the methods to be employed. If the data are to be collected from a widespread population by face-to-face interviews, it will usually be advisable to arrange for the sample to be selected in clusters of compact geographic areas, so that an interviewer can carry out several interviews within a cluster with limited travel. This consideration leads to the need for *cluster* or *multistage sampling,* which is described later. Third, the sample design should be formed to provide precise estimators of the population parameters being investigated. Often a good deal of information is known about the population, such as the class of job conducted by each of the factory workers and their numbers of years service. This information may be utilized in the sample design for *stratification,* discussed later; alternatively, it may be used to adjust estimates in the analysis in one of a number of ways—poststratification, ratio, or regression estimation. Finally, the sample design needs to be practicable. Sophisticated procedures that would in theory improve the sample design are best avoided if there is a risk that they may not be carried out correctly by those responsible for their implementation. The final selection of a sample often has to be left to the survey field workers (usually the interviewers), and they need to be given simple, clear, and workable instructions on how to proceed.

Probability Versus Nonprobability Sampling

A fundamental issue in sample design is whether or not the sample is selected by a probability mechanism. With probability sampling all the elements in the population have nonzero probabilities of being selected, and the relative selection probabilities are calculable; the elements selected for the sample are often determined by taking numbers from a table of random numbers. As the subsequent discussion will indicate, in the past half century many different varieties of probability sample designs have been developed.

Nonprobability sampling covers a range of sampling procedures that fail to satisfy the conditions needed for probability sampling. It includes samples of volunteers, samples chosen purposively for the survey, and samples chosen by human judgment to be "representative." It also includes quota sampling, a method widely used in market research in which the final selections of individuals within defined subgroups (e.g., within sex, age, and employment-status subgroups) are left to the survey interviewers, with the number of individuals to be interviewed in each subgroup being specified by the researcher (see Stephan and McCarthy, 1958; Moser and Kalton, 1971, Sec. 6.4). In one type of quota sampling, known as probability sampling with quotas (Sudman, 1966; Stephenson, 1979), areas are chosen by probability sampling methods, and within areas interviewers are given exact instructions on how to select households at which to call. If a person fitting an unfilled quota is available at the time of call, an interview is conducted; otherwise, the interviewer proceeds to the next household. Although, in theory, interviewers have no discretion in their choice of households, this scheme still does not fully satisfy the conditions for probability sampling.

The strength of perfectly executed probability sampling is that statistical theory can be applied to derive the sampling biases involved in the sample estimators (estimators are usually chosen to have no or negligible bias) and to provide measures of the estimators' sampling variabilities. With nonprobability sampling no model-free theoretical development is possible, and the quality of sample estimators can be assessed only by judgment and past experience. With large numbers of selections the security provided by probability sampling is a forceful argument for its use, but the case is less clear for very small samples. If, say, a survey had to be restricted to one or two locations (towns in a survey of the general population or schools for a student survey), a purposive selection of the locations would almost certainly be prefera-

ble. Most surveys, however, employ many selections for large samples. For this reason we will henceforth consider only probability sample designs.

Probability sampling requires a randomization process for selecting the sample elements. A possible system would be a lottery in which disks identifying all the elements in the population are thoroughly mixed in an urn and then the required number of disks is picked. This system is, however, inadequate because it would be excessively time-consuming with a large population and because of the impossibility of mixing the disks into a random arrangement. In its place the standard procedure for choosing random selections is by means of a carefully constructed table of random numbers, such as the Rand Corporation's (1955) table, *A Million Random Digits*. All the elements in the population are associated with specified numbers (not necessarily on a one-to-one basis), so the random numbers selected unambiguously specify the elements to be included in the sample.

A feature brought out by this description of a random-selection procedure is the need to be able to form linkages between all the elements in the population and a set of numbers. In a straightforward case where a list of the population is available, this linkage may be readily achieved by simply numbering the elements; for instance, in the factory example the payroll list may provide a full coverage of all the workers. In other cases no such list may be available; for instance, there exists no list of all the residents in the United States. In these cases the linkages have to be made in a more complex way. One widely used method is known as *area sampling;* in this method the elements are associated with the areal unit in which they are located (in the case of samples of persons, the area of their main residence). The areas are numbered, and a random selection of areas is selected. All the elements in the selected areas may then be drawn, or elements in selected areas may be numbered and a sample of them may be selected (see the later discussion of multistage sampling). The term *sampling frame* is used to denote a population list or an equivalent procedure for identifying the population elements.

Sampling Frames and Frame Problems

When the population has been defined for a survey, the next step in sample design is to discover what sampling frames are available. The nature of the chosen frame exerts a considerable influence on the structure of the sample. If, say, the payroll list of factory workers separated the workers by job classification, this information could be used in stratified sampling to give a sample with the desired distribution of job classes. If a widespread population is listed by geographic areas, these areas may be used in multistage sampling to give the desired clustering of the final interviews. The arrangement of the frame and the information it contains about the elements in the population are thus major factors in sample design.

In practice, it is a rarity for a sampling frame to cover the population in an ideal way with a one-to-one correspondence between the frame listings and the population elements. Kish (1965) has developed a fourfold classification of frame problems. A common problem is that of *missing elements,* when the frame fails to cover some of the elements in the defined population. The payroll list may, for instance, exclude the recently employed workers or certain part-time workers. One solution to this problem is to redefine the survey population to exclude such workers. This solution is reasonable in some, but not all, circumstances, depending on the size and importance of those missed. A second solution is to find a supplement frame for the missing elements; such frames are, however, often unavailable. A further solution is some form of linking procedure, linking the missing elements by clearly defined rules to those elements already listed in the frame. One possible sampling scheme would then be to include in the sample the elements for the selected listing and all the missing elements linked to them. A well-known linking scheme is the half-open interval for sampling elements that follow a specified order: The scheme involves taking the element selected from the frame and any elements that are found after it but before the next listed element. This scheme is sometimes employed with samples of dwelling units in street order (e.g., so as to include recently constructed houses), but the scheme is usually imperfectly executed because of practical difficulties in implementing it.

A second frame problem is that of *clusters of elements,* when one listing represents more than one element of the population. Dealing with missing elements by linking, in fact, creates this problem. The problem also arises in a variety of other ways, as when the population is one of individuals while the listings are addresses. One solution is to take all the elements for a selected listing. This solution has the attraction of keeping the selection probability of the elements the same as that of the listing, but in some circumstances it has disadvantages. If, say, an address is selected and all its individuals are included in the sample, there is a risk of a contamination ef-

fect in the responses of later respondents who may have listened to or been told about the earlier interviews. In addition, if the individuals at an address tend to give similar responses to the survey questions, the sample design may be a statistically inefficient one (see the later discussion of cluster sampling). An alternative solution that avoids these disadvantages is to randomly select one of the elements in a cluster. In this case the selection probability of an element is no longer the same as that of its listing, and account needs to be taken of this fact in the survey analysis.

The third frame problem in Kish's classification is that of *blanks or foreign elements,* when there are listings that do not correspond to population elements. These listings may occur because of withdrawals from the population (e.g., demolished houses, people who have died or emigrated) or because the frame covers a broader population than the survey is interested in (e.g., a list of all students at a university when the survey relates only to undergraduates). The solution for blanks and foreign elements is simply to reject them from the sample if selected, without making substitutions. To allow for these rejections, one needs to initially select a sample larger than ultimately required.

The final problem is that of *duplicate listings,* when some elements have more than one listing on the frame. Unless account is taken of duplications, the elements involved have greater probabilities of appearing in the sample. One way to handle this problem is to correct for the unequal probabilities by adjustments in the analysis. A second way is to remove all the duplicate listings from the frame, but this is often impractical. A third way is to use what is known as unique identification, whereby a rule is established associating each element with only one of its listings (perhaps the first one recorded on the list) and treating the other listings as blanks.

The four frame problems described above occur regularly in practice, and the sampling statistician has to keep them constantly in mind. In some cases considerable ingenuity is needed to handle them. A particularly difficult situation often arises when a survey is concerned with a small subgroup of the total population, called a rare population. Consider, for instance, a survey of persons who have had a severe illness (rigorously defined) in the past year. One approach would be to try to obtain lists of patients hospitalized during the year, but these lists may be inadequate because not all persons with serious illnesses are hospitalized—i.e., there would be many missing elements. Another approach would be to take a sample of the general population to screen for those who had had severe illnesses. This screening would be very expensive because of the many foreign elements on the frame—people who had not had a serious illness in the past year—and because it would be costly to find out which persons were ineligible for the survey. For reasons such as these designing a sample of a rare population poses a special challenge.

With the background that we have established, we are now in a position to review several varieties of probability sample designs. We start with the simplest design, simple random sampling, and successively modify it to take account of various practical and theoretical considerations that determine the choice of an efficient sample design.

SIMPLE RANDOM SAMPLING

We will use the example of the sample of factory workers to illustrate some simple types of sample design. Suppose that the total number of workers in the factory is $N = 2560$, and for simplicity we assume that a complete list of these workers is available to serve as a sampling frame and that there are no other frame problems. The workers are assigned numbers serially from 1 to 2560. Let the required sample size be $n = 400$.

One possible sampling scheme would be to select 400 four-digit random numbers within the range 0001 to 2560 from a table of random numbers and to include the workers associated with these numbers in the sample. This scheme is known as *unrestricted sampling,* or *simple random sampling with replacement.* The term *with replacement* refers to the fact that a worker may be selected more than once for the sample. If the sample had been selected by drawing disks from an urn, after each draw the selected disk would be replaced before the next draw was made.

An alternative scheme would be to draw the sample without replacement. If the random number selected at a particular draw picks an element already included in the sample, the draw is rejected and another one is made. Since it ensures that the sample contains *n different* elements, this scheme is preferable to unrestricted sampling. It is known as simple random sampling without replacement, or just *simple random sampling* (SRS). Formally defined, simple random sampling is a sample design in which each possible set of *n* distinct elements from the *N* elements in the population is equally likely to be the chosen sample. It follows from this definition that each ele-

ment has the same probability (n/N) of being selected for the sample. This property also applies with unrestricted sampling and a number of other designs; such designs are designated as *epsem designs,* with epsem standing for "equal-probability selection method."

Suppose that one purpose of the survey is to estimate the mean value of some variable in the population, say $\bar{Y} = \Sigma Y_i/N$, using the sample estimator $\bar{y} = \Sigma y_i/n$. The sampling error of the sample mean may be measured by its *standard error,* denoted by $\text{SE}(\bar{y})$, or by its variance $V(\bar{y})$, where $V(\bar{y}) = [\text{SE}(\bar{y})]^2$; sample estimators of these quantities are denoted by $\text{se}(\bar{y})$ and $v(\bar{y})$. For a large sample the estimated standard error of $\bar{y}$ may be used, for instance, in computing a 95% confidence interval for $\bar{Y}$ as $\bar{y} \pm 1.96\text{se}(\bar{y})$.

The form of the standard error or variance of a sample estimator depends on the sample design employed. In the case of an unrestricted sample the variance of the sample mean $\bar{y}_u$ (where the subscript u denotes the fact that unrestricted sampling is being used) is given by the following formula:

$$V(\bar{y}_u) = \frac{\sigma^2}{n},$$

where $\sigma^2 = \Sigma(Y_i - \bar{Y})^2/N$, but this formula does not hold for other designs. Indeed, it is generally true that the standard errors and variances of estimators given in standard statistics texts hold only for unrestricted sampling. Another example is the variance of a sample proportion p given by $V(p) = PQ/n$, where P is the population proportion and $Q = (1 - P)$; this formula also holds only for unrestricted sampling. Different formulas are needed for other designs.

In the case of an SRS the variance of $\bar{y}_0$ (subscript 0 for SRS) is given by

$$V(\bar{y}_0) = \frac{N - n}{N - 1}\frac{\sigma^2}{n} = \frac{N - n}{N - 1}V(\bar{y}_u).$$

This variance is clearly smaller than $V(\bar{y}_u)$ for the same sample size, confirming that sampling without replacement yields a more precise estimator in this situation. A more convenient expression for $V(\bar{y}_0)$ is

$$V(\bar{y}_0) = \frac{(1 - f)S^2}{n},$$

where $f = n/N$ is the sampling fraction and $S^2 = \Sigma(Y_i - \bar{Y})^2/(N - 1)$. For large populations S^2 and σ^2 will be virtually equivalent. Then $V(\bar{y}_0)$ is smaller than $V(\bar{y}_u)$ by approximately $(1 - f)$, a factor that is termed the finite population correction (fpc). When the sample size is small relative to the population size, as it mostly is in practice, the fpc is close to 1, and the gains of sampling without replacement are negligible. It is common practice to ignore the fpc term if the sampling fraction is less than 0.1.

In a practical application $V(\bar{y}_u)$ or $V(\bar{y}_0)$ cannot be computed directly because they depend on unknown population parameters, σ^2 for $V(\bar{y}_u)$ and S^2 for $V(\bar{y}_0)$. In the analysis of the survey's data these quantities may both be estimated by $s^2 = \Sigma(y_i - \bar{y})^2/(n - 1)$. In the design of a survey estimates of σ^2 or S^2 may be required in order to calculate the sample size needed to give an estimator of the mean with a desired level of precision. Such estimates have to be based on past surveys or other sources.

Suppose that an SRS is proposed, that the estimator of the population mean is required to have a variance of 0.9, and that S^2 is estimated at 625. Then ignoring the fpc term, the sample size n′ can be obtained from

$$\frac{S^2}{n'} = \frac{625}{n'} = 0.9,$$

or n′ = 562.5, or, on rounding, 563. With $N = 2560$ the sampling fraction is not negligible, and the required sample size is modified according to the formula

$$n = \frac{n'}{1 + (n'/N)}$$

to give

$$n = \frac{562.5}{1 + (562.5/2560)}$$

$$= 461.2, \text{ or } 462.$$

In practice, a further modification is needed to allow for nonresponse—i.e., responses will not be obtained for all elements selected for the sample. With an anticipated response rate of 80 percent, the required size for the selected sample would need to be raised to 461.2/0.8 = 576.5, or 577. Of course, this modification does not correct for nonresponse bias (see the later discussion of nonresponse).

While this example outlines a basic approach to sample size determination, it is clearly oversimplified in a number of respects. In the first place, it assumes that the researcher is able to specify the level of precision required for the survey estimator, but this is no easy task. In practice, the level is nearly always arbitrary in some degree, and at best the researcher will be able to make only a rough-and-ready assessment of the precision he or she requires. Second, surveys are multipurpose, providing many different estimates, both for the total sample and a range of subclasses, and all these estimates need to be considered in determining the sample size. One reason that survey samples are often large is to provide subclass estimates of adequate precision. Finally, the resources available also affect the choice of sample size; in the face of limited resources the researcher may well reduce the required levels of precision. Fuller discussions of sample size determination are provided by Cochran (1977, Chap. 4) and Sudman (1976, Chap. 5).

SYSTEMATIC SAMPLING

It will be apparent that the task of selecting an SRS by using a table of random numbers in the procedure described above is a time-consuming and tedious one when the sample and population sizes are large. In cases where the population list is available as a computer file, the task can be performed by the computer, using computer-generated random numbers. In other cases the labor needed to draw an SRS is usually avoided by modifying the sample design to a systematic sample.

To illustrate the selection of a systematic sample, we will continue with the example from the previous section concerning a sample of 400 workers, but for simplicity we will start by taking the population size as 2400. The sampling fraction is $n/N = 400/2400 = 1/6$, so on average one worker is to be sampled for every 6 in the population. A systematic sample is then selected by drawing a random number between 1 and 6 to determine the first member of the sample and then taking every sixth worker thereafter; if, say, the random number were 4, the sample would comprise workers numbered 4, 10, 16, 22, etc., in the population list.

The reason for changing to a population size of 2400 in this example was to make the sampling interval—the inverse of the sampling fraction—an integer, 6. With the population size of 2560 from the original example, the sampling interval is 2560/400 = 6.4. Several procedures are available for handling noninteger intervals (Kish, 1965, Sec. 4.1), one of which is to employ fractional intervals. For this example a random number from 1 to 6.4 is chosen by taking a number from 10 to 64 from a table of random numbers and inserting a decimal point, with numbers from 1.0 to 1.9 being associated with the first population element, those from 2.0 to 2.9 with the second, etc. The sampling interval 6.4 is then added repeatedly to this number to identify the remaining selections, which are determined by rounding the numbers down to the integer values. Suppose, say, the random start is 4.3; adding 6.4 successively gives 10.7, 17.1, 23.5, etc. The sample would therefore comprise workers numbered 4, 10, 17, 23, etc.

Like SRS, systematic sampling is an epsem design. It differs from SRS in the joint inclusion probabilities of pairs of elements, probabilities that affect the variances of survey estimators. With SRS all pairs of elements in the population are equally likely to appear together in the sample, whereas with systematic sampling this is not so. With the integer sampling interval in our first example, for instance, the probability of two workers appearing together in a sample is $\frac{1}{6}$ if their population numbers differ by a multiple of 6 but 0 if they do not.

A problem arising with the use of systematic sampling is that the sample is nonmeasurable; i.e., an estimate of the sampling error of a survey estimate cannot be calculated from the sample data without making some assumptions about the population. This point may be illustrated with a simple example in which the first six workers have different values for the variable under study, and these values are then repeated exactly in cycles of six throughout the rest of the population. Whichever random start is chosen, a one-in-six systematic sample would then show no variability of values within the sample; thus the sample's internal variability does not provide an indication of the precision of the survey estimator. For estimation of sampling error some assumption about the order of the population listing is needed. One assumption is that the population is listed in a random order with regard to the variable under study; under this assumption the sample is equivalent to an SRS. If, say, the workers in the factory were listed alphabetically and the survey variable under consideration is a score on an attitude scale of identification with the factory, this assumption is probably a reasonable approximation. Examples like this are often met in practice.

Another commonly encountered situation is when the variable under study is likely to be monotonically related to the order of listing. Thus if the workers were listed by seniority or length of service, it may well be that the ordering would be monotonically related to their degree of identification with the factory. In this case by providing an even spread of the sample over the population listings, systematic sampling would yield a more precise estimator than a simple random sample. In many cases sampling statisticians deliberately arrange the order of a population list in order to gain this increased precision.

Systematic sampling from a list ordered by a variable thought to be monotonically related to the survey variable is sometimes called *implicit stratification*. It will be discussed further in the next section.

The risk with using systematic sampling is that the sampling interval employed may coincide with a multiple of some periodicity in the list, for if this occurs the selected sample may be a poor one. Moser and Kalton (1971, p. 84) illustrate this point by a list of married couples, listed in pairs with husbands always first. A systematic sample with an even sampling interval would then yield a sample of either all men or all women; such a sample would be an undesirable one for any survey variable related to the sex of the respondent. Thus when there is a risk that the list is arranged in a cyclical order, systematic sampling should be used with caution or avoided. However, since this risk is extremely unlikely with the majority of population lists, systematic sampling is widely used in practice, without undue concern for undetected periodicities.

STRATIFICATION

In addition to providing a means of selecting elements for the sample, sampling frames generally contain a range of information about the population. For area samples the geographic position of the area is known and various characteristics of the areas may be available from the census and other sources. List samples are often compiled in parts corresponding to different sections of the population: School students may be listed by class, university students by major and year, hospital patients by ward, etc. Stratification can make use of such supplementary information in sample design to produce a more efficient sample, as described below.

The essence of stratification is the division of the population into a number of subgroups, or strata, and then the selection of separate probability samples within the strata. In this section we will consider only sampling by SRS within strata, but the sampling could be of any form. The sampling fractions in the various strata need not be the same, although in practice they often are; when they are not, adjustments are needed in the analysis to correct for the over- and underrepresentations of the different strata in the sample. When a uniform sampling fraction is used for all strata, the sample distribution across the strata is proportional to the population distribution and the design is termed a *proportionate stratified sample*. When variable sampling fractions are used, the design is called a *disproportionate stratified sample*.

Since a proportionate stratified sample with SRS within strata is an epsem design, the simple sample mean $\bar{y}_p = \Sigma\, y_i/n$ (subscript p for proportionate stratification) can be used to estimate the overall population mean $\bar{Y}$. The variance of $\bar{y}_p$ is given by

$$V(\bar{y}_p) = \frac{(1-f)S_W^2}{n},$$

where S_W^2 is the average within-stratum element variance, i.e., $S_W^2 = \Sigma\, W_h S_h^2$, where W_h is the proportion of the population in stratum h and S_h^2 is the element variance in that stratum. The variance of $\bar{y}_p$ is the same as that for the sample mean of a simple random sample, $V(\bar{y}_0)$, except that S_W^2 replaces S^2, the overall element variance. Using the well-known analysis-of-variance result that the overall variance is the sum of the within- and between-group (strata) variances, $\sigma^2 = \sigma_W^2 + \sigma_b^2$, and approximating $S^2 \simeq \sigma^2$ and $S_W^2 \simeq \sigma_W^2$, it follows that S_W^2 cannot be larger than S^2. Thus the mean of a proportionate stratified sample has a variance no larger than that of an SRS of the same size, and its variance will be smaller to the extent that there is variance between the strata means. In other words, the mean of a proportionate stratified sample will be more precise than that of an SRS to the extent that there is homogeneity in the survey variables within strata or, equivalently, heterogeneity between strata. The gains in precision from proportionate stratification arise from the fact that this form of sampling makes the distribution of the sample across the strata exactly the same as that of the population, while with SRS these two distributions may deviate because of random fluctuations. To attain gains in precision, the stratification factors used to determine the strata need to be related to the survey variables. In a survey of factory workers' attitudes toward management, for instance, length of service and seniority might well be related to these attitudes, and hence, providing information on them is available, they might be used as effective stratification factors.

The standard way of selecting a stratified sample is to separate the population into explicit strata and then to draw separate samples within each stratum; if the elements are selected directly within the strata, systematic sampling may well be used. With a proportionate stratified sample a close approximation to this explicit stratification is to order the population list by strata and then take a systematic sample throughout the population. This procedure allocates the sample proportionately across the strata (apart from rounding effects), and for this reason it is sometimes termed implicit stratification.

We have been using simple random sampling as a yardstick against which to assess the proportionate stratified design, and this is just one example of a general procedure for assessing complex designs. The index of assessment commonly used is known as the *design effect*, which is defined as the ratio of the variance of the estimator for the complex design to the variance of that estimator for an SRS of the same size. Sometimes, the square root of the design effect—i.e., the ratio of standard errors—is used in place of the design effect. We will denote the design effect by D^2 and its square root by D. If D^2 is less than 1, the estimator based on the complex design has greater precision than that based on an SRS of the same size; if $D^2 = 1$, the two estimators are of equal precision; and if D^2 is greater than 1, the estimator based on the complex design is less precise. In the case of the mean from a proportionate stratified sample, the design effect is given by $D^2 = S_W^2/S^2$, which, as shown above, is less than or equal to 1.

Proportionate allocation is widely used in practice because it leads to simple estimators and because it ensures that sample means and percentages are no less precise than they would have been had an SRS been used. There are, however, several reasons for using a disproportionate allocation in particular circumstances. One reason is that a disproportionate allocation may yield a more precise estimator of the population mean. A second is that estimates may be required for certain strata taken separately, and a proportionate allocation may not provide a large enough sample in those strata to produce estimators of adequate precision. A third is that the survey may be concerned with measuring the difference between the means for two strata; in this case a disproportionate allocation may be called for if the strata are of unequal size. We will return to some of these points later, but first we will give a simple example of a disproportionate stratified sample.

Suppose, in the survey of factory workers, that we divide the population into four strata by skill level and length of service: unskilled workers with less than three years' service (stratum 1), unskilled workers with three or more years' service (2), skilled workers with under five years' service (3), and skilled workers with five or more years' service (4). The aims of the survey are to estimate the average score of all the workers in the factory on a scale of attitudes toward management and to estimate the average scores for the four strata separately. The details of the sample and the results obtained are presented in Table 3. In this table N_h denotes the total number of workers in stratum h, $W_h = N_h/N$ is the proportion of workers in stratum h, n_h is the sample size in stratum h,

TABLE 3
Results from a Hypothetical Survey of Factory Workers

STRATUM	N_h	W_h	n_h	$\bar{y}_h$	s_h^2
1	1280	0.50	160	18	36
2	384	0.15	80	23	26
3	640	0.25	100	20	35
4	256	0.10	60	28	24
Total	$N = 2560$	1.00	400		

and $\bar{y}_h$ and s_h^2 are the sample mean and variance in stratum h. For accommodation of the survey's various aims the sample size of 400 has been allocated somewhat arbitrarily between the strata; the sample sizes in the smaller strata (2 and 4) have been increased above those that would have been obtained from a proportionate allocation to give more precise estimates for their stratum means, and the sample size in the largest stratum (stratum 1) has been correspondingly reduced. Simple random samples of the specified sizes were drawn within each stratum.

The estimates of the stratum means and their standard errors are calculated straightforwardly, using the SRS formulas. For instance, the variance of the sample mean for stratum 1, $\bar{y}_1 = 18$, is estimated by

$$v(\bar{y}_1) = \frac{(1 - f_1)s_1^2}{n_1}$$

$$= \left(1 - \frac{160}{1280}\right)\frac{36}{160} = 0.1969,$$

so that $se(\bar{y}_1) = 0.44$. In estimating the population mean, however, one has to adjust for the disproportionate allocation. The simple mean of the 400 sampled values, $\bar{y} = \Sigma n_h \bar{y}_h / n = 21$, ends to overestimate the population mean because of the overrepresentation of the strata with high means in the sample. The population mean needs to be estimated by weighting the sample stratum means according to the population distribution over the strata, by

$$\bar{y}_d = \frac{\Sigma N_h \bar{y}_h}{N} = \Sigma W_h \bar{y}_h = 20.25.$$

The variance of $\bar{y}_d$ (d for disproportionate stratification) may be estimated by

$$v(\bar{y}_d) = \Sigma \frac{W_h^2(1 - f_h)s_h^2}{n_h} = 0.07653,$$

so $se(\bar{y}_d) = 0.28$. The estimated variance for a sample mean of an SRS of 400 workers is 0.08974. The estimated design effect is thus 0.85, or a 15 percent reduction in variance resulting from the use of this disproportionate design. While in this case the disproportionate design yields a more precise estimator than an SRS of the same size, it should be noted that unlike the situation with proportionate allocation, it is possible for the estimator from the disproportionate stratified design to be less precise.

A natural issue to raise is, What is the optimum allocation of the sample for estimating the population mean? Allowing for the possibility that the costs of collecting responses may vary between strata (data collection may, for instance, be by face-to-face interview in some strata and by telephone interview in others), the optimum allocation is given by making the sampling fraction in a stratum proportional to the stratum's element standard deviation and inversely proportional to the square root of the cost of including an element from that stratum in the sample (c_h), that is, $f_h \propto S_h/\sqrt{c_h}$. If, as is often the case, the costs do not differ between strata, the rule reduces to making the sampling fraction proportional to the element standard deviation, $f_h \propto S_h$; this allocation is known as Neyman allocation. If, furthermore, the strata standard deviations are the same, the optimum allocation reduces to proportionate allocation. With the example given in Table 3, the estimated standard deviations s_h vary only between 4.9 (i.e., $\sqrt{24}$) and 6 ($\sqrt{36}$), so proportionate allocation is close to Neyman allocation. The multipurpose nature of surveys can create problems for the use of optimum allocation in practice, for what may be the optimum allocation for one estimator may be a poor allocation for another; conflicts of this sort generate the need for compromise allocations.

Another factor influencing the sample allocation across strata is that separate estimates and analyses may be needed for the individual strata. Thus, for example, under the proportionate allocation the sample sizes for strata 2 and 4 would have been only 60 and 40, respectively, and as already noted, these sample sizes were increased to 80 and 60 in the allocation in Table 3 to provide more precise estimates for their stratum means.

A different form of optimum allocation arises when the objective of the survey is to make comparisons between strata, examining the differences between the stratum means. In the case of only two strata the optimum allocation for estimating the difference between the stratum means, $\bar{y}_1 - \bar{y}_2$, is to make the stratum sample sizes proportional to the stratum element standard deviations and inversely proportional to the square root of the cost of including an element from the stratum in the sample, or $n_h \propto S_h / \sqrt{c_h}$. This allocation is the same as that for estimating the population mean, except that it is the sample size (n_h) not the sampling fraction ($f_h = n_h / N_h$) that is proportional to $S_h / \sqrt{c_h}$. In the estimation of the difference between two stratum means, it does not matter what the population sizes of the strata are. In the special case that the costs and standard deviations in the two strata are the same, the optimum allocation is $n_1 = n_2$, a widely used allocation in experimental studies.

CLUSTER AND MULTISTAGE SAMPLING

Like stratification, cluster sampling involves the division of the population into groups. However, the two designs serve entirely different purposes: Stratification is concerned with improving precision of the survey estimators; cluster sampling is concerned with securing economies in sampling and data collection. The essential difference between the two designs is that a sample is selected from each stratum in a stratified design, whereas only a sample of clusters is selected in cluster sampling. In stratified sampling the elements sampled in a stratum represent only that stratum, while the elements selected in the sampled clusters of a cluster sample have to represent elements in unselected clusters. In consequence, while stratum homogeneity gives a gain in precision, cluster homogeneity causes a loss of precision. Since, in practice, clusters are usually homogeneous to some extent, the mean of a cluster sample is usually less precise than that of an SRS of the same size. The case for cluster sampling generally resides in the reduced element costs associated with its use, which means that a larger sample can be taken for a given budget. Cluster sampling is advantageous when the gain in precision resulting from the in-

crease in sample size outweighs the loss in precision from cluster homogeneity.

Under a strict definition the term *cluster sampling* is reserved for the design in which the population is divided into clusters, a sample of clusters is selected, and all the elements in the selected clusters are included in the sample. A cluster sample therefore involves only a single stage of selection. Often sample designs employ several stages of selection: A sample of clusters is selected at the first stage, the selected clusters are subdivided into smaller clusters, a sample of these smaller clusters is selected, and so on for as many stages as required. Such designs are called multistage samples; they are also often loosely called cluster samples. As an illustration of this type of design, a sample of students in a school might be selected by taking a sample of homerooms and then including all or only a sample of the students in the selected homerooms. If the survey population were extended to cover all the students in a state, an extra sampling stage might be added: At the first stage a sample of schools might be selected, then a sample of homerooms within selected schools, and finally a sample of students within selected homerooms.

The clusters used for sampling are mostly groupings of the population that exist or are formed for other purposes. In consequence, they are seldom of the same size in terms of the numbers of elements they contain; on the contrary, they often exhibit a substantial variability in size. Despite this fact we will, for simplicity, consider only equal-sized clusters in this section. The problems created by unequal-sized clusters, and methods of dealing with them, are taken up in the next section.

Consider a population of N elements composed of A clusters each containing B elements ($N = AB$), and suppose that an SRS of a clusters is selected with all B elements in the selected clusters being included in the sample, thus producing a sample size of $n = aB$. The sample design is an epsem one, and the population mean can be estimated by $\bar{y}_c = \Sigma y_i / n$. The mean for the n sampled elements is the same as the mean of the a sampled cluster means, or $\bar{y}_c = \Sigma \bar{y}_\alpha / a$, where $\bar{y}_\alpha$ is the mean for the B elements in sampled cluster α. With regard to using $\bar{y}_c$ to estimate the population mean, the sample design can be simply viewed as an SRS of size a from the A cluster means in the population. In consequence, the variance of $\bar{y}_c$ is obtained immediately from SRS theory as

$$V(\bar{y}_c) = \frac{(1 - f)S_a^2}{a},$$

where $f = a/A = n/N$ and S_a^2 is the variance between the cluster means. Thus the design effect for $\bar{y}_c$ is, with $n = aB$,

$$D^2 = \frac{nS_a^2}{aS^2} = \frac{BS_a^2}{S^2}.$$

If the clusters of B elements were formed at random, the variance of the cluster means S_a^2 would be equal to S^2/B, and hence $D^2 = 1$. In practice, the clusters are likely to be internally homogeneous, so their means will differ more than by chance alone and D^2 will be greater than 1.

The effect of cluster homogeneity on the design effect can be seen more clearly by expressing D^2 in an alternative approximate form as

$$D^2 \simeq 1 + (B - 1)\rho,$$

where ρ is the intraclass correlation coefficient measuring the homogeneity of the clusters. The intraclass correlation can take values between $-1/(B + 1)$ and $+1$. A value of approximately $\rho = 0$ means that the clusters are formed at random, in which case $D^2 = 1$. If $\rho < 0$, the clusters are more hetergeneous than would arise with a random formation of clusters; while such negative values of ρ are possible, they almost never occur in practice. A negative value of ρ implies a design effect of less than 1, i.e., the cluster sample is more precise than an SRS of the same size. In most applications ρ is positive but small in magnitude, generally being less than 0.1 and in many cases less than 0.05; larger values do, however, occur in special circumstances. When ρ is positive, the design effect exceeds 1, and even a small value of ρ will generate a large design effect when B is large. For example, with the homeroom class as the cluster in the school sample and with each class containing 31 students, the design effect for the mean of a variable with a ρ-value of 0.05 would be $D^2 = 1 + (30 \times 0.05) = 2.5$, while that for a variable with a ρ-value of 0.1 would be 4. In other words, a sample of $2\frac{1}{2}$ times as many students would be needed to estimate the mean of the first variable from a cluster sample with the same precision as an SRS; in the case of the second variable 4 times as many students would be needed.

Since, in practice, ρ is virtually always positive, a cluster sample will be less precise than an SRS with the same number of sample elements. But the cluster sample may be more efficient than a nonclustered sample of the same *cost* because the reduced cost of administration to elements within a cluster, and sometimes a reduced cost of sampling, enable the investigator to increase the total sample size. In the school sample, for instance, if the sur-

vey data are obtained by means of self-completion questionnaires, it may be as cheap and simple (or even simpler) to have an entire class complete the questionnaires as to ask only some of them to do so. With geographically dispersed populations and data collection by face-to-face interviews, cluster sampling provides considerable economies in interviewers' travel times to call on sample members, economies that usually fully justify the use of clustering. On the other hand, if the survey data are collected by telephone or by mail questionnaires, or if the population resides in a compact area, the case for clustering on the grounds of travel costs disappears, and a nonclustered sample may turn out to be preferable; however, even in these cases cluster sampling may be needed to facilitate sample selection.

The magnitude of the design effect for cluster sampling depends on two factors, B and ρ, and as shown above, it will be large if B is large even if ρ is small. In many cases the clusters available for use in sampling are large, often a great deal larger than the classrooms discussed with the student sample. Consider, for instance, the sample of high school students in a state. The survey sampler may have only a list of high schools available, so the schools are the smallest clusters that he or she can consider initially. A cluster sample of 3000 students made up of all the students in a sample of three high schools each with 1000 students would almost certainly be an inefficient one. Multistage sampling can be used in such cases to provide the advantages of clustering without the disadvantages of complete enumeration of large clusters.

To start with, we will consider a simple two-stage sample, in which a out of A equal-sized clusters are sampled by SRS at the first stage and b out of B elements are selected by SRS at the second stage. This design is an epsem one, and the population mean may be estimated by the simple sample mean $\bar{y}_m = \Sigma y_i/n$, where $n = ab$. Providing a is small compared with A, the design effect of $\bar{y}_m$ is approximately

$$D^2 \simeq 1 + (b - 1)\rho,$$

which is of the same form as that for a complete cluster sample but with B replaced by b. For a complete cluster sample of high schools of 1001 students each, the design effect for a mean of a variable with $\rho = 0.05$ is 51. For a two-stage sample of schools at the first stage, and 101 students per school at the second stage, the corresponding design effect is 6, while for a two-stage sample with 21 students per selected school, the design effect falls to 2.

The flexibility of two-stage sampling leaves open the choice of the combination of number of schools to be selected (a) and the number of students to be selected per sampled school (b). The optimum choice depends on the homogeneity of the variable in the schools and on various cost considerations. Useful guidance on this optimum choice is provided by considering a simple cost function of the form $c_1 a + c_2 n$, where c_1 is the cost of including a school in the sample and c_2 is the cost of including a student. With this cost function the optimum value of b for estimating the population mean is approximately

$$b = \left(\frac{c_1}{c_2} \frac{1 - \rho}{\rho} \right)^{1/2},$$

and a is then determined to give the degree of precision specified for $\bar{y}_m$ or to fit the budget available. Thus, for example, if the cost of including a school in the sample is the same as the cost of including 16 students, and if $\rho = 0.1$, the optimum value of b is 12.

In the two-stage sample of schools the students are selected unclustered within the sampled schools. However, as pointed out earlier, it may be wise to take all the students in selected classes or, alternatively, perhaps to take samples of students from selected classes. These requirements may be met by the use of a three-stage sample, schools being selected at the first stage, classes being selected at the second stage within sampled schools, and students being selected at the third stage within sampled classes. The first-stage units in a multistage design (here schools) are called *primary sampling units* and are widely known as PSUs.

SAMPLING WITH PROBABILITIES PROPORTIONAL TO SIZE

In the preceding section we made the unrealistic assumption that the clusters used in sampling all contained the same number of elements. In practice, clusters vary in size and often to a considerable extent. Homeroom classes may be of roughly the same size, but high schools vary more, perhaps from under 500 to over 3000 students; the variability in the sizes of other types of clusters may be much greater. In this section we examine the problems arising from this variability, and we describe a method of sampling with probabilities proportional to size, commonly known as PPS sampling, that overcomes these problems.

We will illustrate the problems by considering a two-stage sample in which the PSUs vary in size, with B_α ele-

ments in PSU α. Suppose that an epsem sample of elements is required, with each element having a probability f, the overall sampling fraction, of being included in the sample. The inclusion probability for element β in PSU α is given by the multiplication rule of probabilities:

$$P(\alpha\beta) = P(\alpha)P(\beta|\alpha),$$

where $P(\alpha)$ is the probability that PSU α is selected, $P(\beta|\alpha)$ is the conditional probability that element β is selected given that PSU α has been chosen, and $P(\alpha\beta) = f$. In survey sampling this rule is sometimes termed the *selection equation*.

Suppose that the PSUs are chosen at the first stage with equal probabilities, $P(\alpha) = a/A$. Then with the overall epsem requirement, the selection equation becomes

$$f = \frac{a}{A} P(\beta|\alpha),$$

so $P(\beta|\alpha) = fA/a$, a constant. Thus for an overall epsem design the sampling fraction used at the second stage must be the same for all selected PSUs. The consequence of a constant subsampling fraction is that a large subsample will be drawn from a large PSU selected at the first stage and a small sample from a small PSU. This variability in subsample sizes has a number of undesirable features. In the first place, the total sample size cannot be fixed prior to sampling since it depends on the random choice of PSUs: If the sample happens by chance to select a preponderance of large PSUs, the sample will be unduly large; if mostly small PSUs are selected, it will be unduly small. While survey researchers do not need to be able to specify the sample size exactly—and indeed cannot do so—they do need to be able to control it within reasonable limits for reasons of budget and precision. A second unattractive feature of the variability in subsample sizes is that the data collection work load in the different PSUs will vary; it is often both economical and practically convenient to have roughly the same interviewer work load in each selected PSU. Third, the variability in subsample sizes leads to a lack of statistical efficiency and can also cause other statistical difficulties with the survey estimators. For all these reasons it is desirable to limit the variability in subsample sizes.

There are often two conditions that the sample should ideally satisfy: One is that it should be an epsem one, and the other is that the same subsample size, say b, should be taken from each selected PSU. These conditions translate into $P(\alpha\beta) = f = n/N = ab/N$ and $P(\beta|\alpha) = b/B_\alpha$. Substituting these values in the selection equation gives

$$\frac{ab}{N} = P(\alpha)\frac{b}{B_\alpha},$$

which implies that $P(\alpha) = aB_\alpha/N$ or that PSU α is selected with probability proportional to its size, B_α. Thus the ideal conditions can both be satisfied if the PSUs are sampled not with equal probabilities but with probabilities proportional to their sizes.

A method for selecting the PSUs with PPS, using systematic sampling, can best be described through an example. Suppose that a PPS sample of two PSUs is required from a set of six, labeled A to F, with sizes B_α as given in Table 4. The first step is to form the cumulative totals, as given in the last column of the table. The overall total is divided by the number of PSUs to be selected to give $676/2 = 338$, and a random number is selected between 001 and 338. If the random number is between 001 and 094, PSU A is selected; if it is between 095 and 202, PSU B is selected; if between 203 and 234, PSU C is selected; if between 235 and 259, PSU D is selected; and if between 260 and 338, PSU E is taken as the first selection. The second selection is determined by adding the sampling interval of 338 to the random number; thus random numbers of 001 to 061 would lead to PSU E being chosen as the second selection, and random numbers between 062 and 338 would lead to PSU F. Inspection of this procedure shows that the number of random numbers leading to the selection of a PSU is equal to the size of the PSU, so the PSUs are being selected by PPS (in the case of PSU E, its 140 numbers are made up of two parts, the 79 numbers from 260 to 338 for the first selection and the 61 numbers from 01 to 61 for the second selection).

TABLE 4
PPS Selection of PSUs

PSU	B_α	CUMULATIVE B_α
A	94	94
B	108	202
C	32	234
D	25	259
E	140	399
F	277	676

A difficulty with the practical application of PPS sampling is that the exact sizes of the PSUs are rarely known. Instead, usually only some estimates of them, perhaps based on out-of-date information, are available. These estimates are known as measures of sizes. Providing they are reasonable estimates, they may be satisfactorily used in selecting the PSUs with probabilities proportional to measures of sizes (M_α) in the epsem selection equation

$$f = \frac{aM_\alpha}{\Sigma M_\alpha}\frac{b}{M_\alpha}.$$

The important point to note about this equation is that when the PSUs are selected with probabilities proportional to measures of size, the subsampling rate within a selected PSU has to be inversely related to its measure of size. This requirement means that the subsample size will vary between PSUs, but providing the measures of size are fairly accurate, the variability will be tolerable. Care is needed to ensure that the measures of sizes are reasonable estimates, for otherwise difficulties can arise; in particular, the use of an out-of-date measure of size for a PSU that has experienced recent sizable growth may lead to an unacceptably large subsample size if that PSU is selected.

Complications can arise in the application of PPS sampling when some of the PSUs are very large or small. These complications can be seen in the selection equation for a two-stage design:

$$f = \frac{aM_\alpha}{\Sigma M_\alpha}\frac{b}{M_\alpha}.$$

The problem with very large clusters is that their selection probabilities at the first stage may exceed 1, that is, $aM_\alpha > \Sigma M_\alpha$. With the systematic PPS procedure illustrated in Table 4, this problem would have occurred if, say, PSUs E and F had been a single PSU with a size measure of 417. With a sampling interval of 338, this PSU is certain to appear once in the sample and has a probability of 79/338 of appearing twice. One way to handle this problem is to put the PSU into a separate stratum and to apply the overall sampling fraction f within it. The PSUs treated in this way become strata; they are frequently termed self-representing PSUs.

The problem with very small clusters is that the selection probabilities at the second stage may exceed 1, i.e., the size measure for the PSU, M_α, is smaller than the desired subsample size b. This would occur, for instance, with PSU D in Table 4 if the desired subsample size had been set at thirty. A simple procedure for dealing with this problem is to link small PSUs to adjacent ones before selection so that all the combined PSUs are at least of the minimum size. Kish (1965, Sec. 7.5E) discusses alternative procedures for handling oversized and undersized units.

ESTIMATION OF SAMPLING ERRORS

The various variance formulas given in the preceding sections indicate that the precision of sample estimators depends on the sample design employed. In consequence, sampling errors need to be estimated in a way that takes account of the sample design. Proportionate stratification usually gives more precise estimators than a simple random sample of the same size, but cluster sampling (using the term to include multistage sampling) usually gives less precise estimators. In other words, design effects are usually less than one for the former design but greater than 1 for the latter. National surveys generally employ complex sample designs involving both stratification and clustering. The loss in precision from clustering normally outweighs the gain from stratification, with the net outcome of a design effect greater than 1.

No simple universal rule can be given to predict the magnitude of a design effect with a national probability sample since it depends on aspects of the sample design, especially the subsample size taken from each PSU, the variable under study, and the estimator being computed. With a straightforward epsem national probability sample, using a design like that of the Survey Research Center at the University of Michigan as described below, design effects for estimates of means and proportions for the total sample often lie within the range from 1 to 2 (e.g., Kish, 1965, Table 14.1.IV); this means that the standard errors of these estimates are from 1 to 1.4 (i.e., $\sqrt{2}$) times as large as the SRS formulas would suggest. These design effects relate to samples with average subsample sizes of about twenty per primary area, and they would generally be greater with larger subsample sizes. They also relate to epsem samples, and they would also generally be greater with nonepsem designs.

Many of the results reported from surveys are not concerned with the total sample but with various subclasses. If a subclass comprises all the elements in a subset of the PSUs—for instance, a geographic region—the design effects for means and proportions can often be expected to be about the same as those for the total sample. If, however, the subclass is fairly evenly spread across the PSUs (termed a crossclass)—for instance, an age or sex subclass—the design effect tends to be less than that for the total sample; the smaller the crossclass, the closer to 1 the design effect is likely to be.

Design effects for analytic statistics, such as regression coefficients and differences between means and proportions, are also generally less than those for means and proportions based on the total sample (e.g., see Kish and Frankel, 1974). Nevertheless, they are still usually greater than 1, so the use of the sampling error formulas found in regular statistics texts and included in standard programs—which relate to unrestricted sampling (SRS with replacement)—tend to underestimate the true sampling errors. Sometimes, the underestimation is small enough to be safely ignored, in which case the standard programs may be used satisfactorily, but this should not be assumed uncritically. Before reliance is placed on standard programs, some checks should be made to examine the adequacy of the unrestricted sampling approximation.

In recent years several computer programs have been developed to calculate sampling errors for estimates based on complex sample designs. In preparing survey records for computer analysis, researchers should ensure that each record contains the necessary sampling information, in particular, indicators of the PSU and stratum from which it was selected, for otherwise these programs cannot be applied. The estimation of sampling errors by methods that take account of the complex sample design employed should be a routine part of survey analysis.

SAMPLE DESIGNS IN PRACTICE

The aim of the preceding treatment of sampling issues has been to acquaint the reader with the major components involved in most sample designs. For a fuller coverage of these components and also of other sample designs and estimation procedures not discussed here (such as multiphase and replicated sampling, rotating panel designs, poststratification, ratio and regression estimation), reference should be made to one of the sampling texts.

Skillful sample design involves combining the separate components in a way that produces a sample to satisfy the survey's objectives efficiently, taking into account the methods of data collection being used. In this section we briefly review three sample designs, one to indicate some of the necessary considerations involved in even a simple design and the other two to show how various components are combined in more complex face-to-face and telephone designs.

A Student Sample

Our first example illustrates some of the practical decisions involved in designing the sample for a small survey of University of Michigan students in the college of Literature, Science, and Arts (LS&A). A final sample of about 460 was desired out of the college's total enrollment of approximately 13,000. Two alternative sampling frames were considered: one was the registrar records that listed separately all LS&A students in alphabetical order, and the other was the published student directory that gave a single alphabetical listing of all 40,000 University of Michigan students. The directory had the important practical advantage of being more readily accessible. It was, however, subject to a serious frame problem: Some checks of the directory against the registrar records showed the former to be missing (for unknown reasons) about 15 percent of the registered LS&A students. In addition, about two-thirds of the listings in the directory were non-LS&A students, i.e., foreign elements in the sampling frame. These frame problems—particularly the missing elements—were considered too serious to tolerate, and a decision was therefore made to use the registrar records as the sampling frame.

A systematic sampling scheme was adopted for sampling students from the registrar records. From past experience a response rate of 80 percent was assumed, and therefore an initial sample of 575 (i.e., 460/0.8) was needed to yield the required 460 respondents. The sampling interval was thus 13,000/575 = 22.6. For simplification of the selection process the sampling interval was reduced to 20, and a sample of 1 in 20 students was selected by taking a random start between 1 and 20 and every twentieth name thereafter. The approximately 75 extra names produced by reducing the sampling interval from 22.6 to 20 were randomly withdrawn from the sample and held in reserve for use in case the response rate proved to be seriously overestimated.

Several further points may be noted about this sample. First, since names were accompanied by class year in the registrar records, it would have been possible to stratify by year, but this was not done because it would have complicated the selection too much for the gain involved.

Second, the actual size obtained was not exactly 460, since it was affected by the final response rate and the exact population size for which only estimates were available at the time of sampling. Departures from the desired sample size occur with nearly all forms of survey sampling, but with careful design and large samples, they can be kept relatively small and hence are not a cause for concern. Third, the sample design contained a small amount of implicit stratification, since extreme samples of alphabet letters (e.g., many O'Gradys) were prevented by the systematic procedure. As noted earlier, however, it can be assumed that the final sample is close to that of an SRS design, and therefore SRS calculations of standard errors were used for convenience (a conservative procedure in this case).

A Face-to-Face National Survey

Our second example is the national sample of dwellings of the Survey Research Center (SRC) at the University of Michigan. The details given relate to the sample design used with a number of surveys in the 1970s. The area probability sample was designed for general-purpose use in interview surveys of the population of the United States; the elements under study could be all persons with specified characteristics (e.g., persons over eighteen, heads of households), families, spending units, or households depending on the survey's objectives. For practical reasons survey populations were usually confined to the conterminous United States and to persons living in dwelling units not on military reservations; the population living in non–dwelling units such as student dormitories, correctional institutions, hospitals, and other institutions were excluded unless the survey objectives determined otherwise. The sample was carried out in up to five stages with PPS selections and stratification; for many surveys the sample was designed to give each element an equal probability of selection. The PSUs were counties, groups of contiguous counties, or standard metropolitan statistical areas (SMSAs). They were stratified by geographic region, SMSA classification (the twelve largest SMSAs, other SMSAs, and non-SMSAs), size of largest city, primary area population, rate of population growth, major industry or type of farming, and the proportion of the nonwhite population. Primary sampling units were then selected with PPS, where the measure of size was the area's population in the 1970 census. The 1970 national sample included seventy-four primary areas, of which twelve were self-representing and sixty-two non-self-representing areas.

The selected primary areas were next divided into second-stage units, which consisted of cities, towns, census tracts, civil divisions, or rural areas. Within each primary area these units were stratified along an urban/rural dimension, and somewhere between three and ten second-stage selections were made by PPS, where the size measure was the unit's number of housing units. For the third stage of the design the second-stage units were divided into urban blocks or chunks of rural areas, which were then sampled with PPS. Interviewers were sent to the selected third-stage units to scout them and prepare listings of the housing units they contained. The information collected by the interviewers was then used to divide the third-stage units into clusters containing an expected sixteen to forty housing units, one of the clusters then being selected with equal probability. The selected clusters were next divided into small segments of an expected four housing units each; these could be compact segments of adjacent housing units or they could be distributed systematically throughout a cluster. At the time that the sample for a particular survey was being prepared, interviewers updated the list of housing units for the selected segments to be used for that survey. Finally, within the households in the selected housing units, persons eligible for the survey were listed by the interviewer; either the information being collected in the survey was obtained for all of them, or one of them was chosen to be the respondent by an objective, random selection procedure known as the Kish selection grid (Kish, 1965, Sec. 11.3B). Further details on the SRC national sample are provided by Kish and Hess (1965) and Kish (1965, Chaps. 9 and 10).

A Telephone National Survey
Our third example concerns the sample design for a national telephone survey and serves to illustrate the importance of the sampling frame in sample design. An initial concern when considering the use of the telephone for data collection is the frame problem of missing elements, for not all households have telephones. Nowadays, however, telephone penetration is high in the United States, with 92 percent of households having telephones within their housing units (Thornberry and Massey, 1983).

Given that a high proportion of households is accessible by telephone, the next issue is what frame should be used for sample selection. The published telephone directories are an obvious possibility, but they turn out to be unsuitable because about 25 percent of residential numbers are unlisted. This deficiency has stimulated the de-

velopment of what are known as random-digit-dialing (RDD) methods of telephone sampling.

Telephone numbers in the United States are composed of ten digits in three parts, such as 313–555–1234, where the first three digits are the area code, the next three digits are the central office code, and the last four digits are the suffix. Up-to-date lists of working area code–central office code combinations are available and can be used as the basis of a sampling frame. Adding all the suffixes from 0000 to 9999 to these combinations will then provide a complete coverage of the population of residential numbers. It will, however, also include many nonworking and nonresidential numbers, which constitute blanks and foreign elements on the sampling frame; we return to them later.

With face-to-face interview surveys clustering is introduced to reduce interviewers' travel costs, but this consideration does not apply with surveys in which all the data are collected by telephone. A single-stage sample may therefore be used for telephone surveys. The frame of working area code–central office code combinations available from the Long Lines Department of AT&T contains little information for use in stratification, essentially only the exchange to which the combination is assigned and the vertical and horizontal coordinates of the exchange (which are used in calculating long-distance charges). In addition, an index of the size of an exchange is provided by the number of central office codes it covers. Thus, in effect, the sample can be stratified only geographically—by area code, exchange, and geographic coordinates—and by the index of exchange size. A simple sample design is to order area code–central office code combinations according to the stratification variables and then take a systematic sample for implicit stratification throughout the frame (e.g., see Groves and Kahn, 1979).

As noted above, the sampling frame constructed to include all the suffixes from 0000 to 9999 within each area code–central office code combination contains many blanks and foreign elements; just over one-fifth of numbers are, in fact, residential numbers. The standard solution for dealing with blanks and foreign elements is simply to reject them, and the rest of the sample remains a valid sample of the survey population. The disadvantage of this solution is, however, that it is costly to make the calls needed to find out that a number does not link up with a residential unit. For this reason sampling methods have been sought to reduce the number of unproductive calls. One widely used scheme employs a cluster sampling procedure for this purpose (Waksberg, 1978). This scheme treats the suffixes for each area code–central office code combination as 100 clusters of 100 numbers each; the first cluster comprises the numbers 0000 to 0099, the next cluster those from 0100 to 0199, etc. The clusters are sampled with equal probability, say along the lines described above, and one number is selected at random within each cluster. If that number is not a residential number, the cluster is rejected. If it is a working residential number, an interview is taken, and a predetermined number of additional households are selected at random from the cluster. The clusters are in effect sampled by PPS, since the probability of a cluster yielding a residential number with the initial random number is proportional to the number of residential numbers in the cluster. This scheme substantially increases the proportion of residential numbers sampled, from about one in five overall to about two in three in selected clusters.

For more details on telephone sampling the reader is referred to Frankel and Frankel (1977), Groves and Kahn (1979), and Frey (1983).

NONRESPONSE

The preceding discussion has been concerned with drawing a probability sample for a survey. In this process great care is taken to ensure that the sampling frame covers the total survey population and that the selections are made to give every element a known and nonzero probability of selection; sampling theory depends on these features to establish the properties of sample estimators. In the operation of a survey, however, the achieved sample falls short of the selected sample because of a failure to obtain the survey data for some of the sampled elements. The missing data may come about because no information is collected for a sampled element or because while some items of data are collected, others are not; the former situation is termed *element, unit,* or *total nonresponse* and the latter *item nonresponse.*

Total Nonresponse

Nonresponse is a major concern to survey researchers because of the risk that it may cause serious bias in the survey results. If the nonrespondents differ systematically from the respondents, the achieved sample will fail to represent the total population adequately. Thus, for instance, if a greater proportion of wealthy persons than of poor persons fail to respond in an income survey, the survey will tend to underestimate the population's aver-

age income. The extent of nonresponse bias depends on two factors: the proportion of nonrespondents in the sample—the *nonresponse rate*—and the difference between the respondents and nonrespondents in the survey variables. Since survey researchers can never be confident that there is no or little systematic difference between respondents and nonrespondents, the only way to be certain that there is no serious nonresponse bias is to keep the nonresponse rate to a low level. For this reason a major consideration in practical survey design is the control of nonresponse.

Care needs to be taken in interpreting reported response rates since there is some variation in the ways in which they are calculated, which leads to noncomparability among surveys. The response rate is simply defined as

$$\frac{\text{number of interviews completed with eligible elements}}{\text{number of eligible elements in the sample}},$$

with the denominator comprising all sample elements remaining after ineligible ones (blanks and foreign elements, e.g., vacant houses) are removed, and the numerator comprising all usable interviews. However, a number of complications are encountered in practice. For example, a household survey where the target population is black Americans must decide how to treat not-at-home units where race cannot be determined: Treating them all as ineligibles probably leads to an overestimation of the response rate, and treating them all as eligibles leads to an underestimation. In addition, the number of eligible persons in these units is unknown and has to be estimated in some way. Another example concerns non-English-speaking persons in a survey of the population of the United States. Assuming that such persons cannot be interviewed (as is usually the case in an attitude survey where translation would be impractical), such persons may or may not be defined as "eligible" depending upon one's theoretical conception of the American population. In one case their inclusion in the survey population lowers the response rate; in the other case their exclusion raises the response rate but it restricts the population about which inferences are made. In view of such complexities users of survey data should investigate carefully how the response rate is calculated in a particular study.

In face-to-face surveys the two main reasons for total nonresponse are refusals (usually close to two-thirds of all nonresponse) and failures to contact respondents because they are not at home when the interviewers call (usually close to one-third). There are also diverse other reasons, usually of minor importance, such as respondents' ill health or senility, language problems, and lost questionnaires. The proportion of refusals varies considerably from survey to survey, depending on the subject matter under study and the general survey design and administration. The avoidance of refusals exerts a strong influence on the choice of data collection method, on questionnaire design, and on interviewer training. Not-at-homes are reduced by vigorous efforts in field work, specifying a minimum number of calls that interviewers must make on not-at-homes before accepting them as nonrespondents. A minimum of four callbacks is often stipulated, with a requirement that they be made on different days and at different times of day, including one or more evening calls. In assessing the effect of nonresponse on survey results, one must take account of the different sources of nonresponse, for the biasing effects of refusals may be quite different from those of not-at-homes and other sources (Stinchcombe *et al.,* 1981). The composition of nonresponse may also differ considerably from one survey to another.

Although intensive efforts to reduce nonresponse are common practice and undoubtedly valuable, it should be noted that their use may give rise to other problems. There is some indirect evidence that such efforts sometimes manage to convert a sampled person only from a nonrespondent to a reluctant and unwilling respondent who provides responses of poorer quality and more item nonresponses than other respondents (Singer, 1978).

Nonresponse rates for straightforward, national face-to-face surveys conducted by nongovernment survey organizations run nowadays at about 25–30 percent but can vary around these limits depending on such factors as the subject matter, length of interview, respondent eligibility criteria, and length of time allocated to field work. Surveys conducted by the U.S. Bureau of the Census usually achieve appreciably lower levels of nonresponse than nongovernment surveys, perhaps partly because the Bureau is assumed to be a more legitimate source for requesting interviews and partly because many of the Bureau's surveys accept any responsible adult as a household respondent, whereas other surveys (particularly attitude surveys) designate a specific respondent. Nonresponse rates increase with urbanization and are especially high in inner cities, perhaps in good part because fear of crime discourages opening doors to strangers (House and Wolf, 1978). There has been a considerable concern in recent years that nonresponse rates have been increasing, and this does indeed appear to be the case. Steeh (1981) reports analyses of the nonresponses rates in two series of surveys conducted by the Survey Research Center at the University of Michigan in the period 1952–1979 that clearly establish that substantial increases have occurred, with increases in refusals being the dominant cause.

With telephone surveys not-at-homes are more readily handled because of the ease with which repeated calls can be made at different times to secure a response. The main cause of nonresponse is therefore refusal, either by the sampled person or by another household member on his or her behalf. Another type of telephone nonresponse is a break-off interview where the respondent starts to respond but terminates the interview prematurely. In face-to-face surveys such breaks-off are rare, but they occur more frequently with telephone surveys: Groves and Kahn (1979) report that almost 5 percent of their telephone sample terminated the interview in this way.

With telephone surveys using RDD methods there is a further problem of determining exactly what the nonresponse rate is, for a sizable proportion of numbers will ring with no answer on repeated calls. The vast majority of these are probably nonworking numbers, but a few will be persistent not-at-homes. In the Groves and Kahn (1979) study 16.7 percent of sample numbers fell in this category. Treating them all as not-at-homes gave a nonresponse rate of 41 percent; treating them all as nonworking numbers gave a rate of 30 percent. Nowadays, checks are often made with the telephone company business offices to identify the nonworking numbers, and the ambiguous cases can thus be greatly reduced.

Mail surveys avoid the problem of not-at-homes, except in the case of those who are away for the entire period of survey data collection. Nonresponse may occur because the questionnaire fails to reach a sampled person as a result of an inadequate or out-of-date address on the sampling frame; some, but not all, of these questionnaires will be returned by the post office. Some questionnaires may also be returned unanswered or with a refusal, and some may be returned blank by relatives or others because the sampled person is sick or otherwise incapacitated. However, most nonresponses are reflected by a failure to send back any reply at all. Further issues related to response in mail surveys are discussed below.

Item Nonresponse

Even when a respondent has been persuaded to participate in a survey, there remains the problem of obtaining responses to all the survey questions that that respondent should answer. Item nonresponse may arise because the respondent lacks the information necessary to answer the question, fails to make the effort required to retrieve the information from memory or to consult records, finds the question to be too sensitive or embarrassing, or considers it irrelevant to his or her perception of the survey objectives. Another source of item nonresponse is due to the interviewer's failure to ask the question or to record the answer—errors that are particularly likely to occur when the questionnaire is a complex one with different sections applicable to different sets of respondents. Finally, a recorded response may be rejected at an edit check because it is inconsistent with other responses.

The level of item nonresponse depends on the nature of the item: Some simple items may suffer no or negligible missing data, while other, more complex or sensitive ones may have item nonresponse rates of 10–15 percent or even greater. The level also depends on the questionnaire design and other aspects of the survey procedures employed. In some surveys, for instance, proxy informants are asked to provide responses for sampled persons who are unavailable for interview; this procedure avoids some total nonresponse, but it increases the risk of item nonresponses.

Nonresponse Adjustments

In an attempt to reduce nonresponse biases, adjustments can be made to compensate for missing data in the survey analysis. Often some form of weighting adjustment is used to compensate for total nonresponse and some form of imputation is used for item nonresponse. Chapman (1976) and Kalton (1983b) review weighting adjustments and imputation procedures, and Bailar *et al.* (1978) describe the procedures used with the Current Population Survey. Smith (1983) reviews a variety of approaches for assessing and adjusting for total nonresponse, and describes how the application of four of them with the General Social Survey met with very limited success.

As a simple illustration of a weighting adjustment, suppose that in a survey about frequency of air travel, those living in large cities take more flights than those living elsewhere, and the response rate is 60 percent in large cities and 80 percent elsewhere. Assuming that the sample selected was an equal-probability one, the achieved sample underrepresents residents of large cities, and in consequence, the simple mean of the number of flights taken is probably an underestimate. A weighting adjustment can, however, be made in an attempt to correct for this, giving respondents in large cities a weight of $8\%_0 = 1.33$ (the ratio of the response rates) in the analysis to compensate for their relative underrepresentation. Although this procedure adjusts for the imbalance in the achieved sample between large cities and elsewhere, there can be no assurance that it corrects for nonresponse bias, for there may well remain other undetected and uncorrected imbalances. In practice, more complex weighting adjustments involving several auxiliary variables are often used, but even so, there can be no guarantee that they adequately compensate for the missing responses.

Item nonresponses may be treated by imputation, in which values are inserted for the missing responses (see Kalton and Kasprzyk, 1982, for a review of imputation procedures). One common type of procedure starts by dividing the sample into a number of classes on the basis of information available for both records with responses and records without responses to the item in question; the classes are chosen in such a way that the responses to the item are relatively homogeneous within them. Then within a class a record with a response is chosen, and its value is assigned to a record with a missing response. As with weighting adjustments for total nonresponse, imputation procedures aim to correct for the biases in survey estimators, but there can be no guarantee that they will be successful.

MODES OF GATHERING SURVEY DATA

There are currently three major methods of joining questioning and sampling in order to gather survey data: face-to-face interviewing, telephone interviewing, and the mail (self-administered) survey.

FACE-TO-FACE OR PERSONAL INTERVIEWING

In face-to-face surveys interviewers contact potential respondents, usually at their homes, and carry out the interviews in person. Such face-to-face interviewing fits well with area probability sampling, where individuals are located via their housing units, which can be sampled in small geographic clusters. It also allows maximum motivation of respondents, since the presence of a friendly interviewer at the door (often preceded by an identifying letter to the same address) encourages participation, and this can then be sustained throughout the interview. Visual scales and show cards listing multiple-response categories can be employed easily to clarify questions, and the interviewer can also be expected to probe unclear responses and to provide observational data. For all these reasons face-to-face or personal interviewing has traditionally been the favored mode, and it is still the standard method for such major efforts as the General Social Survey and the National Election Studies, though the latter now includes a telephone component as well.

The major drawbacks of face-to-face interviewing are costs and time. The field work on a national probability sample ordinarily takes two to four months to complete, and special efforts are required if more immediate reactions to events are needed. Costs of national surveys using full callback procedures can easily run at present to over $150 per interview when supervisor and interviewer salary and travel are combined. Efficiency is also low, with interviewers spending much of their time seeking respondents, as against the time spent actually interviewing (Sudman, 1967).

TELEPHONE INTERVIEWING

Within the past few years telephone surveys have become the most widely used survey method in the United States, and there is good reason to expect this predominance to increase. With over 90 percent of American households estimated to have telephones and with recently developed random-digit-dialing (RDD) methods of sampling unlisted as well as listed phone numbers, it is generally believed that coverage of the population by telephone is only slightly inferior to that provided through area sampling and face-to-face interviewing (Groves and Kahn, 1979). The field costs of high quality telephone surveys with adequate callbacks are half or less those of similar quality personal interviews, and the time needed to complete a telephone survey can be compressed into a month or even a matter of days, taking advantage of the nearly round-the-clock interviewing possibilities allowed by different time zones. (If the need for callbacks is disregarded and interviews are restricted to a few minutes, both time and costs can be cut much further, but this, of course, reduces both quality and efficiency.)

Another major advantage of telephone surveys is the fact that all interviewers can be located in one place and therefore much more readily monitored and supervised. In addition, telephone interviewing allows maximum utilization of computing and related developments, so with CATI (computer-assisted telephone interviewing) systems the "questionnaire" is read from a cathode

ray terminal (CRT), and respondent answers are entered directly into a computer file, bypassing the traditional need for later transfer to the computer, except in the case of open responses. Complex variations in question sequence (including randomized versions) become relatively simple to arrange, and the pattern of answers is likewise relatively easy to check for respondent inconsistencies or interviewer recording error while the interview is taking place. Until recently, it was thought that telephone interviews had to be kept quite brief because of respondent impatience [no more than five minutes in length according to Simon (1969)], but it is now clear that such interviews can be nearly as long as most face-to-face interviews, though the maximum length consistent with adequate cooperation and good quality remains uncertain. Thus on-line telephone surveys seem likely to become standard for large organizations within a short time.

It was also hoped intially that telephone surveys would allow reductions in nonresponse, since it is easier to reach respondents at all hours and there should be less fear of physical threat via the telephone. However, telephone nonresponse rates are generally a few percentage points higher than those for face-to-face interviewing (Singer, 1979), perhaps in part because of the absence of legitimizing letters for RDD samples and in part because of the fact that it is easier for potential respondents to hang up on someone than to close the door in their face. Furthermore, the composition of the nonresponse category is somewhat different from that in face-to-face surveys, with disproportionate losses by telephone of low-educated and older persons (Groves and Kahn, 1979). In themselves these differences are not large enough to have much indirect impact on other variables associated with age and education, since (as is typical in social research) all the correlations are modest in absolute size and thus their products tend to become quite small. Some studies do report direct effects of mode of administration on responses, such as less willingness to answer sensitive questions on the telephone or greater social desirability pressures in face-to-face situations. But these findings are not large or consistent enough thus far to provide a convincing reason for choosing one mode rather than the other.

One clear disadvantage of the telephone is the fact that it ordinarily restricts questions and response categories to those that can be communicated orally, and this is bound to change the nature of future survey data in many subtle ways. Equally clear is the finding that both respondents and interviewers enjoy telephone surveys less than face-to-face surveys (Fleishman and Berk, 1979; Groves and Kahn, 1979). But in the face of the substantial differential in costs and time, it is unlikely that either of these arguments against reliance on the telephone will prevail in the future for most surveys.

MAIL SURVEYS

Mail surveys dispense with interviewers altogether and thus lead to a major saving in costs for both salary and travel. They are particularly useful where a list of names and addresses is available and where the purpose of the survey has a direct connection to the group surveyed (e.g., a sample of American Psychological Association members surveyed on a topic having to do with professional problems of psychologists). Assuming the questionnaire does not require extensive probing or a set order of questions, there is little reason to regard such an approach by mail as inferior to telephone or face-to-face modes. In fact, it is sometimes claimed that the absence of an interviewer provides a more anonymous atmosphere and therefore encourages frankness, but despite some isolated results supporting this proposition (see Sudman and Bradburn, 1974), no really adequate comparison seems ever to have been carried out.

For the study of attitudes and other subjective variables, mail surveys have the disadvantage of lack of control over how and when respondents fill out questionnaires. Scott (1961) provides evidence that some 14 percent of the returned questionnaires in one mail survey were not answered by the intended respondent, and this doubtless does not include the proportion of respondents who consulted others at some point in the course of answering—a possible advantage for factual questions but probable disadvantage for attitude questions. In addition, it is impossible in mail surveys to preserve a desired question order, to probe ambiguous responses, or to control the pace of answering.

Traditionally, mail surveys have been regarded as problematic because of lower total response rates plus greater nonresponse on individual items. However, Heberlein and Baumgartner (1978) conclude from an analysis of ninety-eight mail questionnaire experiments that it is a mistake to think of such surveys as having response rates that are *inevitably* low, since when a mail questionnaire has obvious importance to respondents (e.g., a Vet-

erans Administration survey of the educational plans of veterans who had expressed an interest in VA educational assistance programs), the response rate can be quite high (over 80 percent). However, this does not answer the question of how high a response rate can be obtained in a mail survey of the general American population, especially given the difficulty of obtaining a list of names and addresses for mailing purposes.

Heberlein and Baumgartner (1978) argue further that the investigator's efforts must be put into increasing the perceived importance of the survey (e.g., by using special forms of mailings) and decreasing the effort needed to comply. The subtlety of the interaction of these two forces is illustrated by their finding that questionnaire length does not have a zero-order correlation with response rate but does have a negative effect when other variables are controlled. They argue that longer questionnaires are perceived to be more important by respondents, as well as more arduous, and that these two factors tend to cancel out except where other indicators of importance can be measured and held constant.

Two variables that do clearly have substantial effects on final response rates are follow-up reminders of any kind and cash incentives (Kanuk and Berenson, 1975; Linsky, 1975). In one careful review of eighteen empirical studies, prepaid monetary incentives appeared to decrease nonresponse by about a third, and the larger the incentive, the larger the decrease (Armstrong, 1975). Promised monetary incentives seem to have a less simple impact than prepaid ones but also show some effect (Schewe and Cournoyer, 1976). All reviews of mail questionnaire studies show follow-up letters to be of major importance in raising response rates substantially (Scott, 1961; Heberlein and Baumgartner, 1978).

Recently, Dillman (1978) has argued that careful administration of mail surveys can yield appreciably higher response rates than previously thought possible, although he does not claim that the rates will reach the levels of comparable face-to-face or telephone surveys. Proceeding from consideration of why people respond or fail to respond to mail questionnaires, Dillman develops an extensive set of practical rules for how to prepare questionnaires, letters, envelopes, follow-up requests, etc., all of which he terms the total design method. Since most of the steps are not tested separately and the response rate data are not based on general-population national surveys, it is difficult to evaluate the various recommendations. However, many of the steps seem reasonable on a commonsense basis, and investigators planning mail surveys will benefit from reviewing Dillman's recommendations. (He also offers a parallel set of suggestions for telephone surveys.) Another good source on the design and administration of mail surveys is Erdos (1970).

MIXED MODES

Variations between answers to questions in face-to-face, telephone, and mail surveys are usually not large, and those that do occur are at least partly traceable to differences in coverage and response rates rather than to mode of administration itself. For this reason it is probably sensible for some purposes to combine two or three of the methods in the interest of cutting costs and increasing coverage and response. Thus the decennial census uses mail questionnaires where possible but supplements these with face-to-face contact when necessary to obtain responses.

Thornberry (1977) carried out an experimental health survey in Rhode Island, where each mode was supplemented by the other two as needed, yielding three survey strategies. For example, the mail strategy consisted of two mailings followed by telephone interviews where possible and face-to-face interviews where necessary. Final response rates for all three strategies were noticeably higher than usual, though the mail strategy was about 8 percent lower than the other two. Thornberry also found that when the primary method of data collection was face to face, no other supplement was needed to obtain a high response rate; when the telephone contact was primary, about one-third of the eventual respondents required follow-up face-to-face interviewing; for the mail strategy about half the eventual respondents required telephone or face-to-face interviewing. (The telephone sampling was from lists containing addresses and therefore allowed preliminary letters; "cold contacts" required by random-digit dialing might have been somewhat less successful.) Costs for telephone and mail strategies, even allowing for each being a combination, were about half that of face-to-face interviewing, with the mail strategy only a little cheaper than the telephone strategy.

Analysis of the quality of reported data showed few differences among the three strategies. (Strategies rather than distinct modes were compared because the latter confound response differences and sampling differences.

Thornberry assumes, however, that differences between strategies are due primarily to mode differences, not to variations in sampling designs or response rates.) The mail strategy showed a higher rate of missing data, but answers to the most sensitive health questions appeared to be franker than for either the telephone or the face-to-face strategies. Differences between telephone and face-to-face strategies themselves were slight. Overall, the author concludes that given considerations of cost, quality, and speed, a telephone strategy supplemented by mail and face-to-face interviewing has much to recommend it as the primary means of gathering survey data. However, the implications of these conclusions for other types of content, such as surveys where attitudes and beliefs are focal, remain uncertain. Moreover, a major obstacle to combining all three modes in general population surveys is the absence of preexisting lists containing both addresses and telephone numbers. Of course, for certain types of surveys there may be other ways to exploit dual or triple modes, as when face-to-face interviewing is used for an initial contact and then further data are obtained at a later point by telephone or mail.

VARIATIONS IN SETTING

For reasons having to do with both sampling requirements and the convenience of respondents, most surveys use the home as the site of the interview or questionnaire. But for certain sensitive subjects, say reports by adolescents of deviant behavior, other locations might be assumed (as by Belson, 1978) to be better for encouraging frankness of response. A study by Zanes and Matsoukas (1979) provides qualified support for such a hypothesis. Students in the eleventh grade of a middle-class neighborhood were randomly assigned to home or classroom administration of questionnaires. Questions on drug use produced only a small trend for higher reports in the presumably anonymous classroom setting for the sample as a whole, but the difference was significant and much larger for the subset of students who had less regular attendance at school. There was also the unexpected finding that students in the school setting expressed more negative feelings about school, a result that is more difficult to attribute to a concern over anonymity, since feelings toward home and parents did not differ by setting.

A more complicated experiment by McKennell (1980) varied both setting and mode of administration in a British study of smoking among young people. Five modes of data collecting were compared: (1) face-to-face interviews at home, (2) self-completion questionnaires at home, (3) face-to-face interviews at school, (4) self-completion questionnaires at school administered individually, and (5) self-completion questionnaires at school administered in a group. For girls no significant differences in the proportion claiming to smoke one or more cigarettes per week were found between any of the five modes. For boys the reported incidence was higher when the questionnaire was self-administered rather than completed by the interviewer, when the data were collected at school rather than at home, and when the school self-completion questionnaire was administered to a group rather than individually. These effects were more pronounced for the younger (eleven- to thirteen-year-old) rather than the older (fourteen- to sixteen-year-old) boys. McKennell hypothesizes that the differences may be explained by children perceiving the school as more permissive than the home with respect to smoking and by the greater anonymity of the group administration. He notes that the high incidence reported by the younger boys in the group situation may contain an element of boasting.

The theoretical issues raised in such experiments pose good problems for further research by social psychologists. In addition to the practical value for decisions on survey administration, experimental variation of setting should afford insight into the nature and extent of situational influences on attitudes.

INTERVIEWING

Let us assume that a survey is carried out by means of interviewing, either telephone or face-to-face. The interviewer's initial task is to encourage potential respondents to take part in the survey and thus provides a bridge between completing the sample and beginning the interview. Second, the interviewer must ask the questions correctly, assess the adequacy of the responses, probe where necessary, and record answers accurately. Third comes editing the interviews for legibility and completeness. The first and third of these tasks are readily checked, the one by the interviewer's response rate and the other by examination of completed questionnaires. The middle stage, which is obviously crucial to the quality of the final data, is much more difficult to scrutinize, and for this reason it often receives the least attention in

practical situations. It is this middle stage that we concentrate on here, after saying what little we can about initiation of an interview.

PERSUADING PEOPLE TO BECOME RESPONDENTS

All interviewers, but especially new ones, are preoccupied with refusals, not only because they represent a loss to the sample but because it is hard not to take them personally. Other than selecting personable individuals and encouraging their confidence, survey investigators can do little to help interviewers in the crucial first few seconds of interaction at the door or on the telephone. Usually, the main advice offered is simply to keep the introduction as brief as possible initially, noting only essential points about sponsorship, content (usually in quite general terms), confidentiality, and perhaps the fact that the person was selected randomly. (It is not usual to script these points to the word, since this would make the interviewer sound too artificial.) When the addresses are available in advance, the investigator can also send prior letters explaining and legitimizing the study. There is a rather widespread belief that advance letters improve response rates, if only by increasing interviewer confidence. Evidence for the belief is slight, but there are two small studies that suggest that advance letters may help when they come from a well-respected organization (Brunner and Carroll, 1969; Cartwright and Tucker, 1969).

Prior letters cannot be used with random digit dial telephone sampling at present, since addresses are not known ahead of time. One approach attempted by Groves and Magilavy (1981) to increase RDD response rates was an adaptation of the foot-in-the-door technique (Freedman and Fraser, 1966; DeJong, 1979). Households in an RDD health survey were called, asked two short questions regarding their health, and told they might be contacted later as part of a larger survey. The authors found that those *who granted the first request* did indeed grant a second long interview more often than a control group not receiving the first request. However, the technique did not raise the *overall* response rate because a substantial number of people refused or could not be reached on first contact, and these people had a very low rate of granting the long interview, thus reducing the overall rate for the experimental sample to the same level as the control group. Two other factors were the fairly high response rate for the survey as a whole, which reduced the proportion of the sample in need of any special inducement, and the fact that the survey could not omit any eligible households from their calculations, unlike the more casual sampling procedures in some earlier investigations. Although it is possible that a greater attempt at persuasion at the first contact for the experimental group might have retained some advantage for the foot-in-the-door technique, the more basic problem may be that past experiments with this technique have not been forced to face this type of test, which requires accounting for all parts of a total sample. There is perhaps a larger implication here for the value of real-world applications in revealing otherwise unrecognized limits to an experimental finding.

BEHAVIOR DURING THE INTERVIEW

In the early days of surveys it was often argued that the main ingredient of a good interview was rapport and that interviewers needed a great deal of freedom to structure the interview in a way that suited the respondent and allowed optimal inquiry. The model was really the clinical interview, or perhaps the intimate conversation between close friends, with flexibility and good feeling seen as necessary to promote candor. For collecting statistics in China, one writer (Lieu, 1948, quoted by Hyman *et al.*, 1954, pp. 1–2) asserted that the information must

> be obtained in the course of general conversation. . . . It will not do for the interviewer to ask one question after another even when the respondent has shown a willingness to talk.

Unstructured interviewing continues to be a source of insight when used by sensitive humanists (e.g., Isaacs, 1965), and it is important as part of the initial pilot work in clarifying survey goals and developing survey measures. But the dominant position among most experienced investigators has long and increasingly favored efforts to standardize interviewer behavior in the final production phase of a large-scale survey (Hyman *et al.*, 1954; Cannell *et al.*, 1981). One reason for this is the recognition that survey interviewers cannot be expected to have the training and skills of the best clinicians. A second reason is the belief that standardization of the stimuli is preferable to highly variable and uncontrolled attempts by interviewers to adapt these to each respondent. A third reason is the sense that a more neutral approach

may in fact yield more honest answers than one that strives for personal closeness, because the latter makes a respondent too concerned about his or her relationship to the interviewer (see Weiss, 1968–1969; Dohrenwend *et al.*, 1969).

Flexibility is still required, of course, to cope with the unique pressures of each interviewing situation, and it is important for researchers to appreciate what some of these pressures are—an appreciation best gained through firsthand experience at interviewing, since it is difficult for academicians reviewing a questionnaire in the calmness of their own offices to realize the problems of administering the same questions in real-life situations. The following sample of interviewer accounts provides a picture that is worth keeping in mind as we proceed to a more analytic view of the interview. [Quotations are from papers by graduate students in the University of Michigan's Detroit Area Study practicum, as recorded in Converse and Schuman (1974). The papers were written after an intensive field period in which each student completed some fifteen face-to-face interviews in metropolitan Detroit.]

> It was a three-ring circus—the respondent had five children ranging from one to eight years and they all had a great time climbing all over the furniture. One child stood on her head on the couch next to me. I managed to hang onto my pencil, the questionnaire, my purse—but it wasn't easy! (p. 3)

> I couldn't see him for the most part, so I couldn't tell from facial expressions how he reacted to the questions. He answered straightforwardly, however, and had many strong opinions. I had suggested that I come back later when it might be more convenient, but he said No, *Now*. So I conducted the interview in the unheated garage, talking mostly to his legs, as he scooted around on a dolly, painting the bottom of his boat. (p. 2)

> From *my* standpoint, the interview took place in total chaos. There was the radio, a record player—both on. The respondent's small son, her daughter's little girl, her husband and son (both embarking on what seemed like some rather dedicated drinking) were all there. A neighbor came in to use the phone, and there were two incoming phone calls. Except for the last few questions, she did the interview well. Chaos seemed an everyday occur-

rence, and my respondent knew how to deal with it. (p. 3)

He was in terrible shape. He sat at the kitchen table drinking beer and was absolutely bleary-eyed, muttering and slurring his words, hardly able to focus his eyes. At the end of the interview he *congratulated* me. He said I was sure lucky that he'd been drinking because he never would have given me the interview when he was sober. His wife heartily agreed: "When he's sober, he hardly says a word." As I left, they both assured me again of my good fortune in finding him drunk—I still haven't decided. (p. 5)

Not that all experiences are quite so difficult, though even the most positive ones can interrupt the structure of the questionnaire:

Her home, modest enough, was one of the most pleasant atmospheres I have ever entered: she just seemed to light up the whole room. She was such an interesting person: when our conversations branched away from the questions in the schedule, I had to remind myself why I was there and get back to the questionnaire. (p. 6)

Although the setting and the respondent are the source of many interviewer problems, poor questions or incongruous questions or simply the frequency with which answers do not fit alternatives add considerably to the difficulties:

They resisted the either/or alternative; they qualified their answers; they rejected the cliché or the stereotype. Many of my respondents showed much greater information and sophistication than the question choices permitted, and not only the highly-educated respondents at that. When I asked one young woman the question on political efficacy, she said, "Well, I guess I'll agree that the average person can 'get what he wants'—as long as he doesn't *want* very much." She had no great stock of formal education, but I'd be hard-pressed to give a shrewder answer than that. I wonder how it will be coded. (pp. 68–69)

You sit in a lady's living room, look through cracked, broken-out windows at blocks and blocks of gutted "has-been" homes. You walk across a sag-

ging creaking floor, and look into narrow eyes peering at you from beneath a dresser. Not a dog, nor a cat—no, a child. Now you ask the big question in the neighborhood problem section: "Have you had any trouble because of neighbors not keeping up their property?" (p. 27)

PROBLEMS IN CARRYING OUT THE ROLE

No doubt in part because of the difficulties exemplified by all of the previous quotations, interviewers make more elementary errors in reading questions than is commonly realized. Bradburn *et al.* (1979) analyzed a sample of 372 tape-recorded interviews from a national survey. Reading errors (adding, omitting, or substituting words) occurred on the average in one out of every three questions, and there were numerous other reading variations (e.g., false starts) as well. Moreover, the errors showed a tendency to be more frequent for more experienced interviewers. Since the interviewers were chosen for excellence and knew they were being recorded, it is fair to assume that errors were, if anything, fewer than in most surveys. Bradburn *et al.* did not find any clear-cut effects from the reading errors, but it must be assumed that they introduce a certain amount of noise into survey data.

These and other forms of interviewer behavior have also been studied in depth by Cannell and his colleagues. For example, Marquis and Cannell (1969) employed tape recordings to code the various acts exhibited by interviewers. Most frequent (other than asking the questions) was feedback to respondents in the form of positive reinforcement ("Um-hum, I see," "That's interesting," "All right"). Furthermore, the feedback was found to be indiscriminate, given to undesirable behavior (such as refusal to answer a question) as much as or more than to desirable behavior. Interviewers apparently provided such feedback in their attempt to maintain a positive relationship with the respondent, but it seemed likely that it also often provided the wrong reinforcement at the wrong time.

These observations led Cannell and his associates (e.g., 1981) to program such positive feedback so that it reinforced only desirable behavior and to add negative feedback for use where a response was deemed inadequate (e.g., "Sometimes it's easy to forget all the things you felt or noticed here. Could you think about it again?"). As we saw earlier, programmed feedback sometimes increased the number of health conditions mentioned, including especially those of an embarrassing nature. The efficacy of programmed feedback as against the other techniques reviewed earlier (instructions, commitment, long questions) is not clear from the experiments performed thus far, and there are obvious dangers of encouraging overreporting by respondents. But the approach does, at the least, encourage us to look more analytically within the interview and to try to use its dynamics in a more deliberate way to provide better data. Furthermore, the telephone mode of survey allows interviews to be monitored much more systematically for these various types of interviewer behavior.

BIAS BY INTERVIEWERS

Just as rapport was long regarded as the prime factor in good interviewing, so interviewer bias along ideological lines was initially feared as a serious threat to good data. The two concerns fit together naturally, since both assume that interviewers are allowed a great deal of freedom to probe or even reword and rearrange questions. Often cited as a warning about bias was an early study of destitute men by Rice (1929) in which an interviewer who was a prohibitionist produced interviews showing alcoholism to be a major source of poverty, whereas an interviewer who was a socialist ended up with interviews implicating economic conditions. Yet in more standardized surveys and with training that stresses neutrality, it seems unlikely that Rice's example has much force. A careful study by Feldman *et al.* (1951–1952) found little evidence of bias due to interviewer ideology, and the same was true of a more general summary review by Hyman *et al.* (1954).

By the 1940s the emphasis had shifted from influence due to interviewer attitudes to more subtle effects flowing from interviewer expectations. In their classic volume on *Interviewing in Social Research*, Hyman *et al.* (1954) described three such types of expectations: role expectations, which were essentially stereotypes of social categories (e.g., all businessmen assumed to be Republicans); probability expectations, based on beliefs about overall response distributions; and attitude structure expectations, which lead the interviewer to expect later responses in an interview to be consistent with those given earlier. A compelling experimental demonstration is provided for the last type: Mildly ambiguous responses were categorized differently by interviewers depending upon what answers had preceded them. Because of the plau-

sibility of Hyman's conceptualization and the force of his experimental results, the assumption that expectations rather than direct ideological influence constitute the main source of interviewer bias has been widely accepted in survey research. It is not known, however, to what extent such expectations actually play an important role in survey data, especially where interviewers are more limited in their control over questioning. Recent studies of interviewer expectations concerning self-reports to sensitive questions (Bradburn *et al.*, 1979; Singer and Kohnke-Aquirre, 1979) do not find it a particularly powerful variable, but these are not close replications of Hyman's work, and the issue merits further research. It certainly does no harm to acquaint interviewers with the possibility that rigid expectations can bias data, and, indeed, one personal gain to students when they take part in interviewing is the discovery that respondents often do violate one's expectations of consistency.

INTERVIEWER CHARACTERISTICS

No matter how neutral an interviewer may appear in behavior, there are obvious physical characteristics that can influence interaction. We noted before that respondents probably project on to interviewers their own attitudes and beliefs to a considerable extent. An exception to this rule is most likely to occur where physical features or appearance signify a distinction in views. Black-white differences offer exactly such an example in American society at present, since they are immediately salient when strangers meet and they represent dividing lines with regard to a number of attitudes and beliefs. Thus it is no surprise that a considerable body of research indicates that race of interviewer has a substantial impact on certain types of responses.

Studies of the American soldier in World War II showed that the answers of black enlisted men to black interviewers were more critical of the army and less enthusiastic about the war than a comparable sample interviewed by whites (Stouffer *et al.,* 1949). Hyman *et al.* (1954) also report large race-of-interviewer effects on blacks in the South, including underreporting to questions about car ownership and education, suggesting that blacks at that point in time felt constrained to present a passive self-image to white interviewers. Effects continued to appear well after the height of the civil rights movement (Schuman and Hatchett, 1974) but seem to have been largely restricted to questions about racial issues, primarily those dealing with distrust of whites or with other obviously antiwhite sentiments. Furthermore, at present it seems simpler to interpret such effects as due mainly to general norms of politeness: Having invited a pleasant-looking white interviewer into one's home, one refrains from expressing hostility to that person's racial or ethnic group. Such an interpretation is supported by the discovery that similar effects occur when whites are the respondents: Significantly fewer antiblack answers are given to black than to white interviewers, for example, a 46 percent difference on a question about tolerance for racial intermarriage (Hatchett and Schuman, 1975–1976).

From the perspective of a situational view of behavior, it can be argued that all of these results may be valid, since each tells us how respondents would behave (verbalize) in a particular type of racial interaction. However, from a perspective on attitudes as representative of "true feelings," matching respondent and interviewer by race will probably seem reasonable to most investigators. We know of no studies of white racial attitudes that rely on black interviewers, and it does not seem sensible to proceed otherwise when black respondents are involved. Most national survey organizations do carry out such matching on an approximate basis, since interviewers are assigned mainly to areas close to their own homes, but neither complete matching nor controlled variation is ordinarily employed, and this confounding of interviewer effects with other effects makes tracking change over time difficult on racial issues. With the move to telephone interviewing the situation becomes even more problematic, since perceptions of race are more uncertain over the telephone and matching is also hard to arrange in the absence of substantial clustering by area. Fortunately, it is only the measurement of certain racial and related political attitudes that are seriously compromised by these interviewing problems. On most other issues neither blacks nor whites show response effects due to race of interviewer.

There is little information on whether sex, age, or other visible interviewer characteristics have the same effects as race. It seems likely that they may whenever respondents classify the interviewer into a larger category and believe they know what would offend or please persons in that category. Even when appearance provides no cue, information given by interviewers can have the same effect, as in one study showing less anti-Jewish responses to interviewers with Jewish-sounding names (Robinson and Rohde, 1946) and in another showing less suspicion

of the U.S. Census Bureau when the interviewers were identified as from the Census rather than from the Survey Research Center (National Research Council, 1979). In Hyman *et al.*'s (1954) terms role expectations operate for respondents as well as for interviewers, and when such expectations are joined to the norm of politeness, this leads to changes in responses to minimize discourtesy toward the interviewer. As already emphasized, however, on *most* issues most respondents have no idea how interviewers feel and probably assume that they do not differ markedly from themselves in views. In some other cases respondents may feel no special pressure to agree with interviewers because disagreement is not viewed as a breach of courtesy. Thus variation due to the characteristics of interviewers is important, but it is also delimitable.

INTERVIEWER VARIANCE

Having reviewed various ways in which interviewers can influence the responses they obtain, we consider now the measurement of systematic differences of any kind among interviewers. Such effects occur when, say, one interviewer tends to influence responses strongly in one direction, another tends to influence them weakly in that direction, and perhaps a third tends to influence them in the other direction. Even where such systematic differences among interviewers tend to cancel out, they introduce variability into the data collection process. Note that not all interviewing errors necessarily give rise to such systematic differences; isolated reading or recording errors, for instance, may be of a haphazard nature and lead to no overall differences among interviewers.

The ideal way to investigate interviewer effects is to carry out a validity study in which recorded responses are compared with true values. By this means both individual interviewer biases and haphazard errors can be measured. In practice, however, such validity studies are rarely feasible, and a less informative but simpler way to proceed is by means of a reliability study. This type of study does not permit measurement of the individual interviewer biases, but it does provide valuable evidence on the variability in these biases. Thus by comparing the responses obtained by a set of interviewers from comparable samples of respondents, one can measure the variability in their individual biases, or the *interviewer variance*. Interviewer variance is that part of the total variance in responses for a variable that is accounted for by systematic differences among interviewers. It should be noted that such variability is not usually captured by standard significance tests and therefore can lead to unexpected failures to replicate supposedly "significant" survey results.

It needs to be emphasized that the measurement of interviewer variance requires that interviewers interview comparable samples; otherwise, the differences in the results obtained will confound interviewer effects with differences between respondents. A simple design is to build up the total sample as a combination of a set of subsamples, or replicates, each based on the identical sample design—this procedure is known as replicated or interpenetrating sampling—and then to assign a separate replicate to each interviewer. This simple design may serve well for a face-to-face survey in a compact geographic area, but it needs to be modified for a widely dispersed population because of the excessive traveling it would entail for the interviewers in contacting their respondents. Restricted replication designs have been developed to handle this problem, but there still remain some serious practical obstacles to conducting interviewer variance studies with face-to-face surveys. In consequence, such studies are as a rule conducted only as special methodological investigations. With centralized telephone surveys the situation is different, however, and it is possible to incorporate interviewer variance studies as a routine procedure.

Studies of interviewer variance are probably most useful as a way of assessing the standardizing effect of selection and training of interviewers; i.e., the more successful the selection and training, the smaller the interviewer variance should be. Linked to systematic monitoring of interviewing, interviewer variance studies also provide a criterion for ratings or judgments of interviewer behavior. Groves *et al.* (1981) have carried out exploratory investigations along these lines but thus far without being able to tie monitored interviewer behavior to variations in interviewer item means. Interviewer variance calculations are also helpful in identifying problem questions and in considering the strengths and weaknesses of particular questions; for example, a count of the sheer number of responses to an open question shows greater interviewer variance than does the frequency of use of specific open or closed codes (Groves and Kahn, 1979), doubtless because the latter leave less scope for differences among interviewers in probing and recording. Finally, in some cases interviewer variance can be explained by such factors as interviewer race or sex, as discussed earlier. In all these uses it must be kept in mind that interviewer variance bears directly only on estimates of reliability. As always, low reliability places limits on validity, but high reliability does not necessarily imply high validity.

EDITING, CODING, AND DATA PROCESSING

After questionnaire data have been collected, there are still a number of time-consuming stages prior to analysis: The questionnaires must be edited for completeness, consistency, and legibility; responses must be converted to numerical codes; these in turn must be keypunched; and the resulting data must be placed on tapes or other forms of storage accessible by computer. Final steps are then taken to "clean" the data, i.e., to discover and correct "wild codes" (e.g., a case punched 3 when only categories 1 and 2 are possible for the variable) and resolve apparent inconsistencies [e.g., cases coded 10 for age and widowed for marital status; see Coale and Stephan (1962) for a more complex set of examples]. As with many parts of survey research, direct experience is the most useful teacher here, but an extensive discussion of these and related steps can be found in Sonquist and Dunkelberg (1977). Recent developments in computing promise to shorten the time needed for some of the stages; for example, coding can now be done directly into terminals without separate keypunching, and as already noted, it is possible to move from respondent answers to final data by means of direct terminal entry. In these cases edit checks can be programmed ahead of time and carried out by computer as the data are entered.

At each stage of the total process, error can be introduced through human mistakes of a clerical nature. Investigators must decide how much time and money to invest in reducing this error, always realizing that new mistakes may be introduced in the course of attempting to remove old ones. Almost always some errors remain despite fairly extensive efforts, but they can usually be kept to low "nuisance" levels for closed questions. The goal in cleaning data should ordinarily be to avoid, as far as possible, later problems in analysis but to prevent the effort in cleaning from absorbing so much time and other resources that it distracts and detracts from the scope of the final analysis. It is also well to keep in mind that although the clerical error being discussed here is highly visible, it is usually much less important than errors of measurement that are not visible at all.

With closed questions the coding stage itself is fairly straightforward, involving perhaps the insertion of two or three extra codes to classify responses that do not fit into the categories offered to respondents. With open questions the coding problem is quite different. First, a coding frame of the categories of answers has to be developed from a sample of responses (often around a hundred) and from the theoretical goals of the research; then the survey responses have to be classified according to these categories. It is often difficult to arrive at a fully adequate set of categories, and there are always some vague and ambiguous responses that are hard to allocate, a combination of factors that can lead to disagreement between coders. The coding task is tedious, and coders can easily make haphazard errors. In addition, they may interpret codes differently from one another, so systematic differences may occur between their codings; these differences result in coder variance, similar to the interviewer variance discussed earlier. For complex codings the levels of agreement between independent codings may be only moderate; Kalton and Stowell (1979) and Collins and Kalton (1980), for instance, report experiments in which the pairwise agreement between coders on the exact categorization of a sample of responses to a number of open questions was around 70 percent. As these authors conclude, coder unreliability can cause a substantial loss of precision in survey estimates based on open responses.

No simple rules can be given for the creation of open codes, other than that they be exhaustive (each response codable into some category), mutually exclusive, and as operationally clear as possible. Experienced investigators ordinarily try to avoid having coders make complex judgments, preferring to leave more theoretical inferences to the analysis stage. For example, for an open question on parental punishment of children, it would probably be better to code actual behavior (e.g., sending the child to his or her room for a period of time) rather than more interpretive judgments (e.g., withdrawal of love). The former emphasis is sometimes called empirical coding and is believed to lead to higher coder reliability. Where more conceptual codes are used, the judgments are more subjective, and there is a considerable danger that interpretations will shift markedly over time, thus creating problems in studying change through replication. This seems to have happened in an investigation by Duncan *et al.* (1973) where what at first appeared to be a change in parental values turned out to be due to systematic differences in coder judgments.

The preceding discussion of more standard open coding is not meant to limit the types of categorization applied to free responses. One important social psychological example of open coding was carried out by Converse (1964) in an attempt to gauge the degree to which the political thinking of respondents showed abstract ideological organization, and this involved quite general judgments by the investigator. At the other extreme Cramer and Schuman (1975) coded simply the use of the pronouns *we* and *they* in respondent references to the American government, although even this turned out to have some unforeseen problems. Still another quite different approach to free answers is to code them for the presence or absence of a set of themes, so that the same answer is considered repeatedly over a series of independent codes rather than forced into one of a set of mutually exclusive categories. There is really no end to the variety of ways that open responses can be categorized, depending upon one's goals. Indeed, one of the beauties of open responses, if they have been adequately recorded and stored, is the possibility that they can be evaluated from many different angles. It is probable that future social scientists will recode answers given today in ways that we are unable even to imagine.

ANALYSIS OF SURVEY DATA

We make no attempt to discuss survey data analysis in detail, but we refer the reader to Chapter 9, to texts on the logic of survey analysis such as Rosenberg (1968), and perhaps most helpful of all to good examples of social psychological survey analysis such as found in Campbell *et al.* (1976) and Duncan and Duncan (1978).

What may be useful, however, is to note certain differences between analyzing survey data and analyzing experimental data. Whereas an experiment ordinarily involves a set of prior predictions about the relations among a small number of variables, a survey often consists of a hundred or more variables about which only a few of the possible hypotheses can have been stated in advance. Moreover, the independent and dependent variables in an experiment are usually sharply distinguished, and the former type are ordinarily structured so as to be uncorrelated; in a set of survey data the status of variables as independent, dependent, or intervening is less clear, and many of the independent variables are themselves intercorrelated.

Perhaps the most important difference in analysis is the fact that the potentially vast number of relations, partial relations, and interactions in survey data lead to a more inductive approach than is the case for the single experiment. In this sense the analysis of a single survey is more like carrying out a sequence of experiments: In both cases hypotheses are stated, tested, reformulated, tested again, etc. For the same reason the analysis of a single survey often takes months or even years, which is the time frame not for a single experiment but for a program of experiments. Moreover, even when the primary analysis is completed, there is usually much left untouched, and the tradition of secondary analysis of data sets collected by others is well established, facilitated by large and growing archival collections (Hyman, 1972).

An associated problem in survey analysis is that the multiple testing of hypotheses within the same data set leads to some capitalizing on chance, and there is less possibility than in experimentation for sheer replication as such. Often a survey is not replicated for some years, by which time enough events have usually occurred so that differences in results are apt to be interpreted as due to real change, with simple unreliability sometimes not sufficiently allowed for. On the other hand, as already emphasized, the fact that survey samples can be said to represent natural populations permits more direct inferences to the real world, as well as facilitating systematic investigations of social and psychological trends.

All these differences are relative, to be sure, and one can find examples of survey and experimental reports that look more similar than this brief discussion suggests.

ETHICAL PROBLEMS BEARING ON SURVEY RESEARCH

In addition to the ethical problems that attend all science—the integrity of the scientific process and the uses of the knowledge obtained—survey research shares with other behavioral and biological sciences the additional problem of treating human beings as objects of investigation. Moreover, this problem is especially acute for survey research because it cannot rely on self-selected volunteers: The goal of generalizing to natural populations makes it essential to try to obtain responses from all members of a selected sample. Yet survey researchers recognize that in principle they should not—and in practice they cannot—require persons to take part in a survey or force them to answer particular questions within it.

This tension between the scientific needs of survey research and the obligations to the public has itself been the subject of research. Results bearing on two important issues will be presented here, along with more general observations.

Informed consent refers to the right of respondents to know ahead of time the content and purpose of a survey (or other investigation) and then to decide whether or not to take part. As noted earlier, however, interviewers usually believe it is best to minimize introductions and move quickly into the interview, avoiding mention ahead of time of topics that might be threatening to respondents. Singer (1978) found experimentally, in a face-to-face survey, that a somewhat fuller explanation of the content of the study, including mention that it included questions on drinking and sex, did not lower the response rate in comparison with a brief and uninformative introduction. A similar lack of effect occurred in a later replication by telephone (Singer and Frankel, 1982). In both cases the experimental variation occurred after gaining initial access and selecting the appropriate respondent within the household, and thus there was not a complete conflict with the desire of investigators and experienced interviewers to keep initial contacts brief and general. At the same time Singer also showed that a request for a signature to *document* consent reduces the response rate significantly (a drop of 7 percent for her face-to-face sample). There was some evidence that the nonsigners would have given less complete and valid responses, so their loss may not have been as serious as the 7 percent suggests.

Singer's experiments deal with the manifest content of a survey, but there is also the issue of what might be called the latent content of a study, i.e., the underlying purposes of the questionnaire and sample design. In the case of Singer's own survey this involved not mainly learning about the respondent's drinking and sexual practices but learning about how people responded to knowing that such questions would be asked. Fully informed consent, therefore, would have required a description of the experimental design itself, which would probably have destroyed much of the value of carrying it out. In other cases, as when *F*-scale or similar questions are administered, there is also a sharp difference between manifest content and the investigator's planned use of the data. Moreover, the informed consent rule might be taken to mean that respondents should be told in advance when their income will be asked at the end of the interview, since questions on income are known to be objectionable to many people (National Research Council, 1979). Taken to its logical extreme, the informed consent rule would probably prevent many surveys from being carried out at all. A better approach, as Singer suggests and as is now becoming standard in most surveys, is an introductory statement such as the following: "Of course, this interview is completely voluntary. If we should come to any question you don't want to answer, just let me know and we'll skip over it" (National Research Council, 1979). Emphasis on the voluntary nature of the interview plus sensitivity about what can be asked and how best it should be introduced seem more appropriate than a literal attempt to apply the informed consent rule to surveys, especially where the dangers of injury to respondents are essentially nonexistent.

Confidentiality of answers is widely assumed to be a major concern of respondents, and survey organizations normally promise not to release individual answers in any form. Both Singer (1978) and a panel of the National Research Council (1979) carried out experiments in which random subsamples received varying degrees of assurance about confidentiality. In the former case no effects and in the latter only trivial effects on initial cooperation were discovered. However, there is evidence in both studies that assurances of confidentiality decreased item nonresponse on sensitive questions such as income and sexual behavior and also, less certainly, decreased underreporting on the sensitive questions, although both types of effects seem to be small.

Perhaps the main reason that all these effects are not larger is that most respondents seem neither terribly worried ahead of time about breaches in confidentiality nor greatly impressed by promises of it. It appears that many respondents assume confidentiality has been promised even when it has not been, yet few believe that the Census Bureau—which is trusted more than nongovernment survey organizations—really protects individual records from non-Census use (National Research Council, 1979). Probably those people who are *most* concerned about the confidentiality of their responses do not consider taking part in surveys at all. One should note that a large part of the refusal component of survey nonresponse occurs before the interviewer has an opportunity to say more than a few words, and this component presumably includes those persons unwilling to accept *any* assurances at all with regard to confidentiality.

Whatever the degree of public desire for or trust in the confidentiality of individual records, survey investigators should certainly take steps to protect confidentiality by separating names and identifying information from other survey responses, using only a connecting set of reference numbers. If complete confidentiality is desired, identifying information must be destroyed, since the legal status of all promises by a nongovernment orga-

nization is uncertain at best. Complete protection is not possible in ongoing panel studies because of the need to identify respondents for later contact, but all practical steps should be taken to minimize a breach of confidentiality. Boruch and Cecil (1979) provide a discussion of confidentiality issues and methods.

The ethical problems discussed above by no means exhaust those that might be considered. There are issues of intrusiveness arising from the increasing number of surveys, especially by telephone, although this is perhaps less of a problem than the variety of sales and political pitches masquerading as surveys. There are also questions about the adequacy of reporting of survey procedures and results, including occasional suppression or distortion for political purposes. These and other issues arise in good part because the survey is an all-purpose tool, valuable not only to social scientists in pursuit of knowledge but also to commercial firms in pursuit of sales, politicians seeking votes, newspapers trying to attract readers, and all manner of other organizations. Unlike the social psychological experiment, the survey method has never been restricted to any one discipline or even to academicians as such. This can be seen as a mark of its versatility and success in obtaining useful information, as Davis (1975) concludes, but it also gives rise to a range of problems that extend well beyond those involving use and misuse by social scientists.

ELABORATIONS OF THE SURVEY METHOD

This chapter has focused on the cross-sectional survey, with some mention of implications when change over time is of concern. It is useful to end by noting examples of types of studies that draw or build on the basic survey method but extend it in valuable ways.

PERIODIC SURVEYS

Some surveys of social psychological change draw independent samples of a defined population at different points in time. This can be done at frequent intervals, as with SRC's Consumer Expectations surveys, intended to chart change in public confidence on a monthly basis, or Smith's (1979) analysis of seasonal vicissitudes in happiness. Over longer periods of time changes can be analyzed into those reflecting shifts in individual attitudes and beliefs and those due to changes in the composition of the total population. Problems of separating the two, and further of distinguishing age, cohort, and period effects, are discussed by Mason *et al.* (1973), Converse (1976), and Glenn (1977). A general consideration of problems that arise in monitoring trends in social indicators appears in Martin (1983).

PANEL STUDIES

Panel studies have come to refer to repeated surveys of the same sample, not simply repeated samples from the same population. Such studies allow identification of change at the individual level, and when first popularized in survey research (e.g., Lazarsfeld and Fiske, 1938), they were seen as a way of allowing strong causal inferences approaching those possible from experimentation. For example, data collected on current smoking and health at several points in the life cycle provide more dependable evidence on the time sequence for these events and hence on the smoking-illness causal connection than do retrospective data collected at some later point of time. In addition, shifts at the individual level (e.g., in voting preferences) can be directly studied by using a panel, even though they may cancel out when aggregated. Experience with panel studies has reduced somewhat the early high expectations because of both theoretical and practical difficulties that confront the analyst (cf. Tanur, 1981). For recent treatments of panel analysis, see Markus (1979) and Duncan (1984), and for an important example of a long-term panel study, see Duncan *et al.* (1984). Rotating panels attempt to combine the advantages of the continuing panel with the advantages of introducing new samples at regular intervals.

ELITE-MASS CONTRASTS

We use the term *elite-mass contrasts* to refer to studies that supplement a cross-sectional sample with a special sample of persons in positions of leadership relative to the cross section. For example, Stouffer's (1955) addition of community leaders to his larger survey and Miller and Stokes's (1963) interviews with both the electorate and their Representatives can be seen as ways of dealing with criticisms that surveys lose contact with the true structure of public opinion (Blumer, 1948), which is more than the sum of individual attitudes. By sampling those in leadership positions, researchers can provide more realistic "weighting" of attitudes, as well as study the mutual perceptions of leaders and led. Elite-mass contrasts are, of course, only one way of supplementing

cross-sectional samples with other data that will enrich standard surveys. Inclusion of other types of contrast samples and of entirely different sources of data [e.g., content analysis of media (MacKuen, 1981)] can also be very useful.

EXPERIMENTS AND QUASI EXPERIMENTS

We have already presented examples of how experiments can be built into surveys by varying questionnaire content, interviewer behavior, or mode of administration. Surveys are also often used as parts of larger experiments, where the survey is constant and provides measures of treatment effects. The Negative Income Tax experiments, one of the largest set of experiments ever carried out in a rigorous way, depended heavily on surveys for outcome measures (for one account, see Rossi and Lagall, 1976). When true field experiments are executed fully, they combine the two main ways in which randomization enters social research: random selection of elements from a larger population and random assignment of the sample elements to treatments. Both procedures are needed when one attempts to evaluate the way a policy change will affect a real population. The many problems that occur in such large-scale social experiments are discussed briefly by Tanur (1981), and there is a large and growing literature on experiments for program evaluation.

SURVEYS OF BEHAVIOR

Although we have treated the survey as resulting from joint use of sampling and questioning, the two components are not necessarily bound together. Obviously, questioning can be a valuable supplement to other social psychological approaches, and probability sampling likewise can be conjoined with other methods of data collection. In particular, probability sampling of natural behavior in natural populations should probably be more widely attempted, with careful description of procedures in order to allow later replication for studies of change. There have been a number of surveys of behavior along this line (e.g., Melbin, 1978), but they rarely are done in a way that would allow exact replication. A study that involved not only observation of behavior but also both experimental manipulation and the use of questionnaires for reporting was Selltiz's (1955) account of discrimination in New York restaurants: The population of restaurants and the sampling procedures were well enough described so that replication within the same area 31 years later was possible (Schuman *et al.* 1983b.) Thus the survey need not be thought of as only one among several competing methods available to social psychologists. It can also be seen as contributing certain of the components to a larger approach that draws on the strengths of all the different ways in which an empirical social psychology can learn about the social world.

REFERENCES

Abelson, R. P. (1982). Three modes of attitude-behavior consistency. In M. P. Zanna, E. T. Higgins, and C. P. Herman (Eds.), *Consistency in social behavior.* The Ontario Symposium. Vol. 2. Hillsdale, N.J.: Erlbaum.

Abernathy, J. R., B. G. Greenberg, and D. C. Horvitz (1970). Estimates of induced abortions in urban North Carolina. *Demography, 7,* 19–29.

Adorno, T. W., E. Frenkel-Brunswik, D. J. Levinson, and R. N. Sanford (1950). *The authoritarian personality.* New York: Harper.

Ajzen, I., and M. Fishbein (1977). Attitude-behavior relations: a theoretical analysis and review of empirical research. *Psychol. Bull., 84,* 888–918.

Allport, G. W. (1954). The historical background of modern social psychology. In G. Lindzey (Ed.), *Handbook of social psychology.* Cambridge, Mass.: Addison-Wesley.

Anderson, R., J. Kasper, M. R. Frankel, and Associates (1979). *Total survey error.* San Francisco: Jossey-Bass.

Andrews, F. M., and S. B. Withey (1976). *Social indicators of well-being.* New York: Plenum.

Armstrong, J. S. (1975). Monetary incentives in mail surveys. *Publ. Opin. Quart., 39,* 111–116.

Babbie, E. R. (1973). *Survey research methods.* Belmont, Calif.: Wadsworth Publishing.

Bailar, B. A., L. Bailey, and C. Corby (1978). A comparison of some adjustment and weighting procedures for survey data. In N. K. Namboodiri (Ed.), *Survey sampling and measurement.* New York: Academic Press.

Bailar, B. A., and N. D. Rothwell (1984). Measuring employment and unemployment. In C. F. Turner and E. Martin (Eds.), *Surveying subjective phenomena.* Vol. 2., Chap. 5. New York: Russell Sage.

Barton, A. J. (1958). Asking the embarrassing question. *Publ. Opin. Quart., 22,* 67–68.

Becker, S. L. (1954). Why an order effect. *Publ. Opin. Quart., 18,* 271–278.

Belson, W. A. (1981). *The design and understanding of survey questions.* London: Gower Publishing Co.

———— (1978). Investigating causal hypotheses concerning delinquent behaviour, with special reference to new strategies in data collection and analysis. *Statistician, 27,* 1–25.

Belson, W. A., and J. A. Duncan (1962). A comparison of the check-list and the open response questioning systems. *Appl. Statist., 11,* 120–132.

Bishop, G. F., R. W. Oldendick, and A. J. Tuchfarber (1983). Effects of filter questions in public opinion surveys. *Publ. Opin. Quart., 47,* 528–546.

Bishop, G. F., R. W. Oldendick, A. J. Tuchfarber, and S. E. Bennett (1980). Pseudo-opinions on public affairs. *Publ. Opin. Quart., 44,* 198–209.

Bishop, G. F., A. J. Tuchfarber, and R. W. Oldendick (1978). Change in the structure of American political attitudes: the nagging question of question wording. *Amer. J. Polit. Sci., 22,* 250–269.

Bishop, Y. M. M., S. E. Fienberg, and P. W. Holland (1975). *Discrete multivariate analysis: theory and practice.* Cambridge, Mass.: M.I.T. Press.

Blalock, H. M. (1961). *Causal inference in nonexperimental research.* Chapel Hill: Univ. of North Carolina Press.

Blumer, H. (1948). Public opinion and public opinion polling. *Amer. Sociol. Rev., XIII,* 542–555.

Boruch, R. F., and J. S. Cecil (1979). *Assuring the confidentiality of social research data.* Philadelphia: Univ. of Pennsylvania Press.

Bowley, A. L., and A. R. Burnett-Hurst (1915). *Livelihood and poverty.* London: Bell & Sons.

Bradburn, N. M., and W. M. Mason (1964). The effect of question order on responses. *J. Marketng. Res., 1,* 57–61.

Bradburn, N. M., S. Sudman, and Associates (1979). *Improving interview method and questionnaire design.* San Francisco: Jossey-Bass.

Brunner, G. A., and S. J. Carroll, Jr. (1969). The effect of prior notification on the refusal rate in fixed address surveys. *J. Advertising, 9,* 42–44.

Cain, P. S., and D. J. Treiman (1981). The dictionary of occupational titles as a source of occupational data. *Amer. Sociol. Rev., 46,* 253–278.

Campbell, A., P. E. Converse, and W. L. Rodgers (1976). *The quality of American life: perceptions, evaluations, and satisfactions.* New York: Russell Sage.

Campbell, D. T., and D. W. Fiske (1959). Convergent and discriminant validation by the multitrait-multimethod matrix. *Psychol. Bull., 56,* 81–105.

Cannell, C. F., and F. J. Fowler (1963). *Comparison of hospitalization reporting in three survey procedures.* U. S. National Center for Health Statistics, Series D–8. Washington, D. C.: Government Printing Office.

Cannell, C. F., K. H. Marquis, and A. Laurent (1977). *A summary of studies of interviewing methodology.* Vital and Health Statistics, Series 2–69. Washington, D. C.: Government Printing Office.

Cannell, C. F., P. V. Miller, and L. Oksenberg (1981). Research on interviewing techniques. In S. Leinhardt (Ed.), *Sociological methodology.* San Francisco: Jossey-Bass.

Cantril, H., Ed. (1944). *Gauging public opinion.* Princeton, N.J.: Princeton Univ. Press.

Cartwright, A., and W. Tucker (1969). An experiment with an advance letter on an interview inquiry. *Brit. J. Prev. Soc. Med., 23,* 241–243.

Chapman, D. W. (1976). A survey of nonresponse imputation procedures. *Proceedings of the social statistics section.* Washington, D.C. American Statistical Association. 245–251.

Coale, A. J., and F. F. Stephan (1962). The case of the Indians and the teen-age widows. *J. Amer. Statist. Assoc., 57,* 338–347.

Cochran, W. G. (1977). *Sampling techniques* (3rd ed.). New York: Wiley.

Collins, M., and G. Kalton (1980). Coding verbatim answers to open questions. *J. Market. Res. Soc., 22,* 239–247.

Converse, J. M. (forthcoming). Survey research in the United States: roots and emergence, 1890–1955. Berkeley: Univ. of California Press.

Converse, J. M., and H. Schuman (1974). *Conversations at random: survey research as interviewers see it.* New York: Wiley.

Converse, P. E. (1964). The nature of belief systems in mass publics. In D. E. Apter (Ed.), *Ideology and discontent.* New York: Free Press.

———— (1970). Attitudes and non-attitudes: continuation of a dialogue. In E. R. Tufte (Ed.), *The quantitative analysis of social problems.* Reading, Mass.: Addison-Wesley.

———— (1972). Change in the American electorate. In A. Campbell and P. E. Converse (Eds.), *The human meaning of social change.* New York: Russell Sage.

———— (1976). *The dynamics of party support.* Beverly Hills, Calif.: Sage.

Converse, P. E., J. D. Dotson, W. J. Hoag, and W. H. McGee, III. (1980). *American social attitudes data source book, 1947–1978.* Cambridge, Mass.: Harvard Univ. Press.

Cowan, C. D., L. R. Murphy, and J. Wiener (1978). Effects of supplemental questions on victimization estimates from the National Crime Survey. *Proceedings of the section on survey research methods.* Washington, D.C.: American Statistical Association. 277–282.

Cramer, M. R., and H. Schuman (1975). We and they: pronouns as measures of political identification and estrangement. *Soc. Sci. Res., 4,* 231–240.

Davis, J. A. (1975). On the remarkable absence of nonacademic implications in academic research: an example from ethnic studies. In N. J. Demerath, III, O. Larsen, and K. F. Schuessler (Eds.), *Social policy and sociology.* New York: Academic Press.

DeJong, W. (1979). An examination of self-perception mediation of the foot-in the-door effect. *J. Pers. Soc. Psychol., 37,* 2221–2239.

Dijkstra, W. and J. van der Zouwen, Eds. (1982). *Response behavior in the survey-interview.* New York: Academic Press.

Dillman, D. A. (1978). *Mail and telephone surveys: the total design method.* New York: Wiley.

Dohrenwend, B. S., J. A. Williams, Jr., and C. H. Weiss (1969). Interviewer biasing effects: toward a reconciliation of findings—comments. *Publ. Opin. Quart., 33,* 121–129.

Duncan, B., and O. D. Duncan (1978). *Sex typing and social roles: a research report.* New York: Academic Press.

Duncan, G. J., R. J. Coe, M. E. Corcoran, M. S. Hill, S. Hoffman, and J. N. Morgan (1984). *Years of Poverty, Years of Plenty.* Ann Arbor, Mich.: Institute for Social Research.

Duncan, O. D. (1966). Path analysis: sociological examples. *Amer. J. Sociol., 72,* 1–16.

———— (1978). Multiway contingency analysis. *Contemporary Sociol., 7,* 403–405.

———— (1984). Measurement and structure. In C. F. Turner and E. Martin (Eds.), *Surveying subjective phenomena.* Vol. 1: Chapter 6. New York: Russell Sage.

Duncan, O. D., H. Schuman, and B. Duncan (1973). *Social change in a metropolitan community.* New York: Russell Sage.

Erdos, P. L. (1970). *Professional mail surveys.* New York: McGraw-Hill.

Ewbank, D. C. (1981). *Age misreporting and age-selective underenumeration: sources, patterns, and consequences for demographic analysis,* Report No. 4. Committee on Population and Demography. Assembly of Behavioral and Social Sciences, National Research Council. Washington, D.C.: National Academy Press.

Farley, R., H. Schuman, S. Bianchi, D. Colasanto, and S. Hatchett (1978). Chocolate city, vanilla suburbs: will the trend toward racially separate communities continue? *Soc. Sci. Res., 7,* 319–344.

Fazio, R. H., and M. P. Zanna (1981). Direct experience and attitude—behavior consistency. In L. Berkowitz (Ed.) *Advances in experimental social psychology.* Vol. 14. New York: Academic Press.

Feldman, J. J., H. Hyman, and C. W. Hart (1951–52). A field study of interviewer effects on the quality of survey data. *Publ. Opin. Quart., 15,* 734–761.

Fields, J. M., and H. Schuman (1976–77). Public beliefs about the beliefs of the public. *Publ. Opin. Quart., 40,* 427–448.

Fishbein, M., and I. Ajzen (1975). *Belief, attitude, intention and behavior.* Reading, Mass.: Addison-Wesley.

Fleishman, E., and M. Berk (1979). *Survey of interviewer attitudes toward selected methodological issues in the National Medical Care Expenditure Survey.* National Center for Health Services Research Proceedings Series, Third Biennial Conference. Hyattsville, Md.: U.S. Dept. of Health and Human Services (PHS) 81–3268. Pp. 249–256.

Frankel, M. R., and L. R. Frankel (1977). Some recent developments in sample survey design. *J. Marketng. Res., 14,* 280–293.

Freedman, J. L., and S. C. Fraser (1966). Compliance without pressure: The foot-in-the-door technique. *J. Pers. soc. Psychol., 4,* 195–202.

Frey, J. H. (1983). *Survey research by telephone.* Beverly Hills, Calif.: Sage.

Gergen, K. J. (1973). Social psychology as history. *J. Pers. soc. Psychol., 26,* 309–320.

Gibson, C., G. M. Shapiro, L. R. Murphy, and G. J. Stanko (1978). Interaction of survey questions as it relates to interviewer-respondent bias. *Proceedings of the section on survey research methods.* Washington, D.C.: American Statistical Association. 251–256.

Glenn, N. D. (1977). *Cohort analysis.* Beverly Hills, Calif.: Sage.

Goodman, L. A. (1972). A modified multiple regression approach to the analysis of dichotomous variables. *Amer. Sociol. Rev., 39,* 28–46.

Goodstadt, M. S., and V. Gruson (1975). The randomized response technique: a test on drug use. *J. Amer. Statist. Assoc., 70,* 814–818.

Gove, W. R., and M. R. Geerken (1977). Response bias in surveys of mental health: an empirical investigation. *Amer. J. Sociol., 82,* 1289–1317.

Groves, R. M., and R. L. Kahn (1979). *Surveys by telephone: a national comparison with personal interviews.* New York: Academic Press.

Groves, R. M., and L. J. Magilavy (1981). Increasing response rates to telephone surveys: A door in the face for foot-in-the-door? *Publ. Opin. Quart., 45,* 346–358.

Groves, R. M., L. J. Magilavy, and N. A. Mathiowetz (1981). The process of interviewer variability: evidence from telephone surveys. *Proceedings of the Section on Survey Research Methods.* Washington, D.C.: American Statistical Association. 438–443.

Hansen, M. H., W. N. Hurwitz, and W. G. Madow (1953). *Sample survey methods and theory. Vol. I. Methods and applications. Vol. II. Theory.* New York: Wiley.

Hatchett, S., and H. Schuman (1975–76). White respondents and race-of-interviewer effects. *Publ. Opin. Quart., 39,* 523–528.

Heberlein, T. A., and R. Baumgartner (1978). Factors affecting response rates to mailed questionnaires: a quantitative analysis of the published literature. *Amer. Sociol. Rev., 43,* 447–462.

Hodge, R. W., P. M. Siegel, and P. H. Rossi (1964). Occupational prestige in the United States, 1925–63. *Amer. J. Sociol., 70,* 286–302.

Hollingshead, A. B. (1949). *Elmstown's youth.* New York: Wiley.

House, J. S., and S. Wolf (1978). Effects of urban residence on interpersonal trust and helping behavior. *J. Pers. soc. Psychol., 36,* 1029–1043.

Hyman, H. H. (1955). *Survey design and analysis.* Glencoe, Ill.: Free Press.

_____ (1972). *Secondary analysis of sample surveys: principles, procedures, and potentialities.* New York: Wiley.

Hyman, H. H., W. J. Cobb, J. J. Feldman, C. W. Hart, and C. H. Stember (1954). *Interviewing in social research.* Chicago: Univ. of Chicago Press.

Hyman, H. H., and P. B. Sheatsley (1950). The current status of American public opinion. In J. C. Payne (Ed.), *The teaching of contemporary affairs.* Twenty-first Yearbook of the National Council of Social Studies, 11–34.

Isaacs, H. R. (1965). *India's ex-untouchables.* New York: John Day Co.

Joreskog, K. G., and D. Sorbom (1979). *Advances in factor analysis and structural equation models.* Cambridge, Mass.: ABT.

Judd, C. M., and J. A. Krosnick (1981). Attitude centrality, organization, and measurement. *J. Pers. soc. Psychol.*

Kalton, G. (1983a). *Introduction to survey sampling.* Beverly Hills, Calif.: Sage.

_____ (1983b). *Compensating for missing survey data.* Ann Arbor, Mich.: Survey Research Center, Univ. of Michigan.

Kalton, G., M. Collins, and L. Brook (1978). Experiments in wording opinion questions. *J. R. Statist. Soc. C, 27,* 149–161.

Kalton, G., and D. Kasprzyk (1982). Inputing for missing survey responses. *Proceedings of the section on survey research methods.* Washington, D.C.: American Statistical Association. 22–31.

Kalton, G., J. Roberts, and D. Holt (1980). The effects of offering a middle response option with opinion questions. *Statistician, 29,* 11–24.

Kalton, G., and R. Stowell (1979). A study of coder variability. *Appl. Statist., 27,* 276–289.

Kanuk, L., and C. Berenson (1975). Mail surveys and response rates: a literature review. *J. Marketng. Res., 12,* 440–453.

Katz, D. (1967). The practice and potential of survey methods in psychological research. In C. Y. Glock (Ed.), *Survey research in the social sciences.* New York: Russell Sage.

Kelley, S., and T. W. Mirer (1974). The simple act of voting. *Amer. Polit. Sci. Rev., 68,* 572–591.

Kendall, P. L., and P. F. Lazarsfeld (1950). Problems of survey analysis. In R. K. Merton and P. F. Lazarsfeld (Eds.), *Continuities in social research: studies in the scope and method of the American soldier.* Glencoe, Ill.: Free Press.

Kish, L. (1965). *Survey sampling.* New York: Wiley.

Kish, L., and M. R. Frankel (1974). Inference from complex samples. *J. R. Statist. Soc. B, 36,* 1–37.

Kish, L., and I. Hess (1965). *The Survey Research Center's national sample of dwellings.* Ann Arbor, Institute for Social Research, Univ. of Michigan.

Krosnick, J. A. (1984). Attitude extremity, stability and self-report: the effects of attitude centrality. Paper given at the American Association for Public Opinion Research annual meetings.

Kruskal, W., and F. Mosteller (1980). Representative sampling, IV: the history of the concept in statistics, 1895–1939. *Int. Statist. Rev., 48,* 169–195.

LaPiere, R. T. (1934). Attitudes versus actions. *Social Forces, 13,* 230–237.

Lazarsfeld, P. F. (1944). The controversy over detailed interviews—an offer for negotiation. *Publ. Opin. Quart., 8,* 38–60.

Lazarsfeld, P. F., and M. Fiske (1938). The panel as a new tool for measuring opinion. *Publ. Opin. Quart., 2,* 596–612.

Lewin, K. (1951). *Field theory in social science.* New York: Harper & Row.

Lieu, D. K. (1948). Collecting statistics in China. *Amer. Statistician.* Vol. 2: 12–13.

Lindzey, G. E., and L. Guest (1951). To repeat—check lists can be dangerous. *Publ. Opin. Quart., 15,* 355–358.

Linsky, A. S. (1975). Stimulating responses to mailed questionnaires: a review. *Publ. Opin. Quart., 39,* 82–101.

Loftus, E. F. (1982). Interrogating eyewitnesses—good questions and bad. In R. M. Hogarth (Ed.), *Question framing and response consistency.* San Francisco: Jossey-Bass.

McFarland, S. G. (1981). Effects of question order on survey responses. *Publ. Opin. Quart., 45,* 208–215.

McKennell, A. C. (1974). *Surveying attitude structures.* Amsterdam: Elsevier.

_____ (1980). Bias in the reported incidence of smoking by children. *Int. J. Epidemiology, 9,* 167–177.

MacKuen, M. (1981). Social communication and the mass policy agenda. In M. MacKuen and S. L. Coombs (Eds.), *More than news.* Beverly Hills, Calif.: Sage.

McNemar, Q. (1946). Opinion-attitude methodology. *Psychol. Bull., 43,* 289–374.

Mahalanobis, P. C., and A. Das Gupta (1954). The use of sample surveys in demographic studies in India. *Proceedings* of the United Nations world population conference. Vol. 6, 363–384.

Markus, G. B. (1979). *Analyzing panel data.* Beverly Hills, Calif.: Sage.

Marquis, K. H. (1978). *Record check validity of survey responses: a reassessment of bias in reports of hospitalization.* Santa Monica, Calif.: Rand Corp. R–2319-HEW.

Marquis, K. H., and C. F. Cannell (1969). *A study of interviewer-respondent interaction in the urban employment survey.* Ann Arbor: Survey Research Center, Univ. of Michigan.

Marquis, K. H., N. Duan, M. S. Marquis, and J. M. Polich (1981). *Response errors in sensitive topic surveys.* Santa Monica, Calif.: Rand Corp. R–1710/1–HHS Executive Summary. R–1710/2-HHS Estimates, Effects, and Correction Options.

Martin, E. (1983). Surveys and social indicators: problems in monitoring trends. In P. H. Rossi, J. D. Wright, and A. B. Anderson (Eds.), *Handbook of Survey Research.* New York: Academic Press.

Mason, K. O., W. Mason, H. H. Winsborough, and W. K. Poole (1973). Some methodological issues in the cohort analysis of archival data. *Amer. Soc. Rev., 38,* 242–258.

Melbin, M. (1978). Night as frontier. *Amer. Sociol. Rev., 43,* 3–22.

Miller, J. D. (1984). A new survey technique for studying deviant behavior. Unpublished doctoral dissertation, The George Washington University.

Miller, P. V., and C. F. Cannell (1977). Communicating measurement objectives in the survey interview. In P. V. Miller and G. Kline (Eds.), *Strategies for communication research.* Vol. 6. Beverly Hills, Calif.: Sage.

Miller, P. V., and C. F. Cannell (1982). A study of experimental techniques for telephone interviewing. *Publ. Opin. Quart., 46,* 250–269.

Miller, W. E., and D. E. Stokes (1963). Constituency influence in congress. *Amer. Polit. Sci. Rev., 57,* 45–56.

Moser, C. A., and G. Kalton (1971). *Survey methods in social investigation* (2nd ed.). London: Heinemann.

Mosteller, F. (1968). Errors: I. Nonsampling errors. *International encyclopedia of the social sciences.* Vol. 5. New York: Macmillan and Free Press.

Mueller, J. E. (1973). *War, presidents and public opinion.* New York: Wiley.

National Opinion Research Center (1947). Jobs and occupations: a popular evaluation. *Opinion News, 9,* 3–13.

National Research Council (1979). *Privacy and confidentiality as factors in survey response.* Washington, D.C.: National Academy of Sciences.

Neter, J., and J. Waksberg (1964). A study of response errors in expenditures data from household interviews. *J. Amer. Statist. Assoc., 59,* 18–55.

Nunnally, J. C. (1978). *Psychometric theory.* New York: McGraw-Hill.

Parry, H. J., and H. M. Crossley (1950). Validity of responses to survey questions. *Publ. Opin. Quart., 14,* 61–80.

Parten, M. (1950). *Surveys, polls, and samples.* New York: Harper.

Payne, S. L. (1951). *The art of asking questions.* Princeton: Princeton Univ. Press.

Pepitone, A. and M. DiNubile (1976). Contrast effects in judgments of crime severity and the punishment of criminal violators. *J. Pers. soc. Psychol., 33,* 448–459.

Piazza, T. (1980). The analysis of attitude items. *Amer. J. Sociol., 86,* 584–603.

Powers, E. A., W. J. Goudy, and P. M. Keith (1978). Congruence between panel and recall data in longitudinal research. *Publ. Opin. Quart., 42,* 380–389.

Presser, S. (1984). The use of survey data in basic research in the social sciences. In C. F. Turner and E. Martin (Eds.) *Surveying subjective phenomena.* Vol. 2. Chap. 5. New York: Russell Sage.

Raghavarao, D., and W. T. Federer (1979). Block total response as an alternative to the randomized response method in surveys. *J.R. Statist. Soc. B, 41,* 40–45.

Rand Corporation (1955). *A million random digits with 100,000 normal deviates.* Glencoe, Ill.: Free Press.

Rice, S. A. (1929). Contagious bias in the interview: a methodological note. *Amer. J. Sociol., 35,* 420–423.

Robinson, D., and S. Rohde (1946). Two experiments with an anti-semitism poll. *J. abnorm. soc. Psychol., 41,* 136–144.

Robinson, J. P., J. G. Rusk, and K. B. Head (1968). *Measures of political attitudes.* Ann Arbor, Mich.: Institute for Social Research, Univ. of Michigan.

Robinson, J. P., and P. R. Shaver (1973). *Measures of social psychological attitudes.* (Rev. ed.) Ann Arbor.: Institute for Social Research, Univ. of Michigan.

Rosenberg, M. (1968). *The logic of survey analysis.* New York: Basic Books.

Ross, L. (1977). The intuitive psychologist and his shortcomings: distortions in the attribution process. In L. Berkowitz (Ed.), *Advances in experimental social psychology.* Vol. 10. New York: Academic Press.

Ross, L., D. Greene, and P. House (1977). The "false consensus effect": an egocentric bias in social perception and attribution processes. *J. exp. soc. Psychol., 13,* 279–301.

Rossi, P. H., and K. C. Lagall (1976). *Reforming public welfare: a critique of the Negative Income Tax experiment.* New York: Russell Sage.

Rossi, P. H., J. D. Wright and A. B. Anderson, Eds. (1983). *Handbook of survey research,* New York: Academic Press.

Rugg, D. (1941). Experiments in wording questions: II. *Publ. Opin. Quart., 5,* 91–92.

Rugg, D., and H. Cantril (1944). The wording of questions. In H. Cantril (Ed.), *Gauging public opinion.* Princeton: Princeton Univ. Press.

Schewe, C. D., and N. G. Cournoyer (1976). Prepaid versus promised monetary incentives to questionnaire response: further evidence. *Publ. Opin. Quart., 40,* 105–107.

Schuessler, K., D. Hittle, and J. Cardascia (1978). Measuring responding desirably with attitude-opinion items. *Soc. Psychol., 41,* 224–235.

Schuman, H. (1966). The random probe: a technique for evaluating the validity of closed questions. *Amer. Sociol. Rev., 21,* 218–222.

Schuman, H., and S. Hatchett (1974). *Black racial attitudes: trends and complexities.* Ann Arbor: Institute for Social Research, Univ. of Michigan.

Schuman, H., and M. Johnson (1976). Attitudes and behavior. *Ann. rev. of Sociol.* Vol. 2. 161–207.

Schuman, H., G. Kalton, and J. Ludwig (1983). Context and contiguity in survey questionnaires. *Publ. Opin. Quart., 47,* 112–115.

Schuman, H., and J. Ludwig (1983). The norm of even-handedness in surveys as in life. *Amer. Sociol. Rev., 48,* 112–120.

Schuman, H., and S. Presser (1981). *Questions and answers in attitude surveys: experiments on question form, wording, and context.* New York: Academic Press.

Schuman, H., E. Singer, R. Donovan, and C. Selltiz (1983). Discriminatory behavior in New York restaurants: 1950 and 1981. *Social Indicators Research. 13,* 69–83.

Schwartz, S. H. (1978). Temporal instability as a moderator of the attitude-behavior relationship. *J. Pers. soc. Psychol., 36,* 715–724.

Scott, C. (1961). Research on mail surveys. *J. R. Statist. Soc. A, 124,* 143–205.

Selltiz, C. (1955). The use of survey methods in a citizen's campaign against discrimination. *Hum. Organiz. 13,* 19–25.

Sigelman, L. (1981). Question-order effects on presidential popularity. *Publ. Opin. Quart., 45,* 199–207.

Silverman, B. I. (1974). Consequences, racial discrimination, and the principle of belief congruence. *J. Pers. soc. Psychol., 29,* 497–508.

Simon, J. L. (1969). *Basic research methods in social science.* New York: Random House.

Singer, E. (1978). Informed consent: consequences for response rate and response quality in social surveys. *Amer. Sociol. Rev., 43,* 144–162.

———— (1979). *Telephone interviewing as a black box—discussion: response styles in telephone and household interviewing.* National Center for Health Services Research Series. Health Survey Research Methods, Third Biennial Conference. Hyattsville, Md.: U.S. Dept. H&HS (PHS) 81–3268.

Singer, E., and M. R. Frankel (1982). Informed consent procedures in telephone interviews. *Amer. Sociol. Rev., 47,* 416–426.

Singer, E., and L. Kohnke-Aquirre (1979). Interviewer expectation effects: a replication and extension. *Publ. Opin. Quart., 43,* 245–260.

Skogan, W. G. (1981). *Issues in the measurement of victimization.* Washington, D.C.: Bureau of Justice Statistics, U.S. Department of Justice (NCJ-74682).

Smith, T. W. (1979). Happiness: time trends, seasonal variations, intersurvey differences, and other mysteries. *Soc. Psychol. Quart., 42,* 18–30.

———— (1980a). Ethnic measurement and identification. *Ethnicity, 7,* 78–95.

———— (1980b). The 75% solution: an analysis of the structure of attitudes on gun control, 1959–1977. *J. criminal Law Criminology, 71,* 300–316.

———— (1983). The hidden 25 percent: an analysis of nonresponse on the 1980 General Social Survey. *Publ. Opin. Quart.,* 47, 386–404.

Sonquist, J. A., and W. C. Dunkelberg (1977). *Survey and opinion research: procedures for processing and analysis.* Englewood Cliffs, N.J.: Prentice-Hall.

Sparks, R. (forthcoming). *Methodological problems of retrospective social surveys: with special reference to surveys of criminal victimization.* Washington, D.C.: Bureau of Justice Statistics, U.S. Department of Justice Technical Report.

Srole, L. (1956). Social integration and certain corollaries: an exploratory study. *Amer. Sociol. Rev., 21,* 709–716.

Steeh, C. G. (1981). Trends in nonresponse rates, 1952–1979. *Publ. Opin. Quart., 45,* 40–57.

Stephan, F. F., and P. J. McCarthy (1958). *Sampling opinions: an analysis of survey procedures.* New York: Wiley.

Stephenson, C. B. (1979). Probability sampling with quotas: an experiment. *Publ. Opin. Quart., 43,* 477–496.

Stinchcombe, A. L., C. Jones, and P. Sheatsley (1981). Nonresponse bias for attitude questions. *Publ. Opin. Quart. 45,* 359–375.

Stocking, C. (1979). Marlowe-Crowne scale in survey research: a sociological interpretation. Unpublished doctoral dissertation, University of Chicago.

Stouffer, S. A. (1955). *Communism, conformity, and civil liberties.* Garden City, N.Y.: Doubleday.

Stouffer, S. A., L. Guttman, E. A. Suchman, P. F. Lazarsfled, S. A. Star, and J. A. Clausen (1950). *Measurement and prediction.* Princeton: Princeton Univ. Press.

Stouffer, S. A., E. A. Suchman, L. C. DeVinney, S. A. Star, and R. M. Williams, Jr., Eds. (1949). *The American soldier: adjustment during army life.* Princeton: Princeton Univ. Press.

Stuart, A. (1976). *Basic ideas of scientific sampling* (2nd ed.). London: Griffin.

Sudman, S. (1966). Probability sampling with quotas. *J. Amer. Statist. Assoc., 61,* 749–771.

———— (1967). *Reducing the cost of surveys.* Chicago: Aldine.

———— (1976). *Applied sampling.* New York: Academic Press.

———— (1980). Reducing response error in surveys. *Statistician, 29,* 237–273.

Sudman, S., and N. M. Bradburn (1974). *Response effects in surveys.* Chicago: Aldine.

———— 1982. *Asking questions: a practical guide to questionnaire design.* San Francisco: Jossey-Bass.

Sudman, S., and R. Ferber (1971). Experiments in obtaining consumer expenditures by diary methods. *J. Amer. Statist. Assoc., 66,* 725–735.

Sullivan, J. L., J. E. Pierson, and G. E. Marcus (1978). Ideological constraint in the mass public: a methodological critique and some new findings. *Amer. J. polit. Sci., 22,* 233–249.

Tanur, J. M. (1983). Methods for large-scale surveys and experiments. In S. Leinhardt (Ed.) *Sociological Methodology 1983–84,* Chap. 1. San Francisco: Jossey-Bass.

Thornberry, O. T., Jr. (1977). An evaluation of three strategies for the collection of health interview data from households. Unpublished doctoral dissertation, Brown University.

Thornberry O. T., Jr., and J. T. Massey (1983). Coverage and response in random digit dialed national surveys. *Proceedings of the section on survey research methods.* Washington, D.C.: American Statistical Association, 654–659.

Tracy, P. E., and J. A. Fox (1981). The validity of randomized response for sensitive measurements. *Amer. Sociol. Rev., 46,* 187–200.

Turner, A. G. (1972). *The San Jose methods test of known crime victims.* Washington, D.C.: National Criminal Justice Information and Statistics Service, Law Enforcement Assistance Administration, U.S. Department of Justice.

Turner, C. F., and E. Krauss (1978). Fallible indicators of the subjective state of the nation. *Amer. Psychol., 33,* 456–470.

Turner, C. F., and E. Martin, Eds. (1981). *Surveys of subjective phenomena: summary report.* Panel on Survey Measurement of Subjective Phenomena, National Research Council. Washington, D.C.: National Academy Press.

Turner, C. F., and E. Martin (1984). *Surveying subjective phenomena.* Vol. 1. New York: Russell Sage.

U.S. Bureau of the Census (1978). *The Current Population Survey: design and methodology.* Technical Paper No. 40. Washington, D.C.: U.S. Government Printing Office.

VanDusen, R. A., and N. Zill, Eds. (1975). *Basic background items for U.S. household surveys.* Washington, D.C.: Center for Coordination of Research on Social Indicators, Social Science Research Council.

Waksberg, J. (1978). Sampling methods for random digit dialing. *J. Amer. Statist. Assoc., 73,* 40–46.

Warner, S. L. (1965). Randomized response: a survey technique for eliminating evasive answer bias. *J. Amer. Statist. Assoc., 60,* 63–69.

Weaver, C. N., and C. L. Swanson (1974). Validity of reported date of birth, salary, and seniority. *Publ. Opin. Quart., 38,* 69–80.

Weiss, C. H. (1968–69). Validity of welfare mothers' interview responses. *Publ. Opin. Quart., 32,* 622–633.

Yates, F. (1981). *Sampling methods for censuses and surveys* (4th ed.). London: Griffin.

Zanes, A., and E. Matsoukas (1979). Different settings, different results? A comparison of school and home responses. *Publ. Opin. Quart., 43,* 550–557.

Zarkovich, S. S. (1966). *Quality of statistical data.* Rome: Food and Agriculture Organization of the United Nations.

Zdep, S. M., and I. N. Rhodes (1976–77). Making the randomized response technique work. *Publ. Opin. Quart., 40,* 531–537.

CHAPTER 13

Program Evaluation

Thomas D. Cook
Northwestern University

Laura C. Leviton
University of Pittsburgh

William R. Shadish, Jr.
Memphis State University

FUNCTIONS OF PROGRAM EVALUATION

The origins of program evaluation lie in the rapid growth of social welfare spending during the 1960s (Levine, 1970; Levitan, 1969; Levitan and Taggart, 1976). Programs were launched in haste, and the need arose to assess how well they ameliorated the social problems that justified their funding. This need was all the more acute because the public sector does not have as readily available some souces of feedback found in the private sector (Cook, 1984). In the latter setting, accountants scrutinize revenues, expenditures, and inventories and periodically determine an organization's profitability in order to summarize what has been achieved and to infer whether the organization has been effective in furthering shareholders' interests. Accountants also work in the public sector. But there they examine expenditures in order to deter and detect fraud, not to summarize achievements or determine how effective a program has been in promoting the "public interest." Indeed, with social programs the determination of effectiveness depends on many criteria other than profit, most of which are less well understood and less readily measured than the dollars taken in and disbursed that loom so large in the private sector.

When an accountant provides financial information, it is often broken down by department or some other form of organizational unit within a company. Like the advice given by management consultants, such information can help pinpoint where problems and achievements lie, and may be most useful when performance is regularly monitored so that changes can be detected. The information collected by in-house auditors and management consultants will in many instances also suggest obvious modifications to practice that might improve functioning. Just as within the private sector, organizations in the public sector need feedback on internal operations so as to detect problems and suggest possible improvements.

In the private sector several forces work to identify novel ideas that might be developed into new practices or products that, if useful, can eventually be disseminated throughout a company or beyond. Established companies have their own research and development divisions to conceptualize and develop products and their own marketing departments to test each product's likely impact. Newer companies have to rely on banks and venture capitalists to provide funds for developing new products and for hiring market research firms to test the commercial viability of what they have developed. Novel ideas also need to be tested in the public sector, and knowledge about demonstrably effective new practices has to be disseminated to potential users.

Scriven (1980) has pointed to the immense range of objects that can be evaluated in either the public or private sectors, including products, personnel, policies, and evaluations themselves. However, most of this chapter deals with social programs funded by federal, state, and local governments to help ameliorate social problems. Evaluation is intended to contribute to social problem solving through summarizing the past achievements of programs, providing feedback to improve program operations, and testing ideas for new programs or new features that could be added to existing programs. Thus, evaluation serves many of the same functions that accountants, management consultants, in-house bookkeepers, research and development specialists, and advertising professionals fulfill in the private sector.

Within the domain of social programs evaluators deal with a wide range of substantive topics. This can be most clearly seen from the table of contents of the *Evaluation Studies Review Annuals* (ESRA) that have been published since 1976. The first volume (Glass, 1976) had sections devoted to the evaluation of programs in education, physical and mental health, public welfare, social services, and criminal justice. Volume two (Guttentag, 1977) added policy and labor studies to this list. Volume three (Cook and Associates, 1978) added evaluations of income maintenance and evaluations in the "public interest." Volume four (Sechrest and Associates, 1979) added studies on the utilization of evaluation and on unanticipated findings. Volume five (Stromsdorfer and Farkas, 1980) added studies of public housing, public safety, finance, and energy. Volume six (Freeman and Solomon, 1981) contributed evaluations in the areas of law, substance abuse, and the environment. Volume seven (House and Associates, 1982) added an extensive discussion of ethical issues, while volume eight (Light, 1983) was almost exclusively concerned with syntheses of multiple evaluations of a single program or a program element. Evaluation is clearly multisectoral and multidisciplinary, although disproportionately concerned with social welfare programs. The field is also attempting to develop its own theories and methods, and nearly every volume in the ESRA series included sections on these topics.

The purpose of this chapter is to discuss these theories and methods, albeit within the context of our own theory, which assumes that program evaluation is sup-

posed to contribute to solving social problems by assigning merit to programs, and providing suggestions about how to improve program performance. Consequently, we have to deal explicitly with how evaluation is—and should be—related to the logic of problem solving, the logic of assigning merit, and the ways social programs can be improved. We turn now to these issues, discussing them as three necessary components of any theory of evaluation.

THREE NECESSARY COMPONENTS OF A THEORY OF EVALUATION

EVALUATION AND RATIONAL PROBLEM SOLVING

Evaluation is a crucial phase in any sequence of rational decision making or problem solving. Problem solving requires, first, that a problem has been identified; second, that options have been generated that might solve the problem; third, that at least one of these options has been implemented; fourth, that the implemented option has been evaluated; and finally, that a decision has been made about whether the tested option is worth adopting because it reduces the magnitude of the problem on hand. If a negative decision is reached about the option tested, then in the rational model a second option can be tested. If that should also fail to provide a satisfactory solution, the sequence can be repeated again until a solution is eventually found that, while not optimal, is at least satisfactory (Simon, 1959). In this particular model, problem-solving will only be useful if the initial problem is important, novel and feasible options have been generated, tests have been powerful and unbiased, logically correct conclusions have been drawn from the test evidence that are then used to guide the choice of actions designed to solve the problem.

Being concerned mostly with how well potential solutions are tested, evaluation is only one part of this interdependent problem-solving sequence. Indeed, evaluation can never be meaningfully abstracted from the larger sequence on which its utility—but not its validity—depends. That is, one can perfectly evaluate a puny attempt to solve an important problem. But what good is this? One can also perfectly evaluate an apparently bold attempt to ameliorate a trivial problem. But what good is this? Finally, one can also perfectly evaluate a bold solution to a major problem, but if the persons responsible for acting on the basis of the evaluative information choose to ignore it, what immediate impact will the evaluation have?

The restricted role of evaluation in rational models of problem solving presents evaluators with a dilemma. Most of them want their work to be useful, but they have little control over the way problems and potential solutions are chosen or over the way their own evaluative results are used. Consequently, if pressures exist in the world of social programs to select problems that are less important, to choose options for change that are less bold, or to make decision making more dependent on political or ideological criteria than on empirical evidence, then evaluation will necessarily play less of a role in problem solving than it could. We shall later see that many such pressures operate and force theorists of evaluation to ask: Should the appropriate role for evaluators be as servants of the political processes that select problems, potential solutions, and changes in practice? Or should evaluators be more active and try to influence the processes whereby problems, potential solutions, and proposals for practical action are selected? If they choose the latter route, should they restrict themselves to balanced commentary, or should they seek to advocate particular conceptions of a problem and particular options for improvement? If the last is preferred, how can it be carried out in ways that are both feasible and ethical? We deal with these issues of role later.

EVALUATION AND THE LOGIC OF ASSIGNING MERIT

The logic of evaluation is extremely general and quite simple (Scriven, 1980). Consider what *Consumer Reports* does to evaluate automobiles. First, it decides on criteria of judgment (purchase price, maintenance costs, miles per gallon, interior space, interior noise, luggage capacity, etc.). Then it decides on comparison standards. In the case of automobiles models are explicitly contrasted. Thus the Honda Accord is contrasted with other subcompacts in the same price, size, and performance range (e.g., the Mazda 626 or the Oldsmobile Firenza). Next, engineers conduct a battery of tests in order to take measures from each of the comparison models on each of the criteria. Finally, the results are synthesized across the criteria to give a summary judgment about the best model to buy in general or the best model to buy if one has a particular need (e.g., for large amounts of luggage space).

The same process is repeated when we evaluate students. First, we decide on criteria of successful students' performance. Second, we decide on standards for assigning merit. These may be relative, as when we grade on a curve and compare students with each other; or they

may appear to be more absolute, as when we use criterion-referenced tests and assign an A to scores greater than, say, 50, a B grade to scores between 40 and 49, and so on. Third, we measure the performance of each student to see how well he or she does in exams, on papers, and in class discussion. Finally, we synthesize the results by putting the performance measures onto a common scale before weighting them and summing them so that the exams are worth, say, 40 percent of the final grade, the papers 50 percent, and in-class performance 10 percent.

This four-step logic is of general relevance and applicability and can be used to assign merit to all things. The problems with it concern how it can be practically implemented. Who is to say which automobiles are to be compared? Why should some criteria be chosen and not others? On what basis should criteria be given different weights? In order to make judgments about an automobile model, how many samples of that model should be tested? How can one measure interior room so as to capture utilizable room, given the shape and size of human bodies? Sophisticated evaluators have to make decisions about these issues, as when *Consumer Reports* gives data about each feature of each model so that families with special needs can draw their own conclusion about the cary to buy—a conclusion that might be at odds with the magazine's overall conclusion because the family assigns a quite different weight to, say, reliability of performance. Problems with implementing evaluation logic apply whatever the object being evaluated (the evaluand). However, the problems are not always sufficiently grave as to cast doubts on the utility of evaluation. *Consumer Reports* has, after all, a loyal following and is financially self-sustaining.

The logic of assigning merit and the role evaluation plays in rational problem solving suggest that the utility of program evaluation depends on a number of factors:

1. The original social problem is important and has been clearly defined.

2. A wide range of heterogeneous and novel options have been developed that will plausibly impact on the problem.

3. The options chosen for implementation can be clearly defined.

4. The criteria for judging options are clear, relevant, and agreed upon.

5. The standards against which an option is to be compared are clear, relevant, and agreed upon.

6. It is possible to estimate the operations and causal consequences of the options being compared.

7. It is possible to synthesize the results to arrive at overall judgments about the utility of an option.

8. Once information about the worth of options has been generated, it will be used to make decisions about actions to be taken.

Of these assumptions, items 4 through 7 pertain to how well the logic of assigning merit can be implemented when social programs are under study. The remainder pertain to the problem-solving context in which the evaluation of social programs is inevitably embedded. We have to describe, therefore, what we mean by social programs.

EVALUATION AND THE NATURE OF SOCIAL PROGRAMS

Omnipresent Political Realities

Evaluation is a political event (Cronbach *et al.,* 1980) that takes place in a context where diverse stakeholder groups have an interest in the program, many of which are keen to preserve or promote their interests. Most groups want to see certain issues on action agendas and not others; they want to see problems defined their own way and not in some different way; and they routinely prefer that some solutions be tried over others (Bryk, 1983). If they want evaluation at all, they typically prefer that some criteria are measured over others, that some standards of comparision are chosen over others, and that some techniques of measuring performance and integrating information are selected rather than others. Most stakeholders will also want the right to be heard in the formal and informal deliberations from which decisions about program changes emerge. They want to be able to represent their interests—and perhaps influence decisions—irrespective of what the evaluative data seem to say.

In nearly all sectors the stakeholder groups are numerous and powerful. In the health sector, the relevant groups include hospital administrators, physicians, nurses, social workers, congressional committees, federal and state agencies that pay for Medicare and Medicaid, insurance companies, pharmaceutical manufacturers, public interest groups, and academics interested in health

policy. All want to participate in the formulation of health policy, influencing how problems are defined, how solutions are selected and evaluated, and how the evaluative results are disseminated and used. Health is not unique. In every sector multiple stakeholder groups are part of the formal and informal system that influences decision making.

In addition to organized interest groups, the political system includes individuals and organizations at the federal, state and local levels who have the ultimate, formal responsibility for making decisions. In government most decisions are taken not by individuals but by committees composed of people with heterogeneous values and interests who identify with different stakeholder groups. These heterogeneous decison-making bodies are supposed to provide the best representation—however imperfect—of the public interest for the following reasons:

1. They are composed of elected representatives and their staffs.

2. The representatives of the majority party speak for more voting citizens and usually control more committee assignments.

3. Deliberations are to some extent open so that the logic and factual basis of support for proposed actions can be critically examined.

4. Formal checks and balances exist between various congressional bodies and between the three branches of American government.

However, these forces do not perfectly represent the "public interest." Legislators are humans and are quite capable of using guile and temporary coalition formation to try to equate the public interest with their own interest. Nonetheless, the system of formal responsibility for decision making is supposed to represent, however imperfectly, the public interest, ultimately derived from popular votes.

Elected officials are not the only persons with formal decison-making responsibility. Members of the executive branch are responsible for overseeing the state and local activities that legislators' decisions are designed to influence and they are responsible for ensuring that program funds are spent in ways that further legislative aims and are not diverted by state and local officials or local service providers to meet their own aims (Bardach, 1977). When difficulties arise in interpreting program goals and regulations, local officials turn for advice and authorization to members of the executive branch, who adjudicate in ways that are supposed to further the legislative intent. In normative conceptions of political decision making, then, the executive and legislative branches have unique but interdependent roles to play in formulating, implementing, and interpreting policy that has to be acted upon locally.

Formal decision making is characterized by more than constant exposure to diverse and conflicting interests. It is also characterized by a high level of turnover in actors and issues. In the legislative branch turnover arises because legislators are not reelected, they switch committee assignments, or they hire new staff members who have their own concerns and interests. Turnover in the executive branch is rapid and arises because senior civil servants and political appointees leave government or transfer jobs within government. In each case their replacements tend to work on new agendas because they want to leave their own mark rather than continue what their predecessors began. Even when the actors do not change, political issues can still wax and wane in importance—often for seemingly accidental reasons as unexpected events occur at home and abroad or the Zeitgeist invents new preoccupations (F. L. Cook, 1981). In such a volatile setting it is not surprising that by the time some evaluations are completed, the persons who commissioned them are no longer in office or no longer care about the issue. Their successors are likely to care even less.

The formal political system is open at nearly all times to the informal pressure of the many diverse parties seeking to further their own interests. In such a system support for preferred agendas usually has to be built from multiple diverse interests. Building such support is not easy. Sometimes, it is achieved by being indirect or misleading about one's intentions, since clarity often makes conflicts of interest salient. Thus, Social Security was originally marketed as an insurance scheme, which it is not, on grounds that the public would approve a system that promises to return to individuals what they have paid in over a system where the generations at work support the retirement of the elderly (Kutza, 1981). Since building coalitions from divergent stakeholder groups constitutes such a large part of the art of politics, it is not surprising that some social problems are not seriously tackled. The difficulties of building a consensus seem too great. For the same reason it is also not surprising that some social problems and program objectives are vaguely defined and cast in terms of the dominant symbols and priorities of the day (Lindblom and Cohen, 1979). Pro-

gram objectives are political statements designed to build support. They are not meant to be precise explications of how a program might reduce the severity of a social problem or to provide evaluators with explicit program rationales that can be easily translated into evaluation objectives or criteria (Cronbach *et al.,* 1980; Scriven, 1980).

Politics always reflects a blend of the ideological and pragmatic that influences not only which social problems are and are not targetted for serious attack but also which potential solutions are and are not chosen to be implemented. Indeed, the options selected for testing usually have to be *both* immediately practical *and* consonant with a nation's dominant value system. In the United States, for instance, no one in the foreseeable future will give serious attention to a proposed social program that seeks to identify geniuses so as to force them to go to state-run boarding schools that attempt to cultivate their special talents. And no one will give serious attention to proposals to reform television entertainment by setting up a federal office to censor the content of entertainment or current affairs programs. Other solutions are less in conflict with dominant ideology but are instead not commensurate with current definitions of what is desirable—such as proposals to reduce crime by making heroin legal, to reduce smoking through limiting tobacco acreage, or to reduce teenage pregnancies either by refusing AFDC aid to unmarried mothers or by providing each high school with an abortion counselor.

Although most of the solutions tested will not challenge the conventional wisdom, a mechanism does exist within the federal system of research and development for identifying a small number of more radical variants. Demonstration projects test on a small scale novel ideas that are being considered for possible wider dissemination. Some seem genuinely bold in conception, as with the negative income tax experiments designed to replace most of the current social service–based welfare system with cash payments to the poor (for summaries of the evaluations, see Cook *et al.,* 1978; Stromsdorfer and Farkas, 1980). Another example would be Fairweather's Lodge designed to provide a viable noninstitutional residential setting for the chronically mentally ill (Fairweather, Sanders, and Tornatzky, 1974). This last case is particularly instructive, for despite positive evalutations and explicit attempts at widespread dissemination, the Lodge has not been widely adopted in the United States. This is probably because, unlike its competitors—mental hospitals, nursing homes, and halfway houses—the Lodge assigns no role to physicians or other mental health professionals, no one makes a profit, and the chronic mental patients who benefit most from the Lodge are not organized to represent their own interests in the political process. Also, legislators and civil servants probably worry about how voters and taxpayers might react if chronic mental patients came to live close to them. For all these reasons the Lodge has low implementability as current policy, despite favorable evaluations (Shadish, 1984). Although demonstrations of bold new ideas may sometimes increase the acceptability of options that deviate from the mainstream, we do not yet understand when this occurs or how often. Evaluators have to understand that most of the options they study involve marginal changes in the status quo and that, if a more fundamental change is studied, it may be less likely to be implemented as eventual policy.

The political context of program evaluation is also made more difficult because stakeholders who are so motivated can nearly always generate a reasoned attack that presents evaluation results as biased, incompetent, incomplete, or all three. Their ability to do this arises from the inherent limitations of social science methods when used to discover the effects of interventions that are only marginally different from the status quo so that only modest results can be expected from them (Cook, 1984a). In addition, every evaluation can be attacked in terms of the constructs not measured or in terms of the questionable quality with which services were implemented (Lindblom and Cohen, 1979). And once findings are attacked, they lose in decision-influencing potency since it is difficult in the political process to assign much weight to disputed scholarly findings (Boeckmann, 1976). But even if evaluation findings were beyond dispute, they would still have to contend with the powerful roles that ideology, pragmatism, interests, and values play in influencing political decision making, as well as with the powerful influence exerted by incidental knowledge—for example, what formal decision makers have personally seen, were told about by friends, or have read about in newspapers (Weiss and Bucuvalas, 1983). For all these reasons evaluations will rarely be used as *the* major input into decisions about social programs. More often, they should add a little weight to the arguments supporting some points of view and should provide one more source of opposition with which antagonists have to deal, forcing them somewhat more onto the defensive.

Although evaluation results are sometimes used in the policy world to mold decisions about programs, Weiss and Weiss (1981) note that this is far from routine

and that results more commonly create "enlightenment." This is a difficult construct, but it includes influencing how social problems are defined or prioritized and how tractable various classes of solution are seen to be. It can even involve the results from the evaluation of one program influencing later decisions about a different program. Indeed, evaluations of "Sesame Street" (Cook *et al.*, 1975) have been invoked when considering whether to fund new educational television programs also aimed at nationwide audiences of young children.

Evaluation results need not influence program performance only through government decisions. Evidence from textbooks in education and social work (Leviton and Cook, 1983) suggests that evaluation results are sometimes incorporated into recommendations for professional practice where they may influence incoming generations of service providers as well as established professionals who read or hear about the research findings. If this happens often, the practices legitimized through evaluation may become more available to people working at the point of service delivery. This is quite different from the point of program administration in a national or state capital. While the central government may propose changes, practitioners at the local level have considerable freedom to decide in which ways they will comply with government proposals, if at all. If they do not comply with changes suggested by evaluators, the evaluative knowledge will not improve the program, however sophisticated and research-based are the prescriptions contained in government regulations designed to influence local practitioners (Williams, 1980). To ameliorate social problems requires either that evaluations help central managers arrive at "better" decisions *that are then acted upon locally* or that evaluations change the information base used to train local managers and service providers.

The Diffuse and Heterogeneous Structure of Programs

Once a social problem has become visible and political forces have coalesced around it, *social policies* are determined. This is true whether the problem concerns poverty, stimulating economic growth, or improving the quality of the physical environment. Policies specify a general line of attack on a problem and imply that other approaches should not be taken. For instance, policy in 1983 dictates that rising health care costs should be contained by slowing the growth of hospital costs and implementing nationwide health promotion campaigns.

Policy is less clearly directed at containing physician costs, making the sale of tobacco or alcohol illegal, or nationalizing the pharmaceutical industry. In the 1960s and 1970s policies to deal with poverty were salient (Levine, 1970; Leviton, 1969) and were based on action to facilitate the purchase of basics, as with Food Stamps and Medicaid, or to improve educational opportunities for economically disadvantaged children so that they might become financially independent in the future. This two-pronged policy can be contrasted with less frequently considered options: policies to alleviate poverty through redistributing wealth, changing tax laws, or guaranteeing jobs for all who want to work. Policies draw attention to priorities and set general guidelines for action. But they are not themselves the blueprints that specify action.

Programs serve as such blueprints, for they coordinate the local projects that use program resources to meet policy goals. Thus when universal literacy and numeracy were important policy goals as part of the War on Poverty, several different programs were funded, including the Elementary and Secondary Education Act, "Sesame Street," Head Start, and Follow Through. Many state programs were also designed and implemented. When the revitalization of cities was a salient policy, Community Development Block Grants were let, General Revenue Sharing became a reality, and individual states developed programs for their cities (Dommel *et al.,* 1978, 1980; Van Horn, 1979). Programs form the administrative link between policies and services through the funds they provide for local service delivery and the regulations they issue that specify permissible and non-permissible activities. However, it is rare for program goals and regulations to be totally explicit or to take all professional discretion from service providers. Moreover, many local personnel know that federal and state authorities rarely have the resources to monitor service delivery closely. Hence in most social programs considerable variability exists from site to site, from service provider to service provider, and from client to client in the quantity, quality, and mix of services for which a particular social program pays. With the exception of some income transfer programs like Social Security, heterogeneity of services is more of a reality than standardization.

In our usage, *projects* are local centers that coordinate the activities for which program funds are received. For example, we consider each of the Community Mental Health Centers financed and regulated under the auspices of the (now defunct) Community Mental Health Center Program to be projects. So, also, is a local

school district's Chapter I office funded under the Elementary and Secondary Education Act. Since most projects have unique characteristics, it would be unrealistic to expect a great deal of similarity between, say, a Community Mental Health Center in Northeast Memphis that serves the downtown complex of hospitals, and a center serving a nearby rural community. Compared with programs, projects are goegraphically more circumscribed, are coordinated locally rather than centrally, and are closer to the persons receiving and delivering services. In addition, the services are *relatively* more homogeneous than the total set of services provided in the program as a whole. We should also note that projects can receive funds from many programs simultaneously; that program funds may represent only part of a project's total budget, with additional revenue coming from local fund-raising activities or fees for services; and that, as in the case of private schools, it may sometimes be useful to consider as projects some organizations that receive few or even no funds from national or state programs.

Elements are components within a project or program that the evaluator's critical analysis suggests may be necessary or sufficient for bringing about desired effects. The emphasis here is on forces that are under human control and that, when deliberately varied, can bring about changes that may contribute to solving a problem. Thus as part of its project-level activities, a community mental health center might provide such elements as psychotherapy, chemotherapy, and alcohol detoxification. It will also have certain intake, outreach, and record-keeping procedures that are also capable of modification and may contribute to improving the welfare of program beneficiaries. In a similar vein, a compensatory education project might have such project-level elements as tutoring by teachers, the use of computer-assisted instruction, peer coaching, or the availability of teacher aides from the community. In a job-training project the elements might include teaching students the specific skills required for particular jobs, teaching them general work skills relating to absenteeism, lateness, demeanor with superiors, or dress, or teaching them what it takes to do well in job interviews.

Service elements are most numerous at the project level where direct contact with clients is most likely to occur. But there are also elements at the program level, though these are more likely to be administrative- than service-oriented. Thus they might deal with whether a program is implemented as a categorical or block grant, whether the annual reports from projects are filed for manual or computerized retrieval, whether local monitoring is done via site visits or written reports, and so on.

The program, project, and element levels differ in heterogeneity. Social programs are typically the most heterogeneous, especially in nations like the United States where traditions of local control and professional autonomy justify local variability in the services actually implemented and where local services cannot be monitored in detail (Cook and Buccino, 1979). Projects are usually less heterogeneous and elements the most homogeneous. The importance of homogeneity follows from the assumption that the easier it is to implement and test treatments (i.e., evaluands) the more homogeneous they are. Treatment heterogeneity forces evaluators to conceptualize and measure the major sources of variance in the evaluand and then to estimate how much each source has contributed to an effect. If this is not done, evaluators run the risk of treating an evaluand as a single entity when it might be more usefully understood as several distinct entities that have quite different, and sometimes even countervailing, effects.

The distinction between programs, projects, and elements is also important because the ultimate rationale for social programs is that they will contribute to the amelioration of important social problems. Since most social problems in the United States are defined as problems of individual behavior (Caplan and Nelson, 1973), local services are usually targeted at individuals and take the form of elements or mixes of elements delivered through a local project. A long chain of interdependent, and sometimes problematic, causal connections has to be postulated in order to link the definition of a social problem to:

1. The development of a relevant policy;

2. The design of a particular program;

3. The implementation of that program in the form of many local projects;

4. The implementation within each project of elements that individuals actually receive; and

5. The receipt of elements that do indeed modify behaviors which are manifestly linked to the social problem that gave rise to program funding in the first place.

Since ameliorating a social problem requires that a program is effective by criteria that are demonstrably—or at the least, defensibly—relevant to the initial problem, it is not enough to identify elements or combinations of elements that modify these criteria. To have a general impact on a problem, the elements so identified must be implemented—or potentially implementable—across many of the projects that constitute a social program. This means that the elements have to be acceptable to those who manage or provide services locally. If government officials decree what is not locally acceptable, their decrees are not likely to be acted upon in ways that lead to high-quality service implementation and to the subsequent reduction of a recognized social problem.

There is often a fundamental difference in perspective and priorities between the program and project levels. Consider drug abuse centers. They are funded at the program level to provide services that will reduce the number of addicts. The hope is that this will lower the incidence of crime, family instability, and unemployment. These last outcomes probably appear more desirable and feasible to politicians than to the administrators of local drug abuse projects who realize all too well that crime, household separations, and employment rates are hardly under their control! Even getting many more people drug-free must seem difficult to most project administrators—if not impossible. If they had to be judged in terms of outcome criteria, they would probably prefer those that relate to their project's ability to reduce the amount of drugs the average client uses. But more important to them than outcome criteria are concerns about maintaining client and revenue flows and administering the project in ways that seem efficient to funders and directors. These are the activities for which project administrators are most directly accountable, and poor performance might threaten their jobs or even the project itself. Consequently, at the project level the smooth functioning of administrative and treatment processes are weighted more than improvements in clients' performance or changes in distal indicators of neighborhood or city functioning. Indeed, practitioners who deliver services usually assume the effectiveness of what they do. If they value research at all, it is probably to improve practice at the margin rather than to summarize project-wide achievements or to assess their own effectiveness. There is here an obvious conflict of priorities. Project employees tend to value the study of elements and proximal criteria over the study of programs and more distal criteria, while government officials tend to have the opposite priorities.

More than accountability is involved in the central decision maker's emphasis on social programs as the unit of study. The likelihood of impacting on national problems also inclines them in that direction. After all, to study a single project inevitably means that relatively few persons can be shown to benefit; and although some elements reach many individuals, few promise much of an impact on individual lives when they are considered by themselves. To make this clear, imagine once again a drug abuse center. On analysis, the elements that constitute it might seem to be an outreach component to attract clients, a management system for record keeping and billing, and the provision of methadone, personal counseling, legal aid, and so on. Some of these elements have only an indirect link to becoming drug-free; many are presumably not sufficient to bring this about; and we do not yet know which mix is sufficient for which kinds of clients. If we were to evaluate any one of these elements by itself, we would expect it to have less of an impact on individual lives and national social problems than would be the case if we evaluated the total set of elements in a project or in all of the projects that constitute a program.

IMPLICATIONS OF THE CONTEXTS INTO WHICH EVALUATION HAS TO BE FIT

We earlier outlined eight factors that would make it easier for evaluation to influence social problem solving. The first was that the social problems targeted for action are important and clearly specified. However, politicians sometimes find it useful to select social problems for reasons of opportunism rather than importance, particularly items on the secondary national agenda that tend to come and go—e.g., elder abuse—rather than those that tend to persist—e.g., crime, poverty, or national defense. (See F. L. Cook, 1981.) Further, the need to build support for a particular program can entail defining the problems at which it is directed so globally that the exact relevance of the program to the problem is unclear. While such vagueness is quite rational from the perspective of the operating politicians who need support to survive and operate (Weiss, 1975), it can obscure the objectives that local projects are supposed to pursue with their program resources.

The second factor stressed in the rational decision-making model was that a social program is decided on only after considering a wide range of heterogeneous and bold options. Yet the U.S. political system operates within a restricted range of values regulating what should be done and is highly pragmatic about what can be done. Consequently, the options incorporated into the design of programs and projects are rarely bold and innovative, and evaluators usually study a restricted range of potential solutions. As a result, only effects of modest size can be expected. Detecting these will be all the more difficult the more imperfect are the evaluative methods used.

The third factor was that the program implemented to solve problems is clearly detailed and uniformly implemented. Yet most social programs involve multiple sites that are typically distributed across the length and breadth of the nation or state. Moreover, the professionals who provide services expect to exercise some discretion in the services they provide, and they often know that the monitoring of services is perfunctory. Consequently, the program-funded activities that take place vary considerably from site to site and even from client to client within sites. Such diffusion and heterogeneity make it difficult to assume either that a clear "program" entity exists to be evaluated or that the results from a small number of project-level evaluations can be easily aggregated to create an unbiased picture of effects at the program level.

The fourth factor was that evaluative criteria could be selected that are important and widely agreed to. Yet stakeholders often disagree about the criteria to be used in evaluating programs, projects, and elements. This is because of their different assessments of what a program should influence and of what it can realistically be expected to influence. Even when agreement is reached about key constructs, this does not mean that agreement will be forthcoming on their priority ordering or on the actual measures to be used in an evaluation.

The fifth factor was that clear comparison standards could be agreed upon. Yet stakeholders also often disagree about the standards with which any program, project, or element should be compared, for they know that merit depends on what one is evaluated against. They all know that a Honda Accord may outrank a Plymouth Horizon on almost every criterion on which measurement is made; but if it is compared to a Rolls Royce, Mercedes, or Cadillac, it will generally be seen as less meritorious.

The sixth factor was that evaluation results can be clearly synthesized and the results of the synthesis agreed to. Yet stakeholders typically differ in their interpretation of evaluation results. Some results are likely to be clearer than others, and some questions of importance to particular stakeholders will not even have been asked. Since sins of omission and commission are inevitable, when completed evaluations enter into debates, they are more likely to be greeted with dispute and contention than with applause and approval (Lindblom and Cohen, 1979).

Finally, it is naive to assume that the information generated from evaluations of program options will be used as the sole or even major criterion for deciding on a course of action. This is because decision making in political systems is not routinely technocratic. It depends largely on values, interests, power advantages, incidental knowledge, the turnover of issues and people, and on the constraints imposed by past decisions. Evaluative knowledge is used; and in many different ways. But by itself it rarely leads directly to major decisions about the course of a program or project. Since evaluation has to function in the context provided by the current political system and a requirement that it "somehow" contribute to social problem-solving, we can easily see that a major issue is how it can fit into such a context and still be useful. The constraints in the context are more obvious than the opportunities.

The contextual factors that affect the utility of evaluation also have important implications for the content of a theory of evaluation. We assume that it will be easier, in general, to improve the more technical aspects of evaluation that relate to its logic for assigning merit (i.e., specifying criteria and standards of comparison, collecting relevant data, and integrating results) than it will be to deal with the complications arising from:

1. The political and administrative realities of social programs over which evaluators have little control;

2. Evaluation being only one part of a complex and interdependent system of problem solving, over most of which evaluators again have little control;

3. The many technical difficulties associated with studying the long-term consequences of social interventions that tend to be multivariate, dynamically changing over time, and unstandardized across the projects and clients within a program.

To be useful, evaluation theories have to deal with these constraints while remaining true to the logic of evaluation and to the commitment that evaluation should help ameliorate social problems through informing decisions about program options. Theories of evaluation should also specify methods for evaluation practice that are epistemologically defensible. But it makes little sense to discuss such methods until one has determined the types of evaluative questions that promise most payoff (leverage is the term we use) because they have taken into account the constraints imposed on evaluation by the nature of social programs and the limited place of evaluation in rational models of problem solving.

DETERMINANTS OF THE LEVERAGE OF EVALUATIONS

In this section we analyze the types of questions from which the persons who commission evaluations (evaluation policymakers) can anticipate most leverage in contributing to program improvement and hence, potentially, to social problem solving. Such policymakers play a decisive role in deciding what is to be evaluated, by which criteria, and relative to which standards. They set the parameters for evaluative work. In a later section we adopt a more microlevel perspective and ask how individual evaluators, who normally begin their work only after others have set the guiding parameters, can increase the utility of what they do. To discuss these issues we need a descriptive language that captures most of the objects evaluated in social programs as well as most of the standards and procedures used to evaluate the programs. The language presented below creates a map on which we later plot the options among which evaluation policymakers usually have to decide in determining what and how to evaluate.

A DESCRIPTIVE LANGUAGE FOR PROGRAM EVALUATION

Terms for Describing the Evaluand

Programs, projects and elements.   We have already referred to three important levels at which evaluation can take place—the program, project, or element level. At the program level, evaluators examine, say, the National School Lunch Program (NSLP) or federal revenue sharing. At the project level, they examine the school lunch project in, say, Greenwood, Mississippi, or revenue sharing in Lubbock, Texas. (Note that in Greenwood and Lubbock officials and practitioners probably call their local project a program.) At the element level, evaluators might compare school lunches that are cooked on the school premises with lunches shipped in and heated or with lunches served as cold snacks and prepared centrally. Of these three levels elements are typically the most homogeneous, the closest to service delivery, and the most easily modified in fundamental ways. But they are also likely to be the most puny in potential impact and may not be widely available across the projects in a program. The program level involves the most clients and often the most powerful mixes of elements. But it also includes the most diffuse set of activities; program officials are remote from service delivery; and the program level is the most difficult to modify in fundamental ways because programs are so politically impacted (Suchman, 1967; Cronbach *et al.,* 1980).

But since programs consist of projects and projects of elements, the three levels of evaluation are not mutually exclusive. Inferences about programs are based upon aggregation across projects, while inferences about a project are based upon aggregation across elements. Moreover, if inferences about elements are not to be specific to a single project and the ways it combines elements, inferences about the general effectiveness of elements require aggregation across the projects where the elements in question are available. This interdependence of levels is most evident when asking why a program or project has the effects attributed to it. If NSLP were effective at the program level in getting children to eat a more balanced diet, the evaluator might then probe to identify the school districts or schools (i.e., projects) that were most successful, asking: "What do they do that makes them so effective?" She might discover they have nutrition education classes, or they provide food that is cooked on the premises rather than shipped in. These would be elements that might explain why the overall program is effective.

However, the interdependence of the three levels should not blind evaluation policymakers to the reality that they usually have to choose one level as a priority and that important consequences follow once the choice has been made. In this regard, consider the decision to reach conclusions about NSLP as a program. To do so with confidence requires a large representative sample of school districts, schools, and participating children. To collect data first-hand from such a sample would almost certainly be very expensive. However, the sampling design would be much less extensive and expensive if conclusions were desired about a single project (i.e., a single school district) and would be even less extensive if only a single element in a single district was at issue (e.g., letting children select their own foods versus providing them with already heaped plates).

Instances or classes. Sometimes, evaluators want to make statements that apply not to a single program, project, or element but to a class. At the program level such a class might be income transfer programs in general, which includes Social Security, Aid for Families with Dependent Children, etc.; at the project level a class might be all education projects whose design assumes that bilingual instruction should be in English but at a level commensurate with the command of English that students actually have; while at the element level conclusions might be desired about the class of elements called teacher aides—a class that includes paid auxiliaries, community volunteers, and other non-teachers.

Cronbach (1982) uses a set of symbols for generalizing from instances to classes. In his terminology u refers to the units of study (e.g., person, classrooms, or psychotherapists), t refers to the treatment (or evaluand) being studied, o refers to the observations or measures collected, and s refers to the setting of an evaluation. When not capitalized, $utos$ refers to the samples of units, treatments, observations, and settings actually observed. When capitalized, $UTOS$ refers to the target class (or population) of persons, treatments, measures, and settings around which an evaluation was conceptualized and to which generalization is desired. When preceded by an asterisk, $*UTOS$ refers to other populations to which generalization is desired but around which the evaluation was not designed.

To illustrate the distinctions, imagine an evaluation designed to test how a new job corps training program (T) affects earnings (O) among young males (U) in Massachusetts (S). To examine this question, we might purposively sample some training centers in the state that agree to cooperate. This would be the observed sample of settings (s). We might then discover that the treatment is implemented in different ways at different sites, corresponding to multiple t's. We might further discover that data on earnings are only available from verbal reports by attendees (a single o) rather than from, say, wage slips. Finally, the directors of training might insist that the evaluation be restricted to males who have attended a project on a regular basis for at least six months (u), omitting the many persons who attended less often but who are nonetheless part of the total population of attendees (U). In this example the samples belong to the classes of interest—that is, job corps centers, earnings, and males in Massachusetts. But the instances would not represent the classes in any formal sense, since there has been no sampling with known probabilities. Nonetheless, data from unrepresentative observed samples (*utos*) are often all one has in order to try to draw inferences about more general classes of interest—that is, *UTOS*—or even about other **UTOS*—for example, programs to train the elderly (**U*) in volunteer work (**T*) to see how this affects their self concept (**O*) in all parts of the United States (**S*).

Evaluators always generalize from observed samples to general classes, even if only implicitly. Reports are almost always couched in general terms. They are more likely to conclude, for example, that chemotherapy with chronic mental patients reduces recidivism than they are to state that injections of 5 milligrams of Haldol in 52 mental patients who were severely deficient in social skills as measured by the Inpatient Scale of Minimal Functioning (Paul *et al.,* 1976) resulted in a mean difference of 5.2 days subsequent rehospitalization in a one-year follow-up. The typical report generalizes from injections of Haldol (*t*) to the construct of chemotherapy (*T*), from the 52 mental patients with low social skills (*u*) to chronic mental patients (*U*), and from the data on rehospitalization (*o*) to recidivism (*O*). Less frequently, evaluators generalize from *utos* to **UTOS*, as would happen if they speculated from the previous example to the effects of Haldol on self-reports of well-being (**O*) in geriatric patients (**U*).

Cronbach (1982) argues that generalization from *utos* to **UTOS* ought to be the central concern of evaluation. This is because, in his opinion, policy decisions are more often concerned with the transfer of findings to unsampled sites and related policy issues than with sample-specific results or with generalization to specific populations. Our notion that projects are heterogeneous and that many of them have to be influenced if the overall program is to make a dent in recognized social problems emphasizes that with restricted budgets and ever-changing futures it is indeed desirable to be able to generalize to nonstudied sites, measures, types of people, and realizations of a treatment. Consider the difference in utility between the conclusion "Having students do more homework increases achievement" and the conclusion "Increasing the time spent on academic tasks increases achievement" (Wiley and Harnischfeger, 1978). Knowledge about the class "time on task" (*T*) is more useful because the concept can be operationalized in many ways that are assumed to have comparable results—for example, as hours of homework, the number of school days per year, the number of hours per school day, the number of non-academic classes taken, or the degree of attention during school lessons. A corresponding difference at the project level might be between discovering that a particular drug abuse center in, say, Tampa reduces drug use by 15 percent on the average versus learning that drug abuse centers that use methadone to maintain clients' functioning decrease use by 15 percent on the average, wherever they are. The latter information is obviously more useful because it refers to a class of projects with a core element (providing methadone) that in our hypothetical example is generally effective and easily manipulable.

Inferences about classes of treatment necessarily depend on demonstrating that comparable effects have occurred across most of the units and settings in which instances of the treatment have been implemented. Consequently, inferences about treatment classes point to treatments that are likely to be transferable from project to project. This might explain why in addition to evaluations of programs, projects, and elements as instances, there have also been some past evaluations aimed at identifying *classes* of presumptively *manipulable* elements (e.g., time on task), projects (e.g., the models of preschool education probed in *Follow Through* by Stebbins, et al., 1978), and even programs (e.g., the class of programs designed to rehabilitate repeat criminal offenders as opposed to incapacitating them). Knowledge about classes promises greater generality and dissemination through a heterogeneous nation than does knowledge about instances.

Describing Evaluative Criteria

In many contexts we want to learn about the *units a program, project, or element has reached.* These may be nations, states, cities, or individuals, and in the case of individuals the emphasis can be on those who provide or receive services. The need for information about units is especially striking with categorical programs that specify target populations of eligible persons or institutions: for example, the Special Supplemental Food Program for Women, Infants, and Children (WIC) specifies that only pregnant and postpartum women are to be served, and the Job Corps specifies inner-city youth. For such programs some stakeholders will ask: How many persons have received program services? Of these, how many were ineligible? And how many eligibles are not receiving the services due them? It is sometimes important to describe personal characteristics other than those determining program eligibility. In compensatory education, for example, some stakeholders want to know whether a particular program is disproportionately reaching the best and the brightest among the economically disadvantaged (and is therefore "creaming"), while others want to know whether it is reaching more of the very lowest achievers from the poorest home backgrounds (and is therefore "lifting the floor").

Describing the characteristics of service providers (e.g., teachers or therapists) is also useful, for it is surprising how often central program managers have no realistic conception not only of who is receiving services but also of who is providing them (Nathan *et al.*, 1981). A description of service providers is also necessary for estimating whether an effect is robust across providers and so is likely to be replicated in other settings with the types of service providers found there. This would be important, for instance, in assessing community mental health centers, for the work of psychiatrists, psychologists, social workers, nurse practitioners, and paraprofessionals may differ in cost-effectiveness, even if not in effectiveness (Durlak, 1979; Kiesler, Cummings, and Van Den Bos, 1979; Nimh, 1980). Moreover, within all of these professional groups, providers vary by age, sex, race, years of experience, and type of training. Analysis of such variables will often suggest attributes of service providers that should be added to a profile of desirable provider characteristics.

It is one thing to decree that a program, project, or element should be introduced, and it is quite another to have the services *implemented* with the anticipated quantity and quality (Bardach, 1977; Berman, 1980; Pressman and Wildavsky, 1973; Williams, 1980). For example, Navasky and Paster (1976) found that few planned activities of the Law Enforcement Assistance Administration (LEAA) were actually implemented, thus illustrating a gap between plan and reality. But their negative findings about implementation should also caution against using data on crime rates to conclude that the idea behind LEAA was necessarily a failure. To use such data for this purpose logically requires that LEAA had been "adequately" implemented or that the poor implementation resulted from the very conceptualization of LEAA rather than for reasons of historical or political accident.

More is at issue with implementation than program services being delivered in any shape or form. Sometimes, services are made available in attenuated form, as when less is spent per client than was originally envisaged. This suggests that simple cost data can provide clues about the quantity and quality of what is im-plemented (Levin, 1975, 1983; Thompson, 1980), permitting one to go beyond the simplistic binary classification of whether a client was in a program or not. Even when resources are plentiful, considerable variability may still arise in the quantity, quality, and appropriateness of services from client to client and from provider to provider. For example, Mullen, Chazin, and Feldstein (1972) discovered that over fourteen months the median number of visits by welfare recipients to counselors was 15, but the range was from 1 to 129! An insensitive evaluation will result if the persons who received few services are always treated as though they had received as much as others. It is only through studying differences in implementation that one can learn:

1. How the quality, quantity, and mix of services codetermine effects.

2. Which types of clients and service deliverers are associated with higher-quality implementation.

3. Why the implementation of services is sporadic.

4. What might be done to make the services more attractive to clients and service personnel in the future.

Much of the novelty of modern evaluation lies in the commitment to make valuing partly dependent on the *effects* a social intervention has on those who experience it (Campbell, 1969). Many effects are possible, both intended and unintended, with some of the latter being at least as important as the former. For example, a series of evaluations demonstrated that in families guaranteed an annual income for three years, few men dropped out of the labor force. This implies that income guarantees do not reduce the work ethic among men. But this "positive" effect is given a different slant if one believes that the guaranteed income also caused about a quarter of the working women studied to leave the labor force and also increased the rate of separations among men and women who had previously lived together (Tuma, Hannon, and Groeneveld, 1979). In addition to probing program goals that are clear and to discovering unplanned effects, evaluation should also be concerned with exploring the extent to which demonstrated effects are general in application or are restricted to particular subgroups of respondents, settings, and even measures (Scriven, 1976; Cronbach *et al.*, 1980). In such a broad conception evaluators *explore* for effects. They do not limit themselves to testing preformulated hypotheses about possible effects (Tukey, 1977), particularly not those outlined in documents listing program or project objectives.

Impacts are like effects in that they are causal consequences of a program, project, or element. However, in our definition impacts occur in the social systems of which prospective program beneficiaries are a part and not in the beneficiaries themselves. That is, they occur in beneficiaries' families, neighborhoods, and cities, or even in programs and projects other than the one under analysis. Thus if a local drug abuse project succeeded in reducing drug use among its clientele, some stakeholders would want to know how this affected indicators of drug use for the city at large, since increased attendance at the center where evaluation took place might have reduced attendance at other centers!

Impact analyses tend to involve constructs that are linked to program or project services by a longer and more diffuse presumptive causal chain than is the case with effects. Thus for the drug project example attendance at the project might be postulated to cause such individual-level effects as decreased drug use, which might in its turn be presumed to cause such remote impacts as reduced criminal activity or decreased unemployment. Being later in the causal chain, impacts are less likely than effects to be under the control of personnel who work for the drug abuse project. After all, citywide drug rates depend on the price and availability of drugs, and employment rates depend in part on the state of the local economy. Impacts are also more likely than effects to be measured at an aggregate level. Thus they usually have in their base many persons who were never exposed to the project or element being studied. For instance, a drug abuse center will probably contact only a miniscule percentage of the total population that determines local labor force or crime statistics. And it will probably contact only a small percentage of all addicts. Of those it contacts, many will refuse to attend the center or will attend it only once. Any project targeted at a subset of individuals in the community will be at a disadvantage if it is held accountable in terms of statistical indicators whose base is the community at large Meidinger and Schnaiberg, 1980).

One reason for distinguishing between evaluative questions that concern clients, implementation, effects, or impacts is that important trade-offs follow from the priority assigned to each. While it is desirable to select evaluative questions from within each of the four categories, restricted budgets usually entail that some categories have to be assigned a higher priority than others. Thus if it were important to study how much WIC influenced the birth weight of babies whose mothers had attended WIC centers since the first trimester of pregnancy, an extensive study of the services actually implemented with these women might use project records, face-to-face interviews, or on-site observation. The expense of collecting such data would drain resources away from creating a more extensive sample of WIC centers or from creating large control groups of women who had not attended such centers. Yet sample size and control groups might be crucial for a sensitive study of effectiveness. Similarly, if impact questions were paramount, evaluators might expend considerable resources checking how a WIC center had influenced women's work relationships, status in other federal programs, family relationships, and the like. To answer these questions would require sampling a broader range of people than WIC attendees alone. Indeed, other members of their families and officials from other social programs would almost certainly have to be interviewed.

The second reason for the distinctions between question types is to highlight that they have different priorities for different stakeholder groups. Decision makers in central government incline more toward questions of effectiveness and impact. This is because their usual mandate is to monitor social programs whose goals specify, however unclearly, some effects and impacts that, if realized, would suggest that a recognized social problem is being ameliorated. Administrators of local projects are less concerned with effectiveness (unless they are sure it will be demonstrated). Their major concern is to ensure the fiscal health of the project, which depends more heavily on a continuous flow of clients and reimbursable services. Hence client and implementation issues tend to loom largest for local administrators. The priorities are not quite the same with service providers, who look to implementation and effectiveness data to ascertain the effective elements of practice they can easily adopt into their repertoire. The assumption here is that practitioners value evaluative knowledge more if it suggests practical improvements they can make to the services they deliver to clients.

The priorities we attribute to practitioners indicate a further distinction that needs to be made about question types. This is that we can ask questions about clients, implementation, effects, or impacts in either a *descriptive* mode, to find out what happened, or in an *explanatory* mode, to find out why something happened as it did. Descriptively, we know that flicking a light switch nearly always illuminates a room at night. We can know about this useful, dependable causal connection, even though we might not know why manipulating the switch has this effect. Indeed, full causal knowledge of the lighting system might require the equivalent of an electrician's diagram that shows the wires into a home, the circuits in it, and where bulbs are located. Also needed would be knowledge of what happens to electricity in this system, why bulbs have filaments, and how circuit breakers operate. Such knowledge would have many advantages if the light were to go out. Since the explanatory knowledge specifies that a functioning light bulb is necessary for light, we might check the bulb. If we found it to be functioning, but the light still did not go on, we might then check the fuse. If we discovered that the fuse was working, we might then check the source of electricity into the house, then the wiring in the house, and so on. Explanation facilitates transferable problem solving, since knowing how electricity makes bulbs burn can be used anywhere electricity can be generated.

Explanatory causal statements specify the dimensions of the evaluand that are causally efficacious, the dimensions of the outcome measures that have been influenced by the cause, and the micromediating mechanisms through which the causally efficacious component of the independent variable changed the influenced parts of the dependent variable (Bhaskar, 1979). To be more specific, imagine that an evaluation of, "Sesame Street" had indicated that animal figures teach most (i.e., they constitute the efficacious components of the global cause "Sesame Street" programming); their effect is mostly on number and letter recognition (i.e., these are causally impacted components of the dependent variable); and the causal connection between animal figures and recognition arises because the figures enhance attention to the televised material and also cause the material to be spontaneously rehearsed at a later date. If more letter and number recognition were desired, the explanatory knowledge just listed could be used to justify putting more animal figures into the programming and presenting humans only when other aspects of the televised material will hold the attention of children.

Some theorists believe that explanation is a task for basic research and that pursuing it in evaluations takes resources away from the more pragmatic and important task of identifying useful options for action (Cook and Campbell, 1979; Scriven, 1980). However, other theorists (e.g., Chen and Rossi, 1980, 1983; Cronbach, 1982) advocate explanatory goals for evaluation because of the clues explanation can provide to guide efforts at program improvement, both in the setting under study *and else-*

where. If evaluation is to improve programs that are made up of heterogeneous local projects, many of which have to be influenced if social problems are to be ameliorated on any practical scale, then there can be little doubt that explanatory knowledge is useful because it identifies specific causal agents and also facilitates transfer. However, explanation is not the only means of achieving knowledge of transferable projects or elements. Knowledge of project or element classes has logically to be based on having demonstrated that particular relationships are so dependable that they hold over a heterogeneous sample of the projects in a program. The identification of transferable causal agents through demonstrated heterogeneous replication may be potentially as powerful as the identification of such agents through demonstrated explanation.

As far as criteria are concerned, evaluation policymakers have to decide on:

1. The level at which to evaluate, the program, the project, or the element.

2. The degree of emphasis to be given to each level as a specific instance or general class.

3. The degree of emphasis to be assigned to particular types of criteria involving clients, implementation, effectiveness, or impact.

4. The emphasis to be given to descriptive or explanatory analyses.

We are not denying the desirability of including all the options above when deciding on the gross outlines of an agency's evaluation policy or for the approach to be taken in evaluating a single heterogeneous program. We are merely stressing the reality that because of limited evaluation resources, emphasizing some options will lower the quality of answers about other options and can also further the interests of some stakeholders over others.

Describing Standards of Comparison

Absolute standards of desired performance can be specified for every criterion, as when one predetermines that a project should provide services to at least 20 percent of the physically disabled in a particular city (a client criterion); that each of these persons should receive an average of at least two home visits per month (an implementation criterion); that the visits should improve client functioning by at least 10 percent over a six-month period (an effect specification); and that this improvement should reduce by at least 20 percent the strain felt by the family members principally responsible for the care of the disabled person (an impact criterion). Although it is sometimes possible to induce stakeholders to set absolute performance standards (Wholey, 1979)—and many management techniques encourage it (e.g., management by objectives)—veteran politicians and bureaucrats are often reluctant to specify any level of performance by which their efforts could be judged. They know that if they promise to reduce inflation 5 percent, but it only drops 4 percent, then they run the danger that the 4 percent "victory" will be overlooked and may be considered a failure. Despite this, absolute levels of desired performance are sometimes made public and used for evaluative purposes.

More often specified are *relative* standards of comparison. The most common instance is the situation when an evaluand is compared with what would have happened had it not been available. Some form of "no-treatment control group" usually makes it possible to claim that one has assessed the marginal difference the evaluand has made in the number and type of clients reached, the quantity and quality of services implemented, and the effects or impacts obtained. Scriven (1980) has convincingly argued that such a no-treatment comparison is nearly always less useful than explicit comparison with alternative means of bringing about comparable ends, for most decision making takes place in the context of weighing the relative utility of multiple alternatives. Thus the question "What difference does 'Sesame Street' make to school achievement by age 8?" might be less meaningful to someone concerned with decisions about funding for educational television than the question "Does 'Sesame Street' make more of a difference than 'Mr. Rogers' Neighborhood'?" To practitioners in mental health centers it might be less useful to know "Is behavior therapy successful with long-term schizophrenics?" than to know whether behavior therapy is better than the drug Haldol. For policymakers who want to improve children's knowledge about health, it is less meaningful to ask: "How effective is the health education curriculum supplied by the Heart Health Association?" than to ask: "Is the curriculum of the Heart Health Association more meritorious than the curriculum of the School Health Education Program?"

Explicit comparison is often resisted because, while each evaluand has some goals that appear to overlap with those of other evaluands, it typically has other goals that

are manifestly unique. The issue then arises of how the nonoverlapping components can be factored into a fair comparison of alternatives. Even the shared goals may seem less similar on analysis than at first glance, for the developers of different programs may attach different priorities to the same objectives or may differ in the time they think is required before a particular effect can be manifest. For these reasons it is more difficult to implement evaluations that explicitly compare policy alternatives than to implement evaluations where a single alternative is compared to what would have happened had there been nothing—not even the current levels of services for which individuals are eligible. Yet the direct comparison of alternatives is much closer to a consumer-centered model of evaluation and to how decisions are made in the political world than is asking whether an evaluand is better than nothing at all.

Integrating Evaluation Findings

In the logic of evaluation once the evaluand, the evaluation criteria, and the standards of comparison have been set, measurement occurs to determine the levels of performance achieved on each criterion. However, we leave consideration of measurement until later, anticipating the difficulty that more is involved with social programs than passive measurement alone. Indeed, if a decision has been made to evaluate using relative standards of comparison, then the principal task is not to test whether a preordained performance level has been attained. Rather, it is to measure how much of the change in performance has been *caused* by a program, a project, or an element. Fortunately, since social scientists have devoted so much attention to measurement and causal analysis in the past, much of the terminology we need for describing measurement in evaluation is already standard.

Not standard are the terms needed to describe how evaluation findings can be synthesized or integrated into global judgments of merit. One option is to halt the integration process at a *summary of discrete findings*. This involves describing the various findings and critically judging the degree of validity that can be attributed to each of them based on an explicit logic for making inferences about causation and generalization. Since most evaluations have multiple findings that may be associated with different levels of presumed validity, in all summary statements it is desirable to be explicit about evidential gaps. Where possible, the gaps should be filled in from what is already known in the research literature or professional practice. In this, apparent conflicts between studies will have to be explicitly confronted and, to the extent possible, reconciled.

To summarize is not to be explicit about *the assignment of worth or value*. Etymologically, the assignment of value or merit is the sine qua non of evaluation. Yet not all government agencies or evaluators are keen to see worth attributed to programs or their constituent parts. This is partly because, with multiple criteria, the findings often constitute an interpretative hodgepodge that cannot be easily integrated. Some findings may seem positive in their implications, others negative, and the implications for valuing may not be at all clear in yet other cases. Also, some findings may appear so large that they deserve special weighting, while others may involve smaller effects that nonetheless deserve special weighting because of their policy relevance. But what should these importance weights be? Nearly all judgments of importance, magnitude, and validity will have their critics because no universally accepted methods exist to deal with these matters. Yet if they are not dealt with, no global overall assessments of merit are possible, and preferences cannot appear to be scientific or objective.

It is perhaps for this reason that benefit-cost analysis has great appeal to central policymakers as a method of synthesis, the more so since financial considerations play such a large role for them in determining the worth of program options (Levin, 1983; Thompson, 1980). However, benefit-cost analysis requires translating all the assumed inputs and outputs of the evaluand into a common monetary metric so that a ratio can be computed that represents the extent to which the total benefits exceed (or fall below) the total costs. The many unrealistic assumptions required to do this make benefit-cost analysis dubious as a summary method for assigning worth (see Stokey and Zeckhauser, 1978). In particular, it is not easy to define a credible universe of possible benefits or costs; to relate cost estimates to each individual input; to impute costs or benefits to ephemeral outcomes (e.g., some attitude changes); or to impute costs or benefits to effects whose meaning depends on later changes that might or might not occur (e.g., a reduction in drug use of 15 percent obtains its financial relevance through an unclear causal link to eventual reductions in crime and unemployment, among other things).

These problems with benefit-cost analysis have led some economists to prefer cost-effectiveness analyses. These require only that program inputs be translated into dollars so that different components can be compared with each other in order to ascertain the relative cost of bringing about a particular unit of change in a particular outcome variable or index. Since the outcomes remain in the original metric, evaluators might be able to conclude that one alternative outperforms another in bringing about, say, academic achievement, while a different option might be better for enhancing, say, school attendance. Because it does not require aggregation across outcomes, a cost-effectiveness analysis with such results would leave readers with the consciousness-raising puzzle of working through the relative importance of increasing attendance rather than achievement by the amounts observed over the period studied.

A final task that the synthesis of evaluation findings could include is the *explicit drawing of policy recommendations*. Many evaluators are reluctant to include such recommendations in reports and many evaluation policymakers do not want to see them. This reflects the belief that Congress and government agencies are responsible for recommending changes and in so doing may consider a broader range of relevant concerns than evaluators would (Wholey, 1979). However, other evaluators are less management-oriented (e.g., Chen and Rossi, 1980; Cronbach, 1982) and believe that each stakeholder group should be encouraged to assign merit and to suggest action based on its own preferences for criteria and standards. This point of view is based partly on considerations of fairness and partly also on the frank recognition that different stakeholder groups attach different utilities to outcomes and may be more likely to buy into the evaluation results if they see that some of their preferences have been taken into account by the evaluators (Leviton and Hughes, 1981). In pluralist formulations of the evaluator's role, she is supposed to help others assign worth and help them work through for themselves the policy implications of what is known.

Yet if evaluation is to contribute to the reduction of social problems through the improvement of social programs, the integration of results might go one step further than presenting action recommendations or helping others formulate them. Evaluators might also review the arguments relevant to each recommendation as they have emerged from stakeholder analysis, knowledge of program objectives and resources, and the relevant value concerns discussed in the relevant scholarly literature. Policy analysts spend much of their time reviewing different options for action through a similiar process in which they develop arguments in favor of and against the set of options initially deemed to be feasible. For some theorists (e.g., Wholey, 1983) the evaluator's task is to contribute information that may help in this process. Why not, then, commission evaluators to organize arguments for and against each identified option, leaving readers free to make their own judgments about an action? If it is feared that too much bias may result if a single person generates all the arguments, why not develop different sets of arguments from different value or interest perspectives?

Implications of these Terminological Distinctions
The foregoing discussion allows us to describe the major options for deciding on the broad approaches to be taken in formulating evaluation objectives. The issues are:

1. What shall be emphasized more in evaluations—programs, projects, or elements?

2. Should the emphasis be more on single instances or general classes?

3. Which *criteria* should be emphasized more—those relevant to variables about clients and service providers, implementation, effect, or impact?

4. Should the criteria be examined more in a descriptive than an explanatory mode?

5. Which *standards of comparison* should be emphasized more—absolute or relative ones?

6. How far should evaluators go in *integrating* evaluation results?

7. What methods should they select for measuring performance?

The options above are not mutually exclusive. For instance, one could evaluate a program instance (e.g., the National School Lunch Program) concentrating on a particular class of projects (e.g., schools that prepare food from scratch on the premises) and on the elements within this class that might explain a desired effect of importance (e.g., if plate waste is reduced, is it because of staff concern to create meals that children particularly like?). One can also evaluate a project in terms of client, implementation, effect, *and* impact criteria, using absolute standards of comparison with some criteria (e.g., Do at least 80 percent of the children eligible for free lunches attend on the average school day?) and relative criteria with others (e.g., Is the average daily plate waste less in schools that prepare their own food than in schools that heat meals prepared elsewhere?). It is therefore possible in the abstract to imagine a single study of such comprehensiveness that it includes all six evaluands (programs,

projects, and elements as both classes and single instances); all eight types of questions (about units, implementation, effectiveness, and impact in both a descriptive and an explanatory mode); both absolute and relative criteria; and in this single comprehensive study conclusions are reached that summarize findings, assign merit from multiple perspectives, and develop arguments for and against a number of action options that seem to be consonant with the data.

However, no evaluator has yet produced such a comprehensive evaluation. This may be because evaluation theory has not yet adequately sensitized evaluation funders to the full range of alternatives. But it may also reflect concerns about the risks inherent in incorporating so many options into a single large and expensive study, for a few mistakes or chance misfortunes could seriously detract from the utility of the whole. A large study might also fail to provide evaluators with the opportunity to become "insiders" about the substantive issues and sites under study, leaving them deficient in much of the contextual knowledge that improves the design and implementation of studies as well as the interpretation of results. A single comprehensive study may also not be logically desirable. Evaluative criteria are sequentially ordered. It often does not make sense to explore how well a program is being implemented if it is not reaching its intended beneficiaries; nor does it make sense to probe a program's impacts if effects are not occurring; or to ask about cost-effectiveness if there are no demonstrated effects or impacts. It is also worth remembering that evaluators are often called in to examine programs, projects, or elements when they are novel and are undergoing a "shakedown" period that may not reflect the quality of functioning attained once a steady state has been reached. In this situation, evaluators often prefer to provide feedback about how services are targeted and implemented rather than about effects and impacts. Given all the above, it is not surprising that some evaluation theorists are now calling for programmatic sequences of smaller studies instead of single large studies with multiple purposes (Cook and Gruder, 1978; Cronbach, 1982).

It is not only completed evaluations that are noncomprehensive. Evaluation theories are too. Indeed, one of the major implications of our descriptive terminology is that it helps illustrate the implicit priorities in the work of different theorists. For example, social experimentation as discussed by Riecken and Boruch (1974) tends to emphasize programs and projects over elements, instances over classes, effect and impact criteria over client and implementation criteria, descriptive over explanatory analyses, and relative levels of desired performance over absolute ones. Guba and Lincoln (1981), on the other hand, emphasize projects and elements over programs, instances over classes, criteria relevant to service providers/recipients and implementation over effects in impacts, and explanatory questions over descriptive ones. Cronbach (1982) emphasizes projects and elements over programs, classes more than instances, criteria of implementation and effect over other criteria, and causal explanations over descriptive information; and absolute over relative standards of comparison. Thus many of the disagreements among evaluation theorists are about what should be evaluated, which criteria should be emphasized, and which standards of comparison are more relevant.

The major implication of our terminological distinctions is to raise the crucial issue of where among these options for evaluation design policymakers should place their priorities for individual evaluation studies so that the selection of evaluands, criteria, standards of comparison, and modes of synthesis will have more leverage in generating evaluation results that contribute to social problem solving. It is to this we now turn.

A THEORY OF DETERMINANTS OF LEVERAGE

The Leverage in Different Characteristics of the Evaluand

An evaluand can be presumed to increase in leverage: 1., the greater the influence it promises to have on individual lives in ways that obviously relate to ameliorating a social problem; and 2., the more the evaluand is distributed—that is, the greater the number of persons to whom it is available, or might be made so, across the heterogeneous collection of projects in a program.

To understand the crucial role of the distribution of effective evaluands, imagine evaluating attempts to deal with fraud and abuse among applicants to the Food Stamp Program. Preevaluative work should establish that many millions of Americans receive such stamps, that expenditures for them run into many billions of dollars each year, and that claims of fraud and abuse are widespread. Knowing this, evaluators might then want to learn how much abuse there is, who is committing it, why it is being committed, and what can be done to reduce it. However, these options differ in the likelihood they will lead to knowledge about manipulable options that could be widely implemented within the program. A valid profile of the persons most likely to apply fraudulently to the

program could be used to target income verification checks on any applicant anywhere who fits the profile. It would also be possible to implement nationwide any strategies to reduce false applications that depended on printing a warning on the application form—for example, a warning that the applicant's reported income will be verified from government records or wage slips. However, to learn why people lie on their food stamp applications would be less useful, for it is not clear how such knowledge could be used to bring about practical changes that could be widely implemented throughout the program.

Important consequences follow from determining the amount of leverage in different types of evaluands. Programs promise the largest and most widespread effects and are therefore generally more significant than projects or elements. But they cannot be as easily manipulated, since their political impactedness entails that programs rarely die. Projects are more manipulable because their number waxes and wanes with program budgets as new projects are started and old ones phased out, and because existing projects can change their philosophies, leaders, and models of service delivery (Larsen and Werner, 1979). But each project normally reaches few persons. Elements are the most readily manipulated, for many can be added without disruption to the repertoire of service providers in many of the projects in a program. Yet most elements are quite weak in impact by themselves. To exemplify the above, consider the difference in potential manipulability between a national program like Headstart, a local project such as the Headstart Center in a single school district, or an element such as individual tutoring in reading skills for 15 minutes per day. Which can be started or discontinued more easily? Now consider their potential impact on lives. In general, the potential manipulability and social significance of evaluands are negatively related.

Nonetheless, some effective policy options can be widely implemented without undue difficulty, especially those that have many of the characteristics of elements. Some effective drugs and vaccines fall into this category, as may the fluoridation of drinking water. In a similar vein, Applied Management Sciences (1983) discovered that a minor and inexpensive change on the form for reporting parental income reduced the number of subsidized school lunches served to ineligible children. Because it applied to so many children nationally and did not scare away children who were truly eligible, this minor modification of a program element saved millions of dollars. Evaluation policymakers need to be especially sensitized to atypical cases where the anticipated significance for individual lives and manipulability across a wide range of program participants are both thought to be high, for there the payoff from evaluation is particularly promising.

In the 1960s most policymakers interested in evaluation seem to have emphasized questions about the causal effects and impacts of national programs that reached millions of clients and that, at the time, held promise of radical changes in individual lives. In the same era many demonstrations were launched to test options that radically differed from the policy of the times and that some hoped might be the foundation for innovative national programs. Thus the negative income tax experiments were begun in the hope of providing the poor with more cash instead of professional services; an experiment was designed in Kansas to test whether patrolling police cars are really needed (Larson 1978); and experiments were undertaken to test whether providing citizens with vouchers for services they could buy in the private sector would reform public schools or provide better housing for the poor. Campbell (1969) was particularly associated with this position as part of his call for an "Experimenting Society." It was a call clearly predicated on discovering novel approaches to problem solving that might have a particularly large effect on individual lives and might form new widely available programs.

But the ambiguity of results from these demonstrations, the growing realization that current programs are highly resistant to fundamental changes, and an ideological trend in the second half of the 1970s to de-emphasize the government's role in domestic social change led some evaluators to stress the need for knowledge about more modest evaluands that could perhaps be more readily introduced into practice. These were nearly always elements. One area where this new priority became apparent was in the call for in-house evaluations conducted by project employees in response to the information needs of project management. Crucial assumptions behind this advocacy were that local personnel know better than central program officials which local elements need improving; as project employees, in-house evaluators are trusted by project personnel and so may collect better data and may be are more likely to get their evaluation results used to improve the project. This decentralized model of evaluation was so attractive that it was advanced for congressionally mandated evaluation in compensatory education (David, 1981), community mental health (Cook and Shadish, 1982), and local law enforcement (Feeley and Sarat, 1980). A second area where the primacy of evaluating manipulable elements became apparent was in the work of Wholey (1983) and Patton (1978), who developed theories and procedures designed to help program and project officials manage better, almost irrespective of the significance of the program aspect they wanted to see improved. A shift occurred, then, from a concern with present or future programs to a more modest concern with project or program elements that might affect functioning in many of the projects within a program.

Whatever the evaluand, more leverage lies in generating knowledge about it as a class than as a single instance. This is because inferences about classes depend on demonstrating that relationships remain stable across most instances of an evaluand, each of which will have its own unique characteristics. Thus inferences about classes presuppose having demonstrated the potential for transfer—having shown that larger numbers of individuals have been affected than is the case with a single project. The leverage offered by such empirical generalization is related to the leverage afforded by explanatory knowledge, since the latter allows planners to identify the causal powers that need to be present from one site to the next if a desired effect is to come about. These powers will typically consist of a mix of elements that is considered sufficient to bring about desired effects. Identifying this mix helps overcome the chronic weakness of research on individual elements, which is their restricted ability by themselves to bring about much change in individual lives.

Leverage and the Nature of Evaluative Information

The foregoing discussion concerned determinants of the leverage *in the evaluand* and suggested that greater leverage is associated with evaluands that promise larger effects, reach more people in need, and have the potential to reach even more people because they are manipulable and can be transferred to other sites. These three determinants are related in complex ways to the evaluands we defined. The leverage associated with transfer gives more leverage to classes than instances, whatever the evaluand. The leverage associated with manipulability gives more leverage to elements than projects and to projects than programs. But the leverage associated with the size of effects and the number of people served gives more leverage to programs than to projects or elements. A major task for evaluation policymakers is to come to grips both with the countervailing relationships implicit in how particular evaluands are related to determinants of leverage, and with the conceptual and practical problems inherent in evaluating general classes rather than individual instances. But before discussing these matters we have to detail other determinants of leverage—in the nature of the information obtained and in the roles the evaluator plays vis-a-vis stakeholder groups.

Such leverage presumably depends on how the nature of the information collected affects the likelihood that it will enter into deliberations about program or project change and will come to play an important role in these deliberations. It is obvious that evaluative information need not be published or disseminated vigorously, for government agencies can consign evaluations to gather dust on shelves or can use the findings for their own internal purposes without ever publicizing them. It is not known how often these situations arise. But it is the case in the United States that the commitment to freedom of information facilitates access to nonsecret documents and that many stakeholder groups continuously track the production of knowledge relevant to their interests so that they can cooperate in determining whether program changes are needed, what changes are possible, and how attempts at change should be evaluated.

In a lengthy review of the relevant theory and case study findings on determinants of the use of evaluation findings, Leviton and Hughes (1981) concluded that the likelihood of evaluative information entering formal and informal policy deliberations depends on evaluators generating information that major stakeholders see as relevant and credible. Credibility is thought to depend on the nature of the findings (especially their fit with conventional wisdom, past research findings, and other forms of existing knowledge) and on the nature of the methods used to generate the information. In practice, the methodological requirement is that evaluations use state-of-the-art methods, preferably quantitative, and that they be backed by a consensus of experts.

Turning to relevance, Leviton and Hughes (1981) suggest that it depends on evaluation results being available in time for important meetings, being clearly presented, and having their presumed action implications spelled out. Other work indicates that relevance depends on findings and action implications being publicly debated and a consensus emerging about what is known and what to do (Leviton and Boruch, 1983). We can also hypothesize that the degree to which findings are relevant also depends on the criteria used for evaluation. To know that clients have received program services is necessary for inferring that social problems might be ameliorated.

But such knowledge is rarely sufficient for this purpose since inefficient services are sometimes implemented and services that are generally effective can in some instances be implemented so poorly that effectiveness is precluded. Effectiveness and impact variables constitute more direct indicators of problem-related change, with the latter suggesting that the change has been so large and so prevalent that accepted indicators of a social problem have been influenced (e.g., indicators of drug abuse or crime rates). The implication is that for purposes of ameliorating social problems, causal effects and impacts are closer to problem solution than criteria related to clients and implementation.

Yet the last two are far from trivial, being necessary conditions for problem solving. Hence a premature focus on outcomes can lead to research with minimal leverage. Imagine discovering that a project was not effective by the criteria examined. Without data on clients and implementation it would not be clear whether the resources reached the wrong people or were poorly administered or whether the theoretical rationale for the design of the whole project was flawed. If negative-appearing results are available and deal only with effect or impact criteria, this will almost always generate fierce opposition from affected stakeholders. They will tend to argue that the evaluand was still in a state of development when it was tested or that it was better implemented at sites that were not studied than at those studied, and so on. For these reasons many evaluation theorists counsel that efforts always be made to assess both the clients that an evaluand reaches and the quality with which its services are delivered, even if this entails fewer resources being devoted to measuring and analyzing data on effects and impacts (Wholey, 1983). Of course, the need for client and implementation data is less if prior research has consistently indicated high levels of performance; and the need is greater if such variables have never before been measured or if past performance was shown to be disappointing or highly variable. The point is that it will usually be advantageous to devote some resources to the study of client and implementation variables, even if this is not the major focus.

Leverage and Evaluator Roles

Evaluation results are also considered more credible when they come from sources independent of the evaluand (Campbell, 1969; Scriven, 1980). Bias is usually presumed to be more likely when employees of the organization under study conduct an evaluation, the more so if funding decisions, future salaries, or employment status are thought to depend on results. The possibility of such bias explains why, when the Department of Education wanted to decide which self-evaluated projects should be financially supported so as to disseminate their activities to new sites, an independent panel of substantive and methodological experts was set up to examine the evaluation results presented by the projects. Scriven (1972) goes further than any other theorist with respect to evaluator bias, believing that even external evaluators can inadvertently adopt pro-program biases when they consult with program or project personnel. He contends that in this situation evaluators may adopt the others' frame of reference, steering them toward criteria and standards of evaluation that will make projects and programs look good. To prevent such co-optation and make his case dramatically clear, Scriven favors goal-free evaluation in which evaluators do not even talk to program personnel to understand their goals for the evaluand. Instead, they generate evaluative issues from their own analysis of knowledge needs.

A stark contrast to Scriven is offered by Campbell's (1969) advocacy of a servant role for evaluators. Campbell argues that evaluators should do no more than elicit central administrators' questions and try to answer them. Patton (1978) and Wholey (1983) adopt a similar position. But they also recognize that evaluators will sometimes have to raise the consciousness of those who commission their work in order for evaluation issues to be specified clearly and for measures to be agreed upon. Chen and Rossi (1983), Cronbach *et al.* (1980), and House (1980), go even further and view evaluation as being in the service of multiple stakeholder groups. They see evaluators as information brokers who educate different stakeholder groups about both the questions worth asking and the implications of subsequent findings, helping them integrate the information for themselves. Leviton and Hughes (1981) suggest that adopting such an information broker role will result in more use of evaluation findings because more stakeholder groups will come to learn of the findings and their implications. Indeed, they claim that if evaluators have been actively engaged with the various stakeholder groups before, during, and after data collection, evaluation results will be particularly salient and action-relevant. Salient examples of evaluations where leverage increased because of evaluators or adopting an active information broker role include Hill (1980), Bauman (1976), and Berman and McLaughlin (1978).

One problem with conceptualizing the evaluator's role as an active information broker is that frequent consultation with multiple stakeholder groups may have unanticipated and undesired consequences (Bryk, 1983). For instance, it might increase the political profile of an evaluation to the point where evaluators develop a counterproductive sense of others monitoring their actions; unreasonably prolonged debates might ensue about the selection of criteria and standards of comparison; stakeholder analyses require time and money that some think might be better used for other evaluative purposes; and finally, practical and technical difficulties arise if consulting with stakeholders generates a large number of evaluative questions and issues that then have to be prioritized in order to attain a final and more manageable set. A second problem with conceptualizing evaluators as information brokers is that the role could detract attention from other ways in which the use of findings can be stimulated, although it need not necessarily do so. For instance, use might be enhanced if evaluators and policymakers use media contacts to disseminate result, or if they report findings at conventions, in books, or in journal articles. The evaluators might even eschew multiple stakeholder groups and consider a single person, agency, or office as the sole client (Patton, 1978; Wholey, 1979), thereby avoiding the front-end problems of politics and coordination that follow when multiple stakeholder groups are involved in question formulation and follow-up activities. Indeed, the single-client model may under some (as yet unknown) conditions lead to more use than occurs with multiple stakeholders.

Conclusions

The leverage of program evaluations depends on considerations that include, but are not limited to, the logic of evaluation as it touches on the specification of criteria and standards of evaluation, the measurement of performance, and the integration of results. Leverage also depends on the other determinants of problem solving—namely, the importance of the original problem, the potential that proposed solutions are thought to have for causing important changes in individual lives, and the likelihood that any option that has been tested and shown to be effective is, or can be, widely implemented across most or all of the projects that make up a program. Leverage also depends on the nature of the evaluator's role relationships with major stakeholder groups, for this may facilitate use of the evaluation results by keeping an evaluation visible and helping stakeholders analyze for themselves the credibility and relevance of questions and findings. Finally, leverage is presumably greater if the information is collected in ways that seem "scientific," if it is internally consistent and is consistent with other knowledge, and if it is presented in timely, clear, and relevant fashion to audiences with a stake in the issue under investigation.

THE IDENTIFICATION AND JUSTIFICATION OF SPECIFIC SOURCES OF LEVERAGE

In the above formulation, much leverage depends on the potential power and transferability of the options explored in an evaluation. But programs are diffuse and offer multiple options at either the program, the project, or the element level; stakeholders often differ in evaluand, criteria, and standards of evaluation they consider most important; and the level of greatest presumed transferability and most direct contact with beneficiaries—the element—will often be the least powerful in terms of its potential effects on individuals. On the other hand, the level that promises to reach most people and that holds the greatest promise for powerful effects—the program—is the least manipulable, and the persons with responsibility at that level are particularly remote from the local level where services are actually delivered. Given these countervailing relationships, one of the most crucial issues facing evaluation policy is to identify specific points where evaluation might have most coverage in the social sector. We discuss this below, asking: Which types of evaluative question have the most leverage when programs, projects, or elements are the evaluands as either individual instances or classes?

Monitoring Client and Implementation Criteria within Ongoing Programs

Most social programs are heterogeneous in the persons served and the services implemented, with millions of dollars and clients, thousands of practitioners, and many different mixes of service involved. Systematic and up-to-date descriptive information about program activities is not always available to policymakers and program managers who, unlike project-level personnel, are quite remote from day-to-day operations at the local level (Nathan *et al.,* 1981). Yet a major responsibility of policymakers and program managers is to oversee the quality of service implementation and to control it through issuing regulations and monitoring how well they are complied with. In the United States they have to do this in a context where local personnel want to further their own goals—which may or may not be consonant with national objectives (Bardach, 1977)—and where both major political parties are committed to preventing the growth of the federal bureaucracy (Cook and Buccino, 1979). Consequently, many local personnel know that central government officials rarely have the resources for intensive monitoring.

It would be wrong to think that program managers and policymakers are in a total void about program activities. In some sectors management information systems (MIS) have been developed that contain reliable and recent information that projects have supplied and to which program managers have easy access. But such systems are not always available; and when they are, they are more likely to contain information about gross expenditures, the numbers of clients served, and billings rather than information about the quantity, quality, relevance, and efficacy of the services actually delivered. Senior program officials also get information about implementation and effects from gossip in Washington and state capitals, from media stories, and from selected feedback by interested parties, including lobbyists (Downs, 1967). However, such sources are likely to be biased in what they report, and their knowledge base is likely to be incomplete. Some policymakers and program managers also conduct site visits and local hearings in order to collect implementation data for themselves. But once again, the sampling base is limited, and the visitors are likely to be exposed to show-and-tell performances. Finally, program managers control research funds that can be given to contract research firms for studying the implementation of program services. However, this process provides feedback only slowly and still puts the manager at one stage removed from direct contact with activities at the project level. Political restrictions on the size of the federal bureaucracy mean that few program managers have the time for systematic personal observation at the local level.

We assume that considerable leverage will often result from evaluations aimed at describing the targeting, implementation, and costs of services within a program. Indeed, implementation studies of this type often led to results being used in education in the 1970s (Leviton and Boruch, 1983). Such descriptive information has many uses. Foremost among them is the identification of problems of service delivery and management. Some of the identified problems may be tractable and have known solutions that could be implemented across many of the projects in a program. Some of the other problems may have less obvious solutions unless explanations can be offered of why the problems occur. It is for this reason that studies of program-level implementation, while primarily descriptive, should also include explanatory components when resources of time and money permit.

Even when descriptions of the targeting, implementation, and costs do not lead to recommendations about action, our guess is that providing central decision makers with feedback about the conditions that pertain locally will allow then to respond to requests for information from Congress and the public. Also, the feedback should "enlighten" (Weiss and Weiss, 1981) them about what to expect in terms of effects and impacts. Thus if monitoring reveals that certain services are not being implemented at all, or are being implemented at a level professional practice generally believes to be inadequate, it would usually be unrealistic to expect to find effects or impacts, and evaluators might spend more of their time trying to explain why service delivery is so substandard. For instance, Gunter *et al.*, (1983) studied the implementation of emergency medical service planning and development across the nation, and they concluded that in many locations the planning did not improve performance. They then tried to explain why this was the case, noting that where planning and development efforts failed, the needs and interests of service providers had not been taken into account. Finally, we can expect descriptive information about clients, implementation, and cost to help in developing cost projections for the future so that there can be some forewarning of large increases such as happened in the 1970s with Food Stamps and Medicaid. The necessary conditions for such projections are, of course, that data about participation in a program or project are available for several years and that the extent of unmet demand can be estimated for both the present and the future.

If monitoring reveals that program services are being implemented widely and well, this is encouraging since implementation is a necessary condition for effectiveness. Although evidence of high-quality implementation is not usually sufficient to justify conclusions about effects, such conclusions are warranted when other evidence clearly indicates that the services in question are mostly effective *when delivered*. Screening for cancer is a case in point. Since we know it is effective in detecting most cancers, the major evaluative concern with a screening program would be whether screening materials are available and whether prospective victims are reached. If they are, determining the effectiveness of the materials in discovering cancers should constitute a low research priority.

The Assessment of Effects and Impacts for Individual Ongoing Programs

Evaluators originally assumed that programs would live or die on the basis of evaluation findings. Indeed, Campbell (1969) proposed that programmatic reforms should be seen as experiments "in which we retain, imitate, modify, or discard on the basis of apparent effectiveness on the multiple imperfect criteria available" (p. 409). However, at the program level currently under discussion, we have seen no ongoing programs terminated because of negative evaluation and no programs begun or retained because of positive evaluation. Programs need strong political support to be funded initially, and they generate even more support from their dependents as time goes by (Kaufman, 1976). Indeed, even multisite demonstration programs, clearly labeled as such, often come to be viewed as service programs, with organized groups of clients and service providers bringing political pressure to bear if unpopular decisions seem imminent (Leviton and Boruch, 1983). The presence of such support means that evaluative results rarely have much leverage over stop-and-go decisions about programs.

Although individual programs do not often die, their budgets do rise and fall, and information about effects and impacts may sometimes contribute to decisions about budget levels. At appropriations hearings administrators often back up their requests for funds with information from evaluations, and congressional committees routinely question administrators about the consequences of their programs. But while evaluations are sometimes cited as the reason for budget changes, many of the citations are designed to justify decisions that have already been made on more political grounds (Knorr, 1977; Leviton and Boruch, 1983).

This is not to deny that feedback about program effectiveness might sometimes be assimilated with many other types of information in such a way that incremental changes are eventually created in individual programs or in programs similar to those that have already been evaluated. But while such enlightenment may be important in transforming programs, it is less immediate and less directly linked to ensuing action than is the feedback provided from monitoring program activities. Indeed, our experience suggests that causal studies of individual programs are more likely than descriptive monitoring studies to produce results that are hotly disputed and so take longer to fit into a political context that facilitates program change. Like Cronbach *et al.* (1980), we doubt whether it is reasonable to expect much short-term use from cause-probing studies of ongoing social programs. Consequently, we are willing to conclude that little leverage can be expected from studies that take the program as their evaluand and descriptions of effectiveness and impact as the principal criteria of merit.

Monitoring Client and Implementation Criteria in Individual Projects

Descriptive information about projects is used by local managers in planning, budgeting, and negotiations with funders. Consequently, they usually have reasonably good information about expenditure patterns, the number of clients served, and the services provided. Their information comes from many sources, including their own day-to-day operational knowledge of the project, the reports put out by their own accounting systems, and discussions with colleagues and clients who have also had firsthand experiences with project activities. Since such informal sources of knowledge often seem to be preferred over more formal evaluative knowledge (Sproull and Zubrow, 1981), it may well be that local managers use monitoring data to modify project operations *but do not need evaluators to generate such data.* Indeed, few project managers ask evaluators they employ for new knowledge about effective practices (Cook and Shadish, 1982; Feeley and Sarat, 1980). Thus while there is clearly some leverage in monitoring individual projects, it is not clear that formal evaluations can provide much more leverage than the information currently collected by project officials.

The rationale for mandated evaluation by in-house evaluation specialists is superficially persuasive, because senior project officials have control over their projects and are in a unique position to implement options for project improvement. Their freedom to do so is not unlimited, for they have to consider staff willingness to change and the financial costs of change. Nonetheless, when their power to implement changes at the project level is contrasted with the difficulties that central program managers face at this level, it would seem reasonable to adopt an evaluation policy in which in-house evaluators are financially supported in each of the projects constituting a program (Davis, Windle, and Scharfstein, 1977). However, a policy of mandated evaluation by in-house specialists assumes that most of the project directors in a program want evaluative information and that evaluators can provide the kinds of information they need. Because experience in criminal justice (Feeley and Sarat, 1980), community mental health (Cook and Shadish, 1982), and education (David, 1981), belies these core assumptions, we cannot be sanguine that in-house evaluations throughout a program will lead to significant improvement in many of the projects constituting the program.

Assessing Effectiveness and Impact Criteria for Individual Projects

At the local level evaluations of effectiveness are usually carried out to meet program-level reporting requirements rather than to provide feedback to project-level personnel. Indeed, project officials and local service deliverers usually assume the effectiveness of their efforts. They generally see little purpose to judgments of effectiveness offered by external evaluators who, in their eyes, rarely appreciate the real-world constraints operating at the point of service delivery. If project personnel want causal information at all, it is for improving day-to-day operations. So they would emphasize identifying successful elements of practice rather than judging the effectiveness of a global project.

A further argument against assessing the effectiveness and impact of individual projects is that when such information is eventually received by personnel at the central program level, they seldom do anything with it to improve project functioning. The exception is where major problems have been clearly identified in a particular project, at which point program personnel usually offer technical assistance (Boruch *et al.,* 1980; Davis, Windle, and Scharfstein, 1977). However, many problems at the project level will not be detected by project staff or, if detected, will not be reported to program officials for fear that exposure of the problems may affect future funding levels and employment security. Many project employees presumably believe that project evaluations of effectiveness could have such consequences, since there are so few other rationales for why program officials would request such information. We doubt, therefore, whether evaluations of the effectiveness or impact of individual projects constitute an efficient means for identifying the subset of projects that might benefit from technical assistance.

Nonetheless, there are arguments for studying the effectiveness of individual projects under certain conditions. First, some projects are located within powerful centralized organizations where the evaluator is linked to the central administration rather than the project. For instance, some evaluators work for the central administration of a school district, and through this link they can help put pressure on individual schools that are not performing well so that they change particular practices. Second, there are many externally funded projects set up as demonstrations to probe some novel idea. These are usually evaluated by researchers from universities or large contract research firms, and the evaluations often capture so much attention in the worlds of scholarship and policy, that a particularly high level of attention is focussed on the new policy thrust. Third, in many ongoing programs, projects turn over as program budget vary (Cook, 1981; Cronbach, *et al.,* 1980), internal enthusiasm changes (Berman and McLaughlin, 1978; Glaser, 1976; Far West Laboratories, 1979), or the local client pool shifts. The issue is, What kind of knowledge about project effects can best be used to take advantage of this turnover when it is high enough that introducing new projects and/or phasing out established ones could significantly enhance program performance within reasonable time periods?

Evaluating the Effectiveness and Impact of Project Classes Rather Than Project Instances

Knowledge about effective project classes can be used to upgrade a program in ways that are not logically relevant when the only knowledge available is about the effects of individual projects. Knowledge about classes is essential if evaluations are to inform central *program* managers about the types of projects their programs should contain. In times of program expansion such information could be used to add to a program more projects whose major implemented activities correspond with a type that evaluation has shown to be robustly successful by important criteria. In times of diminishing budgets the program manager could use information about project classes to cut out more of the projects belonging to classes that are not usually effective. In this strategy program managers make decisions on the basis of what is implemented at each project and its fit to what independent research suggests is generally effective. This is quite different from using reports from each project about how effective it is, for such reports are likely to be biased. Alternatively, if independent evaluators were asked to evaluate each project in a program for effectiveness and impact, this would be exceedingly expensive and time-consuming if done sensitively. If done less well, important decisions would be made on the basis of dubious findings. The way to avoid this dilemma is to base decisions on what projects implement, since we believe that such information can be collected more quickly and inex-

pensively than information about project effects. The necessary condition for using implementation data in this way is, of course, that research is already available which provides knowledge about the likely consequences of different patterns of implemented activities. Research on project types provides just such knowledge.

If project classes are evaluated both to describe *and explain* their operations and consequences, this should provide considerable insight into the project-level elements that promote success or failure. This insight will help achieve generalized knowledge about the project-level elements of greatest importance, some of which might be added to quite different types of projects in order to bolster their effectiveness. Moreover, the focus on elements will prove extremely advantageous if there is little evidence for the classes evaluators thought they would find, or if the instances are so variable that it is not clear whether to concentrate on differences between or within classes. Thus while it is an important task for program evaluation to identify classes of projects that are successful, it is also desirable to try to identify the project-level elements that are necessary and sufficient for bringing about the observed effects.

It is not a new idea to concentrate on changing programs through disseminating information about successful projects or successful project-level practices. However, past attempts to do this suffered because knowledge of effectiveness came from single evaluations of single projects, as with the Department of Education's Dissemination Review Panel (Tallmadge, 1977) and similar efforts in health, mental health, and criminal justice (Beck, 1978; Larsen, 1979). Basing knowledge of successful practices on studies of a single project means that one cannot sensitively assess the roles played in producing the results by transferable project characteristics, chance, or characteristics unique to the project (e.g., the charisma of a particular local leader or project developer). Transfer to other sites is less problematic when knowledge is available about project classes, for such knowledge has logically to result from demonstrations of effectiveness that were reliably repeated across a group of projects that had similar implemented activities but dissimilar locations, clients, service providers, and marginalia of service composition and delivery. Such heterogeneity helps probe the conditions under which a project type is effective and so reduces the risk of inappropriate generalization.

But what is a project class/type/model—concepts we use interchangeably? Our preference is to infer a class

TABLE 1
Exemplars of a Single Project Type for Home Health Services to the Elderly

SOUTH HILLS HEALTH SYSTEM (SHHS)

This is a multi-hospital system through which a comprehensive range of home health services are provided. At the present time five hospitals and two health systems participate in the home health care program at the SHHS. Participating hospitals function as branch units of the home health agency and provide identical services within the overall geographic area served by the agency. The base unit of the SHHS Home Health Agency is at the Homestead Center. There are two regional supervisors at the base unit for the eastern and western regions of the service area respectively.

Home care services include professional nursing care, speech therapy, occupational therapy, physical therapy, social services, home health-aide services, pharmacy services, dietary guidance, and health education. This is the only agency which provides psychiatric nursing service.

A nursing co-ordinator monitors the operations and other management activities at each of the participating hospitals. A special services coordinator at the base co-ordinates and monitors the operations of all special services such as physical therapy, occupational therapy, respiratory therapy, and social services. (p. 14)

NORTHWEST ALLEGHENY HOME CARE PROGRAM

This is a multi-hospital system which began providing services in 1967. (The program trains its own RN's,

LPN's, and physical therapists.) The central office is located at Allegheny General Hospital. Ohio Valley General Hospital and North Hills Passavant Hospital have home care nursing units and are called the satellite divisions. The other three hospitals which do not have home care nursing units are called referral hospitals which function with a nurse coordinator who refers patients to the appropriate satellite division.

A regional manager in the central office monitors the operations of all the participating hospitals. There is a nurse coordinator at each hospital except Allegheny General Hospital, which has the only patient referral nurses. The nurse co-ordinators and the referral nurses channel the patient referrals through an intake nurse at the central office.

Since more than 10% of the patients served by home care are cancer cases, there is an oncology team to provide the specialized services necessary for these cases. Home care services include professional nursing, physical speech, occupational and respiratory therapies, social service, home health-aide services, dietary guidance, health education, and arrangements for lab tests including blood work. The most significant expansion has been in the services provided by home health-aides. Other services which have been added in response to patient's needs are I.V. Chemotherapy and I.V. Hydration (pp. 10–11).

SOURCE: Sainsbury, T., Sharma, R. K., Iyengar, S., and Overman, B., 1982, pp. 10 and 14.

---

from the degree of overlap between the theory implicit (or hopefully explicit) in the activities actually carried out in two or more projects. Consider *hospital-based home care* for the frail elderly. Table 1 provides a description of the care activities planned for two settings. The plans overlap considerably, each being multihospital based, targeted at comparable physical and psychological problems, and involving comparable services. Such projects potentially belong in the same class. Contrast this with *adult day care* for the frail elderly based either on custodial care in a social setting outside of the home but not in a hospital or on rehabilitation confined to a day hospital. The objectives, services, and organizational contexts are distinctly different in the case of adult day care and hospital-based home care (Weissert, 1976, 1977). But our

definition of class requires a further distinction. To constitute a class, the common activities outlined in theory have to be to a large extent implemented in practice. Thus confident knowledge of classes always depends upon a grounded analysis of what actually happens at the project level; it is not sufficient to detail what is supposed to happen. A project class is a behavioral and not a normative construct, though we might surmise that the likelihood of behavioral overlap is highest when two or more projects have followed the same model of what the project activities should be.

As another example, consider attempts to educate children who are deficient in English because it is not their native language. Normatively, most projects aimed at teaching such children English can be classified as following a strategy based on immersion (all substantive classes are in English and there is no opportunity to learn English in one's native language); submersion (all substantive classes are in English but there is some tutoring in the English language, often outside regular class hours); English as a second language (i.e., all content classes are in English, but the level of English is specially geared to the language ability of the children); and transmission (all content classes are in the dominant language of the surrounding neighborhood so that its culture can be transmitted; English is taught only in English classes). If these normative models correspond to some extent with school practice, they suggest that constructing project classes depends on the availability of a restricted number of practical theories that specify both the services clients should receive and the factors on which the efficacy of these services is thought to depend. It also depends on the ability to assign many of the projects in a program to one of the theory-based classes without unreasonable strain.

To infer project classes from published descriptions, from interviews with project directors or program developers, or even from professional labels such as "behavior therapy," "psychotherapy," "Montessori preschool," or "Bank Street preschool" is less adequate than basing inferences about classes on the direct observation of project activities. This is mostly because similar sets of activities can occur in projects with quite different labels (House, 1980) and because projects with similar labels can differ fundamentally in what actually occurs (Larson, 1976). In this last context it is important to distinguish between project differences that are more or less fundamental to the definition of a type or class. The ultimate criterion in constructing classes is to assess whether the overlap in fundamental activities is extensive enough to hypothesize that *despite theoretically irrelevant local variations in other activities and in peripheral aspects of the fundamental activities*, a set of projects can be arrived at that constitute instances of a single class. Although evaluators should want as much homogeneity as possible in the activities that define a class, generalizability is enhanced when the instances making up a class are heterogeneous on conceptual irrelevancies that might influence success criteria. But given the low predictive power of most social science theories, we can rarely be sure that all such irrelevancies have been identified or made truly heterogeneous. Hence, the realistic evaluator should look more to whether instances of a postulated

class are *generally* effective than to whether they are invariably effective.

Which research techniques should be used to construct classes and assign particular projects to a given class? When quantitative data on projects are available, a wide variety of relevant multivariate techniques exists, which we discuss later in some detail. But while we recommend using these as part of a strategy, we would be loathe to see them used exclusively. Instead, we prefer that they be complemented by qualitative assessments that critically use the project labels most commonly found in a substantive field, as well as direct observation or practitioner knowledge that can help identify sites where the crucial aspects of a particular project type have been implemented well.

A second problem that could occur when constructing project classes is that too many may be found. However, we are prepared to assume that in most cases the number of concepts practitioners use to organize the delivery of services is restricted by training, experience, and the limits of human inventiveness, even though practitioners do not adopt wholesale the practices they learn elsewhere. Rather, they adapt them to their circumstances (Larson and Agarwala-Rogers, 1977). Nonetheless, we are not alone in assuming that the core of practice usually conforms to one or another set of prescribed practices and arrangements that include many adaptations to fit local circumstances (e.g., Fisher, Penoi, and Wesley, 1980; Haney, 1977).

A third problem is that not all project classes will have identical objectives. Consequently, it will be difficult to arrive at a set of performance criteria that the proponents of each class would consider equally relevant to their project. Indeed, if the selection of performance measures is deliberately or inadvertently tailored to favor one class of project over others, then the evaluation will be criticized as unfair. As an example, consider stressing speed of integration into regular classrooms as a major success criterion for bilingual education projects. This would inevitably predispose an evaluation to discover that transmission—teaching all substantive courses in a child's native language—is the least effective class. Yet children's lower proficiency in English might be offset by a greater proficiency in mathematics because children in transmission classes have always been taught math in their native language, and so have never had to learn it in a language they hardly understand.

Once multiple stakeholder interests have been considered and multiple criteria measured, we no longer have a horse race between project classes with different approaches to solving a common social problem (House *et al.,* 1978). Instead, the metaphor of a yacht race might be more appropriate, for in a yacht race there are multiple prizes depending on the length of the yachts. Following the yacht race analogy, immersion or submersion might best facilitate mainstreaming into regular classrooms, but transmission might teach mathematics better and increase academic motivation by a larger amount. Such findings would force readers to ponder whether transmission's advantages in mathematics and academic motivation outweigh the disadvantage of learning English later and perhaps eventually less well. But most yacht races also have a single overall winner as well as a winner in each class, with the overall winner being the yacht that outperformed the expectations for its class by the largest amount. In having multiple winners *and* a single winner, the comparison of project classes is very much like the *Consumer Reports* model of product evaluation in which multiple criteria are used to provide knowledge about options with similar, but not necessarily identical, aims. Some cars win for gas mileage, luggage space, or repair record, while one model typically stands out from the others in terms of the way its benefits accumulate across multiple criteria. Yet no one need accept the judgment about an overall winner if they can justify assigning unique utilities to particular criteria.

Assessing the Effectiveness and Impact of Classes of Elements

Some leverage is offered by information that identifies effective classes of elements that occur or could be implemented across many of the projects within a program. The elements that constitute a class can often take many forms, as when time on task is measured or manipulated as the number of school days per year, the amount of homework, the length of school days, the number of study breaks, the degree of application in class, and so on. However, element types can also be more concrete than time on task. Consider the neighborhood nonprofessionals who work as aides in local health departments and hospitals where they may be used in community outreach and health education efforts, in rat control drives, and in many other quite disparate health projects. Would it not be helpful to evaluate the efficacy of such paraprofessionals across many different health projects to try to assess the kinds of tasks that they can and cannot

FIGURE 1
Two Follow Through Models

HIGH/SCOPE MODEL	BEHAVIORAL ANALYSIS MODEL
Teacher and aide are available ↓	Teacher, aide and parents are present ↓
Individual instruction provided ↓	Individual instruction ↓
Sequenced materials available ↓	Sequenced materials available ↓
Child plans work ↓	Child exhibits appropriate behavior ↓
Plan discussed with teacher ↓	Teacher/aides recognize behavior as appropriate ↓
Child carries out work ↓	Child receives tokens ↓
Child evaluates own work in group	Child spends tokens on special activities
Learns language skills ／＼ Learns intended concepts	↓
Child's mental growth increases	Child takes pleasure in learning (to decrease external reinforcement) ↓
	Child learns material ↓
	Careful record keeping of child's learning.

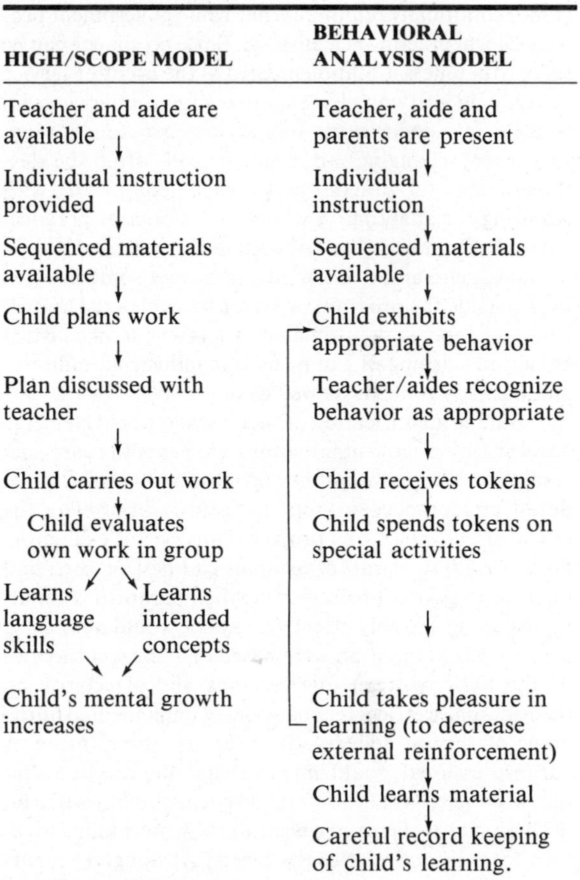

SOURCE: Stallings, 1973, p. 153 and 166.

perform well? The Follow Through Program presents another example. Two Follow Through models derived from Stallings (1973) are illustrated in Fig. 1. Although quite different, they nonetheless share some common elements including the presence of aides, individual instruction, and sequenced instructional materials. These are elements *that education theorists repeatedly reinvent,* and their use should be evaluated so that conclusions can be reached about the contexts in which they are more or less useful.

From the perspective of ameliorating social problems through program improvement, identifying classes of elements that are both effective and transferable has a major advantage. Theorists of implementation like Berman (1980), Bardach (1977), Fullan (1982) and Williams (1980) continually remind us that while government proposes, local practitioners dispose. Since no change can be successful unless it is implemented at the point of service delivery, identifying elements that practitioners can introduce into their work should improve functioning. Moreover, changing an element will often be less threatening to practitioners when compared with adopting (or adapting) a whole new model of practice. An added bonus is that knowledge about a class of elements is generalized knowledge that can sometimes be used outside the program or sector for which the knowledge was generated. If time on task is a general cause of enhanced learning, it can be used in industrial, military, and business contexts as well as in schools.

But the identification of successful types of elements has a major disadvantage. Many elements that are successful in achieving what they propose to do can be introduced into practice without necessarily improving the global effectiveness of a project. Thus even if evaluators discovered how paraprofessionals can best be used and then induced some projects to use their paraprofessionals in such demonstrably effective ways, it would not help if the projects in question were based on incorrect theories of the links between interventions and effects or on theories that were correct but poorly implemented at the point of service delivery. In either of these instances paraprofessionals could improve what they do. But what they do would have little effect on client outcomes if, say, the majority of clients of a drug abuse project failed to return for a second visit to the center. Although elements constitute projects, improvements in elements will only improve the overall effectiveness of a project if the elements are necessary or sufficient for project-level effects or if they are the only elements in the project to malfunction. Some elements undoubtedly meet these specifications, and a crucial part of the evaluation policymaker's role is to explicate such classes of elements so that they can be sensitively evaluated.

Assessing Effectiveness and Impact Criteria with Specific Elements in Individual Projects

Managers and service deliverers who work in projects often want to know how well elements in their particular project are being implemented, for knowing this can help them pinpoint where performance needs improving. But it is not clear how much they need formal evaluation for this task. They have their own impressions about what is going wrong, and colleagues typically proffer theirs.

Managers and practitioners at the local level may also want to know whether a new practice they have heard about in other settings would be effective in the specific setting where they work. An answer to this question logically requires testing whether the potential new element is more effective than current practice or other feasible alternatives to current practice. While it would often be possible to conduct such tests at the project level—especially if elements are changed that do not disequilibrate individual practice in general (Glaser, 1976)—it is not clear how often project officials actually request information about the efficacy of novel elements. Certainly, they do not seem to request it often in community mental health settings (Cook and Shadish, 1982), though they may sometimes in education (Boruch *et al.*, 1980).

Central program managers are rarely interested in studies of elements at a single site unless the elements promise a particularly large impact and might be inexpensively transferred elsewhere. If so, a demonstration project may result to test whether different elements with overlapping aims have different consequences. When a demonstration involves testing different variants of a single element, the element in question is likely to be only one of the many links that constitute the causal theory of a project, and its utility cannot be divorced from the other links. For instance, a local health director might seek to discover a more effective way to screen people for hypertension. But improving this element in a health center would not have much effect on the local incidence of hypertension since identified hypertensives are not likely to comply with suggested medical regimens (Weinstein and Stason, 1976). From the perspective of central program managers, only a few elements loom important.

For reasons enumerated earlier it seems that few in-house evaluators are willing or able to conduct the cause-probing studies most likely to discover successful elements—causal modeling or some form of experimentation (Cook and Shadish, 1982; David, 1981). Evaluators external to a project rarely conduct element-level studies in a single local project, though they do examine single elements across many projects in order to aggregate the resulting information into program-level judgments. But these higher-order judgments provide little or no feedback about individual projects. It does not seem reasonable to us either to expect that external researchers will often be called upon to evaluate seriously elements in a single project or that many local projects will suddenly transform themselves into self-critical organizations that aggressively seek to improve their functioning through evaluation (Wildavsky, 1979). For all the foregoing reasons we postulate that causal studies of elements within a single project are not likely to have much payoff for evaluation policy.

Conclusions About Sources of Leverage in Evaluation Questions

We are prepared to assume that program improvement can come about through changes at the program, project, and element levels. When the evaluand is a social program, information will play a useful role in ameliorating the underlying social problem only if a genuine need for the program exists, if the theory underlying program design is correct, and if activities take place in most of the program-funded projects that either are consonant with the theory or are inadvertently effective in meeting needs. Since evaluations of a program depend on generalizations abstracted from an analysis of multiple projects, monitoring a heterogeneous sample of projects is likely to provide program managers with a realistic sense of which services are reaching their intended beneficiaries, how well these services are being implemented, and what their current costs are. Also, monitoring will provide clues to practical actions that can be taken to improve targeting, implementation, and cost control. Thus for programs where little descriptive data is routinely collected, monitoring may have important practical consequences.

It is much less clear whether significant short-term leverage is provided by evaluations at the program level that emphasize effectiveness and impact criteria. This is mostly because programs are politically impacted and decisions about them are largely made on political grounds. The last is especially true of decisions about whether a program should exist but is probably also true of changes in the program funding level.

Although programs rarely die, there is some turnover of projects within most programs. This creates potential leverage if studies of manipulable and transferable classes of projects can be used to modify the mix of projects in a program. The crucial assumptions on which the utility of this leverage point depends are, first, that the rate of project turnover is reasonably high, and, second, that central program managers have some control over which new projects are added to a program and which are dropped. If either of these assumptions is false, knowledge about effective project classes will not improve the mix of projects within a program.

When the evaluation of project classes is conducted in explanatory fashion, it has the further advantage that

it may furnish local administrators and service providers with clues about practical elements that may be successfully introduced into their own work. Focussing on the identification of successful and transferable project elements will also provide useful "fallback" knowledge should it be more difficult to discover project classes than is implied by the restricted set of categorical labels used to describe practice in nearly all service sectors. However, for assessment of the implementability and effectiveness of individual elements to be useful in modifying overall project performance, the elements in question cannot be trivial. But since many elements are quite trivial, evaluators need a practical way to identify those that may be either necessary or sufficient for project effectiveness and may also be relevant to a wide variety of project settings (e.g., time on task as a means to improve educational achievement).

METHODS FOR STUDYING EVALUATION QUESTIONS WITH GREATER LEVERAGE

We turn now to an analysis of the methods most applicable to the major leverage points identified above—namely, monitoring ongoing programs and identifying effective classes of projects and elements that promise to be transferable across many of the projects in a program. We present several methods relevant to each leverage point, noting their strengths and weaknesses from both technical and practical perspectives. The latter concern mostly budget, time lines, and the expertise of available evaluation staffs.

METHODS FOR MONITORING CLIENTS AND IMPLEMENTATION IN AN ONGOING PROGRAM

Monitoring serves several functions for improving decision makers' control at the program level, each of which also applies at the project level for those administrators and service providers who want to rely on more formal sources of knowledge than those they currently use. Where little is already known, monitoring will help central decision makers understand what happens throughout the program in the many sites they can never visit; it should also help detect anticipated and unanticipated problems that occur with the targeting, quality, and costs of services; and finally, when the same problem is repeatedly identified, steps can be taken to recommend solutions. Some of the recommended solutions may be obvious from what is currently known in common sense, professional practice, or social science theory. In other cases recommendations will be less obvious, and more thinking will be needed to generate novel solutions with which to experiment in the future.

As with all types of evaluation, monitoring requires choosing publicly justified standards of comparison, performance criteria, performance measures, and techniques for synthesizing results. Standards of comparison are often derived from (1) norms, as when the Environmental Protection Agency (EPA) determines that a numerically specified level of pollution is "unacceptably high" implying that obtained levels should be lower than this standard; from (2) past experience, as when evaluators estimate whether the crime rate has risen over the same month last year and the implication once again is that it should be reduced; or from (3) intergroup comparisons, as when life expectancy data show that blacks die sooner than whites (DHHS, 1981) and the implication here is that the gap should be narrowed or eliminated.

The performance criteria used in monitoring are invariably value-laden (Ezrahi, 1978) and depend on a priori judgments. For instance, attempts to measure how many people are poor depend on many assumptions, including what percentage of family income should be spent on food and what on other needs (DeNeufville, 1975). Evaluators need to explicate the values implicit in each criterion and standard of comparison they consider. Where possible, they should subject each possible choice to critical examination from a variety of perspectives provided by persons other than members of an evaluation team. Having briefly dealt with criteria and standards, we turn now to issues of measurement that arise in monitoring.

Monitoring by Means of Indicators from State or National Archives

Many federal, state, and local agencies routinely collect data on such community-level indicators as age, sex, ethnicity, labor force participation, health status, average property value, home ownership rate, and crime rate. Such measures are primarily intended to indicate the extent to which recognized problems are becoming more or less serious. It is also hoped that in rare cases the indicators will detect new problems as they emerge.

Since indicators should be communicable, difficulty arises whenever the definition of an indicator does not closely correspond with the ordinary language meanings implicit in the construct that is supposedly being indicat-ed. For instance, official measures of poverty are based on the absolute level of material well-being, although ordinary language may also connote "a relative condition, or a state of mind" (DeNeufville, 1975). Since it is impossible for a single measure to capture all the connotations of a construct from ordinary language, and since each measure inevitably contains variance irrelevant to the construct (Cook and Campbell, 1979), multiple indicators are required for monitoring. There are now, for example, several indicators of the money supply because legitimate controversies arose among economists about how to conceptualize the liquidity of funds.

Indicators should also meet standard psychometric requirements. They should, for instance, be reliable, equivalent for different social groups, and distributed so that floor or ceiling effects do not arise (Elinson, 1974). They should also be flexible and relevant to changing social circumstances. For example, there is now no need to include the cost of buggy whips in the Consumer Price Index (CPI). Indeed, the change in the CPI in 1982 to de-emphasize housing costs was a response to the criticism that such costs had played a disproportionate role in the aggregate CPI, which was used to set increases in Social Security even though the elderly who receive such payments are more likely than others to own their own homes and so are less affected by housing costs (Gordon, 1980). Indicator data should also be carefully collected, and anyone seeking to use such data is well advised to check how the basic data were collected. Sechrest (1984) has documented too many instances of sophisticated analyses conducted on data that were invented or were so sloppily collected as to be worthless. Finally, whenever the data from formal reporting systems are used to allocate resources, the possibility of corruption arises. Celebrated examples are described by Blau (1954), Cochran (1978) and Campbell (1975). The last of these has even noted how the use of body counts during the Vietnam War led some soldiers to kill civilians in order to advance their careers. When an indicator leads to behavior that corrupts its intended function, it is obviously of little use in evaluation.

The appeal of national indicator data is that they can often be made available quickly and inexpensively, and they sometimes provide useful background information about programs or policy. For example, national data on the unemployment rate over several years may, when carefully interpreted, shed general light on the status of whatever mix of programs had been undertaken to stimulate the national economy. However, the relevance of the data for evaluating *specific* programs and projects is limited. For example, while changes in the national unemployment rate could be related to the performance of job-training programs in general, to draw inferences about a particular program requires disentangling its effects from those of other job-relevant programs or market forces that may have influenced employment. Archives tend to contain data that are too distal for most stakeholders' purposes. Indeed, they are rarely disaggregated finely enough. Thus if the managers of a program for youth employment wanted to examine unemployment among their target population—urban males under twenty-one living in a particular city who did not graduate from high school and had been in the program long enough to have been influenced by it—they would not be helped by archival data at the state or national level. Such data do not refer to unemployment for so specific a group. At most, we might be able to get data on males under twenty-one for certain larger cities.

However, social indicators can help detect problems worth further attention, especially if some kinds of disaggregation are possible. If the indicators suggested that unemployment was declining among Hispanic youth but not black youth, evaluators might then choose to turn their attention to discovering whether special obstacles exist in training projects where blacks are the major clients. Or if an indicator allows for disaggregation by geographical area, as with many indicators of health status, it might be possible to monitor individual projects whose catchment area roughly corresponds with the area for which the statistics are reported (Campbell, 1976). To do this might help in locating projects that are performing especially well or poorly so that they can be studied in greater detail. However, fulfilling such functions assumes that state or national data can be disaggregated by group or neighborhood characteristics and that there is a very close correspondence between the persons surveyed in the data-collection effort and the actual recipients of program services. Since these assumptions are not often met, our belief is that state and national archives will rarely be relevant to the evaluation of specific programs.

Using Local Management Information Systems (MIS)

A second form of monitoring has emerged in MIS kept by projects, the data from which are sometimes sent for central storage at the program level. Management information systems are becoming increasingly computer-based (Attkisson *et al.,* 1978) and, unlike social indicators, are directly relevant to project-level operation. This

is because they typically include information about clients and not whole geographic areas and because the data refer to such important constructs as client numbers and characteristics, the dates and nature of services provided, and the sums of money billed. Less common in such local systems is information about effects or impacts. However, data relevant to effects and impacts do sometimes occur, as with achievement data in school district records or birth weights in WIC nutrition project files, each of which can be sent in to program headquarters.

When it is locally believed that the data might be used to influence project welfare, an obvious potential problem arises with MIS—the possibility that corrupt data will enter the system or be sent from the system to the program central office (Cochran, 1978). A second set of problems arises in creating a profile of program activities or accomplishments. To do this logically requires aggregating across the projects in a program. When all of the projects provide valid data, a census results, and a program can be described from its parts, though mail questionnaires or site visits to a random sample of projects may be required to collect information not in the reporting system. To create a program profile in this way depends on the absence of bias in who files reports and on uniformity in how the information is reported across projects in a program. Many programs try to mandate uniformity. For example, the Department of Education (DE) requires all school districts to report in the same way about educational achievement among students in compensatory education projects, and DE has even developed technical assistance centers to help school districts that have difficulty in this task (Boruch *et al.,* 1980). Yet the reporting of student achievement data is still far from uniform, though enough similarity is apparent to make the data useful for many purposes if they are critically handled and some types of data are more likely to be uniform than others (e.g., the number of people attending a school and the total amount billed to the state). But these do not exhaust all the services delivered; nor are they relevant to issues about the quality or appropriateness of services, or about the effects of services on client functioning or on the social systems with which clients interact.

In cases where the data are neither comparable across projects nor centrally archived, program-level inferences depend on detecting problems of implementation that repeatedly occur across a purposive (i.e., formally nonrepresentative) but heterogeneous sample of projects that have good records and are willing to make them available. However, for many statisticians this type of sampling permits weak inferences about the program at large; and from a practical perspective it takes longer to get data from projects themselves than from some central archive to which the projects have already sent information.

Management information systems are probably more useful for providing feedback to individual projects than to program officials. Thus when they were assisting the new superintendent of a large school district, Bickell and Cooley (1982) obtained districtwide achievement data and noted that many children were leaving the third grade without knowing how to read and write and that attendance was atypically low at some schools. The information served to narrow and focus attention on some grades but not others and on some schools but not others. It also led to action recommendations that were later implemented and resulted in better reading by the third grade and higher attendance at the problem schools. All this happened because the external evaluators used districtwide MIS data to detect some of the more serious and common operational problems in the school district.

Program Audits

When compared with setting up a new MIS in all the projects that receive funds from a program, audits can be brief, focused, and relatively inexpensive. They also help locate potential problems of cost, management, and service provision in a sample of projects and can generate suggestions about better internal controls.The audit concept has recently expanded beyond the context where external accountants review financial records. It now includes any method of making project staff accountable to central office management (Sawyer, 1979). In the public sector this means that inspector generals, the General Accounting Office (GAO), and state audit departments now function on behalf of legislatures to maintain and enhance the interests of the general public in programs and projects (Mosher, 1979), reducing the difference between audits and evaluation. Indeed, GAO now has an Division of Methodology and Program Evaluation. But despite this obfuscation of functions, accounting for expenditures and ensuring their appropriateness still play larger roles in auditing than in most other forms of evaluation where, if financial data play any role at all, it is as a means for characterizing total expenditures or for conducting cost-effectiveness and cost-benefit analysis. Finances do not serve in these other forms of evaluation as a means of holding individual projects accountable for

how much has been spent, what has been purchased, and whether regulations have been followed in soliciting bids and paying staff.

A casebook of examples by the GAO (Kloman, 1979) reveals several key features of good auditing practice. It is not considered necessary for auditors to be specialists in substantive areas related to the program under investigation, for good management and financial practices are considered universal. But when substantive knowledge is required, auditors are urged to supplement their critical review of documents at a sample of projects with the advice of expert consultants. When the documentation at a project is not comprehensive or trustworthy enough, auditors are also invited to survey recipients, conduct site visits, observe clients directly, and measure physical output. A case in point is the GAO investigation of fraud in the National Grain Inspection System. Because Congress wanted a complete investigation from the farm to the foreign buyer, the GAO administered questionnaires to a sample of farmers and county grain elevator operators, and it also tested the amount and quality of grain before, during, and after unloading at the foreign ports. The GAO also held in-depth discussions with grain importers in nine foreign countries, interviewed state and federal inspectors, and studied the Canadian grain marketing and inspection system to provide a basis of comparison with the American system (Manchir, Goldsmith, and Kloman, 1979).

Audits are mostly used to describe how projects are internally organized and how money has been disbursed. Such description can help identify and publicize particularly grave or recurrent problems, as is apparent when the decision to audit occurs because of public outcries, media investigations, or internal government suspicions. But the decision to audit particular projects or clients can also reflect routine operating procedures that are not triggered by specific suspicions. When done on a random basis with a sufficient number of projects, routine selection generates a program profile whose sampling error is known and permits individual instances of irregularity to be detected. These irregularities can then be publicized in the hope of deterring administrators at other projects who do not follow regulations or might even be tempted into irregularity. When used in this way, program audits resemble the procedures used by the Internal Revenue Service (IRS) to audit individual tax returns. That is, the IRS chooses some individuals for closer inspection on a random basis and others because clues in the returns or knowledge from informants suggest that a malpractice may have occurred. The review of randomly selected cases permits a small audit staff with limited resources to detect and publicize poor management practices, perhaps inducing some project officials to adhere to regulations *in case* auditing/evaluation should take place later.

The major problem with audits requiring site visits to a random sample of projects is that the visits are likely to be short if the number of sampled projects has to be "large". Consequently, subtle problems in the targeting and implementation of services may not be detected, and auditors may not develop a subtle appreciation of possible side effects. Our guess is that audits are more useful when financial questions are paramount and strong suspicion already exists about particular problems in particular projects. If subtler knowledge is required, methods are called for that require more intensive on-site observation, making the research expense correspondingly higher per site. On a fixed evaluation budget this means fewer sites and the possibility that a program profile may be less stable.

Qualitative Methods

In programs where little is known about the nature of the clients actually reached and about the services actually delivered, participant observation by substantive experts will provide an in-depth description of local activities. For instance, Nathan and his colleagues (1977, 1981) recruited about twenty social scientists who had previously studied particular local governments and asked them to describe and comment on how block grants were implemented in the cities they knew. Such grants give local governments considerable discretion over how funds are spent, and politicians and foundation officials wanted to learn how the money would be disbursed (see also Dommel *et al.,* 1978, 1980). Each observer used his own observation, whatever documents he could get hold of, and his own sources inside and outside local government to probe how much was spent for different purposes (e.g., for capital improvements versus social services), to learn how local government functions, and to assess how local political power configurations had changed because of the new system for awarding grants. Nathan's use of local informants with acknowledged expertise in the politics of the cities studied strikes us as an important step toward understanding how the extremely heterogeneous block grant programs actually operate (Eggers, 1981) and what some of their planned and unplanned effects might be. But since the focus was largely budgetary, administrative, and political, infor-

mation was noticeably lacking on the criteria with which social program evaluators are traditionally concerned—specification of the services delivered to clients and of their effectiveness. (We presume, however, that the social scientist observers probably formed grounded hypotheses about these matters, but they were not a major focus.)

Hendricks (1981) has developed a system called service delivery assessment (SDA) that emphasizes observers gaining information about the quality of local service delivery in heterogeneous social service programs. The SDA involves a preevaluative assessment phase in which the crucial service delivery issues are provisionally identified through documents, interviews, and a small number of pilot site visits. Then data gatherers visit a purposively selected sample of local agencies where they observe and interview clients, service providers, and agency managers in order to "see" the agency from all perspectives. Part of the purpose of the visit is to probe the issues identified at the preevaluative stage, but part is also to let unforeseen issues emerge. After data collection the investigators come together and try to synthesize their impressions in order to arrive at a consensus about how services are being delivered and how the service delivery can be improved. These deliberations are then summarized and debated with policymakers within five or six months of beginning the assessment, making for a more rapid provision of feedback than is the case with Nathan's method. In Hendrick's case he and his staff report to the Secretary of Health and Human Services and have no personal stake in the action programs they evaluate. However, the logic of his procedures transfers readily to any sector where officials are in danger of being so insulated from the local level that irrealism may result (Blau, 1954). What is not clear at this time is how implementable Hendrick's procedures would be if the data collection and integration were not directly undertaken by agency personnel. In many agencies the size of the evaluation staff and the limited capacity for rapid staff changes may require that contracts for descriptive evaluation be let to outsiders. How such outside help would affect access to projects, the speed of conducting evaluations, and the credibility—and hence use—of the evaluation results from SDA are issues worth further exploration.

With SDA the purposive sampling of a heterogeneous collection of projects and the interviewing of different stakeholder groups at each site help discriminate common problems of implementation from those that are restricted to a few visible sites or are perceived to be problematic by a single stakeholder group. Bringing together observers with intensive experience at different local projects also helps generate a more informed and potentially critical debate about what can be done to solve identified problems. The validity of conclusions about problems and solutions depends in part on the nature of the projects sampled. For some purposes evaluators would like to sample projects at random from the program list, while for other purposes they would like to sample at random from within strata—for example, from within strata containing sites that are known or suspected to be among the very best or worst in terms of causing changes in more important outcomes. But while sensitive to different rationales for stratification, Hendricks is adamant that random selection is not required at the last level of sampling. Instead, he advocates that projects be chosen purposively rather than with known probability, subject to the important restriction that the sampled sites are heterogeneous in size, location, and other factors. His belief is that the costs of random selection are not worth the marginal decrement in bias and precision that the procedure offers.

A study of science instruction in high schools (Stake and Easley, 1978) provides a third example of monitoring which uses data that are more qualitative than quantitative. This example, designed to let crucial issues emerge rather than to probe prespecified questions, involved sending participant observers to schools. They spent many months there developing their own scheme for describing events and inferring their impact. Unstructured research of this type is most useful when little prior knowledge is available about the issues worth probing or when there is reason to suspect that contextual variables of which no one is yet aware may play a powerful role in mediating the most important outcomes. Under such conditions intensive participant observation at a small number of sites is probably more useful than other forms of monitoring because it makes fewer initial assumptions.

However, on a per-site basis such studies can be expensive; moreover, the choice of method is sometimes associated with an ideological belief in the power of contextual variables to influence the provision and effectiveness of services. Such ideology, with or without the small-sample problem that arises from high costs per site, can paralyze the process of integrating findings across sites. Indeed, in the study in question the ethnographer/observers were so convinced of the uniqueness of the schools they each visited that no generalizations could be made about the amount, quality, and relevance of science instruction in the schools. The picture painted was of between-school variance so extreme that it made no sense to construct common classes of projects or elements. Even the few commonly noted elements were held to exist in such unique contexts that their meaning differed to each observer of the science classes. Such an inability to generalize does not inevitably result from studies using intensive on-site observation, and common problems of implementation can be discovered across many of the sampled projects. However, some commitments to ethnography may create an intellectual climate that is hostile to generalizing across local differences that are inevitably there and that help explain behavior in the setting studied but that do not help in the task of identifying transferable practices that might improve program performance.

Activities Surveys

Where high-quality information is needed to profile implementation, costs, service providers, and service recipients in a broadly dispersed population, activities surveys are warranted. These are telephone or, more normally, mail questionnaires designed to measure the overt and covert goals of projects, to analyze the rationale for activities, to describe the project-level activities that actually occur, to identify the client groups actually served, to estimate the costs per client, and to create a provisional model of project activities. Of all monitoring methods, the activities survey is potentially the most useful for achieving a large random sample of sites, the data from which can help generate valid program profiles and can help construct a typology of project classes. The activities survey has these advantages because the mail or telephone survey is usually less expensive per site than audits or qualitative observational methods and so more projects can be sampled, and because the survey is also more comprehensive in the information it can generate when compared with MIS or social indicator archives.

To achieve a national profile, one could collect data about project activities from a census of projects. This is not always feasible and is rarely desirable if all that is desired is to create a program profile (as opposed to, say, categorizing each project as belonging to a certain class of project). A better option for creating a program profile is to select a substantial random sample of projects. In this respect, consider a study of cost containment in hospitals. There are about 7000 hospitals in the United States, most of which are trying in some way to contain costs (Daughety *et al.,* 1979). If we surveyed only 10 percent of them, we would still have about 700 on which to create a national profile or even to begin identifying the different classes or types of cost containment strategies being implemented. If we had strongly grounded a priori expectations about the classes, we could supplement the random selection by stratifying on factors highly correlated with presumed class membership. Stratification would enable the evaluator to test prespecified ideas about project classes, reducing the dependence on techniques that are more inductive.

While evaluators have to use whatever means they can to become intimately acquainted with what actually happens at the project level, our suggestion is that activities surveys will often provide the desired comprehensiveness in sampling and measurement at relatively low cost. However, it should not take place unless there has been some pilot research using document review, intensive interviews with a small sample of persons who are particularly knowledgeable about local circumstances, and some pilot visits to observe operations at a small number of projects (e.g., Hendricks, 1981). Such pilot work will improve a questionnaire in many ways, foremost among which is that the evaluator will become more sensitive to local-level responses that may reflect bias or ignorance on the part of respondents. After all, if administrators respond, they are likely to outline what is supposed to happen in their project, and they may not be well informed about all that actually does happen. Pilot work is crucial if activities surveys are to go to the right respondents, if the information they contain is to be grounded in real local events, and if the responses are not to be corrupted.

General Methodological Issues When Monitoring Programs

Considerations in sampling projects. Since the evaluation of a program requires aggregating observations across projects, it is inevitable that projects will usually have to be sampled in order to draw conclusions about a program. When resources are limited, evaluators face a choice between the intensive, prolonged study of a small number of sites and the less extensive study of a larger number of sites. When the creation of a program profile is paramount, the latter strategy is clearly preferable, especially when there is a clear consensus about the information most worth collecting. When the emphasis is on detecting problems of implementation or arriving at grounded hypotheses about possible side effects, inten-

sive studies are initially preferable at a smaller number of heterogeneous sites. In the best of possible worlds evaluators would move freely from the more intensive study of a small number of sites to the less intensive study of a larger number, proceeding in a programmatic fashion that would be optimal for generating an extensive program profile that detailed common problems of implementation and allowed evaluators to define project classes and to assign some of the individual projects to each of the classes. In practice, however, neither the time nor money is usually available for such programmatic research, and a choice has to be made along the intensive/extensive, small-sample/large-sample axes.

Textbooks on sampling theory point out that if we want to generalize to an entity (say a particular social program), we have to sample projects at random from a list of all program-funded projects. Such random selection can be quite elaborate, especially if multiple stratification and clustering takes place; but at all stages the selection of projects has to be random. Yet, in the basic sciences it is rare for random selection to be used in testing the generalizability of propositions (St. Pierre and Cook, 1984). Rather, they are tested by examining whether a particular relationship is found across many time intervals, in many different settings, and despite all the different irrelevancies associated with how constructs are manipulated or measured in individual studies. Random selection occurs to estimate how large a relationship is; whereas sampling for heterogeneity occurs in order to assess how robust a relationship is across a set of irrelevancies. The greater the heterogeneity in the irrelevancies known or suspected to be related to outcome measures, the more confident we can be that we are dealing with a robust relationship. However, we are not likely to know its average size in any formal sense. We are more likely to have a reasonable estimate of the likelihood of an association with a particular sign.

It is not clear whether random sampling is ever needed if problem detection is the major purpose of monitoring. A heterogeneous set of sites is usually adequate. But since random selection also creates heterogeneity within limits imposed by the population variance, it is one of the procedures that creates heterogeneity. But relative to purposive sampling, random selection can entail practical drawbacks largely because of the marginally greater time and money involved in drawing up a sampling frame. Moreover, participation in research can rarely be coerced, and much random selection occurs from populations of projects and clients who are willing to be studied rather than from target populations of research interest. For problem detection Hendricks (1981) clearly believes that the marginal gains in bias and precision to which random selection leads are not worth their additional cost, largely because an unbiased estimate of the target population is rarely possible and because no precise unbiased estimate of the prevalence of implementation problems is needed. Rather, the need is to identify problems that lower the likelihood of effects and that occur so often and so obviously that they stand out once one begins to look for them.

A census or random sampling is desirable, however, if the evaluator has already provisionally identified project classes and is looking for sites that conform most closely with the activities defining a class. However, if random sampling is not feasible for this purpose, a purposive sample of projects would usually still be acceptable. The rationale for selecting a heterogeneous sample—whether through random or purposive sampling—is paramount when little prior evidence exists about the nature of classes or the identification of particular examples of each class. When such knowledge is already available, sampling is easiest of all. One goes only to relevant sites (St. Pierre and Cook, 1984), picking them at random if many instances of each class have been found.

Selecting qualitative methods.   We have previously advocated the use of qualitative methods for describing program operations. However, some evaluation theorists have recently questioned the conventional wisdom that such methods are inferior to quantitative techniques for causal inference (e.g., Guba and Lincoln, 1981; Patton, 1978). Such scholars note the frequency in the past with which quantitative methods, primarily experimental and quasi-experimental, have failed to reach causal conclusions that were beyond dispute on methodological grounds, and they contend that it is now time to explore more qualitative methods of causal analysis. The implication is that methods for describing program operations can be used for learning about the effects and impact of programs, making artificial the distinction between analyses of clients and implementation versus analyses of effects and impacts.

This advocacy has been legitimized by Campbell's (1975) apparent revocation of the hard-line against one-shot case studies taken in Campbell and Stanley (1966), for Campbell now argues that case studies can under

some conditions provide strong causal inferences. His argument is based on an analogy with the degrees-of-freedom concept in statistics. He contends that case studies usually generate multiple sources of cause-relevant evidence that, when linked to background knowledge from experience, prior research, or grounded theory, can permit all the identified threats to internal validity to be ruled out. As part of this revocation, Cook and Campbell (1979) cite the hypothetical case of anthropological research on the effects of introducing an axe into a remote jungle tribe, contending that cause can be inferred if wood is suddenly cut in ways that are widely regarded locally as novel and that are commensurate with the shape of an axe but not with the shape of the implements previously used. Also, the remote jungle location specified in the example makes it unlikely that other technological advances for woodcutting could have become available at the same time the axe was introduced.

An epistemological framework much like Campbell's buttresses Scriven's (1976) thinking about the relevance of *modus operandi* methods in evaluation. Scriven (1976) uses the analogy of the detective who, at the scene of a crime, carefully notes all the specific details associated with the event to be explained. She then relates those details to the preferred *modus operandi* of known criminals, ruling out some of the contenders as causal agents because their preferred way of operating differs from the pattern used in the crime under investigation. This list is further refined through interviews and record searches to find out who has credible alibis until, it is hoped, only a single contender remains. Of course, several contenders may still remain even after all reasonable efforts have been extended. But even in this case the level of uncertainty will have been reduced over what it originally was. Guba and Lincoln (1981) use investigative journalists rather than detectives as a stimulus to thinking about how causal inferences are made. They invoke the journalists' use of networks of contacts with known credibility, their persistent questioning of sources, the requirement that all information be validated across more than one source, and the further requirement that it pass the critical scrutiny of senior (and experienced) editorial staff.

In the relevant work of Campbell, Scriven, and Guba and Lincoln, the starting point is a clearly demarcated event or effect for which a cause has to be found (Straw *et al.,* 1982). This is quite different from the modal case in evaluation where the starting point is an independent variable whose effects are to be discovered. Evaluators are more prone to ask: "What are the effects of Program X on A, B, and C?" than to ask: "What caused the observed change in Y?" Moreover, it is rare in evaluation for the major outcome variables (e.g., changes in recidivism, academic achievement, or drug arrests) to be singly, determined. Multiple causes are more common that operate at the same time, making it difficult to keep their unique contributions distinct.

In the monitoring context hardly anyone would dispute that qualitative methods are useful for generating hypotheses about causal agents, for outlining possible explanatory processes, and for uncovering more obvious project effects. This is particularly true when clients, service providers, and managers can be interviewed and public records critically appraised. In a similar vein, good investigative journalists probably learn to distinguish the testimonials of the interested or the duped from the more valid testimonials of persons with firsthand knowledge of a project who have critically reflected on their experiences. Nonetheless, some empty testimonials will go undetected; some persons offering honest testimony may not know how they have changed or may not be able to distinguish among the many possible causes of change they have validly noted; and few respondents can precisely estimate how much an intervention has influenced them. Moreover, the factors that facilitate causal inference in case studies—abrupt effects with single causes and causes with known *modus operandi*—rarely occur in social programming. Consequently, while the arguments in favor of case study methods complementing quantitative methods are compelling, the arguments for qualitative methods substituting for quantitative ones are more questionable (see Reichardt and Cook, 1979, 1981). This is not to deny, though, that qualitative methods will normally facilitate inferences about causal agents by uncovering some possible unanticipated effects and by making some interpretations of the cause seem implausible. Indeed, in a small minority of cases only a single cause will remain in contention and strong causal inference will be warranted.

This discussion illustrates three different functions of causal analysis to which qualitative methods speak with different degrees of probable success. The first concerns whether the usual techniques for monitoring will regularly allow the evaluator to examine client and implementation criteria and from these draw inferences about effects. The answer is asymmetrical. Where compelling evidence indicates poor targeting or low levels of implementation, negative conclusions about intended effectiveness will usually be warranted. But where the evidence indicates successful targeting and implementation, causal conclusions about changes in effectiveness and impact criteria are only warranted when considerable independent information exists indicating that the services in question are effective whenever they are delivered. The second function concerns the extent to which qualitative methods can identify the causes of problems in the delivery of program services. This identification depends on the extent to which critical analysis of the observed effects reveals a pattern so unique that only one causal agent fits the data. If this does not occur, the pattern of effects should be at least unique enough that some possible causes can be ruled out and a choice can be made from among the remainder using plausibility judgments based on logic, the existing literature, and practitioner knowledge. The final causal issue concerns the extent to which qualitative methods help suggest remedies to the organizational problems they reveal. Much depends here on how clearly the problem is diagnosed and on the availability of well-tested remedies in common sense, the substantive literature, and professional practice. Where no remedies are available in these sources, diagnosing the problem will not suggest a remedy; where many are available, the reverse should be true. Our guess is that the qualitative methods used in monitoring will usually do better in advancing a restricted number of possible remedial actions than in thrusting a single action to the fore as the only one known to be both effective and implementable in the projects requiring amelioration. Nonetheless, when action has to be taken in a hurry, the partial editing that monitoring provides should create a better justification for what to do than having no study at all, particularly when the reasons for selecting the action are publicly detailed and withstand critical scrutiny.

IDENTIFYING CLASSES OF PROJECTS AND ELEMENTS THAT ARE GENERALLY SUCCESSFUL BY IMPORTANT CRITERIA

Identifying successful classes requires first determining the classes represented in a program and then evaluating them according to a heterogeneous set of success criteria. From this results the evaluation model preferred by *Consumer Reports,* Campbell (1969), Scriven (1980), and all cost-effectiveness analysts (e.g., Levin, 1983) in which different ways of achieving comparable ends are contrasted. As with nearly all method choices in the social sciences, many techniques are available for inferring classes and then evaluating their effects, with each involving different trade-offs of time, resources, precision, and staff familiarity. We detail some relevant techniques below, beginning with those that require fewest resources.

Literature Reviews, Especially Meta-analysis

It is sometimes possible to secure information from many completed studies of projects in order to infer classes, assign projects to classes, assess the success of each project, aggregate the results across all the projects in a particular class, and then to compare the average results across the classes. This is basically the procedure followed by meta-analysts (Glass, McGaw, and Smith, 1981). They first determine the population of conceptually relevant studies (e.g., of psychotherapy). Then they divide the psychotherapies into types (e.g, behavioral, psychoanalytic). Next, they develop effect sizes for each relevant study or comparison. They do this through a standardization procedure that computes the difference between treatment and control group means and then divides this difference by a standard deviation measure that puts each difference onto the same standardized scale irrespective of the original metric. Smith and Glass (1977) followed this general procedure when they located psychotherapy studies, used multidimensional scaling to create classes of psychotherapy, computed mean effect sizes for each class based on data from all the relevant studies, and then contrasted the difference between the means for each class. Their conclusion was that while the average psychotherapy client is better off than 75 percent of controls, there is little difference in outcome between the various types of therapy examined.

Using meta-analysis to identify successful project classes in not without its difficulties. One concerns the validity of classes, given the limited information typically available from existing studies about what was actually implemented. As a result, evaluators have to depend heavily on verbal labels and other forms of incomplete reporting, so that Smith and Glass may have found no differences between classes of psychotherapy because there may be less difference in what actually transpires during therapy than the various therapy labels suggest. In fact, relationships between what psychotherapists say they do and what they actually do have often been found

to be low (Garfield, 1980; Lieberman, Yalom, and Miles, 1973), entailing not only less sharp class distinctions but also the likelihood of considerable variability within classes. Inferences about class membership are better if they are based on direct observation or intensive interviews. This was certainly not the case in the Smith and Glass (1977) study, where graduate students were used to rate the similarities between supposedly different therapies on the basis of very incomplete information.

Another problem arises with meta-analysis when the available studies share a methodological bias in one causal direction, as Director (1979) has suggested for job-training projects and Campbell and Erlebacher (1970) for compensatory education. Evaluators will then draw an erroneous conclusion about the average size of effects (Cook and Leviton, 1980) because they will have cumulated the same bias across studies. This gives an impressive convergence of results—but a convergence on the wrong answer. The crucial assumption of meta-analysis is that the bias across all the studies being aggregated is zero. When classes are being contrasted, the corresponding assumption is that the average bias is equal across the classes. Note that the bias in question refers to bias of all kinds and not just threats to internal validity. If nearly all the studies in a meta-analysis of school desegregation come from school districts that have voluntarily desegregated, then it would be wrong to draw conclusions from these studies either about desegregation in general, or about desegregation that has been court-mandated (Cook, 1984c).

As a partial test of the zero-bias assumption, meta-analysts try to examine separately all the available studies where the bias is assumed to be zero. In the case of threats to internal validity this typically means a separate analysis of those randomized experiments where there has not been differential attrition (Devine and Cook, 1983). The average effect for such studies is then compared with the estimate from the remainder. Should there be no difference, the assumption of zero bias is accepted. Should there be a difference, the assumption is rejected. In the absence of enough studies to provide a stable and presumptively unbiased estimate, the evaluator has to make and defend judgments about the methodological characteristics of studies that should provide better, although not perfect, estimates. Sometimes these judgments result in a scale measuring the degree of presumed bias, and this scale is used for weighting studies. But such a scale will inevitably have practical limitations that depend on the plausibility of the assumptions it contains. Moreover, it is often used to accept the null hypothesis that studies differing in methodological quality do not differ in average effect size. But to use scales in this way assumes high levels of statistical power and probably large sample sizes. Indeed, it is usually difficult to compare effect sizes directly, not only for reasons of statistical power but also because errors are not independent of each other if some studies have provided more effect size estimates than others. Finally, it is wrong to assume with meta-analysis that only threats to internal validity need consideration. As the school desegregation example illustrates, threats to external validity remain problematic even when multiple studies with high internal validity exist that all deal with a single population of persons, settings, or times.

The comparison of therapy types illustrates another problem. By standardizing, meta-analysts can compare studies with different outcomes so that a study to prevent biting fingernails can be combined with a study to remedy character disorder. But these outcomes may not be equally important, and some types of psychotherapy might be targeted at one of these outcomes but not others. Meta-analysts can only learn about specific outcomes of special importance if the outcomes are treated separately in the analysis rather than as alternative measures of the same construct. In concluding that each class of psychotherapy has effects of comparable magnitude, meta-analysis could inadvertently lead the reader to the unfounded conclusion that psychotherapies are interchangeable. This would only be true if several therapies were evaluated by identical criteria and were found not to differ.

Not all literature reviews use meta-analysis (Light and Pillemer, in press). One can find analyses of *archives of completed evaluations* for which no average effect sizes are computed. Many programs have developed such archives, particularly in education, where Hawkridge *et al.* (1969) used local evaluation reports to try to identify compensatory education projects that raised achievement and seemed transferable. They located more than 2000 such evaluations, from which only 21 projects emerged as beneficial by all their stringent criteria. In theory, these projects could have been grouped by class (or presumed class). However, the small number of presumably successful instances—and the likely dependence on verbal labels to indicate project activities and theories—would not in this case lead to confident inferences about the preferred ways to carry out compensatory education. Since 1968 the Department of Education has funded other studies to locate successful individual projects rather than classes of project (Hawkridge *et*

al., 1969; Wargo, Campeau, and Tallmadge, 1971; Campeau *et al.,* 1979; Hamilton and Mitchell, 1979).

Simultaneous Replication Across Multiple Projects

If key informants or past research has led to developing a credible set of project classes, projects can then be sampled within classes and studies conducted to measure the level of performance on client, implementation, effect, and impact variables. If information about classes is not available, classes have to be discovered. This is done by sampling projects, measuring the elements and activities that occur in each of them, and inferring classes from observed commonalities. Once classes have been constructed, individual projects or elements can then be assigned to a class on the basis of the activities data, though there will inevitably be many cases where the activities are so mixed or the records so deficient that no confident assignment can be made. Note, though, that the purpose in selecting projects is not to assign all projects to a class. It is to identify those projects that reflect, in the purest possible way, the theory of activities implicit or explicit in project design, provided that critical analysis suggests these activities are likely to be transferable.

Unlike meta-analysis, the above approach uses a two-stage primary data collection effort to construct classes and assess performance. However, it is expensive to collect extensive data from a large sample of heterogeneous projects, and the temptation exists to use cross-sectional surveys *both* to assign to classes *and* to probe the consequences of different classes. However, practical problems beset anyone who wants to identify successful classes of projects or elements in a single, large-scale, cross-sectional study. Logistics are invariably complex, and it is difficult to perform well all the interdependent tasks necessary for such multi-purpose research; and when prior knowledge is not well developed, underinformed conceptualizations of project classes, relevant outcomes, potential mediator variables, and the reasons for group nonequivalence can result. Witness in this regard the extensive controversy that accompanied Coleman's studies of desegregation (Coleman *et al.,* 1966) and of public versus private schools (Coleman *et al.,* 1981), each of which used a one-shot heterogeneous sampling design to make inferences both about project classes and about their differential causal effects. Multiple-regression techniques are often used in this situation to control statistically for third-variable causes. But such techniques rely heavily on the (usually untestable) validity of assumptions about the selection processes that caused different types of people to receive different treatments (Campbell and Erlebacher, 1970; Campbell and Boruch, 1975). Adding pretest information on the same measures that provide posttest information aids considerably in developing more plausible selection models, but even this is not perfect (Cook and Campbell, 1979). Partial solutions to the selection problem are now on the horizon, with the analysis of latent constructs being recommended for problems due to unreliability in measurement (Joreskog and Sorbom, 1979) and with econometric modeling techniques being recommended for the specification of theoretical selection processes (Stromsdorfer and Farkas, 1980). However, the practicality of these solutions is still in question, especially with respect to algorithms for computing parameters (Cronbach, 1982).

Another set of proposed solutions requires the use of a few randomized experiments to complement the more primitive quasi-experimental designs available to cross-sectional researchers (Boruch, 1975). But this solution may not always be possible. If it were, there would be no obvious need for one-wave quasi experiments in the first place. We are not optimistic, therefore, about the use of large-scale, cross-sectional surveys for generating, *by themselves,* the kind of information that is required for conclusions about successful classes of projects or elements.

Programmatic Studies

The method we prefer for identifying successful project classes requires three logical steps in sequence:

1. Using descriptive data about project activities to infer a limited set of policy-relevant and potentially transferable project and element classes.

2. Using methods that are inexpensive per site, imprecise in causal inference, but extensive in reach to identify a small and manageable number of project and element classes that *might* be successful by the more important and widely acknowledged criteria of success.

3. Using more precise methods of causal analysis and explanation in a smaller number of sites of the sort that step 2 indicated might be successful in order to confirm or disconfirm the success of the classes provisionally identified and to probe why some classes are more successful than others, paying particular attention to the identification of effective elements.

If the steps are followed in this sequence, evaluation becomes a funnel, using inexact methods of low cost per site to define classes and to locate the most promising projects, and restricting the use of more precise and more expensive cause-probing methods to a small number of projects that belong to well-validated classes for which there is reason to believe they may be successful by some of the criteria widely believed to be important

Not all of these steps are necessary in every attempt to identify successful project or element classes. Nor are the steps always necessary in the order given. Project activities need not be described, for example, if a great deal is already known about the major activities and implicit theories being followed in a wide range of projects. If practitioners are convinced that there are not many clearly distinct types and that they are being implemented in something close to planned fashion, then the evaluator might move directly to step 3 where the planned verification of provisionally successful classes takes place along with a more open-ended probe of the mechanisms that might have mediated the successful outcomes. We are more concerned that attempts be made to identify successful project classes than that the three steps above be followed in sequence. However, when one wrongly infers a class, the consequences can be disastrous. In the case of Follow Through, over $20 million was spent to discriminate between different types of preschool education. But according to House *et al.* (1982) there was no prior assurance that despite different developer labels, unique types existed that could be clearly discriminated from each other. (For a dissenting view, see Rhine, 1983.)

Many techniques are available for creating the knowledge needed at each of the three steps. It is important to know several of the major ones, for practical pressures often force a choice between techniques. Moreover, some major stakeholders of an evaluation see the more descriptive first and second stages as only a prelude to the more important generalized, causal knowledge generated at step 3. They prefer, therefore, that the speediest methods are selected at the two earliest stages.

Step 1: Inferring project classes. An activities survey provides evaluators with a description of each local project that identifies its overt and covert goals, the means it uses to meet them, and the assumptions on which the choice of means depends. Partly on the basis of this information, a decision can be made to concentrate on projects or elements as the major object of study. The former emphasis is warranted when the turnover in projects is high or plans exist to make a significant change in a program's budget. An emphasis on elements is warranted when the number and structure of projects is stable and many projects in a program seem to be experiencing the same important difficulty. For example, most alcohol and drug abuse centers and smoking clinics have difficulty maintaining participation after the client's first visit, and it would be useful to identify transferable elements that increase the rate at which clients return for a more complete course of treatment.

Descriptions of project activities can be obtained by using many methods, including the monitoring methods outlined earlier. Sometimes, reviews of the literature on project activities and goals can also provide the information for inferring types, as can how-to-do-it manuals (Rutman, 1980). When nominal labels exist about unique treatment models, it is possible to follow the lead of Stallings (1973) who had Follow Through sponsors list the activities they believed were critical to their models, thus providing her with lists of what was supposed to differentiate the models. However, there should be some independent, behavioral validation of such lists from interviews and observational studies at a small number of convenient sites. It is dangerous to rely only on the nominal distinctions practitioners. This is, first, because there may be too many models—there are claims of over 200 psychotherapies (Kiesler, 1979) and 22 models of Follow Through; and second, because some category labels will turn out, upon subsequent investigation, to be ill-founded, usually because the project activities that actually occur do not closely correspond with what advocates claim are the distinctive manipulable elements that constitute the class or type in question.

A superior method is to have experts rate the extent to which project activities define project or element types. Since there is probably considerable overlap in psychotherapies, Smith and Glass (1977) asked graduate students in a psychotherapy seminar to rate the similarity of ten nominal categories of psychotherapy, and a multidimensional scaling of their responses revealed only four distinct types. (One has to wonder in this case, of course, just how expert the graduate students were. Other mental health professionals with more experience might have reached different conclusions). Similar multivariate approaches to defining project and element types are based on expert ratings of directly observed behavior at the project level. This is clearly preferable to the use of expert opinion. Stallings (1973) and Soar (1973) used factor analysis to examine observational data on Follow Through classroom activities. Fairweather, Sanders, and Tornatzky (1974) employed a related multivariate tech-

nique, cluster analysis, to characterize mental hospitals that were and were not receptive to an innovation, while Shadish *et al.* (1981) employed profile analysis to identify two types of nursing homes that they then validated against an independent external criterion. Finally, discriminant analysis (Cooley and Lohnes, 1971) can be used with expert ratings or direct observational data to maximize the differences among a particular set of projects or elements on as many dimensions as are necessary to describe the differences. Some of the work on identifying successful schools that we describe below uses discriminant analysis.

These multivariate quantitative techniques help identify commonalities from among the diverse activities occurring within and between projects. They therefore cluster projects into groups. However, the techniques are particularly susceptible to mindless use, and so it is important to be critical when using them to draw inferences about project types. Indeed, we would counsel the use of multiple quantitative and qualitative techniques in order to achieve cross-validation. Where cross-validation cannot be achieved, we would caution against an exclusive reliance on quantitative techniques, preferring data sources that are more grounded in comprehensive observation and less dependent on questionnaires with their a priori categories. But whichever techniques are relied upon most heavily, the reality is that the instances belonging to any one class or type will still be heterogeneous in many activities. They will not be replicates. They will be related to each other because they overlap on a small set of presumably transferable elements that constitute the conceptual core of an inferred type; but they will differ from each other many other factors.

Step 2: Provisional identification of successful project classes. The techniques available for provisionally determining the success of various project types also apply to detecting which types of elements seem successful. The techniques we outline are all usually flawed as means for drawing conclusions about causal effects or impacts, and some of the types provisionally identified as successful at step 2 will be discarded by the more rigorous methods of step 3. Step 2 is concerned with gaining *provisional* information about successful project types in order to arrive at a restricted set of types that can be more deeply probed at step 3.

Given knowledge about types from one of the techniques used at step 1, the evaluator may ask knowledgeable individuals to *nominate* those types they believe are particularly effective by criteria that are widely agreed upon to be important. If time and resources permit, the evaluators should complement the nominations by using interviews and existing reports to eliminate some false positives and to gain a firsthand impression of the classes. St. Pierre, Cook, and Straw (1982) used such a nomination method to select a number of states with nutrition education curricula that were highly regarded, and their subsequent probing led them to rate Nebraska's curriculum as the most promising. This was because the curriculum seemed transferable (other states were considering adopting it) and it enjoyed a high reputation among professionals in the field. Thus it was selected for later, more intensive study as a model of nutrition education that stood a high chance of being successful when rigorously evaluated. It would have been preferable in this case had several curricula been selected for more intensive and rigorous study, but resources permitted examining only one project class.

The nomination method is usually speedy, easy to implement, inexpensive, and politically acceptable, and it can be comprehensive if evaluators ask about all available classes and check with a wide range of stakeholders. However, evaluators tend to go to central administrators for their initial information, running the risk of building a proadministration filter into the initial selection of reportedly successful projects worth closer study. Also, the project types most likely to be nominated are the most visible ones, and their visibility may be due to their developers being better promoters than innovators (Boruch *et al.,* 1980). Such arguments strengthen the case for consulting multiple stakeholder groups about both project types and the criteria of success they use in nominating types. It also argues for the evaluator doing all that is possible to subject the nominations to critical scrutiny.

Multiple-regression analysis has often been used to identify elements associated with effective projects. However, it can also be adapted for detecting successful project types by entering client and other project characteristics into a regression equation, along with a dummy variable representing a project class or a vector of project characteristics. Project types would be considered provisionally successful the higher were the residual scores on variables believed to be important. However, a serious problem in all regression analyses of this sort is collinearity between client and treatment variables, as when students with lower social class backgrounds attend schools associated with lower achievement gains. Such collinearity makes it difficult to differentiate variation due to schools (the treatment) from variation due to student characteristics (Mayeske *et al.,* 1972). This problem is not currently solvable, rendering the regression approach questionable as the last step in any procedure for determining successful project types. But in the present formulation its function is as an intermediate means designed only to probe the original list of classes so as to reduce their number to a smaller list that can be probed in more detail later. The false positives that multiple regression can identify should be weeded out at the next step. The false negatives, of course, are lost from further consideration.

The multiple-regression approach is similar to some of the more inductive techniques that have been used to identify "outliers"—projects that on major outcome variables lie near or under the positively valenced tail of the distribution of project outcomes. These outliers are then examined to determine what they have in common in terms of project or element activities. To detect outliers requires accepting some variables as indicative of success and then using multiple regression to assign each project a set of scores after account has been taken of selection differences between the kinds of people exposed to different projects. Evaluators then treat the projects associated with higher residual scores as more successful, and examine to what extent they are characterized by similar objectives and activities. If some are, the conclusion is drawn that they represent a class and that the class is worth further exploration because it may cause desired effects. If the successful projects are not characterized by similar mixes of implemented activities, a search is then made to discover any individual elements they might have in common. Such techniques have often been used in studies of school effectiveness. In an evaluation by the California State Department of Education (1977), regressions of academic achievement on school and home background characteristics were computed and then validated with data from the next school year (see McPartland, 1980). This technique gave each school an achievement mean purportedly free of the influence of student body characteristics. Observers blind to the adjusted school achievement levels then visited classrooms, interviewed teachers and principals, and examined fiscal data. They did this in order to establish what distinguished schools achieving more than would be predicted for them from those achieving less than predicted.

Identifying outliers is inherently problematic whenever cross-sectional data are used . This is mostly because of the distortions that may arise due to chance or inadequate selection models. However, the detection of outliers can sometimes take place in an interrupted-time-series context that permits evaluators to identify projects where an improvement in performance suddenly occurs and persists over time. Such improvements are more likely to indicate valid and stable effects than is the case with cross-sectional methods. However, a stable shift in a time series does not by itself permit one to conclude what caused the change. To get at possible causes, one has to collect additional data from projects to see whether new activities were implemented at the time of change and to test whether these activities were similar to those implemented at a different time in other projects that might have shown time-series shifts. In essence, one first discovers the effect and then probes whether a common cause can be found across most instances of the effect. (For an example, see Straw *et al.,* 1982).

The third method for detecting provisionally successful projects is based on *review committees.* The Department of Education and the National Institute of Justice have developed committees to which project developers can present evidence of effectiveness in the hope of receiving additional funds to disseminate their projects more widely. While such committees have been used in the past to detect individual projects that are successful by the criteria agreed upon, once a set of classes is available they can obviously be used to identify successful project classes. Committees could also prioritize the classes in terms of cost, likelihood of success by different criteria, and relevance to target populations, prior to inviting known projects of a particular class to submit evaluations of effectiveness that are then critically assessed by the committee.

Advantage of such review methods is that purportedly successful projects are identified at low expense by using locally generated data that required minimal investment on the part of program-level officials. However, a disadvantage is that few evaluations are repeated, and so some of the identified successes may be due to chance (Wargo *et al.,* 1971). The likelihood of chance is less, of course, when *several* projects of a presumed common class have been evaluated and found to be successful. A second disadvantage of the review method is that many of the local sponsors who volunteer their projects for review have a strong desire to see their ideas disseminated, and this desire may influence how they write evaluation reports. The reverse side is that projects managed by more modest sponsors are less likly to get a hearing, whatever their success. It is desirable, therefore, that committees play an active role in locating

projects. This will not always be easy. A third disadvantage is that locally conducted evaluations are often of low technical quality. Consequently, many successful projects may be screened out of reviews at an early date on grounds that the evaluative data do not make it possible to determine how successful they are. Indeed, some committee reviews in the past have used traditional, quantitative, and experimental criteria for judging whether a project was successful, throwing out those that used different methods. Such standards would be too stringent in our current conceptualization, which assumes that reviews are used to identify classes of elements or projects that can be considered *provisionally* successful.

Step 3: Confirmation/disconfirmation of success together with the probing of causal mediating processes. Step 3 is designed to detect the true positives from among the provisional positives discovered in step 2. Since the detection of valid causal relationships lies at the heart of step 3, it is also the step of most relevance to demonstration projects, most of which are set up to test new ideas for projects and elements. Demonstration projects permit evaluators maximal control over the research setting. This means that causal propositions are better tested since the control can often be translated into a greater likelihood of random assignment to treatments representing different elements or projects as instances or classes. Control also makes it easier to probe causal mediation to determine *why* effects come about. Such knowledge is largely achieved through collecting data on what is implemented and on the processes that substantive theory says should occur to bring about effects (Cook, 1983b). Implementation and process data are then related to outcomes to determine the conditions under which effects occur.

Since inferences about classes depend on replication across projects that are somewhat homogeneous in the services implemented but are heterogeneous in everything else, it is naive to expect that all instances of a class will perform similarly. They will not, and evaluators should look for the general but not invariant replication of results. This has important implications for the number of instances of each class and for the number of classes that can be compared. The more classes there are, the larger is the potential smorgasbord from which individual project directors or policymakers can select activities that interest them because of the results they generally cause. But for a given research budget, the more classes there are, the fewer will be the instances of each class and the greater is the likelihood that project-specific heterogeneity will reduce the statistical power to detect true differences between classes. Including many instances of a class helps avoid this last problem but at the cost of comparing fewer classes or increasing the budget and logistical headaches.

At step 3, causal analysis ought to be as rigorous as possible, which is why random assignment is preferred. Random assignment facilitates causal inference by creating probabilistically equivalent groups, thereby ruling out nearly all the internal-validity threats associated with group nonequivalence. However, even with random assignment, treatment groups can differ in attrition rates or in the degree of resentful demoralization or compensatory rivalry that arises from respondents comparing the treatment they have received with what others have received (Cook and Campbell, 1979). Hence random assignment is no panacea. Moreover, it is not always possible. The circumstances when it is possible are not yet totally clear, with Boruch (1975) arguing that it is more widely applicable than many of its critics have assumed. Nonetheless, there are clearly some contexts where it is impossible (Cook and Campbell, 1979; Cronbach, 1982). In contexts where random assignment is practical, procedures have recently become available for minimizing differential attrition by paying individuals who receive less desirable treatments a small sum per interview (Hausman, 1981) or by gaining close and continuous contact with respondents (Fairweather and Tornatzky, 1977). Randomized experiments should be designed to include features likely to reduce differential attrition. However, attrition rates should also be directly measured so that problems detected early, or fallback quasi-experiments can be salvaged from the original design. Yet even when differential attrition occurs, the resulting selection bias may be less in magnitude and more easily modeled than would have been the case if random assignment had never taken place and the original assignment of units had been based on self-selection or administrators' decisions about who was to receive particular services.

Since the primary purpose of cause-probing studies is to ascertain the relative efficacy of different project or element classes on a variety of different criteria, it is advisable to conduct a demonstration study where random assignment occurs and several options are explicitly compared. Such a demonstration is better technically if the units cannot communicate with each other and is ethically and politically superior if all the alternatives promise amelioration (Cook and Campbell, 1979). Sometimes, logistics prevent random assignment to the various classes and instead require that the kinds of people who are assigned to one treatment class differ from those assigned to another. This procedure makes the direct comparison of alternatives more difficult, since treatments are confounded with types of clients. However, a number of design and statistical procedures can be taken to unconfound them as much as possible (Cook and Campbell, 1979). Though not perfect, they are often the only viable approach if projects offering the various services under comparison cannot be set up in the same catchment area.

When random assignment is not feasible, or when considerable differential attrition occurs, fallback quasi-experimental design features have to be used to facilitate causal inference (Cook and Campbell, 1979). Such features include the use of pretests, control groups (including cohorts), nonequivalent dependent variables, repeated presentations of a treatment, and switching replications of a treatment. To be used well, quasi experiments demand that evaluators be intimately knowledgeable about the subject matter under investigation as well as with the types of design that generally yield stronger causal inferences. Foremost among the latter are interrupted-time-series and regression-discontinuity designs (Cook and Campbell, 1979). But their feasibility is somewhat limited in evaluation by the restricted availability of extended, relevant times-series data, on the one hand, and by the infrequency with which individuals receive treatments solely on the basis of measured selection variables, on the other hand. Nonetheless, interrupted-time-series methods are feasible when one is studying some elements, especially in controlled settings using single-subject designs that can be repeated across respondents (Hayes, 1981; Kazdin, 1981). And regression-discontinuity designs have occasionally been successfully used in compensatory education (Trochim, 1982).

If causal inference at stage 3 depends on studies with nonequivalent groups, and if powerful quasi-experimental designs are not available, then statistical-adjustment procedures have to be used to "equate" groups. Analysis of covariance (ANCOVA) ought probably not to be relied on by itself, owing to the problems that follow from unreliable measurement of the covariates (Reichardt, 1979) and the assumptions one is forced to accept about the validity of the selection model implicit in ANCOVA. The model postulates that the nonequivalent groups receiving different treatments are growing apart over time in exactly the same way that units are growing apart within groups (Campbell and Erlebacher, 1970; Cronbach *et al.*, 1977). Recent developments in modeling latent variables by means of multiple fallible indicators of each theoretically selected construct (Joreskog and Sorbom, 1979) get around the unreliability problem, while some progress is being made with strategies for modeling selection processes from econometrics (Heckman, 1979). We would suggest, therefore, that a LISREL framework be used in the data analysis and that multiple causal models be probed, each of which specifies a different, plausible selection model.

One of the main problems in evaluation has been the trade-off between the extensive samples needed for confident generalization and the intensive on-site observation needed for ensuring that treatment assignment has been maintained, for assessing how well services have been implemented, for discovering side effects, and for explaining why particular effects and impact have come about. With a fixed evaluation budget the extensive nature of sampling and the intensive nature of process measurement are at odds (Cook, 1981). One of the major advantages of step 3 is that intensive on-site analysis is more likely to take place since the number of sites can be many fewer than in step 2. Moreover, it is always possible to restrict intensive study to a subset of the step 3 sites, selected so that causal explanatory processes can be examined with instances of each class. Knowledge of such processes can then be used to decide about the likelihood of transfer to other projects. The appropriate data collection and data analysis techniques for exploring explanatory processes are either qualitative and logical (Guba and Lincoln, 1981) or quantitative, requiring causal modeling (Dwyer, 1983). They always depend on measurement and observation, so that a crucial issue involves developing an adequate set of process theories prior to data collection or during the course of protracted observation. It is the measurement framework that will primarily influence explanatory power, and it can be grafted onto any experimental framework designed to provide clear inferences about causal connections.

A Critique of This Three-Step Approach
One objection to this three-step approach to identifying successful project or element classes is that it may be difficult to develop classes. While this objection is true, the problem may not be insurmountable once it is frankly recognized that decisions about classes can be based upon a combination of nominational, observational, and quantitative methods; that while all members of a class have to share nearly all the activities defining that class, they do not have to be identical on these activities and they will anyway differ on many attributes that are irrelevant to the defining activities, but are correlated with the outcome criteria of greatest importance. Consequently, not all instances of a class are expected to have the same effect. Since policymakers usually have only a limited capacity to tailor interventions to the peculiarities of individual sites, they often have to mandate or encourage changes that they hope will influence many of the projects in a program without having much realistic hope of influencing all of them. Policymakers seek coarsegrained knowledge about factors they can change, however varied are the local contexts in which these factors are embedded, and on which their efficacy might depend. This does not totally deny the utility of evaluators probing the conditions under which a class of elements or projects is effective, since policymakers can sometimes prescribe different interventions for different settings, and local project managers sometimes have the discretion to choose the activities they will implement. But when changes have to be made across the board, program managers or policymakers can rarely do much with the more fine-grained (and often more explanatory) information that statistical interactions or complex causal models provide.

A second objection to our three-step approach is that social programs are not expanding in the early 1980s, and so it makes more sense to concentrate on the evaluation of transferable elements than on projects. While reasonable, this objection fails to consider that one way to manage a budget decline is to eliminate projects whose operating models are ineffective, at least as indicated by evaluation. Also, even when budget reductions are the norm, budgets may still increase for some programs that seek to improve the mix of projects. And finally, strategies for identifying successful project classes may become useful in the future if national priorities are different from those of the early 1980s and emphasize increased social welfare budgets.

A third objection notes that much evaluation is internal to projects and is conducted by project employees rather than outside consulting firms or university-based researchers. Compared to external evaluators, many project employees have little incentive to generalize beyond the settings where they are employed, and tend to have been less well trained in evaluation and to have less freedom to ask pointed questions. Is it realistic to expect these persons to conduct the sequence of studies just outlined? Is it not more realistic to expect in-house evaluators to count heads and write reports on the basis of simple cross-tabulations without doing much more? To a large extent these objections are warranted. We should not, in general, look to local evaluators to identify successful, transferable projects and elements, even in those sectors where there are strong technical traditions at the local level, as in education where most school districts employ well-trained professionals in tests, measurement, and evaluation. But while these evaluators could use some of the methods discussed under step 3 to identify elements that are successful in local schools, our speculation is that they rarely do so and instead concentrate on periodic testing and single evaluation studies rather than programmatic evaluation research.

A fourth objection is that knowledge about transfer is better achieved through literature reviews or the development of substantive theory than through planned programs of evaluation that first identify project or element classes and then evaluate to what extent they produce replicated findings on important criteria of success. We agree that reviews and substantive theory are also paths to generalized knowledge. However, literature reviews need a large set of studies that do not share common biases, and the quality of substantive theory needed for applying basic research findings with confidence across a large number of local sites has not yet emerged in the social sciences (Chen and Rossi, 1980). Rarely are we in a position to know all—or even most—of the manipulable factors that are necessary and sufficient for bringing about particular results and can be incorporated into the design of novel projects or can be used to restructure part of the operations of extant projects.

A fifth objection is that the political system in which evaluation is embedded will not wait the time required to move from the exploration of diverse program inputs in step 1 to the more fine-grained analysis of a restricted number of projects in step 3. Results are needed sooner. This objection was partially anticipated when we detailed some less valid but speedier techniques for identifying manipulable project and element classes and for conducting coarse-grained evaluations of outcomes and processes so as to provisionally identify the classes that might be successful. By choosing options that provide more rapid feedback, evaluators can, within a few months, have a restricted set of element classes on which confirmatory research can then be conducted. However, such speed is achieved at the cost of lower confidence in the validity of the information needed for step 3 as can be made clear by conceptualizing the speediest method to step 3. This entails experts and practitioners first nominating classes and then also nominating projects where the activities are commensurate with class membership, seem to have been implemented well, and seem to have led to successful outcomes. The projects identified by such a two-step nomination procedure could then be studied in the detail outlined for stage 3, perhaps with new demonstration sites or through the detailed study of existing exemplary sites or through a combination of new and existing projects, as Connell and Turner (1983) arranged in comparing different health education curricula. But should the original nomination of classes or of sites with high-quality implementation be wrong, the rest of the evaluation program is worth little, and it may be regretted that more expensive and time-consuming methods were not used at steps 1 and 2. In responding to pressures to get to step 3 as quickly as possible, evaluators should remind those who pressure them that the slower methods provide useful information at each step. Much enlightenment is created by describing program activities and assessing commonalities in service across sites (step 1) and in exploring the projects and project or element classes that seem to be most successful (step 2). A the very least step 2 will set up lively debates about what constitutes success. It is not the case that useful information comes only at step 3.

A sixth objection touches on difficulties in specifying the criteria by which projects should be judged. The stakeholders are not likely to agree on all criteria. Even when they do agree, they may nonetheless differ about each criteria's relative importance. Consider the evaluation of Follow Through. Some of the contractors had models emphasizing preschool achievement skills and were prepared to be judged primarily by achievement criteria. But other contractors emphasized social skills or the development of self-concept on grounds that these were intrinsically important to children and would, at a later (but unspecified) date, contribute to faster achievement gains. Such contractors were loathe to see achievement skills stressed so heavily. However, their preference for measures of social skills and affective development was not easy to accommodate, since these constructs are not as easily measured as achievement. The relatively poor quality of such measures meant that if contractors stressing nonachievement goals had done no better on these measures than contractors who stressed achievement, it would not have been clear whether their poorer performance reflected low-quality measurement or inadequate curricula.

These reflections illustrate the importance in evaluations of selecting some measures that are tailored to the unique goals of each element or project class as well as other measures that are considered relevant across classes (Cook, 1974). Thus in an evaluation of health education curricula currently underway (Connell and Turner, 1983), the developers of different curricula rated a large set of items and selected those they considered most closely tailored to what their curriculum actually taught about health. Each curriculum is to be evaluated by these criteria. But each will also be evaluated by criteria its developers may not have emphasized that experts believe are important in any health curriculum. The evaluation results can then be displayed in different ways, with each project being compared with others by some criteria and being uniquely evaluated by other criteria. This procedure should force readers to reflect more than usual on the utility they wish to assign to various criteria.

A final objection is that attempts have already been made to use evaluation for identifying successful project classes, and such attempts have failed (Guba and Lincoln, 1981; House, 1980). Critics point here to all the "planned variations" studies of the late 1960s and early 1970s and conclude, with Rivlin and Timpane (1975), that they helped policy little, although they may have helped identify the major difficulties in conceptualizing and implementing studies that contrast projects with overlapping aims. Many of the recommendations in the preceding pages reflect knowledge of the mistakes of the past. Foremost among these was the assumption that project classes could be confidently inferred without behavioral observation or critical analysis (House *et al.,* 1978). Our call, on the other hand, was that project classes should only be inferred if activities data showed convergent validity between instances of the same class and also discriminant validity between instances of different classes. We also note that the competition between classes should not be in the form of a horse race. Rather, a yacht race should take place from which many winners might emerge, each by different criteria to which different stakeholders might attach different utilities.

Little differentiates the search for effective project classes and for effective element classes. This is because the three-step sequence we have outlined contains a general model for inferring general knowledge. It begins by informing evaluators about what actually happens at the level of service delivery (part of step 1), allowing them to detect problems of implementation, to develop classes, and to arrive at a large array of potential solutions (the end result of step 1). The list of potential solutions is then reduced in coarse ways that are inexpensive per site and cover many sites (step 2). The reduced array of potential solutions is finally tested in more exact and intensive ways at a relatively small number of sites over which there can be considerable logistical supervision by the evaluators (step 3). Such supervision helps with inferences about causal connections and causal explanatory processes. Following such a sequence, evaluators become increasingly familiar with the substantive issues they are studying. Consequently, when more experience is required to complete the more complex research tasks of the later steps, they are more likely to have it. One of the major mistakes of the past has been to issue contracts to researchers who have considerable methodological expertise but little sustained experience of large-scale research in the substantive area under study. Thus they were bound to be less sensitive than they should have been to the particular forms of sampling, measurement, experimental design, data collection, data analysis, evaluation management, and disciplinary politics that were required by the substantive area under study. To be carried out effectively, each research task has to be informed, not only by knowledge of relevant methods, but also by prior substantive knowledge and prior experience conducting research on the type of program being evaluated.

CONCLUSIONS ABOUT EVALUATION POLICY

Taking the broad perspective of national policy on evaluation, the preceding section discussed both the objects most worth evaluating (programs, projects, and elements as individual cases or general types) and the questions most worth asking about such objects (questions about describing or also explaining the targeting, implementation, effectiveness, and impact of services). We concluded that when an ongoing social program is to be studied, evaluation policy is best directed toward monitoring activities in a wide range of projects in order to describe problems with the targeting, implementation, and costs of services so that managers and practitioners can use this information to suggest practical ways to improve operations in many of the projects in a program. But if such knowledge was eventually implemented in many local projects, it would still not guarantee that the program would be improved, for its underlying rationale may be theoretically flawed or it may have negative side effects of consequence. By itself, monitoring is usually mute about effectiveness, unless it reveals that few activities have taken place and so ineffectiveness can be assumed.

As far as effectiveness, impact, and cost-effectiveness are concerned, we suggested that social programs are so politically impacted that it makes little sense to evaluate their effectiveness and impact. Instead, we suggested that it may be more useful to identify the classes of projects and project activities that are demonstrably successful and transferable. The assumptions driving this recommendation are as follows:

1. Sometimes, new projects can be adopted within a social program or old ones eliminated.

2. Many new elements can be locally adopted or adapted because they do not radically alter service delivery.

3. Some projects and elements have effects that are so dependable they continue to be found in a large subset of the sites to which they have been transferred.

We assume that successful transfer is more likely from knowledge about effects or impacts if this knowledge is based on demonstrations that the same pattern of results has been obtained across a heterogeneous collection of sites and if explanatory analyses have helped identify the causally efficacious components of any demonstrably effective classes.

The prior discussion spoke more to evaluation policymakers than to practicing evaluators who mostly begin their work after the evaluand has been specified as a program, project, or element in the form of a single instance or a class. However, in our experience individual evaluators are still likely to have some discretion in deciding the following issues:

1. What the evaluand will be compared with.

2. Which categories of question will be stressed more heavily (about client characteristics, implementation, effects, or impacts).

3. Which individual criteria will be selected in each of the four categories.

4. What emphasis will be given to description and explanation.

5. What the choice of methods of data collection and analysis will be.

6. What level of detail will be provided in summarizing and integrating findings.

7. What the role of the evaluator will be *vis-à-vis* stakeholders and the agencies providing funds for evaluation.

We turn now to these issues. The discussion will mostly be general since a vast range of programs is evaluated in each human service sector; a wide range of time, budget, and intellectual constraints operate from one evaluation study to the next; and many different types of questions could have priority. However, to make issues of question and method choice salient, we will sometimes discuss one example in detail. However, we want to stress that the following section is about the design of single evaluative studies of all kinds, not just those conducted in a single project instance, as with the example we explore.

THE DESIGN OF INDIVIDUAL EVALUATIVE STUDIES

ISSUE AND QUESTION CHOICE

At the preevaluative stage evaluators have to generate a catholic array of questions so as to avoid slipping into those that first come to their own, or their funder's, mind. Then this array has to be reduced to a smaller list of high-priority questions for which it is reasonable to expect an answer within the constraints of time, money, and staff skills and preferences that pertain.

Mechanisms for Generating Specific Evaluation Issues and Questions

Needs analysis.   A precondition for generating evaluation questions is an understanding of the importance of the social need to which the program, project, or element is directed. Scriven (1980) has emphasized this precondition, being convinced that some interventions are targeted at problems of lesser importance. For instance, in evaluating a project to raise the achievement of the severely mentally handicapped, a needs analysis would have to grapple with the problem of estimating how important it is to raise their already minimal achievement levels as opposed to, say, teaching them skills to keep them out of institutions or to decrease the custodial strain on parents and other care givers. Since evaluators usually come onto the scene after a need has been assumed, their leverage for retargeting needs is limited. Nonetheless, we know of instances where the evaluator's questioning of needs has led to refocusing an evaluation—and even of instances where evaluators have refused to evaluate projects they believed were based on trivial needs.

When a needs analysis is conducted prior to an evaluation, it is more likely to result in additions to the measurement framework than to anything else. In the example of the project for severely mentally handicapped children, we could envisage a needs analysis resulting in the addition of measures of the strains and gratifications associated with caring for the children. A needs analysis conducted even later may still be useful (Scriven, 1980). Consider "Sesame Street." The show was originally funded to help all children, especially disadvantaged ones. The original evaluators (Ball and Bogatz, 1970) interpreted this aim to mean that disadvantaged children should learn from the show, and their evaluation was designed to test whether such learning took place. Cook *et al.* (1975) provided a second interpretation of the needs of disadvantaged children, reasoning that because educational and occupational structures in the United States are pyramidal, advancement necessitates competition between individuals. Under this set of assumptions two major needs of economically disadvantaged children are to know more and to narrow gaps in achievement, which exist as early as age four, between their achievement levels and those of children from more advantaged homes. The original conceptualization of needs led—quite understandably—to an evaluation with many economically disadvantaged but few advantaged children, making it difficult with such a sampling design to probe sensitively the second need based on gaps. Had the second interpretation of need been sharply posed when the original evaluation was designed, the sample of economically advantaged children would presumably have been larger and of Ball and Bogatz' analysis of the gap issue improved. Even so, data from other archived sources are relevant to the gap issue and were used by Cook *et al.* to explore the issue in ways that the data of Ball and Bogatz did not permit. The option to pursue other relevant data sources is open to all evaluators who question the assumptions about needs that are explicit or implicit in a particular evaluation design. Even when secondary data sources are not available, just raising the issue of

an alternative definition of need can raise policymakers' consciousness. In the "Sesame Street" case merely raising the issue probably impacted on decisions about future educational television programs for national audiences of young children.

The literature review. Literature reviews have many functions for evaluators, including assistance in assessing the needs of program clients and in understanding the kinds of information that would be helpful to different stakeholder groups. Mostly, however, the review will help build a set of questions about the intervention itself. To illustrate this, imagine that your hometown decided to imitate a certain East Coast city that has set up special volunteer police squads to target persons who repeatedly cause crimes. The hope is to capture more repeat offenders, both those for whom new arrest warrants are outstanding and those who can be observed committing crimes thanks to surveillance or sting operations. The causal assumptions here are that arresting repeat offenders will reduce the city's crime rate because known repeat offenders commit a disproportionate number of crimes, because arresting them will remove them from the streets, and/or because their arrest will deter other persons—including repeat offenders—from committing crimes.

When one is asked to evaluate the repeat-offenders squads, one of the first tasks should be to consult the relevant literature in books, articles, and unpublished documents and to consult with relevant academics and police officials. In this way one learns more about previous police efforts based on a similar philosophy. A literature review would quickly acquaint evaluators with the relevant academic theories of deterrence and incapacitation that buttress the design of the intervention; with what is known about the determinants of arrest and incarceration; with the methods that can be used to measure relevant input, implementation and effect constructs; with the logistical problems that can be anticipated in conducting demonstrations in the criminal justice system; and with some of the questions worth asking about the intervention.

One question likely to emerge quickly is: How does the existence of the new unit affect the behavior of other police? In particular, do regular police now leave the arresting and surveillance of known criminals to the new squads? Another question touches on whether the new squads go after easy targets for arrest in an attempt to bolster their arrest rate. Still another would be whether criminals with long arrest records are more frequent or merely less cautious offenders. One might also ask how realistic it is to expect the new squads to lower crime rates when some of the judges who could jail offenders are reluctant to incarcerate. Even if we restrict ourselves to the narrower set of question about the squads' effectiveness in arresting repeat offenders, we could still ask: Do the arrests of persons with no previous record decrease because of the emphasis on multiple offenders? Which is more effective for increasing the arrest rate of multiple offenders, to seek out criminals for whom an arrest warrant is already outstanding, to conduct surveillance operations, or to set up sting operations aimed at the fences and drug dealers with whom repeat offenders have frequent contact? We might also ask: Are the new squads cost-effective when compared with existing detective squads or to certain specialized squads, such as vice or burglary? More global questions might also emerge. Do the new squads increase the arrest of repeat offenders more than a crackdown on drug dealing or fences would? How often do the new squads violate the rights of suspected criminals? Are the cases they bring to the courts more or less likely to lead to conviction and imprisonment?

While literature reviews might suggest questions like the foregoing, they will probably also indicate that some questions have already been satisfactorily answered or are less important than might have been believed on lesser acquaintance with the project. Reviews should also raise consciousness about the implications of operationalizing a particular question one way versus another. For instance, the cost-effectiveness of the new repeat-offenders squads will presumably differ depending on whether they are compared with police officers in general (many of whom work in offices), police officers who mostly work outdoors, or special squads that target particular types of criminal, location, or offense—for example, vice or burglary squads. Reviews can further suggest questions for which it is not reasonable to expect an answer. Thus if an evaluation has to be completed within six months, and a review tells the evaluator that it takes an average of ten months to go from arrest to sentencing, it would be foolish to try to assess how the new squads affect prison sentences.

Literature reviews can also provide clues about the conditions under which an intervention is likely to be more or less successful. For instance, we might learn from a review that the effectiveness of newly formed specialized squads depends on recruiting officers with previous experience in plainclothes work who are willing to work considerable amounts of overtime on occasions when most people would prefer to be at home. In addition, reviews can provisionally enlighten evaluators about the relative priority of issues. For instance, evaluators would be forced to assign a high priority to any questions that a review suggested most stakeholder groups believed to be important—for example, whether, in light of their large budgets for overtime, payments to informants, and the purchase of special equipment, the new units are more cost-effective than existing detective squads. And last of all, careful reading should provide evaluators with initial hypotheses about the unique questions that different stakeholder groups might consider most important.

In examining the documentation and published literature on a particular program, project, or element, the evaluator will usually come to realize how much prior knowledge exists. In cases where the prior information is meager, evaluators should seriously consider designing research to ask questions in the order previously used to describe evaluation criteria. That is, begin by describing the recipients and service providers; then describe implementation; then try to describe effects; and finally, describe impacts. Next, try to explain why the results came about as they did. We are not suggesting that this order is always appropriate; only that target groups have to be reached before services can be delivered; services have to be delivered at some "reasonable" level of quality before effects can appear; effects are necessary for impacts; and causal explanation depends on there being clear effects and impacts to be explained. There is a logical sequence in building knowledge about a program. Detailed analysis of the existing literature allows evaluators to structure what is already known and to decide where to enter the sequence of question formulation.

Stakeholder information needs.   Many people and organizations have a stake in programs, projects, or elements, and they do not all have the same stake. Indeed, they often have different agendas for the same program, different views on what it is accomplishing, and different expectations about what it should be expected to accomplish. Evaluators should never assume that they understand from the literature and discussions with funders who all the stakeholders are and what they want to learn. They must be sought out and, if possible, some of them personally interviewed. If circumstances do not permit consultation with representatives of all stakeholder groups, evaluators should at least try to read about their views or deduce them from background knowledge. Failure to consult stakeholders often means not only a basic lack of fairness (House, 1980) but also later complications, especially in trying to get the results used.

It is important to realize that the representatives of some stakeholder groups may not be able to formulate their information needs at a high level of consciousness. For instance, the officer commanding the new repeat-offenders project might well maintain that his squad's primary task is to arrest more repeat offenders. But the evaluator needs to explore with him which criteria he means: (1) by increasing the number of repeat offenders arrested over the number his men caught before they volunteered for the new squads; (2) increasing, citywide, the number of arrestees who are multiple offenders; or (3) increasing the citywide percentage of all arrestees who are multiple offenders. These are not identical criteria of success, and each has unique implications. For instance, if the regular police leave the pursuit of repeat offenders to the new squads, this action will decrease the number of repeat offenders the regular police catch. Consequently, the new squads might catch more repeat offenders (criterion 1), but citywide the total number of repeat offenders arrested might stay the same (criterion 2), and the percentage of arrestees who are repeat offenders might even go down if the regular police concentrate on persons never before arrested (criterion 3).

Stakeholder groups will also vary in their level of interest in some questions. For example, senior officials in the police department might be less interested in the number and percentage of repeat offenders caught and more interested in relative cost-effectiveness. City police department budgets are getting tighter. Given the level of investment necessary for repeat-offender squads, senior officials may want to learn whether they are more cost-effective than ordering existing plainclothes units to step up their search for repeat offenders or ordering the burglary squad to go after fences more vigorously. If relative efficiency is a concern to senior police officials, one of the evaluator's tasks is to help them think through appropriate standards of comparison (should the new squads be compared with all detective squads, with burglary squads, or with some other type of squad?), as well as the appropriate criteria of performance (e.g., an increase in the number of repeat offenders arrested, a drop in the crime rate, or higher cost-effectiveness relative to other specialized squads).

Local politicians and citizen groups probably have yet another stake in repeat-offender squads, wanting most of all to learn whether they reduce local crime rates. Such groups would not be impressed if the squads arrested more repeat offenders but judges set bail at nominal sums and offenders returned to the streets where they were as active as before in committing crimes. The evaluator could probe how political officials and citizen crime-fighting groups value different questions by asking them what actions they think they would take if the evaluation showed that more repeat offenders were arrested but crime rates did not go down. How worthwhile would politicians and citizen groups see such an outcome?

As evaluators interview and "educate" stakeholders (Cronbach, 1982) in order to draw up a list of questions based on different evaluands, different standards of comparison, different conceptual criteria of success and failure, and different ways of measuring each criterion, they should also probe to discover what stakeholders think the unanticipated positive and negative effects of the intervention might be. Many stakeholders should be informative on this score since they have firsthand experience of the evaluand and have financial or ideological interests that dispose them to seek out the positive or the negative. Indeed, program critics are probably the best source for identifying possible negative side effects and for generating qualifications about the range of persons, settings, and times in which positive effects might be found. Evaluators should also try to have stakeholders consider how realistic it is to expect specific levels of performance from the new squads, since unrealistic expectations are endemic in the world of social policy due to the frequency with which program advocates use overblown rhetoric to justify initial funding.

The stakeholders who pay for an evaluation usually expect that their own knowledge needs will take precedence. While recognizing this, evaluators have to be careful lest the power of funders (or any other single group, for that matter) co-opts them into asking a restricted set of questions. Co-optation is sometimes manifest as censorship, especially when funders forbid evaluators to speak to particular stakeholder groups. But more prevalent is the indirect co-optation that occurs when evaluators adopt the perspective of funders and formulate research questions in ways that will make a program or project appear more successful than it is (Scriven, 1973, 1976). When the most powerful stakeholders put pressure on evaluators, their questions and interests have to be taken into account. There are no difficulties in doing this when the stakeholders' needs coincide with the evaluator's independent analysis of knowledge needs; but when the analyses do not coincide, evaluators should inform the more powerful stakeholders of the problems

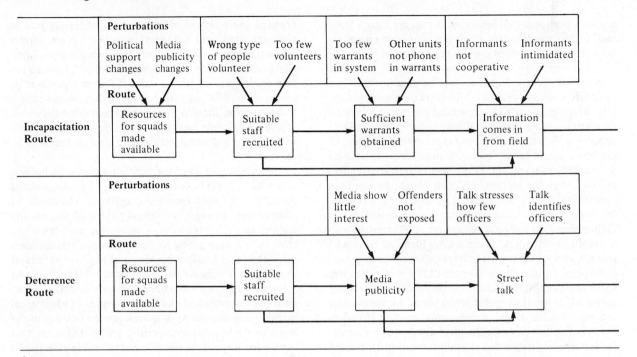

FIGURE 2

they may later face if the information needs of other groups are ignored and the evaluation results are seen as biased when they enter policy debates. They will then become controversial, and the political system will find it difficult to assign them much weight. In the rare cases where powerful stakeholders want compromised results or insist on questions that cannot be justified as important, evaluators face a classic role conflict. Resignation is then appropriate, either from the job or to spending one's time conducting a co-opted evaluation with little leverage.

Stakeholder analyses are not easy to conduct (Cook and Gruder, 1978; Hill, 1980; Bryk, 1983). They require planning time and funds. And because they raise the saliency of the evaluation with most stakeholder groups, evaluators have to use time and psychic energy maintaining contacts, fielding inquiries, and anticipating stakeholder reactions to everything they do. In addition, it is not easy to synthesize the information needs of different stakeholders to arrive at a small, manageable list, particularly when different groups have sharply different needs and make a strong (or loud) claim that their needs be

met. While quantitative procedures for refining lists of information needs exist (see Edwards, Guttentag, and Snapper, 1975), they have to be complemented by qualitative methods that may have the added advantage of generating a provisional list of possible side effects and of contextual variables on which effectiveness might depend.

Stakeholder analyses should be aimed at raising evaluators' consciousnesses about the research issues to be probed, not at supplanting their need to prioritize evaluation issues. Stakeholder analysis is not meant to remove the responsibility for ultimate question formulation from the shoulders of evaluators and those who fund them. It is meant to make the process of question formulation less parochial through a consideration of others' needs. In this context it is important when one is contacting stakeholders to make clear in advance that a set of interviews is expected to help formulate questions for possible inclusion in the final evaluation plan. The important concept is "possible inclusion." Evaluators cannot guarantee to diverse stakeholders that their questions will definitely be included.

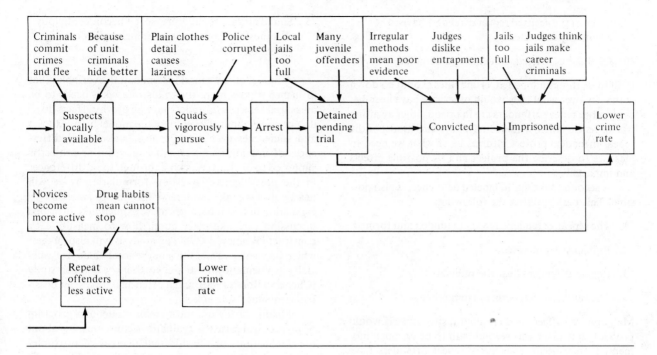

The system model of the program, project, or element. Documentation, interviews with planners, practitioners, and clients, and direct observation during a pilot test period can, singly or in combination, help evaluators understand how an intervention is supposed to operate and how it may, in fact, be operating. Such procedures should elicit information about the nature of the theory behind the program, project, or element, about the way the theory is realized in program design, and about some of the factors to be measured to examine the presumed flow of causal influence from the intervention to impacts (Chen and Rossi, 1980; Wholey, 1979).

Take the repeat-offenders project as an example. The systems flow model in Fig. 2 describes what is supposed to happen if the project is to impact on crime rates, either by incapacitating repeat offenders or by deterring them. It also illustrates some of the outside forces that could operate either to obscure a true impact or to cause a spurious one. The figure indicates that for the incapacitation of repeat offenders to occur the following requirements must be met:

1. Funds have to be available for the repeat-offenders squads.

2. The desired police personnel has to be recruited, organized, and motivated.

3. Sufficient arrest warrants have to be available to keep the officers busy.

4. Information has to be available about targets for surveillance.

5. Officers have to seek offenders vigorously and skillfully.

6. The offenders have to be in or near the city.

7. The police in the new squads have to arrest the repeat offenders when they find them.

8. The arrests have to entail removing some offenders from the streets because they are detained without bail or because bail is set so high that few offenders can afford to put down the 10 percent required.

9. Some of the accused repeat offenders have to be eventually convicted.

10. Of those convicted some have to be jailed.

If all these things happened, crime rates should go down in the city over what they would otherwise have been because more repeat offenders are in prison either awaiting trial or serving their sentences. This systems model of the repeat-offenders project informs us of what we need to measure to describe the project and its possible effects and impacts.

A second causal path, labeled deterence, is also possible. This path specifies the following:

1. The repeat-offender squads are funded and formed.

2. Publicity is generated.

3. Repeat offenders hear the publicity.

4. The publicity deters them from crime.

Many police officers and criminal justice experts would probably not judge this second path to be of much moment, largely because so many repeat offenders have drug habits that they cannot support except through crime. This fact argues for, at most, a weak relationship between the new squads, deterrence, and a reduced crime rate, and it makes the causal path from the new squads to incapacitation and a reduced crime rate all the more important.

Presuming a valid underlying theory, the model in Fig. 2 also helps conceptualize some of the outside forces that could impinge on the system to increase or decrease effectiveness. These forces are detailed in Fig. 2 as "perturbations" that lead into the presumed causal flow. Among these perturbations are the following:

1. Sometime during the project, funding levels might change because of publicity about the project or changes in the support provided by the mayor or police chief.

2. Too few warrants might be outstanding.

3. Potential informants might be reluctant to come forward because of street-level intimidation.

4. The hours worked by the special squads might go down since undercover work makes it easier for police to go home or do personal chores during duty hours.

5. Squad morale might decrease if it becomes obvious that judges are reluctant to set high bail or to send repeat offenders to prison.

A model of the causal system and the variables that influence it does more than illustrate what needs to be measured for a causal understanding of why effects do or do not come about. Developing the model helps expose, and sometimes eventually resolve, stakeholder differences of opinion about how the program or project is supposed to operate. Working through these differences in the preevaluative, question formulation stage will nearly always make the intervention more amenable to evaluation in that it becomes more explicit and informed discussion can take place about how to measure each construct (Wholey, 1979). The analysis will also suggest which particular causal links in the total chain are especially problematic and so are worth more detailed study (Chen and Rossi, 1980), and it often also forces out possible unintended side effects.

Finally, laying out the systems model of a program or project will raise the evaluator's consciousness about the implications of the different degrees of proximity associated with the different dependent variables in the presumed causal chain of influence. In general, it is more realistic to expect that effects will be detected on variables closest to the intervention (e.g., the number of repeat offenders arrested), since project personnel have more control over proximal variables than distal ones like the crime rate (Cook, 1974). Also, the more proximal variables change sooner, with the lag period for distal variables being so unpredictable that it is often difficult to determine. Indeed, if no effects are found, it will not be clear whether this result occurs because there are truly no effects or because the final measurement took place too soon. Premature final measurement is likely in evaluation, especially with the more distal outcomes by government officials who tend to be held accountable by which the general public. Thus while members of the repeat-offender squads would prefer to be evaluated in terms of the number of repeat offenders arrested, officials holding public office would probably prefer the squad's work to be evaluated in terms of city-wide crime rates, which are not easily influenced. Constructing a systems model of a program or project is highly advantageous because it raises consciousness about the feasibility of achieving such distal outcomes and emphasizes the large number of assumptions on which the hope of distal impacts depends.

On-site pilot testing. Preevaluative work designed to ask questions with greater leverage is always improved by on-site pilot tests that allow evaluators to observe project operations directly. Such on-site observation should include interviewing some clients and treatment providers so as to gain a better understanding of possible side effects and of the contextual forces on which effectiveness might depend. On-site observation can also be used for estimating the feasibility of planned data collection procedures and for assessing the validity of measures. Such pilot testing usually occurs in a very small number of purposively selected sites, often those known to be particularly cooperative.

Methods for Generating the List of Evaluative Questions and Issues

Constraints of time, budget, role relationships with funders, and intellectual preference will determine how much preevaluative work is carried out and what form it takes. There is a growing realization among evaluation theorists that more effort should be devoted to preevaluation planning; but there is also the realization that if the most accurate means were used to develop needs assessments, literature reviews, systems models, stakeholder analyses, and pilot tests, preevaluative work could go on forever.

Fortunately, the functions implicit in each of the above methods can be fulfilled many ways, some less expensive and time-consuming than others. With more mature programs a literature review might be sufficient by itself to justify needs, elicit stakeholder views, and develop systems models. In other cases comprehensive literature reviews will not be practical or possible, and more preevaluative data collection might have to take place. Even so, the same set of interviews conducted during site visits can generate both a stakeholder analysis and a model of the project or program system. Five separate data collection activities are not needed to carry out the major preevaluative functions.

Stakeholder analysis is most easily imagined as face-to-face, open-ended interviews, which also might include ratings of the priority of those research issues that have already been identified. But sometimes, the interviews can be conducted by telephone, or questionnaires can be mailed out. If none of these are possible, evaluators can still seek relevant information from reports and documents published by stakeholder groups, from the scholarly literature, and from questions about the presumed knowledge needs asked of third persons who are particularly knowledgeable about the groups and programs under study. Finally, if none of these is possible, evaluators should, at a minimum, try to imagine what the different groups' needs might be so that evaluators can at least modestly probe in more critical fashion the evaluation questions that come most easily to mind. Practical constraints influence the choice of preevaluative methods, tugging the evaluator to prefer some preevaluative goals over others and some techniques for meeting these goals over others. The important point is not to slip into selecting a list of questions without considering alternatives that might have more leverage for identifying crucial research questions or issues.

Refining the List of Questions

Although needs analysis, literature reviews, stakeholder interviews, systems models and pilot tests are principally intended to generate a list of issues, they also contribute to refining the lists they generate. Literature reviews inform evaluators about the questions already answered that need not be asked again and can also reveal that some questions are of high importance to nearly all stakeholders while others are of interest to few. Also, system models can indicate causal links that are problematic but are of great logical importance to the theory behind a program or project. These deserve special research attention (Chen and Rossi, 1980). But while the refinement offered by such preevaluative techniques is considerable, it is not systematic. Evaluators need explicit criteria by which to reduce the questions to an even more limited set that they might realistically be expected to answer.

The number of evaluation questions has to be reduced because the technical quality of answers usually decreases with the number of questions asked. Quality is still a concern, however, when few questions are asked, for the sampling and experimental design frameworks that would be chosen if one question had highest priority could be quite different if another were paramount (Cook and Campbell, 1979; Cronbach, 1982). We will discuss this issue in detail later. For the present it is sufficient to note that when one question is clearly paramount, that should obviously be the major determinant of method choice. However, when several questions have emerged as important, the methods chosen to answer one question will usually constrain the methods available for answering others. Question and method choices are therefore interdependent—not in the simple sense that question choice should drive method choice, but in the more complex sense that choosing to answer one question one way influences the manner in which other questions can be answered and the quality of the answers. In the usual situation where multiple questions are asked in an evaluation, it is important that evaluators *explore different ways of fitting different methods and questions together.*

Prioritizing questions for anticipated leverage would not be problematic if the identified stakeholder groups agreed on the crucial questions and prioritized them similarly. However, this will seldom be the case. Cook (1984) has argued:

1. Policymakers and senior-level bureaucrats are typically more interested in issues of effectiveness, impact, and cost-effectiveness—and then at the program rather than the project or element level.

2. The managers of federal and state programs are more interested in issues of client targeting, implementation, and total cost—and then also at the program level.

3. Practitioners are interested in how to improve service delivery but only at the element level and then for their project.

4. Clients and project administrators are mostly interested in issues concerning the convenience of services and their future fiscal viability.

5. Academics with a professional interest in a particular topic are most interested in accumulating knowledge about the theory buttressing the design of local projects.

Given such differences in the evaluand and type of question preferred, obtaining a final list of feasible questions requires either prioritizing the stakeholders or complementing stakeholder analysis with other techniques for determining priorities.

The stakeholders to whom highest priority will be most readily accorded are those who set the evaluation parameters. Usually, this group will be congressional committees or senior bureaucrats who pay the piper and expect to call the tune. And perhaps they should, for theories of representational democracy make them the best guardians of the "public interest," however imperfectly they may play the role (Cohen, 1983; Cook, 1984b). Moreover, these policymakers must at some level be responsive to other stakeholder groups (for an explicit example of this, see Hill, 1980). Yet precisely because they are imperfect representatives of the public interest

and function in a political environment that encourages vagueness in goals and comprehensiveness in the interests satisfied, evaluators need to bring a critical perspective to bear on senior officials' preliminary questions and need to complement them by eliciting others' information needs. Although evaluation can, and should, be in the interests of multiple groups, this is not to deny that it should be more in the interests of those groups that are closest to the hypothetical public interest.

Does this mean, then, that consulting with multiple stakeholders is an empty charade, designed to manipulate the less powerful into cooperating with the information needs of the more powerful? Not at all. Evaluations can usually provide answers to many questions, albeit not all with the same degree of confidence. But not all knowledge requires the same degree of confidence. Sometimes, it is enough to provide clues rather than "truths" and gross indications of association rather than specific magnitude estimates. As we will see shortly, multiple techniques exist for providing an answer to nearly every type of research question. Since some techniques require little expense, time, or technical sophistication, part of the art of question selection consists in choosing methods so that most stakeholder groups can have some sort of an answer to one or more of their major information needs. This task is made all the easier because sometimes the ability to provide more knowledge may entail little more than adding items to a questionnaire that is to be given anyway, collecting additional observational data, or providing feedback from a literature review. We are continually amazed by the modest information needs of some stakeholders, by the low level of uncertainty reduction they require, and by the many uses they can find for almost any piece of information (Leviton and Boruch, 1983; Rich, 1975). Stakeholder analysis is not conducted to give everyone the same stake in an evaluation; it is conducted to provide critical perspectives concerning the questions first formulated about a program, and to engage the interest of the different stakeholders by letting them know that an evaluation is occurring in which they may have some stake.

Prioritizing questions and issues is not a process that can be routinized through the use of a single method. Evaluators have to use informants to help them with decisions both about question priorities and about how realistic it is to expect an intervention to impact on particular outcome variables. Consider in this last respect the national nutrition-education-training program evaluated in Nebraska by St. Pierre, Cook, and Straw (1982). They asked how the state's realization of the program—a realization widely reputed among nutritionists to be exemplary—influenced children's knowledge and attitudes about nutrition and their selection of food in the school cafeteria during lunch. Since it is expensive to measure what children actually select and eat and then to classify their consumption in terms of nutritional value, St. Pierre, Cook, and Straw decided not to make the behavioral study of food consumption their highest priority and instead concentrated on the more proximal knowledge and attitude changes that teachers were trying to bring about in children. The issue for question selection concerns the weight to be given to questions about effects that might occur early or late in a presumed casual chain. Remote impacts are harder to influence because they depend on many more factors over which program personnel have no control. But they are also more important because they indicate that recognized social problem (i.e., poor nutritional practices by school children) have been to some extent ameliorated. Changes in the more proximal constructs (e.g., attitudes about food) usually indicate only that variables have been affected that *might* ameliorate problems (poor eating habits) at a later date, depending on whether other things also occur.

It is difficult to take a general stand on how the proximal-distal issue should influence question selection. There are, though, some specific contexts where deciding is easier. One is when the existing literature indicates that questions at a particular level of proximity/distality have already been answered for the program or project under analysis or for programs like it. Usually, it will be the more proximal outcomes for which knowledge is available. For example, much research suggests that education projects can increase knowledge and inculcate desired beliefs in children if they have little or no prior information on the topic. Since few children have much systematic knowledge about good nutritional practices, with the wisdom of hindsight it seems that St. Pierre, Cook, and Straw (1982) probably would have done better to devote fewer resources to examining how Nebraska's nutrition program affected knowledge and beliefs and should have instead concentrated more on how the program affected children's food choices in school and at home.

A second context where choice is easier is when a program, project, or element has not been evaluated before. Then, all things being equal, we prefer to concentrate on more proximal issues of how well services are targeted and implemented and perhaps on what immediate effects they have. To go beyond these issues can be misleading. When no distal impacts are detected, one cannot logically distinguish between several possibilities: Has the project been implemented poorly? Has not enough time elapsed for impacts to appear? Was the idea behind the project faulty? Was the idea behind the project generally appropriate but was a single causal link in its systems model misspecified? Was the evaluation designed or implemented poorly?

In planning an evaluation, one should never forget that new questions and issues will be discovered, and they should be. Indeed, if one were to accept the rationale that evaluation should be directed at enlightenment rather than the purposeful testing of means designed to improve programs, then a major goal of evaluation would be the discovery of new issues to ponder on. For some theorists such discovery is of the highest importance (e.g., Stake and Easley, 1978; Weiss, 1977). However, we prefer to view evaluation as a field inevitably and perennially caught in a tension between probing preordained issues and discovering new ones. Each evaluation should include some techniques that may facilitate discovery; otherwise, side effects and restrictions to the generality of findings would go undetected. Consequently, there should be some direct on-site observation if possible; if it is not possible, interviews are required with supporters and critics of a program who have spent considerable time on-site.

Unfortunately, no algorithm exists for deciding how much of the evaluation resources should be devoted to answering preformulated questions or discovering new ones. That decision has to be made on a case-by-case basis that depends, to some extent, on how much prior knowledge is available. Similarly, no algorithm exists for prioritizing among the preordained questions. That, too, involves a case-by-case decision that depends largely on the evaluator's judgment and his or her relationship with those who fund the evaluation. Some techniques are available to help prioritize, such as Delphi groups or multiattribute utility scaling (Edwards, Guttentag, and Snapper, 1975) or multidimensional preference scaling (Shadish, Thomas, and Bootzin, 1982). However, these *contribute* to decisions about priorities; they can rarely constitute such decisions.

METHOD CHOICE

Once the final list of evaluative questions has been agreed upon, multiple methods exist to probe each question (Cook, in press, Shadish, in press). They differ in the degree to which they rule out various sources of bias and in the demands they make on time, money, and technical expertise. The multiplicity of methods relevant to any one evaluation issue suggests that it should be possible to answer the questions of highest priority using more valid methods that are also likely to be costly while answering some of the lower-priority questions using methods that are less valid but also less costly. Of course, some low-priority questions will be dropped once the costs of an answer become clear. Method choice involves juggling a list of questions and question priorities together with the known constraints and the methodological preferences of the evaluation team. Out of this juggling act results a research design that is then implemented, inevitably imperfectly. Indeed, some fine tuning of the research design often takes place after an evaluation has already begun.

Once the preformulated evaluative criteria and standards of comparison have been decided on, the overall research design still lacks two of the logical requirements of evaluation—a specification of how measurement is to occur and how the results of the measurement process are to be synthesized. In research design it is standard to specify plans for the following functions:

1. Sampling at many levels (e.g., states, school districts, schools, grades within schools, classes within grades, and children within classes).

2. Measuring client implementation, effect, and contextual variables.

3. Inferring causal relationships impact, from an experimental design composed of various measurement waves and treatment groups.

4. Managing field operations (St. Pierre, 1983).

5. Analyzing the descriptive and explanatory data.

6. Writing reports.

7. Disseminating the results.

For each of these functions an evaluation plan should:

1. Specify the methods chosen.

2. Outline why they were chosen.

3. Detail the problems expected to occur in implementing the plan.

4. Discuss the steps to be taken to prevent the identified problems from actually arising.

5. Outline realistic fallback options in case the planned designs for sampling, measurement, cause probing, and data collection break down.

The content of such plans varies enormously, depending on which features of a program (and the projects and elements that constitute it) are involved in the principle evaluation questions; the extent to which the evaluators are interested in cases or general types; the degree of emphasis given to description or explanation; and the extent to which the major criteria touch on service providers and recipients, the implementation of services, and their effectiveness or their impact. The variety in evaluands and criteria makes it difficult to discuss method choice in ways that are not so general as to be of marginal relevance to particular evaluations or so specific that their general relevance is unclear. Our strategy in discussing methods is to highlight debates that have occurred in the evaluation literature on the assumption that they reflect frequently occurring dilemmas for individual evaluations. To be consistent with the logic of evaluation, we structure the debates so that they consider the measurement of performance and the synthesizing of evaluation results; inevitably, they also touch on issues of sampling, measurement, experimental design, and techniques for data collection and analysis. To be consistent with the primacy of getting evaluative information used, we also discuss debates about the dissemination of evaluation findings.

Debates About Measuring Performance

Answering the major types of evaluation questions

Sampling to answer questions about service providers and clients. If one is to draw a profile of service providers and clients, the technically superior method would be to contact everyone—that is, to conduct a census. To do so, evaluators might use program or project files, mail questionnaires, or face-to-face interviews—data collection methods that vary in expense, flexibility, and expected response rate. In many cases it is more reasonable to sample service recipients at random rather than conduct a census, since random selection allows one to arrive at an unbiased estimate of the population at much lower cost. In practice, biases of usually unknown magnitude creep into most sample surveys because some units (states, projects, or people) refuse to cooperate with a study and because in multiwave studies some individuals cannot be recontacted.

Although sampling theory provides the only formal theory of representativeness and generalization, it is not the only mechanism for generalizing to populations of persons and projects. When it is not possible to sample with known probabilities, evaluators can sometimes select a purposive sample of projects on grounds of convenience and heterogeneity. Some might come, say, from cooperative states in the Northeast, the Southeast, the Southwest, the West, or the Midwest, with the choice being made within states on grounds that some projects are bigger than the state average while others are smaller. With a purposive sampling plan like this one, the evaluator would probe how similar service providers and recipients are *despite* the variability between states and between projects of different sizes. Should there be little similarity, the evaluator would then try to identify systematic regional or size differences in the persons served or the services implemented. A related purposive sampling technique is to select not for heterogeneity but for presumptive modality (Cook and Campbell, 1979; St. Pierre and Cook, 1984), as when one chooses for study sites that, on the basis of background information about the population, seem representative of it. The variables on which one might want to choose modal sites could include project size, funding levels, and years in existence.

These four methods of sampling sites in a program or clients within sites—the census, random selection, purposive selection of heterogeneous instances, and the purposive selection of presumptive modal instances—differ in the validity of the answers they provide. The first two are clearly superior and the latter two inferior. That is not the major point, though. The major point is that the evaluator has a choice among options for sampling. Hence if questions about clients are paramount, technically superior methods can be selected where they are feasible; but if such questions are less important, technically inferior methods might be chosen that make less of a demand on resources.

Measurement to answer questions about implementation. Implementation is best measured continuously, using direct observational measures on a sample of projects, service providers, or days of operations. Most evaluations eventually involve a subanalysis in which each unit is classified by the amount of treatment it receives. This is not to probe how well project services are implemented in general or how effective a global project is. Rather, it is to probe how effective project services are when received at various levels of quality.

Observational methods have the great advantage of comprehensiveness, groundedness, and an enhanced likelihood of detecting unexpected implementation-related behaviors. But they are so expensive and obtrusive (Webb *et al.*, 1966) that many administrators prefer implementation to be assessed from interviews and questionnaires given to clients and/or service providers. However, such techniques run the risk of decreased reliability due to judgments being based on the most recent occurrences that may not be the most typical. If interviews or questionnaires are not possible, case records can sometimes be consulted to check on the services each client has received. However, these records are the least likely to permit discovery or to answer the entire range of questions one would like to ask about the quantity, quality, and appropriateness of services. Moreover, if records are used for billing or evaluation purposes, the possibility of overestimating treatment provision arises. Once again, though, many techniques exist that differ in technical adequacy and cost, but negatively so. Depending on priorities and constraints, evaluators can choose how they want to measure implementation.

Experimental design to answer questions about effectiveness. Many techniques exist for testing whether a possible solution has caused any of the changes noted in program clients. The randomized experiment is perhaps the best known, having been deliberately invented for probing causal relationships. Although not perfect (see Cook and Campbell, 1979; Cronbach, 1982), it is probably still better than the alternatives. When it is not feasible, or its implementation has been unsuccessful because of treatment-related attrition or treatment-related comparison processes, other methods are available. Quasi experiments are the most widely advocated alternatives, nearly all of which have pretests and control groups, and mimic the logic of randomized experiments, but without assuming that the treatment groups are probabilistically equivalent. However, causal inference can also be based on structural equation techniques (Joreskog and Sorbum, 1979), although compared with some of the stronger quasi-experimental designs (such as interrupted time series), these modeling techniques place a heavier burden on valid measurement and substantive theory, including theory about why different people are exposed to different programs, projects, or elements. Still, such techniques are similar to many of the data analysis techniques suggested for the most frequent quasi-experimental design—the nonequivalent-groups design with pretests and posttest—where problems of unreliability of measurement and the validity of selection models need to be struggled with. Recently, a number of theorists have explored qualitative methods for drawing causal inferences. These methods are now at an early stage of development [see the earlier discussion of Campbell (1974, 1975), Guba and Lincoln's (1981) analogy with investigative journalism, and Scriven's (1976) work on the *modus operandi* technique].

Although evaluators have many techniques to choose from in inferring effects, the methods tend to be related such that the least feasible are the most precise technically (randomized experiments, the better quasi experiments, structural-equation models, and qualitative methods, in that order). However, causal inference ultimately depends on the plausibility with which alternative interpretations can be ruled out rather than on experimental design per se. Indeed, the rankings above are based on the implicit argument that the stronger designs usually permit more of the frequently occurring sources of bias to be ruled out. There are cases, though, where prior knowledge or common sense rules out most threats without complex designs. For this reason, in instances where an effect is unique (say an American child speaking Azeri Turkish), it is not at all necessary to do experiments. To know that the child has playmates who come from Azerbaijan is enough to detect the cause, since maturation, testing, instrumentation, history, and the like (Campbell and Stanley, 1966) are not plausible in the context. Similarly, if substantive theory is well developed and we know all (or most) of the causes of some event, all that may be required for causal inference is structural-equation modeling designed to estimate the strength of relationships that prior research has indicated are causal.

Methods for impact analysis. Impact involves causal inference, and so its methods are much like those just reviewed for effectiveness. Thus the random assignment of neighborhoods has been used to evaluate the impact of different degrees of police patrolling on crime rates (Kelling *et al.,* 1976); interrupted-time-series analysis has been used to evaluate how crime rates have been affected by the introduction of television (Hennigan *et al.,* 1982) or by changes in gun control laws (Deutsch and Alt, 1977; Hay and McCleary, 1979), while multiwave panel studies have been used to assess the impact of television suicides on subsequent suicides (Kessler and Stipp, 1984; Philips, 1982) and to evaluate the impact of community-level health promotion campaigns on the risk of heart attack (Farquhar *et al.,* 1977). Also, posttest-only questionnaire methods have been used to assess the impact of the Concorde (Dintzer and Soderstrom, 1980), while qualitative techniques based on experts' intensive, insider knowledge of communities have also been utilized (Dommel *et al.,* 1980).

Next to the use of secondary data sources, the questionnaire method is among the least expensive for impact

assessment. Thus in an impact study of school desegregation one might want to learn how respondents of different kinds believe that desegregation has affected flight to the suburbs, home prices, trust in local government, and stereotyping and prejudice among adults in the community (Cook, 1983a). Note, though, that the issue is no longer the direct assessment of impact through the mechanism of ruling out alternative interpretations. Rather, the research issue is about perceptions of cause-effect relationships. Nonetheless, if there is an impressive consensus in responses and the evaluator's critical analysis fails to make alternative causes of any plausibility emerge, then the perception of causation is very similar to traditional scientific inferences about causation. As with the other question types, then, many methods exist for inferring impact; they differ in the time, money, and skills required; and in general, the technically superior methods are less feasible.

Descriptive questions about cost. Although cost is part of analyses of implementation and effects, we single it out for attention because of its salience for policy. Cost analysis is more standard than the other techniques mentioned above. But great variation in precision is possible, depending on how one treats opportunity costs, determines depreciation rates, or collects the original data (Levin, 1975, 1983; Stokey and Zeckhauser, 1978). For instance, one might be able to tap directly into expenditure records. But in many cases it is only possible to get access to the resources used. These then have to be converted to costs by multiplying each resource used by its average cost. Of even greater importance is the universe of costs one chooses to measure and how one chooses to assign dollar values to benefits in benefit-cost analysis. The degree of precision of cost analyses should primarily depend on the priority of fine-grained cost information; but once again, many options are clearly available as to how comprehensive and precise one wants to be (Levin, 1983).

The debate about questions and methods. One serious debate in the evaluation literature is about the extent to which particular types of questions *require* particular research techniques for a useful answer. Most of the focus has been on the extent to which, in practice, causal inference requires randomized experiments. Campbell (1969) and Boruch (1975) argue for randomized experiments even when they entail restrictions to the sampling and measurement frameworks of a study. Their case rests on the beliefs, first, that other techniques of causal inference are more fallible and, second, that the consequences of being wrong about causal connections are greater than the consequences of being wrong about other features of research design. One can be wrong either by concluding that a relationship is causal when it is not, which might lead to unwarranted program change, or by concluding that a relationship is not causal when it is, which might result in beneficial changes not being made. In either case Campbell and Boruch see serious negative consequences. They contend that the consequences are less serious if one correctly concludes that a relationship is causal but misspecifies its range of application—that is, one is correct about internal but not external validity. To implement a policy change on the basis of such results would still be beneficial in the aggregate, though not to the extent anticipated if the misspecification of external validity exaggerated the true realm of applicability. Similarly, if a valid causal connection generalized to some types of crime but not to others, ignorance of this restriction on the part of evaluators would not be as serious for policy as would be falsely concluding that there is an association between a treatment and a general reduction in crime. Campbell's view is that the consequences of being right about cause but wrong about its universality are less than the consequences of being wrong about cause but right about the generality of the wrong association.

This position has come under considerable attack, with critics arguing that randomized experiments are not universally implementable and often suffer from treatment-related attrition that makes them ultimately little different from quasi experiments (Cook and Campbell, 1979); that policymakers are less compulsively concerned wth causal inference then scholars and so assign it a lower utility (Cronbach, 1982); that structural-equation models are better than claimed for inferring cause (Heckman, 1979); and that investigative journalists, detectives, and ordinary mortals have for years been drawing causal conclusions from experience without conducting formal experiments (Guba and Lincoln, 1981). Another trenchant criticism has been that restricting external validity in order to increase internal validity prioritizes on confident knowledge about causes in the past to the detriment of generalization about causes in the future (Cronbach, 1982). Internal validity is indeed retrospective. It asks: "Was an observed relationship due to a causal connection between X and Y?" Cronbach sees greater utility in the prospective question: "If we do X in the future, will Y probably result?" To answer Cronbach's question, to which most of policy analysis is addressed, depends on either demonstrating that a causal relationship is empiri-

cally robust or on specifying what mediated the obtained effect. Consequently, Campbell's critics place more weight on extensive sampling and on explanation-enhancing measurement than on experimental design. Indeed, they would often be prepared to sacrifice some experimental design features for the enhanced capacity to generalize and explain.

The issue is delicate and situation-specific. But it should be noted that a randomized experiment will rarely be restricted to a single site, a single population of respondents, and a single operationalization of outcome measures. Also, the substantive literature may contain past studies or well-tested theories that facilitate inferences about generalization. And most experimenters will be able to collect some information that helps causal explanation merely by extending the measurement framework. Thus evaluators who share Campbell's priorities will not be totally powerless to generalize and explain. Nonetheless, randomized experiments do frequently degenerate into quasi experiments because of differential attrition, and nonexperiments are not totally irrelevant for inferring cause since some alternative interpretations can typically be ruled out. Consequently, it is not easy to estimate the marginal gain in the quality of causal inference that usually results from randomized experiments. Moreover, there is usually a trade-off between internal and external validity, entailing that any marginal benefits for causal inference are partially offset by losses in generalization. How this tradeoff should affect the evaluator's behavior probably depends on the extent of prior knowledge about the evaluand and on the degree of consensus between stakeholders in their needs for confident knowledge about causal connections or for more generalized knowledge that may warrant less certainty about the causal conclusions drawn.

The debate about whether particular types of questions require particular techniques has led to greater awareness of the multiple methods available for answering each of the questions evaluators pose and to an enhanced realization that any one method can be used to answer several different types of questions. The old link between questions and methods has been weakened—a link that led scholars interested in causal relationships to advocate only randomized experiments, that led scholars interested in population estimates to advocate only formal sampling techniques, and that led scholars interested in causal explanation to prefer only theory-testing laboratory experiments or causal modeling. The breakdown between questions and methods has an important implication that can be brought out by conceiving of methods in the traditional sense of survey, experimental, and qualitative methods.

Especially in multiwave form, surveys can be used to answer questions about all eight of our types of questions, that is, questions about service recipients, implementation, effects, and impacts when posed descriptively ("What happened?") or in explanatory fashion ("Why did it happen this way?"). Qualitative methods have a similar plasticity of function, especially if based on on-site observation and in-depth interviews where unanticipated events and relationships may also be detected. Experimentation is much less plastic than surveys or qualitative research, particularly when random assignment is involved. Indeed, in many contexts random assignment can artificially influence who receives services because of the need for control groups and because assignment by chance is less common than assignment by merit, need, or administrator decision. Implementation can be studied in experiments but often in an environment redolent with perceptions that something "unusual" is taking place. Experiments do serve to study effects and impacts well, and it is for this reason they were designed. But they render cost analysis more difficult since unusual expenses are often incurred in order to mount an intervention experimentally, and these cannot always be foreseen and measured so as to subtract them from the overall costs. It seems, then, that survey and qualitative methods have greater flexibility for question asking than experimentation. Consequently, they promise evaluations in which more questions can be answered. A rationale like the foregoing has been part of the attack on experimental methods.

To refute it requires justifying the cardinal importance of causal relationships in evaluation and making the case that the marginal-gain experiments usually provide for causal inference is therefore worth the costs associated with a reduced ability to answer questions about clients, implementation, and perhaps explanation. Note that the case is not built on either/or arguments, for none of the methods we have analyzed is totally deficient for answering any type of question. At issue are judgments of relative merit. Our belief (Cook and Campbell, 1979; Cook, Kendzierski, and Thomas, 1983) is that multiwave survey studies (i.e., panel studies) will rarely produce convincing causal inferences in light of the many plausible causal models that will be left untested, although in some contexts—especially where much prior research exists—the inferences will be much stronger. Our further belief (Reichardt and Cook, 1981) is that in many qualitative studies it is difficult to isolate the par-

ticular changes attributable to program inputs. But in cases where the observed changes are clear, evaluators who prefer qualitative methods can adopt the detective or investigative journalist role to try to reduce the number of causal contenders. But since causal inferences are generally less certain in surveys and qualitative research than in experiments, the old problem remains: Is the marginal increment in uncertainty reduction about causal connections that randomized experiments provide enough for stakeholders to want to use the resulting data more often in debates, especially since experimental results will never be beyond reasonable challenge for reasons of both internal and external validity?

Debates about methods for explanation.   There is debate about the utility of explanation in evaluation, with both Scriven (1980) and Campbell (1969) arguing that evaluation should be pragmatic and should aim at detecting and solving problems and not at explaining why problems occur and why some solutions are effective and others not. Cronbach *et al.* (1980) and Chen and Rossi (1980) make the opposite argument, contending that explanation is crucial for formulating novel programs and improving programs that already exist because explanation provides information about changes that can be transferred to many program sites.

It should be clearly understood what the debate is not about. If the issue were whether there should be measures of the extent to which an intervention is correctly targeted and implemented, all the theorists would reply in the affirmative, knowing that implementation measures provide some clues as to why a particular effect is or is not coming about. But full explanation is a different matter. If we adopt Bhaskar's (1979) theory of explanation, it involves four tasks: decomposing the global treatment into its potential causal components; decomposing the effect into its affected components; analyzing the processes whereby the causally efficacious components of the treatment could have impinged on the causally impacted components of the effect; and then testing the explanations from the third stage to ascertain those that can be logically and empirically justified.

The distinction between programs, projects, and elements is an attempt to begin the process of causal decomposition. Thus if we found that a project to provide psychoeducational services to surgical patients was effective in getting them out of the hospital sooner (cf. Mumford, Schlesinger, and Glass, 1982; Devine and Cook, 1983), we would ask: "What were the causally efficacious components? Was it providing patients with *infor-*

mation about what would happen to them each day in the hospital so that their uncertainty was reduced? Was it training in body movement *skills* they could carry out to reduce pain? Or was it the *social support* provided by the nurses?'' With respect to the outcome, one might ask: ''What influenced the physician's decision to discharge patients earlier? Was it a surgical wound that healed faster? Were the patients' moods better? Or did the patients make more references to support systems at home that made the physicians believe they were ready for discharge?''

Let us imagine that it was information about hospital practices and their rationales that primarily caused patients to be in a better mood, and that it was this mood that doctors used as a basis for their decision to discharge. We have now isolated a major causal element (information about hospital practices and the rationales for them). But we still do not know the micromediating mechanisms. They might be that the greater uncertainty reduction the information causes leads to less muscle tension, a greater tolerance for pain, and to physicians hearing their patients say more often that they feel fine. Alternatively, asking for information may increase the respect of the medical staff and lead to patients having a more pronounced sense of individuation and less sense of needing to play the ''patient'' role. These more active behaviors may then cue the physician to discharge the patient. Once elicited, these two explanations would then have to be tested through observation, thereby completing Bhaskar's four-step process of explanation. For Scriven and Campbell such explanatory analyses seem too much like basic research, consume too many resources, and are not required as guides to practical action. It is enough that one can dependably reproduce the relationship between patient education and fewer days in the hospital or the more refined, and even more dependable, relationship between information about hospital procedures and fewer days in the hospital. But for Cronbach and Rossi knowing the causal explanatory process promotes theory and helps transfer findings, perhaps to sectors that have nothing to do with health directly.

However, there is a point at which explanation becomes so reductionist that it is counterproductive for evaluators. For most evaluations of single cases the bounds of reduction should, in our opinion, be set by the system model of a program, project, or element, for this is supposed to represent an explanatory model of how one gets from elements to outcomes at different points along a causal chain. Systems models rarely specify

intrapersonal unobservables. Typically, they specify overt behaviors and the availability of physical resources at different points in the model. It is this grounded concreteness, this emphasis on manipulable elements and the contextual variables on which their effectiveness might depend, that makes system models so practical for action and opens up the possibility of analyses of transfer to other sites. Thus we would prefer to see explanation at no level lower than is incorporated into the typical systems model of an evaluand. Lower levels border on basic research and begin to evoke (for us at least) the fears expressed by Scriven and Campbell.

While a systems model should determine the level of desired explanation, it should also indicate the constructs that have to be measured if the desired explanation is to be attained. In quantitative research traditions systems models are most amenable to path analysis or structural-equation modeling (Bentler and Woodward, 1978; Joreskog and Sorbom, 1979)—a technique designed for explanation that is more accurate the more measures there are of each latent construct, the more models are pitted against each other, and the more null relationships are built into the models. The implication is that evaluators need to specify several plausible models of a program, project, or element system and need to operationalize each construct in each model in several different ways. Within qualitative research traditions systems models are tested by means of field observations and critical analysis to reconstruct plausible patterns of causal influence. Useful also is recourse to the published scholarly literature and unpublished prior evaluations. These can be invaluable means to discipline explanatory analyses since the preferred explanation will have to fit past findings as well as those achieved in any current evaluation.

Debates about methods for empirical generalization. We have previously discussed the role of sampling models in ensuring that an achieved sample either formally represents a known population or at least includes instances from that population. The previous discussion concerned sampling populations of persons and settings, rather than times and operational representations of cause, effect, and mediator constructs. The problem with sampling time is that there are no concrete populations of interest, and we are anyway usually restricted to the limited time span over which a study is conducted or to the only slightly longer time span, historically speaking, over which the literature on a topic has accumulated. For sampling operational instances of constructs, there is also no concrete target population, and formal sampling theory is only appropriate where multi-item tests can be constructed as with achievement tests in education. Mostly, therefore, we are forced to select on a purposive basis those particular instances of a construct that past validity studies, conventional practice, individual intuition, or consultation with critically minded persons suggest offer the closest correspondence to the construct of interest. Alternatively, we can use the same procedures to select multiple operational representations of each construct, chosen because they overlap in representing the critical theoretical components of the construct and because they differ from each other on irrelevant dimensions. This second form of sampling is called multiple operationalism (Webb *et al.,* 1966), and it depends more heavily on individual judgment than does the random sampling of persons from a well-designated, target population. Yet such judgments, while inevitable, are less well understood than formal sampling methods and are largely ignored by sampling experts.

Part of the detective skill in data analysis consists in probing the ways in which potential solutions can interact with characteristics of persons, settings, times, and construct definitions to limit the generality of conclusions about the evaluand. If the preevaluative question formulation stage suggested a high priority for examining particular statistical interactions, the important moderator variables specified in the interaction should be included in the sampling plan, preferably as stratification variables. But if stratification has not taken place, it is often possible to take advantage of natural variation on the variables in question in order to probe for statistical interactions. The debate in the evaluation literature on this score appears to be ontological: Is the external world "composed" of many powerful main effects (Campbell, 1969) or is it shaped like a pretzel, full of complex interactions and reciprocal feedback loops (Cronbach *et al.,* 1980)? However, the debate is also pragmatic. Being more concerned with policymakers than practitioners as the audience for evaluation, Campbell notes that policymakers can rarely accomplish the fine tuning necessary to implement a change with one type of child but not another or in one kind of city but not another. Politics pushes toward universal programs or categorical programs where the eligibility criterion is easily measured (e.g., age) or is socially compelling (e.g., income). Politicians are reluctant to support programs for groups when it is difficult to measure reliably who belongs in them or when it is difficult to make the case that the services are absolutely needed. It is also worth noting that from

Campbell's policy-centered perspective interactions are only problematic when a treatment has positive benefits for some persons and negative benefits for others. This is quite different from the case with statistical interactions of such a form that everyone benefits by different amounts or some benefit and others neither benefit nor are harmed. Having mostly policymakers in mind, Campbell desires coarse tuning; but having practitioners as his major target group for knowledge—especially teachers in school settings—Cronbach is more concerned with fine-tuning and statistical interactions, since professional practice often requires tailoring services to individual needs. In any event, without analyses by subpopulation, type of setting, year of study, pattern of treatment exposure, and type of outcome measure, little can be done to probe restrictions to the generality of findings.

As with explanation, generalization is furthered by literature reviews. The ultimate review seems to be the meta-analysis of hundreds of studies conducted with many types of people in many settings using many realizations of a treatment and many measures at many points in recent history. The bottom-line numerical estimates of effect that result from such metanalyses are eagerly sought after in the world of policy, not only because they appear to be so simple and communicable, but also because they are the product of so much generalization across irrelevancies that policymakers cannot easily take into account from their position in central management. Our guess is that the warm reception metanalysis has had among evaluators and policymakers is due to its aspiration to discover robust main effects that cut across valid statistical interactions whose relevance to practical action is often unclear to government officials (Cook and Leviton, 1980; Leviton and Cook, 1981).

Debates about methods for discovery. However sophisticated the preevaluative planning, a capacity is almost always required in evaluation for discovering unanticipated problems in implementing a study, unanticipated side effects that affect the targeting, implementation, and effects of services, unanticipated restrictions to the generality of findings, and unanticipated solutions to the above problems that may have been generated in some local projects.

The debate within evaluation has been about the extent to which questions and issues should be emergent as opposed to formulated prior to data collection (House,

1980). The argument in favor of targeting more resources at letting issues emerge is that substantive theory is generally too weak to provide valid system models, that unanticipated side effects are prevalent, and that individual sites are so unique that a cross-site research plan is bound to lose much of what happens at each site. The argument is buttressed by noting that close, open-ended monitoring will permit evaluators to see the program or project through client's and practitioners' eyes (House, 1980; Patton, 1978; Stake and Easley, 1978), thus enlightening researchers about the shared phenomenal world at the project level that determines how practitioners and clients behave. This world can be quite different from what formal decision makers believe it is like. In conducting such open-ended research, evaluators should sample all interested parties: those who authorize, administer, provide, and receive services, as well as those who interface with each of these groups. By seeing a program or project as all the implicated groups do, the evaluators may see its unanticipated benefits and problems more clearly, and evaluators and their sponsors will be enlightened about what the program means in people's lives.

No evaluation theorist would dispute the need for some capacity to discover the unanticipated. The issue is, What should determine the amount of resources spent on discovery as opposed to testing? The answer depends, in part, on stakeholder information needs but also on the amount of relevant information already available in books, documents, and informed minds. The less information there is, the greater will be the need for open-ended methods. Even when voluminous prior information is available, evaluators should, at a minimum, personally interview their contact persons at each site, tell their site coordinators to keep their eyes and ears open whenever they visit sites, and should include some open-ended questions about side effects in otherwise closed-ended measurement instruments.

Debates about epistemological foundations. The advocacy of open-ended methods designed to facilitate discovery is often linked to an epistemology that rejects various versions of realism and positivism in favor of idealism and hemeneutics (Cook and Reichardt, 1979; Cook, in press). However, the link is not necessary. It is easy to advocate participant observation or in-depth interviews to discover what a program means in the lives of those it touches without rejecting the realist assumption that an ordered world exists independently of our senses. However, it may not be easy to observe this world in per-

fect fashion for, as Karl Marx and Kuhn (1962) have asserted, all observations are impregnated with the bias-inducing wishes, category systems, and expectations of observers that follow from their social class interests or scientific paradigms. All individual observations are necessarily fallible entry points into reality. Yet most of those who commission evaluations want them to be objective. For this reason they prefer external evaluators over in-house evaluators, scientific over other methods, and evaluations with external advisory boards composed of methodologists and substantive experts over evaluations without such boards. However, it is important to realize that while the above strategies may reduce bias, they will not eliminate it. In the basic sciences confident knowledge depends on the accumulation of related findings across laboratories, with single studies rarely providing powerful probes of hypotheses. Objectivity is a system-level concept dependent on replication and open debate about the interpretation of results; it is not an inevitable attribute of particular methods or individuals, even though some individuals or methods may be more critical than others in identifying biases and trying to overcome them. Yet they will inevitably fail in an absolute sense, since it is always logically possible that an as yet unknown source of bias is shared by all researchers.

Evaluation aims to reach the truth (Guba and Lincoln, 1981). While many evaluators differ as to how it is reached, nearly all agree that the methods selected should be empirical and critical. By *empirical* we understand that substantive conclusions should be intersubjectively testable, even conclusions based on the meanings given to a program by service providers and recipients. Excluded are all inferences based on the evaluator's subjective experience or feelings of conviction (Popper, 1968). However, since the truth cannot be directly perceived by our fallible senses and cognitive apparatus (Cook and Campbell, 1979), evaluation has to be critical. By this term we understand that steps have to be taken to force out and test all the assumptions that are implicit in the design of a program, in the questions funders want to ask, in the methods they want used and that evaluators finally decide upon, and in any conclusions that are eventually reached about a program's achievements. In considering as provisionally true only those statements about a program that have withstood rigorous attempts to falsify the assumptions on which they are based, all assertions are rejected that are based on the proposition that a particular substantive conclusion must be true because a particular method was used to generate it.

A statement withstands critical examination only when all the identified diverse perspectives converge on a single interpretation, a process called triangulation (Cook, 1984; Webb *et al.,* 1966). In measurement theory triangulation involves assessing a construct several ways, each of which is presumed to share variance with the other measures but also to have unique and theoretically irrelevant sources of variance associated with it. The hope is to make inferences about the shared variance that do not depend on any measure-specific irrelevancies. In experimental design triangulation involves first implementing testing sessions and comparisons that require as few assumptions as possible (e.g., about selection, maturation, statistical regression, etc.); second, using statistical analysis to probe assumptions that cannot be falsified through experimental design; and then cross-checking any remaining assumptions with the results of other studies on the same topic that used different designs with different latent assumptions. In data analysis triangulation requires conducting multiple analyses on the basis of different models about how the dependent variables might have been influenced by the intervention and the plausible alternative causes that have been identified. In the interpretation of evaluations triangulation involves submitting statements about research plans and tentative conclusions to the scrutiny of theorists and practitioners who are known to hold diverse points of view about the program or project. Their heterogeneity in perspective is likely to ferret out any implicit assumptions behind the questions chosen and the provisional answers offered. While such a consistently critical posture inevitably overlooks paradigmatic assumptions shared by all the investigators, it nonetheless reduces the level of parochialism in issue formulation, research design, and the interpretation of findings.

Evaluation is scientific because the essence of science is empiricism (Popper, 1968). However, it is not scientific if science is understood in terms of a particular methodological approach or paradigm. A wide array of methods can, and should, characterize evaluation, including the randomized experiment, the case study, structural modeling, and participant observation. This is not to deny that different methods have different strengths and weaknesses of which the evaluator needs to be aware. It is merely to point out that no method is universally perfect or imperfect. Indeed, our definition of critical empiricism is broad enough to include investigative journalism and government audits. In the former case, think back to the investigation of Watergate, where leads were not published unless they were corroborated by multiple sources (i.e., they were intersubjectively verified) and editors and lawyers approved of them after logical analysis, a search for counterfactual information, and consideration of the law (i.e., the leads were to some extent critically examined).

It is less clear whether other methods would qualify as both empirical and critical. It has been suggested that evaluation might adopt some of the methods of the legal/judicial process (Popham and Carlson, 1977). For example, rules might be formulated about the admissibility of evidence and conditions of testimony, and a hearing could be held, after which an evaluative judgment about a program is rendered. While the rules for evidence and testimony are conducive to intersubjective corroboration to establish the "facts," it is not clear whether such hearings are concerned with reaching the truth or with presenting a convincing argument. Of course, argumentation has a role in public policy (Dunn, 1982). Indeed, the tradition of congressional hearings is based upon it, partly because the apparently objective reports of scientists are inevitably infused with inadvertent biases. Yet evaluators try to keep biases to a minimum, while the lawyer begins with a case to make and then seeks evidence to develop an argument for her case and against the opposing case.

Methods for Synthesizing Results and Attributing Worth

When the results of an evaluation have been provisionally analyzed, they typically constitute many findings of uneven certainty and disparate implications (Datta, 1977; Lindblom and Cohen, 1979). Some findings will withstand most critical scrutiny, others little. Some findings will make a program, project, or element seem advantageous in the eyes of most beholders, while others will make it seem harmful or disappointing. Other findings will simply seem confusing in their implications, as when we learn that a repeat-offenders project catches more repeat offenders but we do not know how it impacts on local crime rates. Other findings will be extremely interesting without having any apparent immediate implications for action. The complexity is potentially greater when programs or projects are explicitly contrasted, with some doing better than others on some criteria but less well on others. Moreover, many of the criteria will differ in their relevance to the goals of particular programs. But despite such confusion, it is tempting to summarize all the findings into a single judgment of value or merit. Such a summary aids in communication, particularly with journalists and politicians who are usually more interested in summarizing achievements to estimate merit than in using complex feedback to diagnose problems and solutions that may improve program performance. The issue which we broached earlier (p. 714) is: Should evaluators summarize, and if so, how?

Most evaluation theorists counsel evaluators to resist the urge to summarize (e.g., Chen and Rossi, 1983; Cronbach, 1982). They prefer evaluators to check their provisional findings, one by one, with stakeholder groups and professional critics in order to increase the level of critical awareness. In addition, some of the individual findings may be useful in their own right to some groups and would lose their utility when aggregated into a global (and inevitably challenged) bottom-line estimate of merit. Indeed, in most evaluations that result in cantankerous public debate, there are usually some minor but still useful findings that remain unchallenged and deserve to be singled out so that their implications can be explored. In concentrating on individual findings and their implications, the evaluator functions more like an educator than an advocate.

But when evaluators try to discuss each finding separately, someone is sooner or later likely to ask: "But tell me, is the program a good idea?" This question calls not for description, explanation, and interpretation but for the assignment of value—surely a crucial part of evaluation. Yet most evaluators prefer to leave the explicit assignment of value to readers who assign their own utilities to criteria and standards of comparison. Among evaluation theorists Cronbach and Rossi would side with evaluators who are reluctant to assign value, while Scriven (1980) would accuse them of neglecting a logically justified and necessary evaluative task that is routinely carried out in the type of product evaluation that most closely relates to his own conception of evaluation.

Our own preference is that the sanctity of individual findings always be respected and that the evaluator, in responding to pressures to come up with a single value judgment, adopt the role of someone who, by making explicit the logic of evaluation, will usually complicate rather than simplify. Hence an answer to someone who asked: "Tell me, is 'Sesame Street' a good idea?" might be: " 'Sesame Street' is a good idea if you think greater rote knowlede of letters and numbers at age four and five is useful, even though we do not yet know how schools capitalize on such speeded learning or how such learning is related to more complex information-processing skills. But do not forget that the show seems to be viewed more

often in homes with economically advantaged children than in homes with less advantaged children. This makes it difficult to estimate how much the advantages of many children knowing a little more are offset by the disadvantages associated with the widening of achievement gaps even before children of different racial and class groups begin their formal schooling. Moreover, if you value social development over cognitive development it seems that 'Mister Rogers' may be better than 'Sesame Street.' " This is not a simple answer and it invites debate about the value of different criteria and standards of comparison, *as it is supposed to*. The answer is designed to prevent premature closure, to create grounded uncertainty about the assignment of value, and to enlighten listeners and readers about issues in the choice of evaluation criteria and comparison standards that deserve more thought.

Evaluators can also stimulate synthesis and the assignment of merit by taking the claimed findings and inviting stakeholder groups to outline what they make of them, detailing the values they assign and the rationales they offer for their judgments (Scriven, 1980). All this can then be reproduced in evaluation reports, with or without commentary on the logic and veracity of the rationales. Thus some defenders of "Sesame Street" might claim that it is important to raise the preliterate and prenumerical skills of economically disadvantaged four-year-olds even if achievement gaps are widened because 1.) some especially talented poor children will benefit from the show and will become models of achievement to their cohorts; or 2.) because if first-grade curricula do not change because of the show, the disadvantaged will be better prepared for school and the economically advantaged will not be able to capitalize on the extra knowledge the show has caused since school curricula have not changed. Checks can then be made in the literature both to estimate the viability of such a modeling theory and to discover whether first-grade curricula have become more advanced since "Sesame Street." Critics of "Sesame Street" might claim, on the other hand, that the show is less helpful to preschoolers than shows directed at social and affective development, offering the rationale that social and affective gains are more powerful causes of later cognitive gains than early cognitive gains are of later social or affective gains. This rationale can also be explored in the existing literature and through the understandings of diverse experts.

The foregoing are qualitative techniques designed to bring critical perspectives to bear in deciding on the general implications of multiple findings that differ in certainty and implication and are never comprehensive enough. Quantitative techniques also exist in the decision-making literature for ascertaining the utility attached to different criteria and standards of comparison and for using these utilities to weight findings so as to arrive at a composite assignment of value (e.g., multiattribute utility theory). Such methods can and should be used with different stakeholder groups so as to contrast differences in how value is assigned. But such quantitative methods also depend on discovering the major unanticipated side effects since they have to be included in any comprehensive list of results. Moreover, as with the other major quantitative-synthesis technique, benefit-cost analysis, the apparent precision of the final judgments can be illusory unless a meaningful universe of benefits and costs has been tapped into and the performance measures reflect the gains and losses causally attributable to a program rather than the gains and losses correlated with being in a program.

A major objection to all quantitative weight-and-sum methods, the foregoing aside, is that in most instances of use no convincing rationale is offered for the weights attached to findings. Yet if rationales are available, they can be examined. And even if the examination suggests that the rationales reflect self-interest or dubious assumptions, it should force readers to estimate the weights they want to attach to specific findings, thereby possibly modifying their overall impression of how successful the evaluand is. The process of assigning explicit value to programs, projects, and elements is underresearched, and it is clear that no simple techniques can be adequate in light of the uncertainty of most findings, stakeholder differences in utilities, and the difficulty of tapping *all* relevant outcomes. Yet the process of assigning merit can be extremely enlightening to potential consumers and users of evaluations, provided that the sanctity of individual findings is not violated and the exploration of implications reflects multiple interests and perspectives.

Methods for Dissemination

If we are correct that most of the problems of program evaluation stem from the limited role of evaluation in rational models of problem solving and from the nature and context of social programs—rather than from the logic of evaluation—then it follows that evaluation is more likely to contribute to program improvement and the alleviation of social problems if it is also concerned with the postevaluative processes of disseminating and using results as well as with the preevaluative processes of question formulation and relationship-building with stakeholders. Thus, we now step outside of the purely evaluative framework to consider ways of increasing the availability and use of evaluation findings.

A key to successful dissemination is the availability of a clear, concise summary written in simple English that evaluators can easily present verbally to interested parties. As an aid in communications to lay audiences, it is also desirable to translate estimates of the size of effects into metrics that are widely understood. Thus academic achievement gains of X raw points are less well understood than grade-equivalent scores or months of academic gain per year; the number of repeat offenders arrested is less well understood than a percentage reduction in the rate of burglaries; a change in occupation prestige ranking is less well understood than a change in dollar income per month. Some of these transformations are easy to make because there has been extensive prior research on, say, the relationship between achievement test gains and at what age children typically learn particular curriculum content in language arts and mathematics. But other translations are more heavily dependent on assumptions that may be poorly tested or not tested at all (e.g., about the relationship between the number of repeat offenders arrested and changes in the rate of burglaries throughout a city). Nonetheless, such translations provide a specificity that aids memorability. Thus in evaluation of "Sesame Street" the most remembered result from Cook *et al.* (1975) seems to have been the increase the show caused in the number of letters of the alphabet that children could recite in sequence—A, B, C, D, E, and so on. Other measures were less well calibrated with the experience of readers and have been cited less often.

Leviton and Hughes (1981) have emphasized the importance of multiple written and verbal summaries that speak to the different vocabularies and information needs of different stakeholder groups. If budget resources permit multiple summaries, they are obviously desirable. Leviton and Hughes particularly stressed the utility of verbal briefings so as to explore with stakeholder groups their understanding of what the findings are, their estimates of how valid each finding is, and their beliefs about the action implications of the results. The advocacy of evaluators playing a close and continuous role with stakeholders, particularly those with formal decision-making responsibilities, reflects the beliefs that this increases stakeholders' commitment to use the results for action. Acquaintance with a few well-known "fixers" can also help. These are people personally committed to the public policy issue at hand who are also intimately acquainted with the relevant political systems. So, they can make things happen. The senior author remembers a Senate-authorized committee of which he was a member in whose results a "fixer" was very interested. On many occasions during the course of the committee's work, the fixer opened doors to Senators, congressmen, and the heads of large federal departments, with the result that when the study was completed, it was high in saliency and action resulted (Cook, 1983c). In addition to doing such networking, evaluators can work with their sponsors to issue press releases, give presentations at conventions, or even write scholarly articles and books.

Like the extensive preevaluative work we outlined, postevaluative activities enlarge the scope of the evaluator's role to take account of the realities of the political problem-solving system in which evaluation is inevitably embedded. Few federal or state agencies are willing to provide the funds necessary for more than perfunctory question reformulation or dissemination efforts. The latter is especially true before agencies know of an evaluation's results. Government agencies have their own interests to promote and defend, even though not everyone within the agency will agree what they are. Without funds and social support from sponsors, the task of dissemination is more difficult. Nonetheless, there are documented cases of evaluators who called press conferences to issue results that were not popular with those employing them (Campbell, 1973). Such whistle-blowing is a dramatic last resort that often has dire professional consequences. While courage to disseminate the undesirable should be part of every evaluator's repertoire, we do not think it will be exercised often—both because few agencies seek to forbid the dissemination of results and because evaluators may fear that whistle-blowing will harm their ability to win future research contracts.

CONCLUSION

Scriven's (1980) logic of evaluation applies to all objects. Consequently, product evaluation is like program evaluation in requiring an evaluand, criteria of merit, standards of comparison, the measurement of performance, and the synthesis of performance results into judgments of value. Yet despite these similarities there are many differences between the evaluation of products and programs, and explicating them highlights the major problematic aspects of program evaluation on which work still needs to be done and from which global assessments of the generic potential of program evaluation can be derived.

To facilitate the discussion, let us take the evaluation of automobiles as an example of product evaluation. As an evaluand, an automobile is tangible and circumscribed in form. Although variability exists between examples of the same model, quality-control practices during manufacture are designed to minimize these differences so as to standardize the evaluand for a particular period, the model year. Although changes are made from year to year, these are not usually major, adding further to continuity. Social programs, though, are not like automobiles. Consider the National School Lunch Program (NSLP). The food offered, the manner of its production, and the circumstances of its consumption vary from school to school and from day to day within schools. Diffuseness of activities over a large area, local differences in activities, dynamic changes in activities from time to time within sites—all these characterize social programs and make them more difficult to describe and understand as entities. Moreover, designers and quality-control experts may work together extensively to determine the form of an automobile. But with many social programs federal, state, and local officials have to cooperate without much face-to-face contact, relying often on written directives and telephone conversations that can never be totally clear in all their applications and probably speak to some of these groups' interests more than others. Consistency and constancy of purpose hardly characterize most social programs.

Programs are typically more complex in composition than are automobiles in the sense that the workings of each part (element or project) are less well understood theoretically and are more open to perturbation from outside forces. With automobiles the parts are the result of a century or more of knowledge in engineering and physics and of practice on the roads. Moreover, all of the parts are enclosed within a small system called the chassis and body, while many of the most important ones are further enclosed within a subsystem called the engine that is placed under the hood to protect it from outside perturbations. The open systems and imperfect theory that characterize social programs make them more problematic to conceptualize than automobiles and lead to many of the dilemmas of question choice with which this chapter primarily dealt.

The evaluation of both automobiles and social programs requires specifying criteria of merit. Presumably, engineers and managers at *Consumer Reports* once argued over the criteria to be used in judging cars, and it may well be that feedback from readers, manufacturers, and other groups led to revisions in the original list of criteria. But a common set of criteria is consistently used today in evaluating automobiles, and there seems to be little overt disagreement with the set. Most evaluations of social programs also involve multiple criteria. But the criteria are much more controversial than those for automobiles in ways that engage stakeholder values and interests. Moreover, with social programs it is not always clear how criteria specified at different levels of distality in program plans are indeed related to each other, or how long it takes to go from, say, issuing new guidelines about a program to observing changes in the severity of social problems. However, with cars, we know the exact sequence of operations and the time frames involved from turning the ignition key to reaching fifty-five miles per hour. The specification of criteria and their relationships to each other is clearly more pragmatic and less theoretical with social programs than with automobiles. For this reason, we had to be concerned in this chapter with the multiple disputed criteria needed for assessing implementation, process, and outcome, with the low probabiltiy of some distal events even occurring, and with the consequences of politically specified and unclear program objectives that are sometimes at variance with agendas at the project level.

The national market for automobiles is clearly segmented. We all know that a Ferrari has different characteristics from a Mercedes, a Mercedes from a Honda Accord, a Honda Accord from a Chevette, a Chevette from a van, and a van from a truck. This segmentation implies that we know which models should be compared with each other in terms of the functions they promise to perform and the costs of such performance. We know the brackets within which comparison is meaningful. Disagreements in ascertaining the bracket do occur with some automobile models; but the disagreements are far less widespread and virulent than those that occur when one is ascertaining standards of comparison for social programs or projects. The specification of absolute standards is widely resisted by politically sophisticated administrators, while the credibility of direct comparisons is frequently undermined by those who point to the lack of correspondence between the objectives, procedures, priorities, and time frames of different programs that might be directly compared. While product evaluation logically leads to a preference decision between alternative ways of achieving the same end or ends (e.g., moving from place to place in comfort and style), the political context of program evaluation makes it difficult to determine standards of comparison. Moreover, the multivariate, unstandardized, and dynamically changing nature of programs and projects makes it difficult to think that direct comparisons are ever *fully* warranted in terms of program overlap, however much such direct comparison may be needed.

Where the evaluation of social programs differs most from the evaluation of consumer products is in the third step of any evaluative effort—the measurement of performance. This difference is, in part, due to the following:

1. Intrinsic difficulties of measurement with social concepts (e.g., attitudes, crime rates) that surpass the problems in measuring physical performance.

2. The social nature of research with humans, who, unlike inert objects, are active, questioning agents responsive to research settings and demands.

3. The corruptibility of most social indicators.

4. The long causal chains of influence that operate with social programs where the distal events of most policy relevance are multiply determined, are not closely related to program content, and occur with time delays that cannot be easily specified in advance (Flay and Cook, 1981).

5. With social programs we measure, not performance alone, but *changes* in performance.

6. Also, we need to isolate that part of a change which can be causally attributed to a program or its constituent components. This requires the availability of obvious and stable no-cause conditions, but these are rare in the social world where much is in flux and every change can be multiply determined.

Consequently, the difficulties in isolating changes in performance *caused* by a program clearly differentiate product from program evaluation.

The process of summarizing results and assigning merit is broadly similar for programs and products, but there are some important differences of emphasis. Social programs typically engage more fundamental social values in more obvious ways than is the case with most products. Also, when compared with the stakeholders for most products, the stakeholder groups that a program affects are typically more in number, more heterogeneous in perspectives and interests, more passionate in defending their interests, and more knowledgeable about how to defend them. This creates an environment in which evaluators know that they can be challenged for what they do and do not do, for what they find and do not find. Their difficulties are exacerbated because of the absence of widely recognized techniques of synthesis and because the results they claim to have generated come from social research methods that are far from flawless in theory and in the ways they are implemented. While *Consumer Reports* reaches its overall conclusions about best buys in ways that are not always clear, they seem nonetheless to be less frequently challenged than the summary verdicts of most evaluations of social programs or policies.

Most of the factors that make the evaluation of programs more problematic than the evaluation of products stem from the nature of programs and the complexity of their political and administrative contexts. But other difficulties follow from the logical dependence of evaluation on the selection of important social problems and of bold options for program improvement as well as on the willingness of political actors to use evaluation results in deliberations about programs. For many reasons evaluation runs the risk of working on less serious and less clear problems and of studying change attempts that can only ameliorate these problems at the margin. Also, the results of their efforts have to be disseminated to political actors who, in deciding on action, usually weigh values, interests, opportunism, and other forms of knowledge over the results of formal evaluations. And there is not much evaluators can do to change this state of affairs.

What they can most readily do relates to the roles evaluators choose for themselves. The writers and editors of *Consumer Reports* know who their audience is, and so they can work hard to write articles that their audience wants to read and can read. As a result of this audience knowledge, the magazine has, over the years, developed a long list of satisfied subscribers who represent many interests but come together in the need for accurate and honest information about products they are likely to purchase. However, program evaluators have many potential audiences with quite different knowledge needs and interests. Unlike *Consumer Reports* journalists, evaluators cannot cease work with the publication of their efforts, secure in the knowledge that their work will be disseminated and used. Evaluators have to adopt a more active and extensive role that fits them into the political structure that commissions and uses evaluations. This system is powerful, complex, and volatile, with a need to control knowledge agendas, with a love-hate relationship with formal knowledge, and with an ingrained habit to place cultural values and power relationships over social science findings. Thus it is not easy to gain attention for plans to reformulate the definition of a social problem or for the critical scrutiny of suggestions for reform and improvement. Nor is it easy to gain attention for completed research findings and to have them be used in any of the ways *use* is commonly defined. It is only by adopting a more active and comprehensive conceptualization of the evaluator's role that many of the limitations can be reduced that are inherent in evaluation's relationship both to problem solving and to the political context in which evaluation occurs. These limitations will never be transcended, though, as this exposition of the difference between program and product evaluations has, we hope, made clear.

REFERENCES

Applied Management Sciences, Inc. (1984). Income verification pilot project. Phase II: Results of quality assurance evaluation, 1982–83 school year. January. 962 Wayne Avenue, Suite 701, Silver Spring, Md. 20910.

Attkisson, C. C., W. A, Hargreaves, M. J., Horowitz, and J. E. Sorensen Eds. (1978). *Evaluation of human service programs.* New York: Academic Press.

Ball, S., and G. A. Bogatz (1970). *The first year of "Sesame Street": an evaluation.* Princeton, N.J.: Educational Testing Service.

Bardach, E. (1977). *The implementation game: what happens after a bill becomes a law.* Cambridge, Mass.: M.I.T. Press.

Bauman, P. (1976). The formation of the health maintenance organization policy, 1970–1973. *Social science and medicine.* Vol. 10. Pp. 129–142.

Beck, M. A. (1978). Effecting the research to action linkage: the research utilization program of NILECJ. Washington, D.C.: National Center for Law Enforcement and Criminal Justice, September.

Bentler, P. M., and J. A. Woodward (1978). A Head Start reevaluation: positive effects are not yet demonstrable. *Evaluation Quart., 2,* 493–510.

Berman, P. (1980). Thinking about programmed and adaptive implementation: matching strategies to situations. In H. M. and D. E. Mann (Eds.), *Why policies succeed or fail.* Beverly Hills, Calif.: Sage. Pp. 205–227.

Berman P., and M. W. McLaughlin (1978). *Federal programs supporting educational change. Vol. VIII: implementing and sustaining innovations.* Santa Monica, Calif.: The Rand Corporation. (ED 159 289).

Bhaskar, R. (1979). *The possibility of naturalism: a philosophical critique of the contemporary human sciences.* Great Britain: The Harvest Press Limited.

Bickell, E., and W. W. Cooley (1982). *The utilization of a district-wide needs assessment.* Pittsburgh, Penn. Univ. of Pittsburgh Learning Research and Development Center.

Boeckmann, M. E. (1976). Policy impacts of the New Jersey income maintenance experiment. *Policy Sci., 7,* 53–76.

Boruch, R. F. (1975). On common contentions about randomized experiments. In R. F. Boruch and H. W. Riecken (Eds.), *Experimental tests of public policy.* Boulder, Colo.: Westview Press.

Boruch, R. F., L. C. Leviton, D. S. Cordray, and G. Pion (1980). How are evaluations used? In R. F. Boruch and D. S. Cordray (Eds.), *An appraisal of educational program evaluations: federal, state and local levels.* Washington, D. C.: Department of Education.

Blau, P. M. (1954). *The dynamics of bureaucracy.* Chicago: Univ. of Chicago Press.

Bryk, A. S. (Ed.). (1983). *Stakeholder-based evaluation.* San Francisco: Jossey-Bass.

California State Department of Education. (1977). *California school effectiveness study, the first year, 1974-1975. A report to the California State Legislature as required by Education Code Section 12851.* Sacramento: California State Dept. of Educ.

Campbell, D. T. (1969). Reforms as experiments. *Amer. Psychologist, 24,* 409–429.

_____ (1973). The social scientist as methodological servant of the experimenting society. *Policy Studies, 2,* 72–75.

_____ (1974). Qualitative knowing in action research. Kurt Lewin Award Address, Society for the Psychological Study of Social Issues, Meeting of the American Psychological Association, New Orleans, La., September 1.

_____ (1975). "Degrees of freedom" and the case study. *Compara. Politic. Studies,* September, 178–193.

_____ (1976). Focal local indicators for social program evaluation. *soc. indicators Res., 3,* 237–256.

Campbell, D. T., and R. F. Boruch (1975). Making the case for randomized assignment to treatments by considering the alternatives: six ways in which quasi-experimental evaluations tend to underestimate effects. In C. A. Bennett and A. A. Lumsdaine (Eds.), *Evaluation and experiment: some critical issues in assessing social programs.* New York: Academic Press.

Campbell, D. T., and A. E. Erlebacher (1970). How regression artifacts can mistakenly make compensatory education programs look harmful. In J. Hellmuth (Ed.), *Compensatory education: a national debate.* Vol. 3 of *The disadvantaged child.* New York: Brunner/Mazel.

Campbell, D. T., and J. C. Stanley (1966). *Experimental and quasi-experimental designs for research.* Chicago: Rand McNally.

Campeau, P. L. *et al.* (1975). *The identification and description of exemplary bilingual programs.* Palo Alto, Calif.: American Institutes for Research.

Chebinsky, E. (1979). Evaluating broad-aim large-scale demonstration programs. In F. M. Zweig, (Ed.), *Evaluation in legislation.* Beverly Hills, Calif.: Sage.

Chen, H., and P. H. Rossi (1980). The multi-goal, theory-driven approach to evaluation: a model linking basic and applied social science. *Soc. Forces, 59,* 106–122.

_____ (1983). Evaluating with sense: the theory-driven approach. *Evaluation Rev. 7,* 283–302.

Cicirelli, V. G. and Associates (1969). *The impact of Head Start: an evaluation of the effects of Head Start on children's cognitive and affective development* (Vol. 1 and 2). A report to the Office of Economic Opportunity. Athens: Ohio Univ. and Westinghouse Learning Corporation.

Cochran, N. (1978). Grandma Moses and the "corruption" of data. *Evaluation quart., 2,* 5–51.

Cohen, D. K. (1983). Evaluation and reform. In A. S. Bryk (Ed.), *Stakeholder-based evaluation.* San Francisco: Jossey-Bass.

Coleman, J. S., E. Q. Campbell, C. J. Hobson, J. McPartland, A. M. Mood, F. D. Weinfeld, and R. L. York (1966). *Equality of educational opportunity.* Washington, D.C.: U.S. Government Printing Office.

Coleman, J. S., T. Hoffer, and S. Kilgore (1981). *Public and private schools.* Draft Report, National Opinion Research Center, Chicago.

Connell, L., and G. Turner (1983). *The evaluation of school health curricula.* Cambridge, Mass.: Abt Associates, Inc.

Cook, F. L. (1981). Crime and the elderly: the emergence of a policy issue. In D. A. Lewis (Ed.), *Reactions to crime.* Beverly Hills, Calif.: Sage. P. 772.

Cook, T. D. (1974). The medical and tailored models of evaluation research. In J. G. Albert and M. Kamrass (Eds.), *Social experiments and social program evaluation.* Cambridge, Mass.: Ballinger.

_____ (1981). Dilemmas in evaluation of social programs. In M. B. Brewer and B. E. Collins (Eds.), *Scientific inquiry and the social sciences: a volume in honor of Donald T. Campbell.* San Francisco: Jossey-Bass.

_____ (1983a). Quasi-experimental research on the desegregation question. *Advancing the art of inquiry in school desegregation research.* Santa Monica, Calif.: Systems Development Corporation, April.

_____ (1983b). Quasi-experimentation: its ontology, epistemology and methodology. In G. Morgan (Ed.), *Beyond method: strategies for social research.* Beverly Hills, Calif.: Sage.

_____ (1983c). Research, program development and the education of native Hawaiians: a conversation with Myron Thompson. *Amer. Psychologist. 38.* Pp. 1015–1021.

_____ (1984a). Opportunities for evaluation in the next few years. *Evaluation News, 5,* Pp. 20–45.

_____ (1984b). Evaluation: whose questions should be answered? In G. R. Gilbert (Ed.), *Making and managing* policy: formulation, analysis, evaluation. New York: Marcel Dekker, Inc.

_____ (1984c). What have black children gained academically from school desegregation: A review of the meta-analytic evidence. In *School Desegregation*. Washington, D.C.: National Institute of Education.

_____ (1984). Post-positivist critical multiplism. In L. Shotland and M. M. Mark (Eds.), *Social science and social policy*. Beverly Hills, Calif.: Sage.

Cook, T. D., H. Appleton, R. Conner, A. Shaffer, G. Tamkin, and S. J. Weber (1975). *"Sesame Street" revisited*. New York: Russell Sage Foundation.

Cook, T. D., and A. Buccino (1979). The social scientist as a provider of consulting services to the federal government. In J. J. Platt and R. J. Wicks (Eds.), *The psychological consultant*. New York: Grune and Stratton.

Cook, T. D., and D. T. Campbell (1979). *Quasi-experimentation: design and analysis issues for field settings*. Chicago: Rand McNally.

Cook, F. L., and T. D. Cook (1976). Evaluating the rhetoric of crisis: a case study in victimization of the elderly. *Soc. Serv. Rev., 50* (4), 632–646.

Cook, T. D., M. Del Rosario, K. Hennigan, M. M. Mark, and W. M. K. Trochim (Eds.) (1978). *Evaluation studies review annual*, Vol. 3. Beverly Hills, Calif.: Sage Publications.

Cook, T. D., and C. L. Gruder (1978). Metaevaluation research. *Evaluation Quart. 2* (1), 5–51.

Cook, T. D., D. Kendzierski, and S. V. Thomas (1983). The implicit assumptions of television research: an analysis of the NIMH report on television and behavior. *Public Opinion Quart., 47,* 161–201.

Cook, T. D., and L. C. Leviton (1980). Reviewing the literature: a comparison of traditional methods with meta-analysis. *J. Pers. 48,* 449–472.

Cook, T. D., and C. S. Reichardt, Eds. (1979). *Qualitative and quantitative methods in evaluation*. Beverly Hills, Calif.: Sage.

Cook, T. D., and W. R. Shadish (1982). Metaevaluation: an evaluation of the CMCH congressionally-mandated evaluation system. In G. Stahler and W. R. Tash (Eds.), *Innovative approaches to mental health evaluation*. New York: Academic Press.

Cooley, L. J., and P. R. Lohnes (1971). *Multivariate data analysis*. New York: Wiley-Interscience.

Cronbach, L. J. (1982). *Designing evaluations of educational and social programs*. San Francisco: Jossey-Bass.

Cronbach, L. J., S. R. Ambron, S. M. Dornbusch, R. D. Hess, R. C. Hornik, D. C. Phillips, D. F. Walker, and S. S. Weiner (1980). *Toward reform of program evaluation*. San Francisco: Jossey-Bass.

Cronbach, L. J., D. R. Rogosa, R. E. Floden, and G. G. Price (1977). *Analysis of covariance in nonrandomized experiments: parameters affecting bias*. (Occasional paper.) Stanford Univ., Stanford Evaluation Consortium.

Datta, L. E. (1977). Has it worked when it has been tried? And half full or half empty? In M. Guttentag (Ed.), *Evaluation studies review annual*, Vol. 2. Beverly Hills, Calif.: Sage.

Daughety, V., B. Friedman, P. J. Held, E. F. X. Hughes, L. C. Leviton, B. Longest, and M. V. Pauly (1979). A conceptual framework for a "micro-analysis" of the voluntary effort. Evanston, Ill.: Northwestern Univ. Center for Health Services and Policy Research.

David, J. L. (1981). Local uses of Title I evaluations. *Educational evaluation and policy analysis, 3,* 27–39.

Davis, H. R., C. Windle, and S. S. Scharfstein (1977). Developing guidelines for program evaluation in community mental health centers. *Evaluation, 4,* 25–29.

DeNeufville, J. I. (1975). *Social indicators and public policy: interactive processes of design and application*. Amsterdam: Elsevier Scientific.

Department of Health and Human Services. *Health, United States, 1981*. Washington, D.C.: Deparment of Health and Human Services.

Deutsch, S. J., and F. B. Alt (1977). The effect of Massachusetts' gun control law on gun-related crimes in the city of Boston. *Evaluation Quart., 1,* 543–68.

Devine, E. C., and T. D. Cook (1983). Effects of psychoeducational Interventions on length of post-surgical hospital stay: a meta-analytic review of 49 studies. *Nursing Res., 1,* 267–274.

Dintzer, I., and J. E. Soderstrom (1978). Making a case for an interface between quasi-experimental designs and social impact analyses. *Evaluation and program Plan., 1,* 309–318.

Director, S. M. (1978). Underadjustment bias in the evaluation of manpower training. *Evaluation Quart., 3,* 196–218.

Dommel, P. R., R. P. Nathan, S. F. Liebschutz, M. T. Wrightson, *et al.* (1978). *Decentralizing community development*. Washington, D.C.: The Brookings Institute.

Dommel, P. R., V. E. Bach, S. F. Liebschutz, L. S. Rubinowitz, *et al.* (1980). *Targeting community development*. Washington, D.C.: U.S. Department of Housing and Urban Development, January.

Dommel, P. R. and Associates (1982). *Decentralizing urban policy*. Washington, D.C.: The Brookings Institute.

Downs, A. (1967). *Inside bureaucracy*. Boston: Little, Brown and Company.

Dunn, W. N. (1982). Reforms as arguments. *Knowledge: creation, diffusion, utilization, 3* (3), 293–326.

Durlak, J. A. (1979). Comparative effectiveness of paraprofessional and professional helpers. *Psychol. Bull., 86,* 80–92.

Dwyer, J. H. (1983). *Statistical models for the social and behavorial sciences*. New York: Oxford University Press.

Edwards, W., M. Guttentag, and K. Snapper (1975). A decision-theoretic approach to evaluation research. In M. Guttentag and E. L. Struening (Eds.), *Handbook of evaluation research*. Beverly Hills, Calif.: Sage.

Eggers, F. (1981). Evaluating block grants: lessons learned from the Community Development Block Grant experience. Presented at the annual meeting of the Evaluation Research Society, Austin, Tex.

Elinson, J. (1974). Toward sociomedical health indicators. *Soc. Indicators Res., 1,* 59–71.

Ezrahi, Y. (1978). Political contexts of science indicators. In Y. Elkana *et al.* (Eds.), *Toward a metric of science indicators*. New York: Wiley-Interscience.

Fairweather, G. W., D. H. Sanders, and L. G. Tornatzky (1974). *Creating change in mental health organizations.* New York: Pergamon Press.

Fairweather, G. W., and L. G. Tornatzky (1977). *Experimental methods for social policy research.* New York: Pergamon Press.

Far West Laboratories. (1979). *Educational programs that work.* (6th ed.). San Francisco, Calif.: Far West Laboratories.

Farquhar, J. W., N. Maccoby, P. D. Wood, J. Alexander, H. Breitrose, B. J. Brown, W. L. Haskell, A. L. McAlister, A. J. Meyer, J. D. Nash, and M. P. Stern (1977). Community education for cardiovascular health. *The Lancet,* June 4, 1192-95.

Feeley, M. M., and A. D. Sarat (1980). *The policy dilemma: federal crime policy and the Law Enforcement Assistance Administration 1968-1978.* Minneapolis: Univ. of Minnesota Press.

Fisher, E., J. Penoi, and W. Wesley (1980). *Analysis of LRDC follow through model.* Pittsburgh, Penn: Univ. of Pittsburgh.

Freeman, H. E., and M. A. Solomon (1981). Introduction: evaluation and the uncertain 1980s. In H. E. Freeman and M. A. Solomon (Eds.), *Evaluation studies review annual,* Vol. 6. Beverly Hills, Calif.: Sage.

Fullan, M. (1982). *The meaning of educational change.* New York: Teachers College Press.

Garfield, S. L. (1980). *Psychotherapy: an eclectic approach.* New York: Wiley-Interscience.

Gilbert, J. P., B. McPeek, and F. Mosteller (1978). Statistics and ethics in surgery and anesthesia. *Science, 78,* 684-689.

Glaser, E. M. (1976). *Putting knowledge to use: a distillation of the literature regarding knowledge transfer and change.* Beverly Hills, Calif.: Human Interaction Research Institute.

Glass, G. V., Ed. (1976). *Evaluation studies review annual,* Vol. 1. Beverly Hills, Calif.: Sage.

Glass, G. V., B. McGaw, and M. L. Smith (1981). *Meta-analysis in social research.* Beverly Hills, Calif.: Sage.

Goldsmith, J., and N. Tomas (1974). Crimes against the elderly: a continuing national crisis. *Aging,* June-July, 236-237.

Gordon, R. J. (1981). The consumer price index: measuring inflation and causing it. *Public Interest, 63,* Pp. 112-134.

Guba, E. G., and Y. S. Lincoln (1981). *Effective evaluation.* San Francisco, Calif.: Jossey-Bass.

Gunter, M., L. Shulman, E. Esposito, and E. Ricci (1981). *Organizing, financing, and managing pre-hospital care systems.* Pittsburgh, Pa.: Health Services Research Unit, Univ. of Pittsburgh Press.

Guttentag, M. (Ed.). (1977). *Evaluation studies review annual,* Vol. 2. Beverly Hills, Calif.: Sage Publications.

Hamilton, J. A., and A. M. Mitchell (1979). *Final technical report: identification of evaluated examplary activities in career education.* Palo Alto, Calif.: American Institutes for Research.

Haney, W. (1977). *A technical history of the national Follow Through evaluation.* Cambridge, Mass.: Huron Institute.

Hawkridge, D. G., P. L. Campeau, K. M. DeWitt, and P. K. Trickett (1969). *A study of further selected examplary programs for the education of disadvantaged children.* Palo Alto, Calif.: American Institute for Research.

Hay, R. A., and R. McCleary (1979). On the specification of Box-Tiao time series models for impact assessment: a comment on the recent work of Deutsch and Alt. *Evaluation Quart., 3* (2), 277-314.

Hayes, S. C. (1981). Single case experimental design and empirical clinical practice. *J. consult. clinic. Psychol., 49,* 193-211.

Heckman, J. J. (1979). Sample selection bias as a specification error. *Econometrica, 47,* 153-161.

Hendricks, M. (1981). Service delivery assessment: qualitative evaluations at the cabinet level. In N. L. Smith (Ed.), *New directions for program evaluation: federal efforts to develop new evaluation methods,* No. 12. San Francisco: Jossey-Bass.

Hennigan, K. M., M. L. Del Rosario, L. Heath, T. D. Cook, J. D. Wharton, and B. J. Calder (1982). The impact of the introduction of television on crime in the United States: empirical findings and theoretical implications. *J. Per. soc. Psychol., 42* (3), 461-477.

Hill, P. (1980). Evaluating education programs for federal policy makers: lessons from the NIE Compensatory Education Study. In J. Pincus *et al., Educational evaluation in the public policy setting.* Santa Monica, Calif.: Rand Corporation (R-2502-RC).

House, E. R. (1980). *Evaluating with validity.* Beverly Hills, Calif.: Sage.

House, E. R., G. V. Glass, L. D. McLean, and D. F. Walker (1978). No simple answer: critique of the "Follow Through" evaluation. *Harvard educat. Rev., 48,* 128-160.

House, E. R., S. Mathison, J. A. Pearsol, and H. Preskill (1982). *Evaluation studies review annual,* Vol. 7. Beverly Hills, Calif.: Sage.

Joreskog, K. G., and D. Sorbom (1979). *Advances in factor analysis and in structural equation models.* Cambridge, Mass.: ABT Books.

Kaufman, H. (1976). *Are federal agencies immortal?* Washington, D. C.: The Brookings Institute.

Kazdin, A. E. (1981). Drawing valid inferences from case studies. *J. Consult. clinic. Psychol. 49,* 183-192.

Kelling, G. L., T. Pate, D. Dieckman, and C. E. Brown (1976). The Kansas City preventive patrol experiment. In G. V. Glass (Ed.), *Evaluation studies review annual,* Vol. 1. Beverly Hills, Calif.: Sage.

Kessler, R. C., and H. Stipp (In press). The impact of fictional television suicide stories on U.S. fatalities: a replication. *Amer. J. Sociol.*

Kiesler, C. A., N. A. Cummings, and G. R. Van den Bos (Eds.) (1979). *Psychology and national health insurance.* Washington, D.C.: American Psychological Association.

Klitgaard, R. E. (1978). Identifying exceptional performers. *Policy Analysis, 4,* 529-547.

Kloman, E. H., Ed. (1979). *Cases in accountability: the work of the GAO.* Boulder, Colo.: Westview Press.

Knorr, K. (1977). Policymakers' use of social science knowledge: symbolic or instrumental? In C. H. Weiss (Ed.), *Using social research in public policy making.* Lexington, Mass.: Lexington Books.

Kristein, M. M. (1977). Economic issues in prevention. *Prev. Med. 6*, 252–264.

Kuhn, T. S. (1962). *The structure of scientific revolutions.* Chicago: Univ. of Chicago Press.

Kutza, E. A. (1981). *The benefits of old age: social welfare policy for the elderly.* Chicago: Univ. of Chicago Press.

Larsen, J. K., and R. Agarwala-Rogers (1977). Reinvention of innovative ideas: modified? adopted? none of the above? *Evaluation, 4,* 136–140.

Larsen, J. K., and P. D. Werner (1981). Measuring utilization of mental health program consultation. In J. A. Ciarlo (Ed.) *Utilizing evaluation.* Beverly Hills, Calif.: Sage.

Larson, R. C. (1976). What happened to patrol operations in Kansas City? *Evaluation, 3,* 117–23.

Levin, H. M. (1975). Cost-effectiveness analysis in evaluation research. In M. Guttentag and E. L. Struening (Eds.), *Handbook of evaluation research.* Beverly Hills, Calif.: Sage.

Levin, H. M. (1983). *Cost-effectiveness: a primer.* Beverly Hills, Calif.: Sage.

Levine, R. A. (1970). *The poor ye need not always have with you: lessons from the war on poverty.* Cambridge, Mass.: the M.I.T. Press.

Levitan, S. A. (1969). *The great society's poor law: a new approach to poverty.* Baltimore: The Johns Hopkins Press.

Levitan, S. A., and R. Taggart (1976). *The promise of greatness.* Cambridge, Mass.: Harvard Univ. Press.

Leviton, L. C., and R. F. Boruch (1983). Contributions of evaluation to education programs and policy. *Evaluation Rev., 7,* 563–598.

Leviton, L. C., and R. F. Boruch (1984). Why the compensatory education evaluation was useful. *J. policy Analysis Manage., 3,* 299–305.

Leviton, L. C., and T. D. Cook (1981). What differentiates meta-analysis from other forms of review? *J. Pers., 49,* 31–36.

———— (1983). Evaluation findings in education and social work textbooks. *Evaluation Rev., 7,* 497–518.

Leviton, L. C., and E. F. X. Hughes (1981). Research on the utilization of evaluations: a review and synthesis. *Evaluation Rev., 5,* 525–548.

Lieberman, M. A., I. D. Yalom, and M. B. Miles (1973). *Encounter groups: First facts.* New York: Basic Books.

Light, R. J., Ed (1983). *Evaluation studies review annual,* vol. 8. Beverly Hills, Calif.: Sage Publications.

Lindblom, C. E. (1977). *Politics and markets: the world's political-economic systems.* New York: Basic Books.

———— (1980). *The policy-making process.* Englewood Cliffs, N.J.: Prentice-Hall.

Lindblom, C. E., and D. K. Cohen (1979). *Usable knowledge: social science and social problem solving.* New Haven: Yale Univ. Press.

Manchir, J., L. A. Goldsmith, and E. H. Kloman (1979). The national grain inspection system. In E. H. Kloman (Ed.), *Cases in accountability: the work of the GAO.* Boulder, Colo.: Westview Press.

Mayeske, G. W. *et al.* (1972). *A study of our nation's schools.* Washington, D.C.: U.S. Office of Education, Office of Planning, Budget and Evaluation (ED 082 312).

Meidinger, E., and A. Schnaiberg (1980). Social impact assessment as evaluation research: claimants and claims. *Evaluation Rev., 4* (4), 507–35.

Mosher, F. C. (1979). *The GAO: the quest for accountability in American government.* Boulder, Colo.: Westview Press.

Mullen, E. J., R. M. Chazin, and D. M. Feldstein (1972). Services for the newly dependent: an assessment. *Soc. Serv. Rev., 46,* 309–322.

Mumford, E., H. S. Schlesinger, and G. V. Glass (1982). The effects of psychological intervention on recovery from surgery and heart attack: an analysis of the literature. *Amer. J. pub. Health, 72,* 141–151.

Nathan, R. P. (1979). Federal grants-in-aid: how are they working in 1978? Presented at a conference on "Cities in Stress," sponsored by the Center for Urban Policy Research, Rutgers University, March 1979.

Nathan, R. P., and C. F. Adams *et al.* (1977). *Revenue sharing: the second round.* Washington, D.C.: The Brookings Institute.

Nathan, R. P. *et al.* (1981). *Public service employment: a field evaluation.* Washington, D.C.: The Brookings Institute.

National Institute of Mental Health. (1980). Provisional data from federally funded mental health centers. Washington, D.C.: Survey and Reports Branch, Division of Biometry and Epidemiology, NIMH.

Nevasky, V. S., and D. Paster (1976). Background paper. In *Law enforcement: the federal role.* Report of the Twentieth Century Fund Task Force on the Law Enforcement Assistance Administration. New York: McGraw Hill.

Patton, M. Q. (1978). *Utilization—focused evaluation,* Beverly Hills, Calif.: Sage Publications.

Paul, G. L., J. P. Redfield, and R. J. Lentz (1976). The inpatient scale of minimal functioning: a revision of the social breakdown syndrome gradient index. *J. Consult. clinic. Psychol., 44,* 1021–1022.

Popham, J. W., and D. Carlson (1977). Deep, dark deficits of the adversary evaluation model. *Education Research. 6,* 3–6.

Popper, K. R. (1972). *Objective knowledge: an evolutionary approach.* Oxford: Oxford Univ. Press.

Pressman, J., and A. Wildavsky (1973). *Implementation.* Berkeley: Univ. of California Press.

Reichardt, C. S., and T. D. Cook (1979). Beyond qualitative versus quantitative methods. In T. D. Cook and C. S. Reichardt (Eds.), *Qualitative and quantitative methods in evaluation.* Beverly Hills, Calif.: Sage Publications.

———— (1981). "Paradigms lost": some thoughts on choosing methods in evaluation research. *Evaluation and Program Planning, 1,* 229–236.

Ricci, E., L. Shuman, G. Esposito, *et al.* (1980). *Case studies in community decision making: the emergency medical services experience.* Pittsburgh: Univ. of Pittsburgh Health Services Research Unit.

Riecken, H. W., and R. F. Boruch (Eds.). (1974). *Social experimentation: a method for planning and evaluating social intervention.* New York: Academic Press.

Rivlin, M., and P. M. Timpane (Eds.). (1975). *Planned variation in education.* Washington, D.C.: The Brookings Institute.

Rossi, P. H. (1982). Some dissenting comments on Stake's review. In E. R. House *et al.* (Eds.), *Evaluation studies review annual,* Vol. 7. Beverly Hills, Calif.: Sage Publications.

Rutman, L. (1980). *Planning Useful Evaluations.* Beverly Hills, Calif.: Sage Publications.

St. Pierre, R. G. (1983). *Management and organization of program evaluation.* San Francisco: Jossey-Bass.

St. Pierre, R. G. and T. D. Cook (1984). Sampling strategy in the design of program evaluations. In R. F. Conner, D. E. Altman, and C. Jackson (Eds.), *Evaluation Studies Review Annual,* Vol. 9. Beverly Hills, Calif.: Sage.

St. Pierre, R. G., T. D. Cook, and R. B. Straw (1982). An evaluation of the nutrition education and training program: findings from Nebraska. *Evaluation and Program Planning, 4,* 335–344.

Sackett, D. L. *et. al.* (1975). Randomized clinical trial of strategies for improving medication compliance in primary hypertension. *Lancet,* 1205–1207.

Sainsbury, T., R. K. Sharma, S. Iyengar, and B. Overman (1982). *A Preliminary Study of Home Health Care in Allegheny County, Pennsylvania.* Pittsburgh: University of Pittsburgh.

Sawyer, L. B. (1979). The manager and the modern internal auditor. New York: AMACOM.

Scriven, M. (1972). Pros and cons about goal-free evaluation. *Evaluation Comment, 3,* 1–4.

———— (1976). Maximizing the power of causal investigation: the modus operandi method. In G. V. Glass (Ed.), *Evaluation studies review annual,* Vol. 1. Beverly Hills, Calif.: Sage Publications.

———— (1980). *The logic of evaluation.* Inverness, Calif.: Edgepress.

Sechrest, L. (1984). Social science and social policy: will our numbers ever be good enough? In L. Shotland and M. M. Mark (Eds.), *Social science and social policy.* Beverly Hills, Calif.: Sage.

Sechrest, L., S. G. West, M. A. Phillips, R. Redner, and W. Yeaton (1982). *Evaluation studies review annual,* Vol. 4. Beverly Hills, Calif.: Sage.

Shadish, W. R., Jr. (1983). A review and critique of controlled studies of the effectiveness of preventive child health care. In R. J. Light (Ed.), *Evaluation studies review annual,* Vol. 8. Beverly Hills, Calif.: Sage. Pp. 507–535.

———— (1984). Policy research: lessons from the implementation of deinstitutionalization. *Amer. Psychologist., 39,* 725–738.

———— (in press). Sources of method choices: needs, purposes, questions, and technology. In L. Bickman and D. L. Weatherford (Eds.), *Evaluating early intervention programs for severely handicapped children and their families.* Baltimore: Univ. Park Press.

Shadish, W. R., Jr., R. B. Straw, A. J. McSweeney, D. L. Koller, and R. R. Bootzin (1981). Nursing home care for mental patients: descriptive data and some propositions. *Amer. J. Community Psychol., 9,* 617–633.

Shadish, W. R., S. Thomas, and R. R. Bootzin (1982). Criteria for success in deinstitutionalization: perceptions of nursing homes by different interest groups. *Amer. J. Community Psychol., 10,* 553–566.

Simon, H. A. (1959). Theories of decision-making in economics and behavorial science. *Amer. Economic Rev., 49,* 253–83.

Smith, M. L., and G. V. Glass (1977). Meta-analysis of psychotherapy outcome studies. *Amer. Psychologist, 32,* 752–760.

Soar, R. S. (1973). *Final report: follow through process measurement and pupil growth,* (1970–1971). Gainesville, Fla.: College of Education, Univ. of Florida.

Sproull L. S., and D. Zubrow, Standardized testing in the educational organization administrative performance system. Presented at AERA annual meeting, Boston, April, 1980.

Stake, R. E., and J. A. Easley (1978). Case studies in science education. Champaign: Univ. of Illinois Center for Instructional Research and Curriculum Evaluation and Committee on Culture and Cognition.

Stallings, J. A. (1973). *Follow Through program classroom observation evaluation, 1971–1972.* Menlo Park, Calif.: Stanford Research Institute. (ED 085 100).

Stebbins, L. B., R. G. St. Pierre, E. C. Proper, R. B. Anderson, and T. R. Cerva (1978). An evaluation of Follow Through. In T. D. Cook *et al.* (Eds.), *Evaluation studies review annual,* Vol. 3. Beverly Hills, Calif.: Sage Publications. Pp. 571–610.

Stokey, E., and R. Zeckhauser (1978). *A primer for policy analysis.* New York: W. W. Norton.

Straw, R. B., N. M. Fitzgerald, T. D. Cook, and S. V. Thomas (1982). Using routine monitoring data to identify effects and their causes. In G. Forehand (Ed.), *New directions for program evaluation: applications of time series analysis to evaluation.* San Francisco: Jossey-Bass.

Stromsdorfer, E. W., and G. Farkas, Eds. (1980). *Evaluation studies review annual,* Vol. 5. Beverly Hills, Calif.: Sage.

Suchman, E. A. (1967). *Evaluative research.* New York: Russell Sage Foundation.

Tallmadge, G. K. (1977). *Ideabook: the joint dissemination review panel.* Washington, D.C.: U.S. Office of Education and National Institute of Education.

Thompson, M. (1980). *Benefit-cost analysis for program evaluation.* Beverly Hills, Calif.: Sage.

Trochim, W. M. K. (1982). Methodologically based discrepancies in compensatory education evaluation. *Evaluation Rev., 6,* 443–480.

Tukey, J. W. (1977). *Exploratory data analysis.* Reading, Mass.: Addison-Wesley.

Tuma, N. B., M. T. Hannon, and L. P. Groeneveld (1979). Dynamic analysis of event histories. *Amer. J. Sociol., 84,* 820–54.

Van Horn, C. E. (1979). *Policy implementation in the federal system.* Lexington, Mass.: D. C. Heath.

Wargo, M. J., P. L. Campeau, and G. K. Tallmadge (1971). *Further examination of exemplary programs for educating disadvantaged children.* Palo Alto, Calif.: American Institutes for Research. (EC 055 128).

Webb, E. G., D. T. Campbell, R. D. Schwartz, and L. Sechrest (1966). *Unobtrusive measures: nonreactive research in the social sciences.* Skokie, Ill.: Rand McNally.

Weinstein, M. D., and W. B. Stason (1976). *Hypertension: a policy perspective.* Cambridge, Mass.: Harvard Univ. Press.

Weiss, C. H. (1973). Where politics and evaluation meet. *Evaluation, 1,* 37–45.

Weiss, C. H. (1975). Evaluation research in the political context. In E. L. Struening and M. Guttentag (Eds.), *Handbook of evaluation research,* Vol. 1. Beverly Hills, Calif. Sage.

_____ (1977). Research for policy's sake: the enlightment function of evaluations. *Policy Analysis, 3,* 531–45.

Weiss, C. H., and M. J. Bucuvalas (1980). *Social science research and decision-making.* New York: Columbia University Press.

Weiss, J. A., and C. H. Weiss (1981). Social scientists and decision makers look at the usefulness of mental health research. *Amer. Psychologist, 36,* 837–847.

Weissert, W. G. (1976). Two models of geriatric day care: findings from a comparative study. *The Gerontologist, 16,* 420–27.

_____ (1977). Adult day care programs in the United States: Current research projects and a survey of ten centers. *Public Health Reports, 92,* 49–56.

Wholey, J. S. (1979). *Evaluation: promise and performance.* Washington, D.C. The Urban Institute.

_____ (1983). *Evaluation and effective public management.* Boston: Little, Brown.

Wildavsky, A. (1979). *Speaking truth to power: the art and craft of policy analysis.* Boston: Little, Brown.

Williams, W. (1980). *The implementation perspective.* Berkeley, Calif.: Univ. of California Press.

Yin, R. K. (1980). Creeping federalism: the federal impact on the structure and function of local government. In N. J. Glickman (Ed.), *The urban impacts of federal policies.* Baltimore: The Johns Hopkins Univ. Press.

Zweig, F. M. (Ed.), (1979). *Evaluation in legislation.* Beverly Hills, Calif.: Sage.

Index

Names

Abell, P., 409
Abelson, R. P., 76, 89, 143, 148, 164, 171, 172, 200, 209, 235, 257, 271, 272, 279, 285, 286, 291, 295, 456, 483, 532, 559, 560, 652
Aberle, D. F., 24, 330
Abernathy, J. R., 654
Ablrecht, S. L., 353
Abrahams, D., 482
Abramson, L. Y., 91
Ach, N., 36
Achen, C., 496
Acito, F., 264
Adams, E. W., 516, 517, 531
Adams, J. S., 69
Adams, N., 156
Adams, R. N., 591
Adelbratt, T., 267, 268
Adelman, L., 239
Aderman, D., 470
Adewole, A., 200
Adler, A., 9
Adorno, T. W., 51, 73, 94, 140, 183, 535, 636
Agar, M., 569, 604
Agarwala-Rogers, R., 726

Ager, J. W., 504
Aiken, M., 408
Ainslee, G., 262
Ajzen, I., 71, 180, 187, 196, 283, 500, 557, 560, 561, 647, 653
Albers, W. A., 231
Aldag, R. J., 387, 409
Alderfer, C. P., 383, 386
Aldous, J., 352
Aldrich, H. E., 409, 415, 416, 417, 418
Alevizos, P. N., 597–599
Alexander, C. N., 343, 344, 363, 365, 427
Alexander, E. R., 272–273, 274
Alexander, J. L., 597
Ali, M. M., 246
Allais, M., 245, 251
Allen, A., 52
Allen, M. P., 420
Allen, R. B., 159, 208
Allen, V. L., 313, 323, 335, 336, 339, 349, 352, 365
Allison, G. T., 280, 384, 393, 394
Allport, F. H., 15, 16, 19, 31, 34, 39, 40, 47, 50, 58, 77, 85, 139, 140, 144

Allport, G. W., 8, 9, 15, 35, 37, 47, 49, 50, 51, 52, 61, 63, 83, 94, 130, 138, 140, 176, 184, 185, 195, 510, 581, 649
Alpender, G. G., 349
Alpert, M., 295
Altman, I., 95–96
Altstatt, L., 118
Amabile, M., 283
Amabile, T. M., 182, 190, 191
Anderson, C., 181
Anderson, C. A., 293
Anderson, J. C., 391
Anderson, J. R., 137, 142, 145, 165
Anderson, L. R., 504
Anderson, N., 56, 568
Anderson, N. H., 88, 166, 167, 171, 180, 182, 201, 209, 237, 251, 252, 253, 254, 517, 533, 541
Anderson, R., 610, 642
Anderson, T. R., 407
Andrews, F. M., 659, 660
Aneshensel, C. S., 353, 362
Anmerikaner, M., 596
Anthony, D., 592
Appelbaum, M. I., 495

Appelman, D. J., 195
Arabie, B., 523–524
Araji, S., 349, 353
Aram, J. D., 337, 338
Argyle, M., 503
Argyris, C., 338, 381, 382, 430
Aristippus, 4
Aristotle, 2
Arkes, H. R., 191
Arkin, R. M., 182, 195
Armour, H. O., 406
Armstrong, J. S., 583, 680
Arnold, H. J., 240, 392
Arnold, S., 586, 587
Arnold, S. E., 204
Aronfreed, J., 71, 116
Aronson, E., 56, 64, 70, 71, 79, 89,
    139, 141, 203, 314, 441, 445–448,
    449, 450, 452, 453, 454–455,
    457–458, 459, 460, 462, 465, 467,
    479, 480, 482, 484, 596
Arrow, K., 245
Arvey, R. D., 390
Aschner, M. J., 335
Asch, S. E., 16, 21, 33, 49, 54, 56, 79,
    83, 87, 88, 97, 130, 139, 166, 171,
    176, 202, 207, 209, 210, 212, 450,
    455, 467, 482–283
Ashby, R. W., 581
Ashenfelter, O., 412
Ashley-Montagu, M. F., 10, 12
Ashton, R. H., 283, 242, 609
Asumi, K., 339
Attkisson, C. C., 731
Attneave, F., 246
Attridge, C., 588, 603
Atwood, R. W., 544
Austin, G. A., 263, 604
Austin, J. G., 189
Avery, R. K., 578
Ax, A. F., 455
Axelrod, R., 273, 280, 288, 385, 423,
    609
Ayeroff, F., 291
Aziza, C., 205

Babbie, E. R., 642
Baccino, A., 721
Back, K. W., 62, 68, 453, 576
Backman, W., 474
Bacon, F. T., 179
Bacon, L., 339
Bagehot, W., 14, 17
Bagozzi, R. P., 510

Bailar, B. A., 678
Bakeman, R., 505
Baker, F. B., 542
Baker, H., 4
Baker, S. H., 404
Baldes, J. J., 390, 391
Baldridge, J. V., 393
Baldwin, J. M., 14, 17
Bale, R. E., 62
Bales, R. F., 77, 332, 350, 613–617
Balke, W. M., 239
Ball, D. W., 327
Ball, S., 749
Balling, S. S., 124
Baltes, M. M., 122
Bandura, A., 71, 73, 74, 110–111,
    116, 118, 119, 121, 122, 137, 210,
    212, 334, 391, 398, 569
Banks, C., 442, 466
Baratta, P., 246
Barber, B., 337
Barber, E., 337
Barber, T. X., 98
Barbour, F., 265, 268, 269
Bardach, E., 702, 711, 721, 728
Bard, L., 69
Bargh, J. A., 173
Bar-Hillel, M., 187, 283
Baritz, J. H., 380
Barker, L. S., 610–611
Barker, R., 63, 68, 95
Barker, R. G., 576, 584, 587,
    593–594, 610–611, 612, 613
Barnard, C. I., 77, 380
Barnes, H. E., 3
Barnlund, D. C., 505
Baron, J. N., 412
Baron, R. A., 114, 115
Baron, R. M., 574
Baron, R. S., 125
Barrios, A. A., 166
Barron, F. H., 258
Bartlett, F. C., 27, 30, 36, 63, 64, 65,
    83, 84, 144, 164
Barton, A. H., 569, 575, 608
Barton, A. J., 655
Barton, E. M., 122
Barwick, K. D., 397
Barzun, J., 624
Baskett, G. A., 544
Bassok, M., 163, 190
Bastian, A., 27
Bates, F. L., 336, 340
Bateson, G., 336, 584, 596, 601, 609

Battit, G. E., 483
Baty, G., 416, 419
Bauer, R. A., 27, 40
Baum, C. G., 586
Baumann, D. J., 117
Bauman, P., 720
Bauman, W. S., 240
Baumeister, R., 205
Baumgartner, R., 680
Baumol, W., 403
Baumrind, D., 97, 549–550
Beach, L. R., 177, 266, 273, 274, 277,
    281
Bear, G., 200
Beattie, G. W., 624
Bechterew, V. W., 19, 39, 40
Beck, E. M., 411, 412
Beck, H. P., 125
Beck, M. A., 724
Becker, G. M., 245
Becker, H., 3, 13
Becker, H. K., 483
Becker, H. S., 319, 320, 349, 596,
    624
Becker, S. L., 647
Beckman, L. J., 529
Beebe, M., 582
Bell, C. H., 390, 402
Bellack, A. S., 578
Bellamy, G. T., 586
Bellezza, F. S., 154, 165
Bellows, N., 258
Bellugi, U., 74
Belson, W. A., 643, 647, 681
Bem, D. J., 52, 90, 91, 92, 140, 203,
    204, 212, 314, 327, 389, 393, 396,
    562
Bem, S., 154, 161, 164, 336, 353
Beman, P., 720
Benedict, R., 339
Benjamin, L. S., 608, 617–620
Bennett, H. S., 624
Bentham, J., 3, 4, 5, 6, 7, 8, 42
Bentler, P. M., 498, 501, 502, 519,
    763
Benware, C., 204
Ben Zur, H., 262, 274
Berck, P. L., 597–599
Berelson, B., 41
Berenson, C., 680
Berger, C. J., 397
Berger, J., 357, 358, 360, 362
Berger, P., 352
Berger, P. H., 326

Berger, P. L., 422
Berger, S., 119
Berger, S. M., 109, 112, 120–121
Berk, M., 680
Berk, S. F., 339
Berkowitz, L., 41, 73, 82, 95, 109, 110–112, 113, 114, 116–117
Berle, A. A., 403
Berlin, B., 211
Berlyne, D. E., 140, 198
Berman, J. J., 562
Berman, P., 711, 724, 728
Bernal, G., 119
Bernard, H. R., 624
Bernard, J., 339, 353
Bernard, L. L., 3, 15, 33
Bernheim, H., 18, 19, 20
Bernieri, F. J., 194
Berning, C. A. K., 262, 263
Bernoulli, D., 244
Bernstein, A. G., 180
Bernstein, S., 112, 580
Berry, D. C., 294
Berry, W., 625
Berscheid, E., 123, 162, 212, 460
Bertalanffy, L. von, 26
Bettman, J. R., 255, 256, 257, 258, 259, 264, 265, 267
Bezimbinder, T. C., 517
Bhaskar, R., 713, 762–763
Bibb, R., 412
Biblarz, A., 319
Bickell, E., 732
Biddle, B. J., 312
Bidwell, C. E., 382
Bielby, W. T., 412
Bierbrauer, G., 142, 195
Biglan, A., 391
Bigus, O. E., 580
Binet, A., 18, 20, 39
Binkhorst, D., 385, 423
Birnbaum, M., 182
Bishop, G. F., 648, 649, 660
Bishop, Y. M. M., 502, 638
Bittner, E., 320, 582
Bitzine, K. W., 128
Blacher-Dixon, J., 335
Black, J. B., 148, 151, 153, 155
Black, J. S., 560
Blai, B., 388
Blalock, H. M., 400, 498, 637
Blanchard, E. B., 121
Blankenship, D. A., 166
Blanton, M., 15, 16

Blanton, S., 15, 16
Blau, P. M., 336, 338, 380, 394, 400, 407, 418, 730, 733
Blau, Z. S., 349
Blauner, R., 413
Bleda, P. R., 128
Bloch, F. E., 412
Block, J., 52
Blood, M. R., 387
Blood, R. O., 338, 339
Bloom, J. R., 388, 389
Blum, E. R., 122
Blumberg, P., 338
Blumenfeld, W. E., 391
Blumer, H., 312, 313, 315, 317–318, 319, 328, 341, 342, 355, 361, 364, 422, 691
Bobbitt, H. R., 269
Bobrow, D. G., 145
Bock, E. W., 339
Boeckmann, M. E., 704
Bogatz, G. A., 749
Bogdan, R., 575, 594, 624
Boggiano, A. K., 205
Boje, D. M., 422, 429
Bolen, D., 116
Bolstad, O. D., 586, 587, 603
Bolster, B., 182
Bolton, G. M., 544
Bonacich, E., 412
Bonacich, P., 62, 596
Bonhan, G. S., 552
Bonjean, C. M., 596
Bonnett, D. G., 502
Bonoma, T. V., 205
Boodman, C. C., 63
Booker, A., 113, 114
Bootzin, R. R., 757
Borden, R. J., 113
Borgadus, E. S., 519
Borgatta, E. F., 335
Borgida, E., 168, 181, 187, 190, 283
Boring, E. G., 4, 17, 28, 40, 597
Boruch, R. F., 690, 717, 719, 721, 722, 723, 728, 731, 740, 742, 744, 760
Bosanquet, B., 27
Bosk, C. L., 624
Bosley, J. J., 145
Bott, E., 352, 366
Bouchard, T. J., 572
Bougon, M., 384, 423
Bourgeois, L. J., 430

Bower, G. H., 137, 148, 151, 153, 154, 155, 165, 166, 175, 208
Bower, J. L., 429
Bowers, K. S., 51, 123, 384
Bowley, A. L., 636
Bowman, E. H., 242
Boyer, J. L., 118
Bradburn, N. M., 349, 350, 552, 642, 653, 654, 657, 680, 684, 685
Bradley, G. W., 195
Brady, D., 239
Brady, J., 483
Braid, J., 17, 19
Braly, K. W., 94
Bramel, D., 194
Branck, T., 556
Brand, E., 185
Branden, J. L., 505
Brandt, R. M., 593, 595–596
Bransford, J. D., 151
Braun, S. H., 119–120
Braunstein, M. L., 255, 256, 257, 262
Braver, S. L., 205
Braverman, H., 413
Braybrooke, D., 294, 384
Brehm, J. W., 57, 70, 76, 91, 182, 201, 203, 205, 206, 277, 288, 456
Brehm, R. A., 201
Brehm, S. S., 206
Brehmer, B., 233, 234, 236, 239, 293
Brekke, N., 283
Brewer, J. F., 397
Brewer, M. B., 182, 463, 472
Breznitz, S. J., 262, 274
Brickman, P., 116, 276
Bridgeman, D., 484
Bridgman, P. W., 509
Bridwell, L. G., 388
Brief, A. P., 387
Brigham, J. C., 94
Brim, O. G., 320, 352
Brinker, D. J., 119
Britt, D. W., 119
Britt, S. H., 23
Brittain, J. W., 415, 417
Broadbent, D. E., 82, 255, 294
Brock, T. C., 170, 175
Brody, C., 427
Brooks, C., 582
Brown, C. E., 194
Brown, D., 186
Brown, H. W., 582
Brown, P., 112
Brown, R., 74

Brown, R. C., 128
Brown, R. E., 397
Brown, R. H., 385, 386, 422, 423, 424
Brown, T., 19
Brown, T. A., 294
Brown, W., 425
Bruner, J. S., 63, 85, 86, 87, 139, 140, 143, 144, 153, 189, 197, 210, 263, 605
Brunett, S. A., 255
Brunner, G. A., 682
Brunswik, E., 47, 88, 235, 236, 481
Bryan, J. H., 116
Bryant, C. D., 583
Bryk, A. S., 702, 720, 752
Bryson, G., 315
Buccino, A., 706
Buchanan, W., 118, 128
Bucher, R., 342, 395
Buckholdt, D. R., 575
Buckley, W., 581
Bucuvalas, M. J., 704
Buff, S. A., 590
Burchard, W.W., 337
Burger, J. M., 195
Burgess, E. W., 318
Burgess, G. C., 50
Burhstein, E., 166
Burke, M., 264
Burke, P. J., 319, 345, 347, 354, 366, 367, 368
Burke, R. J., 338
Burlin, F. D., 350
Burnett-Hurst, A. R., 636
Burnett, S. A., 269
Burns, T., 408
Burnstein, E., 157, 165, 171, 186, 199, 200, 201
Burrell, G., 421, 423
Burroughs, W. A., 397
Burstyn, J. N., 335
Burt, R. S., 399, 420
Bushell, D., 50
Bushnell, M. M., 624
Bushyhead, J. B., 294
Buss, A. H., 112, 113, 114, 175
Buss, E., 113, 114
Bussey, K., 120, 121
Butler, M. C., 339, 350
Butler, S. R., 591
Butzin, C. A., 166
Bybee, J. A., 174
Byrne, D., 74, 127, 128, 567

Cacioppo, J. T., 176, 200
Cain, P. S., 644
Calconico, J. M., 320
Calder, B. J., 400, 557, 562
Caldwell, B. M., 610
Caldwell, D., 389, 401, 402
Camerer, C., 242
Cameron, N., 335
Campbell, A., 660, 688
Campbell, B. H., 163
Campbell, C., 551
Campbell, D., 415, 416
Campbell, D. T., 64, 71, 253, 426, 472–473, 477, 481, 488, 504, 510, 541, 543, 557, 582, 583, 602, 603, 659, 711, 713, 718, 719, 720, 722, 730, 731, 736, 737, 738, 740, 744, 745, 755, 759, 761, 762, 763, 764, 765, 769
Campbell, J. P., 399
Campeau, P. L., 739
Cannell, C. F., 645, 646, 647, 653, 683, 684
Canon, L. K., 143
Cantor, N., 143, 147, 148, 151, 157, 164, 165, 169, 173, 208, 209
Cantril, H., 20, 23, 181, 655, 657
Capon, N., 264
Carbonell, J. G., 272
Carey, M. S., 597, 601
Carli, L. L., 119
Carlsmith, J. M., 64, 70, 79, 204, 291, 441–442, 450, 452, 455, 456, 457, 460, 461, 462, 482, 596
Carlson, C. C., 126, 129
Carlson, D., 766
Carlston, D. E., 150, 152, 176, 208, 209
Carroll, J. B., 523–524
Carroll, J. S., 181, 194, 208, 256, 257, 258, 265, 282
Carroll, L., 592
Carroll, S. J., 389, 390, 391, 682
Carter, E. E., 275
Carter, L., 62
Carter, L. H., 571
Carter, L. R., 498
Carter, P. L., 238
Cartwright, A., 682
Cartwright, D., 2, 3, 47, 53, 54, 58, 89, 94, 207, 381, 489
Carver, C. S., 175
Cassirer, E., 51
Castellan, N. J., 237, 293

Catlin, H., 4
Cattin, P., 243
Cavan, R. S., 319, 339, 340, 349, 622
Cecil, J. S., 122, 125, 690
Chaffee, E. E., 386, 395
Chaiken, A. L., 123
Chaires, W. M., 185
Chambers, J. D., 205
Chammah, A., 294
Chan, D. W., 501
Chandler, A. D., 416
Chapanis, A., 202
Chapanis, N. P., 202
Chapman, D. W., 678
Chapman, J. P., 190, 191, 282
Chapman, L. J., 190, 191, 282
Charcot, J. M., 14, 17, 18, 19, 20, 23
Charmaz, K. C., 567
Chartier, G. M., 12
Chase, S., 13
Chave, E. J., 60
Chazin, R. M., 711
Chen, H., 713, 715, 720, 746, 753–755, 762, 767
Cherkoff, J. M., 505
Cherlin, A., 339
Chick, G. E., 624
Child, J., 407, 408, 410
Chiu, J. S. Y., 404
Choo, G., 602
Christensen, A., 586
Christensen-Szalanski, J. J. J., 177, 266–267, 273, 277, 294
Christie, R., 51, 58
Christman, K. P., 420
Cialdini, R. B., 117, 128, 129, 176, 205, 473
Cicourel, A. V., 315, 340–341, 422
Ciscel, D. H., 404
Citron, C. C., 123
Clark, H. H., 492
Clark, L. F., 154, 165
Clark, L. V., 119
Clark, M., 262
Clark, R. E., 578
Clarke, H. M., 36
Clarkson, G., 257
Clarkson, G. P. E., 427
Clary, E. G., 160
Claudy, J. G., 242
Clausen, J. A., 325
Clazebrook, A. H., 182
Cleckley, H. M., 537
Clegg, S., 430

Cleveland, S. E., 535, 536, 539
Cliff, N., 521–522
Clore, G. L., 127, 128, 596
Coburn, D., 336–337
Cochran, N., 730, 731
Cochran, W. G., 665
Cofer, C. N., 126
Coffey, H. S., 62
Cohen, A. K., 326, 363, 365
Cohen, A. R., 70, 76, 170, 201, 288, 453
Cohen, C. E., 147, 151, 152, 154, 159, 164, 167, 168, 170, 172
Cohen, D. K., 568, 703, 704, 708, 756, 766
Cohen, J., 109, 283, 489, 496, 497, 500
Cohen, K. J., 419, 427, 428
Cohen, L. J., 180, 233, 234, 283
Cohen, M. D., 385, 427
Cohen, P., 496, 500
Cohen, S. P., 613, 616–617
Coker, R. E., 338
Cole, A. H., 456
Coleman, J. S., 380, 739
Colley, C. H., 341
Collins, B., 288
Collins, B. E., 204, 461
Collins, M., 688
Collins, R., 341
Colson, E., 584
Combs, A., 174
Comstock, D. E., 403
Comte, A., 1, 2, 10, 40, 42
Conant, R. C., 581
Condry, J. C., 205
Cone, J. D., 587, 601, 602
Conger, A. J., 243
Connell, L., 746, 747
Conner, T. L., 357
Connolley, E. S., 204
Connor, J. M., 123
Connor, T. L., 358, 360
Connor, W. H., 117
Conrath, D. W., 255, 270
Converse, J. M., 636, 648
Converse, M. R., 683
Converse, P. E., 38, 510, 649–650, 657–658, 659–660, 688, 691
Cook, F. L., 703, 707
Cook, R. L., 240
Cook, S. W., 545
Cook, T. D., 472, 477, 488, 699, 703, 704, 706, 713, 716, 718, 721, 723,

724, 728, 730, 735–736, 737, 738, 739, 740, 742, 743–744, 745, 747, 749, 752, 754–755, 756–757, 759, 760, 761, 762, 764, 765, 766, 768, 769, 770
Cooley, C. H., 15, 17, 69, 311, 312, 314, 317, 328, 329, 355, 359
Cooley, L. J., 741
Cooley, W. W., 732
Coombs, C. H., 245, 253, 254, 259, 512–513, 515, 517, 518, 526–528, 529–530
Coombs, L. C., 529–530
Coons, A. E., 399
Cooper, H., 195
Cooper, J., 76, 91, 140, 204, 205, 319
Cooper, J. B., 545
Cope, V. M., 455, 459
Copeland, R. E., 397
Corbin, D., 596
Corbin, R. M., 271, 274, 275
Corrigan, B., 238, 241, 242, 559, 561
Corsaro, W. A., 317, 351
Coser, R. L., 364
Cottrell, L. S., 3, 60, 318–319, 335, 349
Cottrell, N. B., 70, 124, 125, 140, 200, 204, 455
Couch, A., 183
Couch, C., 318, 319
Cournoyer, N. G., 680
Coutu, W., 38, 319
Cowan, C. D., 656
Cowan, C. L., 143, 160
Cowen, E. L., 535
Cox, M. G., 164
Cox, S. D., 182
Coyle, V. W., 542
Craft, E. A., 368
Cramer, E. M., 495
Cramer, M. R., 688
Cramer, R. E., 124
Crandal, V. J., 291
Crane, K. A., 206
Crecine, J. P., 427
Crespi, L. P., 182, 560
Cressey, D. R., 319, 349
Crocker, J., 148, 150, 151, 165, 283
Cronbach, L. J., 51, 72, 87, 702, 703, 709–710, 711, 713, 715, 716–717, 720, 723, 724, 740, 744, 745, 751, 755, 761, 762, 763, 764, 767

Cronkite, R. C., 352, 362
Crossley, H. M., 643, 653
Crow, T., 127
Crowley, L. R., 594
Croyle, R. T., 204
Crozier, M., 336, 394
Crutchfield, R. S., 49, 138, 510
Cumming, E., 349
Cummings, L. L., 351, 392, 397, 409
Cummings, N. A., 711
Cuncan, R. B., 409
Cuneo, D. O., 166
Cunningham, M. R., 117
Curti, M. E., 4
Curtis, M. I., 390
Curtis, T. E., 592
Cyert, R. M., 275, 380, 384, 416, 419, 427, 428

Dabbs, J. M., 505, 591, 602
Dachler, H. P., 389, 390, 391
Daft, R. L., 385, 421, 582
D'Agostino, J., 151
Dahl, R. A., 394
Dahrendorf, R., 331
Dalton, G. K., 338
Dalton, M., 577
Damico, S., 338
D'Andrade, R. G., 172
Danehy, J. J., 608
Danheiser, P., 160, 161
Daniels, A., 336
Darley, J., 390
Darley, J. A., 185
Darley, J. M., 95, 162
Darlington, R. B., 116, 239, 496
Darrough, W. D., 579
Darwin, C., 12, 33
Das Gupta, A., 645
Dashiell, J. F., 40, 63, 77
Datta, L. E., 766
Daughety, V., 734
David, J. L., 718, 723, 728
Davis, F., 592, 624
Davis, H. R., 723
Davis, J. A., 400, 690
Davis, K. E., 90, 92, 140, 141, 142, 211, 312, 331
Davis, L. E., 547
Davis, M. H., 205
Davis, M. S., 573
Davol, S. H., 200
Dawe, H. C., 595, 624
Dawes, R. B., 466

Dawes, R. M., 238, 241, 242, 243, 254, 255, 294, 512, 519, 521, 527, 540, 546, 550, 551, 552, 553–555, 559–560, 561
Dawes-Saraga, R. M., 541
Daws, R. M., 245
Dean, J. P., 577
Deaux, K., 573
DeCastro, J., 573
deCharmes, R., 35, 39, 89
Deci, E. L., 204, 205
Deegan, M. J., 578
DeFazio, V. J., 568
DeFinette, B., 245
DeFleur, M. L., 560
DeGroot, A. D., 272, 273
DeJong, W., 682
deLange, M., 40
Dem, D. J., 142
Dembo, T., 63, 68
DeNeufville, J. I., 730
Denny, T., 585
Denzin, N. K., 320, 342, 354, 574
Descartes, 33
DeSilva, A. M., 165
Deslauriers, B. C., 397
DeSmet, A. A., 294
DeSoto, C. B., 52, 145, 186, 199
deSoto, C. D., 541
Deutsch, M., 68, 80–81, 139, 288
Deutschberger, P., 319, 325, 327, 334
Deutscher, I., 349
DeVellis, B. M., 129
Devine, E. C., 738, 762
Devlega, V. J., 123
DeWaele, J. P., 578
Dewey, J., 6, 33, 35, 312, 316, 328
Dickens, C., 6
Diener, E., 396
Diesing, P., 280, 604, 624
Dijkstra, W., 642
Dill, W. R., 380
Dillehay, R. C., 558
Dillman, D. A., 680–681
Dinitz, S., 319
Dintzer, I., 760
Dintzer, L., 91
DiNubile, M., 657
Dittman, A. T., 612
Ditton, J., 577
Dobbs, J. M., 122
Dodge, K. A., 161
Dohrenwend, B. P., 349

Dohrenwend, B. S., 349, 683
Dolby, R. G. A., 568
Dollard, J., 6, 16, 35, 50, 71, 72, 73, 94, 118, 130, 139
Domhoff, G. W., 414
Dommel, P. R., 705, 733, 760
Donahue, G., 319
Doob, A. N., 206, 572
Doob, L. W., 13, 22, 72, 126, 127, 130
Dooling, D. J., 151, 153
Dorfman, D. D., 185
Dorfman, P. W., 238
Dornbusch, S. M., 319, 327
Dosher, B. A., 256, 264, 267, 268
Dossett, D. L., 390
Dougherty, T. W., 578
Douglas, J. D., 570–572, 576, 577, 581, 585, 586, 588
Dowling, J., 426
Downey, H. K., 409
Downey, R. G., 596
Downing, L. L., 160
Downs, A., 721
Dreben, E. K., 171
Droba, D. D., 37
Duberman, L., 339
Dubin, R., 319, 352
Ducamp, A., 518, 519, 528
Dudycha, A. L., 236, 237
Duffey, J., 601
Dulany, D. E., 392
Dull, V., 463
Duncan, B., 502, 688
Duncan, B. L., 161
Duncan, J. A., 647
Duncan, O. D., 498, 502, 637, 638, 659, 688, 691
Duncan, R. B., 408
Dunham, R. B., 388, 402
Dunkelberg, W. C., 687
Dunkerly, D., 430
Dunlap, K., 34
Dunn, D. S., 174
Dunn, M. G., 414
Dunn, W. N., 766
Dunnette, M. D., 399, 603
Durkheim, E., 14, 29, 30, 40, 332
Durlak, J. A., 711
Duval, S., 175, 182, 212, 470
Dwyer, J. H., 745
Dyckman, T. R., 275
Dyer, L., 392
Dyer, W. G., 399

Eagly, A. H., 205
Easley, J. A., 734, 757, 765
Ebbesen, E. B., 152, 159, 167, 170, 172, 204, 208, 265
Ebbinghaus, H., 64
Eckberg, D. L., 583
Eddy, D. M., 294
Edelman, M., 381, 423, 424
Edens, R., 601
Edlow, W. D., 194
Edrich, H., 545
Edstrom, A., 419
Edwards, A. L., 183
Edwards, R. C., 412
Edwards, R. E., 206
Edwards, W., 233, 236, 243, 245, 294, 296, 752, 757
Egbert, L. D., 483
Eggers, F., 733
Ehrlich, D., 203
Ehrlich, H. J., 337
Einhorn, H. J., 196, 231, 232, 233, 235, 238, 239, 240, 241, 242, 243, 255, 257, 259, 266, 281, 292, 293, 561
Eisen, S. V., 160
Eiser, J. R., 196
Eisman, B., 126
Ekland-Olson, S., 601
Elbing, A. O., 404
Elder, G. H., 363
Elinson, J., 730
Eliot, T. S., 455
Elkin, F., 352, 365
Elliot, D. N., 185
Ellis, D. G., 578
Ellsworth, P. C., 64, 208, 596
Ellwood, C. A., 41
Elmore, R., 200
Elms, A. C., 76, 97, 99, 202
El Salmi, A. M., 351
Elstein, A. S., 238
Elster, J., 289, 583
Emerson, J. P., 585
Emerson, R. M., 394
Endler, N., 52
Endler, N. S., 119
Engel, G. V., 337
Engelmann, G., 4
Engels, F., 6
Englander, T., 275
Eno, B., 578
Epicurus, 4
Epstein, C. F., 363

Epstein, S., 143, 576
Erdelyi, M. H., 86, 149
Erdos, P. L., 681
Erez, M., 390
Erickson, E. H., 50, 85
Erickson, F., 594
Ericsson, K. A., 257, 258, 259
Eriksen, C. W., 74, 86
Erlebacher, A. E., 493, 738, 740, 745
Eskilson, A., 362
Espinas, A., 27
Estes, W. K., 84, 192, 231, 281
Ettlie, J. E., 573
Etzioni, A., 285
Evan, W., 416, 418, 419
Evans, J., 180, 295
Evans, M., 151, 154, 167
Evans, M. G., 393
Everett, P. B., 397
Ewall, W., 113
Ewbank, D. C., 644
Ezrahi, Y., 730

Faber, M. D., 264
Fagot, R. F., 516, 517, 531
Fairweather, G. W., 703, 741, 744
Fallding, H. G., 318
Fanshel, D., 608
Faraday, M., 18
Farberman, H. A., 342
Farkas, A. J., 166
Farkas, G., 700, 703, 740
Farley, R., 655
Farquhar, J. W., 760
Farr, R. M., 63
Farris, E., 573
Fazio, R. H., 91, 162, 179, 204, 205,
    206, 285, 652
Feather, N. T., 200
Featherman, D. L., 411
Feeley, M. M., 718, 723
Fehrenbach, P. A., 121
Feigelman, W., 592
Feinberg, R. A., 122, 124
Feld, S., 200, 363
Feldman, D. C., 240
Feldman, J. J., 685
Feldman, R. S., 180
Feldman, S., 182
Feldstein, D. M., 711
Feller, W., 189, 244
Fellner, W., 276
Felson, R. B., 319
Fenigstein, A., 175

Fenkel-Brunswik, E., 51
Ferber, R., 647
Féré, C., 35, 39
Ferguson, A., 312, 315
Ferster, C. B., 396
Feshbach, S., 95
Festinger, L., 59, 63, 68, 69, 70, 71,
    72, 74–75, 76, 78, 79, 89, 90, 97,
    121, 177, 199, 201, 202, 205, 207,
    276, 288, 289, 332, 388, 400, 442,
    450, 453, 456, 457, 461, 535, 576
Fichte, 27
Fiddler, D. S., 551, 552
Fiedler, F. E., 506
Fields, J. M., 655
Fienberg, S. E., 502, 503
Fischer, G. W., 200
Fischhoff, B., 180, 190, 191, 192,
    231, 236, 247, 275, 283, 284, 285
Fisek, M. H., 357, 358, 360
Fishbein, M., 41, 71, 166, 187, 500,
    510, 557, 560, 561, 647, 653
Fishburn, P. C., 245, 253, 259
Fisher, E., 726
Fisher, I., 245
Fisher, S. D., 272
Fiske, D. W., 541, 659
Fiske, M., 691
Fiske, S. T., 148, 150, 155, 164, 167,
    168, 171, 173, 182, 272, 282, 285,
    470
Fitz, D., 115
Flaherty, M. G., 354
Flamange, J. C., 518, 519, 528
Flanagan, C. A., 577
Flanagan, R. J., 413, 430
Flavell, J. H., 144
Fleishman, E., 393, 680
Fleissner, D., 240
Fleming, I., 443
Fletcher, D. J., 240
Floyd, J., 449, 452, 458
Fogarty, M., 336
Foley, J. P., 126
Folkins, C. H., 568
Fondacaro, R., 170, 212
Foner, A., 339
Fong, G. T., 163, 233
Foote, N. N., 319
Forehand, R., 586, 587
Forgas, J. P., 174, 208, 211, 212
Form, W. H., 412
Foster, S. L., 586, 603
Fouillée, A., 30

Fouraker, L. E., 294
Fowler, F. J., 645
Fox, J. A., 654
Fox, R. C., 584
Frager, R., 459, 461
Frankel, M. R., 673, 676, 689
Frankel, R. L., 676
Frankie, G., 120
Franks, D. D., 320
Fraser, C. D., 501
Fraser, S. C., 472, 682
Frauenfelder, K., 186
Freedman, J. L., 56, 95, 206, 289,
    460, 472, 682
Freedman, M. B., 62
Freedman, H. E., 700
Freeman, J. H., 380, 382, 383, 407,
    408, 415, 416, 417, 420–421, 429
Freidson, E., 342
Freud, S., 3, 6, 7, 9, 11, 16, 18, 21, 24,
    27, 33, 37, 73
Frey, D., 204, 206
Friedland, E. I., 384, 393
Friedman, M., 246, 404
Friedman, S., 191
Fried, M. L., 568
Friesen, P., 624
Frodi, A., 114
Froming, W. J., 470
Fromkin, H. L., 170, 569
Fromm, E., 79
Fuggle, F. D., 258
Fulero, S., 151, 154, 167
Fullan, M., 728
Funder, D. C., 52, 396
Funk, S. G., 524
Furedy, J. J., 206

Gaebelein, J., 495
Gaes, G. G., 204
Gagnon, J. P., 544
Galanter, E., 82, 172, 192, 522
Galbraith, J., 392
Galbraith, J. R., 419
Gallagher, J. J., 335
Gallagher, R., 3, 60
Gallo, P. S., 81
Galper, R. E., 171
Galton, F., 40
Gamboa, V. U., 397
Gange, J. J., 125
Gard, J. W., 201
Gardiner, P. C., 296
Gardner, R. A., 192

Garfield, S. L., 738
Garfinkel, H., 99, 327, 422, 579, 592, 601
Gass, W. H., 596
Gati, I., 168
Gecas, V., 319
Geen, R. G., 73, 112, 113, 114, 115, 125
Geer, J. H., 118, 121
Geerken, M. R., 658
Geertz, C., 601, 624
Gehlke, C. E., 30
Geis, F. L., 51
Gellert, E., 603
Geoffrey, W., 590
George, A. L., 272, 273, 274, 287
George, H., 4
Gephart, R. P., 423, 425, 575
Gerard, H. A., 288
Gerard, H. B., 69, 79, 150, 151, 204, 276, 453, 479, 480
Gerbing, D. W., 201
Gergen, K., 99
Gergen, K. G., 314, 315, 367
Gergen, K. J., 51, 381, 429, 442, 583, 639
Gerhardt, U., 337
Gerow, J. R., 185
Gerth, H., 357
Gerwin, D., 427
Gettys, C. F., 272, 275
Getzels, J. W., 337
Gewirtz, J. L., 118
Ghiselli, E. E., 561
Gibson, C., 656
Gibson, J. J., 148
Giddings, F. H., 12
Gifford, R. K., 190, 191
Gifford, W. E., 269, 270
Gilbert, L. A., 351
Gilligan, S. G., 175, 208
Gillig, P. M., 176
Gillin, C. T., 367
Gilmore, J., 76
Gilovich, T., 195, 272, 286
Ginosar, Z., 187, 283
Ginsberg, E., 182
Gladwin, T., 592
Glaser, B. G., 319, 320, 343, 575, 600
Glaser, E. M., 724, 728
Glass, D. C., 95, 484
Glass, G. V., 505, 700, 738, 741, 763
Glassman, R. B., 569
Glavis, L. R., 578

Glenn, N. D., 349, 691
Glick, W., 382, 387
Gmelch, G., 581
Goale, A. J., 687
Goethals, G. R., 205
Goffman, E., 49, 99, 292, 319, 320, 327, 342, 343, 349, 355, 359, 363, 365, 366, 422, 425, 574, 597
Goldberg, L. R., 238, 241, 242, 492, 542
Goldberg, V. P., 413
Golden, M. P., 588
Golden, R. R., 551
Goldenweiser, A., 27, 30
Golder, T. V., 624
Goldiamond, I., 86, 184
Goldin, S. E., 272, 273
Goldman, P., 411
Goldsmith, L. A., 732
Goldstein, D., 179
Gollob, H. F., 200, 201
Gonos, G., 363, 422, 575
Good, K. J., 125
Goode, F., 517
Goode, W. J., 312, 336, 337, 339
Goodman, C. C., 85
Goodman, C. D., 140, 210
Goodman, L. A., 521, 637
Goodman, N., 320, 325, 522
Goodman, R. A., 388
Goodnow, J. J., 189, 263, 605
Goodstadt, M. S., 552, 654
Gordon, D. F., 592
Gordon, F. E., 350
Gordon, F. R., 119
Gordon, G., 395
Gordon, S. E., 155
Gordon, S. F., 155, 170
Gordon, S. L., 354, 355
Gordon, X., 730
Gorman, B., 578
Goslin, D. A., 335, 352, 365
Gottdiener, M., 596
Gottlieb, A., 315, 320, 322
Gottman, J. M., 488, 505
Gouldner, A. W., 329, 336, 340, 380
Gove, W. E., 339
Gove, W. R., 362, 658
Graesser, A. C., 155
Graesser, C. C., 254
Graff, H. F., 624
Graham, N. C., 182
Greeley, A. M., 349
Greenberg, B. C., 550, 551, 552

Greenberg, J., 195
Green, B. F., 254, 520–521, 561
Green, D., 194, 204
Green, D. M., 157, 184, 231
Green, G., 392
Green, T. H., 27
Green, V. E., 517
Greene, D., 92, 204
Greenwald, A. G., 140, 166, 175, 176, 182, 204, 205–206
Gregory, W. L., 282
Grev, R., 117
Grice, G. R., 182
Grice, P., 168, 169, 188, 189, 194
Griffin, M., 157
Griffith, R. M., 246
Griffitt, W. B., 128
Groeneveld, L. P., 711
Gross, A. E., 443, 456, 572
Gross, E., 355
Gross, M. C., 126, 129
Gross, N., 336, 337, 349, 398
Groves, R. M., 638, 676, 677, 679, 680, 682, 687
Gruder, C. L., 716, 752
Grusec, J. E., 119, 120, 121
Grusky, O., 425, 596
Gruson, V., 552, 654
Guay, P. F., 126, 129
Guba, E. G., 337, 585, 717, 736, 745, 747, 761, 765
Gubrium, J. F., 575
Guest, L., 647
Gillikson, H., 56
Gump, P. V., 613
Gumplowicz, L., 2
Gunter, M., 722
Gurwitz, S. B., 161
Guterman, N., 22
Guttentag, M., 700, 752, 757

Haas, H., 578
Haas, J., 407, 568, 592
Hackman, J. R., 383, 387, 388, 389, 392, 401
Haddon, A. C., 3
Haga, W. J., 337
Hage, G., 339
Hage, J., 408
Hagstrom, W., 336
Haines, G. H., 258
Haines, H., 63
Halford, L. J., 578
Hall, D. J., 624

Hall, D. T., 336, 338, 350, 388, 339
Hall, G. S., 40
Hall, P. M., 342
Hall, R., 336
Hall, R. H., 407
Hall, R. V., 397
Hamill, R., 181
Hamilton, D. L., 94, 151, 156, 166, 170, 171, 176, 182, 190, 191, 208, 234, 463
Hamilton, J. A., 739
Hamilton, W., 19
Hammersla, K. S., 119
Hammerton, M., 187
Hammond, K. A., 239
Hammond, K. R., 233, 234, 235, 236, 237, 238, 239, 288, 293, 295
Hamner, E. P., 397
Hamner, W. C., 238, 390, 391, 397
Handa, J., 246
Handel, S., 541
Handel, W., 312, 341, 361, 363, 364, 365
Haney, C., 442, 466, 467
Haney, W., 726
Hannan, M. T., 4–8, 382, 383, 415, 416, 417, 711
Hanratty, M. A., 115
Hanson, D. L., 602
Hanson, L., 182
Hanson, M. H., 661
Hansson, R. O., 262, 274
Harary, F., 89
Harburg, E., 199
Hargens, L. L., 395
Harkins, S. G., 170, 185
Harkness, A. R., 191
Harré, R., 98, 99, 314, 384, 578
Harris, J. E., 405
Harris, R. J., 491
Harris, V. A., 193
Harrison, A. O., 350, 351
Harrison, M. L., 592
Harry, J., 350
Hart, H., 2
Hart, J. D., 601
Harter, S., 352, 543
Hartley, E. L., 94
Hartup, W. W., 121
Harvey, J. H., 88, 92, 170, 171
Harvey, O. J., 62
Hasher, L., 157, 179
Hass, H., 596

Hastie, R., 144, 148, 150, 155, 156, 166, 168, 169, 171, 176, 208, 209, 282
Hastings, R., 355
Hastorf, A. H., 195, 208
Hatch, E., 584
Hatchett, S., 685–686
Hauser, R. M., 383, 400, 411
Haven, C., 339, 349
Havens, E. M., 338
Hawes, L. C., 578
Hawkins, C., 96
Hawkins, R. P., 587, 601, 602
Hawkins, W. F., 184
Hawkridge, D. G., 739
Hawley, A. H., 416
Hayano, D. M., 568
Hay, R. A., 488, 760
Hayes, J. R., 225, 258, 293
Hayes, S. C., 744
Hayes-Roth, B., 165
Haynes, S. N., 578, 604
Hays, W. L., 533
Head, H., 144
Heberlein, T. A., 680
Heckman, J. J., 745, 761
Heckman, N. A., 338
Hedley, J., 596
Heerboth, J., 274
Hegel, G. W. F., 2, 26, 27, 28, 29
Heider, F., 23, 47, 54, 70, 83, 88, 89, 90, 92, 93, 139, 142, 145, 161, 198, 199, 200, 209, 210, 212, 314, 611
Heider, K. G., 596, 601
Heilman, M. E., 206
Heilman, S. C., 601
Heise, D. R., 347, 356–357, 367, 498
Heiss, J., 311, 330, 341
Heizer, J., 397
Hellriegel, D., 409
Helmich, D., 425
Helmreich, R., 164, 204, 288, 461
Helson, H., 180
Helson, R., 51
Hendrick, C., 166, 210
Hendricks, M., 733, 735, 736
Heneman, N. G., 397
Henley, N. M., 145
Henninger, M., 201
Henry, W. E., 337, 349
Henshel, R. L., 442, 575
Henslin, J. M., 292
Hepburn, C., 187
Herb, T. R., 362

Herbart, J. F., 17, 28, 29
Herberlein, T. A., 560
Herbert, J., 588, 603
Herman, C., 208
Herman, J. B., 388, 402
Herr, D. G., 495
Hershey, J. C., 244, 246, 251, 252, 296
Herson, M., 578
Herzberg, F., 387
Hess, E. H., 544
Hess, I., 675
Hetherington, E. M., 120, 335
Hewitt, J. P., 311, 326, 352, 353, 361, 363, 365, 368
Heyns, R. W., 568, 594
Hicks, J. M., 253
Hickson, D. J., 394, 408, 410
Higa, W. R., 126
Higbee, K. L., 122
Higgins, E. T., 140, 161, 167, 170, 171, 173, 185, 204, 208, 212, 470
Hill, L., 583
Hill, M. K., 602
Hill, P., 720, 752, 756
Hill, R., 319, 340, 352
Hills, F. S., 393, 394
Hilton, I., 122
Himmelfarb, S., 185, 205
Hinings, C. R., 394
Hinkle, S., 193
Hirschman, A. O., 413, 583
Hirshleifer, S., 290
Hitler, A., 27, 47
Hobbes, T., 2, 4, 8, 9, 10, 25
Hochschild, A. R., 355
Hockett, C. F., 608
Hocking, W. E., 31
Hodge, R. W., 644
Hodges, B., 182
Hodun, A., 200
Hoelter, J., 346
Hoffman, L., 609
Hoffman, L. R., 179
Hoffman, L. W., 338
Hoffman, P. J., 236, 238, 239, 240, 254
Hoga, D. P., 339
Hogan, R., 52
Hogarth, R. M., 188, 196, 231, 232, 233, 235, 242, 243, 266, 269, 270, 276, 277–278, 279, 281, 293
Hohenfeld, J. A., 595
Holahan, C. K., 351

Holdaway, S., 608
Holder, O., 517
Holland, P. M., 503
Hollingshead, A. B., 644
Hollingworth, H. L., 19
Holly, R., 573
Holmes, D. S., 466
Holmstrom, L., 336
Holt, E. B., 15, 16, 34
Holton, G., 511
Holtzner, B., 422
Homans, G. C., 74, 77, 78, 97, 624
Honigman, J. J., 604
Hood, W., 62
Hoppe, F., 8, 9, 68
Horan, P. M., 412
Horner, M., 353, 362
Horney, K., 9, 50
Horowitz, M. W., 199
Horsfall, R., 145
Horwitz, M., 68
House, E. R., 700, 726, 747, 751, 764–765
House, F. N., 3
House, J., 49
House, J, S., 677
House, P., 194
House, R. J., 393, 399
Houseknecht, S. K., 338, 350
Hovland, C. I., 20, 22, 74, 75, 76, 122, 281, 476, 482, 510, 545
Howard, J. W., 154
Howard-Pitney, B., 168
Howell, R. J., 544
Howell, W. C., 255, 269
Howes, D. H., 183, 184
Hoy, E., 119
Hoyt, M. F., 204
Hsu, F. L. K., 588
Huang, L. C., 245, 254
Hubbard, M., 161, 181
Huber, G. P., 243, 409
Huber, J., 329
Huber, O, 267
Hubert, L. J., 542
Hubert, S., 166, 171, 180
Hudis, P. M., 338
Hughes, E., 584
Hughes, E. C., 317, 333, 349, 624
Hughes, E. F. X., 715, 719, 720, 768
Hughes, M., 339
Hugo, R., 582
Hulin, C. L., 383, 387, 388, 402

Hull, C. L., 19, 67, 68, 71, 72, 75, 84, 109, 110, 126, 128, 130
Hull, J. G., 174
Humboldt, K. W. von, 27
Hume, D., 312, 315–316
Humphrey, G., 15, 16
Humphrey, J. A., 335
Humphreys, L., 577
Humphreys, P., 358
Hunt, W. A., 596
Hunter, J. E., 201, 501
Hunter, R., 166
Huntsman, B., 404
Hursch, C., 236
Hursch, C. J., 237
Hursch, J., 236
Huson, C., 400
Hutcheson, F., 315, 354
Hutt, C., 597
Hutt, S. J., 587
Hutte, H. A., 199
Huxley, A., 29
Hyman, D. B., 174
Hyman, H. H., 58, 637, 656, 683, 685, 686, 689

Ickes, W. J., 88, 92, 349
Ingham, G. K., 401
Inglis, G. B., 602
Inkeles, A., 336
Insko, C. A., 128, 200, 201, 203, 505
Irle, M., 204
Irwin, D. M., 624
Irwin, F. W., 291
Isaacs, H. R., 683
Isen, A. M., 117, 208, 290
Isenberg, D. J., 613
Itskhokin, A., 367
Ivancevich, J., 390, 391
Iyengar, S., 725
Izard, C. E., 210

Jacklin, C. N., 505
Jackson, D. N., 183, 501
Jackson, J., 335, 340, 341
Jackson, S. E., 364
Jacobs, D., 418
Jacobs, J., 576, 578, 583, 587, 592, 610, 621, 624
Jacobs, R. C., 426, 504
Jacobsen, L., 335
Jacobson, A., 88, 166
Jacobson, J., 411
Jacobson, L., 212

Jacoby, J., 256, 259, 262, 263
Jaeger, A. M., 403, 430
Jagacinski, C. M., 264
Jahoda, M., 58
Jain, A. K., 263
Jais, I. L., 289
James, R. M., 96
James, W., 15, 18, 26, 29, 33, 34, 36, 38, 40, 69, 312, 316, 355
Janet, P., 18
Janis, I. L., 20, 22, 75, 76, 128, 202, 233, 234, 255, 271, 274, 276, 277, 278, 279, 280, 285, 288, 289, 292, 296, 297, 335, 483
Janisse, M. P., 544–545
Jarmecky, L., 118
Jarvie, I. C., 624
Jaspers, J. M. E., 200
Jeffrey, K. M., 170, 171
Jeffreys, H., 245
Jehenson, R., 609
Jemmott, J., 462
Jenkins, H. M., 191, 281
Jennings, D. L., 190, 191, 195, 283
Jennings, S., 195
Jensen, A. R., 533
Jepson, C., 233
Jepson, D., 295
Jersild, A., 186
Jervis, R., 272, 280, 288, 289, 292
Jick, T. D., 601
Johnson, E. J., 264
Johnson, E. L., 231
Johnson, G. A., 129
Johnson, G. E., 412
Johnson, J., 174
Johnson, J. B., 386
Johnson, J. E., 267, 484
Johnson, J. M., 582, 586, 588
Johnson, L. C., 601
Johnson, M., 652
Johnson, M. K., 151
Johnson, M. P., 558, 560
Johnson, N. J., 407
Johnson, S. M., 586, 587, 603
Johnson-Laird, P. N., 189, 293, 296
Joiner, B. L., 551
Jones, A. P., 339, 350
Jones, C. R., 167, 173, 470
Jones, E. E., 52, 69, 76, 79, 82, 89, 90, 92, 140, 141, 142, 143, 160, 161, 167, 170, 175, 193, 204, 211, 389, 462, 547, 575
Jones, L. V., 253

Jones, R. A., 91, 609
Jordan, N., 89, 199, 202
Joreskog, K. G., 501, 638, 740, 745, 763
Judd, C. H., 27, 31
Judd, C. M., 155, 164, 488, 499, 658
Jung, C. G., 26
Junker, B. H., 591

Kafry, D., 238, 239, 240
Kagan, J., 334-335
Kagenhiro, D. K., 170
Kahle, L. R., 562
Kahn, L. M., 412
Kahn, R. L., 336, 337, 338, 398, 418, 638, 676, 677, 679, 680, 687
Kahneman, D., 92, 177, 179, 180, 187, 190, 194, 233, 234, 236, 245, 246, 247, 248-250, 251-253, 255, 263, 267, 276, 281, 282, 283, 284, 286-287, 293-296, 396
Kakkar, P., 264, 265
Kalberg, S., 597
Kalle, R. J., 205, 547
Kalleberg, A. L., 349
Kalton, G., 648, 651, 657, 661, 662, 666, 678, 688
Kalven, H., 96
Kammeyer, K., 335
Kando, T., 353, 362
Kanfer, F. H., 116, 484
Kanouse, D., 182
Kant, I., 17
Kanter, R. M., 289, 329, 363
Kanuk, L., 680
Kaplan, A., 99
Kaplan, H. B., 175
Kaplan, M. F., 167
Karmarkar, U. S., 246, 250-251
Karph, F. B., 3
Karshmer, J. F., 119
Kasarda, J. D., 382, 408
Kaspryzk, D., 678
Katkin, E. S., 124
Katona, G., 5, 47
Katz, D., 38, 51, 94, 158, 337, 338, 510, 640
Katz, E., 504
Katz, L. B., 156, 170, 171, 182
Katzev, R., 474
Kaufman, H., 416, 722
Kaufman, S., 388
Kay, E., 389-390, 391
Kay, P., 211

Kaye, D., 128
Kazdin, A. E., 572, 744
Kearney, M., 624
Keating, J. P., 262
Keats, J. A., 185
Keen, P. G. W., 273
Keeney, R. L., 233, 243, 296
Kees, W., 596
Keeve, S., 185
Keller, C. M., 574
Kelley, H. H., 68, 69, 74, 75, 76, 78, 80, 81, 82, 90, 92, 99, 142, 144, 160, 162, 177, 204, 259, 335, 389, 419, 489, 577
Kelley, K. A., 123
Kelley, S., 652
Kellner, H., 352
Kellogg, J. A., 174
Kelly, C. W., 275
Kelly, G. A., 141, 147, 174, 522
Kelman, H. C., 71, 98, 560
Kemper, T. D., 334, 355
Kendall, P. L., 637
Kendon, A., 596
Kendrick, D. T., 129
Kendzierski, D., 179, 739, 762
Keniston, K., 183
Kennedy, W. A., 122
Kennedy, R. L., 236
Kenny, D. A., 156, 182, 282, 488, 492, 498, 499-500, 504, 505, 521, 542, 562
Kenrick, D. T., 117
Kent, R. N., 586, 603
Keppel, G., 493
Kerbo, H. R., 573
Kerchhoff, A. C., 62
Keren, G., 243, 494
Kerns, C. D., 120
Kessler, R. C., 760
Khandwalla, P., 409
Kiaer, A. N., 636
Kian, M., 129
Kidd, R. F., 88, 92
Kiesler, C. A., 91, 140, 194, 204, 288, 388, 399, 400, 470, 711, 741
Kiesler, S. B., 388, 399, 400
Kihlstrom, J. F., 208
Kilburn, H. C., 420
Killian, L. M., 319, 355
Killworth, P. D., 624
Kilmann, R. H., 589
Kim, J., 390, 391
Kimbel, G. A., 72

Kimberly, J. R., 406, 408
Kimmel, M. J., 80, 81, 232
Kinch, J. W., 319
Kinchla, R. A., 185
Kinder, D. R., 155, 272, 279
King, B. T., 335
King, G. A., 161
Kinne, S. B., 390, 391
Kintsch, W., 153
Kirker, W. S., 154
Kirkpatrick, C., 319, 355
Kirschner, P., 128
Kish, L., 661, 663, 673, 675
Kitt, A. S., 212, 335
Klapp, O. E., 357
Klein, V., 336
Kleinhesselink, R. R., 206
Kleinke, C. A., 186
Kleinknecht, R. E., 551, 552
Kleinmuntz, B., 238, 241, 257
Kleinmuntz, D. N., 238
Klineberg, O., 63
Kloman, E. H., 732
Kluckhohn, C., 3, 7, 29
Kluckhohn, F. R., 27
Knight, G., 344, 427
Knorr, K., 722
Koch, H. L., 186
Koch, S., 624
Koffka, K., 37, 67, 83, 88, 199
Kogan, N., 58, 200
Kohen, E., 242
Köhler, W., 16, 83, 199
Kohn, C. A., 262, 263
Kohnke-Aquirre, L., 685
Koivumaki, J. H., 193
Kolb, W. L., 328, 367
Kolditz, T., 195
Komaki, J., 397
Komarovsky, M., 335, 340, 350, 352, 353, 362
Konecni, V. J., 265
Koopmans, T. C., 275
Koos, E. L., 340
Kopelman, R. E., 382
Koriat, A., 296, 297
Kornhauser, W., 336
Kort, F., 238
Korte, C., 612
Kosa, J., 338
Koslowski, M., 519-520
Kraemer, H. C., 505
Kraft, P., 413

Kramer, B. M., 184, 185
Krantz, D. H., 233, 295, 512, 515, 517
Krantz, D. S., 484
Krauss, E., 655
Krauss, R. M., 81
Krebs, D., 117
Krech, D., 49, 138, 140, 510
Kreitman, N., 601
Kreitner, R., 396, 397
Krieger, S., 601
Kris, M., 185, 282
Kroeber, A. L., 3, 29
Kronenfeld, J. E., 407
Kropotkin, P. A., 10, 12
Krosnick, J. A., 658
Kruglanski, A. W., 196
Kruskal, J. B., 488, 524
Kruskal, W., 636
Ksander, M., 575
Kuethe, J. L., 145, 146, 186
Kuhn, L. L., 577
Kuhn, M. H., 312, 317–318, 328, 341, 346
Kuhn, T. S., 99, 379, 424, 429, 765
Kuiper, N. A., 154
Kulik, J. A., 155, 164
Kumar, P. A., 155, 208, 282
Kunreuther, H. C., 242, 246
Kunst-Wilson, W. R., 149
Kunz, P. R., 574
Kurskel, W. H., 521
Kuskin, M. S., 412
Kutza, E. A., 703

Labov, W., 608
Lachman, R. S., 151
Ladd, E. C., 381
Lagakos, S. W., 263
Lagall, K. C., 691
Lahey, M. A., 596
Lally, J. J., 337
Lambert, W. W., 109, 112
Lamn, H., 247
Landis, C., 596
Landy, D., 453
Lane, D. M., 238, 239
Lang, P. J., 601
Langan, C. J., 125
Lange, L., 36
Langer, E. J., 167, 169, 171, 267, 279, 285, 291, 463, 473, 474, 484
Lanzetta, J. T., 191
LaPiere, R. T., 94, 556–558, 652

Larner, R. J., 404
Larntz, K., 503
Larsen, J. K., 717, 724, 726
Larson, R. C., 718, 726
Larsson, S., 247
Larter, W. M., 155
Latané, B., 95, 591
Latham, G. P., 390, 391
Latour, B., 575
Lau, R. R., 595
Lauderdale, P., 344
La Voie, L., 504, 505
Lawler, E. E., 387, 388, 392
Lawrence, D. H., 70, 71, 201
Lawrence, P. R., 387, 409, 576
Laws, J. L., 336, 353
Lawson, N. C., 601
Lazarsfeld, P. F., 504, 637, 648, 691
Lazarsfeld, P. H., 569, 575, 608
Lazarus, M., 2, 27, 28
Lazarus, R. S., 149
Leary, M. R., 192
Leary, T., 617
Leary, T. F., 62
Leavitt, H. J., 380
Leblebici, H., 393, 395, 409, 416, 419
Le Bon, G., 14, 17, 18, 22, 23, 24
Lecky, P., 9, 70
La Dantec, F., 9–10
Lee, J. A., 601, 624
Lee, W., 245, 259, 269
Leiberman, S., 399
Leidy, T. E., 391
Leigh, D. E., 412
Leightin, A. H., 13
Leirer, V. O., 156, 170, 171
Leiter, K., 579
LeMasters, E. E., 352
Lemert, E. M., 319
Lemons, F., 546
Leon, M., 167
Leone, C., 160
Leong, A., 393, 394, 395
LePage, A., 73, 114
Lepper, M. R., 92, 181, 204
Lepper, R., 181
Lerner, L., 119
Lesey, M., 596
Lester, M., 367, 579
Leventhal, H., 93, 122, 170, 289, 484
Lever, J., 567
Levi, A. S., 234, 249
Levin, H. M., 711, 715, 738, 760
Levin, I. P., 167

Levin, P. F., 117
Levine, M., 577
Levine, M. E., 268, 395
Levine, R. A., 699, 705
Levine, R. L., 239
Levine, R. V., 573
Levinson, D. J., 51
Levitan, S. A., 699, 705
Leviton, L. C., 704, 715, 719, 720, 721, 738, 756, 764, 768
Levy, H., 253
Levy-Bruhl, L., 30
Lewellen, W. G., 403–404
Lewicka, M., 155
Lewin, K., 33, 39, 40, 47, 51, 54, 60, 63, 65, 66, 67, 68, 69, 71, 74–75, 76, 77, 78, 83, 84, 85, 88, 90, 93, 98, 255, 442, 484, 646
Lewis, C., 494
Lewis, H. B., 139, 176
Lewis, J. D., 317, 328, 359, 367
Lewis, R. A., 350
Lewis, R. E. F., 596
Lewis, S. K., 205
Lewit, D. W., 199
Libby, R., 253
Lichtenstein, S., 177, 182, 231, 235, 236, 238, 240, 247, 253, 294
Licke, E. A., 391
Lieberman, D. A., 258
Lieberman, M. A., 738
Liebow, E., 352, 362
Lieu, D. K., 683
Light, D., 582, 586
Light, J., 62
Light, R. J., 505, 700, 739
Liker, J., 363
Likert, R., 60, 526, 648
Lin, T. J., 205
Lincoln, J. R., 383, 430
Lincoln, Y. S., 717, 736, 745, 747, 761, 765
Lindblom, C. E., 294, 384, 568, 703, 704, 708, 766
Linder, D. E., 56, 76, 91, 204, 206, 459
Lindesmith, A. R., 319, 355
Lindzey, E., 141
Lindzey, G., 34, 77, 139, 185
Lindzey, G. E., 647
Lingle, J. H., 143, 152, 153, 158, 161, 170, 171
Lingoes, J. C., 524
Linn, R. L., 542

Linsky, A. S., 680
Linton, R., 312, 332, 333, 335
Linville, P. W., 148, 161
Lipman-Blumen, J., 339, 341
Lippitt, R., 40, 63, 65, 68, 71, 442, 568, 594
Lipps, T., 15, 16
Lipset, S. M., 380, 381
Lipsitz, A. A., 200
Lirtzman, S. I., 399
Little, K. B., 146
Locander, W., 552
Locke, E. A., 389, 390, 397
Lockhead, G. R., 231
Locksley, A. E., 166, 187
Lodahl, J., 395
Loew, C. A., 113
Lofland, J., 320, 326, 567, 579, 580, 584, 588, 624
Lofland, L. 320
Loftus, E. F., 649
Lohnes, P. R., 741
Lombardo, J. P., 118, 123, 124, 128
London, I. D., 609
London, M., 390, 391, 541
Lopes, L. L., 238, 244, 253
Lord, C., 296
Lord, C. G., 154
Lord, C. J., 52
Lord, R. G., 595
Lorge, I., 140, 176
Loroch, J. W., 409
Loscocco, K. A., 349
Lott, A. J., 126, 127, 129
Lott, B., 110, 126
Lott, B. E., 127, 129, 202
Love, R. L., 612
Lowenthal, L., 22
Lowenthal, M. F., 339, 349, 352
Lowe, R. C., 602, 624
Lowin, A., 206
Lowry, D. H., 182
Lubin, A., 601
Luce, R. D., 78, 259, 269, 516
Luchins, A. S., 185, 267, 293
Luckey, E. B., 350
Luckman, T., 326, 422
Ludwig, J., 656
Lui, L., 463
Lumsden, J., 583
Luria, Z., 536–539
Lussier, D. A., 262
Luthans, F., 397
Luthans, R., 396

Lyman, S. M., 368
Lynch, B. P., 408
Lyon, D., 187
Lyons, J., 199

McAllister, D. W., 266–267, 430
McArdle, J. J., 501
McArthur, L. Z., 160, 167, 168, 182, 191, 282
Macauley, J., 95
McCall, G., 311, 345, 346, 354, 359, 363, 366, 367
McCall, M. W., 272, 274
McCann, C. D., 170, 212
McCann, J. M., 238
McCarthy, P. J., 662
McCleary, R., 488, 760
McClelland, D. C., 50, 82, 85, 387
McClelland, G. H., 235, 529–530
McClelland, L., 182
MacCleod, R. B., 84
McCoach, W. P., 243
Maccoby, N., 285
McCord, J., 596
MacCrimmon, K. R., 247, 255, 270, 271
McDermott, G., 397
McDonald, R. P., 501
McDougall, W., 3, 4, 7, 8, 9, 12, 13, 15, 16, 17, 18, 19, 20, 25, 27, 31, 32, 33, 34, 38, 41, 47, 77
McDowell, J. J., 596
McEachern, W. A., 404
McFarland, S. G., 656
Mcgarvey, W., 201
McGaw, B., 505, 738
McGee, M. G., 573
McGillis, D., 160
McGlothin W. H., 249
McGrath, J. E., 602, 624
MacGregor, D., 180
McGuire, C. V., 168
McGuire, J. W., 404
McGuire, W. J., 75, 76–77, 89, 168, 288, 290
Machiavelli, 42
Machina, M. J., 246, 251
Machlup, F., 404
McHugh, P., 326, 579–580
Macke, A. S., 326, 337, 338, 349, 350, 363, 366
McKennell, A. C., 648, 681–682
McKenney, J. L., 273
Mackenzie, K. D., 385

Macker, C. E., 116
Mackie, M., 338
Mackinnon, A. J., 294
MacKuen, M., 691
McLaughlin, M. W., 720, 724
McLeary, R. A., 149
McLemore, C. W., 617
McLemore, S. D., 596
McLeod, J. M., 199
McLeod, R., 582
McNeil, L. M., 624
MacNeil, M. K., 547–548
McNemar, Q., 648
McPartland, T. S., 318, 742
McPhail, C., 318
MacPhillamy, D. J., 264
McTavish, J., 466
McVicar Hunt, J., 537
Maddux, J. E., 122
Maehr, M. L., 123
Magidson, J., 503
Magilavy, L. J., 682
Magnuson, D., 52
Mahalanobis, P. C., 645
Mahoney, M. J., 295
Mahoney, T. A., 393, 395
Maier, N. R. F., 13, 178, 179, 190
Maier, S. F., 292
Maines, D. R., 342, 343
Maki, J., 256, 258, 259, 261
Makridakis, S., 270
Malhotra, N. K., 261, 263
Malinowski, B., 27, 588, 590, 624
Malone, T. W., 505
Malpass, R. S., 151, 153
Manchir, J., 732
Mandler, J., 144
Manis, M., 145, 180, 187, 283
Manis, R. B., 49
Mann, C. H., 335
Mann, J. H., 335
Mann, L., 233, 234, 271, 274, 276, 277, 278, 279, 285, 288, 289, 290, 292, 296, 543
Mann, M., 206
Mann, R. W., 194
Mannheim, K., 6
Manning, P. K., 574, 577, 584, 624
Manns, C. L., 393
Marceil, J. C., 590
Marcel, A., 149
March, J. G., 233, 255, 275, 280, 380, 384, 385, 393, 394, 395, 403, 416, 427, 428

Markowitz, H. M., 246, 253
Marks, R., 185
Marks, R. W., 291
Marks, S. R., 339, 351, 366
Markus, G. B., 691
Markus, H., 125, 126, 142, 146, 147, 154, 161, 163, 164, 172, 175, 208, 209
Markus, J., 153
Marlowe, D., 51, 459, 461
Marques, T. E., 238, 239
Marquis, K. H., 646, 653, 684
Marris, R., 403
Marshall, K., 573
Marshall, R., 411
Martin, C. H., 126
Martin, E., 643, 691
Martin, E. D., 24
Martindale, D., 312
Martinez, J., 171
Maruyama, M., 429, 609
Marx, J. H., 422
Marx, K., 6, 27, 765
Mash, E. J., 586, 597
Masling, M., 166
Maslow, A. H., 367, 383, 386, 388
Mason, K. O., 350, 691
Mason, W. M., 657
Massad, C. M., 161, 181
Massey, J. T., 657
Masson, R. T., 404
Masters, J. C., 119
Mathews, S., 585
Mathewson, G. C., 453, 479, 480
Matlin, M., 185, 186, 290
Matsoukas, E., 681
Matsui, T., 392
Mausner, B., 387
Mavin, G. H., 161
May, E. R., 272, 273
May, M. A., 13
Mayer, A., 39
Mayeske, G. W., 742
Mazur, A., 608
Mead, G. H., 14–15, 17, 49, 69, 210, 311, 312, 314, 316, 317, 318, 319, 321, 324, 325, 328, 341, 346, 355, 359, 363, 364, 366, 367, 422
Mead, M., 13, 83, 596
Means, G. C., 403
Mechanic, D., 349, 405
Medin, D. L., 143
Meehl, P. E., 241, 551
Meeker, B. F., 353, 362

Mehan, H., 577, 578, 591, 592
Meichenbaum, D. H., 123
Meidinger, E., 712
Meissner, M., 408
Melamed, B. G., 601
Melbin, M., 332, 624, 691
Meltzer, B. M., 49, 317–318, 328
Meltzer, H., 8, 140, 186
Meltzer, R., 262
Menlove, F. L., 121
Merleau-Ponty, M., 210, 212
Merry, R., 182
Merton, R. K., 162, 212, 312, 333, 335, 336, 337, 351, 363, 365, 380, 398
Mesmer, F. A., 17
Messick, S., 183
Mettee, D. R., 186, 467
Meyer, D. E., 253
Meyer, G. D., 239
Meyer, J. W., 382, 425–426
Meyer, M. W., 383, 407
Meyer, T. P., 115
Michaelis, A. R., 596
Michela, J. L., 259
Midlarsky, E., 116
Mietzsche, F., 9
Mika, S., 167
Miles, M. B., 738
Miles, R. H., 337, 339, 351, 366
Milgram, S., 24, 55, 79–80, 97, 207, 332, 442, 450, 455, 456, 466, 467, 478–480, 483, 543, 549–550
Mill, J. S., 5, 6, 7, 8
Miller, A. G., 193, 194
Miller, D., 195, 208, 624
Miller, D. J., 121
Miller, D. T., 142, 175
Miller, D. W., 270
Miller, E., 200
Miller, F. G., 125
Miller, G. A., 82, 172, 255, 279
Miller, H., 338, 390
Miller, J. C., 456, 483
Miller, J. D., 654
Miller, J. G., 238
Miller, J. J., 492
Miller, N., 115
Miller, N. E., 6, 16, 35, 50, 71, 72, 73, 118, 130, 139, 480, 481
Miller, P. V., 647, 653
Miller, R. L., 116
Miller, T. I., 601
Miller, W. E., 110, 691

Millman, M., 624
Mills, C. W., 319, 357, 414
Mills, J., 262, 445–448, 450, 453, 454, 479, 480
Mills, R. T., 484
Milord, J. T., 261
Mindlin, S., 409
Miner, J. B., 397
Minke, K. A., 126
Minor, J. H., 350, 351
Minsky, M., 143
Mintzberg, H., 270, 271, 273, 274, 275
Mirels, H., 205
Mirer, T. W., 652
Mischel, W., 50, 51, 52, 71, 120, 121, 143, 147, 148, 151, 157, 164, 165, 169, 170, 171, 208, 209, 290, 396
Mishler, E. G., 579
Mitchell, A. M., 739
Mitchell, S. K., 603
Mitchell, T. R., 266, 273, 274, 277, 390, 391, 392, 401, 402, 430
Mitchell, V., 51
Mitchell, W. C., 337
Mitroff, I. I., 429, 575, 589
Miyamoto, S. F., 319
Mobley, W. H., 389, 390, 391, 429
Modigliani, A., 355
Moede, W., 39, 40
Mohr, L., 408
Monteverde, K., 405
Montgomery, H., 256, 257, 258, 259, 261, 264, 266, 267, 268
Montgomery, K. C., 140
Mook, D. G., 442
Moor, L. F., 380
Moore, B. S., 470
Moore, D., 125
Moore, G., 414
Moore, H. T., 40, 79
Moore, M., 551, 552, 553–555
Moore, W. L., 394, 395
Moos, R. H., 612
Morehead, J., 584
Moreland, R. L., 153, 172, 181
Moreno, J. L., 41, 61, 332
Morgan, C., 38
Morgan, G., 421, 422, 423, 583
Morgan, W., 338
Morgenstern, O., 80, 235, 245
Moriarity, M., 552
Morier, D. M., 190

Morrissette, J. O., 89, 199
Mortimore, G. W., 285
Moscovici, S., 58, 143, 211, 212
Moser, C. A., 661, 662, 666
Mosher, F. C., 732
Moskowitz, H., 238
Mosteller, F., 488, 636, 642
Mount, M. K., 602
Mowday, R. T., 387
Mower-White, C. J., 200
Mowrer, O. H., 71, 72, 118, 126, 128, 130, 202, 349
Mueller, J. E., 652
Mullen, B., 194
Mullen, E. J., 711
Müller, G. E., 36
Mullet, R. L., 151, 153
Mumford, E., 762
Mumpower, J., 82, 235, 288
Mundy, D., 74
Münsterberg, H., 35
Murchison, C., 61, 63
Murphy, A. H., 294
Murphy, G., 4, 41, 51, 61, 85, 195
Murphy, K. R., 239
Murphy, L., 13
Murphy, L. B., 41, 61
Murphy, T. G., 282
Murray, E., 319
Murray, H. A., 7, 38, 50, 476, 482
Murray, M., 338
Mussen, P. H., 120
Mutran, E., 319, 347
Myers, C. S., 27
Myers, D. G., 247
Myrdal, A., 336
Myrdal, G., 556, 558

Nadler, D. A., 390
Naficy, A., 205
Nagel, E., 404
Nagel, J. H., 394
Namboodiri, N. K., 498
Nappe, G. W., 182
Nash, J., 578
Nathan, R. P., 711, 721, 733
Navasky, V. S., 711
Nay, W. R., 601, 603
Naylor, J. C., 236, 237, 238, 239
Neale, M. S., 578
Nehrbass, R. G., 380-381
Neisser, U., 82, 86, 143, 164, 165
Nelson, D., 127
Nelson, H. M., 337

Nelson, R. O., 578, 586
Nemeth, C., 362
Neter, J., 646, 647
Neugarten, B. L., 339, 349, 352
Newman, M. R., 602
Nevill, D., 338
Newcomb, T. M., 38, 41, 47-48, 61, 70, 89, 199, 576
Newcomb, T. N., 510
Newell, A., 255, 257, 258, 267, 273
Newhams, T., 397
Newman, J. E., 401
Newman, J. R., 243
Newman, L. S., 500, 561
Newtson, D., 62-63, 152, 161, 181
Nisbett, R. E., 52, 74, 90, 92, 93, 142, 174, 175, 177, 178, 181, 187, 191, 193, 195, 196, 197, 204, 208, 233, 234, 240, 258-259, 269, 282, 283, 284, 286, 295, 289, 457, 470, 575, 593
Noble, D. F., 413
Nord, W., 396
Norman, D. A., 145
Norman, R. M., 200
Norris-Baker, C., 578
Nottenburg, G., 148
Nougaim, K. E., 388
Nowak, P., 419, 420
Nunnally, J. C., 642
Nutt, L. E., 578
Nuttal, R. L., 459, 461
Nuttin, J. M., 204, 205
Nye, F. I., 335, 353, 354

Oakes, M., 191
O'Connell, M. J., 409
Oden, G. C., 167, 253
Ofshe, R., 320
O'Gorman, H. J., 655
Ohtsuka, Y., 392
O'Kelly, L. J., 186
Oldfield, R. C., 144
Oldham, G. R., 383, 387, 388, 390, 391, 401
Oldman, D., 292
Olesen, V. L., 320
Olsen, J. P., 255, 427, 428
Olshavsky, R. W., 262, 264
Olson, C. L., 187
Olson, J. M., 206
Ondrack, D. A., 574
O'Neal, E., 115

Oppenheimer, V. K., 350
Orden, S. R., 349, 350
O'Reilly, C. A., 388, 389, 391, 397, 401, 402
Orne, M. T., 98, 201, 427, 454, 465
Orr, S. P., 191
Ortiz, V., 187
Ortony, A., 144, 162, 163-164, 165, 167, 169, 583
Orzech, M. J., 122
Osgood, C. E., 5, 56, 70, 89, 126, 207, 210, 535, 536-539
Osherow, N., 484
Ossorio, A. G., 62
Ossorio, P., 98
Ostrom, T. M., 143, 151-152, 153, 161, 164, 167, 168, 171, 175, 180, 510
O'Toole, R., 319, 352
Ouchi, W. G., 386, 403, 430
Overman, B., 725
Owens, J., 151

Pace, D. J., 547
Padgett, J. F., 384, 386, 396
Padilla, A. M., 185
Pagano, D. F., 183
Page, M. M., 114
Page, R., 462, 547
Pallak, M. S., 124, 140, 204
Palmer, D. A., 420
Palmer, S., 335
Pancer, S. M., 591
Parelius, A., 353, 362
Pareto, V., 5
Park, C. W., 256, 257, 258, 264, 265
Park, R. E., 317, 332, 333
Parke, R. D., 113
Parker, A. L., 120
Parker, D. F., 392
Parker, S. D., 472
Parlette, G. N., 388, 389
Parmenter, R., 597
Parry, H, J., 643, 653
Parsons, T., 5, 30, 32, 312, 331, 332-333, 334, 336, 350
Parten, M., 655
Pasamanick, B., 182
Paster, D., 711
Patterson, G. R., 519
Patton, M. B., 575
Patton, M. Q., 594, 718, 720, 736, 765
Pavlov, I. P., 15, 72

Payne, J. S., 208
Payne, J. W., 255, 256, 257, 258, 259, 261, 262, 263, 264
Payne, S. L., 642, 651
Peake, P. K., 52
Pear, T. H., 13
Pearce, J. L., 388
Pearce, P. L., 591
Pedalino, E., 397
Peitromonaco, P., 173
Pelz, D., 337, 338
Pennings, J. M., 382, 420
Penoi, J., 726
Pepinsky, H. B., 575
Pepitone, A., 657
Perkins, J., 519
Perkins, S. C., 195
Perlmutter, H. V., 199
Perrow, C., 336, 382, 394, 408
Perrucci, C. C., 338
Perrucci, R., 336, 337
Perry, D. G., 120, 121
Perry, R. B., 31
Perry, R. R., 261
Peters, D. R., 393
Peters, L. H., 392
Peters, T. J., 401
Peterson, C. R., 177, 281
Peterson, D. F., 275
Peterson-Hardt, S., 350
Petras, J. W., 317
Petrinovich, L., 236, 237
Petrowsky, M., 349
Petrullo, L., 147
Pettigrew, A. M., 393, 395
Pettigrew, T., 195
Petty, R. E., 175, 176, 200
Pfeffer, J., 381, 383, 384, 385, 387, 388, 389, 393, 394, 395, 399, 401, 402, 409, 410, 412, 413, 415, 416, 417–419, 420, 423, 424–425, 426, 573
Phelps, R. H., 238, 239, 255
Phillips, J. L., 201
Phillips, K., 608
Piaget, J., 30, 144
Piazza, T., 659
Picek, J. S., 151, 200
Pichevin, M., 201
Piliavin, I. M., 470, 568
Piliavin, J. A., 470, 568
Piliavin, J. M., 473
Pilzecker, A., 36
Pinder, C. G., 380

Pittenger, R. E., 608
Pittman, T. S., 82, 124, 204, 205
Pitz, G. F., 274, 275
Plant, M. A., 601
Plato, 2, 11, 25
Platt, H., 407
Plott, C. R., 268, 395
Podell, L., 519
Poitou, J., 201
Polansky, N., 587
Polefka, J., 195, 208
Pollack, D., 545
Pollio, H. R., 185
Pollner, M., 579
Polly, S., 142, 195
Polsby, N. W., 394
Pondy, L. R., 422, 423, 424–425, 429, 575, 585
Poole, K. T., 529
Popham, J. W., 766
Popper, K. R., 765, 766
Porter, L. W., 387, 392
Posner, M. I., 149, 197
Post, D., 282
Postman, L., 63, 85, 186, 210
Potts, G. R., 145
Poulton, E. C., 180
Pounds, W., 271
Powers, C., 341, 361, 364–365, 366
Powers, E. A., 658
Powers, P. C., 115
Powers, W. T., 347, 356, 367
Prasad, J. A., 63
Pratt, G. L., 519–520
Pratt, J. W., 245
Preiss, J. J., 591
Presser, S., 640, 647, 648–652, 655, 656–658, 660
Pressman, J., 711
Preston, M. G., 246
Pribram, K. H., 82, 172
Price, K. O., 199
Prince, M., 18, 19, 50
Pritchard, R. D., 390, 397
Progoff, I., 578
Proshansky, H. M., 41, 85, 96
Provan, K. G., 394
Pruitt, D. G., 58, 80, 81, 232, 253
Pryor, J. B., 168, 282
Pugh, D. S., 406
Pugh, M. D., 359
Punch, M., 608
Pyszczynski, T., 195, 291

Quanty, M. B., 185
Quarantelli, E. L., 319
Quattrone, G. A., 193, 284
Quigley, B., 547
Quigley-Fernandez, B., 205

Rabinow, P., 569
Rabinowitz, L., 419
Raden, D., 557
Radloff, R., 69, 74
Raiffa, H., 78, 231, 233, 236, 243, 269, 295, 296
Rainer, T., 569, 578
Rainwater, L., 352
Ramsey, F. P., 245
Ramsey, J. O., 524
Ranck, K. H., 340
Randall, R., 418
Raphael, E., 338, 407
Raphael, R., 624
Rapoport, A., 81, 259, 294
Rapoport, R., 350, 365
Rappaport, R. A., 584
Rappoport, L., 239
Rasmussen, P. K., 577
Ratcliff, R. E., 414
Rausch, C. N., 290
Rausch, H. L., 612, 624
Rauschenberger, J., 388
Ravetz, J., 231
Ray, J. J., 183
Read, S. J., 154, 156
Reber, A. S., 189
Reckless, W., 319
Reed, P., 612
Reed, T., 127
Reeder, G. D., 182
Reeder, L. G., 319
Regan, D. R., 171
Reich, M., 411
Reichardt, C. S., 737, 744, 762, 765
Reicken, H. W., 89
Reinharz, S., 578, 588
Reis, H. T., 498, 573
Reiss, A. J., 569, 587
Reiter, L. A., 129
Reitman, W. R., 270
Reitzes, D. C., 319, 347, 368
Reizler, K., 355
Renzaglia, G. A., 587
Rettig, S., 182
Rexroat, C., 318
Reynolds, H. T., 502
Reynolds, L. T., 317

Rheingold, H. L., 352
Rhodes, I. N., 654
Rhodewalt, F., 204
Rholes, W. S., 167, 173, 470
Ribot, T., 12, 13
Rice, D. G., 601
Rice, S. A., 3, 685
Rich, R. F., 756
Richardson, D. C., 112
Richardson, J. G., 350
Richey, M., 182
Richmond, J. B., 285
Riecken, H. W., 59, 70, 97, 201, 717
Riegel, K. F., 576
Riemer, J. W., 578, 592
Riesman, D., 79
Riess, M., 195
Riggs, J. M., 193
Riley, M. W., 339
Rip, P., 259
Rips, L. J., 168
Riskin, S. R., 583
Ritter, B., 121
Ritzer, G., 337, 422, 429
Rivers, W. H. R., 27
Rivlin, M., 747
Rizzo, J. R., 399
Robbins, T., 592
Roberts, D. R., 403, 404
Roberts, F. S., 512, 515
Roberts, J. M., 624
Roberts, K. H., 382, 383, 387, 388,
    402, 429
Roberts, R. R., 587
Robertson, D. R., 145–146, 157
Robertson, J. F., 349
Robinson, D., 625, 686
Robinson, J., 182
Robinson, J. P., 660
Robinson, R. E., 531
Rocha, R. F., 115
Rodin, J., 90, 470, 474, 484, 568
Rodrigues, A., 199
Rodrigues, J., 210
Roe, A., 336, 338
Rogers, C. R., 147, 174, 175
Rogers, E., 112
Rogers, R. W., 113, 115, 122
Rogers, T. B., 154
Rogolsky, S., 185
Rohde, S., 686
Roheim, G., 27
Roistacher, R. C., 399
Rokeach, M., 140, 182, 550

Romanczyk, R. G., 603
Ronis, D. L., 205–206
Roper, E., 648, 651
Rorer, L. G., 183, 193, 236
Rosa, E., 608
Rosch, E. H., 143, 147, 168, 211
Rose, A. M., 321
Rose, T. L., 190, 463
Rosekrans, M. A., 12, 121
Rosen, C. B., 353, 362
Rosen, L. D., 256, 257, 264, 265
Rosen, S., 129, 567
Rosenberg, B. G., 335, 352
Rosenberg, M., 76, 175, 367, 368, 688
Rosenberg, M. J., 89, 128, 202, 510
Rosenberg, S., 209
Rosenblatt, R. M., 419
Rosenfield, D., 195
Rosenhan, D. L., 116, 470
Rosenholtz, S. J., 357, 358
Rosenkoetter, P., 256
Rosenthal, R., 98, 162, 212, 335, 454,
    479, 505
Rosenzweig, S., 98
Rosnow, R. L., 97
Rosow, I., 350, 365
Ross, C. E., 353
Ross, E. A., 2, 4, 11, 20, 24, 41, 47
Ross, J., 412
Ross, L., 52, 90, 92, 93, 142, 177,
    178, 181, 190, 191, 194, 195, 196,
    197, 208, 233, 234, 269, 282, 283,
    284, 286, 293, 296, 396, 403, 593,
    652, 655
Ross, M., 142, 175, 195, 204, 208,
    557, 562
Ross, R. R., 123
Rossi, A. S., 339
Rossi, P. H., 642, 644, 691, 713, 715,
    720, 746, 753–755, 762, 763, 767
Rossman, B. B., 201
Roth, J. A., 320, 578
Rothbart, M., 151, 154, 157, 167, 176
Rothermel, T., 416, 419
Rothman, R., 336, 337
Rotondo, A., 174
Rotter, J. B., 50, 71
Rousseau, D. M., 383
Rowan, B., 425–426
Royce, J., 28
Rubin, D. C., 521
Rubin, D. M., 501
Rubinstein, J., 624
Ruble, D. N., 205

Rubovitz, P. C., 123
Ruesch, J., 596
Rugg, D., 181, 651, 657
Ruiz, R. A., 185
Rummelhart, D. E., 144, 162,
    163–164, 165, 167, 169
Rushing, W. A., 407, 408
Russell, B., 4, 9, 556, 610
Russle, D., 595
Russo, J. E., 256, 257, 261, 263, 264,
    265, 267, 268
Rutman, L., 741
Ryder, R. G., 339

Saal, T. E., 596
Saaty, T. L., 243
Sabine, G. H., 4
Sable, A., 468
Sachs, N. J., 274
Sadalla, E., 452, 456
Safilios-Rothschild, C., 338, 365
Sagatun, I., 344
Sainsbury, T., 725
St. Pierre, R. G., 735–736, 742,
    756–757, 758
Saks, M. J., 167
Salancik, G. R., 383, 384, 385, 387,
    389, 393, 394, 395, 396, 399, 401,
    402, 409, 410, 413, 416, 418–419,
    420, 573–574, 583
Saloner, G., 406
Samph, T., 587
Sampson, E. E., 20
Samuelson, P. H., 244
Sanchez, M. E., 119
Sanders, C. R., 568
Sanders, D. H., 703, 741
Sanders, G. S., 125
Sandy, P. R., 569
Sanford, R. N., 51
Santa, J. L., 492
Santee, R. T., 364
Sarason, I. G., 396
Sarat, A. D., 718, 723
Sarbin, T., 323, 335, 336, 339, 349,
    352
Sarbin, T. R., 174, 313, 341, 349, 365
Sarri, D. B., 542
Saslow, C., 185
Sattath, S., 260, 268
Savage, L. J., 245, 246
Sawyer, J., 241
Sawyer, J. D., 155
Sawyer, L. B., 732

Scanzoni, J., 337, 338, 339
Schachter, S., 12, 13, 56, 59, 62, 68, 69, 70, 90, 91, 97, 141, 201, 212, 355, 400, 450, 451, 453, 456, 576, 601
Schaeffle, A., 27
Schafe, M., 552
Schafer, E., 85
Schafer, R., 590
Schaffer, D. R., 204
Schanck, R. L., 194
Schaninger, C. M., 256
Schank, R. C., 148, 164, 172, 209, 271
Scharfstein, S. S., 723
Schatzman, L., 594
Schauble, P., 596
Scheff, T. J., 319, 365
Schegloff, E., 608
Scheidt, R. J., 114
Scheier, M. F., 175
Scheler, M., 13
Schelling, T. C., 80, 289, 609
Schenk, E. A., 239
Schewe, C. D., 680
Schiffrin, D., 353
Schimizu, I. M., 552
Schlenker, B. R., 49–50, 99, 128, 183, 192, 205, 206, 442
Schlenker, S. R., 82
Schlesinger, H. S., 762
Schmidt, C. J., 578
Schmidt, F. L., 392
Schmidt, N., 542
Schmidt, P., 578
Schmitt, N., 239
Schnaiberg, A., 712
Schneider, D. J., 195, 208
Schneider, W., 266
Schoemaker, P. J. H., 243, 244, 245, 246, 251–252, 286
Schoengerr, R. S., 349, 407
Schoggen, M., 612
Schoggen, P., 584, 610, 612–613
Schorr, D., 156
Schuessler, K., 654
Schul, Y., 158, 171
Schuler, R. S., 337
Schultz, D. P., 24
Schuman, H., 558, 560, 643, 647, 648–652, 655, 656, 660, 683, 685–686, 688, 692
Schurr, P. H., 400
Schustack, M., 281

Schutz, A., 213, 422
Schwalbe, M., 319
Schwartz, H., 576, 578, 583, 587, 592, 610, 621, 624
Schwartz, J., 147, 164, 165, 169
Schwartz, M., 179, 319, 346, 363, 368
Schwartz, P., 336, 353, 567
Schwartz, S. H., 652
Schwarz, G., 526, 531
Schweder, R. A., 172
Schwing, R., 231
Sciglimpaglia, D., 256
Scott, C., 680
Scott, L. R., 397
Scott, M., 594
Scott, M. B., 368
Scott, W. A., 200
Scott, W. R., 336, 338, 380, 400, 403, 410, 584
Scriven, M., 700, 701, 703, 711, 713, 714, 719–720, 736, 737, 748–749, 751, 762, 763, 767, 769
Sears, D. O., 186, 206, 289
Sears, P., 68
Sears, R. R., 71, 72, 200, 334, 335
Seashore, S. E., 401
Seaver, D. A., 243
Sechrest, L., 51, 572, 700, 730
Secord, P. F., 98, 161, 314, 384
Sedlak, A. J., 200, 209
Seeman, M., 413
Seery, J. B., 524
Segal, B. E., 337
Seidenberg, B., 41
Seidner, M. L., 116, 484
Seligman, C., 390
Seligman, M., 292
Seligman, M. E. P., 91, 92
Selltiz, C., 545, 691
Seltzer, A. L., 544
Selznick, P., 337, 380, 395
Sentis, K., 147, 165, 175, 200
Serbin, L. A., 123
Serpe, R. T., 319, 325, 346
Seta, J. J., 125
Seymore, J. D., 397
Shadish, W. R., 718, 723, 728, 741, 757
Shafer, G., 283
Shaklee, H., 466
Shand, A., 38
Shanteau, J. C., 167, 238, 239, 251, 252–253, 255

Shapira, Z., 205, 267
Shapiro, T. C., 595
Shapley, L. S., 244
Sharma, R. K., 725
Shaver, P. R., 660
Shaw, J. B., 401
Shaw, M. L., 231, 492
Sheatsley, P. B., 58, 656
Shefrin, H. M., 290
Shepard, R. N., 524–525
Sherif, C. W., 62, 545
Sherif, M., 62, 63, 64–65, 76, 79, 83, 84, 98, 176, 332, 426, 545
Sherman, S. J., 151, 200
Sherwood, J. J., 319
Shibutani, T., 319, 354, 355, 359, 364
Shiffrin, R. M., 151, 200, 266
Shimkunas, A., 182
Shlien, J. M., 544
Shoben, E. J., 148, 168
Shope, G. L., 112
Shott, S., 354, 355
Shoup, L. H., 414
Shrader, E. G., 199
Shuford, E. H., 269
Shugan, S. M., 267
Shulman, R. F., 204
Shure, G. H., 82
Shuval, J. T., 338
Shweder, R. A., 293
Sicoly, F., 175, 195
Sidis, B., 17, 18, 23
Sidowski, J. B., 74
Sieber, S. D., 339, 351, 366
Siegal, S., 294
Siegel, P. M., 644
Sigall, H., 454, 460, 462, 547
Sigelman, L., 657
Sighele, S., 17, 23
Sigler, E., 123
Silver, M. J., 98
Silverman, B. I., 655
Silverman, D., 429
Silverman, I., 207, 550
Simeonsson, J. J., 335
Simmel, G., 23, 312, 332, 362, 365
Simmel, M., 161
Simmelhag, V. L., 292, 293
Simmons, J. L., 311, 345, 346, 354, 359, 363, 366, 367
Simon, H. A., 232, 233, 254, 255, 257, 258, 259, 260, 267, 270, 273, 275, 281, 293, 380, 383, 384, 403, 700

Simon, J. L., 679
Simon, L. C., 200
Simpson, D. D., 168
Singer, D., 546
Singer, E., 679, 685, 689–690
Singer, J., 141, 400, 484
Singer, J. E., 91, 95, 456
Singer, R. C., 95
Singer, R. P., 122
Sinha, D., 63
Siu, R. G. H., 577
Skinner, B. F., 50, 71, 72, 73, 78, 90, 109, 116, 130, 137, 140–141, 292, 396, 567
Skogan, W. G., 645
Slaby, R. G., 113
Slocum, J. W., 269, 409
Slocum, W. L., 353, 362
Slovic, P., 177, 182, 187, 231, 233, 235, 236, 238, 240, 253, 256, 264, 267, 285, 288, 295
Smead, R. J., 258
Smedslund, J., 191
Smelser, N. J., 24
Smircich, L., 421, 422
Smith, A., 4, 11, 13, 315–316, 354
Smith, B., 58
Smith, C., 337
Smith, D., 596
Smith, D. L., 329, 624
Smith, E. E., 143, 156, 168
Smith, E. R., 492, 499
Smith, J., 147, 172
Smith, L. M., 590
Smith, M. B., 84, 314
Smith, M. D., 601
Smith, M. L., 505, 738, 741
Smith, P. B., 400
Smith, P. V., 505
Smith, R. E., 396
Smith, S., 115
Smith, T. W., 195, 644, 651, 657, 660, 678, 690
Smith, W. A., 192
Smith, W. P., 92
Smithers, J. A., 585
Smith-Lovin, L., 356, 621
Snapper, K., 752, 757
Snizek, W. E., 591
Snoek, J. D., 336, 351
Snow, D. A., 601
Snyder, C. R., 195
Snyder, G. H., 280

Snyder, M., 51, 123, 154, 157, 162, 163, 165, 167, 171, 179, 180, 204, 212, 460, 573
Snyder, M. L., 195, 206
Snyderman, B., 387
Snygg, D., 174
Soar, R. S., 741
Sobieczek, B., 357, 359–360
Soderstrom, J. E., 760
Soelberg, P. O., 274, 275, 276, 277
Solano, C., 52
Solem, A. R., 178
Solomon, L., 81
Solomon, M. A., 700
Solomon, R. L., 183, 184
Solomon, S., 195
Sommer, B. B., 596
Sommer, R., 596
Songer, E., 201
Sonquist, J. A., 687
Sorbom, D., 501, 638, 740, 745, 763
Sorokin, P. A., 3, 10, 13
Spaeth, H. J., 518, 519
Spaeth, J. L., 400
Spanier, G. B., 350
Sparks, R., 646
Speck, F. G., 584
Speller, D. E., 262, 263
Spence, J., 164
Spence, K. W., 72
Spence, M. A., 382
Spencer, D. G., 387
Spencer, H., 2, 3, 5, 6, 11, 13, 25, 35, 40
Spencer, J. R., 472
Spenner, K., 413
Spiegelberg, H., 586
Spiro, R. J., 157, 200
Spitzer, S., 318
Spradley, J. P., 570, 593, 594, 605–607, 621–622, 624
Spreitzer, E., 339, 349
Springbett, B., 182
Sproull, L. S., 723
Sprowls, J. W., 3
Sprowls, R. C., 246
Squyres, E. M., 573
Srinivasan, V., 517
Srole, L., 642
Srull, T. K., 156, 157, 167, 172, 208
Staats, A. W., 126, 127, 129
Staats, C. K., 126
Staddon, J. E. R., 292, 293
Staelin, R., 263

Stager, S., 319
Stagner, R., 186
Stahelski, A. J., 162, 577
Stake, R. E., 734, 757, 765
Staley, J. C., 473
Stalker, G. M., 408
Stallings, J. A., 727, 741
Stang, D., 185, 186, 290
Stanley, J. C., 64, 477, 543, 736
Stapert, J. C., 128
Starbuck, E. D., 40
Starr, M. K., 270
Stason, W. B., 728
Stava, P., 428
Staw, B. M., 409
Stebbins, L. B., 710
Stebbins, R. A., 609
Steckle, L. C., 186
Stedry, A. C., 389–390, 391
Steeh, C. G., 638, 677
Steele, C. M., 205
Steer, R. M., 390
Steers, R. M., 387, 389, 391
Steigleder, M. K., 124
Steinbeck, J., 582
Steinberg, J., 117
Steinbruner, J. D., 270, 274, 275, 279, 280, 288
Steiner, G. A., 41
Steiner, I. D., 41, 78
Steinthal, H., 2, 27, 28
Steinzor, B., 62
Stenson, H. H., 237
Stephan, C., 484
Stephan, F. F., 662, 687
Stephan, W. G., 195
Stephens, M. A. P., 578, 612
Stephens, T. A., 397
Stephenson, C. B., 662
Sternbach, R. A., 601
Sternberg, R., 281
Stevens, S. S., 510, 515, 531, 533
Stevenson, R. L., 18
Stewart, G. L., 592
Stewart, T. R., 239, 240
Stich, M. H., 118, 123
Stillwell, W. G., 243
Stinchcombe, A. L., 416, 677
Stingle, K. G., 118
Stipp, H., 760
Stirner, M., 9
Stocking, C., 654
Stogdill, R. M., 393, 399
Stokes, D. E., 691

Stokes, R., 352, 353, 361, 363, 365, 368
Stokey, E., 715, 760
Stokols, D., 612
Stolzenberg, R. M., 337, 338
Stone, E. F., 387
Stone, G. P., 319, 345, 355
Stoner, J. A. F., 58
Stonner, D., 112
Storey, R., 409
Storms, M., 491
Stotland, E., 38, 143
Stouffer, S. A., 337, 349, 519, 637, 685, 691
Stowell, R., 688
Strahan, R. F., 602
Stratton, J., 318
Strauss, A., 319, 320, 323, 326, 342, 343, 355, 575, 594
Strauss, G., 413
Straw, R. B., 736, 742, 743, 756, 757
Strehl, K., 395
Streufert, S., 570
Stricker, G., 146
Strodtbeck, F. L., 27, 96
Stromsdorfer, E. W., 700, 703, 740
Strong, S., 357
Stryker, S., 49, 311, 312, 313, 314, 315, 319, 320, 322, 324, 325, 326, 328, 334, 344–345, 346, 354, 357, 360, 361, 363, 364, 366, 367, 368
Stuart, R. B., 578
Styles, J., 588, 592
Suchman, E. A., 709
Suci, D. J., 535, 536
Sudman, S., 552, 642, 645, 647, 661, 662, 665, 679, 680
Sudnow, D., 592
Suling, R. A., 151
Sullivan, H. S., 50
Sullivan, J. L., 660
Sullivan, W. M., 569
Suls, J., 69, 175
Sulzer, J. L., 115
Sumner, W. G., 2, 332
Summers, D. A., 237, 240
Summers, J. O., 261, 263
Suter, L., 338
Sutherland, E. H., 319
Suttie, I. D., 10, 14
Sutton-Smith, B., 335

Svenson, O., 255, 256, 259, 261, 262, 264, 266
Swann, W. B., 154, 163, 180, 204
Swanson, C. L., 643
Swart, C., 114
Sweeney, P., 181
Sweet, J., 338
Swets, J. A., 157, 184, 231
Swidler, A., 568
Syert, R. M., 403
Sykes, M. P., 535, 536, 539
Sykes, R. E., 568, 587
Szucko, J. J., 241
Szwajkowski, E., 409

Tabori, L., 74
Taggast, R., 699
Tagiuri, R., 87, 147, 200
Tajfel, H., 208, 211
Taliaferro, J. D., 240
Tallmadge, G. K., 724, 739
Tanke, E. D., 96, 123, 162, 212, 460
Tanke, T. J., 96
Tannenbaum, P. H., 70, 89, 207, 535, 536
Tanur, J. M., 348, 354, 691
Tappenbeck, J., 210
Tarde, G., 2, 14, 17, 23, 40
Tashakkori, A., 200
Tatnall, P. A., 338
Taves, P. A., 140, 204
Taylor, R. N., 255, 270, 271
Taylor, S., 151
Taylor, S. E., 96, 148, 150, 165, 167, 173, 176, 182, 193, 196, 208, 255, 282, 285, 470
Taylor, S. J., 594, 624
Taylor, S. P., 112
Taylor, T. J., 612
Teasdale, J. D., 91
Tedeschi, J. T., 128, 205, 547
Teece, D. J., 405, 406
Teger, A. I., 58
Terborg, J., 390
Terdal, L. G., 597
Terrell, K., 338
Terry, C., 262
Terwillinger, R., 285, 289
Tesser, A., 129, 143, 159–160, 161, 567, 578
Tetlock, P. E., 181
Tetlock, R., 234

Thaler, R. H., 286, 290
Thayer, D. T., 501
Thelen, M. H., 121
Thibaut, J. W., 56, 68, 69, 74, 77, 78, 80, 82, 143, 160, 170, 335, 453
Thigpen, C. H., 537
Thissen, D., 242
Thistlethwaite, D. L., 200
Thoits, P. A., 339, 351
Thomas, D., 62, 84
Thomas, D. L., 320, 328
Thomas, D. S., 83, 317, 341
Thomas, E. A. C., 505
Thomas, E. J., 312
Thomas, S., 757
Thomas, S. V., 739, 762
Thomas, W. I., 35, 37, 75, 83, 317, 328, 341, 342, 574–575
Thompson, E. G., 201
Thompson, J. D., 408, 418
Thompson, M., 711, 715
Thompson, S. C., 167, 182, 282
Thomson, R., 83
Thomson, R. H., 186
Thornberry, O. T., 675
Thorndike, E. L., 8, 33, 72, 190
Thorndyke, P. W., 144, 165
Thorngate, W., 256, 258, 259, 261, 268, 601
Thronberry, O. T., 681
Thurnwald, R., 27
Thurstone, L. L., 41, 60, 61, 253, 513, 515, 523, 560
Tiller, M. G., 206
Timpane, P. M., 747
Titchener, E. B., 5, 7, 19, 36, 258
Toby, J., 337, 349
Toda, M., 269, 279
Todd, F. J., 237
Todd, J. B., 602
Toffler, B. L., 206
Tognacci, L. N., 545
Tolbert, C. M., 412
Tomkins, S. S., 93, 289
Toppen, A., 612
Toppino, T., 179
Torbert, W. R., 578
Torgerson, W., 239, 523
Tornatzky, L. G., 703, 741, 744
Tosi, H. L., 389, 390, 391, 407, 409
Toten, J., 171
Touhey, J. C., 344

Tracy, P. E., 654
Travis, L. E., 40
Treiman, D. J., 644
Treiman, P. J., 338
Triplett, N., 39, 40, 47, 63
Trochim, W. M. K., 744
Trocki, K., 338
Troland, L. T., 7
Trope, Y., 163, 187, 190, 283
Trotter, W., 12, 33
Trow, D., 275
Trow, M. A., 380
Truzzi, M., 624
Trzebinski, J., 164, 173
Tsujimoto, R. N., 145–146, 157
Tucker, L. R., 237, 241
Tucker, W., 682
Tuggle, F. D., 421
Tukey, D. W., 516
Tukey, J., 532, 559
Tukey, J. W., 191, 488, 506, 711
Tully, J., 345, 347, 366
Tuma, N. B., 711
Tundorf, H., 483
Turner, A. G., 645
Turner, A. N., 387
Turner, C. F., 643, 655
Turner, G., 746, 747
Turner, J., 455
Turner, J. H., 340–341
Turner, R., 347–348
Turner, R. H., 38, 319, 323, 324, 333, 341, 352, 354, 355, 358, 361, 362, 510
Turner, T. J., 148, 153, 155
Turteltaub, A., 121
Tversky, A., 92, 168, 177, 179, 180, 187, 189, 190, 233, 234, 236, 245, 246, 247, 248–250, 251–253, 255, 256, 257, 259, 260, 264, 268, 269, 276, 281, 283, 284, 286–287, 293–296, 396, 511, 517, 526, 531, 2882
Tyszka, T., 275

Ugwyebu, D. C. E., 161
Ulman, L., 413
Ulrich, R., 578
Underber, R. P., 535
Underwood, B., 470, 473
Unger, R. M., 381
Upshaw, H. S., 180
Upton, G. J. G., 502

Uranowitz, S. W., 154, 157, 165, 167
Useem, M., 414

Valens, S., 535
Valins, S., 90
Vallacher, R. R., 175
Van Den Bos, G. R., 711
Van der Pligt, J., 196
Van Dijk, T. A., 153
Van Dusen, R. A., 644
Van Hoose, T., 454, 460
Van Horn, C. E., 705
Van Kreveld, D., 201
Van Maanen, J., 574, 584, 585, 624
Van Raaij, W. F., 261
Vaughan, C. E., 4
Vaughan, G. M., 63
Vaught, C., 624
Veevers, J. E., 338
Verbrugge, L., 349
Verillo, R. T., 535
Vico, G., 1
Videbeck, R., 319
Vidmar, N., 503
Vincent, C. E., 352
Vinokur, A., 180
Voltaire, 9
von Bertalanffy, L., 26
Von Briesen Raz, J., 193
von Humboldt, K. W., 27
von Neumann, J., 80, 235, 245
Von Winterfeldt, D., 270
Vroom, V. H., 391, 392

Wachter, M. L., 405
Wack, D. L., 124, 140, 204
Waelder, R., 21
Wagner, J., 596
Wahba, M. A., 388
Wahrman, R., 359
Waid, C. C., 243
Wainer, H., 242, 561
Waite, L. J., 337, 338
Waksberg, J., 646, 647, 676
Walker, C. J., 205
Walker, S. G., 272
Wallace, B., 210
Wallace, J., 452, 456
Wallach, H., 211
Wallach, N. W., 58
Wallas, G., 33
Waller, W., 318, 319, 335
Wallis, W. D., 31

Wallsten, T. S., 235, 256, 259, 262
Wallston, B., 338
Walsh, M. L., 127
Walster, E., 56, 82, 181, 276, 277, 482
Walster, G. W., 276
Walters, R. H., 73–74
Ward, H. D., 191
Ward, W. C., 281
Wargo, M. J., 739, 743
Warheit, G. J., 362
Warkov, S., 407
Warner, L. G., 560
Warner, S. L., 184, 550, 653
Warren, D. R., 123
Warren, H. C., 19, 37
Warren, R. P., 582
Warshay, L., 327
Washburn, M. F., 37
Washburn, W. E., 573
Wason, P. C., 189, 281, 295, 296
Waterman, C. K., 124
Waterman, D., 257, 258
Watson, D., 141
Watson, G., 39
Watson, J. B., 34, 75
Watts, J., 289
Wax, M. L., 588
Wearing, A. J., 294
Weary, G., 195
Weaver, C. N., 349, 643
Webb, E., 572
Webb, E. G., 764, 766
Webb, E. J., 473, 543, 572
Webb, F. B., 760
Webber, I. L., 339
Webbt, Pierre, R. G., 758
Weber, A., 182
Weber, M., 312, 332, 380, 406
Webster, M., 357, 359–360
Wegner, D. M., 175
Weick, K. E., 62, 382, 383, 385, 389, 416, 423, 424, 425, 568, 569, 570, 572, 575, 609
Weigel, R. H., 500, 561
Weigert, A. J., 320, 355
Weill, M., 351
Weiner, B., 92
Weiner, S. S., 428
Weinstein, E., 319, 320, 325, 327, 334
Weinstein, E. A., 348, 352, 354
Weinstein, K. K., 349
Weinstein, M. D., 728

Weir, T., 338
Weisman, F., 552
Weiss, C. H., 683, 704, 707, 722, 757
Weiss, H. M., 401
Weiss, J., 287
Weiss, J. A., 272, 279, 704, 722
Weiss, J. H., 704
Weiss, R. F., 118, 122, 123, 124, 125, 128
Weiss, R. L., 119, 120
Weiss, R. S., 571
Weiss, W., 281, 476
Weissert, W. G., 725
Weitz, B., 262
Weitzel-O'Neil, P. A., 353, 362
Weitzman, L., 335
Welch, F., 411
Weldon, D. E., 151, 153
Wellens, A. R., 200
Welles, O., 23
Wells, F. L., 190
Wender, P. H., 609
Wenninger, V. L., 124
Werner, C., 167
Werner, P. D., 717
Wertheimer, M., 67, 79, 185
Werts, C. E., 542
Wesley, W., 726
West, L. J., 573
West, S. G., 74
Wetzel, C. G., 196
Wexley, K. N., 397
Weyant, J. M., 117
Wheeler, L., 115, 121
Wherry, R. J., 238
Whitaker, E. W., 320
White, B., 62, 63
White, D., 396
White, G. M., 116
White, J. K., 387
White, L., 573
White, L. A., 30
White, R., 40
White, R. K., 65, 68, 71, 442
White, R. W., 16
White, S. E., 390, 401, 402
Whitney, R., 186
Whittemore, I. C., 40
Whitt, J. A., 414
Wholey, J. S., 714, 715, 718, 719, 720, 753–754
Whyte, W. F., 576, 577, 583, 585–586, 609–610

Whyte, W. H., 596, 597
Wicker, A. W., 559–560, 605, 612
Wicklund, R. A., 57, 74, 175, 201, 203, 205, 206, 212, 277, 470
Widmer, M. L., 601
Wieder, D. L., 578
Wiener, N., 26
Wiest, W. M., 200
Wietz, B. A., 397
Wiggins, J. S., 241
Wiggins, N., 238, 242
Wigginton, J. C., 385, 421, 582
Wilcox, J. B., 258
Wildavsky, A., 384, 395, 711, 729
Wilde, J., 145–146, 157
Wilder, H., 176
Wiley, M. G., 343, 362, 363, 365, 710
Wilhelmy, R. A., 204
Wilkes, R. E., 258
Wilkie, W. L., 263
Wilkinson, L., 497
Willems, E. P., 570, 584, 594, 610, 612, 624
Willerman, B., 449, 452, 458
Williams, K. R., 578
Williams, L. P., 600
Williams, W., 9, 704, 711, 728
Williamson, O. E., 395, 396, 403, 404–405, 406, 414
Wills, T. A., 182
Wilson, C. C., 578
Wilson, D. T., 174
Wilson, T. D., 74, 174, 181, 240, 258–259, 457
Wilson, T. P., 581
Windelband, W., 4
Windle, C., 723
Winer, B. J., 491
Winett, R. A., 578
Winkler, R. L., 294
Winter, S. G., 404, 416
Wintrob, R. N., 519–520
Wiseman, J. P., 604, 624
Wish, M., 488
Wishner, J., 87
Wispe, L. G., 337, 584
Wissler, C., 16
Withey, S. B., 659, 660
Witte, E., 272
Wittenberg, B. H., 185
Witz, S., 556
Wofford, J. C., 388
Wolf, S., 677

Wolfe, D. W., 338, 339
Wolfe, J. C., 388
Wolfenstein, M., 596
Wolfson, M., 201
Wolin, S. S., 4
Woll, S. B., 151, 154, 165
Wollen, K. A., 182
Wood, H., 577, 578, 591, 592
Wood, V., 349
Woodmansee, J. J., 545
Woodward, J., 408
Woodward, J. A., 763
Woodworth, R. S., 33, 143
Woolgar, S., 575
Wooton, A., 580
Worchel, S., 204, 206
Worchel, S. L., 76
Wortman, C. B., 91
Wright, H. F., 568, 576, 587, 593–594, 602, 612, 613
Wright, P., 259, 262, 263, 265, 267, 268, 269, 274
Wright, R. A., 206
Wright, W. F., 240
Wrong, D., 340
Wundt, W., 3, 5, 20, 27, 28, 29, 36, 38
Wyer, R. S., 155, 156, 160, 166, 167, 170, 171, 172, 201, 208
Wykoff, L. B., 74

Yaari, M. E., 246
Yalom, I. D., 738
Yates, J. F., 264, 269, 276
Yates, R., 661
Yntema, D. B., 239
Yoels, W. C., 395
Yoma, I., 612
Yopp, H., 151
Youmans, K. C., 412
Young, F. W., 524
Young, K., 37
Yukl, G. A., 390, 397

Zadny, J., 150, 151
Zajonc, R. B., 74, 82, 93, 99, 124, 125, 126, 139, 142, 144, 149, 158, 160, 169, 172, 173, 186, 199, 200, 201, 203, 205, 212
Zald, M. N., 393
Zanes, A., 681
Zangwill, G. L., 144
Zanna, M. P., 91, 140, 182, 204, 205, 206, 208, 285, 470, 652
Zarkovich, S. S., 645, 646

Zavalloni, M., 58
Zdep, S. M., 654
Zeckhauser, R., 715, 760
Zedeck, S., 238, 239, 240
Zegiob, L. E., 586, 587
Zeigarnik, B., 68
Zeisel, H., 96
Zeitz, G., 383, 430
Zelditch, M., 357, 358, 359
Zeleny, M., 235
Zenker, S., 180

Zifferblatt, S. M., 397
Zigarmi, D., 588
Zigarmi, P., 588
Zigler, E. F., 352
Zill, N., 644
Ziller, R. C., 596
Zimbardo, P. G., 90, 206, 212, 442, 453, 466, 568
Zimmerman, D. H., 578
Zins, M. A., 264
Zito, J. M., 568

Znaniecki, F., 35, 37, 75, 333
Zoleno, R. N., 544
Zouwen, J., 642
Zobrow, D., 723
Zucker, L. G., 383, 422–423, 426–427
Zuckerman, M., 194, 195
Zurcher, L. A., 337, 339, 578, 601, 624
Zwerman, W. L., 408

Index

SUBJECT

Abnormal suggestibility, 18
Absicht, 36
Abstracted role segments, 32
Academy of Management Journal,
    380
Acceptance of goals, 390
Accessibility, 86
Accident procedure, 456
Accumulation of role, 351
Accuracy
    of judgments, 87
    of recall, 157
Achievement motivation, 92
Acquiescence, 183
Action
    aligning, 352
    alternative, 272
    ego-defensive, 205
    ideas and tendencies to, 36
    perspectives on, 386
    threshold of, 271
Activation of schemas, 150
Active search, 273
Actors' attributions, 196
Addition-of-utilities rule, 261
Administrative Science Quarterly,
    380

Affect, 93
    participation of, 210–211
Affect-control theory, 356
Affection, 11, 17, 25
Affective imitation, 16
Affiliation, 69
Affirmation and paraphrasing,
    582–583
Agentic state, 80
Aggression, 57, 72, 110–115
    anxiety related to, 114
    imitation of, 114–115
    inhibition of, 114
    justified, 115
    reinforcement of, 112–113
    stimuli evoking, 113–114
Aggression-frustration theory, 72,
    207
Akosmistische Person- und
    Gottesliebe, 13
Aligning actions, 352
Altercasting, 319, 325
Alter ego, 32
Alternatives
    cognitive representation of, 256
    evaluation of, 274–276, 277
    identification of, 271–274, 277

reevaluation of, 203
rejected, 203
selected, 203
Altruism, 13, 116–118
    reward for, 116
Ambiguity, 198
    in stimulus, 167
American Dilemma, The, 556
American Journal of Sociology, 380,
    513
American pragmatic philosophers,
    316
American Psychological Association
    (APA), 468–469, 550
    guidelines of, 469
American Social Psychology, 3
American Sociological Review,
    380
Analogical doctrines, 25–26
Analysis
    causal, 498
    cost, 760
    exploratory data, 488
    factor, 488
    internal, 451, 452
    Marxist, 410–414
    meta-, 505

methodical, 605–607
needs, 748–749
organizational, 393–396
path, 498
personality, 171
survey data, 688–689
unit of, 33, 382, 383, 386, 393, 504
unweighted-means, 495–496
variance, 66
Anchoring, 180, 284
Anger, 111
Animal magnetism, 17
Annual Review of Psychology, 51, 523
Anomie, 30, 332
Anticipated regret, 290
Anticipatory goal responses, 128
Anticipatory socialization, 325, 335
Anxiety, 112
APA. *See* American Psychological Association
Application error, 296
Applied settings for field experimentation, 484
Approach response, 73
Arousal
   and dissonance, 204
   of drive, 129
   factors in, 116–117
Art of Asking Questions, The, 642
Artifacts and experimenter effects, 98
Artificiality, 480
Aspiration level, 68, 207
Association
   blocking of normal, 19
   of ideas, 17
Associationism, 19
Atmosphere
   group, 40
   leadership, 63, 65
Attention to stimuli, 138
Attitude, 33, 35–38, 126–127, 175–176, 318, 647–652
   and behavior, 555–563
   change in, 57, 70, 75–77, 128
   defined, 36, 37, 509–510
   group, 515
   interpersonal, 127
   latent, 37
   measurement of, 60, 555–563
   task, 36
Attitude-congruent behavior, 204

Attitude-discrepant behavior, 204
Attraction
   consequences of, 127
   interpersonal, 126–130
Attributes, 262
   See also specific types
   of worth, 766
Attribution, 140
   actors' and observers', 196
   causal, 204
Attribution-based research, 59
Attribution error, 52, 193–194
   fundamental, 193–194
   ultimate, 195
Attribution theory, 88, 141, 143, 236, 314
Attributive projection, 195
Audits of programs, 732–733
Aufgabe, 36
Authoritarian personality, The, 183
Authoritarian personality, 51, 73
Autochthonous factors, 139
Autocratic leadership, 65
Availability, 179–180, 191
   bias of, 182, 184, 191, 193
   effects of, 282
Availability heuristic, 194, 246–247
Aversive drive, 129
Avoidance, 73
   defensive, 278
   of value trade-offs, 287–288
Awareness, 174
   contexts of, 319
   learning without, 74
   perception without, 197
   subject, 454–456

Balance theory, 198–201
Bargaining, 81
Base rates, 187–188
Basic and Applied Social Psychology, 49
Behavior. *See also* specific types
   aggressive. *See* Aggression
   altruistic. *See* Altruism
   attitude-congruent, 204
   attitude-discrepant, 204
   and attitude measures, 555–563
   external control of organizational, 414–421
   helping, 95
   in interaction, 361–364
   interview, 683–684
   organizational, 414–421, 423–425

past, 644–647
proattitudinal, 204–205
problem, 257–258
prophesied, 123
streams of, 505
surveys of, 691–692
Behavioral confirmation, 163
Behavioral decision theory, 236
Behavioral factors, 139
Behavioral thresholds, 557
Behavior of Crowds, The, 24
Behaviorism, 140–141
Behavioroid measures, 459, 473
Beitrage, 27
Beliefs, 647–652
Betweenness property, 254
Bewusstseinslage, 36
Beyond the Pleasure Principle, 7
Bezugsvorstellung, 36
Bias, 178–180, 181–182, 196, 233
   availability, 182, 184, 191, 193
   defined, 178
   input, 178–182
   interviewer, 685
   negativity, 182, 186
   operational, 178, 186–197
   output, 183–186
   positivity, 185–186
   representativeness, 189, 191
   response, 183–184
   self-serving, 195–196
   subject awareness, 454–456
Black box, 415
Blanks, 663
Blocking of normal associations, 19
Bogus pipeline, 205
Bootstrapping, 72, 242
Bottom-up matching process, 271
Bounded rationality, 233, 384
Break points, 62
British Association for the Advancement of Science, 515–516
British linguistic philosophy, 98

California State Department of Education, 742
Cancellation, 250, 516–518
Capturing of policy, 238
Categorization, 176
Category, 197
   selection of, 602–603
Catharsis, 73

Causal analysis, 498
Causal attribution, 204
Causality
  perception of, 198
  phenomenal, 89
Causal modeling, 498
Causal primacy effect, 180
Causation vs. correlation, 447
Cell sizes, 493–496
Central-tendency schemas, 144
Change
  attitude, 57, 70, 75–77, 128
  role, 339–340
  unconflicted, 278
Character, 38, 346
  dynamic, 198
Checklists, 595–596
Choice rules, 259–269
Chronometry, 200–201
Classical conditioning, 16, 127
Classical projection, 195
Clinical vs. statistical judgment,
  240–242
Cluster sampling, 661, 669–671
Clusters of elements, 663
Coarse-grained environment, 417
Coating groups, 39
Coding, 249, 687–688
  imaginal, 118
Coefficients
  path, 499
  Pearson product-moment
    correlation, 559
  of reproducibility, 520–521
  structural, 499
Cognition, 11, 17, 25
  hot, 141
  social, 208, 213
Cognitive analysis, 139
Cognitive approach
  vs. dominant approach, 137–139
  and organizational behavior,
    423–425
  vs. psychoanalytic approach,
    137–139
  vs. stimulus-response approach,
    137–139
Cognitive balance theory, 88
Cognitive category, 86
Cognitive chronometry, 200–201
Cognitive dissonance, 57, 123–124,
  201–207
Cognitive least effort principle, 266

Cognitive Psychology, 82
Cognitive representation of
  alternatives, 256
Cognitive response theory, 176
Cognitive restructuring, 17, 21–22
Cognitive schemas, 143
Cognitive social psychology, 82
Cognitive structures, 16, 138
  defined, 143
Cohesiveness of groups, 62, 453
Cold information processing, 141
Collective consciousness, 25–26, 27,
  29
Collective representations, 25,
  29–30
Combination, 249
Coming of Age in Samoa, 83
Commensurabililty, 263–264
Commitment, 276, 277, 288–289,
  319, 345, 646
Common-dimension effect, 264
Common-segment doctrines, 25,
  31–32
  and role, 32
Communication, 212, 316
  informal, 69
Communication and Persuasion,
  75–76
Comparative judgment law, 60
Comparison
  aspiration, 68
  paired, 513–515
  social, 207
  standards of, 713–714
Compensatory rules, 260–261
Competition, 124
Complexity of tasks, 261
Compliance, 76
Component variable, 238
Comprehension, 16
  error in, 296
Computer models, 257
  of information processing, 141
Comte's theory of three stages, 2
Conation, 11, 17, 25
Conceptual memory, 208–209
Conceptual replication, 480,
  481–483
Conceptual training for decision
  makers, 294–296
Conceptual variable, 477
Conditionally monotone
  relationship, 241

Conditioned reflex, 14, 15
Conditioned response, 19, 34
Conditioning, 17
  classical, 16, 127
  instrumental, 16
  operant, 16, 396–398
Confidentiality, 163
Confirmation
  behavioral, 163
  processing of, 275
Conflict, 198, 207
  models of, 277–279
  paradigm, 429
  role, 398–399
  social, 78
Conformity, 50, 335–336, 400
  research on, 207
  social, 78
Confused individuating information,
  189–190
Congruent stimulus, 167
Conjunction, 193, 284
  fallacy of, 189–190
Conjunctive probabilities, 283–284
Conjunctive rule, 259–260
Consciousness
  collective, 25–26, 27, 29
  dissociation of, 17, 18–19
  posture of, 36
Conscious purpose, 36
Consensual prototypes, 147
Consensus, 193–195
Consistency theories, 207–208
Consistent information schema,
  155–156
Constraints, 293–297
  on decision making, 280–297
  interpersonal, 362–363
  macrosocial structural, 363
  microstructural, 363–364
Constructionists, 421–428
Construct validation, 477, 479, 499
Contagion, 62, 121–122
Context, 620–624
  awareness, 319
  as cultural categories, 622
  decision, 296–297
  defined, 172–173
  dependence on, 579
  as goals, 173
  as higher-order themes, 622–624
  information-processing, 172–174
  as subgoals, 173

Contingency approach, 265–267
Contrient interdependence, 81
Control, 476
    illusion of, 291–292
    organizational, 403
    organizational behavior, 414–421
    vs. realism, 476
    subject, 544–545
    theory of, 175
Control-affect theory, 356
Controlled observation, 40–41
Conventions
    conversational, 180–181, 194
    linguistic, 198
Convergent validity, 541–543
Conversation, 123
    conventions in, 180–181, 194
    of gestures, 321
Cooperative interaction, 77
Copying, 118
    See also Imitation
Correlation, 489
    vs. causation, 447
    form-resistant, 658–659
    heterogeneity of, 491–492
    illusory, 176, 186, 190–191, 193,
        282
    multiple, 496
Corrigible rationalisms, 233
COSAN, 501
Cost
    long-term vs. short-term gain, 290
    of thinking, 267
    transaction, 404–406
Cost analysis, 760
Cost-benefit contingency model,
    266–267
Counter-attitudinal behavior, 204
Counterbalancing, 490–491
Cover story, 449–450
Creativity, 359–360
Creeping determinism, 192
Crisis, 148–149
Criteria
    impact, 723–724, 728–729
    implementation, 723
Cross-modality matching, 515
Crowd, 22–24
Crowd, The, 18
Crowding, 95–96
Crowd man, 22
Crowne-Marlowe Social Desirability
    Scale, 654

Cue weights, 239–240, 241, 242
Cultural categories, 622
Cultural determinism, 25, 30–31
Culture, 24, 312
    personality in, 29
Custom, 316
Cybernetics, 26, 279–280
Cyrenaic hedonism, 7

Darwinism, 12, 33
Data
    See also Information
    analysis of, 488
    gathering of survey, 678–682
    individuating, 192
    protocol, 257–258
Data processing, 687–688
Debriefing, 296, 465
Deception, 442–446, 464
    research on, 98
    self-, 195
Decision research, 207
Decisions
    conceptual training for, 294–296
    constraints on, 280–297
    context of, 296–297
    integrated views of, 277–280
    problems in, 255–280
    quality of and information load,
        263
    riskless, 235–243
    risky, 243–254
    structuring of, 271
    theory of, 82, 236
Default schema, 160
Defense, 85, 197
Defensive avoidance, 278
    and stress, 289–290
Defensive mechanism, 9
Definitional bootstraping, 72
Definitional crisis, 148–149
Degrees of freedom, 501
Deliberate vs. nondeliberate
    imitation, 14
Demand characteristics, 454,
    479–480
Democratic leaders, 65
Dependence, 78
    context, 579
Dependent variables, 449, 450,
    458–463, 473–474
Deprivation, 94
Descent law, 14

Descriptive vs. normative models,
    232
Descriptive psychology, 98
Design effect, 667
Design of jobs, 386–389
Desirability, 184
Detection
    dominance, 250
    signal, 184, 185
Determinierende Tendenz, 36
Determining tendencies, 17
Determinism
    creeping, 192
    cultural, 25, 30–31
Dictionary of Occupational Titles,
    413
Dictionary of Psychology, 19
Differentiation of roles, 62
Diffusionists, 16
Dimensional commensurability,
    263–264
Direction, 36
Directive state theory, 85
Disagreement, 128
Disconfirmed expectations, 203
Discovery, 575, 764
Discriminant validity, 500
Disjunctive rule, 260
Dislike, 129
Disorganization, 312
Displacement, 73
Dispositionism, 51
Disproportionate stratified sample,
    666
Dissemination, 768–769
Dissociation of consciousness, 17,
    18–19
Dissonance
    and arousal, 204
    cognitive, 57, 123–124, 201–207
    motivational consequences of,
        206
    postdecision, 203
Dissonance theory, 63
    and self, 203, 205
    vs. self-perception theory, 90–91
Dissonant states, 140
Distance of role, 319
Distraction, 125
Disturbance, 498
Documentary method of
    paraphrasing, 579–581
Dominance detection, 250

Dominant vs. cognitive approach, 137–139
Drama of small events, 608–609
Drive
arousal of, 129
factors in, 115
Duplicate listings, 663
Dynamic character, 198
Dynamic Psychology, 33
Dynamics
group, 67
motivational, 139
structural, 139, 197–198
Dynamogenesis, 18, 39

Echo principle, 15
Ecology, 415–418, 420
Economic man, 5
Editing, 249–250, 687–688
Ego, 32
Ego-defensive mechanisms, 9, 205
Ego and His Own, The, 9
Egoism, 8–10
Einfuhlung, 13
Einsfuhlung, 13
Einstellung, 36, 267, 293
EIP. *See* Elementary information processes
Ejective stage, 14
Electromyograph (EMG), 547
Elementargedanken, 27
Elementary information processes (EIP), 267
Elements, 705–707
classes of, 727–728, 737–747
clusters of, 663
Elimination-by-aspects rule, 260
Elite-mass contrasts, 691
Embracement of role, 319
Emergence of role, 352–354
EMG. *See* Electromyograph
Emotions, 329, 354–357
See also specific emotions
sympathetic induction of, 12
Empathy, 13, 15, 16
Empirical generalization, 763–764
Empirical realization, 480
Empirical relation system, 511
Encoding, 151–152, 153, 156, 158, 166, 168, 171
Encounters, 342
End effects, 646
Endogenous variables, 498
Engrossment, 342

Environment, 409–410
coarse-grained, 417
fine-grained, 417
Epicurean hedonism, 7
Epistemological foundations, 765–766
EQS, 501
Equal-appearing intervals, 60
Equity, 82
Eros, 7
Error
application, 296
attribution. *See* Attribution error
comprehension, 296
fundamental attribution, 193–194
"halo," 190
measurement, 501
sampling, 673
Error-prone intuitive scientists, 233–234
Error term, 491
ESRA. *See* Evaluation Studies Review Annuals
Estimation, 487
maximum-likelihood, 501
ratio, 515
Ethical hedonism, 5
Ethics, 466–469, 549–550, 689–690
in field research, 474–475
utilitarian, 5–6
Ethnic identification, 184
Ethnographic records, 594
Ethno-methodology, 98
Ethogenic approach, 98–99
Euclidean distance, 524
Evaluand leverage, 718
Evaluation, 158–162
of alternatives, 274–276, 277
fear of, 125
findings of, 714–716
implications of, 707–708
leverage of, 708–729
leverage in questions for, 729–748
policy on, 747–748
social program, 702
theory of, 700–708
Evaluation Studies Review Annuals (ESRA), 700
Evaluative criteria, 710–713
Evaluative information, 718–719
Evaluative questions and issues, 755
Evaluative studies, 748–769
Evaluator roles, 719–720
Event memory, 208–209

Events
drama of, 608–609
structures of, 32
unfolding of, 617–620
Event schemas, 148
Evolution, 5
Exchange, 80
Expectancy theory, 391–393
Expectations
disconfirmed, 203
role, 335
Expectations states theory, 357
Expected-utility principle, 244–245
Expected-value models, 243–246
Experimental vs. correlational approaches, 51
Experimental manipulation, 451
Experimental realism, 482–483
Experimental Social Psychology, 41, 61
Experimentelle Massenpsychologie, 39
Experiments, 38–40, 691
field, 470, 483–484
followup to, 449, 463–466
impact, 450, 452–453, 455
judgment, 443, 449
Explanation negotiation, 98
Explicit information search, 256–257
Explicitness, 587–597
Explicit preconceptions, 588–591
Explicit roles, 591–592
Exploratory data analysis, 488
Exposure after decisions, 57
Extensional basis for probability judgments, 283
External predictability, 512
External validity, 478–480, 483
Eye movements, 256

Face-to-face groups, 39
Facial response mediation, 93
Facilitation, 39, 63, 124–126
Fact vs. opinion, 643–653
Factor analysis, 488
Factorial design, 490–491
Failures in market, 404–406
False consensus, 193–195
Far West Laboratories, 724
Fear
appeals to, 122
of evaluation, 125
Feedback, 57, 647
Fellow-feeling, 13

Field experimentation, 470
  and application, 483–484
Field research, 474–475
Field settings, 443
Field stimulation, 573–574
Field theory, 139
  Lewinian, 67–68
Fine-grained environment, 417
First Principles, 35
Fixedness, 185
Focused gatherings, 342
Folk mind, 25, 27–29
Followup to experiments, 449,
  463–466
Foreign elements, 663
Formal representation system, 511
Format of information, 261, 264
Form-resistant correlations, 658–659
Frames of reference, 64
Framing effects on value accounting,
  286–287
Freedom, 501
Frustration, 111
Frustration-aggression theory, 72,
  207
F-statistic, 489
Functional fixedness, 185
Functionalistic position, 85
Fundamental attribution error, 52,
  178, 193–194
Fundamental measurement, 517
Future hedonism, 7

Gambler's fallacy, 192
Game theory, 80
Gamma statistic, 521–522
Garbage can model, 427–428
Gatherings, 342
Gefühlsansteckung, 13
Geist, 28
Generalized other, 317
Generalized reinforcers, 129
General person memory model, 209
Generations design, 504
Geography of social psychology, 53
Geometrical progression law, 14
Gestures, 320–321
Global representation, 159
Goals
  acceptance of, 390
  context as, 173
  group, 77
  idea of, 36
  information-processing, 170, 172

information-seeking, 171
  and memory, 156
  personality analysis, 171
  setting of, 389–391
Good-figure forces, 199
Graphs of problem behavior,
  257–258
Gregariousness, 12
Group Mind, The, 31, 77
Group mind, 24–33
Groups, 128
  atmosphere of, 40
  attitude scales of, 515
  coacting, 39
  cohesiveness of, 453
  dynamics of, 67
  face-to-face, 39
  fallacy of, 31
  goals of, 77
  influence of, 62, 64–65
  locomotion of, 79
  participation rates in, 62
  polarization of, 58
  problem-solving in, 77
  small, 504–505
Groupthink, 292–293, 296
  defined, 292
Growing Up in New Guinea, 83
Growth of American Thought, The, 4
Guttman Scales, 518–522, 526, 528,
  531, 552–555, 557

Habit, 33, 34–35, 38, 316
Habit-family hierarchy, 35
"Halo error," 190
Haltung, 36
Handbook of Social Psychology, 61,
  62, 77, 510, 568
Hedonism, 4–8, 11
Hedonistic calculus, 5
Helping behavior, 95
Helplessness model, 91
Heterogeneity of correlation,
  491–492
Heuristics, 186–197, 233
  availability, 194, 246–247
  defined, 178
  self-serving, 193, 195–196
Hierarchy
  habit-family, 35
  response, 34–35
Higher-order themes and context,
  622–624
Hindsight, 191–192

Hot cognition, 141
Hull-Spence position, 109–110, 139
Human Group, The, 78
*Human Inference: Strategies and
  Shortcomings of Social
  Judgment,* 177
Human Nature and Politics, 33
Human solidarity, 12
Hypervigilance, 278
Hypnotism, 17, 18, 20
Hypothesis generation, 272
Hypothesis theory, 86
Hysterical contagion, 62

"I," 317, 324, 346, 359, 366, 367
Id, 18
Ideas, 17
Idees-forces, 30
Identification, 16, 17, 18, 20–21, 118,
  487–488
  of alternatives, 271–274, 277
  ethnic, 184
  with group goals, 77
Identity, 345
  role, 346
  salience of, 345
  situated, 319, 343
  theory of, 312, 345
Ideology, 6
Ideomotor response, 17
Ideomotor theory, 15
Idiosyncratic knowledge, 405
Ignorance
  of own values, 285
  pluralistic, 194
Ill-defined decision problems,
  269–280
Illness management, 96
Illusion
  of control, 291–292
  of validity, 196
Illusion of Attitude Change, The,
  204
Illusory conditionals, 282–283
Illusory correlation, 176, 186,
  190–191, 193, 282
Imaginal coding, 118
Imitation, 10–11, 14–16, 17, 73,
  118–122
  affective, 16
  of aggression, 114–115
  defined, 16
  instinct of, 15
  learning of, 119

Imitation (*continued*)
learning through, 121
nondeliberate vs. deliberate, 14
Imitation and Social Learning, 73
Impact, 442, 448, 449, 450, 476, 483,
712–713
Impact criteria, 723–724, 728–729
Impact experiment, 450, 452–453,
455
Implementation criteria, 721–722,
723
Implicit personality schemas, 147
Implied presence, 3
Imposition, 361
determinants of, 364–367
Impression formation, 87
Impression management, 183, 192,
205, 206
Impression-personality schema, 160
Improper vs. proper linear models,
242
Improvisation, 361
determinants of, 364–367
Incongruity, 198
Inconsistent information schema,
155–156, 203
Incrementalism, defined, 384
Independence, 122–123, 516
Independent variable, 449, 450–458,
470–471
Indexicality, 579
Indirect measures, 462–463, 543–550
Individuality, 359–360
Individual norm, 65
Individuating information, 187–188,
192
confused, 189–190
Induced compliance paradigm, 76
Industrial psychology, 380, 386
Inertia, 278
Inferences, 140, 158–162, 176–178
Inferential errors, 177–179
Influence of groups, 62, 64–65
Informal communication, 69
Information
See also Data
consistent, 155–156
evaluative, 718–719
format of, 261, 264
gathering of, 281–288
inconsistent, 155–156, 203
individuating. See individuating
information
leverage of, 718

load of, 261–263
problems in combining, 287
search for, 256–257, 262
stakeholder needs for, 750–752
transformation of, 141
Informational social influence, 400
Information integration theory, 166,
180, 236, 237, 252–253, 281–288
Information processing
cold, 141
computer model of, 141
context of, 172–174
defined, 150
goals of, 170, 172
probabilistic, 86
and schemas, 150–174
Information-seeking goals, 171
Informed consent, 689–690
In-group, 195
cohesion of, 62
Inhibition, 114
Innate motor scripts, 93
Innate tendency, 15
Innovators, 56
Inpatient Scale of Minimal
Functioning (ISMF), 710
Input biases, 178–182
Inquiry, 584–587
Insensitivity to base rates, 282–283
Insightful reflex, 14
Instinct, 7, 33–34, 38
of imitation, 15
submissive, 18
transitoriness of, 34
*Instincts of the Herd in Peace and
War,* 12, 23
Institutional Behavior, 31
Institutionalization theory, 425–427
Instrumental conditioning, 16
Insufficient justification, 203, 206
Integrated views of decision process,
277–280
Integration of information, 166, 180,
236, 237, 252–253, 281–288
Intellectualized sympathy, 13
Intensional basis for probability
judgments, 283
Intentions, 652–653
Interaction, 490
behavior in, 361–364
cooperative, 77
social, 312, 503
symbolic, 312
Interactional role theory, 330

Interactionism, 52, 422–423
Interaction Process Analysis, 62
Interattribute vs. intraattribute
processing, 264
Interdependence, 78
contrient, 81
defined, 398
promotive, 81
Interdimensional vs.
intradimensional, 259
Interface of personality, 50–53
Interlocking techniques, 518–522
Internal analysis, 451, 452
Internal before exotic law, 14
Internalization, 334
of prohibitions, 70
Internal predictability, 512
Internal validity, 477–478, 480
Interpersonal attitudes, 127
Interpersonal attraction, 126–130
Interpersonal constraints, 362–363
*Interpersonal Relations: A theory of
Interdependence,* 78
Interpretation, 539–540
Intersubjectivity, 210, 213
Interval scales, 532
Interview, 460, 682–687
behavior in, 683–684
personal, 687–679
Interviewer
bias of, 685
characteristics of, 685–686
variance in, 686–687
Interviewing in Social Research, 685
Intraattribute vs. interattribute
processing, 264
Intradimensional vs.
interdimensional, 259
Intrinsic motivation, 205
Introduction to Social Psychology,
33
Introspection, 317
Intrusions, 157
Intuitive scientists, 233–234
Irrationalists, 10
ISMF. *See* Inpatient Scale of Minimal
Functioning
Isomorphism, 83

Job design, 386–389
Journal of Abnormal Psychology,
19, 50
*Journal of Abnormal and Social
Psychology,* 19, 50, 537

*Journal of Applied Social
    Psychology,* 49, 94
Journal of Conflict Resolution, 80
*Journal of Experimental Social
    Psychology,* 49, 489
Journal of Personality, 49, 51
*Journal of Personality and
    Psychology,* 489
*Journal of Personality and Social
    Psychology,* 19, 49, 50, 96
Journal of Social Issues, 49
Journal of Social Psychology, 49
Judgment, 236–237, 448, 449
    accuracy of, 87
    clinical vs. statistical, 240–242
    comparative, 60
    probability, 283
    social, 236
    stereotyped, 191
Judgment experiment, 443, 449, 452
Jury stimulation experiments, 96
Justification, 203, 206
Justified aggression, 115

Knowledge
    idiosyncratic, 405
    structures of, 143
KYST, 524

Laboratory research efforts, 484
La foule criminelle, 23
Laissez-faire, 5, 6, 7, 11, 40, 65
La mentalité primitive, 30
Latent attitudes, 37
Latent variables, 500–502
Law of affective evolution, 10
Law of comparative judgment, 60
Law of descent, 14
Law of effect, 8
Law of geometrical progression, 14
Law of the internal before the exotic,
    14
Leader Behavior Description
    Questionnaire, 399
Leadership
    See also specific types
    atmosphere of, 63, 65
    autocratic, 65
    democratic, 65
    laissez-faire, 65
    path-goal theory of, 393
Learning
    without awareness, 74
    probability, 188, 192

of tasks, 129
    through imitation, 121
    to imitate, 119
    to like, 127
    vicarious, 73
    Yale theory of, 34
Learning theory, 109
    liberalized, 130
Least effort principle, 266
Le crime à deux, 23
L'Egoisme, 9
Leverage
    determinants of, 717
    of evaluand, 718
    in evaluation questions, 729–748
    of information, 718
    sources of, 721–729
Leviathan, 8
Lewinian field theory, 67–68
Lexicographic rule, 260
Liberalized learning theory, 130
Liberalized stimulus-response theory,
    110
Life space, 84
Likert Scale, 536
Liking, 127
    role of, 585
Linear combinations of probability
    and utility, 253–254
Linear models, 237–243
    proper vs. improper, 242
Linear-ordering schema, 146
Linear regression models, 255
Linguistic conventions, 198
LISREL, 501
Literal interpretation fallacy,
    539–540
Literature reviews, 738–739, 749–750
Load of information, 261–263
Locomotion of groups, 79
Log-linear models, 502–503
Long-term vs. short-term cost gain,
    290

Machiavellianism, 51, 56
Macrosocial structural constraints,
    363
Magnitude, 515
Mail surveys, 680
Management information systems
    (MIS), 731–732, 734
Managerial Psychology, 380
Manipulation
    checks on, 451

of decision context, 296–297
    of experiments, 451
Market failures approach, 404–406
Marxist analysis, 410–414
Mass Communication, 75
Masses, 22–33
Matched-dependent relationship, 16
Matching, 271
    bottom-up, 271
    cross-modality, 515
    strategy in, 193
    structuring by, 271–272
    template, 52
    theory-driven, 271
    top-down, 271
MAUM. *See* Multiattribute utility
    measurement
Maximum-likelihood estimation, 501
"Me," 317, 324
Meaning, 314, 320–321
    multiple, 476–477
Measurement, 510–513
    See also specific types
    attitude, 60, 555–563
    behavioroid, 459, 473
    of cost of thinking, 267
    defined, 510–511
    error in, 501
    fundamental, 517
    indirect, 462–466, 541
    multiattribute utility (MAUM),
        243, 296
    nonrepresentational, 512, 531–534
    performance, 758–766
    representational, 511, 531–534
    simultaneous conjoint, 515–518
    unobtrusive, 473–474, 572–573
Mediating processes, 743–745
Mediational models, 499
Memory, 645–646
    conceptual, 208–209
    event, 208–209
    and goals, 156
    organization of, 153
    person, 208, 209
    recognition, 147–148
    selective, 197
    social, 63
Memory research, 208
Memory search, 273
Menschenliebe, 13
Mental attitudes, 35
Mentalism, 83
Mental organization, 20

Mere presence, 125
Merger of role and person, 348
Mesmerism, 17
Metaanalysis, 505, 738–739
Metaphysical absolutes, defined, 9
Metaphysical stage of social science, 2
Metastrategy, 265
    defined, 266
Method choice, 757–769
Methodical analysis, 605–607
Methodical category systems, 602–605
Methodical multiples, 601–602
Methodical work, 597–607
Methodology, 149, 381, 385, 421–422, 428
    See also specific types
    of program monitoring, 735–737
    qualitative, 733–734
    simulation, 427
M-form structure, 406
Micro-sociology, 98
Microstructural constraints, 363–364
Mimicry, 119
Mind
    folk, 25, 27–29
    group, 24–33
    objective, 25–27
    one, 26
    social, 25
Mindless processing, 169
Minimal social situation, 74
MIS. *See* Management information systems
Misattribution, 91, 204
Missing elements, 663
Miteinanderfühlung, 13
Mitgefühl, 13
Mixed-motive situations, 80
Model characteristics, 120
Model-observer similarity, 120
Mohs scale, 511, 532
Monitoring
    of clients, 729–737
    of explicit information search, 256–257
    of programs, 735–737
    self-, 51
Monoideism, 17, 19
Monotone relationship, 241
Morale, 94
Moral realism, 30

Motivation
    achievement, 92
    and dissonance, 206
    dynamics of, 139
    factors in, 288–293
    forces in, 234
    intrinsic, 205
    vocabulary of, 319
Motor attitudes, 35
Motor mimicry, 119
Multiattribute utility measurement (MAUM), 243, 296
Multicollinearity, 488
Multidimensional scaling, 488
Multidimensional unfolding, 531
Multidivisional structure, 406
Multiple correlation, 496
Multiple indicators, 659
Multiple meaning, 476–477
Multiple methods, 601
Multiple regression, 496–498, 742
Multiple-response modes, 601–602
Multiple-role involvement, 336–337
MULTI-SCALE, 524
Multistage models, 264–265
Multistage sampling, 661, 669–671
Multitrait, multimethod method, 541
Mundane realism, 79, 482–483
Mutual Aid, 12

Nachfühlung, 13
Naive estimates of value, 285–286
Nancy school, 18, 19, 20
Nation, 24
Naturalness, 591
Nature of Prejudice, The, 94
"Nay-sayers," 183
Needs analysis, 748–749
Needs theory, 386–389
Negative hedonism, 7
Negative vs. positive outcome probabilities, 281–282
Negative reinforcers, 129
Negativity bias, 182
    vs. positivity bias, 186
Negotiated orders, 343
Negotiation, 81, 343
    of explanations, 98
New Directions in Attribution Research, 92
New Look, 86, 139, 144, 149, 197
Noncompensatory rules, 259–260

Nondeliberate vs. deliberate imitation, 14
Nonindependence, 504
Nonprobability vs. probability sampling, 662
Nonrepresentational measurement, 512, 531–534
Nonresponse, 676–678
Nonspecific innate tendency, 15
Non-zero-sum games, 80
Normal associations, 19
Normal suggestibility, 18
Normative models, 234
    vs. descriptive models, 232
Norms
    individual's, 65
    of procedure, 296–297

Obedience, 79, 207
Object, 316
Objective mind, 25–27
Objective self-awareness, 175
Objective vs. subjective weights, 240
Objektiver geist, 26
Observation, 572–579
    controlled, 40–41
    self, 577–579
    systematic, 62–63, 568–572
Observers' attributions, 196
Occupancy of role, 399
On Being Human, 12
One mind, 26
Operant conditioning, 16, 396–398
Operational bias, 178, 186–197
Operational codes, 272
Opinion, 128
    vs. fact, 643–653
Optimality of choice rules, 268
Order effects, 57
Orders, 343
Ordinal scales, 532
Organization
    memory, 153
    personal, 312
    social, 312
Organizational analysis, 393–396
Organizational behavior
    cognitive perspectives on, 423–425
    external control of, 414–421
Organizational control, 403
Organizational level rational action, 402–414
Organizational set, 418

Organizational size, 406–408
Original Nature of Man, The, 33
Others
  generalized, 317
  significant, 325
  taking roles of, 319
Outcome debriefing, 296
Outcome probabilities, 281–282
Out-group, 195
Outline of Psychology, 36
Output biases, 178, 183–186
Overjustification, 91, 204
Overload, 287

PACKAGE, 501–502
Paired comparisons, 513–515
Panel studies, 691
Paradigm
  conflict in, 429
  defined, 424
Paramorphic representation,
  238–240
Paraphrasing, 579–583
Participation
  of affect, 210–211
  in groups, 62
Passive search, 273
Passive sympathy, 12, 15
Past behavior, 644–647
Past hedonism, 8
Path analysis, 498
Path coefficients, 499
Path-goal theory of leadership, 393
Payoff matrixes, 78
PBG. *See* Problem behavior graph
Pearson product-moment correlation
  coefficient, 559
Perceiver
  and social perception, 212
  state of, 169
Perception
  without awareness, 197
  of causality, 198
  of choice rules, 267–268
  person, 87–89, 209, 210
  selective, 142
  self-, 140–141, 203–206
  social, 212, 213
Perception and Communication,
  82
Perceptive vs. receptive individuals,
  273
Perceptual defense, 85, 197

Performance
  on learning tasks, 129
  measurement of, 758–766
Performance feedback, 57
Permissible transformations, 531
Perseverance, 181
Personal disorganization, 313
Personality, 32
  analysis goals of, 171
  authoritarian, 73
  in culture, 29
  interface of, 50–53
  scales of, 51
  schemas of, 147
Personality-impression schema, 160
*Personality and Social Psychology
  Bulletin,* 49, 50
Personal organization, 312, 313
Person memory, 208
Person perception, 87–89, 209, 210
Person schemas, 148
Persuasibility, 20
Persuasion, 122
Phenomenal causality, 89
Phenomenology, 12–13, 84
Philanthropy, 13
Pilot testing, 755
Plans and the Structure of Behavior,
  82
Platonic trichotomy, 11
Pleasure-seeking hedonism, 7
Pluralistic explanations, 4
Pluralistic ignorance, 194
Polarization, 160
  group, 58
Policy capturing, 238
Political perspectives on
  organizational analysis, 393–396
*Political Philosophy from Plato to
  Jeremy Bentham,* 4
Pollyanna principle, 185, 290–291
Polymorphism, 417
Population, 661
  ecology of, 415–418, 420
  target, 661
Portfolio theory, 253–254
Position language category, 323
Positive vs. negative outcome
  probabilities, 281–282
Positive reinforcers, 129
Positivist stage of social science, 2
Positivity bias, 185–186
  vs. negativity bias, 186

Postdecisional exposure, 57
Postdecisional regret, 277
Postdecision dissonance, 203
Postexperimental followup, 449,
  463–466
Posture of consciousness, 36
Power, 8–10, 78, 394, 395, 396,
  410–411, 412, 413, 418, 420, 425
  strategy of, 82
PPS. *See* Probabilities proportional
  to size
Pragmatic philosophers, 316
Pragnanz, 83
Prebriefing, 296
Preconceptions, 588–591
Predictability, 512
Predictions, 158–162
Preference methods, 526
Preference spaces, 526
Prejudice, 94–95, 176
Presentative sympathy, 11
Present hedonism, 7
Pressures of roles, 398
Prestige of innovators, 56
Pretest, 457
Primacy, 180–181
Primary sampling units (PSU),
  671–673
Priming, 185
Primitive passive sympathy, 12, 15
Principle of Utility, 4
Prior expectancy in response to
  performance feedback, 57
Prisoner's Dilemma game, 294
Proattitudinal behavior, 204–205
Probabilistic information processing,
  86
Probabilities
  conjunctive, 283–284
  size, 671–673
Probabilities proportional to size
  (PPS), 617–672, 674–675
Probability judgments, 283
Probability learning, 188, 192, 193
Probability vs. nonprobability
  sampling, 662
Probability statistics, 66–67
Probability and utility, 253–254
Probability-weighting function,
  246–247
Problem behavior graph (PBG),
  257–258
Problem recognition, 270–271, 277

Problem solving in groups, 77
Problem space, 255
Procedural norms, 296–297
Procedural schemas, 144
Process debriefing, 296
Processing
    goals of, 173
    of information. *See* Information
        processing
    mindless, 169
Process models, 235, 254–280,
    427–428
Process prebriefing, 296
Process vs. structure, 232
Process-tracing methods, 256–259
Program evaluation, 708–717,
    722–723, 732–733
Programmatic research, 475–484
Program structure, 704–707
Prohibitions, 70
Project classes, 724–727
    identification of, 737–747
    infering, 740–741
Projection, 195
Projective stage, 14
Promotive interdependence, 81
Propaganda, 20, 94
Propensities, 34
Proper vs. improper linear models,
    242
Prophesied behavior, 123
Proportionate stratified sample, 666
Prospect theory, 246
    criticisms of, 250–252
Protocols
    reliability and validity of, 258–259
    uses of data of, 257–258
    verbal, 257–259
Prototypes, 197
    consensual, 147
    defined, 147
Proximity techniques, 522–526
Pseudosympathy, 13
PSU. *See* Primary sampling units
Psychicactuality, 28
Psychoanalytic vs. cognitive
    approach, 137–139
Psychological account, defined, 286
Psychological decision theory, 236
Psychological reactance, 277
Psychological vs. sociological social
    psychologies, 49
Psychologie des sectes, 23

Psychology of the Emotions, 12
*Psychology of Interpersonal
    Relations, The,* 89
Psychophysical function, 513
Psychophysics, 83
Public opinion research, 61
Purpose, 36
P-value, 489

Qualitative methods, 733–734
Quasi-concepts, 68
Quasi-experimental designs, 488
Quasi-*F*-ratio, 492–493
Questionnaires, 459
Questions
    adequacy of, 645
    choice of, 748–757
    constraint on, 647
    constructing survey, 659–660
    evaluative, 755
    length of, 646
    leverage of in evaluation, 729–748
    refining of, 755–757
    sensitive, 653–655
    specificity of, 650–652

Radical behaviorism, 140–141
RAM, 501
Random assignment, 446–447
Random-digit-dialing (RDD), 675,
    677, 679, 682
Randomized responding, 550–555
Random response effects, 657–658
Rating scales, 540–541
Ratio estimation, 515
Rationalistic hedonism, 5
Rationalists, 233
Rationality, 21, 232–235
    bounded, 384
    organization-level, 402–414
Rational problem solving, 700–701
Ratio scales, 531
RDD. *See* Random-digit-dialing
Reactance, 206
    psychological, 277
Reactivity, 473, 586–587
Realism, 476
    vs. control, 476
    experimental, 482–483
    mundane, 79, 482–483
Realistic social experiences, 476
Reality, 79
Realization, 480

Recall accuracy, 157
Receptive vs. perceptive individuals,
    273
Reciprocal nature of social
    perception, 212
Reciprocal relation, 31
Reciprocity, 213
    of roles, 31
Recognition memory method,
    147–148
Recognition of problems, 270–271,
    277
Recording of eye movements, 256
Records
    ethnographic, 594
    explicit, 593–597
Redintegration, 17, 19
Reduction
    of determining tendencies, 17
    uncertainty, 275
Reevaluation of alternatives, 203
Reference frames, 64
Reference-point shifts, 248–249
Reflection effect, 248, 251
Reflective sympathy, 13
Refex, 14, 15
Regression, 68
    coefficients of, 489
    multiple, 496–498
    stepwise, 497
Regret
    anticipated, 290
    postdecisional, 277
Reinforcement, 6–7, 8, 16, 647
    of aggressive behavior, 112–113.
    consequences of, 110, 119
    generalized, 129
    negative, 129
    positive, 129
    secondary, 128
    self-, 117–118
Rejected alternative, 203
Rejection-inducing dimensions, 265
Relationships
    conditionally monotone, 241
    interdependent, 78
    matched-dependent, 16
    monotone, 241
    reciprocal, 31
    sentiment, 198
    social, 505
    unit, 198
Relative deprivation, 94

Relative-preference dimensions, 265
Reliability, 603–604
  of verbal protocols, 258–259
Remembering, 63, 64, 83
Repeated-measures designs, 491
Repetition as function of truth value, 179
Replication
  conceptual, 480, 481–483
  simultaneous, 739–740
Representation
  defined, 141–142
  global, 159
  paramorphic, 238–240
  specific, 159
Representational events, 142
Representational measurement, 511, 531–534
Representativeness, 187–189, 192–193
  bias of, 189, 191
Representative sympathy, 11
Repression sensitization, 205, 206
Reproducibility coefficient, 520–521
Requisite variety and paraphrasing, 581–582
Rerepresentative sympathy, 11
Research
  See also specific types
  attribution-based, 59
  conformity, 207
  deception, 98
  decision, 207
  dominating themes of, 54
  field, 474–475
  laboratory, 484
  memory, 208
  person perception, 87–89
  public opinion, 61
  survey, 635–640
Resolution of role conflict, 350–351
Response
  approach, 73
  bias in, 183–184
  conditioned, 19, 34
  heirarchy of, 34–35
  ideomotor, 17
  random effects of, 657–658
  randomized, 550–555
  stimulation produced by, 71
  systematic effects of, 657–658
Restructuring, 17, 21–22

Retention, 153–158
Retrieval, 153–158, 171
Revue de métaphysique, 29
Rewards
  for altruism, 116
  secondary, 127
  sources of, 127
Richtungsvorstellung, 36
Rigidly structured mental organization, 20
Riskless decisions, 235–243
  vs. risky decisions, 232
Risky decisions
  models of, 243–254
  vs. riskless decisions, 232
Risky shift, 58
Role conflict, 336–337, 398–399
  resolution of, 337–339, 350–351
Role effects perspective, 399
Roles, 312, 323, 326
  See also specific types
  abstracted, 32
  accumulation of, 351
  change in, 339–340
  and common segment, 32
  differentiation of, 62
  distance of, 319
  embracement of, 319
  emergence of, 352–354
  expectations of, 335
  explicit, 591–592
  identity of, 346
  making of, 319, 324
  merger of person with, 348
  occupancy of, 399
  pressures of, 398
  reciprocity of, 31
  satisfaction in, 349–350
  schemas of, 148
  strain of, 336
  taking of, 317, 324–325
  taking of others', 319
Role set, 398, 399
Role theory, 312, 398–399
  interactional, 330
  structural, 330
Rotation design, 505
Rules
  choice, 267–268
  compensatory, 260–261
  conjunctive, 259–260
  disjunctive, 260
  elimination-by-aspects, 260

  lexicographic, 260
  noncompensatory, 259–260
  stopping, 279
Salience, 191, 282
  defined, 167
  identity, 345
Salpetriere School, 18
Sample designs, 673–676
Sample space, 190
Sampling
  cluster, 669–671
  disproportionate stratified, 666
  errors in, 673
  frames in, 662–664
  multistage, 661, 669–671
  primary units in (PSU), 671–673
  probability vs. nonprobability, 662
  process of, 661–664
  proportionate stratified, 666
  survey, 660–678
  systematic, 665–666
Satisfaction in roles, 349–350
Saturated model, 503
Scale types, 532–534
Scapegoating, 65
Schemas, 64, 144–147, 148, 196, 197
  See also specific types
  activation of, 150
  cognitive, 143
  as computer format, 164
  consistent information, 155–156
  default, 160
  defined, 164
  event, 148
  implicit personality, 147
  impression-personality, 160
  inconsistent information, 155–156
  and information processing, 150–174
  linear-ordering, 146
  person, 148
  procedural, 144
  role, 148
  self-, 146–147, 153, 154
  template, 144
Scottish Moral Philosophers, 312, 315–316, 328
Script, defined, 148
SDA. *See* Service delivery assessment
Search
  active, 273
  information, 262

Search (*continued*)
  memory, 273
  passive, 273
  trap, 273
Search-design continuum, 272–274
Secondary reinforcers, 128
Segregation, 249–250
Selected alternative, 203
Selection, 276, 277
Selective control of stimuli, 138
Selective exposure hypothesis, 206, 289
Selective memory, 197
Selective perception, 142
Self, 311, 316, 317, 324, 325–326, 327, 348, 350, 354–359
  and dissonance theory, 203, 205
  observing of, 577–579
  stability of, 318
Self-awareness, 175
Self-concept, 174–175
Self-deception, 195, 203
Self-esteem, 9, 57, 316
Self-monitoring, 51
Self-perception, 140–141, 203–206
  vs. dissonance theory, 90–91
Self-persuasion, 76
Self-presentation, 82
Self-regulation, 175
Self-reinforcement, 117–118
Self-relations, 36
Self-schemas, 146–147, 153, 154
Self-serving bias, 195–196
Self-serving heuristic, 193, 195–196
Semantic differential, 536–539
Sensitive questions, 653–655
Sensitization, 205, 206
Sensitizing concepts, 318
Sentiment, 33, 38, 198
  self-regarding, 38
Service delivery assessment (SDA), 733
Set, 36, 148–149
  role, 399
Setting
  field, 443
  variations in, 681–682
Setting of goals, 389–392
Setting the stage, 449–451
Shifts, 248–249
Short-term vs. long-term cost gain, 290
Signal detection, 184, 185
Significance tests, 506

Significant others, 325
Significant symbols, 316–317, 321
Simple association, 19
Simple multiattribute-rating technique (SMART), 296
Simple random sampling (SRS), 664–670
Simplicist fallacy, 4
Simplification, 249
Simulation techniques, 427–428
Simultaneous conjoint measurement, 515–518
Simultaneous feeling, 13
Simultaneous replication, 739–740
Situated activity systems, 342
Situated identity, 319, 343
Situation definitions, 317, 322–323, 326
Situationism, 35, 51, 384–385
Size of cells, 493–496
Size of organization, 406–408
Size probabilities, 671–673
Small events
  drama of, 608–609
  unfolding of, 617–620
Small groups, 504–505
SMART. *See* Simple multiattribute-rating technique
SMSA. *See* Standard metropolitan statistical areas
Social act, 320
Social categorization, 176, 643–644
Social climate, 40
Social Cognition, 49
Social cognition, 208, 213
Social comparison, 68–69, 121, 207
Social conflict, 78
Social conformity, 78
Social constructionist views, 421–428
Social contract, 8
Social desirability, 184
Social exchange, 80
Social facilitation, 39, 63, 124–126
Social factors, 288–293
Social increment, 40
Social influence, 400
Social institution, 24
Social interaction, 312, 321–322, 503
Social invention, 2
Socialization, 15, 312, 313, 320, 325
  anticipatory, 325, 335
Social judgment theory, 236
Social Learning and Imitation, 16
Social legislation, 6

Social memory, 63
Social mind, 25
Social organization, 312
Social perception, 212, 213
Social person, 311
Social process, 314
Social program evaluation, 702
Social psychology, defined, 2–3, 35, 47, 138
Social Psychology, 3, 23
Social Psychology Quarterly, 49, 489
Social reality, 79
Social relations model, 505
Social science stages, 2
Social situations, 607–620
Social stimulation, 40
Social structure, 311
Social subvaluent, 40
Social Thought from Lore to Science, 3
Social value, defined, 37
Society, 311
Sociometry, 489
Sociometry, 49, 61–62
Sociorationalistic, 99
Solidarity, 12
Solipsism, 574–575
Sophistication, 295
Sources of rewards, 127
Specification, 487
Specific representation, 159
S-R. *See* Stimulus-response
SRA, 669
SRC, 675
SRS. *See* Simple random sampling
Stability of self, 318
Stages of social science, 2
Stakeholder information needs, 750–752
Standardization, 496
Standard metropolitan statistical areas (SMSA), 674
State of perceiver, 169
Static movement systems, 37
Statistical vs. clinical judgment, 240–242
Statistics, 66–67
Statuses, 333
Stepwise regression, 497
Stereotyping, 65, 94–95, 176, 188, 191
Stigma, 94
Stimulation
  attention to, 138

congruent vs. ambiguous, 167
  field, 573–574
  response-produced, 71
  selective control of, 138
Stimulus-response (S-R) theory,
    71–75, 109, 421
  vs. cognitive approach, 137–139
  liberalized, 110
Stopping rule, 279
Strange Case of Dr. Jekyll and Mr.
    Hyde, The, 18
Strategy
  matching, 193
  power, 82
Stratificaton, 666–669
Stratified sample, 666
Streams of behavior, 505
Stress and defensive avoidance,
    289–290
Structural approach, 422–423
Structural balance, 198
Structural coefficients, 499
Structural constraints, 363
Structural contingency theory,
    406–410
Structural dynamics, 139, 197–198
Structural equation, 498–502
Structural-functionalism, 330
Structural models, 235–254
Structural role theory, 330
Structure
  cognitive, 16, 138, 143
  decision, 271
  event, 32
  by hypothesis generation, 272
  knowledge, 143
  by matching, 271–272
  M-form, 406
  multidivisional, 406
  vs. process, 232
  social, 311
Structure of Appearance, The, 522
Structured mental organization, 20
Subadditivity effect, 252–253
Subception, 197
Subject awareness biases, 454–456
Subject control, 544–545
Subjectively expected utility, 245–246
Subjective vs. objective weights, 240
Subjective stage, 14
Subjectivism, 83–84
Submission, 17, 18
Subvaluent, 40
Suggestibility, 18

Suggestion, 10–11, 14, 17, 18
Suggestion-imitation principle, 11
Suicide, 30
Survey research, 635–640
Surveys
  activities, 734–735
  analysis of data from, 688–689
  components of, 640–642
  gathering of data for, 678–682
  limitations of, 638
  mail, 680
  periodic, 690–691
  population for, 661
  questions for, 642–660
  sampling for, 660–678
Suspicion, 576–577
Sustained inquiry, 584–587
Sustaining, 583–587
Symbolic interaction theory, 312
Symbols, 316–317, 321
Sympathetic induction of emotion,
    12
Sympathetic introspection, 317
Sympathy, 10–14, 15, 17
Synthesizing of results, 766
Systematic observation, 62–63
  defined, 568–572
Systematic response effects, 658–659
Systematic sampling, 665–666
System model, 753–754

Taking role of others, 319
Target population, 661
Task attitude, 36
Task complexity, 261
Technology, 408, 410
Telescoping, 646
Template matching, 52
Template schemas, 144
Tension reduction, 7
Textbook of Psychology, 36
Thanatos, 7
Thematic intrusions, 157
Theological stage of social science, 2
Theory-driven matching process, 271
Theory of Moral Sentiments, 11
Thinking
  measuring cost of, 267
  wishful, 290–291
Thought, 575–576
Threat, 81
Three Faces of Eve, The, 537
Three faces of social psychology, 49

Thresholds
  action, 271
  behavioral, 557
Time and information load, 262
Time-series designs, 488
Time to Speak, A, 98
Top-down matching process, 271
Transaction cost approach, 404–406
Transformation
  of information, 141
  permissible, 531
Transitoriness of instinct, 34
Translation effect, 248–249
Transpathy, 13
Trap search, 273
Trichotomy, 11
Trust, 586
Truth value, 179
T-test, 66

Ubiquitous rating scale, 534–541
Ultimate attribution error, 195
Uncertainty, 198
  defined, 269–270
  reduction of, 275
Unconflicted change, 278
Unconflicted inertia, 278
Underidentification, 494
Unequal cell sizes, 493–496
Unfolding, 526–528
  of small events, 617–620
Unidimensional unfolding, 526–528
Unipathy, 13
Unit of analysis, 33, 382, 383, 386,
    393, 504
Unitary explanation, 4
Unit formation, 198
Unitizing, 152–153
Unit relations, 198
Unobtrusive measurements, 473–474,
    572–573
Unobtrusive Measures: Non-Reactive
    Research in the Social Sciences,
    543
Unrestricted sampling, 664
Unstructured mental organization, 20
Unweighted-means analysis, 495–496
Utilitarian ethics, 5–6
Utilitarianism, 4–8
Utility models, 243–246

Validity, 604–605
  construct, 477, 479, 499
  convergent, 541–543

Validity (*continued*)
  discriminant, 500
  external, 478–480, 483
  illusion of, 196
  internal, 477–478, 480
  of verbal protocols, 258–259
Value accounting, 286–287
Value function, 247–248
Values, 647–652
  avoidance of trade-offs in, 287–288
  difficulties in applying, 284–287
  failure to consider relevant, 285
  ignorance of own, 285
  naive estimates of, 285–286
  social, 37
Variables
  component, 238
  conceptual, 477
  dependent, 449, 458–463, 473–474

endogenous, 498
independent, 449, 450–458,
  470–471
latent, 500–502
Variance analysis, 66
Varieties of Religious Experience, 40
Verbal protocols, 257–259
Vicarious learning, 73
Vigilance, 85, 278
Vividness, 181–182, 191
Vocabulary of motives, 319
Volk, 27, 29
Völkerpsychologie, 27
Volksgeist, 27, 28
Volksseel, 28

Warmth, 120
War of the Worlds, The, 23
Weapons effect, 114

Weighted average model, 88
Weights, 238, 494
  objective vs. subjective, 240
Welfare state, 6
Wesen und Formen der Sympathie,
  13
Will to Power, The, 9
Wishful thinking, 290–291
Worth, 766
Wurzburg school, 36–37

Yale learning theory, 34
"Yea-sayers," 183, 186

Zeilvorstellung, 36
Zeitgeist, 54, 95
*Zeitschrift fur Volkerpsychologie
  und Sprachwissenschaft*, 27
Zero-sum games, 80